OUR NATIONAL INCOME ACCOUNTS AND REAL GDP SINCE 1929*

In this table we see historical data for the various components of nominal GDP. These are given in the first four columns. We then show the rest of the na[tional] income accounts going from GDP to NDP to NI to PI to DPI. The last colu[mn] real GDP.

	The Sum of These Expenditures				Equals	Less	Equals	Plus	Less	Equals	Less			Plus	Equals	Less	Equals	
Year	Personal Consumption Expenditures	Gross Private Domestic Investment	Government Purchases of Goods and Services	Net Exports	Gross Domestic Product	Depreciation	Net Domestic Product	Net U.S. Income Earned Abroad	Indirect Business Taxes, Transfers, Adjustments	National Income	Undistributed Corporate Profits	Social Security Taxes	Corporate Income Taxes	Transfer Payments and Net Interest Earnings	Personal Income	Personal Income Taxes and Nontax Payments	Disposable Personal Income	Real GDP (2005 dollars)
1985	2720.3	736.2	879.0	-115.2	4220.3	506.7	3713.6	26.5	16.7	3723.4	133.4	281.4	99.4	317.5	3526.7	417.4	3109.3	6839.7
1986	2899.7	746.5	949.3	-132.7	4462.8	531.1	3931.7	17.8	47.2	3902.3	103.7	303.4	109.7	336.9	3722.4	437.3	3285.1	7076.0
1987	3100.2	785.0	999.5	-145.2	4739.5	561.9	4177.6	17.9	21.8	4173.7	126.1	323.1	130.4	353.3	3947.4	489.1	3458.3	7316.0
1988	3353.6	821.6	1039.0	-110.4	5103.8	597.6	4506.2	23.6	-19.6	4549.4	161.1	361.5	141.6	368.5	4253.7	505.0	3748.7	7618.0
1989	3598.5	874.9	1099.1	-88.2	5484.4	644.3	4840.1	26.2	39.7	4826.6	122.6	385.2	146.1	415.1	4587.8	566.1	4021.7	7887.8
1990	3839.9	861.0	1180.2	-78.0	5803.1	682.5	5120.6	34.8	66.3	5089.1	123.3	410.1	145.4	468.3	4878.6	592.8	4285.8	8034.8
1991	3986.1	802.9	1234.4	-27.5	5995.9	725.9	5270.0	30.4	72.5	5227.9	131.9	430.2	138.6	523.8	5051.0	586.7	4464.3	8022.3
1992	4235.3	864.8	1271.0	-33.2	6337.9	751.9	5586.0	29.7	102.9	5512.8	142.7	455.0	148.7	595.6	5362.0	610.6	4751.4	8288.7
1993	4477.9	953.4	1291.2	-65.0	6657.5	776.4	5881.1	31.9	139.6	5773.4	168.1	477.7	171.0	601.9	5558.5	646.6	4911.9	8511.0
1994	4743.3	1097.1	1325.5	-93.6	7072.3	833.7	6238.6	26.2	142.5	6122.3	171.8	508.2	193.7	593.9	5842.5	690.7	5151.8	8853.5
1995	4975.8	1144.0	1369.2	-91.4	7397.6	878.4	6519.2	35.8	101.1	6453.9	223.8	532.8	218.7	673.7	6152.3	744.1	5408.2	9075.0
1996	5256.8	1240.3	1416.0	-96.2	7816.9	918.1	6898.8	35.0	93.7	6840.1	256.9	555.2	231.7	724.3	6520.6	832.1	5688.5	9411.0
1997	5547.4	1389.8	1468.7	-101.6	8304.3	974.4	7329.9	33.0	70.7	7292.2	287.9	587.2	246.1	744.1	6915.1	926.3	5988.8	9834.9
1998	5879.5	1509.1	1518.3	-159.9	8747.0	1030.2	7716.8	21.3	-14.7	7752.8	201.7	624.2	248.3	744.4	7423.0	1027.1	6395.9	10245.6
1999	6342.8	1641.5	1631.3	-262.1	9353.5	1101.3	8252.2	33.8	-72.0	8358.0	255.3	661.4	258.6	728.1	7910.8	1107.5	6803.3	10779.8
2000	6830.4	1772.2	1731.0	-382.1	9951.5	1187.8	8763.7	39.0	-136.2	8938.9	174.8	691.7	265.2	752.2	8559.4	1232.2	7327.2	11226.0
2001	7148.8	1661.9	1846.4	-371.0	10286.1	1281.5	9004.6	43.6	-137.0	9185.2	192.3	717.5	204.1	812.0	8883.3	1234.8	7648.5	11347.2
2002	7439.2	1647.0	1983.3	-427.2	10642.3	1292.0	9350.3	30.7	-27.5	9408.5	294.5	734.3	192.6	873.0	9060.1	1050.4	8009.7	11553.0
2003	7804.0	1729.7	2112.6	-504.1	11142.2	1336.5	9805.7	68.1	33.6	9840.2	325.1	758.9	243.3	865.2	9378.1	1000.3	8377.8	11840.7
2004	8285.1	1968.6	2232.8	-618.7	11867.8	1436.1	10431.7	53.7	-48.6	10534.0	384.4	805.2	307.4	900.2	9937.2	1047.8	8889.4	12263.8
2005	8819.0	2172.2	2369.9	-722.7	12638.4	1609.5	11028.9	68.5	-176.4	11273.8	456.9	850.0	413.7	932.7	10485.9	1208.6	9277.3	12638.4
2006	9322.7	2327.2	2518.4	-769.4	13398.9	1615.2	11783.7	58.0	-189.5	12031.2	497.5	902.4	468.9	1105.7	11268.1	1352.4	9915.7	12976.2
2007	9826.4	2288.5	2676.5	-713.8	14077.6	1720.5	12357.1	64.4	-26.7	12448.2	403.4	942.3	450.4	1242.0	11894.1	1491.0	10403.1	13254.1
2008	10129.9	2136.1	2883.2	-707.8	14441.4	1847.1	12594.3	141.9	288.0	12448.2	322.4	974.5	292.2	1379.7	12238.8	1107.6	10806.4	13312.1
2009[a]	10089.1	1628.8	2930.8	-392.4	14256.3	1863.7	12392.6	122.1	-120.5	12635.2	350.9	942.1	449.2	1179.1	12072.1	1107.6	10964.5	12987.4
2010[a]	10356.2	1577.3	3214.1	-512.6	14635.0	2243.1	12391.9	66.3	-244.4	12702.6	360.8	946.3	451.3	1413.8	12358.0	1257.6	11100.4	13190.4
2011[a]	10421.1	1743.7	3514.2	-611.5	15067.5	2210.2	12857.3	71.0	77.7	12850.6	365.1	980.2	453.2	1704.2	12756.3	1132.3	11624.0	13405.8

[a]Author's estimates.

**Note:* Some rows may not add up due to rounding errors.

MACROECONOMIC PRINCIPLES

Nominal versus Real Interest Rate

$i_n = i_r$ + expected rate of inflation

where i_n = nominal rate of interest
i_r = real rate of interest

Marginal versus Average Tax Rates

$$\text{Marginal tax rate} = \frac{\text{change in taxes due}}{\text{change in taxable income}}$$

$$\text{Average tax rate} = \frac{\text{total taxes due}}{\text{total taxable income}}$$

GDP—The Expenditure and Income Approaches

$\text{GDP} = C + I + G + X$

where C = consumption expenditures
I = investment expenditures
G = government expenditures
X = net exports

GDP = wages + rent + interest + profits

Say's Law

Supply creates its own demand, or *desired* aggregate expenditures will equal *actual* aggregate expenditures.

Saving, Consumption, and Investment

Consumption + saving = disposable income

Saving = disposable income − consumption

Average and Marginal Propensities

$$\text{APC} = \frac{\text{real consumption}}{\text{real disposable income}}$$

$$\text{APS} = \frac{\text{real saving}}{\text{real disposable income}}$$

$$\text{MPC} = \frac{\text{change in real consumption}}{\text{change in real disposable income}}$$

$$\text{MPS} = \frac{\text{change in real saving}}{\text{change in real disposable income}}$$

The Multiplier Formula

$$\text{Multiplier} = \frac{1}{\text{MPS}} = \frac{1}{1 - \text{MPC}}$$

Multiplier × change in autonomous real spending = change in equilibrium real GDP

Relationship Between Bond Prices and Interest Rates

The market price of existing (old) bonds is inversely related to "the" rate of interest prevailing in the economy.

Government Spending and Taxation Multipliers

$$M_g = \frac{1}{\text{MPS}}$$

$$M_t = -\text{MPC} \times \frac{1}{\text{MPS}}$$

Economics Today

Sixteenth Edition

Roger LeRoy Miller

Research Professor of Economics
University of Texas–Arlington

Addison-Wesley

Boston Columbus Indianapolis New York San Francisco Upper Saddle River
Amsterdam Cape Town Dubai London Madrid Milan Munich Paris Montreal Toronto
Delhi Mexico City Sao Paulo Sydney Hong Kong Seoul Singapore Taipei Tokyo

The Pearson Series in Economics

Abel/Bernanke/Croushore
*Macroeconomics**

Bade/Parkin
*Foundations of Economics**

Berck/Helfand
The Economics of the Environment

Bierman/Fernandez
Game Theory with Economic Applications

Blanchard
*Macroeconomics**

Blau/Ferber/Winkler
The Economics of Women, Men and Work

Boardman/Greenberg/Vining/Weimer
Cost-Benefit Analysis

Boyer
Principles of Transportation Economics

Branson
Macroeconomic Theory and Policy

Brock/Adams
The Structure of American Industry

Bruce
Public Finance and the American Economy

Carlton/Perloff
Modern Industrial Organization

Case/Fair/Oster
*Principles of Economics**

Caves/Frankel/Jones
World Trade and Payments: An Introduction

Chapman
Environmental Economics: Theory, Application, and Policy

Cooter/Ulen
Law & Economics

Downs
An Economic Theory of Democracy

Ehrenberg/Smith
Modern Labor Economics

Ekelund/Ressler/Tollison
*Economics**

Farnham
Economics for Managers

Folland/Goodman/Stano
The Economics of Health and Health Care

Fort
Sports Economics

Froyen
Macroeconomics

Fusfeld
The Age of the Economist

Gerber
*International Economics**

Gordon
*Macroeconomics**

Greene
Econometric Analysis

Gregory
Essentials of Economics

Gregory/Stuart
Russian and Soviet Economic Performance and Structure

Hartwick/Olewiler
The Economics of Natural Resource Use

Heilbroner/Milberg
The Making of the Economic Society

Heyne/Boettke/Prychitko
The Economic Way of Thinking

Hoffman/Averett
Women and the Economy: Family, Work, and Pay

Holt
Markets, Games and Strategic Behavior

Hubbard/O'Brien
*Economics**
*Money, Banking, and the Financial System**

Hughes/Cain
American Economic History

Husted/Melvin
International Economics

Jehle/Reny
Advanced Microeconomic Theory

Johnson-Lans
A Health Economics Primer

Keat/Young
Managerial Economics

Klein
Mathematical Methods for Economics

Krugman/Obstfeld/Melitz
*International Economics: Theory & Policy**

Laidler
The Demand for Money

Leeds/von Allmen
The Economics of Sports

Leeds/von Allmen/Schiming
*Economics**

Lipsey/Ragan/Storer
*Economics**

Lynn
Economic Development: Theory and Practice for a Divided World

Miller
*Economics Today**

Understanding Modern Economics

Miller/Benjamin
The Economics of Macro Issues

Miller/Benjamin/North
The Economics of Public Issues

Mills/Hamilton
Urban Economics

Mishkin
*The Economics of Money, Banking, and Financial Markets**

*The Economics of Money, Banking, and Financial Markets, Business School Edition**

*Macroeconomics: Policy and Practice**

Murray
Econometrics: A Modern Introduction

Nafziger
The Economics of Developing Countries

O'Sullivan/Sheffrin/Perez
*Economics: Principles, Applications and Tools**

Parkin
*Economics**

Perloff
*Microeconomics**

*Microeconomics: Theory and Applications with Calculus**

Perman/Common/McGilvray/Ma
Natural Resources and Environmental Economics

Phelps
Health Economics

Pindyck/Rubinfeld
*Microeconomics**

Riddell/Shackelford/Stamos/Schneider
Economics: A Tool for Critically Understanding Society

Ritter/Silber/Udell
*Principles of Money, Banking & Financial Markets**

Roberts
The Choice: A Fable of Free Trade and Protection

Rohlf
Introduction to Economic Reasoning

Ruffin/Gregory
Principles of Economics

Sargent
Rational Expectations and Inflation

Sawyer/Sprinkle
International Economics

Scherer
Industry Structure, Strategy, and Public Policy

Schiller
The Economics of Poverty and Discrimination

Sherman
Market Regulation

Silberberg
Principles of Microeconomics

Stock/Watson
Introduction to Econometrics
Introduction to Econometrics, Brief Edition

Studenmund
Using Econometrics: A Practical Guide

Tietenberg/Lewis
Environmental and Natural Resource Economics

Environmental Economics and Policy

Todaro/Smith
Economic Development

Waldman
Microeconomics

Waldman/Jensen
Industrial Organization: Theory and Practice

Weil
Economic Growth

Williamson
Macroeconomics

Dedication

To the memory of Gaylord Jentz,

A true professional as well as a good friend. I will miss you.

— R. L. M.

Editorial Director: Sally Yagan
Editor in Chief: Donna Battista
Acquisitions Editor: Noel Seibert
Assistant Editor: Carolyn Terbush
Editorial Assistant: Megan Cadigan
Director of Marketing: Patrice Jones
AVP/Executive Marketing Manager: Lori DeShazo
Marketing Assistant: Kim Lovato
Managing Editor: Nancy H. Fenton
Senior Production Project Manager: Kathryn Dinovo
Senior Manufacturing Buyer: Carol Melville
Creative Director: Christy Mahon
Senior Art Director: Jonathan Boylan
Interior Designer: Delgado and Co.
Cover Designer: Jonathan Boylan
Manager, Visual Research: Karen Sanatar
Manager, Rights and Permissions: Zina Arabia
Permissions Project Supervisor: Michael Joyce
Media Director: Susan Schoenberg
Senior Media Producer: Melissa Honig
MyEconLab Content Lead: Noel Lotz
Supplements Editor: Alison Eusden
Full-Service Project Management: Orr Book Services
Composition: Nesbitt Graphics, Inc.
Art Studio: ElectraGraphics, Inc.
Printer/Binder: Courier / Kendallville
Cover Printer: Lehigh-Phoenix Color / Hagerstown
Text Font: 10/12 Janson

Photo credits appear on page xxix, which constitutes a continuation of the copyright page.

Library of Congress Cataloging-in-Publication Data

Miller, Roger LeRoy.
Economics today / Roger LeRoy Miller. —16th ed.
p. cm. — (The pearson series in economics)
Includes index.
ISBN 978-0-13-255461-9 (single volume edition; chapters 1-33) — ISBN 978-0-13-255451-0 (the macro view; chapters 1–18; 32–33) — ISBN 978-0-13-255441-1 (the micro view; chapters 1–6; 19–33)
1. Economics. 2. Microeconomics. 3. Macroeconomics. I. Title.
HB171.5.M642 2012
330—dc22 2010049938

10 9 8 7 6 5 4 3 2 1

Addison-Wesley is an imprint of

www.pearsonhighered.com

ISBN 10: 0-13-255485-2
ISBN 13: 978-0-13-255485-5

Brief Contents

Contents

One-Semester Course Outline

MACROECONOMIC EMPHASIS

THE MACRO VIEW

1. The Nature of Economics
2. Scarcity and the World of Trade-Offs
3. Demand and Supply
4. Extensions of Demand and Supply Analysis
5. Public Spending and Public Choice
6. Funding the Public Sector
7. The Macroeconomy. Unemployment, Inflation, and Deflation
8. Measuring the Economy's Performance
9. Global Economic Growth and Development
10. Real GDP and the Price Level in the Long Run
11. Classical and Keynesian Macro Analyses
12. Consumption, Real GDP, and the Multiplier
13. Fiscal Policy
14. Deficit Spending and the Public Debt
15. Money, Banking, and Central Banking
16. Domestic and International Dimensions of Monetary Policy
17. Stabilization in an Integrated World Economy
18. Policies and Prospects for Global Economic Growth
32. Comparative Advantage and the Open Economy
33. Exchange Rates and the Balance of Payments

MICROECONOMIC EMPHASIS

THE MICRO VIEW

1. The Nature of Economics
2. Scarcity and the World of Trade-Offs
3. Demand and Supply
4. Extensions of Demand and Supply Analysis
5. Public Spending and Public Choice
6. Funding the Public Sector
19. Demand and Supply Elasticity
20. Consumer Choice
21. Rents, Profits, and the Financial Environment of Business
22. The Firm: Cost and Output Determination
23. Perfect Competition
24. Monopoly
25. Monopolistic Competition
26. Oligopoly and Strategic Behavior
27. Regulation and Antitrust Policy in a Globalized Economy
28. The Labor Market: Demand, Supply, and Outsourcing
29. Unions and Labor Market Monopoly Power
30. Income, Poverty, and Health Care
31. Environmental Economics
32. Comparative Advantage and the Open Economy
33. Exchange Rates and the Balance of Payments

BALANCED MICRO-MACRO

1. The Nature of Economics
2. Scarcity and the World of Trade-Offs
3. Demand and Supply
4. Extensions of Demand and Supply Analysis
5. Public Spending and Public Choice
6. Funding the Public Sector
20. Consumer Choice
21. Rents, Profits, and the Financial Environment of Business
22. The Firm: Cost and Output Determination
23. Perfect Competition
24. Monopoly
28. The Labor Market: Demand, Supply, and Outsourcing
29. Unions and Labor Market Monopoly Power
7. The Macroeconomy. Unemployment, Inflation, and Deflation
10. Real GDP and the Price Level in the Long Run
11. Classical and Keynesian Macro Analyses
12. Consumption, Real GDP, and the Multiplier
13. Fiscal Policy
14. Deficit Spending and the Public Debt
15. Money, Banking, and Central Banking
16. Domestic and International Dimensions of Monetary Policy
32. Comparative Advantage and the Open Economy
33. Exchange Rates and the Balance of Payments

Preface

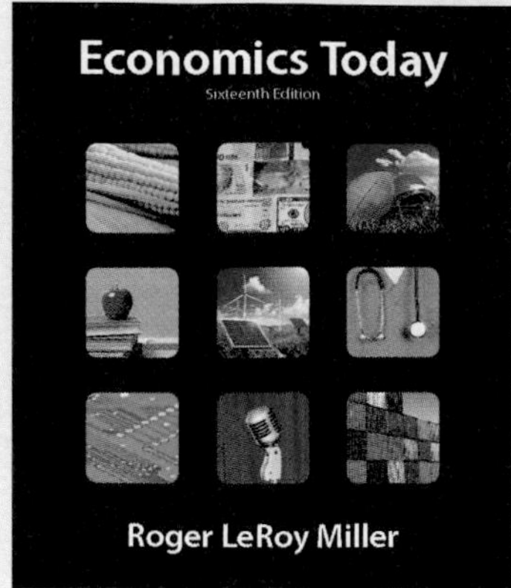

Economics Today—Encouraging Students to Read, Study, and Learn

In today's fast-paced, multitasking environment, students must be convinced that there is a concrete payoff from taking the time to read a text, utilize all of its study features, and learn the fundamental concepts it presents. Thus, we, as professional economists, must constantly search for new ways to demonstrate to our students how powerful the tools of economic analysis can be. We have to persuade them that economic tools are useful not only for economists, businesspeople, and policymakers, but also for them.

Over the years that I have devoted to helping students learn about our fascinating field, I have consistently found that presenting students with current and relevant examples is the most successful means of motivating them to read an economics textbook and to learn the essential tools that economists have to offer. Thus, you will find that this latest edition of *Economics Today* contains a wide array of student-oriented examples showing students how relevant our discipline is to domestic, policy, and global issues.

"Presenting students with current and relevant examples is the most successful means of motivating them."

You will notice a new feature in every chapter called "Why Not ... ?" This new feature addresses the types of questions that occur to students as they encounter daily media coverage of real-world events involving economic decision making by households, businesses, and government policymakers. Thinking about how the concepts they encounter in each chapter apply in addressing such questions enables students to see the relevance of the tools of economic analysis.

"This latest edition of *Economics Today* contains a wide array of student-oriented examples showing students how relevant our discipline is."

As always, I have revised significant sections of this text. For instance, you will find that the coverage of fiscal policymaking, the federal deficits and the public debt, and new Federal Reserve policy approaches and macroeconomic policymaking contained in Chapters 14 through 17 has been thoroughly restructured and updated. In addition, Chapter 30 provides a carefully organized explanation of the key features of the new federal health care program slated to go into effect during the next few years, along with a discussion of the program's likely economic impacts.

Consistent with the growing emphasis on assessment of learning in higher education today, I continue to facilitate assessment of student learning by means of "Quick Quiz" boxes that appear throughout each chapter and Clicker/Personal Response System questions available for use by instructors in PowerPoint presentations that accompany the book. Pearson and I continue to expand the assessment aspect of MyEconLab, our online course management and tutorial system. As in the last edition, 100 percent of end-of-chapter exercises are assignable in MyEconLab for greater flexibility in assessing students. We also strive to continue to provide students with current events coverage and analysis through weekly news and ABC News clips.

In this new edition of *Economics Today*, I have sought to impart to students concepts that they will be able to apply to every aspect of their lives. I am convinced that once students are empowered by the tools of economic analysis, they will appreciate their classroom experiences for years to come.

—Roger LeRoy Miller

New to This Edition

This new edition of *Economics Today* addresses today's most pressing issues while seeking to lower learning obstacles that students sometimes confront. The text's fundamental goals remain firmly in place: demonstrating to students the relevance of economics to *their* lives and offering them numerous opportunities in every chapter to confirm that they understand key concepts before continuing on.

Cutting-edge developments have been incorporated throughout. These include:

- Evaluation of the **U.S. government deficit and public debt:** Chapter 14 provides a thorough discussion of the exploding U.S. government deficit, the upswing in the U.S. public debt, and prospects for eventually reducing both annual deficit flows and the outstanding stock of government debt.
- A full revision of the nuts and bolts of **modern monetary policy:** Chapters 15 and 16 have been thoroughly updated to take into account the considerably altered nature of Federal Reserve monetary policymaking since 2008.
- Evaluation of the recent **performance of the U.S. stock market:** Chapter 21 compares the behavior of average stock prices during and after the 2008 meltdown with stock price behavior during the Great Depression and other periods in which significant declines in stock prices occurred.
- Coverage of the economic effects of the **new federal health care legislation:** Chapter 30 provides an organized discussion of the key features of the health care law passed in 2010 and evaluates fundamental economic implications of the legislation.

ISSUES & APPLICATIONS

Is Your College Degree Worth $1 Million?

CONCEPTS APPLIED

▶ Income

▶ Determinants of Income

▶ Distribution of Income

Ads placed by a number of colleges across the United States include the claim that a college degree can be expected to yield $1 million more in lifetime income than would be earned with only a high school diploma. As you have learned in this chapter, the amount of education and training that people obtain does indeed have a significant influence on their incomes and, consequently, the distribution of incomes across society. But from the perspective of an entering college student, is a college degree really worth $1 million?

The macro portion of the text now includes the following:

- Chapter 7 explains the concept of the **misery index,** evaluates why its value has increased in recent years, and compares its current level with those of previous years.
- Chapter 11 provides an analysis of the **consumption decline** that occurred during the late 2000s.
- Chapter 13 offers an explanation of why the federal government's provision of one-time **tax rebates** failed to boost household consumption spending and combat the economic downturn.
- Chapter 17 evaluates how the widespread use of a measure of expected future inflation in financial markets is consistent with key implications of the **new Keynesian theory.**

In the micro portion of the text, I have added analyses of the following:

- Chapter 20 explains why some proponents of **behavioral economics** suggest that many U.S. consumers do not benefit from using credit cards.
- Chapter 22 discusses why many energy experts suggest that the use of smaller reactors may fuel a future resurgence in the use of **nuclear power.**
- Chapter 25 evaluates why the concepts of **product differentiation and trademarks** help to explain the unusual names chosen by rock bands.
- Chapter 26 provides an explanation for why **vertical mergers** have made a comeback in U.S. industry.
- Students often have trouble visualizing "gains from trade" and "losses from monopoly." To assist them in developing a concrete understanding of these concepts, new to this edition is Appendix B following Chapter 4, entitled "Consumer Surplus, Producer Surplus, and Gains from Trade Within a Price System." In addition, following Chapter 24 is Appendix G, entitled "Consumer Surplus and the Deadweight Loss Resulting from Monopoly."

Making the Connection—from the Classroom to the Real World

Economics Today provides current examples with critical analysis questions that show students how economic theory applies to their diverse interests and lives. For the Sixteenth Edition, **more than 90 percent** of the examples are new.

Domestic topics and events are presented through thought-provoking discussions, such as:

- Why Even Low-Income Households Are Rushing to Buy iPhones
- Does Consuming More Expensive Items Make People Happier?

EXAMPLE **How Much Might "Going Green" Reduce U.S. Economic Growth?**

President Obama and leaders in the U.S. Congress have agreed that reduction of greenhouse gas emissions should be a national priority. Their near-term goal is to reduce such emissions to 2005 levels by no later than 2014. Their longer-term goal is to reduce emissions by an additional 30 percent by 2030.

Attainment of these goals would constrain the ability of businesses to use resources at lowest cost. As a consequence, production of capital goods would decline, and that would reduce future economic growth. Economists at the Environmental Protection Agency (EPA) have estimated that these efforts to cut emissions of greenhouse gases likely would lead to a cumulative reduction in real GDP of about 4 percent by 2030. Based on the current level of U.S. real GDP, this estimated eventual decrease in annual real GDP would be equivalent to the reduction that occurred during the Great Recession of the late 2000s. Instead of being a short-term decrease in real GDP as in the recession, however, the reduction generated by the proposed emissions regulations would be permanent.

FOR CRITICAL ANALYSIS

Why do you think that economists suggest that any regulatory policies that generate cuts in production of capital goods will tend to reduce the nation's long-run growth rate for real GDP?

Important policy questions help students understand public debates, such as:

- Moderating the Great Recession Is Harder Than Anticipated
- Congress Decides to License Tax Preparers

POLICY EXAMPLE **Can Minimum Wage Laws Ever Boost Employment?**

How does a monopsony respond to a minimum wage law that sets a wage floor above the wage rate it otherwise would pay its workers? Figure 29-7 on the facing page provides the answer to this question. In the figure, the entire upward-sloping curve labeled S is the labor supply curve in the absence of a minimum wage. Given the associated MFC curve and the firm's MRP curve, Q_m is the quantity of labor hired by a monopsony in the absence of a minimum wage law. The profit-maximizing wage rate is W_m.

If the government establishes a minimum wage equal to W_{min}, however, then the supply of labor to the firm becomes horizontal at the minimum wage and includes only the upward-sloping portion of the curve S above this legal minimum. In addition, the wage rate W_{min} becomes the monopsonist's marginal factor cost along the horizontal portion of this new labor supply curve, because when the firm hires one more unit of labor, it must pay each unit of labor the same wage rate, W_{min}.

To maximize its economic profits under the minimum wage, the monopsony equalizes the minimum wage rate with marginal revenue product and hires Q_{min} units of labor. This quantity exceeds the amount of labor, Q_m, that the monopsony would have hired in the absence of the minimum wage law. Thus, establishing a minimum wage can generate a rise in employment at a monopsony firm.

FOR CRITICAL ANALYSIS

If a government establishes a minimum wage law covering all firms within its jurisdiction, including firms operating in both perfectly competitive and monopsonistic labor markets, will overall employment necessarily increase?

INTERNATIONAL EXAMPLE **What Economic Growth Success Stories Have in Common**

A commission funded by grants from the World Bank, the Hewlett Foundation, and several national governments recently studied 13 nations that, at some time since 1950, experienced 25-year periods of annual growth rates of at least 7 percent. The countries were Botswana, Brazil, China, Hong Kong, Indonesia, Japan, Malaysia, Malta, Oman, Singapore, South Korea, Taiwan, and Thailand. The commission found that all 13 nations shared five characteristics. The first four were (1) macroeconomic stability, (2) high levels of saving and investment, (3) relatively unregulated domestic industries, and (4) gover

The fi

mists: All

growth periods, none of the countries' governments erected significant barriers to flows of imports and exports across national borders. Furthermore, the periods of high economic growth ended for several nations when their governments began restricting flows of international trade.

FOR CRITICAL ANALYSIS

Given the evidence that low trade barriers promote higher economic growth, why do you think that some residents of every country favor signifi-

INTERNATIONAL POLICY EXAMPLE **Freedom of Information and Growth in Developing Nations**

The Indian government requires farmers to sell soybeans to middlemen who, in turn, resell the beans in wholesale markets. In years past, this restriction has given the middlemen an advantage in price negotiations because they always have up-to-the-minute data about wholesale soybean prices. As a consequence, many Indian farmers who might otherwise produce soybeans have been dissuaded from doing so, for fear of being "taken" by middlemen. This has depressed the rate of increase of agricultural production in a nation in which a significant fraction of the population suffers from malnourishment.

Recently, ITC Limited, a wholesale buyer of soybeans in India, has established a network of more than 1,700 Internet kiosks in villages in key agricultural regions of the country. At these kiosks, farmers can obtain the current day's minimum and maximum wholesale soybean prices paid to market middlemen. With this information in their possession, farmers are able to bargain for better prices on their crops. In areas served by ITC's kiosks, the result has been a 33 increase in Indian soybean farmers' profits and a 19 percent increase in soybean production. The resulting boost in the supply of soybeans has contributed to lower prices and an increase in soybean consumption by the nation's residents.

FOR CRITICAL ANALYSIS

What do you suppose has happened to the profits of soybean market middlemen?

Global and international policy examples emphasize the continued importance of international perspectives and policy, such as:

- How Cellphones Are Fueling Economic Development
- Globalization of Tasks and the Elasticity of U.S. Labor Demand
- Does the Spread of Regional Trade Blocs Reduce Protectionism?

Helping Students Focus and Think Critically

New and revised pedagogical tools engage students and help them focus on the central ideas in economics today.

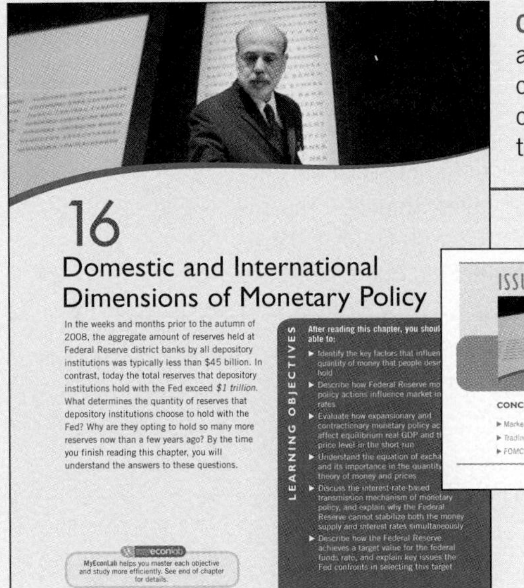

16

Domestic and International Dimensions of Monetary Policy

In the weeks and months prior to the autumn of 2008, the aggregate amount of reserves held at Federal Reserve district banks by all depository institutions was typically less than $45 billion. In contrast, today the total reserves that depository institutions hold with the Fed exceed *$1 trillion*. What determines the quantity of reserves that depository institutions choose to hold with the Fed? Why are they opting to hold so many more reserves now than a few years ago? By the time you finish reading this chapter, you will understand the answers to these questions.

Chapter Openers tie to the **Issues & Applications** feature at the end of each chapter. A current application captures students' attention at the beginning of the chapter and is revisited in more depth at the end using the concepts they have just learned.

ISSUES & APPLICATIONS

Explaining the Rise in the Quantity of Bank Reserves

CONCEPTS APPLIED

- Market for Bank Reserves
- Trading Desk
- FOMC Directive

In the late summer of 2008, the equilibrium quantity of reserves determined in the U.S. market for bank reserves was no higher than $45 billion. As you can see in Figure 16-11 on the next page, however, since then the total reserves of depository institutions have increased by nearly 25 times, to a level exceeding $1 trillion.

-GDP Ratio

...g page displays the ...P for the same set of ...ebt in Greece, Italy, and Japan are more than 100 percent of GDP. This means that even if Greek, Italian, and Japanese residents were to transmit all the incomes they earn in a full year to their governments, their nations' net public debts still would not be fully repaid. In Japan, people would have to give up *two* full years' worth of GDP to pay off the Japanese government's net public debt.

Thus, the U.S. ratio is not the highest among industrialized nations. Nevertheless, the U.S. net public debt–GDP ratio is now about 70 percent, which is more than twice as high as it was as recently as 2000.

For Critical Analysis

1. Why does the fact that the U.S. government's deficit-GDP ratio is now so high help to explain why its debt-GDP ratio has increased?

Web Resources

1. To take a look at the latest government deficit and net public debt statistics for Europe, go to www.econtoday.com/ch14.
2. For the latest data on the U.S. budget deficit and net public debt, go to www.econtoday.com/ch14.

Research Project

Explain why it is important, when evaluating a nation's government deficit and net public debt, to relate both figures to the size of the country's economy.

myeconlab

For more questions on this chapter's Issues & Applications, go to **MyEconLab**. In the Study Plan for this chapter, select Section N: News.

Critical Analysis questions, Web Resources, and a **Research Project** provide further opportunities for discussion and exploration. Suggested answers for Critical Analysis questions are in the *Instructor's Manual.* Visit **MyEconLab** for additional practice and assignable questions for each chapter topic as well as abc NEWS video clips on concepts covered.

The **end-of-chapter summary** shows students what they need to know and where to go in **MyEconLab** for more practice.

A variety of end-of-chapter problems offer students opportunities to test their knowledge and review chapter concepts. Answers for odd-numbered questions are provided in the back of the text, and **all questions** are assignable in **MyEconLab.**

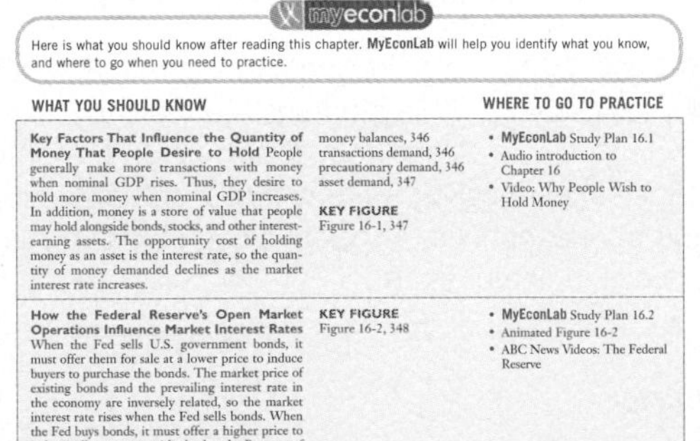

myeconlab

Here is what you should know after reading this chapter. **MyEconLab** will help you identify what you know, and where to go when you need to practice.

WHAT YOU SHOULD KNOW		WHERE TO GO TO PRACTICE
Key Factors That Influence the Quantity of Money That People Desire to Hold People generally make more transactions with money when nominal GDP rises. Thus, they desire to hold more money when nominal GDP increases. In addition, money is a store of value that people may hold alongside bonds, stocks, and other interest-earning assets. The opportunity cost of holding money as an asset is the interest rate, so the quantity of money demanded declines as the market interest rate increases.	money balances, 346 transactions demand, 346 precautionary demand, 346 asset demand, 347 **KEY FIGURE** Figure 16-1, 347	• **MyEconLab** Study Plan 16.1 • Audio introduction to Chapter 16 • Video: Why People Wish to Hold Money
How the Federal Reserve's Open Market Operations Influence Market Interest Rates When the Fed sells U.S. government bonds, it must offer them for sale at a lower price to induce buyers to purchase the bonds. The market price of existing bonds and the prevailing interest rate in the economy are inversely related, so the market interest rate rises when the Fed sells bonds. When the Fed buys bonds, it must offer a higher price to induce sellers to part with the bonds. Because of the inverse relationship between the market price of existing bonds and the prevailing rate of interest, the market interest rate declines when the Fed purchases bonds.	**KEY FIGURE** Figure 16-2, 348	• **MyEconLab** Study Plan 16.2 • Animated Figure 16-2 • ABC News Videos: The Federal Reserve

Quick Quizzes encourage student interaction and provide an opportunity for them to check their understanding before moving on. Answers are at the end of the chapter, and more practice questions can be found in **MyEconLab.**

QUICK QUIZ See page 16 for the answers. Review concepts from this section in MyEconLab.

Economics is a social science that involves the study of how individuals choose among alternatives to satisfy their _________, which are what people would buy if their incomes were _________.

_________, the study of the decision-making processes of individuals (or households) and firms, and _________, the study of the performance of the economy as a whole, are the two main branches into which the study of economics is divided.

The three basic economic questions ask what and how much will be produced, how will items be produced, and for whom will items be produced. The two opposing answers are provided by the type of economic system: either _________ _________ _________ _________ or the _________ _________.

In economics, we assume that people do not intentionally make decisions that will leave them worse off. This is known as the _________ assumption.

You Are There discusses real people making real personal and business decisions. Topics include:

- Stopping Students' Thursday Night Parties with Friday Classes
- Apple Puts Adobe on Hold

You Are There How Zimbabwe Undercut Collectors' Hopes of Profits

Donald MacTavish, a collector of and dealer in currency notes, has acquired notes that he hopes eventually may be prized by money collectors: one-trillion-dollar notes printed during Zimbabwe's *hyperinflation*—an inflation rate so high that the Zimbabwe dollar often lost more than half its value in a single day. MacTavish bought each note at a price of less than 20 U.S. dollars for each one-trillion-dollar Zimbabwe bill. He hopes that only a limited number of the bills will make their way into collectors' hands. Some collectors, he has observed, think that the price of the notes might eventually rise to more than 100 U.S. dollars.

Shortly after acquiring the Zimbabwe notes, however, MacTavish reads some bad news. Zimbabwe's government printed and distributed the notes in very large volumes. Indeed, so many notes were issued that economists have concluded that this helps to explain why Zimbabwe's inflation rate became the second highest in recorded history. To MacTavish's dismay, experts on the values of moneys that have gone out of circulation are suggesting that Zimbabwe's one-trillion-dollar notes are so abundant that their market values may never exceed what he paid for them.

Critical Analysis Questions

1. How did printing and distributing one-trillion-dollar notes help fuel Zimbabwe's hyperinflation?
2. Why do you think that during the hyperinflation, Zimbabwe's residents used currency notes to buy goods and services as rapidly they possibly could?

New! Why Not ... ? boxes help students think about how the concepts in the book apply to key economic questions, enabling them to see the relevance of economic analysis. Topics include:

- Why Not ... eliminate nearly all U.S. carbon emissions?
- Why Not ... promote innovation by giving out more patents?

Why Not ... prohibit U.S. firms from outsourcing?

Barring U.S. companies from engaging in international labor outsourcing likely would have two negative consequences for the U.S. economy. First, with outsourcing prohibited, the equilibrium wages that U.S. firms would have to pay to obtain labor that they had previously outsourced would increase, which would boost their operating costs. These firms would respond by reducing the quantities of goods and services supplied at any given prices, and the reduction in supply in affected markets would lead to higher equilibrium prices for consumers. Second, other nations' governments probably would respond by prohibiting their own companies from outsourcing to U.S. workers. This response would generate a decrease in the demand for U.S. labor, which would result in lower market clearing wages and reduced equilibrium employment in the affected U.S. labor markets.

MyEconLab: The Power of Practice

is an online assessment system that gives students the tools they need to learn from their mistakes—right at the moment they are struggling. With comprehensive homework, quiz, test, and tutorial options, instructors can also manage all assessment needs in one program.

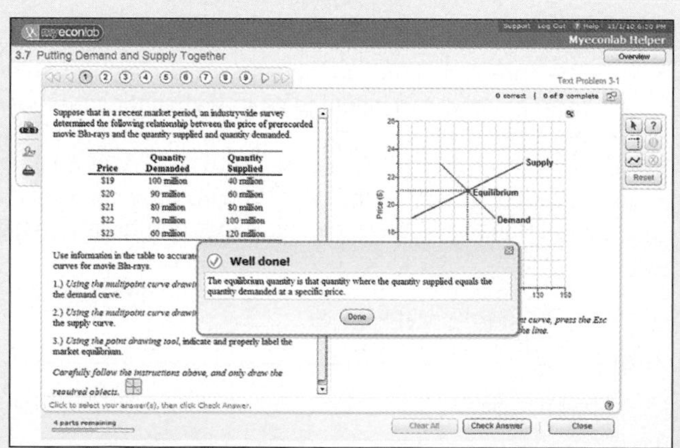

For the Instructor

- Instructors can now select a preloaded course option, which creates a ready-to-go course with homework, quizzes, and tests already set up, or they can choose to create their own assignments.

- All end-of-chapter problems are assignable and automatically graded in MyEconLab, and for most chapters, additional algorithmic, draw-graph, and numerical exercises are available to choose among.
- Instructors can also choose questions from the Test Item File or use the Custom Exercise Builder to create their own problems for assignment.
- The powerful Gradebook records each student's performance and time spent on the Tests and Study Plan, and generates reports by student or by chapter.

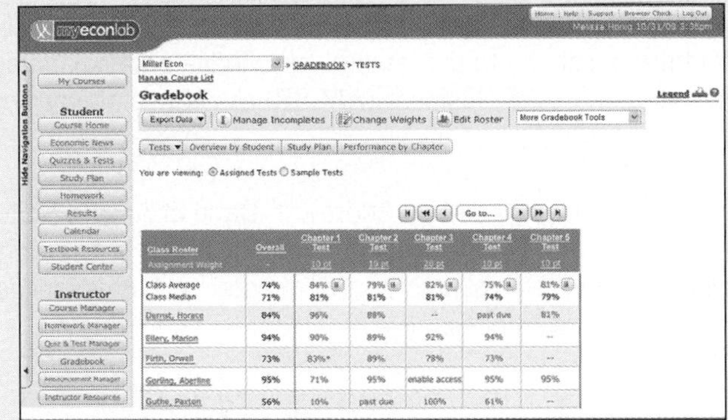

- Economics in the News is a turn-key solution to bringing current news into the classroom. Updated weekly during the academic year, this feature posts news articles with questions for further discussion.
- A comprehensive suite of ABC news videos, which address current topics, is available for classroom use. Video-specific exercises are available for instructor assignment. Videos tied to the "Issues & Applications" features in the text are also available with assignable questions.
- Experiments in MyEconLab are a fun and engaging way to promote active learning and mastery of important economic concepts. Pearson's experiments program is flexible and easy for instructors and students to use.
  - Single-player experiments allow your students to play an experiment against virtual players from anywhere at any time with an Internet connection.
  - Multiplayer experiments allow you to assign and manage a real-time experiment with your class.

  In both cases, pre- and post-questions for each experiment are available for assignment in MyEconLab.

For the Student

Students are in control of their own learning through a collection of tests, practice, and study tools. Highlights include:

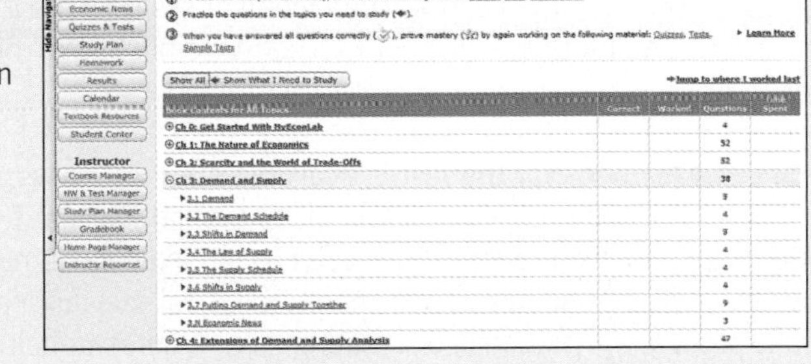

- Two Sample Tests per chapter are preloaded in MyEconLab, enabling students to practice what they have learned, test their understanding, and identify areas for further work.
- Based on each student's performance on homework, quizzes, and tests, MyEconLab generates a Study Plan that shows where the student needs further study.
- Learning Aids, such as step-by-step guided solutions, a graphing tool, content-specific links to the eText, animated graphs, video clips of the author, and glossary flashcards, help students master the material.

Please visit www.myeconlab.com for more information.

Supplemental Resources

Student and instructor materials provide tools for success.

Test Item Files 1, 2, and 3 offer more than 10,000 multiple choice and short answer questions, all of which are available in computerized format in the TestGen software. The significant revision process by authors Paul Graf of Indiana University–Bloomington and Jim Lee of Texas A&M–Corpus Christi ensures the accuracy of problems and solutions in these revised and updated Test Item Files. The Test Item File authors have connected the questions to the general knowledge and skill guidelines found in the Association to Advance Collegiate Schools of Business (AACSB) assurance of learning standards.

The Instructor's Manual, prepared by Andrew J. Dane of Angelo State University, includes lecture-ready examples; chapter overviews, objectives, and outlines; points to emphasize; answers to all critical analysis questions; answers to even-numbered end-of-chapter problems; suggested answers to "You Are There" questions; and selected references.

PowerPoint lecture presentations for each chapter, revised by Jim Lee of Texas A&M–Corpus Christi, include graphs from the text and outline key terms, concepts, and figures from the text.

Clicker PowerPoint slides, prepared by Rick Pretzsch of Lonestar College–CyFair, allow professors to instantly quiz students in class and receive immediate feedback through Clicker Response System technology.

The Instructor's Resource Disk offers all instructor supplements conveniently packaged on a CD-ROM.

The Instructor Resource Center puts supplements right at instructors' fingertips. Visit www.pearsonhighered.com/irc to register.

The Study Guide offers the practice and review that students need to excel. Written by Roger LeRoy Miller and updated by David VanHoose of Baylor University, the Study Guide has been thoroughly revised to take into account changes to the Sixteenth Edition.

Blackboard and WebCT Pearson course management systems are offered for fully customizable course content that includes a link to the MyEconLab software hosting all of the course materials.

The CourseSmart eTextbook for the text is available through www.coursesmart.com. CourseSmart goes beyond traditional expectations by providing instant, online access to the textbooks and course materials you need at a lower cost to students. And, even as students save money, you can save time and hassle with a digital textbook that allows you to search the most relevant content at the very moment you need it. Whether you're evaluating textbooks or creating lecture notes to help students with difficult concepts, CourseSmart can make life a little easier. See how when you visit www.coursesmart.com/instructors.

Acknowledgments

I am the most fortunate of economics textbook writers, for I receive the benefit of literally hundreds of suggestions from those of you who use *Economics Today*. There are some professors who have been asked by my publisher to participate in a more detailed reviewing process of this edition. I list them below. I hope that each one of you so listed accepts my sincere appreciation for the fine work that you have done.

Ercument Aksoy, *Los Angeles Valley College*
Fatma Antar, *Manchester Community College*
Len Anyanwu, *Union Community College*
John Atkins, *Pensacola Junior College*
John Bockino, *Suffolk County Community College*
Sowjanya Dharmasankar, *Waubonsee Community College*
Diana Fortier, *Waubonsee Community College*
Robert Gentenaar, *Pima Community College*
Tori Knight, *Carson–Newman College*
Jim Lee, *Texas A&M University–Corpus Christi*
Laura Maghoney, *Solano Community College*
Fred May, *Trident Technical College*
Kevin McWoodson, *Moraine Valley Community College*
Mohammed Partapurwala, *Monroe Community College*
Steven Pressman, *Monmouth University*
Rick Pretzsch, *Lonestar College*
Marina Rosser, *James Madison University*
Basel Saleh, *Radford University*
Gail Shields, *Central Michigan University*
Terry Sutton, *Rogers State University*
Deborah Thorsen, *Palm Beach Community College*
Anthony Uremovic, *Joliet Junior College*
Charles Zalonka, *Oklahoma State University*
George Zestos, *Christopher Newport University*

I also thank the reviewers of the previous editions:

Rebecca Abraham
Cinda J. Adams
Esmond Adams
John Adams
Bill Adamson
Carlos Aguilar
John R. Aidem
John W. Allen
Mohammed Akacem
E. G. Aksoy
M. C. Alderfer
John Allen
Ann Al-Yasiri
Charles Anderson
Leslie J. Anderson
Fatma W. Antar
Rebecca Arnold
Mohammad Ashraf
Ali A. Ataiifar
Aliakbar Ataiifar
Leonard Atencio
John M. Atkins
Glen W. Atkinson
Thomas R. Atkinson
James Q. Aylesworth
John Baffoe-Bonnie
Kevin Baird
Maurice B. Ballabon
Charley Ballard
G. Jeffrey Barbour
Robin L. Barlett
Daniel Barszcz
Kari Battaglia
Robert Becker
Charles Beem
Glen Beeson
Bruce W. Bellner
Daniel K. Benjamin
Emil Berendt
Charles Berry
Abraham Bertisch
John Bethune
R. A. Blewett
Scott Bloom
John Bockino
M. L. Bodnar
Mary Bone
Karl Bonnhi
Thomas W. Bonsor
John M. Booth
Wesley F. Booth
Thomas Borcherding
Melvin Borland
Tom Boston
Barry Boyer
Maryanna Boynton
Ronald Brandolini
Fenton L. Broadhead
Elba Brown
William Brown
Michael Bull
Maureen Burton
Conrad P. Caligaris
Kevin Carey
James Carlson
Robert Carlsson
Dancy R. Carr
Scott Carson
Doris Cash
Thomas H. Cate
Richard J. Cebula
Catherine Chambers
K. Merry Chambers
Richard Chapman
Ronald Cherry
Young Back Choi
Marc Chopin
Carol Cies
Joy L. Clark
Curtis Clarke
Gary Clayton
Marsha Clayton
Dale O. Cloninger
Warren L. Coats
Ed Coen
Pat Conroy
James Cox
Stephen R. Cox
Eleanor D. Craig
Peggy Crane
Jerry Crawford
Patrick M. Crowley
Joanna Cruse
John P. Cullity
Will Cummings
Thomas Curtis
Margaret M. Dalton
Andrew J. Dane
Mahmoud Davoudi
Diana Denison
Edward Dennis
Julia G. Derrick
Carol Dimamro
William Dougherty
Barry Duman
Diane Dumont
Floyd Durham
G. B. Duwaji
James A. Dyal
Ishita Edwards
Robert P. Edwards
Alan E. Ellis
Miuke Ellis
Steffany Ellis
Frank Emerson
Carl Enomoto
Zaki Eusufzai
Sandy Evans
John L. Ewing-Smith
Frank Falero
Frank Fato
Abdollah Ferdowsi
Grant Ferguson
Victoria L. Figiel
Mitchell Fisher
David Fletcher
James Foley
John Foreman
Diana Fortier
Ralph G. Fowler
Arthur Friedberg
Peter Frost
Timothy S. Fuerst
Tom Fullerton
E. Gabriel
James Gale
Byron Gangnes
Steve Gardner
Peter C. Garlick
Neil Garston
Alexander Garvin
Joe Garwood
Doug Gehrke
J. P. Gilbert
Otis Gilley
Frank Glesber
Jack Goddard
Michael G. Goode
Allen C. Goodman
Richard J. Gosselin
Paul Graf
Anthony J. Greco
Edward Greenberg
Gary Greene
Peter A. Groothuis
Philip J. Grossman
Nicholas Grunt
William Gunther
Kwabena Gyimah-Brempong
Demos Hadjiyanis
Martin D. Haney
Mehdi Haririan
Ray Harvey
Michael J. Haupert
E. L. Hazlett
Sanford B. Helman
William Henderson
Robert Herman
Gus W. Herring
Charles Hill
John M. Hill
Morton Hirsch
Benjamin Hitchner
Charles W. Hockert
R. Bradley Hoppes
James Horner
Grover Howard
Nancy Howe-Ford
Yu-Mong Hsiao
Yu Hsing
James Hubert
George Hughes
Joseph W. Hunt Jr.
Scott Hunt
John Ifediora
R. Jack Inch
Christopher Inya
Tomotaka Ishimine
E. E. Jarvis
Parvis Jenab
Allan Jenkins
John Jensel
Mark Jensen
S. D. Jevremovic
J. Paul Jewell
Nancy Jianakoplos
Frederick Johnson
David Jones
Lamar B. Jones
Paul A. Joray
Daniel A. Joseph
Craig Justice
M. James Kahiga
Septimus Kai Kai
Devajyoti Kataky
Timothy R. Keely
Ziad Keilany
Norman F. Keiser
Brian Kench
Randall G. Kesselring
Alan Kessler
E. D. Key
Saleem Khan
M. Barbara Killen
Bruce Kimzey
Terrence Kinal
Philip G. King
E. R. Kittrell
David Klingman
Charles Knapp
Jerry Knarr
Faik Koray
Janet Koscianski
Dennis Lee Kovach
Marie Kratochvil
Peter Kressler
Paul J. Kubik
Michael Kupilik

Margaret Landman
Larry Landrum
Richard LaNear
Keith Langford
Theresa Laughlin
Anthony T. Lee
Loren Lee
Bozena Leven
Donald Lien
George Lieu
Stephen E. Lile
Lawrence W. Lovick
Marty Ludlum
G. Dirk Mateer
Robert McAuliffe
James C. McBrearty
Howard J. McBride
Bruce McClung
John McDowell
E. S. McKuskey
James J. McLain
John L. Madden
Mary Lou Madden
John Marangos
Dan Marburger
Glen Marston
John M. Martin
Akbar Marvasti
Paul J. Mascotti
James D. Mason
Paul M. Mason
Tom Mathew
Warren Matthews
Warren T. Matthews
Pete Mavrokordatos
G. Hartley Mellish
Mike Melvin
Diego Mendez-Carbajo
Dan C. Messerschmidt
Michael Metzger
Herbert C. Milikien
Joel C. Millonzi
Glenn Milner
Daniel Mizak
Khan Mohabbat
Thomas Molloy
William H. Moon
Margaret D. Moore
William E. Morgan
Stephen Morrell
Irving Morrissett
James W. Moser
Thaddeaus Mounkurai
Martin F. Murray
Densel L. Myers
George L. Nagy
Solomon Namala
Ronald M. Nate
Jerome Neadly
James E. Needham
Claron Nelson
Douglas Nettleton
William Nook
Gerald T. O'Boyle
Greg Okoro
Richard E. O'Neill
Lucian T. Orlowski
Diane S. Osborne
Joan Osborne
Melissa A. Osborne
James O'Toole
Jan Palmer
Zuohong Pan
Gerald Parker
Ginger Parker
Randall E. Parker
Kenneth Parzych
Norm Paul
Wesley Payne
Raymond A. Pepin
Martin M. Perline
Timothy Perri
Jerry Petr
Maurice Pfannesteil
James Phillips
Raymond J. Phillips
I. James Pickl
Bruce Pietrykowski
Dennis Placone
Mannie Poen
William L. Polvent
Robert Posatko
Greg Pratt
Leila J. Pratt
Reneé Prim
Robert E. Pulsinelli
Rod D. Raehsler
Kambriz Raffiee
Sandra Rahman
Jaishankar Raman
John Rapp
Richard Rawlins
Gautam Raychaudhuri
Ron Reddall
Mitchell Redlo
Charles Reichhelu
Robert S. Rippey
Charles Roberts
Ray C. Roberts
Richard Romano
Judy Roobian-Mohr
Duane Rosa
Richard Rosenberg
Larry Ross
Barbara Ross-Pfeiffer
Philip Rothman
John Roufagalas
Stephen Rubb
Henry Ryder
Basel Saleh
Patricia Sanderson
Thomas N. Schaap
William A. Schaeffer
William Schamiel
David Schauer
A. C. Schlenker
David Schlow
Scott J. Schroeder
William Scott
Dan Segebarth
Paul Seidenstat
Swapan Sen
Augustus Shackelford
Richard Sherman Jr.
Liang-rong Shiau
David Shorow
Vishwa Shukla
R. J. Sidwell
David E. Sisk
Alden Smith
Garvin Smith
Howard F. Smith
Lynn A. Smith
Phil Smith
William Doyle Smith
Lee Spector
George Spiva
Richard L. Sprinkle
Alan Stafford
Amanda Stallings-Wood
Herbert F. Steeper
Diane L. Stehman
Columbus Stephens
William Stine
Allen D. Stone
Osman Suliman
J. M. Sullivan
Rebecca Summary
Joseph L. Swaffar
Thomas Swanke
Frank D. Taylor
Daniel Teferra
Lea Templer
Gary Theige
Dave Thiessen
Robert P. Thomas
Deborah Thorsen
Richard Trieff
George Troxler
William T. Trulove
William N. Trumbull
Arianne K. Turner
Kay Unger
Anthony Uremovic
John Vahaly
Jim Van Beek
David VanHoose
Lee J. Van Scyoc
Roy Van Til
Sharmila Vishwasrao
Craig Walker
Robert F. Wallace
Henry C. Wallich
Milledge Weathers
Ethel Weeks
Roger E. Wehr
Robert G. Welch
Terence West
James Wetzel
Wylie Whalthall
James H. Wheeler
Everett E. White
Michael D. White
Mark A. Wilkening
Raburn M. Williams
James Willis
George Wilson
Travis Wilson
Mark Wohar
Ken Woodward
Tim Wulf
Peter R. Wyman
Whitney Yamamura
Donald Yankovic
Alex Yguado
Paul Young
Shik Young
Mohammed Zaheer
Ed Zajicek
Sourushe Zandvakili
Paul Zarembka
George K. Zestos
William J. Zimmer Jr.

Revising *Economics Today* this time around was challenging, given that the changes in the economy within the United States and the world were so rapid. I was helped by my fantastic editorial team at Pearson. I was pushed hard by Noel Seibert, my editor. I was also dependent on Carolyn Terbush, the assistant editor on this project.

On the production side, I was again fortunate enough to have as my production supervisor Kathryn Dinovo. The designer, Jon Boylan, succeeded in creating a new look that still kept the traditional feel of this text. As always, I benefited from the years of experience of John Orr of Orr Book Services. I appreciate the copyediting and proofing services that Pat Lewis again provided. For this edition on the supplements side, Alison Eusden guaranteed revised error-free ancillaries. I would also like to thank Lori DeShazo and Kim Lovato for continued marketing efforts.

As you can imagine, more emphasis for each edition has been placed on online and other media materials. Melissa Honig and Susan Schoenberg worked overtime to make sure that MyEconLab was fully functional. I also was lucky to have the services of Noel Lotz who helped develop new content for MyEconLab.

This time around, Jim Lee of Texas A&M–Corpus Christi and Paul Graf of Indiana University–Bloomington authored the three Test Item Files. David VanHoose of Baylor University continued to create not only accurate but useful study guides. Similarly, Andrew J. Dane of Angelo State University has kept the *Instructor's Manual* in sync with the latest revisions, while Jim Lee of Texas A&M–Corpus Christi provided the PowerPoint presentations and Rick Pretzsch of Lonestar College–CyFair provided the Clicker PowerPoint slides.

Finally, there are two individuals I must thank for their work above and beyond the call of duty. The first is Professor Dan Benjamin of Clemson University, who continues to act as my "super reviewer" and "super proofreader." Finally, Sue Jasin, my longtime assistant, could probably teach a course in economics after all of the typing and retyping of various drafts.

I welcome comments and ideas from professors and students alike and hope you enjoy the new edition of *Economics Today.*

R. L. M.

Photo Credits

Cover images (in order, from top left): ©Shutterstock/Kiselev Andrey Valerevich; ©Shutterstock/TRINACRIA PHOTO; ©Shutterstock/Tyler Hartl; ©Shutterstock/Morgan Lane Photography; ©Shutterstock/imagestalk; ©Shutterstock/123stocks; ©Shutterstock/Wutthichai; ©Shutterstock/Nikolai Pozdeev; ©Shutterstock/Claude Beaubien

Chapter 1	Kiyoshi Ota/Bloomberg via Getty Images	1, 12
Chapter 2	Joe Belanger/Alamy	26, 42
Chapter 3	Adams Picture Library t/a ap/Alamy	48, 68
Chapter 4	Sajjad Hussain/AFP/Getty Images	74, 88
Chapter 5	Kimberly White/Reuters/Landov	98, 114
Chapter 6	Words and Meanings/Mark Sykes/Alamy	121, 134
Chapter 7	Mark Ralston/AFP/Getty Images	139, 155
Chapter 8	Zuma Wire World Photos/Newscom	161, 180
Chapter 9	Imaginechina via AP Photos	187, 204
Chapter 10	Kiyoshi Ota/Bloomberg via Getty Images	209, 222
Chapter 11	Teri Stratford	229, 245
Chapter 12	Jack Smith/Bloomberg via Getty Images	250, 270
Chapter 13	Scott J. Ferrell/Congressional Quarterly/Getty Images	277, 289
Chapter 14	Photodisc/Getty Images	298, 312
Chapter 15	Rick Wilking/Reuters/Corbis	317, 340
Chapter 16	Arne Dedert/EPA/Corbis	345, 363
Chapter 17	© Teri Stratford/Six-Cats Research Inc.	373, 392
Chapter 18	Image Source/Getty Images	397, 409
Chapter 19	Huntstock/Getty Images	415, 430
Chapter 20	Ed Bock/Getty Images	435, 448
Chapter 21	Radius Images/Getty Images	462, 477
Chapter 22	iStockphoto	483, 501
Chapter 23	Phil Schermeister/Corbis	507, 526
Chapter 24	JG Photography/Alamy	532, 548
Chapter 25	© Teri Stratford/Six-Cats Research Inc.	555, 568
Chapter 26	Karin Duthie/Alamy	573, 589
Chapter 27	Press Association via AP Photos	594, 612
Chapter 28	Evelyn Hockstein/The New York Times/Redux	618, 636
Chapter 29	Mario Laporta/AFP/Getty Images	642, 657
Chapter 30	Thomas M. Barwick/Getty Images	663, 682
Chapter 31	David Barnes/Getty Images	688, 699
Chapter 32	Kevin Lee/Bloomberg/Getty Images	705, 721
Chapter 33	Medioimages/Photodisc/Getty Images	726, 744

1 The Nature of Economics

Today, the U.S. government plays a much larger role in the nation's economy than it did before the Great Recession of the late 2000s. A prominent example is the level of government involvement in the nation's banking industry. Prior to the late 2000s, owners of private banks decided how much to pay the managers that they hired. Now government agencies overrule salary offers that bank owners extend to prospective managers and adjust the salaries of existing managers. The U.S. government has even become part owner of a number of U.S. banks. Thus, the U.S. government exercises considerably more direct control over financial companies than it did before the onset of the Great Recession. In this chapter, you will learn what greater government control means for decision making in the United States about what and how much to produce, how to organize production, and who obtains the items produced.

LEARNING OBJECTIVES

After reading this chapter, you should be able to:

- ▶ Discuss the difference between microeconomics and macroeconomics
- ▶ Evaluate the role that rational self-interest plays in economic analysis
- ▶ Explain why economics is a science
- ▶ Distinguish between positive and normative economics

myeconlab

MyEconLab helps you master each objective and study more efficiently. See end of chapter for details.

Did You Know That ?

the number of college students majoring in economics rose by more than 40 percent during the past decade? One reason that students opt for extensive study of economics is that they find the subject fascinating. Another reason, however, is self-interest. On average, students who major in economics earn 13 percent more than business management majors, 26 percent more than chemistry majors, and 50 percent more than psychology majors. Thus, students have a strong incentive to consider majoring in economics.

In this chapter, you will learn why contemplating the nature of self-interested responses to **incentives** is the starting point for analyzing choices people make in all walks of life. After all, how much time you devote to studying economics in this introductory course depends in part on the incentives established by your instructor's grading system. As you will see, self-interest and incentives are the underpinnings for all the decisions you and others around you make each day.

Incentives
Rewards for engaging in a particular activity.

The Power of Economic Analysis

Simply knowing that self-interest and incentives are central to any decision-making process is not sufficient for predicting the choices that people will actually make. You also have to develop a framework that will allow you to analyze solutions to each economic problem—whether you are trying to decide how much to study, which courses to take, whether to finish school, or whether the U.S. government should provide more grants to universities or raise taxes. The framework that you will learn in this text is the *economic way of thinking*.

This framework gives you power—the power to reach informed judgments about what is happening in the world. You can, of course, live your life without the power of economic analysis as part of your analytical framework. Indeed, most people do. But economists believe that economic analysis can help you make better decisions concerning your career, your education, financing your home, and other important matters. In the business world, the power of economic analysis can help you increase your competitive edge as an employee or as the owner of a business. As a voter, for the rest of your life you will be asked to make judgments about policies that are advocated by political parties. Many of these policies will deal with questions related to international economics, such as whether the U.S. government should encourage or discourage immigration, prevent foreign residents and firms from investing in port facilities or domestic banks, or restrict other countries from selling their goods here.

Finally, just as taking an art, music, or literature appreciation class increases the pleasure you receive when you view paintings, listen to concerts, or read novels, taking an economics course will increase your understanding and pleasure when watching the news on TV or reading articles in the newspaper or on the Internet.

Defining Economics

Economics
The study of how people allocate their limited resources to satisfy their unlimited wants.

Economics is part of the social sciences and, as such, seeks explanations of real events. All social sciences analyze human behavior, as opposed to the physical sciences, which generally analyze the behavior of electrons, atoms, and other nonhuman phenomena.

Economics is the study of how people allocate their limited resources in an attempt to satisfy their unlimited wants. As such, economics is the study of how people make choices.

Resources
Things used to produce goods and services to satisfy people's wants.

Wants
What people would buy if their incomes were unlimited.

To understand this definition fully, two other words need explaining: *resources* and *wants*. **Resources** are things that have value and, more specifically, are used to produce goods and services that satisfy people's wants. **Wants** are all of the items that people would purchase if they had unlimited income.

Whenever an individual, a business, or a nation faces alternatives, a choice must be made, and economics helps us study how those choices are made. For example, you have to choose how to spend your limited income. You also have to choose how to spend your limited time. You may have to choose how much of your company's limited funds to spend on advertising and how much to spend on new-product research. In economics, we examine situations in which individuals choose how to do things, when to do things, and with whom to do them. Ultimately, the purpose of economics is to explain choices.

Microeconomics versus Macroeconomics

Economics is typically divided into two types of analysis: **microeconomics** and **macroeconomics.**

Microeconomics
The study of decision making undertaken by individuals (or households) and by firms.

Macroeconomics
The study of the behavior of the economy as a whole, including such economywide phenomena as changes in unemployment, the general price level, and national income.

> ***Microeconomics is the part of economic analysis that studies decision making undertaken by individuals (or households) and by firms. It is like looking through a microscope to focus on the small parts of our economy.***

> ***Macroeconomics is the part of economic analysis that studies the behavior of the economy as a whole. It deals with economywide phenomena such as changes in unemployment, in the general price level, and in national income.***

Microeconomic analysis, for example, is concerned with the effects of changes in the price of gasoline relative to that of other energy sources. It examines the effects of new taxes on a specific product or industry. If price controls were reinstituted in the United States, how individual firms and consumers would react to them would be in the realm of microeconomics. The effects of higher wages brought about by an effective union strike would also be analyzed using the tools of microeconomics.

In contrast, issues such as the rate of inflation, the amount of economywide unemployment, and the yearly growth in the output of goods and services in the nation all fall into the realm of macroeconomic analysis. In other words, macroeconomics deals with **aggregates,** or totals—such as total output in an economy.

Aggregates
Total amounts or quantities; aggregate demand, for example, is total planned expenditures throughout a nation.

Be aware, however, of the blending of microeconomics and macroeconomics in modern economic theory. Modern economists are increasingly using microeconomic analysis—the study of decision making by individuals and by firms—as the basis of macroeconomic analysis. They do this because even though macroeconomic analysis focuses on aggregates, those aggregates are the result of choices made by individuals and firms.

The Three Basic Economic Questions and Two Opposing Answers

In every nation, three fundamental questions must be addressed irrespective of the form of its government or who heads that government, how rich or how poor the nation may be, or what type of **economic system**—the institutional mechanism through which resources are utilized to satisfy human wants—has been chosen. The three questions concern the problem of how to allocate society's scarce resources:

Economic system
A society's institutional mechanism for determining the way in which scarce resources are used to satisfy human desires.

1. *What and how much will be produced?* Some mechanism must exist for determining which items will be produced while others remain inventors' pipe dreams or individuals' unfulfilled desires.
2. *How will items be produced?* There are many ways to produce a desired item. It is possible to use more labor and less capital, or vice versa. It is possible, for instance, to produce an item with an aim to maximize the number of people employed. Alternatively, an item may be produced with an aim to minimize the

total expenses that members of society incur. Somehow, a decision must be made about the mix of resources used in production, the way in which they are organized, and how they are brought together at a particular location.

3. *For whom will items be produced?* Once an item is produced, who should be able to obtain it? People use scarce resources to produce any item, so people value access to that item. Thus, determining a mechanism for distributing produced items is a crucial issue for any society.

Now that you know the questions that an economic system must answer, how do current systems actually answer them?

Two Opposing Answers

At any point in time, every nation has its own economic system. How a nation goes about answering the three basic economic questions depends on that nation's economic system.

CENTRALIZED COMMAND AND CONTROL Throughout history, one common type of economic system has been *command and control* (also called *central planning*) by a centralized authority, such as a king or queen, a dictator, a central government, or some other type of authority that assumes responsibility for addressing fundamental economic issues. Under command and control, this authority decides what items to produce and how many, determines how the scarce resources will be organized in the items' production, and identifies who will be able to obtain the items.

For instance, in a command-and-control economic system, a government might decide that particular types of automobiles ought to be produced in certain numbers. The government might issue specific rules for how to marshal resources to produce these vehicles, or it might even establish ownership over those resources so that it can make all such resource allocation decisions directly. Finally, the government will then decide who will be authorized to purchase or otherwise utilize the vehicles.

THE PRICE SYSTEM The alternative to command and control is the *price system* (also called a *market system*), which is a shorthand term describing an economic system that answers the three basic economic questions via decentralized decision making. Under a pure price system, individuals and families own all of the scarce resources used in production. Consequently, choices about what and how many items to produce are left to private parties to determine on their own initiative, as are decisions about how to go about producing those items. Furthermore, individuals and families choose how to allocate their own incomes to obtain the produced items at prices established via privately organized mechanisms.

In the price system, which you will learn about in considerable detail in Chapters 3 and 4, prices define the terms under which people agree to make exchanges. Prices signal to everyone within a price system which resources are relatively scarce and which resources are relatively abundant. This *signaling* aspect of the price system provides information to individual buyers and sellers about what and how many items should be produced, how production of items should be organized, and who will choose to buy the produced items.

Thus, in a price system, individuals and families own the facilities used to produce automobiles. They decide which types of automobiles to produce, how many of them to produce, and how to bring scarce resources together within their facilities to generate the desired production. Other individuals and families decide how much of their earnings they wish to spend on automobiles.

MIXED ECONOMIC SYSTEMS By and large, the economic systems of the world's nations are *mixed* economic systems that incorporate aspects of both centralized command and control and a decentralized price system. At any given time, some nations lean toward centralized mechanisms of command and control and allow relatively little scope for decentralized decision making. At the same time, other nations limit the extent to which a central authority dictates answers to the three basic economic questions, leaving people mostly free to utilize a decentralized price system to generate their own answers.

A given country may reach different decisions at different times about how much to rely on command and control versus a price system to answer its three basic economic questions. Until 2008, for instance, the people of the United States preferred to rely mainly on a decentralized price system to decide which and how many automobiles to produce, how to marshal scarce resources to produce those vehicles, and how to decide who should obtain them. Today, the U.S. government is the majority owner of a large portion of the facilities used to manufacture automobiles and hence has considerable command-and-control authority over U.S. vehicle production.

The Economic Approach: Systematic Decisions

Economists assume that individuals act *as if* they systematically pursue self-motivated interests and respond predictably to perceived opportunities to attain those interests. This central insight of economics was first clearly articulated by Adam Smith in 1776. Smith wrote in his most famous book, *An Inquiry into the Nature and Causes of the Wealth of Nations*, that "it is not from the benevolence of the butcher, the brewer, or the baker that we expect our dinner, but from their regard to their own interest." Thus, the typical person about whom economists make behavioral predictions is assumed to act *as though* he or she systematically pursues self-motivated interest.

How has U.S. economic stagnation altered the marriage incentives of Indian women?

INTERNATIONAL EXAMPLE

Indian Men Living in the United States Become Ineligible Bachelors

At Web sites that help Indian men working in the United States find matrimonial matches back home in India, locating brides has become more difficult. In years past, many career-oriented Indian women were willing to marry Indian men employed by U.S. companies. Today, however, an increasing number of Indian women balk at this idea. In light of weak economic conditions in the United States, where the unemployment rate has recently exceeded 10 percent, these women worry that their prospective husbands' current jobs might disappear and that their own employment prospects might be poor. In contrast, Indian economic activity has been growing at an annual rate of nearly 8 percent, and jobs are plentiful. Thus, more Indian women are opting for married life in India instead.

FOR CRITICAL ANALYSIS

Why do you suppose that fewer young men from India are seeking U.S. employment?

The Rationality Assumption

The **rationality assumption** of economics, simply stated, is as follows:

Rationality assumption The assumption that people do not intentionally make decisions that would leave them worse off.

> ***We assume that individuals do not intentionally make decisions that would leave themselves worse off.***

The distinction here is between what people may think—the realm of psychology and psychiatry and perhaps sociology—and what they do. Economics does *not* involve itself in analyzing individual or group thought processes. Economics looks at what people actually do in life with their limited resources. It does little good to criticize the rationality assumption by stating, "Nobody thinks that way" or "I never think that way" or "How unrealistic! That's as irrational as anyone can get!" In a world in which people can be atypical in countless ways, economists find it useful to concentrate on discovering the baseline. Knowing what happens on average is a good place to start. In this way, we avoid building our thinking on exceptions rather than on reality.

Take the example of driving. When you consider passing another car on a two-lane highway with oncoming traffic, you have to make very quick decisions: You must estimate the speed of the car that you are going to pass, the speed of the oncoming cars, the distance between your car and the oncoming cars, and your car's potential rate of acceleration. If we were to apply a model to your behavior, we would use the rules of calculus. In actual fact, you and most other drivers in such a situation do not actually think of using the rules of calculus, but to predict your behavior, we could make the prediction *as if* you understood those rules.

Responding to Incentives

If it can be assumed that individuals never intentionally make decisions that would leave them worse off, then almost by definition they will respond to changes in incentives. Indeed, much of human behavior can be explained in terms of how individuals respond to changing incentives over time.

Schoolchildren are motivated to do better by a variety of incentive systems, ranging from gold stars and certificates of achievement when they are young, to better grades with accompanying promises of a "better life" as they get older. Of course, negative incentives affect our behavior, too. Penalties, punishments, and other forms of negative incentives can raise the cost of engaging in various activities.

How have U.S. state and federal governments given people who do not play golf a positive incentive to buy golf carts?

You Are There

To contemplate why the location that a producer chooses for filming a movie can depend on incentives offered by governments, take a look at **A Movie Producer Responds to Incentives,** on page 11.

POLICY EXAMPLE **The Government Gives Everyone an Incentive to Own a Golf Cart**

Both the U.S. government and a number of state governments offer tax credits to people who buy electric vehicles, including road-ready golf carts. Many people have discovered that these tax credits are sufficient to fund more than two-thirds of the purchase price of a qualifying golf cart. Dealers of golf carts have been quick to use the tax credits as a key selling point. One Florida dealer offers to lease back a road-worthy golf cart from a buyer at $100 per month—so that the dealer can rent the cart at a higher rate to people who will actually use it—and then buy the cart back after 27 months at a price of $2,000. Thus, as the dealer's banner ad declares, the buyer of a golf cart qualifying for the government's tax credit can either "GET A FREE GOLF CART, or make $2,000 doing absolutely nothing!!" In Florida and many other states, golf cart sales have soared.

FOR CRITICAL ANALYSIS

Why do you suppose that many people who previously purchased non-road-worthy golf carts to drive on golf courses now drive road-worthy golf carts instead?

Defining Self-Interest

Self-interest does not always mean increasing one's wealth measured in dollars and cents. We assume that individuals seek many goals, not just increased wealth measured in monetary terms. Thus, the self-interest part of our economic-person assumption includes goals relating to prestige, friendship, love, power, helping others, creating works of art, and many other matters. We can also think in terms of enlightened self-interest, whereby individuals, in the pursuit of what makes them better off, also achieve the betterment of others around them. In brief, individuals are assumed to want the ability to further their goals by making decisions about how things around them are used. The head of a charitable organization usually will not turn down an additional contribution, because accepting the funds yields control over how they are used, even though it is for other people's benefit.

Thus, self-interest does not rule out doing charitable acts. Giving gifts to relatives can be considered a form of charity that is nonetheless in the self-interest of the giver. But how efficient is such gift giving?

EXAMPLE **The Perceived Value of Gifts**

Every holiday season, aunts, uncles, grandparents, mothers, and fathers give gifts to their college-aged loved ones. Joel Waldfogel, an economist at the University of Pennsylvania, has surveyed several thousand college students after Christmas to find out the value of holiday gifts. He finds that recorded music and outerwear (coats and jackets) have a perceived intrinsic value about equal to their actual cash equivalent. By the time he gets down the list to socks, underwear, and cosmetics, the students' valuation is only about 82 percent of the cash value of the gift. He find that aunts, uncles, and grandparents give the "worst" gifts and friends, siblings, and parents give the "best."

FOR CRITICAL ANALYSIS

What argument could you use against the idea of substituting cash or gift cards for physical gifts?

QUICK QUIZ See page 16 for the answers. Review concepts from this section in MyEconLab.

Economics is a social science that involves the study of how individuals choose among alternatives to satisfy their __________, which are what people would buy if their incomes were __________.

__________, the study of the decision-making processes of individuals (or households) and firms, and __________, the study of the performance of the economy as a whole, are the two main branches into which the study of economics is divided.

The three basic economic questions ask what and how much will be produced, how will items be produced, and for whom will items be produced. The two opposing answers are provided by the type of economic system: either __________ __________ __________ __________ or the __________ __________.

In economics, we assume that people do not intentionally make decisions that will leave them worse off. This is known as the __________ assumption.

Economics as a Science

Economics is a social science that employs the same kinds of methods used in other sciences, such as biology, physics, and chemistry. Like these other sciences, economics uses models, or theories. Economic **models,** or **theories,** are simplified representations of the real world that we use to help us understand, explain, and predict economic phenomena in the real world. There are, of course, differences between sciences. The social sciences—especially economics—make little use of laboratory experiments in which changes in variables are studied under controlled conditions. Rather, social scientists, and especially economists, usually have to test their models, or theories, by examining what has already happened in the real world.

Models, or **theories** Simplified representations of the real world used as the basis for predictions or explanations.

Models and Realism

At the outset it must be emphasized that no model in *any* science, and therefore no economic model, is complete in the sense that it captures *every* detail or interrelationship that exists. Indeed, a model, by definition, is an abstraction from reality. It is conceptually impossible to construct a perfectly complete realistic model. For example, in physics we cannot account for every molecule and its position and certainly not for every atom and subatomic particle. Not only is such a model impossibly expensive to build, but working with it would be impossibly complex.

The nature of scientific model building is that the model should capture only the *essential* relationships that are sufficient to analyze the particular problem or answer the particular question with which we are concerned. *An economic model cannot be faulted as unrealistic simply because it does not represent every detail of the real world.* A map of a city that shows only major streets is not faulty if, in fact, all you need to know is how to pass through the city using major streets. As long as a model is able to shed light on the *central* issue at hand or forces at work, it may be useful.

A map is the quintessential model. It is always a simplified representation. It is always unrealistic. But it is also useful in making predictions about the world. If the model—the map—predicts that when you take Campus Avenue to the north, you always run into the campus, that is a prediction. If a simple model can explain observed behavior in repeated settings just as well as a complex model, the simple model has some value and is probably easier to use.

Assumptions

Every model, or theory, must be based on a set of assumptions. Assumptions define the array of circumstances in which our model is most likely to be applicable. When some people predicted that sailing ships would fall off the edge of the earth, they used the *assumption* that the earth was flat. Columbus did not accept the implications of such a model because he did not accept its assumptions. He assumed that the world was round. The real-world test of his own model refuted the flat-earth model. Indirectly, then, it was a test of the assumption of the flat-earth model.

Is it possible to use our knowledge about assumptions to understand why driving directions sometimes contain very few details?

EXAMPLE Getting Directions

Assumptions are a shorthand for reality. Imagine that you have decided to drive from your home in San Diego to downtown San Francisco. Because you have never driven this route, you decide to use a travel-planner device such as global-positioning-system equipment.

When you ask for directions, the electronic travel planner could give you a set of detailed maps that shows each city through which you will travel—Oceanside, San Clemente, Irvine, Anaheim, Los Angeles, Bakersfield, Modesto, and so on—and then, opening each map, show you exactly how the freeway threads through each of these cities. You would get a nearly complete description of reality because the GPS travel planner will not have used many simplifying assumptions. It is more likely, however, that the travel planner will simply say, "Get on Interstate 5 going north. Stay on it for about 500 miles. Follow the signs for San Francisco. After crossing the toll bridge, take any exit marked 'Downtown.'" By omitting all of the trivial details, the travel planner has told you all that you really need and want to know. The models you will be using in this text are similar to the simplified directions on how to drive from San Diego to San Francisco—they focus on what is relevant to the problem at hand and omit what is not.

FOR CRITICAL ANALYSIS

In what way do small talk and gossip represent the use of simplifying assumptions?

***Ceteris paribus* [KAY-ter-us PEAR-uh-bus] assumption**
The assumption that nothing changes except the factor or factors being studied.

THE *CETERIS PARIBUS* ASSUMPTION: ALL OTHER THINGS BEING EQUAL Everything in the world seems to relate in some way to everything else in the world. It would be impossible to isolate the effects of changes in one variable on another variable if we always had to worry about the many other variables that might also enter the analysis. Similar to other sciences, economics uses the ***ceteris paribus* assumption.** *Ceteris paribus* means "other things constant" or "other things equal."

Consider an example taken from economics. One of the most important determinants of how much of a particular product a family buys is how expensive that product is relative to other products. We know that in addition to relative prices, other factors influence decisions about making purchases. Some of them have to do with income, others with tastes, and yet others with custom and religious beliefs. Whatever these other factors are, we hold them constant when we look at the relationship between changes in prices and changes in how much of a given product people will purchase.

Deciding on the Usefulness of a Model

We generally do not attempt to determine the usefulness, or "goodness," of a model merely by evaluating how realistic its assumptions are. Rather, we consider a model "good" if it yields usable predictions that are supported by real-world observations. In other words, can we use the model to predict what will happen in the world around us? Does the model provide useful implications about how things happen in our world?

Once we have determined that the model does predict real-world phenomena, the scientific approach to the analysis of the world around us requires that we consider evidence. Evidence is used to test the usefulness of a model. This is why we call economics

Why Not . . . try to increase blood donations by offering small payments to donors?

Donating blood is a time-consuming, often tiring, and sometimes even painful activity that provides scarce, life-saving human plasma. To try to encourage more people to give blood, some governments now provide small financial payments to blood donors. Empirical studies by economists, however, suggest that many people make fewer charitable contributions when others know that the donors are rewarded for their contributions. Most individuals who make charitable donations derive satisfaction from the fact that others see them sacrifice to do a good deed, such as giving blood. When some people who previously had regularly donated blood learn that they will receive small financial payments for their blood, they presume that others seeing them offer their blood will assume that they are "greedily" selling it. As a consequence, they become less likely to respond to blood drives, even though they now could receive a payment for doing so.

an **empirical** science. *Empirical* means that evidence (data) is looked at to see whether we are right. Economists are often engaged in empirically testing their models.

Empirical
Relying on real-world data in evaluating the usefulness of a model.

Models of Behavior, Not Thought Processes

Take special note of the fact that economists' models do not relate to the way people *think*. Economic models relate to the way people *act*, to what they do in life with their limited resources. Normally, the economist does not attempt to predict how people will think about a particular topic, such as a higher price of oil products, accelerated inflation, or higher taxes. Rather, the task at hand is to predict how people will behave, which may be quite different from what they *say* they will do (much to the consternation of poll takers and market researchers). Thus, people's *declared* preferences are generally of little use in testing economic theories, which aim to explain and predict people's *revealed* preferences. The people involved in examining thought processes are psychologists and psychiatrists, not typically economists.

Behavioral Economics and Bounded Rationality

In recent years, some economists have proposed paying more attention to psychologists and psychiatrists. They have suggested an alternative approach to economic analysis. Their approach, which is known as **behavioral economics,** examines consumer behavior in the face of psychological limitations and complications that may interfere with rational decision making.

Behavioral economics
An approach to the study of consumer behavior that emphasizes psychological limitations and complications that potentially interfere with rational decision making.

BOUNDED RATIONALITY Proponents of behavioral economics suggest that traditional economic models assume that people exhibit three "unrealistic" characteristics:

1. *Unbounded selfishness*. People are interested only in their own satisfaction.
2. *Unbounded willpower*. Their choices are always consistent with their long-term goals.
3. *Unbounded rationality*. They are able to consider every relevant choice.

Instead, advocates of behavioral economics have proposed replacing the rationality assumption with the assumption of **bounded rationality,** which assumes that people cannot examine and think through every possible choice they confront. As a consequence, behavioral economists suggest, people cannot always pursue their best long-term personal interests. From time to time, they must also rely on other people and take into account other people's interests as well as their own.

Bounded rationality
The hypothesis that people are *nearly,* but not fully, rational, so that they cannot examine every possible choice available to them but instead use simple rules of thumb to sort among the alternatives that happen to occur to them.

RULES OF THUMB A key behavioral implication of the bounded rationality assumption is that people should use so-called *rules of thumb:* Because every possible choice cannot be considered, an individual will tend to fall back on methods of making decisions that are simpler than trying to sort through every possibility.

A problem confronting advocates of behavioral economics is that people who *appear* to use rules of thumb may in fact behave *as if* they are fully rational. For instance, if a person faces persistently predictable ranges of choices for a time, the individual may rationally settle into repetitive behaviors that an outside observer might conclude to be consistent with a rule of thumb. The bounded rationality assumption indicates that the person should continue to rely on a rule of thumb even if there is a major change in the environment that the individual faces. Time and time again, however, economists find that people respond to altered circumstances by fundamentally changing their behaviors. Economists also generally observe that people make decisions that are consistent with their own self-interest and long-term objectives.

BEHAVIORAL ECONOMICS: A WORK IN PROGRESS It remains to be seen whether the application of the assumption of bounded rationality proposed by behavioral economists will truly alter the manner in which economists construct models intended to better predict human decision making. So far, proponents of behavioral economics have not conclusively demonstrated that paying closer attention to psychological thought processes can improve economic predictions.

As a consequence, the bulk of economic analysis continues to rely on the rationality assumption as the basis for constructing economic models. As you will learn in Chapter 20, advocates of behavioral economics continue to explore ways in which psychological elements might improve analysis of decision making by individual consumers.

Positive versus Normative Economics

Economics uses *positive analysis,* a value-free approach to inquiry. No subjective or moral judgments enter into the analysis. Positive analysis relates to statements such as "If A, then B." For example, "If the price of gasoline goes up relative to all other prices, then the amount of it that people buy will fall." That is a positive economic statement. It is a statement of *what is*. It is not a statement of anyone's value judgment or subjective feelings.

Distinguishing Between Positive and Normative Economics

For many problems analyzed in the "hard" sciences such as physics and chemistry, the analyses are considered to be virtually value-free. After all, how can someone's values enter into a theory of molecular behavior? But economists face a different problem. They deal with the behavior of individuals, not molecules. That makes it more difficult to stick to what we consider to be value-free or **positive economics** without reference to our feelings.

Positive economics
Analysis that is *strictly* limited to making either purely descriptive statements or scientific predictions; for example, "If A, then B." A statement of *what is*.

Normative economics
Analysis involving value judgments about economic policies; relates to whether outcomes are good or bad. A statement of *what ought to be*.

When our values are interjected into the analysis, we enter the realm of **normative economics,** involving *normative analysis*. A positive economic statement is "If the price of gas rises, people will buy less." If we add to that analysis the statement "so we should not allow the price to go up," we have entered the realm of normative economics—we have expressed a value judgment. In fact, any time you see the word *should*, you will know that values are entering into the discussion. Just remember that positive statements are concerned with *what is*, whereas normative statements are concerned with *what ought to be*.

Each of us has a desire for different things. That means that we have different values. When we express a value judgment, we are simply saying what we prefer, like, or desire. Because individual values are diverse, we expect—and indeed observe—that people express widely varying value judgments about how the world ought to be.

A Warning: Recognize Normative Analysis

It is easy to define positive economics. It is quite another matter to catch all unlabeled normative statements in a textbook, even though an author goes over the manuscript many times before it is printed. Therefore, do not get the impression that a textbook author will be able to keep all personal values out of the book. They will slip through. In fact, the very choice of which topics to include in an introductory textbook involves normative economics. There is no value-free way to decide which topics to use in a textbook. The author's values ultimately make a difference when choices have to be made. But from your own standpoint, you might want to be able to recognize when you are engaging in normative as opposed to positive economic analysis. Reading this text will help equip you for that task.

QUICK QUIZ See page 16 for the answers. Review concepts from this section in MyEconLab.

A ________, or ________, uses assumptions and is by nature a simplification of the real world. The usefulness of a ________ can be evaluated by bringing empirical evidence to bear on its predictions.

Most models use the ________ ________ assumption that all other things are held constant, or equal.

________ economics emphasizes psychological constraints and complexities that potentially interfere with rational decision making. This approach utilizes the ________ ________ hypothesis that people are not quite rational, because they cannot study every possible alternative but instead use simple rules of thumb to decide among choices.

________ economics is value-free and relates to statements that can be refuted, such as "If A, then B." ________ economics involves people's values and typically uses the word *should*.

You Are There

A Movie Producer Responds to Incentives

Initially, movie producer Ingo Vollkammer planned to film the action movie *Velocity,* starring Halle Berry, in North America. Then he found that by filming in Madrid, he could obtain several million dollars in subsidies from the Spanish government. Before screenwriters could finish rewriting scenes to be set in Madrid, however, the German government told Vollkammer that if he shot *Velocity* in Berlin, Germany would cover more than $10 million of the film's $25 million production cost. Soon thereafter, the euro's value rose sharply, which raised the dollar-denominated cost of filming in Berlin sufficiently to offset the German subsidies offered.

Vollkammer has responded to this additional change in his incentives by negotiating a new arrangement with the German government. By agreeing to hire a German director and production crew, he has retained most of the German government's financial assistance. Vollkammer has also put screenwriters back to work returning the climactic scenes to North America. By adjusting his script and personnel in response to altered incentives, Vollkammer has reduced the total cost of making the movie to just $15 million.

Critical Analysis Questions

1. What do you suppose was the Spanish government's incentive to offer to subsidize the filming of *Velocity* in Madrid?
2. Why do changes in currency exchange rates affect incentives for U.S. firms to do business with residents of other nations?

ISSUES & APPLICATIONS

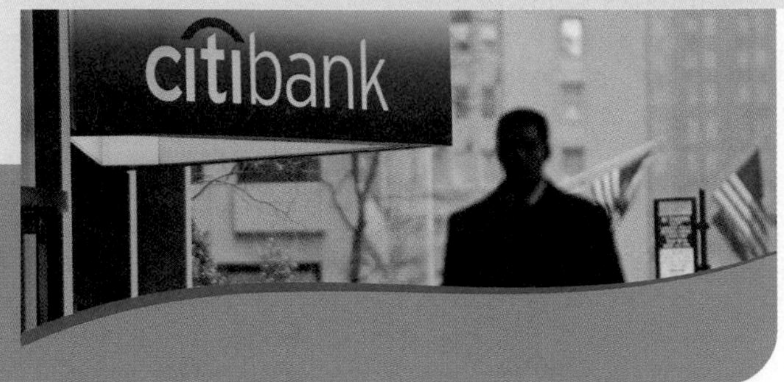

In Many U.S. Industries, Command and Control Rules

CONCEPTS APPLIED

- Economic Systems
- Price System
- Command and Control

Before the late 2000s, the U.S. economic system was mixed but primarily relied on the price system. Recently, in contrast, the U.S. government has opted for more command and control. The expansion of a command-and-control approach began with the U.S. banking system in 2008. Since then, this approach has spread to a number of U.S. industries and ultimately may spread to others.

Command, Control, and the U.S. Banking Industry

In 2008, the U.S. government decided to require a number of U.S. banks to accept taxpayer-funded purchases of ownership shares in those banks. Figure 1-1 below shows the banks at which the government expended the largest amounts for this purpose.

Since then, several banks, such as JPMorgan Chase and Bank of America, have bought back the government's shares. Nevertheless, the government likely will remain the single largest shareholder at Citigroup and a handful of other banks indefinitely. Furthermore, the government has granted itself veto power over management decisions at every bank in the United States. In particular, government agencies oversee the process by which salaries of bank managers are determined. If a bank's owners try to hire a top manager by offering a salary that the bank's regulating agency deems "too high," the agency can void the agreement.

FIGURE 1-1 Banks Receiving the Largest Amounts of U.S. Government Funding

In the late 2000s, the U.S. government purchased billions of dollars of stocks and bonds issued by many banking institutions.

Source: U.S. Treasury Department.

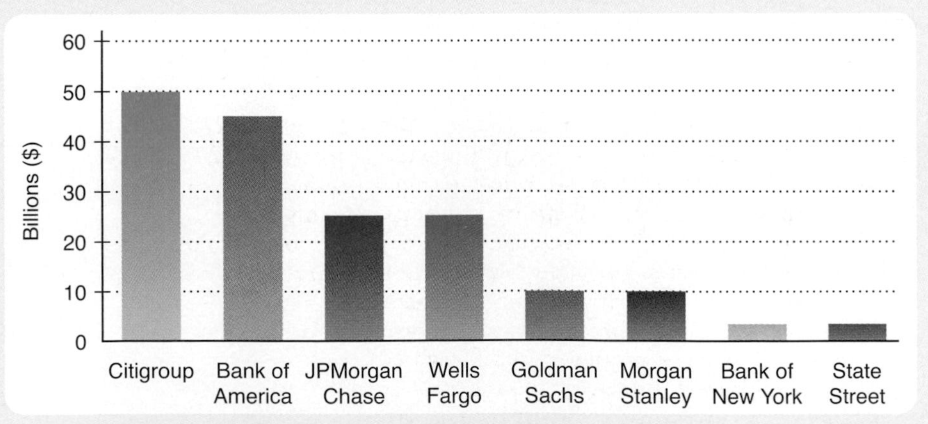

Command and Control Spreads Across U.S. Industries

In the spring of 2009, the government expanded its powers after a sharp decline in auto sales pushed General Motors and Chrysler into bankruptcy. The government assumed control of both firms at a taxpayer cost exceeding $70 billion. A "czar" appointed by President Obama began to oversee operations at the two firms. In addition, Congress dictated where the companies could open new plants, which old plants could be closed, and which auto dealerships the firms could retain. Congress also began discussing what types of vehicles the companies would be permitted to build.

By 2010, the health care industry was also the target of command-and-control policies. After much debate, Congress ultimately passed legislation establishing government authority over the process by which every U.S. resident obtains health care. Congress gave the secretary of health and human services the power to determine what types of care could and could not be consumed by U.S. residents.

Will government command and control replace the U.S. price system? A complete replacement seems unlikely. Nevertheless, congressional expansions of economywide government regulations increasingly have empowered government agencies to decide what and how much to produce, how to produce, and for whom to produce.

For Critical Analysis

1. How does the fact that individuals' decisions under a price system are oriented toward their own self-interest affect the price system's answers to the three basic economic questions?
2. How does the fact that a government's decisions under a command-and-control system are heavily influenced by political considerations affect its answers to the three basic economic questions?

Web Resources

1. Learn about the U.S. government's recent regulations of private firms' management compensation at www.econtoday.com/ch01.
2. For a timeline of the history of General Motors and of its emergence as a government-directed company, go to www.econtoday.com/ch01.

Research Project

Make a list of all of the U.S. government agencies you can think of that regulate U.S. industries. Can you think of reasons why the government might have created these agencies to oversee U.S. companies instead of allowing the companies' decisions to be governed solely by the self-interest of the firms' owners? Explain briefly.

For more questions on this chapter's Issues & Applications, go to **MyEconLab**. In the Study Plan for this chapter, select Section N: News.

Here is what you should know after reading this chapter. **MyEconLab** will help you identify what you know, and where to go when you need to practice.

WHAT YOU SHOULD KNOW		WHERE TO GO TO PRACTICE
Answering the Three Basic Economic Questions Economics is the study of how individuals make choices to satisfy wants. Microeconomics is the study of decision making by individual households and firms, and macroeconomics is the study of nationwide phenomena such as inflation and unemployment. The three basic economic questions ask what and how much will be produced, how will items be produced, and for whom will items be produced. The two opposing answers to these questions are provided by the type of economic system: either centralized command and control or the price system.	incentives, 2 economics, 2 resources, 2 wants, 2 microeconomics, 3 macroeconomics, 3 aggregates, 3 economic system, 3	• **MyEconLab** Study Plans 1.1, 1.2, 1.3 • Audio introduction to Chapter 1 • Video: The Difference Between Microeconomics and Macroeconomics

(*continued*)

MyEconLab continued

WHAT YOU SHOULD KNOW		WHERE TO GO TO PRACTICE
Self-Interest in Economic Analysis Rational self-interest is the assumption that people never intentionally make decisions that would leave them worse off. Instead, they are motivated mainly by their self-interest, which can relate to monetary and nonmonetary goals, such as love, prestige, and helping others.	rationality assumption, 5	• **MyEconLab** Study Plan 1.3 • Video: The Economic Person: Rational Self-Interest • ABC News Video: The Economics of Higher Education
Economics as a Science Economic models, or theories, are simplified representations of the real world. Economic models are never completely realistic because by definition they are simplifications using assumptions that are not directly testable. Nevertheless, economists can subject the predictions of economic theories to empirical tests in which real-world data are used to decide whether or not to reject the predictions.	models, or theories, 7 *ceteris paribus* assumption, 8 empirical, 9 behavioral economics, 9 bounded rationality, 9	• **MyEconLab** Study Plan 1.5 • ABC News Video: Coca-Cola in India
Positive and Normative Economics Positive economics deals with *what is*, whereas normative economics deals with *what ought to be*. Positive economic statements are of the "if . . . then" variety; they are descriptive and predictive. In contrast, statements embodying values are within the realm of normative economics, or how people think things ought to be.	positive economics, 10 normative economics, 10	• **MyEconLab** Study Plan 1.6 • Video: Difference Between Normative and Positive Economics

Log in to MyEconLab, take a chapter test, and get a personalized Study Plan that tells you which concepts you understand and which ones you need to review. From there, MyEconLab will give you further practice, tutorials, animations, videos, and guided solutions.
Log in to www.myeconlab.com

PROBLEMS

All problems are assignable in myeconlab. *Answers to odd-numbered problems appear at the back of the book.*

1-1. Define economics. Explain briefly how the economic way of thinking—in terms of rational, self-interested people responding to incentives—relates to each of the following situations.

a. A student deciding whether to purchase a textbook for a particular class

b. Government officials seeking more funding for mass transit through higher taxes

c. A municipality taxing hotel guests to obtain funding for a new sports stadium

1-2. Some people claim that the "economic way of thinking" does not apply to issues such as health care. Explain how economics does apply to this issue by developing a "model" of an individual's choices.

1-3. Does the phrase "unlimited wants and limited resources" apply to both a low-income household and a middle-income household? Can the same phrase be applied to a very high-income household?

1-4. In a single sentence, contrast microeconomics and macroeconomics. Next, categorize each of the following issues as either a microeconomic issue, a macroeconomic issue, or not an economic issue.

a. The national unemployment rate

b. The decision of a worker to work overtime or not

c. A family's choice to have a baby

d. The rate of growth of the money supply

e. The national government's budget deficit

f. A student's allocation of study time across two subjects

1-5. One of your classmates, Sally, is a hardworking student, serious about her classes, and conscientious about her grades. Sally is also involved, however, in volunteer activities and an extracurricular sport. Is Sally displaying rational behavior? Based on what you read in this chapter, construct an argument supporting the conclusion that she is.

1-6. Recently, a bank was trying to decide what fee to charge for "expedited payments"—payments that the bank would transmit extra-speedily to enable customers to avoid late fees on cable TV bills, electric bills, and the like. To try to determine what fee customers were willing to pay for expedited payments, the bank conducted a survey. It was able to determine that many of the people surveyed already paid fees for expedited payment services that *exceeded* the maximum fees that they said they were willing to pay. How does the bank's finding relate to economists' traditional focus on what people do, rather than what they *say* they will do?

1-7. Explain, in your own words, the rationality assumption, and contrast it with the assumption of bounded rationality proposed by adherents of behavioral economics.

1-8. Why does the assumption of bounded rationality suggest that people might use rules of thumb to guide their decision making instead of considering every possible choice available to them?

1-9. Under what circumstances might people appear to use rules of thumb, as suggested by the assumption of bounded rationality, even though they really were behaving in a manner suggested by the rationality assumption?

1-10. Which of the following predictions appear(s) to follow from a model based on the assumption that rational, self-interested individuals respond to incentives?

a. For every 10 exam points Myrna must earn in order to pass her economics course and meet her graduation requirements, she will study one additional hour for her economics test next week.

b. A coin toss will best predict Leonardo's decision about whether to purchase an expensive business suit or an inexpensive casual outfit to wear next week when he interviews for a high-paying job he is seeking.

c. Celeste, who uses earnings from her regularly scheduled hours of part-time work to pay for her room and board at college, will decide to buy a newly released DVD this week only if she is able to work two additional hours.

1-11. Consider two models for estimating, in advance of an election, the shares of votes that will go to rival candidates. According to one model, pollsters' surveys of a randomly chosen set of registered voters before an election can be used to forecast the percentage of votes that each candidate will receive. This first model relies on the assumption that unpaid survey respondents will give truthful responses about how they will vote and that they will actually cast a ballot in the election. The other model uses prices of financial assets (legally binding IOUs) issued by the Iowa Electronic Markets, operated by the University of Iowa, to predict electoral outcomes. The final payments received by owners of these assets, which can be bought or sold during the weeks and days preceding an election, depend on the shares of votes the candidates actually end up receiving. This second model assumes that owners of these assets wish to earn the highest possible returns, and it indicates that the market prices of these assets provide an indication of the percentage of votes that each candidate will actually receive on the day of the election.

a. Which of these two models for forecasting electoral results is more firmly based on the rationality assumption of economics?

b. How would an economist evaluate which is the better model for forecasting electoral outcomes?

1-12. Write a sentence contrasting positive and normative economic analysis.

1-13. Based on your answer to Problem 1–12, categorize each of the following conclusions as being the result of positive analysis or normative analysis.

a. A higher minimum wage will reduce employment opportunities for minimum wage workers.

b. Increasing the earnings of minimum wage employees is desirable, and raising the minimum wage is the best way to accomplish this.

c. Everyone should enjoy open access to health care at no explicit charge.

d. Heath care subsidies will increase the consumption of health care.

1-14. Consider the following statements, based on a positive economic analysis that assumes that all other things remain constant. For each, list one other thing that might change and thus offset the outcome stated.

a. Increased demand for laptop computers will drive up their price.

b. Falling gasoline prices will result in additional vacation travel.

c. A reduction of income tax rates will result in more people working.

ECONOMICS ON THE NET

The Usefulness of Studying Economics This application helps you see how accomplished people benefited from their study of economics. It also explores ways in which these people feel others of all walks of life can gain from learning more about the economics field.

Title: How Taking an Economics Course Can Lead to Becoming an Economist

Navigation: Go to **www.econtoday.com/ch01** to visit the Federal Reserve Bank of Minneapolis publication, *The Region*. Select the last article of the issue, "Economists in *The Region* on Their Student Experiences and the Need for Economic Literacy."

Application Read the interviews of the six economists, and answer the following questions.

1. Based on your reading, which economists do you think other economists regard as influential? What educational institutions do you think are the most influential in economics?
2. Which economists do you think were attracted to microeconomics and which to macroeconomics?

For Group Study and Analysis Divide the class into three groups, and assign the groups the Blinder, Yellen, and Rivlin interviews. Have each group use the content of its assigned interview to develop a statement explaining why the study of economics is important, regardless of a student's chosen major.

ANSWERS TO QUICK QUIZZES

p. 7: (i) wants . . . unlimited; (ii) Microeconomics . . . macroeconomics; (iii) centralized command and control . . . price system; (iv) rationality

p. 11: (i) model . . . theory . . . model; (ii) *ceteris paribus;* (iii) Behavioral . . . bounded rationality; (iv) Positive . . . Normative

Reading and Working with Graphs

APPENDIX A

A graph is a visual representation of the relationship between variables. In this appendix, we'll deal with just two variables: an **independent variable,** which can change in value freely, and a **dependent variable,** which changes only as a result of changes in the value of the independent variable. For example, even if nothing else is changing in your life, your weight depends on your intake of calories. The independent variable is caloric intake, and the dependent variable is weight.

Independent variable
A variable whose value is determined independently of, or outside, the equation under study.

Dependent variable
A variable whose value changes according to changes in the value of one or more independent variables.

A table is a list of numerical values showing the relationship between two (or more) variables. Any table can be converted into a graph, which is a visual representation of that list. Once you understand how a table can be converted to a graph, you will understand what graphs are and how to construct and use them.

Consider a practical example. A conservationist may try to convince you that driving at lower highway speeds will help you conserve gas. Table A-1 shows the relationship between speed—the independent variable—and the distance you can go on a gallon of gas at that speed—the dependent variable. This table does show a pattern. As the data in the first column get larger in value, the data in the second column get smaller.

TABLE A-1

Gas Mileage as a Function of Driving Speed

Miles per Hour	Miles per Gallon
45	25
50	24
55	23
60	21
65	19
70	16
75	13

Now let's take a look at the different ways in which variables can be related.

Direct and Inverse Relationships

Two variables can be related in different ways, some simple, others more complex. For example, a person's weight and height are often related. If we measured the height and weight of thousands of people, we would surely find that taller people tend to weigh more than shorter people. That is, we would discover that there is a **direct relationship** between height and weight. By this we simply mean that an *increase* in one variable is usually associated with an *increase* in the related variable. This can easily be seen in panel (a) of Figure A-1 below.

Let's look at another simple way in which two variables can be related. Much evidence indicates that as the price of a specific commodity rises, the amount purchased decreases—there is an **inverse relationship** between the variable's price per unit and quantity purchased. Such a relationship indicates that for higher and higher prices, smaller and smaller quantities will be purchased. We see this relationship in panel (b) of Figure A-1.

Direct relationship
A relationship between two variables that is positive, meaning that an increase in one variable is associated with an increase in the other and a decrease in one variable is associated with a decrease in the other.

Inverse relationship
A relationship between two variables that is negative, meaning that an increase in one variable is associated with a decrease in the other and a decrease in one variable is associated with an increase in the other.

Constructing a Graph

Let us now examine how to construct a graph to illustrate a relationship between two variables.

FIGURE A-1 **Direct and Inverse Relationships**

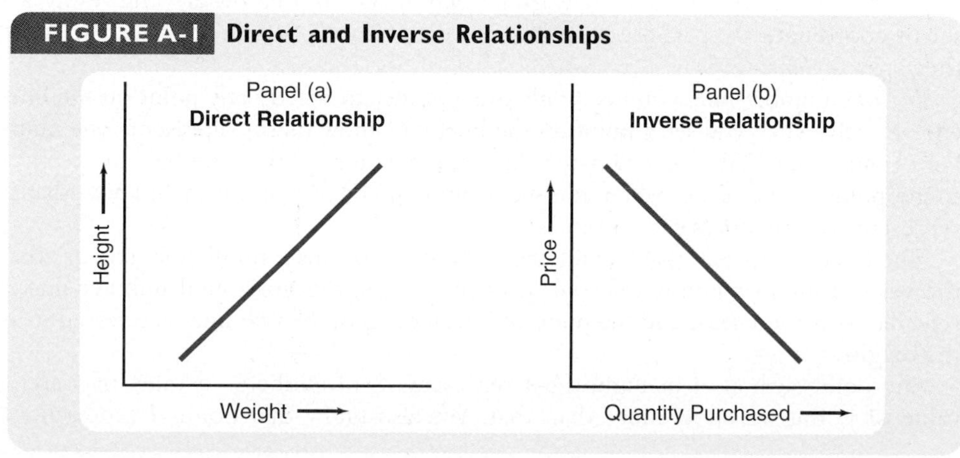

FIGURE A-2 **Horizontal Number Line**

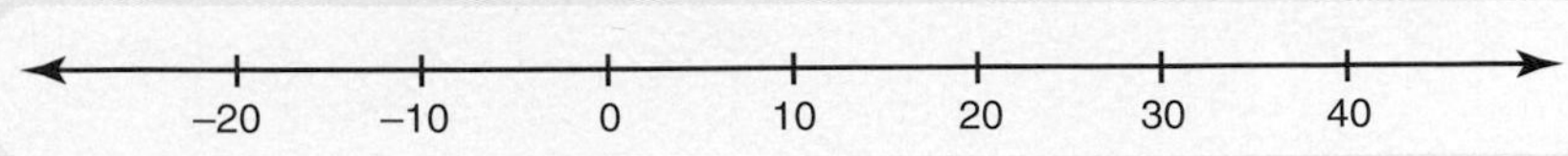

Number line
A line that can be divided into segments of equal length, each associated with a number.

FIGURE A-3

Vertical Number Line

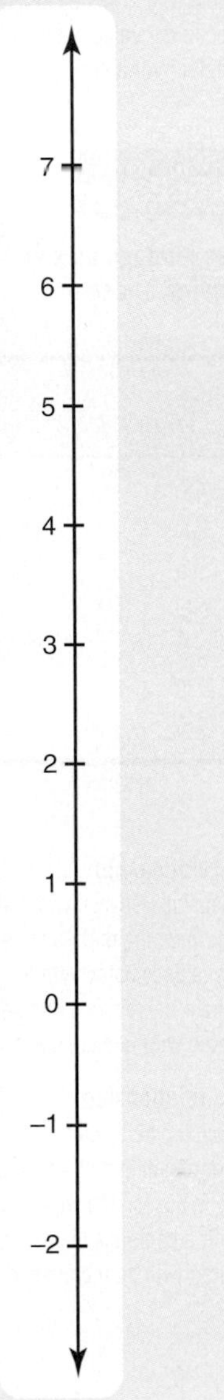

A Number Line

The first step is to become familiar with what is called a **number line.** One is shown in Figure A-2 above. You should know two things about it:

1. The points on the line divide the line into equal segments.
2. The numbers associated with the points on the line increase in value from left to right. Saying it the other way around, the numbers decrease in value from right to left. However you say it, what you're describing is formally called an *ordered set of points*.

On the number line, we have shown the line segments—that is, the distance from 0 to 10 or the distance between 30 and 40. They all appear to be equal and, indeed, are each equal to $\frac{1}{2}$ inch. When we use a distance to represent a quantity, such as barrels of oil, graphically, we are *scaling* the number line. In the example shown, the distance between 0 and 10 might represent 10 barrels of oil, or the distance from 0 to 40 might represent 40 barrels. Of course, the scale may differ on different number lines. For example, a distance of 1 inch could represent 10 units on one number line but 5,000 units on another. Notice that on our number line, points to the left of 0 correspond to negative numbers and points to the right of 0 correspond to positive numbers.

Of course, we can also construct a vertical number line. Consider the one in Figure A-3 alongside. As we move up this vertical number line, the numbers increase in value; conversely, as we descend, they decrease in value. Below 0 the numbers are negative, and above 0 the numbers are positive. And as on the horizontal number line, all the line segments are equal. This line is divided into segments such that the distance between –2 and –1 is the same as the distance between 0 and 1.

Combining Vertical and Horizontal Number Lines

By drawing the horizontal and vertical lines on the same sheet of paper, we are able to express the relationships between variables graphically. We do this in Figure A-4 on the facing page. We draw them (1) so that they intersect at each other's 0 point and (2) so that they are perpendicular to each other. The result is a set of coordinate axes, where each line is called an *axis*. When we have two axes, they span a *plane*.

For one number line, you need only one number to specify any point on the line; equivalently, when you see a point on the line, you know that it represents one number or one value. With a coordinate value system, you need two numbers to specify a single point in the plane; when you see a single point on a graph, you know that it represents two numbers or two values.

The basic things that you should know about a coordinate number system are that the vertical number line is referred to as the ***y* axis,** the horizontal number line is referred to as the ***x* axis,** and the point of intersection of the two lines is referred to as the **origin.**

Any point such as A in Figure A-4 represents two numbers—a value of x and a value of y. But we know more than that: We also know that point A represents a

***y* axis**
The vertical axis in a graph.

***x* axis**
The horizontal axis in a graph.

Origin
The intersection of the *y* axis and the *x* axis in a graph.

FIGURE A-4 A Set of Coordinate Axes

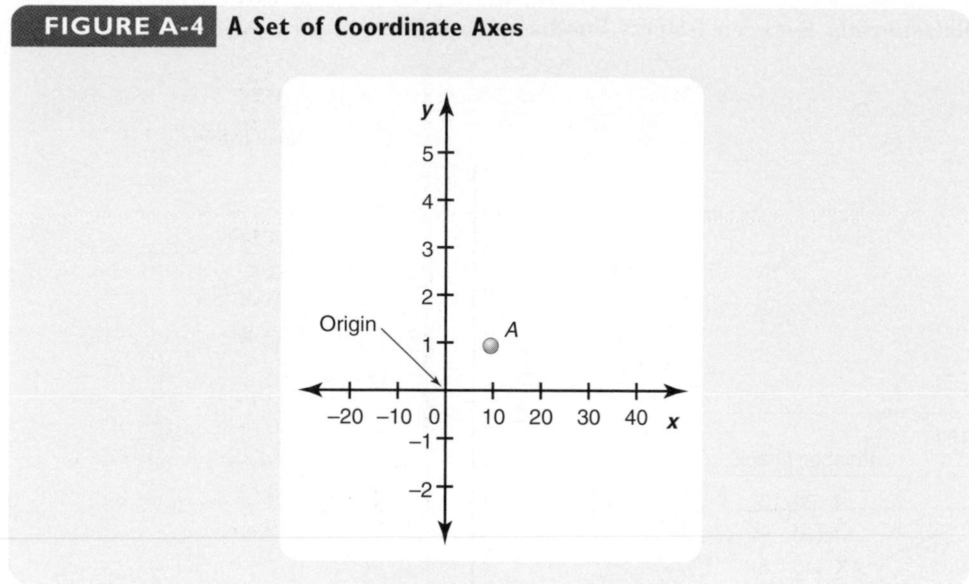

positive value of y because it is above the x axis, and we know that it represents a positive value of x because it is to the right of the y axis.

Point A represents a "paired observation" of the variables x and y; in particular, in Figure A-4, A represents an observation of the pair of values $x = 10$ and $y = 1$. Every point in the coordinate system corresponds to a paired observation of x and y, which can be simply written (x, y)—the x value is always specified first and then the y value. When we give the values associated with the position of point A in the coordinate number system, we are in effect giving the coordinates of that point. A's coordinates are $x = 10$, $y = 1$, or (10, 1).

Graphing Numbers in a Table

Consider Table A-2 alongside. Column 1 shows different prices for T-shirts, and column 2 gives the number of T-shirts purchased per week at these prices. Notice the pattern of these numbers. As the price of T-shirts falls, the number of T-shirts purchased per week increases. Therefore, an inverse relationship exists between these two variables, and as soon as we represent it on a graph, you will be able to see the relationship. We can graph this relationship using a coordinate number system—a vertical and horizontal number line for each of these two variables. Such a graph is shown in panel (b) of Figure A-5 on the top of the following page.

TABLE A-2

T-Shirts Purchased

(1) Price of T-Shirts	(2) Number of T-Shirts Purchased per Week
$10	20
9	30
8	40
7	50
6	60
5	70

In economics, it is conventional to put dollar values on the y axis and quantities on the horizontal axis. We therefore construct a vertical number line for price and a horizontal number line, the x axis, for quantity of T-shirts purchased per week. The resulting coordinate system allows the plotting of each of the paired observation points; in panel (a), we repeat Table A-2, with a column added expressing these points in paired-data (x, y) form. For example, point J is the paired observation (30, 9). It indicates that when the price of a T-shirt is $9, 30 will be purchased per week.

If it were possible to sell parts of a T-shirt ($\frac{1}{2}$ or $\frac{1}{20}$ of a shirt), we would have observations at every possible price. That is, we would be able to connect our paired observations, represented as lettered points. Let's assume that we can make T-shirts perfectly divisible so that the linear relationship shown in Figure A-5 also holds for fractions of dollars and T-shirts. We would then have a line that connects these points, as shown in the graph in Figure A-6 on the bottom of the following page.

FIGURE A-5 Graphing the Relationship Between T-Shirts Purchased and Price

Panel (a)

Price per T-Shirt	T-Shirts Purchased per Week	Point on Graph
$10	20	*I* (20, 10)
9	30	*J* (30, 9)
8	40	*K* (40, 8)
7	50	*L* (50, 7)
6	60	*M* (60, 6)
5	70	*N* (70, 5)

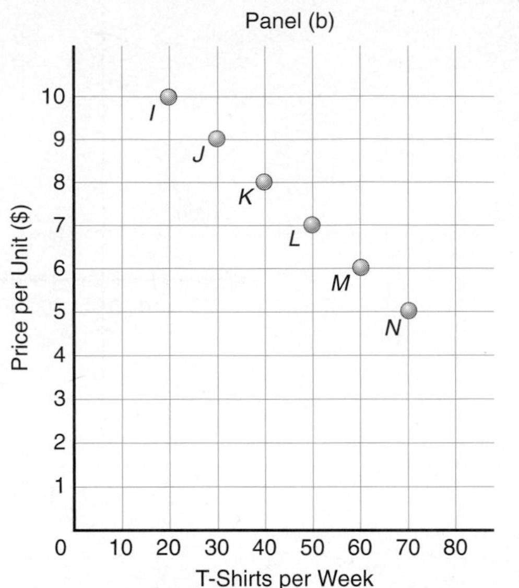

In short, we have now represented the data from the table in the form of a graph. Note that an inverse relationship between two variables shows up on a graph as a line or curve that slopes *downward* from left to right. (You might as well get used to the idea that economists call a straight line a "curve" even though it may not curve at all. Economists' data frequently turn out to be curves, so they refer to everything represented graphically, even straight lines, as curves.)

FIGURE A-6 Connecting the Observation Points

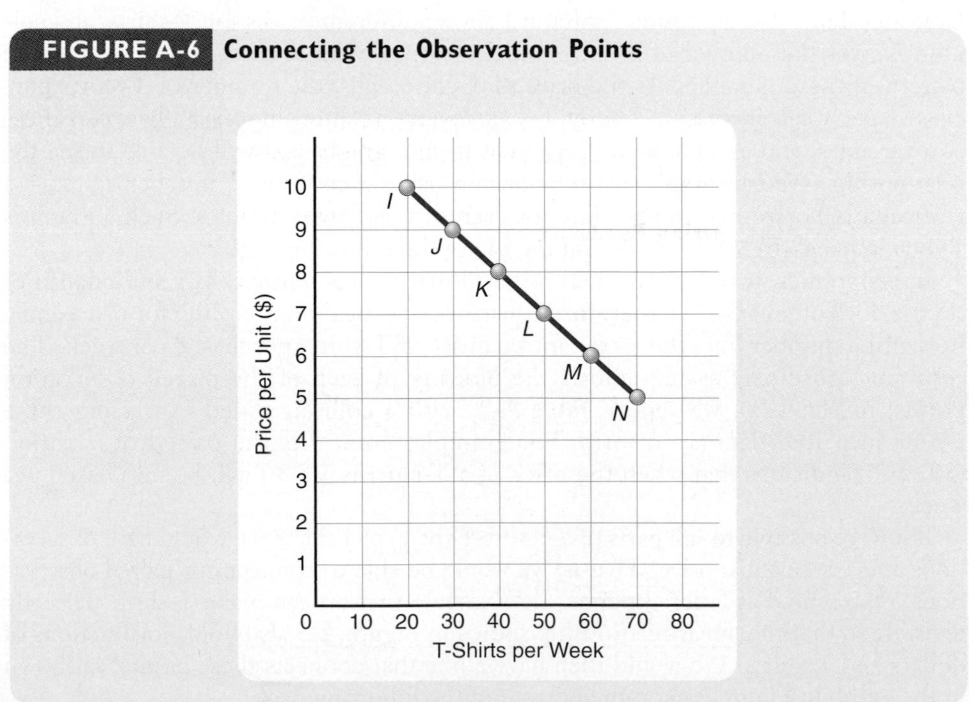

FIGURE A-7 **A Positively Sloped Curve**

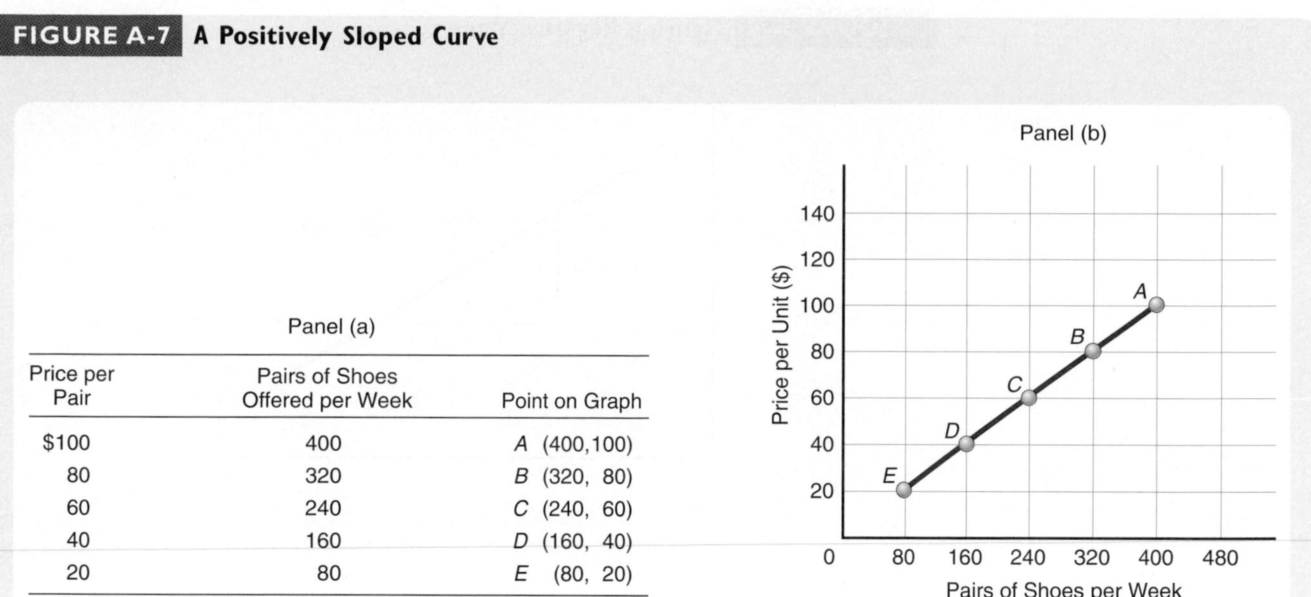
Panel (a)

Price per Pair	Pairs of Shoes Offered per Week	Point on Graph
$100	400	*A* (400,100)
80	320	*B* (320, 80)
60	240	*C* (240, 60)
40	160	*D* (160, 40)
20	80	*E* (80, 20)

The Slope of a Line (A Linear Curve)

An important property of a curve represented on a graph is its *slope*. Consider Figure A-7 above, which represents the quantities of shoes per week that a seller is willing to offer at different prices. Note that in panel (a) of Figure A-7, as in Figure A-5, we have expressed the coordinates of the points in parentheses in paired-data form.

The **slope** of a line is defined as the change in the y values divided by the corresponding change in the x values as we move along the line. Let's move from point E to point D in panel (b) of Figure A-7. As we move, we note that the change in the y values, which is the change in price, is +$20, because we have moved from a price of $20 to a price of $40 per pair. As we move from E to D, the change in the x values is +80; the number of pairs of shoes willingly offered per week rises from 80 to 160 pairs. The slope, calculated as a change in the y values divided by the change in the x values, is therefore

Slope
The change in the y value divided by the corresponding change in the x value of a curve; the "incline" of the curve.

$$\frac{20}{80} = \frac{1}{4}$$

It may be helpful for you to think of slope as a "rise" (movement in the vertical direction) over a "run" (movement in the horizontal direction). We show this abstractly in Figure A-8 below. The slope is the amount of rise divided by the amount of run.

FIGURE A-8 **Figuring Positive Slope**

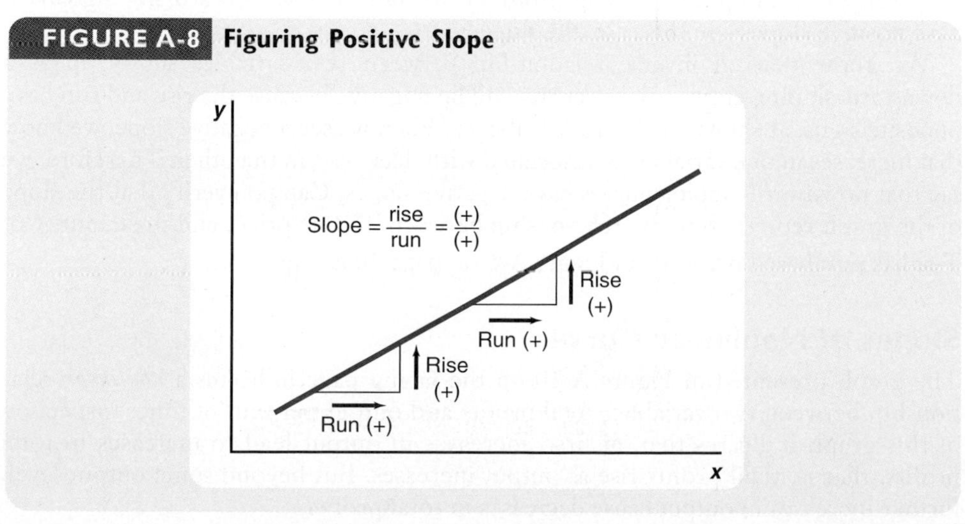

FIGURE A-9 **Figuring Negative Slope**

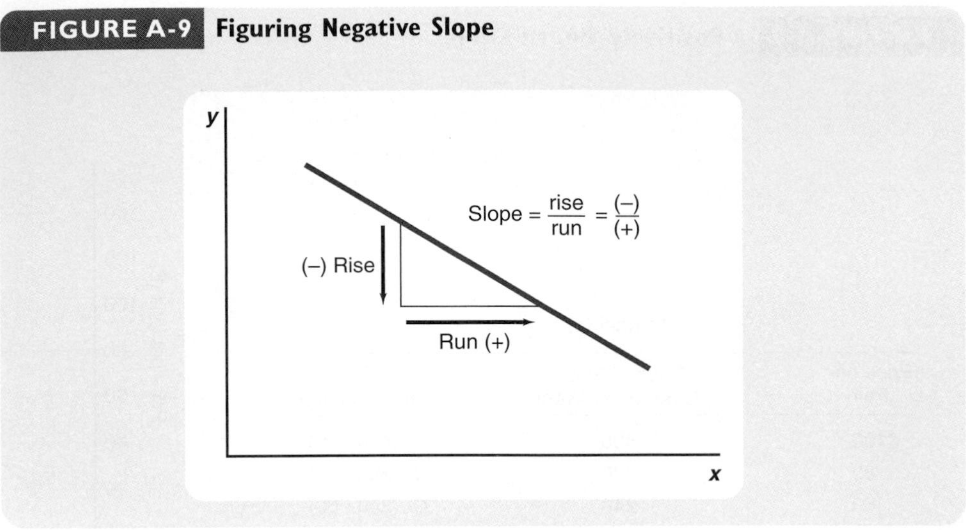

In the example in Figure A-8 on page 21, and of course in Figure A-7 on the previous page, the amount of rise is positive and so is the amount of run. That's because it's a direct relationship. We show an inverse relationship in Figure A-9 above. The slope is still equal to the rise divided by the run, but in this case the rise and the run have opposite signs because the curve slopes downward. That means that the slope is negative and that we are dealing with an inverse relationship.

Now let's calculate the slope for a different part of the curve in panel (b) of Figure A-7. We will find the slope as we move from point *B* to point *A*. Again, we note that the slope, or rise over run, from *B* to *A* equals

$$\frac{20}{80} = \frac{1}{4}$$

A specific property of a straight line is that its slope is the same between any two points. In other words, the slope is constant at all points on a straight line in a graph.

We conclude that for our example in Figure A-7, the relationship between the price of a pair of shoes and the number of pairs of shoes willingly offered per week is *linear*, which simply means "in a straight line," and our calculations indicate a constant slope. Moreover, we calculate a direct relationship between these two variables, which turns out to be an upward-sloping (from left to right) curve. Upward-sloping curves have positive slopes—in this case, the slope is $+\frac{1}{4}$.

We know that an inverse relationship between two variables shows up as a downward-sloping curve—rise over run will be negative because the rise and run have opposite signs, as shown in Figure A-9 above. When we see a negative slope, we know that increases in one variable are associated with decreases in the other. Therefore, we say that downward-sloping curves have negative slopes. Can you verify that the slope of the graph representing the relationship between T-shirt prices and the quantity of T-shirts purchased per week in Figure A-6 on page 20 is $-\frac{1}{10}$?

Slopes of Nonlinear Curves

The graph presented in Figure A-10 on the facing page indicates a *nonlinear* relationship between two variables, total profits and output per unit of time. Inspection of this graph indicates that, at first, increases in output lead to increases in total profits; that is, total profits rise as output increases. But beyond some output level, further increases in output cause decreases in total profits.

FIGURE A-10 The Slope of a Nonlinear Curve

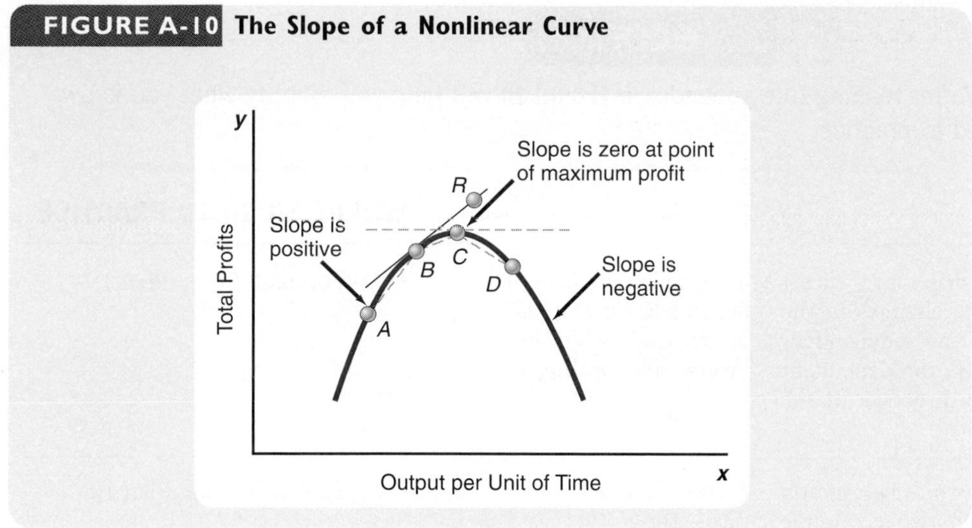

Can you see how this curve rises at first, reaches a peak at point *C*, and then falls? This curve relating total profits to output levels appears mountain-shaped.

Considering that this curve is nonlinear (it is obviously not a straight line), should we expect a constant slope when we compute changes in *y* divided by corresponding changes in *x* in moving from one point to another? A quick inspection, even without specific numbers, should lead us to conclude that the slopes of lines joining different points in this curve, such as between *A* and *B*, *B* and *C*, or *C* and *D*, will *not* be the same. The curve slopes upward (in a positive direction) for some values and downward (in a negative direction) for other values. In fact, the slope of the line between any two points on this curve will be different from the slope of the line between any two other points. Each slope will be different as we move along the curve.

Instead of using a line between two points to discuss slope, mathematicians and economists prefer to discuss the slope *at a particular point*. The slope at a point on the curve, such as point *B* in the graph in Figure A-10 above, is the slope of a line tangent to that point. A tangent line is a straight line that touches a curve at only one point. For example, it might be helpful to think of the tangent at *B* as the straight line that just "kisses" the curve at point *B*.

To calculate the slope of a tangent line, you need to have some additional information besides the two values of the point of tangency. For example, in Figure A-10, if we knew that the point *R* also lay on the tangent line and we knew the two values of that point, we could calculate the slope of the tangent line. We could calculate rise over run between points *B* and *R*, and the result would be the slope of the line tangent to the one point *B* on the curve.

Here is what you should know after reading this appendix. **MyEconLab** will help you identify what you know, and where to go when you need to practice.

WHAT YOU SHOULD KNOW		WHERE TO GO TO PRACTICE
Direct and Inverse Relationships In a direct relationship, a dependent variable changes in the same direction as the change in the independent variable. In an inverse relationship, the dependent variable changes in the opposite direction of the change in the independent variable.	independent variable, 17 dependent variable, 17 direct relationship, 17 inverse relationship, 17	• **MyEconLab** Study Plan 1.7
Constructing a Graph When we draw a graph showing the relationship between two economic variables, we are holding all other things constant (the Latin term for which is *ceteris paribus*).	number line, 18 *y* axis, 18 *x* axis, 18 origin, 18	• **MyEconLab** Study Plan 1.8
Graphing Numbers We obtain a set of coordinates by putting vertical and horizontal number lines together. The vertical line is called the *y* axis; the horizontal line, the *x* axis.		• **MyEconLab** Study Plan 1.9
The Slope of a Linear Curve The slope of any linear (straight-line) curve is the change in the *y* values divided by the corresponding change in the *x* values as we move along the line. Otherwise stated, the slope is calculated as the amount of rise over the amount of run, where rise is movement in the vertical direction and run is movement in the horizontal direction.	slope, 21 **KEY FIGURES** Figure A-8, 21 Figure A-9, 22	• **MyEconLab** Study Plan 1.10 • Animated Figures A-8, A-9
The Slope of a Nonlinear Curve The slope of a nonlinear curve changes; it is positive when the curve is rising and negative when the curve is falling. At a maximum or minimum point, the slope of the nonlinear curve is zero.	**KEY FIGURE** Figure A-10, 23	• **MyEconLab** Study Plan 1.10 • Animated Figure A-10

Log in to MyEconLab, take an appendix test, and get a personalized Study Plan that tells you which concepts you understand and which ones you need to review. From there, MyEconLab will give you further practice, tutorials, animations, videos, and guided solutions.
Log in to www.myeconlab.com

PROBLEMS

All problems are assignable in myeconlab. Answers to odd-numbered problems appear at the back of the book.

A-1. Explain which is the independent variable and which is the dependent variable for each of the following examples.

a. Once you determine the price of a notebook at the college bookstore, you will decide how many notebooks to buy.

b. You will decide how many credit hours to register for this semester once the university tells you how many work-study hours you will be assigned.

c. You anticipate earning a higher grade on your next economics exam because you studied more hours in the weeks preceding the exam.

A-2. For each of the following items, state whether a direct or an inverse relationship is likely to exist.

a. The number of hours you study for an exam and your exam score

b. The price of pizza and the quantity purchased

c. The number of games the university basketball team won last year and the number of season tickets sold this year

A-3. Review Figure A-4 on page 19, and then state whether each of the following paired observations is on, above, or below the x axis and on, to the left of, or to the right of the y axis.

a. (−10, 4)

b. (20, −2)

c. (10, 0)

A-4. State whether each of the following functions specifies a direct or an inverse relationship.

a. $y = 5x$

b. $y = 10 - 2x$

c. $y = 3 + x$

d. $y = -3x$

A-5. Given the function $y = 5x$, complete the following schedule and plot the curve.

y	x
	−4
	−2
	0
	2
	4

A-6. Given the function $y = 8 - 2x$, complete the following schedule and plot the curve.

y	x
	−4
	−2
	0
	2
	4

A-7. Calculate the slope of the function you graphed in Problem A-5.

A-8. Calculate the slope of the function you graphed in Problem A-6.

2 Scarcity and the World of Trade-Offs

Since 1918, people in most U.S. states have set their clocks forward one hour in the spring and then turned them back one hour in the autumn. Traditionally, proponents of daylight saving time claim that its adoption saves energy that otherwise would be expended on lighting in the evenings under standard time. Recently, however, some economists have suggested that adding an extra hour of daylight in the evenings may actually generate an *increase* in energy expenses. In this chapter, you will learn that making a choice to obtain something, such as an extra hour of daylight, entails incurring an *opportunity cost*—the highest-valued, next-best alternative that must be sacrificed to obtain that choice. If these economists are correct, then the opportunity cost of switching to daylight saving time may be too high to justify the departure from standard time each spring.

LEARNING OBJECTIVES

After reading this chapter, you should be able to:

- Evaluate whether even affluent people face the problem of scarcity
- Understand why economics considers individuals' "wants" but not their "needs"
- Explain why the scarcity problem induces individuals to consider opportunity costs
- Discuss why obtaining increasing increments of any particular good typically entails giving up more and more units of other goods
- Explain why society faces a trade-off between consumption goods and capital goods
- Distinguish between absolute and comparative advantage

MyEconLab helps you master each objective and study more efficiently. See end of chapter for details.

the Institute of Medicine has estimated that U.S. teaching hospitals would face a combined $1.6 billion annual price tag if they were to limit medical residents' shifts to 16 hours or include 5-hour naps in shifts exceeding 16 hours? Even these proposed changes would only reshuffle the schedules of U.S. medical residents to provide more rest breaks, in hopes that less bleary eyes would lead to fewer errors in treating patients. The residents would nonetheless work 80 hours per week, which is 33 percent more than European medical residents work.

At U.S. teaching hospitals, however, rearranging residents' schedules to allow for shorter shifts or for naps would require the hospitals to hire more residents or other medical personnel to cover the scheduling gaps that would result. The Institute of Medicine's study concluded that the implications for patient care of either scheduling change were unknown. The one certainty was that the proposed alternative use of residents' time—getting some rest—would be very costly for the nation's teaching hospitals. The lengthy blocks of time that medical residents currently devote to treating patients are, like all other resources, scarce.

Did You Know That ?

Scarcity

Whenever individuals or communities cannot obtain everything they desire simultaneously, they must make choices. Choices occur because of *scarcity*. **Scarcity** is the most basic concept in all of economics. Scarcity means that we do not ever have enough of everything, including time, to satisfy our *every* desire. Scarcity exists because human wants always exceed what can be produced with the limited resources and time that nature makes available.

Scarcity
A situation in which the ingredients for producing the things that people desire are insufficient to satisfy all wants at a zero price.

What Scarcity Is Not

Scarcity is not a shortage. After a hurricane hits and cuts off supplies to a community, TV newscasts often show people standing in line to get minimum amounts of cooking fuel and food. A news commentator might say that the line is caused by the "scarcity" of these products. But cooking fuel and food are always scarce—we cannot obtain all that we want at a zero price. Therefore, do not confuse the concept of scarcity, which is general and all-encompassing, with the concept of shortages as evidenced by people waiting in line to obtain a particular product.

Scarcity is not the same thing as poverty. Scarcity occurs among the poor and among the rich. Even the richest person on earth faces scarcity. For instance, even the world's richest person has only limited time available. Low income levels do not create more scarcity. High income levels do not create less scarcity.

Scarcity is a fact of life, like gravity. And just as physicists did not invent gravity, economists did not invent scarcity—it existed well before the first economist ever lived. It has existed at all times in the past and will exist at all times in the future.

Scarcity and Resources

Scarcity exists because resources are insufficient to satisfy our every desire. Resources are the inputs used in the production of the things that we want. **Production** can be defined as virtually any activity that results in the conversion of resources into products that can be used in consumption. Production includes delivering things from one part of the country to another. It includes taking ice from an ice tray to put it in your soft-drink glass. The resources used in production are called *factors of production*, and some economists use the terms *resources* and *factors of production* interchangeably. The total quantity of all resources that an economy has at any one time determines what that economy can produce.

Production
Any activity that results in the conversion of resources into products that can be used in consumption.

Factors of production can be classified in many ways. Here is one such classification:

1. *Land.* **Land** encompasses all the nonhuman gifts of nature, including timber, water, fish, minerals, and the original fertility of land. It is often called the *natural resource*.

Land
The natural resources that are available from nature. Land as a resource includes location, original fertility and mineral deposits, topography, climate, water, and vegetation.

Labor
Productive contributions of humans who work.

2. *Labor.* **Labor** is the *human resource*, which includes productive contributions made by individuals who work, such as Web page designers, iPad applications creators, and professional football players.

Physical capital
All manufactured resources, including buildings, equipment, machines, and improvements to land that are used for production.

3. *Physical capital.* **Physical capital** consists of the factories and equipment used in production. It also includes improvements to natural resources, such as irrigation ditches.

Human capital
The accumulated training and education of workers.

4. *Human capital.* **Human capital** is the economic characterization of the education and training of workers. How much the nation produces depends not only on how many hours people work but also on how productive they are, and that in turn depends in part on education and training. To become more educated, individuals have to devote time and resources, just as a business has to devote resources if it wants to increase its physical capital. Whenever a worker's skills increase, human capital has been improved.

Entrepreneurship
The component of human resources that performs the functions of raising capital, organizing, managing, and assembling other factors of production, making basic business policy decisions, and taking risks.

5. *Entrepreneurship.* **Entrepreneurship** (actually a subdivision of labor) is the component of human resources that performs the functions of organizing, managing, and assembling the other factors of production to create and operate business ventures. Entrepreneurship also encompasses taking risks that involve the possibility of losing large sums of wealth on new ventures. It includes new methods of doing common things and generally experimenting with any type of new thinking that could lead to making more income. Without entrepreneurship, hardly any business organizations could operate.

Goods versus Economic Goods

Goods
All things from which individuals derive satisfaction or happiness.

Economic goods
Goods that are scarce, for which the quantity demanded exceeds the quantity supplied at a zero price.

Goods are defined as all things from which individuals derive satisfaction or happiness. Goods therefore include air to breathe and the beauty of a sunset as well as food, cars, and iPhones.

Economic goods are a subset of all goods—they are scarce goods, about which we must constantly make decisions regarding their best use. By definition, the desired quantity of an economic good exceeds the amount that is available at a zero price. Almost every example we use in economics concerns economic goods—cars, Blu-ray disc players, computers, socks, baseball bats, and corn. Weeds are a good example of *bads*—goods for which the desired quantity is much *less* than what nature provides at a zero price.

Services
Mental or physical labor or help purchased by consumers. Examples are the assistance of physicians, lawyers, dentists, repair personnel, housecleaners, educators, retailers, and wholesalers; items purchased or used by consumers that do not have physical characteristics.

Sometimes you will see references to "goods and services." **Services** are tasks that are performed for someone else, such as laundry, Internet access, hospital care, restaurant meal preparation, car polishing, psychological counseling, and teaching. One way of looking at services is to think of them as *intangible goods*.

Wants and Needs

Wants are not the same as needs. Indeed, from the economist's point of view, the term *needs* is objectively undefinable. When someone says, "I need some new clothes," there is no way to know whether that person is stating a vague wish, a want, or a lifesaving requirement. If the individual making the statement were dying of exposure in a northern country during the winter, we might conclude that indeed the person does need clothes—perhaps not new ones, but at least some articles of warm clothing. Typically, however, the term *need* is used very casually in conversation. What people mean, usually, is that they desire something that they do not currently have.

Humans have unlimited wants. Just imagine that every single material want that you might have was satisfied. You could have all of the clothes, cars, houses, downloadable movies, yachts, and other items that you want. Does that mean that nothing else could add to your total level of happiness? Undoubtedly, you might continue to think of new goods and services that you could obtain, particularly as they came to market. You would also still be lacking in fulfilling all of your wants for compassion, friendship, love, affection, prestige, musical abilities, sports abilities, and the like.

In reality, every individual has competing wants but cannot satisfy all of them, given limited resources. This is the reality of scarcity. Each person must therefore make choices. Whenever a choice is made to produce or buy something, something else that is also desired is not produced or not purchased. In other words, in a world of scarcity, every want that ends up being satisfied causes one or more other wants to remain unsatisfied or to be forfeited.

QUICK QUIZ See page 47 for the answers. Review concepts from this section in MyEconLab.

__________ is the situation in which human wants always exceed what can be produced with the limited resources and time that nature makes available.

We use scarce resources, such as __________, __________, __________ and __________ capital, and __________, to produce economic goods—goods that are desired but are not directly obtainable from nature to the extent demanded or desired at a zero price.

__________ are unlimited; they include all material desires and all nonmaterial desires, such as love, affection, power, and prestige.

The concept of __________ is difficult to define objectively for every person; consequently, we simply consider every person's wants to be unlimited. In a world of **scarcity**, satisfaction of one want necessarily means nonsatisfaction of one or more other wants.

Scarcity, Choice, and Opportunity Cost

The natural fact of scarcity implies that we must make choices. One of the most important results of this fact is that every choice made means that some opportunity must be sacrificed. Every choice involves giving up an opportunity to produce or consume something else.

Valuing Forgone Alternatives

Consider a practical example. Every choice you make to study economics for one more hour requires that you give up the opportunity to engage in any of the following activities: study more of another subject, listen to music, sleep, browse at a local store, read a novel, or work out at the gym. The most highly valued of these opportunities is forgone if you choose to study economics an additional hour.

Because there were so many alternatives from which to choose, how could you determine the value of what you gave up to engage in that extra hour of studying economics? First of all, no one else can tell you the answer because only *you* can put a value on the alternatives forgone. Only you know the value of another hour of sleep or of an hour looking for the latest digital music downloads—whatever one activity *you* would have chosen if you had not opted to study economics for that hour. That means that only you can determine the highest-valued, next-best alternative that you had to sacrifice in order to study economics one more hour. Only you can determine the value of the next-best alternative.

Opportunity Cost

The value of the next-best alternative is called **opportunity cost.** The opportunity cost of any action is the value of what is given up—the next-highest-ranked alternative—because a choice was made. When you study one more hour, there may be many alternatives available for the use of that hour, but assume that you can do only one other thing in that hour—your next-highest-ranked alternative. What is important is the choice that you would have made if you hadn't studied one more hour. Your opportunity cost is the *next-highest-ranked* alternative, not *all* alternatives.

Opportunity cost
The highest-valued, next-best alternative that must be sacrificed to obtain something or to satisfy a want.

In economics, cost is always a forgone opportunity.

You Are There

To consider why some universities are reshuffling their class schedules to raise students' opportunity costs of drinking alcohol on weeknights, read **Stopping Students' Thursday Night Parties with Friday Classes,** on page 41.

One way to think about opportunity cost is to understand that when you choose to do something, you lose something else. What you lose is being able to engage in your next-highest-valued alternative. The cost of your chosen alternative is what you lose, which is by definition your next-highest-valued alternative. This is your opportunity cost.

Which nation's residents face the lowest—compared with those of other advanced countries—average opportunity cost of time spent eating and sleeping?

INTERNATIONAL EXAMPLE **France Is the Sleeping Giant**

The Organization for Economic Cooperation and Development (OECD) conducts surveys on social habits that track how people in the OECD's 30 member countries allocate their time. These surveys indicate that, consistent with the cliché, residents of France allocate the most time to eating—an average of two hours per day, about twice as much time as U.S. residents devote to their meals. In addition, the French also sleep more than people in any other OECD country—a daily average of 530 minutes, compared with 518 for U.S. residents. Based on how they allocate their time, French residents face the lowest opportunity cost, compared with residents of other OECD nations, of time devoted to eating and to sleeping.

FOR CRITICAL ANALYSIS

How does a French government mandate of six weeks of paid vacation in addition to traditional paid holidays affect the opportunity cost of eating and sleeping?

The World of Trade-Offs

Whenever you engage in any activity using any resource, even time, you are *trading off* the use of that resource for one or more alternative uses. The extent of the trade-off is represented by the opportunity cost. The opportunity cost of studying economics has already been mentioned—it is the value of the next-best alternative. When you think of *any* alternative, you are thinking of trade-offs.

Let's consider a hypothetical example of a trade-off between the results of spending time studying economics and mathematics. For the sake of this argument, we will assume that additional time studying either economics or mathematics will lead to a higher grade in the subject to which additional study time is allocated. One of the best ways to examine this trade-off is with a graph. (If you would like a refresher on graphical techniques, study Appendix A at the end of Chapter 1 before going on.)

Graphical Analysis

In Figure 2-1 on the facing page, the expected grade in mathematics is measured on the vertical axis of the graph, and the expected grade in economics is measured on the horizontal axis. We simplify the world and assume that you have a maximum of 12 hours per week to spend studying these two subjects and that if you spend all 12 hours on economics, you will get an A in the course. You will, however, fail mathematics. Conversely, if you spend all of your 12 hours studying mathematics, you will get an A in that subject, but you will flunk economics. Here the trade-off is a special case: one to one. A one-to-one trade-off means that the opportunity cost of receiving one grade higher in economics (for example, improving from a C to a B) is one grade lower in mathematics (falling from a C to a D).

The Production Possibilities Curve (PPC)

The graph in Figure 2-1 illustrates the relationship between the possible results that can be produced in each of two activities, depending on how much time you choose to devote to each activity. This graph shows a representation of a **production possibilities curve (PPC).**

Production possibilities curve (PPC)
A curve representing all possible combinations of maximum outputs that could be produced assuming a fixed amount of productive resources of a given quality.

Consider that you are producing a grade in economics when you study economics and a grade in mathematics when you study mathematics. Then the line that goes from A on one axis to A on the other axis therefore becomes a production

FIGURE 2-1 Production Possibilities Curve for Grades in Mathematics and Economics (Trade-Offs)

We assume that only 12 hours can be spent per week on studying. If the student is at point *x*, equal time (6 hours a week) is spent on both courses, and equal grades of C will be received. If a higher grade in economics is desired, the student may go to point *y*, thereby receiving a B in economics but a D in mathematics. At point *y*, 3 hours are spent on mathematics and 9 hours on economics.

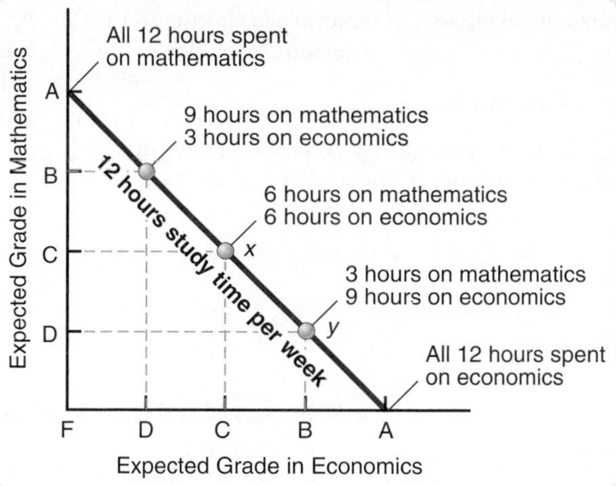

possibilities curve. It is defined as the maximum quantity of one good or service that can be produced, given that a specific quantity of another is produced. It is a curve that shows the possibilities available for increasing the output of one good or service by reducing the amount of another. In the example in Figure 2-1, your time for studying was limited to 12 hours per week. The two possible outputs were your grade in mathematics and your grade in economics. The particular production possibilities curve presented in Figure 2-1 is a graphical representation of the opportunity cost of studying one more hour in one subject. It is a *straight-line production possibilities curve*, which is a special case. (The more general case will be discussed next.)

If you decide to be at point *x* in Figure 2-1, you will devote 6 hours of study time to mathematics and 6 hours to economics. The expected grade in each course will be a C. If you are more interested in getting a B in economics, you will go to point *y* on the production possibilities curve, spending only 3 hours on mathematics but 9 hours on economics. Your expected grade in mathematics will then drop from a C to a D.

Note that these trade-offs between expected grades in mathematics and economics are the result of *holding constant* total study time as well as all other factors that might influence your ability to learn, such as computerized study aids. Quite clearly, if you were able to spend more total time studying, it would be possible to have higher grades in both economics and mathematics. In that case, however, we would no longer be on the specific production possibilities curve illustrated in Figure 2-1. We would have to draw a new curve, farther to the right, to show the greater total study time and a different set of possible trade-offs.

Why does every inch of cabin space have value on a passenger airliner?

EXAMPLE Airlines Confront the Opportunity Cost of Legroom on Planes

Recently, American Airlines reduced the "seat pitch"—the distance from a point on one seat on a plane to the same point on the seat in the next row—to 31 inches. Previously, the seat pitch had been 32 to 33 inches, so the airline effectively removed 1 to 2 inches of legroom available to a typical passenger. Seat pitch reductions, which were implemented by Continental, Delta, and other airlines as well, enabled at least 10 more coach seats to be added to each plane without making the planes any larger. For these airlines, the few thousand dollars generated by squeezing at least 10 or more ticketed passengers onto each plane was an opportunity cost too high to justify an inch or two of extra passenger legroom.

FOR CRITICAL ANALYSIS

Why do you suppose that on many of its planes, American Airlines also decided to eliminate service-cart storage cabinets behind the last row of seats, an action that enabled it to add two more seats to those planes?

QUICK QUIZ See page 47 for the answers. Review concepts from this section in MyEconLab.

Scarcity requires us to choose. Whenever we choose, we lose the ___________-___________-valued alternative.

Cost is always a forgone ___________.

Another way to look at **opportunity cost** is the trade-off that occurs when one activity is undertaken rather than the ___________-___________ alternative activity.

A ___________ ___________ curve graphically shows the trade-off that occurs when more of one output is obtained at the sacrifice of another. This curve is a graphical representation of, among other things, opportunity cost.

The Choices Society Faces

The straight-line production possibilities curve presented in Figure 2-1 on the previous page can be generalized to demonstrate the related concepts of scarcity, choice, and trade-offs that our entire nation faces. As you will see, the production possibilities curve is a simple but powerful economic model because it can demonstrate these related concepts.

A Two-Good Example

The example we will use is the choice between the production of electronic book readers (e-readers) and netbook computers (netbooks). We assume for the moment that these are the only two goods that can be produced in the nation.

Panel (a) of Figure 2-2 on the facing page gives the various combinations of e-readers and netbooks that are possible. If all resources are devoted to e-reader production, 50 million per year can be produced. If all resources are devoted to production of netbooks, 60 million per year can be produced. In between are various possible combinations.

Production Trade-Offs

The nation's production combinations are plotted as points *A*, *B*, *C*, *D*, *E*, *F*, and *G* in panel (b) of Figure 2-2. If these points are connected with a smooth curve, the nation's production possibilities curve (PPC) is shown, demonstrating the trade-off between the production of e-readers and netbooks. These trade-offs occur *on* the PPC.

Go to www.econtoday.com/ch02 for one perspective, offered by the National Center for Policy Analysis, on whether society's production decisions should be publicly or privately coordinated.

Notice the major difference in the shape of the production possibilities curves in Figure 2-1 on the previous page and Figure 2-2 on the facing page. In Figure 2-1, there is a constant trade-off between grades in economics and in mathematics. In Figure 2-2, the trade-off between production of e-readers and netbook production is not constant, and therefore the PPC is a *bowed* curve. To understand why the production possibilities curve for a society is typically bowed outward, you must understand the assumptions underlying the PPC.

Assumptions Underlying the Production Possibilities Curve

When we draw the curve that is shown in Figure 2-2, we make the following assumptions:

1. Resources are fully employed.
2. Production takes place over a specific time period—for example, one year.
3. The resource inputs, in both quantity and quality, used to produce e-readers or netbooks are fixed over this time period.
4. Technology does not change over this time period.

FIGURE 2-2 Society's Trade-Off Between E-Readers and Netbooks

The production of electronic book readers and netbook computers is measured in millions of units per year. The various combinations are given in panel (a) and plotted in panel (b). Connecting the points *A*–*G* with a relatively smooth line gives society's production possibilities curve for e-readers and netbooks.

Point *R* lies outside the production possibilities curve and is therefore unattainable at the point in time for which the graph is drawn. Point *S* lies inside the production possibilities curve and therefore entails unemployed or underemployed resources.

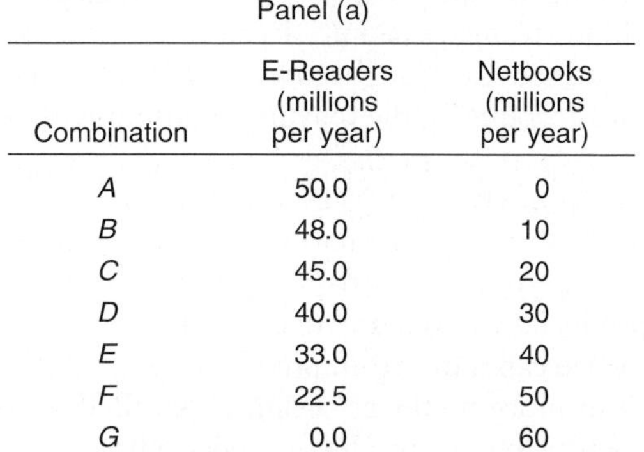

Panel (a)

Combination	E-Readers (millions per year)	Netbooks (millions per year)
A	50.0	0
B	48.0	10
C	45.0	20
D	40.0	30
E	33.0	40
F	22.5	50
G	0.0	60

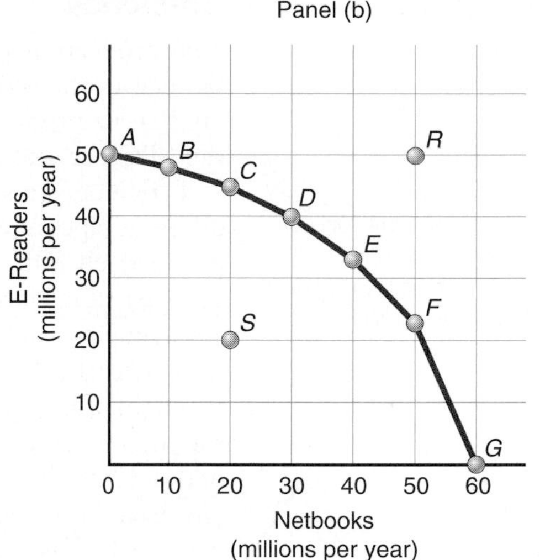

Technology is defined as society's pool of applied knowledge concerning how goods and services can be produced by managers, workers, engineers, scientists, and artisans, using land, physical and human capital, and entrepreneurship. You can think of technology as the formula or recipe used to combine factors of production. (When better formulas are developed, more production can be obtained from the same amount of resources.) The level of technology sets the limit on the amount and types of goods and services that we can derive from any given amount of resources. The production possibilities curve is drawn under the assumption that we use the best technology that we currently have available and that this technology doesn't change over the time period under study.

Technology
Society's pool of applied knowledge concerning how goods and services can be produced.

Why Not . . . provide "free" health care to everyone in the United States?

The production of any good or service requires the allocation of resources that otherwise could be used to produce other goods and services given the available technology. Thus, additional health care services can be provided only by incurring an opportunity cost. Additional health care provided through government programs is never really free. The fact that the new U.S. government health care program has a 10-year price tag exceeding $1 trillion indicates that resources valued at this amount by society would be allocated to producing more health care instead of other items.

Being off the Production Possibilities Curve

Look again at panel (b) of Figure 2-2 above. Point *R* lies *outside* the production possibilities curve and is *impossible* to achieve during the time period assumed. By definition, the PPC indicates the *maximum* quantity of one good, given the quantity produced of the other good.

It is possible, however, to be at point *S* in Figure 2-2 on the previous page. That point lies beneath the PPC. If the nation is at point *S*, it means that its resources are not being fully utilized. This occurs, for example, during periods of relatively high unemployment. Point *S* and all such points inside the PPC are always attainable but imply unemployed or underemployed resources.

Efficiency

The production possibilities curve can be used to define the notion of efficiency. Whenever the economy is operating on the PPC, at points such as *A*, *B*, *C*, or *D*, we say that its production is efficient. Points such as *S* in Figure 2-2, which lie beneath the PPC, are said to represent production situations that are not efficient.

Efficiency
The case in which a given level of inputs is used to produce the maximum output possible. Alternatively, the situation in which a given output is produced at minimum cost.

Efficiency can mean many things to many people. Even in economics, there are different types of efficiency. Here we are discussing *productive efficiency*. An economy is productively efficient whenever it is producing the maximum output with given technology and resources.

A simple commonsense definition of efficiency is getting the most out of what we have. Clearly, we are not getting the most out of what we have if we are at point *S* in panel (b) of Figure 2-2. We can move from point *S* to, say, point *C*, thereby increasing the total quantity of e-readers produced without any decrease in the total quantity of netbooks produced. Alternatively, we can move from point *S* to point *E*, for example, and have both more e-readers and more netbooks. Point *S* is called an **inefficient point,** which is defined as any point below the production possibilities curve.

Inefficient point
Any point below the production possibilities curve, at which the use of resources is not generating the maximum possible output.

The Law of Increasing Additional Cost

In the example in Figure 2-1 on page 31, the trade-off between a grade in mathematics and a grade in economics was one to one. The trade-off ratio was constant. That is, the production possibilities curve was a straight line. The curve in Figure 2-2 is a more general case. We have re-created the curve in Figure 2-2 as Figure 2-3 below. Each combination, *A* through *G*, of e-readers and netbooks is represented on the PPC. Starting with the production of zero netbooks, the nation can produce 50 million e-readers with its available resources and technology.

INCREASING ADDITIONAL COSTS When we increase production of netbooks from zero to 10 million per year, the nation has to give up in e-readers an amount shown by that

FIGURE 2-3 The Law of Increasing Additional Cost

Consider equal increments of production of netbooks, as measured on the horizontal axis. All of the horizontal arrows—*aB, bC*, and so on—are of equal length (10 million). In contrast, the length of each vertical arrow—*Aa, Bb*, and so on—increases as we move down the production possibilities curve. Hence, the opportunity cost of going from 50 million netbooks per year to 60 million (*Ff*) is much greater than going from zero units to 10 million (*Aa*). The opportunity cost of each additional equal increase in production of netbooks rises.

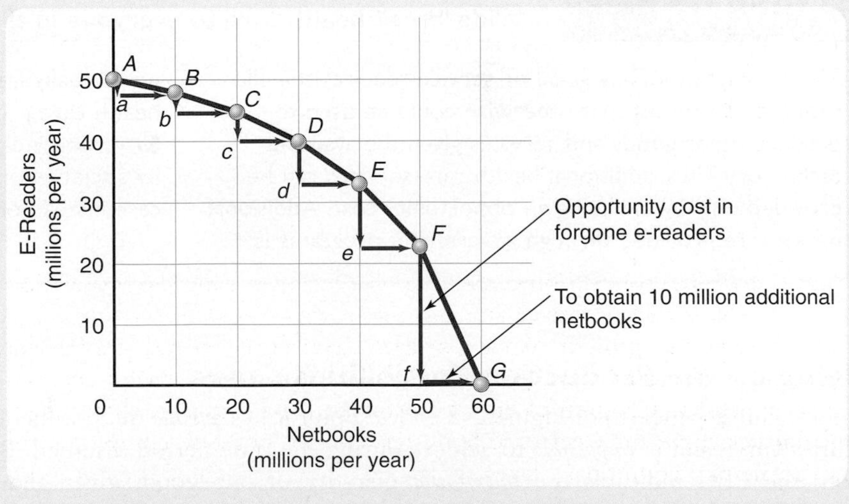

first vertical arrow, *A*a. From panel (a) of Figure 2-2 on page 33 you can see that this is 2 million per year (50 million minus 48 million). Again, if we increase production of netbooks by another 10 million units per year, we go from *B* to *C*. In order to do so, the nation has to give up the vertical distance *Bb*, or 3 million e-readers per year. By the time we go from 50 million to 60 million netbooks, to obtain that 10 million increase, we have to forgo the vertical distance *Ff*, or 22.5 million e-readers. In other words, we see that the opportunity cost of the last 10 million netbooks has increased to 22.5 million e-readers, compared to 2 million e-readers for the same increase in netbooks when we started with none at all being produced.

What we are observing is called the **law of increasing additional cost.** When society takes more resources and applies them to the production of any specific good, the opportunity cost increases for each additional unit produced.

Law of increasing additional cost
The fact that the opportunity cost of additional units of a good generally increases as society attempts to produce more of that good. This accounts for the bowed-out shape of the production possibilities curve.

EXPLAINING THE LAW OF INCREASING ADDITIONAL COST The reason that as a nation we face the law of increasing additional cost (shown as a production possibilities curve that is bowed outward) is that certain resources are better suited for producing some goods than they are for other goods. Generally, resources are not *perfectly* adaptable for alternative uses. When increasing the output of a particular good, producers must use less suitable resources than those already used in order to produce the additional output. Hence, the cost of producing the additional units increases.

With respect to our hypothetical example here, at first the computing specialists at e-reader firms would shift over to producing netbooks. After a while, though, the workers who normally design and produce e-readers would be asked to help design and manufacture netbook components. Clearly, they would be less effective at making netbooks than the people who previously specialized in this task.

In general, *the more specialized the resources, the more bowed the production possibilities curve*. At the other extreme, if all resources are equally suitable for e-reader production or production of netbooks, the curves in Figures 2-2 (p. 33) and 2-3 (p. 34) would approach the straight line shown in our first example in Figure 2-1 on page 31.

QUICK QUIZ See page 47 for the answers. Review concepts from this section in MyEconLab.

Trade-offs are represented graphically by a __________ __________ curve showing the maximum quantity of one good or service that can be produced, given a specific quantity of another, from a given set of resources over a specified period of time—for example, one year.

A **production possibilities curve** is drawn holding the quantity and quality of all resources __________ over the time period under study.

Points __________ the **production possibilities curve** are unattainable; points __________ are attainable but represent an inefficient use or underuse of available resources.

Because many resources are better suited for certain productive tasks than for others, society's production possibilities curve is bowed __________, reflecting the **law of increasing additional cost.**

Economic Growth and the Production Possibilities Curve

At any particular point in time, a society cannot be outside the production possibilities curve. *Over time*, however, it is possible to have more of everything. This occurs through economic growth. (An important reason for economic growth, capital accumulation, is discussed next. A more complete discussion of why economic growth occurs appears in Chapter 9.) Figure 2-4 on the following page shows the production possibilities curve for electronic book readers and netbook computers shifting outward. The two additional curves shown represent new choices open to an economy that has experienced economic growth. Such economic growth occurs because of

FIGURE 2-4 Economic Growth Allows for More of Everything

If the nation experiences economic growth, the production possibilities curve between e-readers and netbooks will move out as shown. This takes time, however, and it does not occur automatically. This means, therefore, that we can have more of both e-readers and netbooks only after a period of time during which we have experienced economic growth.

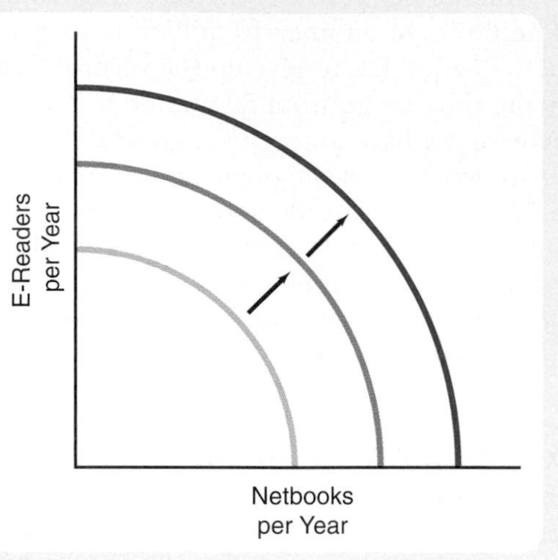

many things, including increases in the number of workers and productive investment in equipment.

Scarcity still exists, however, no matter how much economic growth there is. At any point in time, we will always be on some production possibilities curve; thus, we will always face trade-offs. The more we have of one thing, the less we can have of others.

If economic growth occurs in the nation, the production possibilities curve between e-readers and netbooks moves outward, as shown in Figure 2-4. This takes time and does not occur automatically. One reason it will occur involves the choice about how much to consume today.

The Trade-Off Between the Present and the Future

Consumption
The use of goods and services for personal satisfaction.

The production possibilities curve and economic growth can be combined to examine the trade-off between present **consumption** and future consumption. When we consume today, we are using up what we call consumption or consumer goods—food and clothes, for example.

Why We Make Capital Goods

Why would we be willing to use productive resources to make things—capital goods—that we cannot consume directly? The reason is that capital goods enable us to produce larger quantities of consumer goods or to produce them less expensively than we otherwise could. Before fish are "produced" for the market, equipment such as fishing boats, nets, and poles is produced first. Imagine how expensive it would be to obtain fish for market without using these capital goods. Catching fish with one's hands is not an easy task. The cost per fish would be very high if capital goods weren't used.

Forgoing Current Consumption

Whenever we use productive resources to make capital goods, we are implicitly forgoing current consumption. We are waiting for some time in the future to consume the rewards that will be reaped from the use of capital goods. In effect, when we forgo

FIGURE 2-5 Capital Goods and Growth

In panel (a), the nation chooses not to consume $1 trillion, so it invests that amount in capital goods. As a result, more of all goods may be produced in the future, as shown in the right-hand diagram in panel (a). In panel (b), society chooses even more capital goods (point *C*). The result is that the production possibilities curve (PPC) moves even more to the right on the right-hand diagram in panel (b).

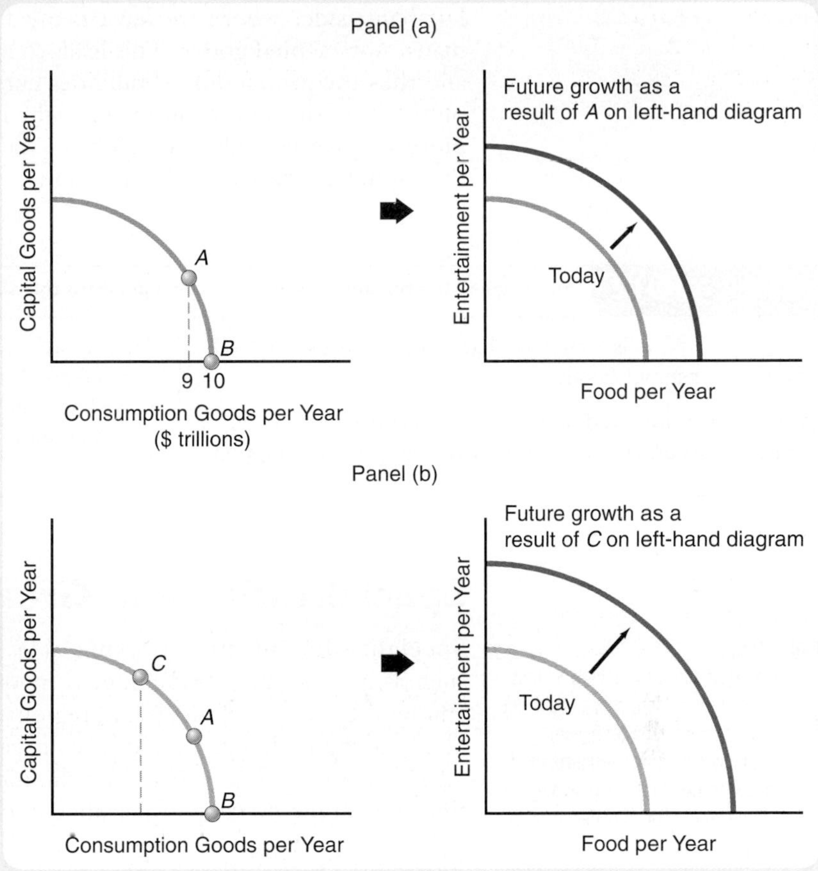

current consumption to invest in capital goods, we are engaging in an economic activity that is forward-looking—we do not get instant utility or satisfaction from our activity.

The Trade-Off Between Consumption Goods and Capital Goods

To have more consumer goods in the future, we must accept fewer consumer goods today, because resources must be used in producing capital goods instead of consumer goods. In other words, an opportunity cost is involved. Every time we make a choice of more goods today, we incur an opportunity cost of fewer goods tomorrow, and every time we make a choice of more goods in the future, we incur an opportunity cost of fewer goods today. With the resources that we don't use to produce consumer goods for today, we invest in capital goods that will produce more consumer goods for us later. The trade-off is shown in Figure 2-5 above. On the left in panel (a), you can see this trade-off depicted as a production possibilities curve between capital goods and consumption goods.

Assume that we are willing to give up $1 trillion worth of consumption today. We will be at point *A* in the left-hand diagram of panel (a). This will allow the economy to grow. We will have more future consumption because we invested in more capital goods today. In the right-hand diagram of panel (a), we see two consumer goods represented, food and entertainment. The production possibilities curve will move outward if we collectively decide to restrict consumption now and invest in capital goods.

In panel (b) in Figure 2-5 on the previous page, we show the results of our willingness to forgo even more current consumption. We move to point C in the left-hand side, where we have many fewer consumer goods today but produce many more capital goods. This leads to more future growth in this simplified model, and thus the production possibilities curve in the right-hand side of panel (b) shifts outward more than it did in the right-hand side of panel (a). In other words, the more we give up today, the more we can have tomorrow, provided, of course, that the capital goods are productive in future periods.

QUICK QUIZ See page 47 for the answers. Review concepts from this section in MyEconLab.

__________ goods are goods that will later be used to produce consumer goods.

A trade-off is involved between current consumption and capital goods or, alternatively, between current consumption and future consumption. The __________ we invest in capital goods today, the greater the amount of consumer goods we can produce in the future and the __________ the amount of consumer goods we can produce today.

Specialization and Greater Productivity

Specialization
The organization of economic activity so that what each person (or region) consumes is not identical to what that person (or region) produces. An individual may specialize, for example, in law or medicine. A nation may specialize in the production of coffee, e-book readers, or digital cameras.

Specialization involves working at a relatively well-defined, limited endeavor, such as accounting or teaching. It involves the organization of economic activity among different individuals and regions. Most individuals do specialize. For example, you could change the oil in your car if you wanted to. Typically, though, you take your car to a garage and let the mechanic change the oil. You benefit by letting the garage mechanic specialize in changing the oil and in doing other repairs on your car. The specialist normally will get the job finished sooner than you could and has the proper equipment to make the job go more smoothly. Specialization usually leads to greater productivity, not only for each individual but also for the nation.

Comparative Advantage

Specialization occurs because different individuals experience different costs when they engage in the same activities. Some individuals can accurately solve mathematical problems at lower cost than others who might try to solve the same problems. Thus, those who solve math problems at lower cost sacrifice production of fewer alternative items. Some people can develop more high-quality iPad applications than others while giving up less production of other items, such as clean houses and neatly manicured yards.

Comparative advantage
The ability to produce a good or service at a lower opportunity cost compared to other producers.

Comparative advantage is the ability to perform an activity *at a lower opportunity cost*. You have a comparative advantage in one activity whenever you have a lower opportunity cost of performing that activity. Comparative advantage is always a *relative* concept. You may be able to change the oil in your car. You might even be able to change it faster than the local mechanic. But if the opportunity cost you face by changing the oil exceeds the mechanic's opportunity cost, the mechanic has a comparative advantage in changing the oil. The mechanic faces a lower opportunity cost for that activity.

You may be convinced that everybody can do more of everything than you can during the same period of time and using the same resources. In this extreme situation, do you still have a comparative advantage? The answer is yes. You do not have to be a mathematical genius to figure this out. The market tells you so very clearly by offering you the highest income for the job for which you have a comparative advantage. Stated differently, to find your comparative advantage, simply find the job that maximizes your income.

Absolute Advantage

Suppose that, conversely, you are the president of a firm and are convinced that you have the ability to do every job in that company faster than everyone else who works there. You might be able to enter data into a spreadsheet program faster than any of the other employees, file documents in order in a file cabinet faster than any of the file clerks, and wash windows faster than any of the window washers. Furthermore, you are able to manage the firm in less time more effectively than anyone else in the company—and in less time than you would have to spend in any alternative function.

If all of these self-perceptions were really true, then you would have an **absolute advantage** in all of these endeavors. In other words, if you were to spend a given amount of time in any one of them, you could produce more than anyone else in the company. Nonetheless, you would not spend your time doing these other activities. Why not? Because your time advantage in undertaking the president's managerial duties is even greater. Therefore, you would find yourself specializing in that particular task even though you have an *absolute* advantage in all these other tasks. Indeed, absolute advantage is irrelevant in predicting how you will allocate your time. Only *comparative advantage* matters in determining how you will allocate your time, because it is the relative cost that is important in making this choice.

Absolute advantage
The ability to produce more units of a good or service using a given quantity of labor or resource inputs. Equivalently, the ability to produce the same quantity of a good or service using fewer units of labor or resource inputs.

The coaches of sports teams often have to determine the comparative advantage of an individual player who has an absolute advantage in every aspect of the sport in question. Babe Ruth, who could hit more home runs and pitch more strikeouts per game than other players on the Boston Red Sox, was a pitcher on that professional baseball team. After he was traded to the New York Yankees, the owner and the manager decided to make him an outfielder, even though he could also hurl more strikeouts per game than other Yankees. They wanted "The Babe" to concentrate on his hitting because a home-run king would bring in more paying fans than a good pitcher would. Babe Ruth had an absolute advantage in both aspects of the game of baseball, but his comparative advantage was clearly in hitting homers rather than in practicing and developing his pitching game.

Scarcity, Self-Interest, and Specialization

In Chapter 1, you learned about the assumption of rational self-interest. To repeat, for the purposes of our analyses we assume that individuals are rational in that they will do what is in their own self-interest. They will not consciously carry out actions that will make them worse off. In this chapter, you learned that scarcity requires people to make choices. We *assume* that they make choices based on their self-interest. When they make these choices, they attempt to maximize benefits net of opportunity cost. In so doing, individuals choose their comparative advantage and end up specializing.

The Division of Labor

In any firm that includes specialized human and nonhuman resources, there is a **division of labor** among those resources. The best-known example comes from Adam Smith (1723–1790), who in *The Wealth of Nations* illustrated the benefits of a division of labor in the making of pins, as depicted in the following example:

Division of labor
The segregation of resources into different specific tasks; for example, one automobile worker puts on bumpers, another doors, and so on.

> One man draws out the wire, another straightens it, a third cuts it, a fourth points it, a fifth grinds it at the top for receiving the head; to make the head requires two or three distinct operations; to put it on is a peculiar business, to whiten the pins is another; it is even a trade by itself to put them into the paper.

Making pins this way allowed 10 workers without very much skill to make almost 48,000 pins "of a middling size" in a day. One worker, toiling alone, could have made perhaps 20 pins a day; therefore, 10 workers could have produced 200.

Division of labor allowed for an increase in the daily output of the pin factory from 200 to 48,000! (Smith did not attribute all of the gain to the division of labor but credited also the use of machinery and the fact that less time was spent shifting from task to task.)

What we are discussing here involves a division of the resource called labor into different uses of labor. The different uses of labor are organized in such a way as to increase the amount of output possible from the fixed resources available. We can therefore talk about an organized division of labor within a firm leading to increased output.

Comparative Advantage and Trade Among Nations

Most of our analysis of absolute advantage, comparative advantage, and specialization has dealt with individuals. Nevertheless, it is equally applicable to groups of people.

Trade Among Regions

Consider the United States. The Plains states have a comparative advantage in the production of grains and other agricultural goods. Relative to the Plains states, the states to the east tend to specialize in industrialized production, such as automobiles. Not surprisingly, grains are shipped from the Plains states to the eastern states, and automobiles are shipped in the reverse direction. Such specialization and trade allow for higher incomes and standards of living.

If both the Plains states and the eastern states were separate nations, the same analysis would still hold, but we would call it international trade. Indeed, the European Union (EU) is comparable to the United States in area and population, but instead of one nation, the EU has 27. What U.S. residents call *interstate* trade, Europeans call *international* trade. There is no difference, however, in the economic results—both yield greater economic efficiency and higher average incomes.

Why does the time required to export an item help to determine whether a nation develops a comparative advantage in producing that item?

INTERNATIONAL EXAMPLE **Time as a Determinant of Comparative Advantage**

During the past decade, firms in an increasing number of industries began to utilize "just-in-time inventory management," which focuses on keeping inventories low by moving items quickly in response to consumer orders. Technological improvements in production processes, shipping, and delivery have enabled firms using this technique to substantially reduce the time required to transmit a newly produced item to consumers. Most firms that have implemented just-in-time inventory management experience significantly lower costs.

Nations where firms have implemented just-in-time inventory management are more likely to develop a comparative advantage over nations where firms have not. In a study of export industries in 64 developing countries, World Bank economists Yue Li and John Wilson found that the time required to export items is an important determinant of comparative advantage. They estimate that a nation's industry is substantially more likely to gain a comparative advantage if it can significantly reduce the time required to export an item.

FOR CRITICAL ANALYSIS

Why might developing the capability to provide a particular service via the Internet help a nation develop a comparative advantage in providing that service?

International Aspects of Trade

Political problems that normally do not occur within a particular nation often arise between nations. For example, if California avocado growers develop a cheaper method of producing avocados than growers in southern Florida use, the Florida growers will lose out. They cannot do much about the situation except try to lower their own costs of production or improve their product.

If avocado growers in Mexico, however, develop a cheaper method of producing avocados, both California and Florida growers can (and likely will) try to raise political barriers that will prevent Mexican avocado growers from freely selling their product in the United States. U.S. avocado growers will use such arguments as "unfair" competition and loss of U.S. jobs. Certainly, avocado-growing jobs may decline in the United States, but there is no reason to believe that U.S. jobs will decline overall. Instead, former U.S. avocado workers will move into alternative employment—something that 1 million people do every *week* in the United States. If the argument of U.S. avocado growers had any validity, every time a region in the United States developed a better way to produce a product manufactured somewhere else in the country, U.S. employment would decline. That has never happened and never will.

Go to **www.econtoday.com/ch02** to find out from the World Trade Organization how much international trade takes place. Under "Resources," click on "Trade statistics" and then click on "International Trade Statistics" for the most recent year.

When nations specialize where they have a comparative advantage and then trade with the rest of the world, the average standard of living in the world rises. In effect, international trade allows the world to move from inside the global production possibilities curve toward the curve itself, thereby improving worldwide economic efficiency. Thus, all countries that engage in trade can benefit from comparative advantage, just as regions in the United States benefit from interregional trade.

QUICK QUIZ See page 47 for the answers. **Review concepts from this section in MyEconLab.**

With a given set of resources, specialization results in __________ output; in other words, there are gains to specialization in terms of greater material well-being.

Individuals and nations specialize in their areas of __________ advantage in order to reap the gains of specialization.

Comparative advantages are found by determining which activities have the __________ opportunity costs—that is, which activities yield the highest return for the time and resources used.

A __________ of labor occurs when different workers are assigned different tasks. Together, the workers produce a desired product.

You Are There

Stopping Students' Thursday Night Parties with Friday Classes

Thomas Rocklin, provost at the University of Iowa, has been trying to determine how to confront a problem facing many university administrators: average rates of alcohol consumption by Iowa students on Thursday nights have jumped dramatically. Rocklin has learned that a recent study suggested that half of male students and more than 40 percent of female students who consume alcoholic beverages on Thursday nights would choose not to do so if they had Friday classes to attend. He also knows that the University of Iowa holds about 40 percent fewer classes on Fridays than on Mondays through Thursdays.

Based on this information, Rocklin has decided to offer each academic department an extra $20 for each student rescheduled into a course that includes a Friday class. When announcing the new policy, Rocklin states, "It's always more effective to offer more incentives to do the right thing." Thus, by inducing departments to boost the number of Friday classes, Rocklin has decided to try to raise students' opportunity cost of attending parties and drinking alcohol—sometimes to excess—on Thursday nights.

Critical Analysis Questions

1. Why might university administrators judge that the opportunity cost of trying to cut binge drinking on Friday nights by offering Saturday classes would be too high?
2. How might requiring students to enroll in 8 a.m. classes help to reduce weekday alcohol consumption by students?

ISSUES & APPLICATIONS

Is Daylight Saving Time Efficient?

CONCEPTS APPLIED

- Efficiency
- Opportunity Cost
- Trade-Offs

A key resource utilized in the production of a nation's goods and services is time. There are always 24 hours in each day, so society must decide how to utilize those hours most efficiently. Back in 1784, Benjamin Franklin proposed daylight saving time as a way to produce the same quantity of goods and services while using fewer candles. The U.S. government did not put his idea into effect until early in the twentieth century. Since then, economists have debated whether implementation of Franklin's idea has really led to greater efficiency.

Assessing the Opportunity Cost of Daylight Saving Time

Recall that the opportunity cost associated with a choice is the value of the next-best alternative. The next-best alternative to daylight saving time would seem to be to keep clock settings unchanged throughout the year. Thus, economists consider the value of this alternative when evaluating whether daylight saving time is efficient.

In the 1970s, the U.S. Department of Transportation conducted a detailed study of daylight saving time and determined that, compared with standard time, it trimmed national electricity usage by about 1 percent. This conclusion indicated that the opportunity cost of using standard time was sufficiently high that daylight saving time was society's better choice.

Is Daylight Saving Time Inefficient?

Since the 1970s, air-conditioning and new household electronic items have come into use, so patterns of U.S. electricity usage have changed considerably. To reassess the efficiency implications of daylight saving time in light of the altered configuration of electricity usage, Matthew Kotchen and Laura Grant of the University of California at Santa Barbara examined a recent time switch. Indiana, which previously had kept its clocks unchanged throughout the year, switched to daylight saving time in 2006.

Kotchen and Grant found that, consistent with Benjamin Franklin's prediction, Indiana residents saved from decreasing their use of electric lights. Nevertheless, today air-conditioning use also affects the energy-use trade-off associated with daylight saving time versus standard time. Households and businesses in Indiana made greater use of their air conditioners to maintain lower temperatures during longer summer evenings. Kotchen and Grant found that, on net, switching to daylight saving time led to *greater* use of electricity, resulting in *higher*, rather than lower, energy expenses in Indiana.

Thus, they concluded that switching to daylight saving time each year may make the U.S. economy *less* efficient than it otherwise would be if the nation remained on standard time.

For Critical Analysis

1. Why does inefficiency mean *either* incurring a higher expense to produce the same number of items *or* producing fewer items at the same level of expenses?
2. Why is it possible that remaining on standard time is not necessarily the next-best alternative to switching to daylight saving time? (Hint: Are there alternatives to moving clocks ahead by exactly one hour in the spring?)

Web Resources

1. For more information about the implementation of daylight saving time in the United States, go to www.econtoday.com/ch02.
2. To learn more about various relative costs of daylight saving time versus standard time, go to www.econtoday.com/ch02.

Research Project

Make a list of possible pros and cons associated with switching to daylight saving time each year instead of keeping clocks on standard time. Based on your list, what issues must be taken into account in trying to assess whether daylight saving time is more or less efficient than standard time?

For more questions on this chapter's Issues & Applications, go to **MyEconLab**. In the Study Plan for this chapter, select Section N: News.

Here is what you should know after reading this chapter. **MyEconLab** will help you identify what you know, and where to go when you need to practice.

WHAT YOU SHOULD KNOW		WHERE TO GO TO PRACTICE
The Problem of Scarcity, Even for the Affluent Even the richest people face scarcity because they have to make choices among alternatives. Despite their high levels of income or wealth, affluent people, like everyone else, want more than they can have (in terms of goods, power, prestige, and so on).	scarcity, 27 production, 27 land, 27 labor, 28 physical capital, 28 human capital, 28 entrepreneurship, 28 goods, 28 economic goods, 28 services, 28	• **MyEconLab** Study Plan 2.1 • Audio introduction to Chapter 2 • Video: Scarcity, Resources, and Production • ABC News Video: The Economics of Higher Education
Why Economists Consider Individuals' Wants but Not Their "Needs" Goods are all things from which individuals derive satisfaction. Economic goods are those for which the desired quantity exceeds the amount that is available at a zero price. The term *need* is undefinable, whereas humans have unlimited *wants*, which are the items on which we place a positive value.		• **MyEconLab** Study Plan 2.2
Why Scarcity Leads People to Evaluate Opportunity Costs Opportunity cost is the highest-valued alternative that one must give up to obtain an item. The trade-offs society faces can be represented by a production possibilities curve (PPC). Along a PPC, all available resources and technology are being used, so to obtain more of one good, resources must be shifted to production of that good and away from production of another. Thus, moving along a PPC from one point to another entails incurring an opportunity cost of allocating scarce resources toward the production of one good instead of another good.	opportunity cost, 29 production possibilities curve (PPC), 30 **KEY FIGURE** Figure 2-1, 31	• **MyEconLab** Study Plans 2.3, 2.4 • Animated Figure 2-1 • ABC News Video: Incentives for Perfect Attendance • Economics Video: Cash for Trash • Economics Video: Myth: Outsourcing Is Bad for America • Economics Video: Stashing Your Cash

(*continued*)

MyEconLab continued

WHAT YOU SHOULD KNOW		WHERE TO GO TO PRACTICE
Why Obtaining Increasing Increments of a Good Requires Giving Up More and More Units of Other Goods When society allocates additional resources to producing more units of a good, it must increasingly employ resources that would be better suited for producing other goods. As a result, the law of increasing additional cost holds. Each additional unit of a good can be obtained only by giving up more and more of other goods, which means that the production possibilities curve is bowed outward.	technology, 33 efficiency, 34 inefficient point, 34 law of increasing additional cost, 35 **KEY FIGURES** Figure 2-3, 34 Figure 2-4, 36	• **MyEconLab** Study Plan 2.5 • Animated Figures 2-3, 2-4 • ABC News Video: The Economics of Energy
The Trade-Off Between Consumption Goods and Capital Goods If we allocate more resources to producing capital goods today, then the production possibilities curve will shift outward by a larger amount in the future, which means that we can have more consumption goods in the future. The trade-off, however, is that producing more capital goods today entails giving up consumption goods today.	consumption, 36	• **MyEconLab** Study Plans 2.6, 2.7 • ABC News Video: The Economics of Energy
Absolute Advantage versus Comparative Advantage A person has an absolute advantage if she can produce more of a good than someone else who uses the same amount of resources. An individual can gain from specializing in producing a good if she has a comparative advantage in producing that good, meaning that she can produce the good at a lower opportunity cost than someone else.	specialization, 38 comparative advantage, 38 absolute advantage, 39 division of labor, 39	• **MyEconLab** Study Plans 2.8, 2.9 • Video: Absolute versus Comparative Advantage • Economics Video: International Trade: DHL

Log in to MyEconLab, take a chapter test, and get a personalized Study Plan that tells you which concepts you understand and which ones you need to review. From there, MyEconLab will give you further practice, tutorials, animations, videos, and guided solutions.
Log in to www.myeconlab.com

PROBLEMS

All problems are assignable in myeconlab. *Answers to odd-numbered problems appear at the back of the book.*

2-1. Define opportunity cost. What is your opportunity cost of attending a class at 11:00 a.m.? How does it differ from your opportunity cost of attending a class at 8:00 a.m.?

2-2. If you receive a ticket to a concert at no charge, what, if anything, is your opportunity cost of attending the concert? How does your opportunity cost change if miserable weather on the night of the concert requires you to leave much earlier for the concert hall and greatly extends the time it takes to get home afterward?

2-3. Recently, a woman named Mary Krawiec attended an auction in Troy, New York. At the auction, a bank was seeking to sell a foreclosed property: a large Victorian house suffering from years of neglect in a neighborhood in which many properties had been on the market for years yet remained unsold. Her $10 offer was the highest bid in the auction, and she handed over a $10 bill for a title to ownership. Once she acquired the house, however, she became responsible for all taxes on the property and for an overdue water bill of $2,000. In addition, to make the house habitable, she and her husband devoted months of time and unpaid labor to renovating the property. In the process, they incurred explicit expenses totaling $65,000. Why do you suppose that the bank was willing to sell the house to Ms. Krawiec for only $10? (Hint: Contemplate the bank's expected gain, net of all explicit and opportunity costs, if it had attempted to make the house habitable.)

2-4. The following table illustrates the points a student can earn on examinations in economics and biology if the student uses all available hours for study.

Economics	Biology
100	40
90	50
80	60
70	70
60	80
50	90
40	100

Plot this student's production possibilities curve. Does the PPC illustrate the law of increasing additional cost?

2-5. Based on the information provided in Problem 2-4, what is the opportunity cost to this student of allocating enough additional study time on economics to move her grade up from a 90 to a 100?

2-6. Consider a change in the table in Problem 2-4. The student's set of opportunities is now as follows:

Economics	Biology
100	40
90	60
80	75
70	85
60	93
50	98
40	100

Does the PPC illustrate the law of increasing additional cost? What is the opportunity cost to this student for the additional amount of study time on economics required to move her grade from 60 to 70? From 90 to 100?

2-7. Construct a production possibilities curve for a nation facing increasing opportunity costs for producing food and video games. Show how the PPC changes given the following events.

a. A new and better fertilizer is invented.

b. Immigration occurs, and immigrants' labor can be employed in both the agricultural sector and the video game sector.

c. A new programming language is invented that is less costly to code and is more memory-efficient, enabling the use of smaller game cartridges.

d. A heat wave and drought result in a 10 percent decrease in usable farmland.

Consider the following diagram when answering Problems 2-8, 2-9, and 2-10.

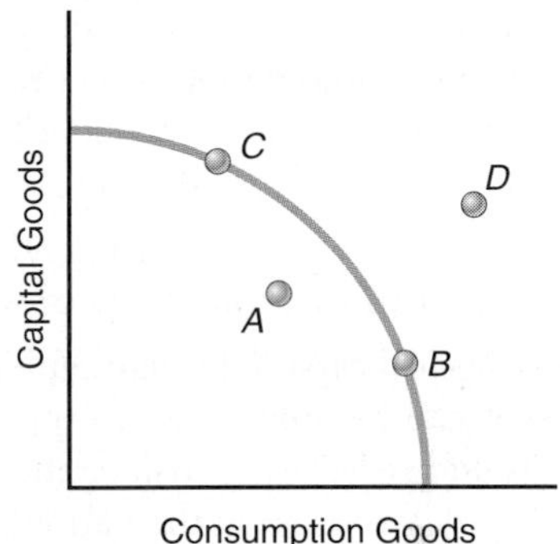

2-8. During a debate on the floor of the U.S. Senate, Senator Creighton states, "Our nation should not devote so many of its fully employed resources to producing capital goods because we already are not producing enough consumption goods for our citizens." Compared with the other labeled points on the diagram, which one could be consistent with the *current* production combination choice that Senator Creighton believes the nation has made?

2-9. In response to Senator Creighton's statement reported in Problem 2-8, Senator Long replies, "We must remain at our current production combination if we want to be able to produce more consumption goods in the future." Of the labeled points on the diagram, which one could depict the *future* production combination Senator Long has in mind?

2-10. Senator Borman interjects the following comment after the statements by Senators Creighton and Long reported in Problems 2-8 and 2-9: "In fact, both of my esteemed colleagues are wrong, because an unacceptably large portion of our nation's resources is currently unemployed." Of the labeled points on the diagram, which one is consistent with Senator Borman's position?

2-11. A nation's residents can allocate their scarce resources either to producing consumption goods or to producing human capital—that is, providing themselves with training and education. The following table displays the production possibilities for this nation:

Production Combination	Units of Consumption Goods	Units of Human Capital
A	0	100
B	10	97
C	20	90
D	30	75
E	40	55
F	50	30
G	60	0

a. Suppose that the nation's residents currently produce combination A. What is the opportunity cost of increasing production of consumption goods by 10 units? By 60 units?

b. Does the law of increasing additional cost hold true for this nation? Why or why not?

2-12. Like physical capital, human capital produced in the present can be applied to the production of future goods and services. Consider the table in Problem 2-11, and suppose that the nation's residents are trying to choose between combination C and combination F. Other things being equal, will the future production possibilities curve for this nation be located farther outward if the nation chooses combination F instead of combination C? Explain.

2-13. You can wash, fold, and iron a basket of laundry in two hours and prepare a meal in one hour. Your roommate can wash, fold, and iron a basket of laundry in three hours and prepare a meal in one hour. Who has the absolute advantage in laundry, and who has an absolute advantage in meal preparation? Who has the comparative advantage in laundry, and who has a comparative advantage in meal preparation?

2-14. Based on the information in Problem 2-13, should you and your roommate specialize in a particular task? Why? And if so, who should specialize in which task? Show how much labor time you save if you choose to "trade" an appropriate task with your roommate as opposed to doing it yourself.

2-15. Using only the concept of comparative advantage, evaluate this statement: "A professor with a Ph.D. in physics should never mow his or her own lawn, because this would fail to take into account the professor's comparative advantage."

2-16. Country A and country B produce the same consumption goods and capital goods and currently have *identical* production possibilities curves. They also have the same resources at present, and they have access to the same technology.

a. At present, does either country have a comparative advantage in producing capital goods? Consumption goods?

b. Currently, country A has chosen to produce more consumption goods, compared with country B. Other things being equal, which country will experience the larger outward shift of its PPC during the next year?

ECONOMICS ON THE NET

Opportunity Cost and Labor Force Participation Many students choose to forgo full-time employment to concentrate on their studies, thereby incurring a sizable opportunity cost. This application explores the nature of this opportunity cost.

Title: College Enrollment and Work Activity of High School Graduates

Navigation: Go to **www.econtoday.com/ch02** to visit the Bureau of Labor Statistics (BLS) home page. Select A–Z Index and then click on *Educational attainment (Statistics)*. Under "School Enrollment," click on *College Enrollment and Work Activity of High School Graduates*.

Application Read the abbreviated report on college enrollment and work activity of high school graduates. Then answer the following questions.

1. Based on the article, explain who the BLS considers to be in the labor force and who it does not view as part of the labor force.
2. What is the difference in labor force participation rates between high school students entering four-year universities and those entering two-year universities? Using the concept of opportunity cost, explain the difference.
3. What is the difference in labor force participation rates between part-time college students and full-time college students? Using the concept of opportunity cost, explain the difference.

For Group Study and Analysis Read the last paragraph of the article. Then divide the class into two groups. The first group should explain, based on the concept of opportunity cost, the difference in labor force participation rates between youths not in school but with a high school diploma and youths not in school and without a high school diploma. The second group should explain, based on opportunity cost, the difference in labor force participation rates between men and women not in school but with a high school diploma and men and women not in school and without a high school diploma.

ANSWERS TO QUICK QUIZZES

p. 29: (i) Scarcity; (ii) land . . . labor . . . physical . . . human . . . entrepreneurship; (iii) Wants; (iv) need

p. 32: (i) next-highest; (ii) opportunity; (iii) next-best; (iv) production possibilities

p. 35: (i) production possibilities; (ii) fixed; (iii) outside . . . inside; (iv) outward

p. 38: (i) Capital; (ii) more . . . smaller

p. 41: (i) higher; (ii) comparative; (iii) lowest; (iv) division

3 Demand and Supply

When people's incomes rise, they usually consume more of most items. Likewise, when their incomes fall, they typically reduce their consumption of the large majority of goods and services. As the recent Great Recession helped to reveal, however, this normally positive relationship between consumers' incomes and their purchases of goods and services does not hold true for all items. When most consumers' incomes fell during the economic downturn, they responded by purchasing *more* shoe repair services, electric hair clippers, and dial-up Internet access services. Why does an income decline lead to an increase in desired purchases of these and certain other goods and services? To understand the answer to this question, you must first learn about all of the determinants—including income—of the amounts of goods and services that people wish to buy.

LEARNING OBJECTIVES

After reading this chapter, you should be able to:

- Explain the law of demand
- Discuss the difference between money prices and relative prices
- Distinguish between changes in demand and changes in quantity demanded
- Explain the law of supply
- Distinguish between changes in supply and changes in quantity supplied
- Understand how the interaction of the demand for and supply of a commodity determines the market price of the commodity and the equilibrium quantity of the commodity that is produced and consumed

MyEconLab helps you master each objective and study more efficiently. See end of chapter for details.

after world gasoline prices jumped in the late 2000s, global bicycle sales rose to more than 1 million per month? Higher fuel prices induced many individuals to substitute away from gasoline-powered vehicles in favor of bikes powered by human muscles. Thus, these people responded to higher gasoline prices by increasing their purchases of bicycles.

Did You Know That ?

If we use the economist's primary set of tools, *demand* and *supply*, we can develop a better understanding of why we sometimes observe relatively large increases in the purchase, or consumption, of items such as bicycles. We can also better understand why a persistent increase in the price of a good such as gasoline ultimately induces an increase in bicycle consumption. Demand and supply are two ways of categorizing the influences on the prices of goods that you buy and the quantities available. Indeed, demand and supply characterize much economic analysis of the world around us.

As you will see throughout this text, the operation of the forces of demand and supply takes place in *markets*. A **market** is an abstract concept summarizing all of the arrangements individuals have for exchanging with one another. Goods and services are sold in markets, such as the automobile market, the health care market, and the market for high-speed Internet access. Workers offer their services in the labor market. Companies, or firms, buy workers' labor services in the labor market. Firms also buy other inputs in order to produce the goods and services that you buy as a consumer. Firms purchase machines, buildings, and land. These markets are in operation at all times. One of the most important activities in these markets is the determination of the prices of all of the inputs and outputs that are bought and sold in our complicated economy. To understand the determination of prices, you first need to look at the law of demand.

Market
All of the arrangements that individuals have for exchanging with one another. Thus, for example, we can speak of the labor market, the automobile market, and the credit market.

Demand

Demand has a special meaning in economics. It refers to the quantities of specific goods or services that individuals, taken singly or as a group, will purchase at various possible prices, other things being constant. We can therefore talk about the demand for microprocessor chips, french fries, multifunction digital devices, children, and criminal activities.

Demand
A schedule showing how much of a good or service people will purchase at any price during a specified time period, other things being constant.

The Law of Demand

Associated with the concept of demand is the **law of demand,** which can be stated as follows:

Law of demand
The observation that there is a negative, or inverse, relationship between the price of any good or service and the quantity demanded, holding other factors constant.

> ***When the price of a good goes up, people buy less of it, other things being equal. When the price of a good goes down, people buy more of it, other things being equal.***

The law of demand tells us that the quantity demanded of any commodity is inversely related to its price, other things being equal. In an inverse relationship, one variable moves up in value when the other moves down. The law of demand states that a change in price causes a change in the quantity demanded in the *opposite* direction.

Notice that we tacked on to the end of the law of demand the statement "other things being equal." We referred to this in Chapter 1 as the *ceteris paribus* assumption. It means, for example, that when we predict that people will buy fewer Blu-ray disc players if their price goes up, we are holding constant the price of all other goods in the economy as well as people's incomes. Implicitly, therefore, if we are assuming that no other prices change when we examine the price behavior of Blu-ray disc players, we are looking at the *relative* price of Blu-ray disc players.

The law of demand is supported by millions of observations of people's behavior in the marketplace. Theoretically, it can be derived from an economic model based on rational behavior, as was discussed in Chapter 1. Basically, if nothing else changes and the price of a good falls, the lower price induces us to buy more over a certain period of time because we can enjoy additional net gains that were unavailable at the higher price. If you examine your own behavior, you will see that it generally follows the law of demand.

How did an error in posting the price of gasoline help to illustrate the law of demand?

EXAMPLE A Mistaken Price Change Confirms the Law of Demand

In Wisconsin Rapids, Wisconsin, employees at a Citgo station intending to change the posted price of gasoline from $3.43 per gallon to $3.49 per gallon accidentally changed the price to $0.349 per gallon. A station attendant said that, within minutes, "people were coming so fast that everything was crowded, like a fairground." During the few minutes between the error and correction of the mistake, customers used self-serve pumps to buy hundreds of gallons of gasoline, filling up their vehicles and any cans they had readily available. Thus, a significant, albeit mistaken, decrease in the price of gasoline induced a substantial increase in the quantity of gasoline demanded.

FOR CRITICAL ANALYSIS

What do you think would have happened if the gas station's pricing error had shifted the decimal point in the opposite direction, yielding a posted price of $34.9 per gallon?

Relative Prices versus Money Prices

Relative price
The money price of one commodity divided by the money price of another commodity; the number of units of one commodity that must be sacrificed to purchase one unit of another commodity.

Money price
The price expressed in today's dollars; also called the *absolute* or *nominal price*.

The **relative price** of any commodity is its price in terms of another commodity. The price that you pay in dollars and cents for any good or service at any point in time is called its **money price.** You might hear from your grandparents, "My first new car cost only fifteen hundred dollars." The implication, of course, is that the price of cars today is outrageously high because the average new car may cost $32,000. But that is not an accurate comparison. What was the price of the average house during that same year? Perhaps it was only $12,000. By comparison, then, given that the average price of houses today is close to $190,000, the price of a new car today doesn't sound so far out of line, does it?

The point is that money prices during different time periods don't tell you much. You have to calculate relative prices. Consider an example of the price of 350-gigabyte flash memory drives versus the price of 350-gigabyte external hard drives from last year and this year. In Table 3-1 below, we show the money prices of flash memory drives and external hard drives for two years during which they have both gone down.

That means that in today's dollars we have to pay out less for both flash memory drives and external hard drives. If we look, though, at the relative prices of flash memory drives and external hard drives, we find that last year, 350-gigabyte flash memory drives were twice as expensive as 350-gigabyte external hard drives, whereas this year they are only one and a half times as expensive. Conversely, if we compare external hard drives to flash memory drives, last year the price of external hard drives was 50 percent of the price of external hard drives, but today the price of external hard drives is about 67 percent of the price of flash memory drives. In the one-year period, although both prices have declined in money terms, the relative price of external hard drives has risen relative to that of flash memory drives.

TABLE 3-1

Money Price versus Relative Price

The money prices of both 350-gigabyte flash memory drives and 350-gigabyte external hard drives have fallen. But the relative price of external hard drives has risen (or conversely, the relative price of flash memory drives has fallen).

	Money Price		Relative Price	
	Price Last Year	Price This Year	Price Last Year	Price This Year
350-gigabyte flash memory drives	$300	$210	$\frac{\$300}{\$150} = 2.0$	$\frac{\$210}{\$140} = 1.50$
350-gigabyte external hard drives	$150	$140	$\frac{\$150}{\$300} = 0.50$	$\frac{\$140}{\$210} = 0.67$

Sometimes relative price changes occur because the quality of a product improves, thereby bringing about a decrease in the item's effective *price per constant-quality unit*. Or the price of an item may decrease simply because producers have reduced the item's quality. Thus, when evaluating the effects of price changes, we must always compare *price per constant-quality unit*.

What has recently happened to the quality-adjusted price of cellphones?

EXAMPLE **Why Even Low-Income Households Are Rushing to Buy iPhones**

Increasingly, "smart" cellphones, such as Apple's iPhone, provide broadband Internet connectivity. Many observers have been surprised to see consumers across all ranges of income rushing to purchase these relatively high-priced digital devices. Indeed, surveys show that for some low-income consumers, an Internet-ready cellphone is their first-ever cellphone purchase. When asked why they are buying the gadgets, most of these consumers respond that they can obtain *both* phone *and* Internet services at a relatively low price. Many say that they plan to use the cellphones as their exclusive means of access to phone services, e-mail, and the Internet. In this way, they can avoid separate payments for phone and Internet service. From their point of view, therefore, the arrival of smart cellphones has caused the *quality-adjusted* cellphone price to drop sufficiently to justify purchasing the device.

FOR CRITICAL ANALYSIS

As the prices of personal computers have steadily declined since their introduction in the late 1970s, what do you think has happened to their quality-adjusted *prices?*

QUICK QUIZ See page 73 for the answers. Review concepts from this section in MyEconLab.

The **law of demand** posits an __________ relationship between the quantity demanded of a good and its price, other things being equal.

The law of __________ applies when other things, such as income and the prices of all other goods and services, are held constant.

The Demand Schedule

Let's take a hypothetical demand situation to see how the inverse relationship between the price and the quantity demanded looks (holding other things equal). We will consider the quantity of titanium batteries—used in various electronic gadgets and other digital devices—demanded *per year*. Without stating the *time dimension*, we could not make sense out of this demand relationship because the numbers would be different if we were talking about the quantity demanded per month or the quantity demanded per decade.

In addition to implicitly or explicitly stating a time dimension for a demand relationship, we are also implicitly referring to *constant-quality units* of the good or service in question. Prices are always expressed in constant-quality units in order to avoid the problem of comparing commodities that are in fact not truly comparable.

In panel (a) of Figure 3-1 on the following page, we see that if the price is $1 apiece, 50 titanium batteries will be bought each year by our representative individual, but if the price is $5 apiece, only 10 batteries will be bought each year. This reflects the law of demand. Panel (a) is also called simply demand, or a *demand schedule*, because it gives a schedule of alternative quantities demanded per year at different possible prices.

The Demand Curve

Tables expressing relationships between two variables can be represented in graphical terms. To do this, we need only construct a graph that has the price per constant-quality titanium battery on the vertical axis and the quantity measured in constant-quality titanium batteries per year on the horizontal axis. All we have to do is take combinations *A* through *E* from panel (a) of Figure 3-1 and plot those points in panel (b).

FIGURE 3-1 The Individual Demand Schedule and the Individual Demand Curve

In panel (a), we show combinations *A* through *E* of the quantities of titanium batteries demanded, measured in constant-quality units at prices ranging from \$5 down to \$1 apiece. These combinations are points on the demand schedule. In panel (b), we plot combinations *A* through *E* on a grid. The result is the individual demand curve for titanium batteries.

Panel (a)

Combination	Price per Constant-Quality Titanium Battery	Quantity of Constant-Quality Titanium Batteries per Year
A	\$5	10
B	4	20
C	3	30
D	2	40
E	1	50

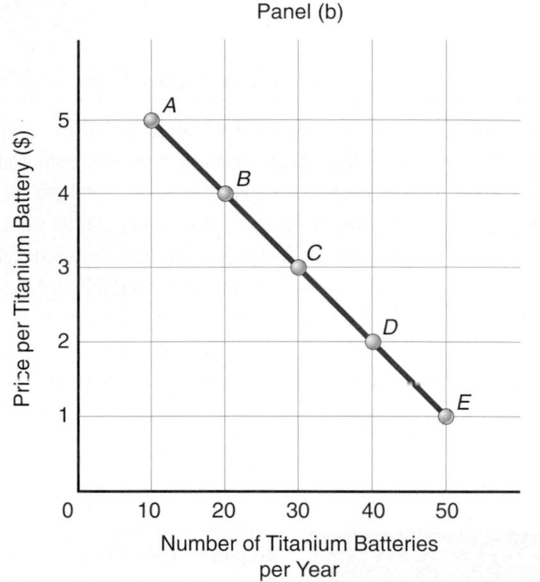

Demand curve
A graphical representation of the demand schedule; a negatively sloped line showing the inverse relationship between the price and the quantity demanded (other things being equal).

Now we connect the points with a smooth line, and *voilà*, we have a **demand curve.** It is downward sloping (from left to right) to indicate the inverse relationship between the price of titanium batteries and the quantity demanded per year. Our presentation of demand schedules and curves applies equally well to all commodities, including dental floss, bagels, textbooks, credit, and labor. Remember, the demand curve is simply a graphical representation of the law of demand.

Individual versus Market Demand Curves

Market demand
The demand of all consumers in the marketplace for a particular good or service. The summation at each price of the quantity demanded by each individual.

The demand schedule shown in panel (a) of Figure 3-1 above and the resulting demand curve shown in panel (b) are both given for an individual. As we shall see, the determination of price in the marketplace depends on, among other things, the **market demand** for a particular commodity. The way in which we measure a market demand schedule and derive a market demand curve for titanium batteries or any other good or service is by summing (at each price) the individual quantities demanded by all buyers in the market. Suppose that the market demand for titanium batteries consists of only two buyers: buyer 1, for whom we've already shown the demand schedule, and buyer 2, whose demand schedule is displayed in column 3 of panel (a) of Figure 3-2 on the facing page. Column 1 shows the price, and column 2 shows the quantity demanded by buyer 1 at each price. These data are taken directly from Figure 3-1 above. In column 3, we show the quantity demanded by buyer 2. Column 4 shows the total quantity demanded at each price, which is obtained by simply adding columns 2 and 3. Graphically, in panel (d) of Figure 3-2, we add the demand curves of buyer 1 [panel (b)] and buyer 2 [panel (c)] to derive the market demand curve.

There are, of course, numerous potential consumers of titanium batteries. We'll simply assume that the summation of all of the consumers in the market results in a demand schedule, given in panel (a) of Figure 3-3 on page 54, and a demand curve, given in panel (b). The quantity demanded is now measured in millions of units per year.

FIGURE 3-2 The Horizontal Summation of Two Demand Curves

Panel (a) shows how to sum the demand schedule for one buyer with that of another buyer. In column 2 is the quantity demanded by buyer 1, taken from panel (a) of Figure 3-1 on the facing page. Column 4 is the sum of columns 2 and 3. We plot the demand curve for buyer 1 in panel (b) and the demand curve for buyer 2 in panel (c). When we add those two demand curves horizontally, we get the market demand curve for two buyers, shown in panel (d).

Panel (a)

(1) Price per Titanium Battery	(2) Buyer 1's Quantity Demanded	(3) Buyer 2's Quantity Demanded	(4) = (2) + (3) Combined Quantity Demanded per Year
$5	10	10	20
4	20	20	40
3	30	40	70
2	40	50	90
1	50	60	110

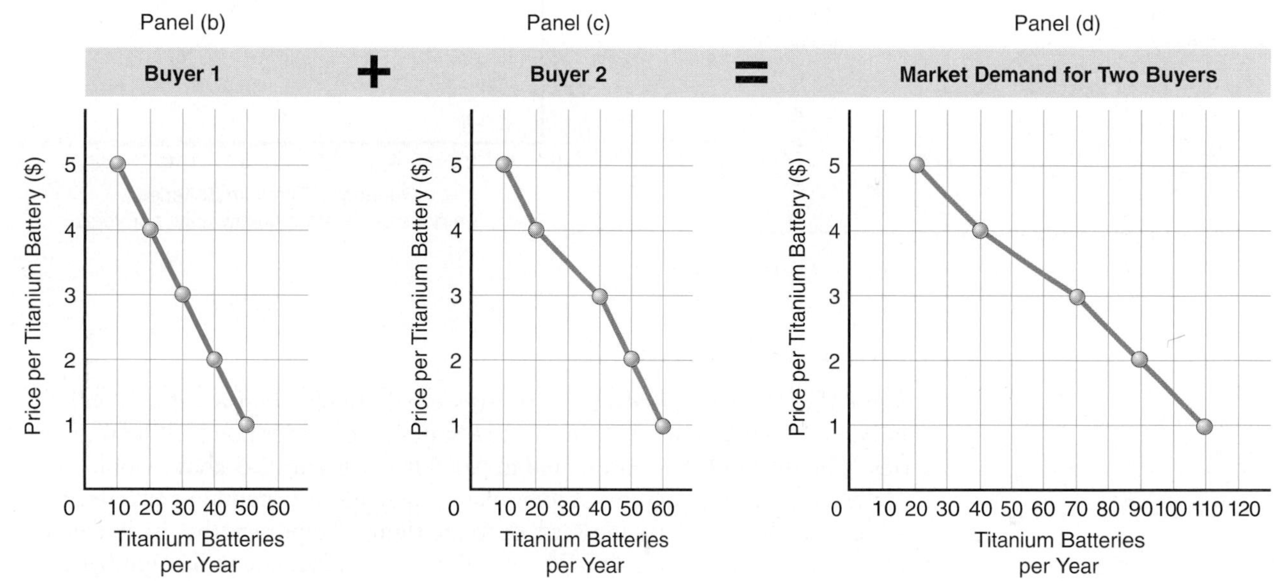

Remember, panel (b) in Figure 3-3 on the following page shows the market demand curve for the millions of buyers of titanium batteries. The "market" demand curve that we derived in Figure 3-2 above was undertaken assuming that there were only two buyers in the entire market. That's why we assume that the "market" demand curve for two buyers in panel (d) of Figure 3-2 is not a smooth line, whereas the true market demand curve in panel (b) of Figure 3-3 is a smooth line with no kinks.

QUICK QUIZ See page 73 for the answers. Review concepts from this section in MyEconLab.

We measure the **demand schedule** in terms of a time dimension and in __________-quality units.

The __________ __________ curve is derived by summing the quantity demanded by individuals at each price. Graphically, we add the individual demand curves horizontally to derive the total, or market, demand curve.

FIGURE 3-3 The Market Demand Schedule for Titanium Batteries

In panel (a), we add up the existing demand schedules for titanium batteries. In panel (b), we plot the quantities from panel (a) on a grid; connecting them produces the market demand curve for titanium batteries.

Panel (a)

Price per Constant-Quality Titanium Battery	Total Quantity Demanded of Constant-Quality Titanium Batteries per Year (millions)
$5	2
4	4
3	6
2	8
1	10

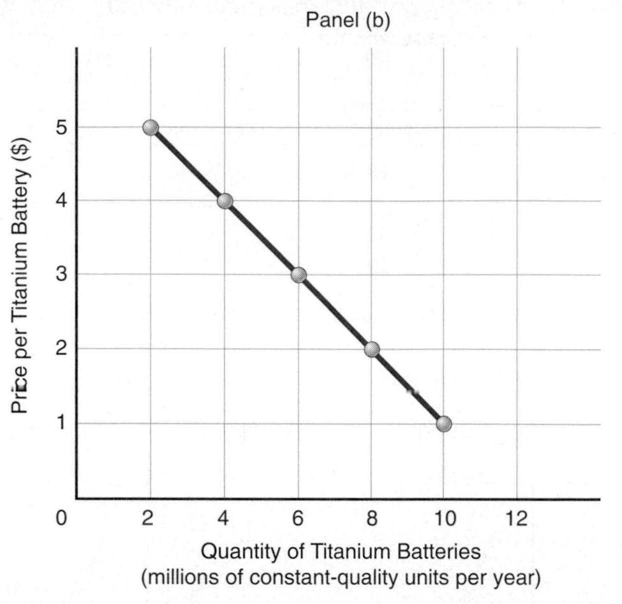

Shifts in Demand

Assume that the federal government gives every student registered in a college, university, or technical school in the United States an e-reader powered by titanium batteries. The demand curve presented in panel (b) of Figure 3-3 above would no longer be an accurate representation of total market demand for titanium batteries. What we have to do is shift the curve outward, or to the right, to represent the rise in demand that would result from this program. There will now be an increase in the number of batteries demanded at *each and every possible price*. The demand curve shown in Figure 3-4 below will shift from D_1 to D_2. Take any price, say, $3 per battery. Originally, before

FIGURE 3-4 Shifts in the Demand Curve

If some factor other than price changes, we can show its effect by moving the entire demand curve, say, from D_1 to D_2. We have assumed in our example that this move was precipitated by the government's giving an e-reader to every registered college student in the United States. Thus, at *all* prices, a larger number of titanium batteries would be demanded than before. Curve D_3 represents reduced demand compared to curve D_1, caused by a prohibition of e-readers on campus.

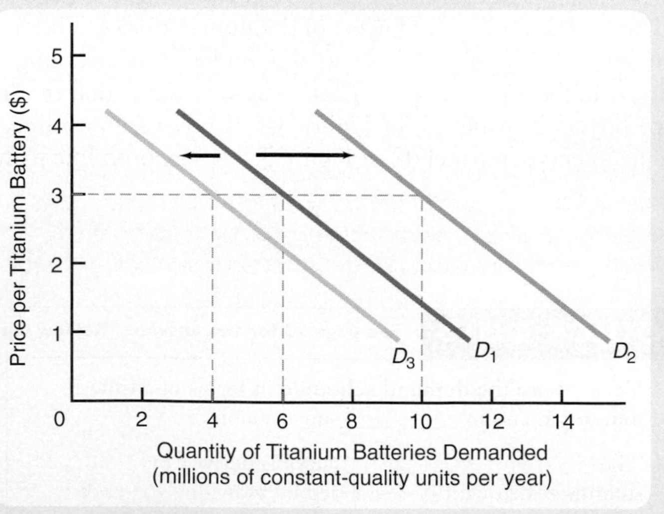

the federal government giveaway of e-readers, the amount demanded at $3 was 6 million batteries per year. After the government giveaway of e-readers, however, the new amount demanded at the $3 price is 10 million titanium batteries per year. What we have seen is a shift in the demand for titanium batteries.

Under different circumstances, the shift can also go in the opposite direction. What if colleges uniformly prohibited the use of e-readers by any of their students? Such a regulation would cause a shift inward—to the left—of the demand curve for titanium batteries. In Figure 3-4 on the bottom of the facing page, the demand curve would shift to D_3. The number demanded would now be less at each and every possible price.

The Other Determinants of Demand

The demand curve in panel (b) of Figure 3-3 on the top of the facing page is drawn with other things held constant, specifically all of the other factors that determine how many titanium batteries will be bought. There are many such determinants. We refer to these determinants as ***ceteris paribus* conditions,** and they include consumers' income; tastes and preferences; the prices of related goods; expectations regarding future prices and future incomes; and market size (number of potential buyers). Let's examine each of these determinants more closely.

***Ceteris paribus* conditions**
Determinants of the relationship between price and quantity that are unchanged along a curve. Changes in these factors cause the curve to shift.

INCOME For most goods, an increase in income will lead to an increase in demand. That is, an increase in income will lead to a rightward shift in the position of the demand curve from, say, D_1 to D_2 in Figure 3-4. You can avoid confusion about shifts in curves by always relating a rise in demand to a rightward shift in the demand curve and a fall in demand to a leftward shift in the demand curve. Goods for which the demand rises when consumer income rises are called **normal goods.** Most goods, such as shoes, computers, and flash memory drives, are "normal goods." For some goods, however, demand *falls* as income rises. These are called **inferior goods.** Beans might be an example. As households get richer, they tend to purchase fewer and fewer beans and purchase more and more fish. (The terms *normal* and *inferior* are merely part of the economist's lexicon. No value judgments are associated with them.)

Normal goods
Goods for which demand rises as income rises. Most goods are normal goods.

Inferior goods
Goods for which demand falls as income rises.

Remember, a shift to the left in the demand curve represents a decrease in demand, and a shift to the right represents an increase in demand.

How did the recent downturn in yearly national income affect the demand for divorce services provided by attorneys and personal financial advisers?

EXAMPLE An Income Drop Reveals That Divorce Services Are a Normal Good

During the Great Recession of the late 2000s, U.S. divorce filings dropped by nearly 4 percent nationwide. A study by the Institute for Divorce Financial Analysts (IDFA), an organization of professionals who work on divorce cases, reported that numerous couples decided that their individual incomes had dropped to levels too low to feel that they could "afford" to live apart. The IDFA study found an upsurge in "creative divorce solutions," in which couples continued to occupy the same lodgings and divide associated expenses but no longer shared a marital relationship. In many other cases, couples who concluded that their incomes were too low to divorce found ways to work through their marital problems and salvage their marriages. Thus, as married couples' incomes declined, so did their demand for divorce services, an indication that these services are a normal good.

FOR CRITICAL ANALYSIS
Why do you think that the demand for services provided by divorce professionals gradually increased as U.S. consumers' incomes slowly recovered in the 2010s?

TASTES AND PREFERENCES A change in consumer tastes in favor of a good can shift its demand curve outward to the right. When Pokémon trading cards became the rage, the demand curve for them shifted outward to the right. When the rage died out, the demand curve shifted inward to the left. Fashions depend to a large extent on people's tastes and preferences. Economists have little to say about the determination of tastes; that is, they don't have any "good" theories of taste determination or why people buy one brand of product rather than others. (Advertisers, however, have various theories that they use to try to make consumers prefer their products over those of competitors.)

PRICES OF RELATED GOODS: SUBSTITUTES AND COMPLEMENTS Demand schedules are always drawn with the prices of all other commodities held constant. That is to say, when deriving a given demand curve, we assume that only the price of the good under study changes. For example, when we draw the demand curve for butter, we assume that the price of margarine is held constant. When we draw the demand curve for home cinema speakers, we assume that the price of surround-sound amplifiers is held constant. When we refer to *related goods*, we are talking about goods for which demand is interdependent. If a change in the price of one good shifts the demand for another good, those two goods have interdependent demands. There are two types of demand interdependencies: those in which goods are *substitutes* and those in which goods are *complements*. We can define and distinguish between substitutes and complements in terms of how the change in price of one commodity affects the demand for its related commodity.

Substitutes
Two goods are substitutes when a change in the price of one causes a shift in demand for the other in the same direction as the price change.

Butter and margarine are **substitutes.** Either can be consumed to satisfy the same basic want. Let's assume that both products originally cost $2 per pound. If the price of butter remains the same and the price of margarine falls from $2 per pound to $1 per pound, people will buy more margarine and less butter. The demand curve for butter shifts inward to the left. If, conversely, the price of margarine rises from $2 per pound to $3 per pound, people will buy more butter and less margarine. The demand curve for butter shifts outward to the right. In other words, an increase in the price of margarine will lead to an increase in the demand for butter, and an increase in the price of butter will lead to an increase in the demand for margarine. For substitutes, a change in the price of a substitute will cause a change in demand *in the same direction*.

How do you suppose that the dropping price of renting computer "clouds" via Internet connections has affected desired purchases of traditional computer hardware?

EXAMPLE Computer Hardware Consumers Substitute in Favor of "Clouds"

In the midst of the U.S. house price meltdown of the late 2000s, executives at the real estate Web site Zillow wanted to track how the market values of 67 million houses had fared during the decade. They determined that to do so, they would have to purchase millions of dollars of traditional computers and put them to work for six months. Instead of pursuing this approach, they rented 500 computer servers from the Internet retailer Amazon and performed the calculations using Web links among the servers at a rental price of $50,000. In so doing, Zillow joined firms across the globe that are substituting away from buying traditional computer hardware in favor of "cloud computing"—renting clusters of hardware that can perform complex calculations over the Internet. As the rental price of Web-based cloud computing has declined, the demand for computer hardware also has decreased.

FOR CRITICAL ANALYSIS

In what direction has the demand curve for computer hardware shifted as the rental price of computer clouds has decreased?

Complements
Two goods are complements when a change in the price of one causes an opposite shift in the demand for the other.

For **complements,** goods typically consumed together, the situation is reversed. Consider desktop computers and printers. We draw the demand curve for printers with the price of desktop computers held constant. If the price per constant-quality unit of computers decreases from, say, $500 to $300, that will encourage more people to purchase computer peripheral devices. They will now buy more printers, at any given printer price, than before. The demand curve for printers will shift outward to the right. If, by contrast, the price of desktop computers increases from $250 to $450, fewer people will purchase computer peripheral devices. The demand curve for printers will shift inward to the left. To summarize, a decrease in the price of computers leads to an increase in the demand for printers. An increase in the price of computers leads to a decrease in the demand for printers. Thus, for complements, a change in the price of a product will cause a change in demand *in the opposite direction* for the other good.

EXPECTATIONS Consumers' expectations regarding future prices and future incomes will prompt them to buy more or less of a particular good without a change in its current money price. For example, consumers getting wind of a scheduled 100 percent increase in the price of titanium batteries next month will buy more of them today at today's prices. Today's demand curve for titanium batteries will shift from D_1 to D_2 in Figure 3-4 on page 54. The opposite would occur if a decrease in the price of titanium batteries was scheduled for next month (from D_1 to D_3).

Expectations of a rise in income may cause consumers to want to purchase more of everything today at today's prices. Again, such a change in expectations of higher future income will cause a shift in the demand curve from D_1 to D_2 in Figure 3-4.

Finally, expectations that goods will not be available at any price will induce consumers to stock up now, increasing current demand.

MARKET SIZE (NUMBER OF POTENTIAL BUYERS) An increase in the number of potential buyers (holding buyers' incomes constant) at any given price shifts the market demand curve outward. Conversely, a reduction in the number of potential buyers at any given price shifts the market demand curve inward.

Changes in Demand versus Changes in Quantity Demanded

We have made repeated references to demand and to quantity demanded. It is important to realize that there is a difference between a *change in demand* and a *change in quantity demanded.*

Demand refers to a schedule of planned rates of purchase and depends on a great many *ceteris paribus* conditions, such as incomes, expectations, and the prices of substitutes or complements. Whenever there is a change in a *ceteris paribus* condition, there will be a change in demand—a shift in the entire demand curve to the right or to the left.

A *quantity demanded* is a specific quantity at a specific price, represented by a single point on a demand curve. When price changes, quantity demanded changes according to the law of demand, and there will be a movement from one point to another along the same demand curve. Look at Figure 3-5 on the following page. At a price of \$3 per titanium battery, 6 million batteries per year are demanded. If the price falls to \$1, quantity demanded increases to 10 million per year. This movement occurs because the current market price for the product changes. In Figure 3-5, you can see the arrow pointing down the given demand curve D.

When you think of demand, think of the entire curve. Quantity demanded, in contrast, is represented by a single point on the demand curve.

> ***A change or shift in demand is a movement of the entire curve. The* only *thing that can cause the entire curve to move is a change in a determinant* other than the good's own price.**

In economic analysis, we cannot emphasize too much the following distinction that must constantly be made:

> ***A change in a good's own price leads to a change in quantity demanded for any given demand curve, other things held constant. This is a movement* along *the curve.***

> ***A change in any of the* ceteris paribus *conditions for demand leads to a change in demand. This causes a* shift *of the curve.***

FIGURE 3-5 Movement Along a Given Demand Curve

A change in price changes the quantity of a good demanded. This can be represented as movement along a given demand schedule. If, in our example, the price of titanium batteries falls from $3 to $1 apiece, the quantity demanded will increase from 6 million to 10 million units per year.

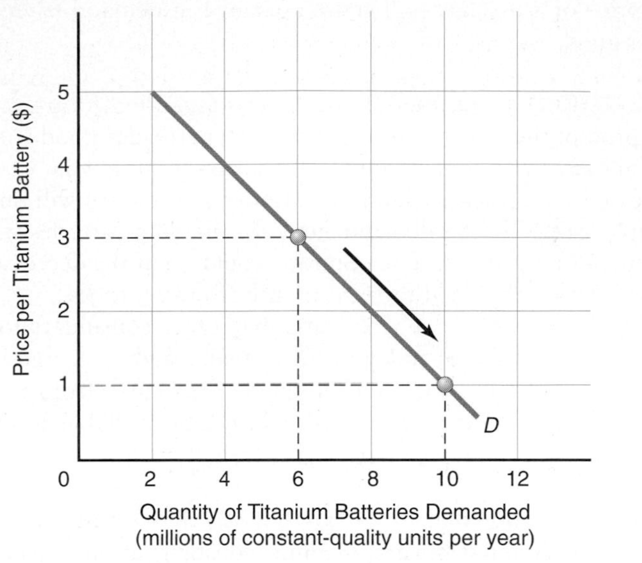

QUICK QUIZ See page 73 for the answers. Review concepts from this section in MyEconLab.

Demand curves are drawn with determinants other than the price of the good held constant. These other determinants, called ***ceteris paribus* conditions,** are (1) __________; (2) __________; (3) __________; (4) __________; and (5) __________ at any given price. If any one of these determinants changes, the demand curve will shift to the right or to the left.

A change in demand comes about only because of a change in the __________ __________ conditions of demand. This change in demand is a shift in the demand curve to the left or to the right.

A change in the quantity demanded comes about when there is a change in the price of the good (other things held constant). Such a change in quantity demanded involves a __________ __________ a given demand curve.

The Law of Supply

Supply
A schedule showing the relationship between price and quantity supplied for a specified period of time, other things being equal.

Law of supply
The observation that the higher the price of a good, the more of that good sellers will make available over a specified time period, other things being equal.

The other side of the basic model in economics involves the quantities of goods and services that firms will offer for sale to the market. The **supply** of any good or service is the amount that firms will produce and offer for sale under certain conditions during a specified time period. The relationship between price and quantity supplied, called the **law of supply,** can be summarized as follows:

At higher prices, a larger quantity will generally be supplied than at lower prices, all other things held constant. At lower prices, a smaller quantity will generally be supplied than at higher prices, all other things held constant.

There is generally a direct relationship between price and quantity supplied. As the price rises, the quantity supplied rises. As the price falls, the quantity supplied also falls. Producers are normally willing to produce and sell more of their product at a higher price than at a lower price, other things being constant. At $5 per titanium battery, manufacturers would almost certainly be willing to supply a larger quantity than at $1 per battery, assuming, of course, that no other prices in the economy had changed.

As with the law of demand, millions of instances in the real world have given us confidence in the law of supply. On a theoretical level, the law of supply is based on a model in which producers and sellers seek to make the most gain possible from their activities. For example, as a manufacturer attempts to produce more and more titanium batteries over the same time period, it will eventually have to hire more workers, pay overtime wages (which are higher), and overutilize its machines. Only if offered a higher price per battery will the manufacturer be willing to incur these higher costs. That is why the law of supply implies a direct relationship between price and quantity supplied.

How does the law of supply apply to an increase in China's "bride price"?

INTERNATIONAL EXAMPLE **Why the Quantity of Brides Supplied Is Rising in China**

In China, a prospective groom and his family traditionally provide the prospective bride with a fixed payment called *cai li*—which in English roughly translates into "bride price"—when the couple marries. During the 2000s, the bride price rose from about $300 to as much as $1,500. As a consequence, the number of Chinese women accepting marriage proposals and receiving *cai li* increased considerably. Thus, the quantity of marriage acceptances supplied by Chinese women has increased as the bride price has risen. Indeed, China has recently experienced a problem of "runaway brides." Some women have accepted *cai li* from multiple grooms but have failed to appear for any of their scheduled weddings.

FOR CRITICAL ANALYSIS

If Chinese couples were to abandon tradition and cease the payment of cai li *to brides, what would you predict would happen to the quantity of marriage acceptances by Chinese women, other things being unchanged?*

The Supply Schedule

Just as we were able to construct a demand schedule, we can construct a *supply schedule*, which is a table relating prices to the quantity supplied at each price. A supply schedule can also be referred to simply as *supply*. It is a set of planned production rates that depends on the price of the product. We show the individual supply schedule for a hypothetical producer in panel (a) of Figure 3-6 below. At a price of $1 per

FIGURE 3-6 The Individual Producer's Supply Schedule and Supply Curve for Titanium Batteries

Panel (a) shows that at higher prices, a hypothetical supplier will be willing to provide a greater quantity of titanium batteries. We plot the various price-quantity combinations in panel (a) on the grid in panel (b). When we connect these points, we create the individual supply curve for titanium batteries. It is positively sloped.

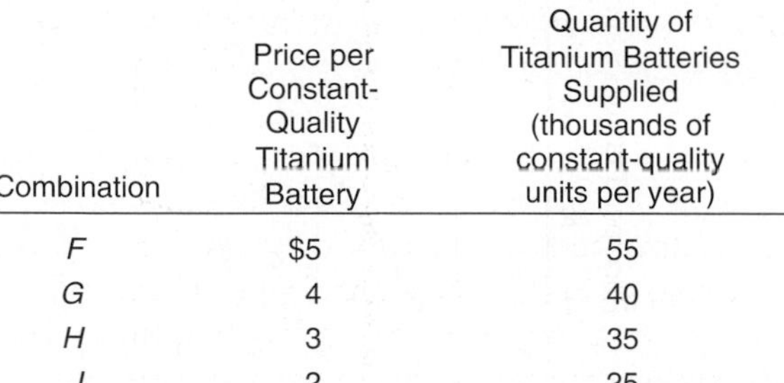

Panel (a)

Combination	Price per Constant-Quality Titanium Battery	Quantity of Titanium Batteries Supplied (thousands of constant-quality units per year)
F	$5	55
G	4	40
H	3	35
I	2	25
J	1	20

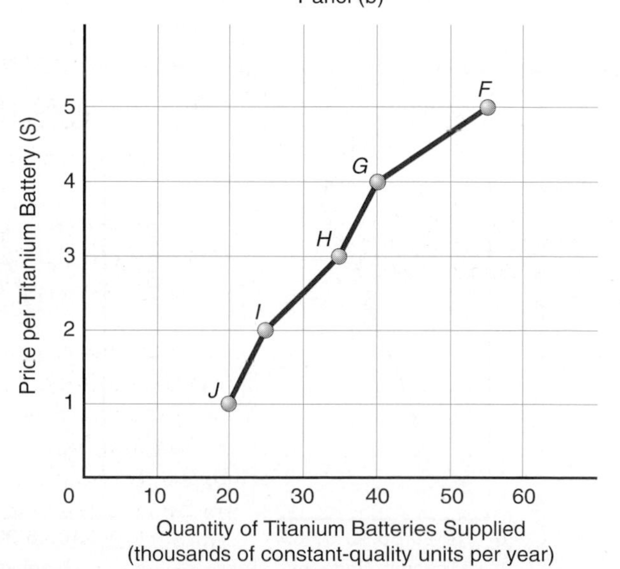

titanium battery, for example, this producer will supply 20,000 titanium batteries per year. At a price of $5 per battery, this producer will supply 55,000 batteries per year.

The Supply Curve

Supply curve
The graphical representation of the supply schedule; a line (curve) showing the supply schedule, which generally slopes upward (has a positive slope), other things being equal.

We can convert the supply schedule from panel (a) of Figure 3-6 on the previous page into a **supply curve,** just as we earlier created a demand curve in Figure 3-1 on page 52. All we do is take the price-quantity combinations from panel (a) of Figure 3-6 and plot them in panel (b). We have labeled these combinations *F* through *J*. Connecting these points, we obtain an upward-sloping curve that shows the typically direct relationship between price and quantity supplied. Again, we have to remember that we are talking about quantity supplied *per year*, measured in constant-quality units.

The Market Supply Curve

Just as we summed the individual demand curves to obtain the market demand curve, we sum the individual producers' supply curves to obtain the market supply curve. Look at Figure 3-7 below, in which we horizontally sum two typical supply curves for manufacturers of titanium batteries. Supplier 1's data are taken from Figure 3-6 on page 59. Supplier 2 is added. The numbers are presented in panel (a). The graphical representation of supplier 1 is in panel (b), of supplier 2 in panel (c), and of the summation in panel (d). The result, then, is the supply curve for titanium batteries for

FIGURE 3-7 Horizontal Summation of Supply Curves

In panel (a), we show the data for two individual suppliers of titanium batteries. Adding how much each is willing to supply at different prices, we come up with the combined quantities supplied in column 4. When we plot the values in columns 2 and 3 on grids from panels (b) and (c) and add them horizontally, we obtain the combined supply curve for the two suppliers in question, shown in panel (d).

Panel (a)

(1) Price per Titanium Battery	(2) Supplier 1's Quantity Supplied (thousands)	(3) Supplier 2's Quantity Supplied (thousands)	(4) = (2) + (3) Combined Quantity Supplied per Year (thousands)
$5	55	35	90
4	40	30	70
3	35	20	55
2	25	15	40
1	20	10	30

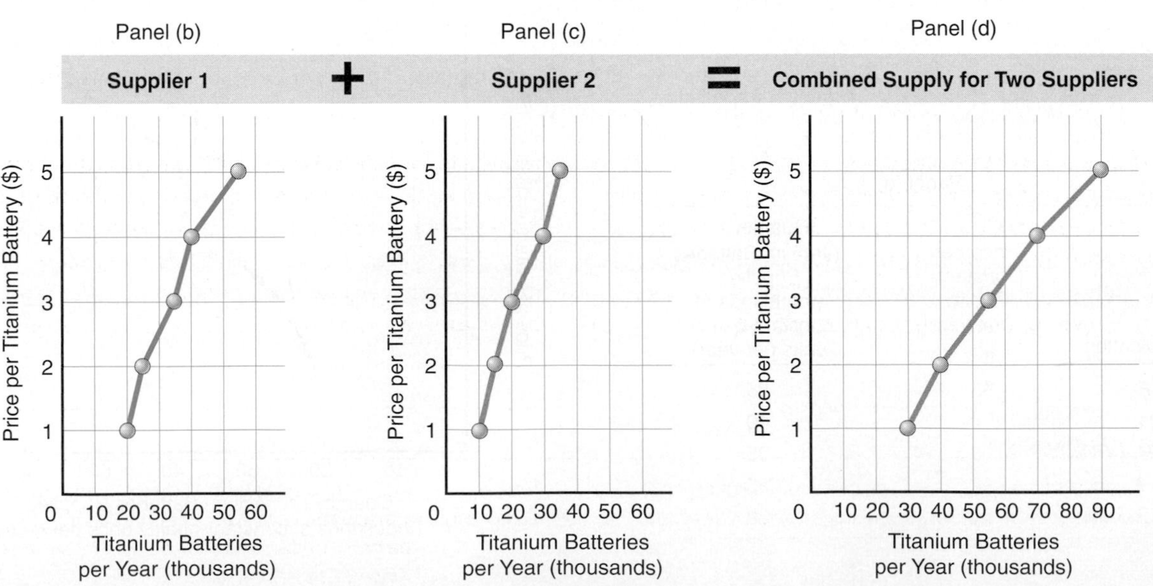

FIGURE 3-8 The Market Supply Schedule and the Market Supply Curve for Titanium Batteries

In panel (a), we show the summation of all the individual producers' supply schedules. In panel (b), we graph the resulting supply curve. It represents the market supply curve for titanium batteries and is upward sloping.

Panel (a)

Price per Constant-Quality Titanium Battery	Quantity of Titanium Batteries Supplied (millions of constant-quality units per year)
$5	10
4	8
3	6
2	4
1	2

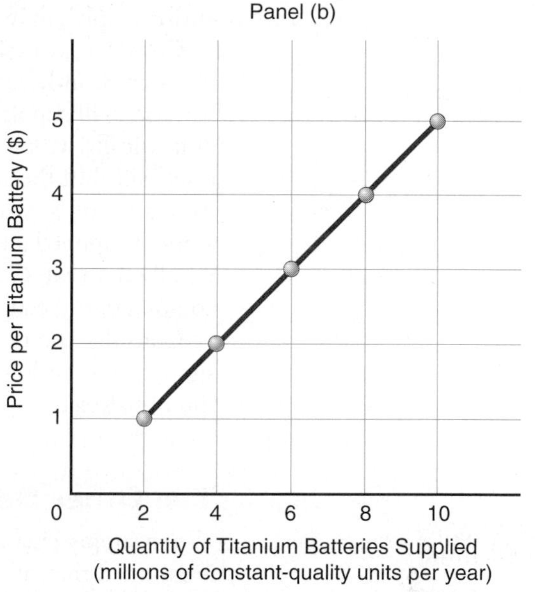

suppliers 1 and 2. We assume that there are more suppliers of titanium batteries, however. The total market supply schedule and total market supply curve for titanium batteries are represented in Figure 3-8 above, with the curve in panel (b) obtained by adding all of the supply curves such as those shown in panels (b) and (c) of Figure 3-7 (p. 60). Notice the difference between the market supply curve with only two suppliers in Figure 3-7 and the one with many suppliers—the entire true market—in panel (b) of Figure 3-8. (For simplicity, we assume that the true total market supply curve is a straight line.)

Note what happens at the market level when price changes. If the price is $3, the quantity supplied is 6 million. If the price goes up to $4, the quantity supplied increases to 8 million per year. If the price falls to $2, the quantity supplied decreases to 4 million per year. Changes in quantity supplied are represented by movements along the supply curve in panel (b) of Figure 3-8.

You Are There

To learn how the law of supply applies to the market for solar cells used to generate solar power, read **Adjusting to a Lower Market Clearing Price of Solar Cells,** on page 68.

Why Not . . . help college students by requiring publishers to reduce prices of all of the textbooks they currently supply?

Certainly, the government could require publishers to charge lower textbook prices, and recently some in Congress have proposed implementing such a policy. But publishers would no longer provide the quantity of textbooks that they *currently* supply. The *current* quantity of supplied textbooks would no longer exist following a government action to require lower textbook prices. If the government were to impose legally enforced reductions in textbook prices, the quantity of textbooks supplied by publishers would decline. Thus, such a policy action would not necessarily "help" college students, because publishers would make fewer textbooks available for college students to purchase.

QUICK QUIZ **See page 73 for the answers. Review concepts from this section in MyEconLab.**

There is normally a __________ relationship between price and quantity of a good supplied, other things held constant.

The __________ curve normally shows a direct relationship between price and quantity supplied. The __________ __________ curve is obtained by horizontally adding individual supply curves in the market.

Shifts in Supply

When we looked at demand, we found out that any change in anything relevant besides the price of the good or service caused the demand curve to shift inward or outward. The same is true for the supply curve. If something besides price changes and alters the willingness of suppliers to produce a good or service, we will see the entire supply curve shift.

Consider an example. There is a new method of manufacturing titanium batteries that significantly reduces the cost of production. In this situation, producers of titanium batteries will supply more product at *all* prices because their cost of so doing has fallen dramatically. Competition among manufacturers to produce more at each and every price will shift the supply curve outward to the right from S_1 to S_2 in Figure 3-9 below. At a price of \$3, the number supplied was originally 6 million per year, but now the amount supplied (after the reduction in the costs of production) at \$3 per battery will be 9 million a year. (This is similar to what has happened to the supply curve of personal computers and cellphones in recent years as computer memory chip prices have fallen.)

Consider the opposite case. If the cost of making titanium batteries increases, the supply curve in Figure 3-9 will shift from S_1 to S_3. At each and every price, the quantity of batteries supplied will fall due to the increase in the price of raw materials.

The Other Determinants of Supply

When supply curves are drawn, only the price of the good in question changes, and it is assumed that other things remain constant. The other things assumed constant are the *ceteris paribus* conditions of supply. They include the prices of resources (inputs) used to produce the product, technology and productivity, taxes and subsidies, producers' price expectations, and the number of firms in the industry. If *any* of these *ceteris paribus* conditions changes, there will be a shift in the supply curve.

COST OF INPUTS USED TO PRODUCE THE PRODUCT If one or more input prices fall, production costs fall, and the supply curve will shift outward to the right; that is, more will be supplied at each and every price. The opposite will be true if one or more inputs become more expensive. For example, when we draw the supply curve of new laptop computers, we are holding the price of microprocessors (and other inputs) constant. When we draw the supply curve of blue jeans, we are holding the cost of cotton fabric fixed.

FIGURE 3-9 Shifts in the Supply Curve

If the cost of producing titanium batteries were to fall dramatically, the supply curve would shift rightward from S_1 to S_2 such that at all prices, a larger quantity would be forthcoming from suppliers. Conversely, if the cost of production rose, the supply curve would shift leftward to S_3.

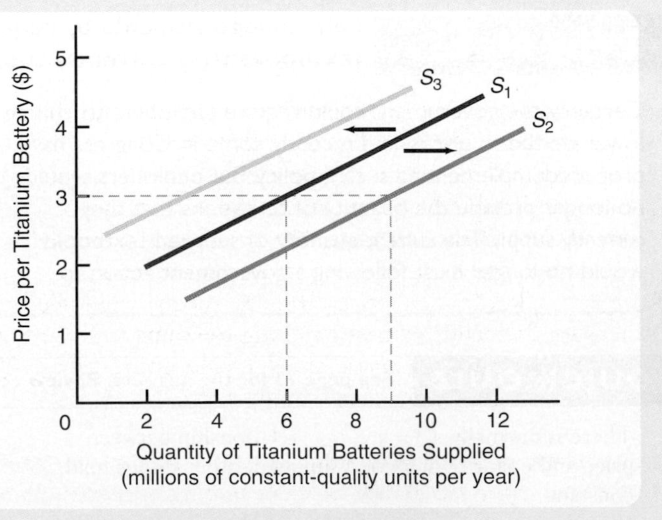

TECHNOLOGY AND PRODUCTIVITY Supply curves are drawn by assuming a given technology, or "state of the art." When the available production techniques change, the supply curve will shift. For example, when a better production technique for titanium batteries becomes available, production costs decrease, and the supply curve will shift to the right. A larger quantity will be forthcoming at each and every price because the cost of production is lower.

How do you think that the supply of natural gas has responded to a technological improvement in drilling for natural gas?

EXAMPLE How "Fracking" for Natural Gas Has Affected Its Supply

Hydraulic fracturing, often called "fracking" (or "fraccing"), is a method of drilling for natural gas that entails drilling *sideways* into the ground to cut *horizontal* wells. Previous drilling methods entailed drilling straight down to cut vertical wells, but these wells usually slashed through rock called shale laid out in roughly horizontal layers. By fracking into those layers horizontally, companies that extract natural gas tap into the methane pockets and extract much more natural gas than had been possible by drilling vertical wells. This technological improvement in extracting natural gas has boosted proven U.S. natural gas reserves—the known stock of gas available to use in heating homes and businesses—by more than 50 percent since 2000.

FOR CRITICAL ANALYSIS

Has the direct effect of fracking on the U.S. supply of natural gas generated a movement along the natural gas supply curve or a shift in that curve?

TAXES AND SUBSIDIES Certain taxes, such as a per-unit tax, are effectively an addition to production costs and therefore reduce the supply. If the supply curve is S_1 in Figure 3-9 on the facing page, a per-unit tax increase would shift it to S_3. A per-unit **subsidy** would do the opposite. It would shift the curve to S_2. Every producer would get a "gift" from the government for each unit produced.

Subsidy
A negative tax; a payment to a producer from the government, usually in the form of a cash grant per unit.

PRICE EXPECTATIONS A change in the expectation of a future relative price of a product can affect a producer's current willingness to supply, just as price expectations affect a consumer's current willingness to purchase. For example, suppliers of titanium batteries may withhold from the market part of their current supply if they anticipate higher prices in the future. The current amount supplied at each and every price will decrease.

NUMBER OF FIRMS IN THE INDUSTRY In the short run, when firms can change only the number of employees they use, we hold the number of firms in the industry constant. In the long run, the number of firms may change. If the number of firms increases, supply will increase, and the supply curve will shift outward to the right. If the number of firms decreases, supply will decrease, and the supply curve will shift inward to the left.

Changes in Supply versus Changes in Quantity Supplied

We cannot overstress the importance of distinguishing between a movement along the supply curve—which occurs only when the price changes for a given supply curve—and a shift in the supply curve—which occurs only with changes in *ceteris paribus* conditions. A change in the price of the good in question always (and only) brings about a change in the quantity supplied along a given supply curve. We move to a different point on the existing supply curve. This is specifically called a *change in quantity supplied*. When price changes, quantity supplied changes—there is a movement from one point to another along the same supply curve.

When you think of *supply*, think of the entire curve. Quantity supplied is represented by a single point on the supply curve.

A change, or shift, in supply is a movement of the entire curve. The* only *thing that can cause the entire curve to move is a change in one of the* ceteris paribus *conditions.

Consequently,

> ***A change in price leads to a change in the quantity supplied, other things being constant. This is a movement* along *the curve.***

> ***A change in any* ceteris paribus *condition for supply leads to a change in supply. This causes a* shift *of the curve.***

QUICK QUIZ See page 73 for the answers. Review concepts from this section in MyEconLab.

If the price changes, we __________ __________ a curve—there is a change in quantity demanded or supplied. If some other determinant changes, we __________ a curve—there is a change in demand or supply.

The **supply curve** is drawn with other things held constant. If these *ceteris paribus* conditions of supply change, the supply curve will shift. The major *ceteris paribus* conditions are (1) __________, (2) __________, (3) __________, (4) __________, and (5) __________.

Putting Demand and Supply Together

In the sections on demand and supply, we tried to confine each discussion to demand or supply only. But you have probably already realized that we can't view the world just from the demand side or just from the supply side. There is interaction between the two. In this section, we will discuss how they interact and how that interaction determines the prices that prevail in our economy and other economies in which the forces of demand and supply are allowed to work.

Let's first combine the demand and supply schedules and then combine the curves.

Go to www.econtoday.com/ch03 to see how the U.S. Department of Agriculture seeks to estimate demand and supply conditions for major agricultural products.

Demand and Supply Schedules Combined

Let's place panel (a) from Figure 3-3 (the market demand schedule) on page 54 and panel (a) from Figure 3-8 (the market supply schedule) on page 61 together in panel (a) of Figure 3-10 on the facing page. Column 1 shows the price; column 2, the quantity supplied per year at any given price; and column 3, the quantity demanded. Column 4 is the difference between columns 2 and 3, or the difference between the quantity supplied and the quantity demanded. In column 5, we label those differences as either excess quantity supplied (called a *surplus,* which we shall discuss shortly) or excess quantity demanded (commonly known as a *shortage,* also discussed shortly). For example, at a price of $1, only 2 million titanium batteries would be supplied, but the quantity demanded would be 10 million. The difference would be −8 million, which we label excess quantity demanded (a shortage). At the other end, a price of $5 would elicit 10 million in quantity supplied, but quantity demanded would drop to 2 million, leaving a difference of +8 million units, which we call excess quantity supplied (a surplus).

Now, do you notice something special about the price of $3? At that price, both the quantity supplied and the quantity demanded per year are 6 million. The difference then is zero. There is neither excess quantity demanded (shortage) nor excess quantity supplied (surplus). Hence the price of $3 is very special. It is called the **market clearing price**—it clears the market of all excess quantities demanded or supplied. There are no willing consumers who want to pay $3 per titanium battery but are turned away by sellers, and there are no willing suppliers who want to sell titanium batteries at $3 who cannot sell all they want at that price. Another term for the market clearing price is the **equilibrium price,** the price at which there is no tendency for change. Consumers are able to get all they want at that price, and suppliers are able to sell all they want at that price.

Market clearing, or equilibrium, price The price that clears the market, at which quantity demanded equals quantity supplied; the price where the demand curve intersects the supply curve.

Equilibrium

We can define **equilibrium** in general as a point at which quantity demanded equals quantity supplied at a particular price. There tends to be no movement of the price or the quantity away from this point unless demand or supply changes. Any movement away from this point will set into motion forces that will cause movement back to it.

Equilibrium The situation when quantity supplied equals quantity demanded at a particular price.

FIGURE 3-10 Putting Demand and Supply Together

In panel (a), we see that at the price of $3, the quantity supplied and the quantity demanded are equal, resulting in neither an excess quantity demanded nor an excess quantity supplied. We call this price the equilibrium, or market clearing, price. In panel (b), the intersection of the supply and demand curves is at *E*, at a price of $3 and a quantity of 6 million per year. At point *E*, there is neither an excess quantity demanded nor an excess quantity supplied. At a price of $1, the quantity supplied will be only 2 million per year, but the quantity demanded will be 10 million. The difference is excess quantity demanded at a price of $1. The price will rise, so we will move from point *A* up the supply curve and from point *B* up the demand curve to point *E*. At the other extreme, a price of $5 elicits a quantity supplied of 10 million but a quantity demanded of only 2 million. The difference is excess quantity supplied at a price of $5. The price will fall, so we will move down the demand curve and the supply curve to the equilibrium price, $3 per titanium battery.

Panel (a)

(1) Price per Constant-Quality Titanium Battery	(2) Quantity Supplied (titanium batteries per year)	(3) Quantity Demanded (titanium batteries per year)	(4) Difference (2) − (3) (titanium batteries per year)	(5) Condition
$5	10 million	2 million	8 million	Excess quantity supplied (surplus)
4	8 million	4 million	4 million	Excess quantity supplied (surplus)
3	6 million	6 million	0	Market clearing price—equilibrium (no surplus, no shortage)
2	4 million	8 million	–4 million	Excess quantity demanded (shortage)
1	2 million	10 million	–8 million	Excess quantity demanded (shortage)

Panel (b)

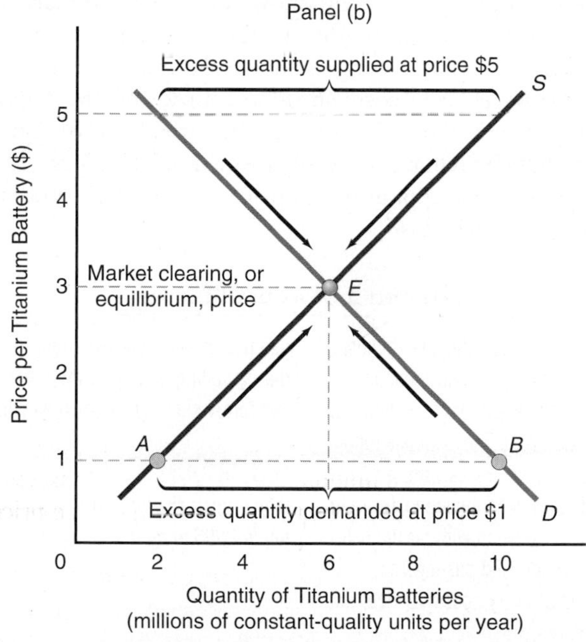

Therefore, equilibrium is a stable point. Any point that is not an equilibrium is unstable and will not persist.

The equilibrium point occurs where the supply and demand curves intersect. The equilibrium price is given on the vertical axis directly to the left of where the supply and demand curves cross. The equilibrium quantity is given on the horizontal axis directly underneath the intersection of the demand and supply curves.

Panel (b) in Figure 3-3 (p. 54) and panel (b) in Figure 3-8 (p. 61) are combined as panel (b) in Figure 3-10 above. The demand curve is labeled *D*, the supply curve *S*. We have labeled the intersection of the supply curve with the demand curve as point *E*, for equilibrium. That corresponds to a market clearing price of $3, at which both the quantity supplied and the quantity demanded are 6 million units per year. There is neither excess quantity supplied nor excess quantity demanded. Point *E*, the equilibrium point, always occurs at the intersection of the supply and demand curves. This is the price *toward which* the market price will automatically tend to gravitate, because there is no outcome better than this price for both consumers and producers.

Shortages

The price of $3 depicted in Figure 3-10 on the previous page represents a situation of equilibrium. If there were a non-market-clearing, or disequilibrium, price, this would put into play forces that would cause the price to change toward the market clearing price at which equilibrium would again be sustained. Look again at panel (b) in Figure 3-10. Suppose that instead of being at the equilibrium price of $3, for some reason the market price is $1. At this price, the quantity demanded of 10 million per year exceeds the quantity supplied of 2 million per year. We have a situation of excess quantity demanded at the price of $1. This is usually called a **shortage.** Consumers of titanium batteries would find that they could not buy all that they wished at $1 apiece. But forces will cause the price to rise: Competing consumers will bid up the price, and suppliers will increase output in response. (Remember, some buyers would pay $5 or more rather than do without titanium batteries.) We would move from points *A* and *B* toward point *E*. The process would stop when the price again reached $3 per battery.

Shortage
A situation in which quantity demanded is greater than quantity supplied at a price below the market clearing price.

At this point, it is important to recall a distinction made in Chapter 2:

Shortages and scarcity are not the same thing.

A shortage is a situation in which the quantity demanded exceeds the quantity supplied at a price that is somehow kept *below* the market clearing price. Our definition of scarcity was much more general and all-encompassing: a situation in which the resources available for producing output are insufficient to satisfy all wants. Any choice necessarily costs an opportunity, and the opportunity is lost. Hence, we will always live in a world of scarcity because we must constantly make choices, but we do not necessarily have to live in a world of shortages.

How did dropping house prices in the late 2000s and early 2010s contribute to a shortage of sawdust?

EXAMPLE How the Housing Bust Created a Sawdust Shortage

Between 2006 and 2010, U.S. housing prices plummeted, which led builders to reduce construction of new housing. A direct result of this reduction in home building was a cutback in the amount of wood sawed for use in houses, which in turn led to a reduction in the supply of sawdust. The sawdust supply curve shifted leftward, but farmers still wanted to purchase sawdust as bedding for horses and chickens. Auto parts manufacturers continued to desire to obtain pulverized sawdust—called "wood flour"—to blend with plastic polymers to make lightweight coverings for steering wheels and dashboards. Even though the quantity of sawdust supplied declined at every possible price, the quantity of sawdust demanded remained unchanged at each price. Thus, at the prevailing price just after the decrease in sawdust supply, there was a temporary shortage of sawdust while its price adjusted upward.

FOR CRITICAL ANALYSIS

Why do you think that the equilibrium price of sawdust rose from $25 per ton in 2006 to more than $100 per ton today?

Surpluses

Now let's repeat the experiment with the market price at $5 rather than at the market clearing price of $3. Clearly, the quantity supplied will exceed the quantity demanded at that price. The result will be an excess quantity supplied at $5 per unit. This excess quantity supplied is often called a **surplus.** Given the curves in panel (b) in Figure 3-10, however, there will be forces pushing the price back down toward $3 per titanium battery: Competing suppliers will cut prices and reduce output, and consumers will purchase more at these new lower prices. If the two forces of supply and demand are unrestricted, they will bring the price back to $3 per battery.

Surplus
A situation in which quantity supplied is greater than quantity demanded at a price above the market clearing price.

Shortages and surpluses are resolved in unfettered markets—markets in which price changes are free to occur. The forces that resolve them are those of competition: In the case of shortages, consumers competing for a limited quantity supplied drive up the price; in the case of surpluses, sellers compete for the limited quantity demanded, thus driving prices down to equilibrium. The equilibrium price is the only stable price, and the (unrestricted) market price tends to gravitate toward it.

What happens when the price is set below the equilibrium price? Here come the scalpers.

POLICY EXAMPLE Should Shortages in the Ticket Market Be Solved by Scalpers?

If you have ever tried to get tickets to a playoff game in sports, a popular Broadway play, or a superstar's rap concert, you know about "shortages." The standard Super Bowl ticket situation is shown in Figure 3-11 below. At the face-value price of Super Bowl tickets ($800), the quantity demanded (175,000) greatly exceeds the quantity supplied (80,000). Because shortages last only as long as prices and quantities do not change, markets tend to exhibit a movement out of this disequilibrium toward equilibrium. Obviously, the quantity of Super Bowl tickets cannot change, but the price can go as high as $6,000.

Enter the scalper. This colorful term is used because when you purchase a ticket that is being resold at a price higher than face value, the seller is skimming profit off the top ("taking your scalp"). If an event sells out and people who wished to purchase tickets at current prices were unable to do so, ticket prices by definition were lower than market clearing prices. People without tickets may be willing to buy high-priced tickets because they place a greater value on the entertainment event than the face value of the ticket. Without scalpers, those individuals would not be able to attend the event. In the case of the Super Bowl, various forms of scalping occur nationwide. Tickets for a seat on the 50-yard line have been sold for as much as $6,000 apiece. In front of every Super Bowl arena, you can find ticket scalpers hawking their wares.

In most states, scalping is illegal. In Pennsylvania, convicted scalpers are either fined $5,000 or sentenced to two years behind bars. For an economist, such legislation seems strange. As one New York ticket broker said, "I look at scalping like working as a stockbroker, buying low and selling high. If people are willing to pay me the money, what kind of problem is that?"

FOR CRITICAL ANALYSIS

What happens to ticket scalpers who are still holding tickets after an event has started?

FIGURE 3-11 Shortages of Super Bowl Tickets

The quantity of tickets for a Super Bowl game is fixed at 80,000. At the price per ticket of $800, the quantity demanded is 175,000. Consequently, there is an excess quantity demanded at the below-market clearing price. In this example, prices can go as high as $6,000 in the scalpers' market.

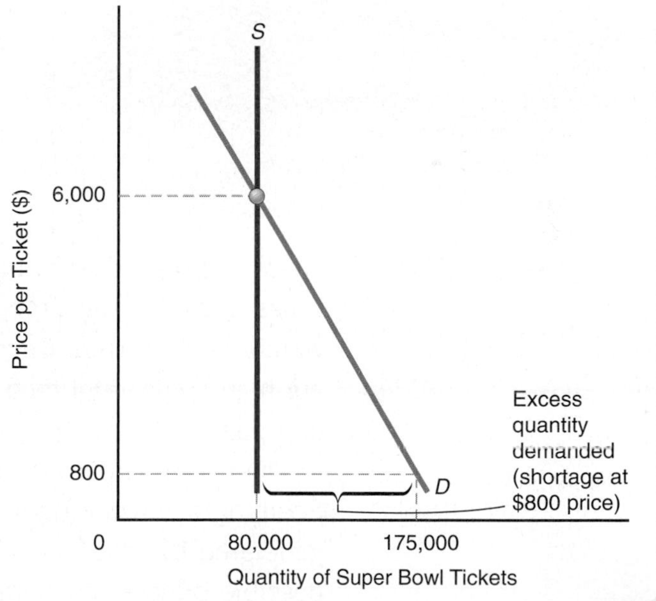

QUICK QUIZ

See page 73 for the answers. Review concepts from this section in MyEconLab.

The market clearing price occurs at the ________ of the market demand curve and the market supply curve. It is also called the ________ price, the price from which there is no tendency to change unless there is a change in demand or supply.

Whenever the price is ________ than the equilibrium price, there is an excess quantity supplied (a **surplus**).

Whenever the price is ________ than the equilibrium price, there is an excess quantity demanded (a **shortage**).

You Are There

Adjusting to a Lower Market Clearing Price of Solar Cells

Anton Milner, chief executive of Q-Cells, the company that produces the largest volume of solar cells—microchips used in solar-power systems—in the world, has never witnessed such a sudden and substantial drop in the market clearing price. So far, the prevailing equilibrium price for a solar cell generating one watt of electrical power has declined from $4 in 2008 to less than $2 today—a price reduction of more than 50 percent.

In response to this price change, Milner has directed other executives at Q-Cells to cut production of solar cells by 7 percent this year, which is very close to the industrywide percentage reduction in quantity of solar cells supplied. In addition, he has reduced the company's staff by 10 percent and postponed for six months the planned construction of a new factory. If solar-cell prices do not recover, Milner realizes, additional staff cuts may be required, and plans for the new factory may have to be scrapped. The company likely will be producing even fewer solar cells.

Critical Analysis Questions

1. Has the solar-cell industry experienced a decrease in supply or a decrease in quantity supplied?
2. Has there been a movement along the market supply curve for solar cells or a shift in this supply curve?

ISSUES & APPLICATIONS

How the Great Recession Identified Inferior Goods

CONCEPTS APPLIED

- ▶ Inferior Good
- ▶ Demand
- ▶ Shifts in Demand

When put on the spot, both economics instructors and students sometimes have trouble thinking of examples of inferior goods, or items for which demand rises when consumers' incomes fall. Standard examples are high-cholesterol food items such as hamburger, macaroni and cheese, and peanut butter.

The recent Great Recession reduced the incomes of most consumers. Seemingly unusual rightward shifts in demand in some markets that were generated by lower incomes—increases in the amount demanded at each possible price as consumers' incomes declined—helped to highlight prominent examples of inferior goods.

Cobbler Services

At the 7,000 shoe-repair shops in the United States, the decline in household incomes that occurred during the recession was a boon for business. Shops that had previously experienced so little business that their owners had contemplated closing them up suddenly saw sales of their services increase as much as 50 percent.

Many people responded to falling incomes by trying to make used shoes last longer rather than buying new shoes. This led to an increase in the demand for cobbler services. Thus, these services are an inferior good.

Electric Hair Clippers

Most U.S. residents obtain haircuts at one of the hundreds of thousands of hair salons and barbershops operating throughout the nation. When their incomes fell during the economic downturn, however, many households decided to perform their own haircutting chores. To do so, they had to obtain haircutting equipment.

In 2008, U.S. purchases of electric hair clippers increased by 10 percent. Purchases rose by another 11 percent in 2009. Consequently, the economywide decline in household incomes during these years led to an increase in the demand for electric hair clippers, implying that these devices also are inferior goods.

Dial-Up Internet Access

As most people's incomes rose from 2000 through 2006, they increasingly opted to purchase broadband—cable, dedicated-service-line (DSL), or satellite—Internet access services. Most people who continued using dial-up Internet access services were low-income consumers willing to sacrifice connection speed for the lower fees charged by dial-up providers such as Earthlink, NetZero, and Juno.

During the Great Recession, a number of people dropped into the low-income category. A number of them opted to purchase dial-up Internet access services. Thus, the demand for this now relatively old-fashioned mechanism for accessing the Web increased when household incomes fell. Dial-up Internet access service, therefore, is another inferior good revealed by the Great Recession.

For Critical Analysis

1. Diagrammatically and in words, what do we mean when we say that following a fall in consumers' incomes, there is an increase in demand for an inferior good?
2. What would you expect to happen to the demands for cobbler services, electric hair clippers, and dial-up Internet access services if consumers' incomes rise in the 2010s?

Web Resources

1. To see a list of examples of inferior goods, go to www.econtoday.com/ch03.
2. To think about why transit services such as those provided by city and inter-city bus lines often appear to be inferior goods, go to www.econtoday.com/ch03.

Research Project

Propose three items, other than those mentioned in this textbook or at the Web sites noted above, that you think are likely to be inferior goods. Search the Web to determine if there is (or is not) evidence supporting your list.

For more questions on this chapter's Issues & Applications, go to **MyEconLab**. In the Study Plan for this chapter, select Section N: News.

Here is what you should know after reading this chapter. **MyEconLab** will help you identify what you know, and where to go when you need to practice.

WHAT YOU SHOULD KNOW		WHERE TO GO TO PRACTICE
The Law of Demand According to the law of demand, other things being equal, individuals will purchase fewer units of a good at a higher price, and they will purchase more units of a good at a lower price.	market, 49 demand, 49 law of demand, 49	• **MyEconLab** Study Plan 3.1 • Audio introduction to Chapter 3
Relative Prices versus Money Prices People determine the quantity of a good to buy based on its relative price, which is the price of the good in terms of other goods. Thus, in a world of generally rising prices, you have to compare the price of one good with the general level of prices of other goods in order to decide whether the relative price of that one good has gone up, gone down, or stayed the same.	relative price, 50 money price, 50	• **MyEconLab** Study Plan 3.1 • Video: The Difference Between Relative and Absolute Prices and the Importance of Looking at Only Relative Prices

(continued)

MyEconLab continued

WHAT YOU SHOULD KNOW		WHERE TO GO TO PRACTICE
A Change in Quantity Demanded versus a Change in Demand The demand schedule shows quantities purchased per unit of time at various possible prices. Graphically, the demand schedule is a downward-sloping demand curve. A change in the price of the good generates a change in the quantity demanded, which is a movement along the demand curve. Factors other than the price of the good that affect the amount demanded are (1) income, (2) tastes and preferences, (3) the prices of related goods, (4) expectations, and (5) market size (the number of potential buyers). If any of these *ceteris paribus* conditions of demand changes, there is a change in demand, and the demand curve shifts to a new position.	demand curve, 52 market demand, 52 *ceteris paribus* conditions, 55 normal goods, 55 inferior goods, 55 substitutes, 56 complements, 56 **KEY FIGURES** Figure 3-2, 53 Figure 3-4, 54 Figure 3-5, 58	• **MyEconLab** Study Plans 3.2, 3.3 • Video: The Importance of Distinguishing Between a Shift in a Demand Curve and a Move Along the Demand Curve • Animated Figures 3-2, 3-4, 3-5 • ABC News Video: What Drives the Market: Supply and Demand • Economics Video: Kraft Leading the Way • Economics Video: Rust Belt City's Brighter Future • Economics Video: Stashing Your Cash • Economics Video: The Return of Zeppelin
The Law of Supply According to the law of supply, sellers will produce and offer for sale more units of a good at a higher price, and they will produce and offer for sale fewer units of the good at a lower price.	supply, 58 law of supply, 58	• **MyEconLab** Study Plan 3.4
A Change in Quantity Supplied versus a Change in Supply The supply schedule shows quantities produced and sold per unit of time at various possible prices. On a graph, the supply schedule is a supply curve that slopes upward. A change in the price of the good generates a change in the quantity supplied, which is a movement along the supply curve. Factors other than the price of the good that affect the amount supplied are (1) input prices, (2) technology and productivity, (3) taxes and subsidies, (4) price expectations, and (5) the number of sellers. If any of these *ceteris paribus* conditions changes, there is a change in supply, and the supply curve shifts to a new position.	supply curve, 60 subsidy, 63 **KEY FIGURES** Figure 3-6, 59 Figure 3-7, 60 Figure 3-9, 62	• **MyEconLab** Study Plans 3.5, 3.6 • Video: The Importance of Distinguishing Between a Change in Supply versus a Change in Quantity Supplied • Animated Figures 3-6, 3-7, 3-9 • Economics Video: Kraft Leading the Way • Economics Video: Rust Belt City's Brighter Future • Economics Video: Stashing Your Cash • Economics Video: The Return of Zeppelin
Determining the Market Price and the Equilibrium Quantity The equilibrium price of a good and the equilibrium quantity of the good that is produced and sold are determined by the intersection of the demand and supply curves. At this intersection point, the quantity demanded by buyers of the good just equals the quantity supplied by sellers, so there is neither an excess quantity of the good supplied (surplus) nor an excess quantity of the good demanded (shortage).	market clearing, or equilibrium, price, 64 equilibrium, 64 shortage, 66 surplus, 66 **KEY FIGURE** Figure 3-11, 67	• **MyEconLab** Study Plan 3.7 • Animated Figure 3-11 • ABC News Video: The Ripple Effects of Oil Prices • Economics Video: No Frills Grocery Shopping

Log in to MyEconLab, take a chapter test, and get a personalized Study Plan that tells you which concepts you understand and which ones you need to review. From there, MyEconLab will give you further practice, tutorials, animations, videos, and guided solutions. Log in to www.myeconlab.com

PROBLEMS

All problems are assignable in myeconlab. Answers to odd-numbered problems appear at the back of the book.

3-1. Suppose that in a recent market period, the following relationship existed between the price of Blu-ray discs and the quantity supplied and quantity demanded.

Price	Quantity Demanded	Quantity Supplied
$19	100 million	40 million
$20	90 million	60 million
$21	80 million	80 million
$22	70 million	100 million
$23	60 million	120 million

Graph the supply and demand curves for Blu-ray discs using the information in the table. What are the equilibrium price and quantity? If the industry price is $20, is there a shortage or surplus of Blu-ray discs? How much is the shortage or surplus?

3-2. Suppose that in a later market period, the quantities supplied in the table in Problem 3-1 are unchanged. The quantity demanded, however, has increased by 30 million at each price. Construct the resulting demand curve in the illustration you made for Problem 3-1. Is this an increase or a decrease in demand? What are the new equilibrium quantity and the new market price? Give two examples of changes in *ceteris paribus* conditions that might cause such a change.

3-3. Consider the market for high-speed satellite Internet access service, which is a normal good. Explain whether the following events would cause an increase or a decrease in demand or an increase or a decrease in the quantity demanded.

a. Firms providing cable (an alternative to satellite) Internet access services reduce their prices.

b. Firms providing high-speed satellite Internet access services reduce their prices.

c. There is a decrease in the incomes earned by consumers of high-speed satellite Internet access services.

d. Consumers' tastes shift away from using cable lines for Internet access in favor of satellite Internet access services.

3-4. In the market for flash memory drives (a normal good), explain whether the following events would cause an increase or a decrease in demand or an increase or a decrease in the quantity demanded. Also explain what happens to the equilibrium quantity and the market clearing price.

a. There are increases in the prices of storage racks and boxes for flash memory drives.

b. There is a decrease in the price of computer drives that read the information contained on flash memory drives.

c. There is a dramatic increase in the price of secure digital cards that, like flash memory drives, can be used to store digital data.

d. A booming economy increases the income of the typical buyer of flash memory drives.

e. Consumers of flash memory drives anticipate that the price of this good will decline in the future.

3-5. Give an example of a complement and a substitute in consumption for each of the following items.

a. Bacon

b. Tennis racquets

c. Coffee

d. Automobiles

3-6. At the beginning of the 2000s, the United States imposed high import taxes on a number of European goods due to a trade dispute. One of these goods was Roquefort cheese. Show how this tax affects the market for Roquefort cheese in the United States, shifting the appropriate curve and indicating a new equilibrium quantity and market price.

3-7. Consider the following diagram of a market for one-bedroom rental apartments in a college community.

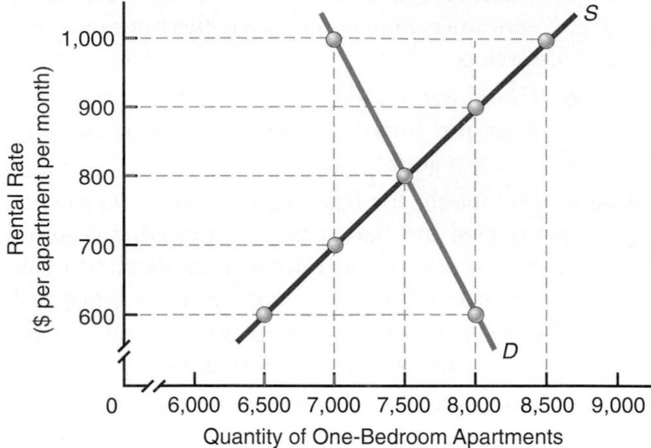

a. At a rental rate of $1,000 per month, is there an excess quantity supplied, or is there an excess quantity demanded? What is the amount of the excess quantity supplied or demanded?

b. If the present rental rate of one-bedroom apartments is $1,000 per month, through what mechanism will the rental rate adjust to the equilibrium rental rate of $800?

c. At a rental rate of $600 per month, is there an excess quantity supplied, or is there an excess quantity demanded? What is the amount of the excess quantity supplied or demanded?

d. If the present rental rate of one-bedroom apartments is $600 per month, through what mechanism will the rental rate adjust to the equilibrium rental rate of $800?

3-8. Consider the market for economics textbooks. Explain whether the following events would cause an increase or a decrease in supply or an increase or a decrease in the quantity supplied.

a. The market price of paper increases.

b. The market price of economics textbooks increases.

c. The number of publishers of economics textbooks increases.

d. Publishers expect that the market price of economics textbooks will increase next month.

3-9. Consider the market for laptop computers. Explain whether the following events would cause an increase or a decrease in supply or an increase or a decrease in the quantity supplied. Illustrate each, and show what would happen to the equilibrium quantity and the market price.

a. The price of memory chips used in laptop computers declines.

b. The price of machinery used to produce laptop computers increases.

c. The number of manufacturers of laptop computers increases.

d. There is a decrease in the demand for laptop computers.

3-10. The U.S. government offers significant per-unit subsidy payments to U.S. sugar growers. Describe the effects of the introduction of such subsidies on the market for sugar and the market for artificial sweeteners. Explain whether the demand curve or the supply curve shifts in each market, and if so, in which direction. Also explain what happens to the equilibrium quantity and the market price in each market.

3-11. Platinum's white luster has made the rare metal the chic look in engagement rings and wedding bands. Recently, however, the price of palladium, a more abundant metal with virtually identical characteristics, has declined considerably. Explain the likely effects that the drop in the price of palladium will have on the market for platinum.

3-12. Ethanol is a motor fuel manufactured from corn, barley, or wheat, and it can be used to power the engines of many autos and trucks. Suppose that the government decides to provide a large per-unit subsidy to ethanol producers. Explain the effects in the markets for the following items:

a. Corn

b. Gasoline

c. Automobiles

3-13. If the price of processor chips used in manufacturing personal computers decreases, what will happen in the market for personal computers? How will the equilibrium price and equilibrium quantity of personal computers change?

3-14. Assume that the cost of aluminum used by soft-drink companies increases. Which of the following correctly describes the resulting effects in the market for soft drinks distributed in aluminum cans? (More than one statement may be correct.)

a. The demand for soft drinks decreases.

b. The quantity of soft drinks demanded decreases.

c. The supply of soft drinks decreases.

d. The quantity of soft drinks supplied decreases.

ECONOMICS ON THE NET

The U.S. Nursing Shortage For some years media stories have discussed a shortage of qualified nurses in the United States. This application explores some of the factors that have caused the quantity of newly trained nurses demanded to tend to exceed the quantity of newly trained nurses supplied.

Title: Nursing Shortage Resource Web Link

Navigation: Go to the Nursing Shortage Resource Web Link at **www.econtoday.com/ch03**, and click on *Nursing Shortage Fact Sheet*.

Application Read the discussion, and answer the following questions.

1. What has happened to the demand for new nurses in the United States? What has happened to the supply of new nurses? Why has the result been a shortage?

2. If there is a free market for the skills of new nurses, what can you predict is likely to happen to the wage rate earned by individuals who have just completed their nursing training?

For Group Study and Analysis Discuss the pros and cons of high schools and colleges trying to factor predictions about future wages into student career counseling. How might this potentially benefit students? What problems might high schools and colleges face in trying to assist students in evaluating the future earnings prospects of various jobs?

ANSWERS TO QUICK QUIZZES

p. 51: (i) inverse; (ii) demand

p. 53: (i) constant; (ii) market demand

p. 58: (i) income . . . tastes and preferences . . . prices of related goods . . . expectations about future prices and incomes . . . market size (the number of potential buyers in the market); (ii) *ceteris paribus;* (iii) movement along

p. 61: (i) direct; (ii) supply; (iii) market supply

p. 64: (i) move along . . . shift; (ii) input prices . . . technology and productivity . . . taxes and subsidies . . . expectations of future relative prices . . . the number of firms in the industry

p. 67: (i) intersection . . . equilibrium; (ii) greater; (iii) less

4

Extensions of Demand and Supply Analysis

According to the chief executive of Dow Chemical, "Water is the oil of the twenty-first century." What he means is that as the global demand for water for drinking, washing, irrigation, and other uses doubles every 20 years, there likely will be pressure for its equilibrium price to rise. If so, this adjustment would mirror the way in which the price of oil rose in the twentieth century. In fact, however, inflation-adjusted prices of water have barely increased in recent years. This is because government controls keep water prices lower than they otherwise would be in unregulated markets. In this chapter, you will learn why such regulations have contributed to more than 1.2 billion people, or about 20 percent of the world's population, experiencing shortages of water. You will also learn how progress in turning seawater into water usable by humans could help to ease these shortages.

LEARNING OBJECTIVES

After reading this chapter, you should be able to:

- Discuss the essential features of the price system
- Evaluate the effects of changes in demand and supply on the market price and equilibrium quantity
- Understand the rationing function of prices
- Explain the effects of price ceilings
- Explain the effects of price floors
- Describe various types of government-imposed quantity restrictions on markets

myeconlab

MyEconLab helps you master each objective and study more efficiently. See end of chapter for details.

nearly 90,000 U.S. residents seek kidney transplants each year, but only about 20,000 kidney transplants occur? Selling a kidney is illegal, so the maximum price of a kidney—called a *price ceiling*—is $0. To assist donors in helping their loved ones *and* others, economists have organized exchanges to match kidneys of loved ones. For instance, a father of a young woman requiring a transplant may donate his kidney that is a match for a woman who has a son with a kidney that is a match for the man's daughter. Much more complicated swaps have occurred. On one day in Washington, D.C., a chain of exchanges involved 13 donations—hence, 26 surgeries. Nevertheless, on net more than 70,000 people in the United States fail to receive transplants annually, up from 60,000 a few years ago.

Did You Know That?

What effects can a price ceiling have on the availability and consumption of a good or service? As you will learn in this chapter, we can use the supply and demand analysis developed in Chapter 3 to answer this question. You will find that when a government sets a ceiling below the equilibrium price, the result will be a *shortage,* in which quantity supplied remains below quantity demanded. Similarly, you will learn how we can use supply and demand analysis to examine the "surplus" of various agricultural products, the "shortage" of apartments in certain cities, and many other phenomena. All of these examples are part of our economy, which we characterize as a *price system.*

The Price System and Markets

In a **price system,** otherwise known as a *market system,* relative prices are constantly changing to reflect changes in supply and demand for different commodities. The prices of those commodities are the signals to everyone within the price system as to what is relatively scarce and what is relatively abundant. In this sense, prices provide information.

Price system
An economic system in which relative prices are constantly changing to reflect changes in supply and demand for different commodities. The prices of those commodities are signals to everyone within the system as to what is relatively scarce and what is relatively abundant.

Indeed, it is the *signaling* aspect of the price system that provides the information to buyers and sellers about what should be bought and what should be produced. In a price system, there is a clear-cut chain of events in which any changes in demand and supply cause changes in prices that in turn affect the opportunities that businesses and individuals have for profit and personal gain. Such changes influence our use of resources.

Exchange and Markets

The price system features **voluntary exchange,** acts of trading between individuals that make both parties to the trade subjectively better off. The prices we pay for the desired items are determined by the interaction of the forces underlying supply and demand. In our economy, exchanges take place voluntarily in markets. A market encompasses the exchange arrangements of both buyers and sellers that underlie the forces of supply and demand. Indeed, one definition of a market is that it is a low-cost institution for facilitating exchange. A market increases incomes by helping resources move to their highest-valued uses.

Voluntary exchange
An act of trading, done on an elective basis, in which both parties to the trade expect to be better off after the exchange.

Transaction Costs

Individuals turn to markets because markets reduce the cost of exchanges. These costs are sometimes referred to as **transaction costs,** which are broadly defined as the costs associated with finding out exactly what is being transacted as well as the cost of enforcing contracts. If you were Robinson Crusoe and lived alone on an island, you would never incur a transaction cost. For everyone else, transaction costs are just as real as the costs of production. Today, high-speed computers have allowed us to reduce transaction costs by increasing our ability to process information and keep records.

Transaction costs
All of the costs associated with exchange, including the informational costs of finding out the price and quality, service record, and durability of a product, plus the cost of contracting and enforcing that contract.

Consider some simple examples of transaction costs. A club warehouse such as Sam's Club or Costco reduces the transaction costs of having to go to numerous specialty stores to obtain the items you desire. Financial institutions, such as commercial banks, have reduced the transaction costs of directing funds from savers to borrowers. In general, the more organized the market, the lower the transaction costs. Among those who constantly attempt to lower transaction costs are the much maligned middlemen.

The Role of Middlemen

As long as there are costs of bringing together buyers and sellers, there will be an incentive for intermediaries, normally called middlemen, to lower those costs. This means that middlemen specialize in lowering transaction costs. Whenever producers do not sell their products directly to the final consumer, by definition, one or more middlemen are involved. Farmers typically sell their output to distributors, who are usually called wholesalers, who then sell those products to retailers such as supermarkets.

How has a firm altered the transaction costs faced by Indian emigrants residing in other nations who wish to assist relatives still in India?

INTERNATIONAL EXAMPLE **Assisting Scattered Emigrants Who Want to Help Kin at Home**

About 25 million people have left India to work in other nations around the globe. These emigrants transmit about $30 billion per year to their families back home—more than any other emigrant group.

To assist Indian emigrants who desire to help family members back home, a company called Sahara Care House offers a suite of 60 products and services. The firm's more than 3,000 India-based "relationship ambassadors" perform a variety of tasks for emigrants' families. For example, an ambassador might deliver flowers, shop for and drop off food and clothing, or accompany loved ones to physicians' visits. Thus, this company specializes in performing tasks for family members on behalf of Indian expatriates, thereby acting as a middleman.

FOR CRITICAL ANALYSIS

Why do you suppose that Indian emigrants are willing to pay Sahara Care House the fees that it charges to perform its middleman services?

Changes in Demand and Supply

A key function of middlemen is to reduce transaction costs of buyers and sellers in markets for goods and services, and it is in markets that we see the results of changes in demand and supply. Market equilibrium can change whenever there is a *shock* caused by a change in a *ceteris paribus* condition for demand or supply. A shock to the supply and demand system can be represented by a shift in the supply curve, a shift in the demand curve, or a shift in both curves. Any shock to the system will result in a new set of supply and demand relationships and a new equilibrium. Forces will come into play to move the system from the old price-quantity equilibrium (now a disequilibrium situation) to the new equilibrium, where the new demand and supply curves intersect.

Effects of Changes in Either Demand or Supply

You Are There

To consider market adjustments to an increase in demand, read **"Cash for Clunkers" Subsidies and the Market for "Liquid Glass,"** on page 88.

In many situations, it is possible to predict what will happen to both equilibrium price and equilibrium quantity when demand or supply changes. Specifically, whenever one curve is stable while the other curve shifts, we can tell what will happen to both price and quantity. Consider the possibilities in Figure 4-1 on the facing page. In panel (a), the supply curve remains unchanged, but demand increases from D_1 to D_2. Note that the results are an increase in the market clearing price from P_1 to P_2 and an increase in the equilibrium quantity from Q_1 to Q_2.

In panel (b) in Figure 4-1, there is a decrease in demand from D_1 to D_3. This results in a decrease in both the equilibrium price of the good and the equilibrium quantity. Panels (c) and (d) show the effects of a shift in the supply curve while the demand curve is unchanged. In panel (c), the supply curve has shifted rightward. The equilibrium price of the product falls, and the equilibrium quantity increases. In panel (d), supply

FIGURE 4-1 Shifts in Demand and in Supply: Determinate Results

In panel (a), the supply curve is unchanged at S. The demand curve shifts outward from D_1 to D_2. The equilibrium price and quantity rise from P_1, Q_1 to P_2, Q_2, respectively. In panel (b), again the supply curve is unchanged at S. The demand curve shifts inward to the left, showing a decrease in demand from D_1 to D_3. Both equilibrium price and equilibrium quantity fall. In panel (c), the demand curve now remains unchanged at D. The supply curve shifts from S_1 to S_2. The equilibrium price falls from P_1 to P_2. The equilibrium quantity increases, however, from Q_1 to Q_2. In panel (d), the demand curve is unchanged at D. Supply decreases as shown by a leftward shift of the supply curve from S_1 to S_3. The market clearing price increases from P_1 to P_3. The equilibrium quantity falls from Q_1 to Q_3.

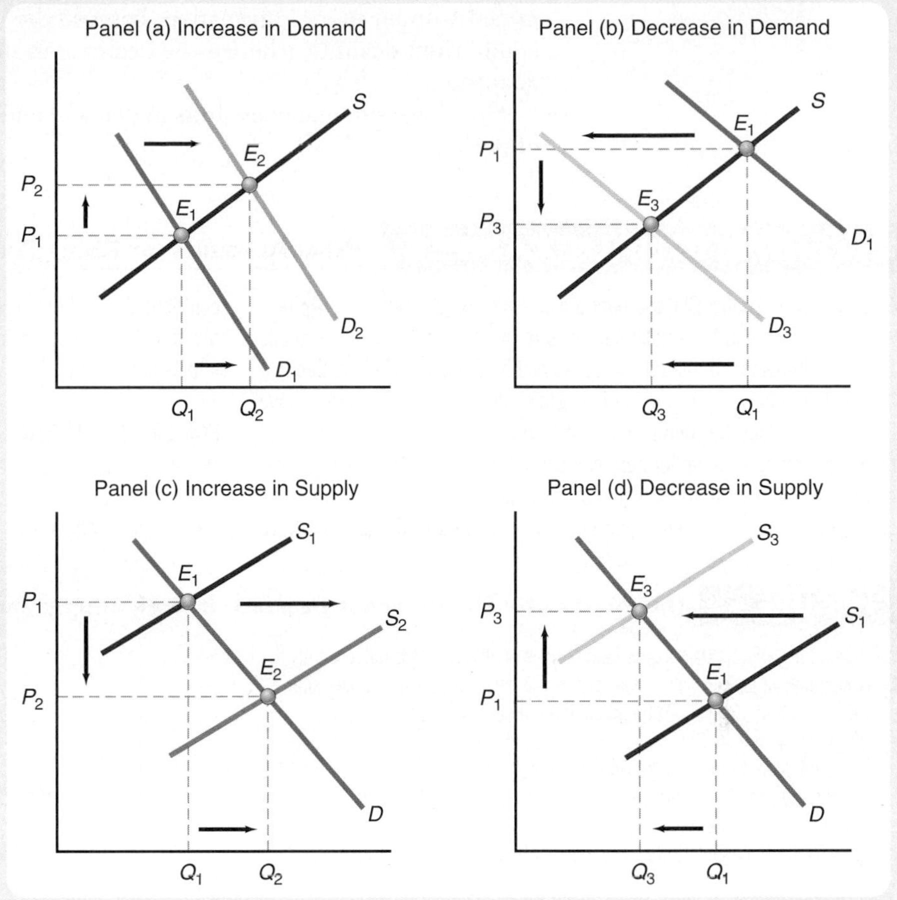

has shifted leftward—there has been a supply decrease. The product's equilibrium price increases, and the equilibrium quantity decreases.

Situations in Which Both Demand and Supply Shift

The examples in Figure 4-1 show a theoretically determinate outcome of a shift either in the demand curve, holding the supply curve constant, or in the supply curve, holding the demand curve constant. When both the supply and demand curves change, the outcome is indeterminate for either equilibrium price or equilibrium quantity.

When both demand and supply increase, the equilibrium quantity unambiguously rises, because the increase in demand and the increase in supply *both* tend to generate a rise in quantity. The change in the equilibrium price is uncertain without more information, because the increase in demand tends to increase the equilibrium price, whereas the increase in supply tends to decrease the equilibrium price. Decreases in both demand and supply tend to generate a fall in quantity, so the equilibrium quantity falls. Again, the effect on the equilibrium price is uncertain without additional information, because a decrease in demand tends to reduce the equilibrium price, whereas a decrease in supply tends to increase the equilibrium price.

We can be certain that when demand decreases and supply increases at the same time, the equilibrium price will fall, because *both* the decrease in demand and the increase in supply tend to push down the equilibrium price. The change in the equilibrium quantity is uncertain without more information, because the decrease in demand tends to reduce the equilibrium quantity, whereas the increase in supply tends to increase the equilibrium quantity. If demand increases and supply decreases at the same time, both occurrences tend to push up the equilibrium price, so the equilibrium price definitely rises. The change in the equilibrium quantity cannot be determined without more information, because the increase in demand tends to raise the equilibrium quantity, whereas the decrease in supply tends to reduce the equilibrium quantity.

How have simultaneous shifts in demand and supply affected the equilibrium price of pork in China?

INTERNATIONAL EXAMPLE What Accounts for Rising Pork Prices in China?

Since the early 2000s, Chinese pork prices have surged. There are two reasons for the jump in the equilibrium price of this food item, which accounts for about 65 percent of the protein consumed by China's residents. One is a booming economy: Pork is a normal good, so as Chinese incomes have increased, so has the demand for pork. Hence, as shown in Figure 4-2 below, the demand curve for pork has shifted rightward. At the same time, rising prices of feed for hogs, higher prices of land to raise hogs, and a "blue ear disease" epidemic that wiped out large numbers of the animals have contributed to a reduction in the supply of pork. On net, the equilibrium quantity of pork produced and consumed has risen, and the market clearing price of pork has increased.

FOR CRITICAL ANALYSIS

How do you suppose that a recent decision by the Chinese government to open the nation's pork market to foreign imports is likely to affect the equilibrium price of pork?

FIGURE 4-2 The Effects of a Simultaneous Decrease in Pork Supply and Increase in Pork Demand

Since the early 2000s, various factors have contributed to a reduction in the supply of pork in China, depicted by the leftward shift in the pork supply curve from S_1 to S_2. At the same time, there was an increase in the demand for pork by Chinese consumers, as shown by the shift in the pork demand curve from D_1 to D_2. On net, the equilibrium quantity of pork produced and consumed rose, from 8 billion pounds per year at point E_1 to 10 billion pounds per year at point E_2, and the equilibrium price of pork increased from about \$3.25 per pound to about \$3.50 per pound.

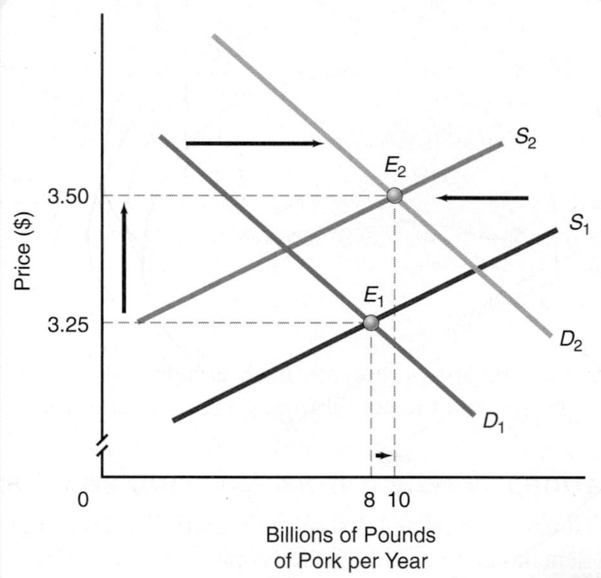

Price Flexibility and Adjustment Speed

We have used as an illustration for our analysis a market in which prices are quite flexible. Some markets are indeed like that. In others, however, price flexibility may take the form of subtle adjustments such as hidden payments or quality changes. For example, although the published price of bouquets of flowers may stay the same, the freshness of the flowers may change, meaning that the price per constant-quality unit changes. The published price of French bread might stay the same, but the quality could go up or down, perhaps through use of a different recipe, thereby changing the price per constant-quality unit. There are many ways to implicitly change prices without actually changing the published price for a *nominal* unit of a product or service.

We must also note that markets do not always return to equilibrium immediately. There may be a significant adjustment time. A shock to the economy in the form of an oil embargo, a drought, or a long strike will not be absorbed overnight. This means that even in unfettered market situations, in which there are no restrictions on changes in prices and quantities, temporary excess quantities supplied or excess quantities demanded may appear. Our analysis simply indicates what the market clearing price and equilibrium quantity ultimately will be, given a demand curve and a supply curve. Nowhere in the analysis is there any indication of the speed with which a market will get to a new equilibrium after a shock. The price may even temporarily overshoot the new equilibrium level. Remember this warning when we examine changes in demand and in supply due to changes in their *ceteris paribus* conditions.

QUICK QUIZ **See page 93 for the answers. Review concepts from this section in MyEconLab.**

When the __________ curve shifts outward or inward with an unchanged __________ curve, equilibrium price and quantity increase or decrease, respectively. When the __________ curve shifts outward or inward given an unchanged __________ curve, equilibrium price moves in the direction opposite to equilibrium quantity.

When there is a shift in demand or supply, the new equilibrium price is not obtained __________. Adjustment takes __________.

The Rationing Function of Prices

The synchronization of decisions by buyers and sellers that leads to equilibrium is called the *rationing function of prices*. Prices are indicators of relative scarcity. An equilibrium price clears the market. The plans of buyers and sellers, given the price, are not frustrated. It is the free interaction of buyers and sellers that sets the price that eventually clears the market. Price, in effect, rations a good to demanders who are willing and able to pay the highest price. Whenever the rationing function of prices is frustrated by government-enforced price ceilings that set prices below the market clearing level, a prolonged shortage results.

Methods of Nonprice Rationing

There are ways other than price to ration goods. *First come, first served* is one method. *Political power* is another. *Physical force* is yet another. Cultural, religious, and physical differences have been and are used as rationing devices throughout the world.

RATIONING BY WAITING Consider first come, first served as a rationing device. We call this *rationing by queues*, where *queue* means "line." Whoever is willing to wait in line the longest obtains the good that is being sold at less than the market clearing price. All who wait in line are paying a higher *total outlay* than the money price paid for the good. Personal time has an opportunity cost. To calculate the total outlay expended on the good, we must add up the money price plus the opportunity cost of the time spent waiting.

Rationing by waiting may occur in situations in which entrepreneurs are free to change prices to equate quantity demanded with quantity supplied but choose not to do so. This results in queues of potential buyers. It may seem that the price in the market is being held below equilibrium by some noncompetitive force. That is not true, however. Such queuing may arise in a free market when the demand for a good is subject to large or unpredictable fluctuations, and the additional costs to firms (and ultimately to consumers) of constantly changing prices or of holding sufficient inventories or providing sufficient excess capacity to cover peak demands are greater than the costs to consumers of waiting for the good. Common examples are waiting in line to purchase a fast-food lunch and queuing to purchase a movie ticket a few minutes before the next showing.

RATIONING BY RANDOM ASSIGNMENT OR COUPONS *Random assignment* is another way to ration goods. You may have been involved in a rationing-by-random-assignment scheme in college if you were assigned a housing unit. Sometimes rationing by random assignment is used to fill slots in popular classes.

Rationing by *coupons* has also been used, particularly during wartime. In the United States during World War II, families were allotted coupons that allowed them to purchase specified quantities of rationed goods, such as meat and gasoline. To purchase such goods, they had to pay a specified price *and* give up a coupon.

The Essential Role of Rationing

In a world of scarcity, there is, by definition, competition for what is scarce. After all, any resources that are not scarce can be had by everyone at a zero price in as large a quantity as everyone wants, such as air to burn in internal combustion engines. Once scarcity arises, there has to be some method to ration the available resources, goods, and services. The price system is one form of rationing. The others that we mentioned are alternatives. Economists cannot say which system of rationing is "best." They can, however, say that rationing via the price system leads to the most efficient use of available resources. As explained in Appendix B, this means that generally in a freely functioning price system, all of the gains from mutually beneficial trade will be captured.

QUICK QUIZ See page 93 for the answers. Review concepts from this section in MyEconLab.

Prices in a market economy perform a rationing function because they reflect relative scarcity, allowing the market to clear. Other ways to ration goods include __________ __________, __________ __________ __________; __________ __________; __________ __________ __________; __________ __________; and __________.

Even when businesspeople can change prices, some rationing by waiting may occur. Such __________ arises when there are large changes in demand coupled with high costs of satisfying those changes immediately.

The Policy of Government-Imposed Price Controls

Price controls
Government-mandated minimum or maximum prices that may be charged for goods and services.

Price ceiling
A legal maximum price that may be charged for a particular good or service.

Price floor
A legal minimum price below which a good or service may not be sold. Legal minimum wages are an example.

The rationing function of prices is prevented when governments impose price controls. **Price controls** often involve setting a **price ceiling**—the maximum price that may be allowed in an exchange. The world has had a long history of price ceilings applied to product prices, wages, rents, and interest rates. Occasionally, a government will set a **price floor**—a minimum price below which a good or service may not be sold. Price floors have most often been applied to wages and agricultural products. Let's first consider price ceilings.

Price Ceilings and Black Markets

As long as a price ceiling is below the market clearing price, imposing a price ceiling creates a shortage, as can be seen in Figure 4-3 on the facing page. At any price below the market clearing, or equilibrium, price of $1,000, there will always be a larger quantity demanded than quantity supplied—a shortage, as you will recall from Chapter 3. Normally, whenever quantity demanded exceeds quantity supplied—that is, when a shortage exists—there is a tendency for the price to rise to its equilibrium level. But with a price ceiling, this tendency cannot be fully realized because everyone is forbidden to trade at the equilibrium price.

Nonprice rationing devices
All methods used to ration scarce goods that are price-controlled. Whenever the price system is not allowed to work, nonprice rationing devices will evolve to ration the affected goods and services.

The result is fewer exchanges and **nonprice rationing devices.** Figure 4-3 illustrates the situation for portable electricity generators after a natural disaster: the equilibrium quantity of portable generators demanded and supplied (or traded) would be 10,000 units, and the market clearing price would be $1,000 per generator. But, if the government essentially imposes a price ceiling by requiring the price of portable generators to remain at the predisaster level, which the government determines was a price of $600,

FIGURE 4-3 Black Markets for Portable Electric Generators

The demand curve is *D*. The supply curve is *S*. The equilibrium price is $1,000. The government, however, steps in and imposes a maximum price of $600. At that lower price, the quantity demanded will be 15,000, but the quantity supplied will be only 5,000. There is a "shortage." The implicit price (including time costs) tends to rise to $1,400. If black markets arise, as they generally will, the equilibrium black market price will end up somewhere between $600 and $1,400. The actual quantity transacted will be between 5,000 and 10,000.

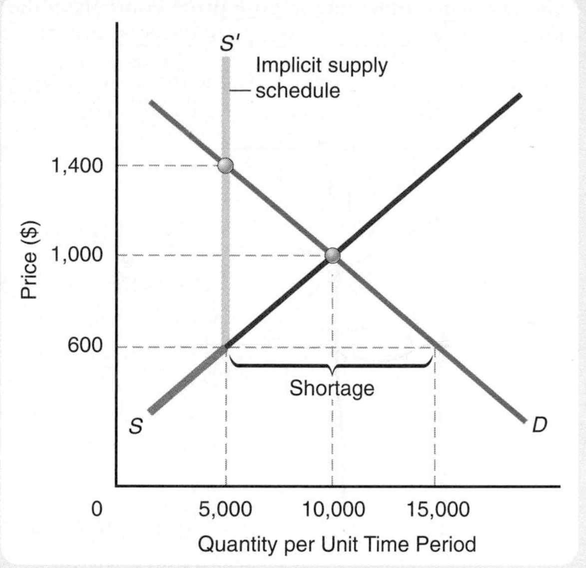

the equilibrium quantity offered is only 5,000. Because frustrated consumers will be able to purchase only 5,000 units, there is a shortage. The most obvious nonprice rationing device to help clear the market is queuing, or physical lines, which we have already discussed. To avoid physical lines, waiting lists may be established.

Typically, an effective price ceiling leads to a **black market.** A black market is a market in which the price-controlled good is sold at an illegally high price through various methods. For example, if the price of gasoline is controlled at lower than the market clearing price, drivers who wish to fill up their cars may offer the gas station attendant a cash payment on the side (as happened in the United States in the 1970s and in China and India in the mid-2000s during price controls on gasoline). If the price of beef is controlled at below its market clearing price, a customer who offers the butcher good tickets to an upcoming football game may be allocated otherwise unavailable beef. Indeed, the true implicit price of a price-controlled good or service can be increased in an infinite number of ways, limited only by the imagination. (Black markets also occur when goods are made illegal.)

Black market
A market in which goods are traded at prices above their legal maximum prices or in which illegal goods are sold.

How have sellers of rice attempted to use nonprice mechanisms to evade Venezuelan price ceilings?

INTERNATIONAL POLICY EXAMPLE

The Rice Must Be White!

In Venezuela, there is a legal ceiling price of white rice of about 1 cent per kilogram (2.2 pounds). Unfortunately for many of the residents of that nation, this is about half of the price at which most Venezuelan rice sellers are willing to offer white rice. As a result, there have been chronic shortages of this staple food item.

In an effort to avoid the government's price controls, firms began to add flavoring and coloring to rice and to sell it in different packaging so that it would not be classified as white rice subject to the ceiling price. Consumers rushed to buy the flavored, colored, and repackaged rice at higher, market clearing prices. The general shortage of rice temporarily disappeared. When the Venezuelan government realized what the sellers were doing, however, it established a new rule mandating that at least 80 percent of all rice offered for sale must be white rice. Soon, consumers again found bare shelves instead of bags of rice at grocery stores.

FOR CRITICAL ANALYSIS

There are ceilings on the prices of most basic food items in Venezuela. Why does this help to explain why there are usually long lines of shoppers waiting to access grocery shelves in that nation's stores?

QUICK QUIZ See page 93 for the answers. Review concepts from this section in MyEconLab.

Governments sometimes impose **price controls** in the form of price ________ and price ________.

An effective price ________ is one that sets the legal price below the market clearing price and is enforced.

Effective price ________ lead to nonprice rationing devices and black markets.

The Policy of Controlling Rents

Rent control
Price ceilings on rents.

More than 200 U.S. cities and towns, including Berkeley, California, and New York City, operate under some kind of rent control. **Rent control** is a system under which the local government tells building owners how much they can charge their tenants for rent. In the United States, rent controls date back to at least World War II. The objective of rent control is to keep rents below levels that would be observed in a freely competitive market.

The Functions of Rental Prices

In any housing market, rental prices serve three functions: (1) to promote the efficient maintenance of existing housing and to stimulate the construction of new housing, (2) to allocate existing scarce housing among competing claimants, and (3) to ration the use of existing housing by current demanders. Rent controls interfere with all of these functions.

RENT CONTROLS AND CONSTRUCTION Rent controls discourage the construction of new rental units. Rents are the most important long-term determinant of profitability, and rent controls artificially depress them. Consider some examples. In a recent year in Dallas, Texas, with a 16 percent rental vacancy rate but no rent control laws, 11,000 new rental housing units were built. In the same year in San Francisco, California, only 2,000 units were built, despite a mere 1.6 percent vacancy rate. The major difference? San Francisco has had stringent rent control laws. In New York City, most rental units being built are luxury units, which are exempt from controls.

EFFECTS ON THE EXISTING SUPPLY OF HOUSING When rental rates are held below equilibrium levels, property owners cannot recover the cost of maintenance, repairs, and capital improvements through higher rents. Hence, they curtail these activities. In the extreme situation, taxes, utilities, and the expenses of basic repairs exceed rental receipts. The result is abandoned buildings from Santa Monica, California, to New York City. Some owners have resorted to arson, hoping to collect the insurance on their empty buildings before the city claims them for back taxes.

RATIONING THE CURRENT USE OF HOUSING Rent controls also affect the current use of housing because they restrict tenant mobility. Consider a family whose children have gone off to college. That family might want to live in a smaller apartment. But in a rent-controlled environment, giving up a rent-controlled unit can entail a substantial cost. In most rent-controlled cities, rents can be adjusted only when a tenant leaves. That means that a move from a long-occupied rent-controlled apartment to a smaller apartment can involve a hefty rent hike. In New York, this artificial preservation of the status quo came to be known as "housing gridlock."

Attempts to Evade Rent Controls

Go to www.econtoday.com/ch04 to learn more about New York City's rent controls from Tenant.net.

The distortions produced by rent controls lead to efforts by both property owners and tenants to evade the rules. These efforts lead to the growth of expensive government bureaucracies whose job it is to make sure that rent controls aren't evaded.

In New York City, because rent on an apartment can be raised only if the tenant leaves, property owners have had an incentive to make life unpleasant for tenants in order to drive them out or to evict them on the slightest pretext. The city has responded by making evictions extremely costly for property owners. Eviction requires a tedious and expensive judicial proceeding. Tenants, for their part, routinely try to sublet all or part of their rent-controlled apartments at fees substantially above the rent they pay to the owner. Both the city and the property owners try to prohibit subletting and often end up in the city's housing courts—an entire judicial system developed to deal with disputes involving rent-controlled apartments. The overflow and appeals from the city's housing courts sometimes clog the rest of New York's judicial system.

Who Gains and Who Loses from Rent Controls?

The big losers from rent controls are clearly property owners. But there is another group of losers—low-income individuals, especially single mothers, trying to find their first apartment. Some observers now believe that rent controls have worsened the problem of homelessness in cities such as New York.

Often, owners of rent-controlled apartments charge "key money" before allowing a new tenant to move in. This is a large up-front cash payment, usually illegal but demanded nonetheless—just one aspect of the black market in rent-controlled apartments. Poor individuals have insufficient income to pay the hefty key money payment, nor can they assure the owner that their rent will be on time or even paid each month. Because controlled rents are usually below market clearing levels, apartment owners have little incentive to take any risk on low-income individuals as tenants. This is particularly true when a prospective tenant's chief source of income is a welfare check. Indeed, a large number of the litigants in the New York housing courts are welfare mothers who have missed their rent payments due to emergency expenses or delayed welfare checks. Their appeals often end in evictions and a new home in a temporary public shelter—or on the streets.

Who benefits from rent control? Ample evidence indicates that upper-income professionals benefit the most. These people can use their mastery of the bureaucracy and their large network of friends and connections to exploit the rent control system. Consider that in New York, actresses Mia Farrow and Cicely Tyson live in rent-controlled apartments, paying well below market rates. So do the former director of the Metropolitan Museum of Art and singer and children's book author Carly Simon.

Why Not . . . require owners of residential buildings to provide low-cost housing so that all U.S. residents can "afford" roofs over their heads?

Calls to require owners of residential buildings to make housing available at "low cost" translate into suggestions to establish ceiling housing prices below equilibrium housing prices. The result of a legal price ceiling for residential housing set lower than the market clearing price would be a shortage of residential housing: More people would want to purchase or rent housing at the ceiling price than owners of residential housing would desire to supply. In fact, less housing would be supplied at the lower price, so fewer people would obtain roofs over their heads than would have been the case without a ceiling price.

QUICK QUIZ

See page 93 for the answers. Review concepts from this section in MyEconLab.

__________ prices perform three functions: (1) allocating existing scarce housing among competing claimants, (2) promoting efficient maintenance of existing houses and stimulating new housing construction, and (3) rationing the use of existing houses by current demanders.

Effective rent __________ impede the functioning of rental prices. Construction of new rental units is discouraged. Rent __________ decrease spending on maintenance of existing ones and also lead to "housing gridlock."

There are numerous ways to evade rent controls. __________ __________ is one.

Price Floors in Agriculture

Another way that government can affect markets is by imposing price floors or price supports. In the United States, price supports are most often associated with agricultural products.

Price Supports

During the Great Depression, the federal government swung into action to help farmers. In 1933, it established a system of price supports for many agricultural products. Since then, there have been price supports for wheat, feed grains, cotton, rice, soybeans, sorghum, and dairy products, among other foodstuffs. The nature of the supports is quite simple: The government simply chooses a *support price* for an agricultural product and then acts to ensure that the price of the product never falls below the support level. Figure 4-4 below shows the market demand for and supply of peanuts. Without a price-support program, competitive forces would yield an equilibrium price of $250 per ton and an equilibrium quantity of 1.4 million tons per year. Clearly, if the government were to set the support price at or below $250 per ton, the quantity of peanuts demanded would equal the quantity of peanuts supplied at point *E*, because farmers could sell all they wanted at the market clearing price of $250 per ton.

But what happens when the government sets the support price *above* the market clearing price, at $350 per ton? At a support price of $350 per ton, the quantity demanded is only 1.0 million tons, but the quantity supplied is 2.2 million tons. The 1.2-million-ton difference between them is called the *excess quantity supplied,* or *surplus*. As simple as this program seems, its existence creates a fundamental question: How can the government agency charged with administering the price-support program prevent market forces from pushing the actual price down to $250 per ton?

If production exceeds the amount that consumers want to buy at the support price, what happens to the surplus? Quite simply, if the price-support program is to work, the government has to buy the surplus—the 1.2-million-ton difference. As a practical matter, the government acquires the 1.2-million-ton surplus indirectly through a government agency. The government either stores the surplus or sells it to foreign countries at a greatly reduced price (or gives it away free of charge) under the Food for Peace program.

FIGURE 4-4 Agricultural Price Supports

Free market equilibrium occurs at *E*, with an equilibrium price of $250 per ton and an equilibrium quantity of 1.4 million tons. When the government sets a support price at $350 per ton, the quantity demanded is 1.0 million tons, and the quantity supplied is 2.2 million tons. The difference is the surplus, which the government buys. Farmers' income from consumers equals $350 × 1.0 million = $350 million.

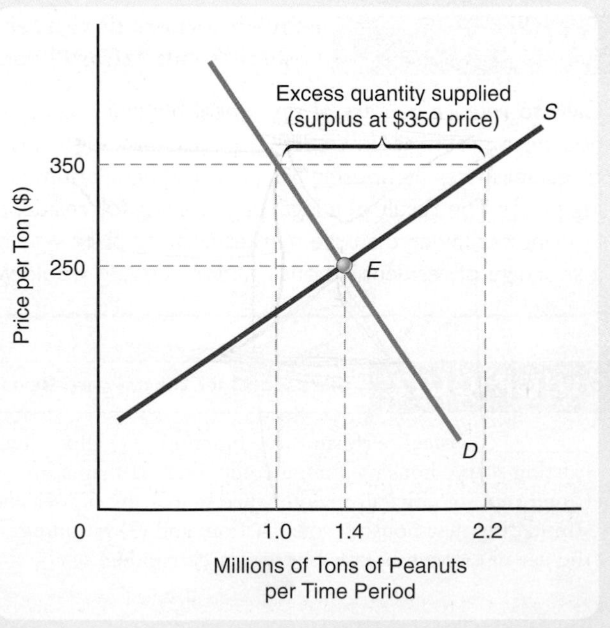

Who Benefits from Agricultural Price Supports?

Although agricultural price supports have traditionally been promoted as a way to guarantee decent earnings for low-income farmers, most of the benefits have in fact gone to the owners of very large farms. Price-support payments are made on a per-bushel basis, not on a per-farm basis. Thus, traditionally, the larger the farm, the bigger the benefit from agricultural price supports. In addition, *all* of the benefits from price supports ultimately accrue to *landowners* on whose land price-supported crops grow.

KEEPING PRICE SUPPORTS ALIVE UNDER A NEW NAME Back in the early 1990s, Congress indicated an intention to phase out most agricultural subsidies by the early 2000s. What Congress actually *did* throughout the 1990s, however, was to pass a series of "emergency laws" keeping farm subsidies alive. Some of these laws aimed to replace agricultural price supports with payments to many farmers for growing no crops at all, thereby boosting the market prices of crops by reducing supply. Nevertheless, the federal government and several state governments have continued to support prices of a number of agricultural products, such as peanuts, through "marketing loan" programs. These programs advance funds to farmers to help them finance the storage of some or all of their crops. The farmers can then use the stored produce as collateral for borrowing or sell it to the government and use the proceeds to repay debts. Marketing loan programs raise the effective price that farmers receive for their crops and commit federal and state governments to purchasing surplus production. Consequently, they lead to outcomes similar to traditional price-support programs.

THE MAIN BENEFICIARIES OF AGRICULTURAL SUBSIDIES In 2002, Congress enacted the Farm Security Act, which has perpetuated marketing loan programs and other subsidy and price-support arrangements for such farm products as wheat, corn, rice, peanuts, and soybeans. All told, the more than $9 billion in U.S. government payments for these and other products amounts to about 25 percent of the annual market value of all U.S. farm production.

The government seeks to cap the annual subsidy payment that an individual farmer can receive at $360,000 per year, but some farmers are able to garner higher annual amounts by exploiting regulatory loopholes. The greatest share of total agricultural subsidies goes to the owners of the largest farming operations. At present, 10 percent of U.S. farmers receive more than 70 percent of agricultural subsidies.

The 2008 Food, Conservation, and Energy Act expanded on the 2002 legislation by giving farmers raising any of a number of crops a choice between subsidy programs. On the one hand, farmers can opt to participate in traditional programs involving a mix of direct payments and marketing loan programs. On the other hand, farmers can choose a program offering guaranteed revenues. If market clearing crop prices end up higher than those associated with the government's revenue guarantee, farmers sell their crops at the higher prices instead of collecting government subsidies. But if equilibrium crop prices end up below a level consistent with the government guarantee, farmers receive direct subsidies to bring their total revenues up to the guaranteed level.

Price Floors in the Labor Market

The **minimum wage** is the lowest hourly wage rate that firms may legally pay their workers. Proponents favor higher minimum wages to ensure low-income workers a "decent" standard of living. Opponents counter that higher minimum wages cause increased unemployment, particularly among unskilled minority teenagers.

Minimum wage
A wage floor, legislated by government, setting the lowest hourly rate that firms may legally pay workers.

Minimum Wages in the United States

The federal minimum wage started in 1938 at 25 cents an hour, about 40 percent of the average manufacturing wage at the time. Typically, its level has stayed at about 40

Go to www.econtoday.com/ch04 for information from the U.S. Department of Labor about recent developments concerning the federal minimum wage.

to 50 percent of average manufacturing wages. After holding the minimum wage at \$5.15 per hour from 1997 to 2007, Congress enacted a series of phased increases in the hourly minimum wage, effective on July 24 of each year, to \$5.85 in 2007, \$6.55 in 2008, and \$7.25 in 2009.

Many states and cities have their own minimum wage laws that exceed the federal minimum. A number of municipalities refer to their minimum wage rules as "living wage" laws. Governments of these municipalities seek to set minimum wages consistent with living standards they deem to be socially acceptable—that is, overall wage income judged to be sufficient to purchase basic items such as housing and food.

Economic Effects of a Minimum Wage

What happens when the government establishes a floor on wages? The effects can be seen in Figure 4-5 below. We start off in equilibrium with the equilibrium wage rate of W_e and the equilibrium quantity of labor equal to Q_e. A minimum wage, W_m, higher than W_e, is imposed. At W_m, the quantity demanded for labor is reduced to Q_d, and some workers now become unemployed. Certain workers will become unemployed as a result of the minimum wage, but others will move to sectors where minimum wage laws do not apply. Wages will be pushed down in these uncovered sectors.

Note that the reduction in employment from Q_e to Q_d, or the distance from *B* to *A*, is less than the excess quantity of labor supplied at wage rate W_m. This excess quantity supplied is the distance between *A* and *C*, or the distance between Q_d and Q_s. The reason the reduction in employment is smaller than the excess quantity of labor supplied at the minimum wage is that the excess quantity of labor supplied also includes the *additional* workers who would like to work more hours at the new, higher minimum wage.

In the long run (a time period that is long enough to allow for full adjustment by workers and firms), some of the reduction in the quantity of labor demanded will result from a reduction in the number of firms, and some will result from changes in the number of workers employed by each firm. Economists estimate that a 10 percent increase in the inflation-adjusted minimum wage decreases total employment of those affected by 1 to 2 percent.

FIGURE 4-5 The Effect of Minimum Wages

The market clearing wage rate is W_e. The market clearing quantity of employment is Q_e, determined by the intersection of supply and demand at point *E*. A minimum wage equal to W_m is established. The quantity of labor demanded is reduced to Q_d. The reduction in employment from Q_e to Q_d is equal to the distance between *B* and *A*. That distance is smaller than the excess quantity of labor supplied at wage rate W_m. The distance between *B* and *C* is the increase in the quantity of labor supplied that results from the higher minimum wage rate.

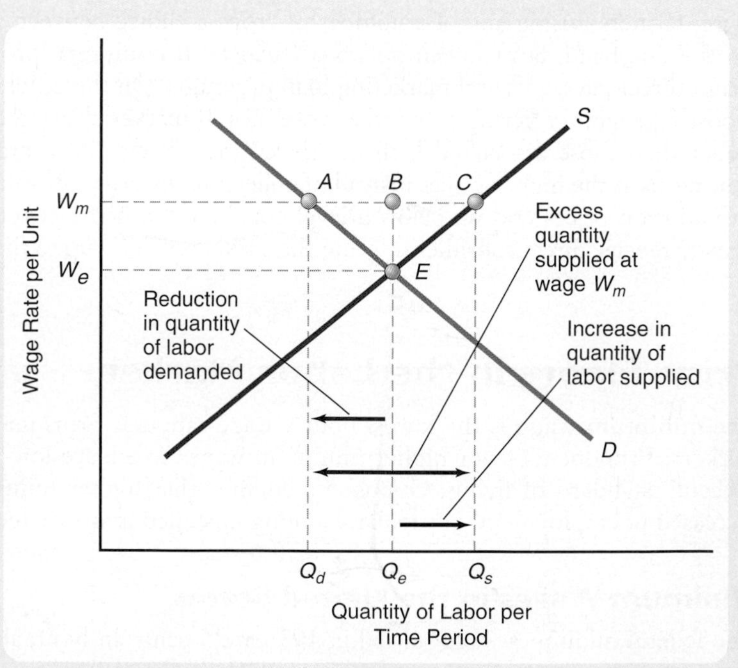

We can conclude from the application of demand and supply analysis that a minimum wage established above the equilibrium wage rate typically has two fundamental effects. On the one hand, it boosts the wage earnings of those people who obtain employment. On the other hand, the minimum wage results in unemployment for other individuals. Thus, demand and supply analysis implies that the minimum wage makes some people better off while making others much worse off.

Why did the minimum wage increases between 2007 and the beginning of 2010 likely contribute to making more people worse off rather than better off?

POLICY EXAMPLE **Bad Timing for Increasing the Minimum Wage**

Congress decided in May 2007 to increase the hourly minimum wage in three steps, from \$5.15 to \$5.85 in 2007, then to \$6.55 in 2008, and then to \$7.25. At that time, the overall U.S. unemployment rate—the ratio of those unemployed to those either employed or seeking work—was 4.5 percent. By 2008, the unemployment rate was 5.8 percent. When the final \$0.70-per-hour increase was added in 2009, the U.S. economy was experiencing its worst downturn since the early 1980s, and the overall unemployment rate was 9.4 percent. Within a few more months, the national unemployment rate exceeded 10 percent.

The increases in unemployment rates among three groups were even more pronounced. Between 2007 and the beginning of 2010, the unemployment rate jumped from 8.3 percent to 15.7 percent among African American workers, from 6.5 percent to 12.9 percent among single women with children, and from 15.7 percent to 27.6 percent among teens. Undoubtedly, the increases in the minimum wage rate contributed to the much higher unemployment rates among these groups.

FOR CRITICAL ANALYSIS

If the imposition of a minimum wage currently generates unemployment, what happens to the unemployment rate when the demand for labor declines?

Quantity Restrictions

Governments can impose quantity restrictions on a market. The most obvious restriction is an outright ban on the ownership or trading of a good. It is currently illegal to buy and sell human organs. It is also currently illegal to buy and sell certain psychoactive drugs such as cocaine, heroin, and methamphetamine. In some states, it is illegal to start a new hospital without obtaining a license for a particular number of beds to be offered to patients. This licensing requirement effectively limits the quantity of hospital beds in some states. From 1933 to 1973, it was illegal for U.S. citizens to own gold except for manufacturing, medicinal, or jewelry purposes.

Some of the most common quantity restrictions exist in the area of international trade. The U.S. government, as well as many foreign governments, imposes import quotas on a variety of goods. An **import quota** is a supply restriction that prohibits the importation of more than a specified quantity of a particular good in a one-year period. The United States has had import quotas on tobacco, sugar, and immigrant labor. For many years, there were import quotas on oil coming into the United States. There are also "voluntary" import quotas on certain goods. For instance, since the mid-2000s, the Chinese government has agreed to "voluntarily" restrict the amount of textile products China sends to the United States and the European Union.

Import quota
A physical supply restriction on imports of a particular good, such as sugar. Foreign exporters are unable to sell in the United States more than the quantity specified in the import quota.

QUICK QUIZ See page 93 for the answers. Review concepts from this section in MyEconLab.

With a price-_________ system, the government sets a minimum price at which, say, qualifying farm products can be sold. Any farmers who cannot sell at that price in the market can "sell" their surplus to the government. The only way a price-_________ system can survive is for the government or some other entity to buy up the excess quantity supplied at the support price.

When a _________ is placed on wages at a rate that is above market equilibrium, the result is an excess quantity of labor supplied at that minimum wage.

Quantity restrictions may take the form of _________ _________, which are limits on the quantity of specific foreign goods that can be brought into the United States for resale purposes.

You Are There

"Cash for Clunkers" Subsidies and the Market for "Liquid Glass"

Auto mechanics have long used a sodium-silicate chemical solution called "liquid glass" to stop leaks in engine gaskets that seal cylinder heads to engine blocks. In Grand Rapids, Michigan, Ron Balk, owner of Cleaning Solutions, found in late July 2009 that his inventory of liquid glass was exhausted and that the market clearing price of that chemical had risen from less than $2.50 per quart to nearly $3.50 per quart.

Why did purchases and the market clearing price of liquid glass increase? In the summer of 2009, mechanics found a new use for the chemical solution. They filled engines of aging gas-guzzling vehicles with liquid glass, which hardened within seconds to make those engines permanently unusable. Energy-inefficient vehicles had to be rendered unusable before people could trade them in for energy-efficient vehicles and receive subsidies under the federal government's "Cash for Clunkers" program. While this subsidy program was in effect, therefore, a substantial increase in the demand for liquid glass took place, which boosted the equilibrium price of the chemical solution.

At Cleaning Solutions, Balk quickly decided how to respond to the price jump. He boosted his firm's production from fewer than 3 gallons per week to about *4,600* gallons per week. Likewise, other firms across the nation that specialize in providing ready-to-order chemical solutions responded to the rise in the price of liquid glass by supplying much more of the engine-killing chemical solution.

Critical Analysis Questions

1. Did the Cash for Clunkers program generate a temporary movement along or a shift in the position of the market demand curve for liquid glass?
2. Did the Cash for Clunkers program generate a temporary movement along or a shift in the position of the market supply curve for liquid glass?

ISSUES & APPLICATIONS

Contemplating Two Ways to Tackle Water Shortages

CONCEPTS APPLIED

- Price Ceiling
- Shortage
- Rationing

More than 97 percent of the water on earth is salty seawater unfit for most human uses, and more than half of usable freshwater is frozen on the planet's poles or in glaciers. Can anything be done, therefore, to help the roughly 20 percent of the world's human population who are unable to obtain as much usable freshwater as they desire?

One Way to Eliminate Shortages: End Price Ceilings

A shortage of any item results whenever the price of the item remains below the equilibrium price. In many nations, government-mandated ceilings on the price of usable freshwater result in shortages. Suppose for instance, as shown in panel (a) of Figure 4-6 on the facing page, that the market clearing price of water within a region is 5 cents per gallon of freshwater, resulting in 200 million gallons being made available and consumed in a typical month. If the region's government mandates a monthly price no higher than 4 cents per gallon, the quantity of water demanded rises to 225 million gallons per month, but the quantity supplied declines to 175 million gallons per month. Thus, there is a water shortage of 50 million gallons.

One way to end such a water shortage, of course, would be for the government of this and other regions to remove price controls. Government leaders around the globe apparently lack the political courage to do so, however.

A Fresh Way to Cut Shortages by Removing Salt from Seawater

In principle, another way to reduce shortages of usable freshwater is to generate an increase in supply. Indeed, as shown in panel (b) below, a 50-million-gallon shortage in a region could be completely eliminated if an additional 50 million gallons of water could be supplied within that region at every price. This would shift the supply curve rightward, from S to S_1, and lead to a new equilibrium at the government's ceiling price of 4 cents per gallon. There would no longer be a shortage at this mandated price.

A new technique holds promise for increasing the supply of freshwater by removing salt from seawater. This is not a novel idea, but the new technique, which involves using electrification methods to break down salt atoms, is much less expensive than methods previously available. Eventually, people really may be drinking ocean water, and at the low prices that governments desire.

For Critical Analysis

1. How would a worldwide increase in water demand affect global water shortages? (Hint: What would be the effects of a rise in demand in panel [a] of Figure 4-6?)
2. How would reductions in government price ceilings affect global water shortages? (Hint: What would be the effects of a decrease in the ceiling price in panel [a] of Figure 4-6?)

Web Resources

1. To learn about global water issues at the Web site of the World Water Council, go to www.econtoday.com/ch04.
2. Read a description of the new technology for stripping atoms of salt from seawater at www.econtoday.com/ch04.

Research Project

Evaluate whether a combination of a higher ceiling price and new technologies that increase the supply of water could eliminate water shortages in various regions of the world. Use a diagram for assistance in thinking through how this combined approach would work.

For more questions on this chapter's Issues & Applications, go to **MyEconLab**. In the Study Plan for this chapter, select Section N: News.

FIGURE 4-6 Two Methods of Eliminating a Water Shortage

As shown in panel (a), if usable freshwater could be produced and bought at an unregulated price of 5 cents per gallon, the equilibrium quantity would be 200 million gallons per month. At a ceiling price of 4 cents per gallon, however, the quantity demanded exceeds the quantity supplied, yielding a monthly shortage of 50 million gallons. Without any other changes, this shortage could be eliminated just by removing the price ceiling. Panel (b) shows that the shortage could also be eliminated if the quantity of freshwater supplied at any price could be increased by 50 million gallons by a technological improvement, such as a better method for extracting salt from seawater.

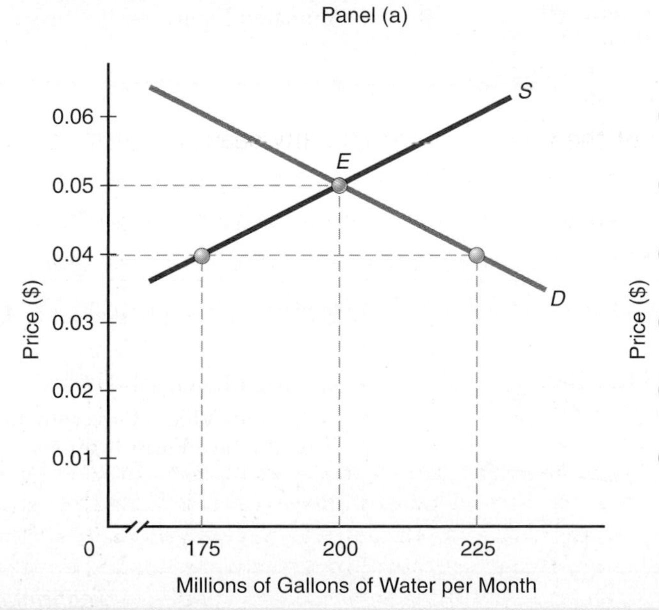

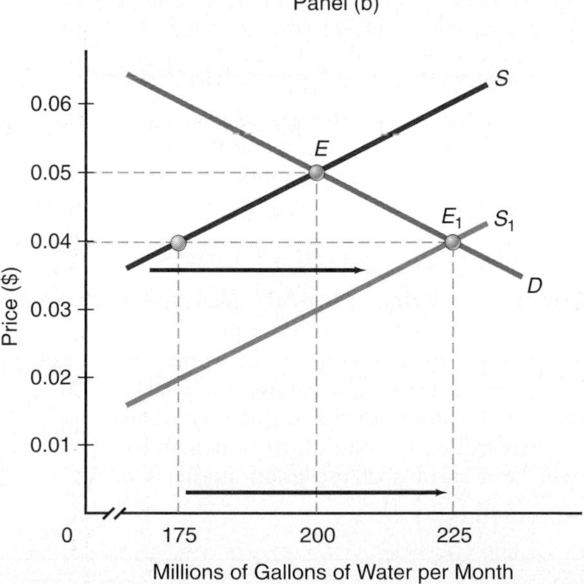

Here is what you should know after reading this chapter. **MyEconLab** will help you identify what you know, and where to go when you need to practice.

WHAT YOU SHOULD KNOW		WHERE TO GO TO PRACTICE
Essential Features of the Price System In the price system, exchange takes place in markets, and prices respond to changes in supply and demand for different commodities. Consumers' and business managers' decisions on resource use depend on what happens to prices. Middlemen reduce transaction costs by bringing buyers and sellers together.	price system, 75 voluntary exchange, 75 transaction costs, 75	• **MyEconLab** Study Plan 4.1 • Audio introduction to Chapter 4
How Changes in Demand and Supply Affect the Market Price and Equilibrium Quantity With a given supply curve, an increase in demand causes a rise in the market price and an increase in the equilibrium quantity, and a decrease in demand induces a fall in the market price and a decline in the equilibrium quantity. With a given demand curve, an increase in supply causes a fall in the market price and an increase in the equilibrium quantity, and a decrease in supply causes a rise in the market price and a decline in the equilibrium quantity. When both demand and supply shift at the same time, we must know the direction and amount of each shift in order to predict changes in the market price and the equilibrium quantity.	**KEY FIGURE** Figure 4-1, 77	• **MyEconLab** Study Plan 4.2 • Animated Figure 4-1 • ABC News Video: What Drives the Market: Supply and Demand
The Rationing Function of Prices In the price system, prices ration scarce goods and services. Other ways of rationing include first come, first served; political power; physical force; random assignment; and coupons.		• **MyEconLab** Study Plan 4.3 • Video: Price Flexibility, the Essential Role of Rationing via Price and Alternative Rationing Systems
The Effects of Price Ceilings Government-imposed price controls that require prices to be no higher than a certain level are price ceilings. If a government sets a price ceiling below the market price, then at the ceiling price the quantity of the good demanded will exceed the quantity supplied. There will be a shortage of the good at the ceiling price. Price ceilings can lead to nonprice rationing devices and black markets.	price controls, 80 price ceiling, 80 price floor, 80 nonprice rationing devices, 80 black market, 81 rent control, 82 **KEY FIGURE** Figure 4-3, 81	• **MyEconLab** Study Plans 4.4, 4.5 • Animated Figure 4-3
The Effects of Price Floors Government-mandated price controls that require prices to be no lower than a certain level are price floors. If a government sets a price floor above the market price, then at the floor price the quantity of the good supplied will exceed the quantity demanded. There will be a surplus of the good at the floor price.	minimum wage, 85 **KEY FIGURES** Figure 4-4, 84 Figure 4-5, 86	• **MyEconLab** Study Plans 4.6, 4.7 • Video: Minimum Wages • Animated Figures 4-4, 4-5 • Economics Video: Government Should Leave Farm Business

(continued)

MyEconLab continued

WHAT YOU SHOULD KNOW		WHERE TO GO TO PRACTICE
Government-Imposed Restrictions on Market Quantities Quantity restrictions can take the form of outright government bans on the sale of certain goods. They can also arise from licensing requirements and import restrictions that limit the number of producers and thereby restrict the amount supplied of a good or service.	import quota, 87	• **MyEconLab** Study Plan 4.8

Log in to MyEconLab, take a chapter test, and get a personalized Study Plan that tells you which concepts you understand and which ones you need to review. From there, MyEconLab will give you further practice, tutorials, animations, videos, and guided solutions.
Log in to www.myeconlab.com

PROBLEMS

All problems are assignable in myeconlab. *Answers to odd-numbered problems appear at the back of the book.*

4-1. In recent years, technological improvements have greatly reduced the costs of producing music CDs, and a number of new firms have entered the music CD industry. At the same time, prices of substitutes for music CDs, such as Internet downloads and music DVDs, have declined considerably. Construct a supply and demand diagram of the market for music CDs. Illustrate the impacts of these developments, and evaluate the effects on the market price and equilibrium quantity.

4-2. Advances in research and development in the pharmaceutical industry have enabled manufacturers to identify potential cures more quickly and therefore at lower cost. At the same time, the aging of our society has increased the demand for new drugs. Construct a supply and demand diagram of the market for pharmaceutical drugs. Illustrate the impacts of these developments, and evaluate the effects on the market price and the equilibrium quantity.

4-3. The following table depicts the quantity demanded and quantity supplied of studio apartments in a small college town.

Monthly Rent	Quantity Demanded	Quantity Supplied
$600	3,000	1,600
$650	2,500	1,800
$700	2,000	2,000
$750	1,500	2,200
$800	1,000	2,400

What are the market price and equilibrium quantity of apartments in this town? If this town imposes a rent control of $650 per month, how many studio apartments will be rented?

4-4. Suppose that the government places a ceiling on the price of Internet access below the equilibrium price.

a. Show why there is a shortage of Internet access at the new ceiling price.

b. Suppose that a black market for Internet providers arises, with Internet service providers developing hidden connections. Illustrate the black market for Internet access, including the implicit supply schedule, the ceiling price, the black market supply and demand, and the highest feasible black market price.

4-5. The table below illustrates the demand and supply schedules for seats on air flights between two cities:

Price	Quantity Demanded	Quantity Supplied
$200	2,000	1,200
$300	1,800	1,400
$400	1,600	1,600
$500	1,400	1,800
$600	1,200	2,000

What are the market price and equilibrium quantity in this market? Now suppose that federal authorities limit the number of flights between the two cities to ensure that no more than 1,200 passengers can be flown. Evaluate the effects of this quota if price adjusts. (Hint: What price per flight are the 1,200 passengers willing to pay?)

4-6. The consequences of decriminalizing illegal drugs have long been debated. Some claim that legalization will lower the price of these drugs and reduce related crime and that more people will use these drugs. Suppose that some of these drugs are legalized so that anyone may sell them and use them. Now consider the two claims—that price will fall and quantity demanded will increase. Based on positive economic analysis, are these claims sound?

4-7. In recent years, the government of Pakistan has established a support price for wheat of about $0.20 per kilogram of wheat. At this price, consumers are willing to purchase 10 billion kilograms of wheat per year, while Pakistani farmers are willing to grow and harvest 18 billion kilograms of wheat per year. The government purchases and stores all surplus wheat.

a. What are annual consumer expenditures on the Pakistani wheat crop?

b. What are annual government expenditures on the Pakistani wheat crop?

c. How much, in total, do Pakistani wheat farmers receive for the wheat they produce?

4-8. Consider the information in Problem 4-7 and your answers to that question. Suppose that the market clearing price of Pakistani wheat in the absence of price supports is equal to $0.10 per kilogram. At this price, the quantity of wheat demanded is 12 billion kilograms. Under the government wheat price-support program, how much more is spent each year on wheat harvested in Pakistan than otherwise would have been spent in an unregulated market for Pakistani wheat?

4-9. Consider the diagram below, which depicts the labor market in a city that has adopted a "living wage law" requiring employers to pay a minimum wage rate of $11 per hour. Answer the questions that follow.

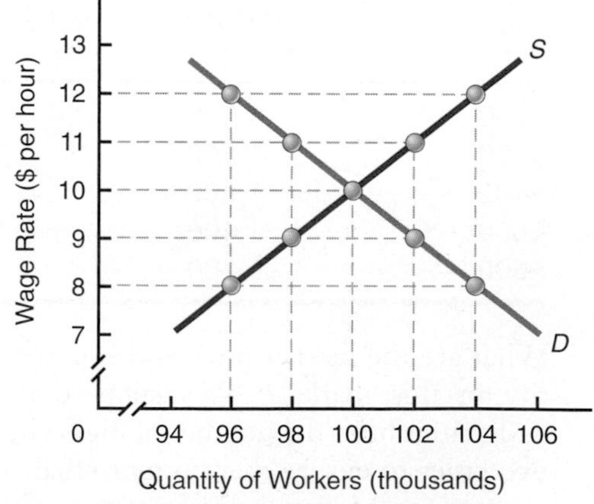

a. What condition exists in this city's labor market at the present minimum wage of $11 per hour? How many people are unemployed at this wage?

b. A city councilwoman has proposed amending the living wage law. She suggests reducing the minimum wage to $9 per hour. Assuming that the labor demand and supply curves were to remain in their present positions, how many people would be unemployed at a new $9 minimum wage?

c. A councilman has offered a counterproposal. In his view, the current minimum wage is too low and should be increased to $12 per hour. Assuming that the labor demand and supply curves remain in their present positions, how many people would be unemployed at a new $12 minimum wage?

4-10. A city has decided to impose rent controls, and it has established a rent ceiling below the previous equilibrium rental rate for offices throughout the city. How will the quantity of offices that building owners lease change?

4-11. In 2009, the government of a nation established a price support for wheat. The government's support price has been above the equilibrium price each year since, and the government has purchased all wheat over and above the amounts that consumers have bought at the support price. Every year since 2009, there has been an increase in the number of wheat producers in the market. No other factors affecting the market for wheat have changed. Predict what has happened every year since 2009 to each of the following:

a. Amount of wheat supplied by wheat producers

b. Amount of wheat demanded by all wheat consumers

c. Amount of wheat purchased by the government

4-12. In advance of the recent increase in the U.S. minimum wage rate, the government of the state of Arizona decided to boost its own minimum wage by an additional $1.60 per hour. This pushed the wage rate earned by Arizona teenagers above the equilibrium wage rate in the teen labor market. What is the predicted effect of this action by Arizona's government on each of the following?

a. The quantity of labor supplied by Arizona teenagers

b. The quantity of labor demanded by employers of Arizona teenagers

c. The number of unemployed Arizona teenagers

ECONOMICS ON THE NET

The Floor on Milk Prices At various times, the U.S. government has established price floors for milk. This application gives you an opportunity to apply what you have learned in this chapter to this real-world issue.

Title: Northeast Dairy Compact Commission

Navigation: Go to **www.econtoday.com/ch04** to visit the Web site of the Northeast Dairy Compact Commission.

Application Read the contents and answer these questions.

1. Based on the government-set price control concepts discussed in Chapter 4, explain the Northeast Dairy Compact that was once in place in the northeastern United States.
2. Draw a diagram illustrating the supply of and demand for milk in the Northeast Dairy Compact and the supply of and demand for milk outside the Northeast Dairy Compact. Illustrate how the compact affected the quantities demanded and supplied for participants in the compact. In addition, show how this affected the market for milk produced by those producers outside the dairy compact.
3. Economists have found that while the Northeast Dairy Compact functioned, midwestern dairy farmers lost their dominance of milk production and sales. In light of your answer to Question 2, explain how this occurred.

For Group Discussion and Analysis Discuss the impact of congressional failure to reauthorize the compact based on your above answers. Identify which arguments in your debate are based on positive economic analysis and which are normative arguments.

ANSWERS TO QUICK QUIZZES

p. 79: (i) demand . . . supply . . . supply . . . demand; (ii) immediately . . . time

p. 80: (i) first come, first served . . . political power . . . physical force . . . random assignment . . . coupons; (ii) queuing

p. 82: (i) ceilings . . . floors; (ii) ceiling . . . controls

p. 83: (i) Rental; (ii) controls . . . controls; (iii) Key money

p. 87: (i) support . . . support; (ii) floor; (iii) import quotas

APPENDIX B Consumer Surplus, Producer Surplus, and Gains from Trade within a Price System

A key principle of economics is that the price system enables people to benefit from the voluntary exchange of goods and services. Economists measure the benefits from trade by applying the concepts of *consumer surplus* and *producer surplus,* which are defined in the sections that follow.

Consumer Surplus

Let's first examine how economists measure the benefits that consumers gain from engaging in market transactions in the price system. Consider Figure B-1 below, which displays a market demand curve, D. We begin by assuming that consumers face a per-unit price of this item given by P_A. Thus, the quantity demanded of this particular product is equal to Q_A at point A on the demand curve.

Typically, we visualize the market demand curve as indicating the quantities that all consumers are willing to purchase at each possible price. But the demand curve also tells us the price that consumers are willing to pay for a unit of output at various possible quantities. For instance, if consumers buy Q_1 units of this good, they will be willing to pay a price equal to P_1 for the last unit purchased. If they have to pay only the price P_A for each unit they buy, however, consumers gain an amount equal to $P_1 - P_A$ for the last of the Q_1 units purchased. This benefit to consumers equals the vertical

FIGURE B-1 Consumer Surplus

If the per-unit price is P_A, then at point A on the demand curve D, consumers desire to purchase Q_A units. To purchase Q_1 units of this item, consumers would have been willing to pay the price P_1 for the last unit purchased, but they have to pay only the per-unit price P_A, so they gain a surplus equal to $P_1 - P_A$ for the last of the Q_1 units purchased. Likewise, to buy Q_2 units, consumers would have been willing to pay the price P_2, so they gain the surplus equal to $P_2 - P_A$ for the last of the Q_2 units purchased. Summing these and all other surpluses that consumers receive from purchasing all Q_A units at the price P_A yields the total consumer surplus at this price, shown by the blue-shaded area.

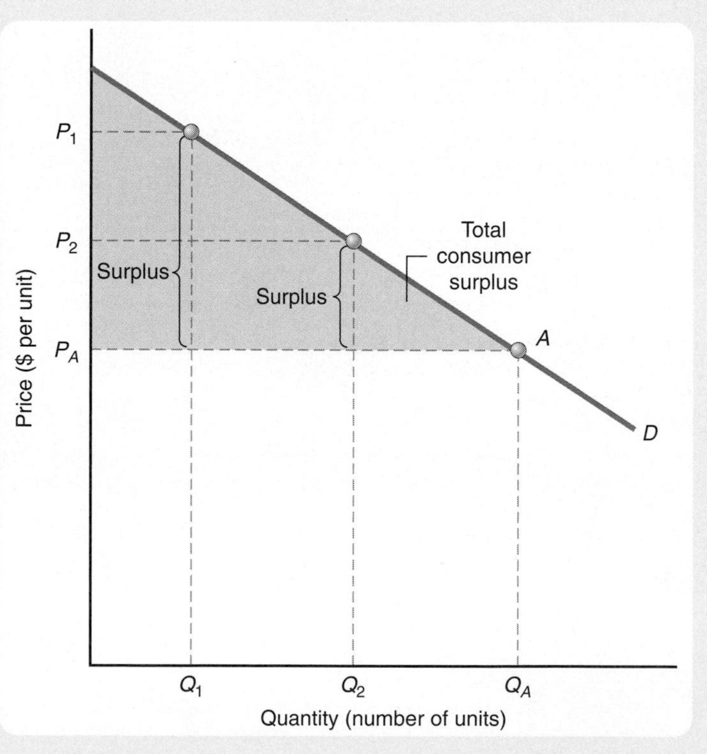

distance between the demand curve and the level of the market clearing price. Economists call this vertical distance a *surplus* value to consumers from being able to consume the last of the Q_1 units at the lower, market clearing price.

Likewise, if consumers purchase Q_2 units of this good, they will be willing to pay a price equal to P_2 for the last unit. Nevertheless, because they have to pay only the price P_A for each unit purchased, consumers gain an amount equal to $P_2 - P_A$. Hence, this is the surplus associated with the last of the Q_2 units that consumers buy.

Of course, when consumers pay the same per-unit price P_A for every unit of this product that they purchase at point A, they obtain Q_A units. Thus, consumers gain surplus values—all of the vertical distances between the demand curve and the level of the market clearing price—for each unit consumed, up to the total of Q_A units. Graphically, this is equivalent to the blue-shaded *area under the demand curve* but above the market clearing price in Figure B-1. This entire area equals the total **consumer surplus,** which is the difference between the total amount that consumers *would have been willing to pay* for an item and the total amount that they actually pay.

Consumer surplus
The difference between the total amount that consumers would have been willing to pay for an item and the total amount that they actually pay.

Producer Surplus

Consumers are not the only ones who gain from exchange. Producers (suppliers) gain as well. To consider how economists measure the benefits to producers from supplying goods and services in exchange, look at Figure B-2 below, which displays a market supply curve, S. Let's begin by assuming that suppliers face a per-unit price of this item given by P_B. Thus, the quantity supplied of this particular product is equal to Q_B at point B on the supply curve.

The market supply curve tells us the quantities that all producers are willing to sell at each possible price. At the same time, the supply curve also indicates the price that producers are willing accept to sell a unit of output at various possible quantities. For example, if producers sell Q_3 units of this good, they will be willing to accept a price equal to P_3 for the last unit sold. If they receive the price P_B for each unit that they supply, however, producers gain an amount equal to $P_B - P_3$ for the last of the Q_3 units sold. This benefit to producers equals the vertical distance between the supply curve and the market clearing price, which is a *surplus* value from being able to provide the last of the Q_3 units at the higher, market clearing price.

FIGURE B-2 Producer Surplus

If the per-unit price is P_B, then at point B on the supply curve S, producers are willing to supply Q_B units. To sell Q_3 units of this item, producers would have been willing to receive the price P_3 for the last unit sold, but instead they receive the higher per-unit price P_B, so they gain a surplus equal to $P_B - P_3$ for the last of the Q_3 units sold. Similarly, producers would have been willing to receive P_4 to provide Q_4 units, so they gain the surplus equal to $P_B - P_4$ for the last of the Q_4 units sold. Summing these and all other surpluses that producers receive from supplying all Q_B units at the price P_B yields the total producer surplus at this price, shown by the red-shaded area.

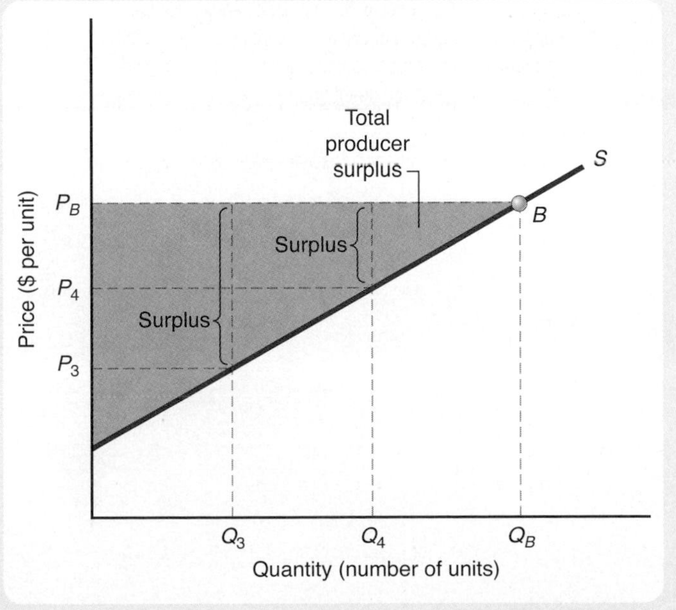

Similarly, if producers supply Q_4 units of this good, they will be willing to accept a price equal to P_4 for the last unit. Producers actually receive the price P_B for each unit supplied, however, so they gain an amount equal to $P_B - P_4$. Hence, this is the surplus gained from supplying the last of the Q_4 units.

Naturally, when producers receive the same per-unit price P_B for each unit supplied at point B, producers sell Q_B units. Consequently, producers gain surplus values—all of the vertical distances between the level of the market clearing price and the supply curve—for each unit supplied, up to the total of Q_B units. In Figure B-2 on page 95, this is equivalent to the red-shaded *area above the supply curve* but below the market clearing price. This area is the total **producer surplus,** which is the difference between the total amount that producers actually receive for an item and the total amount that they *would have been willing to accept* for supplying that item.

Producer surplus
The difference between the total amount that producers actually receive for an item and the total amount that they would have been willing to accept for supplying that item.

Gains from Trade Within a Price System

The concepts of consumer surplus and producer surplus can be combined to measure the gains realized by consumers and producers from engaging in voluntary exchange. To see how, take a look at Figure B-3 below. The market demand and supply curves intersect at point E, and as you have learned, at this point, the equilibrium quantity is Q_E. At the market clearing price P_E, this is both the quantity that consumers are willing to purchase and the quantity that producers are willing to supply.

In addition, at the market clearing price P_E and the equilibrium quantity Q_E, the blue-shaded area under the demand curve but above the market clearing price is the amount of consumer surplus. Furthermore, the red-shaded area under the market clearing price but above the supply curve is the amount of producer surplus. The sum of *both* areas is the total value of the **gains from trade**—the sum of consumer surplus and producer surplus—generated by the mutually beneficial voluntary exchange of the equilibrium quantity Q_E at the market clearing price P_E.

Gains from trade
The sum of consumer surplus and producer surplus.

FIGURE B-3 Consumer Surplus, Producer Surplus, and Gains from Trade

At point E, the demand and supply curves intersect at the equilibrium quantity Q_E and the market clearing price P_E. Total consumer surplus at the market clearing price is the blue-shaded area under the demand curve but above the market clearing price. Total producer surplus is the red-shaded area below the market clearing price but above the supply curve. The sum of consumer surplus and producer surplus at the market clearing price constitutes the total gain to society from voluntary exchange of the quantity Q_E at the market clearing price P_E.

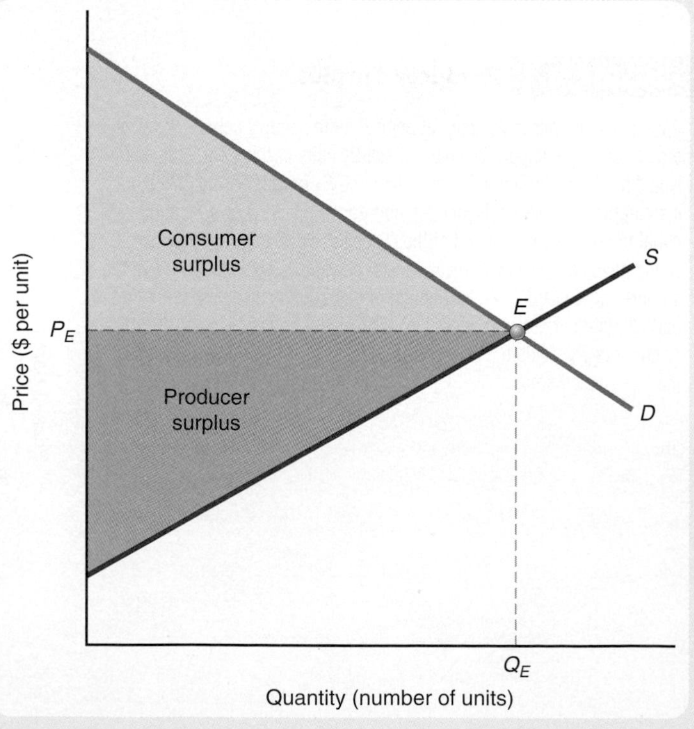

Price Controls and Gains from Trade

How do price controls affect gains from trade? Consider first the effects of imposing a ceiling price that is lower than the market clearing price. As you learned in Chapter 4, the results are an increase in quantity demanded and a decrease in quantity supplied, so a shortage occurs. The smaller quantity supplied by firms is the amount actually produced and available in the market for the item in question. Thus, consumers are able to purchase fewer units, and this means that consumer surplus must be lower than it would have been without the government's price ceiling. Furthermore, because firms sell fewer units, producer surplus must also decrease. Thus, the government's imposition of the price ceiling reduces gains from trade.

Now consider the effects of the establishment of a price floor above the market clearing price of a good. As discussed in Chapter 4, the effects of imposing such a floor price are an increase in the quantity supplied and a decrease in the quantity demanded. The smaller quantity demanded by consumers is the amount actually traded in the market. Thus, consumers purchase fewer units of the good, resulting in a reduction in consumer surplus. In addition, firms sell fewer units, so producer surplus must also decrease. Thus, the establishment of a price floor also reduces gains from trade.

5

Public Spending and Public Choice

For most people, $40 billion is an almost unimaginably large sum. Ignoring interest, a person would have to earn an average of $500 million per year for 80 years to accumulate that much. This translates into more than $40 million per month, nearly $9.2 million per week, or almost $1.4 million per day. Nevertheless, $40 billion is less than 1 percent of the U.S. government's annual budget for expenditures. It is also the amount that the government plans to allocate each year to firms that specialize in "clean-energy" technologies. The government hopes that once such technologies are in place, fewer emissions will enter the atmosphere. What can we learn from economics about possible ways in which the U.S. government might address issues such as atmospheric pollution? This is one of the subjects of the present chapter.

LEARNING OBJECTIVES

After reading this chapter, you should be able to:

- Explain how market failures such as externalities might justify economic functions of government
- Distinguish between private goods and public goods and explain the nature of the free-rider problem
- Describe political functions of government that entail its involvement in the economy
- Analyze how Medicare affects the incentives to consume medical services
- Explain why increases in government spending on public education have not been associated with improvements in measures of student performance
- Discuss the central elements of the theory of public choice

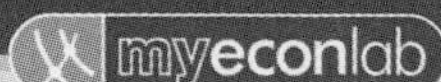

MyEconLab helps you master each objective and study more efficiently. See end of chapter for details.

Did You Know ? That

the French Mediterranean island of Corsica has about 10,000 stray cattle and pigs, or approximately one cow or pig for every four square miles? Most of the stray cattle were abandoned by farmers after the elimination of agricultural subsidies from the French government made it too costly to maintain the animals. Farmers who own the rest of the cattle and pigs allow them to roam wild rather than incurring the expenses required to keep them in fenced lots. Nearly every day the strays cause damage to humans' property. In some recent examples, a bull slipped off an overhanging cliff and destroyed a bar's terrace, pigs roamed onto a runway and halted airline traffic, and several automobile drivers collided with cows crossing the road at night.

Corsica's roaming cattle and pigs constitute a spillover effect onto uninvolved third parties caused by the failure of Corsican farmers to take into account the full costs of their actions. The result is "too much" activity in the Corsican agricultural market generating the spillover effect—too many dangerously rambling beasts. As you will learn in this chapter, a key function of government is to correct for an inability of the price system to prevent such spillover effects, which economists classify among flaws in the price system that they call *market failures.*

What a Price System Can and Cannot Do

Throughout the book so far, we have alluded to the advantages of a price system. High on the list is economic efficiency. In its ideal form, a price system allows all resources to move from lower-valued uses to higher-valued uses via voluntary exchange, by which mutually advantageous trades take place. In a price system, consumers are sovereign. That is to say, they have the individual freedom to decide what they wish to purchase. Politicians and even business managers do not ultimately decide what is produced; consumers decide. Some proponents of the price system argue that this is its most important characteristic. Competition among sellers protects consumers from coercion by one seller, and sellers are protected from coercion by one consumer because other consumers are available.

Sometimes, though, the price system does not generate these results, and too few or too many resources go to specific economic activities. Such situations are **market failures.** Market failures prevent the price system from attaining economic efficiency and individual freedom. Market failures offer one of the strongest arguments in favor of certain economic functions of government, which we now examine.

Market failure
A situation in which the market economy leads to too few or too many resources going to a specific economic activity.

Correcting for Externalities

In a pure market system, competition generates economic efficiency only when individuals know and must bear the true opportunity cost of their actions. In some circumstances, the price that someone actually pays for a resource, good, or service is higher or lower than the opportunity cost that all of society pays for that same resource, good, or service.

Externalities

Consider a hypothetical world in which there is no government regulation against pollution. You are living in a town that until now has had clean air. A steel mill moves into town. It produces steel and has paid for the inputs—land, labor, capital, and entrepreneurship. The price the mill charges for the steel reflects, in this example, only the costs that it incurs. In the course of production, however, the mill utilizes one input—clean air—by simply using it. This is indeed an input because in making steel, the furnaces emit smoke. The steel mill doesn't have to pay the cost of dirtying the air. Rather, it is the people in the community who incur that cost in the form of dirtier clothes, dirtier cars and houses, and more respiratory illnesses. The effect is similar to what would happen if the steel mill could take coal or oil or workers' services without paying for them. There is an **externality,** an external cost. Some of the costs

Externality
A consequence of an economic activity that spills over to affect third parties. Pollution is an externality.

Third parties
Parties who are not directly involved in a given activity or transaction.

Property rights
The rights of an owner to use and to exchange property.

associated with the production of the steel have "spilled over" to affect **third parties,** parties other than the buyer and the seller of the steel.

A fundamental reason that air pollution creates external costs is that the air belongs to everyone and hence to no one in particular. Lack of clearly assigned **property rights,** or the rights of an owner to use and exchange property, prevents market prices from reflecting all the costs created by activities that generate spillovers onto third parties.

How has the absence of property rights beyond the earth's atmosphere contributed to a buildup of orbiting debris?

EXAMPLE **Space Age Litterbugs**

The first U.S. astronaut to engage in a spacewalk, Edward White, lost a glove. More recently, a crew member at work outside a NASA space shuttle accidentally let go of a 30-pound tool bag. Other lost objects circling the earth include a camera lens cap, circuit boards, and clamps. In addition, satellites have collided and broken into pieces, and a few have been blown to bits in antisatellite weapons tests conducted by nations' militaries.

All of this space littering has created a cloud of orbiting space junk that includes 18,000 objects large enough to track with radar as well as millions of smaller bits of junk. After every space shuttle mission since 1981, NASA has spent about $400,000 to replace the shuttle's debris-pitted windows. Astronauts often have to maneuver their spacecraft around objects, and commercial satellite firms must plan launches to avoid the largest swarms of debris. At least once each day, a group of scientists issues warnings of close encounters faced by orbiting commercial satellites. Satellite managers transmit signals to engines that power the satellites out of the way of the oncoming space junk.

FOR CRITICAL ANALYSIS

Why do you suppose that an absence of property rights to positions in near-earth orbit has made space around the planet so crowded with litter?

External Costs in Graphical Form

To consider how market prices fail to take into account external costs in situations in which third-party spillovers exist without a clear assignment of property rights, look at panel (a) in Figure 5-1 on the facing page. Here we show the demand curve for steel as D. The supply curve is S_1. The supply curve includes only the costs that the firms have to pay. Equilibrium occurs at point E, with a price of $800 per ton and a quantity equal to 110 million tons per year.

But producing steel also involves externalities—the external costs that you and your neighbors pay in the form of dirtier clothes, cars, and houses and increased respiratory disease due to the air pollution emitted from the steel mill. In this case, the producers of steel use clean air without having to pay for it. Let's include these external costs in our graph to find out what the full cost of steel production would really be if property rights to the air around the steel mill could generate payments for "owners" of that air. We do this by imagining that steel producers have to pay the "owners" of the air for the input—clean air—that the producers previously used at a zero price.

Recall from Chapter 3 that an increase in input prices shifts the supply curve up and to the left. Thus, in panel (a) of the figure, the supply curve shifts from S_1 to S_2. External costs equal the vertical distance between A and E_1. In this example, if steel firms had to take into account these external costs, the equilibrium quantity would fall to 100 million tons per year, and the price would rise to $900 per ton. Equilibrium would shift from E to E_1. In contrast, if the price of steel does not account for external costs, third parties bear those costs—represented by the distance between A and E_1—in the form of dirtier clothes, houses, and cars and increased respiratory illnesses.

You Are There

To contemplate how parked railcars can create a negative externality, read **A Town Confronts a Parked Externality,** on page 114.

External Benefits in Graphical Form

Externalities can also be positive. To demonstrate external benefits in graphical form, we will use the example of inoculations against communicable disease. In panel (b) of Figure 5-1, we show the demand curve as D_1 (without taking account of any external

FIGURE 5-1 External Costs and Benefits

In panel (a), we show a situation in which the production of steel generates external costs. If the steel mills ignore pollution, at equilibrium the quantity of steel will be 110 million tons. If the steel mills had to pay for the external costs that are caused by the mills' production but are currently borne by nearby residents, the supply curve would shift the vertical distance A–E_1, to S_2. If consumers of steel were forced to pay a price that reflected the spillover costs, the quantity demanded would fall to 100 million tons. In panel (b), we show a situation in which inoculations against communicable diseases generate external benefits to those individuals who may not be inoculated but who will benefit because epidemics will not occur. If each individual ignores the external benefit of inoculations, the market clearing quantity will be 150 million. If external benefits were taken into account by purchasers of inoculations, however, the demand curve would shift to D_2. The new equilibrium quantity would be 200 million inoculations, and the price of an inoculation would rise from $10 to $15.

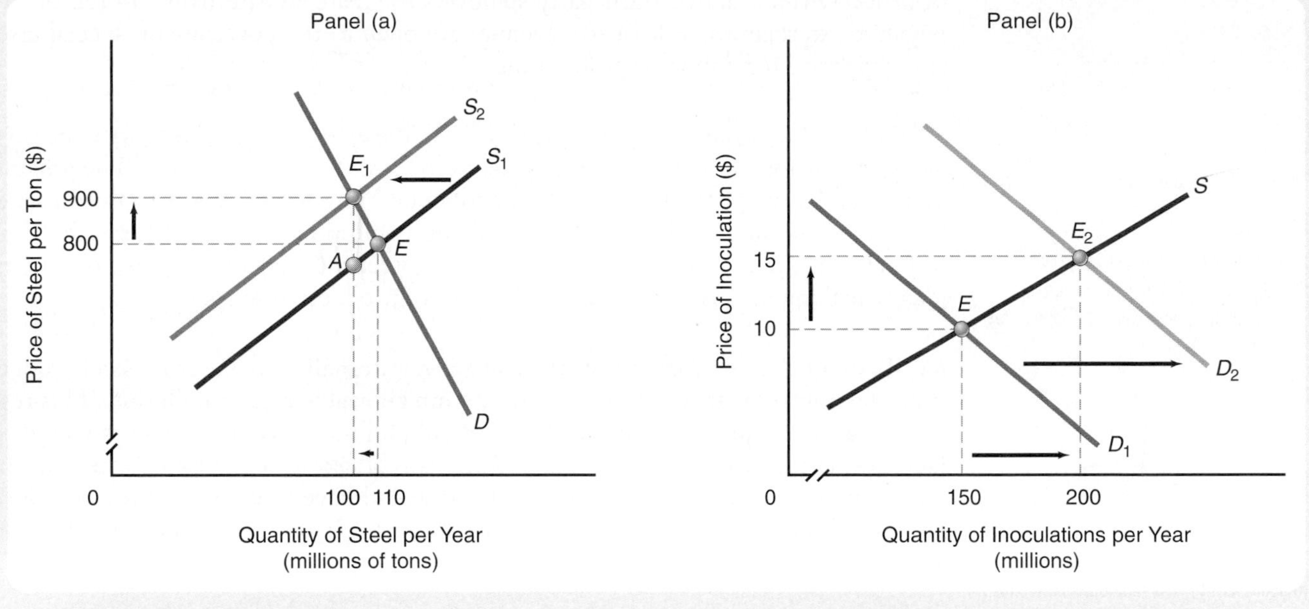

benefits) and the supply curve as S. The equilibrium price is $10 per inoculation, and the equilibrium quantity is 150 million inoculations.

We assume, however, that inoculations against communicable diseases generate external benefits to individuals who may not be inoculated but will benefit nevertheless because epidemics will not break out. If such external benefits were taken into account by those who purchase inoculations, the demand curve would shift from D_1 to D_2.

As a consequence of this shift in demand at point E_2, the new equilibrium quantity would be 200 million inoculations, and the new equilibrium price would be $15 per inoculation. If people who consider getting inoculations fail to take external benefits into account, individuals in society are not devoting enough resources to inoculations against communicable diseases.

Resource Misallocations of Externalities

When there are external costs, the market will tend to *overallocate* resources to the production of the good or service in question, for those goods or services are implicitly priced deceptively low. In the steel example, too many resources will be allocated to steel production, because the steel mill owners and managers are not required to take account of the external cost that steel production is imposing on other individuals. In essence, the full cost of production is not borne by the owners and managers, so the price they charge the public for steel is lower than it would otherwise be. And, of course, the lower price means that buyers are willing and able to buy more. More steel is produced and consumed than if the sellers and buyers were to bear external costs.

In contrast, when there are external benefits, the price is too low to induce suppliers to allocate resources to the production of that good or service (because the demand, which fails to reflect the external benefits, is relatively too low). Thus, the market *underallocates* resources to producing the good or service. Hence, in a market system, too many of the goods that generate external costs are produced, and too few of the goods that generate external benefits are produced.

How the Government Can Correct Negative Externalities

In theory, the government can take action to try to correct situations in which a lack of property rights allows third-party spillovers to create an externality. In the case of negative externalities, at least two avenues are open to the government: special taxes and legislative regulation or prohibition.

SPECIAL TAXES In our example of the steel mill, the externality problem arises because using the air for waste disposal is costless to the firm but not to society. The government could attempt to tax the steel mill commensurate with the cost to third parties from smoke in the air. This, in effect, would be a pollution tax or an **effluent fee.** The ultimate effect would be to reduce the supply of steel and raise the price to consumers, ideally making the price equal to the full cost of production to society.

Effluent fee
A charge to a polluter that gives the right to discharge into the air or water a certain amount of pollution; also called a *pollution tax.*

REGULATION Alternatively, to correct a negative externality arising from steel production, the government could specify a maximum allowable rate of pollution. This regulation would require that the steel mill install pollution abatement equipment at its facilities, reduce its rate of output, or some combination of the two. Note that the government's job would not be simple, for it would have to determine the appropriate level of pollution, which would require extensive knowledge of both the benefits and the costs of pollution control.

Go to www.econtoday.com/ch05 to learn more about how the Environmental Protection Agency uses regulations to try to protect the environment.

How the Government Can Correct Positive Externalities

What can the government do when the production of one good spills *benefits* over to third parties? It has several policy options: financing the production of the good or producing the good itself, subsidies (negative taxes), and regulation.

GOVERNMENT FINANCING AND PRODUCTION If the positive externalities seem extremely large, the government has the option of financing the desired additional production facilities so that the "right" amount of the good will be produced. Again consider inoculations against communicable diseases. The government could—and often does—finance campaigns to inoculate the population. It could (and does) even produce and operate inoculation centers where inoculations are given at no charge.

SUBSIDIES A subsidy is a negative tax. It is a payment made either to a business or to a consumer when the business produces or the consumer buys a good or a service. To generate more inoculations against communicable diseases, the government could subsidize everyone who obtains an inoculation by directly reimbursing those inoculated or by making payments to private firms that provide inoculations. Subsidies reduce the net price to consumers, thereby causing a larger quantity to be demanded.

REGULATION In some cases involving positive externalities, the government can require by law that individuals in the society undertake a certain action. For example, regulations require that all school-age children be inoculated before entering public and private schools. Some people believe that a basic school education itself generates positive externalities. Perhaps as a result of this belief, we have regulations—laws—that require all school-age children to be enrolled in a public or private school.

QUICK QUIZ See page 120 for the answers. Review concepts from this section in MyEconLab.

External ________ lead to an overallocation of resources to the specific economic activity. Two possible ways of correcting these spillovers are ________ and ________.

External ________ result in an underallocation of resources to the specific activity. Three possible government corrections are ________ the production of the activity, ________ private firms or consumers to engage in the activity, and ________.

The Other Economic Functions of Government

Besides correcting for externalities, the government performs many other economic functions that affect the way exchange is carried out. In contrast, the political functions of government have to do with deciding how income should be redistributed among households and selecting which goods and services have special merits and should therefore be treated differently. The economic and political functions of government can and do overlap.

Let's look at four more economic functions of government.

Providing a Legal System

The courts and the police may not at first seem like economic functions of government. Their activities nonetheless have important consequences for economic activities in any country. You and I enter into contracts constantly, whether they be oral or written, expressed or implied. When we believe that we have been wronged, we seek redress of our grievances through our legal institutions. Moreover, consider the legal system that is necessary for the smooth functioning of our economic system. Our system has defined quite explicitly the legal status of businesses, the rights of private ownership, and a method of enforcing contracts. All relationships among consumers and businesses are governed by the legal rules of the game. In its judicial function, then, the government serves as the referee for settling disputes in the economic arena. In this role, the government often imposes penalties for violations of legal rules.

Much of our legal system is involved with defining and protecting property rights. One might say that property rights are really the rules of our economic game. When property rights are well defined, owners of property have an incentive to use that property efficiently. Any mistakes in their decisions about the use of property have negative consequences that the owners suffer. Furthermore, when property rights are well defined, owners of property have an incentive to maintain that property so that if they ever desire to sell it, it will fetch a better price.

Promoting Competition

Many people believe that the only way to attain economic efficiency is through competition. One of the roles of government is to serve as the protector of a competitive economic system. Congress and the various state governments have passed **antitrust legislation.** Such legislation makes illegal certain (but not all) economic activities that might restrain trade—that is, that might prevent free competition among actual and potential rival firms in the marketplace. The avowed aim of antitrust legislation is to reduce the power of **monopolies**—firms that can determine the market price of the goods they sell. A large number of antitrust laws have been passed that prohibit specific anticompetitive actions. Both the Antitrust Division of the U.S. Department of Justice and the Federal Trade Commission attempt to enforce these antitrust laws. Various state judicial agencies also expend efforts at maintaining competition.

Antitrust legislation
Laws that restrict the formation of monopolies and regulate certain anticompetitive business practices.

Monopoly
A firm that can determine the market price of a good. In the extreme case, a monopoly is the only seller of a good or service.

Providing Public Goods

The goods used in our examples up to this point have been **private goods.** When I eat a cheeseburger, you cannot eat the same one. So you and I are rivals for that cheeseburger, just as much as contenders for the title of world champion are. When I use a Blu-ray

Private goods
Goods that can be consumed by only one individual at a time. Private goods are subject to the principle of rival consumption.

player, you cannot play some other disc at the same time. When I use the services of an auto mechanic, that person cannot work at the same time for you. That is the distinguishing feature of private goods—their use is exclusive to the people who purchase or rent them. The **principle of rival consumption** applies to all private goods by definition. Rival consumption is easy to understand. Either you use a private good or I use it.

Principle of rival consumption
The recognition that individuals are rivals in consuming private goods because one person's consumption reduces the amount available for others to consume.

Public goods
Goods for which the principle of rival consumption does not apply. They can be jointly consumed by many individuals simultaneously at no additional cost and with no reduction in quality or quantity. Also no one who fails to help pay for the good can be denied the benefit of the good.

There is an entire class of goods that are not private goods. These are called **public goods.** The principle of rival consumption does not apply to them. They can be consumed *jointly* by many individuals simultaneously, and no one can be excluded from consuming these goods even if they fail to pay to do so. National defense, police protection, and the legal system are examples of public goods.

CHARACTERISTICS OF PUBLIC GOODS Two fundamental characteristics of public goods set them apart from all other goods:

1. *Public goods can be used by more and more people at no additional opportunity cost and without depriving others of any of the services of the goods.* Once funds have been spent on national defense, the defense protection you receive does not reduce the amount of protection bestowed on anyone else. The opportunity cost of your receiving national defense once it is in place is zero because once national defense is in place to protect you, it also protects others.
2. *It is difficult to design a collection system for a public good on the basis of how much individuals use it.* Nonpayers can often utilize a public good without incurring any monetary cost, because the cost of excluding them from using the good is so high. Those who provide the public good find that it is not cost-effective to prevent nonpayers from utilizing it. For instance, taxpayers who pay to provide national defense typically do not incur the costs that would be entailed in excluding nonpayers from benefiting from national defense.

One of the problems of public goods is that the private sector has a difficult, if not impossible, time providing them. Individuals in the private sector have little or no incentive to offer public goods. It is difficult for them to make a profit doing so, because nonpayers cannot be excluded. Consequently, true public goods must necessarily be provided by government. (Note, though, that economists do not categorize something as a public good simply because the government provides it.)

Given that until now human space flight has been provided by governments, why are private companies getting into the space-travel business?

EXAMPLE Countdown to Private Production of Space Travel

The companies have names such as Armadillo Aerospace, Blue Origin, Rocketplane Global, Space Adventures, SpaceX, and Virgin Galactic. These and other private firms are working toward offering the same service: suborbital space flights. Virgin Galactic, for instance, has designed a suborbital spaceship with a wingspan equivalent to that of a Boeing 757. Eventually, Virgin Galactic and other firms hope to offer flights beyond the earth's atmosphere using vehicles capable of escaping the earth's gravitational pull and entering into orbit around the planet.

Virgin Galactic's suborbital ship has only eight seats. Once eight people are on the ship, there is no room for anyone else. Consequently, space travel is subject to the principle of rival consumption. Spaceships cannot be used by more and more people at no additional opportunity cost and without depriving others of the service. Furthermore, owners of Virgin Galactic and other firms providing space-travel services are willing to invest their funds because they anticipate earning profits. Therefore, these private firms do not face any problems with collecting funds on the basis of how much people will use their services.

Private firms that aim to provide space-travel services understand that even though national governments have long organized the production of space travel, it is not a public good. Space travel is a private good that governments alone have chosen to provide—until now.

FOR CRITICAL ANALYSIS

Could the fact that certain uses of space flights relate to national defense potentially lead to the classification of the provision of these particular space-travel services as a public good? Explain your answer.

FREE RIDERS The nature of public goods leads to the **free-rider problem,** a situation in which some individuals take advantage of the fact that others will assume the burden of paying for public goods such as national defense. Suppose that citizens were taxed directly in proportion to how much they tell an interviewer that they value national defense. Some people who actually value national defense will probably tell interviewers that it has no value to them—they don't want any of it. Such people are trying to be free riders. We may all want to be free riders if we believe that someone else will provide the commodity in question that we actually value.

Free-rider problem
A problem that arises when individuals presume that others will pay for public goods so that, individually, they can escape paying for their portion without causing a reduction in production.

The free-rider problem often arises in connection with sharing the burden of international defense. A country may choose to belong to a multilateral defense organization, such as the North Atlantic Treaty Organization (NATO), but then consistently attempt to avoid contributing funds to the organization. The nation knows it would be defended by others in NATO if it were attacked but would rather not pay for such defense. In short, it seeks a free ride.

Ensuring Economywide Stability

Our economy sometimes faces the problems of undesired unemployment and rising prices. The government, especially the federal government, has made an attempt to solve these problems by trying to stabilize the economy by smoothing out the ups and downs in overall business activity. The notion that the federal government should undertake actions to stabilize business activity is a relatively new idea in the United States, encouraged by high unemployment rates during the Great Depression of the 1930s and subsequent theories about possible ways that government could reduce unemployment. In 1946, Congress passed the Full-Employment Act, a landmark law concerning government responsibility for economic performance. It established three goals for government stabilization policy: full employment, price stability, and economic growth. These goals have provided the justification for many government economic programs during the post–World War II period.

The Political Functions of Government

At least two functions of government are political or normative functions rather than economic ones like those discussed in the first part of this chapter. These two areas are (1) the provision and regulation of government-sponsored and government-inhibited goods and (2) income redistribution.

Government-Sponsored and Government-Inhibited Goods

Through political processes, governments often determine that certain goods possess special merit and seek to promote their production and consumption. A **government-sponsored good** is defined as any good that the political process has deemed socially desirable. (Note that nothing inherent in any particular good makes it a government-sponsored good. The designation is entirely subjective.) Examples of government-sponsored goods in our society are sports stadiums, museums, ballets, plays, and concerts. In these areas, the government's role is the provision of these goods to the people in society who would not otherwise purchase them at market clearing prices or who would not purchase an amount of them judged to be sufficient. This provision may take the form of government production and distribution of the goods. It can also take the form of reimbursement for spending on government-sponsored goods or subsidies to producers or consumers for part of the goods' costs. Governments do indeed subsidize such goods as professional sports, concerts, ballets, museums, and plays. In most cases, those goods would not be so numerous without subsidization.

Government-sponsored good
A good that has been deemed socially desirable through the political process. Museums are an example.

Government-inhibited goods are the opposite of government-sponsored goods. They are goods that, through the political process, have been deemed socially undesirable. Heroin, cigarettes, gambling, and cocaine are examples. The government

Government-inhibited good
A good that has been deemed socially undesirable through the political process. Heroin is an example.

exercises its role with respect to these goods by taxing, regulating, or prohibiting their manufacture, sale, and use. Governments justify the relatively high taxes on alcohol and tobacco by declaring that they are socially undesirable. The best-known example of governmental exercise of power in this area is the stance against certain psychoactive drugs. Most psychoactives (except nicotine, caffeine, and alcohol) are either expressly prohibited, as is the case for heroin, cocaine, and opium, or heavily regulated, as in the case of prescription psychoactives.

Why Not . . . classify broadband Internet access as a government-sponsored good and provide it to all U.S. residents?

The key difficulties with governmental provision of broadband service to all are revealed by recent efforts by the federal government to subsidize the extension of broadband access services to rural areas. One stumbling block is that no one knows exactly what "broadband" means because continuing technological improvements keep leading to faster feasible Internet access speeds. A related problem is that the government cannot determine how much taxpayers will have to pay to extend broadband access to rural residents. If the government provides the lowest available broadband speed, the cost to taxpayers will be $20 billion, but if it provides the highest available broadband speed, the price tag could be as high as $350 billion. Only 20 percent of U.S. residents live in rural areas. Providing the highest-speed Internet service to *all* U.S. residents might require a taxpayer expenditure of more than $1.7 trillion—an amount exceeding 10 percent of all income earned by U.S. residents in an entire year!

Income Redistribution

Transfer payments
Money payments made by governments to individuals for which no services or goods are rendered in return. Examples are Social Security old-age and disability benefits and unemployment insurance benefits.

Transfers in kind
Payments that are in the form of actual goods and services, such as food stamps, subsidized public housing, and medical care, and for which no goods or services are rendered in return.

Another relatively recent political function of government has been the explicit redistribution of income. This redistribution uses two systems: the progressive income tax (described in Chapter 6) and transfer payments. **Transfer payments** are payments made to individuals for which no services or goods are rendered in return. The two primary money transfer payments in our system are Social Security old-age and disability benefits and unemployment insurance benefits. Income redistribution also includes a large amount of income **transfers in kind,** rather than money transfers. Some income transfers in kind are food stamps, Medicare and Medicaid, government health care services, and subsidized public housing.

The government has also engaged in other activities as a form of redistribution of income. For example, the provision of public education is at least in part an attempt to redistribute income by making sure that the poor have access to education.

QUICK QUIZ See page 120 for the answers. **Review concepts from this section in MyEconLab.**

The economic activities of government include (1) correcting for __________, (2) providing a __________ __________, (3) promoting __________, (4) producing __________ goods, and (5) ensuring __________ __________.

The principle of __________ __________ does not apply to public goods as it does to private goods.

Public goods have two characteristics: (1) Once they are produced, there is no additional __________ __________ when additional consumers use them, because your use of a public good does not deprive others of its simultaneous use; and (2) consumers cannot conveniently be __________ on the basis of use.

Political, or normative, activities of the government include the provision and regulation of __________-__________ and __________-__________ goods and __________ redistribution.

Public Spending and Transfer Programs

The size of the public sector can be measured in many different ways. One way is to count the number of public employees. Another is to look at total government outlays. Government outlays include all government expenditures on employees, rent, electricity,

FIGURE 5-2 Total Government Outlays over Time

Total government outlays (federal, state, and local combined) remained small until the 1930s, except during World War I. After World War II, government outlays did not fall back to their historical average and quite recently have risen back close to their World War II levels.

Sources: Facts and Figures on Government Finance, various issues; *Economic Indicators*, various issues.

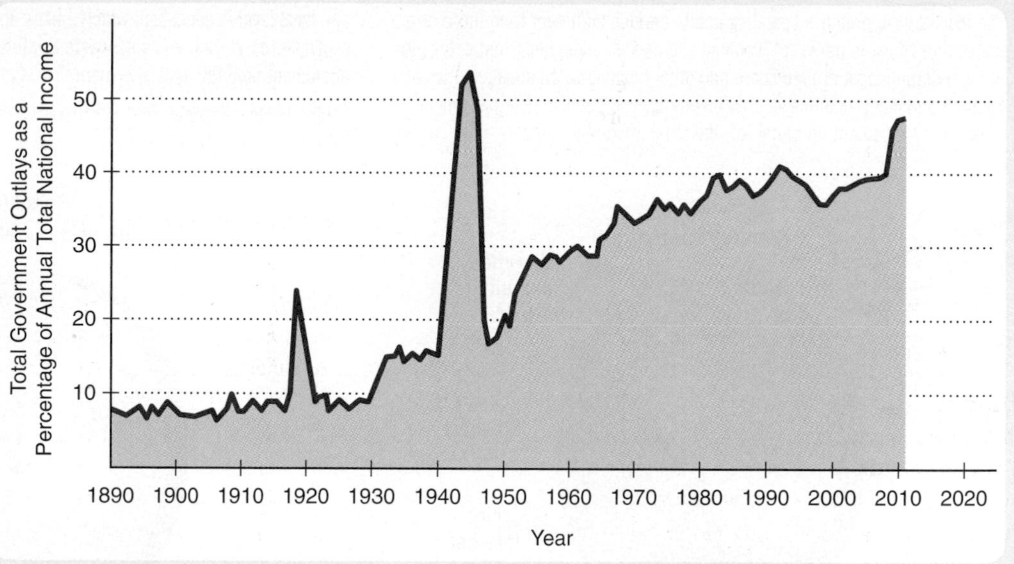

and the like. In addition, total government outlays include transfer payments, such as welfare and Social Security. In Figure 5-2 above, you see that government outlays prior to World War I did not exceed 10 percent of annual national income. There was a spike during World War I, a general increase during the Great Depression, and then a huge spike during World War II. After World War II, government outlays as a percentage of total national income rose steadily before dropping in the 1990s, rising again in the early 2000s, and then jumping sharply in the late 2000s.

How do federal and state governments allocate their spending? A typical federal government budget is shown in panel (a) of Figure 5-3 on the following page. The three largest categories are Medicare and other health-related spending, Social Security and other income-security programs, and national defense, which together constitute 77.6 percent of the total federal budget.

The makeup of state and local expenditures is quite different. As panel (b) shows, education is the biggest category, accounting for 34.2 percent of all expenditures.

Publicly Subsidized Health Care: Medicare

Figure 5-3 shows that health-related spending is a significant portion of total government expenditures. Certainly, medical expenses are a major concern for many elderly people. Since 1965, that concern has been reflected in the existence of the Medicare program, which pays hospital and physicians' bills for U.S. residents over the age of 65 (and for those younger than 65 in some instances). In return for paying a tax on their earnings while in the workforce (2.9 percent of wages and salaries, rising to 3.8 percent of all income for high-income households), retirees are assured that the majority of their hospital and physicians' bills will be paid for with public monies.

Go to **www.econtoday.com/ch05** to visit the U.S. government's official Medicare Web site.

THE SIMPLE ECONOMICS OF MEDICARE To understand how, in fewer than 40 years, Medicare became the second-biggest domestic government spending program in existence, a bit of economics is in order. Consider Figure 5-4 on the bottom of the following page, which shows the demand for and supply of medical care.

The initial equilibrium price is P_0 and equilibrium quantity is Q_0. Perhaps because the government believes that Q_0 is not enough medical care for these consumers,

FIGURE 5-3 Federal Government Spending Compared to State and Local Spending

The federal government's spending habits are quite different from those of the states and cities. In panel (a), you can see that the most important categories in the federal budget are Medicare and other health-related spending, Social Security and other income-security programs, and national defense, which make up 77.6 percent. In panel (b), the most important category at the state and local level is education, which makes up 34.2 percent. "Other" includes expenditures in such areas as waste treatment, garbage collection, mosquito abatement, and the judicial system.

Sources: Budget of the United States Government; government finances.

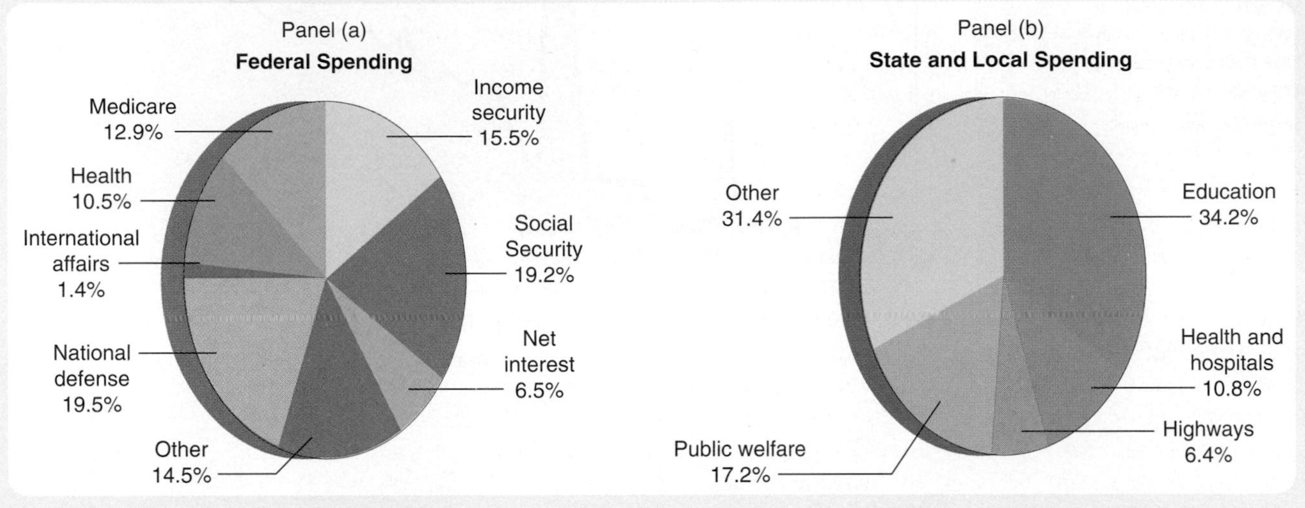

suppose that the government begins paying a subsidy that eventually is set at M for each unit of medical care consumed. This will simultaneously tend to raise the price per unit of care received by providers (physicians, hospitals, and the like) and lower the perceived price per unit that consumers see when they make decisions about how much medical care to consume. As presented in the figure, the price received by providers rises to P_s, while the price paid by consumers falls to P_d. As a result,

FIGURE 5-4 The Economic Effects of Medicare Subsidies

When the government pays a per-unit subsidy M for medical care, consumers pay the price of services P_d for the quantity of services Q_m. Providers receive the price P_s for supplying this quantity. Originally, the federal government projected that its total spending on Medicare would equal an amount such as the area $Q_0 \times (P_0 - P_d)$. Because actual consumption equals Q_m, however, the government's total expenditures equal $Q_m \times M$.

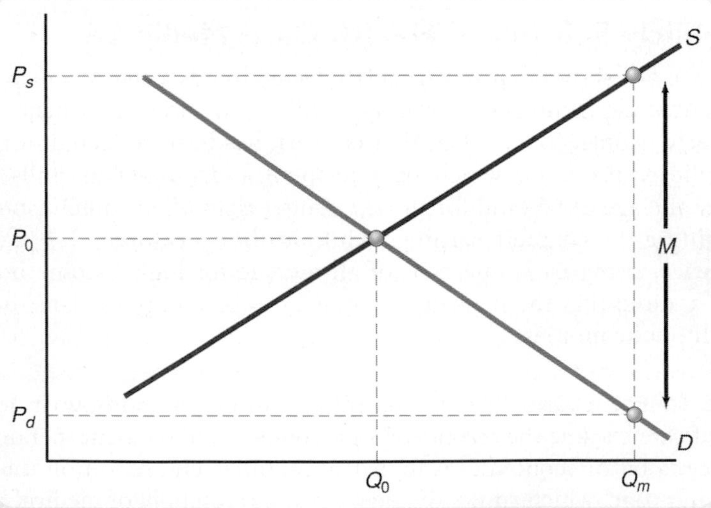

consumers of medical care want to purchase Q_m units, and suppliers are quite happy to provide it for them.

MEDICARE INCENTIVES AT WORK We can now understand the problems that plague the Medicare system today. First, one of the things that people observed during the 20 years after the founding of Medicare was a huge upsurge in physicians' incomes and medical school applications, the spread of private for-profit hospitals, and the rapid proliferation of new medical tests and procedures. All of this was being encouraged by the rise in the price of medical services from P_0 to P_s, as shown on the facing page in Figure 5-4, which encouraged entry into this market.

Second, government expenditures on Medicare have routinely turned out to be far in excess of the expenditures forecast at the time the program was put in place or was expanded. The reasons for this are easy to see. Bureaucratic planners often fail to recognize the incentive effects of government programs. On the demand side, they fail to account for the huge increase in consumption (from Q_0 to Q_m) that will result from a subsidy like Medicare. On the supply side, they fail to recognize that the larger amount of services can only be extracted from suppliers at a higher price, P_s. Consequently, original projected spending on Medicare was an area like $Q_0 \times (P_0 - P_d)$, because original plans for the program only contemplated consumption of Q_0 and assumed that the subsidy would have to be only $P_0 - P_d$ per unit. In fact, consumption rises to Q_m, and the additional cost per unit of service rises to P_s, implying an increase in the per-unit subsidy to M. Hence, actual expenditures turn out to be the far larger number $Q_m \times M$. Every expansion of the program, including the 2004 broadening of Medicare to cover obesity as a new illness eligible for coverage and the extension of Medicare to cover patients' prescription drug expenses beginning in 2006, has followed the same pattern.

Third, total spending on medical services has soared, consuming far more income than initially expected. Originally, total spending on medical services was $P_0 \times Q_0$. In the presence of Medicare, spending rises to $P_s \times Q_m$.

HEALTH CARE SUBSIDIES CONTINUE TO GROW Just how fast are Medicare subsidies growing? Medicare's cost has risen from 0.7 percent of U.S. national income in 1970 to more than 2.8 percent today, which amounts to nearly $400 billion per year. Because Medicare spending is growing much faster than total employer and employee contributions, future spending guarantees far outstrip the taxes to be collected in the future to pay for the system. (The current Medicare tax rate is 2.9 percent on all wages, with 1.45 percent paid by the employee and 1.45 percent paid by the employer. For all income earned above $200,000 for individuals and $250,000 for married couples, a 3.8 percent Medicare tax rate applies.) Today, unfunded guarantees of Medicare spending in the future are estimated at more than $25 trillion (in today's dollars).

These amounts fail to reflect the costs of another federal health program called Medicaid. The Medicaid program is structured similarly to Medicare, in that the government also pays per-unit subsidies for health care to qualifying patients. Medicaid, however, provides subsidies only to people who qualify because they have lower incomes. At present, about 50 million people, or about one out of every six U.S. residents, qualify for Medicaid coverage. Medicaid is administered by state governments, but the federal government pays about 57 percent of the program's total cost from general tax revenues. The current cost of the program is more than $400 billion per year. In recent years, Medicaid spending has grown even faster than expenditures on Medicare, rising by more than 75 percent since 2000 alone. Of course, in legislation enacted in 2010, the U.S. Congress further expanded by more than $100 billion per year the rate of growth of government health care spending, which already has been growing at an average pace of 8 percent per year.

Why is the state of Massachusetts rethinking its Medicare-style approach to government funding of health care spending?

POLICY EXAMPLE **Seeking to Halt "Overuse" of Massachusetts Health Care**

In 2006, the state of Massachusetts adopted a program analogous to Medicare for *all* of its residents. State government projections indicated that implementation of the new program would cut overall health care expenses in that state. In fact, within three years health care spending for a typical Massachusetts resident had risen to 33 percent above the average for other U.S. residents.

The problem was that the state's projections assumed that the quantity of health care services demanded would not rise when residents' out-of-pocket prices decreased. By the end of the 2000s, a special panel asked to recommend how to reduce the program's expense had concluded that the program "rewards overuse of services." The panel unanimously recommended reconsidering the program's Medicare-style structure.

FOR CRITICAL ANALYSIS

What did the state of Massachusetts presume about the shape of the demand curve for health care services when it assumed that a decrease in out-of-pocket prices would generate no change in the quantity of services demanded?

Economic Issues of Public Education

In the United States, government involvement in health care is a relatively recent phenomenon. In contrast, state and local governments have assumed primary responsibility for public education for many years. Currently, these governments spend more than $900 billion on education—in excess of 6 percent of total U.S. national income. State and local sales, excise, property, and income taxes finance the bulk of these expenditures. In addition, each year the federal government provides tens of billions of dollars of support for public education through grants and other transfers to state and local governments.

THE NOW-FAMILIAR ECONOMICS OF PUBLIC EDUCATION State and local governments around the United States have developed a variety of complex mechanisms for funding public education. What all public education programs have in common, however, is the provision of educational services to primary, secondary, and college students at prices well below those that would otherwise prevail in the marketplace for these services.

So how do state and local governments accomplish this? The answer is that they operate public education programs that share some of the features of government-subsidized health care programs such as Medicare. Analogously to Figure 5-4 on page 108, public schools provide educational services at a price below the market price. They are willing to produce the quantity of educational services demanded at this below-market price as long as they receive a sufficiently high per-unit subsidy from state and local governments.

THE INCENTIVE PROBLEMS OF PUBLIC EDUCATION Since the 1960s, various measures of the performance of U.S. primary and secondary students have failed to increase even as public spending on education has risen. Some measures of student performance have even declined.

Many economists argue that the incentive effects that have naturally arisen with higher government subsidies for public education help to explain this lack of improvement in student performance. A higher per-pupil subsidy creates a difference between the relatively high per-unit costs to schools of providing the amount of educational services that parents and students are willing to purchase and the relatively lower valuations of those services. As a consequence, some schools have provided services, such as after-school babysitting and various social services, that have contributed relatively little to student learning.

A factor that complicates efforts to assess the effects of education subsidies is that the public schools often face little or no competition from unsubsidized providers of educational services. In addition, public schools rarely compete against each other. In most locales, therefore, parents who are unhappy with the quality of services provided at the subsidized price cannot transfer their child to a different public school.

What problem has arisen for public schools that offer services for which parents are willing to pay more than the current price?

EXAMPLE Valuable Charter School Services—for Those Who Can Get Them

Charter schools are state-funded schools that have the freedom to offer a variety of learning approaches. Considerable evidence suggests that learning outcomes improve for many students when they attend these schools. In most states with charter schools, students in other public schools can transfer to a charter school offering a different approach to learning, as long as the charter school has room for them. Generally, though, charter schools are full, and transfer applicants face lengthy waiting lists.

Nearly all states with charter schools limit their number. Nevertheless, many parents have come to place higher values on the educational services of charter schools, implying increasing demand for those services. Once students are admitted, though, states set the prices of attending a charter school at close to zero. The result is predictable: The quantity of charter school services demanded exceeds the quantity supplied—hence the waiting lists.

FOR CRITICAL ANALYSIS

What would happen to the number of students enrolled at charter schools if states would allow more charter schools to open and to charge fees?

QUICK QUIZ See page 120 for the answers. Review concepts from this section in MyEconLab.

Medicare subsidizes the consumption of medical care by the elderly, thus increasing the amount of such care consumed. People tend to purchase large amounts of __________-value, __________-cost services in publicly funded health care programs such as Medicare, because they do not directly bear the full cost of their decisions.

Basic economic analysis indicates that higher subsidies for public education have widened the differential between parents' and students' relatively __________ per-unit valuations of the educational services of public schools and the __________ costs that schools incur in providing those services.

Collective Decision Making: The Theory of Public Choice

Governments consist of individuals. No government actually thinks and acts. Instead, government actions are the result of decision making by individuals in their roles as elected representatives, appointed officials, and salaried bureaucrats. Therefore, to understand how government works, we must examine the incentives of the people in government as well as those who would like to be in government—avowed or would-be candidates for elective or appointed positions—and special-interest lobbyists attempting to get government to do something. At issue is the analysis of **collective decision making.** Collective decision making involves the actions of voters, politicians, political parties, interest groups, and many other groups and individuals. The analysis of collective decision making is usually called the **theory of public choice.** It has been given this name because it involves hypotheses about how choices are made in the public sector, as opposed to the private sector. The foundation of public-choice theory is the assumption that individuals will act within the political process to maximize their *individual* (not collective) well-being. In that sense, the theory is similar to our analysis of the market economy, in which we also assume that individuals act as though they are motivated by self-interest.

Collective decision making
How voters, politicians, and other interested parties act and how these actions influence nonmarket decisions.

Theory of public choice
The study of collective decision making.

To understand public-choice theory, it is necessary to point out other similarities between the private market sector and the public, or government, sector; then we will look at the differences.

Similarities in Market and Public-Sector Decision Making

In addition to the assumption of self-interest being the motivating force in both sectors, there are other similarities.

OPPORTUNITY COST Everything that is spent by all levels of government plus everything that is spent by the private sector must add up to the total income available at any point in time. Hence, every government action has an opportunity cost, just as in the market sector.

COMPETITION Although we typically think of competition as a private market phenomenon, it is also present in collective action. Given the scarcity constraint government faces, bureaucrats, appointed officials, and elected representatives will always be in competition for available government funds. Furthermore, the individuals within any government agency or institution will act as individuals do in the private sector: They will try to obtain higher wages, better working conditions, and higher job-level classifications. We assume that they will compete and act in their own interest, not society's.

SIMILARITY OF INDIVIDUALS Contrary to popular belief, the types of individuals working in the private sector and working in the public sector are not inherently different. The difference, as we shall see, is that the individuals in government face a different **incentive structure** than those in the private sector. For example, the costs and benefits of being efficient or inefficient differ in the private and public sectors.

Incentive structure
The system of rewards and punishments individuals face with respect to their own actions.

One approach to predicting government bureaucratic behavior is to ask what incentives bureaucrats face. Take the United States Postal Service (USPS) as an example. The bureaucrats running that government corporation are human beings with IQs not dissimilar to those possessed by workers in similar positions at Google or American Airlines. Yet the USPS does not function like either of these companies. The difference can be explained in terms of the incentives provided for managers in the two types of institutions. When the bureaucratic managers and workers at Google make incorrect decisions, work slowly, produce shoddy programs, and are generally "inefficient," the profitability of the company declines. The owners—millions of shareholders—express their displeasure by selling some of their shares of company stock. The market value, as tracked on the stock exchange, falls. This induces owners of shares of stock to pressure managers to pursue strategies more likely to boost revenues and reduce costs.

But what about the USPS? If a manager, a worker, or a bureaucrat in the USPS gives shoddy service, the organization's owners—the taxpayers—have no straightforward mechanism for expressing their dissatisfaction. Despite the postal service's status as a "government corporation," taxpayers as shareholders do not really own shares of stock in the organization that they can sell.

Thus, to understand purported inefficiency in the government bureaucracy, we need to examine incentives and institutional arrangements—not people and personalities.

Differences Between Market and Collective Decision Making

There are probably more dissimilarities between the market sector and the public sector than there are similarities.

GOVERNMENT GOODS AND SERVICES AT ZERO PRICE The majority of goods that governments produce are furnished to the ultimate consumers without payment required. **Government,** or **political, goods** can be either private or public goods. The fact that they are furnished to the ultimate consumer free of charge does *not* mean that the cost to society of those goods is zero, however. It only means that the price *charged* is zero. The full opportunity cost to society is the value of the resources used in the production of goods produced and provided by the government.

Government, or **political, goods**
Goods (and services) provided by the public sector; they can be either private or public goods.

For example, none of us pays directly for each unit of consumption of defense or police protection. Rather, we pay for all these items indirectly through the taxes that support our governments—federal, state, and local. This special feature of government can be looked at in a different way. There is no longer a one-to-one relationship between consumption of government-provided goods and services and payment for these items. Indeed, most taxpayers will find that their tax bill is the same whether or not they consume government-provided goods.

USE OF FORCE All governments can resort to using force in their regulation of economic affairs. For example, governments can use *expropriation*, which means that if you refuse to pay your taxes, your bank account and other assets may be seized by the Internal Revenue Service. In fact, you have no choice in the matter of paying taxes to governments. Collectively, we decide the total size of government through the political process, but individually, we cannot determine how much service we pay for during any one year.

VOTING VERSUS SPENDING In the private market sector, a dollar voting system is in effect. This dollar voting system is not equivalent to the voting system in the public sector. There are at least three differences:

1. In a political system, one person gets one vote, whereas in the market system, each dollar a person spends counts separately.
2. The political system is run by **majority rule,** whereas the market system is run by **proportional rule.**
3. The spending of dollars can indicate intensity of want, whereas because of the all-or-nothing nature of political voting, a vote cannot.

Majority rule
A collective decision-making system in which group decisions are made on the basis of more than 50 percent of the vote. In other words, whatever more than half of the electorate votes for, the entire electorate has to accept.

Proportional rule
A decision-making system in which actions are based on the proportion of the "votes" cast and are in proportion to them. In a market system, if 10 percent of the "dollar votes" are cast for blue cars, 10 percent of automobile output will be blue cars.

Ultimately, the main distinction between political votes and dollar votes is that political outcomes may differ from economic outcomes. Remember that economic efficiency is a situation in which, given the prevailing distribution of income, consumers obtain the economic goods they want. There is no corresponding situation when political voting determines economic outcomes. Thus, a political voting process is unlikely to lead to the same decisions that a dollar voting process would yield in the marketplace.

Indeed, consider the dilemma every voter faces. Usually, a voter is not asked to decide on a single issue (although this happens). Rather, a voter is asked to choose among candidates who present a large number of issues and state a position on each of them. Just consider the average U.S. senator, who has to vote on several thousand different issues during a six-year term. When you vote for that senator, you are voting for a person who must make thousands of decisions during the next six years.

How does government control over mail delivery affect decisions about the number of post offices in operation?

INTERNATIONAL EXAMPLE So Little Mail, So Little for So Many Post Offices to Do

As more people around the globe transmit information via e-mail instead of physical letters and other documents, government-owned postal firms are experiencing annual declines in mail volume ranging from 5 to 15 percent. In many nations, postal firms have branched out into additional businesses, such as banking and other financial services. Even though every government has been seeking to reduce the number of post offices it operates, economists agree that national governments have been much slower to scale back their postal firms than if the firms were operated privately. The United States still has more than 1.2 post offices for every 10,000 residents—the same as it had more than a decade ago. In contrast, China's Communist government operates only 0.5 post office per 10,000 residents.

Some governments are having an even harder time than the U.S. government in shrinking postal operations. The number of post offices per 10,000 residents is 2.3 in Italy; 2.8 in France, the United Kingdom, and Russia; and 3.3 in Ukraine.

FOR CRITICAL ANALYSIS

In view of the global decline in demand for mail delivery services, why might post office closure rates be lower under government ownership than if postal operations were privately owned?

QUICK QUIZ

See page 120 for the answers. Review concepts from this section in MyEconLab.

The theory of __________ __________ examines how voters, politicians, and other parties collectively reach decisions in the public sector of the economy.

As in private markets, __________ __________ and __________ have incentive effects that influence public-sector decision making. In contrast to private market situations, however, there is not a one-to-one relationship between consumption of a publicly provided good and the payment for that good.

You Are There

A Town Confronts a Parked Externality

Bruce Atkinson, a resident of New Castle, Indiana, has posted another YouTube video showing the dozens of graffiti-covered, 20-foot-tall, yellow railcars lining the streets of the town. "Block after block, 'lovely' yellow cars," he states in one video, as the camera's view takes in a railcar painted with a drawing of a marijuana leaf. "Can you imagine living next to those?" In fact, New Castle schoolchildren play on swings and slides a few yards from a line of railcars covered with spray-painted words that their parents try to teach them not to say. The tall railcars cast shadows across yards of homes only 10 feet from the railroad tracks, killing grass and creating mud pits. To visit next-door neighbors, residents must walk several blocks to get around lines of railcars separating their homes. And for all of the community's residents, the railcars represent a daily eyesore—a negative spillover from the market for rail transport services.

New Castle's visual railcar pollution problem reflects a phenomenon experienced by communities across the nation. When demand for rail shipping services plummeted during the late 2000s, railroad firms had to find a place to store more than 200,000 idled railcars—enough to stretch from New York City to Salt Lake City if placed end to end. In many cases, firms decided to store the railcars on the tracks in communities through which their trains rarely run. Railroad firms own those tracks, and parking the railcars on the tracks is the best available business decision that the firms can make, given the conditions they face in the market for rail services. To residents of New Castle, however, the parked railcars constitute a negative externality.

Critical Analysis Questions

1. What would happen to the market supply curve for rail services—including parked railcars—if the railroad firms took into account all relevant social costs?
2. Can you think of any potential solution to the market failure faced by residents of New Castle and other communities whose streets are lined with railcars?

ISSUES & APPLICATIONS

Uncle Sam Becomes an Investor in Clean-Energy Technology

CONCEPTS APPLIED

- ▶ External Costs
- ▶ Government-Sponsored Good
- ▶ Subsidies

For years, the U.S. federal government has sought to reduce emissions of atmospheric pollutants. In most cases, it has attempted to reduce the external costs associated with such emissions via taxes and regulation. More recently, however, the government has decided to promote a cleaner atmosphere by designating various clean air–promoting technologies and products as government-sponsored goods.

Cash to Burn—Only Figuratively, Though

As the 2010s dawned, the U.S. Department of Energy announced that it hoped to lend or give away more than $40 billion annually to businesses working on "clean technology." It quickly doled out more than $13 billion in low-interest loans and direct subsidies to firms developing technological processes and products such as wind turbines, solar panels, and new types of batteries.

Among the key recipients of government funds have been manufacturers of electric vehicles. In addition to traditional auto manufacturers such as General Motors and Ford Motor Company, new industry startups such as Bright Automotive, Fisker Automotive, and Tesla Motors have obtained federal funding. Using novel forms of battery power—some of them financed, in part, by government loans and subsidies—these companies are working to produce vehicles that emit no pollutants whatsoever. This objective, of course, squares with the U.S. government's efforts to clean up pollution and reduce associated external costs.

Oops, All of Those Clean-Car Batteries Have to Be Charged

There are two difficulties associated with clean electric vehicles, however. One is that the technology for charging all the vehicles' batteries is still undeveloped. Another is that while the vehicles may be clean, production of the energy required to charge their batteries is not.

Although significant headway has been made in developing better batteries to power emission-free vehicles, most batteries continue to suffer from various physical inefficiencies. These inefficiencies translate into higher operating costs and fewer miles that vehicles can remain on the road between charges. Of course, the U.S. government realizes this, which is why companies such as Southern California Edison, Compact Power, and DTE Energy have received billions of dollars in government assistance.

Nevertheless, even if more efficient batteries emerge, it is unclear where many people would charge electric vehicles. Not everyone lives in a house with a garage. Families who live in apartments, students who live in fraternities and dormitories, and others will require access to charging stations of some type. So far, special extension cords and overnight charging kiosks are still on the drawing board for the most part, although government agencies are paying for many drawings.

The second problem may be even harder to solve. The bulk of the electricity transmitted by all of those future vehicle charging stations will continue to be produced by traditional power plants. Many of these power plants run on old-fashioned, pollution-emitting energy sources such as coal and diesel fuel. Thus, producing all the extra electricity required to charge all the proposed vehicle batteries will not involve "clean energy." Even if wider use of electric vehicles reduces certain types of emissions, other types of emissions created by electric power plants will increase.

For Critical Analysis

1. Clean-energy firms have had trouble hiring a sufficient number of specialists in electricity generation. Why do you think that the U.S. government now subsidizes training programs for applied scientists and engineers specializing in electricity?
2. What do you think is the U.S. government's motivation for launching a new $3.4 billion subsidy program aimed at making the nation's power grid more physically efficient in transmitting electricity?

Web Resources

1. Read the U.S. government's guide to electric vehicles at www.econtoday.com/ch05.
2. For information about the top North American manufacturers of electric vehicles, go to www.econtoday.com/ch05.

Research Project

Evaluate the pros and cons of using taxation and regulation to contain the external costs of atmospheric pollution versus subsidies to firms producing government-sponsored clean-energy goods. Which approach makes greater use of the price system to ration goods and services?

For more questions on this chapter's Issues & Applications, go to **MyEconLab**. In the Study Plan for this chapter, select Section N: News.

Here is what you should know after reading this chapter. **MyEconLab** will help you identify what you know, and where to go when you need to practice.

WHAT YOU SHOULD KNOW		WHERE TO GO TO PRACTICE
How Market Failures Such as Externalities Might Justify Economic Functions of Government A market failure occurs when too many or too few resources are directed to a specific form of economic activity. One type of market failure is an externality, which is a spillover effect on third parties not directly involved in producing or purchasing a good or service. In the case of a negative externality, firms do not pay for the costs arising from spillover effects that their production of a good imposes on others, so they produce too much of the good in question. In the case of a positive externality, buyers fail to take into account the benefits that their consumption of a good yields to others, so they purchase too little of the good.	market failure, 99 externality, 99 third parties, 100 property rights, 100 effluent fee, 102 antitrust legislation, 103 monopoly, 103 **KEY FIGURE** Figure 5-1, 101	• **MyEconLab** Study Plans 5.1, 5.2 • Audio introduction to Chapter 5 • Animated Figure 5-1 • ABC News Video: The Economics of Energy
Private Goods versus Public Goods and the Free-Rider Problem Private goods are subject to the principle of rival consumption, meaning that one person's consumption of such a good reduces the amount available for another person to consume. In contrast, public goods can be consumed by many people simultaneously at no additional opportunity cost and with no reduction in quality or quantity. In addition, no individual can be excluded from the benefits of a public good even if that person fails to help pay for it.	private goods, 103 principle of rival consumption, 104 public goods, 104 free-rider problem, 105	• **MyEconLab** Study Plan 5.3 • Video: Private Goods and Public Goods
Political Functions of Government That Lead to Its Involvement in the Economy As a result of the political process, government may seek to promote the production and consumption of government-sponsored goods. The government may also seek to restrict the production and sale of goods that have been deemed socially undesirable, called government-inhibited goods. In addition, the political process may determine that income redistribution is socially desirable.	government-sponsored good, 105 government-inhibited good, 105 transfer payments, 106 transfers in kind, 106	• **MyEconLab** Study Plan 5.4
The Effect of Medicare on the Incentives to Consume Medical Services Medicare subsidizes the consumption of medical services. As a result, the quantity consumed is higher, as is the price sellers receive per unit of those services. Medicare also encourages people to consume medical services that are very low in per-unit value relative to the cost of providing them.	**KEY FIGURES** Figure 5-2, 107 Figure 5-4, 108	• **MyEconLab** Study Plan 5.5 • Video: Medicare • Animated Figures 5-2, 5-4

(continued)

MyEconLab continued

WHAT YOU SHOULD KNOW		WHERE TO GO TO PRACTICE
Why Bigger Subsidies for Public Schools Do Not Necessarily Translate into Improved Student Performance When governments subsidize public schools, the last unit of educational services provided by public schools costs more than its valuation by parents and students. Thus, public schools provide services in excess of those best suited to promoting student learning.		• **MyEconLab** Study Plan 5.5
Central Elements of the Theory of Public Choice The theory of public choice applies to collective decision making, or the process through which voters and politicians interact to influence nonmarket choices. Certain aspects of public-sector decision making, such as scarcity and competition, are similar to those that affect private-sector choices. Others, however, such as legal coercion and majority-rule decision making, differ from those involved in the market system.	collective decision making, 111 theory of public choice, 111 incentive structure, 112 government, or political, goods, 112 majority rule, 113 proportional rule, 113	• **MyEconLab** Study Plan 5.6

Log in to MyEconLab, take a chapter test, and get a personalized Study Plan that tells you which concepts you understand and which ones you need to review. From there, MyEconLab will give you further practice, tutorials, animations, videos, and guided solutions.
Log in to www.myeconlab.com

PROBLEMS

All problems are assignable in myeconlab. *Answers to odd-numbered problems appear at the back of the book.*

5-1. Many people who do not smoke cigars are bothered by the odor of cigar smoke. If private contracting is impossible and in the absence of any government involvement in the market for cigars, will too many or too few cigars be produced and consumed? From society's point of view, will the market price of cigars be too high or too low?

5-2. Suppose that repeated application of a pesticide used on orange trees causes harmful contamination of groundwater. The pesticide is applied annually in almost all of the orange groves throughout the world. Most orange growers regard the pesticide as a key input in their production of oranges.

a. Use a diagram of the market for the pesticide to illustrate the implications of a failure of orange producers' costs to reflect the social costs of groundwater contamination.

b. Use your diagram from part (a) to explain a government policy that might be effective in achieving the amount of orange production that fully reflects all social costs.

5-3. Now draw a diagram of the market for oranges. Explain how the government policy you discussed in part (b) of Problem 5-2 is likely to affect the market price and equilibrium quantity in the orange market. In what sense do consumers of oranges now "pay" for dealing with the spillover costs of pesticide production?

5-4. Suppose that the U.S. government determines that cigarette smoking creates social costs not reflected in the current market price and equilibrium quantity of cigarettes. A study has recommended that the government can correct for the externality effect of cigarette consumption by paying farmers *not* to plant tobacco used to manufacture cigarettes. It also recommends raising the funds to make these payments by increasing taxes on cigarettes. Assuming that the government is correct that cigarette smoking creates external costs, evaluate whether the study's recommended policies might help correct this negative externality.

5-5. A nation's government has determined that mass transit, such as bus lines, helps alleviate traffic congestion, thereby benefiting both individual auto commuters and companies that desire to move products and factors of production speedily along streets and highways. Nevertheless, even though several private bus lines are in service, the country's commuters are failing to take the social benefits of the use of mass transit into account.

a. Discuss, in the context of demand-supply analysis, the essential implications of commuters' failure to take into account the social benefits associated with bus ridership.

b. Explain a government policy that might be effective in achieving the socially efficient use of bus services.

5-6. Draw a diagram of this nation's market for automobiles, which are a substitute for buses. Explain how the government policy you discussed in part (b) of Problem 5-5 is likely to affect the market price and equilibrium quantity in the country's auto market. How are auto consumers affected by this policy to attain the spillover benefits of bus transit?

5-7. Displayed in the diagram below are conditions in the market for residential Internet access in a U.S. state. The government of this state has determined that access to the Internet improves the learning skills of children, which it has concluded is an external benefit of Internet access. The government has also concluded that if these external benefits were to be taken into account, 3 million residences would have Internet access. Suppose that the state government's judgments about the benefits of Internet access are correct and that it wishes to offer a per-unit subsidy just sufficient to increase total Internet access to 3 million residences. What per-unit subsidy should it offer? Use the diagram to explain how providing this subsidy would affect conditions in the state's market for residential Internet access.

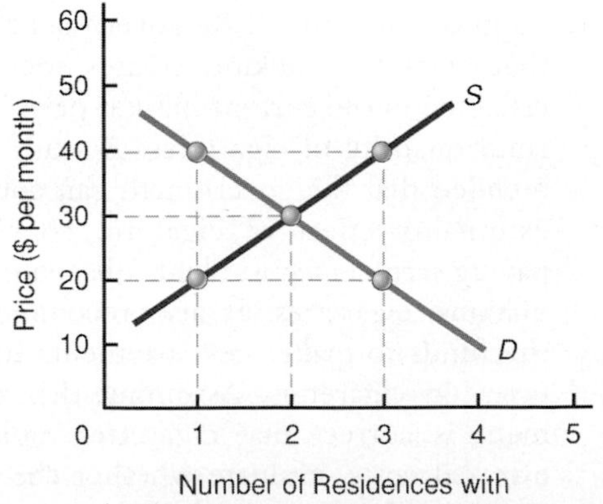

5-8. The French government recently allocated the equivalent of more than $120 million in public funds to *Quaero* (Latin for "I search"), an Internet search engine analogous to Google or Yahoo. Does an Internet search engine satisfy the key characteristics of a public good? Why or why not? Based on your answer, is a publicly funded Internet search engine a public good or a government-sponsored good?

5-9. A government offers to let a number of students at a public school transfer to a private school under two conditions: It will transmit to the private school the same per-pupil subsidy it provides the public school, and the private school will be required to admit the students at a below-market net tuition rate. Will the economic outcome be the same as the one that would have arisen if the government instead simply provided students with grants to cover the current market tuition rate at the private school? (Hint: Does it matter if schools receive payments directly from the government or from consumers?)

5-10. After a government implements a voucher program, granting funds that families can spend at schools of their choice, numerous students in public schools switch to private schools. Parents' and students' valuations of the services provided at both private and public schools adjust to equality with the true market price of educational services. Is anyone likely to lose out nonetheless? If so, who?

5-11. Suppose that the current price of a computer memory storage drive is $100 and that people are buying 1 million drives per year. In order to improve computer literacy, the government decides to begin subsidizing the purchase of new drives. The government believes that the appropriate price is $60 per drive, so the program offers to send people cash for the difference between $60 and whatever the people pay for each drive they buy.

a. If no consumers change their memory-storage-drive-buying behavior, how much will this program cost the taxpayers?

b. Will the subsidy cause people to buy more, fewer, or the same number of drives? Explain.

c. Suppose that people end up buying 1.5 million drives once the program is in place. If the market price of drives does not change, how much will this program cost the taxpayers?

d. Under the assumption that the program causes people to buy 1.5 million drives and also causes the market price of drives to rise to $120, how much will this program cost the taxpayers?

5-12. Scans of internal organs using magnetic resonance imaging (MRI) devices are often covered by subsidized health insurance programs such as Medicare.

Consider the following table illustrating hypothetical quantities of individual MRI testing procedures demanded and supplied at various prices, and then answer the questions that follow.

Price	Quantity Demanded	Quantity Supplied
$100	100,000	40,000
$300	90,000	60,000
$500	80,000	80,000
$700	70,000	100,000
$900	60,000	120,000

a. In the absence of a government-subsidized health plan, what is the equilibrium price of MRI tests? What is the amount of society's total spending on MRI tests?

b. Suppose that the government establishes a health plan guaranteeing that all qualified participants can purchase MRI tests at an effective price (that is, out-of-pocket cost) to the individual of $100 per test. How many MRI tests will people consume?

c. What is the per-unit price that induces producers to provide the amount of MRI tests demanded at the government-guaranteed price of $100? What is society's total spending on MRI tests?

d. Under the government's coverage of MRI tests, what is the per-unit subsidy it provides? What is the total subsidy that the government pays to support MRI testing at its guaranteed price?

5-13. Suppose that, as part of an expansion of its State Care health system, a state government decides to offer a $50 subsidy to all people who, according to their physicians, should have their own blood pressure monitoring devices. Prior to this governmental decision, the market clearing price of blood pressure monitors in this state was $50, and the equilibrium quantity purchased was 20,000 per year.

a. After the government expands its State Care plan, people in this state desire to purchase 40,000 devices each year. Manufacturers of blood pressure monitors are willing to provide 40,000 devices at a price of $60 per device. What out-of-pocket price does each consumer pay for a blood pressure monitor?

b. What is the dollar amount of the increase in total expenditures on blood pressure monitors in this state following the expansion in the State Care program?

c. Following the expansion of the State Care program, what *percentage* of total expenditures on blood pressure monitors is paid by the government? What percentage of total expenditures is paid by consumers of these devices?

5-14. A government agency is contemplating launching an effort to expand the scope of its activities. One rationale for doing so is that another government agency might make the same effort and, if successful, receive larger budget allocations in future years. Another rationale for expanding the agency's activities is that this will make the jobs of its workers more interesting, which may help the government agency attract better-qualified employees. Nevertheless, to broaden its legal mandate, the agency will have to convince more than half of the House of Representatives and the Senate to approve a formal proposal to expand its activities. In addition, to expand its activities, the agency must have the authority to force private companies it does not currently regulate to be officially licensed by agency personnel. Identify which aspects of this problem are similar to those faced by firms that operate in private markets and which aspects are specific to the public sector.

ECONOMICS ON THE NET

Putting Tax Dollars to Work In this application, you will learn about how the U.S. government allocates its expenditures. This will enable you to conduct an evaluation of the current functions of the federal government.

Title: Historical Tables: Budget of the United States Government

Navigation: Go to **www.econtoday.com/ch05** to visit the home page of the U.S. Government Printing Office. Click on "Browse the FY Budget" for the applicable year, and then click on "PDF" next to *Historical Tables*.

Application After the document downloads, examine Section 3, Federal Government Outlays by Function, and in particular Table 3.1, Outlays by Superfunction and Function. Then answer the following questions.

1. What government functions have been capturing growing shares of government spending in recent years? Which of these do you believe are related to the problem of addressing externalities, providing public goods, or dealing with other market failures? Which appear to be related to political functions instead of economic functions?

2. Which government functions are receiving declining shares of total spending? Are any of these related to the problem of addressing externalities, providing public goods, or dealing with other market failures? Are any related to political functions instead of economic functions?

For Group Study and Analysis Assign groups to the following overall categories of government functions: national defense, health, income security, and Social Security. Have each group prepare a brief report concerning long-term and recent trends in government spending on its category. Each group should take a stand on whether specific spending on items in its category is likely to relate to resolving market failures, public funding of government-sponsored goods, regulating the sale of government-inhibited goods, and so on.

ANSWERS TO QUICK QUIZZES

p. 103: (i) costs . . . taxation . . . regulation; (ii) benefits . . . financing . . . subsidizing . . . regulation

p. 106: (i) externalities . . . legal system . . . competition . . . public . . . economywide stability; (ii) rival consumption; (iii) opportunity cost . . . charged; (iv) government-sponsored . . . government-inhibited . . . income

p. 111: (i) low . . . high; (ii) low . . . higher

p. 113: (i) public choice; (ii) opportunity cost . . . competition

6 Funding the Public Sector

During his presidential campaign, Barack Obama stated in an interview that he was open to *doubling* the top tax rate on *capital gains*—increases in the prices of assets at the time they are sold relative to their prices when the assets were purchased. Shortly after taking office, however, President Obama formally proposed raising the top tax rate on capital gains by "only" one-third, from 15 percent to 20 percent. Nevertheless, a number of congressional leaders continue to push for doubling tax rates on capital gains, which they argue would boost the government's tax revenues by many billions of dollars per year. Are there any practical limitations on how high governments can raise tax rates in hopes of obtaining more tax revenues? The relationship between tax rates and tax revenues is a key subject of this chapter.

LEARNING OBJECTIVES

After reading this chapter, you should be able to:

- Distinguish between average tax rates and marginal tax rates
- Explain the structure of the U.S. income tax system
- Understand the key factors influencing the relationship between tax rates and the tax revenues governments collect
- Explain how the taxes governments levy on purchases of goods and services affect market prices and equilibrium quantities

myeconlab

MyEconLab helps you master each objective and study more efficiently. See end of chapter for details.

Did You Know That? the body of laws and rules governing the assessment and collection of U.S. federal taxes—known as the nation's "tax code"—expands at an average rate of 1,000 words per day? To obtain the funds required to finance their operations, governments collect taxes from many different sources—hence, the multitude of words written into a variety of legal statutes governing taxation. State and local governments assess sales taxes, property taxes, income taxes, hotel occupancy taxes, and electricity, gasoline, water, and sewage taxes. At the federal level, there are income taxes, Social Security taxes, Medicare taxes, and so-called excise taxes. When a person dies, state and federal governments also collect estate taxes. Clearly, governments give considerable attention to their roles as tax collectors.

Paying for the Public Sector

There are three sources of funding available to governments. One source is explicit fees, called user *charges*, for government services. The second and main source of government funding is taxes. Nevertheless, sometimes federal, state, and local governments spend more than they collect in taxes. To do this, they must rely on a third source of financing, which is borrowing. A government cannot borrow unlimited amounts, however. After all, a government, like an individual or a firm, can convince others to lend it funds only if it can provide evidence that it will repay its debts. A government must ultimately rely on taxation and user charges, the sources of its own current and future revenues, to repay its debts.

Over the long run, therefore, taxes and user charges are any government's *fundamental* sources of revenues. The **government budget constraint** states that each dollar of public spending on goods, services, transfer payments, and repayments of borrowed funds during a given period must be provided by tax revenues and user charges collected by the government. This long-term constraint indicates that the total amount that a government plans to spend and transfer today and into the future cannot exceed the total taxes and user charges that it currently earns and can reasonably anticipate collecting in future years. Taxation dwarfs user charges as a source of government resources, so let's begin by looking at taxation from a government's perspective.

Government budget constraint
The limit on government spending and transfers imposed by the fact that every dollar the government spends, transfers, or uses to repay borrowed funds must ultimately be provided by the user charges and taxes it collects.

What novel approach have various U.S. state governments recently developed to obtain some additional funds to satisfy their budget constraints?

POLICY EXAMPLE Government Grinches Grab Gifts!

During the Great Recession of the late 2000s, declines in incomes and purchases of goods and services resulted in sharp reductions in payments of income and sales taxes to U.S. state governments. Nearly half of U.S. states responded by seizing unused balances on gift cards. Most of these states now require retailers that issue gift cards to maintain databases that allow government agencies to track all outstanding balances. After a legally mandated interval—which varies from state to state—the agencies impound any unused gift-card balances as user charges and utilize them to help raise more government revenues.

FOR CRITICAL ANALYSIS

Purely from the standpoint of satisfying the government budget constraint, does it matter to states if the funds they raise come from taxes or user charges? Explain.

Systems of Taxation

In light of the government budget constraint, a major concern of any government is how to collect taxes. Jean-Baptiste Colbert, the seventeenth-century French finance minister, said the art of taxation was in "plucking the goose so as to obtain the largest amount of feathers with the least possible amount of hissing." In the United States, governments have designed a variety of methods of plucking the private-sector goose.

The Tax Base and the Tax Rate

To collect a tax, a government typically establishes a **tax base,** which is the value of goods, services, wealth, or incomes subject to taxation. Then it assesses a **tax rate,** which is the proportion of the tax base that must be paid to the government as taxes.

Tax base
The value of goods, services, wealth, or incomes subject to taxation.

Tax rate
The proportion of a tax base that must be paid to a government as taxes.

What new approach might Congress apply to obtain funds from a tax base that is already commonly utilized by state governments?

POLICY EXAMPLE Will U.S. Consumers Pour Their Dollars into a Federal VAT?

For years, U.S. states have levied sales taxes by applying tax rates to the dollar amounts that businesses receive on sales of goods and services. Recently, congressional leaders have suggested a new federal *value-added tax (VAT)* on goods and services. In contrast to sales taxes, which are assessed on final sales of items, with a VAT the tax rates are applied at every stage of an item's production. Under a federal VAT, therefore, the final price that a consumer would pay for each item—before paying any additional state sales taxes—would reflect the various federal VAT rates imposed during the item's production.

Before VATs were implemented in Europe in the late 1960s, taxes collected by European governments amounted to 28 percent of the value of the total annual output of goods and services. Today, European governments collect taxes exceeding 40 percent of the value of all production. Thus, European governments have found that a VAT is a highly effective mechanism for extracting funds from consumers.

FOR CRITICAL ANALYSIS

Why do you think that critics of a federal VAT argue that coupling it with state sales taxes would result in "double taxation" of the dollar value of goods and services?

As we discuss shortly, for the federal government and many state governments, incomes are key tax bases. Therefore, to discuss tax rates and the structure of taxation systems in more detail, let's focus for now on income taxation.

You Are There

To contemplate how marginal income tax rates can affect a person's business decisions, read **A Business Owner Responds to a Marginal Tax Rate Increase,** on page 133.

Marginal and Average Tax Rates

If somebody says, "I pay 28 percent in taxes," you cannot really tell what that person means unless you know whether he or she is referring to average taxes paid or the tax rate on the last dollars earned. The latter concept refers to the **marginal tax rate,** where the word *marginal* means "incremental."

Marginal tax rate
The change in the tax payment divided by the change in income, or the percentage of additional dollars that must be paid in taxes. The marginal tax rate is applied to the highest tax bracket of taxable income reached.

The marginal tax rate is expressed as follows:

$$\text{Marginal tax rate} = \frac{\text{change in taxes due}}{\text{change in taxable income}}$$

It is important to understand that the marginal tax rate applies only to the income in the highest **tax bracket** reached, where a tax bracket is defined as a specified range of taxable income to which a specific and unique marginal tax rate is applied.

Tax bracket
A specified interval of income to which a specific and unique marginal tax rate is applied.

The marginal tax rate is not the same thing as the **average tax rate,** which is defined as follows:

Average tax rate
The total tax payment divided by total income. It is the proportion of total income paid in taxes.

$$\text{Average tax rate} = \frac{\text{total taxes due}}{\text{total taxable income}}$$

What is the "average marginal income tax rate," and how has it changed over time in the United States?

POLICY EXAMPLE **What the Typical Taxpayer Owes Out of the Next Dollar Earned**

Each U.S. taxpayer faces her or his own unique marginal tax rate, depending on that person's income level and other circumstances, such as the state of residence. Nevertheless, economists Robert Barro and Charles Redlick of Harvard University have calculated an "average marginal income tax rate" faced by a typical U.S. resident. In 1920, this rate, which then was simply the marginal federal income tax rate faced by an average individual, was just below 5 percent. Today, in addition to a marginal federal income tax rate of nearly 22 percent, the typical U.S. resident also pays a marginal state income tax rate of about 4 percent and a combined marginal Social Security and Medicare income tax rate exceeding 9 percent. Thus, the current average marginal income tax rate in the United States is nearly 36 percent.

FOR CRITICAL ANALYSIS

How will a recent increase in the Medicare tax rate for individuals earning more than $200,000 per year affect the average marginal income tax rate?

Taxation Systems

No matter how governments raise revenues—from income taxes, sales taxes, or other taxes—all of those taxes fit into one of three types of taxation systems: proportional, progressive, or regressive, according to the relationship between the tax rate and income. To determine whether a tax system is proportional, progressive, or regressive, we simply ask, What is the relationship between the average tax rate and the marginal tax rate?

Proportional taxation
A tax system in which, regardless of an individual's income, the tax bill comprises exactly the same proportion.

PROPORTIONAL TAXATION **Proportional taxation** means that regardless of an individual's income, taxes comprise exactly the same proportion. In a proportional taxation system, the marginal tax rate is always equal to the average tax rate. If every dollar is taxed at 20 percent, then the average tax rate is 20 percent, and so is the marginal tax rate.

Go to **www.econtoday.com/ch06** to learn from the National Center for Policy Analysis about what distinguishes recent flat tax proposals from a truly proportional income tax system. Click on "Flat Tax Proposals."

Under a proportional system of taxation, taxpayers at all income levels end up paying the same *percentage* of their income in taxes. With a proportional tax rate of 20 percent, an individual with an income of $10,000 pays $2,000 in taxes, while an individual making $100,000 pays $20,000. Thus, the identical 20 percent rate is levied on both taxpayers.

Progressive taxation
A tax system in which, as income increases, a higher percentage of the additional income is paid as taxes. The marginal tax rate exceeds the average tax rate as income rises.

PROGRESSIVE TAXATION Under **progressive taxation,** as a person's taxable income increases, the percentage of income paid in taxes increases. In a progressive system, the marginal tax rate is above the average tax rate. If you are taxed 5 percent on the first $10,000 you earn, 10 percent on the next $10,000 you earn, and 30 percent on the last $10,000 you earn, you face a progressive income tax system. Your marginal tax rate is always above your average tax rate.

Regressive taxation
A tax system in which as more dollars are earned, the percentage of tax paid on them falls. The marginal tax rate is less than the average tax rate as income rises.

REGRESSIVE TAXATION With **regressive taxation,** a smaller percentage of taxable income is taken in taxes as taxable income increases. The marginal rate is *below* the average rate. As income increases, the marginal tax rate falls, and so does the average tax rate. The U.S. Social Security tax is regressive. Once the legislative maximum taxable wage base is reached, no further Social Security taxes are paid. Consider a simplified hypothetical example: Suppose that every dollar up to $100,000 is taxed at 10 percent. After $100,000 there is no Social Security tax. Someone making $200,000 still pays only $10,000 in Social Security taxes. That person's average Social Security tax is 5 percent. The person making $100,000, by contrast, effectively pays 10 percent. The person making $1 million faces an average Social Security tax rate of only 1 percent in our simplified example.

QUICK QUIZ See page 138 for the answers. Review concepts from this section in MyEconLab.

Governments collect taxes by applying a tax __________ to a tax __________, which refers to the value of goods, services, wealth, or incomes. Income tax rates are applied to tax brackets, which are ranges of income over which the tax rate is constant.

The __________ tax rate is the total tax payment divided by total income, and the __________ tax rate is the change in the tax payment divided by the change in income.

Tax systems can be __________, __________, or __________, depending on whether the marginal tax rate is the same as, greater than, or less than the average tax rate as income rises.

The Most Important Federal Taxes

What types of taxes do federal, state, and local governments collect? The two pie charts in Figure 6-1 below show the percentages of receipts from various taxes obtained by the federal government and by state and local governments. For the federal government, key taxes are individual income taxes, corporate income taxes, Social Security taxes, and excise taxes on items such as gasoline and alcoholic beverages. For state and local governments, sales taxes, property taxes, and personal and corporate income taxes are the main types of taxes.

The Federal Personal Income Tax

The most important tax in the U.S. economy is the federal personal income tax, which, as Figure 6-1 indicates, accounts for almost 44 percent of all federal revenues. All U.S. citizens, resident aliens, and most others who earn income in the United States are required to pay federal income taxes on all taxable income, including income earned abroad.

FIGURE 6-1 Sources of Government Tax Receipts

As panel (a) shows, about 92 percent of federal revenues comes from income and Social Security and other social insurance taxes. State government revenues, shown in panel (b), are spread more evenly across sources, with less emphasis on taxes based on individual income.

Source: U.S. Department of Commerce, Bureau of Economic Analysis.

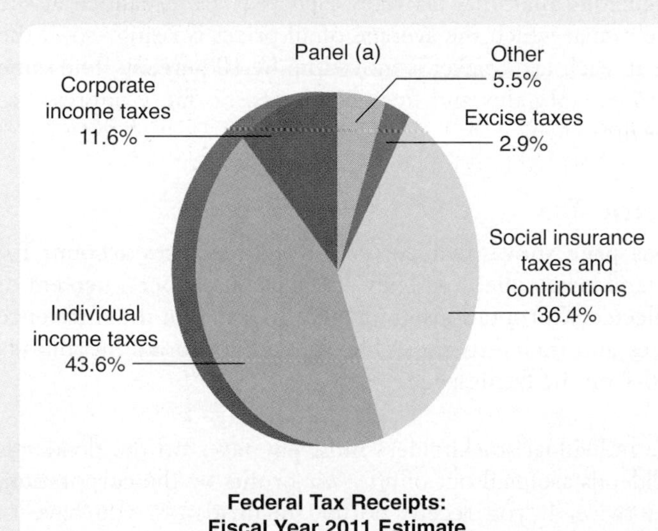

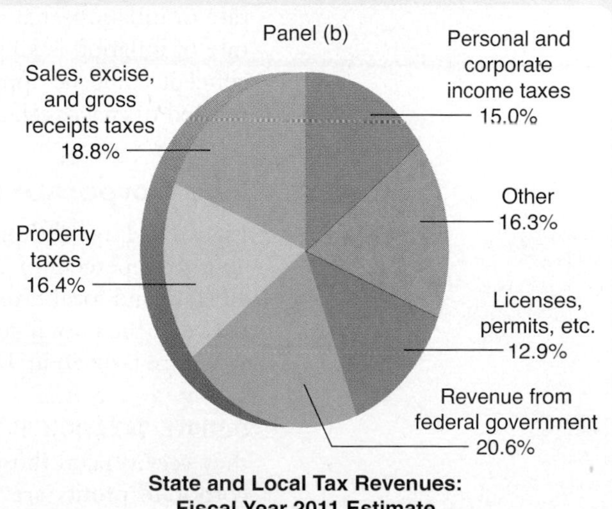

TABLE 6-1

Federal Marginal Income Tax Rates

These rates applied in 2010.

Single Persons		Married Couples	
Marginal Tax Bracket	Marginal Tax Rate	Marginal Tax Bracket	Marginal Tax Rate
$0–$8,375	10%	$0–$16,750	10%
$8,376–$34,000	15%	$16,751–$68,000	15%
$34,001–$82,400	25%	$68,001–$137,300	25%
$82,401–$171,850	28%	$137,301–$209,250	28%
$171,851–$373,650	33%	$209,251–$373,650	33%
$373,651 and up	35%	$373,651 and up	35%

Source: U.S. Department of the Treasury.

The rates that are paid rise as income increases, as can be seen in Table 6-1 above. Marginal income tax rates at the federal level have ranged from as low as 1 percent after the 1913 passage of the Sixteenth Amendment, which made the individual income tax constitutional, to as high as 94 percent (reached in 1944). There were 14 separate tax brackets prior to the Tax Reform Act of 1986, which reduced the number to three (now six, as shown in Table 6-1).

The Treatment of Capital Gains

Capital gain
A positive difference between the purchase price and the sale price of an asset. If a share of stock is bought for $5 and then sold for $15, the capital gain is $10.

Capital loss
A negative difference between the purchase price and the sale price of an asset.

The difference between the purchase price and sale price of an asset, such as a share of stock or a plot of land, is called a **capital gain** if it is a profit and a **capital loss** if it is not. The federal government taxes capital gains, and as of 2011, there were several capital gains tax rates.

What appear to be capital gains are not always real gains. If you pay $100,000 for a financial asset in one year and sell it for 50 percent more 10 years later, your nominal capital gain is $50,000. But what if during those 10 years inflation has driven average asset prices up by 50 percent? Your *real* capital gain would be zero, but you would still have to pay taxes on that $50,000. To counter this problem, many economists have argued that capital gains should be indexed to the rate of inflation. This is exactly what is done with the marginal tax brackets in the federal income tax code. Tax brackets for the purposes of calculating marginal tax rates each year are expanded at the rate of inflation, that is, the rate at which the average of all prices is rising. So, if the rate of inflation is 10 percent, each tax bracket is moved up by 10 percent. The same concept could be applied to capital gains and financial assets. So far, Congress has refused to enact such a measure.

The Corporate Income Tax

Figure 6-1 on the previous page shows that corporate income taxes account for almost 12 percent of all federal taxes collected. They also make up about 2 percent of all state and local taxes collected. Corporations are generally taxed on the difference between their total revenues and their expenses. The federal corporate income tax structure is given in Table 6-2 on the facing page.

DOUBLE TAXATION Because individual stockholders must pay taxes on the dividends they receive, and those dividends are paid out of *after-tax* profits by the corporation, corporate profits are taxed twice. If you receive $1,000 in dividends, you have to declare them as income, and you must normally pay taxes on them. Before the corporation was able to pay you those dividends, it had to pay taxes on all its profits, including any that it put back into the company or did not distribute in the form of dividends.

TABLE 6-2

Federal Corporate Income Tax Schedule

These corporate tax rates were in effect through 2011.

Corporate Taxable Income	Corporate Tax Rate
$0–$50,000	15%
$50,001–$75,000	25%
$75,001–$100,000	34%
$100,001–$335,000	39%
$335,001–$10,000,000	34%
$10,000,001–$15,000,000	35%
$15,000,001–$18,333,333	38%
$18,333,334 and up	35%

Source: Internal Revenue Service.

Eventually, the new investment made possible by those **retained earnings**—profits not given out to stockholders—along with borrowed funds will be reflected in the value of the stock in that company. When you sell your stock in that company, you will have to pay taxes on the difference between what you paid for the stock and what you sold it for. In both cases, dividends and retained earnings (corporate profits) are taxed twice. In 2003, Congress reduced the double taxation effect somewhat by enacting legislation that allowed most dividends to be taxed at lower rates than are applied to regular income through 2010.

Retained earnings
Earnings that a corporation saves, or retains, for investment in other productive activities; earnings that are not distributed to stockholders.

WHO REALLY PAYS THE CORPORATE INCOME TAX? Corporations can function only as long as consumers buy their products, employees make their goods, stockholders (owners) buy their shares, and bondholders buy their bonds. Corporations per se do not do anything. We must ask, then, who really pays the tax on corporate income? This is a question of **tax incidence.** (The question of tax incidence applies to all taxes, including sales taxes and Social Security taxes.) The incidence of corporate taxation is the subject of considerable debate. Some economists suggest that corporations pass their tax burdens on to consumers by charging higher prices. Other economists argue that it is the stockholders who bear most of the tax. Still others contend that employees pay at least part of the tax by receiving lower wages than they would otherwise. Because the debate is not yet settled, we will not hazard a guess here as to what the correct conclusion may be. Suffice it to say that you should be cautious when you advocate increasing corporation income taxes. *People*, whether owners, consumers, or workers, end up paying all of the increase—just as they pay all of any tax.

Tax incidence
The distribution of tax burdens among various groups in society.

Social Security and Unemployment Taxes

Each year, taxes levied on payrolls account for an increasing percentage of federal tax receipts. These taxes, which are distinct from personal income taxes, are for Social Security, retirement, survivors' disability, and old-age medical benefits (Medicare). Today, the Social Security tax is imposed on earnings up to roughly $106,800 at a rate of 6.2 percent on employers and 6.2 percent on employees. That is, the employer matches your "contribution" to Social Security. (The employer's contribution is really paid by the employees, at least in part, in the form of a reduced wage rate.) As Chapter 5 explained, a Medicare tax is imposed on all wage earnings at a combined rate of 2.9 percent. The 2010 federal health care law also added a 3.8 percent Medicare tax on annual incomes above $200,000.

Social Security taxes came into existence when the Federal Insurance Contributions Act (FICA) was passed in 1935. At that time, many more people paid into the Social Security program than the number who received benefits. Currently, however, older people drawing benefits make up a much larger share of the population. Consequently, at some point within the next few years, the outflow of Social Security benefit payments will begin exceeding the inflow of Social Security taxes. Various economists have advanced proposals to raise Social Security tax rates on younger workers or to reduce benefit payouts to older retirees and disabled individuals receiving Social Security payments. So far, however, the federal government has failed to address Social Security's deteriorating funding situation.

There is also a federal unemployment tax, which helps pay for unemployment insurance. This tax rate is 0.8 percent on the first $7,000 of annual wages of each employee who earns more than $1,500. Only the employer makes this tax payment. This tax covers the costs of the unemployment insurance system. In addition to this federal tax, some states with an unemployment system impose their own tax of up to about 3 percent, depending on the past record of the particular employer. An employer who frequently lays off workers typically will have a slightly higher state unemployment tax rate than an employer who never lays off workers.

QUICK QUIZ See page 138 for the answers. Review concepts from this section in MyEconLab.

The federal government raises most of its revenues through __________ taxes and social insurance taxes and contributions, and state and local governments raise most of their tax revenues from __________ taxes, __________ taxes, and income taxes.

Because corporations must first pay an income tax on most earnings, the personal income tax shareholders pay on dividends received (or realized capital gains) constitutes __________ taxation.

Both employers and employees must pay __________ __________ taxes and contributions at rates of 6.2 percent on roughly the first $106,800 in wage earnings, and a 2.9 percent __________ tax rate is applied to all wage earnings. The federal government and some state governments also assess taxes to pay for __________ insurance systems.

Tax Rates and Tax Revenues

For most state and local governments, income taxes yield fewer revenues than taxes imposed on sales of goods and services. Figure 6-1 on page 125 shows that sales taxes, gross receipts taxes, and excise taxes generate almost one-fifth of the total funds available to state and local governments. Thus, from the perspective of many state and local governments, a fundamental issue is how to set tax rates on sales of goods and services to extract desired total tax payments.

Sales Taxes

Sales taxes
Taxes assessed on the prices paid on most goods and services.

***Ad valorem* taxation**
Assessing taxes by charging a tax rate equal to a fraction of the market price of each unit purchased.

Governments levy **sales taxes** on the prices that consumers pay to purchase each unit of a broad range of goods and services. Sellers collect sales taxes and transmit them to the government. Sales taxes are a form of ***ad valorem* taxation,** which means that the tax is applied "to the value" of the good. Thus, a government using a system of *ad valorem* taxation charges a tax rate equal to a fraction of the market price of each unit that a consumer buys. For instance, if the tax rate is 8 percent and the market price of an item is $100, then the amount of the tax on the item is $8.

A sales tax is therefore a proportional tax. The total amount of sales taxes a government collects equals the sales tax rate times the sales tax base, which is the market value of total purchases.

Static Tax Analysis

Static tax analysis
Economic evaluation of the effects of tax rate changes under the assumption that there is no effect on the tax base, meaning that there is an unambiguous positive relationship between tax rates and tax revenues.

There are two approaches to evaluating how changes in tax rates affect government tax collections. **Static tax analysis** assumes that changes in the tax rate have no effect on the tax base. Thus, this approach implies that if a state government desires to increase its sales tax collections, it can simply raise the tax rate. Multiplying the higher tax rate by the tax base thereby produces higher tax revenues.

Governments often rely on static tax analysis. Sometimes this yields unpleasant surprises. Consider, for instance, what happened in 1992 when Congress implemented a federal "luxury tax" on purchases of new pleasure boats priced at $100,000 or more. Applying the 10 percent luxury tax rate to the anticipated tax base—sales of new boats during previous years—produced a forecast of hundreds of millions of dollars in revenues from the luxury tax. What actually happened, however, was an 80 percent plunge in sales of new luxury boats. People postponed boat purchases or bought used boats instead. Consequently, the tax base all but disappeared, and the federal government collected only a few tens of millions of dollars in taxes on boat sales. Congress repealed the tax a year later.

Dynamic Tax Analysis

The problem with static tax analysis is that it ignores incentive effects created by new taxes or hikes in existing tax rates. According to **dynamic tax analysis,** a likely response to an increase in a tax rate is a *decrease* in the tax base. When a government pushes up its sales tax rate, for example, consumers have an incentive to cut back on their purchases of goods and services subjected to the higher rate, perhaps by buying them in a locale where there is a lower sales tax rate or perhaps no tax rate at all. As shown in Figure 6-2, the maximum sales tax rate varies considerably from state to state.

Dynamic tax analysis
Economic evaluation of tax rate changes that recognizes that the tax base eventually declines with ever-higher tax rates, so that tax revenues may eventually decline if the tax rate is raised sufficiently.

Consider someone who lives in a state bordering Oregon. In such a border state, the sales tax rate can be as high as 8 percent, so a resident of that state has a strong incentive to buy higher-priced goods and services in Oregon, where there is no sales tax. Someone who lives in a high-tax county in Alabama has an incentive to buy an item online from an out-of-state firm to avoid paying sales taxes. Such shifts in expenditures in response to higher relative tax rates will reduce a state's sales tax base and thereby result in lower sales tax collections than the levels predicted by static tax analysis.

Dynamic tax analysis recognizes that increasing the tax rate could actually cause the government's total tax collections to *decline* if a sufficiently large number of consumers react to the higher sales tax rate by cutting back on purchases of goods and services included in the state's tax base. Some residents who live close to other states with lower sales tax rates might, for instance, drive across the state line to do more of their shopping. Other residents might place more orders with catalog companies or online firms located in other legal jurisdictions where their state's sales tax does not apply.

FIGURE 6-2 States with the Highest and Lowest Sales Tax Rates

A number of states allow counties and cities to collect their own sales taxes in addition to state sales taxes. This figure shows the maximum sales tax rates for selected states, including county and municipal taxes. Delaware, Montana, New Hampshire, and Oregon have no sales taxes. All other states besides those in the figure and the District of Columbia have maximum sales tax rates between the 4 percent rate of Hawaii and the 9.875 percent rate in Arkansas.

Source: U.S. Department of Commerce.

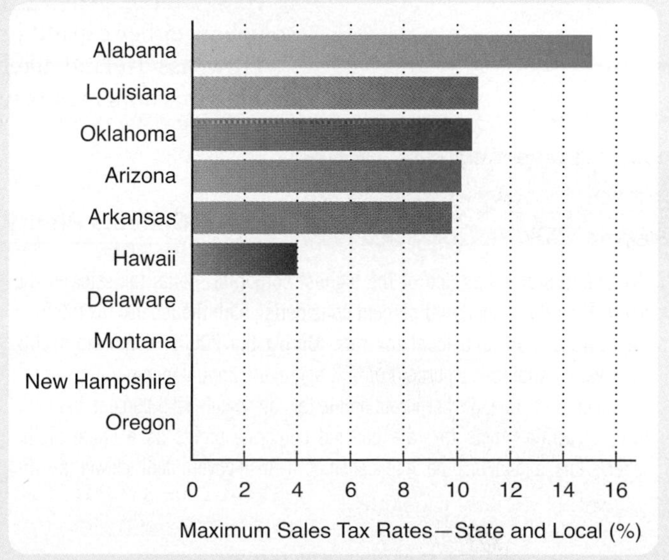

Why Not . . . **follow the example of states such as Maryland by creating a "millionaires" tax bracket with extra-high tax rates applied to incomes exceeding $1 million per year?**

The year after Maryland established a special millionaires tax bracket with a combined state and city tax rate of almost 10 percent, more than one-third of all the millionaires disappeared from the state's tax rolls. Many of those earning annual incomes exceeding $1 million who had paid income taxes to Maryland the previous year already owned second homes in other states, such as Florida or South Carolina. A number of these individuals responded to Maryland's creation of the millionaires tax bracket by switching their formal residences to these or other lower-tax states, thereby ceasing to be Maryland residents for income tax purposes. Thus, instead of collecting a predicted additional $106 million of income taxes following the establishment of the millionaires tax bracket, Maryland received almost $100 million per year *less* in taxes from people who earned annual incomes above $1 million.

Maximizing Tax Revenues

Dynamic tax analysis indicates that whether a government's tax revenues ultimately rise or fall in response to a tax rate increase depends on exactly how much the tax base declines in response to the higher tax rate. On the one hand, the tax base may decline by a relatively small amount following an increase in the tax rate, or perhaps even imperceptibly, so that tax revenues rise. For instance, in the situation we imagine a government facing in Figure 6-3 on the facing page, a rise in the tax rate from 5 percent to 6 percent causes tax revenues to increase. Along this range, static tax analysis can provide a good approximation of the revenue effects of an increase in the tax rate. On the other hand, the tax base may decline so much that total tax revenues decrease. In Figure 6-3, for example, increasing the tax rate from 6 percent to 7 percent causes tax revenues to *decline*.

What is most likely is that when the tax rate is already relatively low, increasing the tax rate causes relatively small declines in the tax base. Within a range of relatively low sales tax rates, therefore, increasing the tax rate generates higher sales tax revenues, as illustrated along the upward-sloping portion of the curve depicted in Figure 6-3. If the government continues to push up the tax rate, however, people increasingly have an incentive to find ways to avoid purchasing taxable goods and services. Eventually, the tax base decreases sufficiently that the government's tax collections decline with ever-higher tax rates.

Consequently, governments that wish to maximize their tax revenues should not necessarily assess a high tax rate. In the situation illustrated in Figure 6-3, the government maximizes its tax revenues at T_{max} by establishing a sales tax rate of 6 percent. If the government were to raise the rate above 6 percent, it would induce a sufficient decline in the tax base that its tax collections would decline. If the government wishes to collect more than T_{max} in revenues to fund various government programs, it must somehow either expand its sales tax base or develop another tax.

How has Ireland likely come closer than the United States to establishing a revenue-maximizing tax rate on corporate profits?

INTERNATIONAL POLICY EXAMPLE

Ireland Collects Plenty of Corporate Taxes with a Low Rate

The United States has one of the highest corporate profits tax rates in the world. The rate is nearly 40 percent considering both the federal tax rate and the average state and local tax rate. During the 2000s, corporate profits taxes were equal to 2.1 percent of U.S. aggregate annual income.

In contrast, Ireland's corporate profits tax rate is only 12.5 percent. Ireland's lower corporate profits tax rate boosted corporate profits as a share of the nation's total annual income. Application of the Irish government's lower tax rate to this larger share of national income yielded higher tax revenues. As a consequence, during the 2000s, the Irish government collected an amount of corporate profits taxes equal to 3.6 percent of Ireland's aggregate annual income.

FOR CRITICAL ANALYSIS

Why can reducing instead of increasing a tax rate sometimes maximize a government's tax revenues?

FIGURE 6-3 Maximizing the Government's Sales Tax Revenues

Dynamic tax analysis predicts that ever-higher tax rates bring about declines in the tax base, so that at sufficiently high tax rates the government's tax revenues begin to fall off. This implies that there is a tax rate, 6 percent in this example, at which the government can collect the maximum possible revenues, T_{max}.

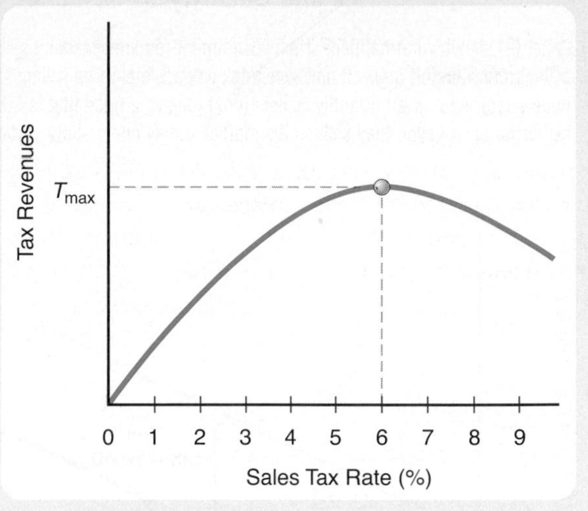

QUICK QUIZ See page 138 for the answers. Review concepts from this section in MyEconLab.

The __________ view of the relationship between tax rates and tax revenues implies that higher tax rates always generate increased government tax collections.

According to __________ tax analysis, higher tax rates cause the tax base to decrease. Tax collections will rise less than predicted by __________ tax analysis.

Dynamic tax analysis indicates that there is a tax rate that maximizes the government's tax collections. Setting the tax rate any higher would cause the tax base to __________ sufficiently that the government's tax revenues will __________.

Taxation from the Point of View of Producers and Consumers

Governments collect taxes on product sales at the source. They require producers to charge these taxes when they sell their output. This means that taxes on sales of goods and services affect market prices and quantities. Let's consider why this is so.

Taxes and the Market Supply Curve

Imposing taxes on final sales of a good or service affects the position of the market supply curve. To see why, consider panel (a) of Figure 6-4 on the next page, which shows a gasoline market supply curve S_1 in the absence of taxation. At a price of $3.35 per gallon, gasoline producers are willing and able to supply 180,000 gallons of gasoline per week. If the price increases to $3.45 per gallon, firms increase production to 200,000 gallons of gasoline per week.

Both federal and state governments assess **excise taxes**—taxes on sales of particular commodities—on sales of gasoline. They levy gasoline excise taxes as a **unit tax,** or a constant tax per unit sold. On average, combined federal and state excise taxes on gasoline are about $0.40 per gallon.

Excise tax
A tax levied on purchases of a particular good or service.

Unit tax
A constant tax assessed on each unit of a good that consumers purchase.

Let's suppose, therefore, that a gasoline producer must transmit a total of $0.40 per gallon to federal and state governments for each gallon sold. Producers must continue to receive a net amount of $3.35 per gallon to induce them to supply 180,000 gallons each week, so they must now receive $3.75 per gallon to supply that weekly quantity. Likewise, gasoline producers now will be willing to supply 200,000 gallons each week only if they receive $0.40 more per gallon, or a total amount of $3.85 per gallon.

FIGURE 6-4 The Effects of Excise Taxes on the Market Supply and Equilibrium Price and Quantity of Gasoline

Panel (a) shows what happens if the government requires gasoline sellers to collect and transmit a $0.40 unit excise tax on gasoline. To be willing to continue supplying a given quantity, sellers must receive a price that is $0.40 higher for each gallon they sell, so the market supply curve shifts vertically by the amount of the tax. As illustrated in panel (b), this decline in market supply causes a reduction in the equilibrium quantity of gasoline produced and purchased. It also causes a rise in the market clearing price, to $3.75, so that consumers pay part of the tax. Sellers pay the rest in lower profits.

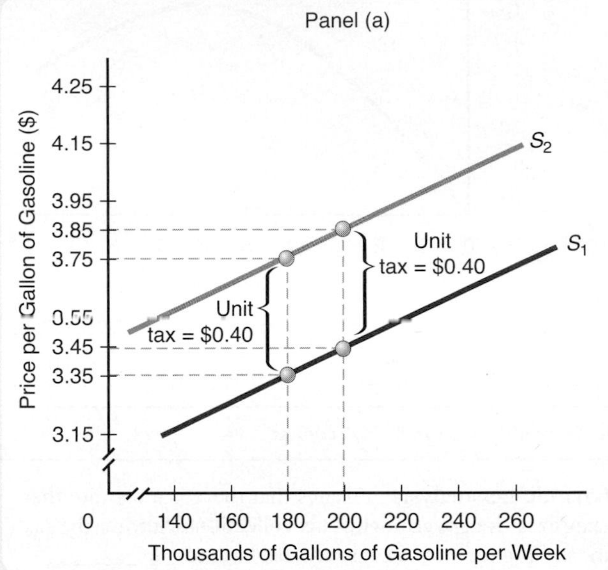

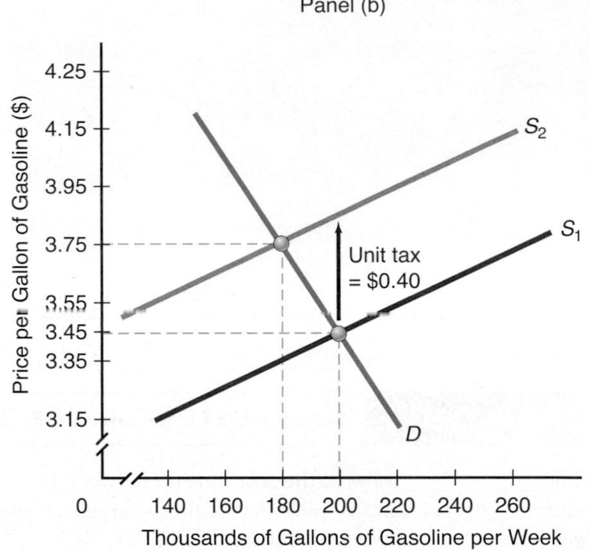

As you can see, imposing the combined $0.40 per gallon excise taxes on gasoline shifts the supply curve vertically by exactly that amount to S_2 in panel (a). Thus, the effect of levying excise taxes on gasoline is to shift the supply curve vertically by the total per-unit taxes levied on gasoline sales. Hence, there is a decrease in supply. (In the case of an *ad valorem* sales tax, the supply curve would shift vertically by a proportionate amount equal to the tax rate.)

How Taxes Affect the Market Price and Equilibrium Quantity

Panel (b) of Figure 6-4 above shows how imposing $0.40 per gallon in excise taxes affects the market price of gasoline and the equilibrium quantity of gasoline produced and sold. In the absence of excise taxes, the market supply curve S_1 crosses the demand curve D at a market price of $3.45 per gallon. At this market price, the equilibrium quantity of gasoline is 200,000 gallons of gasoline per week.

The excise tax levy of $0.40 per gallon shifts the supply curve to S_2. At the original $3.45 per gallon price, there is now an excess quantity of gasoline demanded, so the market price of gasoline rises to $3.75 per gallon. At this market price, the equilibrium quantity of gasoline produced and consumed each week is 180,000 gallons.

What factors determine how much the equilibrium quantity of a good or service declines in response to taxation? The answer to this question depends on how responsive quantities demanded and supplied are to changes in price.

Who Pays the Tax?

In our example, imposing excise taxes of $0.40 per gallon of gasoline causes the market price to rise to $3.75 per gallon from $3.45 per gallon. Thus, the price that each consumer pays is $0.30 per gallon higher. Consumers pay three-fourths of the excise tax levied on each gallon of gasoline produced and sold in our example.

Gasoline producers must pay the rest of the tax. Their profits decline by $0.10 per gallon because costs have increased by $0.40 per gallon while consumers pay $0.30 more per gallon.

In the gasoline market, as in other markets for products subject to excise taxes and other taxes on sales, the shapes of the market demand and supply curves determine who pays most of a tax. The reason is that the shapes of these curves reflect the responsiveness to price changes of the quantity demanded by consumers and of the quantity supplied by producers.

In the example illustrated in Figure 6-4 on the facing page, the fact that consumers pay most of the excise taxes levied on gasoline reflects a relatively low responsiveness of quantity demanded by consumers to a change in the price of gasoline. Consumers pay most of the excise taxes on each gallon produced and sold because in this example the amount of gasoline they desire to purchase is relatively (but not completely) unresponsive to a change in the market price induced by excise taxes.

QUICK QUIZ See page 138 for the answers. **Review concepts from this section in MyEconLab.**

When the government levies a tax on sales of a particular product, firms must receive a higher price to continue supplying the same quantity as before, so the supply curve shifts __________. If the tax is a unit excise tax, the supply curve shifts __________ by the amount of the tax.

Imposing a tax on sales of an item __________ the equilibrium quantity produced and consumed and __________ the market price.

When a government assesses a unit excise tax, the market price of the good or service typically rises by an amount __________ than the per-unit tax. Hence, consumers pay a portion of the tax, and firms pay the remainder.

You Are There

A Business Owner Responds to a Marginal Tax Rate Increase

Wendell Gibby, M.D., is a Utah physician who owns a small company that produces medical imaging software. Since its inception in the 1980s, the firm has earned millions of dollars in revenues. It employs more than 100 people and exports its products worldwide. To hold down expenses so that he can reinvest more funds into the business, Dr. Gibby drives a 1998 sport utility vehicle with more than 200,000 miles on its odometer. Nevertheless, as the owner of a small business, Dr. Gibby is facing an increase in his marginal income tax rate from a little above 40 percent to well over 50 percent.

Dr. Gibby knows that if the higher income tax rate had been in force when he founded his software firm, he would have chosen not to do so. He has decided that he will continue to operate his business in the face of the higher marginal income tax rate, but he will scale back his plans for expansion. Indeed, in the near term he will reduce production and eliminate a few jobs. The resulting reduction in sales will generate lower income for Dr. Gibby, and the result also will be less income for the government to tax.

Critical Analysis Questions

1. Is Dr. Gibby's response to a higher marginal tax rate consistent with the prediction of static tax analysis or dynamic tax analysis?
2. With respect to Dr. Gibby's company only, does it seem likely that the government set the income tax rate at a tax-revenue-maximizing level? Explain your reasoning.

ISSUES & APPLICATIONS

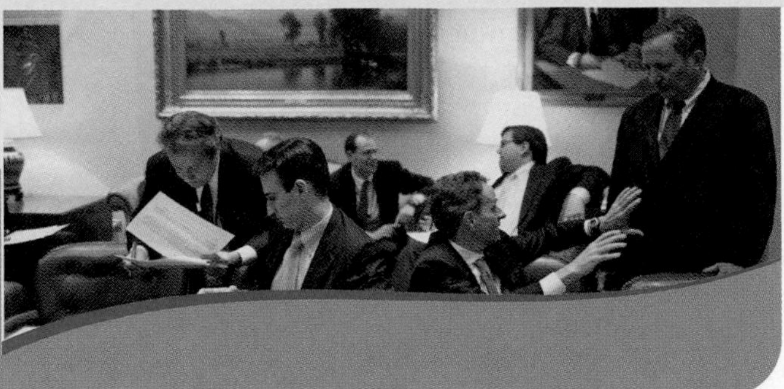

Raising Capital Gains Tax Rates Shrinks the Tax Base

CONCEPTS APPLIED

- Capital Gains
- Tax Base
- Static versus Dynamic Tax Analysis

In recent years, presidential candidates and other politicians have sparred over whether to change tax rates on capital gains. Some have suggested reducing capital gains tax rates in hopes of stimulating more business activity, but others have argued for raising tax rates on capital gains to boost federal tax collections.

Static Analysis of Capital Gains Taxes

According to policymakers pressing for a higher tax rate on capital gains, enacting this policy would generate more federal tax revenues. After all, they argue, the higher tax rates must lead to higher tax revenue.

This perspective, of course, depends on static tax analysis. This analysis assumes that taxable capital gains will remain unaltered if tax rates increase.

Dynamic Analysis of Capital Gains Taxes

According to dynamic tax analysis, collections of capital gains taxes would increase following an increase in tax rates on capital gains only if realized capital gains do not shrink significantly in response. Unfortunately for proponents of higher tax rates on capital gains, however, people who own assets have considerable discretion over when to sell them and realize capital gains that will be taxed. The capital gains tax base, therefore, is likely to be particularly responsive to changes in tax rates.

Figure 6-5 on the facing page illustrates just how responsive the capital gains tax base has been to changes in tax rates on capital gains since the early 1960s. Decreases in realized capital gains are closely associated with increases in capital gains tax rates. Thus, higher tax rates on capital gains induce people to respond by choosing *not* to realize these gains, thereby shrinking the capital gains tax base.

For Critical Analysis

1. Why would actual revenue gains from raising tax rates on capital gains likely be much lower than predicted by static tax analysis?
2. Is it possible that raising tax rates on capital gains could lead to a reduction in collected capital gains taxes? Explain briefly.

Web Resources

1. To see a Congressional Budget Office analysis of the relationship between tax rates on capital gains and collected tax revenues prior to the 1990s, go to www.econtoday.com/ch06.
2. For an evaluation of possible effects of proposed increases in the capital gains tax rates in the 2010s, go to www.econtoday.com/ch06.

Research Project

Proponents of cutting tax rates on capital gains suggest that tax revenues collected on realized capital gains likely would not drop very much as a consequence and even could increase. Evaluate this position.

For more questions on this chapter's Issues & Applications, go to **MyEconLab**. In the Study Plan for this chapter, select Section N: News.

FIGURE 6-5 **Capital Gains Tax Rates and Realized Capital Gains as a Percentage of Aggregate U.S. National Income**

Since the early 1960s, realized capital gains have been inversely related to the top federal tax rate on capital gains.

Source: U.S. Treasury Department.

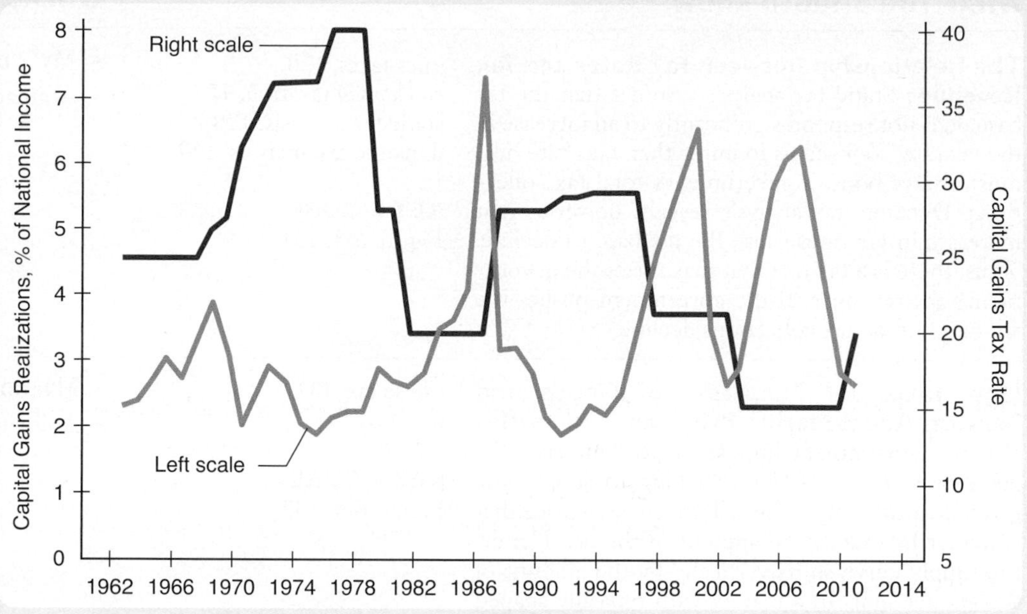

Here is what you should know after reading this chapter. **MyEconLab** will help you identify what you know, and where to go when you need to practice.

WHAT YOU SHOULD KNOW		WHERE TO GO TO PRACTICE
Average Tax Rates versus Marginal Tax Rates The average tax rate is the ratio of total tax payments to total income. In contrast, the marginal tax rate is the change in tax payments induced by a change in total taxable income. Thus, the marginal tax rate applies to the last dollar that a person earns.	government budget constraint, 122 tax base, 123 tax rate, 123 marginal tax rate, 123 tax bracket, 123 average tax rate, 123	• **MyEconLab** Study Plans 6.1, 6.2 • Audio introduction to Chapter 6 • Video: Types of Tax Systems • ABC News Video: Big Government: Who Is Going to Pay the Bill?
The U.S. Income Tax System The U.S. income tax system assesses taxes against both personal and business income. It is designed to be a progressive tax system, in which the marginal tax rate increases as income rises, so that the marginal tax rate exceeds the average tax rate. This contrasts with a regressive tax system, in which higher-income people pay lower marginal tax rates, resulting in a marginal tax rate that is less than the average tax rate. The marginal tax rate equals the average tax rate only under proportional taxation, in which the marginal tax rate does not vary with income.	proportional taxation, 124 progressive taxation, 124 regressive taxation, 124 capital gain, 126 capital loss, 126 retained earnings, 127 tax incidence, 127	• **MyEconLab** Study Plan 6.3 • Video: The Corporate Income Tax

(continued)

MyEconLab continued

WHAT YOU SHOULD KNOW		WHERE TO GO TO PRACTICE
The Relationship Between Tax Rates and Tax Revenues Static tax analysis assumes that the tax base does not respond significantly to an increase in the tax rate, so it seems to imply that a tax rate hike must always boost a government's total tax collections. Dynamic tax analysis reveals, however, that increases in tax rates cause the tax base to decline. Thus, there is a tax rate that maximizes the government's tax revenues. If the government pushes the tax rate higher, tax collections decline.	sales taxes, 128 *ad valorem* taxation, 128 static tax analysis, 128 dynamic tax analysis, 129 **KEY FIGURE** Figure 6-3, 131	• **MyEconLab** Study Plan 6.4 • Animated Figure 6-3
How Taxes on Purchases of Goods and Services Affect Market Prices and Quantities When a government imposes a per-unit tax on a good or service, a seller is willing to supply any given quantity only if the seller receives a price that is higher by exactly the amount of the tax. Hence, the supply curve shifts vertically by the amount of the tax per unit. In a market with typically shaped demand and supply curves, this results in a fall in the equilibrium quantity and an increase in the market price. To the extent that the market price rises, consumers pay a portion of the tax on each unit they buy. Sellers pay the remainder in lower profits.	excise tax, 131 unit tax, 131 **KEY FIGURE** Figure 6-4, 132	• **MyEconLab** Study Plan 6.5 • Animated Figure 6-4

Log in to MyEconLab, take a chapter test, and get a personalized Study Plan that tells you which concepts you understand and which ones you need to review. From there, MyEconLab will give you further practice, tutorials, animations, videos, and guided solutions.
Log in to www.myeconlab.com

PROBLEMS

All problems are assignable in myeconlab. *Answers to odd-numbered problems appear at the back of the book.*

6-1. A senior citizen gets a part-time job at a fast-food restaurant. She earns $8 per hour for each hour she works, and she works exactly 25 hours per week. Thus, her total pretax weekly income is $200. Her total income tax assessment each week is $40, but she has determined that she is assessed $3 in taxes for the final hour she works each week.

a. What is this person's average tax rate each week?

b. What is the marginal tax rate for the last hour she works each week?

6-2. For purposes of assessing income taxes, there are three official income levels for workers in a small country: high, medium, and low. For the last hour on the job during a 40-hour workweek, a high-income worker pays a marginal income tax rate of 15 percent, a medium-income worker pays a marginal tax rate of 20 percent, and a low-income worker is assessed a 25 percent marginal income tax rate. Based only on this information, does this nation's income tax system appear to be progressive, proportional, or regressive?

6-3. Suppose that a state has increased its sales tax rate every other year since 2003. Assume that the state collected all sales taxes that residents legally owed. The table on the facing page summarizes its experience. What were total taxable sales in this state during each year displayed in the table?

Year	Sales Tax Rate	Sales Tax Collections
2003	0.03 (3 percent)	$9.0 million
2005	0.04 (4 percent)	$14.0 million
2007	0.05 (5 percent)	$20.0 million
2009	0.06 (6 percent)	$24.0 million
2011	0.07 (7 percent)	$29.4 million

6-4. The sales tax rate applied to all purchases within a state was 0.04 (4 percent) throughout 2010 but increased to 0.05 (5 percent) during all of 2011. The state government collected all taxes due, but its tax revenues were equal to $40 million each year. What happened to the sales tax base between 2010 and 2011? What could account for this result?

6-5. A city government imposes a proportional income tax on all people who earn income within its city limits. In 2010, the city's income tax rate was 0.05 (5 percent), and it collected $20 million in income taxes. In 2011, it raised the income tax rate to 0.06 (6 percent), and its income tax collections declined to $19.2 million. What happened to the city's income tax base between 2010 and 2011? How could this have occurred?

6-6. An obscure subsidiary of Microsoft Corporation, Ireland-based Round Island One Limited, has only about 1,000 employees. Nevertheless, Microsoft has gradually been shifting more income-generating activities to Ireland, which has a lower corporate tax rate than nations such as the United States and the United Kingdom. In one year alone, shifting more of its operations to Ireland allowed Microsoft to reduce its worldwide corporate income tax rate by 6 percentage points. What happened to Ireland's tax base as a result? What happened to tax bases in nations such as the United States and the United Kingdom?

6-7. The British government recently imposed a unit excise tax of about $154 per ticket on airline tickets applying to flights to or from London airports. In answering the following questions, assume normally shaped demand and supply curves.

a. Use an appropriate diagram to predict effects of the ticket tax on the market clearing price of London airline tickets and on the equilibrium number of flights into and out of London.

b. What do you predict is likely to happen to the equilibrium price of tickets for air flights into and out of cities that are in close proximity to London but are not subject to the new ticket tax? Explain your reasoning.

6-8. To raise funds aimed at providing more support for public schools, a state government has just imposed a unit excise tax equal to $4 for each monthly unit of wireless phone services sold by each company operating in the state. The following diagram depicts the positions of the demand and supply curves for wireless phone services *before* the unit excise tax was imposed. Use this diagram to determine the position of the new market supply curve now that the tax hike has gone into effect.

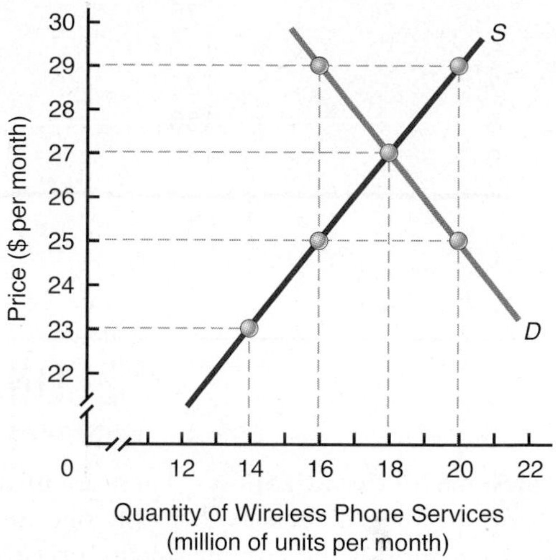

a. Does imposing the $4-per-month unit excise tax cause the market price of wireless phone services to rise by $4 per month? Why or why not?

b. What portion of the $4-per-month unit excise tax is paid by consumers? What portion is paid by providers of wireless phone services?

6-9. Suppose that the federal government imposes a unit excise tax of $2 per month on the monthly rates that Internet service providers charge for providing high-speed Internet access to households and businesses. Draw a diagram of normally shaped market demand and supply curves for Internet access services. Use this diagram to predict how the Internet service tax is likely to affect the market price and market quantity.

6-10. Consider the $2-per-month tax on Internet access in Problem 6-9. Suppose that in the market for Internet access services provided to households, the market price increases by $2 per month after the unit excise tax is imposed. If the market supply curve slopes upward, what can you say about the shape of the market demand curve over the relevant ranges of prices and quantities? Who pays the excise tax in this market?

6-11. Consider once more the Internet access tax of $2 per month discussed in Problem 6-9. Suppose that in the market for Internet access services provided to businesses, the market price does not change after the unit excise tax is imposed. If the market supply curve slopes upward, what can you say about the shape of the market demand curve over the relevant ranges of prices and quantities? Who pays the excise tax in this market?

6-12. The following information applies to the market for a particular item in the *absence* of a unit excise tax:

Price ($ per unit)	Quantity Supplied	Quantity Demanded
4	50	200
5	75	175
6	100	150
7	125	125
8	150	100
9	175	75

a. According to the information in the table, in the *absence* of a unit excise tax, what is the market price? What is the equilibrium quantity?

b. Suppose that the government decides to subject producers of this item to a unit excise tax equal to $2 per unit sold. What is the new market price? What is the new equilibrium quantity?

c. What portion of the tax is paid by producers? What portion of the tax is paid by consumers?

ECONOMICS ON THE NET

Social Security Privatization There are many proposals for reforming Social Security, but only one fundamentally alters the nature of the current system: privatization. The purpose of this exercise is to learn more about what would happen if Social Security were privatized.

Title: Social Security Privatization

Navigation: Go to **www.econtoday.com/ch06** to learn about Social Security privatization. Click on *It's Your Money: A Citizen's Guide to Social Security Reform.*

Application For each of the three entries noted here, read the entry and answer the question.

1. According to this article, when will the system begin to experience difficulties? Why?
2. What does this article contend are the likely consequences of applying the Social Security payroll tax to more of a person's income? Why?
3. Why does this article argue that simply adding personal accounts will not solve Social Security's problems?

For Group Study and Analysis It will be worthwhile for those not nearing retirement age to examine what the "older" generation thinks about the idea of privatizing the Social Security system in the United States. So create two groups—one for and one against privatization. Each group will examine the following Web site and come up with arguments in favor of or against the ideas expressed on it.

Go to **www.econtoday.com/ch06** to read a proposal for Social Security reform. Accept or rebut the proposal, depending on the side to which you have been assigned. Be prepared to defend your reasons with more than just your feelings. At a minimum, be prepared to present arguments that are logical, if not entirely backed by facts.

Taking into account the characteristics of your group as a whole, is it likely to be made better off or worse off if Social Security is privatized? Should your decision to support or oppose privatization be based solely on how it affects you personally? Or should your decision take into account how it might affect others in your group?

ANSWERS TO QUICK QUIZZES

p. 125: (i) rate . . . base; (ii) average . . . marginal; (iii) proportional . . . progressive . . . regressive

p. 128: (i) income . . . sales . . . property; (ii) double; (iii) Social Security . . . Medicare . . . unemployment

p. 131: (i) static; (ii) dynamic . . . static; (iii) fall . . . decline

p. 133: (i) vertically . . . vertically; (ii) reduces . . . raises; (iii) less

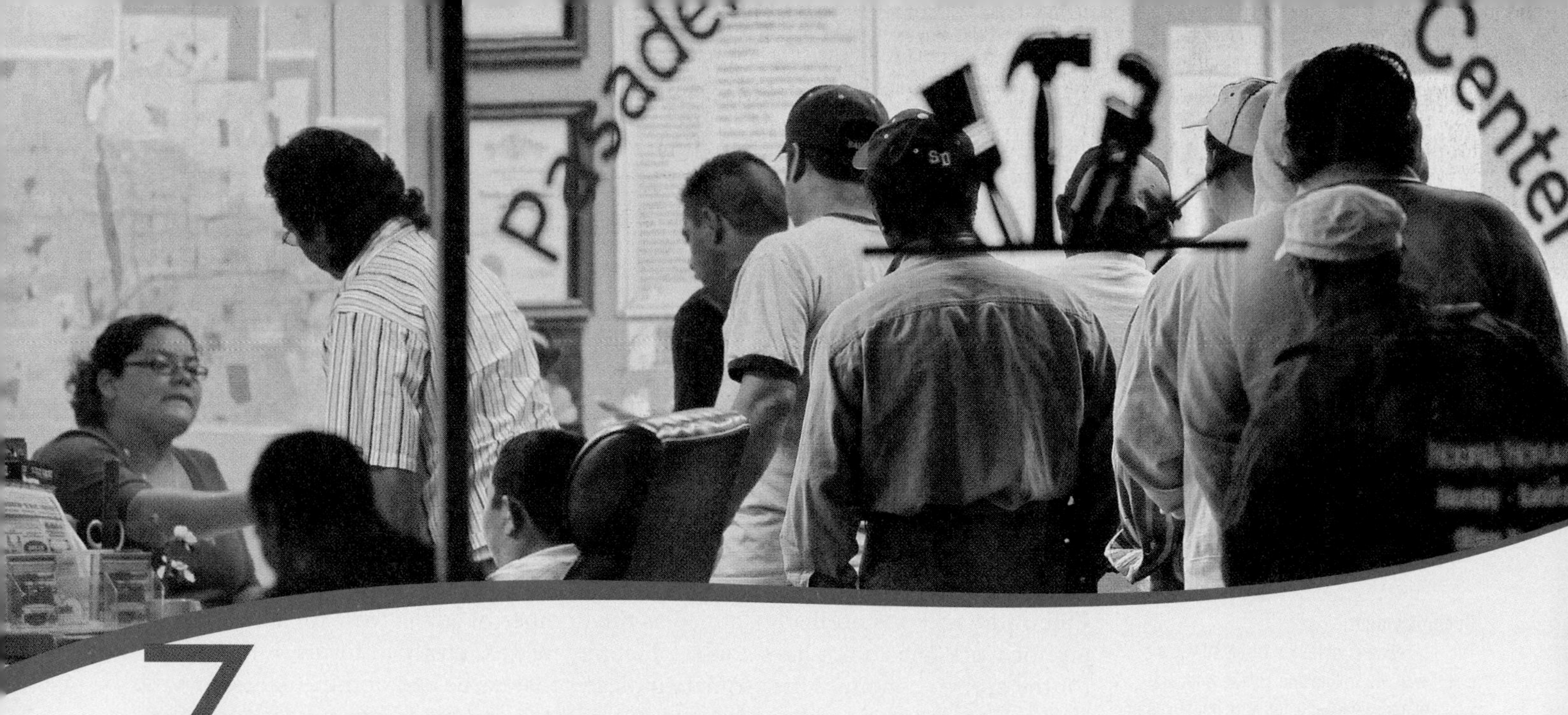

7 The Macroeconomy: Unemployment, Inflation, and Deflation

Because of its emphasis on the roles of scarcity and trade-offs, economics has been called the dismal science. It is perhaps fitting, therefore, that economists track a *misery index*. This measure sums two percentages. One percentage is the *unemployment rate*—the percentage of the labor force out of work. The other percentage is the *inflation rate*—the annual percentage change in the average level of prices of goods and services. What should we make of the sharp upturn in the value of the misery index during the past few years? To answer this question, you must first understand both the unemployment rate and the inflation rate, which are fundamental topics of this chapter.

LEARNING OBJECTIVES

After reading this chapter, you should be able to:

- Explain how the U.S. government calculates the official unemployment rate
- Discuss the types of unemployment
- Describe how price indexes are calculated and define the key types of price indexes
- Distinguish between nominal and real interest rates
- Evaluate who loses and who gains from inflation
- Understand key features of business fluctuations

myeconlab

MyEconLab helps you master each objective and study more efficiently. See end of chapter for details.

Did You Know That ?

during the Great Recession of the late 2000s, about 80 percent of the more than 7 million people who lost their jobs were male? People who had received the most education were more insulated from job losses, and recently women have attained more education than men. About 62 percent of the two- and four-year degrees granted during the past five years were earned by women. As a result of their better training, these women were more likely to hold onto stable positions and thus avoid unemployment.

Trying to understand determinants of unemployment and of the overall performance of the national economy is a central objective of macroeconomics. This branch of economics seeks to explain and predict movements in the average level of prices, unemployment, and the total production of goods and services. This chapter introduces you to these key issues of macroeconomics.

Unemployment

Unemployment
The total number of adults (aged 16 years or older) who are willing and able to work and who are actively looking for work but have not found a job.

Unemployment is normally defined as the number of adults who are actively looking for work but do not have a job. Unemployment is costly in terms of lost output for the entire economy. One estimate indicates that at the end of the 2000s, when the unemployment rate rose by more than 4 percentage points and firms were operating below 80 percent of their capacity, the amount of output that the economy lost due to idle resources was roughly 5 percent of the total production throughout the United States. (In other words, we were somewhere inside the production possibilities curve that we talked about in Chapter 2.) That was the equivalent of more than an inflation-adjusted $700 billion of schools, houses, restaurant meals, cars, and movies that *could have been* produced. It is no wonder that policymakers closely watch the unemployment figures published by the Department of Labor's Bureau of Labor Statistics.

On a more personal level, the state of being unemployed often results in hardship and failed opportunities as well as a lack of self-respect. Psychological researchers believe that being fired creates at least as much stress as the death of a close friend. The numbers that we present about unemployment can never fully convey its true cost to the people of this or any other nation.

Historical Unemployment Rates

Labor force
Individuals aged 16 years or older who either have jobs or who are looking and available for jobs; the number of employed plus the number of unemployed.

The unemployment rate, defined as the proportion of the measured **labor force** that is unemployed, hit a low of 1.2 percent of the labor force at the end of World War II, after having reached 25 percent during the Great Depression in the 1930s. You can see in Figure 7-1 on the top of the facing page what has happened to the unemployment rate in the United States since 1890. The highest level ever was reached in the Great Depression, but the unemployment rate was also high during the Panic of 1893.

Employment, Unemployment, and the Labor Force

Figure 7-2 on the next page presents the population of individuals 16 years of age or older broken into three segments: (1) employed, (2) unemployed, and (3) not in the civilian labor force (a category that includes homemakers, full-time students, military personnel, persons in institutions, and retired persons). The employed and the unemployed, added together, make up the labor force. In 2011, the labor force amounted to 141.3 million + 14.2 million = 155.5 million people. To calculate the unemployment rate, we simply divide the number of unemployed by the number of people in the labor force and multiply by 100: 14.2 million/155.5 million × 100 = 9.1 percent.

You Are There

To contemplate the important role of small businesses in shaping U.S. employment and unemployment statistics, read **A Family Restaurant Regretfully Boosts the Unemployment Rate,** on page 154.

The Arithmetic Determination of Unemployment

Because there is a transition between employment and unemployment at any point in time—people are leaving jobs and others are finding jobs—there is a simple relationship between the employed and the unemployed, as can be seen in Figure 7-3 on page 142.

FIGURE 7-1 More Than a Century of Unemployment

The U.S. unemployment rate dropped below 2 percent during World Wars I and II but exceeded 25 percent during the Great Depression. During the Great Recession following 2007, the unemployment rate rose above 10 percent.

Source: U.S. Department of Labor, Bureau of Labor Statistics.

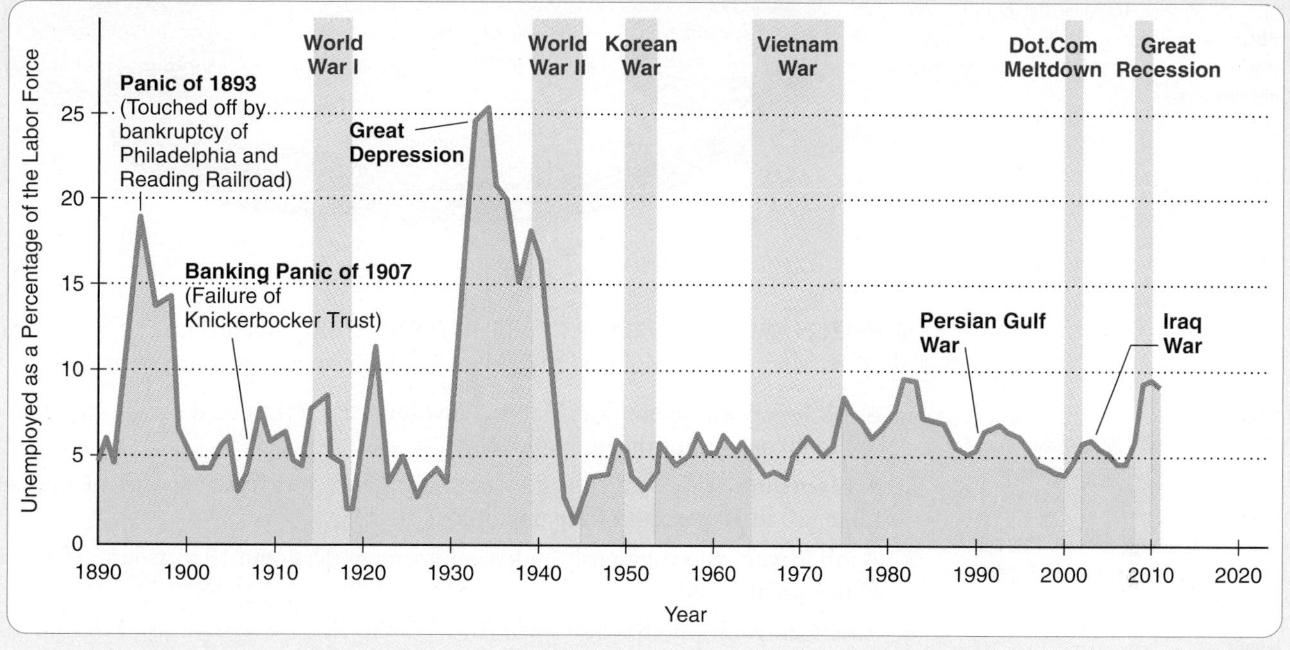

Job departures are shown at the top of the diagram, and job acquisitions are shown at the bottom. If the numbers of job departures and acquisitions are equal, the unemployment rate stays the same. If departures exceed acquisitions, the unemployment rate rises.

The number of unemployed is some number at any point in time. It is a **stock** of individuals who do not have a job but are actively looking for one. The same is true for the number of employed. The number of people departing jobs, whether voluntarily or involuntarily, is a **flow,** as is the number of people acquiring jobs.

Stock
The quantity of something, measured at a given point in time—for example, an inventory of goods or a bank account. Stocks are defined independently of time, although they are assessed at a point in time.

Flow
A quantity measured per unit of time; something that occurs over time, such as the income you make per week or per year or the number of individuals who are fired every month.

FIGURE 7-2 Adult Population

The population aged 16 and older can be broken down into three groups: people who are employed, those who are unemployed, and those not in the labor force.

Source: U.S. Department of Labor, Bureau of Labor Statistics.

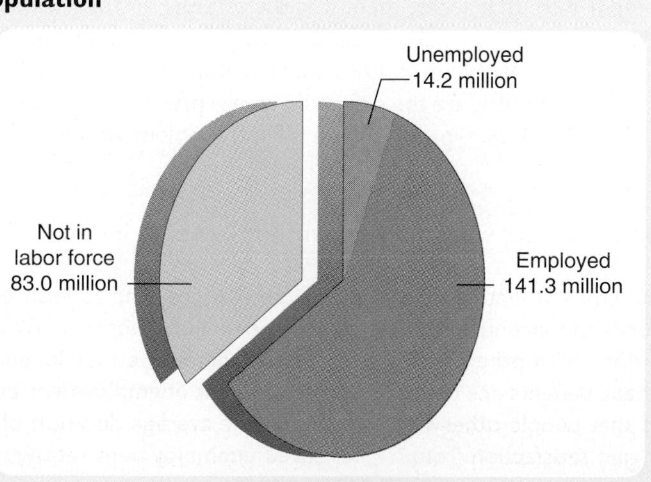

FIGURE 7-3 The Logic of the Unemployment Rate

Individuals who depart jobs but remain in the labor force are subtracted from the employed and added to the unemployed. When the unemployed acquire jobs, they are subtracted from the unemployed and added to the employed. In an unchanged labor force, if both flows are equal, the unemployment rate is stable. If more people depart jobs than acquire them, the unemployment rate increases, and vice versa.

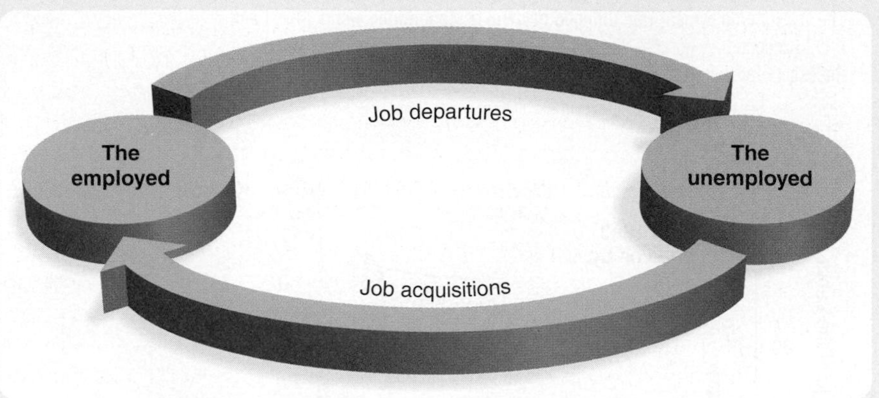

CATEGORIES OF INDIVIDUALS WHO ARE WITHOUT WORK According to the Bureau of Labor Statistics, an unemployed individual will fall into any of four categories:

Job loser
An individual in the labor force whose employment was involuntarily terminated.

Reentrant
An individual who used to work full-time but left the labor force and has now reentered it looking for a job.

Job leaver
An individual in the labor force who quits voluntarily.

New entrant
An individual who has never held a full-time job lasting two weeks or longer but is now seeking employment.

1. A **job loser,** whose employment was involuntarily terminated or who was laid off (40 to 60 percent of the unemployed)
2. A **reentrant,** who worked a full-time job before but has been out of the labor force (20 to 30 percent of the unemployed)
3. A **job leaver,** who voluntarily ended employment (less than 10 to around 15 percent of the unemployed)
4. A **new entrant,** who has never worked a full-time job for two weeks or longer (10 to 15 percent of the unemployed)

DURATION OF UNEMPLOYMENT If you are out of a job for a week, your situation is typically much less serious than if you are out of a job for, say, 14 weeks. An increase in the duration of unemployment can increase the unemployment rate because workers stay unemployed longer, thereby creating a greater number of them at any given time. The most recent information on duration of unemployment paints the following picture: more than a third of those who become unemployed acquire a new job by the end of one month, approximately one-third more acquire a job by the end of two months, and only about a sixth are still unemployed after six months. Since the mid-1960s, the average annual duration of unemployment for all the unemployed has varied between 10 and 20 weeks. The overall average duration for the past 25 years has been at least 16 weeks.

When overall business activity goes into a downturn, the duration of unemployment tends to rise, thereby accounting for much of the increase in the estimated unemployment rate. In a sense, then, it is the increase in the *duration* of unemployment during a downturn in national economic activity that generates the bad news that concerns policymakers in Washington, D.C. Furthermore, the individuals who stay unemployed longer than six months are the ones who create pressure on Congress to "do something." What Congress does, typically, is extend and supplement unemployment benefits.

Why Not . . . provide job losers with unemployment benefits indefinitely?

When the government provides unemployment benefits to unemployed individuals, it reduces the incentive for them to search seriously for positions with other firms. After all, even though unemployment benefits are only a fraction of the wages and salaries that people otherwise could earn, some individuals may gain satisfaction from devoting more time to leisure activities while collecting these benefits. Consequently, these people are willing to remain unemployed for longer periods. Thus, providing government unemployment benefits indefinitely would boost the average duration of unemployment. The measured unemployment rate would rise, too.

THE DISCOURAGED WORKER PHENOMENON Critics of the published unemployment rate calculated by the federal government believe that it fails to reflect the true numbers of **discouraged workers** and "hidden unemployed." Though there is no agreed-on method to measure discouraged workers, the Department of Labor defines them as people who have dropped out of the labor force and are no longer looking for a job because they believe that the job market has little to offer them. To what extent do we want to include in the measured labor force individuals who voluntarily choose not to look for work or those who take only a few minutes a day to scan the want ads and then decide that there are no jobs?

Discouraged workers
Individuals who have stopped looking for a job because they are convinced that they will not find a suitable one.

Some economists argue that people who work part-time but are willing to work full-time should be classified as "semihidden" unemployed. Estimates range as high as 6 million workers at any one time. Offsetting this factor, though, is *overemployment.* An individual working 50 or 60 hours a week is still counted as only one full-time worker. Some people hold two or three jobs but still are counted as just one employed person.

LABOR FORCE PARTICIPATION The way in which we define unemployment and membership in the labor force will affect the **labor force participation rate.** It is defined as the proportion of noninstitutionalized (i.e., not in prisons, mental institutions, etc.) working-age individuals who are employed or seeking employment.

Labor force participation rate
The percentage of noninstitutionalized working-age individuals who are employed or seeking employment.

The U.S. labor force participation rate has risen somewhat over time, from 60 percent in 1950 to about 66 percent today. The gender composition of the U.S. labor force has changed considerably during this time. In 1950, more than 83 percent of men and fewer than 35 percent of women participated in the U.S. labor force. Today, fewer than 70 percent of men and more than 60 percent of women are U.S. labor force participants.

QUICK QUIZ See page 160 for the answers. Review concepts from this section in MyEconLab.

__________ persons are adults who are willing and able to work and are actively looking for a job but have not found one. The unemployment rate is computed by dividing the number of unemployed by the total __________ __________, which is equal to those who are employed plus those who are unemployed.

The unemployed are classified as __________ __________, __________, __________ __________, and __________ __________ to the labor force. The flow of people departing jobs and people acquiring jobs determines the stock of the unemployed as well as the stock of the employed.

The duration of unemployment affects the unemployment rate. If the duration of unemployment increases, the measured unemployment rate will __________, even though the number of unemployed workers may remain the same.

Whereas overall labor force participation has risen only modestly since World War II, there has been a major increase in __________ labor force participation.

The Major Types of Unemployment

Unemployment has been categorized into four basic types: frictional, structural, cyclical, and seasonal.

Frictional Unemployment

Of the more than 155 million people in the labor force, more than 50 million will either change jobs or take new jobs during the year. In the process, in excess of 22 million persons will report themselves unemployed at one time or another. This continuous flow of individuals from job to job and in and out of employment is called **frictional unemployment.** There will always be some frictional unemployment as resources are redirected in the economy, because job-hunting costs are never zero, and workers never have full information about available jobs. To eliminate frictional unemployment,

Frictional unemployment
Unemployment due to the fact that workers must search for appropriate job offers. This activity takes time, and so they remain temporarily unemployed.

we would have to prevent workers from leaving their present jobs until they had already lined up other jobs at which they would start working immediately. And we would have to guarantee first-time job seekers a job *before* they started looking.

Structural Unemployment

Structural unemployment
Unemployment resulting from a poor match of workers' abilities and skills with current requirements of employers.

Structural changes in our economy cause some workers to become unemployed for very long periods of time because they cannot find jobs that use their particular skills. This is called **structural unemployment.** Structural unemployment is not caused by general business fluctuations, although business fluctuations may affect it. And unlike frictional unemployment, structural unemployment is not related to the movement of workers from low-paying to high-paying jobs.

At one time, economists thought about structural unemployment only from the perspective of workers. The concept applied to workers who did not have the ability, training, and skills necessary to obtain available jobs. Today, it still encompasses these workers. In addition, however, economists increasingly look at structural unemployment from the viewpoint of employers, many of whom face government mandates requiring them to take such steps as providing funds for social insurance programs for their employees and announcing plant closings months or even years in advance. There is now considerable evidence that government labor market policies influence how many job positions businesses wish to create, thereby affecting structural unemployment. In the United States, many businesses appear to have adjusted to these policies by hiring more "temporary workers" or establishing short-term contracts with "private consultants." Such measures may have reduced the extent of U.S. structural unemployment in recent years.

Cyclical Unemployment

Cyclical unemployment
Unemployment resulting from business recessions that occur when aggregate (total) demand is insufficient to create full employment.

Cyclical unemployment is related to business fluctuations. It is defined as unemployment associated with changes in business conditions—primarily recessions and depressions. The way to lessen cyclical unemployment would be to reduce the intensity, duration, and frequency of downturns of business activity. Economic policymakers attempt, through their policies, to reduce cyclical unemployment by keeping business activity on an even keel.

Why are "nonregular" workers in Japan particularly susceptible to cyclical unemployment?

INTERNATIONAL EXAMPLE A Source of "Nonregularity" in Japan's Cyclical Unemployment

In Japan, "regular workers" usually have full-time jobs that, in addition to paying full-time wages, offer health care and retirement benefits, bonuses, job training, and even guarantees of employment for life. In contrast, "nonregular workers," who often are contract employees placed with firms by employment agencies, earn wages that may be only 40 percent of those paid to regular workers. Nonregular employees also receive no other benefits. Furthermore, if a company experiences difficult times and must cut labor costs, nonregular workers, who account for more than one-third of Japanese workers, are the first to lose their positions.

When the Great Recession engulfed the Japanese economy in the late 2000s, that nation's unemployment rate rose by 2 percentage points within six weeks. The bulk of the Japanese residents who joined the ranks of the newly unemployed were nonregular workers.

FOR CRITICAL ANALYSIS

Why do you suppose that when regular Japanese employees who have recently lost their positions apply for new jobs, they often have a difficult time beating out applicants who are willing to serve as nonregular workers?

Seasonal Unemployment

Seasonal unemployment comes and goes with seasons of the year in which the demand for particular jobs rises and falls. In northern states, construction workers can often work only during the warmer months. They are seasonally unemployed during the winter. Summer resort workers can usually get jobs in resorts only during the summer season. They, too, sometimes become seasonally unemployed during the winter. The opposite is sometimes true for ski resort workers.

Seasonal unemployment
Unemployment resulting from the seasonal pattern of work in specific industries. It is usually due to seasonal fluctuations in demand or to changing weather conditions that render work difficult, if not impossible, as in the agriculture, construction, and tourist industries.

The unemployment rate that the Bureau of Labor Statistics releases each month is "seasonally adjusted." This means that the reported unemployment rate has been adjusted to remove the effects of variations in seasonal unemployment. Thus, the unemployment rate that the media dutifully announce reflects only the sum of frictional unemployment, structural unemployment, and cyclical unemployment.

Full Employment and the Natural Rate of Unemployment

Does full employment mean that everybody has a job? Certainly not, for not everyone is looking for a job—full-time students and full-time homemakers, for example, are not. Is it always possible for everyone who is looking for a job to find one? No, because transaction costs in the labor market are not zero. Transaction costs are those associated with any activity whose goal is to enter into, carry out, or terminate contracts. In the labor market, these costs involve time spent looking for a job, being interviewed, negotiating the terms of employment, and the like.

Full Employment

We will always have some frictional unemployment as individuals move in and out of the labor force, seek higher-paying jobs, and move to different parts of the country. **Full employment** is therefore a concept that implies some sort of balance or equilibrium in an ever-shifting labor market. Of course, this general notion of full employment must somehow be put into numbers so that economists and others can determine whether the economy has reached the full-employment point.

Full employment
An arbitrary level of unemployment that corresponds to "normal" friction in the labor market. In 1986, a 6.5 percent rate of unemployment was considered full employment. Since the 1990s, it has been assumed to be around 5 percent.

The Natural Rate of Unemployment

To try to assess when a situation of balance has been attained in the labor market, economists estimate the **natural rate of unemployment,** the rate that is expected to prevail in the long run once all workers and employers have fully adjusted to any changes in the economy. If correctly estimated, the natural rate of unemployment should not include cyclical unemployment. When seasonally adjusted, the natural unemployment rate should include only frictional and structural unemployment.

Natural rate of unemployment
The rate of unemployment that is estimated to prevail in long-run macroeconomic equilibrium, when all workers and employers have fully adjusted to any changes in the economy.

A long-standing difficulty, however, has been a lack of agreement about how to estimate the natural unemployment rate. From the mid-1980s to the early 1990s, the President's Council of Economic Advisers (CEA) consistently estimated that the natural unemployment rate in the United States was about 6.5 percent. Even into the 2000s, Federal Reserve staff economists, employing an approach to estimating the natural rate of unemployment that was intended to improve on the CEA's traditional method, arrived at a natural rate just over 6 percent. When the measured unemployment rate fell to 4 percent in 2000, however, economists began to rethink their approach to estimating the natural unemployment rate. This led some to alter their estimation methods to take into account such factors as greater rivalry among domestic businesses and increased international competition, which at that time led to an estimated natural rate of unemployment of roughly 5 percent. In light of the recent upsurge in the unemployment rate, economists are seeking to determine if the natural rate has risen.

QUICK QUIZ See page 160 for the answers. Review concepts from this section in MyEconLab.

__________ **unemployment** occurs because of transaction costs in the labor market. For example, workers do not have full information about vacancies and must search for jobs.

__________ **unemployment** occurs when there is a poor match of workers' skills and abilities with available jobs, perhaps because workers lack appropriate training or government labor rules reduce firms' willingness to hire.

The levels of frictional and structural unemployment are used in part to determine our (somewhat arbitrary) measurement of the __________ rate of unemployment.

Inflation and Deflation

During World War II, you could buy bread for 8 to 10 cents a loaf and have milk delivered fresh to your door for about 25 cents a half gallon. The average price of a new car was less than $700, and the average house cost less than $3,000. Today, bread, milk, cars, and houses all cost more—a lot more. Prices are about 15 times what they were in 1940. Clearly, this country has experienced quite a bit of *inflation* since then. We define **inflation** as an upward movement in the average level of prices. The opposite of inflation is **deflation,** defined as a downward movement in the average level of prices. Notice that these definitions depend on the *average* level of prices. This means that even during a period of inflation, some prices can be falling if other prices are rising at a faster rate. The prices of electronic equipment have dropped dramatically since the 1960s, even though there has been general inflation.

Inflation
A sustained increase in the average of all prices of goods and services in an economy.

Deflation
A sustained decrease in the average of all prices of goods and services in an economy.

To discuss what has happened to prices here and in other countries, we have to know how to measure inflation.

Inflation and the Purchasing Power of Money

By definition, the value of a dollar does not stay constant when there is inflation. The value of money is usually talked about in terms of **purchasing power.** A dollar's purchasing power is the real goods and services that it can buy. Consequently, another way of defining inflation is as a decline in the purchasing power of money. The faster the rate of inflation, the greater the rate of decline in the purchasing power of money.

Purchasing power
The value of money for buying goods and services. If your money income stays the same but the price of one good that you are buying goes up, your effective purchasing power falls, and vice versa.

One way to think about inflation and the purchasing power of money is to discuss dollar values in terms of *nominal* versus *real* values. The nominal value of anything is simply its price expressed in today's dollars. In contrast, the real value of anything is its value expressed in purchasing power, which varies with the overall price level. Let's say that you received a $100 bill from your grandparents this year. One year from now, the nominal value of that bill will still be $100. The real value will depend on what the purchasing power of money is after one year's worth of inflation. Obviously, if there is inflation during the year, the real value of that $100 bill will have diminished. For example, if you keep the $100 bill in your pocket for a year during which the rate of inflation is 3 percent, at the end of the year you will have to come up with $3 more to buy the same amount of goods and services that the $100 bill can purchase today.

What does the fact that inflation has contributed to higher movie ticket prices imply regarding media rankings of top-selling movies?

EXAMPLE **Rethinking Rankings of Top-Selling Films**

Every time a Hollywood moviemaker has a major box office success, the entertainment media compare the new film's sales against those of past movies. These media reports usually put recent movies such as *Titanic* (1997), *The Dark Knight* (2008), and *Avatar* (2009) at the top of the lists.

The problem with such media comparisons is that they fail to differentiate between films' nominal and real ticket sales. When all past films' ticket sales are expressed in terms of the real purchasing power of the dollar, rankings of top-selling movies change dramatically. When sales are adjusted for the real purchasing power of the dollar, the top movies include *Gone with the Wind* from 1939, *The Sound of Music* from 1965, and *Star Wars* from 1977. Thus, more real purchasing power was expended in years past to see these older movies than is expended today to view films that are highly ranked based only on *nominal* sales unadjusted for inflation.

FOR CRITICAL ANALYSIS

Does the fact that the dollar price paid to view a typical film in 2010 was much higher than the price paid to view a movie in 1939 mean that more real purchasing power was required to see a movie in 2010 than in 1939? Explain.

Measuring the Rate of Inflation

How can we measure the rate of inflation? This is a thorny problem for government statisticians. It is easy to determine how much the price of an individual commodity has risen: If last year a light bulb cost 50 cents and this year it costs 75 cents, there has been a 50 percent rise in the price of that light bulb over a one-year period. We can express the change in the individual light bulb price in one of several ways: The price has gone up 25 cents. The price is one and a half (1.5) times as high; the price has risen by 50 percent. An *index number* of this price rise is simply the second way (1.5) multiplied by 100, meaning that the index today would stand at 150. We multiply by 100 to eliminate decimals because it is easier to think in terms of percentage changes using whole numbers. This is the standard convention adopted for convenience in dealing with index numbers or price levels.

Computing a Price Index

The measurement problem becomes more complicated when it involves a large number of goods, especially if some prices have risen faster than others and some have even fallen. What we have to do is pick a representative bundle, a so-called market basket, of goods and compare the cost of that market basket of goods over time. When we do this, we obtain a **price index,** which is defined as the cost of a market basket of goods today, expressed as a percentage of the cost of that identical market basket of goods in some starting year, known as the **base year.**

Price index
The cost of today's market basket of goods expressed as a percentage of the cost of the same market basket during a base year.

Base year
The year that is chosen as the point of reference for comparison of prices in other years.

$$\text{Price index} = \frac{\text{cost of market basket today}}{\text{cost of market basket in base year}} \times 100$$

In the base year, the price index will always be 100, because the year in the numerator and in the denominator of the fraction is the same. Therefore, the fraction equals 1, and when we multiply it by 100, we get 100. A simple numerical example is given in Table 7-1 on the next page. In the table, there are only two goods in the market basket—corn and computers. The *quantities* in the basket are the same in the base year, 2003, and the current year, 2013. Only the *prices* change. Such a *fixed-quantity* price index is the easiest to compute because the statistician need only look at prices of goods and services sold every year rather than observing how much of these goods and services consumers actually purchase each year.

Consumer Price Index (CPI)
A statistical measure of a weighted average of prices of a specified set of goods and services purchased by typical consumers in urban areas.

Producer Price Index (PPI)
A statistical measure of a weighted average of prices of goods and services that firms produce and sell.

GDP deflator
A price index measuring the changes in prices of all new goods and services produced in the economy.

Personal Consumption Expenditure (PCE) Index
A statistical measure of average prices that uses annually updated weights based on surveys of consumer spending.

REAL-WORLD PRICE INDEXES Government statisticians calculate a number of price indexes. The most often quoted are the **Consumer Price Index (CPI)**, the **Producer Price Index (PPI)**, the **GDP deflator,** and the **Personal Consumption Expenditure (PCE) Index.** The CPI attempts to measure changes only in the level of prices of goods and services

TABLE 7-1

Calculating a Price Index for a Two-Good Market Basket

In this simplified example, there are only two goods—corn and computers. The quantities and base-year prices are given in columns 2 and 3. The cost of the 2003 market basket, calculated in column 4, comes to $1,400. The 2013 prices are given in column 5. The cost of the market basket in 2013, calculated in column 6, is $1,650. The price index for 2013 compared with 2003 is 117.86.

(1) Commodity	(2) Market Basket Quantity	(3) 2003 Price per Unit	(4) Cost of Market Basket in 2003	(5) 2013 Price per Unit	(6) Cost of Market Basket in 2013
Corn	100 bushels	$ 4	$ 400	$ 8	$ 800
Computers	2	500	1,000	425	850
Totals			**$1,400**		**$1,650**

$$\textbf{Price index} = \frac{\text{cost of market basket in 2013}}{\text{cost of market basket in base year 2003}} \times 100 = \frac{\$1{,}650}{\$1{,}400} \times 100 = \mathbf{117.86}$$

purchased by consumers. The PPI attempts to show what has happened to the average price of goods and services produced and sold by a typical firm. (There are also *wholesale price indexes* that track the price level for commodities that firms purchase from other firms.) The GDP deflator is the most general indicator of inflation because it measures changes in the level of prices of all new goods and services produced in the economy. The PCE Index measures average prices using weights from surveys of consumer spending.

THE CPI The Bureau of Labor Statistics (BLS) has the task of identifying a market basket of goods and services of the typical consumer. Today, the BLS uses the time period 1982–1984 as its base of market prices. It intends to change the base to 1993–1995 but has yet to do so. It has, though, updated the expenditure weights for its market basket of goods to reflect consumer spending patterns in 2001–2002. All CPI numbers since February 1998 reflect these expenditure weights.

Economists have known for years that the way the BLS measures changes in the CPI is flawed. Specifically, the BLS has been unable to account for the way consumers substitute less expensive items for higher-priced items. The reason is that the CPI is a fixed-quantity price index, meaning that the BLS implicitly ignores changes in consumption patterns that occur between years in which it revises the index. Until recently, the BLS has also been unable to take quality changes into account as they occur. Now, though, it is subtracting from certain list prices estimated effects of qualitative improvements and adding to other list prices to account for deteriorations in quality. An additional flaw is that the CPI usually ignores successful new products until long after they have been introduced. Despite these flaws, the CPI is widely followed because its level is calculated and published monthly.

THE PPI There are a number of Producer Price Indexes, including one for foodstuffs, another for intermediate goods (goods used in the production of other goods), and one for finished goods. Most of the producer prices included are in mining, manufacturing, and agriculture. The PPIs can be considered general-purpose indexes for nonretail markets.

Although in the long run the various PPIs and the CPI generally show the same rate of inflation, that is not the case in the short run. Most often the PPIs increase before the CPI because it takes time for producer price increases to show up in the prices that consumers pay for final products. Much of the time, changes in the PPIs are watched closely as a hint that CPI inflation is going to increase or decrease.

THE GDP DEFLATOR The broadest price index reported in the United States is the GDP deflator, where GDP stands for gross domestic product, or annual total national income. Unlike the CPI and the PPIs, the GDP deflator is *not* based on a fixed market basket of goods and services. The basket is allowed to change with people's consumption and investment patterns. In this sense, the changes in the GDP deflator reflect both price changes and the public's market responses to those price changes. Why? Because new expenditure patterns are allowed to show up in the GDP deflator as people respond to changing prices.

Go to **www.econtoday.com/ch07** to obtain information about inflation and unemployment in other countries from the International Monetary Fund. Click on "World Economic Outlook Databases."

THE PCE INDEX Another price index that takes into account changing expenditure patterns is the Personal Consumption Expenditure (PCE) Index. The Bureau of Economic Analysis, an agency of the U.S. Department of Commerce, uses continuously updated annual surveys of consumer purchases to construct the weights for the PCE Index. Thus, an advantage of the PCE Index is that weights in the index are updated every year. The Federal Reserve has used the rate of change in the PCE Index as its primary inflation indicator because Fed officials believe that the updated weights in the PCE Index make it more accurate than the CPI as a measure of consumer price changes. Nevertheless, the CPI remains the most widely reported price index, and the U.S. government continues to use the CPI to adjust the value of Social Security benefits to account for inflation.

HISTORICAL CHANGES IN THE CPI Between World War II and the early 1980s, the Consumer Price Index showed a fairly dramatic trend upward. Figure 7-4 below shows the annual rate of change in the CPI since 1860. Prior to World War II, there

FIGURE 7-4 Inflation and Deflation in U.S. History

For 80 years after the Civil War, the United States experienced alternating inflation and deflation. Here we show them as reflected by changes in the Consumer Price Index. Since World War II, the periods of inflation have not been followed by periods of deflation. Even during peacetime, the price index has continued to rise. The shaded areas represent wartime.

Source: U.S. Department of Labor, Bureau of Labor Statistics.

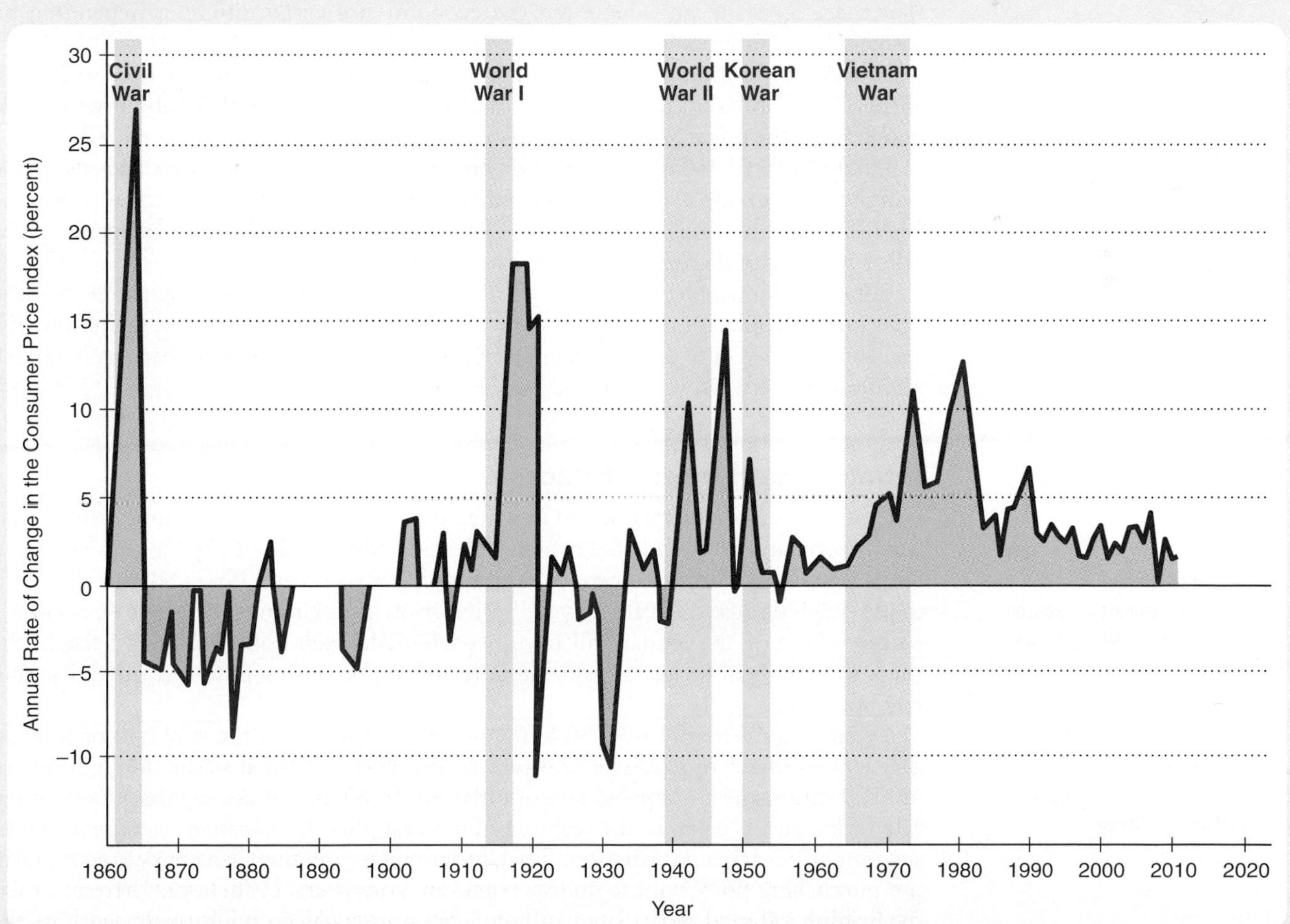

were numerous periods of deflation interspersed with periods of inflation. Persistent year-in and year-out inflation seems to be a post–World War II phenomenon, at least in this country. As far back as before the American Revolution, prices used to rise during war periods but then would fall back toward prewar levels afterward. This occurred after the Revolutionary War, the War of 1812, the Civil War, and to a lesser extent World War I. Consequently, the overall price level in 1940 wasn't much different from 150 years earlier.

QUICK QUIZ See page 160 for the answers. Review concepts from this section in MyEconLab.

Once we pick a market basket of goods, we can construct a **price index** that compares the cost of that market basket today with the cost of the same market basket in a __________ year.

The __________ __________ Index is the most often used price index in the United States. The **Producer Price Index (PPI)** is also widely mentioned.

The __________ __________ measures what is happening to the average price level of *all* new, domestically produced final goods and services in our economy.

The __________ __________ __________ Index uses annually updated weights from consumer spending surveys to measure average prices faced by consumers.

Anticipated versus Unanticipated Inflation

To determine who is hurt by inflation and what the effects of inflation are in general, we have to distinguish between anticipated and unanticipated inflation. We will see that the effects on individuals and the economy are vastly different, depending on which type of inflation exists.

Anticipated inflation
The inflation rate that we believe will occur; when it does, we are in a situation of fully anticipated inflation.

Unanticipated inflation
Inflation at a rate that comes as a surprise, either higher or lower than the rate anticipated.

Anticipated inflation is the rate of inflation that most individuals believe will occur. If the rate of inflation this year turns out to be 5 percent, and that's about what most people thought it was going to be, we are in a situation of fully anticipated inflation.

Unanticipated inflation is inflation that comes as a surprise to individuals in the economy. For example, if the inflation rate in a particular year turns out to be 10 percent when on average people thought it was going to be 3 percent, there was unanticipated inflation—inflation greater than anticipated.

Some of the problems caused by inflation arise when it is unanticipated, because then many people are unable to protect themselves from its ravages. Keeping the distinction between anticipated and unanticipated inflation in mind, we can easily see the relationship between inflation and interest rates.

Inflation and Interest Rates

Nominal rate of interest
The market rate of interest observed on contracts expressed in today's dollars.

Let's start in a hypothetical world in which there is no inflation and anticipated inflation is zero. In that world, you may be able to borrow funds—to buy a house or a car, for example—at a **nominal rate of interest** of, say, 6 percent. If you borrow the funds to purchase a house or a car and your anticipation of inflation turns out to be accurate, neither you nor the lender will have been fooled. Each dollar you pay back in the years to come will be just as valuable in terms of purchasing power as the dollar that you borrowed.

Real rate of interest
The nominal rate of interest minus the anticipated rate of inflation.

What you ordinarily want to know when you borrow is the *real* rate of interest that you will have to pay. The **real rate of interest** is defined as the nominal rate of interest minus the anticipated rate of inflation. In effect, we can say that the nominal rate of interest is equal to the real rate of interest plus an *inflationary premium* to take account of anticipated inflation. That inflationary premium covers depreciation in the purchasing power of the dollars repaid by borrowers. (Whenever there are relatively high rates of anticipated inflation, we must add an additional factor to the inflationary premium—the product of the real rate of interest times the anticipated rate of inflation. Usually, this last term is omitted because the anticipated rate of inflation is not high enough to make much of a difference.)

Does Inflation Necessarily Hurt Everyone?

Most people think that inflation is bad. After all, inflation means higher prices, and when we have to pay higher prices, are we not necessarily worse off? The truth is that inflation affects different people differently. Its effects also depend on whether it is anticipated or unanticipated.

UNANTICIPATED INFLATION: CREDITORS LOSE AND DEBTORS GAIN In most situations, unanticipated inflation benefits borrowers because the nominal interest rate they are being charged does not fully compensate creditors for the inflation that actually occurred. In other words, the lender did not anticipate inflation correctly. Whenever inflation rates are underestimated for the life of a loan, creditors lose and debtors gain. Periods of considerable unanticipated (higher than anticipated) inflation occurred in the late 1960s and all of the 1970s. During those years, creditors lost and debtors gained.

PROTECTING AGAINST INFLATION Lenders attempt to protect themselves against inflation by raising nominal interest rates to reflect anticipated inflation. Adjustable-rate mortgages in fact do just that: The interest rate varies according to what happens to interest rates in the economy. Workers can protect themselves from inflation by obtaining **cost-of-living adjustments (COLAs),** which are automatic increases in wage rates to take account of increases in the price level.

Cost-of-living adjustments (COLAs) Clauses in contracts that allow for increases in specified nominal values to take account of changes in the cost of living.

To the extent that you hold non-interest-bearing cash, you will lose because of inflation. If you have put $100 in a mattress and the inflation rate is 5 percent for the year, you will have lost 5 percent of the purchasing power of that $100. If you have your funds in a non-interest-bearing checking account, you will suffer the same fate. Individuals attempt to reduce the cost of holding cash by putting it into interest-bearing accounts, a wide variety of which often pay nominal rates of interest that reflect anticipated inflation.

THE RESOURCE COST OF INFLATION Some economists believe that the main cost of inflation is the opportunity cost of resources used to protect against distortions that inflation introduces as firms attempt to plan for the long run. Individuals have to spend time and resources to figure out ways to adjust their behavior in case inflation is different from what it has been in the past. That may mean spending a longer time working out more complicated contracts for employment, for purchases of goods in the future, and for purchases of raw materials.

Inflation requires that price lists be changed. This is called the **repricing,** or **menu, cost of inflation.** The higher the rate of inflation, the higher the repricing cost of inflation, because prices must be changed more often within a given period of time.

Repricing, or menu, cost of inflation The cost associated with recalculating prices and printing new price lists when there is inflation.

QUICK QUIZ **See page 160 for the answers.** **Review concepts from this section in MyEconLab.**

Whenever inflation is __________ than anticipated, creditors lose and debtors gain. Whenever the rate of inflation is __________ than anticipated, creditors gain and debtors lose.

Holders of cash lose during periods of inflation because the __________ __________ of their cash depreciates at the rate of inflation.

Households and businesses spend resources in attempting to protect themselves against the prospect of inflation, thus imposing a __________ cost on the economy.

Changing Inflation and Unemployment: Business Fluctuations

Some years unemployment goes up, and some years it goes down. Some years there is a lot of inflation, and other years there isn't. We have fluctuations in all aspects of our macroeconomy. The ups and downs in economywide economic activity are sometimes called **business fluctuations.** When business fluctuations are positive, they are called **expansions**—speedups in the pace of national economic activity. The opposite of an expansion is a **contraction,** which is a slowdown in the pace of national economic activity. The top of an expansion is usually called its *peak*, and the bottom of a contraction is usually called its *trough*. Business fluctuations used to be called *business cycles*, but that term no longer seems appropriate because *cycle* implies regular or automatic recurrence, and we have never had automatic recurrent fluctuations in general business and economic activity. What we have had are contractions and expansions that vary greatly in length. For example, the 10 post–World War II expansions have averaged 57 months, but three of those exceeded 90 months, and two lasted less than 25 months.

Business fluctuations
The ups and downs in business activity throughout the economy.

Expansion
A business fluctuation in which the pace of national economic activity is speeding up.

Contraction
A business fluctuation during which the pace of national economic activity is slowing down.

If the contractionary phase of business fluctuations becomes severe enough, we call it a **recession.** An extremely severe recession is called a **depression.** Typically, at the beginning of a recession, there is a marked increase in the rate of unemployment, and the duration of unemployment increases. In addition, people's incomes start to decline. In times of expansion, the opposite occurs.

Recession
A period of time during which the rate of growth of business activity is consistently less than its long-term trend or is negative.

Depression
An extremely severe recession.

In Figure 7-5 below, you see that typical business fluctuations occur around a growth trend in overall national business activity shown as a straight upward-sloping line. Starting out at a peak, the economy goes into a contraction (recession). Then an expansion starts that moves up to its peak, higher than the last one, and the sequence starts over again.

A Historical Picture of Business Activity in the United States

Figure 7-6 on the facing page traces changes in U.S. business activity from 1880 to the present. Note that the long-term trend line is shown as horizontal, so all changes

FIGURE 7-5 The Idealized Course of Business Fluctuations

A hypothetical business cycle would go from peak to trough and back again in a regular cycle. Real-world business cycles are not as regular as this hypothetical cycle.

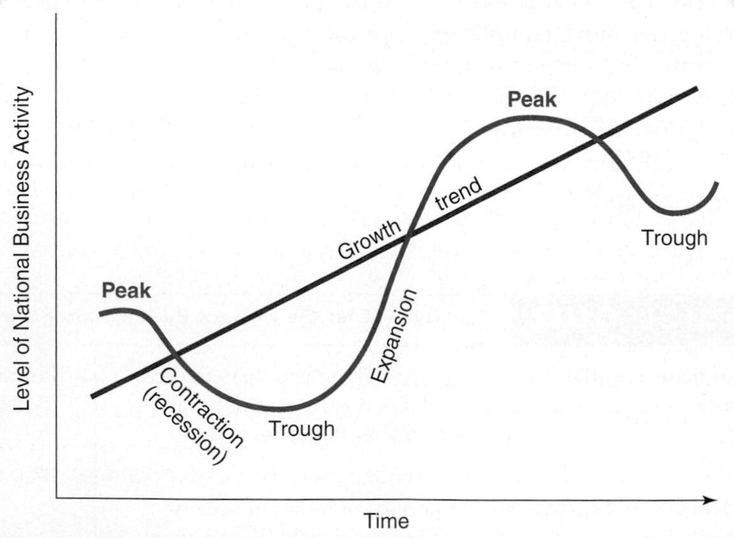

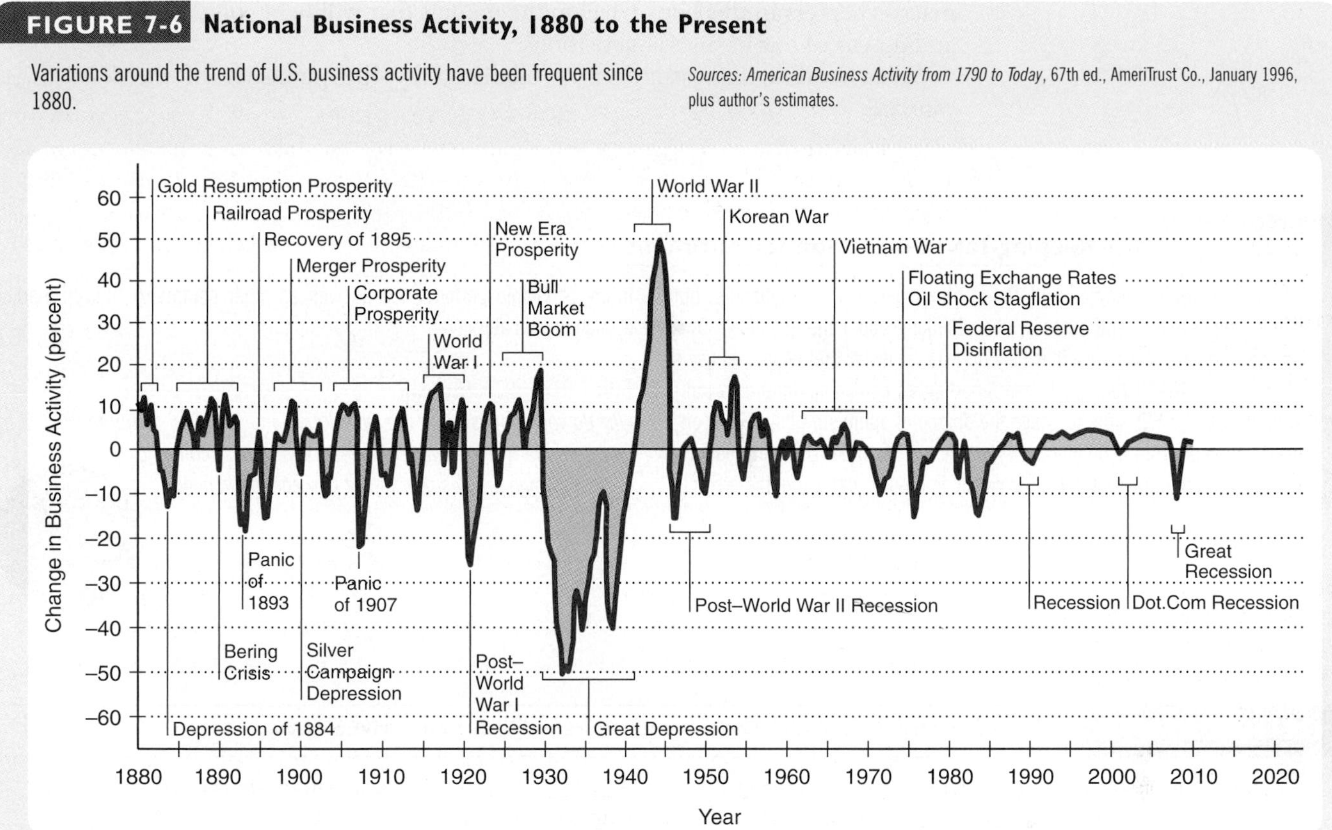

FIGURE 7-6 National Business Activity, 1880 to the Present

Variations around the trend of U.S. business activity have been frequent since 1880.

Sources: American Business Activity from 1790 to Today, 67th ed., AmeriTrust Co., January 1996, plus author's estimates.

in business activity focus around that trend line. Major changes in business activity in the United States occurred during the Great Depression, World War II, and, most recently, the Great Recession of the late 2000s. Note that none of the actual business fluctuations in Figure 7-6 exactly mirror the idealized course of a business fluctuation shown in Figure 7-5 on the facing page.

Go to **www.econtoday.com/ch07** to learn about how economists at the National Bureau of Economic Research formally determine when a recession started.

Explaining Business Fluctuations: External Shocks

As you might imagine, because changes in national business activity affect everyone, economists for decades have attempted to understand and explain business fluctuations. For years, one of the most obvious explanations has been external events that tend to disrupt the economy. In many of the graphs in this chapter, you have seen that World War II was a critical point in this nation's economic history. A war is certainly an external shock—something that originates outside our economy.

To try to help account for shocks to economic activity that may induce business fluctuations and thereby make fluctuations easier to predict, the U.S. Department of Commerce and private firms and organizations tabulate indexes (weighted averages) of **leading indicators.** These are events that economists have noticed typically occur *before* changes in business activity. For example, economic downturns often follow such events as a reduction in the average workweek, an increase in unemployment insurance claims, a decrease in the prices of raw materials, or a drop in the quantity of money in circulation.

Leading indicators
Events that have been found to occur before changes in business activity.

To better understand the role of shocks in influencing business fluctuations, we need a theory of why national economic activity changes. The remainder of the macro chapters in this book develop the models that will help you understand the ups and downs of our business fluctuations.

What leading indicator is now tabulated by the publisher of the *Wall Street Journal*?

EXAMPLE Keeping Tabs on Economic Sentiment

People sometimes become sentimental about personal relationships, but do they really react sentimentally when thinking about the economy? Dow Jones & Company is so sure that they do—or, at least, that economic news reporters do—that it recently began reporting an Economic Sentiment Indicator, or ESI. The ESI aims to gauge the degree of optimism about the economy as gleaned from economic news articles in 15 major U.S. newspapers. Dow Jones contends that the ESI, which it reports each month, predicts future economic performance as well as other commonly utilized leading economic indicators.

FOR CRITICAL ANALYSIS

Why do you suppose that the Dow Jones analysts who compute the ESI try to determine whether daily articles about good economic news outweigh articles that report bad economic news?

QUICK QUIZ

See page 160 for the answers. Review concepts from this section in MyEconLab.

The ups and downs in economywide business activity are called __________ __________, which consist of **expansions** and **contractions** in overall business activity.

The lowest point of a contraction is called the __________; the highest point of an expansion is called the __________.

A __________ is a downturn in business activity for some length of time.

One possible explanation for business fluctuations relates to __________ __________, such as wars, dramatic increases in the prices of raw materials, and earthquakes, floods, and droughts.

You Are There A Family Restaurant Regretfully Boosts the Unemployment Rate

Since 1954, the Roussos Restaurant of Daphne, Alabama, has served a host of customers including the well-known entertainers Jimmy Buffett and Elvis Presley. Like about 90 percent of other U.S. businesses, the restaurant has functioned as a family-operated enterprise. The Great Recession of the late 2000s is now in progress, however, and the restaurant's daily earnings have suddenly dropped by nearly 50 percent. For a year the Roussos have tried to keep the firm operating even though remaining revenues have been insufficient to cover costs, but now they have concluded that they must join the more than 6 million small businesses that have closed since the end of 2007.

The first people to hear the news from the family owners at an emotional meeting are the restaurant's 55 employees, some of whom have been with the firm for more than 35 years. These individuals have now joined the millions of people who have lost their jobs with small businesses. Defined as firms with fewer than 500 employees, small businesses typically provide more than half of all nongovernment jobs in the United States. Thus, as hundreds of thousands of small businesses have disappeared, so have millions of job positions for U.S. workers, an outcome that has contributed to a sustained high U.S. unemployment rate.

Critical Analysis Questions

1. Were the employees of Roussos Restaurant classified as job leavers or job losers? Explain.
2. How do you suppose that a sharp reduction in the rate of small-business startups during the late 2000s and early 2010s has affected the U.S. *employment* rate?

ISSUES & APPLICATIONS

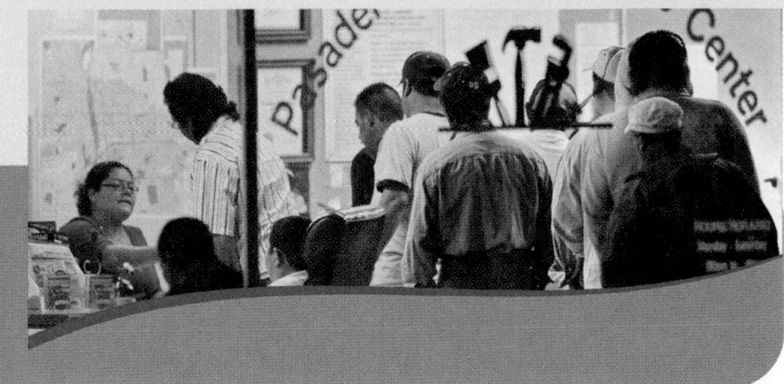

Bad News from the Misery Index

CONCEPTS APPLIED

- Unemployment Rate
- Inflation Rate
- Natural Rate of Unemployment

The sum of the unemployment rate and the annual inflation rate is commonly known as the *misery index*. To obtain the misery index, therefore, Figure 7-7 below adds the annual rate of inflation to the unemployment rate.

The Misery Index Turns Back Upward

Figure 7-7 shows that the misery index was less than 10 percent from the mid-1990s until the mid-2000s. Previously, the longest stretch in which the misery index remained persistently below 10 percent was the 1960s.

Since the early 1950s, the misery index has risen as high as 20 percent during two intervals. The first occurred in 1974, when the unemployment rate rose to 9 percent and the annual inflation rate reached 11 percent. The second occurred during 1980, when the unemployment rate rose above 8 percent and the inflation rate spiked to nearly 14 percent.

Four other upturns in the value of the misery index also stand out: the late 1950s, when it approached 11 percent; the early 1970s, when it was about 12 percent; the early

FIGURE 7-7 The Misery Index Since the Early 1950s

The misery index—the sum of the unemployment rate and the inflation rate—hit its peak values in 1974 and 1980.

Sources: Economic Report of the President and *Economic Indicators,* various issues.

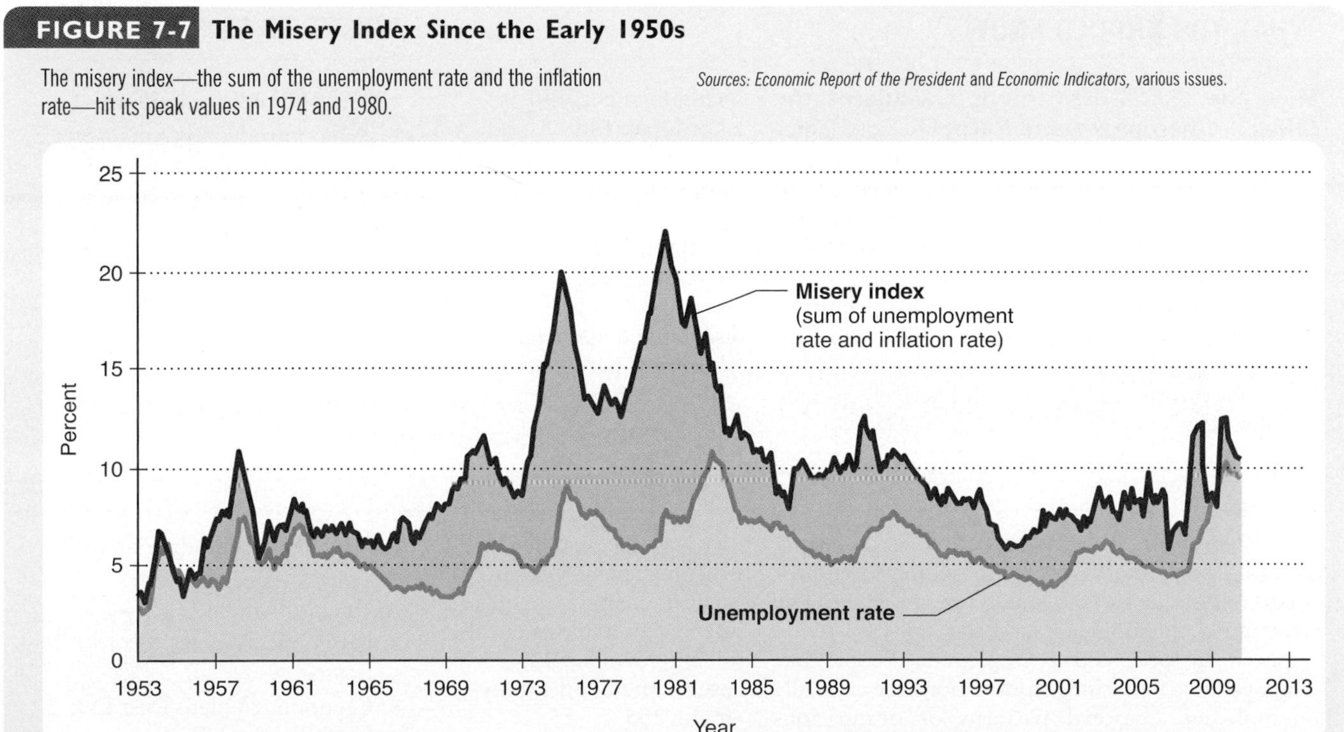

1990s, when it was close to 13 percent; and the late 2000s and early 2010s, when it again approached 13 percent. Thus, during the Great Recession of the late 2000s, the misery index reached a level that ranks among the seven highest of the past six decades.

The Keys to Less "Misery" in the 2010s

So far, the misery index has not attained the heights of 1974 and 1980. Nonetheless, the latest upturn in the misery index resembles the increases during those years in one important respect: like them, the recent rise in the index has involved a substantial increase in the unemployment rate. Indeed, the latest jump in the misery index has been driven *primarily* by a rise in the unemployment rate. The misery-index peaks in 1974 and 1980 occurred during a lengthy period in which the nation experienced *both* a relatively high natural rate of unemployment and significant inflation. Whether the misery index will continue to rise and reach levels rivaling the 1974 or 1980 peaks depends on two factors: (1) whether the recent upsurge in the unemployment rate is mainly cyclical or structural, and (2) whether the rate of inflation remains relatively low or increases.

For Critical Analysis

1. Why is seasonal unemployment unlikely to explain longer-term variations in the misery index?
2. What are two channels through which the natural unemployment rate conceivably could increase and keep the misery index elevated during the 2010s? (Hint: What are the two key components of natural unemployment?)

Web Resources

1. For updates on the misery index, go to www.econtoday.com/ch07.
2. To learn about an alternative type of misery index, go to www.econtoday.com/ch07.

Research Project

It is easy to understand why an increase in the unemployment rate has social costs. Evaluate how a higher inflation rate is costly to society.

For more questions on this chapter's Issues & Applications, go to **MyEconLab**. In the Study Plan for this chapter, select Section N: News.

Here is what you should know after reading this chapter. **MyEconLab** will help you identify what you know, and where to go when you need to practice.

WHAT YOU SHOULD KNOW		WHERE TO GO TO PRACTICE
How the U.S. Government Calculates the Official Unemployment Rate The total number of workers who are officially unemployed consists of noninstitutionalized people aged 16 or older who are willing and able to work and who are actively looking for work but have not found a job. To calculate the unemployment rate, the government determines what percentage this quantity is of the labor force, which consists of all noninstitutionalized people aged 16 years or older who either have jobs or are available for and actively seeking employment.	unemployment, 140 labor force, 140 stock, 141 flow, 141 job loser, 142 reentrant, 142 job leaver, 142 new entrant, 142 discouraged workers, 143 labor force participation rate, 143 **KEY FIGURE** Figure 7-3, 142	• **MyEconLab** Study Plan 7.1 • Audio introduction to Chapter 7 • Animated Figure 7-3 • ABC News Video: The Ripple Effect of Oil Prices • Economics Video: 'Gray Googlers' Work from Home
The Types of Unemployment Temporarily unemployed workers who are searching for appropriate job offers are frictionally unemployed. The structurally unemployed lack the skills currently required by prospective employers. People unemployed due to business contractions are cyclically unemployed. Seasonal patterns of occupations	frictional unemployment, 143 structural unemployment, 144 cyclical unemployment, 144 seasonal unemployment, 145 full employment, 145 natural rate of unemployment, 145	• **MyEconLab** Study Plans 7.2, 7.3 • Video: Major Types of Unemployment • Economics Video: Record Job Losses • Economics Video: Rust Belt City's Brighter Future

(continued)

MyEconLab continued

WHAT YOU SHOULD KNOW		WHERE TO GO TO PRACTICE
within specific industries generate seasonal unemployment. The natural unemployment rate is the seasonally adjusted rate of unemployment including frictional and structural unemployment.		
How Price Indexes Are Calculated and Key Price Indexes To calculate any price index, economists multiply 100 times the ratio of the cost of a market basket of goods and services in the current year to the cost of the same market basket in a base year. The Consumer Price Index (CPI) is computed using a weighted set of goods and services purchased by a typical consumer in urban areas. The Producer Price Index (PPI) is a weighted average of prices of goods sold by a typical firm. The GDP deflator measures changes in the overall level of prices of all goods produced during a given interval. The Personal Consumption Expenditure (PCE) Index is a measure of average prices using weights from surveys of consumer spending.	inflation, 146 deflation, 146 purchasing power, 146 price index, 147 base year, 147 Consumer Price Index (CPI), 147 Producer Price Index (PPI), 147 GDP deflator, 147 Personal Consumption Expenditure (PCE) Index, 147 **KEY FIGURE** Figure 7-4, 149	• **MyEconLab** Study Plan 7.4 • Video: Measuring the Rate of Inflation • Animated Figure 7-4
Nominal Interest Rate versus Real Interest Rate The nominal interest rate is the market rate of interest applying to contracts expressed in current dollars. The real interest rate is net of inflation that borrowers and lenders anticipate will erode the value of nominal interest payments during the period that a loan is repaid. Hence, the real interest rate equals the nominal interest rate minus the expected inflation rate.	anticipated inflation, 150 unanticipated inflation, 150 nominal rate of interest, 150 real rate of interest, 150	• **MyEconLab** Study Plan 7.5 • Video: Inflation and Interest Rates
Losers and Gainers from Inflation Creditors lose as a result of unanticipated inflation that comes as a surprise after they have made a loan, because the real value of the interest payments they receive will turn out to be lower than they had expected. Borrowers gain when unanticipated inflation occurs, because the real value of their interest and principal payments declines. Key costs of inflation include expenses of protecting against inflation, costs of altering business plans because of unexpected changes in prices, and menu costs of repricing goods and services.	cost-of-living adjustments (COLAs), 151 repricing, or menu, cost of inflation, 151	• **MyEconLab** Study Plan 7.5
Key Features of Business Fluctuations Business fluctuations are increases and decreases in business activity. A positive fluctuation is an expansion, which is an upward movement in business activity from a trough, or low point, to a peak, or high point. A negative fluctuation is a contraction, which is a drop in the pace of business activity from a previous peak to a new trough.	business fluctuations, 152 expansion, 152 contraction, 152 recession, 152 depression, 152 leading indicators, 153 **KEY FIGURE** Figure 7-6, 153	• **MyEconLab** Study Plan 7.6 • Animated Figure 7-6 • ABC News Video: The Multipler and the Business Cycle • Economics Video: Record Job Losses • Economics Video: Stashing Your Cash

Log in to MyEconLab, take a chapter test, and get a personalized Study Plan that tells you which concepts you understand and which ones you need to review. From there, MyEconLab will give you further practice, tutorials, animations, videos, and guided solutions.
Log in to www.myeconlab.com

PROBLEMS

All problems are assignable in myeconlab. *Answers to odd-numbered problems appear at the back of the book.*

7-1. Suppose that you are given the following information:

Total population	300.0 million
Adult, noninstitutionalized, nonmilitary population	200.0 million
Unemployment	7.5 million

a. If the labor force participation rate is 70 percent, what is the labor force?

b. How many workers are employed?

c. What is the unemployment rate?

7-2. Suppose that you are given the following information:

Labor force	206.2 million
Adults in the military	1.5 million
Nonadult population	48.0 million
Employed adults	196.2 million
Institutionalized adults	3.5 million
Nonmilitary, noninstitutionalized adults not in labor force	40.8 million

a. What is the total population?

b. How many people are unemployed, and what is the unemployment rate?

c. What is the labor force participation rate?

7-3. Suppose that the U.S. adult population is 224 million, the number employed is 156 million, and the number unemployed is 8 million.

a. What is the unemployment rate?

b. Suppose that there is a difference of 60 million between the adult population and the combined total of people who are employed and unemployed. How do we classify these 60 million people? Based on these figures, what is the U.S. labor force participation rate?

7-4. During the course of a year, the labor force consists of the same 1,000 people. Employers have chosen not to hire 20 of these people in the face of government regulations making it too costly to employ them. Hence, they remain unemployed throughout the year. At the same time, every month during the year, 30 different people become unemployed, and 30 other different people who were unemployed find jobs. There is no seasonal employment.

a. What is the frictional unemployment rate?

b. What is the unemployment rate?

c. Suppose that a system of unemployment compensation is established. Each month, 30 new people (not including the 20 that employers have chosen not to employ) continue to become unemployed, but each monthly group of newly unemployed now takes two months to find a job. After this change, what is the frictional unemployment rate?

d. After the change discussed in part (c), what is the unemployment rate?

7-5. Suppose that a nation has a labor force of 100 people. In January, Amy, Barbara, Carine, and Denise are unemployed. In February, those four find jobs, but Evan, Francesco, George, and Horatio become unemployed. Suppose further that every month, the previous four who were unemployed find jobs and four different people become unemployed. Throughout the year, however, the same three people—Ito, Jack, and Kelley—continually remain unemployed because firms facing government regulations view them as too costly to employ.

a. What is this nation's frictional unemployment rate?

b. What is its structural unemployment rate?

c. What is its unemployment rate?

7-6. In a country with a labor force of 200, a different group of 10 people becomes unemployed each month, but becomes employed once again a month later. No others outside these groups are unemployed.

a. What is this country's unemployment rate?

b. What is the average duration of unemployment?

c. Suppose that establishment of a system of unemployment compensation increases to two months the interval that it takes each group of job losers to become employed each month. Nevertheless, a different group of 10 people still becomes unemployed each month. Now what is the average duration of unemployment?

d. Following the change discussed in part (c), what is the country's unemployment rate?

7-7. A nation's frictional unemployment rate is 1 percent. Seasonal unemployment does not exist in this country. Its cyclical rate of unemployment is 3 percent, and its structural unemployment rate is 4 percent. What is this nation's overall rate of unemployment? What is its natural rate of unemployment?

7-8. In 2010, the cost of a market basket of goods was \$2,000. In 2012, the cost of the same market basket of goods was \$2,100. Use the price index formula to calculate the price index for 2012 if 2010 is the base year.

7-9. Consider the following price indexes: 90 in 2011, 100 in 2012, 110 in 2013, 121 in 2014, and 150 in 2015. Answer the following questions.

a. Which year is likely the base year?

b. What is the inflation rate from 2012 to 2013?

c. What is the inflation rate from 2013 to 2014?

d. If the cost of a market basket in 2012 is $2,000, what is the cost of the same basket of goods and services in 2011? In 2015?

7-10. The real interest rate is 4 percent, and the nominal interest rate is 6 percent. What is the anticipated rate of inflation?

7-11. Currently, the price index used to calculate the inflation rate is equal to 90. The general expectation throughout the economy is that next year its value will be 99. The current nominal interest rate is 12 percent. What is the real interest rate?

7-12. At present, the nominal interest rate is 7 percent, and the expected inflation rate is 5 percent. The current year is the base year for the price index used to calculate inflation.

a. What is the real interest rate?

b. What is the anticipated value of the price index next year?

7-13. Suppose that in 2015 there is a sudden, unanticipated burst of inflation. Consider the situations faced by the following individuals. Who gains and who loses?

a. A homeowner whose wages will keep pace with inflation in 2015 but whose monthly mortgage payments to a savings bank will remain fixed

b. An apartment landlord who has guaranteed to his tenants that their monthly rent payments during 2015 will be the same as they were during 2014

c. A banker who made an auto loan that the auto buyer will repay at a fixed rate of interest during 2015

d. A retired individual who earns a pension with fixed monthly payments from her past employer during 2015

7-14. Consider the diagram below. The line represents the economy's growth trend, and the curve represents the economy's actual course of business fluctuations. For each part below, provide the letter label from the portion of the curve that corresponds to the associated term.

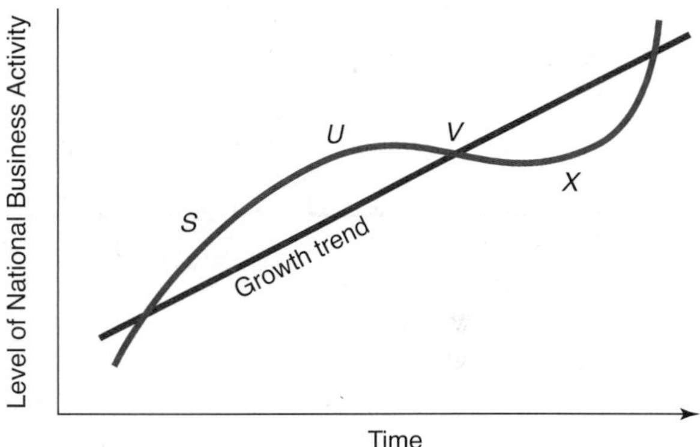

a. Contraction

b. Peak

c. Trough

d. Expansion

ECONOMICS ON THE NET

Looking at the Unemployment and Inflation Data This chapter reviewed key concepts relating to unemployment and inflation. In this application, you get a chance to examine U.S. unemployment and inflation data on your own.

Title: Bureau of Labor Statistics: Employment and Unemployment

Navigation: Use the link at **www.econtoday.com/ch07** to visit the "Employment" page of the Bureau of Labor Statistics (BLS). Click on "Top Picks" next to *Labor Force Statistics (Current Population Survey–CPS)*.

Application Perform the indicated operations, and answer the following questions.

1. Retrieve data for Civilian Labor Force Level, Employment Level, and Unemployment Level. Can you identify periods of sharp cyclical swings? Do they show up in data for the labor force, employment, or unemployment?
2. Are cyclical factors important?

For Group Study and Analysis Divide the class into groups, and assign a price index to each group. Ask each group to take a look at the index for All Years at the link to the BLS statistics on inflation at **www.econtoday.com/ch07**. Have each group identify periods during which their index accelerated or decelerated (or even fell). Do the indexes ever provide opposing implications about inflation and deflation?

ANSWERS TO QUICK QUIZZES

p. 143: (i) Unemployed . . . labor force; (ii) job losers . . . reentrants . . . job leavers . . . new entrants; (iii) increase; (iv) female

p. 146: (i) Frictional; (ii) Structural; (iii) natural

p. 150: (i) base; (ii) Consumer Price; (iii) GDP deflator; (iv) Personal Consumption Expenditure

p. 151: (i) greater . . . less; (ii) purchasing power; (iii) resource

p. 154: (i) business fluctuations; (ii) trough . . . peak; (iii) recession; (iv) external shocks

8

Measuring the Economy's Performance

Does a general increase in the level of a nation's economic activity and the resulting rise in the capability of a typical resident of that country to buy more goods and services tend to make that person happier? During the past four decades, economists have debated whether available evidence supports a yes or no answer to this question. Naturally, to evaluate the evidence, economists have to measure the level of "happiness" of a nation's residents, which is not an easy task. Such an evaluation also requires that the economists be able to measure the level of the country's economic activity. The measurement of a nation's overall economic performance is the main topic of this chapter.

LEARNING OBJECTIVES

After reading this chapter, you should be able to:

- Describe the circular flow of income and output
- Define gross domestic product (GDP)
- Understand the limitations of using GDP as a measure of national welfare
- Explain the expenditure approach to tabulating GDP
- Explain the income approach to computing GDP
- Distinguish between nominal GDP and real GDP

myeconlab

MyEconLab helps you master each objective and study more efficiently. See end of chapter for details.

U.S. economic activity declined by a greater percentage during the first 18 months of the Great Recession of the late 2000s than during any other 18-month period since World War II? To measure the nation's overall economic performance over time, the government utilizes what has become known as **national income accounting.** How this is done is the main focus of this chapter. But first we need to look at the flow of income within an economy, for it is the flow of goods and services from businesses to consumers and of payments from consumers to businesses, that constitutes economic activity.

National income accounting
A measurement system used to estimate national income and its components; one approach to measuring an economy's aggregate performance.

The Simple Circular Flow

The concept of a circular flow of income (ignoring taxes) involves two principles:

1. In every economic exchange, the seller receives exactly the same amount that the buyer spends.
2. Goods and services flow in one direction and money payments flow in the other.

In the simple economy shown in Figure 8-1 on the facing page, there are only businesses and households. It is assumed that businesses sell their *entire* output in the current period to households and that households spend their *entire* income in the current period on consumer products. Households receive their income by selling the use of whatever factors of production they own, such as labor services.

Profits Explained

We have indicated in Figure 8-1 that profit is a cost of production. You might be under the impression that profits are not part of the cost of producing goods and services, but profits are indeed a part of this cost because entrepreneurs must be rewarded for providing their services or they won't provide them. Their reward, if any, is profit. The reward—the profit—is included in the cost of the factors of production. If there were no expectations of profit, entrepreneurs would not incur the risk associated with the organization of productive activities. That is why we consider profits a cost of doing business. Just as workers expect wages, entrepreneurs expect profits.

Total Income or Total Output

Total income
The yearly amount earned by the nation's resources (factors of production). Total income therefore includes wages, rent, interest payments, and profits that are received by workers, landowners, capital owners, and entrepreneurs, respectively.

Final goods and services
Goods and services that are at their final stage of production and will not be transformed into yet other goods or services. For example, wheat ordinarily is not considered a final good because it is usually used to make a final good, bread.

The arrow that goes from businesses to households at the bottom of Figure 8-1 on the facing page is labeled "Total income." What would be a good definition of **total income?** If you answered "the total of all individuals' income," you would be right. But all income is actually a payment for something, whether it be wages paid for labor services, rent paid for the use of land, interest paid for the use of capital, or profits paid to entrepreneurs. It is the amount paid to the resource suppliers. Therefore, total income is also defined as the annual *cost* of producing the entire output of **final goods and services.**

The arrow going from households to businesses at the top of Figure 8-1 represents the dollar value of output in the economy. This is equal to the total monetary value of all final goods and services for this simple economy. In essence, it represents the total business receipts from the sale of all final goods and services produced by businesses and consumed by households. Business receipts are the opposite side of household expenditures. When households purchase goods and services, those payments become a *business receipt.* Every transaction, therefore, simultaneously involves an expenditure and a receipt.

FIGURE 8-1 The Circular Flow of Income and Product

Businesses provide final goods and services to households (upper clockwise loop), who in turn pay for them (upper counterclockwise loop). Payments flow in a counterclockwise direction and can be thought of as a circular flow. The dollar value of output is identical to total income because profits are defined as being equal to total business receipts minus business outlays for wages, rents, and interest. Households provide factor services to businesses and receive income (lower loops).

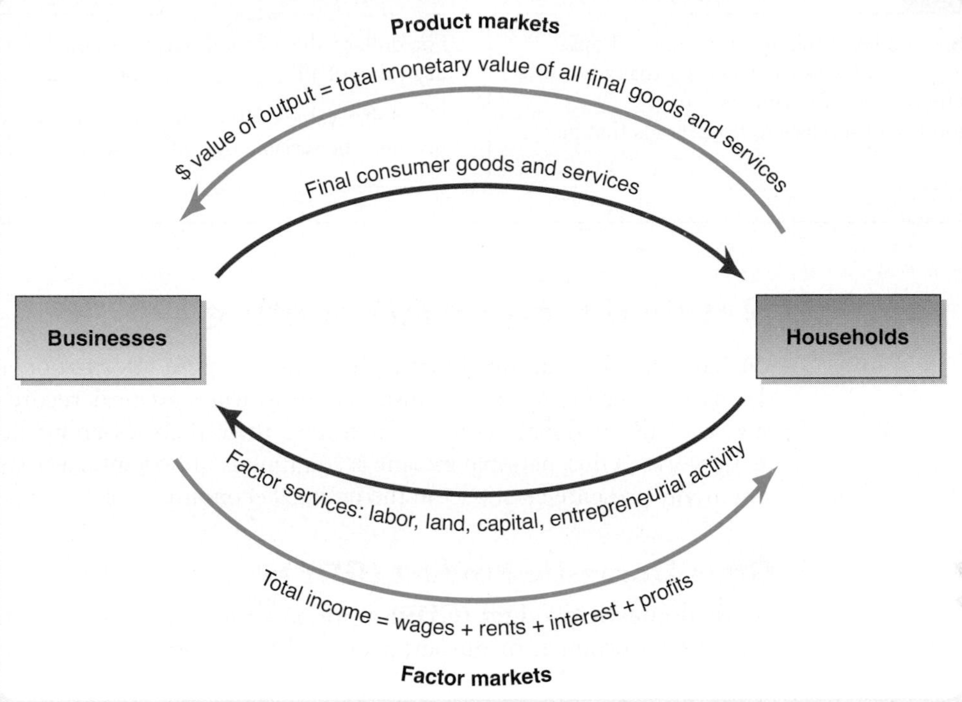

PRODUCT MARKETS Transactions in which households buy goods take place in the product markets—that's where households are the buyers and businesses are the sellers of consumer goods. *Product market* transactions are represented in the upper loops in Figure 8-1 above. Note that consumer goods and services flow to household demanders, while money flows in the opposite direction to business suppliers.

FACTOR MARKETS *Factor market* transactions are represented by the lower loops in Figure 8-1. In the factor market, households are the sellers. They sell resources such as labor, land, capital, and entrepreneurial ability. Businesses are the buyers in factor markets. Business expenditures represent receipts or, more simply, income for households. Also, in the lower loops of Figure 8-1, factor services flow from households to businesses, while the money paid for these services flows in the opposite direction from businesses to households. Observe also the flow of money (counterclockwise) from households to businesses and back again from businesses to households: It is an endless circular flow.

Why the Dollar Value of Total Output Must Equal Total Income

Total income represents the income received by households in payment for the production of goods and services. Why must total income be identical to the dollar value of total output? First, as Figure 8-1 shows, spending by one group is income to another. Second, it is a matter of simple accounting and the economic definition of profit as a cost of production. Profit is defined as what is *left over* from total business receipts after all other costs—wages, rents, interest—have been paid. If the dollar value of total output is $1,000 and the total of wages, rent, and interest for producing that output is $900, profit is $100. Profit is always the *residual* item that makes total income equal to the dollar value of total output.

QUICK QUIZ See page 186 for the answers. Review concepts from this section in MyEconLab.

In the circular flow model of income and output, households sell __________ services to businesses that pay for those services. The receipt of payments is total __________. Businesses sell goods and services to households that pay for them.

The dollar value of total output is equal to the total monetary value of all __________ goods and services produced.

The dollar value of final output must always equal total income. The variable that adjusts to make this so is known as __________.

National Income Accounting

We have already mentioned that policymakers require information about the state of the national economy. Economists use historical statistical records on the performance of the national economy in testing their theories about how the economy really works. Thus, national income accounting is important. Let's start with the most commonly presented statistic on the national economy.

Gross Domestic Product (GDP)

Gross domestic product (GDP)
The total market value of all final goods and services produced during a year by factors of production located within a nation's borders.

Gross domestic product (GDP) represents the total market value of the nation's annual final product, or output, produced by factors of production located within national borders. We therefore formally define GDP as the total market value of all final goods and services produced in an economy during a year. We are referring here to the value of a *flow of production.* A nation produces at a certain rate, just as you receive income at a certain rate. Your income flow might be at a rate of $20,000 per year or $100,000 per year. Suppose you are told that someone earns $5,000. Would you consider this a good salary? There is no way to answer that question unless you know whether the person is earning $5,000 per month or per week or per day. Thus, you have to specify a time period for all flows. Income received is a flow. You must contrast this with, for example, your total accumulated savings, which are a stock measured at a point in time, not over time. Implicit in just about everything we deal with in this chapter is a time period—usually one year. All the measures of domestic product and income are specified as *rates* measured in dollars per year.

Stress on Final Output

Intermediate goods
Goods used up entirely in the production of final goods.

GDP does not count **intermediate goods** (goods used up entirely in the production of final goods) because to do so would be to count them twice. For example, even though grain that a farmer produces may be that farmer's final product, it is not the final product for the nation. It is sold to make bread. Bread is the final product.

Value added
The dollar value of an industry's sales minus the value of intermediate goods (for example, raw materials and parts) used in production.

We can use a numerical example to clarify this point further. Our example will involve determining the value added at each stage of production. **Value added** is the dollar value contributed to a product at each stage of its production. In Table 8-1 on the facing page, we see the difference between total value of all sales and value added in the production of a donut. We also see that the sum of the values added is equal to the sale price to the final consumer. It is the 45 cents that is used to measure GDP, not the 97 cents. If we used the 97 cents, we would be double counting from stages 2 through 5, for each intermediate good would be counted at least twice—once when it was produced and again when the good it was used in making was sold. Such double counting would greatly exaggerate GDP.

TABLE 8-1

Sales Value and Value Added at Each Stage of Donut Production

(1) Stage of Production	(2) Dollar Value of Sales	(3) Value Added
Stage 1: Fertilizer and seed	$.03	$.03
Stage 2: Growing	.07	.04
Stage 3: Milling	.12	.05
Stage 4: Baking	.30	.18
Stage 5: Retailing	.45	.15
	Total dollar value of all sales $.97	Total value added $.45

Stage 1: A farmer purchases 3 cents' worth of fertilizer and seed, which are used as factors of production in growing wheat.

Stage 2: The farmer grows the wheat, harvests it, and sells it to a miller for 7 cents. Thus, we see that the farmer has added 4 cents' worth of value. Those 4 cents represent income over and above expenses incurred by the farmer.

Stage 3: The miller purchases the wheat for 7 cents and adds 5 cents as the value added. That is, there is 5 cents for the miller as income. The miller sells the ground wheat flour to a donut-baking company.

Stage 4: The donut-baking company buys the flour for 12 cents and adds 18 cents as the value added. It then sells the donut to the final retailer.

Stage 5: The donut retailer sells donuts at 45 cents apiece, thus creating an additional value of 15 cents.

We see that the total value of the transactions involved in the production of one donut is 97 cents, but the total value added is 45 cents, which is exactly equal to the retail price. The total value added is equal to the sum of all income payments.

Exclusion of Financial Transactions, Transfer Payments, and Secondhand Goods

Remember that GDP is the measure of the dollar value of all final goods and services produced in one year. Many more transactions occur that have nothing to do with final goods and services produced. There are financial transactions, transfers of the ownership of preexisting goods, and other transactions that should not and do not get included in our measure of GDP.

Go to www.econtoday.com/ch08 for the most up-to-date U.S. economic data at the Web site of the Bureau of Economic Analysis.

FINANCIAL TRANSACTIONS There are three general categories of purely financial transactions: (1) the buying and selling of securities, (2) government transfer payments, and (3) private transfer payments.

Securities. When you purchase shares of existing stock in Apple, Inc., someone else has sold it to you. In essence, there was merely a *transfer* of ownership rights. You paid $100 to obtain the stock. Someone else received the $100 and gave up the stock. No producing activity was consummated at that time, unless a broker received a fee for performing the transaction, in which case only the fee is part of GDP. The $100 transaction is not included when we measure GDP.

Government Transfer Payments. Transfer payments are payments for which no productive services are concurrently provided in exchange. The most obvious government transfer payments are Social Security benefits, veterans' payments, and unemployment compensation. The recipients add nothing to current production in return for such transfer payments (although they may have contributed in the past to be eligible to receive them). Government transfer payments are not included in GDP.

Private Transfer Payments. Are you receiving funds from your parents in order to attend school? Has a wealthy relative ever given you a gift of cash? If so, you have been the recipient of a private transfer payment. This is merely a transfer of funds from one individual to another. As such, it does not constitute productive activity and is not included in GDP.

TRANSFER OF SECONDHAND GOODS If I sell you my two-year-old laptop computer, no current production is involved. I transfer to you the ownership of a computer that was produced years ago; in exchange, you transfer to me $350. The original purchase price of the computer was included in GDP in the year I purchased it. To include the price again when I sell it to you would be counting the value of the computer a second time.

OTHER EXCLUDED TRANSACTIONS Many other transactions are not included in GDP for practical reasons:

- Household production—housecleaning, child care, and other tasks performed by people in their *own* households and for which they receive no payments through the marketplace
- Otherwise legal underground transactions—those that are legal but not reported and hence not taxed, such as paying housekeepers in cash that is not declared as income to the Internal Revenue Service
- Illegal underground activities—these include prostitution, illegal gambling, and the sale of illicit drugs

You Are There

To contemplate why economists may sometimes doubt a nation's official GDP tabulations, read **Questioning China's Official Real GDP Statistics,** on page 180.

Recognizing the Limitations of GDP

Like any statistical measure, gross domestic product is a concept that can be both well used and misused. Economists find it especially valuable as an overall indicator of a nation's economic performance. But it is important to realize that GDP has significant weaknesses. Because it includes only the value of goods and services traded in markets, it excludes *nonmarket* production, such as the household services of homemakers discussed earlier. This can cause some problems in comparing the GDP of an industrialized country with the GDP of a highly agrarian nation in which nonmarket production is relatively more important. It also causes problems if nations have different definitions of legal versus illegal activities. For instance, a nation with legalized gambling will count the value of gambling services, which has a reported market value as a legal activity. But in a country where gambling is illegal, individuals who provide such services will not report the market value of gambling activities, and so they will not be counted in that country's GDP. This can complicate comparing GDP in the nation where gambling is legal with GDP in the country that prohibits gambling.

Furthermore, although GDP is often used as a benchmark measure for standard-of-living calculations, it is not necessarily a good measure of the well-being of a nation. No measured figure of total national annual income can take account of changes in the degree of labor market discrimination, declines or improvements in personal safety, or the quantity or quality of leisure time. Measured GDP also says little about our environmental quality of life. As the now-defunct Soviet Union illustrated to the world, the large-scale production of such items as minerals, electricity, and irrigation for farming can have negative effects on the environment: deforestation from strip mining, air and soil pollution from particulate emissions or nuclear accidents at power plants, and erosion of the natural balance between water and salt in bodies of water such as the Aral Sea. Other nations, such as China and India, have also experienced greater pollution problems as their levels of GDP have increased. Hence, it is important to recognize the following point:

> ***GDP is a measure of the value of production in terms of market prices and an indicator of economic activity. It is not a measure of a nation's overall welfare.***

Why is the government of France rethinking the use of GDP as its primary measure of that nation's economic performance?

INTERNATIONAL POLICY EXAMPLE

The French Government Seeks to De-emphasize GDP

The president of France, Nicolas Sarkozy, recently endorsed a report that concluded that there is an "excessive focus on GDP statistics." The French government, the report argued, should develop an alternative measure of economic performance in which GDP is only one among several criteria.

One possibility, the report suggested, would be for France to adopt a measure similar to the United Nations' Human Development Index, or HDI. The HDI seeks to measure a nation's average achievements in three basic areas: (1) health, measured by life expectancy at birth; (2) knowledge, measured by a combination of school enrollments and adult literacy rates; and (3) standard of living, measured by GDP per person. Thus, even if the French government were to adopt the HDI to track the economic performance of France, it would continue to consider GDP but would also include measures of health and knowledge.

FOR CRITICAL ANALYSIS

Why do you suppose that economists who criticize the French government's efforts to broaden its measure of economic performance argue that life expectancy, school enrollments, and adult literacy rates are not really economic quantities?

Nonetheless, GDP is a relatively accurate and useful measure of the economy's domestic economic activity, measured in current dollars. Understanding GDP is thus an important first step for analyzing changes in economic activity over time.

QUICK QUIZ

See page 186 for the answers. Review concepts from this section in MyEconLab.

__________ __________ __________ is the total market value of final goods and services produced in an economy during a one-year period by factors of production within the nation's borders. It represents the dollar value of the flow of final production over a one-year period.

To avoid double counting, we look only at final goods and services produced or, equivalently, at __________ __________.

In measuring GDP, we must ________ (1) purely financial transactions, such as the buying and selling of securities; (2) government transfer payments and private transfer payments; and (3) the transfer of secondhand goods.

Many other transactions are excluded from measured __________, among them household services rendered by homemakers, underground economy transactions, and illegal economic activities, even though many of these result in the production of final goods and services.

GDP is a useful measure for tracking changes in the __________ __________ of overall economic activity over time, but it is not a measure of the well-being of a nation's residents because it fails to account for nonmarket transactions, the amount and quality of leisure time, environmental or safety issues, labor market discrimination, and other factors that influence general welfare.

Two Main Methods of Measuring GDP

The definition of GDP is the total dollar value of all final goods and services produced during a year. How, exactly, do we go about actually computing this number?

The circular flow diagram presented in Figure 8-1 on page 163 gave us a shortcut method for calculating GDP. We can look at the *flow of expenditures*, which consists of consumption, investment, government purchases of goods and services, and net expenditures in the foreign sector (net exports). In this **expenditure approach** to measuring GDP, we add the dollar value of all final goods and services. We could also use the *flow of income*, looking at the income received by everybody producing goods and services. In this **income approach**, we add the income received by all factors of production.

Expenditure approach
Computing GDP by adding up the dollar value at current market prices of all final goods and services.

Income approach
Measuring GDP by adding up all components of national income, including wages, interest, rent, and profits.

Deriving GDP by the Expenditure Approach

To derive GDP using the expenditure approach, we must look at each of the separate components of expenditures and then add them together. These components are consumption expenditures, investment, government expenditures, and net exports.

Durable consumer goods
Consumer goods that have a life span of more than three years.

Nondurable consumer goods
Consumer goods that are used up within three years.

Services
Mental or physical labor or help purchased by consumers. Examples are the assistance of physicians, lawyers, dentists, repair personnel, housecleaners, educators, retailers, and wholesalers; things purchased or used by consumers that do not have physical characteristics.

Gross private domestic investment
The creation of capital goods, such as factories and machines, that can yield production and hence consumption in the future. Also included in this definition are changes in business inventories and repairs made to machines or buildings.

Investment
Any use of today's resources to expand tomorrow's production or consumption.

CONSUMPTION EXPENDITURES How do we spend our income? As households or as individuals, we spend our income through consumption expenditure (C), which falls into three categories: **durable consumer goods, nondurable consumer goods,** and **services.** Durable goods are *arbitrarily* defined as items that last more than three years. They include automobiles, furniture, and household appliances. Nondurable goods are all the rest, such as food and gasoline. Services are intangible commodities: medical care, education, and the like.

Housing expenditures constitute a major proportion of anybody's annual expenditures. Rental payments on apartments are automatically included in consumption expenditure estimates. People who own their homes, however, do not make rental payments. Consequently, government statisticians estimate what is called the *implicit rental value* of existing owner-occupied homes. It is roughly equal to the amount of rent you would have to pay if you did not own the home but were renting it from someone else.

GROSS PRIVATE DOMESTIC INVESTMENT We now turn our attention to **gross private domestic investment** (I) undertaken by businesses. When economists refer to investment, they are referring to additions to productive capacity. **Investment** may be thought of as an activity that uses resources today in such a way that they allow for greater production in the future and hence greater consumption in the future. When a business buys new equipment or puts up a new factory, it is investing. It is increasing its capacity to produce in the future.

In estimating gross private domestic investment, government statisticians also add consumer expenditures on *new* residential structures because new housing represents an addition to our future productive capacity in the sense that a new house can generate housing services in the future.

The layperson's notion of investment often relates to the purchase of stocks and bonds. For our purposes, such transactions simply represent the *transfer of ownership* of assets called stocks and bonds. Thus, you must keep in mind the fact that in economics, investment refers *only* to *additions* to productive capacity, not to transfers of assets.

Producer durables, or **capital goods**
Durable goods having an expected service life of more than three years that are used by businesses to produce other goods and services.

Fixed investment
Purchases by businesses of newly produced producer durables, or capital goods, such as production machinery and office equipment.

Inventory investment
Changes in the stocks of finished goods and goods in process, as well as changes in the raw materials that businesses keep on hand. Whenever inventories are decreasing, inventory investment is negative. Whenever they are increasing, inventory investment is positive.

FIXED VERSUS INVENTORY INVESTMENT In our analysis, we will consider the basic components of investment. We have already mentioned the first one, which involves a firm's purchase of equipment or construction of a new factory. These are called **producer durables,** or **capital goods.** A producer durable, or a capital good, is simply a good that is purchased not to be consumed in its current form but to be used to make other goods and services. The purchase of equipment and factories—capital goods—is called **fixed investment.**

The other type of investment has to do with the change in inventories of raw materials and finished goods. Firms do not immediately sell off all their products to consumers. Some of this final product is usually held in inventory waiting to be sold. Firms hold inventories to meet future expected orders for their products. When a firm increases its inventories of finished products, it is engaging in **inventory investment.** Inventories consist of all finished goods on hand, goods in process, and raw materials.

The reason that we can think of a change in inventories as being a type of investment is that an increase in such inventories provides for future increased consumption possibilities. When inventory investment is zero, the firm is neither adding to nor subtracting from the total stock of goods or raw materials on hand. Thus, if the firm keeps the same amount of inventories throughout the year, inventory *investment* has been zero.

Why do some economists suggest that *actual* business fixed investment may be considerably higher than *officially reported* business fixed investment?

EXAMPLE Is Failing to Include Hidden Intangibles Depressing Measured Business Fixed Investment?

For purposes of national income accounting, business fixed investment officially consists of purchases of newly produced producer durables, or capital goods. These are material, or *tangible,* goods such as telecommunications equipment and computers. Some economists suggest that because investment is broadly defined as the use of current resources to expand future productive capabilities, business fixed investment should also include *intangible* investment. Such investment includes amounts firms spend on such items as improvements in their organizational structure, research to develop new processes or products, and employee education.

Leonard Nakamura, an economist at the Federal Reserve Bank of Philadelphia, has estimated that since 1959 intangible investment has increased from just below 4 percent of GDP to almost 9 percent of GDP. Thus, Nakamura finds that if intangible investment had been counted as part of business fixed investment, in recent years business fixed investment as a percentage of GDP would have nearly doubled from more than 9 percent to almost 18 percent.

FOR CRITICAL ANALYSIS

Why is tangible investment likely to be easier to measure accurately than intangible investment?

GOVERNMENT EXPENDITURES In addition to personal consumption expenditures, there are government purchases of goods and services (G). The government buys goods and services from private firms and pays wages and salaries to government employees. Generally, we value goods and services at the prices at which they are sold. But many government goods and services are not sold in the market. Therefore, we cannot use their market value when computing GDP. The value of these goods is considered equal to their *cost.* For example, the value of a newly built road is considered equal to its construction cost and is included in the GDP for the year it was built.

NET EXPORTS (FOREIGN EXPENDITURES) To get an accurate representation of GDP, we must include the foreign sector. As U.S. residents, we purchase foreign goods called *imports.* The goods that foreign residents purchase from us are our *exports.* To determine the *net* expenditures from the foreign sector, we subtract the value of imports from the value of exports to get net exports (X) for a year:

$$\text{Net exports } (X) = \text{total exports} - \text{total imports}$$

To understand why we subtract imports rather than ignoring them altogether, recall that we want to estimate *domestic* output, so we have to subtract U.S. expenditures on the goods produced in other nations.

Presenting the Expenditure Approach

We have just defined the components of GDP using the expenditure approach. When we add them all together, we get a definition for GDP, which is as follows:

$$\text{GDP} = C + I + G + X$$

where

$$\begin{aligned} C &= \text{consumption expenditures} \\ I &= \text{investment expenditures} \\ G &= \text{government expenditures} \\ X &= \text{net exports} \end{aligned}$$

THE HISTORICAL PICTURE To get an idea of the relationship among C, I, G, and X, look at Figure 8-2 on the next page, which shows GDP, personal consumption expenditures, government purchases, and gross private domestic investment plus net exports since 1929. When we add up the expenditures of the household, business, government, and foreign sectors, we get GDP.

FIGURE 8-2 GDP and Its Components

Here we see a display of gross domestic product, personal consumption expenditures, government purchases, and gross private domestic investment plus net exports for the years since 1929. (Note that the scale of the vertical axis changes as we move up the axis.) During the Great Depression of the 1930s, gross private domestic investment *plus* net exports was negative because we were investing very little at that time. During the 2000s, gross private domestic investment initially declined and then recovered slowly until the Great Recession when it turned sharply downward. Net exports also became increasingly negative. Hence, the sum of these two items has declined since 2007.

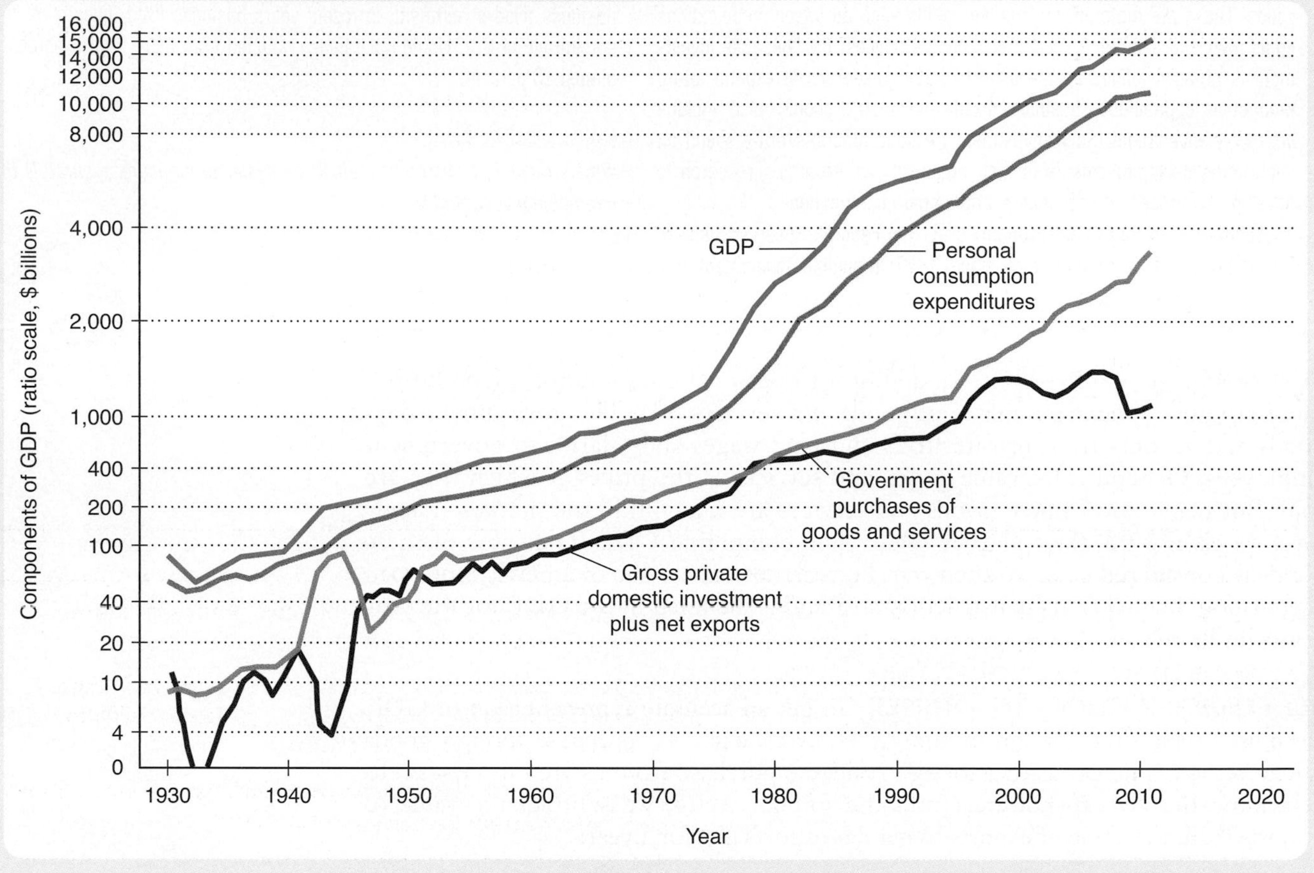

DEPRECIATION AND NET DOMESTIC PRODUCT We have used the terms *gross domestic product* and *gross private domestic investment* without really indicating what *gross* means. The dictionary defines it as "without deductions," the opposite of *net*. Deductions for what? you might ask. The deductions are for something we call **depreciation.** In the course of a year, machines and structures wear out or are used up in the production of domestic product. For example, houses deteriorate as they are occupied, and machines need repairs or they will fall apart and stop working. Most capital, or durable, goods depreciate.

Depreciation
Reduction in the value of capital goods over a one-year period due to physical wear and tear and also to obsolescence; also called *capital consumption allowance.*

An estimate of the amount that capital goods have depreciated during the year is subtracted from gross domestic product to arrive at a figure called **net domestic product (NDP),** which we define as follows:

Net domestic product (NDP)
GDP minus depreciation.

$$\text{NDP} = \text{GDP} - \text{depreciation}$$

Depreciation is also called **capital consumption allowance** because it is the amount of the capital stock that has been consumed over a one-year period. In essence, it equals the amount a business would have to put aside to repair and replace deteriorating machines. Because we know that

Capital consumption allowance
Another name for depreciation, the amount that businesses would have to save in order to take care of deteriorating machines and other equipment.

$$\text{GDP} = C + I + G + X$$

we know that the formula for NDP is

$$\text{NDP} = C + I + G + X - \text{depreciation}$$

Alternatively, because net $I = I -$ depreciation,

$$\text{NDP} = C + \text{net } I + G + X$$

Net investment measures *changes* in our capital stock over time and is positive nearly every year. Because depreciation does not vary greatly from year to year as a percentage of GDP, we get a similar picture of what is happening to our national economy by looking at either NDP or GDP data.

Net investment
Gross private domestic investment minus an estimate of the wear and tear on the existing capital stock. Net investment therefore measures the change in the capital stock over a one-year period.

Net investment is an important variable to observe over time nonetheless. If everything else remains the same in an economy, changes in net investment can have dramatic consequences for future economic growth (a topic we cover in more detail in Chapter 9). Positive net investment by definition expands the productive capacity of our economy. This means that there is increased capital, which will generate even more income in the future. When net investment is zero, we are investing just enough to take account of depreciation. Our economy's productive capacity remains unchanged. Finally, when net investment is negative, we can expect negative economic growth prospects in the future. Negative net investment means that our productive capacity is actually declining—we are disinvesting. This actually occurred during the Great Depression.

QUICK QUIZ See page 186 for the answers. Review concepts from this section in MyEconLab.

The __________ approach to measuring GDP requires that we add up consumption expenditures, gross private investment, government purchases, and net exports. Consumption expenditures include consumer __________, consumer __________, and __________.

Gross private domestic investment *excludes* transfers of asset ownership. It includes only additions to the productive __________ of a nation, repairs on existing capital goods, and changes in business __________.

We value government expenditures at their cost because we usually do not have __________ prices at which to value government goods and services.

To obtain **net domestic product (NDP),** we subtract from GDP the year's ________ of the existing capital stock.

Deriving GDP by the Income Approach

If you go back to the circular flow diagram in Figure 8-1 on page 163, you see that product markets are at the top of the diagram and factor markets are at the bottom. We can calculate the value of the circular flow of income and product by looking at expenditures—which we just did—or by looking at total factor payments. Factor payments are called income. We calculate **gross domestic income (GDI),** which we will see is identical to gross domestic product (GDP). Using the income approach, we have four categories of payments to individuals: wages, interest, rent, and profits.

Gross domestic income (GDI)
The sum of all income—wages, interest, rent, and profits—paid to the four factors of production.

1. *Wages.* The most important category is, of course, wages, including salaries and other forms of labor income, such as income in kind and incentive payments. We also count Social Security taxes (both the employees' and the employers' contributions).
2. *Interest.* Here interest payments do not equal the sum of all payments for the use of funds in a year. Instead, interest is expressed in *net* rather than in gross terms. The interest component of total income is only net interest received by households plus net interest paid to us by foreign residents. Net interest received by households is the difference between the interest they receive (from savings accounts, certificates of deposit, and the like) and the interest they pay (to banks for home mortgages, credit cards, and other loans).

Go to **www.econtoday.com/ch08** to examine recent trends in U.S. GDP and its components.

3. *Rent.* Rent is all income earned by individuals for the use of their real (nonmonetary) assets, such as farms, houses, and stores. As stated previously, we have to include here the implicit rental value of owner-occupied houses. Also included in this category are royalties received from copyrights, patents, and assets such as oil wells.
4. *Profits.* Our last category includes total gross corporate profits plus *proprietors' income.* Proprietors' income is income earned from the operation of unincorporated businesses, which include sole proprietorships, partnerships, and producers' cooperatives. It is unincorporated business profit.

All of the payments listed are *actual* factor payments made to owners of the factors of production. When we add them together, though, we do not yet have gross domestic income. We have to take account of two other components: **indirect business taxes,** such as sales and business property taxes, and depreciation, which we have already discussed.

Indirect business taxes
All business taxes except the tax on corporate profits. Indirect business taxes include sales and business property taxes.

INDIRECT BUSINESS TAXES Indirect taxes are the (nonincome) taxes paid by consumers when they buy goods and services. When you buy a book, you pay the price of the book plus any state and local sales tax. The business is actually acting as the government's agent in collecting the sales tax, which it in turn passes on to the government. Such taxes therefore represent a business expense and are included in gross domestic income.

DEPRECIATION Just as we had to deduct depreciation to get from GDP to NDP, so we must *add* depreciation to go from net domestic income to gross domestic income. Depreciation can be thought of as the portion of the current year's GDP that is used to replace physical capital consumed in the process of production. Because somebody has paid for the replacement, depreciation must be added as a component of gross domestic income.

The last two components of GDP—indirect business taxes and depreciation—are called **nonincome expense items.**

Nonincome expense items
The total of indirect business taxes and depreciation.

Figure 8-3 on the facing page shows a comparison between estimated gross domestic product and gross domestic income for 2011. Whether you decide to use the expenditure approach or the income approach, you will come out with the same number. There are sometimes statistical discrepancies, but they are usually relatively small.

QUICK QUIZ See page 186 for the answers. Review concepts from this section in MyEconLab.

To derive GDP using the income approach, we add up all factor payments, including ___________, ___________, ___________, and ___________.	To get an accurate measure of GDP using the income approach, we must also add ___________ ___________ ___________ and ___________ to those total factor payments.

Other Components of National Income Accounting

Gross domestic income or product does not really tell us how much income people have access to for spending purposes. To get to those kinds of data, we must make some adjustments, which we now do.

National Income (NI)

We know that net domestic product (NDP) is the total market value of goods and services available to consume and to add to the capital stock. NDP, however, includes indirect business taxes and transfers, which should not count as part of income earned

FIGURE 8-3 Gross Domestic Product and Gross Domestic Income, 2011 (in billions of 2005 dollars per year)

By using the two different methods of computing the output of the economy, we come up with gross domestic product and gross domestic income, which are by definition equal. One approach focuses on expenditures, or the flow of product; the other approach concentrates on income, or the flow of costs.

Sources: U.S. Department of Commerce and author's estimates.

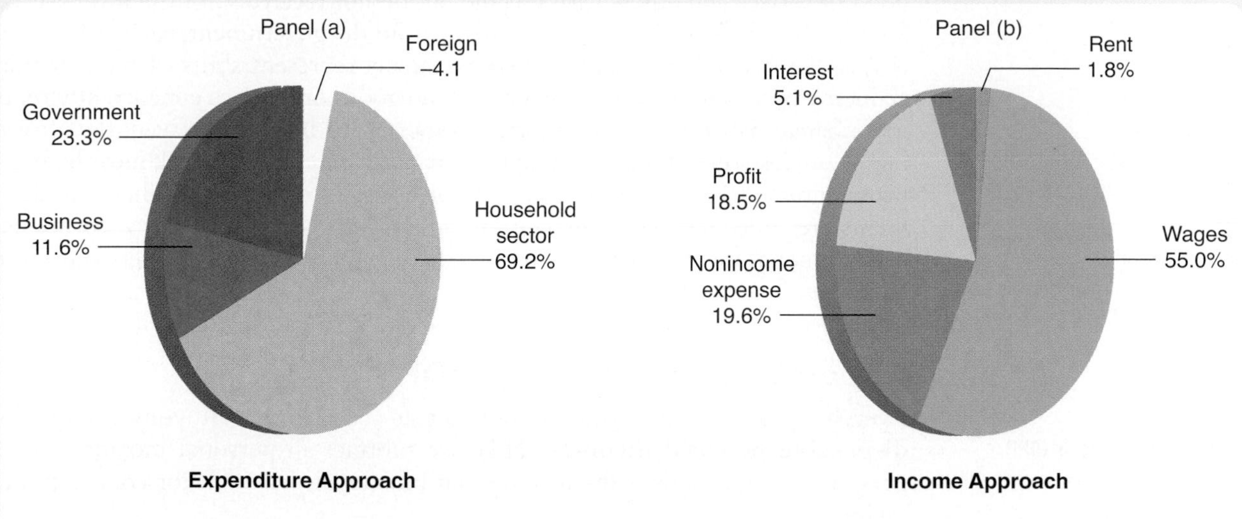

Expenditure Point of View—Product Flow Expenditure by Different Sectors:		Income Point of View—Cost Flow Domestic Income (at Factor Cost):	
Household sector		*Wages*	
Personal consumption expenses	$10,421.1	All wages, salaries, and supplemental employee compensation	$8,287.3
Government sector		*Rent*	
Purchase of goods and services	3,514.2	All rental income of individuals plus implicit rent on owner-occupied dwellings	283.6
Business sector		*Interest*	
Gross private domestic investment (including depreciation)	1,743.7	Net interest paid by business	782.1
Foreign sector		*Profit*	
Net exports of goods and services	–611.5	Proprietorial income	1,301.0
		Corporate profits before taxes deducted	1,495.2
		Nonincome expense items	
		Indirect business taxes	759.9
		Depreciation	2,210.2
		Statistical discrepancy	–51.8
Gross domestic product	$15,067.5	Gross domestic income	$15,067.5

by U.S. factors of production, but does not include various business incomes that should. We therefore subtract from NDP indirect taxes and transfers and add other business income adjustments. Because U.S. residents earn income abroad and foreign residents earn income in the United States, we also add *net* U.S. income earned abroad.

National income (NI)
The total of all factor payments to resource owners. It can be obtained from net domestic product (NDP) by subtracting indirect business taxes and transfers and adding net U.S. income earned abroad and other business income adjustments.

The result is what we define as **national income (NI)**—income earned by all U.S. factors of production.

Personal Income (PI)

National income does not actually represent what is available to individuals to spend because some people obtain income for which they have provided no concurrent good or service and others earn income but do not receive it. In the former category are mainly recipients of transfer payments from the government, such as Social Security, welfare, and food stamps. These payments represent shifts of funds within the economy by way of the government, with no goods or services concurrently rendered in exchange. For the other category, income earned but not received, the most obvious examples are corporate retained earnings that are plowed back into the business, contributions to social insurance, and corporate income taxes. When transfer payments are added and when income earned but not received is subtracted, we end up with **personal income (PI)**—income *received* by the factors of production prior to the payment of personal income taxes.

Personal income (PI)
The amount of income that households actually receive before they pay personal income taxes.

Disposable Personal Income (DPI)

Everybody knows that you do not get to take home all your salary. To get **disposable personal income (DPI),** we subtract all personal income taxes from personal income. This is the income that individuals have left for consumption and saving.

Disposable personal income (DPI)
Personal income after personal income taxes have been paid.

Deriving the Components of GDP

Table 8-2 below shows how to derive the various components of GDP. It explains how to go from gross domestic product to net domestic product to national income to personal income and then to disposable personal income. On the frontpapers of your book, you can see the historical record for GDP, NDP, NI, PI, and DPI for selected years since 1929.

We have completed our rundown of the different ways that GDP can be computed and of the different variants of national income and product. What we have not yet

TABLE 8-2

Going from GDP to Disposable Income, 2011

	Billions of Dollars
Gross domestic product (GDP)	15,067.5
Minus depreciation	–2,210.2
Net domestic product (NDP)	12,857.3
Minus indirect business taxes and transfers	–1,374.4
Plus other business income adjustments	1,296.7
Plus net U.S. income earned abroad	71.0
National income (NI)	12,850.6
Minus corporate taxes, Social Security contributions, corporate retained earnings	–1,881.5
Plus government transfer payments	1,787.2
Personal income (PI)	12,756.3
Minus personal income taxes	–1,132.3
Disposable personal income (DPI)	11,624.0

Sources: U.S. Department of Commerce and author's estimates.

touched on is the difference between national income measured in this year's dollars and national income representing real goods and services.

QUICK QUIZ See page 186 for the answers. Review concepts from this section in MyEconLab.

To obtain __________ __________, we subtract indirect business taxes and transfers from net domestic product and add other business income adjustments and net U.S. income earned abroad.

To obtain __________ __________, we must add government transfer payments, such as Social Security benefits and food stamps. We must subtract income earned but not received by factor owners, such as corporate retained earnings, Social Security contributions, and corporate income taxes.

To obtain disposable personal income, we subtract all personal __________ __________ from personal income. Disposable personal income is income that individuals actually have for consumption or saving.

Distinguishing Between Nominal and Real Values

So far, we have shown how to measure *nominal* income and product. When we say "nominal," we are referring to income and product expressed in the current "face value" of today's dollar. Given the existence of inflation or deflation in the economy, we must also be able to distinguish between the **nominal values** that we will be looking at and the **real values** underlying them. Nominal values are expressed in current dollars. Real income involves our command over goods and services—purchasing power—and therefore depends on money income and a set of prices. Thus, real income refers to nominal income corrected for changes in the weighted average of all prices. In other words, we must make an adjustment for changes in the price level.

Nominal values
The values of variables such as GDP and investment expressed in current dollars, also called *money values;* measurement in terms of the actual market prices at which goods and services are sold.

Real values
Measurement of economic values after adjustments have been made for changes in the average of prices between years.

Consider an example. Nominal income *per person* in 1960 was only about $2,800 per year. In 2011, nominal income per person was about $50,000. Were people really that bad off in 1960? No, for nominal income in 1960 is expressed in 1960 prices, not in the prices of today. In today's dollars, the per-person income of 1960 would be closer to $14,500, or about 30 percent of today's income per person. This is a meaningful comparison between income in 1960 and income today. Next we will show how we can translate nominal measures of income into real measures by using an appropriate price index, such as the Consumer Price Index or the GDP deflator discussed in Chapter 7.

Correcting GDP for Price Changes

If a Blu-ray disc costs $20 this year, 10 Blu-ray discs will have a market value of $200. If next year they cost $25 each, the same 10 Blu-ray discs will have a market value of $250. In this case, there is no increase in the total quantity of Blu-ray discs, but the market value will have increased by one-fourth. Apply this to every single good and service produced and sold in the United States, and you realize that changes in GDP, measured in *current* dollars, may not be a very useful indication of economic activity.

If we are really interested in variations in the *real* output of the economy, we must correct GDP (and just about everything else we look at) for changes in the average of overall prices from year to year. Basically, we need to generate an index that approximates the average prices and then divide that estimate into the value of output in current dollars to adjust the value of output to what is called **constant dollars,** or dollars corrected for general price level changes. This price-corrected GDP is called *real GDP.*

Constant dollars
Dollars expressed in terms of real purchasing power using a particular year as the base or standard of comparison, in contrast to current dollars.

How much has correcting for price changes caused real GDP to differ from nominal GDP during the past few years?

EXAMPLE Correcting GDP for Price Index Changes, 2001–2011

Let's take a numerical example to see how we can adjust GDP for changes in the price index. We must pick an appropriate price index in order to adjust for these price level changes. We mentioned the Consumer Price Index, the Producer Price Index, and the GDP deflator in Chapter 7. Let's use the GDP deflator to adjust our figures. Table 8-3 below gives 11 years of GDP figures. Nominal GDP figures are shown in column 2. The price index (GDP deflator) is in column 3, with base year of 2005, when the GDP deflator equals 100. Column 4 shows real (inflation-adjusted) GDP in 2005 dollars.

The formula for real GDP is

$$\text{Real GDP} = \frac{\text{nominal GDP}}{\text{price index}} \times 100$$

The step-by-step derivation of real (constant-dollar) GDP is as follows: The base year is 2005, so the price index for that year must equal 100. In 2005, nominal GDP was $12,638.4 billion, and so was real GDP expressed in 2005 dollars. In 2006, the price index increased to 103.263. Thus, to correct 2006's nominal GDP for inflation, we divide the price index, 103.263, into the nominal GDP figure of $13,398.9 billion and then multiply it by 100. The rounded result is $12,976.2 billion, which is 2006 GDP expressed in terms of the purchasing power of dollars in 2005. What about a situation when the price index is lower than in 2005? Look at 2001. Here the price index shown in column 3 is only 90.654. That means that in 2001, the average of all prices was just below 91 percent of prices in 2005. To obtain 2001 GDP expressed in terms of 2005 purchasing power, we divide nominal GDP, $10,286.2 billion, by 90.654 and then multiply by 100. The rounded result is a larger number—$11,347.2 billion. Column 4 in Table 8-3 is a better measure of how the economy has performed than column 2, which shows nominal GDP changes.

FOR CRITICAL ANALYSIS

Based on the information in Table 8-3, in what years was the economy in a recession? Explain briefly.

TABLE 8-3

Correcting GDP for Price Index Changes

To correct GDP for price index changes, we first have to pick a price index (the GDP deflator) with a specific year as its base. In our example, the base year is 2005. The price index for that year is 100. To obtain 2005 constant-dollar GDP, we divide the price index into nominal GDP and multiply by 100. In other words, we divide column 3 into column 2 and multiply by 100. This gives us column 4, which (taking into account rounding of the deflator) is a measure of real GDP expressed in 2005 purchasing power.

(1) Year	(2) Nominal GDP (billions of dollars per year)	(3) Price Index (base year 2005 = 100)	(4) = [(2) ÷ (3)] × 100 Real GDP (billions of dollars per year, in constant 2005 dollars)
2001	10,286.2	90.654	11,347.2
2002	10,642.3	92.113	11,553.0
2003	11,142.1	94.099	11,840.7
2004	11,867.8	96.769	12,263.8
2005	12,638.4	100.000	12,638.4
2006	13,398.9	103.263	12,976.2
2007	14,077.6	106.221	13,254.1
2008	14,441.4	108.481	13,312.1
2009	14,256.3	109.745	12,987.4
2010	14,635.0	110.952	13,190.4
2011	15,067.5	112.395	13,405.8

Sources: U.S. Department of Commerce, Bureau of Economic Analysis, and author's estimates.

Plotting Nominal and Real GDP

Nominal GDP and real GDP since 1970 are plotted in Figure 8-4 on the facing page. There is quite a big gap between the two GDP figures, reflecting the amount of inflation that has occurred. Note that the choice of a base year is arbitrary. We have

FIGURE 8-4 Nominal and Real GDP

Here we plot both nominal and real GDP. Real GDP is expressed in the purchasing power of 2005 dollars. The gap between the two represents price level changes.

Source: U.S. Department of Commerce.

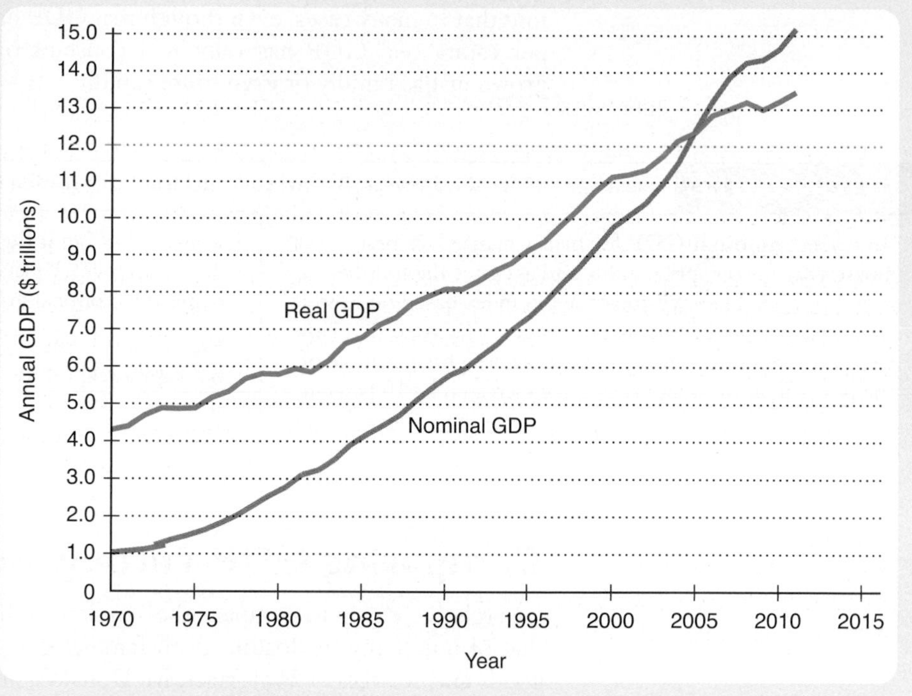

chosen 2005 as the base year in our example. This happens to be the base year that is currently used by the government for the GDP deflator.

Why Not . . . always use the most recent completed calendar year as the base year for computing real GDP?

Every few years, the U.S. government adopts a more recent year to be the base year for real GDP calculations. For instance, in 2004 the government adopted a 2000 base year for its computation of real GDP, and in 2009 the government changed the base year to 2005. In principle, the government could update its base year more often than it does. Even if it did, however, it would not select the most recent completed year as the base year, because that is usually the period for which national income accounting is least likely to have been accurate. Every three months, the government's national income accountants *estimate* real GDP, but typically they revise their figure at least once, often twice, and sometimes as many as three times before settling on a final amount. Thus, the government usually waits until the federal government accountants feel confident that the GDP measurement for a given year is certain before establishing that year as the base year.

Per Capita Real GDP

Looking at changes in real GDP may be deceiving, particularly if the population size has changed significantly. If real GDP over a 10-year period went up 100 percent, you might jump to the conclusion that the real income of a typical person in the economy had increased by that amount. But what if during the same period the population increased by 200 percent? Then what would you say? Certainly, the amount of real GDP per person, or *per capita real GDP*, would have fallen, even though *total* real GDP had risen. To account not only for price changes but also for population changes, we must first deflate GDP and then divide by the total population, doing this for each year. If we were to look at certain less developed countries, we would find that in many cases, even though real GDP has risen over the past several decades, per capita real GDP has remained constant or fallen because the population has grown just as rapidly or even more rapidly.

QUICK QUIZ See page 186 for the answers. Review concepts from this section in MyEconLab.

To correct **nominal GDP** for price changes, we first select a base year for our price index and assign it the number __________. Then we construct an index based on how a weighted average of prices has changed relative to that base year. For example, if in the next year a weighted average of the prices indicates that prices have increased by 10 percent, we would assign it the number __________. We then divide each year's price index, so constructed, into its respective nominal GDP figure (and multiply by 100).

We can divide the __________ into real GDP to obtain per capita real GDP.

Comparing GDP Throughout the World

It is relatively easy to compare the standard of living of a family in Los Angeles with that of one living in Boston. Both families get paid in dollars and can buy the same goods and services at Wal-Mart, McDonald's, and Costco. It is not so easy, however, to make a similar comparison between a family living in the United States and one in, say, Indonesia. The first problem concerns money. Indonesian residents get paid in rupiah, their national currency, and buy goods and services with those rupiah. How do we compare the average standard of living measured in rupiah with that measured in dollars?

Foreign Exchange Rates

Foreign exchange rate
The price of one currency in terms of another.

In earlier chapters, you have encountered international examples that involved local currencies, but the dollar equivalent has always been given. The dollar equivalent is calculated by looking up the **foreign exchange rate** that is published daily in major newspapers throughout the world. If you know that you can exchange $1.25 per euro, the exchange rate is 1.25 to 1 (or otherwise stated, a dollar is worth 0.80 euros). So, if French incomes per capita are, say, 28,944 euros, that translates, at an exchange rate of $1.25 per euro, to $36,180. For years, statisticians calculated relative GDPs by simply adding up each country's GDP in its local currency and dividing by the respective dollar exchange rate.

True Purchasing Power

The problem with simply using foreign exchange rates to convert other countries' GDPs and per capita GDPs into dollars is that not all goods and services are bought and sold in a world market. Restaurant food, housecleaning services, and home repairs do not get exchanged across countries. In countries that have very low wages, those kinds of services are much cheaper than foreign exchange rate computations would imply. Government statistics claiming that per capita income in some poor country is only $300 a year seem shocking. But such a statistic does not tell you the true standard of living of people in that country. Only by looking at what is called **purchasing power parity** can you hope to estimate other countries' true standards of living compared to ours.

Purchasing power parity
Adjustment in exchange rate conversions that takes into account differences in the true cost of living across countries.

Given that nations use different currencies, how can we compare nations' levels of real GDP per capita?

INTERNATIONAL EXAMPLE Purchasing Power Parity Comparisons of World Incomes

A few years ago, the International Monetary Fund accepted the purchasing power parity approach as the correct one. It started presenting international statistics on each country's GDP relative to every other's based on purchasing power parity relative to the U.S. dollar. The results were surprising. As you can see from Table 8-4 below, China's per capita GDP is higher based on purchasing power parity than when measured at market foreign exchange rates.

FOR CRITICAL ANALYSIS

What is the percentage increase in China's per capita GDP when one switches from foreign exchange rates to purchasing power parity?

TABLE 8-4

Comparing GDP Internationally

Country	Annual GDP Based on Purchasing Power Parity (billions of U.S. dollars)	Per Capita GDP Based on Purchasing Power Parity (U.S. dollars)	Per Capita GDP Based on Foreign Exchange Rates (U.S. dollars)
United States	13,886	46,040	46,040
United Kingdom	2,464	34,050	40,660
Germany	3,207	34,740	38,990
France	2,467	33,850	38,810
Japan	4,829	34,750	37,790
Italy	1,988	30,190	33,490
Russia	1,070	14,330	7,530
Brazil	1,122	9,270	5,860
China	3,126	5,420	2,370
Indonesia	373	3,750	1,650

Source: World Bank.

QUICK QUIZ See page 186 for the answers. Review concepts from this section in MyEconLab.

The foreign __________ __________ is the price of one currency in terms of another.

Statisticians often calculate relative GDP by adding up each country's GDP in its local currency and dividing by the dollar __________ __________.

Because not all goods and services are bought and sold in the world market, we must correct exchange rate conversions of other countries' GDP figures to take into account differences in the true __________ of __________ across countries.

You Are There

Questioning China's Official Real GDP Statistics

Paul Cavey of Macquarie Securities is evaluating China's GDP data. Some economists have argued that in years past, China's government has overstated real GDP. In 1989, China's real GDP officially rose by more than 4 percent, but most economists agree that it actually grew by only 1.5 percent. In the late 1990s, China's official annual real GDP growth rate was 7.7 percent, whereas private economists estimate that the true growth rate was between 2 and 5 percent.

Some economists now suggest that China's government may be overstating real GDP growth again. The official average annual real GDP growth rate since 2008 has remained high, yet electricity production has declined. Skeptical economists think that this discrepancy indicates that China's real GDP probably has increased less than reported. Cavey notes, however, that China's steel and aluminum industries accounted for much of the growth in electricity usage between 2000 and 2008 but only a small percentage of the increase in industrial production. Since 2008, China's production of steel and aluminum has dropped significantly. This decline in aluminum and steel production could account for the stagnant electricity usage, while production of other items really might have contributed to a net increase in real GDP. Thus, China's real GDP data may be accurate.

Critical Analysis Questions

1. Why do you think that many observers have argued that the world's GDP statistics would be more believable if private companies tabulated the data?
2. Why do you suppose that the U.S. government leaves official determination of business contractions and expansions to a nonprofit organization?

ISSUES & APPLICATIONS

Can More Per Capita Real GDP Buy Additional Happiness?

CONCEPTS APPLIED

- ▶ Real GDP
- ▶ Per Capita Real GDP
- ▶ Purchasing Power

Most economists view real GDP as the best available measure of a nation's *economic* well-being and per capita real GDP as the most useful indicator of the *economic* well-being of a country's typical resident. There is disagreement, however, about whether higher per capita real GDP is related to greater happiness.

The Easterlin Paradox

In 1974, University of Pennsylvania economist Richard Easterlin studied 14 nations' levels of per capita real GDP and measures of life satisfaction. The measures he considered were answers to a single survey question—"In general, how happy would you say that you are: *very* happy, *fairly* happy, or *not very* happy?"—plus an average of answers to several questions about life satisfaction.

Easterlin reached two conclusions. First, people in poor countries did become happier when per capita real GDP in those nations rose, because their higher purchasing power enabled them to purchase basic items they previously could not readily obtain. Second, in nations in which the typical resident was *not* poor, higher levels of per capita real GDP did not appear to generate greater satisfaction. The latter conclusion was a paradoxical surprise to economists. Consequently, after his study was released, that conclusion became known as the *Easterlin Paradox*: Above a relatively low level of per capita real GDP, further increases in real GDP apparently did not make people happier.

Reassessing the Easterlin Paradox

Recently, two other University of Pennsylvania economists, Betsey Stevenson and Justin Wolfers, have reconsidered Easterlin's conclusions. In a broader study of more than 100 nations, they have found that higher reported levels of life satisfaction accompany increases in per capita real GDP.

Stevenson and Wolfers emphasize that the positive relationship they find between satisfaction and per capita real GDP does not necessarily mean that an increase in a typical person's purchasing power *by itself* makes people happier. Greater purchasing power allows people, for instance, to pay for more visits to family and friends in far-flung locations, to purchase more trips to locales they enjoy, and to opt to work less than before and spend more time enjoying leisure. In addition, people can use increases in per capita real GDP to fund investments in technological improvements and capital goods that enable them to cut their hours of work further and lead more healthful lives. Thus, it is not more per capita real GDP in and of itself that makes people happier. Instead, it is the fact that people are able to allocate the greater purchasing power to activities they enjoy that leads to greater satisfaction.

For Critical Analysis

1. What are some possible reasons why a person might report lower life satisfaction even though her purchasing power has recently increased?
2. Is the availability of greater purchasing power likely to raise an individual's level of satisfaction though he is unable to allocate it to activities he enjoys?

Web Resources

1. For a summary of recent research by Richard Easterlin that supports the existence of his paradox in 13 nations in Eastern Europe, go to www.econtoday.com/ch08.
2. To review the study by Stevenson and Wolfers, go to www.econtoday.com/ch08.

Research Project

Easterlin has suggested that the answers to the poll questions considered by Stevenson and Wolfers might be subject to cultural differences in how people respond to such questions. Can you develop a list of *objective* measures of life satisfaction—that is, measures that can be estimated independently of how happy people say they are rather than depending on how satisfied people report themselves to be? If so, explain how items on your list accomplish this objective. If not, explain why you found composing such a list impossible.

For more questions on this chapter's Issues & Applications, go to **MyEconLab**. In the Study Plan for this chapter, select Section N: News.

Here is what you should know after reading this chapter. **MyEconLab** will help you identify what you know, and where to go when you need to practice.

WHAT YOU SHOULD KNOW		WHERE TO GO TO PRACTICE
The Circular Flow of Income and Output The circular flow of income and output captures two principles: (1) In every transaction, the seller receives the same amount that the buyer spends; and (2) goods and services flow in one direction, and money payments flow in the other direction. Households ultimately purchase the nation's total output of final goods and services. They make these purchases using income—wages, rents, interest, and profits—earned from selling labor, land, capital, and entrepreneurial services, respectively. Hence, income equals the value of output.	national income accounting, 162 total income, 162 final goods and services, 162 **KEY FIGURE** Figure 8-1, 163	• **MyEconLab** Study Plan 8.1 • Audio introduction to Chapter 8 • Animated Figure 8-1

(continued)

MyEconLab continued

WHAT YOU SHOULD KNOW		WHERE TO GO TO PRACTICE
Gross Domestic Product (GDP) A nation's gross domestic product is the total market value of its final output of goods and services produced within a given year using factors of production located within the nation's borders. Because GDP measures the value of a flow of production during a year in terms of market prices, it is not a measure of a nation's wealth.	gross domestic product (GDP), 164 intermediate goods, 164 value added, 164	• **MyEconLab** Study Plan 8.2
The Limitations of Using GDP as a Measure of National Welfare Gross domestic product is a useful measure for tracking year-to-year changes in the value of a nation's overall economic activity in terms of market prices. But it excludes nonmarket transactions that may add to or detract from general welfare. It also fails to account for factors such as environmental quality and the amount and quality of leisure time.		• **MyEconLab** Study Plan 8.2 • Video: What GDP Excludes
The Expenditure Approach to Tabulating GDP To calculate GDP using the expenditure approach, we sum consumption spending, investment expenditures, government spending, and net export expenditures. Thus, we add up the total amount spent on newly produced goods and services to obtain the dollar value of the output produced and purchased during the year.	expenditure approach, 167 income approach, 167 durable consumer goods, 168 nondurable consumer goods, 168 services, 168 gross private domestic investment, 168 investment, 168 producer durables, or capital goods, 168 fixed investment, 168 inventory investment, 168 depreciation, 170 net domestic product (NDP), 170 capital consumption allowance, 170 net investment, 171 **KEY FIGURE** Figure 8-2, 170	• **MyEconLab** Study Plan 8.3 • Video: Investment and GDP • Animated Figure 8-2
The Income Approach to Computing GDP To tabulate GDP using the income approach, we add total wages and salaries, rental income, interest income, profits, and nonincome expense items—indirect business taxes and depreciation—to obtain gross domestic income, which is equivalent to gross domestic product. Thus, the total value of all income earnings (equivalent to total factor costs) equals GDP.	gross domestic income (GDI), 171 indirect business taxes, 172 nonincome expense items, 172 national income (NI), 174 personal income (PI), 174 disposable personal income (DPI), 174	• **MyEconLab** Study Plans 8.3, 8.4 • Video: Investment and GDP • Economics Video: Record Job Losses

MyEconLab continued

WHAT YOU SHOULD KNOW		WHERE TO GO TO PRACTICE
Distinguishing Between Nominal GDP and Real GDP Nominal GDP is the value of newly produced output during the current year measured at current market prices. Real GDP adjusts the value of current output into constant dollars by correcting for changes in the overall level of prices from year to year. To calculate real GDP, we divide nominal GDP by the price index (the GDP deflator) and multiply by 100.	nominal values, 175 real values, 175 constant dollars, 175 foreign exchange rate, 178 purchasing power parity, 178 **KEY FIGURE** Figure 8-4, 177	• **MyEconLab** Study Plans 8.5, 8.6 • Animated Figure 8-4

Log in to MyEconLab, take a chapter test, and get a personalized Study Plan that tells you which concepts you understand and which ones you need to review. From there, MyEconLab will give you further practice, tutorials, animations, videos, and guided solutions.
Log in to www.myeconlab.com

PROBLEMS

All problems are assignable in myeconlab. Answers to odd-numbered problems appear at the back of the book.

8-1. Each year after a regular spring cleaning, Maria spruces up her home a little by retexturing and repainting the walls of one room in her house. In a given year, she spends $25 on magazines to get ideas about wall textures and paint shades, $45 on newly produced texturing materials and tools, $35 on new paintbrushes and other painting equipment, and $175 on newly produced paint. Normally, she preps the walls, a service that a professional wall-texturing specialist would charge $200 to do, and applies two coats of paint, a service that a painter would charge $350 to do, on her own.

a. When she purchases her usual set of materials and does all the work on her home by herself in a given spring, how much does Maria's annual spring texturing and painting activity contribute to GDP?

b. Suppose that Maria hurt her back this year and is recovering from surgery. Her surgeon has instructed her not to do any texturing work, but he has given her the go-ahead to paint a room as long as she is cautious. Thus, she buys all the equipment required to both texture and paint a room. She hires someone else to do the texturing work but does the painting herself. How much would her spring painting activity add to GDP?

c. As a follow-up to part (b), suppose that as soon as Maria bends down to dip her brush into the paint, she realizes that painting will be too hard on her back after all. She decides to hire someone else to do all the work using the materials she has already purchased. In this case, how much will her spring painting activity contribute to GDP?

8-2. Each year, Johan typically does all his own landscaping and yard work. He spends $200 per year on mulch for his flower beds, $225 per year on flowers and plants, $50 on fertilizer for his lawn, and $245 on gasoline and lawn mower maintenance. The lawn and garden store where he obtains his mulch and fertilizer charges other customers $500 for the service of spreading that much mulch in flower beds and $50 for the service of distributing fertilizer over a yard the size of Johan's. Paying a professional yard care service to mow his lawn would require an expenditure of $1,200 per year, but in that case Johan would not have to buy gasoline or maintain his own lawn mower.

a. In a normal year, how much does Johan's landscaping and yard work contribute to GDP?

b. Suppose that Johan has developed allergy problems this year and will have to reduce the amount of his yard work. He can wear a mask while running his lawn mower, so he will keep mowing his yard, but he will pay the lawn and garden center to spread mulch and distribute fertilizer. How much will all the work on Johan's yard contribute to GDP this year?

c. As a follow-up to part (b), at the end of the year, Johan realizes that his allergies are growing worse and that he will have to arrange for all his landscaping and yard work to be done by someone else next year. How much will he contribute to GDP next year?

8-3. Consider the following hypothetical data for the U.S. economy in 2014 (all amounts are in trillions of dollars).

Consumption	11.0
Indirect business taxes	.8
Depreciation	1.3
Government spending	2.8
Imports	2.7
Gross private domestic investment	3.0
Exports	2.5

a. Based on the data, what is GDP? NDP? NI?

b. Suppose that in 2015, exports fall to $2.3 trillion, imports rise to $2.85 trillion, and gross private domestic investment falls to $2.25 trillion. What will GDP be in 2015, assuming that other values do not change between 2014 and 2015?

8-4. Look back at Table 8-3 on page 176, which explains how to calculate real GDP in terms of 2005 constant dollars. Change the base year to 2001. Recalculate the price index, and then recalculate real GDP—that is, express column 4 of Table 8-3 in terms of 2001 dollars instead of 2005 dollars.

8-5. Consider the following hypothetical data for the U.S. economy in 2014 (in trillions of dollars), and assume that there are no statistical discrepancies or other adjustments.

Profit	2.8
Indirect business taxes and transfers	.8
Rent	.7
Interest	.8
Wages	8.2
Depreciation	1.3
Consumption	11.0
Exports	1.5
Government transfer payments	2.0
Personal income taxes and nontax payments	1.7
Imports	1.7
Corporate taxes and retained earnings	.5
Social Security contributions	2.0
Government spending	1.8

a. What is gross domestic income? GDP?

b. What is gross private domestic investment?

c. What is personal income? Personal disposable income?

8-6. Which of the following are production activities that are included in GDP? Which are not?

a. Mr. King performs the service of painting his own house instead of paying someone else to do it.

b. Mr. King paints houses for a living.

c. Mrs. King earns income from parents by taking baby photos in her digital photography studio.

d. Mrs. King takes photos of planets and stars as part of her astronomy hobby.

e. E*Trade charges fees to process Internet orders for stock trades.

f. Mr. Ho spends $10,000 on shares of stock via an Internet trade order and pays a $10 brokerage fee.

g. Mrs. Ho receives a Social Security payment.

h. Ms. Hernandez makes a $300 payment for an Internet-based course on stock trading.

i. Mr. Langham sells a used laptop computer to his neighbor.

8-7. Explain what happens to contributions to GDP in each of the following situations.

a. A woman who makes a living charging for investment advice on her Internet Web site marries one of her clients, to whom she now provides advice at no charge.

b. A tennis player wins two top professional tournaments as an unpaid amateur, meaning the tournament sponsor does not have to pay out his share of prize money.

c. A company that had been selling used firearms illegally finally gets around to obtaining an operating license and performing background checks as specified by law prior to each gun sale.

8-8. Explain what happens to the official measure of GDP in each of the following situations.

a. Air quality improves significantly throughout the United States, but there are no effects on aggregate production or on market prices of final goods and services.

b. The U.S. government spends considerably less on antipollution efforts this year than it did in recent years.

c. The quality of cancer treatments increases, so patients undergo fewer treatments, which hospitals continue to provide at the same price per treatment as before.

8-9. Which of the following activities of a computer manufacturer during the current year are included in this year's measure of GDP?

a. The manufacturer produces a chip in June, uses it as a component in a computer in August, and sells the computer to a customer in November.

b. A retail outlet of the firm sells a computer completely built during the current year.

c. A marketing arm of the company receives fee income during the current year when a buyer of one of its computers elects to use the computer manufacturer as her Internet service provider.

8-10. A number of economists contend that official measures of U.S. gross private investment expenditures are understated. Answer parts (a) and (b) below to determine just how understated these economists believe that officially measured investment spending may be.

a. Household spending on education, such as college tuition expenditures, is counted as consumption spending. Some economists suggest that these expenditures, which amount to 6 percent of GDP, should be counted as investment spending instead. Based on this 6 percent estimate and the GDP computations detailed in Figure 8-3 on page 173, how many billions of dollars would shift from consumption to investment if this suggestion was adopted?

b. Some economists argue that intangible forms of investment—business research spending, educational expenses for employees, and the like—should be included in the official measure of gross private domestic investment. These expenditures, which amount to about 9 percent of GDP, currently are treated as business input expenses and are not included in GDP. Based on this 9 percent estimate and the GDP computations detailed in Figure 8-3 on page 173, how much higher would gross private domestic investment be if intangible investment expenditures were counted as investment spending?

c. Based on your answers to parts (a) and (b), what is the total amount that gross private domestic investment may be understated, according to economists who argue that household education spending and business intangible investments should be added? How much may GDP be understated?

8-11. Consider the following table for the economy of a nation whose residents produce five final goods.

	2011		2015	
Good	Price	Quantity	Price	Quantity
Shampoo	$ 2	15	$ 4	20
External hard drives	200	10	250	10
Books	40	5	50	4
Milk	3	10	4	3
Candy	1	40	2	20

Assuming a 2011 base year:

a. What is nominal GDP for 2011 and 2015?

b. What is real GDP for 2011 and 2015?

8-12. Consider the following table for the economy of a nation whose residents produce four final goods.

	2013		2014	
Good	Price	Quantity	Price	Quantity
Computers	$1,000	10	$800	15
Bananas	6	3,000	11	1,000
Televisions	100	500	150	300
Cookies	1	10,000	2	10,000

Assuming a 2014 base year:

a. What is nominal GDP for 2013 and 2014?

b. What is real GDP for 2013 and 2014?

8-13. In the table for Problem 8-12, if 2014 is the base year, what is the price index for 2013? (Round decimal fractions to the nearest tenth.)

8-14. Suppose that early in a year, a hurricane hits a town in Florida and destroys a substantial number of homes. A portion of this stock of housing, which had a market value of $100 million (not including the market value of the land), was uninsured. The owners of the residences spent a total of $5 million during the rest of the year to pay salvage companies to help them save remaining belongings. A small percentage of uninsured owners had sufficient resources to spend a total of $15 million during the year to pay construction companies to rebuild their homes. Some were able to devote their own time, the opportunity cost of which was valued at $3 million, to work on rebuilding their homes. The remaining people, however, chose to sell their land at its market value and abandon the remains of their houses. What was the combined effect of these transactions on GDP for this year? (Hint: Which transactions took place in the markets for *final* goods and services?) In what ways, if any, does the effect on GDP reflect a loss in welfare for these individuals?

8-15. Suppose that in 2015, geologists discover large reserves of oil under the tundra in Alaska. These reserves have a market value estimated at $50 billion at current oil prices. Oil companies spend $1 billion to hire workers and move and position equipment to begin exploratory pumping during that same year. In the process of loading some of the oil onto tankers at a port, one company accidentally spills some of the oil into a bay and by the end of the year pays $1 billion to other companies to clean it up. The oil spill kills thousands of birds, seals, and other wildlife. What was the combined effect of these events on GDP for this year? (Hint: Which transactions took place in the markets for *final* goods and services?) In what ways, if any, does the effect on GDP reflect a loss in national welfare?

8-16. Consider the diagram in the next column, and answer the following questions.

a. What is the base year? Explain.

b. Has this country experienced inflation or deflation since the base year? How can you tell?

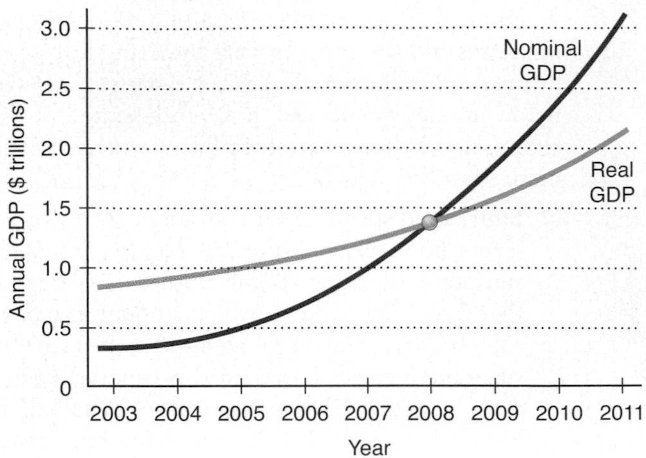

ECONOMICS ON THE NET

Tracking the Components of Gross Domestic Product One way to keep tabs on the components of GDP is via the FRED database at the Web site of the Federal Reserve Bank of St. Louis.

Title: Gross Domestic Product and Components

Navigation: Use the link at **www.econtoday.com/ch08** to visit the home page of the Federal Reserve Bank of St. Louis. Click on *Gross Domestic Product (GDP) and Components.*

Application

1. Click on *GDP/GNP*, and then click a checkmark next to *GDP (Gross Domestic Product)*. Write down nominal GDP data for the past 10 quarters.
2. Back up to *GDPCA (Real Gross Domestic Product) Dollars*. Write down the amounts for the past 10 quarters. Use the formula on page 176 to calculate the price level for each quarter. Has the price level decreased or increased in recent quarters?

For Group Study and Analysis Divide the class into "consumption," "investment," "government sector," and "foreign sector" groups. Have each group evaluate the contribution of each category of spending to GDP and to its quarter-to-quarter volatility. Reconvene the class, and discuss the factors that appear to create the most variability in GDP.

ANSWERS TO QUICK QUIZZES

p. 164: (i) factor . . . income; (ii) final; (iii) profit
p. 167: (i) Gross domestic product; (ii) value added; (iii) exclude; (iv) GDP; (v) market value
p. 171: (i) expenditure . . . durables . . . nondurables . . . services; (ii) capacity . . . inventories; (iii) market; (iv) depreciation
p. 172: (i) wages . . . interest . . . rent . . . profits; (ii) indirect business taxes . . . depreciation
p. 175: (i) national income; (ii) personal income; (iii) income taxes
p. 178: (i) 100 . . . 110; (ii) population
p. 179: (i) exchange rate; (ii) exchange rate; (iii) cost . . . living

9

Global Economic Growth and Development

During the fifteenth century, the Italian city-state of Venice issued the first *patent,* a government protection that gives an inventor the exclusive right to earnings from an invention for a specified period of time. During the twentieth century, patents were not authorized in Communist China until 1985, and the Chinese government issued relatively few patents until the mid-2000s. Since then, however, Chinese firms have obtained thousands of patents, both from the Chinese government and from governments of other nations, such as the United States. A number of economists suggest that increased efforts by Chinese firms to patent their inventions will help China sustain the solid economic performance it has experienced in recent years. How could the use of patents contribute to a nation's economic performance? In this chapter, you will learn the answer to this question.

LEARNING OBJECTIVES

After reading this chapter, you should be able to:

- Define economic growth
- Recognize the importance of economic growth rates
- Explain why productivity increases are crucial for maintaining economic growth
- Describe the fundamental determinants of economic growth
- Understand the basis of new growth theory
- Discuss the fundamental factors that contribute to a nation's economic development

myeconlab

MyEconLab helps you master each objective and study more efficiently. See end of chapter for details.

Did You Know That ? an infrared camera that was originally mounted on military helicopters and used to track potential terrorists at night via heat waves radiated by their bodies now has household applications? The company that makes the camera, FLIR Systems, realized that the technology could be incorporated into automobiles to enable drivers to "see" farther into the dark than was possible with standard headlights. The firm has also fashioned its cameras into handheld viewers that can be used to identify hot spots in houses where energy is escaping behind walls.

This is just one of many examples of inventions originally intended for a specific purpose that companies have directed to alternative uses. Economists refer to this process of adapting inventions to profit-seeking market applications as *innovation*. Today, many economists agree that innovation contributes fundamentally to *economic growth*, which is the topic of this chapter.

How Do We Define Economic Growth?

Recall from Chapter 2 that we can show economic growth graphically as an outward shift of a production possibilities curve, as is seen in Figure 9-1. If there is economic growth between 2013 and 2035, the production possibilities curve will shift outward toward the red curve. The distance that it shifts represents the amount of economic growth, defined as the increase in the productive capacity of a nation. Although it is possible to come up with a measure of a nation's increased productive capacity, it would not be easy. Therefore, we turn to a more readily obtainable definition of economic growth.

Most people have a general idea of what economic growth means. When a nation grows economically, its citizens must be better off in at least some ways, usually in terms of their material well-being. Typically, though, we do not measure the well-being of any nation solely in terms of its total output of real goods and services or in terms of real GDP without making some adjustments. After all, India has a real GDP more than 15 times as large as that of Denmark. The population in India, though, is about 200 times greater than that of Denmark. Consequently, we view India as a relatively poor country and Denmark as a relatively rich country. Thus, when we measure economic growth, we must adjust for population growth. Our formal definition becomes this: **Economic growth** occurs when there are increases in *per capita* real GDP, measured by the rate of change in per capita real GDP per year. Figure 9-2 on page 190 presents the historical record of real GDP per person in the United States.

Economic growth
Increases in per capita real GDP measured by its rate of change per year.

Problems in Definition

Our definition of economic growth says nothing about the *distribution* of output and income. A nation might grow very rapidly in terms of increases in per capita real GDP, while its poor people remain poor or become even poorer. Therefore, in assessing the economic growth record of any nation, we must be careful to pinpoint which income groups have benefited the most from such growth. How much does economic growth differ across countries?

FIGURE 9-1 Economic Growth

If there is growth between 2013 and 2035, the production possibilities curve for the entire economy will shift outward from the blue line labeled 2013 to the red line labeled 2035. The distance that it shifts represents an increase in the productive capacity of the nation.

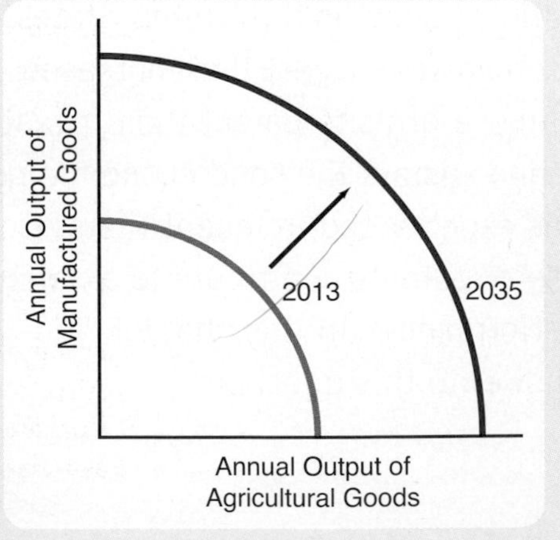

INTERNATIONAL EXAMPLE Growth Rates Around the World

Table 9-1 shows the average annual rate of growth of real GDP per person in selected countries since 1970. During this time period, the United States has been positioned about midway in the pack. Thus, even though we are one of the world's richest countries, our rate of economic growth has been in the middle range. The reason that U.S. per capita real GDP has remained higher than per capita real GDP in most other nations is that, despite the late-2000s downturn, U.S. growth has been sustained over many decades. This is something that most other countries have so far been unable to accomplish.

FOR CRITICAL ANALYSIS

"The largest change is from zero to one." Does this statement have anything to do with relative growth rates in poorer versus richer countries?

TABLE 9-1

Per Capita Real GDP Growth Rates in Various Countries

Country	Average Annual Rate of Growth of Real GDP Per Capita, 1970–2011 (%)
Sweden	1.7
France	1.8
Germany	1.8
United States	1.9
Canada	2.0
Brazil	2.1
Japan	2.1
Turkey	2.1
India	3.2
Indonesia	4.1
Malaysia	4.7
China	7.2

Sources: World Bank, International Monetary Fund, and author's estimates.

Real standards of living can go up without any positive economic growth. This can occur if individuals are, on average, enjoying more leisure by working fewer hours but producing as much as they did before. For example, if per capita real GDP in the United States remained at $45,000 a year for a decade, we could not automatically jump to the conclusion that U.S. residents were, on average, no better off. What if, during that same 10-year period, average hours worked fell from 37 per week to 33 per week? That would mean that during the 10 years under study, individuals in the labor force were "earning" 4 more hours of leisure a week.

Go to **www.econtoday.com/ch09** to get the latest figures and estimates on economic growth throughout the world.

Nothing so extreme as this example has occurred in this country, but something similar has. Average hours worked per week fell steadily until the 1960s, when they leveled off. That means that during much of the history of this country, the increase in per capita real GDP *understated* the actual economic growth that we were experiencing because we were enjoying more and more leisure as time passed.

Is Economic Growth Bad?

Some commentators on our current economic situation believe that the definition of economic growth ignores its negative effects. Some psychologists even contend that economic growth makes us worse off. They say that the more the economy grows, the more "needs" are created so that we feel worse off as we become richer. Our expectations are rising faster than reality, so we presumably always suffer from a sense of disappointment. Also, economists' measurement of economic growth does not take into account the spiritual and cultural aspects of the good life. As with all activities, both costs and benefits are associated with growth. You can see some of those listed in Table 9-2 on the next page.

Any measure of economic growth that we use will be imperfect. Nonetheless, the measures that we do have allow us to make comparisons across countries and over

FIGURE 9-2 The Historical Record of U.S. Economic Growth

The graph traces per capita real GDP in the United States since 1900. Data are given in 2005 dollars.

Source: U.S. Department of Commerce. *Author's estimate.

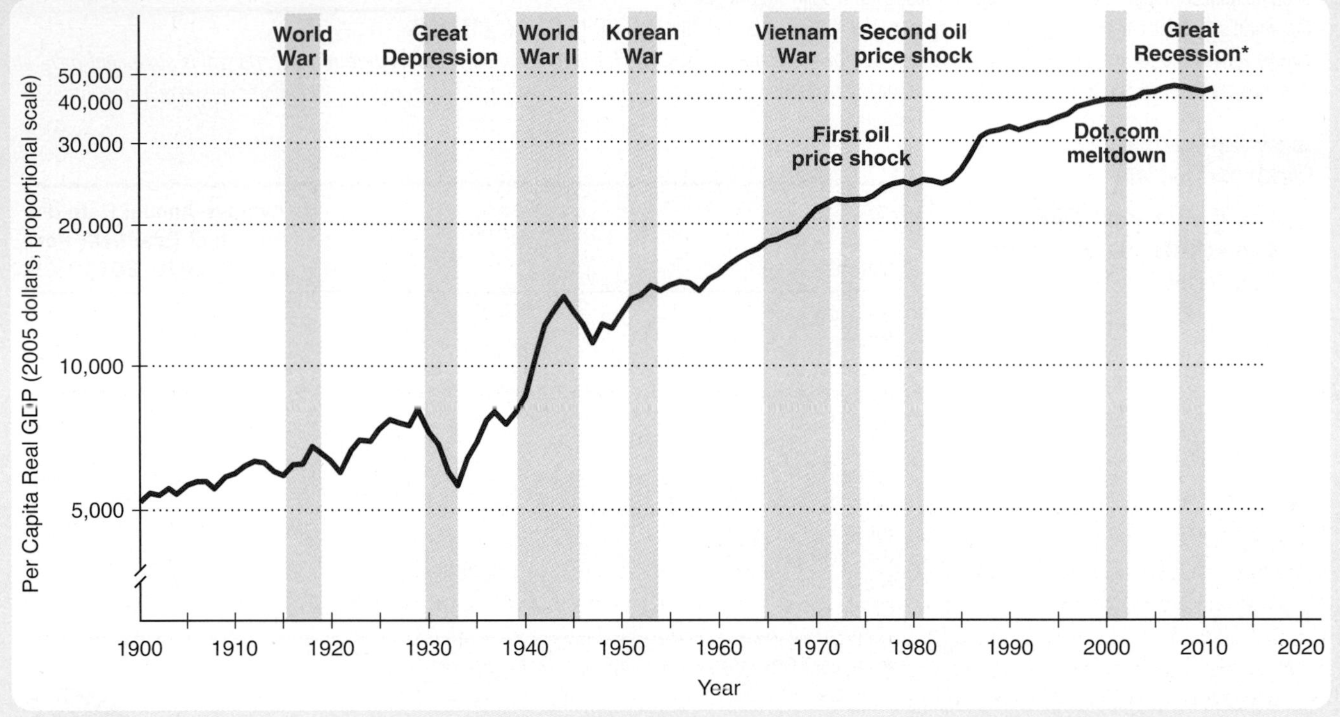

time and, if used judiciously, can enable us to gain important insights. Per capita real GDP, used so often, is not always an accurate measure of economic well-being, but it is a serviceable measure of productive activity.

The Importance of Growth Rates

Notice in Table 9-1 on the previous page that the growth rates in real per capita income for most countries differ very little—generally by only a few percentage points. You might want to know why such small differences in growth rates are important. What does it matter if we grow at 3 percent rather than at 4 percent per year? The answer is that in the long run, it matters a lot.

A small difference in the rate of economic growth does not matter very much for next year or the year after. For the more distant future, however, it makes considerable difference. The power of *compounding* is impressive. Let's see what happens with three different annual rates of growth: 3 percent, 4 percent, and 5 percent. We start with $1 trillion per year of U.S. GDP at some time in the past. We then compound this $1 trillion, or allow it to grow at these three different growth rates. The difference

TABLE 9-2

Costs and Benefits of Economic Growth

Benefits	Costs
Reduction in illiteracy	Environmental pollution
Reduction in poverty	Breakdown of the family
Improved health	Isolation and alienation
Longer lives	Urban congestion
Political stability	

TABLE 9-3

One Dollar Compounded Annually at Different Interest Rates

Here we show the value of a dollar at the end of a specified period during which it has been compounded annually at a specified interest rate. For example, if you took $1 today and invested it at 5 percent per year, it would yield $1.05 at the end of one year. At the end of 10 years, it would equal $1.63, and at the end of 50 years, it would equal $11.50.

	Interest Rate						
Number of Years	3%	4%	5%	6%	8%	10%	20%
1	1.03	1.04	1.05	1.06	1.08	1.10	1.20
2	1.06	1.08	1.10	1.12	1.17	1.21	1.44
3	1.09	1.12	1.16	1.19	1.26	1.33	1.73
4	1.13	1.17	1.22	1.26	1.36	1.46	2.07
5	1.16	1.22	1.28	1.34	1.47	1.61	2.49
6	1.19	1.27	1.34	1.41	1.59	1.77	2.99
7	1.23	1.32	1.41	1.50	1.71	1.94	3.58
8	1.27	1.37	1.48	1.59	1.85	2.14	4.30
9	1.30	1.42	1.55	1.68	2.00	2.35	5.16
10	1.34	1.48	1.63	1.79	2.16	2.59	6.19
20	1.81	2.19	2.65	3.20	4.66	6.72	38.30
30	2.43	3.24	4.32	5.74	10.00	17.40	237.00
40	3.26	4.80	7.04	10.30	21.70	45.30	1,470.00
50	4.38	7.11	11.50	18.40	46.90	117.00	9,100.00

is huge. In 50 years, $1 trillion per year becomes $4.38 trillion per year if compounded at 3 percent per year. Just one percentage point more in the growth rate, 4 percent, results in a real GDP of $7.11 trillion per year in 50 years, almost double the previous amount. Two percentage points' difference in the growth rate—5 percent per year—results in a real GDP of $11.5 trillion per year in 50 years, or nearly three times as much. Obviously, very small differences in annual growth rates result in great differences in cumulative economic growth. That is why nations are concerned if the growth rate falls even a little in absolute percentage terms.

Thus, when we talk about growth rates, we are talking about compounding. In Table 9-3 above, we show how $1 compounded annually grows at different interest rates. We see in the 3 percent column that $1 in 50 years grows to $4.38. We merely multiplied $1 trillion times 4.38 to get the growth figure in our earlier example. In the 5 percent column, $1 grows to $11.50 after 50 years. Again, we multiplied $1 trillion times 11.50 to get the growth figure for 5 percent in the preceding example.

How do economists measure the pace of economic growth for the entire world or for groups of countries?

INTERNATIONAL EXAMPLE Tracking a Global Economic Growth Divergence

To calculate global economic growth, economists must measure global per capita real GDP. To do so, they convert the value of every country's GDP into U.S. dollars by multiplying each nation's GDP by the exchange rate of the dollar for its currency. Then they adjust for the fact that nations' price levels vary relative to the U.S. price level and add the individual nations' GDP figures together to obtain global GDP. Next, they adjust global GDP for inflation by dividing it by the global GDP deflator, thereby obtaining a measure of world *real* GDP. When world real GDP is divided by an estimate of the world's population, the result is global per capita real GDP. By calculating annual percentage changes in this measure, we find that between 2007 and 2009, the rate of growth in world per capita real GDP dropped from nearly 6 percent to about −0.5 percent before rising above 2 percent by 2011.

Countries can also be grouped into advanced nations, such as the United States, and developing nations, such as India, and separate rates of economic growth calculated for the two groups. This reveals a distinct difference in growth rates since 2007. For developing nations, the economic growth rate has remained positive, although it dropped from 8 percent per year in 2007 to about 2 percent per year in 2009 before rising above 4 percent in 2011. In contrast, the rate of economic growth across all advanced nations fell from nearly 3 percent in 2007 to below −3 percent in 2009. By 2011, the overall rate of economic growth for the advanced portion of the world had risen to only about 1 percent.

FOR CRITICAL ANALYSIS

Is the difference between per capita real GDP in advanced countries and per capita real GDP in developing nations increasing or decreasing?

Rule of 70
A rule stating that the approximate number of years required for per capita real GDP to double is equal to 70 divided by the average rate of economic growth.

THE RULE OF 70 Table 9-3 on the preceding page indicates that how quickly the level of a nation's per capita real GDP increases depends on the rate of economic growth. A formula called the **rule of 70** provides a shorthand way to calculate approximately how long it will take a country to experience a significant increase in per capita real GDP. According to the rule of 70, the approximate number of years necessary for a nation's per capita real GDP to increase by 100 percent—that is, to *double*—is equal to 70 divided by the average rate of economic growth. Thus, at an annual growth rate of 10 percent, per capita real GDP should double in about 7 years. As you can see in Table 9-3, at a 10 percent growth rate, in 7 years per capita real GDP would rise by a factor of 1.94, which is very close to 2, or very nearly the doubling predicted by the rule of 70. At an annual growth rate of 8 percent, the rule of 70 predicts that nearly 9 years will be required for a nation's per capita real GDP to double. Table 9-3 verifies that this prediction is correct. Indeed, the table shows that after 9 years an exact doubling will occur at a growth rate of 8 percent.

The rule of 70 implies that at lower rates of economic growth, much more time must pass before per capita real GDP will double. At a 3 percent growth rate, just over 23 (70 ÷ 3) years must pass before per capita real income doubles. At a rate of growth of only 1 percent per year, 70 (70 ÷ 1) years must pass. This means that if a nation's average rate of economic growth is 1 percent instead of 3 percent, 47 more years—about two generations—must pass for per capita real GDP to double. Clearly, the rule of 70 verifies that even very slight differences in economic growth rates are important.

QUICK QUIZ See page 208 for the answers. Review concepts from this section in MyEconLab.

Economic growth can be defined as the increase in _________ _________ real GDP, measured by its rate of change per year.

The _________ of economic growth are reductions in illiteracy, poverty, and illness and increases in life spans and political stability. The _________ of economic growth may include environmental pollution, alienation, and urban congestion.

Small percentage-point differences in growth rates lead to _________ differences in per capita real GDP over time. These differences can be seen by examining a compound interest table such as the one in Table 9-3 on page 191.

Productivity Increases: The Heart of Economic Growth

Let's say that you are required to type 10 term papers and homework assignments a year. You have a computer, but you do not know how to touch-type. You end up spending an average of two hours per typing job. The next summer, you buy a touch-typing tutorial to use on your computer and spend a few minutes a day improving your speed. The following term, you spend only one hour per typing assignment, thereby saving 10 hours a semester. You have become more productive. This concept of productivity summarizes your ability (and everyone else's) to produce the same output with fewer inputs. Thus, **labor productivity** is normally measured by dividing total real domestic output (real GDP) by the number of workers or the number of labor hours. By definition, labor productivity increases whenever average output produced per worker (or per hour worked) during a specified time period increases.

Labor productivity
Total real domestic output (real GDP) divided by the number of workers (output per worker).

Go to www.econtoday.com/ch09 for information about the latest trends in U.S. labor productivity.

Clearly, there is a relationship between economic growth and increases in labor productivity. If you divide all resources into just capital and labor, economic growth can be defined simply as the cumulative contribution to per capita GDP growth of three components: the rate of growth of capital, the rate of growth of labor, and the rate of growth of capital and labor productivity. If everything else remains constant, improvements in labor productivity ultimately lead to economic growth and higher living standards.

Figure 9-3 on the facing page displays estimates of the relative contributions of the growth of labor and capital and the growth of labor and capital productivity to economic

FIGURE 9-3 Factors Accounting for Economic Growth in Selected Regions

In the United States, South Asia, and Latin America, growth in labor resources is the main contributor to economic growth.

Source: International Monetary Fund.

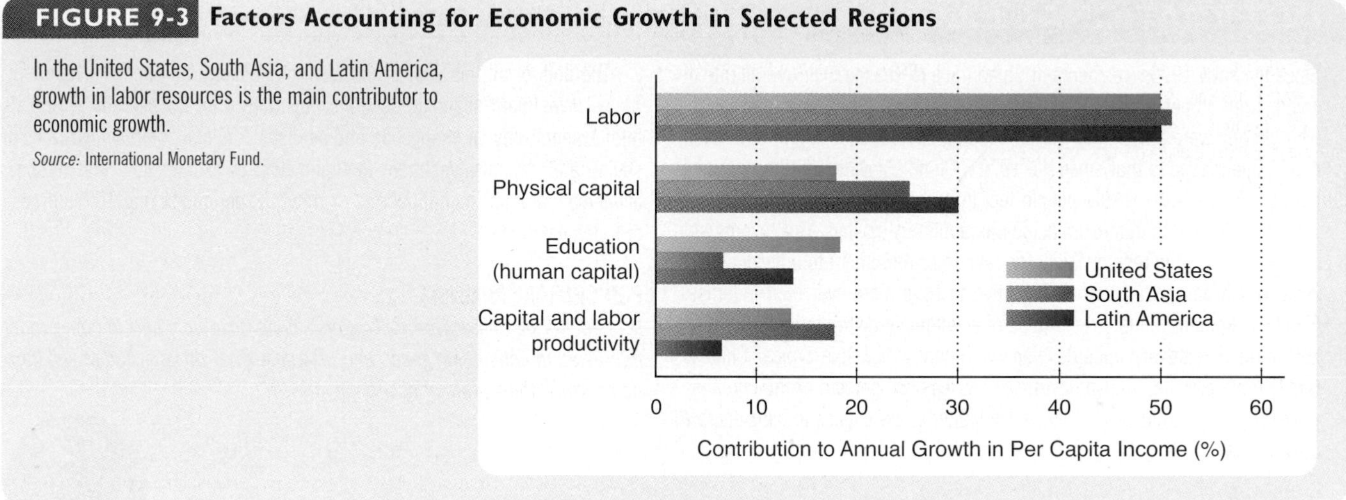

growth in the United States, nations in South Asia, and Latin American countries. The growth of labor resources, through associated increases in labor force participation, has contributed to the expansion of output that has accounted for at least half of economic growth in all three regions. Total capital is the sum of physical capital, such as tools and machines, and human capital, which is the amount of knowledge acquired from research and education. Figure 9-3 above shows the separate contributions of the growth of these forms of capital, which together have accounted for roughly a third of the growth rate of per capita incomes in the United States, South Asia, and Latin America. In these three parts of the world, growth in overall capital and labor productivity has contributed the remaining 7 to 18 percent.

Saving: A Fundamental Determinant of Economic Growth

Economic growth does not occur in a vacuum. It is not some predetermined fate of a nation. Rather, economic growth depends on certain fundamental factors. One of the most important factors that affects the rate of economic growth and hence long-term living standards is the rate of saving.

A basic proposition in economics is that if you want more tomorrow, you have to consume less today.

To have more consumption in the future, you have to consume less today and save the difference between your consumption and your income.

On a national basis, this implies that higher saving rates eventually mean higher living standards in the long run, all other things held constant. Although the U.S. saving rate has recently increased, concern has been growing that we still are not saving enough. Saving is important for economic growth because without saving, we cannot have investment. If there is no investment in our capital stock, there would be much less economic growth.

The relationship between the rate of saving and per capita real GDP is shown in Figure 9-4 on the next page. Among the nations with the highest rates of saving are China, Germany, Japan, and Saudi Arabia.

Why do China's citizens save so much, and how does the high rate of national saving affect the country's economic growth rate?

INTERNATIONAL EXAMPLE The High Chinese Saving Rate and Its Growth Implications

Since the early 1970s, residents of China have increased their overall rate of saving from 35 percent to 47 percent of real GDP. Why are Chinese residents, who already were among the world's leading savers, choosing to save even more? One reason is that since the 1970s, China's government has reduced job guarantees. As a result, people feel less secure about their incomes in the near term and therefore set aside precautionary savings. The government also has shifted the responsibility for saving for retirement to individual citizens, which has added to their incentive to save more over their lifetimes. Finally, in spite of China's rapid pace of economic growth, its financial markets remain relatively underdeveloped. To buy a home, a typical Chinese family must provide a down payment of at least 30 percent of the purchase price. Thus, to purchase a house, a household must engage in considerable advance saving.

The bulk of all this saving has been channeled into capital investment. Today, investment spending accounts for more than 45 percent of China's total expenditures on final goods and services. The consistently high rates of saving and capital investment in China help to explain how that nation's economy maintains an annual rate of growth of per capita real GDP in excess of 6 percent.

FOR CRITICAL ANALYSIS

If residents of China eventually stop saving so much and become more interested in consuming goods and services, what do you predict will happen to the nation's rate of economic growth?

FIGURE 9-4 Relationship Between Rate of Saving and Per Capita Real GDP

This diagram shows the relationship between per capita real GDP and the rate of saving expressed as the average share of annual real GDP saved.

Source: World Bank.

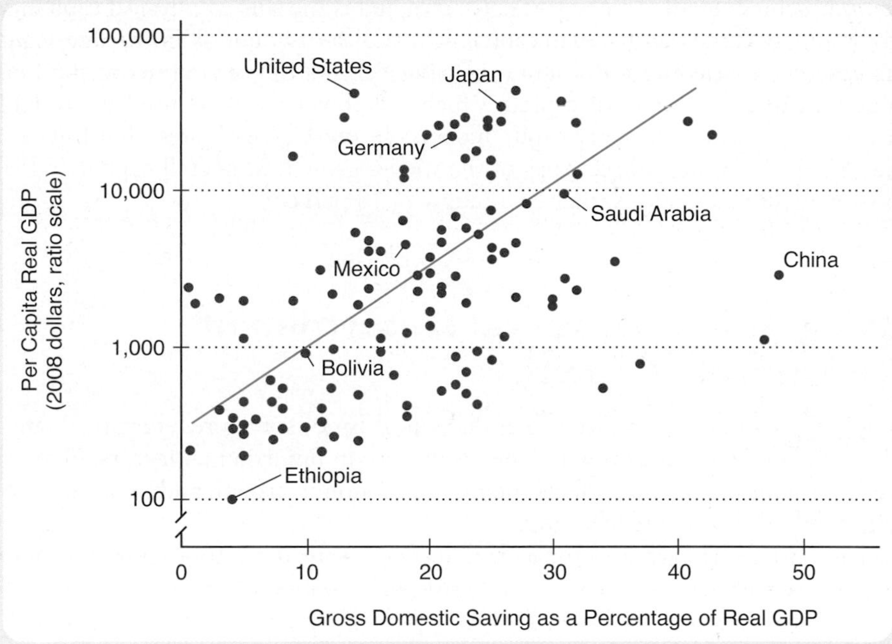

QUICK QUIZ

See page 208 for the answers. Review concepts from this section in MyEconLab.

Economic growth is numerically equal to the rate of growth of __________ plus the rate of growth of __________ plus the rate of growth in the productivity of __________ and of __________. Improvements in labor productivity, all other things being equal, lead to greater economic growth and higher living standards.

One fundamental determinant of the rate of growth is the rate of __________. To have more consumption in the future, we have to __________ rather than consume. In general, countries that have had higher rates of __________ have had higher rates of growth in per capita real GDP.

New Growth Theory and the Determinants of Growth

A simple arithmetic definition of economic growth has already been given. The per capita growth rates of capital and labor plus the per capita growth rate of their productivity constitute the rate of economic growth. Economists have had good data on the growth of the physical capital stock in the United States as well as on the labor force. But when you add those two growth rates together, you still do not get the total economic growth rate in the United States. The difference has to be due to improvements in productivity. Economists typically labeled this "improvements in technology," and that was that. More recently, proponents of what is now called **new growth theory** argue that technology cannot simply be viewed as an outside factor without explanation. Technology must be understood in terms of what drives it. What are the forces that make productivity grow in the United States and elsewhere?

New growth theory
A theory of economic growth that examines the factors that determine why technology, research, innovation, and the like are undertaken and how they interact.

Growth in Technology

Consider some startling statistics about the growth in technology. Microprocessor speeds may increase from 4,000 megahertz to 10,000 megahertz by the year 2020. By that same year, the size of the thinnest circuit line within a transistor may decrease by 90 percent. The typical memory capacity (RAM) of computers will jump from 2 gigabytes, or about 32 times the equivalent text in the Internal Revenue Code, to more than 300 gigabytes. Recent developments in phase-change memory technologies and in new techniques for storing bits of data on molecules and even individual atoms promise even greater expansions of computer memory capacities. Predictions are that computers may become as powerful as the human brain by 2030.

Technology: A Separate Factor of Production

We now recognize that technology must be viewed as a separate factor of production that is sensitive to rewards. Indeed, one of the major foundations of new growth theory is this:

When the rewards are greater, more technological advances will occur.

Let's consider several aspects of technology here, the first one being research and development.

Research and Development

A certain amount of technological advance results from research and development (R&D) activities that have as their goal the development of specific new materials, new products, and new machines. How much spending a nation devotes to R&D can have an impact on its long-term economic growth. Part of how much a nation spends depends on what businesses decide is worth spending. That in turn depends on their expected rewards from successful R&D. If your company develops a new way to produce computer memory chips, how much will it be rewarded? The answer depends on what you can charge others to use the new technique.

PATENTS To protect new techniques developed through R&D, we have a system of **patents,** in which the federal government gives the patent holder the exclusive right to make, use, and sell an invention for a period of 20 years. One can argue that this special protection given to owners of patents increases expenditures on R&D and therefore adds to long-term economic growth. Figure 9-5 on the next page shows that U.S. patent grants fell during the 1970s, increased steadily after 1982, surged following 1995, dropped in 2004 and 2005, and increased again after 2007.

Patent
A government protection that gives an inventor the exclusive right to make, use, or sell an invention for a limited period of time (currently, 20 years).

FIGURE 9-5 U.S. Patent Grants

The U.S. Patent and Trademark Office gradually began awarding more patent grants between the early 1980s and the mid-1990s. Since 1995, the number of patents granted each year has risen in most years, except the mid and late 2000s.

Source: U.S. Patent and Trademark Office.

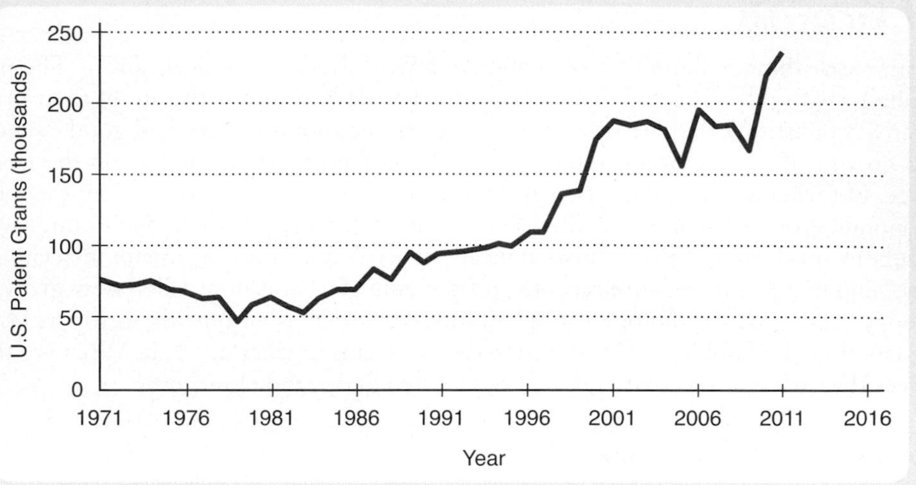

Why Not . . . promote innovation by awarding more patents?

Actually, the U.S. Patent and Trademark Office (USPTO) approves almost 40 percent of the nearly 500,000 patent applications it receives each year. It is already very easy to obtain a patent. Overwhelmed USPTO officials often grant patents for processes that many firms already have utilized for decades. Sometimes the USPTO accidentally awards overlapping patent rights to multiple applicants. Some of these applicants know that patents already exist for nearly identical products and processes. Nevertheless, they hope to be able to establish a property right via the court system instead of through research and development. This helps to explain why total expenditures on patent litigation are now in excess of $10 billion per year. Thus, even though using patents to assign property rights to inventions helps to promote innovative activity, making patents easier to obtain likely would promote more litigation instead of additional innovation.

POSITIVE EXTERNALITIES AND R&D As we discussed in Chapter 5, positive externalities are benefits from an activity that are enjoyed by someone besides the instigator of the activity. In the case of R&D spending, a certain amount of the benefits go to other companies that do not have to pay for them. In particular, according to economists David Coe of the International Monetary Fund and Elhanan Helpman of Harvard University, about a quarter of the global productivity gains of R&D investment in the top seven industrialized countries goes to other nations. For every 1 percent rise in the stock of R&D in the United States alone, for example, productivity in the rest of the world increases by about 0.25 percent. One country's R&D expenditures benefit other countries because they are able to import capital goods—say, computers and telecommunications networks—from technologically advanced countries and then use them as inputs in making their own industries more efficient. In addition, countries that import high-tech goods are able to imitate the technology.

The Open Economy and Economic Growth

People who study economic growth today emphasize the importance of the openness of the economy. Free trade encourages a more rapid spread of technology and industrial ideas. Moreover, open economies may experience higher rates of economic growth because their own industries have access to a bigger market. When trade barriers are erected in the form of tariffs and the like, domestic industries become isolated from global technological progress. This occurred for many years in Communist countries and in most developing countries in Africa, Latin America, and elsewhere. Figure 9-6 on the facing page shows the relationship between economic growth and openness as measured by the level of tariff barriers.

FIGURE 9-6 The Relationship Between Economic Growth and Tariff Barriers to International Trade

Nations with low tariff barriers are relatively open to international trade and have tended to have higher average annual rates of real GDP per capita growth since 1965.

Source: World Bank.

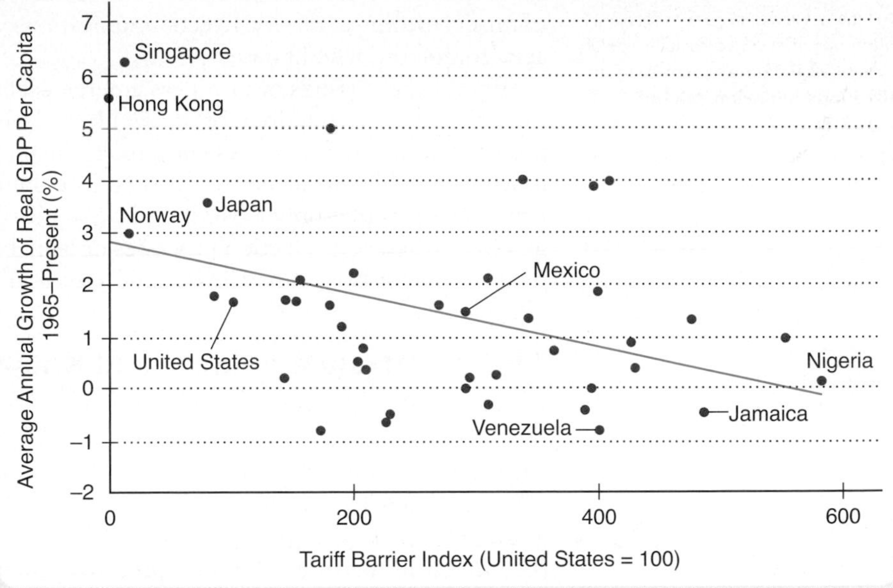

When a commission charged with finding the secrets to economic growth studied countries that have experienced long periods of high growth, what do you think it discovered?

INTERNATIONAL EXAMPLE What Economic Growth Success Stories Have in Common

A commission funded by grants from the World Bank, the Hewlett Foundation, and several national governments recently studied 13 nations that, at some time since 1950, experienced 25-year periods of annual growth rates of at least 7 percent. The countries were Botswana, Brazil, China, Hong Kong, Indonesia, Japan, Malaysia, Malta, Oman, Singapore, South Korea, Taiwan, and Thailand. The commission found that all 13 nations shared five characteristics. The first four were (1) macroeconomic stability, (2) high levels of saving and investment, (3) relatively unregulated domestic industries, and (4) governments that protected property rights.

The fifth characteristic surprised many politicians but very few economists: All 13 countries were open to international trade. During their high-growth periods, none of the countries' governments erected significant barriers to flows of imports and exports across national borders. Furthermore, the periods of high economic growth ended for several nations when their governments began restricting flows of international trade.

FOR CRITICAL ANALYSIS

Given the evidence that low trade barriers promote higher economic growth, why do you think that some residents of every country favor significant barriers to trade?

Innovation and Knowledge

We tend to think of technological progress as, say, the invention of the transistor. But invention means nothing by itself. **Innovation** is required. Innovation involves the transformation of something new, such as an invention, into something that benefits the economy either by lowering production costs or by providing new goods and services. Indeed, the new growth theorists believe that real wealth creation comes from innovation and that invention is but a facet of innovation.

Innovation
Transforming an invention into something that is useful to humans.

Historically, technologies have moved relatively slowly from invention to innovation to widespread use, and the dispersion of new technology remains for the most part slow and uncertain. The inventor of the transistor thought it might be used to make better hearing aids. At the time it was invented, the *New York Times*'s sole reference

You Are There

To contemplate a real-world example of how many years can pass before an invention becomes a successful innovation, consider **A Nonabsorbable Fat Finally Finds a Market Niche,** on page 204.

to it was in a small weekly column called "News of Radio." When the laser was invented, no one really knew what it could be used for. It was initially used to help in navigation, measurement, and chemical research. Today, it is used in the reproduction of music, printing, surgery, telecommunications, and optical data transmittal and storage. Tomorrow, who knows?

Typically, thousands of raw ideas emerge each year at a large firm's R&D laboratories. Only a few hundred of these ideas develop into formal proposals for new processes or products. Of these proposals, the business selects perhaps a few dozen that it deems suitable for further study to explore their feasibility. After careful scrutiny, the firm concludes that only a handful of these ideas are inventions worthy of being integrated into actual production processes or launched as novel products. The firm is fortunate if one or two ultimately become successful marketplace innovations.

The Importance of Ideas and Knowledge

Economist Paul Romer has added at least one other important factor that determines the rate of economic growth. He contends that production and manufacturing knowledge is just as important as the other determinants and perhaps even more so. He considers knowledge a factor of production that, like capital, has to be paid for by forgoing current consumption. Economies must therefore invest in knowledge just as they invest in machines. Because past investment in capital may make it more profitable to acquire more knowledge, there may be an investment-knowledge cycle in which investment spurs knowledge and knowledge spurs investment. A once-and-for-all increase in a country's rate of investment may permanently raise that country's growth rate. (According to traditional theory, a once-and-for-all increase in the rate of saving and therefore in the rate of investment simply leads to a new steady-state standard of living, not one that continues to increase.)

Another way of looking at knowledge is that it is a store of ideas. According to Romer, ideas are what drive economic growth. In fact, we have become an idea economy. Consider Microsoft Corporation. A relatively small percentage of that company's labor force is involved in actually building products. Rather, a majority of Microsoft employees are attempting to discover new ideas that can be translated into computer code that can then be turned into products. The major conclusion that Romer and other new growth theorists draw is this:

Economic growth can continue as long as we keep coming up with new ideas.

The Importance of Human Capital

Knowledge, ideas, and productivity are all tied together. One of the threads is the quality of the labor force. Increases in the productivity of the labor force are a function of increases in human capital, the fourth factor of production discussed in Chapter 2. Recall that human capital consists of the knowledge and skills that people in the workforce acquire through education, on-the-job training, and self-teaching. To increase your own human capital, you have to invest by forgoing income-earning activities while you attend school. Society also has to invest in the form of teachers and education.

According to the new growth theorists, human capital is becoming nearly as important as physical capital, particularly when trying to explain international differences in living standards. It is therefore not surprising that one of the most effective ways that developing countries can become developed is by investing in secondary schooling.

One can argue that policy changes that increase human capital will lead to more technological improvements. One of the reasons that concerned citizens, policymakers, and politicians are looking for a change in the U.S. schooling system is that our educational system seems to be falling behind those of other countries. This lag is greatest in science and mathematics—precisely the areas required for developing better technology.

QUICK QUIZ See page 208 for the answers. Review concepts from this section in MyEconLab.

__________ __________ theory argues that the greater the rewards, the more rapid the pace of technology. And greater rewards spur research and development.

The openness of a nation's economy to international __________ seems to correlate with its rate of economic growth.

Invention and innovation are not the same thing. __________ are useless until __________ transforms them into goods and services that people find valuable.

According to __________ __________ theory, economic growth can continue as long as we keep coming up with new ideas.

Increases in __________ capital can lead to greater rates of economic growth. These come about by increased education, on-the-job training, and self-teaching.

Immigration, Property Rights, and Growth

New theories of economic growth have also shed light on two additional factors that play important roles in influencing a nation's rate of growth of per capita real GDP: immigration and property rights.

Population and Immigration as They Affect Economic Growth

There are several ways to view population growth as it affects economic growth. On the one hand, population growth can result in a larger labor force and increases in human capital, which contribute to economic growth. On the other hand, population growth can be seen as a drain on the economy because for any given amount of GDP, more population means lower per capita GDP. According to Harvard economist Michael Kremer, the first of these effects is historically more important. His conclusion is that population growth drives technological progress, which then increases economic growth. The theory is simple: If there are 50 percent more people in the United States, there will be 50 percent more geniuses. And with 50 percent more people, the rewards for creativity are commensurately greater. Otherwise stated, the larger the potential market, the greater the incentive to become ingenious.

A larger market also provides an incentive for well-trained people to immigrate, which undoubtedly helps explain why the United States attracts a disproportionate number of top scientists from around the globe.

Does immigration help spur economic growth? Yes, according to the late economist Julian Simon, who pointed out that "every time our system allows in one more immigrant, on average, the economic welfare of American citizens goes up. . . . Additional immigrants, both the legal and the illegal, raise the standard of living of U.S. natives and have little or no negative impact on any occupational or income class." He further argued that immigrants do not displace natives from jobs but rather create jobs through their purchases and by starting new businesses. Immigrants' earning and spending simply expand the economy.

Not all researchers agree with Simon, and few studies have tested the theories he and Kremer have advanced. This area is currently the focus of much research.

Property Rights and Entrepreneurship

If you were in a country where bank accounts and businesses were periodically expropriated by the government, how willing would you be to leave your financial assets in a savings account or to invest in a business? Certainly, you would be less willing than if such actions never occurred. In general, the more securely private property rights (see page 100) are assigned, the more capital accumulation there will be. People will be willing to invest their savings in endeavors that will increase their wealth in future years. This requires that property rights in their wealth be sanctioned and enforced by the government. In fact, some economic historians have attempted to show that it was the development of well-defined private property rights and legal structures that allowed Western Europe to increase its growth rate after many centuries of stagnation. The ability and certainty with which they can reap the gains from investing also determine the extent to which business owners in other countries will invest capital in developing countries. The threat of loss of property rights that hangs over some developing nations probably stands in the way of foreign investments that would allow these nations to develop more rapidly.

The legal structure of a nation is closely tied to the degree with which its citizens use their own entrepreneurial skills. In Chapter 2, we identified entrepreneurship as the fifth factor of production. Entrepreneurs are the risk takers who seek out new ways to do things and create new products. To the extent that entrepreneurs are allowed to capture the rewards from their entrepreneurial activities, they will seek to engage in those activities. In countries where such rewards cannot be captured because of a lack of property rights, there will be less entrepreneurship. Typically, this results in fewer investments and a lower rate of growth. We shall examine the implications this has for policymakers in Chapter 18.

QUICK QUIZ **See page 208 for the answers. Review concepts from this section in MyEconLab.**

While some economists argue that population growth reduces __________ growth, others contend that the opposite is true. The latter economists consequently believe that immigration should be encouraged rather than discouraged.

Well-defined and protected __________ rights are important for fostering entrepreneurship. In the absence of well-defined __________ rights, individuals have less incentive to take risks, and economic growth rates suffer.

Economic Development

Development economics
The study of factors that contribute to the economic growth of a country.

How did developed countries travel paths of growth from extreme poverty to relative riches? That is the essential issue of **development economics,** which is the study of why some countries grow and develop and others do not and of policies that might help developing economies get richer. It is not enough simply to say that people in different countries are different and that is why some countries are rich and some countries are poor. Economists do not deny that different cultures have different work ethics, but they are unwilling to accept such a pat and fatalistic answer.

Look at any world map. About four-fifths of the countries you will see on the map are considered relatively poor. The goal of economists who study development is to help the more than 4 billion people today with low living standards join the more than 2 billion people who have at least moderately high living standards.

Putting World Poverty into Perspective

Most U.S. residents cannot even begin to understand the reality of poverty in the world today. At least one-half, if not two-thirds, of the world's population lives at subsistence level, with just enough to eat for survival. Indeed, the World Bank estimates that nearly 20 percent of the world's people live on less than \$1.50 per day. The official poverty line in the United States is above the annual income of at least half the human beings on the planet. This is not to say that we should ignore domestic problems with the poor and homeless simply because they are living better than many people elsewhere in the world. Rather, it is necessary for us to maintain an appropriate perspective on what are considered problems for this country relative to what are considered problems elsewhere.

The Relationship Between Population Growth and Economic Development

The world's population is growing at the rate of about 2.3 people a second. That amounts to 198,720 a day or 72.5 million a year. Today, there are nearly 6.5 billion people on earth. By 2050, according to the United Nations, the world's population will be close to leveling off at around 9.1 billion. Panel (a) of Figure 9-7 on the following page shows population growth. Panel (b) emphasizes an implication of panel (a), which is that almost all the growth in population is occurring in developing nations. Many developed countries are expected to lose population over the next several decades.

Ever since the Reverend Thomas Robert Malthus wrote *An Essay on the Principle of Population* in 1798, excessive population growth has been a concern. Modern-day Malthusians are able to generate great enthusiasm for the concept that population growth is bad. Over and over, media pundits and a number of scientists tell us that rapid population growth threatens economic development and the quality of life.

MALTHUS WAS PROVED WRONG Malthus predicted that population would outstrip food supplies. This prediction has never been supported by the facts, according to economist Nicholas Eberstadt of the American Enterprise Institute for Public Policy Research. As the world's population has grown, so has the world's food supply, measured by calories per person. Furthermore, the price of food, corrected for inflation, has generally been falling for more than a century. That means that the supply of food has been expanding faster than the increase in demand caused by increased population.

GROWTH LEADS TO SMALLER FAMILIES Furthermore, economists have found that as nations become richer, average family size declines. Otherwise stated, the more economic development occurs, the slower the population growth rate becomes. This has certainly been true in Western Europe and in the former Soviet Union, where populations in some countries are actually declining. Predictions of birthrates in developing countries have often turned out to be overstated if those countries experience rapid economic growth. This was the case in Chile, Hong Kong, Mexico, and Taiwan. Recent research on population and economic development has revealed that social and economic modernization has been accompanied by a decline in childbearing significant enough that it might be called a fertility revolution. Modernization reduces infant mortality, which in turn reduces the incentive for couples to have many children to make sure that a certain number survive to adulthood. Modernization also lowers the demand for children for a variety of reasons, not the least being that couples in more developed countries do not need to rely on their children to take care of them in old age.

The Stages of Development: Agriculture to Industry to Services

If we analyze the development of modern rich nations, we find that they went through three stages. First is the agricultural stage, when most of the population is involved in agriculture. Then comes the manufacturing stage, when much of the population becomes involved in the industrialized sector of the economy. And finally there is a shift toward services. That is exactly what happened in the United States: The so-called tertiary, or service, sector of the economy continues to grow, whereas the manufacturing sector (and its share of employment) is declining in relative importance.

Of particular significance, however, is the requirement for early specialization in a nation's comparative advantage (see Chapter 2). The doctrine of comparative advantage is particularly appropriate for the developing countries of the world. If trading is allowed among nations, a country is best off if it produces what it has a comparative advantage in producing and imports the rest (for more details, see Chapter 32). This means that many developing countries should continue to specialize in agricultural production or in labor-intensive manufactured goods.

FIGURE 9-7 Expected Growth in World Population by 2050

Panel (a) displays the percentages of the world's population residing in the various continents by 2050 and shows projected population growth for these continents and for selected nations. It indicates that Asia and Africa are expected to gain the most in population by the year 2050. Panel (b) indicates that population will increase in developing countries before beginning to level off around 2050, whereas industrially advanced nations will grow very little in population in the first half of this century.

Source: United Nations.

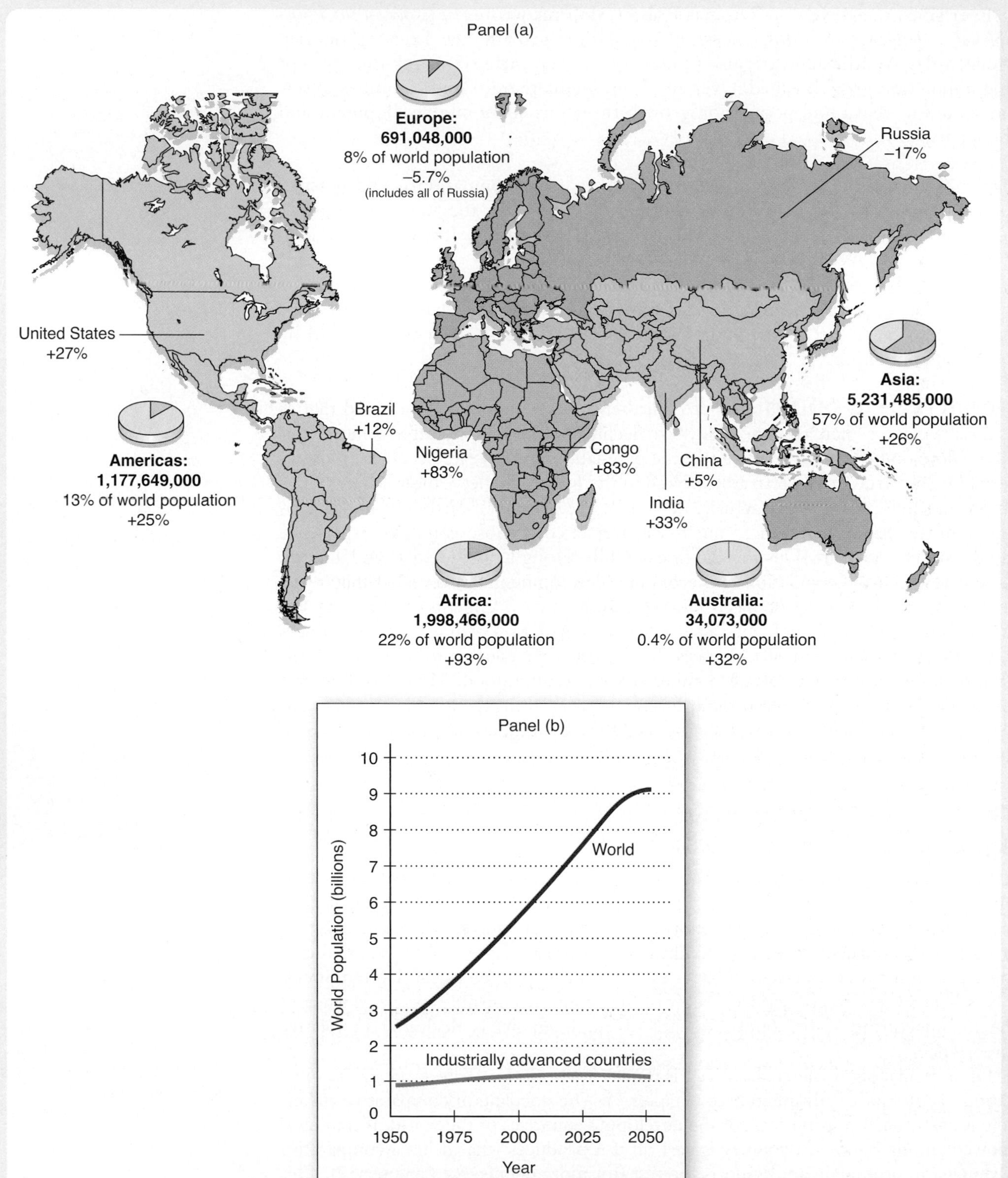

Keys to Economic Development

According to one theory of development, a country must have a large natural resource base in order to develop. This theory goes on to assert that much of the world is running out of natural resources, thereby limiting economic growth and development. Only the narrowest definition of a natural resource, however, could lead to such an opinion. In broader terms, a natural resource is something occurring in nature that we can use for our own purposes. As emphasized by new growth theory, natural resources therefore include human capital—education and experience. Also, natural resources change over time. Several hundred years ago, for example, they did not include hydroelectric power—no one knew that such a natural resource existed or how to bring it into existence.

Go to **www.econtoday.com/ch09** to contemplate whether there may be a relationship between inequality and a nation's growth and to visit the home page of the World Bank's Thematic Group on Inequality, Poverty, and Socioeconomic Performance.

Natural resources by themselves are not a prerequisite for or a guarantee of economic development, as demonstrated by Japan's extensive development despite a lack of domestic oil resources and by Brazil's slow pace of development in spite of a vast array of natural resources. Resources must be transformed into something usable for either investment or consumption.

Economists have found that four factors seem to be highly related to the pace of economic development:

1. *Establishing a system of property rights.* As noted earlier, if you were in a country where bank accounts and businesses were periodically expropriated by the government, you would be reluctant to leave some of your wealth in a savings account or to invest in a business. Expropriation of private property rarely takes place in developed countries. It has occurred in numerous developing countries, however. For example, private property was once nationalized in Chile and still is for the most part in Cuba. Economists have found that other things being equal, the more secure private property rights are, the more private capital accumulation and economic growth there will be.
2. *Developing an educated population.* Both theoretically and empirically, we know that a more educated workforce aids economic development because it allows individuals to build on the ideas of others. Thus, developing countries can advance more rapidly if they increase investments in education. Or, stated in the negative, economic development is difficult to sustain if a nation allows a sizable portion of its population to remain uneducated. Education allows impoverished young people to acquire skills that enable them to avoid poverty as adults.
3. *Letting "creative destruction" run its course.* The twentieth-century Harvard economist Joseph Schumpeter championed the concept of "creative destruction," through which new businesses ultimately create new jobs and economic growth after first destroying old jobs, old companies, and old industries. Such change is painful and costly, but it is necessary for economic advancement. Nowhere is this more important than in developing countries, where the principle is often ignored. Many governments in developing nations have had a history of supporting current companies and industries by discouraging new technologies and new companies from entering the marketplace. The process of creative destruction has not been allowed to work its magic in these countries.
4. *Limiting protectionism.* Open economies experience faster economic development than economies closed to international trade. Trade encourages individuals and businesses to discover ways to specialize so that they can become more productive and earn higher incomes. Increased productivity and subsequent increases in economic growth are the results. Thus, having fewer trade barriers promotes faster economic development.

Go to **www.econtoday.com/ch09** to link to a World Trade Organization explanation of how free trade promotes greater economic growth and higher employment.

QUICK QUIZ See page 208 for the answers. Review concepts from this section in MyEconLab.

Although many people believe that population growth hinders economic development, there is little evidence to support that notion. What is clear is that economic development tends to lead to a reduction in the rate of __________ growth.

Historically, there are three stages of economic development: the __________ stage, the __________ stage, and the __________-__________ stage, when a large part of the workforce is employed in providing services.

Although one theory of economic development holds that a sizable natural resource base is the key to a nation's development, this fails to account for the importance of the human element: The __________ __________ must be capable of using a country's natural resources.

Fundamental factors contributing to the pace of economic development are a well-defined system of __________ __________, training and __________, allowing new generations of companies and industries to __________ older generations, and promoting an open economy by allowing __________ __________.

You Are There

A Nonabsorbable Fat Finally Finds a Market Niche

It is 1968, and two chemists at Procter & Gamble are looking for a way to make a type of fat that the bodies of premature infants can readily absorb. By accident, they invent a new type of fat, which they call *olestra,* that cannot be absorbed at all.

Now fast-forward to 1996. Procter & Gamble launches olestra as a calorie-free fat and forecasts future sales totaling as much as $1 billion per year. Unfortunately, though, the calorie-free fat turns out to have undesirable digestive side effects, and sales dry up rapidly. The company shelves the product.

Fast-forward once more, to today. Procter & Gamble has found another use for olestra—as the base for Sefose, a new type of paint. Olestra, it turns out, possesses a very desirable property: It is much less likely than other paints to vaporize when subjected to heat or electricity. Therefore, unlike oil- and latex-based paints, Sefose can be painted onto almost anything, including hot engines and electrical wiring. Sales of Sefose have taken off, and Procter & Gamble is convinced that, finally, after more than four decades of effort, it has transformed its olestra invention into a market innovation.

Critical Analysis Questions

1. Why do you suppose that many inventions never become market innovations?
2. What advantages might a very large company such as Procter & Gamble have in efforts to transform inventions into successful innovations?

ISSUES & APPLICATIONS

China Discovers the Growth Benefits of Patents

CONCEPTS APPLIED

- Economic Growth
- Innovation
- Patents

Conducting research and development that generate inventions and transforming those inventions into innovations that succeed in the marketplace promote a relatively high rate of economic growth in any nation. Innovation, in turn, expands the set of products traded in a nation's markets and leads to lower-cost productive processes, thereby sustaining economic growth.

FIGURE 9-8 Applications for and Awards of Patents in China Since 1996

The numbers of patents applied for and granted to Chinese and foreign firms by China's government have risen significantly since the early 2000s.

Source: U.S. Department of Commerce.

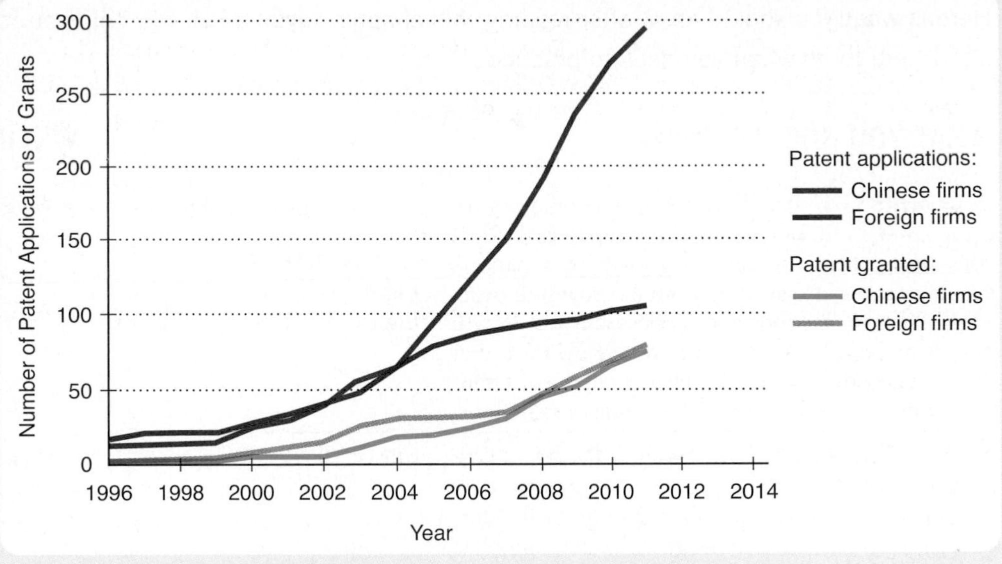

Patents Catch On in China

From the 1980s through the early 2000s, companies throughout the world complained about Chinese firms' alleged thefts of patented products and processes. Since the mid-2000s, however, China's government has worked harder to enforce foreign patents. In addition, in hopes of spurring innovative activity, the government has encouraged Chinese companies to apply for patents to protect their property rights.

Figure 9-8 shows the number of applications for, and awards of, Chinese "invention patents" by Chinese and foreign firms since 1996. Applications for patents by Chinese firms have increased significantly since 2004, and patent grants to Chinese firms have risen at a steady pace.

Chinese Firms Obtain More Foreign Patents

China's government has also encouraged Chinese companies to patent their inventions in other nations. The government anticipates that this move will reduce the net flow of patent payments across China's borders. Today, for instance, Chinese companies pay about $2 billion per year in license and royalty fees to U.S. patent holders but receive very few license and royalty fees from U.S. companies that make use of Chinese-patented products and processes.

Eventually, the net flow of patent payments appears likely to shift more in China's favor. Firms based in China received only 90 U.S. patents in 1999. Since the late 2000s, however, Chinese companies have regularly obtained more than 1,000 U.S. patents per year

For Critical Analysis

1. During the 2000s, China joined many other nations in agreeing to adopt internationally harmonized patent rules. Why do you think that most of the world's nations have agreed to eliminate differences in their patent regulations?
2. Why do you suppose that actions by China's government to strengthen the property rights of patent holders have encouraged more Chinese companies to apply for patents?

Web Resources

1. Visit the Web site of the China Patent and Trademark Office at www.econtoday.com/ch09.
2. For a list of questions and answers about Chinese patents, go to www.econtoday.com/ch09.

Research Project

Discuss the advantages and disadvantages for a developing nation of adopting the patent protections provided by governments of advanced countries.

For more questions on this chapter's Issues & Applications, go to **MyEconLab**. In the Study Plan for this chapter, select Section N: News.

Here is what you should know after reading this chapter. **MyEconLab** will help you identify what you know, and where to go when you need to practice.

WHAT YOU SHOULD KNOW		WHERE TO GO TO PRACTICE
Economic Growth The rate of economic growth is the annual rate of change in per capita real GDP. This measure of the rate of growth of a nation's economy takes into account both its growth in overall production of goods and services and the growth rate of its population. It is an average measure that does not account for possible changes in the distribution of income or various welfare costs or benefits.	economic growth, 188 **KEY FIGURES** Figure 9-1, 188 Figure 9-2, 190	• **MyEconLab** Study Plan 9.1 • Audio introduction to Chapter 9 • Animated Figures 9-1, 9-2 • ABC News Video: Economic Growth: How Much, How Fast?
Why Economic Growth Rates Are Important. Economic growth compounds over time. Thus, over long intervals, relatively small differences in the rate of economic growth can accumulate to produce large disparities in per capita incomes.	rule of 70, 192	• **MyEconLab** Study Plan 9.1 • Video: Growth Rates and Compound Interest
Why Productivity Increases Are Crucial for Maintaining Economic Growth Productivity growth is a fundamental factor influencing near-term changes in economic growth. Higher productivity growth unambiguously contributes to greater annual increases in a nation's per capita real GDP.	labor productivity, 192	• **MyEconLab** Study Plan 9.2 • Economics Video: Rust Belt City's Brighter Future
The Key Determinants of Economic Growth The fundamental factors contributing to economic growth are growth in a nation's pool of labor, growth of its capital stock, and growth in the productivity of its capital and labor. A key determinant of capital accumulation is a nation's saving rate. Higher saving rates contribute to greater investment and hence increased capital accumulation and economic growth.		• **MyEconLab** Study Plan 9.3 • Video: Saving and Economic Growth
New Growth Theory This theory examines why individuals and businesses conduct research into inventing and developing new technologies and how this innovation process interacts with the rate of economic growth. A key implication of the theory is that ideas and knowledge are crucial elements of the growth process.	new growth theory, 195 patent, 195 innovation, 197 **KEY FIGURES** Figure 9-5, 196 Figure 9-6, 197	• **MyEconLab** Study Plan 9.4 • Video: The Importance of Human Capital • Animated Figures 9-5, 9-6 • Economics Video: Cash for Trash • Economics Video: 'Gray Googlers' Work from Home • Economics Video: Rust Belt City's Brighter Future • Economics Video: The Return of Zeppelin
Fundamental Factors That Contribute to a Nation's Economic Development Key features shared by nations that attain higher levels of economic development are protection of property rights, significant opportunities for their residents to obtain training and education, policies that permit new companies and industries to replace older ones, and the avoidance of protectionist barriers that hinder international trade.	development economics, 200 **KEY FIGURE** Figure 9-7, 202	• **MyEconLab** Study Plans 9.5, 9.6 • Animated Figure 9-7

Log in to MyEconLab, take a chapter test, and get a personalized Study Plan that tells you which concepts you understand and which ones you need to review. From there, MyEconLab will give you further practice, tutorials, animations, videos, and guided solutions.
Log in to www.myeconlab.com

PROBLEMS

All problems are assignable in myeconlab. Answers to odd-numbered problems appear at the back of the book.

9-1. The graph below shows a production possibilities curve for 2014 and two potential production possibilities curves for 2015, denoted 2015_A and 2015_B.

a. Which of the labeled points corresponds to maximum feasible 2014 production that is more likely to be associated with the curve denoted 2015_A?

b. Which of the labeled points corresponds to maximum feasible 2014 production that is more likely to be associated with the curve denoted 2015_B?

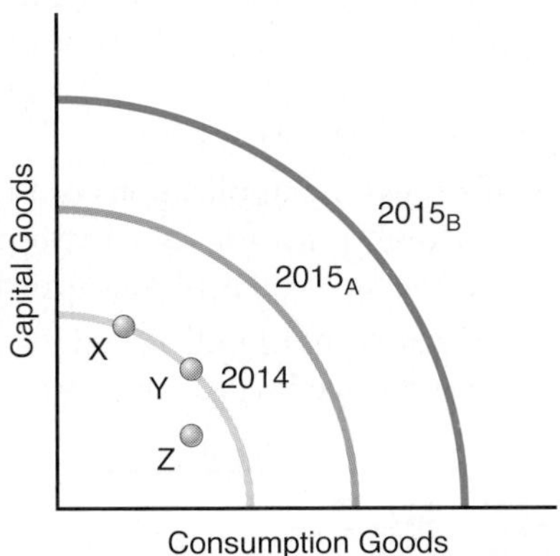

9-2. A nation's capital goods wear out over time, so a portion of its capital goods become unusable every year. Last year, its residents decided to produce no capital goods. It has experienced no growth in its population or in the amounts of other productive resources during the past year. In addition, the nation's technology and resource productivity have remained unchanged during the past year. Will the nation's economic growth rate for the current year be negative, zero, or positive?

9-3. In the situation described in Problem 9-2, suppose that educational improvements during the past year enable the people of this nation to repair all capital goods so that they continue to function as well as new. All other factors are unchanged, however. In light of this single change to the conditions faced in this nation, will the nation's economic growth rate for the current year be negative, zero, or positive?

9-4. Consider the following data. What is the per capita real GDP in each of these countries?

Country	Population (millions)	Real GDP ($ billions)
A	10	55
B	20	60
C	5	70

9-5. Suppose that during the next 10 years, real GDP triples and population doubles in each of the nations in Problem 9-4. What will per capita real GDP be in each country after 10 years have passed?

9-6. Consider the following table displaying annual growth rates for nations X, Y, and Z, each of which entered 2011 with real per capita GDP equal to $20,000:

	Annual Growth Rate (%)			
Country	2011	2012	2013	2014
X	7	1	3	4
Y	4	5	7	9
Z	5	4	3	2

a. Which nation most likely experienced a sizable earthquake in late 2011 that destroyed a significant portion of its stock of capital goods, but was followed by speedy investments in rebuilding the nation's capital stock? What is this nation's per capita real GDP at the end of 2014, rounded to the nearest dollar?

b. Which nation most likely adopted policies in 2011 that encouraged a gradual shift in production from capital goods to consumption goods? What is this nation's per capita real GDP at the end of 2014, rounded to the nearest dollar?

c. Which nation most likely adopted policies in 2011 that encouraged a quick shift in production from consumption goods to capital goods? What is this nation's per capita real GDP at the end of 2014, rounded to the nearest dollar?

9-7. Per capita real GDP grows at a rate of 3 percent in country F and at a rate of 6 percent in country G. Both begin with equal levels of per capita real GDP. Use Table 9-3 on page 191 to determine how much higher per capita real GDP will be in country G after 20 years. How much higher will real GDP be in country G after 40 years?

9-8. Per capita real GDP in country L is three times as high as in country M. The economic growth rate in country M, however, is 8 percent, while country L's economy grows at a rate of 5 percent. Use Table 9-3 on page 191 to determine approximately how many years will pass before per capita real GDP in country M surpasses per capita real GDP in country L.

9-9. Per capita real GDP in country S is only half as great as per capita real GDP in country T. Country T's rate of economic growth is 4 percent. The government of country S, however, enacts policies that achieve a growth rate of 20 percent. Use Table 9-3 on page 191 to determine how long country S must maintain this growth rate before its per capita real GDP surpasses that of country T.

9-10. In 2012, a nation's population was 10 million. Its nominal GDP was $40 billion, and its price index was 100. In 2013, its population had increased to 12 million, its nominal GDP had risen to $57.6 billion, and its price index had increased to 120. What was this nation's economic growth rate during the year?

9-11. Between the start of 2012 and the start of 2013, a country's economic growth rate was 4 percent. Its population did not change during the year, nor did its price level. What was the rate of increase of the country's nominal GDP during this one-year interval?

9-12. In 2012, a nation's population was 10 million, its real GDP was $1.21 billion, and its GDP deflator had a value of 121. By 2013, its population had increased to 12 million, its real GDP had risen to $1.5 billion, and its GDP deflator had a value of 125. What was the percentage change in per capita real GDP between 2012 and 2013?

9-13. A nation's per capita real GDP was $2,000 in 2011, and the nation's population was 5 million in that year. Between 2011 and 2012, the inflation rate in this country was 5 percent, and the nation's annual rate of economic growth was 10 percent. Its population remained unchanged. What was per capita real GDP in 2012? What was the *level* of real GDP in 2012?

9-14. Brazil has a population of about 200 million, with about 145 million over the age of 15. Of these, an estimated 25 percent, or 35 million people, are functionally illiterate. The typical literate individual reads only about two nonacademic books per year, which is less than half the number read by the typical literate U.S. or European resident. Answer the following questions solely from the perspective of new growth theory:

a. Discuss the implications of Brazil's literacy and reading rates for its growth prospects in light of the key tenets of new growth theory.

b. What types of policies might Brazil implement to improve its growth prospects? Explain.

ECONOMICS ON THE NET

Multifactor Productivity and Its Growth Growth in productivity is a key factor determining a nation's overall economic growth.

Title: Bureau of Labor Statistics: Multifactor Productivity Trends

Navigation: Use the link at **www.econtoday.com/ch09** to visit the multifactor productivity home page of the Bureau of Labor Statistics.

Application Read the summary, and answer the following questions.

1. What does multifactor productivity measure? Based on your reading of this chapter, how does multifactor productivity relate to the determination of economic growth?
2. Click on *Multifactor Productivity Trends in Manufacturing*. According to these data, which industries have exhibited the greatest productivity growth in recent years?

For Group Study and Analysis Divide the class into three groups to examine multifactor productivity data for the private business sector, the private nonfarm business sector, and the manufacturing sector. Have each group identify periods when multifactor productivity growth was particularly fast or slow. Then compare notes. Does it appear to make a big difference which sector one looks at when evaluating periods of greatest and least growth in multifactor productivity?

ANSWERS TO QUICK QUIZZES

p. 192: (i) per capita; (ii) benefits . . . costs; (iii) large

p. 194: (i) capital . . . labor . . . capital . . . labor; (ii) saving . . . save . . . saving

p. 199: (i) New growth; (ii) trade; (iii) Inventions . . . innovation; (iv) new growth; (v) human

p. 200: (i) economic; (ii) property . . . property

p. 204: (i) population; (ii) agricultural . . . manufacturing . . . service-sector; (iii) working population; (iv) property rights . . . education . . . replace . . . international trade

10

Real GDP and the Price Level in the Long Run

During the early 2000s, Japan's price level declined at a steady pace. Then, between late 2003 and 2008, the price level went through brief periods in which it oscillated very slightly upward or downward. On net, however, Japan's price level still dropped somewhat during this second period. Then, in the late 2000s, the price level suddenly jumped upward at a rate of more than 2 percent per year before plunging downward at a rate exceeding 2 percent per year. What caused Japan's price level to behave as it did across the 2000s? To answer this question, you must understand how a nation's *equilibrium* price level is determined. Helping you develop an understanding of this concept is a key goal of this chapter.

LEARNING OBJECTIVES

After reading this chapter, you should be able to:

- Understand the concept of long-run aggregate supply
- Describe the effect of economic growth on the long-run aggregate supply curve
- Explain why the aggregate demand curve slopes downward and list key factors that cause this curve to shift
- Discuss the meaning of long-run equilibrium for the economy as a whole
- Evaluate why economic growth can cause deflation
- Evaluate likely reasons for persistent inflation in recent decades

MyEconLab helps you master each objective and study more efficiently. See end of chapter for details.

Did You Know That ?

until the spring of 2008, the U.S. price level had not exhibited a decline during any single 12-month interval since 1955? Thus, the U.S. economy experienced a full year of *deflation,* or a decrease in the price level over time, for the first time in half a century. Why was there such a lengthy period between deflationary bouts in the United States? What can cause deflation to occur? In addition, why did *inflation,* or an increase in the prive level over time, take place during every other 12-month interval following 1955? To answer these questions, you must learn about the causes of both deflation and inflation, which are key topics that this chapter addresses.

Output Growth and the Long-Run Aggregate Supply Curve

In Chapter 2, we showed the derivation of the production possibilities curve (PPC). At any point in time, the economy can be inside or on the PPC but never outside it. Along the PPC, a country's resources are fully employed in the production of goods and services, and the sum total of the inflation-adjusted value of all final goods and services produced is the nation's real GDP. Economists refer to the total of all planned production for the entire economy as the **aggregate supply** of real output.

Aggregate supply
The total of all planned production for the economy.

Long-run aggregate supply curve
A vertical line representing the real output of goods and services after full adjustment has occurred. It can also be viewed as representing the real GDP of the economy under conditions of full employment—the full-employment level of real GDP.

Base-year dollars
The value of a current sum expressed in terms of prices in a base year.

Endowments
The various resources in an economy, including both physical resources and such human resources as ingenuity and management skills.

The Long-Run Aggregate Supply Curve

Put yourself in a world in which nothing has been changing, year in and year out. The price level has not changed. Technology has not changed. The prices of inputs that firms must purchase have not changed. Labor productivity has not changed. All resources are fully employed, so the economy operates on its production possibilities curve, such as the one depicted in panel (a) of Figure 10-1 below. This is a world that is fully adjusted and in which people have all the information they are ever going to have about that world. The **long-run aggregate supply curve** (*LRAS*) in this world is some amount of real GDP—say, \$15 trillion of real GDP—which is the value of the flow of production of final goods and services measured in **base-year dollars.** We can represent long-run aggregate supply by a vertical line at \$15 trillion of real GDP. This is what you see in panel (b) of the figure below. That curve, labeled *LRAS,* is a vertical line determined by technology and **endowments,** or resources that exist in our economy. It is the full-information and full-adjustment level of real output of

FIGURE 10-1 The Production Possibilities Curve and the Economy's Long-Run Aggregate Supply Curve

At a point in time, a nation's base of resources and its technological capabilities define the position of its production possibilities curve (PPC), as shown in panel (a). This defines the real GDP that the nation can produce when resources are fully employed, which determines the position of the long-run aggregate supply curve (*LRAS*) displayed in panel (b). Because people have complete information and input prices adjust fully in the long run, the *LRAS* is vertical.

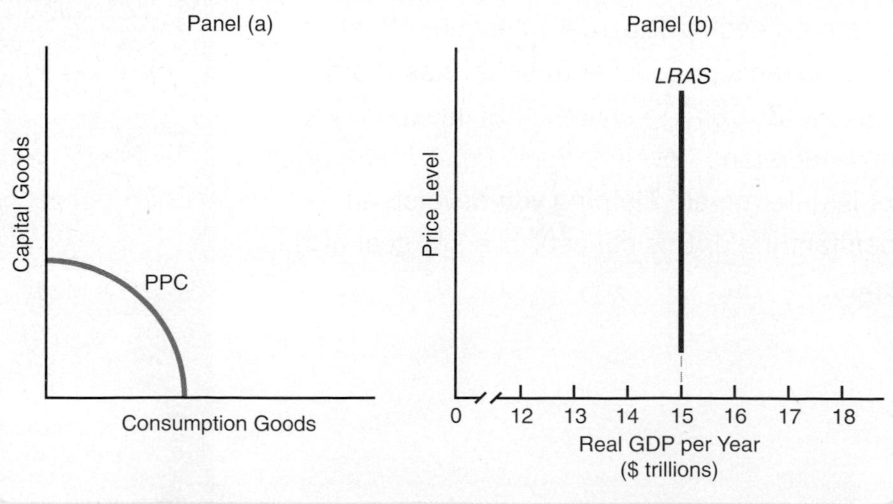

goods and services. It is the level of real GDP that will continue being produced year after year, forever, if nothing changes.

Another way of viewing the *LRAS* is to think of it as the full-employment level of real GDP. When the economy reaches full employment along its production possibilities curve, no further adjustments will occur unless a change occurs in the other variables that we are assuming to be stable. Some economists suggest that the *LRAS* occurs at the level of real GDP consistent with the natural rate of unemployment, the unemployment rate that occurs in an economy with full adjustment in the long run. As we discussed in Chapter 7, many economists like to think of the natural rate of unemployment as consisting of frictional and structural unemployment.

To understand why the *LRAS* is vertical, think about the long run, which is a sufficiently long period that all factors of production and prices, including wages and other input prices, can change. A change in the level of prices of goods and services has no effect on real GDP per year in the long run, because higher prices will be accompanied by comparable changes in input prices. Suppliers will therefore have no incentive to increase or decrease their production of goods and services. Remember that in the long run, everybody has full information, and there is full adjustment to price level changes. (Of course, this is not necessarily true in the short run, as we shall discuss in Chapter 11.)

Go to **www.econtoday.com/ch10** to find out how fast wages are adjusting. Click on "Employment Costs," and then on "Employment Cost Index."

Economic Growth and Long-Run Aggregate Supply

In Chapter 9, you learned about the determinants of growth in per capita real GDP: the annual growth rate of labor, the rate of year-to-year capital accumulation, and the rate of growth of the productivity of labor and capital. As time goes by, population gradually increases, and labor force participation rates may even rise. The capital stock typically grows as businesses add such capital equipment as new information-technology hardware. Furthermore, technology improves. Thus, the economy's production possibilities increase, and as a consequence, the production possibilities curve shifts outward, as shown in panel (a) of Figure 10-2 below.

The result is economic growth: Aggregate real GDP and per capita real GDP increase. This means that in a growing economy such as ours, the *LRAS* will shift outward to the right, as in panel (b) below. We have drawn the *LRAS* for the year 2013 to the right of our original *LRAS* of $14.3 trillion of real GDP. We assume that between now and 2013, real GDP increases to $15 trillion, to give us the position of the $LRAS_{2013}$ curve. Thus, it is to the right of today's *LRAS* curve.

We may conclude that in a growing economy, the *LRAS* shifts ever farther to the right over time. If the *LRAS* happened to shift rightward at a constant pace, real GDP

FIGURE 10-2 The Long-Run Aggregate Supply Curve and Shifts in It

In panel (a), we repeat a diagram that we used in Chapter 2, on page 37, to show the meaning of economic growth. Over time, the production possibilities curve shifts outward. In panel (b), we demonstrate the same principle by showing the long-run aggregate supply curve initially as a vertical line at $14.3 trillion of real GDP per year. As our productive abilities increase, the *LRAS* moves outward to $LRAS_{2013}$ at $15 trillion.

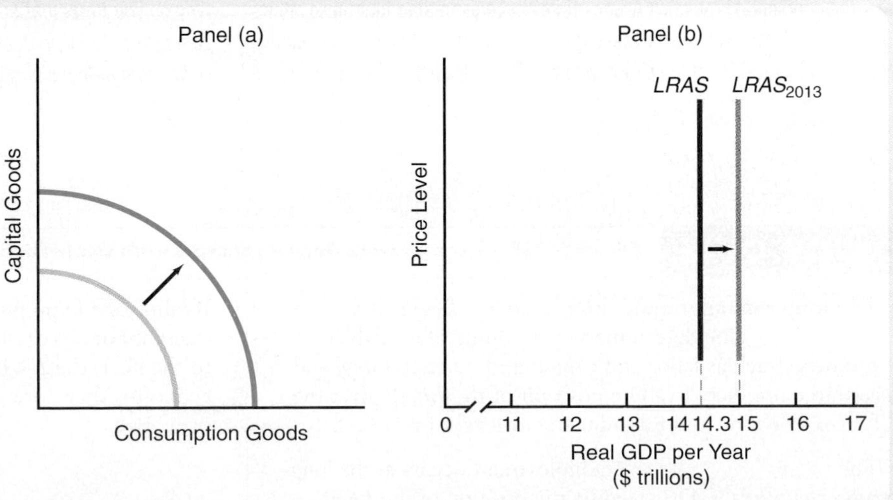

FIGURE 10-3 A Sample Long-Run Growth Path for Real GDP

Year-to-year shifts in the long-run aggregate supply curve yield a long-run trend path for real GDP growth. In this example, from 2013 onward, real GDP grows by a steady 3 percent per year.

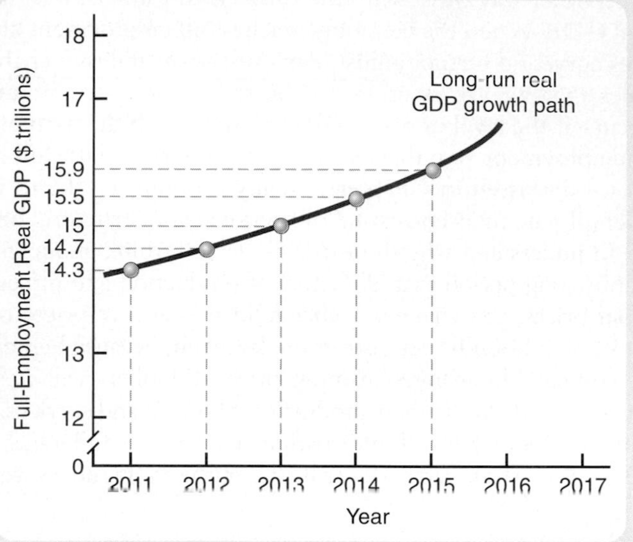

would increase at a steady annual rate. As shown in Figure 10-3 above, this means that real GDP would increase along a long-run, or *trend*, path that is an upward-sloping line. Thus, if the *LRAS* shifts rightward from $14.3 trillion to $15 trillion between now and 2013 and then increases at a steady 3 percent annual rate every year thereafter, in 2014 long-run real GDP will equal $15.5 trillion, in 2015 it will equal $15.9 trillion, and so on.

Why might the U.S. trend growth path become shallower if U.S. leaders follow through on plans to cut greenhouse gas emissions dramatically?

EXAMPLE How Much Might "Going Green" Reduce U.S. Economic Growth?

President Obama and leaders in the U.S. Congress have agreed that reduction of greenhouse gas emissions should be a national priority. Their near-term goal is to reduce such emissions to 2005 levels by no later than 2014. Their longer-term goal is to reduce emissions by an additional 30 percent by 2030.

Attainment of these goals would constrain the ability of businesses to use resources at lowest cost. As a consequence, production of capital goods would decline, and that would reduce future economic growth. Economists at the Environmental Protection Agency (EPA) have estimated that these efforts to cut emissions of greenhouse gases likely would lead to a cumulative reduction in real GDP of about 4 percent by 2030. Based on the current level of U.S. real GDP, this estimated eventual decrease in annual real GDP would be equivalent to the reduction that occurred during the Great Recession of the late 2000s. Instead of being a short-term decrease in real GDP as in the recession, however, the reduction generated by the proposed emissions regulations would be permanent.

FOR CRITICAL ANALYSIS

Why do you think that economists suggest that any regulatory policies that generate cuts in production of capital goods will tend to reduce the nation's long-run growth rate for real GDP?

QUICK QUIZ

See page 228 for the answers. Review concepts from this section in MyEconLab.

The **long-run aggregate supply curve,** *LRAS*, is a __________ line determined by amounts of available resources such as labor and capital and by technology and resource productivity. The position of the *LRAS* gives the full-information and full-adjustment level of real GDP.

The __________ rate of unemployment occurs at the long-run level of real GDP given by the position of the *LRAS*.

If labor or capital increases from year to year or if the productivity of either of these resources rises from one year to the next, the *LRAS* shifts __________. In a growing economy, therefore, real GDP gradually __________ over time.

Total Expenditures and Aggregate Demand

In equilibrium, individuals, businesses, and governments purchase all the goods and services produced, valued in trillions of real dollars. As explained in Chapters 7 and 8, GDP is the dollar value of total expenditures on domestically produced final goods and services. Because all expenditures are made by individuals, firms, or governments, the total value of these expenditures must be what these market participants decide it shall be.

The decisions of individuals, managers of firms, and government officials determine the annual dollar value of total expenditures. You can certainly see this in your role as an individual. You decide what the total dollar amount of your expenditures will be in a year. You decide how much you want to spend and how much you want to save. Thus, if we want to know what determines the total value of GDP, the answer is clear: the spending decisions of individuals like you; firms; and local, state, and national governments. In an open economy, we must also include foreign individuals, firms, and governments (foreign residents, for short) that decide to spend their money income in the United States.

Simply stating that the dollar value of total expenditures in this country depends on what individuals, firms, governments, and foreign residents decide to do really doesn't tell us much, though. Two important issues remain:

1. What determines the total amount that individuals, firms, governments, and foreign residents want to spend?
2. What determines the equilibrium price level and the rate of inflation (or deflation)?

The *LRAS* tells us only about the economy's long-run real GDP. To answer these additional questions, we must consider another important concept. This is **aggregate demand,** which is the total of all *planned* real expenditures in the economy.

Aggregate demand
The total of all planned expenditures in the entire economy.

The Aggregate Demand Curve

The **aggregate demand curve,** *AD*, gives the various quantities of all final commodities demanded at various price levels, all other things held constant. Recall the components of GDP that you studied in Chapter 8: consumption spending, investment expenditures, government purchases, and net foreign demand for domestic production. They are all components of aggregate demand. Throughout this chapter and the next, whenever you see the aggregate demand curve, realize that it is a shorthand way of talking about the components of GDP that are measured by government statisticians when they calculate total economic activity each year. In Chapter 12, you will look more closely at the relationship between these components and, in particular, at how consumption spending depends on income.

Aggregate demand curve
A curve showing planned purchase rates for all final goods and services in the economy at various price levels, all other things held constant.

The aggregate demand curve gives the total amount, measured in base-year dollars, of *real* domestic final goods and services that will be purchased at each price level—everything produced for final use by households, businesses, the government, and foreign residents. It includes iPods, socks, shoes, medical and legal services, computers, and millions of other goods and services that people buy each year.

A graphical representation of the aggregate demand curve is seen in Figure 10-4 on the next page. On the horizontal axis, real GDP is measured. For our measure of the price level, we use the GDP price deflator on the vertical axis. The aggregate demand curve is labeled *AD*. If the GDP deflator is 110, aggregate quantity demanded is $15 trillion per year (point *A*). At the price level 115, it is $14 trillion per year (point *B*). At the price level 120, it is $13 trillion per year (point *C*). The higher the price level, the lower the total real amount of final goods and services demanded in the economy, everything else remaining constant, as shown by the arrow along *AD* in Figure 10-4. Conversely, the lower the price level, the higher the total real GDP demanded by the economy, everything else staying constant.

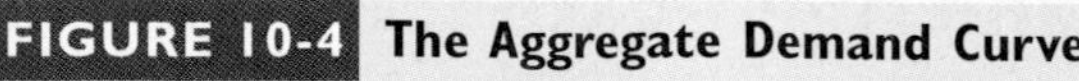

FIGURE 10-4 The Aggregate Demand Curve

The aggregate demand curve, *AD*, slopes downward. If the price level is 110, we will be at point *A* with $15 trillion of real GDP demanded per year. As the price level increases to 115 and to 120, we move up the aggregate demand curve to points *B* and *C*.

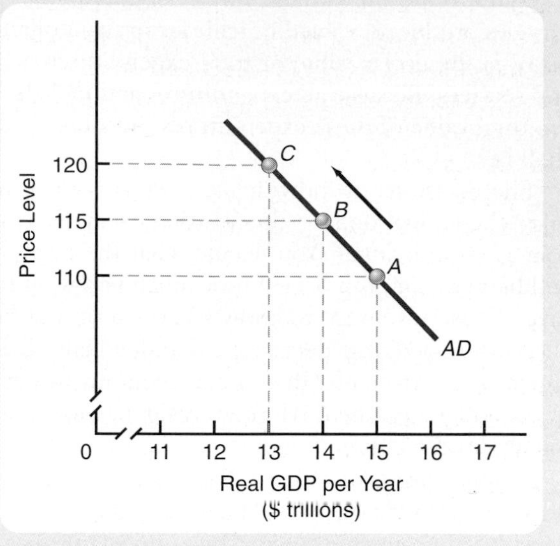

Let's take the year 2011. Estimates based on U.S. Department of Commerce preliminary statistics reveal the following information:

- Nominal GDP was estimated to be $15,067.5 billion.
- The price level as measured by the GDP deflator was about 112.4 (base year is 2005, for which the index equals 100).
- Real GDP was approximately $13,405.8 billion in 2005 dollars.

What can we say about 2011? Given the dollar cost of buying goods and services and all of the other factors that go into spending decisions by individuals, firms, governments, and foreign residents, the total amount of planned spending on final goods and services by firms, individuals, governments, and foreign residents was $13,405.8 billion in 2011 (in terms of 2005 dollars).

What Happens When the Price Level Rises?

What if the price level in the economy rose to 160 tomorrow? What would happen to the amount of real goods and services that individuals, firms, governments, and foreigners wish to purchase in the United States? We know from Chapter 3 that when the price of one good or service rises, the quantity of it demanded will fall. But here we are talking about the *price level*—the average price of *all* goods and services in the economy. The answer is still that the total quantities of real goods and services demanded would fall, but the reasons are different. When the price of one good or service goes up, the consumer substitutes other goods and services. For the entire economy, when the price level goes up, the consumer doesn't simply substitute one good for another, for now we are dealing with the demand for *all* goods and services in the nation. There are *economywide* reasons that cause the aggregate demand curve to slope downward. They involve at least three distinct forces: the *real-balance effect*, the *interest rate effect*, and the *open economy effect*.

THE REAL-BALANCE EFFECT A rise in the price level will have an effect on spending. Individuals, firms, governments, and foreign residents carry out transactions using money, a portion of which consists of currency and coins that you have in your pocket (or stashed away) right now. Because people use money to purchase goods and services, the amount of money that people have influences the amount of goods and services they want to buy. For example, if you find a $100 bill on the sidewalk, the amount of money you have increases. Given your now greater level of money, or cash, balances—currency in this case—you will almost surely increase your spending on goods and services. Similarly, if your pocket is picked while you are at the mall, your desired spending would be affected. For instance, if your wallet had $150 in it when it was stolen, the reduction in your cash balances—in this case, currency—would no doubt cause you to reduce your planned expenditures. You would ultimately buy fewer goods and services.

This response is sometimes called the **real-balance effect** (or *wealth effect*) because it relates to the real value of your cash balances. While your *nominal* cash balances may remain the same, any change in the price level will cause a change in the *real* value of those cash balances—hence the real-balance effect on total planned expenditures.

Real-balance effect
The change in expenditures resulting from a change in the real value of money balances when the price level changes, all other things held constant; also called the *wealth effect.*

When you think of the real-balance effect, just think of what happens to your real wealth if you have, say, a $100 bill hidden under your mattress. If the price level increases by 5 percent, the purchasing power of that $100 bill drops by 5 percent, so you have become less wealthy. You will reduce your purchases of all goods and services by some small amount.

THE INTEREST RATE EFFECT There is a more subtle but equally important effect on your desire to spend. A higher price level leaves people with too few money balances. Hence, they try to borrow more (or lend less) to replenish their real money holdings. This drives up interest rates. Higher interest rates raise borrowing costs for consumers and businesses. They will borrow less and consequently spend less. The fact that a higher price level pushes up interest rates and thereby reduces borrowing and spending is known as the **interest rate effect.**

Interest rate effect
One of the reasons that the aggregate demand curve slopes downward: Higher price levels increase the interest rate, which in turn causes businesses and consumers to reduce desired spending due to the higher cost of borrowing.

Higher interest rates make it more costly for people to finance purchases of houses and cars. Higher interest rates also make it less profitable for firms to install new equipment and to erect new office buildings. Whether we are talking about individuals or firms, a rise in the price level will cause higher interest rates, which in turn reduce the amount of goods and services that people are willing to purchase. Therefore, an increase in the price level will tend to reduce total planned expenditures. (The opposite occurs if the price level declines.)

THE OPEN ECONOMY EFFECT: THE SUBSTITUTION OF FOREIGN GOODS Recall from Chapter 8 that GDP includes net exports—the difference between exports and imports. In an open economy, we buy imports from other countries and ultimately pay for them through the foreign exchange market. The same is true for foreign residents who purchase our goods (exports). Given any set of exchange rates between the U.S. dollar and other currencies, an increase in the price level in the United States makes U.S. goods more expensive relative to foreign goods. Foreign residents have downward sloping demand curves for U.S. goods. When the relative price of U.S. goods goes up, foreign residents buy fewer U.S. goods and more of their own. At home, relatively cheaper prices for foreign goods cause U.S. residents to want to buy more foreign goods instead of domestically produced goods. Thus, when the domestic price level rises, the result is a fall in exports and a rise in imports. That means that a price level increase tends to reduce net exports, thereby reducing the amount of real goods and services purchased in the United States. This is known as the **open economy effect.**

Open economy effect
One of the reasons that the aggregate demand curve slopes downward: Higher price levels result in foreign residents desiring to buy fewer U.S.-made goods, while U.S. residents now desire more foreign-made goods, thereby reducing net exports. This is equivalent to a reduction in the amount of real goods and services purchased in the United States.

What Happens When the Price Level Falls?

What about the reverse? Suppose now that the GDP deflator falls to 100 from an initial level of 120. You should be able to trace the three effects on desired purchases of goods and services. Specifically, how do the real-balance, interest rate, and open economy effects cause people to want to buy more? You should come to the conclusion that the lower the price level, the greater the total planned spending on goods and services.

The aggregate demand curve, *AD*, shows the quantity of aggregate output that will be demanded at alternative price levels. It is downward sloping, just like the demand curve for individual goods. The higher the price level, the lower the real amount of total planned expenditures, and vice versa.

Demand for All Goods and Services versus Demand for a Single Good or Service

Even though the aggregate demand curve, *AD*, in Figure 10-4 on page 214 looks similar to the one for individual demand, *D*, for a single good or service that you encountered in Chapters 3 and 4, the two are not the same. When we derive the aggregate demand curve, we are looking at the entire economic system. The aggregate demand curve, *AD*, differs from an individual demand curve, *D*, because we are looking at total planned expenditures on *all* goods and services when we construct *AD*.

Shifts in the Aggregate Demand Curve

In Chapter 3, you learned that any time a nonprice determinant of demand changes, the demand curve will shift inward to the left or outward to the right. The same analysis holds for the aggregate demand curve, except we are now talking about the non-price-level determinants of aggregate demand. So, when we ask the question, "What determines the position of the aggregate demand curve?" the fundamental proposition is as follows:

> ***Any non-price-level change that increases aggregate spending (on domestic goods) shifts* AD *to the right. Any non-price-level change that decreases aggregate spending (on domestic goods) shifts* AD *to the left.***

The list of potential determinants of the position of the aggregate demand curve is long. Some of the most important "curve shifters" for aggregate demand are presented in Table 10-1 below.

Why did the U.S. aggregate demand curve shift leftward between 2007 and 2009?

TABLE 10-1

Determinants of Aggregate Demand

Aggregate demand consists of the demand for domestically produced consumption goods, investment goods, government purchases, and net exports. Consequently, any change in total planned spending on any one of these components of real GDP will cause a change in aggregate demand. Some possibilities are listed here.

Changes That Cause an Increase in Aggregate Demand	Changes That Cause a Decrease in Aggregate Demand
An increase in the amount of money in circulation	A decrease in the amount of money in circulation
Increased security about jobs and future income	Decreased security about jobs and future income
Improvements in economic conditions in other countries	Declines in economic conditions in other countries
A reduction in real interest rates (nominal interest rates corrected for inflation) not due to price level changes	A rise in real interest rates (nominal interest rates corrected for inflation) not due to price level changes
Tax decreases	Tax increases
A drop in the foreign exchange value of the dollar	A rise in the foreign exchange value of the dollar

EXAMPLE Explaining the Drop in Aggregate Demand in the Late 2000s

In 2006 and 2007, prices of houses, which for many families are major components of their household wealth, began to decline considerably throughout much of the United States. By late 2007 and 2008, the market values of many houses purchased with mortgage loans from banks had fallen below the amounts people had borrowed. Many borrowers decided simply to walk away from their houses, leaving banks with the lower-valued homes. As a consequence, many banks found themselves financially constrained and responded by cutting back on loans to businesses. Firms, in turn, terminated employees and cut back on new hiring. Thus, the bulk of U.S. residents suddenly experienced decreased security about their jobs and their future incomes and wealth, which resulted in a significant decrease in aggregate demand.

FOR CRITICAL ANALYSIS

Why do you suppose that the Federal Reserve responded to the decrease in aggregate demand by trying to engineer reductions in real interest rates? (See Table 10-1.)

QUICK QUIZ

See page 228 for the answers. Review concepts from this section in MyEconLab.

Aggregate demand is the total of all planned __________ in the economy, and **aggregate supply** is the total of all planned __________ in the economy. The aggregate demand curve shows the various quantities of total planned __________ on final goods and services at various price levels; it is downward sloping.

There are three reasons why the aggregate demand curve is downward sloping. They are the __________ - __________ effect, the __________ __________ effect, and the __________ __________ effect.

The __________ - __________ effect occurs because price level changes alter the real value of cash balances, thereby causing people to desire to spend more or less, depending on whether the price level decreases or increases.

The __________ __________ effect is caused by interest rate changes that mimic price level changes. At higher interest rates, people seek to buy __________ houses and cars, and at lower interest rates, they seek to buy __________.

The **open economy effect** occurs because of a shift away from expenditures on __________ goods and a shift toward expenditures on __________ goods when the domestic price level increases.

Long-Run Equilibrium and the Price Level

As noted in Chapter 3, equilibrium occurs where the demand and supply curves intersect. The same is true for the economy as a whole, as shown in Figure 10-5 below: The equilibrium price level occurs at the point where the aggregate demand curve *(AD)*

FIGURE 10-5 Long-Run Economywide Equilibrium

For the economy as a whole, long-run equilibrium occurs at the price level where the aggregate demand curve crosses the long-run aggregate supply curve. At this long-run equilibrium price level, which is 120 in the diagram, total planned real expenditures equal real GDP at full employment, which in our example is a real GDP of $15 trillion.

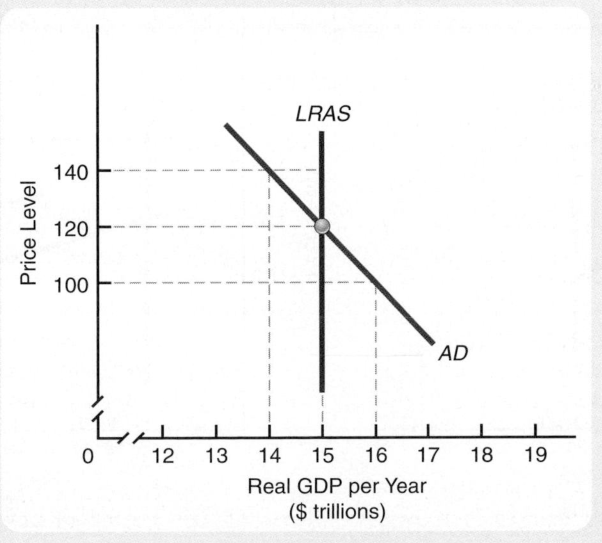

crosses the long-run aggregate supply curve *(LRAS)*. At this equilibrium price level of 120, the total of all planned real expenditures for the entire economy is equal to actual real GDP produced by firms after all adjustments have taken place. Thus, the equilibrium depicted in Figure 10-5 on page 217 is the economy's *long-run equilibrium.*

The Long-Run Equilibrium Price Level

Note in Figure 10-5 on the previous page that if the price level were to increase to 140, actual real GDP would exceed total planned real expenditures. Inventories of unsold goods would begin to accumulate, and firms would stand ready to offer more services than people wish to purchase. As a result, the price level would tend to fall.

In contrast, if the price level were 100, then total planned real expenditures by individuals, businesses, and the government would exceed actual real GDP. Inventories of unsold goods would begin to be depleted. The price level would rise toward 120, and higher prices would encourage firms to expand production and replenish inventories of goods available for sale.

The Effects of Economic Growth on the Price Level

We now have a basic theory of how real GDP and the price level are determined in the long run when all of a nation's resources can change over time and all input prices can adjust fully to changes in the overall level of prices of goods and services that firms produce. Let's begin by evaluating the effects of economic growth on the nation's price level.

ECONOMIC GROWTH AND SECULAR DEFLATION Take a look at panel (a) of Figure 10-6 below, which shows what happens, other things being equal, when the *LRAS* shifts rightward over time. If the economy were to grow steadily during, say, a 10-year interval, the long-run aggregate supply schedule would shift to the right, from $LRAS_1$ to $LRAS_2$. In panel (a), this results in a downward movement along the aggregate demand schedule. The equilibrium price level falls, from 120 to 80.

FIGURE 10-6 Secular Deflation versus Long-Run Price Stability in a Growing Economy

Panel (a) illustrates what happens when economic growth occurs without a corresponding increase in aggregate demand. The result is a decline in the price level over time, known as *secular deflation.* Panel (b) shows that, in principle, secular deflation can be eliminated if the aggregate demand curve shifts rightward at the same pace that the long-run aggregate supply curve shifts to the right.

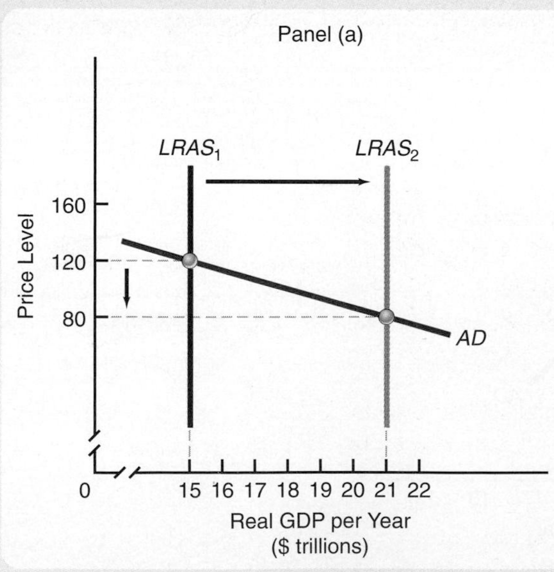

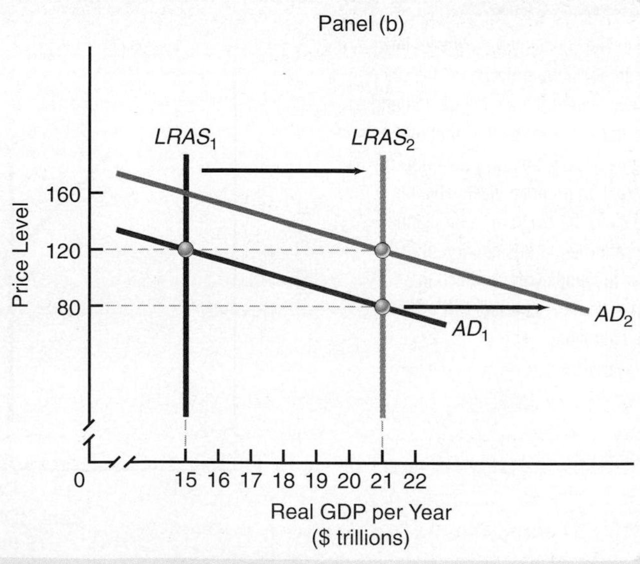

Thus, if all factors that affect total planned real expenditures are unchanged, so that the aggregate demand curve does not noticeably move during the 10-year period of real GDP growth, the growing economy in the example would experience deflation. This is known as **secular deflation,** or a persistently declining price level resulting from economic growth in the presence of relatively unchanged aggregate demand.

Secular deflation
A persistent decline in prices resulting from economic growth in the presence of stable aggregate demand.

SECULAR DEFLATION IN THE UNITED STATES In the United States, between 1872 and 1894, the price of bricks fell by 50 percent, the price of sugar by 67 percent, the price of wheat by 69 percent, the price of nails by 70 percent, and the price of copper by nearly 75 percent. Founders of a late-nineteenth-century political movement called *populism* offered a proposal for ending deflation: They wanted the government to issue new money backed by silver. As noted in Table 10-1 on page 216, an increase in the quantity of money in circulation causes the aggregate demand curve to shift to the right. It is clear from panel (b) of Figure 10-6 on the facing page that the increase in the quantity of money would indeed have pushed the price level back upward, because the *AD* curve would shift from AD_1 to AD_2.

Nevertheless, money growth remained low for several more years. Not until the early twentieth century would the United States put an end to secular deflation, namely, by creating a new monetary system.

Go to www.econtoday.com/ch10 to learn about how the price level has changed during recent years. Then click on "Gross Domestic Product and Components" (for GDP deflators) or "Consumer Price Indexes."

Causes of Inflation

Of course, so far during your lifetime, deflation has not been a problem in the United States. Instead, what you have experienced is inflation. Figure 10-7 on the top of the next page shows annual U.S. inflation rates for the past few decades. Clearly, inflation rates have been variable. The other obvious fact, however, is that inflation rates have been consistently *positive.* The price level in the United States has *risen* almost every year. For today's United States, secular deflation has not been a big political issue. If anything, it is secular *inflation* that has plagued the nation.

Why Not . . . pass a law that prohibits firms from raising their prices?

Between 1971 and 1973, the U.S. government tried to reduce the measured inflation rate by limiting price increases to specific allowed percentages. This policy had two consequences. First, in many markets, the artificially limited price increases led consumers to desire to purchase more items than firms were willing to sell, resulting in shortages. Second, many firms sought to raise quality-adjusted prices by reducing product quality, so items available to consumers were often of lower quality. This experience demonstrates that direct inflation controls generate widespread shortages and reductions in product quality.

Supply-Side Inflation?

What causes such persistent inflation? The model of aggregate demand and long-run aggregate supply provides two possible explanations for inflation. One potential rationale is depicted in panel (a) of Figure 10-8 on the bottom of the next page. This panel shows a rise in the price level caused by a *decline in long-run aggregate supply.* Hence, one possible reason for persistent inflation would be continual reductions in economywide production.

A leftward shift in the aggregate supply schedule could be caused by several factors, such as reductions in labor force participation, higher marginal tax rates on wages, or the provision of government benefits that give households incentives *not* to supply labor services to firms. Tax rates and government benefits have increased during recent decades, but so has the U.S. population. The significant overall rise in real GDP that has taken place during the past few decades tells us that population growth and productivity gains undoubtedly have dominated other factors. In fact, the aggregate

FIGURE 10-7 Inflation Rates in the United States

Annual U.S. inflation rates rose considerably during the 1970s but declined to lower levels after the 1980s. The inflation rate has declined significantly in recent years after creeping upward during the early and middle 2000s.

Sources: Economic Report of the President; Economic Indicators, various issues.

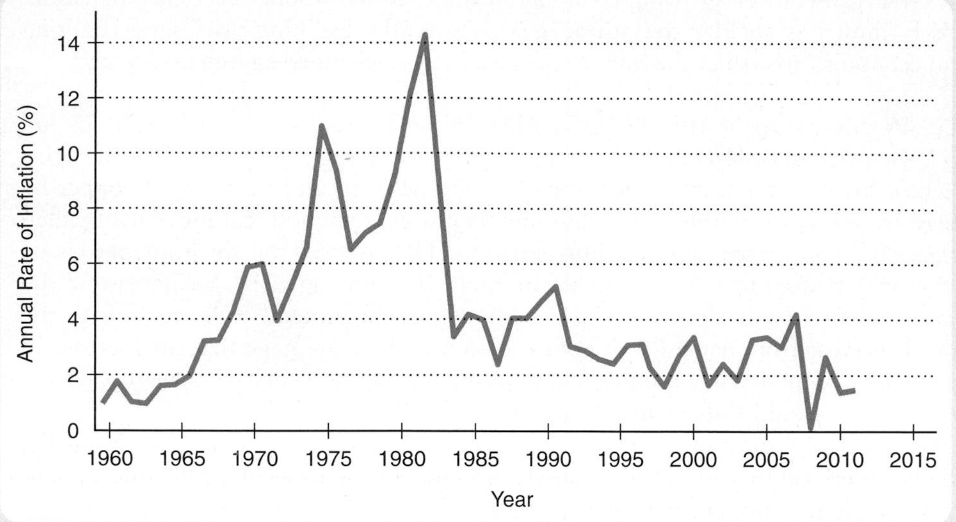

supply schedule has actually shifted *rightward*, not leftward, over time. Consequently, this supply-side explanation for persistent inflation *cannot* be the correct explanation.

Demand-Side Inflation

This leaves only one other explanation for the persistent inflation that the United States has experienced in recent decades. This explanation is depicted in panel (b) of Figure 10-8 below. If aggregate demand increases for a given level of long-run aggregate supply, the price level must increase. The reason is that at an initial price level

FIGURE 10-8 Explaining Persistent Inflation

As shown in panel (a), it is possible for a decline in long-run aggregate supply to cause a rise in the price level. Long-run aggregate supply *increases* in a growing economy, however, so this cannot explain the observation of persistent U.S. inflation. Panel (b) provides the actual explanation of persistent inflation in the United States and most other nations today, which is that increases in aggregate demand push up the long-run equilibrium price level. Thus, it is possible to explain persistent inflation if the aggregate demand curve shifts rightward at a faster pace than the long-run aggregate supply curve.

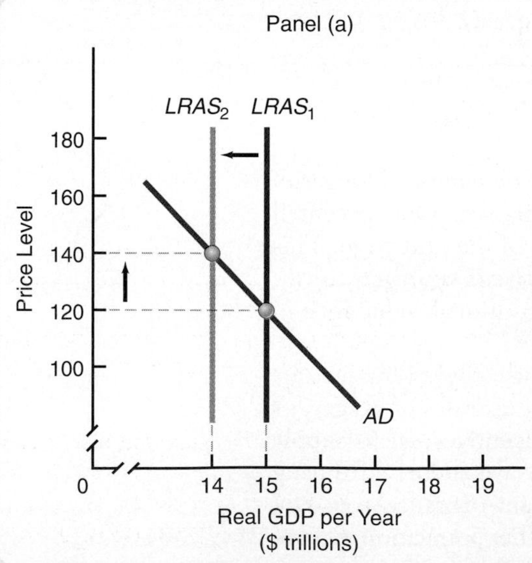

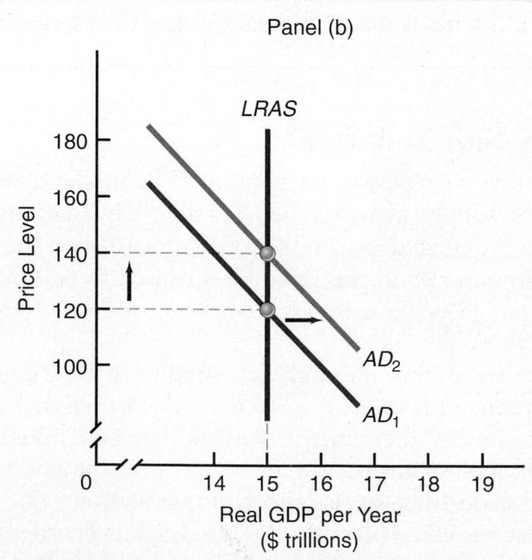

FIGURE 10-9 Real GDP and the Price Level in the United States, 1970 to the Present

This figure shows the points where aggregate demand and aggregate supply have intersected each year from 1970 to the present. The United States has experienced economic growth over this period, but not without inflation.

Sources: Economic Report of the President; Economic Indicators, various issues; author's estimates.

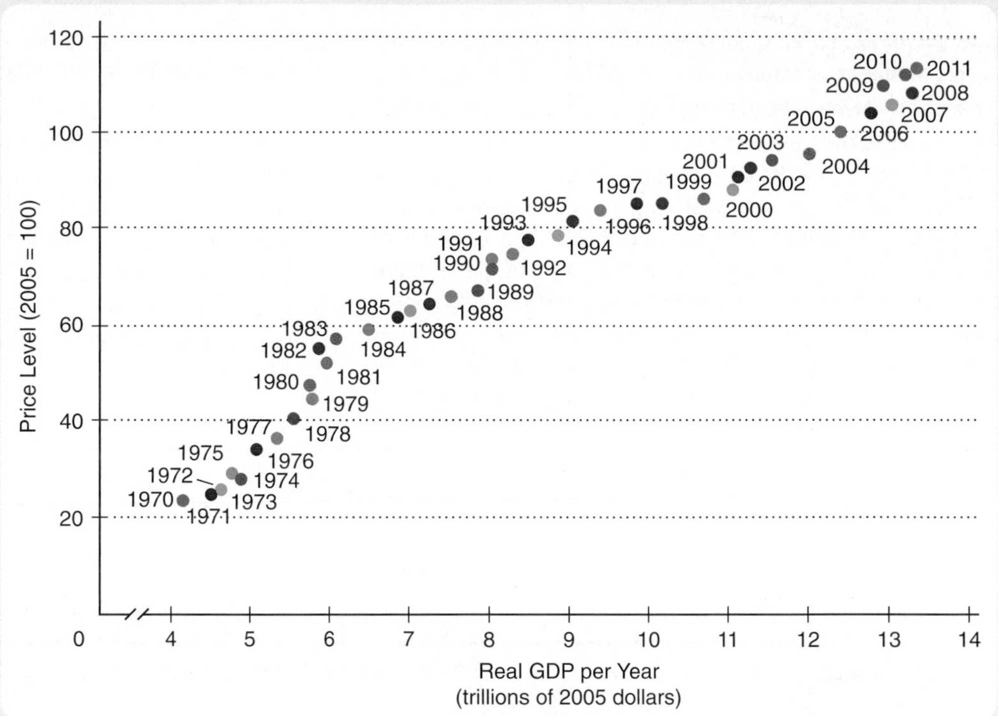

such as 120, people desire to purchase more goods and services than firms are willing and able to produce given currently available resources and technology. As a result, the rise in aggregate demand leads only to a general rise in the price level, such as the increase to a value of 140 depicted in the figure.

From a long-run perspective, we are left with only one possibility: Persistent inflation in a growing economy is possible only if the aggregate demand curve shifts rightward over time at a faster pace than the rightward progression of the long-run aggregate supply curve. Thus, in contrast to the experience of people who lived in the latter portion of the nineteenth century, when aggregate demand grew too slowly relative to aggregate supply to maintain price stability, your grandparents, parents, and you have lived in times when aggregate demand has grown too *speedily.* The result has been a continual upward drift in the price level, or long-term inflation.

Figure 10-9 above shows that U.S. real GDP has grown in most years since 1970. Nevertheless, this growth has been accompanied by higher prices every single year.

You Are There

To contemplate a real-world confrontation with demand-side inflation, read **Fighting Inflation in Pakistan,** on the next page.

QUICK QUIZ See page 228 for the answers. **Review concepts from this section in MyEconLab.**

When the economy is in long-run equilibrium, the price level adjusts to equate total planned real ___________ by individuals, businesses, and the government with total planned ___________ by firms.

Economic growth causes the long-run aggregate supply schedule to shift ___________ over time. If the position of the aggregate demand curve does not change, the long-run equilibrium price level tends to ___________, and there is **secular deflation.**

Because the U.S. economy has grown in recent decades, the persistent inflation during those years has been caused by the aggregate demand curve shifting ___________ at a faster pace than the long-run aggregate supply curve.

You Are There

Fighting Inflation in Pakistan

Shamshad Akhtar, the governor of Pakistan's central bank, the State Bank of Pakistan, has assumed office in the midst of an upsurge in the nation's inflation rate. Although the annual inflation rate has recently dropped from about 22 percent to around 18 percent, her top priority is to reduce the inflation rate further.

Akhtar does not have to look far to determine one reason why Pakistan's inflation rate has increased. The quantity of money in circulation has been rising at an annual rate of more than 16 percent, which has pushed up aggregate demand and boosted the equilibrium price level. Thus, Akhtar has been pressing to significantly reduce the growth rate of the quantity of money. Today, she sees that Pakistan's money growth rate has dropped below 10 percent. For the first time since she took over as the central bank's governor, Akhtar sees glimmers of hope for cutting the nation's annual inflation rate to a single digit.

Critical Analysis Questions

1. What other elements conceivably could cause aggregate demand to continue to rise and thwart Akhtar's efforts to reduce Pakistan's inflation rate? (Hint: Take a look back at Table 10-1 on page 216.)
2. Would an increase in the rate of growth of long-run aggregate supply help or hinder Akhtar's anti-inflation endeavors? Explain briefly.

ISSUES & APPLICATIONS

Japan's Deflation Rate Switches from Steady to Volatile

CONCEPTS APPLIED

- ▶ Aggregate Demand
- ▶ Long-Run Aggregate Supply
- ▶ Secular Deflation

In Japan, the rate of change in the price level during the 2000s was negative more often than it was positive. Consequently, economists have often referred to Japan's rate of average price change during this period as deflation instead of inflation.

Steady but Declining Deflation for Most of the 2000s

Figure 10-10 on the facing page verifies that during the early 2000s Japan experienced a persistent negative rate of change in the price level, or deflation. Most economists agree that during this period, the nation's aggregate demand curve was nearly stationary, but its long-run aggregate supply curve shifted rightward. The consequence was secular deflation. Until late 2003, the annual deflation rate was nearly 1 percent.

From late 2003 through the middle of 2008, Japanese aggregate demand began to grow at a steadier pace. As a result, the rate of change in the price level was periodically positive during this interval, although not as often as it was negative. Thus, on average, there was a lower rate of deflation.

FIGURE 10-10 The Rate of Change of Japanese Prices Since 2000

Between 2000 and 2003, the rate of change in Japan's price level was generally between −0.5 percent and −1.0 percent, so the nation experienced deflation. Its deflation rate dropped during the mid-2000s. Then, during the late 2000s, Japan suddenly experienced inflation, as the rate of change in the price level suddenly jumped to nearly 2.5 percent. This was followed by more significant deflation, as the rate of change in the price level dropped as low as −2.5 percent.

Source: International Monetary Fund.

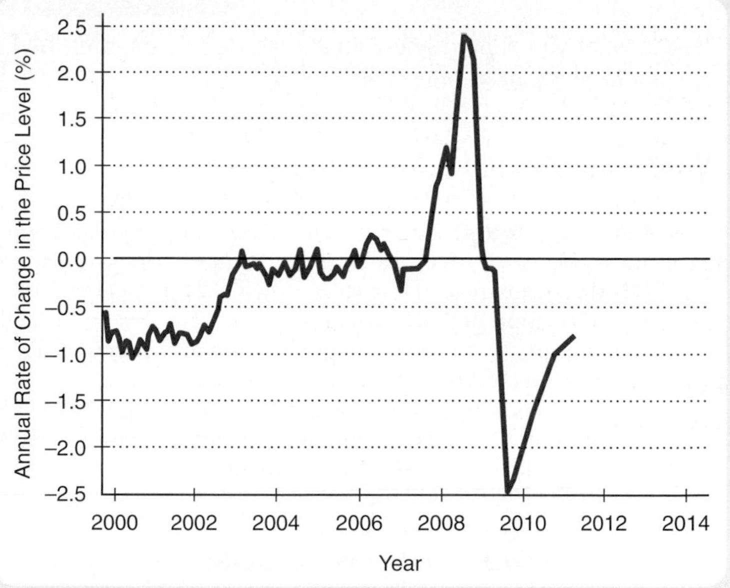

Deflation Volatility Since the Late 2000s

During the latter part of 2008, Japanese aggregate demand rose considerably as U.S. residents and others increased their purchases of Japanese export goods. The rate of change in Japan's price level suddenly turned significantly positive, and the nation briefly experienced a nearly 2.5 percent *inflation* rate.

Then, just as rapidly, purchases of Japanese export goods by residents of the United States and other nations plunged, which caused a sudden drop in aggregate demand. By 2010, Japan's *deflation* rate was 2.5 percent. The deflation rate has moved closer to 1 percent since then.

For Critical Analysis

1. What happened to the equilibrium price level in Japan during the early 2000s?
2. How did Japan's equilibrium price level adjust between the middle of 2008 and early 2010?

Web Resources

1. For a discussion of efforts by Japan's central bank, the Bank of Japan, to battle deflation by boosting the quantity of money in circulation, use the link available at www.econtoday.com/ch10.
2. To learn why Bank of Japan officials perceive that a higher rate of deflation is a problem, go to www.econtoday.com/ch10.

Research Project

Explain why deflation will remain the norm in Japan if the aggregate demand curve once again becomes stationary over time while long-run aggregate supply shifts rightward as a consequence of economic growth.

For more questions on this chapter's Issues & Applications, go to **MyEconLab**. In the Study Plan for this chapter, select Section N: News.

Here is what you should know after reading this chapter. **MyEconLab** will help you identify what you know, and where to go when you need to practice.

WHAT YOU SHOULD KNOW		WHERE TO GO TO PRACTICE
Long-Run Aggregate Supply The long-run aggregate supply curve is vertical at the amount of real GDP that firms plan to produce when they have full information and when complete adjustment of input prices to any changes in output prices has taken place. This is the full-employment level of real GDP, or the economywide output level at which the natural rate of unemployment—the sum of frictional and structural unemployment as a percentage of the labor force—occurs.	aggregate supply, 210 long-run aggregate supply curve, 210 base-year dollars, 210 endowments, 210 **KEY FIGURE** Figure 10-1, 210	• **MyEconLab** Study Plan 10.1 • Audio introduction to Chapter 10 • Video: The Long-Run Aggregate Supply Curve • Animated Figure 10-1
Economic Growth and the Long-Run Aggregate Supply Curve Economic growth is an expansion of a country's production possibilities. Thus, the production possibilities curve shifts rightward when the economy grows, and so does the nation's long-run aggregate supply curve. In a growing economy, the changes in full-employment real GDP defined by the shifting long-run aggregate supply curve define the nation's long-run, or trend, growth path.	**KEY FIGURES** Figure 10-2, 211 Figure 10-3, 212	• **MyEconLab** Study Plan 10.1 • Video: The Long-Run Aggregate Supply Curve • Animated Figures 10-2, 10-3
Why the Aggregate Demand Curve Slopes Downward and Factors That Cause It to Shift The real-balance effect occurs when a rise in the price level reduces the real value of cash balances, which induces people to cut back on planned spending. Higher interest rates typically accompany increases in the price level, and this interest rate effect induces people to cut back on borrowing and spending. Finally, a rise in the price level at home causes domestic goods to be more expensive relative to foreign goods, so there is a fall in exports and a rise in imports, both of which cause domestic planned expenditures to fall. These three factors together account for the downward slope of the aggregate demand curve, which shifts if there is any other change in total planned real expenditures at any given price level.	aggregate demand, 213 aggregate demand curve, 213 real-balance effect, 215 interest rate effect, 215 open economy effect, 215 **KEY FIGURE** Figure 10-4, 214	• **MyEconLab** Study Plans 10.2, 10.3 • Video: The Aggregate Demand Curve and What Happens When the Price Level Rises • Video: Shifts in the Aggregate Demand Curve • ABC News Video: The Multiplier and the Business Cycle • Animated Figure 10-4
Long-Run Equilibrium for the Economy In a long-run economywide equilibrium, the price level adjusts until total planned real expenditures equal actual real GDP. Thus, the long-run equilibrium price level is determined at the point where the aggregate demand curve intersects the long-run aggregate supply curve.	**KEY FIGURE** Figure 10-5, 217	• **MyEconLab** Study Plan 10.4 • Animated Figure 10-5

MyEconLab continued

WHAT YOU SHOULD KNOW		WHERE TO GO TO PRACTICE
Why Economic Growth Can Cause Deflation If the aggregate demand curve is stationary during a period of economic growth, the long-run aggregate supply curve shifts rightward along the aggregate demand curve. The long-run equilibrium price level falls, so there is secular deflation.	secular deflation, 219 **KEY FIGURE** Figure 10-6, 218	• **MyEconLab** Study Plan 10.4 • Animated Figure 10-6
Likely Reasons for Recent Persistent Inflation Inflation can result from a decline in long-run aggregate supply. In a growing economy, however, long-run aggregate supply generally rises. Thus, a much more likely cause of persistent inflation is a pace of aggregate demand growth that exceeds the pace at which long-run aggregate supply increases.	**KEY FIGURES** Figure 10-7, 220 Figure 10-8, 220	• **MyEconLab** Study Plan 10.5 • Economic Video: Whirlpool • Animated Figures 10-7, 10-8

Log in to MyEconLab, take a chapter test, and get a personalized Study Plan that tells you which concepts you understand and which ones you need to review. From there, MyEconLab will give you further practice, tutorials, animations, videos, and guided solutions.
Log in to www.myeconlab.com

PROBLEMS

All problems are assignable in myeconlab. *Answers to odd-numbered problems appear at the back of the book.*

10-1. Many economists view the natural rate of unemployment as the level observed when real GDP is given by the position of the long-run aggregate supply curve. How can there be positive unemployment in this situation?

10-2. Suppose that the long-run aggregate supply curve is positioned at a real GDP level of $15 trillion in base-year dollars, and the long-run equilibrium price level (in index number form) is 115. What is the full-employment level of *nominal* GDP?

10-3. Continuing from Problem 10-2, suppose that the full-employment level of *nominal* GDP in the following year rises to $17.7 trillion. The long-run equilibrium price level, however, remains unchanged. By how much (in real dollars) has the long-run aggregate supply curve shifted to the right in the following year? By how much, if any, has the aggregate demand curve shifted to the right? (Hint: The equilibrium price level can stay the same only if *LRAS* and *AD* shift rightward by the same amount.)

10-4. Suppose that the position of a nation's long-run aggregate supply curve has not changed, but its long-run equilibrium price level has increased. Which of the following factors might account for this event?

a. A rise in the value of the domestic currency relative to other world currencies

b. An increase in the quantity of money in circulation

c. An increase in the labor force participation rate

d. A decrease in taxes

e. A rise in real incomes of countries that are key trading partners of this nation

f. Increased long-run economic growth

10-5. Suppose that during a given year, the quantity of U.S. real GDP that can be produced in the long run rises from $14.9 trillion to $15.0 trillion, measured in base-year dollars. During the year, no change occurs in the various factors that influence aggregate demand. What will happen to the U.S. long-run equilibrium price level during this particular year?

10-6. Assume that the position of a nation's aggregate demand curve has not changed, but the long-run equilibrium price level has declined. Other things being equal, which of the following factors might account for this event?

a. An increase in labor productivity
b. A decrease in the capital stock
c. A decrease in the quantity of money in circulation
d. The discovery of new mineral resources used to produce various goods
e. A technological improvement

10-7. Suppose that there is a sudden rise in the price level. What will happen to economywide planned spending on purchases of goods and services? Why?

10-8. Assume that the economy is in long-run equilibrium with complete information and that input prices adjust rapidly to changes in the prices of goods and services. If there is a rise in the price level induced by an increase in aggregate demand, what happens to real GDP?

10-9. Consider the diagram below when answering the questions that follow.

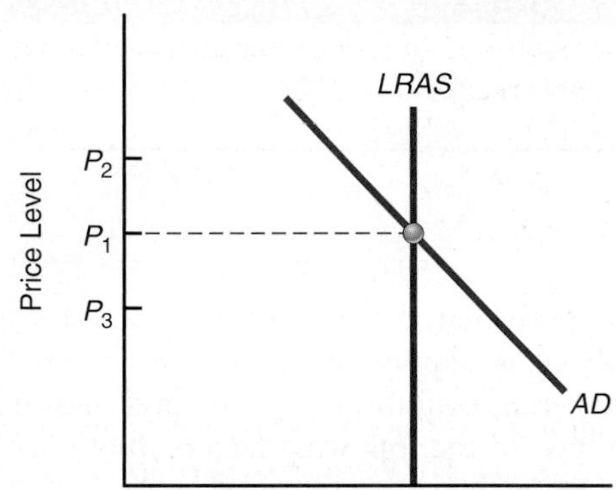

a. Suppose that the current price level is P_2. Explain why the price level will decline toward P_1.
b. Suppose that the current price level is P_3. Explain why the price level will rise toward P_1.

10-10. Explain whether each of the following events would cause a movement along or a shift in the position of the *LRAS* curve, other things being equal. In each case, explain the direction of the movement along the curve or shift in its position.

a. Last year, businesses invested in new capital equipment, so this year the nation's capital stock is higher than it was last year.
b. There has been an 8 percent increase in the quantity of money in circulation that has shifted the *AD* curve.
c. A hurricane of unprecedented strength has damaged oil rigs, factories, and ports all along the nation's coast.
d. Inflation has occurred during the past year as a result of rightward shifts of the *AD* curve.

10-11. Explain whether each of the following events would cause a movement along or a shift in the position of the *AD* curve, other things being equal. In each case, explain the direction of the movement along the curve or shift in its position.

a. Deflation has occurred during the past year.
b. Real GDP levels of all the nation's major trading partners have declined.
c. There has been a decline in the foreign exchange value of the nation's currency.
d. The price level has increased this year.

10-12. This year, a nation's long-run equilibrium real GDP and price level both increased. Which of the following combinations of factors might simultaneously account for *both* occurrences?

a. An isolated earthquake at the beginning of the year destroyed part of the nation's capital stock, and the nation's government significantly reduced its purchases of goods and services.
b. There was a technological improvement at the end of the previous year, and the quantity of money in circulation rose significantly during the year.
c. Labor productivity increased somewhat throughout the year, and consumers significantly increased their total planned purchases of goods and services.
d. The capital stock increased somewhat during the year, and the quantity of money in circulation declined considerably.

10-13. Explain how, if at all, each of the following events would affect equilibrium real GDP and the long-run equilibrium price level.

a. A reduction in the quantity of money in circulation
b. An income tax rebate (the return of previously paid taxes) from the government to households, which they can apply only to purchases of goods and services
c. A technological improvement
d. A decrease in the value of the home currency in terms of the currencies of other nations

10-14. For each question, suppose that the economy *begins* at the long-run equilibrium point *A* in the diagram on the facing page. Identify which of the other points on the diagram—points *B*, *C*, *D*, or *E*—could represent a *new* long-run equilibrium after the described events take place and move the economy away from point *A*.

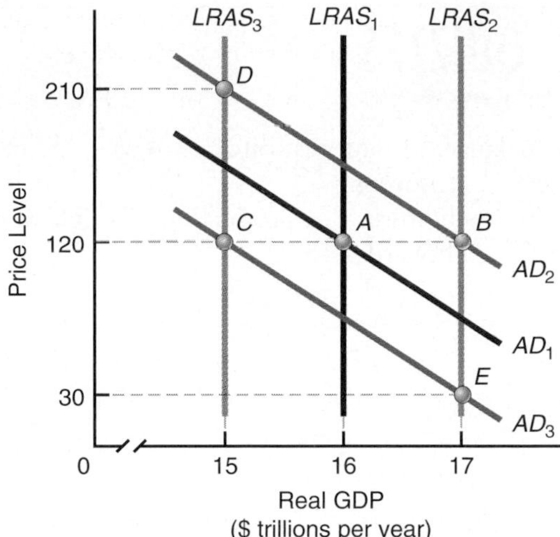

a. Significant productivity improvements occur, and the quantity of money in circulation increases.

b. No new capital investment takes place, and a fraction of the existing capital stock depreciates and becomes unusable. At the same time, the government imposes a large tax increase on the nation's households.

c. More efficient techniques for producing goods and services are adopted throughout the economy at the same time that the government reduces its spending on goods and services.

10-15. In Ciudad Barrios, El Salvador, the latest payments from relatives working in the United States have finally arrived. When the credit unions open for business, up to 150 people are already waiting in line. After receiving the funds their relatives have transmitted to these institutions, customers go off to outdoor markets to stock up on food or clothing or to appliance stores to purchase new stereos or televisions. Similar scenes occur throughout the developing world, as each year migrants working in higher-income, developed nations send around $200 billion of their earnings back to their relatives in less developed nations. Evidence indicates that the relatives, such as those in Ciudad Barrios, typically spend nearly all of the funds on current consumption.

a. Based on the information supplied, are developing countries' income inflows transmitted by migrant workers primarily affecting their economies' long-run aggregate supply curves or aggregate demand curves?

b. How are equilibrium price levels in nations that are recipients of large inflows of funds from migrants likely to be affected? Explain your reasoning.

ECONOMICS ON THE NET

Wages, Productivity, and Aggregate Supply How much firms pay their employees and the productivity of those employees influence firms' total planned production, so changes in these factors affect the position of the aggregate supply curve. This application gives you the opportunity to examine recent trends in measures of the overall wages and productivity of workers.

Title: Bureau of Labor Statistics: Economy at a Glance

Navigation: Use the link at **www.econtoday.com/ch10** to visit the Bureau of Labor Statistics (BLS) Web site.

Application Perform the indicated operations, and answer the following questions.

1. In the "Pay and Benefits" popup menu, click on *Employment Costs.* Choose *Employment Cost Index.* What are the recent trends in wages and salaries and in benefits? In the long run, how should these trends be related to movements in the overall price level?

2. Back up to the home page, and in the "Productivity" popup menu, click on *Labor Productivity and Costs* and then on *PDF* next to "LPC News Releases: Productivity and Costs." How has labor productivity behaved recently? What does this imply for the long-run aggregate supply curve?

3. Back up to the home page, and now in the "Employment" popup menu, click on *National Employment* and then on *PDF* next to "Current CES Economic News Release: Employment Situation Summary." Does it appear that the U.S. economy is currently in a long run growth equilibrium?

For Group Study and Analysis

1. Divide the class into aggregate demand and long-run aggregate supply groups. Have each group search the Internet for data on factors that influence its assigned curve. For which factors do data appear to be most readily available? For which factors are data more sparse or more subject to measurement problems?

2. The BLS home page displays a map of the United States. Assign regions of the nation to different groups, and have each group develop a short report about current and future prospects for economic growth within its assigned region. What similarities exist across regions? What regional differences are there?

ANSWERS TO QUICK QUIZZES

p. 212: (i) vertical; (ii) natural; (iii) rightward . . . increases

p. 217: (i) expenditures . . . production . . . spending; (ii) real-balance . . . interest rate . . . open economy; (iii) real-balance; (iv) interest rate . . . fewer . . . more; (v) domestic . . . foreign

p. 221: (i) expenditures . . . production; (ii) rightward . . . decline; (iii) rightward

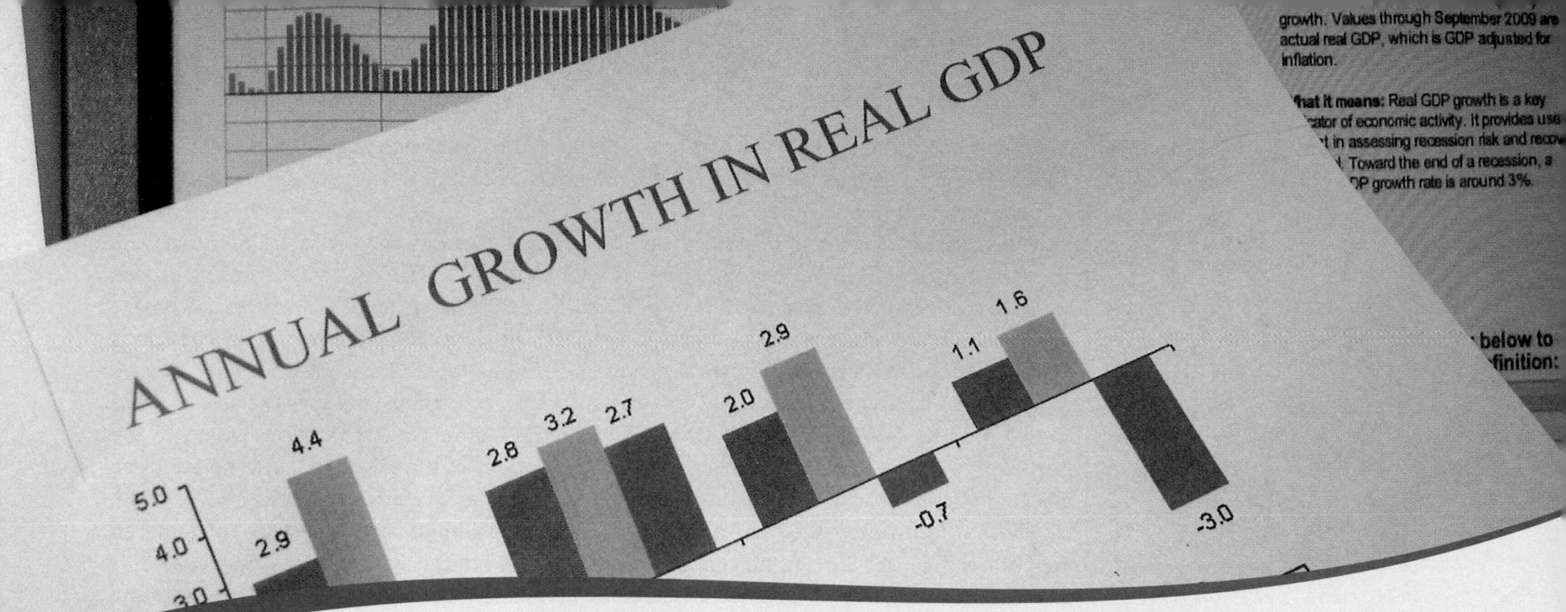

11

Classical and Keynesian Macro Analyses

During the latter half of the 2000s, annual rates of U.S. real GDP growth varied between 3 percent and −3 percent. Annual rates of inflation ranged from 4 percent to 1 percent. Clearly, there was considerable variation in real GDP and the level of prices during this five-year interval. What accounts for such wide swings in real GDP and the price level? Do the variations result mainly from changes in the amounts of goods and services that firms are willing and able to produce? Or are the changes caused mainly by the aggregate amounts that households, firms, and the government are willing and able to spend on goods and services? In this chapter, you will contemplate the answers to these questions.

LEARNING OBJECTIVES

After reading this chapter, you should be able to:

- Discuss the central assumptions of the classical model
- Describe the short-run determination of equilibrium real GDP and the price level in the classical model
- Explain circumstances under which the short-run aggregate supply curve may be either horizontal or upward sloping
- Understand what factors cause shifts in the short-run and long-run aggregate supply curves
- Evaluate the effects of aggregate demand and supply shocks on equilibrium real GDP in the short run
- Determine the causes of short-run variations in the inflation rate

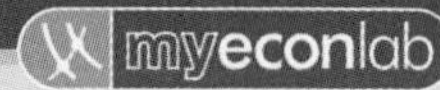

MyEconLab helps you master each objective and study more efficiently. See end of chapter for details.

Did You Know That? the price of a bottle containing 6.5 ounces of Coca-Cola remained unchanged at 5 cents from 1886 to 1959? The prices of many other goods and services changed at least slightly during that 73-year period, and since then the prices of most items, including Coca-Cola, have generally moved in an upward direction. Nevertheless, prices of final goods and services have not always adjusted immediately in response to changes in aggregate demand. Consequently, one approach to understanding the determination of real GDP and the price level emphasizes *incomplete* adjustment in the prices of many goods and services. The simplest version of this approach was first developed by a twentieth-century economist named John Maynard Keynes (pronounced like *canes*). It assumes that in the short run, prices of most goods and services are nearly as rigid as the price of Coca-Cola from 1886 to 1959. Although the modern version of the Keynesian approach allows for greater flexibility of prices in the short run, incomplete price adjustment still remains a key feature of the modern Keynesian approach.

The Keynesian approach does not retain the long-run assumption, which you encountered in Chapter 10, of fully adjusting prices. Economists who preceded Keynes employed this assumption in creating an approach to understanding variations in real GDP and the price level that Keynes called the *classical model.* Like Keynes, we shall begin our study of variations in real GDP and the price level by considering the earlier, classical approach.

The Classical Model

The classical model, which traces its origins to the 1770s, was the first systematic attempt to explain the determinants of the price level and the national levels of real GDP, employment, consumption, saving, and investment. Classical economists—Adam Smith, J. B. Say, David Ricardo, John Stuart Mill, Thomas Malthus, A. C. Pigou, and others—wrote from the 1770s to the 1930s. They assumed, among other things, that all wages and prices were flexible and that competitive markets existed throughout the economy.

Say's Law

Every time you produce something for which you receive income, you generate the income necessary to make expenditures on other goods and services. That means that an economy producing $15 trillion of real GDP, measured in base-year dollars, simultaneously produces the income with which these goods and services can be purchased. As an accounting identity, *actual* aggregate output always equals *actual* aggregate income. Classical economists took this accounting identity one step further by arguing that total national supply creates its own national demand. They asserted what has become known as **Say's law:**

Say's law
A dictum of economist J. B. Say that supply creates its own demand. Producing goods and services generates the means and the willingness to purchase other goods and services.

> ***Supply creates its own demand; hence, it follows that* desired *expenditures will equal* actual *expenditures.***

What does Say's law really mean? It states that the very process of producing specific goods (supply) is proof that other goods are desired (demand). People produce more goods than they want for their own use only if they seek to trade them for other goods. Someone offers to supply something only because he or she has a demand for something else. The implication of this, according to Say, is that no general glut, or overproduction, is possible in a market economy. From this reasoning, it seems to follow that full employment of labor and other resources would be the normal state of affairs in such an economy.

Say acknowledged that an oversupply of some goods might occur in particular markets. He argued that such surpluses would simply cause prices to fall, thereby decreasing production as the economy adjusted. The opposite would occur in markets in which shortages temporarily appeared.

All this seems reasonable enough in a simple barter economy in which households produce most of the goods they want and trade for the rest. This is shown in Figure 11-1 on the facing page, where there is a simple circular flow. But what about a more

FIGURE 11-1 Say's Law and the Circular Flow

Here we show the circular flow of income and output. The very act of supplying a certain level of goods and services necessarily equals the level of goods and services demanded, in Say's simplified world.

sophisticated economy in which people work for others and money is used instead of barter? Can these complications create the possibility of unemployment? And does the fact that laborers receive money income, some of which can be saved, lead to unemployment? No, said the classical economists to these last two questions. They based their reasoning on a number of key assumptions.

Assumptions of the Classical Model

The classical model makes four major assumptions:

1. *Pure competition exists.* No single buyer or seller of a commodity or an input can affect its price.
2. *Wages and prices are flexible.* The assumption of pure competition leads to the notion that prices, wages and interest rates are free to move to whatever level supply and demand dictate (as the economy adjusts). Although no *individual* buyer can set a price, the community of buyers or sellers can cause prices to rise or to fall to an equilibrium level.
3. *People are motivated by self-interest.* Businesses want to maximize their profits, and households want to maximize their economic well-being.
4. *People cannot be fooled by money illusion.* Buyers and sellers react to changes in relative prices. That is to say, they do not suffer from **money illusion.** For example, workers will not be fooled into thinking that doubling their wages makes them better off if the price level has also doubled during the same time period.

Money illusion
Reacting to changes in money prices rather than relative prices. If a worker whose wages double when the price level also doubles thinks he or she is better off, that worker is suffering from money illusion.

The classical economists concluded, after taking account of the four major assumptions, that the role of government in the economy should be minimal. They assumed that pure competition prevails, all prices and wages are flexible, and people are self-interested and do not experience money illusion. If so, they argued, then any problems in the macroeconomy will be temporary. The market will correct itself.

Equilibrium in the Credit Market

When income is saved, it is not reflected in product demand. It is a type of *leakage* from the circular flow of income and output because saving withdraws funds from the income stream. Therefore, total planned consumption spending *can* fall short of total current real GDP. In such a situation, it appears that supply does not necessarily create its own demand.

THE RELATIONSHIP BETWEEN SAVING AND INVESTMENT The classical economists did not believe that the complicating factor of saving in the circular flow model of income

FIGURE 11-2 Equating Desired Saving and Investment in the Classical Model

The schedule showing planned investment is labeled "Desired investment." The desired saving curve is shown as an upward-sloping supply curve of saving. The equilibrating force here is, of course, the interest rate. At higher interest rates, people desire to save more. But at higher interest rates, businesses wish to engage in less investment because it is less profitable to invest. In this model, at an interest rate of 5 percent, planned investment just equals planned saving, which is $2 trillion per year.

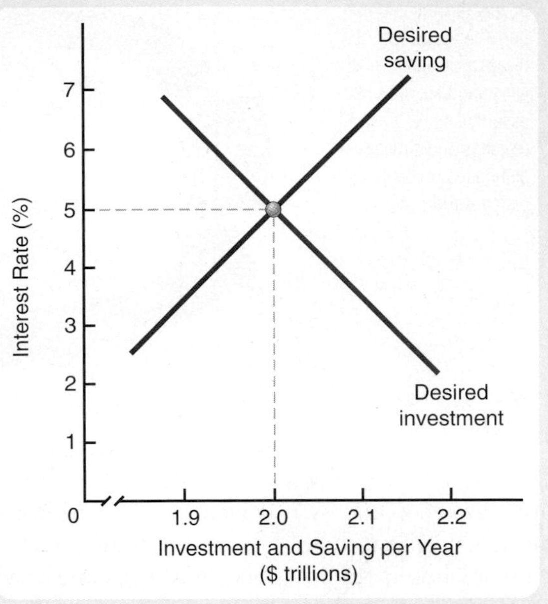

and output was a problem. They contended that each dollar saved would be invested by businesses so that the leakage of saving would be matched by the injection of business investment. *Investment* here refers only to additions to the nation's capital stock. The classical economists believed that businesses as a group would intend to invest as much as households wanted to save.

THE EQUILIBRIUM INTEREST RATE Equilibrium between the saving plans of consumers and the investment plans of businesses comes about, in the classical economists' model, through the working of the credit market. In the credit market, the *price* of credit is the interest rate. At equilibrium, the price of credit—the interest rate—ensures that the amount of credit demanded equals the amount of credit supplied. Planned investment just equals planned saving, so there is no reason to be concerned about the leakage of saving. This is illustrated graphically in Figure 11-2 above.

Go to **www.econtoday.com/ch11** to link to Federal Reserve data on U.S. interest rates.

In the figure, the vertical axis measures the rate of interest in percentage terms, and the horizontal axis measures amounts of desired saving and desired investment per unit time period. The desired saving curve is really a supply curve of saving. It shows that people wish to save more at higher interest rates than at lower interest rates.

In contrast, the higher the rate of interest, the less profitable it is to invest and the lower is the level of desired investment. Thus, the desired investment curve slopes downward. In this simplified model, the equilibrium rate of interest is 5 percent, and the equilibrium quantity of saving and investment is $2 trillion per year.

Why Not . . . always require low interest rates to boost investment spending?

Although artificially lowering the interest rate would generate higher *planned* investment expenditures, it would also cause planned saving to decrease. Consequently, at an artificially low interest rate, the amount of funds provided by savers to finance investment spending would be less than the amount of funds that businesses wished to obtain for investment. Thus, *actual* investment—the feasible amount of investment spending given available saving—would be *reduced* by requiring an artificially low interest rate.

FIGURE 11-3 Equilibrium in the Labor Market

The demand for labor is downward sloping; at higher wage rates, firms will employ fewer workers. The supply of labor is upward sloping. At higher wage rates, more workers will work longer, and more people will be willing to work. The equilibrium wage rate is $18 with an equilibrium employment per year of 160 million workers.

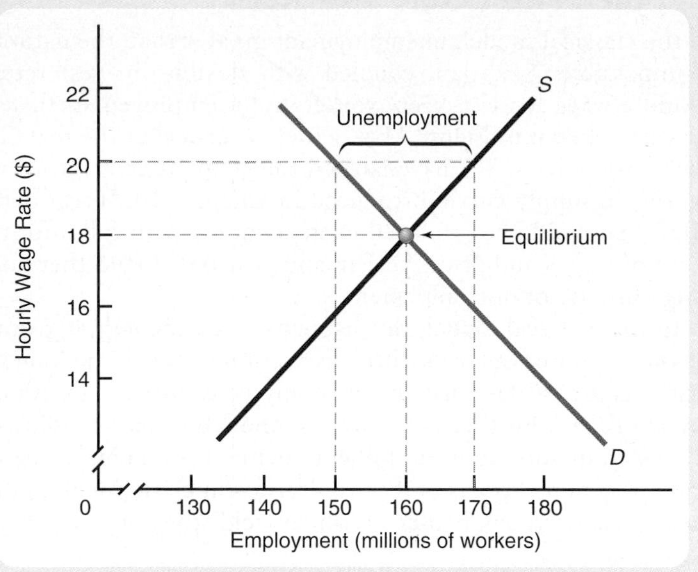

Equilibrium in the Labor Market

Now consider the labor market. If an excess quantity of labor is supplied at a particular wage level, the wage level must be above equilibrium. By accepting lower wages, unemployed workers will quickly be put back to work. We show equilibrium in the labor market in Figure 11-3 above.

Go to **www.econtoday.com/ch11** to find out the latest U.S. saving rate from the Bureau of Economic Analysis. Select "Personal saving as a percentage of disposable personal income."

Assume that equilibrium exists at $18 per hour and 160 million workers employed. If the wage rate were $20 per hour, there would be unemployment—170 million workers would want to work, but businesses would want to hire only 150 million. In the classical model, this unemployment is eliminated rather rapidly by wage rates dropping back to $18 per hour, as seen in Figure 11-3.

THE RELATIONSHIP BETWEEN EMPLOYMENT AND REAL GDP Employment is not to be regarded simply as some isolated figure that government statisticians estimate. Rather, the level of employment in an economy determines its real GDP (output), other things held constant. A hypothetical relationship between input (number of employees) and the value of output (real GDP per year) is shown in Table 11-1 below. The row that has 160 million workers per year as the labor input is highlighted. That might be considered a hypothetical level of full employment, and it is related to a rate of real GDP, in base-year dollars, of $15 trillion per year.

TABLE 11-1

The Relationship Between Employment and Real GDP

Other things being equal, an increase in the quantity of labor input increases real GDP. In this example, if 160 million workers are employed, real GDP is $15 trillion in base-year dollars.

Labor Input per Year (millions of workers)	Real GDP per Year ($ trillions)
150	12
154	13
158	14
160	15
164	16
166	17

Classical Theory, Vertical Aggregate Supply, and the Price Level

In the classical model, unemployment greater than the natural unemployment rate is impossible. Say's law, coupled with flexible interest rates, prices, and wages, would always tend to keep workers fully employed so that the aggregate supply curve, as shown in Figure 11-4 below, is vertical at the real GDP of $15 trillion, in base-year dollars. We have labeled the supply curve *LRAS*, which is the long-run aggregate supply curve introduced in Chapter 10. It was defined there as the real GDP that would be produced in an economy with full information and full adjustment of wages and prices year in and year out. *LRAS* therefore corresponds to the long-run rate of unemployment.

In the classical model, this happens to be the *only* aggregate supply curve. The classical economists made little distinction between the long run and the short run. Prices adjust so fast that the economy is essentially always on or quickly moving toward *LRAS*. Furthermore, because the labor market adjusts rapidly, real GDP is always at, or soon to be at, full employment. Full employment does not mean zero unemployment because there is always some frictional and structural unemployment (discussed in Chapter 7), which yields the natural rate of unemployment.

EFFECT OF AN INCREASE IN AGGREGATE DEMAND IN THE CLASSICAL MODEL In this model, any change in aggregate demand will quickly cause a change in the price level. Consider starting at E_1, at price level 120, in Figure 11-4. If aggregate demand shifts to AD_2, the economy will tend toward point *A*, but because this is beyond full-employment real GDP, prices will rise, and the economy will find itself back on the vertical *LRAS* at point E_2 at a higher price level, 130. The price level will increase as a result of the increase in *AD* because employers will end up bidding up wages for workers, as well as bidding up the prices of other inputs.

The level of real GDP per year clearly does not depend on the level of aggregate demand. Hence, we say that in the classical model, the equilibrium level of real GDP per year is completely *supply determined*. Changes in aggregate demand affect only the price level, not real GDP.

FIGURE 11-4 Classical Theory and Increases in Aggregate Demand

The classical theorists believed that Say's law and flexible interest rates, prices, and wages would always lead to full employment at real GDP of $15 trillion, in base-year dollars, along the vertical aggregate supply curve, *LRAS*. With aggregate demand AD_1, the price level is 120. An increase in aggregate demand shifts AD_1 to AD_2. At price level 120, the quantity of real GDP demanded per year would be $15.5 trillion at point *A* on AD_2. But $15.5 trillion in real GDP per year is greater than real GDP at full employment. Prices rise, and the economy quickly moves from E_1 to E_2, at the higher price level of 130.

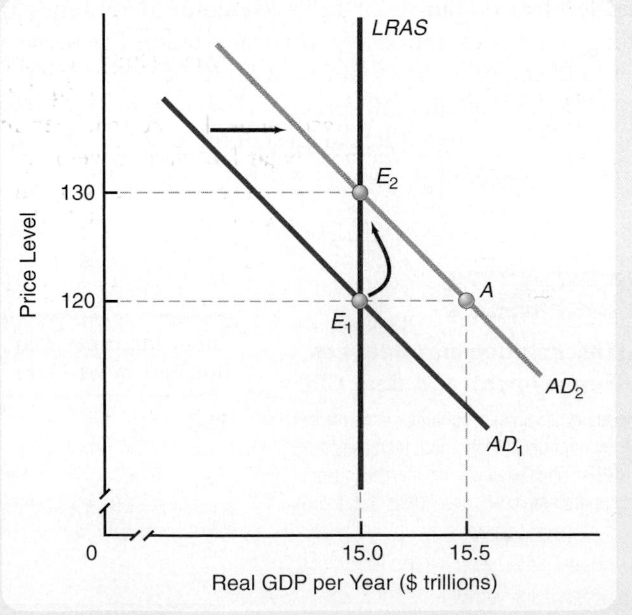

FIGURE 11-5 Effect of a Decrease in Aggregate Demand in the Classical Model

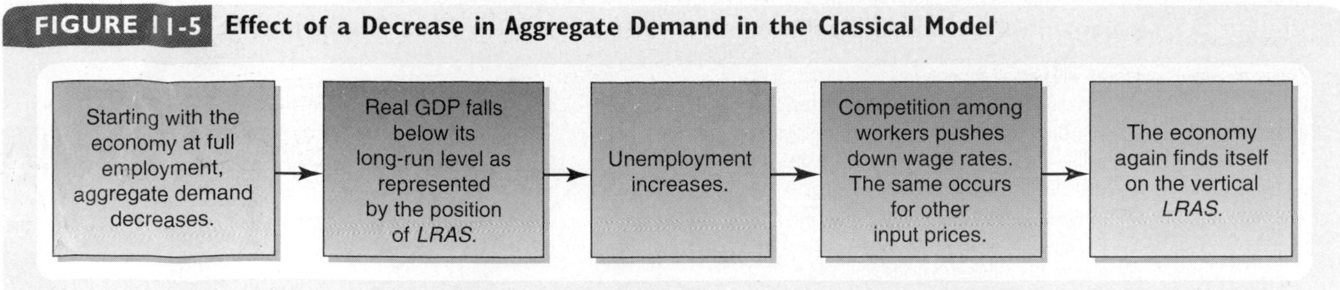

Starting with the economy at full employment, aggregate demand decreases.
Real GDP falls below its long-run level as represented by the position of LRAS.
Unemployment increases.
Competition among workers pushes down wage rates. The same occurs for other input prices.
The economy again finds itself on the vertical LRAS.

EFFECT OF A DECREASE IN AGGREGATE DEMAND IN THE CLASSICAL MODEL The effect of a decrease in aggregate demand in the classical model is the converse of the analysis just presented for an increase in aggregate demand. You can simply reverse AD_2 and AD_1 in Figure 11-4 on the facing page. To help you see how this analysis works, consider the flowchart in Figure 11-5 above.

QUICK QUIZ See page 249 for the answers. Review concepts from this section in MyEconLab.

Say's law states that __________ creates its own __________ and therefore *desired* expenditures will equal *actual* expenditures.

The classical model assumes that (1) __________ __________ exists, (2) __________ and __________ are completely flexible, (3) individuals are motivated by __________-__________, and (4) they cannot be fooled by __________ __________.

When saving is introduced into the model, equilibrium occurs in the credit market through changes in the interest rate such that desired __________ equals desired __________ at the equilibrium rate of interest.

In the labor market, full employment occurs at a __________ __________ at which quantity demanded equals quantity supplied. That particular level of employment is associated with the full-employment level of real GDP per year.

In the classical model, because *LRAS* is __________, the equilibrium level of real GDP is supply determined. Any changes in aggregate demand simply change the __________ __________.

Keynesian Economics and the Keynesian Short-Run Aggregate Supply Curve

The classical economists' world was one of fully utilized resources. There would be no unused capacity and no unemployment. But then in the 1930s Europe and the United States entered a period of economic decline that seemingly could not be explained by the classical model. John Maynard Keynes developed an explanation that has since become known as the Keynesian model. Keynes and his followers argued that prices, especially the price of labor (wages), were inflexible downward due to the existence of unions and long-term contracts between businesses and workers. That meant that prices were "sticky." Keynes contended that in such a world, which has large amounts of excess capacity and unemployment, an increase in aggregate demand will not raise the price level, and a decrease in aggregate demand will not cause firms to lower prices.

Demand-Determined Real GDP

This situation is depicted in Figure 11-6 on the next page. For simplicity, Figure 11-6 does not show the point where the economy reaches capacity, and that is why the *short-run aggregate supply curve* (to be discussed later) never starts to slope upward and is simply the horizontal line labeled *SRAS*. Moreover, we don't show *LRAS* in Figure 11-6 either. It would be a vertical line at the level of real GDP per year that is consistent with full employment. If we start out in equilibrium with aggregate demand at AD_1,

FIGURE 11-6 Demand-Determined Equilibrium Real GDP at Less Than Full Employment

Keynes assumed that prices will not fall when aggregate demand falls and that there is excess capacity, so prices will not rise when aggregate demand increases. Thus, the short-run aggregate supply curve is simply a horizontal line at the given price level, 120, represented by *SRAS.* An aggregate demand shock that increases aggregate demand to AD_2 will increase the equilibrium level of real GDP per year to $15.5 trillion. An aggregate demand shock that decreases aggregate demand to AD_3 will decrease the equilibrium level of real GDP to $14.5 trillion. The equilibrium price level will not change.

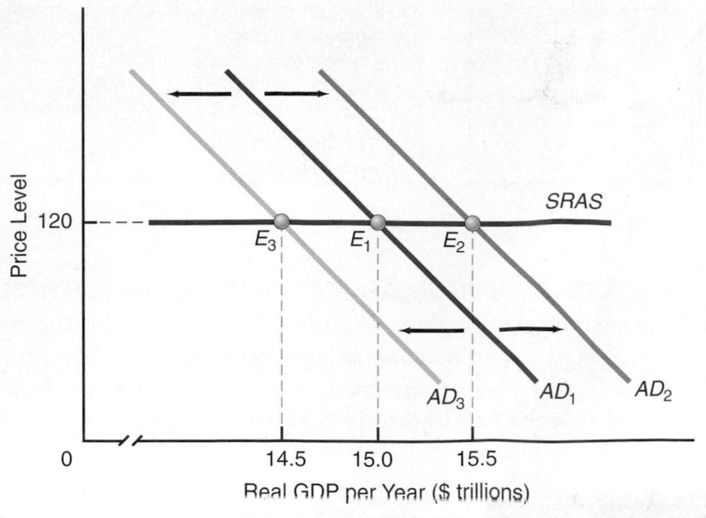

the equilibrium level of real GDP per year, measured in base-year dollars, is $15 trillion at point E_1, and the equilibrium price level is 120. If there is a rise in aggregate demand, so that the aggregate demand curve shifts outward to the right to AD_2, the equilibrium price level at point E_2 will not change; only the equilibrium level of real GDP per year will increase, to $15.5 trillion. Conversely, if there is a fall in aggregate demand that shifts the aggregate demand curve to AD_3, the equilibrium price level will again remain at 120 at point E_3, but the equilibrium level of real GDP per year will fall to $14.5 trillion.

Under such circumstances, the equilibrium level of real GDP per year is completely *demand determined.*

The Keynesian Short-Run Aggregate Supply Curve

Keynesian short-run aggregate supply curve
The horizontal portion of the aggregate supply curve in which there is excessive unemployment and unused capacity in the economy.

The horizontal short-run aggregate supply curve represented in Figure 11-6 above is often called the **Keynesian short-run aggregate supply curve.** According to Keynes, unions and long-term contracts are real-world factors that explain the inflexibility of *nominal* wage rates. Such stickiness of wages makes *involuntary* unemployment of labor a distinct possibility, because leftward movements along the Keynesian short-run aggregate supply curve reduce real production and, hence, employment. The classical assumption of everlasting full employment no longer holds.

Data from the 1930s offer evidence of a nearly horizontal aggregate supply curve. Between 1934 and 1940, the GDP deflator stayed in a range from about 8.3 to less than 9.0, implying that the price level changed by no more than 8 percent. Yet the level of real GDP measured in 2005 dollars varied between nearly $0.7 trillion and close to $1.1 trillion, or by more than 50 percent. Thus, between 1934 and 1940, the U.S. short-run aggregate supply curve was almost flat.

Output Determination Using Aggregate Demand and Aggregate Supply: Fixed versus Changing Price Levels in the Short Run

The underlying assumption of the simplified Keynesian model is that the relevant range of the short-run aggregate supply schedule (*SRAS*) is horizontal, as depicted in panel (a) of Figure 11-7 on the facing page. There you see that short-run aggregate supply is fixed at price level 120. If aggregate demand is AD_1, then the equilibrium

FIGURE 11-7 Real GDP Determination with Fixed versus Flexible Prices

In panel (a), the price level index is fixed at 120. An increase in aggregate demand from AD_1 to AD_2 moves the equilibrium level of real GDP from \$15 trillion per year to \$16 trillion per year in base-year dollars. In panel (b), *SRAS* is upward sloping. The same shift in aggregate demand yields an equilibrium level of real GDP of only \$15.5 trillion per year and a higher price level index at 130.

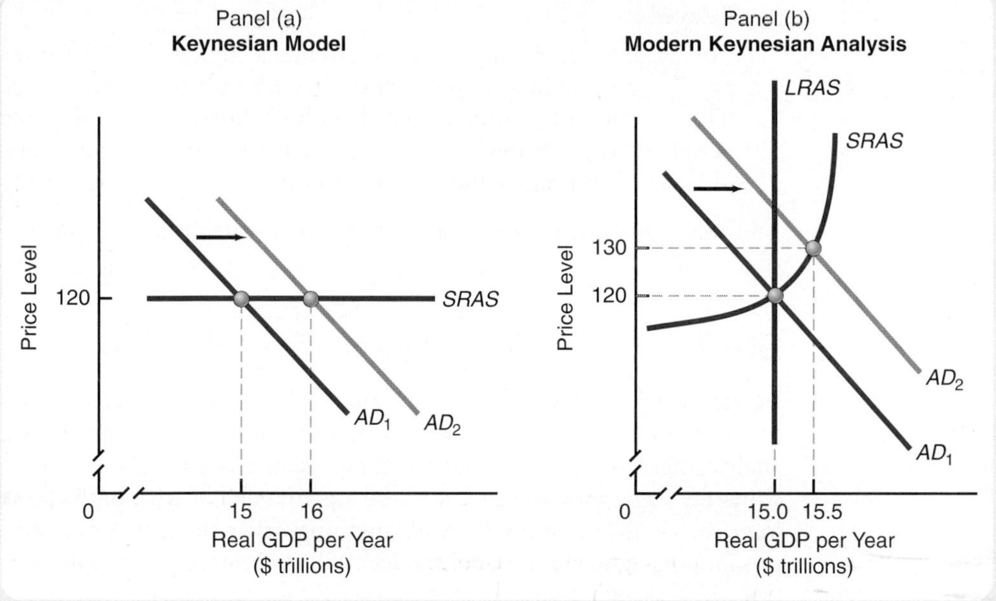

level of real GDP, in base-year dollars, is \$15 trillion per year. If aggregate demand increases to AD_2, then the equilibrium level of real GDP increases to \$16 trillion per year.

As discussed in Chapter 10, the price level has drifted upward during recent decades. Hence, prices are not totally sticky. Modern Keynesian analysis recognizes that *some*—but not complete—price adjustment takes place in the short run. Panel (b) of Figure 11-7 above displays a more general **short-run aggregate supply curve** (*SRAS*). This curve represents the relationship between the price level and real GDP with incomplete price adjustment and in the absence of complete information in the short run. Allowing for partial price adjustment implies that *SRAS* slopes upward, and its slope is steeper after it crosses long-run aggregate supply, *LRAS*. This is because higher and higher prices are required to induce firms to raise their production of goods and services to levels that temporarily exceed full-employment real GDP.

Short-run aggregate supply curve The relationship between total planned economywide production and the price level in the short run, all other things held constant. If prices adjust incompletely in the short run, the curve is positively sloped.

With partial price adjustment in the short run, if aggregate demand is AD_1 then the equilibrium level of real GDP in panel (b) is also \$15 trillion per year, at a price level of 120, too. An increase in aggregate demand to AD_2 such as occurred in panel (a) produces a different short-run equilibrium, however. Equilibrium real GDP increases to \$15.5 trillion per year, which is less than in panel (a) because an increase in the price level to 130 causes planned purchases of goods and services to decline.

In the modern Keynesian short run, when the price level rises partially, real GDP can be expanded beyond the level consistent with its long-run growth path, discussed in Chapter 10, for a variety of reasons:

1. In the short run, most labor contracts implicitly or explicitly call for flexibility in hours of work at the given wage rate. Therefore, firms can use existing workers more intensively in a variety of ways: They can get workers to work harder, to work more hours per day, and to work more days per week. Workers can also be switched from *uncounted* production, such as maintenance, to *counted* production, which generates counted production of goods and services. The distinction between counted and uncounted is what is measured in the marketplace, particularly by

government statisticians and accountants. If a worker cleans a machine, there is no measured output. But if that worker is put on the production line and helps increase the number of units produced each day, measured output will go up. That worker's production has then been counted.

2. Existing capital equipment can be used more intensively. Machines can be worked more hours per day. Some can be made to operate faster. Maintenance can be delayed.
3. Finally, if wage rates are held constant, a higher price level leads to increased profits from additional production, which induces firms to hire more workers. The duration of unemployment falls, and thus the unemployment rate falls. And people who were previously not in the labor force (homemakers and younger or older workers) can be induced to enter it.

All these adjustments cause real GDP to rise as the price level increases.

Shifts in the Aggregate Supply Curve

Just as non-price-level factors can cause a shift in the aggregate demand curve, there are non-price-level factors that can cause a shift in the aggregate supply curve. The analysis here is more complicated than the analysis for the non-price-level determinants for aggregate demand, for here we are dealing with both the short run and the long run—*SRAS* and *LRAS*. Still, anything other than the price level that affects the production of final goods and services will shift aggregate supply curves.

Shifts in Both Short- and Long-Run Aggregate Supply

There is a core class of events that cause a shift in both the short-run aggregate supply curve and the long-run aggregate supply curve. These include any change in our endowments of the factors of production. Any change in factors of production—labor, capital, or technology—that influence economic growth will shift *SRAS* and *LRAS*. Look at Figure 11-8 below. Initially, the two curves are $SRAS_1$ and $LRAS_1$. Now consider a situation in which large amounts of irreplaceable resources are lost *permanently* in a major oil spill and fire. This shifts $LRAS_1$ to $LRAS_2$ at $14.5 trillion of real GDP, measured in base-year dollars. $SRAS_1$ also shifts leftward horizontally to $SRAS_2$.

FIGURE 11-8 Shifts in Long-Run and Short-Run Aggregate Supply

Initially, the two aggregate supply curves are $SRAS_1$ and $LRAS_1$. An event that permanently reduces reserves of a key productive resource such as oil shifts $LRAS_1$ to $LRAS_2$ at $14.5 trillion of real GDP, in base-year dollars, and also shifts $SRAS_1$ horizontally leftward to $SRAS_2$. If, instead, a temporary increase in an input price occurred, $LRAS_1$ would remain unchanged, and only the short-run aggregate supply curve would shift, from $SRAS_1$ to $SRAS_2$.

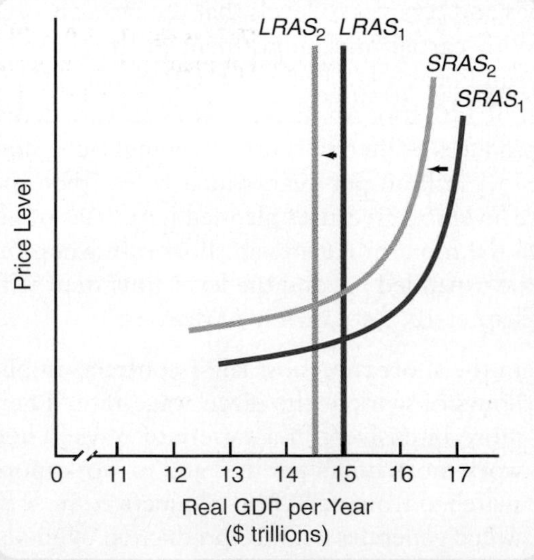

TABLE 11-2

Determinants of Aggregate Supply

The determinants listed here can affect short-run or long-run aggregate supply (or both), depending on whether they are temporary or permanent.

Changes That Cause an Increase in Aggregate Supply	Changes That Cause a Decrease in Aggregate Supply
Discoveries of new raw materials	Depletion of raw materials
Increased competition	Decreased competition
A reduction in international trade barriers	An increase in international trade barriers
Fewer regulatory impediments to business	More regulatory impediments to business
An increase in the supply of labor	A decrease in labor supplied
Increased training and education	Decreased training and education
A decrease in marginal tax rates	An increase in marginal tax rates
A reduction in input prices	An increase in input prices

Shifts in *SRAS* Only

Some events, particularly those that are short-lived, will temporarily shift *SRAS* but not *LRAS*. One of the most obvious is a change in production input prices, particularly those caused by external events that are not expected to last forever. Consider a major hurricane that temporarily shuts down a significant portion of U.S. oil production, as happened after Hurricane Katrina. Oil is an important input in many production activities. The resulting drop in oil production would cause at least a temporary increase in the price of this input. In this case, the long-run aggregate supply curve would remain at $LRAS_1$ in Figure 11-8. The short-run aggregate supply curve *alone* would shift from $SRAS_1$ to $SRAS_2$, reflecting the increase in input prices—the higher price of oil. This is because the rise in the costs of production at each level of real GDP per year would require a higher price level to cover those increased costs.

We summarize the possible determinants of aggregate supply in Table 11-2 above. These determinants will cause a shift in the short-run or the long-run aggregate supply curve or both, depending on whether they are temporary or permanent.

You Are There

To contemplate why a nation might face a trade-off between reducing its exposure to aggregate supply shocks and providing a foundation for aggregate supply growth, consider **Putting More Weight on Stability Than Growth in Denmark,** on page 244.

QUICK QUIZ **See page 249 for the answers. Review concepts from this section in MyEconLab.**

If we assume that the economy is operating on a horizontal short-run aggregate supply curve, the equilibrium level of real GDP per year is completely __________ determined.

The horizontal short-run aggregate supply curve has been called the **Keynesian short-run aggregate supply curve** because Keynes believed that many prices, especially wages, would not be __________ even when aggregate demand decreased.

In modern Keynesian theory, the **short-run aggregate supply curve, *SRAS*,** shows the relationship between the price level and real GDP without full adjustment or full information. It is upward sloping because it allows for only __________ price adjustment in the short run.

Real GDP can be expanded in the short run because firms can use existing workers and capital equipment more __________. Also, in the short run, when input prices are fixed, a higher price level means __________ profits, which induce firms to hire more workers.

Any change in factors influencing long-run output, such as labor, capital, or technology, will shift both *SRAS* and *LRAS*. A temporary change in input prices, however, will shift only __________.

Consequences of Changes in Aggregate Demand

We now have a basic model to apply when evaluating short-run adjustments of the equilibrium price level and equilibrium real GDP when there are shocks to the economy. Whenever there is a shift in the aggregate demand or short-run aggregate supply curves,

FIGURE 11-9 The Short-Run Effects of Stable Aggregate Supply and a Decrease in Aggregate Demand: The Recessionary Gap

If the economy is at equilibrium at E_1, with price level 120 and real GDP per year of $15 trillion, a shift inward of the aggregate demand curve to AD_2 will lead to a new short-run equilibrium at E_2. The equilibrium price level will fall to 115, and the short-run equilibrium level of real GDP per year will fall to $14.8 trillion. There will be a recessionary gap of $200 billion.

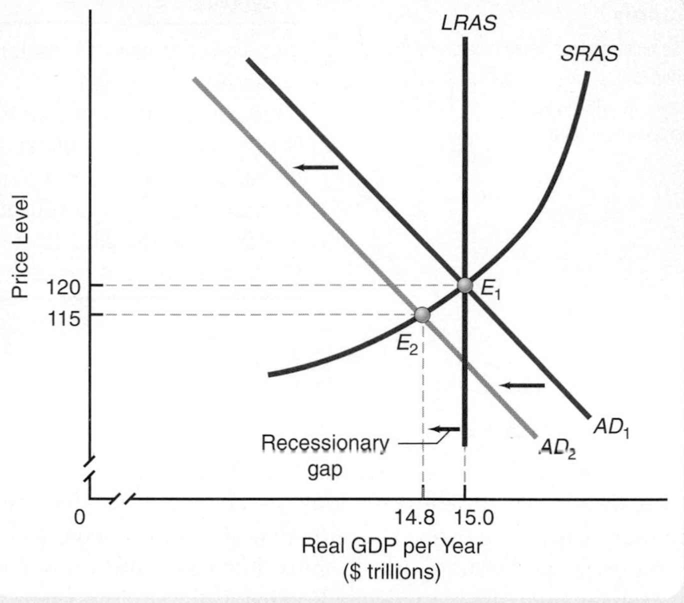

the short-run equilibrium price level or real GDP level (or both) may change. These shifts are called **aggregate demand shocks** on the demand side and **aggregate supply shocks** on the supply side.

Aggregate demand shock
Any event that causes the aggregate demand curve to shift inward or outward.

Aggregate supply shock
Any event that causes the aggregate supply curve to shift inward or outward.

When Aggregate Demand Falls While Aggregate Supply Is Stable

Now we can show what happens in the short run when aggregate supply remains stable but aggregate demand falls. The short-run outcome will be a rise in the unemployment rate. In Figure 11-9 above, you see that with AD_1, both long-run and short-run equilibrium are at $15 trillion (in base-year dollars) of real GDP per year (because *SRAS* and *LRAS* also intersect AD_1 at that level of real GDP). The long-run equilibrium price level is 120. A reduction in aggregate demand shifts the aggregate demand curve to AD_2. The new intersection with *SRAS* is at $14.8 trillion per year, which is less than the long-run equilibrium level of real GDP. The difference between $15 trillion and $14.8 trillion is called a **recessionary gap,** defined as the difference between the short-run equilibrium level of real GDP and real GDP if the economy were operating at full employment on its *LRAS*.

Recessionary gap
The gap that exists whenever equilibrium real GDP per year is less than full-employment real GDP as shown by the position of the long-run aggregate supply curve.

In effect, at E_2, the economy is in short-run equilibrium at less than full employment. With too many unemployed inputs, input prices will begin to fall. Eventually, *SRAS* will have to shift vertically downward. Where will it intersect AD_2?

Short-Run Effects When Aggregate Demand Increases

We can reverse the situation and have aggregate demand increase to AD_2, as is shown in Figure 11-10 on the facing page. The initial equilibrium conditions are exactly the same as in Figure 11-9. The move to AD_2 increases the short-run equilibrium from E_1 to E_2 such that the economy is operating at $15.2 trillion of real GDP per year, which exceeds *LRAS*. This is a condition of an overheated economy, typically called an **inflationary gap.**

Inflationary gap
The gap that exists whenever equilibrium real GDP per year is greater than full-employment real GDP as shown by the position of the long-run aggregate supply curve.

FIGURE 11-10 The Effects of Stable Aggregate Supply with an Increase in Aggregate Demand: The Inflationary Gap

The economy is at equilibrium at E_1. An increase in aggregate demand to AD_2 leads to a new short-run equilibrium at E_2 with the price level rising from 120 to 125 and equilibrium real GDP per year rising from \$15 trillion to \$15.2 trillion. The difference, \$200 billion, is called the inflationary gap.

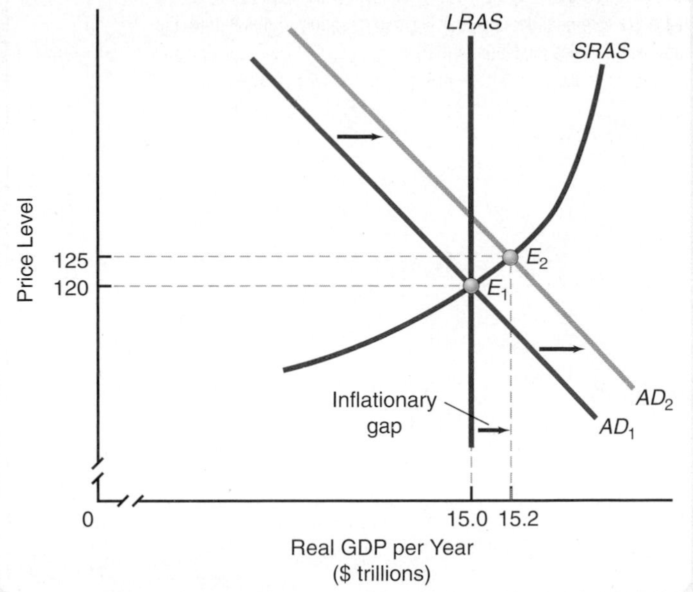

At E_2 in Figure 11-10 above, the economy is at a short-run equilibrium that is beyond full employment. In the short run, more can be squeezed out of the economy than occurs in the long-run, full-information, full-adjustment situation. Firms will be operating beyond long-run capacity. Inputs will be working too hard. Input prices will begin to rise. That will eventually cause *SRAS* to shift vertically upward. At what point on AD_2 in Figure 11-10 will the new *SRAS* stop shifting?

Explaining Short-Run Variations in Inflation

In Chapter 10, we noted that in a growing economy, the explanation for persistent inflation is that aggregate demand rises over time at a faster pace than the full-employment level of real GDP. Short-run variations in inflation, however, can arise as a result of both demand *and* supply factors.

Demand-Pull versus Cost-Push Inflation

Figure 11-10 above presents a demand-side theory explaining a short-run jump in prices, sometimes called *demand-pull inflation.* Whenever the general level of prices rises in the short run because of increases in aggregate demand, we say that the economy is experiencing **demand-pull inflation**—inflation caused by increases in aggregate demand.

Demand-pull inflation
Inflation caused by increases in aggregate demand not matched by increases in aggregate supply.

An alternative explanation for increases in the price level comes from the supply side. Look at Figure 11-11 on the next page. The initial equilibrium conditions are the same as in Figure 11-10. Now, however, there is a leftward shift in the short-run aggregate supply curve, from $SRAS_1$ to $SRAS_2$. Equilibrium shifts from E_1 to E_2. The price level increases from 120 to 125, while the equilibrium level of real GDP per year decreases from \$15 trillion to \$14.8 trillion. Such a decrease in aggregate supply causes what is called **cost-push inflation.**

Cost-push inflation
Inflation caused by decreases in short-run aggregate supply.

As the example of cost-push inflation shows, if the economy is initially in equilibrium on its *LRAS*, a decrease in *SRAS* will lead to a rise in the price level. Thus, any abrupt change in one of the factors that determine aggregate supply will alter the equilibrium level of real GDP and the equilibrium price level. If the economy is for some reason operating to the left of its *LRAS*, an increase in *SRAS* will lead

FIGURE 11-11 Cost-Push Inflation

If aggregate demand remains stable but $SRAS_1$ shifts to $SRAS_2$, equilibrium changes from E_1 to E_2. The price level rises from 120 to 125. If there are continual decreases in aggregate supply of this nature, the situation is called cost-push inflation.

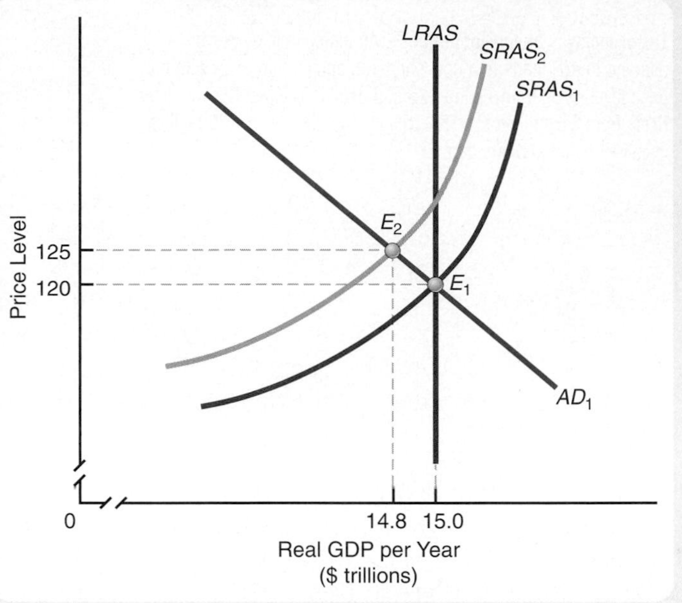

to a simultaneous *increase* in the equilibrium level of real GDP per year and a *decrease* in the price level. You should be able to show this in a graph similar to Figure 11-11 above.

What happened to U.S. aggregate supply at the end of the 2000s?

EXAMPLE The U.S. Economy Experiences a Decline in Aggregate Supply

Federal Reserve economists track the U.S. economy's total capacity to produce goods and services. In 2010, they found that during 2009 the nation's total productive capability dropped by 1 percent. This was the largest percentage decrease since the Federal Reserve began calculating productive capacity in 1967. The decrease resulted primarily from a failure of investment in new productive capital to keep pace with capital depreciation and from an upsurge in business regulation. On net, therefore, the nation's capital stock shrank, and businesses were more heavily regulated. Both of these changes constrained their ability to produce goods and services. Thus, the real value of goods and services that U.S. firms could produce at any price level declined, meaning that the U.S. aggregate supply curve shifted leftward.

FOR CRITICAL ANALYSIS

The U.S. government will raise several marginal tax rates in the coming years. What effects are these tax rate increases likely to have on U.S. aggregate supply?

Aggregate Demand and Supply in an Open Economy

In many of the international examples in the early chapters of this book, we had to translate foreign currencies into dollars when the open economy was discussed. We used the exchange rate, or the dollar price of other currencies. In Chapter 10, you also learned that the open economy effect was one of the reasons why the aggregate demand curve slopes downward. When the domestic price level rises, U.S. residents want to buy cheaper-priced foreign goods. The opposite occurs when the U.S. domestic price level falls. Currently, the foreign sector of the U.S. economy constitutes more than 14 percent of all economic activities.

HOW A WEAKER DOLLAR AFFECTS AGGREGATE SUPPLY Assume that the dollar becomes weaker in international foreign exchange markets. If last year the dollar could buy 150 *naira*, the Nigerian currency, but this year it buys only 100 naira, the dollar has become weaker. To the extent that U.S. companies import raw and partially processed goods from Nigeria, a weaker dollar can lead to higher input prices. For instance, in a typical year, U.S. natural gas distributors purchase about 10,000 million (10 billion) cubic feet of natural gas from suppliers in Nigeria. Suppose that the price of Nigerian natural gas, quoted in Nigerian naira, is 1.5 naira per million cubic feet. At a rate of exchange of 150 naira per dollar, this means that the U.S. dollar price is $0.01 per million cubic feet (1.5 naira divided by 150 naira per dollar equals $0.01), so 10 billion cubic feet of Nigerian natural gas imports cost U.S. distributors $100 million. If the U.S. dollar weakens against the Nigerian naira, so that a dollar purchases only 100 naira, then the U.S. dollar price rises to $0.015 per million cubic feet (1.5 naira divided by 100 naira per dollar equals $0.015). As a consequence, the U.S. dollar price of 10 billion cubic feet of Nigerian natural gas imports increases to $150 million.

Go to **www.econtoday.com/ch11** for Federal Reserve Bank of New York data showing how the dollar's value is changing relative to other currencies.

Thus, a general weakening of the dollar against the naira and other world currencies will lead to a shift inward to the left in the short-run aggregate supply curve as shown in panel (a) of Figure 11-12 below. In that simplified model, equilibrium real GDP would fall, and the price level would rise. Employment would also tend to decrease.

HOW A WEAKER DOLLAR AFFECTS AGGREGATE DEMAND A weaker dollar has another effect that we must consider. Foreign residents will find that U.S.-made goods are now less expensive, expressed in their own currency. Suppose that as a result of the dollar's weakening, the dollar, which previously could buy 0.70 euros, can now buy only 0.67 euros. Before the dollar weakened, a U.S.-produced $10 downloadable music album cost a French resident 7.00 euros at the exchange rate of 0.70 euro per $1. After the dollar weakens and the exchange rate changes to 0.67 euro per $1, that same $10 digital album will cost 6.70 euros. Conversely, U.S. residents will find that the weaker dollar makes imported goods more expensive. The result for U.S. residents is more exports and fewer imports, or higher net exports (exports minus imports). If net exports rise, employment in export industries will rise: This is represented in panel (b) of Figure 11-12. After the dollar becomes weaker, the aggregate demand curve shifts

FIGURE 11-12 The Two Effects of a Weaker Dollar

When the dollar decreases in value in the international currency market, there are two effects. The first is higher prices for imported inputs, causing a shift inward to the left in the short-run aggregate supply schedule from $SRAS_1$ to $SRAS_2$ in panel (a). Equilibrium tends to move from E_1 to E_2 at a higher price level and a lower equilibrium real GDP per year. Second, a weaker dollar can also affect the aggregate demand curve because it will lead to more net exports and cause AD_1 to rise to AD_2 in panel (b). Due to this effect, equilibrium will move from E_1 to E_2 at a higher price level and a higher equilibrium real GDP per year. On balance, the combined effects of the increase in aggregate demand and decrease in aggregate supply will be to push up the price level, but real GDP may rise or fall.

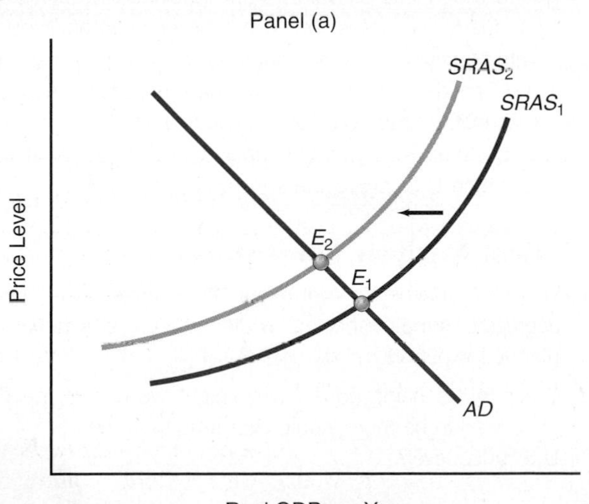

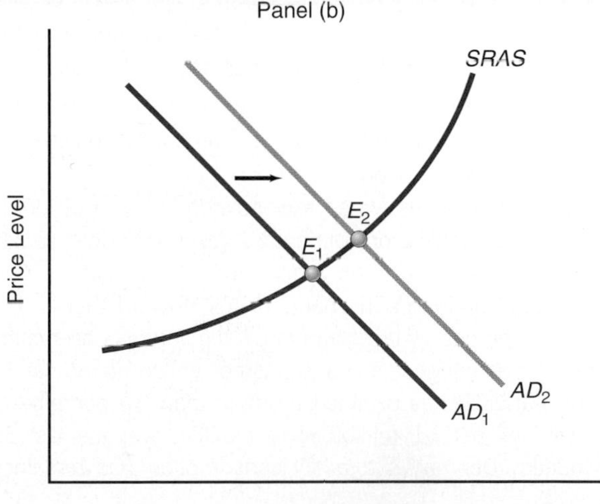

outward from AD_1 to AD_2. The result is a tendency for equilibrium real GDP and the price level to rise and for unemployment to decrease.

THE NET EFFECTS ON INFLATION AND REAL GDP. We have learned, then, that a weaker dollar *simultaneously* leads to a decrease in *SRAS* and an increase in *AD*. In such situations, the equilibrium price level definitely rises. A weaker dollar contributes to inflation.

The effect of a weaker dollar on real GDP depends on which curve—*AD* or *SRAS*—shifts more. If the aggregate demand curve shifts more than the short-run aggregate supply curve, equilibrium real GDP will rise. Conversely, if the aggregate supply curve shifts more than the aggregate demand curve, equilibrium real GDP will fall.

You should be able to redo this entire analysis for a stronger dollar.

QUICK QUIZ See page 249 for the answers. Review concepts from this section in MyEconLab.

__________-run equilibrium occurs at the intersection of the aggregate demand curve, *AD*, and the short-run aggregate supply curve, *SRAS*. __________-run equilibrium occurs at the intersection of *AD* and the long-run aggregate supply curve, *LRAS*. Any unanticipated shifts in aggregate demand or supply are called aggregate demand __________ or aggregate supply __________.

When aggregate demand decreases while aggregate supply is stable, a __________ gap can occur, defined as the difference between how much the economy could be producing if it were operating on its *LRAS* and the equilibrium level of real GDP. An increase in aggregate demand leads to an __________ gap.

With stable aggregate supply, an abrupt outward shift in *AD* may lead to what is called __________-__________ inflation. With stable aggregate demand, an abrupt shift inward in *SRAS* may lead to what is called __________-__________ inflation.

A __________ dollar will raise the cost of imported inputs, thereby causing *SRAS* to shift inward to the left. At the same time, a __________ dollar will also lead to higher net exports, causing the aggregate demand curve to shift outward. The equilibrium price level definitely rises, but the net effect on equilibrium real GDP depends on which shift is larger.

You Are There

Putting More Weight on Stability Than Growth in Denmark

Dalum Papir A/S is almost halfway through its second century as a Danish paper manufacturer. Years ago, the firm was one of many paper companies, but now it constitutes one-half of Denmark's two-firm paper industry. The company utilizes highly energy-efficient techniques to manufacture glossy paper from recycled materials for magazines. Dalum Papir has had little choice but to conserve energy. Government taxation has boosted energy prices more than 45 percent above the U.S. level. In addition, like other Danish firms, Dalum Papir must meet government-mandated standards for energy conservation.

Ever since the 1970s, when a worldwide spike in oil prices set off a prolonged recession, Denmark's government has sought to shield the nation's economy from future aggregate supply shocks induced by jumps in energy prices. Toward that end, it has enacted high energy taxes and tough regulatory conservation measures. A consequence is that Danish oil consumption per $1 million of real GDP has declined by more than 30 percent—to 120 tons of oil per $1 million of real GDP—over the last 30 years. Indeed, Denmark's *total* oil consumption has remained unchanged since the late 1970s. Thus, consistent with the government's intent, whenever oil prices suddenly shoot up, Denmark's economy tends to experience smaller aggregate supply shocks than it did in years past.

As the experience of Dalum Papir and the dwindling Danish paper industry illustrates, however, the government's quest for aggregate supply stability has come at the cost of growth in production of goods and services. Although the Danish economy is less susceptible than the U.S. economy to aggregate supply shocks, Denmark's aggregate supply is growing at about half the pace at which U.S. aggregate supply is expanding.

Critical Analysis Questions

1. Why do unexpected variations in energy prices generate aggregate supply shocks, while sudden changes in total planned expenditures do not?
2. Other things being equal, why might we expect the Danish price level to be more stable over time than the U.S. price level?

ISSUES & APPLICATIONS

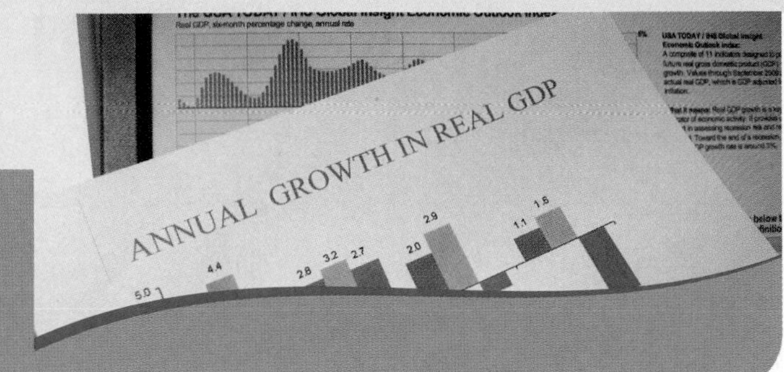

Which Shocks Have the Greatest Effects on the Economy?

CONCEPTS APPLIED

- Aggregate Supply Shocks
- Aggregate Demand Shocks
- Short Run versus Long Run

Classical and Keynesian theories of the determination of real GDP and the price level offer very different predictions about the relative importance of aggregate demand shocks and aggregate supply shocks. According to classical theory, variations in real GDP result primarily from shifts in the vertical long-run aggregate supply curve. In contrast, Keynesian theory suggests that changes in real GDP result mainly from shifts in the aggregate demand curve.

Measuring Aggregate Demand and Supply Shocks

In a recent study, Nathan Balke of Southern Methodist University used an approach to measuring aggregate demand and supply shocks called *principal components analysis*. Under this approach, Balke sought to identify common determinants, called principal components, of variability in real GDP and the price level in the U.S. economy. These common determinants are Balke's aggregate demand and supply shocks.

Which Shock Matters in the Short Run?

Balke found that one type of aggregate demand shock is mainly a consequence of shifts in desired expenditures by households, firms, and the government. This shock, he found, ultimately has meager long-run effects but accounts for much of the short-run variation in real GDP and the price level. This conclusion is consistent with the implications of Keynesian theory in the short run.

Which Shocks Matter in the Long Run?

Balke found evidence that another aggregate demand shock, changes in the quantity of money in circulation, is the main determinant of changes in the price level in the long run. In contrast, an aggregate supply shock arising from variations in aggregate productivity does most to explain changes in real GDP over a long-run time horizon.

These results are consistent with classical theory. Thus, Balke's principal components analysis suggests that the U.S. economy's performance appears to be in harmony with classical theory in the long run.

For Critical Analysis

1. Why do you suppose that changes in the quantity of money eventually must exert long-run effects on the level of prices?
2. Why do you think that all aggregate supply shocks ultimately involve variations in overall productivity?

Web Resources

1. To read past reports by the president's Council of Economic Advisers regarding effects that aggregate demand and supply shocks have had on the U.S. economy, go to www.econtoday.com/ch11.
2. To track data on real GDP and the price level in the United States, go to www.econtoday.com/ch11.

Research Project

Draw three diagrams with aggregate demand, short-run aggregate supply, and long-run aggregate supply curves. Use the first diagram to explain how a temporary increase in aggregate demand, potentially caused by variations in desired spending across sectors of the economy, can generate a short-run change in real GDP. Then, use the second diagram to show how a permanent increase in the quantity of money in circulation can generate a long-run change in the price level. Finally, use the third diagram to explain why changes in long-run aggregate supply generate long-term movements in real GDP.

For more questions on this chapter's Issues & Applications, go to **MyEconLab**. In the Study Plan for this chapter, select Section N: News.

Here is what you should know after reading this chapter. **MyEconLab** will help you identify what you know, and where to go when you need to practice.

WHAT YOU SHOULD KNOW		WHERE TO GO TO PRACTICE
Central Assumptions of the Classical Model The classical model makes four key assumptions: (1) pure competition prevails, so no individual buyer or seller of a good or service or of a factor of production can affect its price; (2) wages and prices are completely flexible; (3) people are motivated by self-interest; and (4) buyers and sellers do not experience money illusion, meaning that they respond only to changes in relative prices.	Say's law, 230 money illusion, 231	• **MyEconLab** Study Plan 11.1 • Audio introduction to Chapter 11 • Video: Say's Law
Short-Run Determination of Equilibrium Real GDP and the Price Level in the Classical Model Under the four assumptions of the classical model, the short-run aggregate supply curve is vertical at full-employment real GDP and thus corresponds to the long-run aggregate supply curve. Real GDP cannot increase in the absence of changes in longer-term economic growth. Variations in the position of the aggregate demand curve along the classical aggregate supply curve generate changes in the equilibrium price level.	**KEY FIGURES** Figure 11-2, 232 Figure 11-3, 233 Figure 11-4, 234 Figure 11-5, 235	• **MyEconLab** Study Plan 11.1 • Audio introduction to Chapter 11 • Animated Figures 11-2, 11-3, 11-4, 11-5
Circumstances Under Which the Short-Run Aggregate Supply Curve May Be Horizontal or Upward Sloping If product prices and wages and other input prices are "sticky," perhaps because of labor and other contracts, the short-run aggregate supply schedule can be horizontal over much of its range. This is the Keynesian short-run aggregate supply curve. More generally, however, to the extent that there is incomplete adjustment of prices in the short run, the short-run aggregate supply curve slopes upward.	Keynesian short-run aggregate supply curve, 236 short-run aggregate supply curve, 237 **KEY FIGURES** Figure 11-6, 236 Figure 11-7, 237	• **MyEconLab** Study Plans 11.2, 11.3 • Video: The Short-Run Aggregate Supply Curve • Animated Figures 11-6, 11-7

MyEconLab continued

WHAT YOU SHOULD KNOW		WHERE TO GO TO PRACTICE
Factors That Induce Shifts in the Short-Run and Long-Run Aggregate Supply Curves Both the long-run aggregate supply curve and the short-run aggregate supply curve shift in response to changes in the availability of labor or capital or to changes in technology and productivity. A widespread temporary change in the prices of factors of production, however, can cause a shift in the short-run aggregate supply curve without affecting the long-run aggregate supply curve.	**KEY TABLE** Table 11-2, 239 **KEY FIGURE** Figure 11-8, 238	• **MyEconLab** Study Plan 11.4 • Video: Shifts in the Short-Run Aggregate Supply Curve • Animated Figure 11-8
Effects of Aggregate Demand and Supply Shocks on Equilibrium Real GDP in the Short Run An aggregate demand shock that causes the aggregate demand curve to shift leftward pushes equilibrium real GDP below the level of full-employment real GDP in the short run, so there is a recessionary gap. An aggregate demand shock that induces a rightward shift in the aggregate demand curve results in an inflationary gap, in which short-run equilibrium real GDP exceeds full-employment real GDP.	aggregate demand shock, 240 aggregate supply shock, 240 recessionary gap, 240 inflationary gap, 240 **KEY FIGURES** Figure 11-9, 240 Figure 11-10, 241	• **MyEconLab** Study Plan 11.5 • Animated Figures 11-9, 11-10
Causes of Short-Run Variations in the Inflation Rate Demand-pull inflation occurs when the aggregate demand curve shifts rightward along an upward-sloping short-run aggregate supply curve. Cost-push inflation occurs when the short-run aggregate supply curve shifts leftward along the aggregate demand curve. A weakening of the dollar shifts the short-run aggregate supply curve leftward and the aggregate demand curve rightward, which causes inflation but has uncertain effects on real GDP.	demand-pull inflation, 241 cost-push inflation, 241 **KEY FIGURE** Figure 11-11, 242	• **MyEconLab** Study Plan 11.6 • Animated Figure 11-11

Log in to MyEconLab, take a chapter test, and get a personalized Study Plan that tells you which concepts you understand and which ones you need to review. From there, MyEconLab will give you further practice, tutorials, animations, videos, and guided solutions.
Log in to www.myeconlab.com

PROBLEMS

All problems are assignable in myeconlab. *Answers to odd-numbered problems appear at the back of the book.*

11-1. Consider a country whose economic structure matches the assumptions of the classical model. After reading a recent best-seller documenting a growing population of low-income elderly people who were ill-prepared for retirement, most residents of this country decide to increase their saving at any given interest rate. Explain whether or how this could affect the following:

a. The current equilibrium interest rate

b. Current equilibrium real GDP

c. Current equilibrium employment

d. Current equilibrium investment

e. Future equilibrium real GDP (see Chapter 9)

11-2. Consider a country with an economic structure consistent with the assumptions of the classical model. Suppose that businesses in this nation suddenly anticipate higher future profitability from investments they undertake today. Explain whether or how this could affect the following:

a. The current equilibrium interest rate

b. Current equilibrium real GDP

c. Current equilibrium employment

d. Current equilibrium saving

e. Future equilibrium real GDP (see Chapter 9)

11-3. "There is *absolutely no distinction* between the classical model and the model of long-run equilibrium discussed in Chapter 10." Is this statement true or false? Support your answer.

11-4. A nation in which the classical model applies experiences a decline in the quantity of money in circulation. Use an appropriate aggregate demand and aggregate supply diagram to explain what happens to equilibrium real GDP and to the equilibrium price level.

11-5. Suppose that the classical model is appropriate for a country that has suddenly experienced an influx of immigrants who possess a wide variety of employable skills and who have reputations for saving relatively large portions of their incomes, compared with native-born residents, at any given interest rate. Evaluate the effects of this event on the following:

a. Current equilibrium employment

b. Current equilibrium real GDP

c. The current equilibrium interest rate

d. Current equilibrium investment

e. Future equilibrium real GDP (see Chapter 9)

11-6. Suppose that the Keynesian short-run aggregate supply curve is applicable for a nation's economy. Use appropriate diagrams to assist in answering the following questions:

a. What are two factors that can cause the nation's real GDP to increase in the short run?

b. What are two factors that can cause the nation's real GDP to increase in the long run?

11-7. What determines how much real GDP responds to changes in the price level along the short-run aggregate supply curve?

11-8. At a point along the short-run aggregate supply curve that is to the right of the point where it crosses the long-run aggregate supply curve, what must be true of the unemployment rate relative to the long-run, full-employment rate of unemployment? Why?

11-9. Suppose that the stock market crashes in an economy with an upward-sloping short-run aggregate supply curve, and consumer and business confidence plummets. What are the short-run effects on equilibrium real GDP and the equilibrium price level?

11-10. Suppose that there is a temporary, but significant, increase in oil prices in an economy with an upward-sloping *SRAS* curve. If policymakers wish to prevent the equilibrium price level from changing in response to the oil price increase, should they increase or decrease the quantity of money in circulation? Why?

11-11. As in Problem 11-10, suppose that there is a temporary, but significant, increase in oil prices in an economy with an upward-sloping *SRAS* curve. In this case, however, suppose that policymakers wish to prevent equilibrium real GDP from changing in response to the oil price increase. Should they increase or decrease the quantity of money in circulation? Why?

11-12. Based on your answers to Problems 11-10 and 11-11, can policymakers stabilize *both* the price level *and* real GDP simultaneously in response to a short-lived but sudden rise in oil prices? Explain briefly.

11-13. For each question that follows, suppose that the economy *begins* at the short-run equilibrium point *A*. Identify which of the other points on the diagram—point *B*, *C*, *D*, or *E*—could represent a *new* short-run equilibrium after the described events take place and move the economy away from point *A*. Briefly explain your answers.

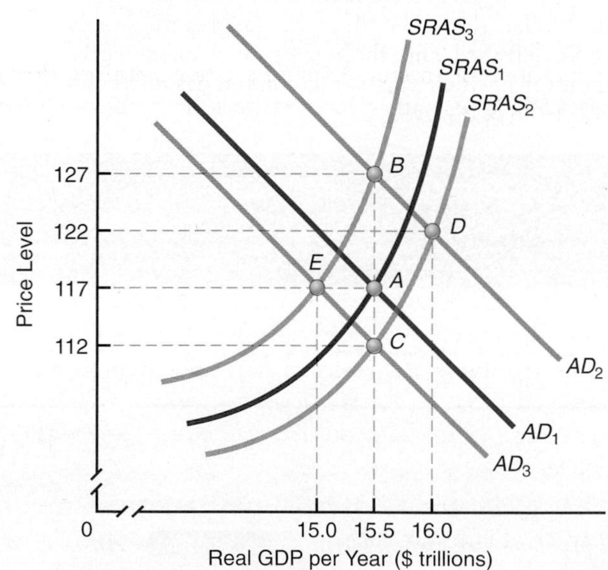

a. Most workers in this nation's economy are union members, and unions have successfully negotiated large wage boosts. At the same time, economic conditions suddenly worsen abroad, reducing real GDP and disposable income in other nations of the world.

b. A major hurricane has caused short-term halts in production at many firms and created major bottlenecks in the distribution of goods and services that had been produced prior to the storm. At the same time, the nation's central bank has significantly pushed up the rate of growth of the nation's money supply.

c. A strengthening of the value of this nation's currency in terms of other countries' currencies affects both the *SRAS* curve and the *AD* curve.

11-14. Consider an open economy in which the aggregate supply curve slopes upward in the short run. Firms in this nation do not import raw materials or any other productive inputs from abroad, but foreign residents purchase many of the nation's goods and services. What is the most likely short-run effect on this nation's economy if there is a significant downturn in economic activity in other nations around the world?

ECONOMICS ON THE NET

Money, the Price Level, and Real GDP The classical and Keynesian theories have differing predictions about how changes in the money supply should affect the price level and real GDP. Here you get to look at data on growth in the money supply, the price level, and real GDP.

Title: Federal Reserve Bank of St. Louis Monetary Trends

Navigation: Use the link at **www.econtoday.com/ch11** to visit the Federal Reserve Bank of St. Louis. Click on *Gross Domestic Product and M2*.

Application Read the article; then answer these questions.

1. Classical theory indicates that, *ceteris paribus*, changes in the price level should be closely related to changes in aggregate demand induced by variations in the quantity of money. Click on *Gross Domestic Product and M2*, and take a look at the charts labeled "Gross Domestic Product Price Index" and "M2." (M2 is a measure of the quantity of money in circulation.) Are annual percentage changes in these variables closely related?
2. Keynesian theory predicts that, *ceteris paribus*, changes in GDP and the quantity of money should be directly related. Take a look at the charts labeled "Real Gross Domestic Product" and "M2." Are annual percentage changes in these variables closely related?

For Group Study and Analysis Both classical and Keynesian theories of relationships among real GDP, the price level, and the quantity of money hinge on specific assumptions. Have class groups search through the FRED database (accessible at **www.econtoday.com/ch11**) to evaluate factors that provide support for either theory's predictions. Which approach appears to receive greater support from recent data? Does this necessarily imply that this is the "true theory"? Why or why not?

ANSWERS TO QUICK QUIZZES

p. 235: (i) supply . . . demand; (ii) pure competition . . . wages . . . prices . . . self-interest . . . money illusion; (iii) saving . . . investment; (iv) wage rate; (v) vertical . . . price level

p. 239: (i) demand; (ii) reduced; (iii) partial; (iv) intensively . . . higher; (v) *SRAS*

p. 244: (i) Short . . . Long . . . shocks . . . shocks; (ii) recessionary . . . inflationary; (iii) demand-pull . . . cost-push; (iv) weaker . . . weaker

12

Consumption, Real GDP, and the Multiplier

During an 18-month period in the depths of the Great Recession of the late 2000s, inflation-adjusted spending on goods and services by U.S. households declined by 2 percent. This drop in household expenditures followed on the heels of significant declines in the levels of wealth and indebtedness of households. The consumption decrease also accompanied a fall in *real disposable income*—real GDP less real tax payments net of transfers—earned by households. Why and how was the 2 percent decrease in U.S. consumption spending related to the declines in inflation-adjusted household wealth and debts and to the fall in real disposable income? After completing this chapter, you will know the answer to this question.

LEARNING OBJECTIVES

After reading this chapter, you should be able to:

- Distinguish between saving and savings and explain how saving and consumption are related
- Explain the key determinants of consumption and saving in the Keynesian model
- Identify the primary determinants of planned investment
- Describe how equilibrium real GDP is established in the Keynesian model
- Evaluate why autonomous changes in total planned expenditures have a multiplier effect on equilibrium real GDP
- Understand the relationship between total planned expenditures and the aggregate demand curve

MyEconLab helps you master each objective and study more efficiently. See end of chapter for details.

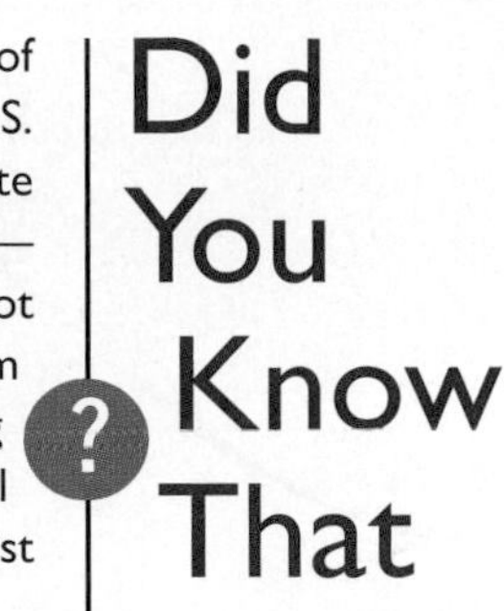

at various times from the late 1990s through the mid-2000s, the U.S. saving rate—the ratio of the flow of real, inflation-adjusted saving to real GDP—was *negative*? In other words, U.S. households spent more overall on consumption of goods and services than the aggregate income they earned. They did this by drawing on their existing wealth and by borrowing—actions that economists call *dissaving*—to help fund their expenditures. The saving rate did not rise significantly above zero until the onset of the Great Recession that stretched from December 2007 into 2009. During that period, U.S. households cut back on their real spending on goods and services and raised their saving rate to above 6 percent. In this chapter, you will learn how an understanding of households' real saving and real consumption spending can assist in evaluating fluctuations in a nation's real GDP.

Some Simplifying Assumptions in a Keynesian Model

Continuing in the Keynesian tradition, we will assume that the short-run aggregate supply curve within the current range of real GDP is horizontal. That is, we assume that it is similar to Figure 11-6 on page 236. Thus, the equilibrium level of real GDP is demand determined. This is why Keynes wished to examine the elements of desired aggregate expenditures. Because of the Keynesian assumption of inflexible prices, inflation is not a concern in this analysis. Hence, real values are identical to nominal values.

To simplify the income determination model that follows, a number of assumptions are made:

1. Businesses pay no indirect taxes (for example, sales taxes).
2. Businesses distribute all of their profits to shareholders.
3. There is no depreciation (capital consumption allowance), so gross private domestic investment equals net investment.
4. The economy is closed—that is, there is no foreign trade.

Given all these simplifying assumptions, **real disposable income,** or after-tax real income, will be equal to real GDP minus net taxes—taxes paid less transfer payments received.

Real disposable income
Real GDP minus net taxes, or after-tax real income.

Another Look at Definitions and Relationships

You can do only two things with a dollar of disposable income: consume it or save it. If you consume it, it is gone forever. If you save the entire dollar, however, you will be able to consume it (and perhaps more if it earns interest) at some future time. That is the distinction between **consumption** and **saving.** Consumption is the act of using income for the purchase of consumption goods. **Consumption goods** are goods purchased by households for immediate satisfaction. (These also include services.) Consumption goods are such things as food and movies. By definition, whatever you do not consume you save and can consume at some time in the future.

Consumption
Spending on new goods and services to be used up out of a household's current income. Whatever is not consumed is saved. Consumption includes such things as buying food and going to a concert.

Saving
The act of not consuming all of one's current income. Whatever is not consumed out of spendable income is, by definition, saved. *Saving* is an action measured over time (a flow), whereas *savings* are a stock, an accumulation resulting from the act of saving in the past.

STOCKS AND FLOWS: THE DIFFERENCE BETWEEN SAVING AND SAVINGS It is important to distinguish between *saving* and *savings*. *Saving* is an action that occurs at a particular rate—for example, $40 per week or $2,080 per year. This rate is a flow. It is expressed per unit of time, usually a year. Implicitly, then, when we talk about saving, we talk about a *flow*, or rate, of saving. *Savings*, by contrast, is a *stock* concept, measured at a certain point or instant in time. Your current *savings* are the result of past *saving*. You may currently have *savings* of $8,000 that are the result of four years' *saving* at a rate of $2,000 per year. Consumption is also a flow concept. You consume from after-tax income at a certain rate per week, per month, or per year.

Consumption goods
Goods bought by households to use up, such as food and movies.

RELATING INCOME TO SAVING AND CONSUMPTION A dollar of take-home income can be allocated either to consumption or to saving. Realizing this, we can see the relationship among saving, consumption, and disposable income from the following expression:

$$\text{Consumption} + \text{saving} \equiv \text{disposable income}$$

This is called an *accounting identity*, meaning that it has to hold true at every moment in time. (To indicate that the relationship is always true, we use the ≡ symbol.)

From this relationship, we can derive the following definition of saving:

$$\text{Saving} \equiv \text{disposable income} - \text{consumption}$$

Hence, saving is the amount of disposable income that is not spent to purchase consumption goods.

Investment
Spending on items such as machines and buildings, which can be used to produce goods and services in the future. The investment part of real GDP is the portion that will be used in the process of producing goods in the future.

Capital goods
Producer durables; nonconsumable goods that firms use to make other goods.

Investment

Investment is also a flow concept. As noted in Chapter 8, *investment* as used in economics differs from the common use of the term. In common speech, it is often used to describe putting funds into the stock market or real estate. In economic analysis, investment is defined to include expenditures on new machines and buildings—**capital goods**—that are expected to yield a future stream of income. This is called *fixed investment.* We also include changes in business inventories in our definition. This we call *inventory investment.*

QUICK QUIZ See page 275 for the answers. Review concepts from this section in MyEconLab.

If we assume that we are operating on a __________ short-run aggregate supply curve, the equilibrium level of real GDP per year is completely demand determined.

__________ is a flow, something that occurs over time. It equals disposable income minus consumption.

__________ is a stock. It is the accumulation resulting from saving.

__________ is also a flow. It includes expenditures on new machines, buildings, and equipment and changes in business inventories.

Determinants of Planned Consumption and Planned Saving

In the classical model discussed in Chapter 11 on pages 230–235, the supply of saving was determined by the rate of interest. Specifically, the higher the rate of interest, the more people wanted to save and therefore the less people wanted to consume.

In contrast, according to Keynes, the interest rate is *not* the most important determinant of an individual's real saving and consumption decisions. In his view, income, not the interest rate, is the main determinant of saving. Thus:

> ***Keynes argued that real saving and consumption decisions depend primarily on a household's present real disposable income.***

Consumption function
The relationship between amount consumed and disposable income. A consumption function tells us how much people plan to consume at various levels of disposable income.

The relationship between planned real consumption expenditures of households and their current level of real disposable income has been called the **consumption function.** It shows how much all households plan to consume per year at each level of real disposable income per year. Columns (1) and (2) of Table 12-1 on the facing page illustrate a consumption function for a hypothetical household.

We see from Table 12-1 that as real disposable income rises, planned consumption also rises, but by a smaller amount, as Keynes suggested. Planned saving also increases

TABLE 12-1

Real Consumption and Saving Schedules: A Hypothetical Case

Column 1 presents real disposable income from zero up to $120,000 per year. Column 2 indicates planned consumption per year. Column 3 presents planned saving per year. At levels of disposable income below $60,000, planned saving is negative. In column 4, we see the average propensity to consume, which is merely planned consumption divided by disposable income. Column 5 lists average propensity to save, which is planned saving divided by disposable income. Column 6 is the marginal propensity to consume, which shows the proportion of *additional* income that will be consumed. Finally, column 7 shows the proportion of *additional* income that will be saved, or the marginal propensity to save. (Δ represents "change in.")

Combination	(1) Real Disposable Income per Year (Y_d)	(2) Planned Real Consumption per Year (C)	(3) Planned Real Saving per Year ($S \equiv Y_d - C$) (1) − (2)	(4) Average Propensity to Consume ($APC \equiv C/Y_d$) (2) ÷ (1)	(5) Average Propensity to Save ($APS \equiv S/Y_d$) (3) ÷ (1)	(6) Marginal Propensity to Consume ($MPC \equiv \Delta C/\Delta Y_d$)	(7) Marginal Propensity to Save ($MPS \equiv \Delta S/\Delta Y_d$)
A	$ 0	$12,000	$–12,000	–	–	–	–
B	12,000	21,600	−9,600	1.8	−0.8	0.8	0.2
C	24,000	31,200	−7,200	1.3	−0.3	0.8	0.2
D	36,000	40,800	−4,800	1.133	−0.133	0.8	0.2
E	48,000	50,400	−2,400	1.05	−0.05	0.8	0.2
F	60,000	60,000	0	1.0	0.0	0.8	0.2
G	72,000	69,600	2,400	0.967	0.033	0.8	0.2
H	84,000	79,200	4,800	0.943	0.057	0.8	0.2
I	96,000	88,800	7,200	0.925	0.075	0.8	0.2
J	108,000	98,400	9,600	0.911	0.089	0.8	0.2
K	120,000	108,000	12,000	0.9	0.1	0.8	0.2

with disposable income. Notice, however, that below an income of $60,000, the planned saving of this hypothetical household is actually negative. The further that income drops below that level, the more the household engages in **dissaving,** either by going into debt or by using up some of its existing wealth.

Dissaving
Negative saving; a situation in which spending exceeds income. Dissaving can occur when a household is able to borrow or use up existing assets.

Graphing the Numbers

We now graph the consumption and saving relationships presented in Table 12-1. In the upper part of Figure 12-1 on the following page, the vertical axis measures the level of planned real consumption per year, and the horizontal axis measures the level of real disposable income per year. In the lower part of the figure, the horizontal axis is again real disposable income per year, but now the vertical axis is planned real saving per year. All of these are on a dollars-per-year basis, which emphasizes the point that we are measuring flows, not stocks.

As you can see, we have taken income-consumption and income-saving combinations *A* through *K* and plotted them. In the upper part of Figure 12-1, the result is called the *consumption function.* In the lower part, the result is called the *saving function.* Mathematically, the saving function is the *complement* of the consumption function because consumption plus saving always equals disposable income. What is not consumed is, by definition, saved. The difference between actual disposable income and the planned rate of consumption per year *must* be the planned rate of saving per year.

How can we find the rate of saving or dissaving in the upper part of Figure 12-1? We begin by drawing a line that is equidistant from both the horizontal and the vertical axes. This line is 45 degrees from either axis and is often called the **45-degree reference line.** At every point on the 45-degree reference line, a vertical line drawn to the income axis is the same distance from the origin as a horizontal line drawn to the

45-degree reference line
The line along which planned real expenditures equal real GDP per year.

FIGURE 12-1 The Consumption and Saving Functions

If we plot the combinations of real disposable income and planned real consumption from columns 1 and 2 in Table 12-1 on the previous page, we get the consumption function.

At every point on the 45-degree line, a vertical line drawn to the income axis is the same distance from the origin as a horizontal line drawn to the consumption axis. Where the consumption function crosses the 45-degree line at *F*, we know that planned real consumption equals real disposable income and there is zero saving. The vertical distance between the 45-degree line and the consumption function measures the rate of real saving or dissaving at any given income level.

If we plot the relationship between column 1 (real disposable income) and column 3 (planned real saving) from Table 12-1 on the previous page, we arrive at the saving function shown in the lower part of this diagram. It is the complement of the consumption function presented above it.

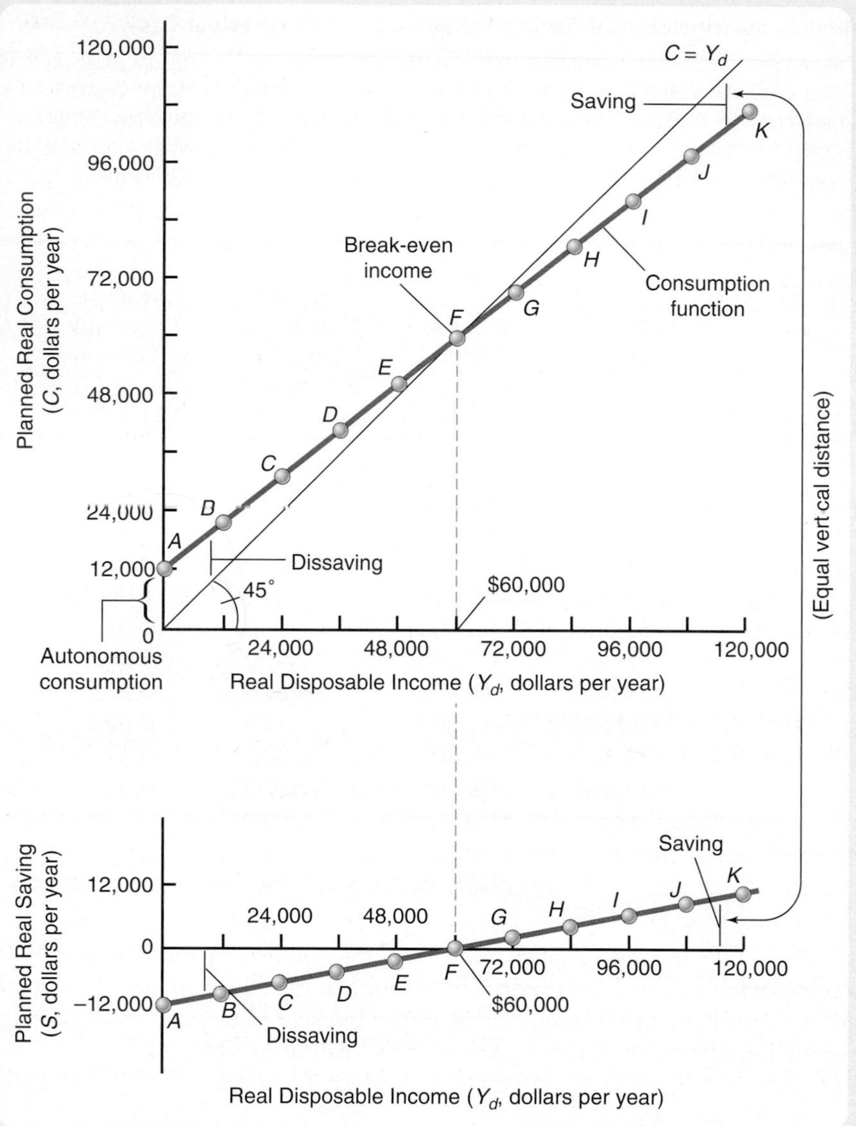

consumption axis. Thus, at point *F*, where the consumption function intersects the 45-degree line, real disposable income equals planned real consumption. Point *F* is sometimes called the *break-even income point* because there is neither positive nor negative real saving. This can be seen in the lower part of Figure 12-1 above as well. The planned annual rate of real saving at a real disposable income level of $60,000 is indeed zero.

Dissaving and Autonomous Consumption

To the left of point *F* in either part of Figure 12-1, this hypothetical family engages in dissaving, either by going into debt or by consuming existing assets. The rate of real saving or dissaving in the upper part of the figure can be found by measuring the vertical distance between the 45-degree line and the consumption function. This simply tells us that if our hypothetical household sees its real disposable income fall to less than $60,000, it will not limit its consumption to this amount. It will instead go into debt or consume existing assets in some way to compensate for part of the lost income.

Now look at the point on the diagram where real disposable income is zero but planned consumption is $12,000. This amount of real planned consumption, which does not depend at all on actual real disposable income, is called **autonomous consumption.** The autonomous consumption of $12,000 is *independent* of disposable income. That means that no matter how low the level of real income of our hypothetical household falls, the household will always attempt to consume at least $12,000 per year. (We are, of course, assuming here that the household's real disposable income does not equal zero year in and year out. There is certainly a limit to how long our hypothetical household could finance autonomous consumption without any income.) That $12,000 of yearly consumption is determined by things other than the level of income. We don't need to specify what determines autonomous consumption; we merely state that it exists and that in our example it is $12,000 per year.

Autonomous consumption
The part of consumption that is independent of (does not depend on) the level of disposable income. Changes in autonomous consumption shift the consumption function.

Just remember that the word *autonomous* means "existing independently." In our model, autonomous consumption exists independently of the hypothetical household's level of real disposable income. (Later we will review some of the determinants of consumption other than real disposable income.) There are many possible types of autonomous expenditures. Hypothetically, we can assume that investment is autonomous—independent of income. We can assume that government expenditures are autonomous. We will do just that at various times in our discussions to simplify our analysis of income determination.

Why does taking into account "consumer sentiment" improve policymakers' forecasts of households' future consumption expenditures?

POLICY EXAMPLE Why Knowing Consumer Sentiment Aids Consumption Forecasts

When government economists seek to forecast total U.S. consumption spending over the coming weeks and months, they always account for the prevailing level of *consumer sentiment* as well as current disposable income. To do this, they use the University of Michigan's Index of Consumer Sentiment, which is based on answers to five questions about how confident people are about their *future* disposable income. Taking this index into account typically improves the consumption forecasts substantially. This is because households' confidence about future disposable income affects *autonomous* consumption. Thus, when people are confident that their flows of disposable income will remain at current levels or increase in the future, they will engage in more consumption spending today at any given level of current disposable income. In contrast, when people are worried that their future flows of disposable income may drop, they will cut back on their autonomous consumption.

FOR CRITICAL ANALYSIS

What are other determinants of autonomous consumption that might improve forecasts of future household consumption? (Hint: What, besides your real disposable income, determines your own consumption spending?)

Average Propensity to Consume and to Save

Let's now go back to Table 12-1 on page 253, and this time let's look at columns 4 and 5: **average propensity to consume (APC)** and **average propensity to save (APS).** They are defined as follows:

Average propensity to consume (APC)
Real consumption divided by real disposable income; for any given level of real income, the proportion of total real disposable income that is consumed.

Average propensity to save (APS)
Real saving divided by real disposable income; for any given level of real income, the proportion of total real disposable income that is saved.

$$\text{APC} \equiv \frac{\text{real consumption}}{\text{real disposable income}}$$

$$\text{APS} \equiv \frac{\text{real saving}}{\text{real disposable income}}$$

Notice from column 4 in Table 12-1 that for this hypothetical household, the average propensity to consume decreases as real disposable income increases. This decrease simply means that the fraction of the household's real disposable income going to consumption falls as income rises. Column 5 shows that the average propensity to save, which at first is negative, finally hits zero at an income level of $60,000 and then becomes positive. In this example, the APS reaches a value of 0.1 at income level $120,000. This means that the household saves 10 percent of a $120,000 income.

It's quite easy for you to figure out your own average propensity to consume or to save. Just divide the value of what you consumed by your total real disposable income for the year, and the result will be your personal APC at your current level of income. Also, divide your real saving during the year by your real disposable income to calculate your own APS.

Marginal Propensity to Consume and to Save

Marginal propensity to consume (MPC) The ratio of the change in consumption to the change in disposable income. A marginal propensity to consume of 0.8 tells us that an additional $100 in take-home pay will lead to an additional $80 consumed.

Marginal propensity to save (MPS) The ratio of the change in saving to the change in disposable income. A marginal propensity to save of 0.2 indicates that out of an additional $100 in take-home pay, $20 will be saved. Whatever is not saved is consumed. The marginal propensity to save plus the marginal propensity to consume must always equal 1, by definition.

Now we go to the last two columns in Table 12-1 on page 253: **marginal propensity to consume (MPC)** and **marginal propensity to save (MPS).** The term *marginal* refers to a small incremental or decremental change (represented by the Greek letter delta, Δ, in Table 12-1). The marginal propensity to consume, then, is defined as

$$\text{MPC} \equiv \frac{\text{change in real consumption}}{\text{change in real disposable income}}$$

The marginal propensity to save is defined similarly as

$$\text{MPS} \equiv \frac{\text{change in real saving}}{\text{change in real disposable income}}$$

MARGINAL VERSUS AVERAGE PROPENSITIES What do MPC and MPS tell you? They tell you what percentage of a given increase or decrease in real income will go toward consumption and saving, respectively. The emphasis here is on the word *change.* The marginal propensity to consume indicates how much you will change your planned real consumption if there is a change in your actual real disposable income.

If your marginal propensity to consume is 0.8, that does *not* mean that you consume 80 percent of *all* disposable income. The percentage of your total real disposable income that you consume is given by the average propensity to consume, or APC. As Table 12-1 indicates, the APC is not equal to 0.8. Instead, an MPC of 0.8 means that you will consume 80 percent of any *increase* in your disposable income. Hence, the MPC cannot be less than zero or greater than one. It follows that households increase their planned real consumption by between 0 and 100 percent of any increase in real disposable income that they receive.

DISTINGUISHING THE MPC FROM THE APC Consider a simple example in which we show the difference between the average propensity to consume and the marginal propensity to consume. Assume that your consumption behavior is exactly the same as our hypothetical household's behavior depicted in Table 12-1. You have an annual real disposable income of $108,000. Your planned consumption rate, then, from column 2 of Table 12-1 is $98,400. So your average propensity to consume is $98,400/$108,000 = 0.911. Now suppose that at the end of the year, your boss gives you an after-tax bonus of $12,000. What would you do with that additional $12,000 in real disposable income? According to the table, you would consume $9,600 of it and save $2,400. In that case, your *marginal* propensity to consume would be $9,600/$12,000 = 0.8 and your marginal propensity to save would be $2,400/$12,000 = 0.2. What would happen to your *average* propensity to consume? To find out, we add $9,600 to $98,400 of planned consumption, which gives us a new consumption rate of $108,000. The average propensity to consume is then $108,000 divided by the new higher salary of $120,000. Your APC drops from 0.911 to 0.9.

In contrast, your MPC remains, in our simplified example, 0.8 all the time. Look at column 6 in Table 12-1 on page 253. The MPC is 0.8 at every level of income. (Therefore, the MPS is always equal to 0.2 at every level of income.) The constancy of MPC reflects the assumption that the amount that you are willing to consume out of additional income will remain the same in percentage terms no matter what level of real disposable income is your starting point.

Some Relationships

Consumption plus saving must equal income. Both your total real disposable income and the change in total real disposable income are either consumed or saved. The sums of the proportions of either measure that are consumed and saved must equal 1, or 100 percent. This allows us to make the following statements:

$$\text{APC} + \text{APS} \equiv 1 \text{ (= 100 percent of total income)}$$

$$\text{MPC} + \text{MPS} \equiv 1 \text{ (= 100 percent of the } \textit{change} \text{ in income)}$$

The average propensities as well as the marginal propensities to consume and save must total 1, or 100 percent. Check the two statements by adding the figures in columns 4 and 5 for each level of real disposable income in Table 12-1 on page 253. Do the same for columns 6 and 7.

Causes of Shifts in the Consumption Function

A change in any other relevant economic variable besides real disposable income will cause the consumption function to shift. The number of such nonincome determinants of the position of the consumption function is almost unlimited. Real household **net wealth** is one determinant of the position of the consumption function. An increase in the real net wealth of the average household will cause the consumption function to shift upward. A decrease in real net wealth will cause it to shift downward. So far we have been talking about the consumption function of an individual or a household. Now let's move on to the national economy.

Net wealth
The stock of assets owned by a person, household, firm, or nation (net of any debts owed). For a household, net wealth can consist of a house, cars, personal belongings, stocks, bonds, bank accounts, and cash (minus any debts owed).

Why Not . . . **help the economy by taking from the rich and giving to the poor?**

Some people think that if the government acted like Robin Hood, the economy would work better. But, in fact, changing the distribution of wealth would not accomplish this. Certainly, redistributing wealth from high-income households to lower-income households would cause the autonomous consumption of lower-income households to rise. But such a redistribution of wealth would cause the autonomous consumption of high-income households to fall. On net, *total* household wealth would be unaffected by the redistribution. Thus, aggregate autonomous consumption would be almost unchanged, and the aggregate consumption function would not shift upward.

QUICK QUIZ **See page 275 for the answers. Review concepts from this section in MyEconLab.**

The **consumption function** shows the relationship between planned rates of real consumption and real __________ __________ per year. The saving function is the complement of the consumption function because real saving plus real __________ must equal real disposable income.

The __________ propensity to consume is equal to real consumption divided by real disposable income. The __________ propensity to save is equal to real saving divided by real disposable income.

The __________ propensity to consume is equal to the change in planned real consumption divided by the change in real disposable income. The __________ propensity to save is equal to the change in planned real saving divided by the change in real disposable income.

Any change in real disposable income will cause the planned rate of consumption to change. This is represented by a __________ __________ the consumption function. Any change in a nonincome determinant of consumption will cause a __________ __________ the consumption function.

Determinants of Investment

Investment, you will remember, consists of expenditures on new buildings and equipment and changes in business inventories. Historically, real gross private domestic investment in the United States has been extremely volatile over the years, relative to real consumption. If we were to look at net private domestic investment (investment after depreciation has been deducted), we would see that in the depths of the Great Depression and at the peak of the World War II effort, the figure was negative. In other words, we were eating away at our capital stock—we weren't even maintaining it by fully replacing depreciated equipment.

If we compare real investment expenditures historically with real consumption expenditures, we find that the latter are less variable over time than the former. Why is this so? One possible reason is that the real investment decisions of businesses are based on highly variable, subjective estimates of how the economic future looks.

The Planned Investment Function

Consider that at all times, businesses perceive an array of investment opportunities. These investment opportunities have rates of return ranging from zero to very high, with the number (or dollar value) of all such projects inversely related to the rate of return. Because a project is profitable only if its rate of return exceeds the opportunity cost of the investment—the rate of interest—it follows that as the interest rate falls, planned investment spending increases, and vice versa. Even if firms use retained earnings (internal financing) to fund an investment, the lower the market rate of interest, the smaller the *opportunity cost* of using those retained earnings.

Thus, it does not matter in our analysis whether the firm must seek financing from external sources or can obtain such financing by using retained earnings. Whatever the method of financing, as the interest rate falls, more investment opportunities will be profitable, and planned investment will be higher.

It should be no surprise, therefore, that the investment function is represented as an inverse relationship between the rate of interest and the value of planned real investment. In Figure 12-2 below, a hypothetical investment schedule is given in panel (a) and plotted in panel (b). We see from this schedule that if, for example, the rate of interest is 5 percent, the dollar value of planned investment will be $2 trillion per year. Notice that planned investment is also given on a per-year basis, showing that it represents a flow, not a stock. (The stock counterpart of investment is the stock of capital in the economy measured in inflation-adjusted dollars at a point in time.)

FIGURE 12-2 Planned Real Investment

As shown in the hypothetical planned investment schedule in panel (a), the rate of planned real investment is inversely related to the rate of interest.

If we plot the data pairs from panel (a), we obtain the investment function, *I*, in panel (b). It is negatively sloped.

Panel (a)

Annual Rate of Interest (%)	Planned Real Investment per Year ($ trillions)
10	1.5
9	1.6
8	1.7
7	1.8
6	1.9
5	2.0
4	2.1
3	2.2
2	2.3
1	2.4

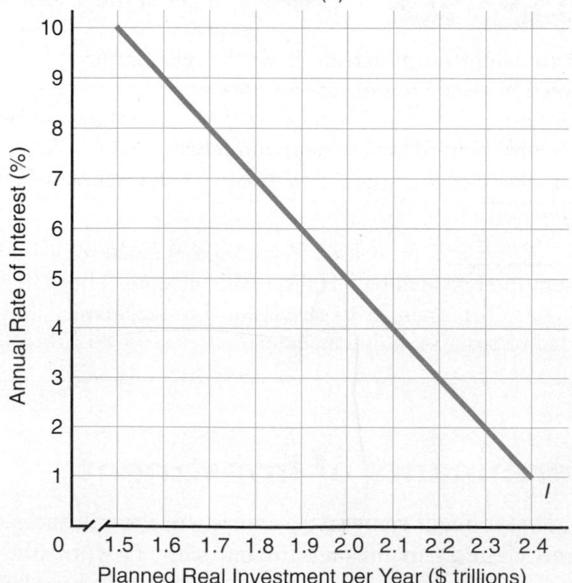

What Causes the Investment Function to Shift?

Because planned real investment is assumed to be a function of the rate of interest, any non-interest-rate variable that changes can have the potential of shifting the investment function. One of those variables is the expectations of businesses. If higher profits are expected, more machines and bigger plants will be planned for the future. More investment will be undertaken because of the expectation of higher profits. In this case, the investment function, *I*, in panel (b) of Figure 12-2, would shift outward to the right, meaning that more investment would be desired at all rates of interest. Any change in productive technology can potentially shift the investment function. A positive change in productive technology would stimulate demand for additional capital goods and shift *I* outward to the right. Changes in business taxes can also shift the investment schedule. If they increase, we predict a leftward shift in the planned investment function because higher taxes imply a lower (after-tax) rate of return.

Go to economic data provided by the Federal Reserve Bank of St. Louis via the link at www.econtoday.com/ch12 to see how U.S. real private investment has varied in recent years.

QUICK QUIZ See page 275 for the answers. **Review concepts from this section in MyEconLab.**

The planned investment schedule shows the relationship between real investment and the ___________ ___________; it slopes ___________.

The non-interest-rate determinants of planned investment are ___________, innovation and technological changes, and ___________ ___________.

Any change in the non-interest-rate determinants of planned investment will cause a ___________ ___________ the planned investment function so that at each and every rate of interest a different amount of planned investment will be made.

Determining Equilibrium Real GDP

We are interested in determining the equilibrium level of real GDP per year. But when we examined the consumption function earlier in this chapter, it related planned real consumption expenditures to the level of real disposable income per year. We have already shown where adjustments must be made to GDP in order to get real disposable income (see Table 8-2 on page 174). Real disposable income turns out to be less than real GDP because real net taxes (real taxes minus real government transfer payments) are usually about 14 to 21 percent of GDP. A representative average is about 18 percent, so disposable income, on average, has in recent years been around 82 percent of GDP.

Consumption as a Function of Real GDP

To simplify our model, assume that real disposable income, Y_d, differs from real GDP by the same absolute amount every year. Therefore, we can relatively easily substitute real GDP for real disposable income in the consumption function.

We can now plot any consumption function on a diagram in which the horizontal axis is no longer real disposable income but rather real GDP, as in Figure 12-3 on the next page. Notice that there is an autonomous part of real consumption that is so labeled. The difference between this graph and the graphs presented earlier in this chapter is the change in the horizontal axis from real disposable income to real GDP per year. For the rest of this chapter, assume that the MPC out of real GDP equals 0.8, suggesting that 20 percent of changes in real disposable income is saved: In other words, of an additional after-tax $100 earned, an additional $80 will be consumed.

The 45-Degree Reference Line

As in the earlier graphs, Figure 12-3 shows a 45-degree reference line. The 45-degree line bisects the quadrant into two equal spaces. Thus, along the 45-degree reference line, planned real consumption expenditures, *C*, equal real GDP per year, *Y*. One can see, then, that at any point where the consumption function intersects the 45-degree reference line, planned real consumption expenditures will be exactly equal to real GDP

FIGURE 12-3 Consumption as a Function of Real GDP

This consumption function shows the rate of planned expenditures for each level of real GDP per year. Autonomous consumption is \$0.2 trillion. Along the 45-degree reference line, planned real consumption expenditures per year, *C*, are identical to real GDP per year, *Y*. The consumption curve intersects the 45-degree reference line at a value of \$1 trillion per year in base-year dollars (the value of current GDP expressed in prices in a base year).

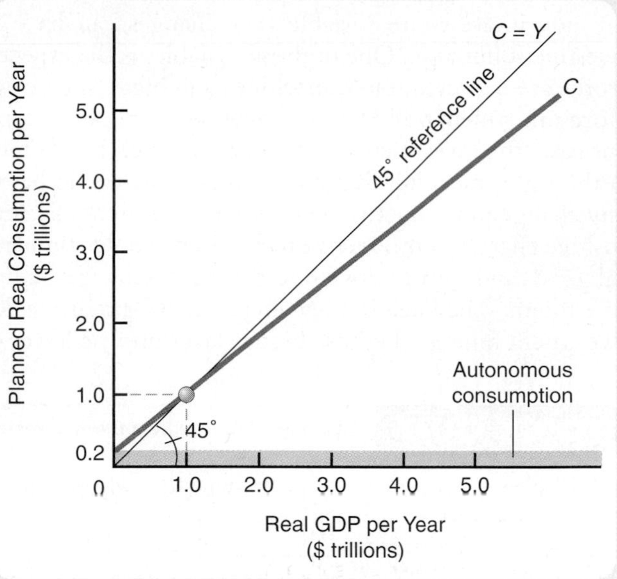

per year, or $C = Y$. Note that in this graph, because we are looking only at planned real consumption on the vertical axis, the 45-degree reference line is where planned real consumption, C, is always equal to real GDP per year, Y. Later, when we add real investment, government spending, and net exports to the graph, *all* planned real expenditures will be labeled along the vertical axis. In any event, real consumption and real GDP are equal at \$1 trillion per year. That is where the consumption curve, C, intersects the 45-degree reference line. At that GDP level, all real GDP is consumed.

Adding the Investment Function

Another component of private aggregate demand is, of course, real investment spending, I. We have already looked at the planned investment function, which related real investment, which includes changes in inventories of final products, to the rate of interest. In panel (a) of Figure 12-4 on the facing page, you see that at an interest rate of 5 percent, the rate of real investment is \$2 trillion per year. The \$2 trillion of real investment per year is *autonomous* with respect to real GDP—that is, it is independent of real GDP. In other words, given that we have a determinant investment level of \$2 trillion at a 5 percent rate of interest, we can treat this level of real investment as constant, regardless of the level of GDP. This is shown in panel (b) of Figure 12-4. The vertical distance of real investment spending is \$2 trillion. Businesses plan on investing a particular amount—\$2 trillion per year—and will do so no matter what the level of real GDP.

How do we add this amount of real investment spending to our consumption function? We simply add a line above the C line that we drew in Figure 12-3 that is higher by the vertical distance equal to \$2 trillion of autonomous real investment spending. This is shown by the arrow in panel (c) of Figure 12-4. Our new line, now labeled $C + I$, is called the *consumption plus investment line*. In our simple economy without real government expenditures and net exports, the $C + I$ curve represents total planned real expenditures as they relate to different levels of real GDP per year. Because the 45-degree reference line shows all the points where planned real expenditures (now $C + I$) equal real GDP, we label it $C + I = Y$. Thus, in equilibrium, the sum of consumption spending (C) and investment spending (I) equals real GDP (Y), which is \$11 trillion per year. Equilibrium occurs when total planned real expenditures equal real GDP (given that any amount of production of goods and services in this model in the short run can occur without a change in the price level).

FIGURE 12-4 Combining Consumption and Investment

In panel (a), we show that at an interest rate of 5 percent, real investment is equal to \$2 trillion per year. In panel (b), investment is a constant \$2 trillion per year. When we add this amount to the consumption line, we obtain in panel (c) the $C + I$ line, which is vertically higher than the C line by exactly \$2 trillion. Real GDP is equal to $C + I$ at \$11 trillion per year where total planned real expenditures, $C + I$, are equal to actual real GDP, for this is where the $C + I$ line intersects the 45-degree reference line, on which $C + I$ is equal to Y at every point. (For simplicity, we ignore the fact that the dependence of saving on income can influence investment.)

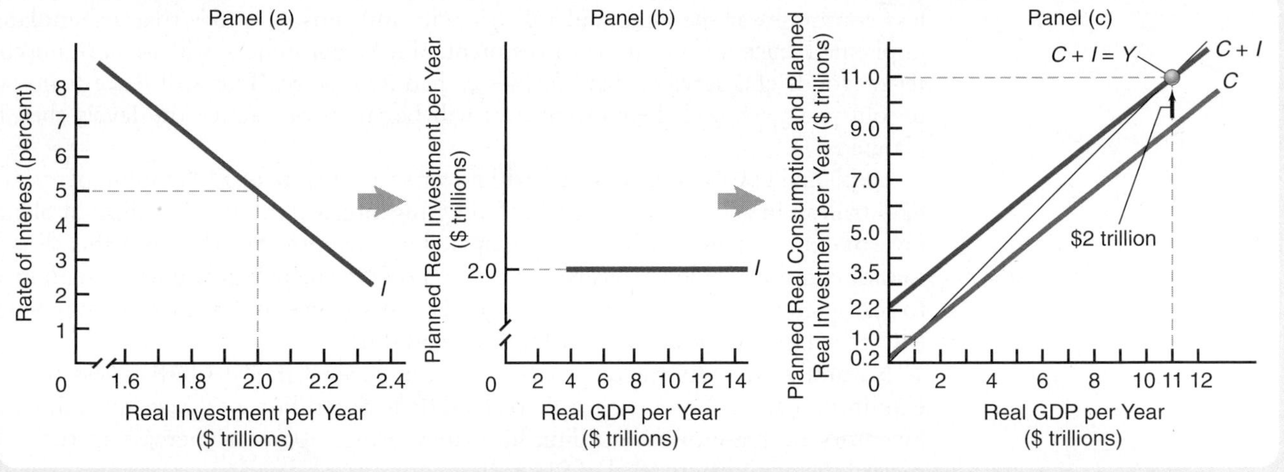

Saving and Investment: Planned versus Actual

Figure 12-5 below shows the planned investment curve as a horizontal line at \$2 trillion per year in base year dollars. Real investment is completely autonomous in this simplified model—it does not depend on real GDP.

The planned saving curve is represented by S. Because in our model whatever is not consumed is, by definition, saved, the planned saving schedule is the complement of the planned consumption schedule, represented by the C line in Figure 12-3 on the facing page. For better exposition, we look at only a part of the saving and investment schedules—annual levels of real GDP between \$9 trillion and \$13 trillion.

Why does equilibrium have to occur at the intersection of the planned saving and planned investment schedules? If we are at E in Figure 12-5, planned saving equals planned investment. All anticipations are validated by reality. There is no tendency

FIGURE 12-5 Planned and Actual Rates of Saving and Investment

Only at the equilibrium level of real GDP of \$11 trillion per year will planned saving equal actual saving, planned investment equal actual investment, and hence planned saving equal planned investment.

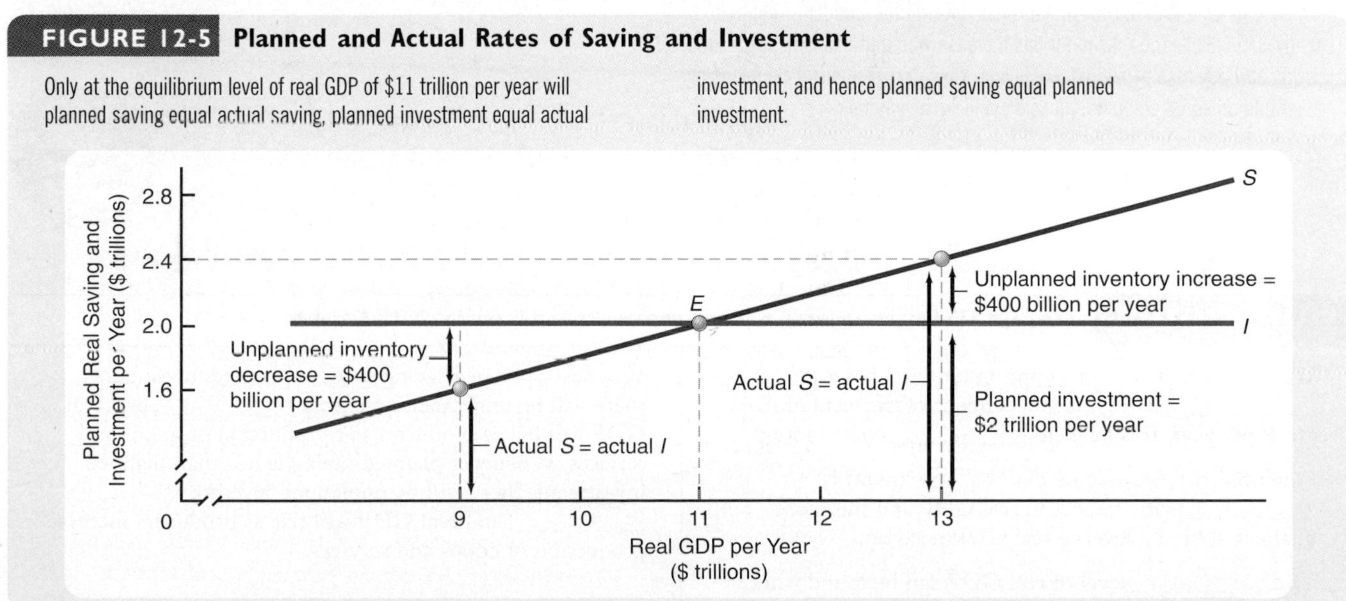

for businesses to alter the rate of production or the level of employment because they are neither increasing nor decreasing their inventories in an unplanned way.

You Are There

To think about why higher planned saving and unplanned inventory buildups often go together, read **In Boise, Idaho, Inventories Accumulate as Desired Saving Rises,** on page 270.

UNPLANNED CHANGES IN BUSINESS INVENTORIES If real GDP is $13 trillion instead of $11 trillion, planned investment, as usual, is $2 trillion per year. It is exceeded, however, by planned saving, which is $2.4 trillion per year. The additional $0.4 trillion ($400 billion) in saving by households over and above planned investment represents less consumption spending and will translate into unsold goods that accumulate as unplanned business inventory investment. Thus, consumers will *actually* purchase fewer goods and services than businesses had *anticipated.* This will leave firms with unsold products, and their inventories will begin to rise above the levels they had planned.

Unplanned business inventories will now rise at the rate of $400 billion per year, or $2.4 trillion in actual investment (including inventories) minus $2 trillion in planned investment by firms that had not anticipated an inventory buildup. But this situation cannot continue for long. Businesses will respond to the unplanned increase in inventories by cutting back production of goods and services and reducing employment, and we will move toward a lower level of real GDP.

Naturally, the adjustment process works in reverse if real GDP is less than the equilibrium level. For instance, if real GDP is $9 trillion per year, an unintended inventory decrease of $0.4 trillion ultimately brings about an increase in real GDP toward the equilibrium level of $11 trillion.

Every time the saving rate planned by households differs from the investment rate planned by businesses, there will be a shrinkage or an expansion in the circular flow of income and output (introduced in Chapter 8) in the form of unplanned inventory changes. Real GDP and employment will change until unplanned inventory changes are again zero—that is, until we have attained the equilibrium level of real GDP.

Why did unplanned business inventories grow rapidly during the latter part of the initial year of the Great Recession of the late 2000s?

EXAMPLE **A Great Inventory Buildup During the Great Recession**

For 10 months following the officially designated start of the Great Recession in December 2007, business inventories behaved as firms had planned. They shrank, reflecting a persistent effort by U.S. corporations and other businesses to manage their inventories at relatively low levels. During the last few weeks of 2008, however, business inventories suddenly jumped by nearly $70 billion. The reason for this increase was that households' desired saving abruptly rose by almost $70 billion. Thus, a cut in household spending generated an equal amount of unsold business inventories.

FOR CRITICAL ANALYSIS

Why do you suppose that a significant decline in real GDP during 2009 helped to equilibrate planned inventories with planned saving? (Hint: Take a look at Figure 12-5 on the previous page.)

QUICK QUIZ See page 275 for the answers. Review concepts from this section in MyEconLab.

We assume that the consumption function has an __________ part that is independent of the level of real GDP per year. It is labeled "__________ consumption."

For simplicity, we assume that real investment is __________ with respect to real GDP and therefore unaffected by the level of real GDP per year.

The __________ level of real GDP can be found where planned saving equals planned investment.

Whenever planned saving exceeds planned investment, there will be unplanned inventory __________, and real GDP will fall as producers cut production of goods and services. Whenever planned saving is less than planned investment, there will be unplanned inventory __________, and real GDP will rise as producers increase production of goods and services.

Keynesian Equilibrium with Government and the Foreign Sector Added

To this point, we have ignored the role of government in our model. We have also left out the foreign sector of the economy. Let's think about what happens when we also consider these as elements of the model.

Government

To add real government spending, G, to our macroeconomic model, we assume that the level of resource-using government purchases of goods and services (federal, state, and local), *not* including transfer payments, is determined by the political process. In other words, G will be considered autonomous, just like real investment (and a certain component of real consumption). In the United States, resource-using federal government expenditures account for almost 25 percent of real GDP.

The other side of the coin, of course, is that there are real taxes, which are used to pay for much of government spending. We will simplify our model greatly by assuming that there is a constant **lump-sum tax** of \$2.3 trillion a year to finance \$2.3 trillion of government spending. This lump-sum tax will reduce disposable income by the same amount. We show this below in Table 12-2 (column 2), where we give the numbers for a complete model.

Lump-sum tax
A tax that does not depend on income. An example is a \$1,000 tax that every household must pay, irrespective of its economic situation.

The Foreign Sector

For years, the media have focused attention on the nation's foreign trade deficit. We have been buying merchandise and services from foreign residents—real imports—the value of which exceeds the value of the real exports we have been selling to them. The difference between real exports and real imports is *real net exports*, which we will label X in our graphs. The level of real exports depends on international economic conditions, especially in the countries that buy our products. Real imports depend on economic conditions here at home. For simplicity, assume that real imports exceed real exports (real net exports, X, is negative) and furthermore that the level of real net exports is autonomous—independent of real national income. Assume a level of X of −\$0.8 trillion per year, as shown in column 8 of Table 12-2.

TABLE 12-2

The Determination of Equilibrium Real GDP with Government and Net Exports Added

Figures are trillions of dollars.

(1) Real GDP	(2) Real Taxes	(3) Real Disposable Income	(4) Planned Real Consumption	(5) Planned Real Saving	(6) Planned Real Investment	(7) Real Government Spending	(8) Real Net Exports (exports minus imports)	(9) Total Planned Real Expenditures (4)+(6)+(7)+(8)	(10) Unplanned Inventory Changes	(11) Direction of Change in Real GDP
9.0	2.3	6.7	6.7	0.0	2.0	2.3	−0.8	10.2	−1.2	Increase
10.0	2.3	7.7	7.5	0.2	2.0	2.3	−0.8	11.0	−1.0	Increase
11.0	2.3	8.7	8.3	0.4	2.0	2.3	−0.8	11.8	−0.8	Increase
12.0	2.3	9.7	9.1	0.6	2.0	2.3	−0.8	12.6	−0.6	Increase
13.0	2.3	10.7	9.9	0.8	2.0	2.3	−0.8	13.4	−0.4	Increase
14.0	2.3	11.7	10.7	1.0	2.0	2.3	−0.8	14.2	−0.2	Increase
15.0	2.3	12.7	11.5	1.2	2.0	2.3	−0.8	15.0	0	Neither (equilibrium)
16.0	2.3	13.7	12.3	1.4	2.0	2.3	−0.8	15.8	+0.2	Decrease
17.0	2.3	14.7	13.1	1.6	2.0	2.3	−0.8	16.6	+0.4	Decrease

FIGURE 12-6 The Equilibrium Level of Real GDP

The consumption function, with no government and thus no taxes, is shown as C. When we add autonomous investment, government spending, and net exports, we obtain $C + I + G + X$. We move from E_1 to E_2. Equilibrium real GDP is $15 trillion per year.

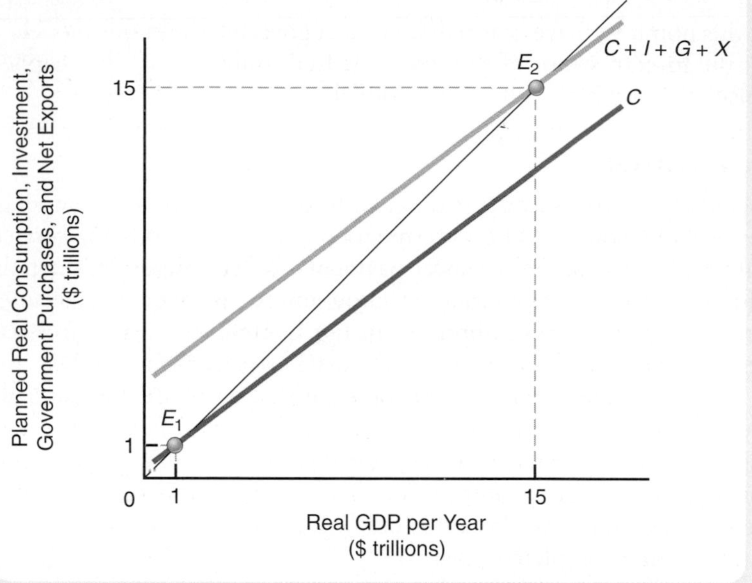

Determining the Equilibrium Level of GDP per Year

We are now in a position to determine the equilibrium level of real GDP per year under the continuing assumptions that the price level is unchanging; that investment, government, and the foreign sector are autonomous; and that planned consumption expenditures are determined by the level of real GDP. As can be seen in Table 12-2 on the preceding page, total planned real expenditures of $15 trillion per year equal real GDP of $15 trillion per year, and this is where we reach equilibrium.

Remember that equilibrium always occurs when total planned real expenditures equal real GDP. Now look at Figure 12-6 above, which shows the equilibrium level of real GDP. There are two curves, one showing the consumption function, which is the exact duplicate of the one shown in Figure 12-3 on page 260, and the other being the $C + I + G + X$ curve, which intersects the 45-degree reference line (representing equilibrium) at $15 trillion per year.

Whenever total planned real expenditures differ from real GDP, there are unplanned inventory changes. When total planned real expenditures are greater than real GDP, inventory levels drop in an unplanned manner. To get inventories back up, firms seek to expand their production of goods and services, which increases real GDP. Real GDP rises toward its equilibrium level. Whenever total planned real expenditures are less than real GDP, the opposite occurs. There are unplanned inventory increases, causing firms to cut back on their production of goods and services in an effort to push inventories back down to planned levels. The result is a drop in real GDP toward the equilibrium level.

QUICK QUIZ **See page 275 for the answers. Review concepts from this section in MyEconLab.**

When we add autonomous investment, I, and autonomous government spending, G, to the consumption function, we obtain the $C + I + G$ curve, which represents total ____________ ____________ for a closed economy. In an open economy, we add the foreign sector, which consists of exports minus imports, or net exports, X. Total planned expenditures are thus represented by the $C + I + G + X$ curve.

Equilibrium real GDP can be found by locating the intersection of the total planned real expenditures curve with the ____________-____________ reference line. At that level of real GDP per year, planned real consumption plus planned real investment plus real government expenditures plus real net exports will equal real GDP.

QUICK QUIZ *(continued)*

Whenever total planned real expenditures exceed real GDP, there will be unplanned __________ in inventories. Production of goods and services will increase, and a higher level of equilibrium real GDP will prevail. Whenever total planned real expenditures are less than real GDP, there will be unplanned __________ in inventories. Production of goods and services will decrease, and equilibrium real GDP will decrease.

The Multiplier

Look again at panel (c) of Figure 12-4 on page 261. Assume for the moment that the only real expenditures included in real GDP are real consumption expenditures. Where would the equilibrium level of real GDP be in this case? It would be where the consumption function (C) intersects the 45-degree reference line, which is at \$1 trillion per year. Now we add the autonomous amount of planned real investment, \$2 trillion, and then determine what the new equilibrium level of real GDP will be. It turns out to be \$11 trillion per year. Adding \$2 trillion per year of investment spending increased equilibrium real GDP by *five* times that amount, or by \$10 trillion per year.

The Multiplier Effect

What is operating here is the multiplier effect of changes in autonomous spending. The **multiplier** is the number by which a permanent change in autonomous real investment or autonomous real consumption is multiplied to get the change in the equilibrium level of real GDP. Any permanent increases in autonomous real investment or in any autonomous component of consumption will cause an even larger increase in real GDP. Any permanent decreases in autonomous real spending will cause even larger decreases in real GDP per year. To understand why this multiple expansion (or contraction) in equilibrium real GDP occurs, let's look at a simple numerical example.

Multiplier
The ratio of the change in the equilibrium level of real GDP to the change in autonomous real expenditures. The number by which a change in autonomous real investment or autonomous real consumption, for example, is multiplied to get the change in equilibrium real GDP.

We'll use the same figures we used for the marginal propensity to consume and to save. MPC will equal 0.8, or $\frac{4}{5}$, and MPS will equal 0.2, or $\frac{1}{5}$. Now let's run an experiment and say that businesses decide to increase planned real investment permanently by \$100 billion a year. We see in Table 12-3 below that during what we'll

TABLE 12-3

The Multiplier Process

We trace the effects of a *permanent* \$100 billion increase in autonomous real investment spending on real GDP per year. If we assume a marginal propensity to consume of 0.8, such an increase will eventually elicit a \$500 billion increase in equilibrium real GDP per year.

Assumption: MPC = 0.8, or $\frac{4}{5}$

(1) Round	(2) Annual Increase in Real GDP (\$ billions)	(3) Annual Increase in Planned Real Consumption (\$ billions)	(4) Annual Increase in Planned Real Saving (\$ billions)
1 (\$100 billion per year increase in I)	100.00	80.000	20.000
2	80.00	64.000	16.000
3	64.00	51.200	12.800
4	51.20	40.960	10.240
5	40.96	32.768	8.192
.	.	.	.
.	.	.	.
.	.	.	.
All later rounds	163.84	131.072	32.768
Totals ($C + I + X$)	500.00	400.000	100.000

call the first round in column 1, investment is increased by $100 billion. This also means an increase in real GDP of $100 billion, because the spending by one group represents income for another, shown in column 2. Column 3 gives the resultant increase in consumption by households that received this additional $100 billion in income. This is found by multiplying the MPC by the increase in real GDP. Because the MPC equals 0.8, real consumption expenditures during the first round will increase by $80 billion.

But that's not the end of the story. This additional household consumption is also spending, and it will provide $80 billion of additional income for other individuals. Thus, during the second round, we see an increase in real GDP of $80 billion. Now, out of this increased real GDP, what will be the resultant increase in consumption expenditures? It will be 0.8 times $80 billion, or $64 billion. We continue these induced expenditure rounds and find that an initial increase in autonomous investment expenditures of $100 billion will eventually cause the equilibrium level of real GDP to increase by $500 billion. A permanent $100 billion increase in autonomous real investment spending has induced an additional $400 billion increase in real consumption spending, for a total increase in real GDP of $500 billion. In other words, equilibrium real GDP will change by an amount equal to five times the change in real investment.

The Multiplier Formula

It turns out that the autonomous spending multiplier is equal to 1 divided by the marginal propensity to save. In our example, the MPC was 0.8, or $\frac{4}{5}$; therefore, because MPC + MPS = 1, the MPS was equal to 0.2, or $\frac{1}{5}$. When we divide 1 by $\frac{1}{5}$, we get 5. That was our multiplier. A $100 billion increase in real planned investment led to a $500 billion increase in the equilibrium level of real GDP. Our multiplier will always be the following:

$$\text{Multiplier} \equiv \frac{1}{1 - \text{MPC}} \equiv \frac{1}{\text{MPS}}$$

You can always figure out the multiplier if you know either the MPC or the MPS. Let's consider an example. If MPS = 0.25 or $\frac{1}{4}$,

$$\text{Multiplier} = \frac{1}{\frac{1}{4}} = 4$$

Because MPC + MPS = 1, it follows that MPS = 1 − MPC. Hence, we can always figure out the multiplier if we are given the marginal propensity to consume. In this example, if the marginal propensity to consume is given as 0.75 or $\frac{3}{4}$,

$$\text{Multiplier} = \frac{1}{1 - \frac{3}{4}} = \frac{1}{\frac{1}{4}} = 4$$

By taking a few numerical examples, you can demonstrate to yourself an important property of the multiplier:

The smaller the marginal propensity to save, the larger the multiplier.

Otherwise stated:

The larger the marginal propensity to consume, the larger the multiplier.

Demonstrate this to yourself by computing the multiplier when the marginal propensity to save equals $\frac{3}{4}$, $\frac{1}{2}$, and $\frac{1}{4}$. What happens to the multiplier as the MPS gets smaller?

When you have the multiplier, the following formula will then give you the change in equilibrium real GDP due to a permanent change in autonomous spending:

$$\text{Change in equilibrium real GDP} = \text{multiplier} \times \text{change in autonomous spending}$$

The multiplier, as noted earlier, works for a permanent increase or a permanent decrease in autonomous spending per year. In our earlier example, if the autonomous component of real consumption had fallen permanently by $100 billion, the reduction in equilibrium real GDP would have been $500 billion per year.

Significance of the Multiplier

Depending on the size of the multiplier, it is possible that a relatively small change in planned investment or in autonomous consumption can trigger a much larger change in equilibrium real GDP per year. In essence, the multiplier magnifies the fluctuations in equilibrium real GDP initiated by changes in autonomous spending.

As was just noted, the larger the marginal propensity to consume, the larger the multiplier. If the marginal propensity to consume is $\frac{1}{2}$, the multiplier is 2. In that case, a $1 billion decrease in (autonomous) real investment will elicit a $2 billion decrease in equilibrium real GDP per year. Conversely, if the marginal propensity to consume is $\frac{9}{10}$, the multiplier will be 10. That same $1 billion decrease in planned real investment expenditures with a multiplier of 10 will lead to a $10 billion decrease in equilibrium real GDP per year.

How a Change in Real Autonomous Spending Affects Real GDP When the Price Level Can Change

So far, our examination of how changes in real autonomous spending affect equilibrium real GDP has considered a situation in which the price level remains unchanged. Thus, our analysis has only indicated how much the aggregate demand curve shifts in response to a change in investment, government spending, net exports, or lump-sum taxes.

Of course, when we take into account the aggregate supply curve, we must also consider responses of the equilibrium price level to a multiplier-induced change in aggregate demand. We do so in Figure 12-7 on the next page. The intersection of AD_1 and *SRAS* is at a price level of 120 with equilibrium real GDP of $15 trillion per year. An increase in autonomous spending shifts the aggregate demand curve outward to the right to AD_2. If the price level remained at 120, the short-run equilibrium level of real GDP would increase to $15.5 trillion per year because, for the $100 billion increase in autonomous spending, the multiplier would be 5, as it was in Table 12-3 on page 265.

The price level does not stay fixed, however, because ordinarily the *SRAS* curve is positively sloped. In this diagram, the new short-run equilibrium level of real GDP is hypothetically $15.3 trillion. The ultimate effect on real GDP is smaller than the multiplier effect on nominal income because part of the additional income is used to pay higher prices. Not all is spent on additional goods and services, as is the case when the price level is fixed.

If the economy is at an equilibrium level of real GDP that is greater than *LRAS*, the implications for the eventual effect on real GDP are even more severe. Look again at Figure 12-7. The *SRAS* curve starts to slope upward more dramatically after $15 trillion of real GDP per year. Therefore, any increase in aggregate demand will lead to a proportionally greater increase in the price level and a smaller increase in equilibrium real GDP per year. The ultimate effect on real GDP of any increase in

FIGURE 12-7 Effect of a Rise in Autonomous Spending on Equilibrium Real GDP

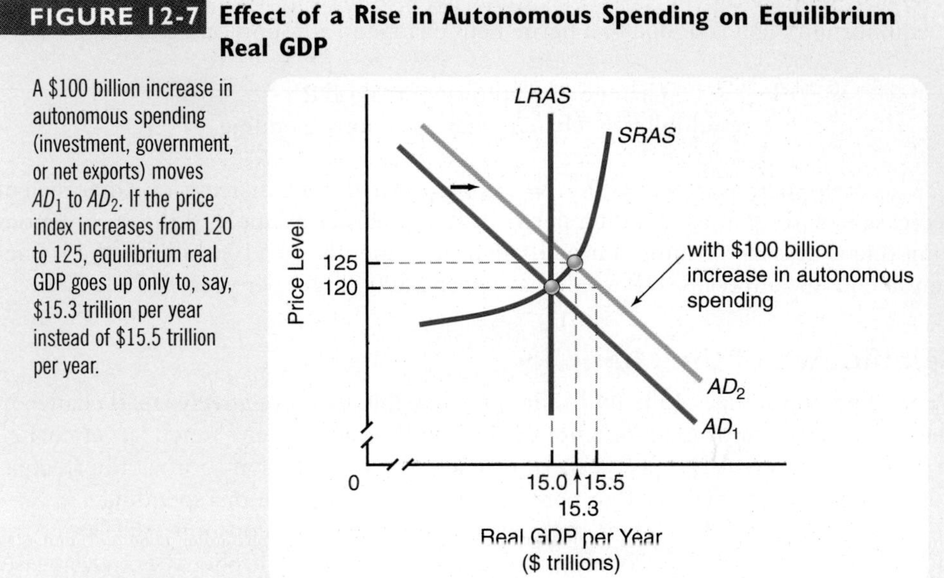

A $100 billion increase in autonomous spending (investment, government, or net exports) moves AD_1 to AD_2. If the price index increases from 120 to 125, equilibrium real GDP goes up only to, say, $15.3 trillion per year instead of $15.5 trillion per year.

autonomous spending will be relatively small because most of the changes will be in the price level. Moreover, any increase in the short-run equilibrium level of real GDP will tend to be temporary because the economy is temporarily above *LRAS*—the strain on its productive capacity will raise the price level.

The Relationship Between Aggregate Demand and the $C + I + G + X$ Curve

There is clearly a relationship between the aggregate demand curves that you studied in Chapters 10 and 11 and the $C + I + G + X$ curve developed in this chapter. After all, aggregate demand consists of consumption, investment, and government purchases, plus the foreign sector of our economy. There is a major difference, however, between the aggregate demand curve, *AD*, and the $C + I + G + X$ curve: The latter is drawn with the price level held constant, whereas the former is drawn, by definition, with the price level changing. To derive the aggregate demand curve from the $C + I + G + X$ curve, we must now allow the price level to change. Look at the upper part of Figure 12-8 on the facing page. Here we see the $C + I + G + X$ curve at a price level equal to 100, and at $15 trillion of real GDP per year, planned real expenditures exactly equal real GDP. This gives us point *A* in the lower graph, for it shows what real GDP would be at a price level of 100.

Now let's assume that in the upper graph, the price level increases to 125. What are the effects?

1. A higher price level can decrease the purchasing power of any cash that people hold (the real-balance effect). This is a decrease in real wealth, and it causes consumption expenditures, *C*, to fall, thereby putting downward pressure on the $C + I + G + X$ curve.
2. Because individuals attempt to borrow more to replenish their real cash balances, interest rates will rise, which will make it more costly for people to buy houses and cars (the interest rate effect). Higher interest rates also make it less profitable to install new equipment and to erect new buildings. Therefore, the rise in the price level indirectly causes a reduction in total planned spending on goods and services.

FIGURE 12-8 **The Relationship Between *AD* and the *C* + *I* + *G* + *X* Curve**

In the upper graph, the $C + I + G + X$ curve at a price level equal to 100 intersects the 45-degree reference line at E_1, or \$15 trillion of real GDP per year. That gives us point *A* (price level = 100; real GDP = \$15 trillion) in the lower graph. When the price level increases to 125, the $C + I + G + X$ curve shifts downward, and the new level of real GDP at which planned real expenditures equal real GDP is at E_2 at \$13 trillion per year. This gives us point *B* in the lower graph. Connecting points *A* and *B*, we obtain the aggregate demand curve.

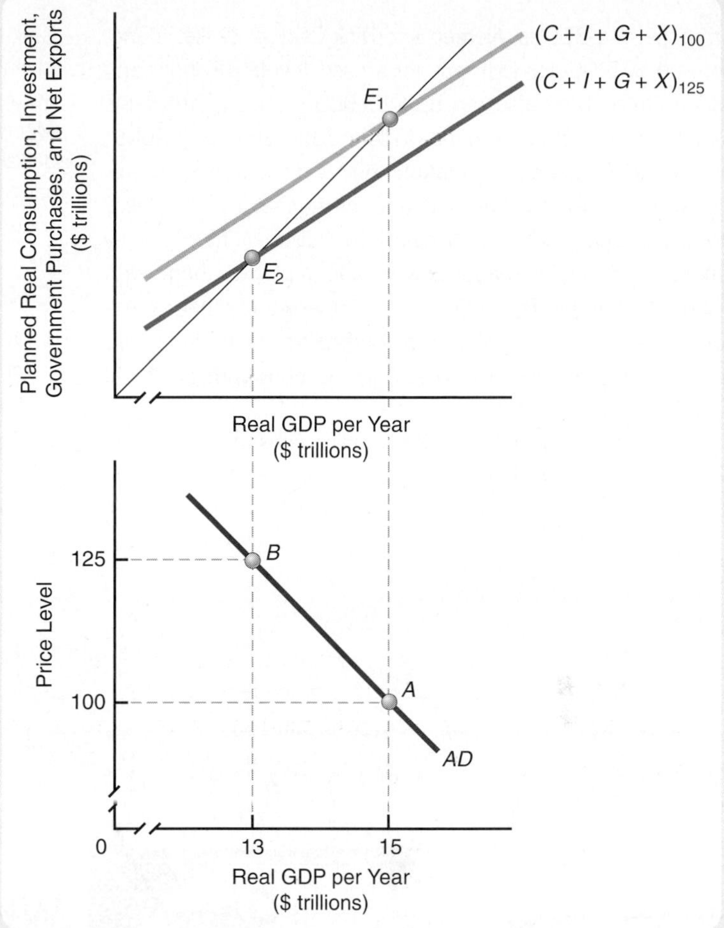

3. In an open economy, our higher price level causes foreign spending on our goods to fall (the open economy effect). Simultaneously, it increases our demand for others' goods. If the foreign exchange price of the dollar stays constant for a while, there will be an increase in imports and a decrease in exports, thereby reducing the size of *X*, again putting downward pressure on the $C + I + G + X$ curve.

The result is that a new $C + I + G + X$ curve at a price level equal to 125 generates an equilibrium at E_2 at \$13 trillion of real GDP per year. This gives us point *B* in the lower part of Figure 12-8 above. When we connect points *A* and *B*, we obtain the aggregate demand curve, *AD*.

QUICK QUIZ **See page 275 for the answers. Review concepts from this section in MyEconLab.**

Any change in autonomous spending shifts the expenditure curve and causes a __________ effect on equilibrium real GDP per year.

The **multiplier** is equal to 1 divided by the __________ propensity to __________.

The smaller the marginal propensity to __________, the larger the **multiplier.** Otherwise stated, the larger the marginal propensity to __________, the larger the **multiplier.**

The $C + I + G + X$ curve is drawn with the price level held constant, whereas the *AD* curve allows the price level to __________. Each different price level generates a new $C + I + G + X$ curve.

You Are There

In Boise, Idaho, Inventories Accumulate as Desired Saving Rises

During the mid-2000s, Noreen and Rick Capp of Boise, Idaho, borrowed $25,000 to help pay for a used Toyota 4Runner and new furniture. They also ran up $11,000 in credit-card debts and $40,000 in student loans. In late 2008 and early 2009, however, the Capps stopped taking their two children to restaurants and tried to cut their spending on utilities by using less natural gas and electricity to heat and cool their home. They even stopped buying paper towels and replaced them with reusable dishcloths. By cutting back on these and other expenditures, the Capps were able to pay off half of their credit-card debt, and they opened a new savings account with an initial $1,000 deposit.

As the Capps and other Boise families consumed less and saved more, local businesses began to experience unintended inventory buildups. At several Boise restaurants, such as Gino's Grill, the 8th Street Wine Company, and Mortimer's Idaho Cuisine, inventories of unsold frozen and other nonperishable food began to accumulate. Inventories of unsold items also grew at Boise's Mervyn's Department Store and at local furniture stores. Thus, decisions by Boise families such as the Capps to increase planned saving were transmitted to businesses as unplanned inventory accumulations.

Critical Analysis Questions

1. When planned saving rose above planned investment in Boise and elsewhere throughout the United States, what do you think happened to equilibrium real GDP?
2. How did business production of new goods and services likely respond to the unintended inventory buildup in 2008 and 2009?

ISSUES & APPLICATIONS

Why U.S. Consumption Spending Dropped in the Late 2000s

CONCEPTS APPLIED

- ▶ Consumption
- ▶ Autonomous Consumption
- ▶ Consumption Function

Between the end of 2007 and mid-2009, aggregate U.S. real consumption spending declined by about $175 billion. Over the 18-month period, this amounted to a decrease in inflation-adjusted consumption expenditures of nearly 2 percent.

Lower Disposable Income Translates into Less Consumption

Take a look at Figure 12-9 on the facing page, which displays index measures of real disposable income and several forms of household wealth. The base year for these index measures is 1960. Hence, the peak index value near 12 for real household debt means that inflation-adjusted household debt reached a high in 2006 at about 12 times its 1960 value. The real housing wealth index's value in 2006 was close to 8, so the inflation-adjusted value of housing wealth was almost 8 times higher in 2006 than in 1960.

FIGURE 12-9 Real Household Debt, Housing Wealth, Disposable Income, and Stock Wealth Indexes Since 1960

Index measures of household debt, housing wealth, disposable income, and stock wealth all decreased after the mid-2000s, which generated lower consumption spending in the late 2000s.

Sources: Reuven Glick and Kevin Lansin, "U.S. Household Deleveraging and Future Consumption Growth," Federal Reserve Bank of San Francisco *Economic Letter* No. 2009–16, May 15, 2009; author's estimates.

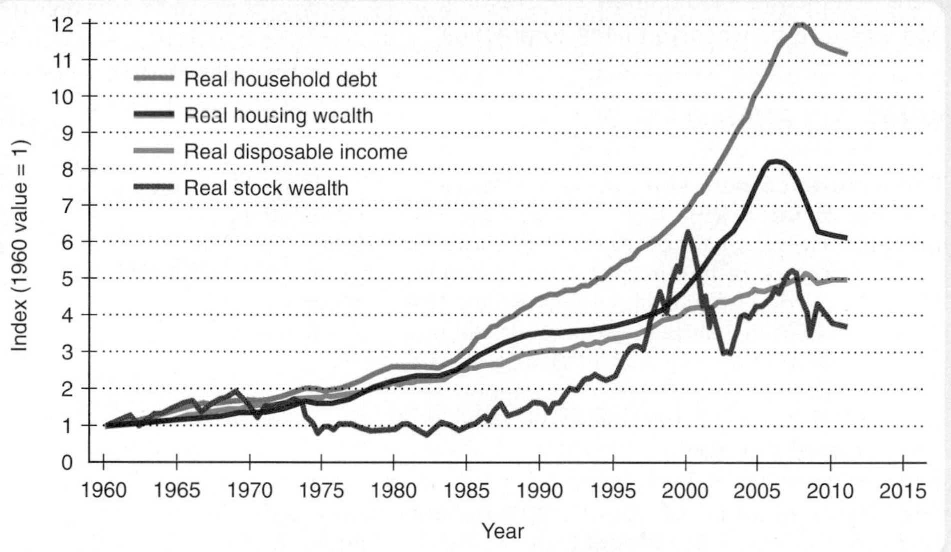

Real disposable income generally has trended upward, aside from a few dips. After 2007, however, the index for real disposable income dropped. This decrease in real disposable income contributed to a drop in real consumption expenditures.

Lower Autonomous Consumption Fuels Further Declines

Figure 12-9 above shows that real housing wealth, real wealth held in firms' stocks, and real household debt doubled or more than doubled between the mid-1990s and the mid-2000s. The additions to wealth and increases in borrowing enabled households to raise their autonomous consumption. Declines in both household wealth and household debt after 2006, however, contributed to lower autonomous consumption, which shifted the U.S. consumption function downward.

Thus, real consumption fell in the late 2000s both because real disposable income decreased and because household wealth and borrowing declined. These are the reasons that real household consumption fell by about 2 percent.

For Critical Analysis

1. In late 2009 and early 2010, the value of corporate stocks held by households rose somewhat. How do you think this affected aggregate real consumption?
2. In late 2009 and early 2010, real disposable income began growing at a slow pace. How do you think aggregate real consumption responded?

Web Resources

1. For the latest data on U.S. consumption spending, go to www.econtoday.com/ch12.
2. To generate a chart plotting U.S. consumption expenditures going back as far as 1947, go to www.econtoday.com/ch12.

Research Project

Evaluate the implications for *real saving* of the downturns in households' inflation-adjusted disposable income, housing and stock wealth, and debt in the late 2000s. Discuss how changes in these quantities generated movements along and shifts in the U.S. saving function. Explain the effects, assuming other things were equal, on unintended inventories and equilibrium real income.

For more questions on this chapter's Issues & Applications, go to **MyEconLab**. In the Study Plan for this chapter, select Section N: News.

Here is what you should know after reading this chapter. **MyEconLab** will help you identify what you know, and where to go when you need to practice.

WHAT YOU SHOULD KNOW		WHERE TO GO TO PRACTICE
The Difference Between Saving and Savings and the Relationship Between Saving and Consumption Saving is a flow over time, whereas savings is a stock of resources at a point in time. Thus, the portion of your disposable income that you do not consume during a week, a month, or a year is an addition to your stock of savings. By definition, saving during a year plus consumption during that year must equal total disposable (after-tax) income earned that year.	real disposable income, 251 consumption, 251 saving, 251 consumption goods, 251 investment, 252 capital goods, 252	• **MyEconLab** Study Plan 12.1 • Audio introduction to Chapter 12
Key Determinants of Consumption and Saving in the Keynesian Model In the Keynesian model, as real disposable income increases, so do real consumption expenditures. The portion of consumption unrelated to disposable income is autonomous consumption. The ratio of saving to disposable income is the average propensity to save (APS), and the ratio of consumption to disposable income is the average propensity to consume (APC). A change in saving divided by the corresponding change in disposable income is the marginal propensity to save (MPS), and a change in consumption divided by the corresponding change in disposable income is the marginal propensity to consume (MPC).	consumption function, 252 dissaving, 253 45-degree reference line, 253 autonomous consumption, 255 average propensity to consume (APC), 255 average propensity to save (APS), 255 marginal propensity to consume (MPC), 256 marginal propensity to save (MPS), 256 net wealth, 257 **KEY FIGURE** Figure 12-1, 254	• **MyEconLab** Study Plan 12.2 • Video: The Marginal Propensity to Consume • Animated Figure 12-1
Key Determinants of Planned Investment Planned investment varies inversely with the interest rate, so the investment schedule slopes downward. Changes in business expectations, productive technology, or business taxes cause the investment schedule to shift. In the basic Keynesian model, changes in real GDP do not affect planned real investment.		• **MyEconLab** Study Plan 12.3 • Video: The Determinants of Investment
How Equilibrium Real GDP Is Established in the Keynesian Model In equilibrium, total planned real consumption, investment, government, and net export expenditures equal real GDP, so $C + I + G + X = Y$. This occurs at the point where the $C + I + G + X$ curve crosses the 45-degree reference line. In a world without government spending and taxes, equilibrium also occurs when planned saving is equal to planned investment, and there is no tendency for business inventories to expand or contract.	lump-sum tax, 263 **KEY FIGURE** Figure 12-5, 261	• **MyEconLab** Study Plans 12.4, 12.5 • Animated Figures 12-5 and 12-6

MyEconLab continued

WHAT YOU SHOULD KNOW		WHERE TO GO TO PRACTICE
Why Autonomous Changes in Total Planned Real Expenditures Have a Multiplier Effect on Equilibrium Real GDP Any increase in autonomous expenditures causes a direct rise in real GDP. The resulting increase in disposable income in turn stimulates increased consumption by an amount equal to the marginal propensity to consume multiplied by the rise in disposable income that results. As consumption increases, so does real GDP, which induces a further increase in consumption spending. The ultimate expansion of real GDP is equal to the multiplier, 1/(1 − MPC), or 1/MPS, times the increase in autonomous expenditures.	multiplier, 265 **KEY TABLE** Table 12-3, 265	• **MyEconLab** Study Plans 12.6, 12.7 • Animated Table 12-3 • Video: The Multiplier • ABC News Video: The Multiplier and the Business Cycle
The Relationship Between Total Planned Expenditures and the Aggregate Demand Curve An increase in the price level induces households and businesses to cut back on spending. Thus, the $C + I + G + X$ curve shifts downward following a rise in the price level, so that equilibrium real GDP falls. This yields the downward-sloping aggregate demand curve.	**KEY FIGURES** Figure 12-7, 268 Figure 12-8, 269	• **MyEconLab** Study Plan 12.8 • Animated Figures 12-7, 12-8

Log in to MyEconLab, take a chapter test, and get a personalized Study Plan that tells you which concepts you understand and which ones you need to review. From there, MyEconLab will give you further practice, tutorials, animations, videos, and guided solutions. Log in to www.myeconlab.com

PROBLEMS

All problems are assignable in myeconlab. *Answers to odd-numbered problems appear at the back of the book.*

12-1. Classify each of the following as either a stock or a flow.

a. Myung Park earns $850 per week.

b. Time Warner purchases $100 million in new computer equipment this month.

c. Sally Schmidt has $1,000 in a savings account at a credit union.

d. XYZ, Inc., produces 200 units of output per week.

e. Giorgio Giannelli owns three private jets.

f. General Motors' production declines by 750 autos per month.

g. Russia owes $25 billion to the International Monetary Fund.

12-2. Consider the table below when answering the following questions. For this hypothetical economy, the marginal propensity to save is constant at all levels of real GDP, and investment spending is autonomous. There is no government.

Real GDP	Consumption	Saving	Investment
$ 2,000	$2,200	$_____	$400
4,000	4,000	_____	_____
6,000	_____	_____	_____
8,000	_____	_____	_____
10,000	_____	_____	_____
12,000	_____	_____	_____

a. Complete the table. What is the marginal propensity to save? What is the marginal propensity to consume?

b. Draw a graph of the consumption function. Then add the investment function to obtain $C + I$.

c. Under the graph of $C + I$, draw another graph showing the saving and investment curves. Note that the $C + I$ curve crosses the 45-degree reference line in the upper graph at the same level of real GDP where the saving and investment curves cross in the lower graph. (If not, redraw your graphs.) What is this level of real GDP?

d. What is the numerical value of the multiplier?

e. What is equilibrium real GDP without investment? What is the multiplier effect from the inclusion of investment?

f. What is the average propensity to consume at equilibrium real GDP?

g. If autonomous investment declines from $400 to $200, what happens to equilibrium real GDP?

12-3. Consider the table below when answering the following questions. For this hypothetical economy, the marginal propensity to consume is constant at all levels of real GDP, and investment spending is autonomous. Equilibrium real GDP is equal to $8,000. There is no government.

Real GDP	Consumption	Saving	Investment
$ 2,000	$ 2,000	_____	_____
4,000	3,600	_____	_____
6,000	5,200	_____	_____
8,000	6,800	_____	_____
10,000	8,400	_____	_____
12,000	10,000	_____	_____

a. Complete the table. What is the marginal propensity to consume? What is the marginal propensity to save?

b. Draw a graph of the consumption function. Then add the investment function to obtain $C + I$.

c. Under the graph of $C + I$, draw another graph showing the saving and investment curves. Does the $C + I$ curve cross the 45-degree reference line in the upper graph at the same level of real GDP where the saving and investment curves cross in the lower graph, at the equilibrium real GDP of $8,000? (If not, redraw your graphs.)

d. What is the average propensity to save at equilibrium real GDP?

e. If autonomous consumption were to rise by $100, what would happen to equilibrium real GDP?

12-4. Calculate the multiplier for the following cases.

a. MPS = 0.25

b. MPC = $\frac{5}{6}$

c. MPS = 0.125

d. MPC = $\frac{6}{7}$

12-5. Assume that the multiplier in a country is equal to 4 and that autonomous real consumption spending is $1 trillion. If current real GDP is $15 trillion, what is the current value of real consumption spending?

12-6. The multiplier in a country is equal to 5, and households pay no taxes. At the current equilibrium real GDP of $14 trillion, total real consumption spending by households is $12 trillion. What is real autonomous consumption in this country?

12-7. At an initial point on the aggregate demand curve, the price level is 125, and real GDP is $15 trillion. When the price level falls to a value of 120, total autonomous expenditures increase by $250 billion. The marginal propensity to consume is 0.75. What is the level of real GDP at the new point on the aggregate demand curve?

12-8. At an initial point on the aggregate demand curve, the price level is 100, and real GDP is $15 trillion. After the price level rises to 110, however, there is an upward movement along the aggregate demand curve, and real GDP declines to $14 trillion. If total autonomous spending declined by $200 billion in response to the increase in the price level, what is the marginal propensity to consume in this economy?

12-9. In an economy in which the multiplier has a value of 3, the price level has decreased from 115 to 110. As a consequence, there has been a movement along the aggregate demand curve from $15 trillion in real GDP to $15.9 trillion in real GDP.

a. What is the marginal propensity to save?

b. What was the amount of the change in autonomous expenditures generated by the decline in the price level?

12-10. Consider the diagram on the top of the facing page, which applies to a nation with no government spending, taxes, and net exports. Use the information in the diagram to answer the following questions, and explain your answers.

a. What is the marginal propensity to save?

b. What is the present level of planned investment spending for the present period?

c. What is the equilibrium level of real GDP for the present period?

d. What is the equilibrium level of saving for the present period?

e. If planned investment spending for the present period increases by $25 billion, what will be the resulting *change* in equilibrium real GDP? What will be the new equilibrium level of real GDP if other things, including the price level, remain unchanged?

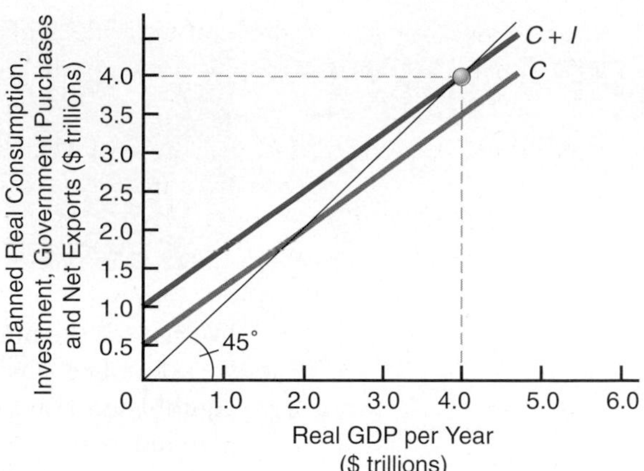

ECONOMICS ON THE NET

The Relationship Between Consumption and Real GDP According to the basic consumption function we considered in this chapter, consumption rises at a fixed rate when both disposable income and real GDP increase. Your task here is to evaluate how reasonable this assumption is and to determine the relative extent to which variations in consumption appear to be related to variations in real GDP.

Title: Gross Domestic Product and Components

Navigation: Use the link at **www.econtoday.com/ch12** to visit the Federal Reserve Bank of St. Louis's Web page on *Gross Domestic Product and Components*. Then click on *Personal Income and Outlays*.

Application

1. Scan down the alphabetical list, and click on *Personal Consumption Expenditure (Bil. of $; Q)*. Then click on "Download Data." Write down consumption expenditures for the past eight quarters. Now back up to *Gross Domestic Product and Components*, click on *Gross Domestic Product, 1 Decimal (Bil. $; Q)*, click on "Download Data," and write down GDP for the past eight quarters. Use these data to calculate implied values for the marginal propensity to consume, assuming that taxes do not vary with income. Is there any problem with this assumption?
2. Back up to *Gross Domestic Product and Components*. Select "Price Indexes & Deflators." Now click on *Gross Domestic Product: Implicit Price Deflator*. Scan through the data since the mid-1960s. In what years did the largest variations in GDP take place? What component or components of GDP appear to have accounted for these large movements?

For Group Study and Analysis Assign groups to use the FRED database to try to determine the best measure of aggregate U.S. disposable income for the past eight quarters. Reconvene as a class, and discuss each group's approach to this issue.

ANSWERS TO QUICK QUIZZES

p. 252: (i) horizontal; (ii) Saving . . . Savings; (iii) Investment

p. 257: (i) disposable income . . . consumption; (ii) average . . . average; (iii) marginal . . . marginal; (iv) movement along . . . shift in

p. 259: (i) interest rate . . . downward; (ii) expectations . . . business taxes; (iii) shift in

p. 262: (i) autonomous . . . autonomous; (ii) autonomous; (iii) equilibrium; (iv) increases . . . decreases

p. 264: (i) planned expenditures; (ii) 45-degree; (iii) decreases . . . increases

p. 269: (i) multiplier; (ii) marginal . . . save; (iii) save . . . consume; (iv) change

APPENDIX C The Keynesian Model and the Multiplier

We can see the multiplier effect more clearly if we look at Figure C-1 below, in which we see only a small section of the graphs that we used in Chapter 12. We start with equilibrium real GDP of \$14.5 trillion per year. This equilibrium occurs with total planned real expenditures represented by $C + I + G + X$. The $C + I + G + X$ curve intersects the 45-degree reference line at \$14.5 trillion per year. Now we increase real investment, I, by \$100 billion. This increase in investment shifts the entire $C + I + G + X$ curve vertically to $C + I' + G + X$. The vertical shift represents that \$100 billion increase in autonomous investment. With the higher level of planned expenditures per year, we are no longer in equilibrium at E. Inventories are falling. Production of goods and services will increase as firms try to replenish their inventories.

Eventually, real GDP will catch up with total planned expenditures. The new equilibrium level of real GDP is established at E' at the intersection of the new $C + I' + G + X$ curve and the 45-degree reference line, along which $C + I + G + X = Y$ (total planned expenditures equal real GDP). The new equilibrium level of real GDP is \$15 trillion per year. Thus, the increase in equilibrium real GDP is equal to five times the permanent increase in planned investment spending.

FIGURE C-1 Graphing the Multiplier

We can translate Table 12-3 on page 265 into graphic form by looking at each successive round of additional spending induced by an autonomous increase in planned investment of \$100 billion. The total planned expenditures curve shifts from $C + I + G + X$, with its associated equilibrium level of real GDP of \$14.5 trillion, to a new curve labeled $C + I' + G + X$. The new equilibrium level of real GDP is \$15 trillion. Equilibrium is again established.

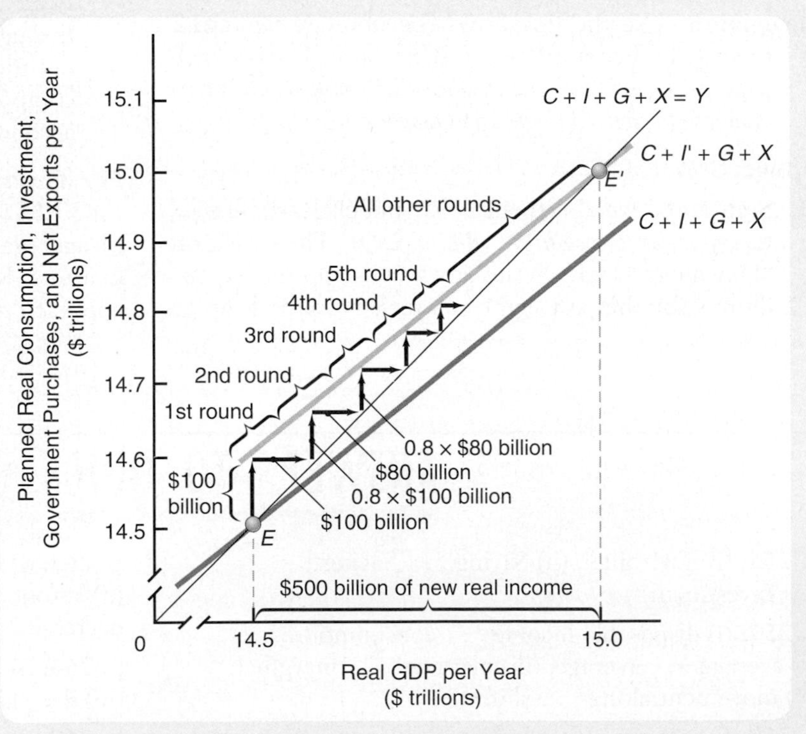

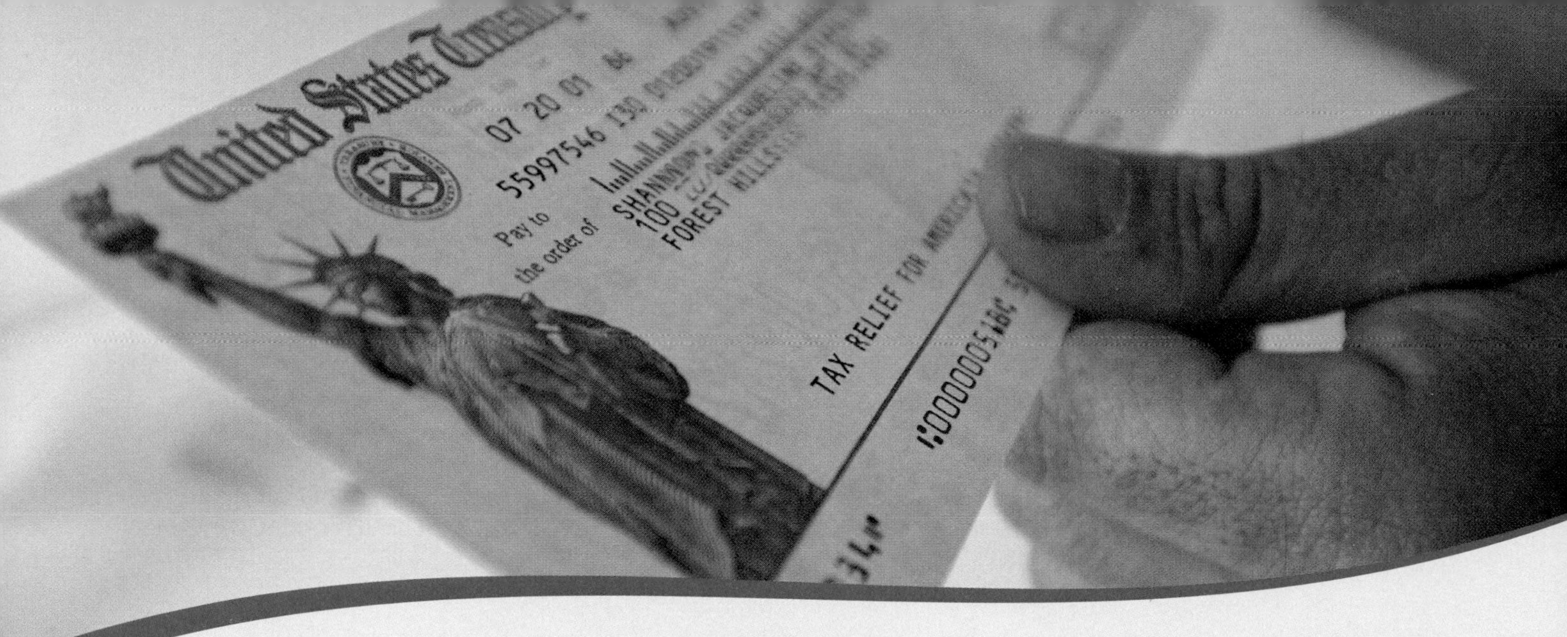

13
Fiscal Policy

When U.S. economic activity began to ebb in early 2008, the U.S. government responded by transferring portions of collected federal taxes to lower- and middle-income households as lump-sum, one-time payments called tax *rebates*. During the spring of 2009, in the depths of the Great Recession, the government authorized a second round of tax rebates. In both years, the government's intent was to boost the after-tax incomes of individuals and families receiving the rebates. The result, so the government hoped, would be greater household spending on final goods and services that would contribute to higher real GDP. In fact, after-tax incomes did increase, but household consumption expenditures responded meagerly—at best. Why and how does the U.S. government sometimes seek to influence economic activity by varying expenditures and tax receipts in its annual fiscal budget? You will find out in this chapter.

LEARNING OBJECTIVES

After reading this chapter, you should be able to:

- Use traditional Keynesian analysis to evaluate the effects of discretionary fiscal policies
- Discuss ways in which indirect crowding out and direct expenditure offsets can reduce the effectiveness of fiscal policy actions
- Explain why the Ricardian equivalence theorem calls into question the usefulness of tax changes
- List and define fiscal policy time lags and explain why they complicate efforts to engage in fiscal "fine-tuning"
- Describe how certain aspects of fiscal policy function as automatic stabilizers for the economy

Did You Know That ?

a massive fiscal stimulus package approved by the U.S. Congress in early 2009 allocated nearly \$600 billion directly to state governments during 2009 and 2010? Many states already had spent more than they were collecting in taxes—together, a total of almost \$300 billion more. Instead of directing the federal funds to *additional* spending in those years, these states used most of the funds to pay off debts generated by spending projects in progress or even completed. As a result, the net effect on *combined* federal *and* state government spending resulting from the federal transfer to the states was very small. Therefore, this portion of the intended congressional stimulus package added little to flows of *total* planned expenditures during 2009 and 2010.

To be sure, the federal government did increase its expenditures in the late 2000s and early 2010s—so much so that each year since 2008, it has spent well in excess of \$1 trillion per year more than it has collected in taxes. Indeed, inflation-adjusted annual federal government expenditures are now about 30 percent higher than they were during 2008. In this chapter, you will learn about how variations in government spending and taxation affect real GDP and the price level.

Discretionary Fiscal Policy

Fiscal policy
The discretionary changing of government expenditures or taxes to achieve national economic goals, such as high employment with price stability.

The making of deliberate, discretionary changes in federal government expenditures or taxes (or both) to achieve certain national economic goals is the realm of **fiscal policy.** Some national goals are high employment (low unemployment), price stability, and economic growth. Fiscal policy can be thought of as a deliberate attempt to cause the economy to move to full employment and price stability more quickly than it otherwise might.

Fiscal policy has typically been associated with the economic theories of John Maynard Keynes and what is now called *traditional* Keynesian analysis. Recall from Chapter 11 that Keynes's explanation of the Great Depression was that there was insufficient aggregate demand. Because he believed that wages and prices were "sticky downward," he argued that the classical economists' picture of an economy moving automatically and quickly toward full employment was inaccurate. To Keynes and his followers, government had to step in to increase aggregate demand. Expansionary fiscal policy initiated by the federal government was the preferred way to ward off recessions and depressions.

Changes in Government Spending

In Chapter 11, we looked at the recessionary gap and the inflationary gap (see Figures 11-9 and 11-10 on pages 240 and 241). The recessionary gap was defined as the amount by which the current level of real GDP falls short of the economy's *potential* production if it were operating on its *LRAS* curve. The inflationary gap was defined as the amount by which the short-run equilibrium level of real GDP exceeds the long-run equilibrium level as given by *LRAS*. Let us examine fiscal policy first in the context of a recessionary gap.

WHEN THERE IS A RECESSIONARY GAP The government, along with firms, individuals, and foreign residents, is one of the spending entities in the economy. When the government spends more, all other things held constant, the dollar value of total spending initially must rise. Look at panel (a) of Figure 13-1 on the facing page. We begin by assuming that some negative shock in the near past has left the economy at point E_1, which is a short-run equilibrium in which AD_1 intersects *SRAS* at \$14.5 trillion of real GDP per year. There is a recessionary gap of \$500 billion of real GDP per year—the difference between *LRAS* (the economy's long-run potential) and the short-run equilibrium level of real GDP per year. When the government decides to spend more (expansionary fiscal policy), the aggregate demand curve shifts to the right to AD_2. Here we assume that the government knows exactly how much more to spend so that AD_2 intersects *SRAS* at \$15 trillion, or at *LRAS*. Because of the upward-sloping *SRAS*, the price level rises from 120 to 130 as real GDP goes to \$15 trillion per year.

FIGURE 13-1 Expansionary and Contractionary Fiscal Policy: Changes in Government Spending

If there is a recessionary gap and short-run equilibrium is at E_1, in panel (a), fiscal policy can presumably increase aggregate demand to AD_2. The new equilibrium is at E_2 at higher real GDP per year and a higher price level. In panel (b), the economy is at short-run equilibrium at E_1, which is at a higher real GDP than the *LRAS*. To reduce this inflationary gap, fiscal policy can be used to decrease aggregate demand from AD_1 to AD_2. Eventually, equilibrium will fall to E_2, which is on the *LRAS*.

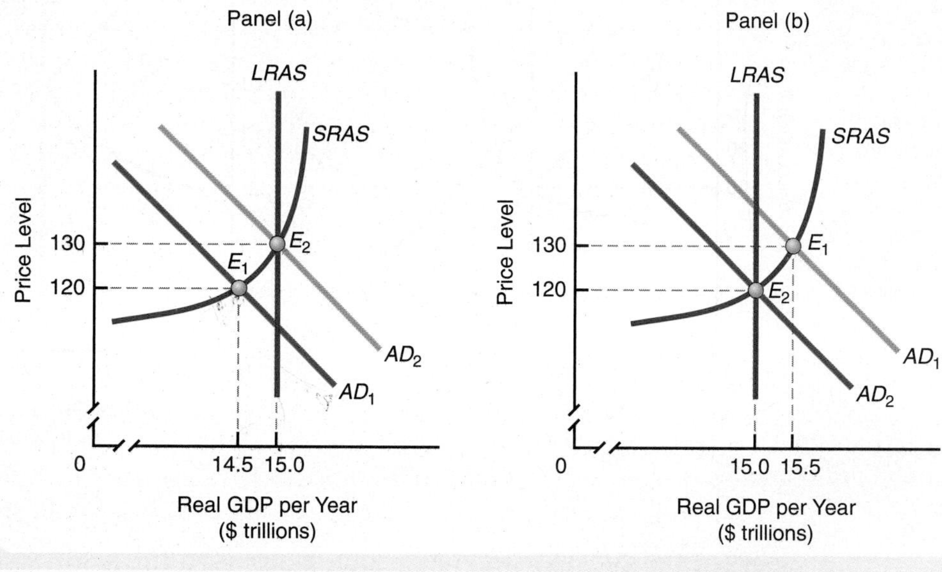

Why Not . . . end our economic troubles by borrowing to finance additional discretionary government spending?

In fact, the government is *already* borrowing to finance the bulk of its discretionary expenditures. Almost all of the federal government's revenues go toward funding nondiscretionary programs such as Social Security, Medicare, and Medicaid. Thus, since 2009, on average, the federal government has had to *borrow* more than 90 cents of *every single dollar* that it has committed to discretionary spending intended to stimulate economic activity—so far with limited success, at best.

WHEN THERE IS AN INFLATIONARY GAP The entire process shown above in panel (a) of Figure 13-1 can be reversed, as shown in panel (b). There, we assume that a recent shock has left the economy at point E_1, at which an inflationary gap exists at the intersection of *SRAS* and AD_1. Real GDP cannot be sustained at $15.5 trillion indefinitely, because this exceeds long-run aggregate supply, which in real terms is $15 trillion. If the government recognizes this and reduces its spending (pursues a contractionary fiscal policy), this action reduces aggregate demand from AD_1 to AD_2. Equilibrium will fall to E_2 on the *LRAS*, where real GDP per year is $15 trillion. The price level will fall from 130 to 120.

Changes in Taxes

The spending decisions of firms, individuals, and other countries' residents depend on the taxes levied on them. Individuals in their role as consumers look to their disposable (after-tax) income when determining their desired rates of consumption. Firms look at their after-tax profits when deciding on the levels of investment per year to undertake. Foreign residents look at the tax-inclusive cost of goods when deciding whether to buy in the United States or elsewhere. Therefore, holding all other things constant, an increase in taxes causes a reduction in aggregate demand because it reduces consumption, investment, or net exports.

FIGURE 13-2 Contractionary and Expansionary Fiscal Policy: Changes in Taxes

In panel (a), the economy is initially at E_1, where real GDP exceeds long-run equilibrium real GDP. Contractionary fiscal policy via a tax increase can move aggregate demand to AD_2 so that the new equilibrium is at E_2 at a lower price level. Real GDP is now consistent with *LRAS*, which eliminates the inflationary gap. In panel (b), with a recessionary gap (in this case of $500 billion), taxes are cut. AD_1 moves to AD_2. The economy moves from E_1 to E_2, and real GDP is now at $15 trillion per year, the long-run equilibrium level.

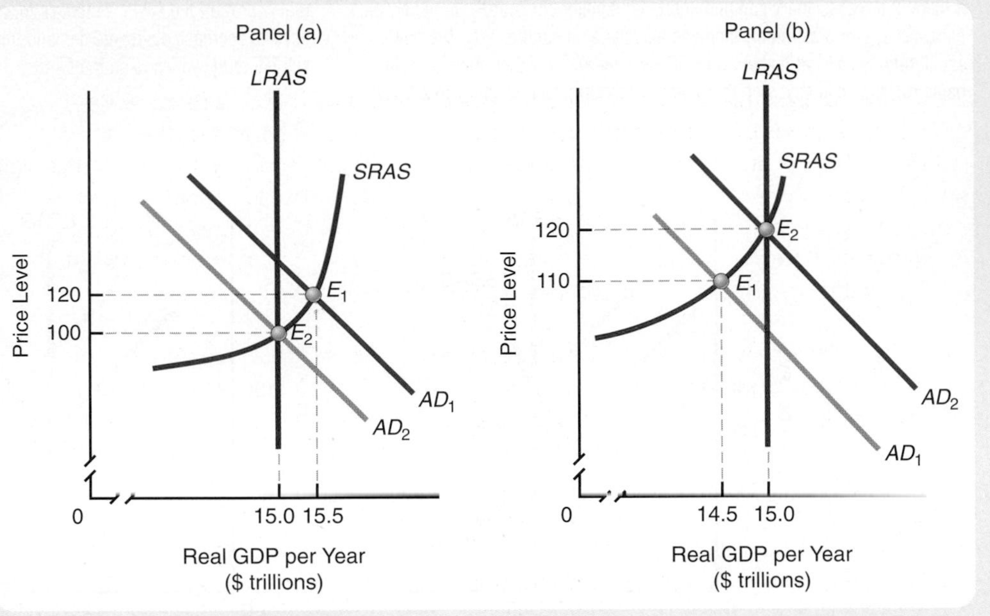

WHEN THE CURRENT SHORT-RUN EQUILIBRIUM IS TO THE RIGHT OF *LRAS* Assume that aggregate demand is AD_1 in panel (a) of Figure 13-2 above. It intersects *SRAS* at E_1, which yields real GDP greater than *LRAS*. In this situation, an increase in taxes shifts the aggregate demand curve inward to the left. For argument's sake, assume that it intersects *SRAS* at E_2, or exactly where *LRAS* intersects AD_2. In this situation, the level of real GDP falls from $15.5 trillion per year to $15 trillion per year. The price level falls from 120 to 100.

WHEN THE CURRENT SHORT-RUN EQUILIBRIUM IS TO THE LEFT OF *LRAS* Look at panel (b) in Figure 13-2. AD_1 intersects *SRAS* at E_1, with real GDP at $14.5 trillion, less than the *LRAS* of $15 trillion. In this situation, a decrease in taxes shifts the aggregate demand curve outward to the right. At AD_2, equilibrium is established at E_2, with the price level at 120 and equilibrium real GDP at $15 trillion per year.

QUICK QUIZ **See page 294 for the answers. Review concepts from this section in MyEconLab.**

Fiscal policy is defined as making discretionary changes in government __________ or __________ to achieve such national goals as high employment or reduced inflation.

To address a situation in which there is a __________ gap and the economy is operating at less than long-run aggregate supply (*LRAS*), the government can __________ its spending and thereby shift the aggregate demand curve to the right, causing the equilibrium level of real GDP per year to increase.

To address a situation in which there is an __________ gap, the government can __________ its spending and cause the aggregate demand curve to shift to the left, which reduces the equilibrium level of real GDP per year.

Changes in taxes can have similar effects on the equilibrium rate of real GDP and the price level. A __________ in taxes can lead to an increase in the equilibrium level of real GDP per year. In contrast, if there is an inflationary gap, an __________ in taxes can decrease equilibrium real GDP.

Possible Offsets to Fiscal Policy

Fiscal policy does not operate in a vacuum. Important questions must be answered: If government spending rises by, say, $300 billion, how is the spending financed, and by whom? If taxes are increased, what does the government do with the taxes? What will happen if individuals anticipate higher *future* taxes because the government is spending more today without raising current taxes? These questions involve *offsets* to the effects of current fiscal policy. We consider them in detail here.

Indirect Crowding Out

Let's take the first example of fiscal policy in this chapter—an increase in government expenditures. If government expenditures rise and taxes are held constant, something has to give. Our government does not simply take goods and services when it wants them. It has to pay for them. When it pays for them and does not simultaneously collect the same amount in taxes, it must borrow. That means that an increase in government spending without raising taxes creates additional government borrowing from the private sector (or from other countries' residents).

INDUCED INTEREST RATE CHANGES If the government attempts to borrow $1.5 trillion more per year from the private sector, as it has since 2009, it will have to offer a higher interest rate to lure the additional funds from savers. This is the interest rate effect of expansionary fiscal policy financed by borrowing from the public. Consequently, when the federal government finances increased spending by additional borrowing, it will push interest rates up. When interest rates go up, it is less profitable for firms to finance new construction, equipment, and inventories. It is also more expensive for individuals to finance purchases of cars and homes.

Thus, a rise in government spending, holding taxes constant (that is, deficit spending), tends to crowd out private spending, dampening the positive effect of increased government spending on aggregate demand. This is called the **crowding-out effect.** In the extreme case, the crowding out may be complete, with the increased government spending having no net effect on aggregate demand. The final result is simply more government spending and less private investment and consumption. Figure 13-3 below shows how the crowding-out effect occurs.

Crowding-out effect
The tendency of expansionary fiscal policy to cause a decrease in planned investment or planned consumption in the private sector. This decrease normally results from the rise in interest rates.

THE FIRM'S INVESTMENT DECISION To understand the crowding-out effect better, consider a firm that is contemplating borrowing $100,000 to expand its business. Suppose that the interest rate is 5 percent. The interest payments on the debt will be 5 percent times $100,000, or $5,000 per year ($417 per month). A rise in the interest rate to 8 percent will push the payments to 8 percent of $100,000, or $8,000 per year ($667 per month). The extra $250 per month in interest expenses will discourage some firms from making the investment. Consumers face similar decisions when they purchase houses and cars. An increase in the interest rate causes their monthly payments to go up, thereby discouraging some of them from purchasing cars and houses.

GRAPHICAL ANALYSIS You see in Figure 13-4 on the next page that the economy is in a situation in which, at point E_1, equilibrium real GDP is below the long-run level consistent with the position of the *LRAS* curve. But suppose that government expansionary fiscal policy in the form of increased government spending (without increasing current taxes) attempts to shift aggregate demand from AD_1 to AD_2. In the

FIGURE 13-3 The Crowding-Out Effect, Step by Step

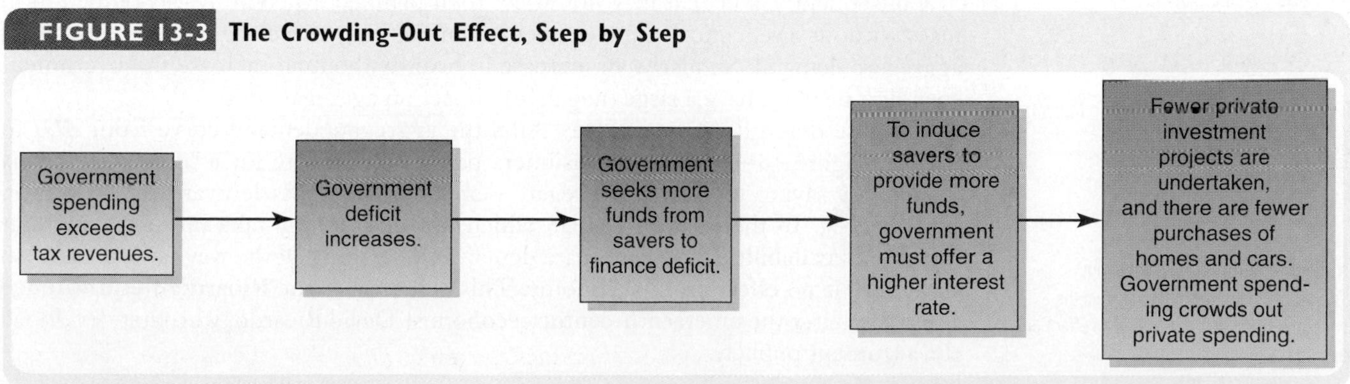

FIGURE 13-4 The Crowding-Out Effect

Expansionary fiscal policy that causes deficit financing initially shifts AD_1 to AD_2. Equilibrium initially moves toward E_2. But expansionary fiscal policy pushes up interest rates, thereby reducing interest-sensitive spending. This effect causes the aggregate demand curve to shift inward to AD_3, and the new short-run equilibrium is at E_3.

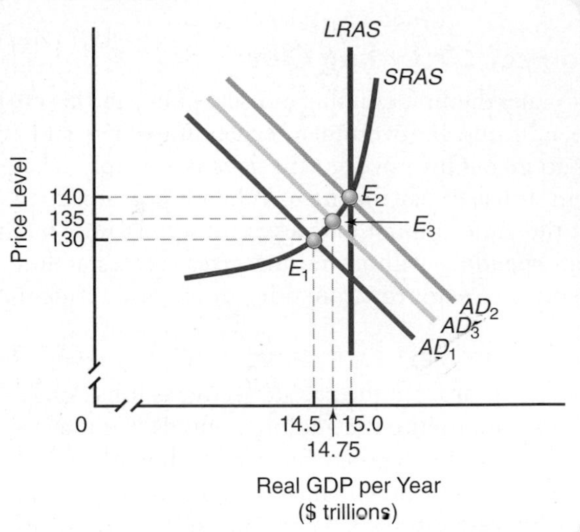

absence of the crowding-out effect, real GDP would increase to $15 trillion per year, and the price level would rise to 140 (point E_2). With the (partial) crowding-out effect, however, as investment and consumption decline, partly offsetting the rise in government spending, the aggregate demand curve shifts inward to the left to AD_3. The new short-run equilibrium is now at E_3, with real GDP of $14.75 trillion per year at a price level of 135. In other words, crowding out dilutes the effect of expansionary fiscal policy, and a recessionary gap remains.

Planning for the Future: The Ricardian Equivalence Theorem

Economists have often implicitly assumed that people look at changes in taxes or changes in government spending only in the present. What if people actually think about the size of *future* tax payments? Does this have an effect on how they react to an increase in government spending with no current tax increases? Some economists believe that the answer is yes. What if people's horizons extend beyond this year? Don't we then have to take into account the effects of today's government policies on the future?

Consider an example. The government wants to reduce taxes by $150 billion today, as it did in 2008 and 2009 via tax "rebate" programs. Assume that government spending remains constant. Assume further that the government initially has a balanced budget. Thus, the only way for the government to pay for this $150 billion tax cut is to borrow $150 billion today. The public will owe $150 billion plus interest later. Realizing that a $150 billion tax cut today is mathematically equivalent to $150 billion plus interest later, people may wish to save the proceeds from the tax cut to meet future tax liabilities—payment of interest and repayment of debt.

Consequently, a tax cut may not affect total planned expenditures. A reduction in taxes without a reduction in government spending may therefore have no impact on aggregate demand. Similarly, an increase in taxes without an increase in government spending may not have a large (negative) impact on aggregate demand.

Ricardian equivalence theorem
The proposition that an increase in the government budget deficit has no effect on aggregate demand.

Suppose that a decrease in taxes shifts the aggregate demand curve from AD_1 to AD_2 in Figure 13-4 above. If consumers partly compensate for a higher future tax liability by saving more, the aggregate demand curve shifts leftward, to a position such as AD_3. In the extreme case in which individuals fully take into account their increased tax liabilities, the aggregate demand curve shifts all the way back to AD_1, so that there is no effect on the economy. This is known as the **Ricardian equivalence theorem,** after the nineteenth-century economist David Ricardo, who first developed the argument publicly.

According to the Ricardian equivalence theorem, it does not matter how government expenditures are financed—by taxes or by borrowing. Is the theorem correct? Research indicates that Ricardian equivalence effects likely exist but has not provided much compelling evidence about their magnitudes.

Direct Expenditure Offsets

Government has a distinct comparative advantage over the private sector in certain activities such as diplomacy and national defense. Otherwise stated, certain resource-using activities in which the government engages do not compete with the private sector. In contrast, some of what government does, such as public education, competes directly with the private sector. When government competes with the private sector, **direct expenditure offsets** to fiscal policy may occur. For example, if the government starts providing milk at no charge to students who are already purchasing milk, there is a direct expenditure offset. Direct household spending on milk decreases, but government spending on milk increases.

Direct expenditure offsets
Actions on the part of the private sector in spending income that offset government fiscal policy actions. Any increase in government spending in an area that competes with the private sector will have some direct expenditure offset.

Normally, the impact of an increase in government spending on aggregate demand is analyzed by implicitly assuming that government spending is *not* a substitute for private spending. This is clearly the case for a cruise missile. Whenever government spending is a substitute for private spending, however, a rise in government spending causes a direct reduction in private spending to offset it.

THE EXTREME CASE In the extreme case, the direct expenditure offset is dollar for dollar, so we merely end up with a relabeling of spending from private to public. Assume that you have decided to spend $100 on groceries. Upon your arrival at the checkout counter, you find a U.S. Department of Agriculture official. She announces that she will pay for your groceries—but only the ones in the cart. Here increased government spending is $100. You leave the store in bliss. But just as you are deciding how to spend the $100, an Internal Revenue Service agent appears. He announces that as a result of the current budgetary crisis, your taxes are going to rise by $100. You have to pay on the spot. Increases in taxes have now been $100. We have a balanced-budget increase in government spending. In this scenario, *total* spending does not change. We simply end up with higher government spending, which directly offsets exactly an equal reduction in consumption. Aggregate demand and GDP are unchanged. Otherwise stated, if there is a full direct expenditure offset, the government spending multiplier is zero.

THE LESS EXTREME CASE Much government spending has a private-sector substitute. When government expenditures increase, private spending tends to decline somewhat (but generally not dollar for dollar), thereby mitigating the upward impact on total aggregate demand. To the extent that there are some direct expenditure offsets to expansionary fiscal policy, predicted changes in aggregate demand will be lessened. Consequently, real GDP and the price level will be less affected.

The Supply-Side Effects of Changes in Taxes

We have talked about changing taxes and changing government spending, the traditional tools of fiscal policy. We have not really talked about the possibility of changing *marginal* tax rates. Recall from Chapter 6 that the marginal tax rate is the rate applied to the last, or highest, bracket of taxable income. In our federal tax system, higher marginal tax rates are applied as income rises. In that sense, the United States has a progressive federal individual income tax system. Expansionary fiscal policy could involve reducing marginal tax rates. Advocates of such changes argue that lower tax rates will lead to an increase in productivity because individuals will work harder and longer, save more, and invest more and that increased productivity will lead to more economic growth, which will lead to higher real GDP. The government, by applying lower marginal tax rates, will not necessarily lose tax revenues, for the lower marginal tax rates will be applied to a growing tax base because of economic growth—after all, tax revenues are the product of a tax rate times a tax base.

FIGURE 13-5 Laffer Curve

The Laffer curve indicates that tax revenues initially rise with a higher tax rate. Eventually, however, tax revenues decline as the tax rate increases.

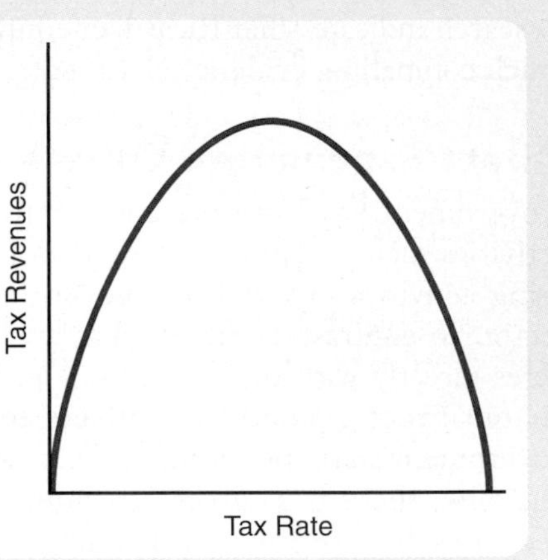

You Are There

To contemplate discretionary fiscal policy choices early in the Obama administration, take a look at **Raising Tax Rates While Emerging from a Severe Recession,** on page 288.

The relationship between tax rates and tax revenues, which you may recall from the discussion of sales taxes in Chapter 6, is sometimes called the *Laffer curve*, named after economist Arthur Laffer, who explained the relationship to some journalists and politicians in 1974. It is reproduced in Figure 13-5 above. On the vertical axis are tax revenues, and on the horizontal axis is the marginal tax rate. As you can see, total tax revenues initially rise but then eventually fall as the tax rate continues to increase after reaching some unspecified tax-revenue-maximizing rate at the top of the curve.

Supply-side economics
The suggestion that creating incentives for individuals and firms to increase productivity will cause the aggregate supply curve to shift outward.

People who support the notion that reducing tax rates does not necessarily lead to reduced tax revenues are called supply-side economists. **Supply-side economics** involves changing the tax structure to create incentives to increase productivity. Due to a shift in the aggregate supply curve to the right, there can be greater real GDP without upward pressure on the price level.

Consider the supply-side effects of changes in marginal tax rates on labor. An increase in tax rates reduces the opportunity cost of leisure, thereby inducing individuals to reduce their work effort and to consume more leisure. But an increase in tax rates will also reduce spendable income, thereby shifting the demand curve for leisure inward to the left, which tends to increase work effort. The outcome of these two effects on the choice of leisure (and thus work) depends on which of them is stronger. Supply-side economists argue that at various times, the first effect has dominated: Increases in marginal tax rates have caused workers to work less, and decreases in marginal tax rates have caused workers to work more.

Is there evidence that tax cuts have larger effects on real GDP than increases in government spending have?

POLICY EXAMPLE Which Affects Real GDP More—Spending or Tax Cuts?

In recent years, several economists have conducted studies of the impacts of changes in discretionary fiscal policy on real GDP, taking into account multiplier effects, crowding out, and changes in the price level. To do so, they have examined the effects on real GDP up to two years following the initial policy actions.

A common finding of these studies is that discretionary increases in government spending have significantly smaller effects on real GDP than do discretionary tax cuts. The studies consistently find that each $1 in real government purchases generates a net increase in real GDP of only about $0.70, whereas each $1 tax cut brings about an increase in real GDP somewhere between $1.40 and $3.00. On a dollar-for-dollar basis, therefore, changes in government spending exert effects on real GDP that are at most half the effects of tax cuts.

FOR CRITICAL ANALYSIS

Why do you think that some economists view the results of these studies as consistent with the predictions of supply-side economics?

QUICK QUIZ See page 294 for the answers. Review concepts from this section in MyEconLab.

Indirect crowding out occurs because of an interest rate effect in which the government's efforts to finance its deficit spending cause interest rates to __________, thereby crowding out private investment and spending, particularly on cars and houses. This is called the **crowding-out effect.**

__________ __________ __________ occur when government spending competes with the private sector and is increased. A direct crowding-out effect may occur.

The __________ __________ theorem holds that an increase in the government budget deficit has no effect on aggregate demand because individuals anticipate that their future taxes will increase and therefore save more today to pay for them.

Changes in marginal tax rates may cause __________-__________ effects if a reduction in marginal tax rates induces enough additional work, saving, and investing. Government tax receipts can actually increase. This is called __________-__________ economics.

Discretionary Fiscal Policy in Practice: Coping with Time Lags

We can discuss fiscal policy in a relatively precise way. We draw graphs with aggregate demand and supply curves to show what we are doing. We could in principle estimate the offsets that we just discussed. Even if we were able to measure all of these offsets exactly, however, would-be fiscal policymakers still face a problem: The conduct of fiscal policy involves a variety of time lags.

Policy Time Lags

Policymakers must take time lags into account. Not only is it difficult to measure economic variables, but it also takes time to collect and assimilate such data. Consequently, policymakers must contend with the **recognition time lag,** the months that may elapse before national economic problems can be identified.

Recognition time lag
The time required to gather information about the current state of the economy.

After an economic problem is recognized, a solution must be formulated. Thus, there will be an **action time lag** between the recognition of a problem and the implementation of policy to solve it. For fiscal policy, the action time lag is particularly long. Such policy must be approved by Congress and is subject to political wrangling and infighting. The action time lag can easily last a year or two. Then it takes time to actually implement the policy. After Congress enacts fiscal policy legislation, it takes time to decide such matters as who gets new federal construction contracts.

Action time lag
The time between recognizing an economic problem and implementing policy to solve it. The action time lag is quite long for fiscal policy, which requires congressional approval.

Finally, there is the **effect time lag:** After fiscal policy is enacted, it takes time for the policy to affect the economy. To demonstrate the effects, economists need only shift curves on a chalkboard, a whiteboard, or a piece of paper, but in the real world, such effects take quite a while to work their way through the economy.

Effect time lag
The time that elapses between the implementation of a policy and the results of that policy.

Problems Posed by Time Lags

Because the various fiscal policy time lags are long, a policy designed to combat a significant recession such as the Great Recession of the late 2000s might not produce results until the economy is already out of that recession and perhaps experiencing inflation, in which case the fiscal policy action would worsen the situation. Or a fiscal policy designed to eliminate inflation might not produce effects until the economy is in a recession. In that case, too, fiscal policy would make the economic problem worse rather than better.

Furthermore, because fiscal policy time lags tend to be *variable* (each lasting anywhere from one to three years), policymakers have a difficult time fine-tuning the economy. Clearly, fiscal policy is more guesswork than science.

Automatic Stabilizers

Not all changes in taxes (or in tax rates) or in government spending (including government transfers) constitute discretionary fiscal policy. There are several types of automatic (or nondiscretionary) fiscal policies. Such policies do not require new legislation on the part of Congress. Specific automatic fiscal policies—called **automatic, or built-in, stabilizers**—include the tax system itself, unemployment compensation, and income transfer payments.

Automatic, or built-in, stabilizers Special provisions of certain federal programs that cause changes in desired aggregate expenditures without the action of Congress and the president. Examples are the federal progressive tax system and unemployment compensation.

The Tax System as an Automatic Stabilizer

You know that if you work less, you are paid less, and therefore you pay fewer taxes. The amount of taxes that our government collects falls automatically during a recession. Basically, as observed in the U.S. economy during the severe recession of the late 2000s, incomes and profits fall when business activity slows down, and the government's tax revenues drop, too. Some economists consider this an automatic tax cut, which therefore stimulates aggregate demand. It reduces the extent of any negative economic fluctuation.

The progressive nature of the federal personal and corporate income tax systems magnifies any automatic stabilization effect that might exist. If your hours of work are reduced because of a recession, you still pay some federal personal income taxes. But because of our progressive system, you may drop into a lower tax bracket, thereby paying a lower marginal tax rate. As a result, your disposable income falls by a smaller percentage than your before-tax income falls.

Unemployment Compensation and Income Transfer Payments

Like our tax system, unemployment compensation payments stabilize aggregate demand. Throughout the course of business fluctuations, unemployment compensation reduces *changes* in people's disposable income. When business activity drops, most laid-off workers automatically become eligible for unemployment compensation from their state governments. Their disposable income therefore remains positive, although at a lower level than when they were employed. During boom periods, there is less unemployment, and consequently fewer unemployment payments are made to the labor force. Less purchasing power is being added to the economy because fewer unemployment checks are paid out. In contrast, during recessions the opposite is true.

Income transfer payments act similarly as an automatic stabilizer. When a recession occurs, more people become eligible for income transfer payments, such as Supplemental Security Income and Temporary Assistance to Needy Families. Therefore, those people do not experience as dramatic a drop in disposable income as they otherwise would have.

Stabilizing Impact

The key stabilizing impact of our tax system, unemployment compensation, and income transfer payments is their ability to mitigate changes in disposable income, consumption, and the equilibrium level of real GDP. If disposable income is prevented from falling as much as it otherwise would during a recession, the downturn will be moderated. In contrast, if disposable income is prevented from rising as rapidly as it otherwise would during a boom, the boom is less likely to get out of hand. The progressive income tax and unemployment compensation thus provide automatic stabilization to the economy. We present the argument graphically in Figure 13-6 on the facing page.

FIGURE 13-6 Automatic Stabilizers

Here we assume that as real GDP rises, tax revenues rise and government transfers fall, other things remaining constant. Thus, as the economy expands from Y_f to Y_1, a budget surplus automatically arises. As the economy contracts from Y_f to Y_2, a budget deficit automatically arises. Such automatic changes tend to drive the economy back toward its full-employment real GDP.

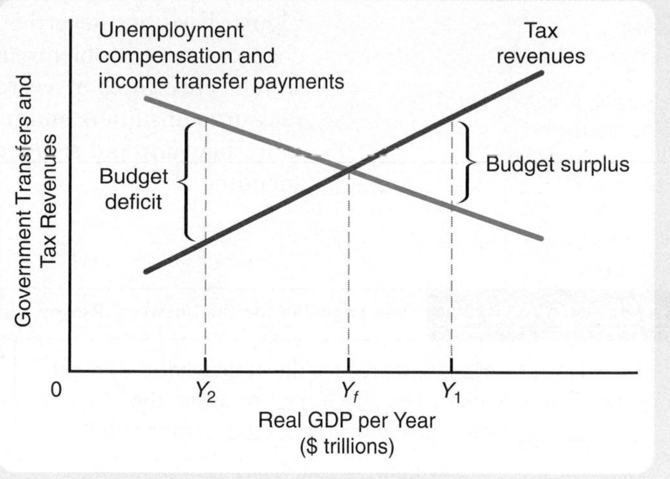

What Do We Really Know About Fiscal Policy?

There are two ways of looking at fiscal policy. One prevails during normal times and the other during abnormal times.

Fiscal Policy During Normal Times

During normal times (without "excessive" unemployment, inflation, or unusual problems in the national economy), we know that due to the recognition time lag and the modest size of any fiscal policy action that Congress will actually take, discretionary fiscal policy is probably not very effective. Congress ends up doing too little too late to help in a minor recession. Moreover, fiscal policy that generates repeated tax changes (as has happened) creates uncertainty, which may do more harm than good. To the extent that fiscal policy has any effect during normal times, it probably achieves this by way of automatic stabilizers rather than by way of discretionary policy.

Go to **www.econtoday.com/ch13** to learn about expanding spending and budget deficits of the U.S. government.

Fiscal Policy During Abnormal Times

During abnormal times, fiscal policy may be effective. Consider some classic examples: the Great Depression and war periods.

THE GREAT DEPRESSION When there is a catastrophic drop in real GDP, as there was during the Great Depression, fiscal policy may be able to stimulate aggregate demand. Because so many people have few assets left and thus are income-constrained during such periods, government spending is a way to get income into their hands—income that they are likely to spend immediately.

WARTIME Wars are in fact reserved for governments. War expenditures are not good substitutes for private expenditures—they have little or no direct expenditure offsets. Consequently, war spending as part of expansionary fiscal policy usually has noteworthy effects, such as occurred while we were waging World War II, when real GDP increased dramatically (though much of the output of new goods and services was expended for military uses).

The "Soothing" Effect of Keynesian Fiscal Policy

One view of traditional Keynesian fiscal policy does not call for it to be used on a regular basis but nevertheless sees it as potentially useful. As you have learned in this chapter, many problems are associated with attempting to use fiscal policy. But if we should encounter a severe downturn, fiscal policy is available. Knowing this may reassure consumers and investors. Thus, the availability of fiscal policy may induce more buoyant and stable expectations of the future, thereby smoothing investment spending.

QUICK QUIZ See page 294 for the answers. Review concepts from this section in MyEconLab.

Time lags of various sorts reduce the effectiveness of fiscal policy. These include the __________ time lag, the __________ time lag, and the __________ time lag.

Two __________, or built-in, stabilizers are the progressive income tax and unemployment compensation.

Built-in stabilizers automatically tend to __________ changes in disposable income resulting from changes in overall business activity.

Although discretionary fiscal policy may not necessarily be a useful policy tool in normal times because of time lags, it may work well during __________ times, such as depressions and wartimes. In addition, the existence of fiscal policy may have a soothing effect on consumers and investors.

You Are There

Raising Tax Rates While Emerging from a Severe Recession

It is early 2010, and White House Budget Director Peter Orszag is anticipating that the government's tax revenues will fall short of its spending every year for the rest of the 2010s. Thus, Orszag is counting on changes in several federal tax rates:

1. A rise in the top personal income tax rate from 35 percent to 39.6 percent.
2. An increase in the top tax rate on corporate dividends from 15 percent to 39.6 percent.
3. An increase in the capital gains tax rate from 15 percent to 20 percent.
4. The imposition of a new tax rate on bank liabilities that is expected to generate almost $10 billion per year.
5. An increase in the tax rate assessed on estates of deceased individuals from 0 percent to at least 45 percent.

In Orszag's view, the only way to bring revenues and spending back into closer balance is to raise these federal tax rates. He and everyone else at the White House are hoping that increased annual government spending will stimulate the economy sufficiently to make up for the contractionary effects of these higher tax rates. Otherwise, the economy's slow recovery from the depths of the most severe recession since the Great Depression of the 1930s could be stopped in its tracks.

Critical Analysis Questions

1. In principle, could the federal budget eventually be balanced by cutting both tax rates and annual government expenditures? Explain briefly.
2. How would proponents of supply-side economics critique Orszag's prescription for fiscal policy?

ISSUES & APPLICATIONS

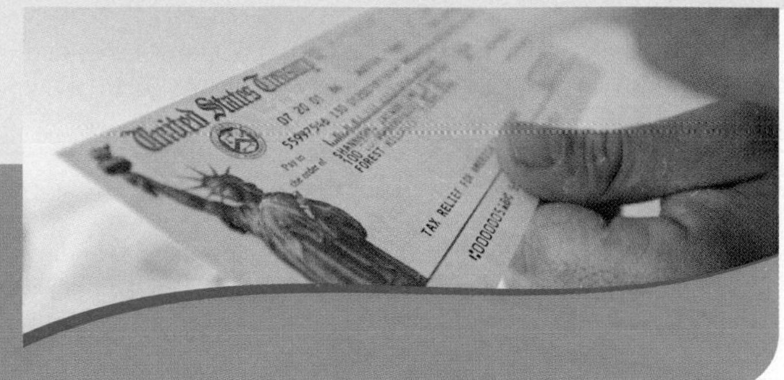

Temporary Tax Rebates Prove to Be Nonstimulating

CONCEPTS APPLIED

- Fiscal Policy
- Ricardian Equivalence Theorem
- Supply-Side Economics

In 2008 and again in 2009, the U.S. government implemented fiscal policy actions in the form of one-time tax *rebates*—lump-sum payments—of between $250 and $800 to millions of low- and middle-income individuals and families. The objective was to raise households' real disposable incomes and real consumption spending, which would boost total planned real expenditures and, ultimately, real GDP.

Higher Disposable Income but Meager Impacts on Consumption

Figure 13-7 below displays inflation-adjusted disposable personal income and personal consumption expenditures since January 2007. The figure shows that real disposable income rose after the federal government transmitted tax rebates to millions of households in the spring of 2008 and again in the spring of 2009.

Figure 13-7 also reveals, however, that significant increases in real consumption expenditures did not materialize. The attempt to stimulate economic activity via higher real consumption expenditures failed.

FIGURE 13-7 U.S. Real Disposable Personal Income and Real Personal Consumption Expenditures Since January 2007

One-time tax rebates distributed during the spring of 2008 and again during the spring of 2009 temporarily pushed up inflation-adjusted disposable personal income but failed to boost real personal consumption expenditures.

Source: Bureau of Economic Analysis.

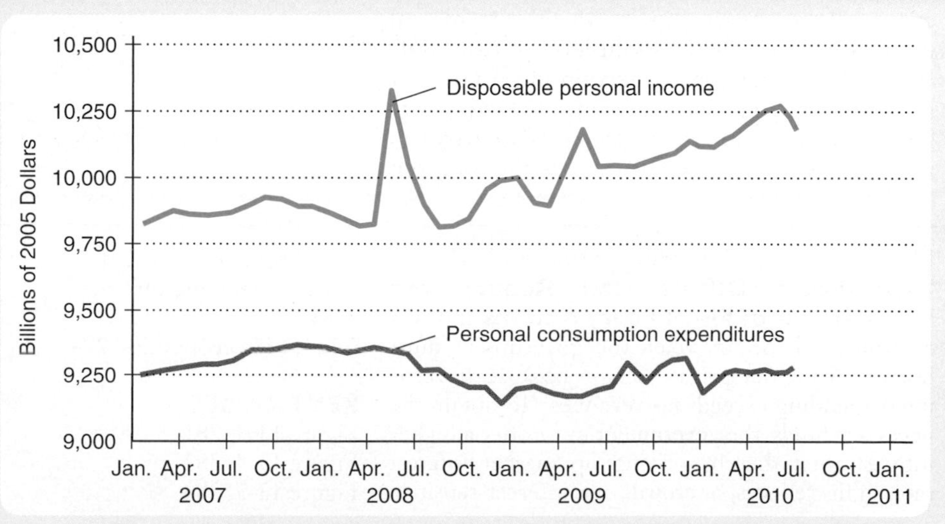

Why the Tax Rebates Fizzled

Economists have advanced three explanations for why the tax rebates failed to boost consumption spending. First, many people who received the rebates used them to pay off debts instead of spending the funds on goods and services.

Second, the government financed the rebates by borrowing, so a number of households responded as predicted by the Ricardian equivalence theorem. They saved the rebates in anticipation of having to pay higher taxes later.

Third, supply-side economics suggests that real GDP would respond to permanent reductions in income tax *rates*. Because the tax rebates were temporary lump sums, their effects on spending were automatically limited, and they failed to provide any incentive for businesses to increase their production of goods and services.

For Critical Analysis

1. How might the threat of higher future taxes to repay a growing net public debt induce people to save tax rebates instead of spending them?
2. Why do you think that reductions in tax rates usually have larger effects on real consumption spending and real GDP than one-time, lump-sum tax rebates?

Web Resources

1. To read a Congressional Budget Office evaluation of the consumption effects of tax rebates, go to www.econtoday.com/ch13.
2. For an analysis of why the 2008 and 2009 tax rebates had such small effects on consumption spending, go to www.econtoday.com/ch13.

Research Project

Evaluate why households tend to increase their annual spending flows more in response to *permanent* tax cuts than to *temporary* tax cuts.

For more questions on this chapter's Issues & Applications, go to **MyEconLab**. In the Study Plan for this chapter, select Section N: News.

Here is what you should know after reading this chapter. **MyEconLab** will help you identify what you know, and where to go when you need to practice.

WHAT YOU SHOULD KNOW		WHERE TO GO TO PRACTICE
The Effects of Discretionary Fiscal Policies Using Traditional Keynesian Analysis In short-run Keynesian analysis, a deliberate increase in government spending or a reduction in taxes shifts the aggregate demand curve outward and thereby closes a recessionary gap in which current real GDP is less than the long-run level of real GDP. Likewise, an intentional reduction in government spending or a tax increase shifts the aggregate demand curve inward and closes an inflationary gap in which current real GDP exceeds the long-run level of real GDP.	fiscal policy, 278 **KEY FIGURES** Figure 13-1, 279 Figure 13-2, 280	• **MyEconLab** Study Plan 13.1 • Audio introduction to Chapter 13 • Economics Video: Cash for Trash • Economics Video: Government Should Leave Farm Business • Animated Figures 13-1, 13-2
How Indirect Crowding Out and Direct Expenditure Offsets Can Reduce the Effectiveness of Fiscal Policy Actions Indirect crowding out occurs when the government must borrow from the private sector because government spending exceeds tax revenues. To obtain the necessary funds, the government must offer a higher interest rate, thereby driving up market interest rates. This reduces, or crowds out, interest-sensitive	crowding-out effect, 281 direct expenditure offsets, 283 supply-side economics, 284 **KEY FIGURES** Figure 13-3, 281 Figure 13-4, 282 Figure 13-5, 284	• **MyEconLab** Study Plan 13.2 • Video: The Crowding-Out Effect • Animated Figures 13-3, 13-4, 13-5

MyEconLab continued

WHAT YOU SHOULD KNOW		WHERE TO GO TO PRACTICE
private spending, thereby reducing the net effect of the fiscal expansion on aggregate demand and equilibrium real GDP. Increased government spending may also substitute directly for private expenditures, and the resulting decline in private spending directly offsets the increase in total planned expenditures that the government had intended to bring about.		
The Ricardian Equivalence Theorem This proposition states that when the government cuts taxes and borrows to finance the tax reduction, people realize that eventually the government will have to repay the loan. Thus, they anticipate that taxes will have to increase in the future. This induces them to save the proceeds of the tax cut to meet their future tax liabilities. Thus, a tax cut fails to induce an increase in aggregate consumption spending and consequently has no effect on total planned expenditures and aggregate demand.	Ricardian equivalence theorem, 282 **KEY FIGURE** Figure 13-4, 282	• **MyEconLab** Study Plan 13.2 • Animated Figure 13-4
Fiscal Policy Time Lags and the Effectiveness of Fiscal "Fine-Tuning" Efforts to engage in fiscal policy actions intended to bring about changes in aggregate demand are complicated by policy time lags. One of these is the recognition time lag, which is the time required to collect information about the economy's current situation. Another is the action time lag, the period between recognition of a problem and implementation of a policy intended to address it. Finally, there is the effect time lag, which is the interval between the implementation of a policy and its having an effect on the economy.	recognition time lag, 285 action time lag, 285 effect time lag, 285	• **MyEconLab** Study Plan 13.3 • Video: Time Lags
Automatic Stabilizers In our tax system, income taxes diminish automatically when economic activity drops, and unemployment compensation and income transfer payments increase. Thus, when there is a decline in real GDP, the automatic reduction in income tax collections and increases in unemployment compensation and income transfer payments tend to minimize the reduction in total planned expenditures that would otherwise have resulted.	automatic, or built-in, stabilizers, 286 **KEY FIGURE** Figure 13-6, 287	• **MyEconLab** Study Plans 13.4, 13.5 • Animated Figure 13-6

Log in to MyEconLab, take a chapter test, and get a personalized Study Plan that tells you which concepts you understand and which ones you need to review. From there, MyEconLab will give you further practice, tutorials, animations, videos, and guided solutions. Log in to www.myeconlab.com

PROBLEMS

All problems are assignable in myeconlab. *Answers to odd-numbered problems appear at the back of the book.*

13-1. Suppose that Congress and the president decide that the nation's economic performance is weakening and that the government should "do something" about the situation. They make no tax changes but do enact new laws increasing government spending on a variety of programs.

a. Prior to the congressional and presidential action, careful studies by government economists indicated that the direct multiplier effect of a rise in government expenditures on equilibrium real GDP is equal to 6. In the 12 months since the increase in government spending, however, it has become clear that the actual ultimate effect on real GDP will be less than half of that amount. What factors might account for this?

b. Another year and a half elapses following passage of the government spending boost. The government has undertaken no additional policy actions, nor have there been any other events of significance. Nevertheless, by the end of the second year, real GDP has returned to its original level, and the price level has increased sharply. Provide a possible explanation for this outcome.

13-2. Suppose that Congress enacts a significant tax cut with the expectation that this action will stimulate aggregate demand and push up real GDP in the short run. In fact, however, neither real GDP nor the price level changes significantly as a result of the tax cut. What might account for this outcome?

13-3. Explain how time lags in discretionary fiscal policymaking could thwart the efforts of Congress and the president to stabilize real GDP in the face of an economic downturn. Is it possible that these time lags could actually cause discretionary fiscal policy to *destabilize* real GDP?

13-4. Determine whether each of the following is an example of a direct expenditure offset to fiscal policy.

a. In an effort to help rejuvenate the nation's railroad system, a new government agency buys unused track, locomotives, and passenger and freight cars, many of which private companies would otherwise have purchased and put into regular use.

b. The government increases its expenditures without raising taxes. To cover the resulting budget deficit, it borrows more funds from the private sector, thereby pushing up the market interest rate and discouraging private planned investment spending.

c. The government finances the construction of a classical music museum that otherwise would never have received private funding.

13-5. Determine whether each of the following is an example of indirect crowding out resulting from an expansionary fiscal policy action.

a. The government provides a subsidy to help keep an existing firm operating, even though a group of investors otherwise would have provided a cash infusion that would have kept the company in business.

b. The government reduces its taxes without decreasing its expenditures. To cover the resulting budget deficit, it borrows more funds from the private sector, thereby pushing up the market interest rate and discouraging private planned investment spending.

c. Government expenditures fund construction of a high-rise office building on a plot of land where a private company otherwise would have constructed an essentially identical building.

13-6. The U.S. government is in the midst of spending more than $1 billion on seven buildings containing more than 100,000 square feet of space to be used for study of infectious diseases. Prior to the government's decision to construct these buildings, a few universities had been planning to build essentially the same facilities using privately obtained funds. After construction on the government buildings began, however, the universities dropped their plans. Evaluate whether the government's $1 billion expenditure is actually likely to push U.S. real GDP above the level it would have reached in the absence of the government's construction spree.

13-7. Determine whether each of the following is an example of a discretionary fiscal policy action.

a. A recession occurs, and government-funded unemployment compensation is paid to laid-off workers.

b. Congress votes to fund a new jobs program designed to put unemployed workers to work.

c. The Federal Reserve decides to reduce the quantity of money in circulation in an effort to slow inflation.

d. Under powers authorized by an act of Congress, the president decides to authorize an emergency release of funds for spending programs intended to head off economic crises.

13-8. Determine whether each of the following is an example of an automatic fiscal stabilizer.

a. A government agency arranges to make loans to businesses whenever an economic downturn begins.

b. As the economy heats up, the resulting increase in equilibrium real GDP immediately results in higher income tax payments, which dampen consumption spending somewhat.

c. As the economy starts to recover from a severe recession and more people go back to work, government-funded unemployment compensation payments begin to decline.

d. To stem an overheated economy, the president, using special powers granted by Congress, authorizes emergency impoundment of funds that Congress had previously authorized for spending on government programs.

13-9. Consider the diagram below, in which the current short-run equilibrium is at point *A*, and answer the questions that follow.

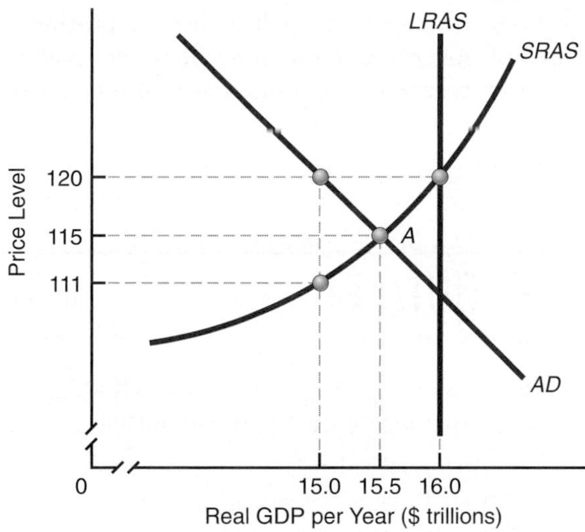

a. What type of gap exists at point *A*?

b. If the marginal propensity to save equals 0.20, what change in government spending financed by borrowing from the private sector could eliminate the gap identified in part (a)? Explain.

13-10. Consider the diagram in the next column, in which the current short-run equilibrium is at point *A*, and answer the questions that follow.

a. What type of gap exists at point *A*?

b. If the marginal propensity to consume equals 0.75, what change in government spending financed by borrowing from the private sector could eliminate the gap identified in part (a)? Explain.

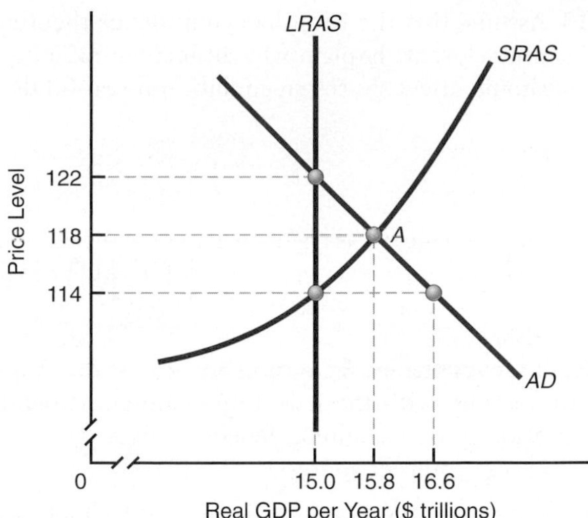

13-11. Currently, a government's budget is balanced. The marginal propensity to consume is 0.80. The government has determined that each additional $10 billion it borrows to finance a budget deficit pushes up the market interest rate by 0.1 percentage point. It has also determined that every 0.1-percentage-point change in the market interest rate generates a change in planned investment expenditures equal to $2 billion. Finally, the government knows that to close a recessionary gap and take into account the resulting change in the price level, it must generate a net rightward shift in the aggregate demand curve equal to $200 billion. Assuming that there are no direct expenditure offsets to fiscal policy, how much should the government increase its expenditures? (Hint: How much private investment spending will each $10 billion increase in government spending crowd out?)

13-12. A government is currently operating with an annual budget deficit of $40 billion. The government has determined that every $10 billion reduction in the amount it borrows each year would reduce the market interest rate by 0.1 percentage point. Furthermore, it has determined that every 0.1-percentage-point change in the market interest rate generates a change in planned investment expenditures in the opposite direction equal to $5 billion. The marginal propensity to consume is 0.75. Finally, the government knows that to eliminate an inflationary gap and take into account the resulting change in the price level, it must generate a net leftward shift in the aggregate demand curve equal to $40 billion. Assuming that there are no direct expenditure offsets to fiscal policy, how much should the government increase taxes? (Hint: How much new private investment spending is induced by each $10 billion decrease in government spending?)

13-13. Assume that the Ricardian equivalence theorem is not relevant. Explain why an income-tax-rate cut should affect short-run equilibrium real GDP.

13-14. Suppose that Congress enacts a lump-sum tax cut of $750 billion. The marginal propensity to consume is equal to 0.75. Assuming that Ricardian equivalence holds true, what is the effect on equilibrium real GDP? On saving?

ECONOMICS ON THE NET

Federal Government Spending and Taxation A quick way to keep up with the federal government's spending and taxation is by examining federal budget data at the White House Internet address.

Title: Historical Tables: Budget of the United States Government

Navigation: Use the link at **www.econtoday.com/ch13** to visit the Office of Management and Budget. Select the most recent budget. Then click on *Historical Tables.*

Application After the document downloads, perform the indicated operations and answer the questions.

1. Go to section 2, "Composition of Federal Government Receipts." Take a look at Table 2.2, "Percentage Composition of Receipts by Source." Before World War II, what was the key source of revenues of the federal government? What has been the key revenue source since World War II?
2. Now scan down the document to Table 2.3, "Receipts by Source as Percentages of GDP." Have any government revenue sources declined as a percentage of GDP? Which ones have noticeably risen in recent years?

For Group Study and Analysis Split into four groups, and have each group examine section 3, "Federal Government Outlays by Function," and in particular Table 3.1, "Outlays by Superfunction and Function." Assign groups to the following functions: national defense, health, income security, and Social Security. Have each group prepare a brief report concerning recent and long-term trends in government spending on each function. Which functions have been capturing growing shares of government spending in recent years? Which have been receiving declining shares of total spending?

ANSWERS TO QUICK QUIZZES

p. 280: (i) expenditures . . . taxes; (ii) recessionary . . . increase; (iii) inflationary . . . decrease; (iv) decrease . . . increase

p. 285: (i) increase; (ii) Direct expenditure offsets; (iii) Ricardian equivalence; (iv) supply-side . . . supply-side

p. 288: (i) recognition . . . action . . . effect; (ii) automatic; (iii) moderate; (iv) abnormal

Fiscal Policy: A Keynesian Perspective

APPENDIX D

The traditional Keynesian approach to fiscal policy differs in three ways from that presented in Chapter 13. First, it emphasizes the underpinnings of the components of aggregate demand. Second, it assumes that government expenditures are not substitutes for private expenditures and that current taxes are the only taxes taken into account by consumers and firms. Third, the traditional Keynesian approach focuses on the short run and so assumes that as a first approximation, the price level is constant.

Changes in Government Spending

Figure D-1 below measures real GDP along the horizontal axis and total planned real expenditures (aggregate demand) along the vertical axis. The components of aggregate demand are real consumption (C), investment (I), government spending (G), and net exports (X). The height of the schedule labeled $C + I + G + X$ shows total planned real expenditures (aggregate demand) as a function of real GDP. This schedule slopes upward because consumption depends positively on real GDP. Everywhere along the 45-degree reference line, planned real spending equals real GDP. At the point Y^*, where the $C + I + G + X$ line intersects the 45-degree line, planned real spending is consistent with real GDP per year. At any income less than Y^*, spending exceeds real GDP, and so real GDP and thus real spending will tend to rise. At any level of real GDP greater than Y^*, planned spending is less than real GDP, and so real GDP and thus spending will tend to decline. Given the determinants of C, I, G, and X, total real spending (aggregate demand) will be Y^*.

The Keynesian approach assumes that changes in government spending cause no direct offsets in either consumption or investment spending because G is not a substitute for C, I, or X. Hence, a rise in government spending from G to G' causes the

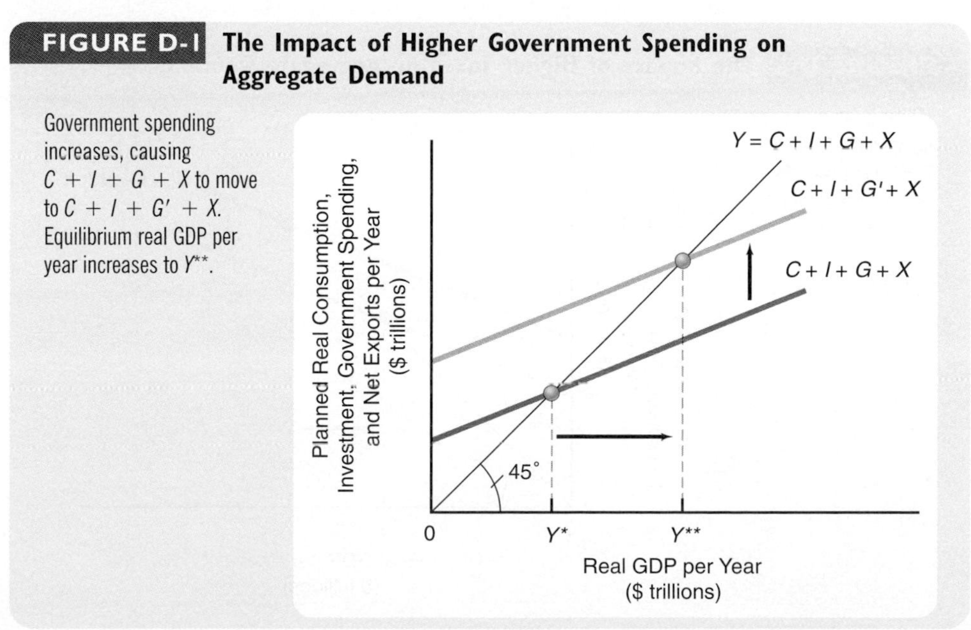

FIGURE D-1 The Impact of Higher Government Spending on Aggregate Demand

Government spending increases, causing $C + I + G + X$ to move to $C + I + G' + X$. Equilibrium real GDP per year increases to Y^{**}.

$C + I + G + X$ line to shift upward by the full amount of the rise in government spending, yielding the line $C + I + G' + X$. The rise in real government spending causes real GDP to rise, which in turn causes consumption spending to rise, which further increases real GDP. Ultimately, aggregate demand rises to Y^{**}, where spending again equals real GDP. A key conclusion of the traditional Keynesian analysis is that total spending rises by *more* than the original rise in government spending because consumption spending depends positively on real GDP.

Changes in Taxes

According to the Keynesian approach, changes in current taxes affect aggregate demand by changing the amount of real disposable (after-tax) income available to consumers. A rise in taxes reduces disposable income and thus reduces real consumption; conversely, a tax cut raises disposable income and thus causes a rise in consumption spending. The effects of a tax increase are shown in Figure D-2 below. Higher taxes cause consumption spending to decline from C to C', causing total spending to shift downward to $C' + I + G + X$. In general, the decline in consumption will be less than the increase in taxes because people will also reduce their saving to help pay the higher taxes.

The Balanced-Budget Multiplier

One interesting implication of the Keynesian approach concerns the impact of a balanced-budget change in government real spending. Suppose that the government increases spending by \$1 billion and pays for it by raising current taxes by \$1 billion. Such a policy is called a *balanced-budget increase in real spending*. Because the higher spending tends to push aggregate demand *up* by *more* than \$1 billion while the higher taxes tend to push aggregate demand *down* by *less* than \$1 billion, a most remarkable thing happens: A balanced-budget increase in G causes total spending to rise by *exactly* the amount of the rise in G—in this case, \$1 billion. We say that the *balanced-budget multiplier* is equal to 1. Similarly, a balanced-budget reduction in government spending will cause total spending to fall by exactly the amount of the government spending cut.

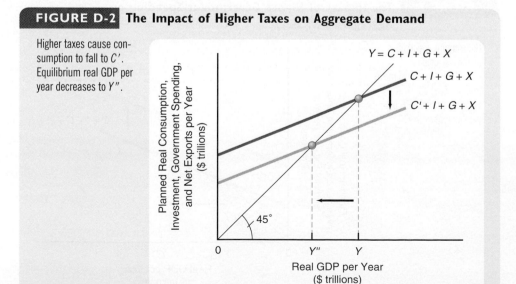

FIGURE D-2 The Impact of Higher Taxes on Aggregate Demand

Higher taxes cause consumption to fall to C'. Equilibrium real GDP per year decreases to Y''.

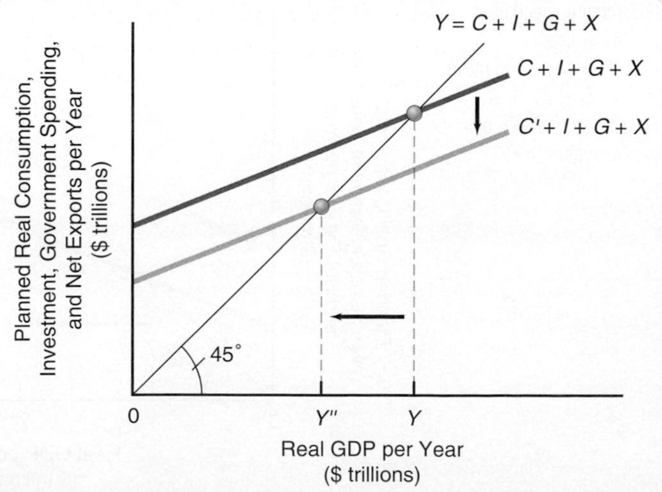

Y = C + I + G + X
C + I + G + X
C' + I + G + X
Planned Real Consumption, Investment, Government Spending, and Net Exports per Year ($ trillions)
45°
0
Y''
Y
Real GDP per Year ($ trillions)

The Fixed Price Level Assumption

The final key feature of the traditional Keynesian approach is that it typically assumes that as a first approximation, the price level is fixed. Recall that nominal GDP equals the price level multiplied by real GDP. If the price level is fixed, an increase in government spending that causes nominal GDP to rise will show up exclusively as a rise in *real* GDP. This will in turn be accompanied by a decline in the unemployment rate because the additional real GDP can be produced only if additional factors of production, such as labor, are utilized.

PROBLEMS

All problems are assignable in myeconlab*. Answers to odd-numbered problems appear at the back of the book.*

D-1. Assume that equilibrium real GDP is \$15.2 trillion and full-employment equilibrium (*FE*) is \$15.55 trillion. The marginal propensity to save is $\frac{1}{7}$. Answer the questions using the data in the following graph.

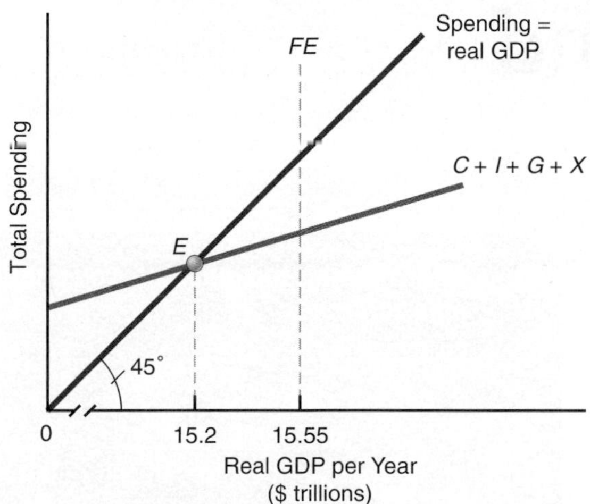

a. What is the marginal propensity to consume?

b. By how much must new investment or government spending increase to bring the economy up to full employment?

c. By how much must government cut personal taxes to stimulate the economy to the full-employment equilibrium?

D-2. Assume that MPC $= \frac{4}{5}$ when answering the following questions.

a. If government expenditures rise by \$2 billion, by how much will the aggregate expenditure curve shift upward? By how much will equilibrium real GDP per year change?

b. If taxes increase by \$2 billion, by how much will the aggregate expenditure curve shift downward? By how much will equilibrium real GDP per year change?

D-3. Assume that MPC $= \frac{4}{5}$ when answering the following questions.

a. If government expenditures rise by \$1 billion, by how much will the aggregate expenditure curve shift upward?

b. If taxes rise by \$1 billion, by how much will the aggregate expenditure curve shift downward?

c. If both taxes and government expenditures rise by \$1 billion, by how much will the aggregate expenditure curve shift? What will happen to the equilibrium level of real GDP?

d. How does your response to the second question in part (c) change if MPC $= \frac{3}{4}$? If MPC $= \frac{1}{2}$?

14

Deficit Spending and the Public Debt

Since 2007, the U.S. government's average annual *budget deficit*—its flow of spending in excess of its flow of tax collections—has increased by about 400 percent. During the same period, the government's accumulated indebtedness, called the *net public debt,* has risen by more than 100 percent, and as a percentage of U.S. GDP, it is at its highest level since World War II. Why have U.S. government budget deficits and the net public debt increased so quickly? Is the United States alone in experiencing substantially greater annual flows of government budget deficits and stocks of indebtedness? To contemplate the answers to these questions, you must first learn about the relationship between government budget deficits and the net public debt, which is a key topic of this chapter.

LEARNING OBJECTIVES

After reading this chapter, you should be able to:

- Explain how federal government budget deficits occur
- Define the public debt and understand alternative measures of the public debt
- Evaluate circumstances under which the public debt could be a burden to future generations
- Analyze the macroeconomic effects of government budget deficits
- Describe possible ways to reduce the government budget deficit

myeconlab

MyEconLab helps you master each objective and study more efficiently. See end of chapter for details.

Did You Know That

the typical baby born somewhere in the United States during the next few minutes already owes about $45,000? This is the baby's share of the U.S. government's debt obligations. Each year since 2008, the government has spent at least $4,000 more per U.S. resident than it has collected in taxes from a typical resident. To finance this extra spending, the government has been borrowing every year and thereby rapidly accumulating additional debts. If the government continues to spend in excess of taxes at the current pace, by 2014 a newborn U.S. resident will arrive owing more than $55,000.

Every year since 2001, the U.S. government has spent more than it collected in taxes. The government anticipates that it will continue to spend more than it receives indefinitely. Should you be worried about this? The answer, as you will see in this chapter, is both yes and no. First, let's examine what the government does when it spends more than it receives.

Public Deficits and Debts: Flows versus Stocks

A **government budget deficit** exists if the government spends more than it receives in taxes during a given period of time. The government has to finance this shortfall somehow. Barring any resort to money creation (the subject matter of Chapters 15 and 16), the U.S. Treasury sells IOUs on behalf of the U.S. government, in the form of securities that are normally called bonds. In effect, the federal government asks U.S. and foreign households, businesses, and governments to lend funds to the government to cover its deficit. For example, if the federal government spends $1 trillion more than it receives in revenues, the Treasury will obtain that $1 trillion by selling $1 trillion of new Treasury bonds. Those who buy the Treasury bonds (lend funds to the U.S. government) will receive interest payments over the life of the bond plus eventual repayment of the entire amount lent. In return, the U.S. Treasury receives immediate purchasing power. In the process, it also adds to its indebtedness to bondholders.

Government budget deficit
An excess of government spending over government revenues during a given period of time.

Distinguishing Between Deficits and Debts

You have already learned about flows. GDP, for instance, is a flow because it is a dollar measure of the total amount of final goods and services produced within a given period of time, such as a year.

The federal deficit is also a flow. Suppose that the current federal deficit is $1.5 trillion. Consequently, the federal government is currently spending at a rate of $1.5 trillion *per year* more than it is collecting in taxes and other revenues.

Of course, governments do not always spend more each year than the revenues they receive. If a government spends an amount exactly equal to the revenues it collects during a given period, then during this interval the government operates with a **balanced budget.** If a government spends less than the revenues it receives during a given period, then during this interval it experiences a **government budget surplus.**

Balanced budget
A situation in which the government's spending is exactly equal to the total taxes and other revenues it collects during a given period of time.

Government budget surplus
An excess of government revenues over government spending during a given period of time.

The Public Debt

You have also learned about stocks, which are measured at a point in time. Stocks change between points in time as a result of flows. The amount of unemployment, for example, is a stock. It is the total number of people looking for work but unable to find it at a given point in time. Suppose that the stock of unemployed workers at the beginning of the month is 15.3 million and that at the end of the month the stock of unemployed workers has increased to 15.5 million. This means that during the month, assuming an unchanged labor force, there was a net flow of 0.2 million individuals away from the state of being employed into the state of being out of work but seeking employment.

Likewise, the total accumulated **public debt** is a stock measured at a given point in time, and it changes from one time to another as a result of government budget deficits or surpluses. For instance, on December 31, 2009, one measure of the public debt was about $7.5 trillion. During 2010, the federal government operated at a

Public debt
The total value of all outstanding federal government securities.

Go to www.econtoday.com/ch14 to learn more about the activities of the Congressional Budget Office, which reports to the legislative branch of the U.S. government about the current state of the federal government's spending and receipts.

deficit of nearly $1.8 trillion. As a consequence, on December 31, 2010, this measure of the public debt had increased to about $9.3 trillion.

Government Finance: Spending More Than Tax Collections

Following four consecutive years—1998 through 2001—of official budget surpluses, the federal government began to experience budget deficits once more beginning in 2002. Since then, government spending has increased considerably, and tax revenues have failed to keep pace. Consequently, the federal government has operated with a deficit. Indeed, since 2009 the federal budget deficit has widened dramatically—to inflation-adjusted levels not seen since World War II.

The Historical Record of Federal Budget Deficits

Figure 14-1 below charts inflation-adjusted expenditures and revenues of the federal government since 1940. The *real* annual budget deficit is the arithmetic difference between real expenditures and real revenues during years in which the government's spending has exceeded its revenues. As you can see, there is nothing out of the ordinary about federal budget deficits. Indeed, the annual budget surpluses of 1998 through 2001 were somewhat out of the ordinary. The 1998 budget surplus was the first since 1968, when the government briefly operated with a surplus. Before the 1998–2001 budget surpluses, the U.S. government had not experienced back-to-back annual surpluses since the 1950s.

Indeed, since 1940 the U.S. government has operated with an annual budget surplus for a total of only 13 years. In all other years, it has collected insufficient taxes and other revenues to fund its spending. Every year this has occurred, the federal government has borrowed to finance its additional expenditures.

FIGURE 14-1 Federal Budget Deficits and Surpluses Since 1940

Federal budget deficits (expenditures in excess of receipts, in red) have been much more common than federal budget surpluses (receipts in excess of expenditures, in green).

Source: Office of Management and Budget.

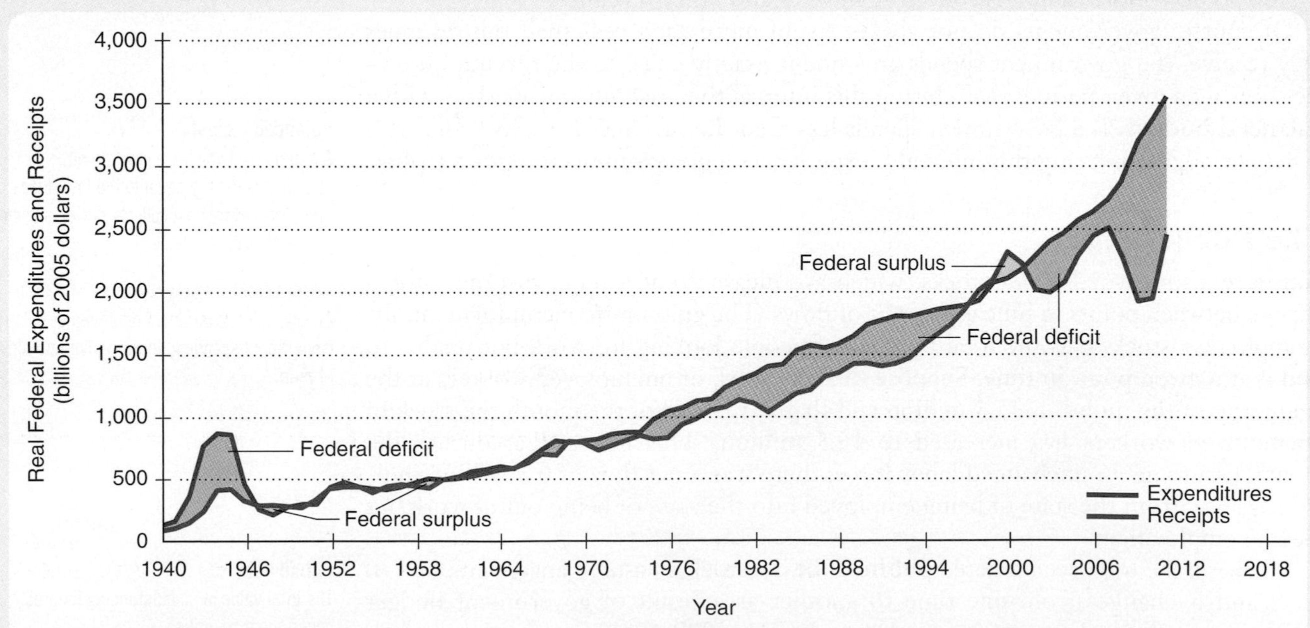

Even though Figure 14-1 on the preceding page accounts for inflation, it does not give a clear picture of the size of the federal government's deficits or surpluses in relation to overall economic activity in the United States. Figure 14-2 below provides a clearer view of the size of government deficits or surpluses relative to the size of the U.S. economy by expressing them as percentages of GDP. As you can see, the federal budget deficit rose to nearly 6 percent of GDP in the early 1980s. It then fell back, increased once again during the late 1980s and early 1990s, and then declined steadily into the budget surplus years of 1998–2001. Since 2001, the government budget deficit has increased to nearly 4 percent of GDP, dropped back below 3 percent of GDP, and then risen rapidly, to nearly 13 percent of GDP.

The Resurgence of Federal Government Deficits

Why has the government's budget slipped from a surplus equal to nearly 2.5 percent of GDP into a deficit of nearly 13 percent of GDP? The answer is that the government has been spending much more than its revenues. Spending has increased at a faster pace since the early 2000s—particularly in light of the ongoing bailout of financial institutions and a sharp rise in discretionary fiscal expenditures—than during any other decade since World War II.

The more complex answer also considers government revenues. In 2001, Congress and the executive branch slightly reduced income tax rates, and in 2003 they also cut federal capital gains taxes and estate taxes. Because tax rates were reduced toward the end of a recession when real income growth was relatively low, government tax revenues were stagnant for a time. When economic activity began to expand into the mid-2000s, tax revenues started rising at a pace closer to the rapid rate of growth of government spending. Then, in the late 2000s, economic activity dropped significantly. Thus, annual tax collections declined at the same time that annual federal expenditures increased. As long as this situation persists, the U.S. government will operate with massive budget deficits such as those observed in the late 2000s.

FIGURE 14-2 The Federal Budget Deficit Expressed as a Percentage of GDP

During the early 2000s, the federal budget deficit rose as a share of GDP and then declined somewhat. Recently, it has increased dramatically. (Note that the negative values for the 1998–2001 period designate budget surpluses as a percentage of GDP during those years.)

Sources: Economic Report of the President; Economic Indicators, various issues.

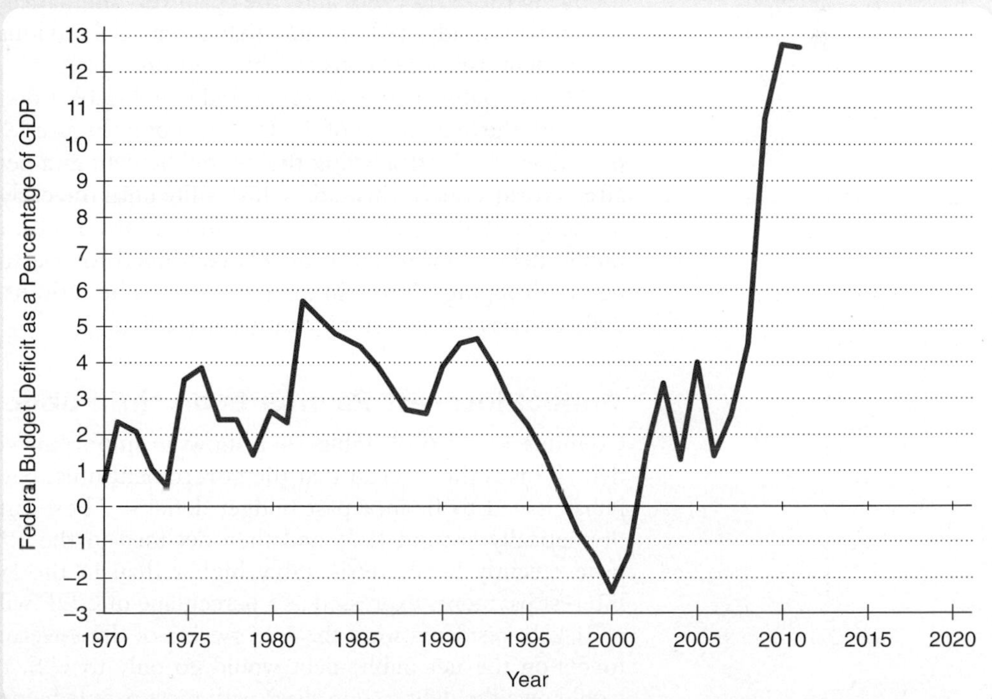

QUICK QUIZ See page 316 for the answers. Review concepts from this section in MyEconLab.

Whenever the federal government spends more than it receives during a given year, it operates with a __________ __________. If federal government spending exactly equals government revenues, then the government experiences a __________ __________. If the federal government collects more revenues than it spends, then it operates with a __________ __________.

The federal budget deficit is a flow, whereas accumulated budget deficits represent a __________, called the **public debt.**

The federal budget deficit expressed as a percentage of GDP rose to around 6 percent in the early 1980s. Between 1998 and 2001, the federal government experienced a budget __________, but since then its budget has once more been in __________. Currently, the budget __________ is nearly 13 percent of GDP.

Evaluating the Rising Public Debt

Gross public debt
All federal government debt irrespective of who owns it.

Net public debt
Gross public debt minus all government interagency borrowing.

All federal public debt, taken together, is called the **gross public debt.** We arrive at the **net public debt** when we subtract from the gross public debt the portion that is held by government agencies (in essence, what the federal government owes to itself). For instance, if the Social Security Administration holds U.S. Treasury bonds, the U.S. Treasury makes debt payments to another agency of the government. On net, therefore, the U.S. government owes these payments to itself.

The net public debt increases whenever the federal government experiences a budget deficit. That is, the net public debt increases when government outlays are greater than total government receipts.

Accumulation of the Net Public Debt

Table 14-1 on the top of the facing page displays, for various years since 1940, real values, in base-year 2005 dollars, of the federal budget deficit, the total and per capita net public debt (the amount owed on the net public debt by a typical individual), and the net interest cost of the public debt in total and as a percentage of GDP. It shows that the level of the real net public debt and the real net public debt per capita grew following the early 1980s and rose again very dramatically in the late 2000s. Thus, the real, inflation-adjusted amount that a typical individual owes to holders of the net public debt has varied considerably over time.

The net public debt levels reported in Table 14-1 do not provide a basis of comparison with the overall size of the U.S. economy. Figure 14-3 on the bottom of the facing page does this by displaying the net public debt as a percentage of GDP. We see that after World War II, this ratio fell steadily until the early 1970s (except for a small rise in the late 1950s) and then leveled off until the 1980s. After that, the ratio of the net public debt to GDP more or less continued to rise to around 50 percent of GDP, before dropping slightly in the late 1990s. The ratio has been rising once again since 2001 and has jumped significantly since 2007.

Annual Interest Payments on the Public Debt

Columns 5 and 6 of Table 14-1 show an important consequence of the net public debt. This is the interest that the government must pay to those who hold the bonds it has issued to finance past budget deficits. Those interest payments started rising dramatically around 1975 and then declined in the 1990s and early 2000s. Deficits have recently been considerably higher than in the late 1990s and early 2000s, so interest payments expressed as a percentage of GDP will rise in the years to come.

If U.S. residents were the sole owners of the government's debts, the interest payments on the net public debt would go only to U.S. residents. In this situation, we would owe the debt to ourselves, with most people being taxed so that the government could pay interest to others (or to ourselves). During the 1970s, however, the share of

TABLE 14-1

The Federal Deficit, Our Public Debt, and the Interest We Pay on It

The inflation-adjusted net public debt in column 3 is defined as total federal debt *excluding* all loans between federal government agencies. Per capita net public debt shown in column 4 is obtained by dividing the net public debt by the population.

(1) Year	(2) Federal Budget Deficit (billions of 2005 dollars)	(3) Net Public Debt (billions of 2005 dollars)	(4) Per Capita Net Public Debt (2005 dollars)	(5) Net Interest Costs (billions of 2005 dollars)	(6) Net Interest as a Percentage of GDP
1940	8.9	97.3	736.2	2.1	0.9
1945	492.9	2,150.7	15,372.8	28.3	1.45
1950	21.1	1,490.7	9,788.0	32.7	1.68
1955	18.0	1,360.8	8,202.8	29.4	1.23
1960	1.6	1,253.5	6,937.0	36.5	1.37
1965	7.9	1,287.7	6,627.5	42.3	1.26
1970	11.5	1,169.1	5,700.1	59.1	1.47
1975	134.1	1,180.0	5,463.1	69.3	1.52
1980	154.3	1,482.6	6,564.3	109.7	1.92
1985	344.1	2,430.0	10,247.4	209.7	3.22
1990	306.5	3,337.4	13,349.4	243.1	3.23
1995	201.2	4,421.6	16,585.2	284.7	3.24
2000	−267.1	3,853.1	13,644.1	252.0	2.34
2005	318.3	4,592.2	15,480.8	184.0	1.38
2008	423.1	5,353.4	17,556.9	226.2	1.35
2009	1,287.8	6,877.6	22,341.7	259.7	1.45
2010	1,411.6	8,437.1	30,040.8	263.5	1.90
2011	1,132.5	9,385.8	30,305.0	286.6	2.00

Sources: U.S. Department of the Treasury; Office of Management and Budget. *Note:* Data for 2011 are estimates.

FIGURE 14-3 **The Official Net U.S. Public Debt as a Percentage of GDP**

During World War II, the officially reported net public debt grew dramatically. After the war, it fell until the 1970s, started rising in the 1980s, and then declined once more in the 1990s. Recently, it has increased significantly.

Source: U.S. Department of the Treasury.

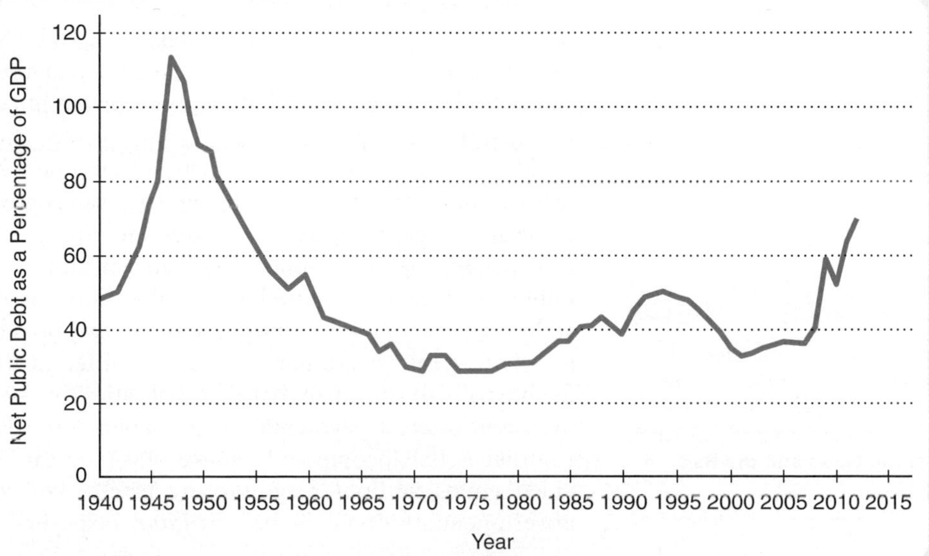

the net public debt owned by foreign individuals, businesses, and governments started to rise, reaching 20 percent in 1978. From there it declined until the late 1980s, when it began to rise rapidly. Today, foreign residents, businesses, and governments hold more than 50 percent of the net public debt. Thus, we do not owe the debt just to ourselves.

Why are several European governments paying higher interest rates on their debts than they did before 2009?

INTERNATIONAL POLICY EXAMPLE

Why European Governments Are Paying More Interest on Debt

Since 2009, bonds issued by several European governments, including those of Greece, Ireland, Italy, Portugal, Spain, and the United Kingdom, have received lower ratings from bond-rating agencies such as Standard & Poor's. This means that these rating agencies perceive a greater likelihood that these nations will be unable to fully meet their future debt responsibilities.

The lower ratings have affected the interest rates that governments of these nations have been required to pay to induce individuals and companies to continue buying their bonds. The United Kingdom's lower rating translated into an interest rate increase of 0.05 percentage point, which translated into $500,000 more in annual interest payments for every $1 billion borrowed. For the Greek government, the lower bond rating boosted its required interest rate by more than a full percentage point, so that it had to pay at least *$10 million* more for each additional $1 billion that it borrowed.

FOR CRITICAL ANALYSIS

Why do you think that people require a higher interest payment to induce them to lend to governments judged to be less likely to honor all of their debt obligations?

Burdens of the Public Debt

Do current budget deficits and the accumulating public debt create social burdens? One perspective on this question considers possible burdens on future generations. Another focuses on transfers from U.S. residents to residents of other nations.

HOW TODAY'S BUDGET DEFICITS MIGHT BURDEN FUTURE GENERATIONS If the federal government wishes to purchase goods and services valued at $300 billion, it can finance this expenditure either by raising taxes by $300 billion or by selling $300 billion in bonds. Many economists maintain that the second option, deficit spending, would lead to a higher level of national consumption and a lower level of national saving than the first option.

The reason, say these economists, is that if people are taxed, they will have to forgo private consumption now as society substitutes government goods for private goods. If the government does not raise taxes but instead sells bonds to finance the $300 billion in expenditures, the public's disposable income remains the same. Members of the public have merely shifted their allocations of assets to include $300 billion in additional government bonds. There are two possible circumstances that could cause people to treat government borrowing differently than they treat taxes. One is that people will fail to realize that their liabilities (in the form of higher future taxes due to increased interest payments on the public debt) have *also* increased by $300 billion. Another is that people will believe that they can consume the governmentally provided goods without forgoing any private consumption because the bill for the government goods will be paid by *future* taxpayers.

You Are There

To think about how rising federal government budget deficits and an increasing net public debt will affect you personally, take a look at **Facing the Good News and the Bad,** on page 311.

THE CROWDING-OUT EFFECT But if full employment exists, and society raises its present consumption by adding consumption of government-provided goods to the original quantity of privately provided goods, then something must be *crowded out*. In a closed economy, investment expenditures on capital goods must decline. As you learned in Chapter 13, the mechanism by which investment is crowded out is an increase in the interest rate. Deficit spending increases the total demand for credit but leaves the total supply of credit unaltered. The rise in interest rates causes a reduction in the growth of investment and capital formation, which in turn slows the growth of productivity and improvement in society's living standard.

This perspective suggests that deficit spending can impose a burden on future generations in two ways. First, unless the deficit spending is allocated to purchases that lead to long-term increases in real GDP, future generations will have to be taxed at a higher rate. That is, only by imposing higher taxes on future generations will the government be able to retire the higher public debt resulting from the present generation's consumption of governmentally provided goods. Second, the increased level of spending by the present generation crowds out investment and reduces the growth of capital goods, leaving future generations with a smaller capital stock and thereby reducing their wealth.

PAYING OFF THE PUBLIC DEBT IN THE FUTURE Suppose that after several more years of running substantial deficits financed by selling bonds to U.S. residents, the public debt becomes so large that each adult person's implicit share of the net public debt liability is $60,000. Suppose further that the government chooses (or is forced) to pay off the debt at that time. Will that generation be burdened with our government's overspending? Assume that a large portion of the debt is owed to ourselves. It is true that every adult will have to come up with $60,000 in taxes to pay off the debt, but then the government will use these funds to pay off the bondholders. Sometimes the bondholders and taxpayers will be the same people. Thus, *some* people will be burdened because they owe $60,000 and own less than $60,000 in government bonds. Others, however, will receive more than $60,000 for the bonds they own. Nevertheless, as a generation within society, they could—if all government debt were issued within the nation's borders—pay and receive about the same amount of funds.

To learn about the agency that manages the public debt, go to **www.econtoday.com/ch14**.

Of course, there could be a burden on some low-income adults who will find it difficult or impossible to obtain $60,000 to pay off the tax liability. Still, nothing says that taxes to pay off the debt must be assessed equally. Indeed, it seems likely that a special tax would be levied, based on the ability to pay.

OUR DEBT TO FOREIGN RESIDENTS So far we have been assuming that we owe all of the public debt to ourselves. But, as we saw earlier, that is not the case. What about the more than 50 percent owned by foreign residents?

It is true that if foreign residents buy U.S. government bonds, we do not owe that debt to ourselves. Thus, when debts held by foreign residents come due, future U.S. residents will be taxed to repay these debts plus accumulated interest. Portions of the incomes of future U.S. residents will then be transferred abroad. In this way, a potential burden on future generations may result.

But this transfer of income from U.S. residents to residents of other nations will not necessarily be a burden. It is important to realize that if the rate of return on projects that the government funds by operating with deficits exceeds the interest rate paid to foreign residents, both foreign residents and future U.S. residents will be better off. If funds obtained by selling bonds to foreign residents are expended on wasteful projects, however, a burden will be placed on future generations.

We can apply the same reasoning to the problem of current investment and capital creation being crowded out by current deficits. If deficits lead to slower growth rates, future generations will be poorer. But if the government expenditures are really investments, and if the rate of return on such public investments exceeds the interest rate paid on the bonds, both present and future generations will be economically better off.

Are U.S. residents obliged to repay more of their net national debt abroad than residents of other nations? (See the following page.)

INTERNATIONAL POLICY EXAMPLE

How Do U.S. Residents' Foreign Debt Obligations Compare?

Today, a typical U.S. resident owes more than $11,000 to people in other nations who hold U.S. government debt obligations. This is about twice as much as is owed abroad by a typical Hungarian or Japanese resident and about three times as much as the typical resident of Israel or Slovenia owes to people in other nations.

At the same time, the foreign debt obligations of an average U.S. resident are less than are owed by residents of a number of other industrialized nations, including Austria, Belgium, Finland, France, Germany, Ireland, and the Netherlands. In Greece, the average resident's foreign indebtedness is almost $30,000.

FOR CRITICAL ANALYSIS

Does the fact that the average resident of China is owed at least $700 by the U.S. government necessarily mean that residents of China will be materially better off than U.S. residents in the long run?

QUICK QUIZ See page 316 for the answers. Review concepts from this section in MyEconLab.

When we subtract the funds that government agencies borrow from each other from the _________ public debt, we obtain the _________ public debt.

The public debt may impose a burden on _________ generations if they have to be taxed at higher rates to pay for the _________ generation's increased consumption of governmentally provided goods. In addition, there may be a burden if the debt leads to crowding out of current investment, resulting in _________ capital formation and hence a _________ economic growth rate.

If foreign residents hold a significant part of our public debt, then we no longer "owe it to ourselves." If the rate of return on the borrowed funds is _________ than the interest to be paid to foreign residents, future generations can be made better off by government borrowing. Future generations will be worse off, however, if the opposite is true.

Federal Budget Deficits in an Open Economy

Many economists believe that it is no accident that foreign residents hold such a large portion of the U.S. public debt. Their reasoning suggests that a U.S. trade deficit—a situation in which the value of U.S. imports of goods and services exceeds the value of its exports—will often accompany a government budget deficit.

Trade Deficits and Government Budget Deficits

Figure 14-4 on the facing page shows U.S. trade deficits and surpluses compared with federal budget deficits and surpluses. In the mid-1970s, imports of goods and services began to consistently exceed exports of those items on an annual basis in the United States. At the same time, the federal budget deficit rose dramatically. Both deficits increased once again in the early 2000s. Then, during the economic turmoil of the late 2000s, the budget deficit exploded while the trade deficit shrank somewhat.

Overall, however, it appears that larger trade deficits tend to accompany larger government budget deficits.

Why the Two Deficits Tend to Be Related

Intuitively, there is a reason why we would expect federal budget deficits to be associated with trade deficits. You might call this the unpleasant arithmetic of trade and budget deficits.

Suppose that, initially, the government's budget is balanced; government expenditures are matched by an equal amount of tax collections and other government revenues. Now

FIGURE 14-4 The Related U.S. Deficits

The United States exported more than it imported until the mid-1970s. Then it started experiencing large trade deficits, as shown in this diagram. The federal budget has been in deficit most years since the 1960s. The question is, has the federal budget deficit created the trade deficit?

Sources: Economic Report of the President; Economic Indicators, various issues; author's estimates.

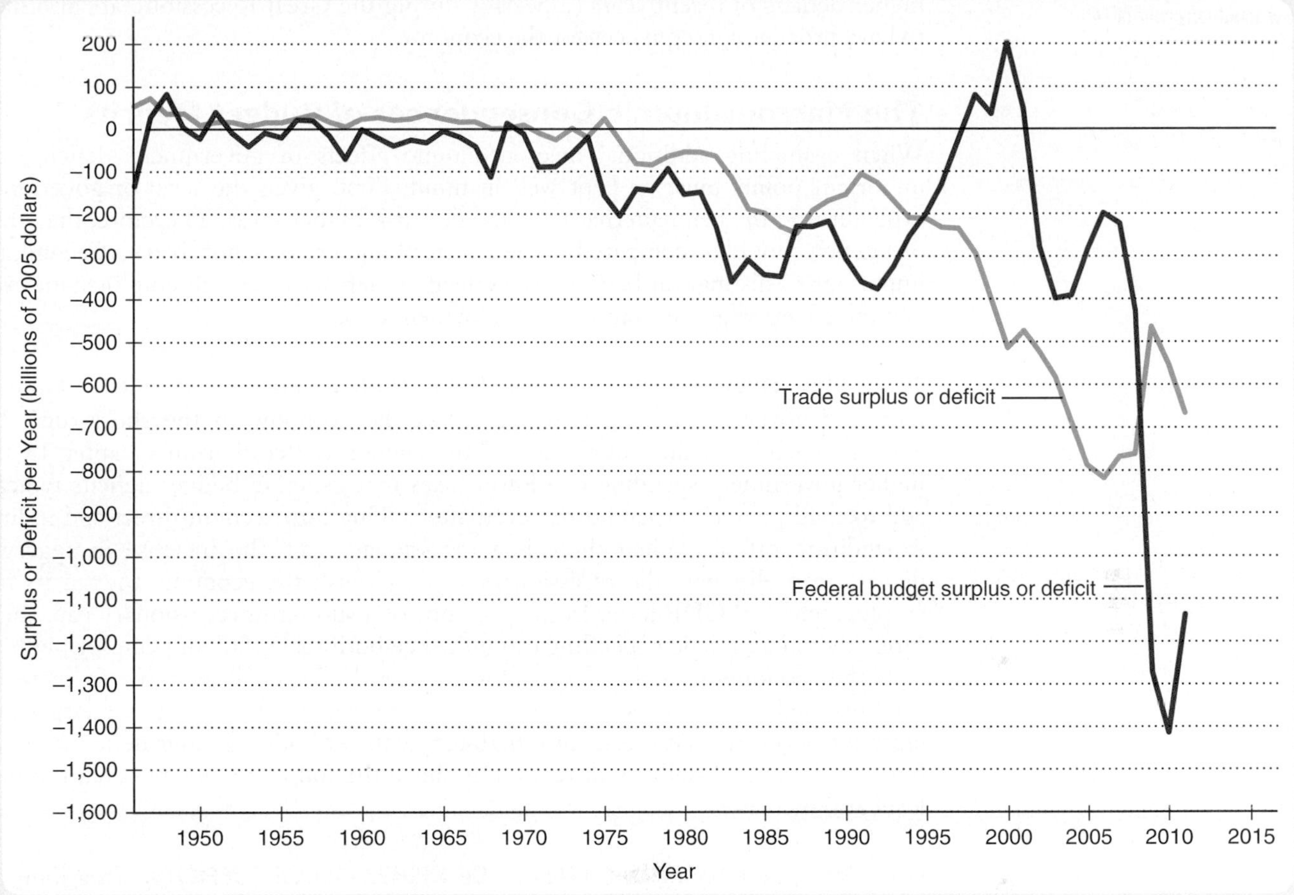

assume that the federal government begins to operate with a budget deficit. It increases its spending, collects fewer taxes, or both. Assume further that domestic consumption and domestic investment do not decrease relative to GDP. Where, then, do the funds come from to finance the government's budget deficit? A portion of these funds must come from abroad. That is to say, dollar holders abroad will have to purchase newly created government bonds.

Of course, foreign dollar holders will choose to hold the new government bonds only if there is an economic inducement to do so, such as an increase in U.S. interest rates. Given that private domestic spending and other factors are unchanged, interest rates will indeed rise whenever there is an increase in deficits financed by increased borrowing.

When foreign dollar holders purchase the new U.S. government bonds, they will have fewer dollars to spend on U.S. items, including U.S. export goods. Hence, when our nation's government operates with a budget deficit, we should expect to see foreign dollar holders spending more on U.S. government bonds and less on U.S.-produced goods and services. As a consequence of the U.S. government deficit, therefore, we should generally anticipate a decline in U.S. exports relative to U.S. imports, or a higher U.S. trade deficit.

Growing U.S. Government Deficits: Implications for U.S. Economic Performance

For more information about the role of the Office of Management and Budget in the government's budgeting process, go to **www.econtoday.com/ch14**.

We have seen that one consequence of higher U.S. government budget deficits tends to be higher international trade deficits. Higher budget deficits, such as the much higher deficits of recent years (especially during the Great Recession), are also likely to have broader consequences for the economy.

The Macroeconomic Consequences of Budget Deficits

When evaluating additional macroeconomic effects of government deficits, two important points must be kept well in mind. First, given the level of government expenditures, the main alternative to the deficit is higher taxes. Therefore, the effects of a deficit should be compared to the effects of higher taxes, not to zero. Second, it is important to distinguish between the effects of deficits when full employment exists and the effects when substantial unemployment exists.

SHORT-RUN MACROECONOMIC EFFECTS OF HIGHER BUDGET DEFICITS How do increased government budget deficits affect the economy in the short run? The answer depends on the initial state of the economy. Recall from Chapter 13 that higher government spending and lower taxes that generate budget deficits typically add to total planned expenditures, even after taking into account direct and indirect expenditure offsets. When there is a recessionary gap, the increase in aggregate demand can eliminate the recessionary gap and push the economy toward its full-employment real GDP level. In the presence of a short-run recessionary gap, therefore, government deficit spending can influence both real GDP and employment.

If the economy is at the full-employment level of real GDP, however, increased total planned expenditures and higher aggregate demand generated by a larger government budget deficit create an inflationary gap. Although greater deficit spending temporarily raises equilibrium real GDP above the full-employment level, the price level also increases.

LONG-RUN MACROECONOMIC EFFECTS OF HIGHER BUDGET DEFICITS In a long-run macroeconomic equilibrium, the economy has fully adjusted to changes in all factors. These factors include changes in government spending and taxes and, consequently, the government budget deficit. Although increasing the government budget deficit raises aggregate demand, in the long run equilibrium real GDP remains at its full-employment level. Further increases in the government deficit via higher government expenditures or tax cuts can only be inflationary. They have no effect on equilibrium real GDP, which remains at the full-employment level in the long run.

The fact that long-run equilibrium real GDP is unaffected in the face of increased government deficits has an important implication:

> ***In the long run, higher government budget deficits have no effect on equilibrium real GDP per year. Ultimately, therefore, government spending in excess of government receipts simply redistributes a larger share of real GDP per year to government-provided goods and services.***

Thus, if the government operates with higher deficits over an extended period, the ultimate result is a shrinkage in the share of privately provided goods and services. By continually spending more than it collects in taxes and other revenue sources, the government takes up a larger portion of economic activity.

How Could the Government Reduce All Its Red Ink?

There have been many suggestions about how to reduce the government deficit. One way to reduce the deficit is to increase tax collections.

QUICK QUIZ See page 316 for the answers. **Review concepts from this section in MyEconLab.**

To obtain the dollars required to purchase newly issued U.S. government bonds, foreign residents must sell __________ goods and services in the United States than U.S. residents sell abroad. Thus, U.S. imports must __________ U.S. exports. For this reason, the federal budget deficit and the international trade __________ tend to be related.

Higher government deficits arise from increased government spending or tax cuts, which raise aggregate demand. Thus, larger government budget deficits can raise real GDP in a __________ gap situation. If the economy is already at the full-employment level of real GDP, however, higher government deficits can only temporarily push equilibrium real GDP __________ the full-employment level.

In the long run, higher government budget deficits cause the equilibrium price level to rise but fail to raise equilibrium real GDP above the full-employment level. Thus, the long-run effect of increased government deficits is simply a redistribution of real GDP per year from __________ provided goods and services to __________-provided goods and services.

INCREASING TAXES FOR EVERYONE From an arithmetic point of view, a federal budget deficit can be wiped out by simply increasing the amount of taxes collected. Let's see what this would require. Projections for 2011 are instructive. The Office of Management and Budget estimated the 2011 federal budget deficit at about $1.3 trillion. To have prevented this deficit from occurring by raising taxes, in 2011 the government would have had to collect almost $9,000 more in taxes from *every worker* in the United States. Needless to say, reality is such that we will never see annual federal budget deficits wiped out by simple tax increases.

TAXING THE RICH Some people suggest that the way to eliminate the deficit is to raise taxes on the rich. What does it mean to tax the rich more? If you talk about taxing "millionaires," you are referring to those who pay taxes on more than $1 million in income per year. There are fewer than 100,000 of them. Even if you were to double the taxes they now pay, the reduction in the deficit would be relatively trivial. Changing marginal tax rates at the upper end will produce similarly unimpressive results. The Internal Revenue Service (IRS) has determined that an increase in the top marginal tax rate from 35 percent to 45 percent would raise, at best, only about $35 billion in additional taxes. (This assumes that people do not figure out a way to avoid the higher tax rate.) Extra revenues of $35 billion per year represent less than 3 percent of the estimated 2011 federal budget deficit.

The reality is that the data do not support the notion that tax increases can completely *eliminate* deficits. Although eliminating a deficit in this way is possible arithmetically, politically just the opposite has occurred. When more tax revenues have been collected, Congress has usually responded by increasing government spending.

Why Not . . . eliminate deficits and the debt by taxing the richest 1 percent more?

Even if the U.S. government imposed a tax rate of *100 percent* on the richest 1 percent of U.S. residents, tax revenues would be increased by only an estimated $1.3 trillion. Thus, a policy that confiscated the incomes of the richest 1 percent of U.S. residents would cover at most the typical budget deficit of a *single year* during the 2010s. Indeed, if the government confiscated the incomes of everyone who earns more than *$75,000* per year, it would bring in just about $4 trillion more tax dollars during that year—enough to pay off only about one-third of the net public debt. Clearly, temporarily raising taxes on the richest 1 percent of U.S. residents could not possibly eliminate all federal budget deficits or come close to paying off the net public debt.

REDUCING EXPENDITURES Reducing expenditures is another way to decrease the federal budget deficit. Figure 14-5 on the next page shows various components of government spending as a percentage of total expenditures. There you see that military spending

FIGURE 14-5 Components of Federal Expenditures as Percentages of Total Federal Spending

Although military spending as a percentage of total federal spending has risen and fallen with changing national defense concerns, national defense expenditures as a percentage of total spending have generally trended downward since the mid-1950s. Social Security and other income security programs and Medicare and other health programs now account for larger shares of total federal spending than any other programs.

Source: Office of Management and Budget.

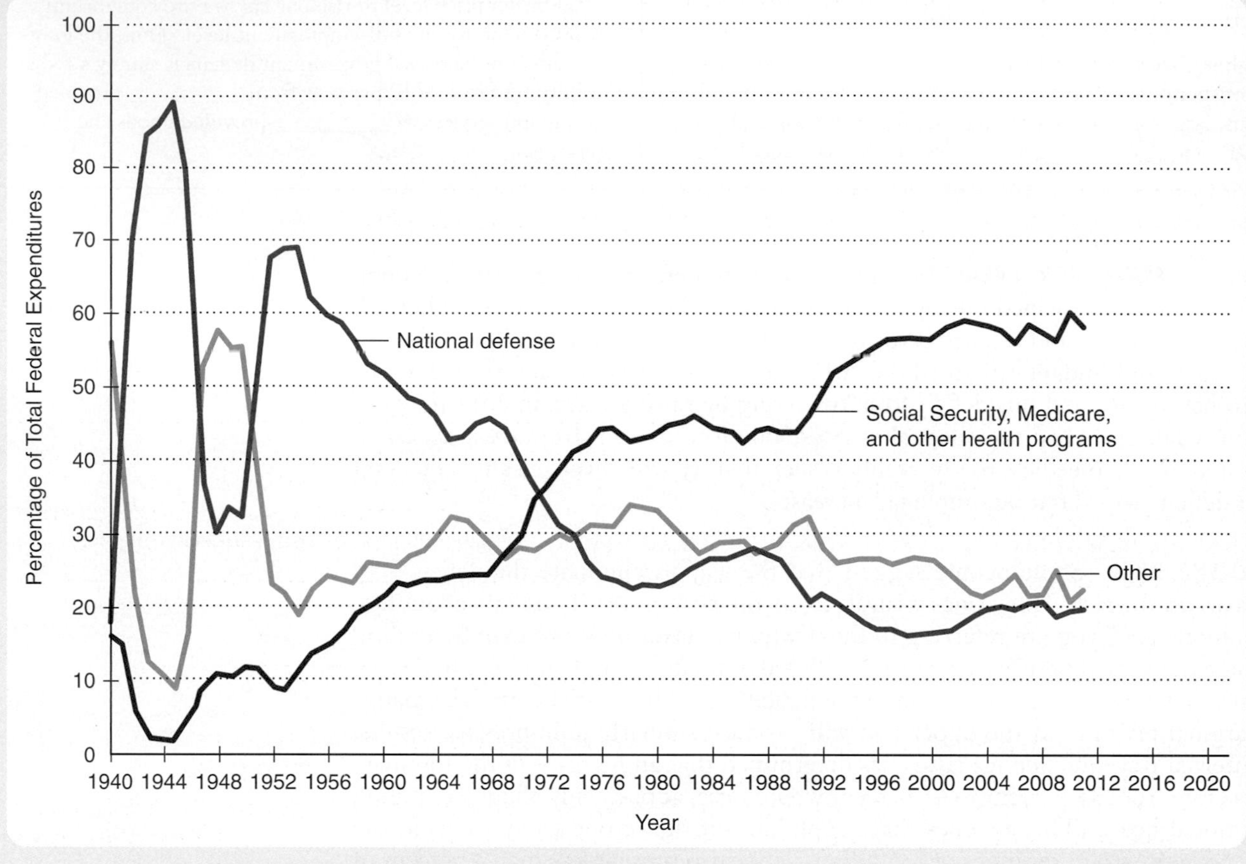

(national defense) as a share of total federal expenditures has risen slightly in some recent years, though it remains much lower than in most previous years.

During the period from the conclusion of World War II until 1972, military spending was the most important aspect of the federal budget. Figure 14-5 above shows that it no longer is, even taking into account the war on terrorism that began in late 2001. **Entitlements,** which are legislated federal government payments that anyone who qualifies is entitled to receive, are now the most important component of the federal budget. These include payments for Social Security and other income security programs and for Medicare and other health programs such as Medicaid. Entitlements are consequently often called **noncontrollable expenditures,** or nondiscretionary expenditures unrelated to national defense that automatically change without any direct action by Congress.

Entitlements
Guaranteed benefits under a government program such as Social Security, Medicare, or Medicaid.

Noncontrollable expenditures
Government spending that changes automatically without action by Congress.

IS IT TIME TO BEGIN WHITTLING AWAY AT ENTITLEMENTS? In 1960, spending on entitlements represented about 20 percent of the total federal budget. Today, entitlement expenditures make up about one-third of total federal spending. Consider Social Security, Medicare, and Medicaid. In constant 2005 dollars, in 2011 Social Security, Medicare, and Medicaid represented about $2,200 billion of estimated federal expenditures. (This calculation excludes military and international payments and interest on the government debt.)

Entitlement payments for Social Security, Medicare, and Medicaid now exceed all other domestic spending. Entitlements are growing faster than any other part of the federal government budget. During the past two decades, real spending on entitlements (adjusted for inflation) grew between 7 and 8 percent per year, while the economy grew less than 3 percent per year. Social Security payments are growing in real terms at about 6 percent per year, but Medicare and Medicaid are growing at double-digit rates. The passage of Medicare prescription drug benefits in 2003 and the new federal health care legislation in 2010 simply added to the already rapid growth of these health care entitlements.

Many people believe that entitlement programs are "necessary" federal expenditures. Interest on the public debt must be paid, but Congress can change just about every other federal expenditure labeled "necessary." The federal budget deficit is not expected to drop in the near future because entitlement programs are not likely to be eliminated. Governments have trouble cutting government benefit programs once they are established. One must conclude that containing federal budget deficits is likely to prove to be a difficult task.

QUICK QUIZ **See page 316 for the answers. Review concepts from this section in MyEconLab.**

One way to reduce federal budget _________ is to increase taxes. Proposals to reduce deficits by raising taxes on the highest-income individuals will not appreciably reduce budget deficits, however.

Another way to decrease federal budget _________ is to cut back on government spending, particularly on _________, defined as benefits guaranteed under government programs such as Social Security and Medicare.

You Are There — Facing the Good News and the Bad

Fast-forward to your life after graduation. You have completed your degree, landed a job, and received your first paycheck. That is clearly good news.

But there is also some bad news in your future. By the time your graduation day arrives, the federal government's share of economic activity will have risen to more than 25 percent, up from a historical average of about 20.5 percent. For the foreseeable future, therefore, one out of every four dollars that the typical U.S. resident earns will fund annual U.S. government expenditures on final goods and services and on interest payments on the federal government's expanding debts. You are one of those typical residents, so about 25 cents of each dollar of pretax earnings you receive henceforth will be put to use by the federal government—rather than by you, the income earner. Today, fewer than 2 of those 25 cents go toward paying interest on accumulated U.S. government debts. By the end of the 2010s, however, at least 5 cents of each dollar you earn will go toward that purpose. One may hope that you will be able to forget this bad news as you celebrate the receipt of your first postcollegiate paycheck.

Critical Analysis Questions

1. Why does the accumulation of higher government debts today necessarily imply that you will pay more taxes in the future than you otherwise would have paid?
2. As the net public debt expands during the 2010s, why will the share of government spending going to debt interest payments also tend to rise?

ISSUES & APPLICATIONS

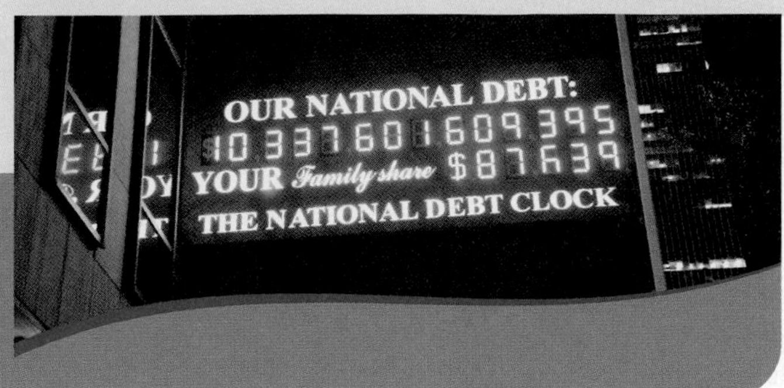

The United States Is Vying for the "Lead" in Deficits and Debt

CONCEPTS APPLIED

- Government Budget Deficit
- Net Public Debt
- Balanced Budget

In several European nations, the government budget deficit and the net public debt have been rising rapidly relative to overall economic activity. But the U.S. deficit has increased so fast that the United States has taken the lead in deficits. Eventually, the U.S. net public debt may also catch up with Europe's levels.

The U.S. Deficit-GDP Ratio Now "Beats" Others' Ratios

Take a look at panel (a) of Figure 14-6 below. It shows that the United States now has a higher budget deficit to GDP ratio than European nations and Japan have. Hence, the U.S. government is borrowing more funds relative to total U.S. economic activity than are other nations' governments. Therefore, for the government to attain a balanced budget U.S. residents would have to give up a larger share of GDP than would other countries' residents.

The government budget deficit as a percentage of GDP is now twice as high in the United States as in the euro area—the region encompassing the European nations that use the euro as a common currency. Compared with the

FIGURE 14-6 Government Budget Deficit and Net Public Debt as Percentages of GDP in Selected Nations

Panel (a) shows that the government budget deficit as a percentage of GDP is higher in the United States than in European nations and Japan. As shown in panel (b), the net public debt as a percentage of GDP currently remains higher in Japan and in several European countries than in the United States.

Sources: European Commission; U.S. Office of Management and Budget.

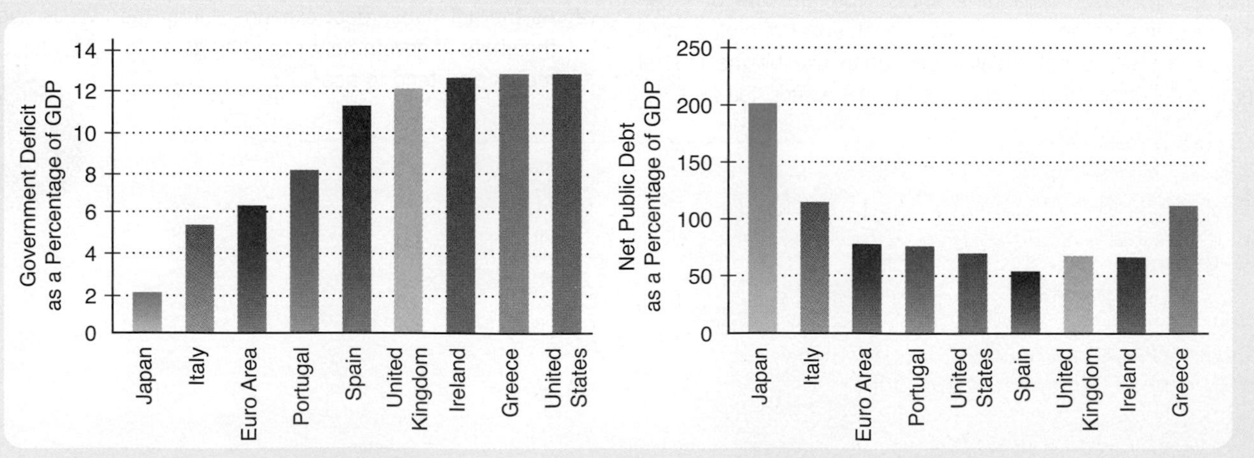

deficits of all 17 nations in the euro area combined, the U.S. budget deficit is now far "ahead."

The U.S. Net Public Debt–GDP Ratio Is Also "Gaining"

Panel (b) of Figure 14-6 on the facing page displays the net public debt as a percentage of GDP for the same set of countries. The levels of net public debt in Greece, Italy, and Japan are more than 100 percent of GDP. This means that even if Greek, Italian, and Japanese residents were to transmit all the incomes they earn in a full year to their governments, their nations' net public debts still would not be fully repaid. In Japan, people would have to give up *two* full years' worth of GDP to pay off the Japanese government's net public debt.

Thus, the U.S. ratio is not the highest among industrialized nations. Nevertheless, the U.S. net public debt–GDP ratio is now about 70 percent, which is more than twice as high as it was as recently as 2000.

For Critical Analysis

1. Why does the fact that the U.S. government's deficit-GDP ratio is now so high help to explain why its debt-GDP ratio has increased?
2. How can it be that the absolute *dollar amounts* of the government deficit and net public debt are substantially greater in the United States than in Ireland?

Web Resources

1. To take a look at the latest government deficit and net public debt statistics for Europe, go to www.econtoday.com/ch14.
2. For the latest data on the U.S. budget deficit and net public debt, go to www.econtoday.com/ch14.

Research Project

Explain why it is important, when evaluating a nation's government deficit and net public debt, to relate both figures to the size of the country's economy.

For more questions on this chapter's Issues & Applications, go to **MyEconLab**. In the Study Plan for this chapter, select Section N: News.

myeconlab

Here is what you should know after reading this chapter. **MyEconLab** will help you identify what you know, and where to go when you need to practice.

WHAT YOU SHOULD KNOW		WHERE TO GO TO PRACTICE
Federal Government Budget Deficits A budget deficit occurs whenever the flow of government expenditures exceeds the flow of government revenues during a period of time. If government expenditures are less than government revenues during a given interval, a budget surplus occurs. The government operates with a balanced budget during a specific period if its expenditures equal its revenues. The deficit recently has risen to nearly 13 percent of GDP.	government budget deficit, 299 balanced budget, 299 government budget surplus, 299 public debt, 299 **KEY FIGURES** Figure 14-1, 300 Figure 14-2, 301	• **MyEconLab** Study Plans 14.1, 14.2 • Audio introduction to Chapter 14 • ABC News Video: Big Government: Who Is Going to Pay the Bill? • Animated Figures 14-1, 14-2
The Public Debt The federal budget deficit is a flow, whereas accumulated budget deficits are a stock, called the public debt. The gross public debt is the stock of total government bonds, and the net public debt is the difference between the gross public debt and the amount of government agencies' holdings of government bonds. In recent years, the net public debt as a share of GDP has exceeded 60 percent of GDP.	gross public debt, 302 net public debt, 302 **KEY FIGURE** Figure 14-3, 303	• **MyEconLab** Study Plan 14.3

(*continued*)

MyEconLab continued

WHAT YOU SHOULD KNOW		WHERE TO GO TO PRACTICE
How the Public Debt Might Prove a Burden to Future Generations People taxed at a higher rate must forgo private consumption as society substitutes government goods for private goods. Any current crowding out of investment as a consequence of additional debt accumulation can reduce capital formation and future economic growth. Furthermore, if capital invested by foreign residents who purchase some of the U.S. public debt has not been productively used, future generations will be worse off.	**KEY FIGURE** Figure 14-4, 307	• **MyEconLab** Study Plans 14.3, 14.4 • Animated Figure 14-4
The Macroeconomic Effects of Government Budget Deficits Because higher government deficits are caused by increased government spending or tax cuts, they contribute to a rise in total planned expenditures and aggregate demand. If there is a short-run recessionary gap, higher government deficits can thereby push equilibrium real GDP toward the full-employment level. If the economy is already at the full-employment level of real GDP, however, then a higher deficit creates a short-run inflationary gap.		• **MyEconLab** Study Plan 14.5
Possible Ways to Reduce the Government Budget Deficit Suggested ways to reduce the deficit are to increase taxes, particularly on the rich, and to reduce expenditures, particularly on entitlements, defined as guaranteed benefits under government programs such as Social Security and Medicare.	entitlements, 310 noncontrollable expenditures, 310 **KEY FIGURE** Figure 14-5, 310	• **MyEconLab** Study Plan 14.5 • Animated Figure 14-5

Log in to MyEconLab, take a chapter test, and get a personalized Study Plan that tells you which concepts you understand and which ones you need to review. From there, MyEconLab will give you further practice, tutorials, animations, videos, and guided solutions.
Log in to www.myeconlab.com

PROBLEMS

All problems are assignable in myeconlab. *Answers to odd-numbered problems appear at the back of the book.*

14-1. In 2013, government spending is $4.3 trillion, and taxes collected are $3.9 trillion. What is the federal government deficit in that year?

14-2. Suppose that the Office of Management and Budget provides the estimates of federal budget receipts, federal budget spending, and GDP at the right, all expressed in billions of dollars. Calculate the implied estimates of the federal budget deficit as a percentage of GDP for each year.

Year	Federal Budget Receipts	Federal Budget Spending	GDP
2013	3,829.8	4,382.6	15,573.2
2014	3,892.4	4,441.6	16,316.0
2015	3,964.2	4,529.3	16,852.1
2016	4,013.5	4,600.1	17,454.4

14-3. It may be argued that the effects of a higher public debt are the same as the effects of a higher deficit. Why?

14-4. What happens to the net public debt if the federal government operates next year with a:

a. budget deficit?

b. balanced budget?

c. budget surplus?

14-5. What is the relationship between the gross public debt and the net public debt?

14-6. Explain how each of the following will affect the net public debt, other things being equal.

a. Previously, the government operated with a balanced budget, but recently there has been a sudden increase in federal tax collections.

b. The federal government had been operating with a very small annual budget deficit until three successive hurricanes hit the Atlantic Coast, and now government spending has risen substantially.

c. The Government National Mortgage Association, a federal government agency that purchases certain types of home mortgages, buys U.S. Treasury bonds from another government agency.

14-7. Explain in your own words why there is likely to be a relationship between federal budget deficits and U.S. international trade deficits.

14-8. Suppose that the share of U.S. GDP going to domestic consumption remains constant. Initially, the federal government was operating with a balanced budget, but this year it has increased its spending well above its collections of taxes and other sources of revenues. To fund its deficit spending, the government has issued bonds. So far, very few foreign residents have shown any interest in purchasing the bonds.

a. What must happen to induce foreign residents to buy the bonds?

b. If foreign residents desire to purchase the bonds, what is the most important source of dollars to buy them?

14-9. Suppose that the economy is experiencing the short-run equilibrium position depicted at point *A* in the diagram at the top of the next column. Then the government raises its spending and thereby runs a budget deficit in an effort to boost equilibrium real GDP to its long-run equilibrium level of $15 trillion (in base-year dollars). Explain the effects of an increase in the government deficit on equilibrium real GDP and the equilibrium price level. In addition, given that many taxes and government benefits vary with real GDP, discuss what change we might expect to see in the budget deficit as a result of the effects on equilibrium real GDP.

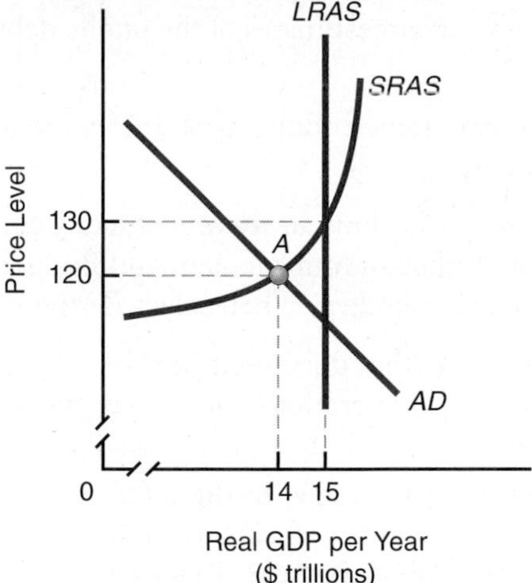

14-10. Suppose that the economy is experiencing the short-run equilibrium position depicted at point *B* in the diagram below. Explain the short-run effects of an increase in the government deficit on equilibrium real GDP and the equilibrium price level. What will be the long-run effects?

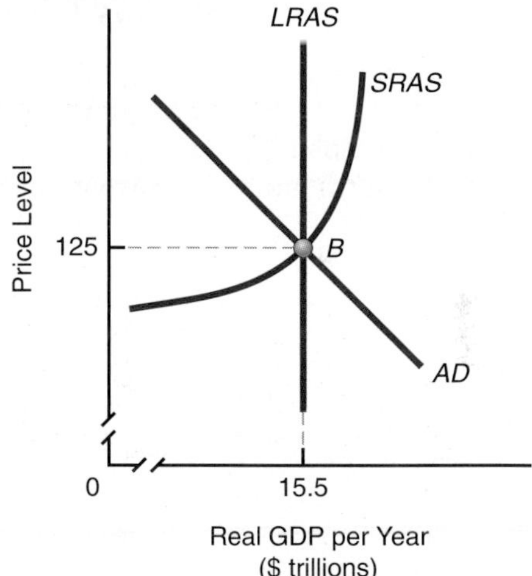

14-11. To reduce the size of the deficit (and reduce the growth of the net public debt), a politician suggests that "we should tax the rich." The politician makes a simple arithmetic calculation in which he applies the higher tax rate to the total income reported by "the rich" in a previous year. He says that this is how much the government could receive from increasing taxes on "the rich." What is the major fallacy in such calculations?

ECONOMICS ON THE NET

The Public Debt By examining the federal government's budget data, its current estimates of the public debt can be determined.

Title: Historical Tables: Budget of the United States Government

Navigation: Use the link at **www.econtoday.com/ch14** to visit the Office of Management and Budget. Select the most recent budget. Then select *Historical Tables*.

Application After the document downloads, perform each of the indicated operations and answer the following questions.

1. In the Table of Contents in the left-hand margin of the Historical Tables, click on Table 7.1, "Federal Debt at the End of the Year, 1940–2015." In light of the discussion in this chapter, which column shows the net public debt? What is the conceptual difference between the gross public debt and the net public debt? Last year, what was the dollar difference between these two amounts?
2. Table 7.1 includes estimates of the gross and net public debt over the next several years. Suppose that these estimates turn out to be accurate. Calculate how much the net public debt would increase on average each year. What are possible ways that the government could prevent these predicted increases from occurring?

For Group Study and Analysis Divide into two groups, and have each group take one side in answering the question, "Is the public debt a burden or a blessing?" Have each group develop rationales for supporting its position. Then reconvene the entire class, and discuss the relative merits of the alternative positions and rationales.

ANSWERS TO QUICK QUIZZES

p. 302: (i) budget deficit . . . balanced budget . . . budget surplus; (ii) stock; (iii) surplus . . . deficit . . . deficit

p. 306: (i) gross . . . net; (ii) future . . . current . . . less . . . lower; (iii) higher

p. 309: (i) more . . . exceed . . . deficit; (ii) recessionary . . . above; (iii) privately . . . government

p. 311: (i) deficits; (ii) deficits . . . entitlements

15

Money, Banking, and Central Banking

Since the 1930s, the U.S. government's Federal Deposit Insurance Corporation (FDIC) has provided taxpayer-guaranteed insurance against risk of loss for individual bank deposit accounts up to a specified limit. In the midst of the financial meltdown and panic that took place in 2008, Congress raised this upper limit to $250,000 (from $100,000) for most deposit accounts. Nevertheless, a number of businesses now compete to provide savers with access to FDIC-insured deposits up to $1 million. At least one firm even promises taxpayer-guaranteed insurance for up to $50 million in deposits. If the limit per account is supposed to be $250,000, how do some people obtain federal insurance covering bank deposits of $1 million or even $50 million? Before you can contemplate the answer to this question, you must first learn about the role of banks in our economy and about the rationales for and structure of the U.S. deposit insurance system.

LEARNING OBJECTIVES

After reading this chapter, you should be able to:

- Define the fundamental functions of money and identify key properties that any good that functions as money must possess
- Explain official definitions of the quantity of money in circulation
- Understand why financial intermediaries such as banks exist
- Describe the basic structure and functions of the Federal Reserve System
- Determine the maximum potential extent that the money supply will change following a Federal Reserve monetary policy action
- Explain the essential features of federal deposit insurance

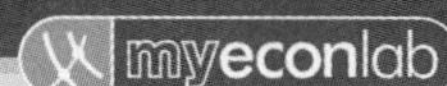

MyEconLab helps you master each objective and study more efficiently. See end of chapter for details.

Did You Know That?

in 2009, the U.S. Senate passed a resolution calling for a first-ever thorough government audit of the Federal Reserve System (the "Fed") and for a complete list of recipients of loans from the Fed? The resolution was nonbinding and lacked the force of law. Nevertheless, this resolution and other recent proposals by some members of Congress to require closer oversight of the Fed reflect congressional concerns about Fed policymaking. In the past, only financial firms had access to loans from the Fed, but since 2007, the Fed has extended credit to nonbanking firms. Furthermore, the Fed has provided funds to prop up some privately owned companies on the brink of bankruptcy while allowing other private firms to collapse. Thus, Federal Reserve officials have taken upon themselves the task of deciding which private firms in the United States will fail and which will not.

Customarily, the primary task of the Federal Reserve System has been to regulate the quantity of money in circulation in the U.S. economy—that is, to conduct *monetary policy*. Money has been important to society for thousands of years. In the fourth century BC, Aristotle claimed that everything had to "be accessed in money, for this enables men always to exchange their services, and so makes society possible." Money is indeed a part of our everyday existence. Nevertheless, we have to be careful when we talk about money. Often we hear a person say, "I wish I had more money," instead of "I wish I had more wealth," thereby confusing the concepts of money and wealth. Economists use the term **money** to mean anything that people generally accept in exchange for goods and services. Table 15-1 below provides a list of some items that various civilizations have used as money. The best way to understand how these items served this purpose is to examine the functions of money.

Money
Any medium that is universally accepted in an economy both by sellers of goods and services as payment for those goods and services and by creditors as payment for debts.

The Functions of Money

Money traditionally has four functions. The one that most people are familiar with is money's function as a *medium of exchange*. Money also serves as a *unit of accounting*, a *store of value* or *purchasing power*, and a *standard of deferred payment*. Anything that serves these four functions is money. Anything that could serve these four functions could be considered money.

Money as a Medium of Exchange

When we say that money serves as a **medium of exchange,** we mean that sellers will accept it as payment in market transactions. Without some generally accepted medium of exchange, we would have to resort to *barter*. In fact, before money was used, transactions took place by means of barter. **Barter** is simply a direct exchange of goods for goods. In a barter economy, the shoemaker who wants to obtain a dozen water glasses must seek out a glassmaker who at exactly the same time is interested in obtaining a pair of shoes. For this to occur, there has to be a high likelihood of a *double*

Medium of exchange
Any item that sellers will accept as payment.

Barter
The direct exchange of goods and services for other goods and services without the use of money.

TABLE 15-1

Types of Money

This is a partial list of items that have been used as money. Native Americans used *wampum,* beads made from shells. Fijians used whale teeth. The early colonists in North America used tobacco. And cigarettes were used in post–World War II Germany and in Poland during the breakdown of Communist rule in the late 1980s.

Iron	Boar tusk	Playing cards
Copper	Red woodpecker scalps	Leather
Brass	Feathers	Gold
Wine	Glass	Silver
Corn	Polished beads (wampum)	Knives
Salt	Rum	Pots
Horses	Molasses	Boats
Sheep	Tobacco	Pitch
Goats	Agricultural implements	Rice
Tortoise shells	Round stones with centers removed	Cows
Porpoise teeth	Crystal salt bars	Paper
Whale teeth	Snail shells	Cigarettes

Source: Roger LeRoy Miller and David D. VanHoose, *Money, Banking, and Financial Markets*, 3rd ed. (Cincinnati: South-Western, 2007), p. 7.

coincidence of wants for each specific item to be exchanged. If there isn't, the shoemaker must go through several trades in order to obtain the desired dozen glasses—perhaps first trading shoes for jewelry, then jewelry for some pots and pans, and then the pots and pans for the desired glasses.

Money facilitates exchange by reducing the transaction costs associated with means-of-payment uncertainty. That is, the existence of money means that individuals no longer have to hold a diverse collection of goods as an exchange inventory. As a medium of exchange, money allows individuals to specialize in producing those goods for which they have a comparative advantage and to receive money payments for their labor. Money payments can then be exchanged for the fruits of other people's labor. The use of money as a medium of exchange permits more specialization and the inherent economic efficiencies that come with it (and hence greater economic growth).

To what lengths does the U.S. government go to ensure that people will be willing to accept U.S. currency in exchange for goods and services?

POLICY EXAMPLE **The Never-Ending Battle Against Counterfeiters**

In all of human history, it has never been easier to counterfeit paper currency. All that is required is a relatively cheap color printer, a computer equipped with graphic design software, and the willingness to risk a lengthy prison term if caught. In an effort to duplicate official U.S. currency notes, many counterfeiters bleach $1 bills and make them look like $100 bills. To replicate the look of holographic markings on authentic government currency, some counterfeiters now utilize holographic wrapping paper commonly available at discount department stores.

If people were to lose faith in the authenticity of currency, it would not circulate as readily as a medium of exchange. Thus, the U.S. government's Bureau of Engraving and Printing (BEP) continually seeks to make U.S. currency more difficult to counterfeit. Its methods include using color-shifting ink that glows under ultraviolet light, embedding watermarks, and making the composition of the bills harder to replicate. Recently, the BEP has been working with a material called Durasafe, which has three distinctive layers on top of a polymer core and a 100 percent cotton outer layer.

Despite all of these efforts, however, counterfeit currency circulates widely. An estimated 1 million counterfeit notes change hands every day.

FOR CRITICAL ANALYSIS

Why is preventing counterfeiting crucial to money's status as a medium of exchange?

Money as a Unit of Accounting

A **unit of accounting** is a way of placing a specific price on economic goods and services. It is the common denominator, the commonly recognized measure of value. The dollar is the unit of accounting in the United States. It is the yardstick that allows individuals easily to compare the relative value of goods and services. Accountants at the U.S. Department of Commerce use dollar prices to measure national income and domestic product, a business uses dollar prices to calculate profits and losses, and a typical household budgets regularly anticipated expenses using dollar prices as its unit of accounting.

Unit of accounting
A measure by which prices are expressed; the common denominator of the price system; a central property of money.

Another way of describing money as a unit of accounting is to say that it serves as a *standard of value* that allows people to compare the relative worth of various goods and services. This allows for comparison shopping, for example.

Money as a Store of Value

One of the most important functions of money is that it serves as a **store of value** or purchasing power. The money you have today can be set aside to purchase things later on. If you have $1,000 in your checking account, you can choose to spend it today on goods and services, spend it tomorrow, or spend it a month from now. In this way, money provides a way to transfer value (wealth) into the future.

Store of value
The ability to hold value over time; a necessary property of money.

Money as a Standard of Deferred Payment

Standard of deferred payment
A property of an item that makes it desirable for use as a means of settling debts maturing in the future; an essential property of money.

The fourth function of the monetary unit is as a **standard of deferred payment.** This function involves the use of money both as a medium of exchange and as a unit of accounting. Debts are typically stated in terms of a unit of accounting, and they are paid with a monetary medium of exchange. That is to say, a debt is specified in a dollar amount and paid in currency (or by debit card or check). A corporate bond, for example, has a face value—the dollar value stated on it, which is to be paid upon maturity. The periodic interest payments on that corporate bond are specified and paid in dollars, and when the bond comes due (at maturity), the corporation pays the face value in dollars to the holder of the bond.

Properties of Money

Money is an asset—something of value—that accounts for part of personal wealth. Wealth in the form of money can be exchanged later for other assets, goods, or services. Although money is not the only form of wealth that can be exchanged for goods and services, it is the most widely and readily accepted one.

Money—The Most Liquid Asset

Liquidity
The degree to which an asset can be acquired or disposed of without much danger of any intervening loss in *nominal* value and with small transaction costs. Money is the most liquid asset.

Money's attribute as the most readily tradable asset is called **liquidity.** We say that an asset is *liquid* when it can easily be acquired or disposed of without high transaction costs and with relative certainty as to its value. Money is by definition the most liquid asset. People can easily convert money to other asset forms. Therefore, most individuals hold at least a part of their wealth in the form of the most liquid of assets, money. You can see how assets rank in liquidity relative to one another in Figure 15-1 below.

When we hold money, however, we incur a cost for this advantage of liquidity. Because cash in your pocket and many checking or debit account balances do not earn interest, that cost is the interest yield that could have been obtained had the asset been held in another form—for example, in the form of stocks and bonds.

The cost of holding money (its opportunity cost) is measured by the alternative interest yield obtainable by holding some other asset.

Monetary Standards, or What Backs Money

Transactions deposits
Checkable and debitable account balances in commercial banks and other types of financial institutions, such as credit unions and savings banks. Any accounts in financial institutions from which you can easily transmit debit-card and check payments without many restrictions.

In the past, many different monetary standards have existed. For example, commodity money, which is a physical good that may be valued for other uses it provides, has been used (see Table 15-1 on page 318). The main forms of commodity money were gold and silver. Today, though, most people throughout the world accept coins, paper currency, and balances held on deposit as **transactions deposits** (debitable and checkable accounts with banks and other financial institutions) in exchange for items sold, including labor services.

FIGURE 15-1 Degrees of Liquidity

The most liquid asset is cash. Liquidity decreases as you move from right to left.

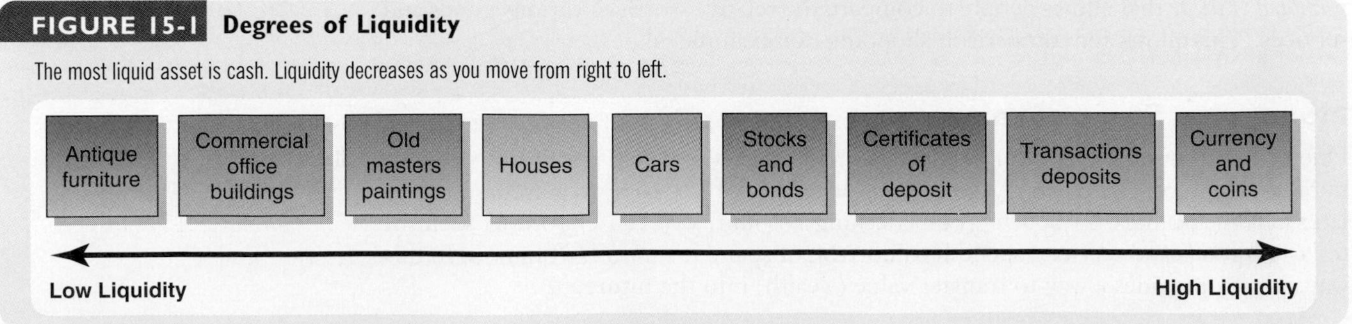

But these forms of money raise a question: Why are we willing to accept as payment something that has no intrinsic value? After all, you could not sell checks or debit cards to very many producers for use as a raw material in manufacturing. The reason is that payments in the modern world arise from a **fiduciary monetary system.** This means that the value of the payments rests on the public's confidence that such payments can be exchanged for goods and services. *Fiduciary* comes from the Latin *fiducia*, which means "trust" or "confidence." In our fiduciary monetary system, there is no legal requirement for money, in the form of currency or transactions deposits, to be convertible to a fixed quantity of gold, silver, or some other precious commodity. The bills are just pieces of paper. Coins have a value stamped on them that today is usually greater than the market value of the metal in them. Nevertheless, currency and transactions deposits are money because of their acceptability and predictability of value.

Fiduciary monetary system
A system in which money is issued by the government and its value is based uniquely on the public's faith that the currency represents command over goods and services.

ACCEPTABILITY Transactions deposits and currency are money because they are accepted in exchange for goods and services. They are accepted because people have confidence that these items can later be exchanged for other goods and services. This confidence is based on the knowledge that such exchanges have occurred in the past without problems.

PREDICTABILITY OF VALUE Money retains its usefulness even if its purchasing power is declining year in and year out, as during periods of inflation, if it still retains the characteristic of predictability of value. If you anticipate that the inflation rate is going to be around 3 percent during the next year, you know that any dollar you receive a year from now will have a purchasing power equal to 3 percent less than that same dollar today. Thus, you will not necessarily refuse to accept money in exchange simply because you know that its value will decline by the rate of inflation during the next year.

You Are There

To learn about how private currencies are catching on in the United States, read **A River Currency for Riverwest, Wisconsin,** on page 339.

Why do governments impose conditions on the use of private currencies?

INTERNATIONAL POLICY EXAMPLE

Venezuela Promotes Private Moneys—with Conditions Attached

Many years ago, Venezuela had a semifeudal society in which landowners paid the serfs on their estates with tokens that they could exchange only for items produced or sold on the landowners' estates. Today, the Venezuelan government is tolerating the use of private currencies, such as a currency called the *cimarrón* that people utilize in the coastal region of Barlovento. Nevertheless, like an old-time landowner, the government imposes restrictions on the legal utilization of these currencies.

For instance, the *cimarrón* and the other nine private currencies used in different parts of Venezuela cannot be exchanged for the *bolívar,* the Venezuelan national currency issued by the central bank, the Bank of Venezuela. In addition, the government restricts the use of the currencies to relatively small organized markets where people can buy items only if they also have items to sell. Thus, the Venezuelan government does not allow the *cimarrón* and other private currencies to be exchanged for units of its own currency or used as media of exchange for *all* goods and services. In this way, the government prevents the private currencies from competing with its own currency, whose general acceptability and predictability of value have decreased amid periodic bursts of inflation.

FOR CRITICAL ANALYSIS

Why do you suppose that private currencies sometimes emerge in nations experiencing significant inflation?

QUICK QUIZ

See page 344 for the answers. Review concepts from this section in MyEconLab.

Money is defined by its functions, which are as a __________ of __________, __________ of __________, __________ of __________, and __________ of __________.

Money is a highly __________ asset because it can be disposed of with low transaction costs and with relative certainty as to its value.

Modern nations have __________ monetary systems—national currencies are not convertible into a fixed quantity of a commodity such as gold or silver.

Money is accepted in exchange for goods and services because people have confidence that it can later be exchanged for other goods and services. In addition, money has __________ value.

Defining Money

Money supply
The amount of money in circulation.

Transactions approach
A method of measuring the money supply by looking at money as a medium of exchange.

Liquidity approach
A method of measuring the money supply by looking at money as a temporary store of value.

Money is important. Changes in the total **money supply**—the amount of money in circulation—and changes in the rate at which the money supply increases or decreases affect important economic variables, such as the rate of inflation, interest rates, and (at least in the short run) employment and the level of real GDP. Economists have struggled to reach agreement about how to define and measure money, however. There are two basic approaches: the **transactions approach,** which stresses the role of money as a medium of exchange, and the **liquidity approach,** which stresses the role of money as a temporary store of value.

The Transactions Approach to Measuring Money: M1

M1
The money supply, measured as the total value of currency plus transactions deposits plus traveler's checks not issued by banks.

Using the transactions approach to measuring money, the money supply consists of currency, transactions deposits, and traveler's checks not issued by banks. One key designation of the money supply, including currency, transactions deposits, and traveler's checks not issued by banks, is **M1.** The various elements of M1 for a typical year are presented in panel (a) of Figure 15-2 below.

CURRENCY The largest component of U.S. currency is paper bills called Federal Reserve notes, which are designed and printed by the U.S. Bureau of Engraving and Printing. U.S. currency also consists of coins minted by the U.S. Treasury. Federal Reserve banks (to be discussed shortly) issue paper notes and coins throughout the U.S. banking system.

Depository institutions
Financial institutions that accept deposits from savers and lend funds from those deposits out at interest.

Thrift institutions
Financial institutions that receive most of their funds from the savings of the public. They include savings banks, savings and loan associations, and credit unions.

TRANSACTIONS DEPOSITS Individuals transfer ownership of deposits in financial institutions by using debit cards and checks. Hence, debitable and checkable transactions deposits are normally acceptable as a medium of exchange. The **depository institutions** that offer transactions deposits are numerous and include commercial banks and almost all **thrift institutions**—savings banks, savings and loan associations (S&Ls), and credit unions.

FIGURE 15-2 Composition of the U.S. M1 and M2 Money Supply, 2011

Panel (a) shows estimates of the M1 money supply, of which the largest component (over 51 percent) is currency. M2 consists of M1 plus three other components, the most important of which is savings deposits at all depository institutions.

Sources: Federal Reserve Bulletin; Economic Indicators, various issues; author's estimates.

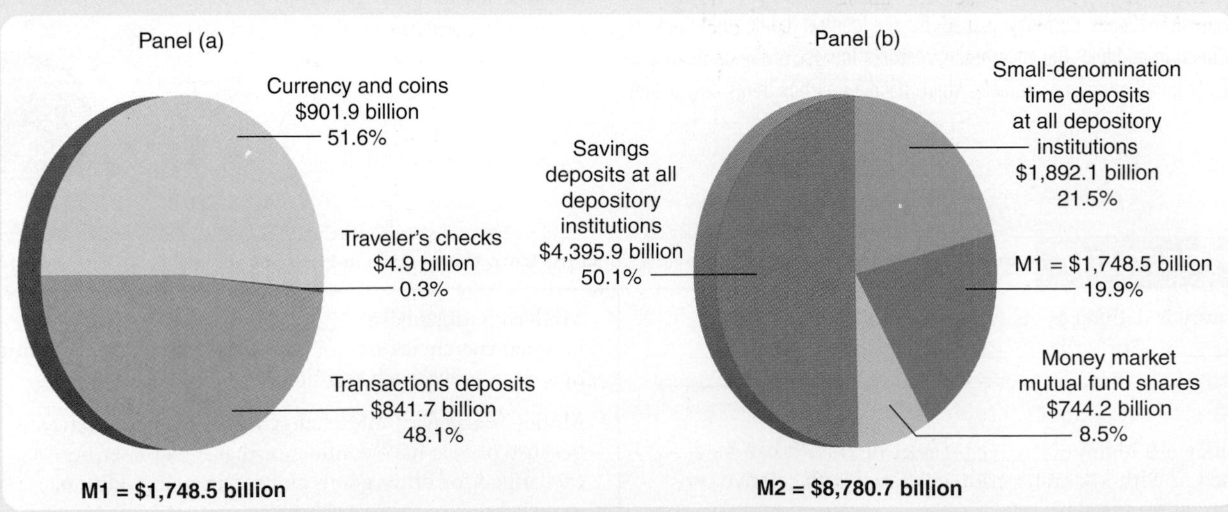

TRAVELER'S CHECKS **Traveler's checks** are paid for by the purchaser at the time of transfer. The total quantity of traveler's checks outstanding issued by institutions other than banks is part of the M1 money supply. American Express and other institutions issue traveler's checks.

Traveler's checks
Financial instruments obtained from a bank or a nonbanking organization and signed during purchase that can be used in payment upon a second signature by the purchaser.

The Liquidity Approach to Measuring Money: M2

The liquidity approach to defining and measuring the U.S. money supply views money as a temporary store of value and so includes all of M1 *plus* several other highly liquid assets. Panel (b) of Figure 15-2 on the facing page shows the components of **M2**—money as a temporary store of value. These components include the following:

M2
M1 plus (1) savings deposits at all depository institutions, (2) small-denomination time deposits, and (3) balances in retail money market mutual funds.

1. ***Savings deposits.*** Total *savings deposits*—deposits with no set maturities—are the largest component of the M2 money supply.
2. ***Small-denomination time deposits.*** With a *time deposit*, the funds must be left in a financial institution for a given period before they can be withdrawn without penalty. To be included in the M2 definition of the money supply, time deposits must be less than $100,000—hence, the designation *small-denomination time deposits*.
3. ***Money market mutual fund balances.*** Many individuals keep part of their assets in the form of shares in *money market mutual funds*—highly liquid funds that investment companies obtain from the public. All money market mutual fund balances except those held by large institutions (which typically use them more like large time deposits) are included in M2 because they are very liquid.

When all of these assets are added together, the result is M2, as shown in panel (b) of Figure 15-2 on the facing page.

OTHER MONEY SUPPLY DEFINITIONS Economists and other researchers have come up with additional definitions of money. Some businesspeople and policymakers prefer a monetary aggregate known as *MZM*. The MZM aggregate is the so-called money-at-zero-maturity money stock. Obtaining MZM entails adding to M1 those deposits without set maturities, such as savings deposits, that are included in M2. MZM includes *all* money market funds but excludes all deposits with fixed maturities, such as small-denomination time deposits.

For Federal Reserve data concerning the latest trends in the monetary aggregates, go to **www.econtoday.com/ch15** and click on "Money Stock Measures–H.6" under Money Stock and Reserve Balances.

QUICK QUIZ See page 344 for the answers. **Review concepts from this section in MyEconLab.**

The **money supply** can be defined in a variety of ways, depending on whether we use the transactions approach or the liquidity approach. Using the __________ approach, the money supply consists of currency, **transactions deposits,** and traveler's checks. This is called __________.

__________ deposits are any deposits in financial institutions from which the deposit owner can transfer funds using a debit card or checks.

When we add savings deposits, small-denomination time deposits, and retail money market mutual fund balances to __________, we obtain the measure known as __________.

Financial Intermediation and Banks

Most nations, including the United States, have a banking system that encompasses two types of institutions. One type consists of privately owned profit-seeking institutions, such as commercial banks and thrift institutions. The other type of institution is a **central bank,** which typically serves as a banker's bank and as a bank for the national treasury or finance ministry.

Central bank
A banker's bank, usually an official institution that also serves as a bank for a nation's government treasury. Central banks normally regulate commercial banks.

Direct versus Indirect Financing

When individuals choose to hold some of their savings in new bonds issued by a corporation, their purchases of the bonds are in effect direct loans to the business. This is an example of *direct finance*, in which people lend funds directly to a business. Business financing is not always direct. Individuals might choose instead to hold a time deposit at a bank. The bank may then lend to the same company. In this way, the same people can provide *indirect finance* to a business. The bank makes this possible by *intermediating* the financing of the company.

Financial Intermediation

Banks and other financial institutions are all in the same business—transferring funds from savers to investors. This process is known as **financial intermediation,** and its participants, such as banks and savings institutions, are **financial intermediaries.** The process of financial intermediation is illustrated in Figure 15-3 below.

Financial intermediation
The process by which financial institutions accept savings from businesses, households, and governments and lend the savings to other businesses, households, and governments.

Financial intermediaries
Institutions that transfer funds between ultimate lenders (savers) and ultimate borrowers.

Asymmetric information
Information possessed by one party in a financial transaction but not by the other party.

Adverse selection
The tendency for high-risk projects and clients to be overrepresented among borrowers.

Moral hazard
The possibility that a borrower might engage in riskier behavior after a loan has been obtained.

ASYMMETRIC INFORMATION, ADVERSE SELECTION, AND MORAL HAZARD Why might people wish to direct their funds through a bank instead of lending them directly to a business? One important reason is **asymmetric information**—the fact that the business may have better knowledge of its own current and future prospects than potential lenders do. For instance, the business may know that it intends to use borrowed funds for projects with a high risk of failure that would make repaying the loan difficult. This potential for borrowers to use the borrowed funds in high-risk projects is known as **adverse selection.** Alternatively, a business that had intended to undertake low-risk projects may change management after receiving a loan, and the new managers may use the borrowed funds in riskier ways. The possibility that a borrower might engage in behavior that increases risk after borrowing funds is called **moral hazard.**

To minimize the possibility that a business might fail to repay a loan, people thinking about lending funds directly to the business must study the business carefully before making the loan, and they must continue to monitor its performance afterward. Alternatively, they can choose to avoid the trouble by holding deposits with financial intermediaries, which then specialize in evaluating the creditworthiness of business borrowers and in keeping tabs on their progress until loans are repaid. Thus, adverse selection and moral hazard both help explain why people use financial intermediaries.

FIGURE 15-3 The Process of Financial Intermediation

The process of financial intermediation is depicted here. Note that ultimate lenders and ultimate borrowers are the same economic units—households, businesses, and governments—but not necessarily the same individuals. Whereas individual households can be net lenders or borrowers, households as an economic unit typically are net lenders. Specific businesses or governments similarly can be net lenders or borrowers. As economic units, both are net borrowers.

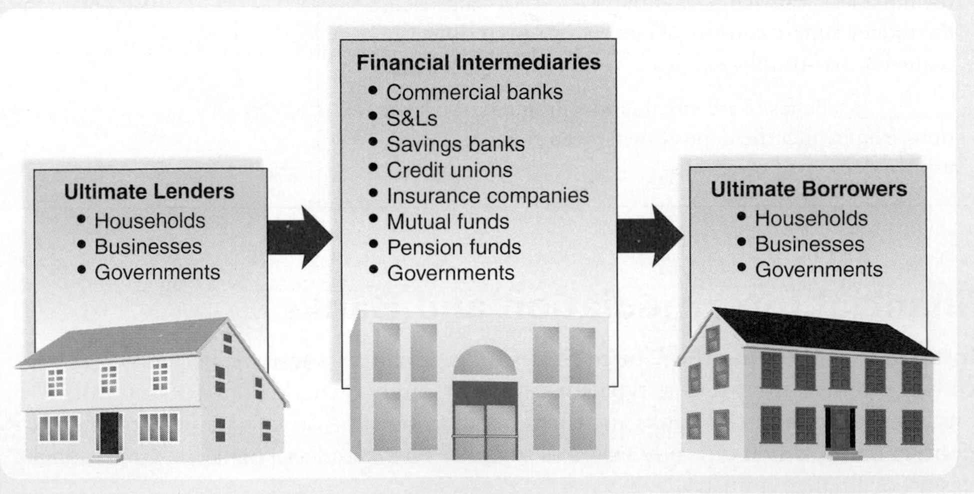

LARGER SCALE AND LOWER MANAGEMENT COSTS Another important reason that financial intermediaries exist is that they make it possible for many people to pool their funds, thereby increasing the size, or *scale*, of the total amount of savings managed by an intermediary. This centralization of management reduces costs and risks below the levels savers would incur if all were to manage their savings alone. *Pension fund companies*, which are institutions that specialize in managing funds that individuals save for retirement, owe their existence largely to their abilities to provide such cost savings to individual savers. Likewise, *investment companies*, which are institutions that manage portfolios of financial instruments called mutual funds on behalf of shareholders, also exist largely because of cost savings from their greater scale of operations. In addition, *government-sponsored financial institutions*, such as the Federal National Mortgage Association, seek to reduce overall lending costs by pooling large volumes of funds from investors in order to buy groups of mortgage loans.

FINANCIAL INSTITUTION LIABILITIES AND ASSETS Every financial intermediary has its own sources of funds, which are **liabilities** of that institution. When you place $100 in your transactions deposit at a bank, the bank creates a liability—it owes you $100—in exchange for the funds deposited. A commercial bank gets its funds from transactions and savings accounts, and an insurance company gets its funds from insurance policy premiums.

Liabilities
Amounts owed; the legal claims against a business or household by nonowners.

Each financial intermediary has a different primary use of its **assets.** For example, a credit union usually makes small consumer loans, whereas a savings bank makes mainly mortgage loans. Table 15-2 below lists the assets and liabilities of typical financial intermediaries. Be aware, though, that the distinctions between different types of financial institutions are becoming more and more blurred. As laws and regulations change, there will be less need to make any distinction. All may ultimately be treated simply as financial intermediaries.

Assets
Amounts owned; all items to which a business or household holds legal claim.

Transmitting Payments via Debit-Card Transactions

Since 2006, the dollar volume of payments transmitted using debit cards has exceeded the value of checking transactions. To see how a debit-card transaction clears, take a look at Figure 15-4 on the next page. Suppose that Bank of America has provided a debit card to a college student named Jill Jones, who in turn uses the card to purchase

TABLE 15-2

Financial Intermediaries and Their Assets and Liabilities

Financial Intermediary	Assets	Liabilities
Commercial banks, savings and loan associations, savings banks, and credit unions	Car loans and other consumer debt, business loans, government securities, home mortgages	Transactions deposits, savings deposits, various other time deposits
Insurance companies	Mortgages, stocks, bonds, real estate	Insurance contracts, annuities, pension plans
Pension and retirement funds	Stocks, bonds, mortgages, time deposits	Pension plans
Money market mutual funds	Short-term credit instruments such as large-denomination certificates of deposit, Treasury bills, and high-grade commercial paper	Fund shares with limited checking privileges
Government-sponsored financial institutions	Home mortgages	Mortgage-backed securities issued to investors

$200 worth of clothing from Macy's, which has an account at Citibank. The debit-card transaction generates an electronic record, which Macy's transmits to Citibank.

The debit-card system automatically uses the electronic record to determine the bank that issued the debit card used to purchase the clothing. It transmits this information to Bank of America. Then Bank of America verifies that Jill Jones is an account holder, deducts $200 from her transactions deposit account, and transmits these funds electronically, via the debit-card system, to Citibank. Finally, Citibank credits $200 to Macy's transactions deposit account, and payment for the clothing purchase is complete.

Do people have to use checks or debit cards to initiate payment transfers from their accounts?

EXAMPLE Mobile Payments Are Catching On

Did you jump into your car and leave your friend's house before remembering to pay back the $25 that you had borrowed a few days ago? If so, instead of turning the car around and driving back to repay her, you can send a mobile payment using your cellphone or some other network-connected device and a person-to-person payment service operated by your bank. Once you have signed up, all you have to do is provide a payment instruction to your bank. The bank handles the payment just as it would if you had used a debit card. In exchange for a small fee—typically about 25 cents per transaction—the bank transfers funds from your account to the account of the person to whom you wish to send a payment. So far, nearly 10 percent of all U.S. residents have used cellphones to transfer payments in this way. Almost 20 percent of young people aged 18 to 25 have done so, a fact that leads most observers to conclude that mobile payments are likely to proliferate during the coming decade.

FOR CRITICAL ANALYSIS

Why is a payment transfer initiated using a cellphone economically indistinguishable from a payment order made using a check or a debit card?

FIGURE 15-4 How a Debit-Card Transaction Clears

A college student named Jill Jones uses a debit card issued by Bank of America to purchase clothing valued at $200 from Macy's, which has an account with Citibank. The debit-card transaction creates an electronic record that is transmitted to Citibank. The debit-card system forwards this record to Bank of America, which deducts $200 from Jill Jones's transactions deposit account. Then the debit-card system transmits the $200 payment to Citibank, which credits the $200 to Macy's account.

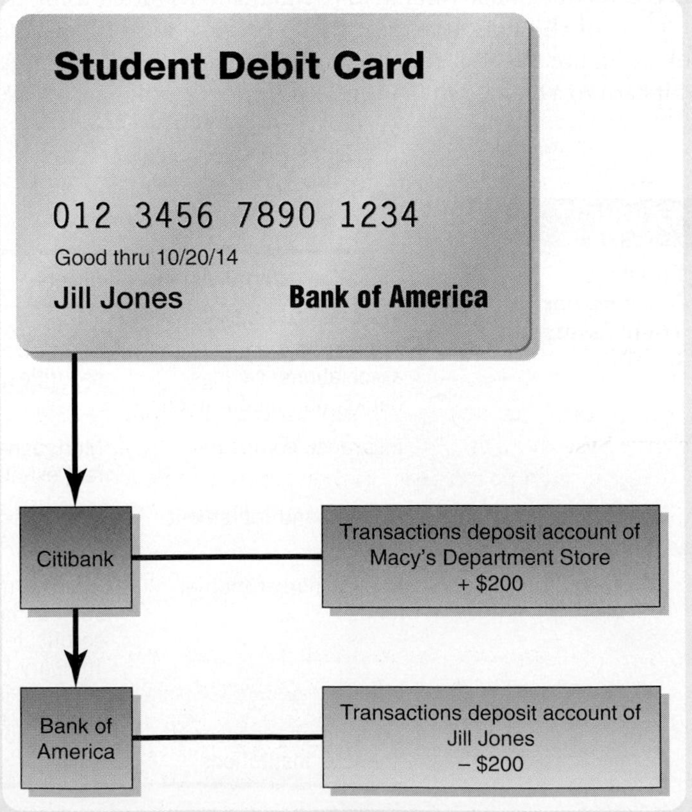

QUICK QUIZ See page 344 for the answers. Review concepts from this section in MyEconLab.

_________ intermediaries, including depository institutions such as commercial banks and savings institutions, insurance companies, mutual funds, and pension funds, transfer funds from ultimate lenders (savers) to ultimate borrowers.

Financial intermediaries specialize in tackling problems of _________ information. They address the _________ _________ problem by carefully reviewing the credit-worthiness of loan applicants, and they deal with the _________ _________ problem by monitoring borrowers after they receive loans. Many financial intermediaries also take advantage of cost reductions arising from the centralized management of funds pooled from the savings of many individuals.

The Federal Reserve System: The U.S. Central Bank

The Federal Reserve System, which serves as the nation's central bank, is one of the key banking institutions in the United States. It is partly a creature of government and partly privately directed.

The Federal Reserve System

The Federal Reserve System, also known simply as **the Fed,** is the most important regulatory agency in the U.S. monetary system and is usually considered the monetary authority. The Fed was established by the Federal Reserve Act, signed on December 13, 1913, by President Woodrow Wilson.

The Fed
The Federal Reserve System; the central bank of the United States.

ORGANIZATION OF THE FEDERAL RESERVE SYSTEM Figure 15-5 on the following page shows how the Federal Reserve System is organized. It is managed by the Board of Governors, composed of seven full-time members appointed by the U.S. president with the approval of the Senate. The chair of the Board of Governors is the leading official of the Board of Governors and of the Federal Reserve System. Since 2006, Ben Bernanke has held this position.

The 12 Federal Reserve district banks have a total of 25 branches. The boundaries of the 12 Federal Reserve districts and the cities in which Federal Reserve banks are located are shown in Figure 15-6 on page 329. The Federal Open Market Committee (FOMC) determines the future growth of the money supply and other important variables. This committee is composed of the members of the Board of Governors, the president of the New York Federal Reserve Bank, and presidents of four other Federal Reserve banks, rotated periodically. The chair of the Board of Governors also chairs the FOMC.

DEPOSITORY INSTITUTIONS Depository institutions—all financial institutions that accept deposits—comprise our monetary system consisting of nearly 6,700 commercial banks, 1,100 savings and loan associations and savings banks, and about 10,000 credit unions. All depository institutions may purchase services from the Federal Reserve System on an equal basis. Also, almost all depository institutions are required to keep a certain percentage of their deposits in reserve at the Federal Reserve district banks or as vault cash. This percentage depends on the bank's volume of business.

FUNCTIONS OF THE FEDERAL RESERVE SYSTEM Here we present in detail what the Federal Reserve does.

1. ***The Fed supplies the economy with fiduciary currency.*** The Federal Reserve banks supply the economy with paper currency called Federal Reserve notes. For example, during holiday seasons, when very large numbers of currency transactions take place, more paper currency is desired. Commercial banks respond to the increased number and dollar amounts of depositors' currency withdrawals by turning to the Federal Reserve banks to replenish vault cash. Hence, the Federal

FIGURE 15-5 Organization of the Federal Reserve System

The 12 Federal Reserve district banks are headed by 12 separate presidents. The main authority of the Fed resides with the Board of Governors of the Federal Reserve System, whose seven members are appointed for 14-year terms by the president of the United States and confirmed by the Senate. Open market operations are carried out through the Federal Open Market Committee (FOMC), consisting of the seven members of the Board of Governors plus five presidents of the district banks (always including the president of the New York bank, with the others rotating).

Source: Board of Governors of the Federal Reserve System, *The Federal Reserve System: Purposes and Functions*, 7th ed. (Washington, D.C., 1984), p. 5.

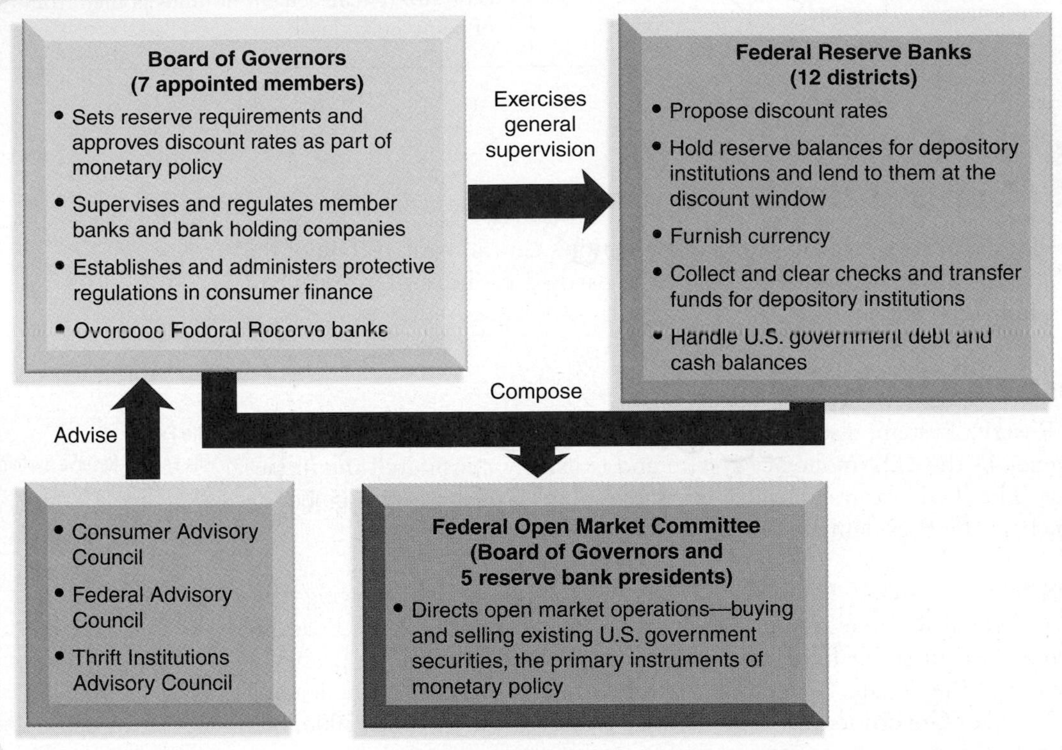

Reserve banks must have on hand a sufficient amount of cash to accommodate the demands for paper currency at different times of the year. Note that even though all Federal Reserve notes are printed at the Bureau of Engraving and Printing in Washington, D.C., each note is assigned a code indicating which of the 12 Federal Reserve banks first introduced the note into circulation. Moreover, each of these notes is an obligation (liability) of the Federal Reserve System, *not* the U.S. Treasury.

2. ***The Fed provides payment-clearing systems.*** The Federal Reserve System has long operated systems for transmitting and clearing payments. Federal Reserve banks all offer check-clearing services to commercial banks, savings institutions, and credit unions. In addition, the Federal Reserve System operates an electronic payments transfer system called *Fedwire*, which U.S. depository institutions use to process interbank payments. For instance, when a bank extends a loan to another institution, it typically transmits the payment using Fedwire. The other institution repays the loan the next day or a few days later by transmitting a payment on the same system. The average payment transfer on Fedwire exceeds $3 million, and the typical daily volume of all payments processed on this system is greater than $1 trillion.
3. ***The Fed holds depository institutions' reserves.*** The 12 Federal Reserve district banks hold the reserves (other than vault cash) of depository institutions. Depository institutions are required by law to keep a certain percentage of their transactions deposits as reserves. Even if they weren't required to do so by law, they would still wish to keep some reserves on which they can draw funds as needed for expected and unexpected transactions.

FIGURE 15-6 The Federal Reserve System

The Federal Reserve System is divided into 12 districts, each served by one of the Federal Reserve district banks, located in the cities indicated. The Board of Governors meets in Washington, D.C.

Source: Board of Governors of the Federal Reserve System.

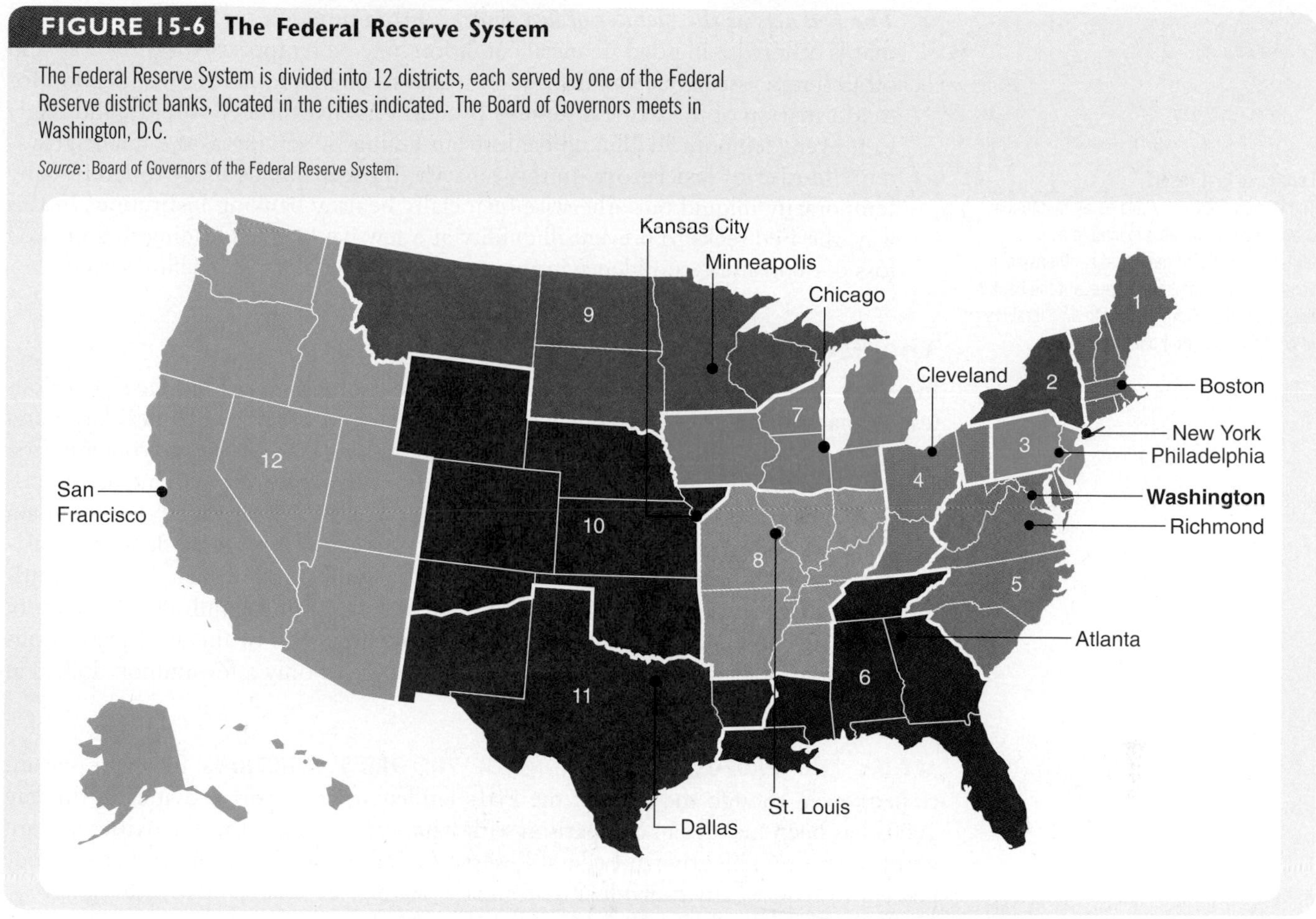

4. ***The Fed acts as the government's fiscal agent.*** The Federal Reserve is the banker and fiscal agent for the federal government. The government, as we are all aware, collects large sums of funds through taxation. The government also spends and distributes equally large sums. Consequently, the U.S. Treasury has a transactions account with the Federal Reserve. Thus, the Fed acts as the government's banker, along with commercial banks that hold government deposits. The Fed also helps the government collect certain tax revenues and aids in the purchase and sale of government securities.
5. ***The Fed supervises depository institutions.*** The Fed (along with the Comptroller of the Currency, the Federal Deposit Insurance Corporation, the Office of Thrift Supervision in the Treasury Department, and the National Credit Union Administration) is a supervisor and regulator of depository institutions. The Fed and other regulators periodically and without warning examine depository institutions to see what kinds of loans have been made, what has been used as security for the loans, and who has received them. Whenever such an examination indicates that a bank is not conforming to current banking rules and standards, the Fed can require the bank to alter its banking practices.
6. ***The Fed conducts monetary policy.*** Perhaps the Fed's most important task is to regulate the nation's money supply. To understand how the Fed manages the money supply, we must examine more closely its reserve-holding function and the way in which depository institutions aid in expansion and contraction of the money supply. We will do this later in this chapter.
7. ***The Fed intervenes in foreign currency markets.*** Sometimes the Fed attempts to keep the value of the dollar from changing. It does this by buying and selling U.S. dollars in foreign exchange markets. You will read more about this important topic in Chapter 33.

8. ***The Fed acts as the "lender of last resort."*** From time to time, an individual bank that is otherwise in good financial condition may be temporarily low on cash and other liquid assets. Such an institution is said to be illiquid. A key justification for the formation of the Federal Reserve System was that the Fed would stand ready to prevent temporarily illiquid banks from failing by serving as the financial system's **lender of last resort.** In this capacity, the Fed stands ready to lend to any temporarily illiquid but otherwise financially healthy banking institution. In this way, the Fed seeks to prevent illiquidity at a few banks from leading to a general loss of depositors' confidence in the overall soundness of the banking system.

Lender of last resort
The Federal Reserve's role as an institution that is willing and able to lend to a temporarily illiquid bank that is otherwise in good financial condition to prevent the bank's illiquid position from leading to a general loss of confidence in that bank or in others.

The Fed in Crisis

In recent years, the Federal Reserve's role as lender of last resort has faced a serious test as many banks, nonbank financial institutions, and other companies, large and small, have struggled with serious financial difficulties. When these problems first surfaced in 2007, the Fed had to determine whether banks were experiencing temporary illiquidity or distress related to other causes. The Fed determined that the main problem was temporary illiquidity, and it responded by providing lender-of-last-resort assistance first to a few banks, then to several banks, and ultimately to a significant number of banks. By early 2009, the Fed was providing hundreds of *billions* of dollars in direct lender-of-last-resort assistance to hundreds of financial institutions and even nonfinancial companies, up from an average of only a few million dollars at any given time earlier in the decade.

ACTUAL AND PROPOSED EXPANSIONS OF THE FED'S FUNCTIONS In an important respect, even though the scale of the Fed's lender-of-last-resort activities in the late 2000s has been massive in comparison with what came before, these activities are not a *new* function. The original Federal Reserve Act of 1913 granted the Fed emergency powers to lend to any individual or company as long as it consulted with Congress. Nevertheless, it is doubtful that its early-twentieth-century congressional founders ever expected the Fed would be offering long-term credit to banks, other financial firms, and even divisions of auto companies as it has since 2007. The founders envisioned a central bank that would provide only short-term loans to avert problems of illiquidity, not extend credit over long periods to keep businesses from collapsing. This is the key sense in which the Fed's functions have broadened since 2007.

Furthermore, legislation signed into law by President Obama in 2010 added to the Federal Reserve's functions by making it the nation's primary *systemic risk regulator*. A *systemic risk* is the potential for a financial breakdown at a large institution to spread throughout banks and other firms and thereby create a crisis such as the one experienced in recent years. Under this law, as the nation's systemic risk regulator, the Fed possesses authority to implement policies aimed at heading off sources of such risks before they can undermine the stability of the nation's financial system.

"MISSION CREEP" AT THE FED? A number of economists, legislators, and other policymakers have expressed reservations about both the expanded scale of the Fed's lender-of-last-resort activities and its new role as regulator of systemic risks. Those who question the magnitude of the Fed's last-resort lending worry that by providing so much credit to so many institutions, the Fed exerts too much control over the distribution of funds throughout the banking system and the broader economy. They contend that Congress intended for the Fed to control the overall money supply, not which firms are able to obtain Fed loans to keep their weakened businesses alive. By controlling flows of funds to firms that it handpicks, the critics argue, the Fed is preventing private markets from directing funds to the best-managed, most creditworthy borrowers.

Analogous concerns have caused some observers to question whether a systemic-regulator function should have been added to the Fed's already long list of responsibilities. They worry that a further empowered Fed may engage in even more interventions in private markets. Systemic risks that might threaten the financial system could originate with any large companies, so ultimately the Fed might become involved in regulating parts of the economy far from the banking system.

Another concern is the potential for the Fed to take on responsibilities that conflict with its primary responsibility of regulating the money supply. Indeed, a few years ago, as a professor, current Fed Chair Ben Bernanke wrote about the potential for such a conflict of interest. A Federal Reserve too heavily involved in trying to assure the success of banks and other institutions, Bernanke noted, might regulate the money supply with an aim to assist these firms and lose sight of broader economic effects. Alternatively, as a systemic regulator, the Fed might be tempted to require the institutions it regulates to engage in activities to further its monetary policy objectives even if those activities were not in those institutions' best interests.

A third concern is that the Fed may become so heavily involved in regulating so many companies that it will become ensnarled in political controversies relating to those firms. Greater exposure to associated pressures, some observers worry, could threaten the Fed's authority to conduct monetary policy independently of politics.

QUICK QUIZ See page 344 for the answers. Review concepts from this section in MyEconLab.

The central bank in the United States is the _________ _________ _________, which was established on December 13, 1913.

There are 12 Federal Reserve district banks, with 25 branches. The Federal Reserve System is managed by the _________ of _________ in Washington, D.C. The Fed interacts with almost all depository institutions in the United States, most of which must keep a certain percentage of their transactions deposits on reserve with the Fed. The Fed serves as the chief regulatory agency for all depository institutions that have Federal Reserve System membership.

The functions of the Federal Reserve System are to supply fiduciary _________, provide payment-clearing services, hold depository institution _________, act as the government's fiscal agent, supervise depository institutions, regulate the supply of money, intervene in foreign currency markets, and act as the _________ of _________ _________.

Fractional Reserve Banking, the Federal Reserve, and the Money Supply

As early as 1000 BC, uncoined gold and silver were being used as money in Mesopotamia. Goldsmiths weighed and assessed the purity of those metals. Later they started issuing paper notes indicating that the bearers held gold or silver of given weights and purity on deposit with the goldsmith. These notes could be transferred in exchange for goods and became the first paper currency. The gold and silver on deposit with the goldsmiths were the first bank deposits. Eventually, goldsmiths realized that inflows of gold and silver for deposit always exceeded the average amount of gold and silver withdrawn at any given time—often by a predictable ratio.

These goldsmiths started making loans by issuing to borrowers paper notes that exceeded in value the amount of gold and silver the goldsmiths actually kept on hand. They charged interest on these loans. This constituted the earliest form of what is now called **fractional reserve banking.** We know that goldsmiths operated this way in Delphi, Didyma, and Olympia in Greece as early as the seventh century BC. In Athens, fractional reserve banking was well developed by the sixth century BC.

Fractional reserve banking
A system in which depository institutions hold reserves that are less than the amount of total deposits.

Depository Institution Reserves

In a fractional reserve banking system, banks do not keep sufficient funds on hand to cover 100 percent of their depositors' accounts. And the funds held by depository institutions in the United States are not kept in gold and silver, as they were with the early goldsmiths. Instead, the funds are held as **reserves** in the form of cash in banks' vaults and deposits that banks hold on deposit with Federal Reserve district banks. The fraction of deposits that banks hold as reserves is called

Reserves
In the U.S. Federal Reserve System, deposits held by Federal Reserve district banks for depository institutions, plus depository institutions' vault cash.

Reserve ratio
The fraction of transactions deposits that banks hold as reserves.

the **reserve ratio.** There are two determinants of the size of this ratio. One is the quantity of reserves that the Federal Reserve requires banks to hold, which are called *required reserves*. The other determinant of the reserve ratio is whatever additional amount of reserves that banks voluntarily hold, known as *excess reserves*.

Balance sheet
A statement of the assets and liabilities of any business entity, including financial institutions and the Federal Reserve System. Assets are what is owned; liabilities are what is owed.

To show the relationship between reserves and deposits at an individual bank, let's examine the **balance sheet,** or statement of assets owned and liabilities (amounts owed to others), for a particular depository institution. Balance Sheet 15-1 below displays a balance sheet for a depository institution called Typical Bank. Liabilities for this institution consist solely of $1 million in transactions deposits. Assets consist of $100,000 in reserves and $900,000 in loans to customers. Total assets of $1 million equal total liabilities of $1 million. Because Typical Bank has $100,000 of reserves and $1 million of transactions deposits, its reserve ratio is 10 percent. Thus, Typical Bank is part of a system of fractional reserve banking, in which it holds only 10 percent of its deposits as reserves.

BALANCE SHEET 15-1

Typical Bank

Assets		Liabilities	
Reserves	$100,000	Transactions deposits	$1,000,000
Loans	$900,000		
Total	$1,000,000	Total	$1,000,000

Fractional Reserve Banking and Money Expansion

Under fractional reserve banking, the Federal Reserve can add to the quantity of money in circulation by bringing about an expansion of deposits within the banking system. To understand how the Fed can create money within the banking system, we must look at how depository institutions respond to Fed actions that increase reserves in the entire system.

Open market operations
The purchase and sale of existing U.S. government securities (such as bonds) in the open private market by the Federal Reserve System.

Let's consider the effect of a Fed **open market operation,** which is a Fed purchase or sale of existing U.S. government securities in the open market—the private secondary market in which people exchange securities that have not yet matured. Assume that the Fed engaged in an *open market purchase* by buying a $100,000 U.S. government security from a bond dealer. The Fed does this by electronically transferring $100,000 to the bond dealer's transactions deposit account at Bank 1. Thus, as shown in Balance Sheet 15-2 below, Bank 1's transactions deposit liabilities increase by $100,000. Let's suppose that the reserve ratio for Bank 1 and all other depository institutions is 10 percent. Thus, as shown in Balance Sheet 15-2, Bank 1 responds to this $100,000 increase in transactions deposits by adding 10 percent of this amount, or $10,000, to its reserves. The bank allocates the remaining $90,000 of additional deposits to new loans, so its loans increase by $90,000.

BALANCE SHEET 15-2

Bank 1

Assets		Liabilities	
Reserves	+$10,000	Transactions deposits	+$100,000
Loans	+$90,000		
Total	+$100,000	Total	+$100,000

EFFECT ON THE MONEY SUPPLY At this point, the Fed's purchase of a $100,000 U.S. government security from a bond dealer has increased the money supply immediately by $100,000. This occurs because transactions deposits held by the public—bond dealers are part of the public—are part of the money supply. Hence, the addition of

$100,000 to deposits with Bank 1, with no corresponding deposit reduction elsewhere in the banking system, raises the money supply by $100,000. (If another member of the public, instead of the Fed, had purchased the bond, that person's transactions deposit would have been reduced by $100,000, so there would have been no change in the money supply.)

The process of money creation does not stop here. The borrower who receives the $90,000 loan from Bank 1 will spend these funds, which will then be deposited in other banks. In this instance, suppose that the $90,000 spent by Bank 1's borrower is deposited in a transactions deposit account at Bank 2. At this bank, as shown in Balance Sheet 15-3 below, transactions deposits and hence the money supply increase by $90,000. Bank 2 adds 10 percent of these deposits, or $9,000, to its reserves. It uses the remaining $81,000 of new deposits to add $81,000 to its loans.

BALANCE SHEET 15-3

Bank 2

Assets		Liabilities	
Reserves	+$9,000	Transactions deposits	+$90,000
Loans	+$81,000		
Total	+$90,000	Total	+$90,000

CONTINUATION OF THE DEPOSIT CREATION PROCESS Look at Bank 3's account in Balance Sheet 15-4 below. Assume that the borrower receiving the $81,000 loan from Bank 2 spends these funds, which then are deposited in an account at Bank 3. Transactions deposits and the money supply increase by $81,000. Reserves of Bank 3 rise by 10 percent of this amount, or $8,100. Bank 3 uses the rest of the newly deposited funds, or $72,900, to increase its loans.

BALANCE SHEET 15-4

Bank 3

Assets		Liabilities	
Reserves	+$8,100	Transactions deposits	+$81,000
Loans	+$72,900		
Total	+$81,000	Total	+$81,000

This process continues to Banks 4, 5, 6, and so forth. Each bank obtains smaller and smaller increases in deposits because banks hold 10 percent of new deposits as reserves. Thus, each succeeding depository institution makes correspondingly smaller loans. Table 15-3 on the top of the following page shows new deposits, reserves, and loans for the remaining depository institutions.

EFFECT ON TOTAL DEPOSITS AND THE MONEY SUPPLY In this example, deposits and the money supply increased initially by the $100,000 that the Fed paid the bond dealer in exchange for a U.S. government security. Deposits and the money supply were further increased by a $90,000 deposit in Bank 2, and they were again increased by an $81,000 deposit in Bank 3. Eventually, total deposits and the money supply increase by $1 million, as shown in Table 15-3. This $1 million expansion of deposits and the money supply consists of the original $100,000 created by the Fed, plus an extra $900,000 generated by deposit-creating bank loans. The deposit creation process is portrayed graphically in Figure 15-7 on the bottom of the following page.

TABLE 15-3

Maximum Money Creation with 10 Percent Reserve Ratio

This table shows the maximum new loans that banks can make, given the Fed's electronic transfer of $100,000 to a transactions deposit account at Bank 1. The reserve ratio is 10 percent.

Bank	New Deposits	New Reserves	Maximum New Loans
1	$100,000 (from Fed)	$10,000	$90,000
2	90,000	9,000	81,000
3	81,000	8,100	72,900
4	72,900	7,290	65,610
.	.	.	.
.	.	.	.
.	.	.	.
All other banks	656,100	65,610	590,490
Totals	$1,000,000	$100,000	$900,000

FIGURE 15-7 **The Multiple Expansion in the Money Supply Due to $100,000 in New Reserves When the Reserve Ratio Is 10 Percent**

The banks are all aligned in decreasing order of new deposits created. Bank 1 receives the $100,000 in new reserves and lends out $90,000. Bank 2 receives the $90,000 and lends out $81,000. The process continues through Banks 3 to 19 and then the rest of the banking system. Ultimately, assuming no leakages into currency, the $100,000 of new reserves results in an increase in the money supply of $1 million, or 10 times the new reserves, because the reserve ratio is 10 percent.

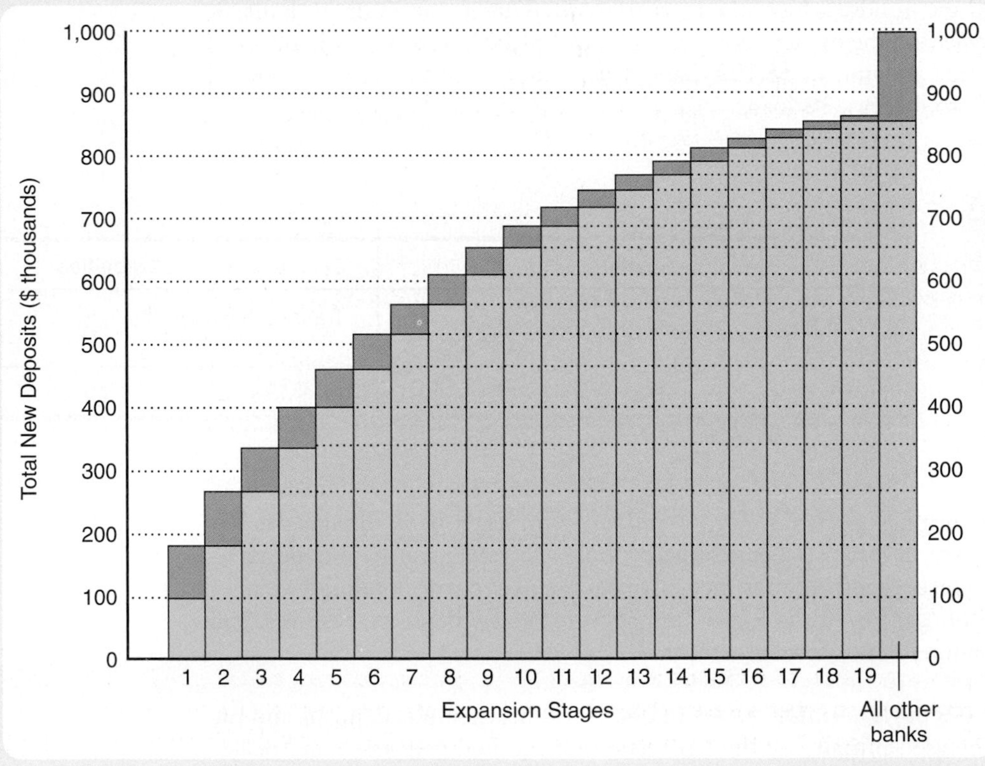

You should be able to work through the foregoing example to show the reverse process when there is a *decrease* in reserves because the Fed engages in an *open market sale* by selling a $100,000 U.S. government security. The result is a multiple contraction of deposits and, therefore, of the total money supply in circulation.

The Money Multiplier

In the example just given, a $100,000 increase in reserves generated by the Fed's purchase of a security yielded a $1 million increase in transactions deposits and, hence, the money supply. Thus, deposits and the money supply increased by a multiple of 10 times the initial $100,000 increase in overall reserves. Conversely, a $100,000 decrease in reserves generated by a Fed sale of a security will yield a decrease in total deposits of $1 million—that is, a multiple of 10 times the initial $100,000 decrease in overall reserves.

We can now make a generalization about the extent to which the total money supply will change when the banking system's reserves are increased or decreased. The **money multiplier** gives the change in the money supply due to a change in reserves. In our example, the value of the money multiplier is 10.

Money multiplier
A number that, when multiplied by a change in reserves in the banking system, yields the resulting change in the money supply.

POTENTIAL VERSUS ACTUAL MONEY MULTIPLIERS If we assume, as in our example, that all loan proceeds are deposited with banks, we obtain the **potential money multiplier**—the *maximum* possible value of the money multiplier:

Potential money multiplier
The reciprocal of the reserve ratio, assuming no leakages into currency. It is equal to 1 divided by the reserve ratio.

$$\text{Potential money multiplier} = \frac{1}{\text{reserve ratio}}$$

That is, the potential money multiplier is equal to 1 divided by the fraction of transactions deposits that banks hold as reserves. In our example, the reserve ratio was 10 percent, or 0.10 expressed as a decimal fraction. Thus, in the example the value of the potential money multiplier was equal to 1 divided by 0.10, which equals 10.

What happens if the entire amount of a loan from a depository institution is not redeposited? When borrowers want to hold a portion of their loans as currency outside the banking system, these funds cannot be held by banks as reserves from which to make loans. The greater the amount of cash leakage, the smaller the *actual* money multiplier. Typically, borrowers do hold a portion of loan proceeds as currency, so the actual money multiplier usually is smaller than the potential money multiplier.

REAL-WORLD MONEY MULTIPLIERS The potential money multiplier is rarely attained for the banking system as a whole. Furthermore, each definition of the money supply, M1 or M2, will yield a different actual money multiplier.

In recent years, the actual M1 multiplier has been in a range between 1.5 and 2.0. The actual M2 multiplier showed an upward trend until recently, rising from 6.5 in the 1960s to over 12 in the mid-2000s. Since then, however, it has dropped to about 5.

Why Not . . . eliminate open market operations?

Open market operations seem complicated and are conducted daily. In principle, the Federal Reserve could engage in monetary policy by varying the reserve ratio. In fact, since 2008, inducing changes in the reserve ratio has been a fundamental way in which the Federal Reserve has been generating variations in the quantity of money in circulation. In 2008, Congress granted the Fed authority to pay interest on reserves that depository institutions hold with Federal Reserve district banks. By paying a higher rate of interest on reserves, the Fed can induce banks to hold more reserves relative to deposits, so the reserve ratio rises. This is why the actual M2 multiplier has recently fallen to less than half of its mid-2000s level. Nevertheless, the Fed has experienced problems in regulating the money supply in this way. Finding the precise change in the interest rate on reserves that will bring about the desired reserve ratio without generating a larger-than-intended multiplier effect on the money supply has proved to be a challenge.

QUICK QUIZ See page 344 for the answers. Review concepts from this section in MyEconLab.

__________ of depository institutions consist of their vault cash and deposits that they hold with __________ __________ district banks.

The fraction of transactions deposit liabilities that depository institutions hold as reserves is the __________ __________.

The __________ __________ __________ is equal to 1 divided by the reserve ratio.

Federal Deposit Insurance

As you have seen, fractional reserve banking enables the Federal Reserve to use an open market purchase (or sale) of U.S. government bonds to generate an expansion (or contraction) of deposits. The change in the money supply is a multiple of the open market purchase (or sale). Another effect of fractional reserve banking is to make depository institutions somewhat fragile. After all, the institutions have only a fraction of reserves on hand to honor their depositors' requests for withdrawals. If many depositors simultaneously rush to their bank to withdraw all of their transactions and time deposits—a phenomenon called a **bank run**—the bank would be unable to satisfy their requests. The result would be the failure of that depository institution. Widespread bank runs could lead to the failure of many institutions.

Bank run
Attempt by many of a bank's depositors to convert transactions and time deposits into currency out of fear that the bank's liabilities may exceed its assets.

Seeking to Limit Bank Failures with Deposit Insurance

When businesses fail, they create hardships for creditors, owners, and customers. But when a depository institution fails, an even greater hardship results, because many individuals and businesses depend on the safety and security of banks. As Figure 15-8 below shows, during the 1920s an average of about 600 banks failed

FIGURE 15-8 Bank Failures

A tremendous number of banks failed prior to the creation of federal deposit insurance in 1933. Thereafter, bank failures were few until the mid-1980s. Annual failure rates jumped again in the early and late 2000s.

Source: Federal Deposit Insurance Corporation.

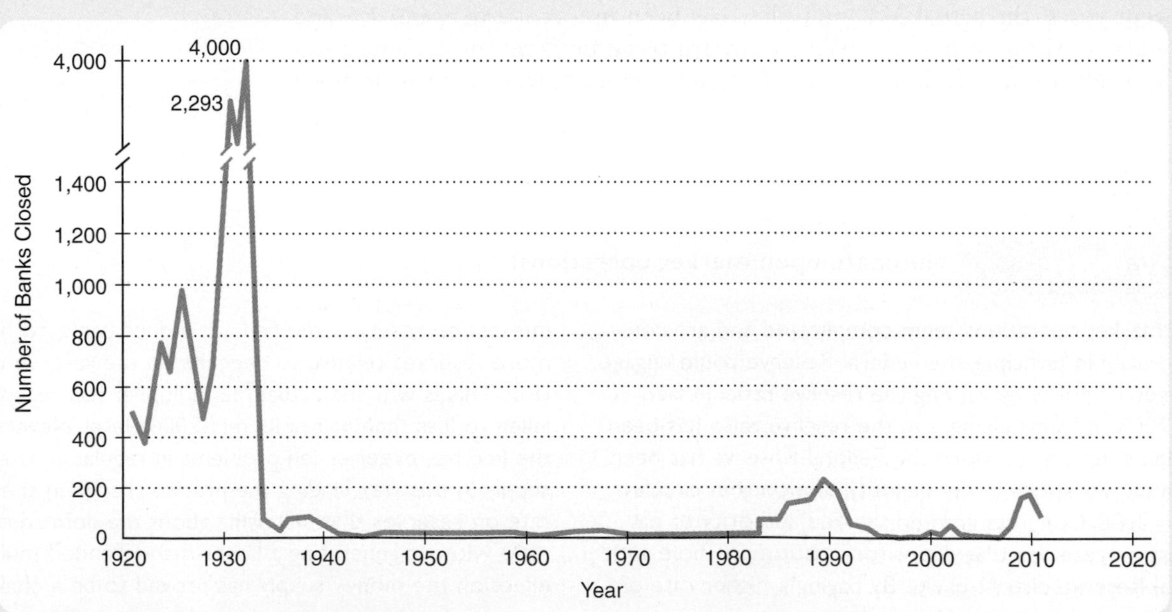

each year. In the early 1930s, during the Great Depression, that average soared to nearly 3,000 failures each year.

In 1933, at the height of these bank failures, the **Federal Deposit Insurance Corporation (FDIC)** was founded to insure the funds of depositors and remove the reason for ruinous runs on banks. In 1934, federal deposit insurance was extended to deposits in savings and loan associations and mutual savings banks, and in 1971 it was offered for deposits in credit unions.

Federal Deposit Insurance Corporation (FDIC)
A government agency that insures the deposits held in banks and most other depository institutions. All U.S. banks are insured this way.

As can be seen in Figure 15-8 on the facing page, bank failure rates dropped dramatically after passage of the early federal legislation. The long period from 1935 until the 1980s was relatively quiet. From World War II to 1984, fewer than nine banks failed per year. From 1995 until 2008, failures again averaged about nine per year. During 2009 and 2010, however, more than 300 banks failed, and hundreds more are still in danger of failing. We will examine the reasons for this shortly. But first we need to understand how deposit insurance works.

The Rationale for Deposit Insurance

Consider the following scenario. A bank begins to look shaky. Its assets do not seem sufficient to cover its liabilities. If the bank has no deposit insurance, depositors in this bank (and any banks associated with it) will all want to withdraw their funds from the bank at the same time. Their concern is that this shaky bank will not have enough assets to return their deposits to them in the form of currency.

Indeed, this is what happens in a bank failure when insurance doesn't exist. Just as when a regular business fails, the creditors of the bank may not all get paid, or if they do, they will get paid less than 100 percent of what they are owed. Depositors are creditors of a bank because their funds are on loan to the bank. As explained earlier, however, banks do not hold 100 percent of their depositors' funds as cash. Instead, banks lend out most of their deposit funds to borrowers. Consequently, all depositors cannot withdraw all their funds simultaneously. Hence, the intent of the legislation enacted in the 1930s was to assure depositors that they could have their deposits converted into cash when they wished, no matter how serious the financial situation of the bank.

To keep up with the latest issues in deposit insurance and banking with the assistance of the FDIC, go to www.econtoday.com/ch15.

Federal deposit insurance provided this assurance. The FDIC charged depository institutions premiums based on their total deposits, and these premiums went into funds that would reimburse depositors in the event of bank failures. By insuring deposits, the FDIC bolstered depositors' trust in the banking system and provided depositors with the incentive to leave their deposits with the bank, even in the face of widespread talk of bank failures. In 1933, it was sufficient for the FDIC to cover each account up to $2,500. The current maximum is $250,000 per depositor per institution.

How Deposit Insurance Causes Increased Risk Taking by Bank Managers

Until the 1990s, all insured depository institutions paid the same small fee for coverage. The fee that they paid was completely unrelated to how risky their assets were. A depository institution that made loans to companies such as Dell, Inc., and Microsoft Corporation paid the same deposit insurance premium as another depository institution that made loans (at higher interest rates) to the governments of developing countries that were teetering on the brink of financial collapse. Although deposit insurance premiums for a while were adjusted somewhat in response to the riskiness of a depository institution's assets, they never reflected all of the relative risk. Indeed, between the late 1990s and the late 2000s, very few depository institutions paid *any* deposit insurance premiums. This lack of correlation between risk and premiums can be considered a fundamental flaw in the deposit insurance scheme. Because bank managers do not have to pay higher insurance premiums when they make riskier loans, they have an incentive to invest in more assets of higher yield, and therefore necessarily higher risk, than they would if there were no deposit insurance.

ARTIFICIALLY LOW INSURANCE PREMIUMS The problem with the insurance scheme is that the premium rate is artificially low. Depository institution managers are able to obtain deposits at less than full cost (because depositors will accept a lower interest payment on insured deposits). Consequently, managers can increase their profits by using insured deposits to purchase higher-yield, higher-risk assets. The gains to risk taking accrue to the managers and stockholders of the depository institutions. The losses go to the deposit insurer (and, as we will see, ultimately to taxpayers).

A REGULATORY SOLUTION To combat these flaws in the financial industry and in the deposit insurance system, a vast regulatory apparatus oversees depository institutions. The FDIC and other federal deposit insurance agencies possess regulatory powers to offset the risk-taking temptations to depository institution managers.

These regulatory powers include the ability to require higher capital investment; to regulate, examine, and supervise bank affairs; and to enforce regulatory decisions. Higher capital requirements were imposed in the early 1990s and then adjusted somewhat beginning in 2000, but the recent jump in bank failures reveals that basic flaws remain.

Deposit Insurance, Adverse Selection, and Moral Hazard

As a deposit insurer, the FDIC effectively acts as a government-run insurance company. This means that the FDIC's operations expose the federal government to the same kinds of asymmetric information problems that other financial intermediaries face.

ADVERSE SELECTION IN DEPOSIT INSURANCE One of these problems is *adverse selection*, which is often a problem when insurance is involved because people or firms that are relatively poor risks are sometimes able to disguise that fact from insurers. It is instructive to examine the way this works with the deposit insurance provided by the FDIC. Deposit insurance shields depositors from the potential adverse effects of risky decisions and so makes depositors willing to accept riskier investment strategies by their banks. Clearly, protection of depositors from risks encourages more high-flying, risk-loving entrepreneurs to become managers of banks. Moreover, because depositors have so little incentive to monitor the activities of insured banks, it is also likely that the insurance actually encourages outright crooks—embezzlers and con artists—to enter the industry. The consequences for the FDIC—and for taxpayers—are larger losses.

MORAL HAZARD IN DEPOSIT INSURANCE Moral hazard is also an important phenomenon in the presence of insurance contracts, such as the deposit insurance provided by the FDIC. Insured depositors know that they will not suffer losses if their bank fails. Hence, they have little incentive to monitor their bank's investment activities or to punish their bank by withdrawing their funds if the bank assumes too much risk. This means that insured banks have incentives to take on more risks than they otherwise would.

Can Deposit Insurance Be Reformed?

The Federal Deposit Insurance Reform Act of 2005 aimed to reform federal deposit insurance. On the one hand, this law expanded deposit insurance coverage and potentially added to the system's moral hazard problems. It increased deposit insurance coverage for Individual Retirement Accounts (IRAs) offered by depository institutions from $100,000 to $250,000 and authorized the FDIC to periodically adjust the insurance limit on all deposits to reflect inflation. On the other hand, the act provided the FDIC with improved tools for addressing moral hazard risks. The law changed a rule that had prevented the FDIC from charging deposit insurance premiums if total insurance funds exceeded 1.25 percent of all insured deposits. This limit had enabled practically all U.S. depository institutions to avoid paying deposit insurance premiums for about a decade. Now the FDIC can adjust deposit insurance premiums at any time.

During the banking troubles of the late 2000s, Congress sought to increase the public's confidence in depository institutions by temporarily extending federal deposit insurance to cover almost all of the deposits in the banking system. While this move succeeded in boosting trust in banks, it also expanded the moral hazard risks of deposit insurance. Nevertheless, the FDIC took advantage of its broadened powers to begin charging insurance premiums again. Indeed, the FDIC has imposed special one-time premiums to replenish its insurance funds after it incurred substantial expenses caused by the failures of numerous banks and savings institutions between 2008 and 2010. Nevertheless, most economists agree that, on net, the federal deposit insurance system's exposure to moral hazard risks has increased considerably in recent years.

QUICK QUIZ See page 344 for the answers. Review concepts from this section in MyEconLab.

To limit the fallout from systemwide failures and bank runs, Congress created the _________ _________ _________ _________ in 1933. Since the advent of federal deposit insurance, there have been no true bank runs at federally insured banks.

Federal insurance of bank deposits insulates depositors from risks, so depositors are _________ concerned about riskier investment strategies by depository institutions. Thus, bank managers have an incentive to invest in _________ assets to make _________ rates of return.

On the one hand, the Federal Deposit Insurance Reform Act of 2005 expanded the _________ hazard risks associated with deposit insurance by increasing limits for insured retirement deposits and indexing limits for other deposits to inflation. On the other hand, the law granted the FDIC greater discretion to assess risk-based deposit insurance _________ intended to restrain _________ hazard risks.

You Are There

A River Currency for Riverwest, Wisconsin

Sura Faraj, a community organizer in Riverwest, Wisconsin, is working on a new project: a novel medium of exchange called River Currency. Under the plan she and other community organizers have developed, two River Currency notes will be tradable for one U.S. dollar. Local businesses, however, will offer price discounts to anyone who uses River Currency to buy their products.

In deciding to introduce River Currency, Riverwest is following dozens of villages and towns in states across the country including Hawaii, Massachusetts, Michigan, New Jersey, and Vermont. The rationale behind most of these currency programs is to encourage people to purchase items from local businesses. Within the local communities, such as Riverwest, such currencies circulate as media of exchange to the extent that people are willing to accept them in trades for goods and services.

Critical Analysis Questions

1. If price tags in Riverwest businesses show prices in terms of River Currency, which of money's functions would River Currency fulfill?
2. If Riverwest banks accept River Currency as a standard of deferred payment and issue deposits and extend loans denominated in River Currency units, could the money multiplier exceed 1 in Riverwest?

ISSUES & APPLICATIONS

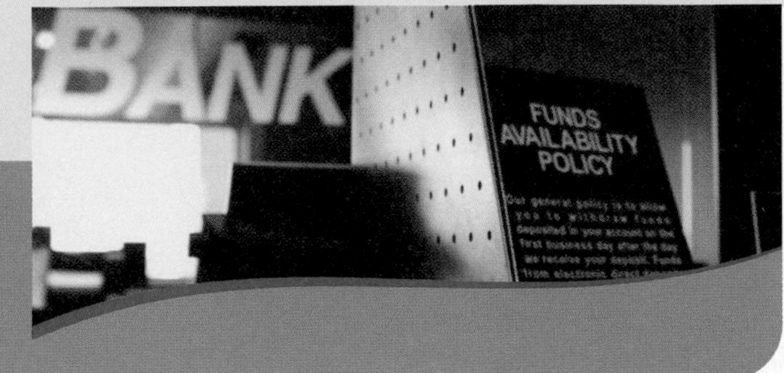

Entrepreneurs Boost FDIC Coverage—and Moral Hazard

CONCEPTS APPLIED

- Federal Deposit Insurance
- Federal Deposit Insurance Corporation
- Moral Hazard in Deposit Insurance

For 75 years, federal deposit insurance coverage was capped at no more than $100,000 per account, but in 2010 Congress permanently expanded most limits for coverage by the Federal Deposit Insurance Corporation (FDIC) to $250,000 per account. Enterprising entrepreneurs have found, however, that they can earn income from helping people obtain FDIC insurance coverage for much larger sums.

Distributing Pools of Funds Across Accounts at Multiple Banks

Just because the FDIC limit per deposit account is $250,000 does not mean that individuals and families cannot receive federal deposit insurance protection for larger pools of funds. For instance, to enable customers to obtain FDIC protection for $500,000, a firm owning two banks can offer a "single FDIC-insured account" that actually consists, behind the scenes, of *two* accounts—one at each bank the firm owns.

A number of entrepreneurs work with large pools of funds. Each customer has a single account with the firm, but the entrepreneurs then deposit the funds in that account into multiple bank accounts on the customer's behalf. The entrepreneurs make sure that no single account contains more than $250,000, so each bank account is fully insured by the FDIC. One company, called Certificate of Deposit Registry Service (CDARS), is headed by entrepreneurs who formerly were a U.S. Comptroller of the Currency, a vice-chair of the Fed's Board of Governors, and an official at the FDIC. CDARS offers to distribute into FDIC-insured bank accounts individually owned pools of funds as large as $50 million!

How the Search for FDIC Protection Expands Moral Hazard

A number of studies by financial economists have demonstrated that in past years, a bank's largest depositors have often done the best job of keeping an eye on how the bank allocates deposit funds. These people, of course, traditionally have had the most to lose if a bank makes too many high-risk loans. When the largest depositors have seen evidence of risky activities by a bank's management, their threats to remove their funds from the bank have helped to induce bank managers to opt for less risky lending strategies.

By helping large depositors obtain taxpayer-guaranteed deposit insurance across many banks, firms such as CDARS remove the incentive for these depositors to pay attention to what bank managers are doing with their funds. The consequence is an increase in the moral hazard problem of deposit insurance—that is, a greater potential for bank managers to direct federally insured deposits to activities that raise taxpayers' risks of loss.

For Critical Analysis

1. If even banks' largest depositors pay no attention to what bank managers are doing with their funds, who is left to look out for taxpayers' interests?
2. Why do you suppose that a few economists argue that society ultimately might be better off on net if federal deposit insurance were eliminated?

Web Resources

1. Learn about a typical program that pools funds into multiple FDIC-insured bank accounts at www.econtoday.com/ch15.
2. For information on the CDARS program, go to www.econtoday.com/ch15.

Research Project

Some economists have suggested that we replace our system of taxpayer-guaranteed federal deposit insurance with a requirement that banks obtain deposit insurance from private insurers. They suggest that because private insurers would have their own funds at stake, they would—in contrast to the FDIC—charge deposit insurance premiums reflecting banks' actual risks and hold large reserves of funds to draw on if insured banks were to fail. Evaluate possible pros and cons of this proposal.

For more questions on this chapter's Issues & Applications, go to **MyEconLab**. In the Study Plan for this chapter, select Section N: News.

Here is what you should know after reading this chapter. **MyEconLab** will help you identify what you know, and where to go when you need to practice.

WHAT YOU SHOULD KNOW		WHERE TO GO TO PRACTICE
The Key Functions and Properties of Money Money is a medium of exchange that people use to make payments for goods, services, and financial assets. It is also a unit of accounting for quoting prices in terms of money values. In addition, money is a store of value, so people can hold money for future use in exchange. Finally, money is a standard of deferred payment, enabling lenders to make loans and buyers to repay those loans with money. A good will function as money only if people are widely willing to accept the good in exchange for other goods and services. Though people may continue to use money even if inflation erodes its real purchasing power, they will do so only if the value of money is relatively predictable.	money, 318 medium of exchange, 318 barter, 318 unit of accounting, 319 store of value, 319 standard of deferred payment, 320 liquidity, 320 transactions deposits, 320 fiduciary monetary system, 321 **KEY FIGURE** Figure 15-1, 320	• **MyEconLab** Study Plans 15.1, 15.2 • Audio introduction to Chapter 15 • Video: The Functions of Money • Video: Monetary Standards, or What Backs Money • Animated Figure 15-1
Official Definitions of the Quantity of Money in Circulation The narrow definition of the quantity of money in circulation, called M1, focuses on money's role as a medium of exchange. It includes only currency, transactions deposits, and traveler's checks. A broader definition, called M2, stresses money's role as a temporary store of value. M2 is equal to M1 plus savings deposits, small-denomination time deposits, and noninstitutional holdings of money market mutual fund balances.	money supply, 322 transactions approach, 322 liquidity approach, 322 M1, 322 depository institutions, 322 thrift institutions, 322 traveler's checks, 323 M2, 323	• **MyEconLab** Study Plan 15.3 • Economics Video: Stashing Your Cash
Why Financial Intermediaries Such as Banks Exist Financial intermediaries help reduce problems stemming from the existence of asymmetric information in financial transactions. Asymmetric information can lead to adverse selection, in which uncreditworthy individuals and firms seek loans, and moral hazard problems, in which an individual or business that has been granted credit begins to	central bank, 323 financial intermediation, 324 financial intermediaries, 324 asymmetric information, 324 adverse selection, 324 moral hazard, 324 liabilities, 325 assets, 325	• **MyEconLab** Study Plan 15.4 • Animated Figures 15-3, 15-4 • Economics Video: Stashing Your Cash

(continued)

MyEconLab continued

WHAT YOU SHOULD KNOW		WHERE TO GO TO PRACTICE
engage in riskier practices. Financial intermediaries may also permit savers to benefit from economies of scale, which is the ability to reduce the costs and risks of managing funds by pooling funds and spreading costs and risks across many savers.	**KEY FIGURES** Figure 15-3, 324 Figure 15-4, 326	
The Basic Structure and Functions of the Federal Reserve System The Federal Reserve System consists of 12 district banks. The governing body of the Fed is the Board of Governors. Decisions about the quantity of money in circulation are made by the Federal Open Market Committee, which is composed of the Board of Governors and five Federal Reserve bank presidents. The Fed's main functions are supplying fiduciary currency, clearing payments, holding banks' reserves, acting as the government's fiscal agent, supervising banks, acting as a lender of last resort, regulating the money supply, and intervening in foreign exchange markets.	The Fed, 327 lender of last resort, 330 **KEY FIGURE** Figure 15-6, 329	• **MyEconLab** Study Plan 15.5 • Animated Figure 15-6 • Video: The Federal Reserve System • ABC News Video: The Federal Reserve
The Maximum Potential Change in the Money Supply Following a Federal Reserve Monetary Policy Action When a bond dealer deposits funds received from the Fed in payment for a security following a Fed open market purchase, there is an immediate increase in the total deposits in the banking system. The money supply increases by the amount of the initial deposit. The depository institution receiving this deposit can lend out funds in excess of those it holds as reserves, which will generate a rise in deposits at another bank. This process continues as each bank receiving a deposit has additional funds over and above those held as reserves. The maximum potential change in deposits throughout the banking system equals the amount of reserves injected (or withdrawn) by the Fed times the potential money multiplier, which is 1 divided by the reserve ratio.	fractional reserve banking, 331 reserves, 331 reserve ratio, 332 balance sheet, 332 open market operations, 332 money multiplier, 335 potential money multiplier, 335 **KEY TABLE** Table 15-3, 334 **KEY FIGURE** Figure 15-7, 334	• **MyEconLab** Study Plans 15.6 • Animated Table 15-3 • Animated Figure 15-7 • ABC News Video: The Federal Reserve
Features of Federal Deposit Insurance To help prevent runs on banks, the U.S. government in 1933 established the Federal Deposit Insurance Corporation (FDIC). This agency charges some depository institutions premiums, and it places these funds in accounts for use in reimbursing failed banks' depositors. Deposit insurance creates an adverse selection problem because its availability can attract risk-taking individuals into banking. A moral hazard problem also exists when deposit insurance premiums fail to reflect the full extent of the risks taken on by bank managers and when depositors have little incentive to monitor the performance of the institutions that hold their deposit funds.	bank run, 336 Federal Deposit Insurance Corporation (FDIC), 337	• **MyEconLab** Study Plan 15.7 • Video: Deposit Insurance and Risk Taking

Log in to MyEconLab, take a chapter test, and get a personalized Study Plan that tells you which concepts you understand and which ones you need to review. From there, MyEconLab will give you further practice, tutorials, animations, videos, and guided solutions.
Log in to www.myeconlab.com

PROBLEMS

All problems are assignable in myeconlab. *Answers to odd-numbered problems appear at the back of the book.*

15-1. Until 1946, residents of the island of Yap used large doughnut-shaped stones as financial assets. Although prices of goods and services were not quoted in terms of the stones, the stones were often used in exchange for particularly large purchases, such as livestock. To make the transaction, several individuals would insert a large stick through a stone's center and carry it to its new owner. A stone was difficult for any one person to steal, so an owner typically would lean it against the side of his or her home as a sign to others of accumulated purchasing power that would hold value for later use in exchange. Loans would often be repaid using the stones. In what ways did these stones function as money?

15-2. During the late 1970s, prices quoted in terms of the Israeli currency, the shekel, rose so fast that grocery stores listed their prices in terms of the U.S. dollar and provided customers with dollar-shekel conversion tables that they updated daily. Although people continued to buy goods and services and make loans using shekels, many Israeli citizens converted shekels to dollars to avoid a reduction in their wealth due to inflation. In what way did the U.S. dollar function as money in Israel during this period?

15-3. During the 1945–1946 Hungarian hyperinflation, when the rate of inflation reached 41.9 *quadrillion* percent per month, the Hungarian government discovered that the real value of its tax receipts was falling dramatically. To keep real tax revenues more stable, it created a good called a "tax pengö," in which all bank deposits were denominated for purposes of taxation. Nevertheless, payments for goods and services were made only in terms of the regular Hungarian currency, whose value tended to fall rapidly even though the value of a tax pengö remained stable. Prices were also quoted only in terms of the regular currency. Lenders, however, began denominating loan payments in terms of tax pengös. In what ways did the tax pengö function as money in Hungary in 1945 and 1946?

15-4. Considering the following data (expressed in billions of U.S. dollars), calculate M1 and M2.

Currency	850
Savings deposits	3,500
Small-denomination time deposits	2,000
Traveler's checks outside banks and thrifts	10
Total money market mutual funds	1,300
Institution-only money market mutual funds	200
Transactions deposits	940

15-5. Identify whether each of the following items is counted in M1 only, M2 only, both M1 and M2, or neither:

a. A $1,000 balance in a transactions deposit at a mutual savings bank

b. A $100,000 time deposit in a New York bank

c. A $10,000 time deposit an elderly widow holds at her credit union

d. A $50 traveler's check not issued by a bank

e. A $50,000 savings deposit

15-6. Match each of the rationales for financial intermediation listed below with at least one of the following financial intermediaries: insurance company, pension fund, savings bank. Explain your choices.

a. Adverse selection

b. Moral hazard

c. Lower management costs generated by larger scale

15-7. Identify whether each of the following events poses an adverse selection problem or a moral hazard problem in financial markets.

a. A manager of a savings and loan association responds to reports of a likely increase in federal deposit insurance coverage. She directs loan officers to extend mortgage loans to less creditworthy borrowers.

b. A loan applicant does not mention that a legal judgment in his divorce case will require him to make alimony payments to his ex-wife.

c. An individual who was recently approved for a loan to start a new business decides to use some of the funds to take a Hawaiian vacation.

15-8. In what sense is currency a liability of the Federal Reserve System?

15-9. In what respects is the Fed like a private banking institution? In what respects is it more like a government agency?

15-10. Take a look at the map of the locations of the Federal Reserve districts and their headquarters in Figure 15-6 on page 329. Today, the U.S. population is centered just west of the Mississippi River—that is, about half of the population is either to the west or the east of a line running roughly just west of this river. Can you reconcile the current locations of Fed districts and banks with this fact? Why do you suppose the Fed has its current geographic structure?

15-11. Draw an empty bank balance sheet, with the heading "Assets" on the left and the heading

"Liabilities" on the right. Then place the following items on the proper side of the balance sheet:

a. Loans to a private company
b. Borrowings from a Federal Reserve district bank
c. Deposits with a Federal Reserve district bank
d. U.S. Treasury bills
e. Vault cash
f. Transactions deposits

15-12. The Federal Reserve purchases $1 million in U.S. Treasury bonds from a bond dealer, and the dealer's bank credits the dealer's account. The reserve ratio is 15 percent. Assuming that no currency leakage occurs, how much will the bank lend to its customers following the Fed's purchase?

15-13. Suppose that the value of the potential money multiplier is equal to 4. What is the reserve ratio?

15-14. Consider a world in which there is no currency and depository institutions issue only transactions deposits. The reserve ratio is 20 percent. The central bank sells $1 billion in government securities. What ultimately happens to the money supply?

15-15. Assume a 1 percent reserve ratio and no currency leakages. What is the potential money multiplier? How will total deposits in the banking system ultimately change if the Federal Reserve purchases $5 million in U.S. government securities?

ECONOMICS ON THE NET

What's Happened to the Money Supply? Deposits at banks and other financial institutions make up a portion of the U.S. money supply. This exercise gives you the chance to see how changes in these deposits influence the Fed's measures of money.

Title: FRED (Federal Reserve Economic Data)

Navigation: Go to **www.econtoday.com/ch15** to visit the Web page of the Federal Reserve Bank of St. Louis.

Application

1. Select the data series for *Demand Deposits at Commercial Banks (Bil. of $; M)*, either seasonally adjusted or not. Scan through the data. Do you notice any recent trend? (Hint: Compare the growth in the figures before 1993 with their growth after 1993.) In addition, take a look at the data series for currency and for other transactions deposits. Do you observe similar recent trends in these series?
2. Back up, and click on *M1 Money Stock (Bil. of $; M)*, again either seasonally adjusted or not. Does it show any change in pattern beginning around 1993?

For Group Study and Analysis FRED contains considerable financial data series. Assign individual members or groups of the class the task of examining data on assets included in M1, M2, and MZM. Have each student or group look for big swings in the data. Then ask the groups to report to the class as a whole. When did clear changes occur in various categories of the monetary aggregates? Were there times when people appeared to shift funds from one aggregate to another? Are there any other noticeable patterns that may have had something to do with economic events during various periods?

ANSWERS TO QUICK QUIZZES

p. 321: (i) medium of exchange . . . unit of accounting . . . store of value . . . standard of deferred payment; (ii) liquid; (iii) fiduciary; (iv) predictable
p. 323: (i) transactions . . . M1; (ii) Transactions; (iii) M1 . . . M2
p. 327: (i) Financial; (ii) asymmetric . . . adverse selection . . . moral hazard
p. 331: (i) Federal Reserve System; (ii) Board . . . Governors; (iii) currency . . . reserves . . . lender of last resort
p. 336: (i) Reserves . . . Federal Reserve; (ii) reserve ratio; (iii) potential money multiplier
p. 339: (i) Federal Deposit Insurance Corporation; (ii) less . . . riskier . . . higher; (iii) moral . . . premiums . . . moral

16 Domestic and International Dimensions of Monetary Policy

In the weeks and months prior to the autumn of 2008, the aggregate amount of reserves held at Federal Reserve district banks by all depository institutions was typically less than $45 billion. In contrast, today the total reserves that depository institutions hold with the Fed exceed *$1 trillion*. What determines the quantity of reserves that depository institutions choose to hold with the Fed? Why are they opting to hold so many more reserves now than a few years ago? By the time you finish reading this chapter, you will understand the answers to these questions.

LEARNING OBJECTIVES

After reading this chapter, you should be able to:

- Identify the key factors that influence the quantity of money that people desire to hold
- Describe how Federal Reserve monetary policy actions influence market interest rates
- Evaluate how expansionary and contractionary monetary policy actions affect equilibrium real GDP and the price level in the short run
- Understand the equation of exchange and its importance in the quantity theory of money and prices
- Discuss the interest-rate-based transmission mechanism of monetary policy, and explain why the Federal Reserve cannot stabilize both the money supply and interest rates simultaneously
- Describe how the Federal Reserve achieves a target value for the federal funds rate, and explain key issues the Fed confronts in selecting this target

myeconlab

MyEconLab helps you master each objective and study more efficiently. See end of chapter for details.

Did You Know That ?

at various times between late 2008 and early 2009, Zimbabwe's *daily* inflation rate exceeded 100 percent, which meant that the nation's price level more than *doubled* within 24-hour periods? These were not the highest daily inflation rates in recorded history, however. During the summer of 1946, the rate of inflation in Hungary reached 195 percent per day. Thus, in Hungary there were 24-hour periods during which the level of prices nearly *tripled*.

In both Zimbabwe in the late 2000s and Hungary in 1946, daily rates of *money supply* growth also exceeded 100 percent. Why are higher rates of inflation associated with higher rates of money growth? Answering this question is one objective of this chapter. Let's begin, however, by considering how people determine the amount of money they wish to hold.

The Demand for Money

In the previous chapter, we saw how the Federal Reserve's open market operations can increase or decrease the money supply. Our focus was on the effects of the Fed's actions on the banking system. In this chapter, we widen our discussion to see how Fed monetary policy actions have an impact on the broader economy by influencing market interest rates. First, though, you must understand the factors that determine how much money people desire to hold—in other words, you must understand the demand for money.

All of us engage in a flow of transactions. We buy and sell things all of our lives. But because we use money—dollars—as our medium of exchange, all *flows* of nonbarter transactions involve a *stock* of money. We can restate this as follows:

To use money, one must hold money.

Given that everybody must hold money, we can now talk about the *demand* to hold it. People do not demand to hold money just to look at pictures of past leaders. They hold it to be able to use it to buy goods and services.

The Demand for Money: What People Wish to Hold

Money balances
Synonymous with money, money stock, money holdings.

People have certain motivations that cause them to want to hold **money balances.** Individuals and firms could try to do without non-interest-bearing money balances. But life is inconvenient without a ready supply of money balances. Thus, the public has a demand for money, motivated by several factors.

Transactions demand
Holding money as a medium of exchange to make payments. The level varies directly with nominal GDP.

THE TRANSACTIONS DEMAND The main reason people hold money is that money can be used to purchase goods and services. People are paid at specific intervals (once a week, once a month, and the like), but they wish to make purchases more or less continuously. To free themselves from having to buy goods and services only on payday, people find it beneficial to hold money. The benefit they receive is convenience: They willingly forgo interest earnings in order to avoid the inconvenience of cashing in nonmoney assets such as bonds every time they wish to make a purchase. Thus, people hold money to make regular, *expected* expenditures under the **transactions demand.** As nominal GDP rises, people will want to hold more money because they will be making more transactions.

Precautionary demand
Holding money to meet unplanned expenditures and emergencies.

THE PRECAUTIONARY DEMAND The transactions demand involves money held to make *expected* expenditures. People also hold money for the **precautionary demand** to make *unexpected* purchases or to meet emergencies. When people hold money for the precautionary demand, they incur a cost in forgone interest earnings that they balance against the benefit of having cash on hand. The higher the rate of interest, the lower the precautionary money balances people wish to hold.

THE ASSET DEMAND Remember that one of the functions of money is to serve as a store of value. People can hold money balances as a store of value, or they can hold bonds or stocks or other interest-earning assets. The desire to hold money as a store of value leads to the **asset demand** for money. People choose to hold money rather than other assets for two reasons: its liquidity and the lack of risk.

Asset demand
Holding money as a store of value instead of other assets such as corporate bonds and stocks.

The disadvantage of holding money balances as an asset, of course, is the interest earnings forgone. Each individual or business decides how much money to hold as an asset by looking at the opportunity cost of holding money. The higher the interest rate—which is the opportunity cost of holding money—the lower the money balances people will want to hold as assets. Conversely, the lower the interest rate offered on alternative assets, the higher the money balances people will want to hold as assets.

The Demand for Money Curve

Assume for simplicity's sake that the amount of money demanded for transactions purposes is proportionate to income. That leaves the precautionary and asset demands for money, both determined by the opportunity cost of holding money. If we assume that the interest rate represents the cost of holding money balances, we can graph the relationship between the interest rate and the quantity of money demanded. In Figure 16-1 below, the demand for money curve shows a familiar downward slope. The horizontal axis measures the quantity of money demanded, and the vertical axis is the interest rate. The rate of interest is the cost of holding money. At a higher interest rate, a lower quantity of money is demanded, and vice versa.

To see this, imagine two scenarios. In the first one, you can earn 20 percent a year if you put your funds into purchases of U.S. government securities. In the other scenario, you can earn 1 percent if you put your funds into purchases of U.S. government securities. If you have $1,000 average cash balances in a non-interest-bearing checking account, in the second scenario over a one-year period, your opportunity cost would be 1 percent of $1,000, or $10. In the first scenario, your opportunity cost would be 20 percent of $1,000, or $200. Under which scenario would you hold more funds in your checking account instead of securities?

QUICK QUIZ See page 369 for the answers. Review concepts from this section in MyEconLab.

To use money, people must hold money. Therefore, they have a __________ for money balances. The determinants of the demand for money balances are the __________ demand, the __________ demand, and the __________ demand.	Because holding money carries an __________ cost—the interest income forgone—the demand for money curve showing the relationship between the quantity of money balances demanded and the interest rate slopes __________.

FIGURE 16-1 The Demand for Money Curve

If we use the interest rate as a proxy for the opportunity cost of holding money balances, the demand for money curve, M_d, is downward sloping, similar to other demand curves.

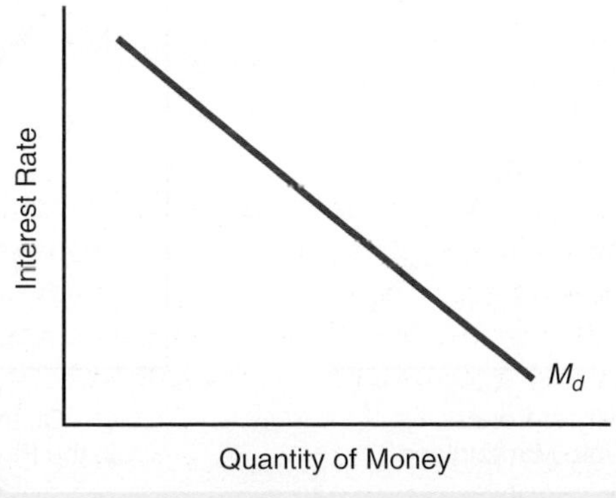

How the Fed Influences Interest Rates

When the Fed takes actions that alter the rate of growth of the money supply, it is seeking to influence investment, consumption, and total aggregate expenditures. In taking these monetary policy actions, the Fed in principle has four tools at its disposal: open market operations, changes in the reserve ratio, changes in the interest rates paid on reserves, and discount rate changes. The first three tools were introduced in Chapter 15. The discount rate will be discussed later in this chapter. Let's consider the effects of open market operations, the tool that the Fed regularly employs on a day-to-day basis.

Open Market Operations

Go to www.econtoday.com/ch16 to learn about the Federal Reserve's current policy regarding open market operations. Scan down the page, and select the "Minutes" for the most recent date.

As we saw in the previous chapter, the Fed changes the amount of reserves in the banking system by its purchases and sales of government bonds issued by the U.S. Treasury. To understand how these actions by the Fed influence the market interest rate, we start out in an equilibrium in which all individuals, including the holders of bonds, are satisfied with the current situation. There is some equilibrium level of interest rate (and bond prices). Now, if the Fed wants to conduct open market operations, it must somehow induce individuals, businesses, and foreign residents to hold more or fewer U.S. Treasury bonds. The inducement must take the form of making people better off. So, if the Fed wants to buy bonds, it will have to offer to buy them at a higher price than exists in the marketplace. If the Fed wants to sell bonds, it will have to offer them at a lower price than exists in the marketplace. Thus, an open market operation must cause a change in the price of bonds.

GRAPHING THE SALE OF BONDS The Fed sells some of the bonds in its portfolio. This is shown in panel (a) of Figure 16-2 below. Notice that the supply of bonds is shown here as a vertical line with respect to price. The demand for bonds is downward sloping. If the Fed offers more bonds it owns for sale, the supply curve shifts from S_1 to S_2. People will not be willing to buy the extra bonds at the initial equilibrium bond price, P_1. They will be satisfied holding the additional bonds at the new equilibrium price, P_2.

THE FED'S PURCHASE OF BONDS The opposite occurs when the Fed purchases bonds. You can view this purchase of bonds as a reduction in the stock of bonds available for

FIGURE 16-2 Determining the Price of Bonds

In panel (a), the Fed offers more bonds for sale. The price drops from P_1 to P_2. In panel (b), the Fed purchases bonds. This is the equivalent of a reduction in the supply of bonds available for private investors to hold. The price of bonds must rise from P_1 to P_3 to clear the market.

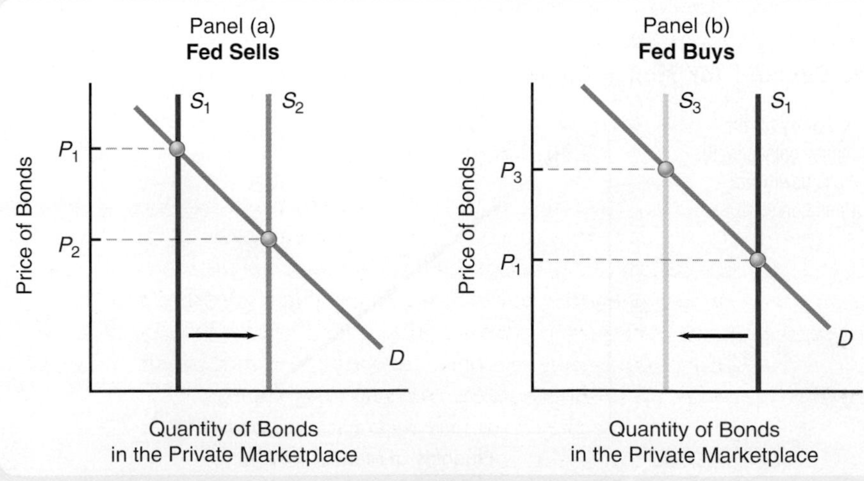

private investors to hold. In panel (b) of Figure 16-2 on the facing page, the original supply curve is S_1. The new supply curve of outstanding bonds will end up being S_3 because of the Fed's purchases of bonds. To get people to give up these bonds, the Fed must offer them a more attractive price. The price will rise from to P_1 to P_3.

Relationship Between the Price of Existing Bonds and the Rate of Interest

The price of existing bonds and the rate of interest are inversely related. Assume that the average yield on bonds is 5 percent. You decide to purchase a bond. A local corporation agrees to sell you a bond that will pay you $50 a year forever. What is the price you are willing to pay for the bond? It is $1,000. Why? Because $50 divided by $1,000 equals 5 percent, which is as good as the best return you can earn elsewhere. You purchase the bond. The next year something happens in the economy, and you can now obtain bonds that have effective yields of 10 percent. (In other words, the prevailing interest rate in the economy is now 10 percent.) What will happen to the market price of the existing bond that you own, the one you purchased the year before? It will fall. If you try to sell the bond for $1,000, you will discover that no investors will buy it from you. Why should they when they can obtain the same $50-a-year yield from someone else by paying only $500? Indeed, unless you offer your bond for sale at a price that is no higher than $500, no buyers will be forthcoming. Hence, an increase in the prevailing interest rate in the economy has caused the market value of your existing bond to fall.

The important point to be understood is this:

The market price of* existing *bonds (and all fixed-income assets) is inversely related to the rate of interest prevailing in the economy.

As a consequence of the inverse relationship between the price of existing bonds and the interest rate, the Fed is able to influence the interest rate by engaging in open market operations. A Fed open market sale that reduces the equilibrium price of bonds brings about an increase in the interest rate. A Fed open market purchase that boosts the equilibrium price of bonds generates a decrease in the interest rate.

QUICK QUIZ **See page 369 for the answers.** **Review concepts from this section in MyEconLab.**

When the Fed sells bonds, it must offer them at a __________ price. When the Fed buys bonds, it must pay a __________ price.

There is an __________ relationship between the prevailing rate of interest in the economy and the market price of *existing* bonds (and all fixed-income assets).

A Federal Reserve open market sale generates a __________ in the price of *existing* bonds and an __________ in the market interest rate. An open market purchase brings about an __________ in the price of *existing* bonds and a __________ in the market rate of interest.

Effects of an Increase in the Money Supply

Now that we've seen how the Fed's monetary policy actions influence the market interest rate, we can ask a broader question: How does monetary policy influence real GDP and the price level? To understand how monetary policy works in its simplest form, we are going to run an experiment in which you increase the money supply in a very direct way. Assume that the government has given you hundreds of millions of dollars in just-printed bills. You then fly around the country in a helicopter, dropping the money out of the window. People pick it up and put it in their pockets. Some deposit the money in their transactions deposit accounts. As a result, they now have too much money—not in the sense that they want to throw it away but rather in relation to other assets that they own. There are a variety of ways to dispose of this "new" money.

Direct Effect

The simplest thing that people can do when they have excess money balances is to go out and spend them on goods and services. Here they have a direct impact on aggregate demand. Aggregate demand rises because with an increase in the money supply, at any given price level people now want to purchase more output of real goods and services.

Indirect Effect

Not everybody will necessarily spend the newfound money on goods and services. Some people may wish to deposit a portion or all of those excess money balances in banks. The recipient banks now discover that they have higher reserves than they wish to hold. As you learned in Chapter 15, one thing that banks can do to get higher-interest-earning assets is to lend out the excess reserves. But banks cannot induce people to borrow more funds than they were borrowing before unless the banks lower the interest rate that they charge on loans. This lower interest rate encourages people to take out those loans. Businesses will therefore engage in new investment with the funds loaned. Individuals will engage in more consumption of durable goods such as housing, autos, and home entertainment centers. Either way, the increased loans generate a rise in aggregate demand. More people will be involved in more spending—even those who did not pick up any of the money that was originally dropped out of your helicopter.

Graphing the Effects of an Expansionary Monetary Policy

Look at Figure 16-3 below. We start out in a situation in which the economy is operating at less than full employment. You see a recessionary gap in the figure, which is measured as the horizontal difference between the long-run aggregate supply curve, *LRAS*, and the current equilibrium. Short-run equilibrium is at E_1, with a price level of 120 and real GDP of $14.5 trillion. The *LRAS* curve is at $15 trillion. Assume now that the Fed increases the money supply. Because of the direct and indirect effects of this increase in the money supply, aggregate demand shifts outward to the right to AD_2. The new equilibrium is at an output rate of $15 trillion of real GDP per year and a price level of 125. Here expansionary monetary policy can move the economy toward its *LRAS* curve sooner than otherwise.

FIGURE 16-3 Expansionary Monetary Policy with Underutilized Resources

If we start out with equilibrium at E_1, expansionary monetary policy will shift AD_1 to AD_2. The new equilibrium will be at E_2.

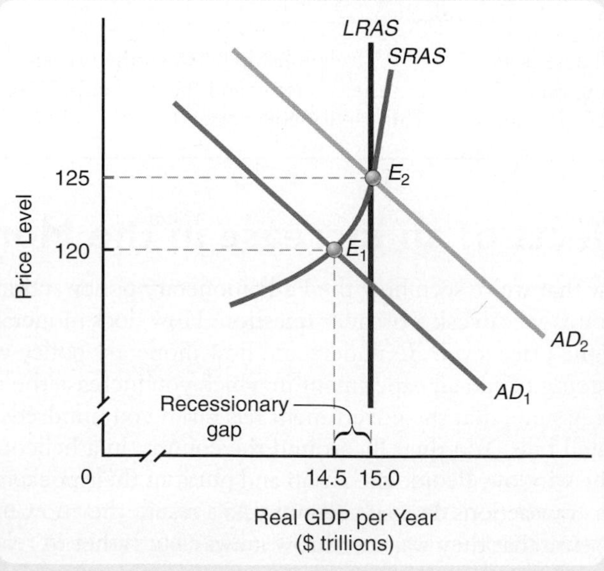

FIGURE 16-4 Contractionary Monetary Policy with Overutilized Resources

If we begin at short-run equilibrium at point E_1, contractionary monetary policy will shift the aggregate demand curve from AD_1 to AD_2. The new equilibrium will be at point E_2.

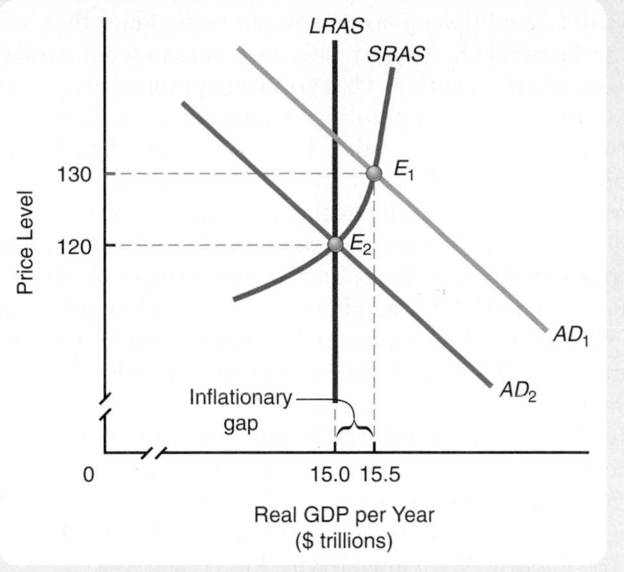

Graphing the Effects of Contractionary Monetary Policy

Assume that there is an inflationary gap as shown in Figure 16-4 above. There you see that the short-run aggregate supply curve, *SRAS*, intersects aggregate demand, AD_1, at E_1. This is to the right of the *LRAS* of real GDP per year of $15 trillion. Contractionary monetary policy can eliminate this inflationary gap. Because of both the direct and indirect effects of monetary policy, the aggregate demand curve shifts inward from AD_1 to AD_2. Equilibrium is now at E_2, which is at a lower price level, 120. Equilibrium real GDP has now fallen from $15.5 trillion to $15 trillion.

Note that contractionary monetary policy involves a reduction in the money supply, with a consequent decline in the price level (deflation). In the real world, contractionary monetary policy more commonly involves reducing the *rate of growth* of the money supply, thereby reducing the rate of increase in the price level (inflation). Similarly, real-world expansionary monetary policy typically involves increasing the rate of growth of the money supply.

QUICK QUIZ **See page 369 for the answers. Review concepts from this section in MyEconLab.**

The __________ effect of an increase in the money supply arises because people desire to spend more on real goods and services when they have excess money balances.

The __________ effect of an increase in the money supply works through a __________ in the interest rate, which encourages businesses to make new investments with the funds loaned to them. Individuals will also engage in more consumption (on consumer durables) because of __________ interest rates.

Open Economy Transmission of Monetary Policy

So far we have discussed monetary policy in a closed economy. When we move to an open economy, with international trade and the international purchases and sales of all assets including dollars and other currencies, monetary policy becomes more complex. Consider first the effect of monetary policy on exports.

Go to **www.econtoday.com/ch16** for links to central banks around the globe, provided by the Bank for International Settlements.

The Net Export Effect of Contractionary Monetary Policy

To see how a change in monetary policy can affect net exports, suppose that the Federal Reserve implements a contractionary policy that boosts the market interest rate. The higher U.S. interest rate, in turn, tends to attract foreign investment in U.S. financial assets, such as U.S. government securities.

If more residents of foreign countries decide that they want to purchase U.S. government securities or other U.S. assets, they first have to obtain U.S. dollars. As a consequence, the demand for dollars goes up in foreign exchange markets. The international price of the dollar therefore rises. This is called an *appreciation* of the dollar, and it tends to reduce net exports because it makes our exports more expensive in terms of foreign currency and imports cheaper in terms of dollars. Foreign residents demand fewer of our goods and services, and we demand more of theirs.

This reasoning implies that when contractionary monetary policy increases the after-tax U.S. interest rate at the current price level, there will be a negative net export effect because foreign residents will want more U.S. financial instruments. Hence, they will demand additional dollars, thereby causing the international price of the dollar to rise. This makes our exports more expensive for the rest of the world, which then demands a smaller quantity of our exports. It also means that foreign goods and services are less expensive in the United States, so we therefore demand more imports. We come up with this conclusion:

> ***Contractionary monetary policy causes interest rates to rise. Such a rise will induce international inflows of funds, thereby raising the international value of the dollar and making U.S. goods less attractive abroad. The net export effect of contractionary monetary policy will be in the same direction as the monetary policy effect, thereby amplifying the effect of such policy.***

The Net Export Effect of Expansionary Monetary Policy

Now assume that the economy is experiencing a recession and the Federal Reserve wants to pursue an expansionary monetary policy. In so doing, it will cause interest rates to fall in the short run, as discussed earlier. Declining interest rates will cause funds to flow out of the United States. The demand for dollars will decrease, and their international price will go down. Foreign goods will now look more expensive to U.S. residents, and imports will fall. Foreign residents will desire more of our exports, and exports will rise. The result will be an increase in net exports. Again, the international consequences reinforce the domestic consequences of monetary policy.

Globalization of International Money Markets

On a broader level, the Fed's ability to control the rate of growth of the money supply may be hampered as U.S. money markets become less isolated. With the push of a computer button, billions of dollars can change hands halfway around the world. If the Fed reduces the growth of the money supply, individuals and firms in the United States can obtain dollars from other sources. People in the United States who want more liquidity can obtain their dollars from foreign residents. Indeed, as world markets become increasingly integrated, U.S. residents, who can already hold U.S. bank accounts denominated in foreign currencies, more regularly conduct transactions using other nations' currencies.

QUICK QUIZ **See page 369 for the answers.** **Review concepts from this section in MyEconLab.**

Monetary policy in an open economy has repercussions for net __________.

If contractionary monetary policy raises U.S. interest rates, there is a __________ net export effect because foreign residents will demand __________ U.S. financial instruments, thereby demanding __________ dollars and hence causing the international price of the dollar to rise.

This makes our exports more expensive for the rest of the world.

When expansionary monetary policy causes interest rates to fall, foreign residents will want __________ U.S. financial instruments. The resulting __________ in the demand for dollars will reduce the dollar's value in foreign exchange markets, leading to an __________ in net exports.

Monetary Policy and Inflation

Most media discussions of inflation focus on the short run. The price index can fluctuate in the short run because of events such as oil price shocks, labor union strikes, or discoveries of large amounts of new natural resources. In the long run, however, empirical studies show that excessive growth in the money supply results in inflation.

If the supply of money rises relative to the demand for money, people have more money balances than desired. They adjust their mix of assets to reduce money balances in favor of other items. This ultimately causes their spending on goods and services to increase. The result is a rise in the price level, or inflation.

The Equation of Exchange and the Quantity Theory

A simple way to show the relationship between changes in the quantity of money in circulation and the price level is through the **equation of exchange,** developed by Irving Fisher (note that ≡ refers to an identity or truism):

Equation of exchange
The formula indicating that the number of monetary units (M_s) times the number of times each unit is spent on final goods and services (V) is identical to the price level (P) times real GDP (Y).

$$M_sV \equiv PY$$

where M_s = actual money balances held by the nonbanking public
V = **income velocity of money,** which is the number of times, on average per year, each monetary unit is spent on final goods and services
P = price level or price index
Y = real GDP per year

Income velocity of money (V)
The number of times per year a dollar is spent on final goods and services; identically equal to nominal GDP divided by the money supply.

Consider a numerical example involving the entire economy. Assume that in this economy, the total money supply, M_s, is \$10 trillion; real GDP, Y, is \$15 trillion (in base-year dollars); and the price level, P, is 1.1134 (111.34 in index number terms). Using the equation of exchange,

$$M_sV \equiv PY$$
$$\$10 \text{ trillion} \times V \equiv 1.1134 \times \$15 \text{ trillion}$$
$$\$10 \text{ trillion} \times V \equiv \$16.7 \text{ trillion}$$
$$V \equiv 1.67$$

Thus, each dollar is spent an average of 1.67 times per year.

THE EQUATION OF EXCHANGE AS AN IDENTITY The equation of exchange must always be true—it is an *accounting identity*. The equation of exchange states that the total amount of funds spent on final output, M_sV, is equal to the total amount of funds *received* for final output, PY. Thus, a given flow of funds can be viewed from either the buyers' side or the producers' side. The value of goods purchased is equal to the value of goods sold.

If Y represents real GDP and P is the price level, PY equals the dollar value of national output of goods and services or *nominal* GDP. Thus,

$$M_sV \equiv PY \equiv \text{nominal GDP}$$

THE QUANTITY THEORY OF MONEY AND PRICES If we now make some assumptions about different variables in the equation of exchange, we come up with the simplified theory of why the price level changes, called the **quantity theory of money and prices.** If we assume that the velocity of money, V, is constant and that real GDP, Y, is also constant, the simple equation of exchange tells us that a change in the money supply can lead only to an equiproportional change in the price level. Continue with our numerical example. Y is \$15 trillion. V equals 1.67. If the money supply increases by 20 percent, to \$12 trillion, the only thing that can happen is that the price level, P, has to go up from 1.113 to 1.336. In other words, the price level must also increase by 20 percent. Otherwise the equation is no longer in balance. An increase in the money supply of 20 percent results in a rise in the price level (inflation) of 20 percent.

Quantity theory of money and prices
The hypothesis that changes in the money supply lead to equiproportional changes in the price level.

FIGURE 16-5 The Relationship Between Money Supply Growth Rates and Rates of Inflation

If we plot rates of inflation and rates of monetary growth for different countries, we come up with a scatter diagram that reveals an obvious direct relationship. If you were to draw a line through the "average" of the points in this figure, it would be upward sloping, showing that an increase in the rate of growth of the money supply leads to an increase in the rate of inflation.

Sources: International Monetary Fund and national central banks. Data are for latest available periods.

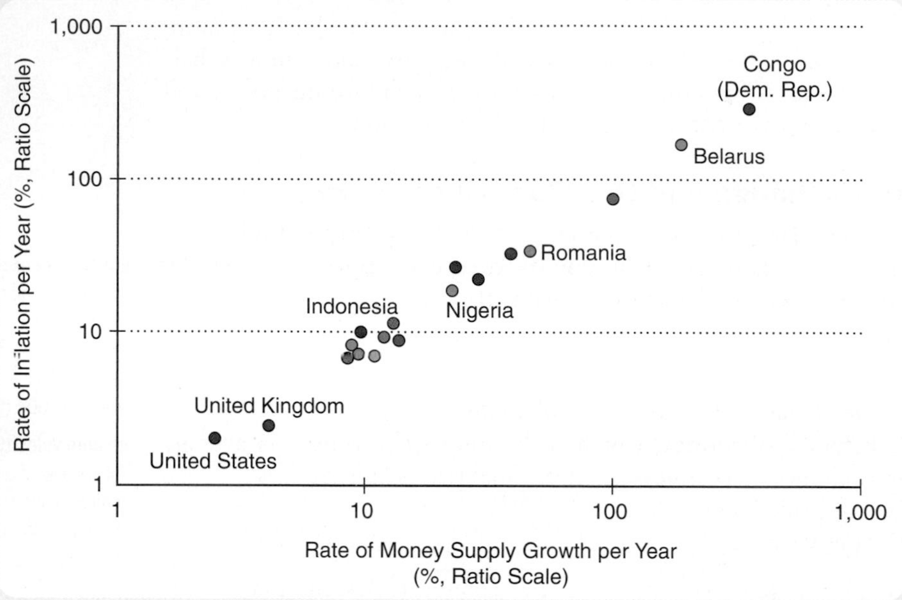

You Are There

To contemplate how Zimbabwe's experience with extremely rapid money supply growth and high inflation during the late 2000s has affected people who collect currencies, read **How Zimbabwe Undercut Collectors' Hopes of Profits,** on page 363.

EMPIRICAL VERIFICATION There is considerable evidence of the empirical validity of the relationship between monetary growth and high rates of inflation. Figure 16-5 above tracks the correspondence between money supply growth and the rates of inflation in various countries around the world.

Why did North Korea recently redefine its currency unit to be a hundred times smaller?

INTERNATIONAL POLICY EXAMPLE

North Korea Divides Its Money by 100

Inflation has been so rampant in North Korea that even the poorest individuals commonly have held thousands of *won,* the nation's currency, and banks have routinely transferred single payments denominated in *trillions* of won. All these extra zeros complicated the task of North Korean accountants and statisticians, who had to spend much of their time making sure they had the right number of digits in financial statements and data spreadsheets.

In an effort to simplify matters, the North Korean government stripped two zeros from the currency. Thus, instead of 5,000 won being equal to 1 euro, only 50 won were equal to 1 euro. With this action, North Korea joined more than 60 nations that have slashed excess zeros from their currencies during the past few years. Other examples include Bulgaria, which recently cut three zeros from its currency; Romania, which cut four zeros; and Turkey, which eliminated six zeros.

FOR CRITICAL ANALYSIS

What do you suppose happened to the measured price level in North Korea, Romania, and Bulgaria after each of these countries redefined its currency unit?

QUICK QUIZ See page 369 for the answers. Review concepts from this section in MyEconLab.

The __________ of __________ states that the expenditures by some people will equal income receipts by others, or $M_sV \equiv PY$ (money supply times velocity equals nominal GDP).

Viewed as an accounting identity, the equation of exchange is always __________, because the amount of funds __________ on final output of goods and services must equal the total amount of funds __________ for final output.

The quantity theory of money and prices states that a change in the __________ __________ will bring about an equiproportional change in the __________ __________.

Monetary Policy in Action: The Transmission Mechanism

Earlier in this chapter, we talked about the direct and indirect effects of monetary policy. The direct effect is simply that an increase in the money supply causes people to have excess money balances. To get rid of these excess money balances, people increase their expenditures. The indirect effect, depicted in Figure 16-6 below as the interest-rate-based money transmission mechanism, occurs because some people have decided to purchase interest-bearing assets with their excess money balances. This causes the price of such assets—bonds—to go up. Because of the inverse relationship between the price of existing bonds and the interest rate, the interest rate in the economy falls. This lower interest rate induces people and businesses to spend more than they otherwise would have spent.

An Interest-Rate-Based Transmission Mechanism

The indirect, interest-rate-based transmission mechanism can be seen explicitly in Figure 16-7 on the following page. In panel (a), you see that an increase in the money supply reduces the interest rate. The economywide demand curve for money is labeled M_d in panel (a). At first, the money supply is at M_s, a vertical line determined by the Federal Reserve. The equilibrium interest rate is r_1. This occurs where the money supply curve intersects the money demand curve.

Now assume that the Fed increases the money supply, say, via open market operations. This will shift the money supply curve outward to the right to M_s'. People find themselves with too much cash (liquidity). They buy bonds. When they buy bonds, they bid up the prices of bonds, thereby lowering the interest rate. The interest rate falls to r_2, where the new money supply curve M_s' intersects the money demand curve M_d. This reduction in the interest rate from r_1 to r_2 has an effect on planned investment, as can be seen in panel (b). Planned investment per year increases from I_1 to I_2. An increase in investment will increase aggregate demand, as shown in panel (c). Aggregate demand increases from AD_1 to AD_2. Equilibrium in the economy increases from real GDP per year of \$14.5 trillion, which is not on the *LRAS*, to equilibrium real GDP per year of \$15 trillion, which is on the *LRAS*.

FIGURE 16-6 The Interest-Rate-Based Money Transmission Mechanism

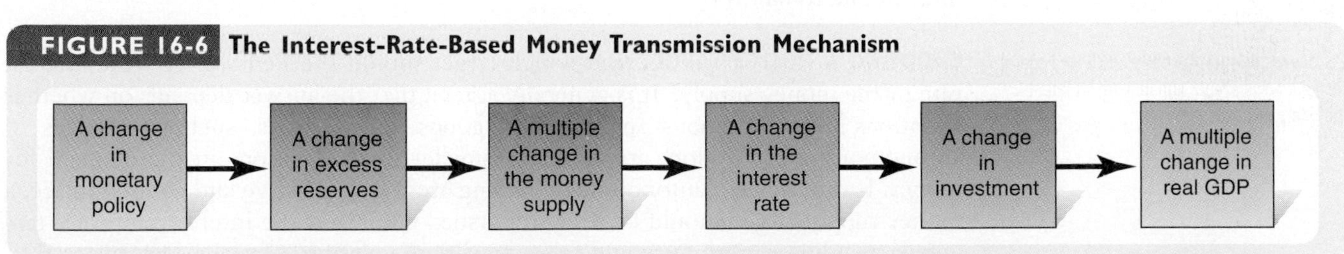

FIGURE 16-7 Adding Monetary Policy to the Aggregate Demand–Aggregate Supply Model

In panel (a), we show a demand for money function, M_d. It slopes downward to show that at lower rates of interest, a larger quantity of money will be demanded. The money supply is given initially as M_s, so the equilibrium rate of interest will be r_1. At this rate of interest, we see from the planned investment schedule given in panel (b) that the quantity of planned investment demanded per year will be I_1. After the shift in the money supply to M_s', the resulting increase in investment from I_1 to I_2 shifts the aggregate demand curve in panel (c) outward from AD_1 to AD_2. Equilibrium moves from E_1 to E_2, at real GDP of $15 trillion per year.

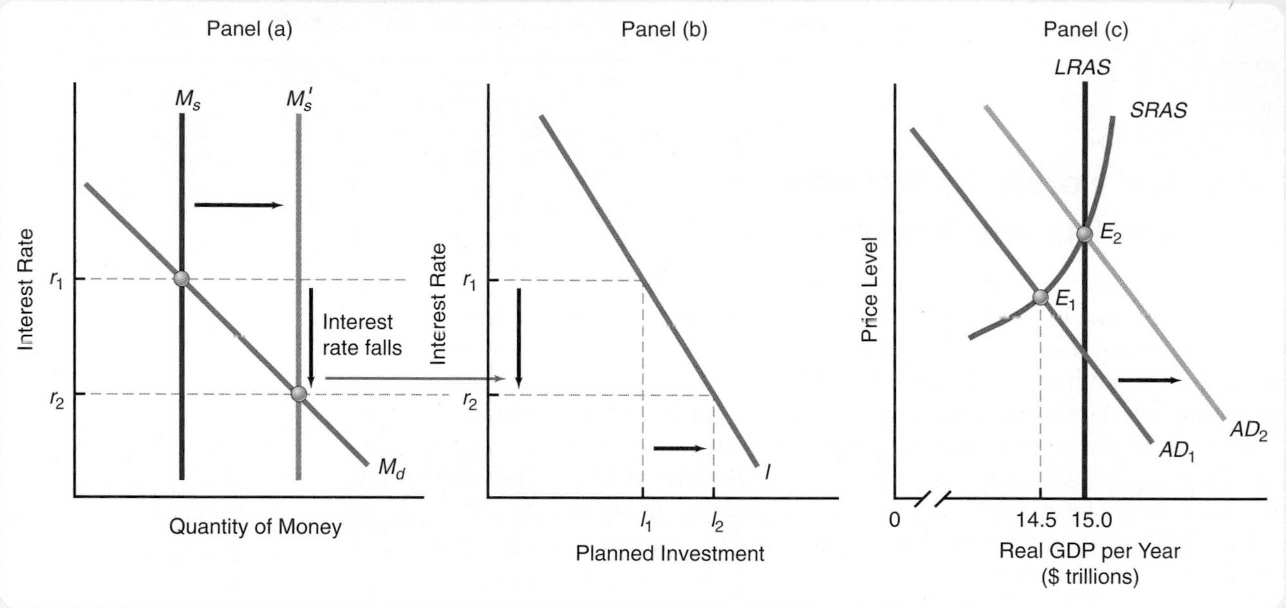

The Fed's Target Choice: The Interest Rate or the Money Supply?

The Federal Reserve has often sought to take advantage of the interest-rate-based transmission mechanism by aiming to achieve an *interest rate target*. There is a fundamental tension between targeting the interest rate and controlling the money supply, however. Targeting the interest rate forces the Fed to abandon control over the money supply. Targeting the money supply forces the Fed to allow the interest rate to fluctuate.

THE INTEREST RATE OR THE MONEY SUPPLY? Figure 16-8 on the facing page shows the relationship between the total demand for money and the supply of money. Note that money supply changes generate movements along the demand for money curve. In the short run, the Fed can choose either a particular interest rate (r_e or r_1) or a particular money supply (M_s or M_s').

If the Fed wants interest rate r_e, it must select money supply M_s. If it desires a lower interest rate in the short run, it must increase the money supply. Thus, by targeting an interest rate, the Fed must relinquish control of the money supply. Conversely, if the Fed wants to target the money supply at, say, M_s', it must allow the interest rate to fall to r_1.

Go to www.econtoday.com/ch16 for Federal Reserve news events announcing its latest monetary policy actions.

CHOOSING A POLICY TARGET But which target should the Fed choose—the interest rate or the money supply? It is generally agreed that the answer depends on whether variations in autonomous spending on goods and services, such as changes in autonomous consumption, are larger or smaller than variations in the demand for money. If variations in autonomous spending are relatively large and commonplace, a money supply target should be set and pursued because if the interest rate were targeted, spending variations would cause maximum volatility of real GDP. To see this,

FIGURE 16-8 Choosing a Monetary Policy Target

The Fed, in the short run, can select an interest rate or a money supply target, but not both. It cannot, for example, choose r_e and M_S'. If it selects r_e, it must accept M_S. If it selects M_S', it must allow the interest rate to fall to r_1. The Fed can obtain point *A* or *B*. It cannot get to point *C* or *D*. It must therefore choose one target or the other.

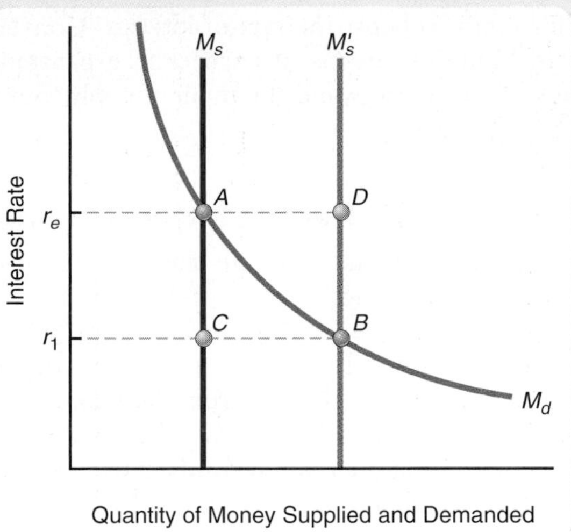

suppose that changed profit expectations induce firms to decrease their flow of autonomous investment spending. The resulting decline in real GDP causes the demand for money curve to shift leftward and pushes down the equilibrium interest rate. To keep the interest rate from falling, the Fed would have to cut the money supply, which would reduce aggregate demand and cause real GDP to fall even farther, thereby destabilizing the economy. Thus, keeping the money supply unchanged at a target level would be preferable to targeting the interest rate.

If the demand for money is highly variable, however, an interest rate target automatically offsets the effect of changes in money demand. For example, suppose that people anticipate significant drops in stock and bond prices. They react to these altered expectations by shifting more of their wealth from holdings of stocks and bonds to holdings of money. This causes the demand for money curve to shift rightward. If the Fed were to keep the money supply unchanged at a target level, the equilibrium interest rate would rise, which would cause total planned expenditures to drop. Real GDP would decline. In this situation, when the demand for money increases, it would be better for the Fed to increase the money supply and keep the interest rate from changing, thereby preventing real GDP from falling.

QUICK QUIZ **See page 369 for the answers.** **Review concepts from this section in MyEconLab.**

According to the interest-rate-based monetary policy transmission mechanism, monetary policy operates through a change in __________ __________, which changes __________, causing a multiple change in the equilibrium level of real GDP per year.

If the Federal Reserve targets the money supply, then the __________ __________ must adjust to an equilibrium at which the quantity of __________ demanded is equal to the quantity of __________ supplied.

The Federal Reserve can attempt to stabilize the __________ __________ or the __________ __________, but not both.

The Way Fed Policy Is Currently Implemented

No matter what the Fed is actually targeting, at present it announces an interest rate target. As we have seen, though, the Fed can influence interest rates only by actively entering the market for federal government securities (usually Treasury bills). So, if the Fed wants to raise "the" interest rate, it essentially must engage in contractionary open market operations. That is to say, it must sell more Treasury securities than it buys, thereby reducing total reserves in the banking system and, hence, the money supply. This tends to boost the rate of interest. Conversely, when the Fed wants to decrease "the" rate of interest, it engages in expansionary open market operations, thereby increasing reserves and the money supply. But what interest rate is the Fed attempting to change?

The Federal Funds Rate and the Discount Rate

In reality, more than one interest rate matters for Fed policymaking. Three interest rates are particularly relevant.

Federal funds market
A private market (made up mostly of banks) in which banks can borrow reserves from other banks that want to lend them. Federal funds are usually lent for overnight use.

Federal funds rate
The interest rate that depository institutions pay to borrow reserves in the interbank federal funds market.

Discount rate
The interest rate that the Federal Reserve charges for reserves that it lends to depository institutions. It is sometimes referred to as the *rediscount rate* or, in Canada and England, as the *bank rate*.

THE FEDERAL FUNDS RATE In normal times, depository institutions wishing to borrow funds rarely seek to borrow directly from the Fed. In years past, this was because the Fed would not lend them all they wanted to borrow. Instead, the Fed encouraged banks to obtain funds in the **federal funds market** when they wanted to expand their reserves. The federal funds market is an interbank market in reserves where one bank borrows the excess reserves—resources held voluntarily over and above required reserves—of another. The generic term *federal funds market* refers to the borrowing or lending of reserve funds that are usually repaid within the same 24-hour period.

Depository institutions that borrow in the federal funds market pay an interest rate called the **federal funds rate.** Because the federal funds rate is a ready measure of the cost that banks must incur to raise funds, the Federal Reserve often uses it as a yardstick by which to measure the effects of its policies. Consequently, the federal funds rate is closely watched as an indicator of the Fed's intentions.

THE DISCOUNT RATE When the Fed does lend reserves directly to depository institutions, the rate of interest that it charges is called the **discount rate.** When depository institutions borrow reserves from the Fed at this rate, they are said to be borrowing through the Fed's "discount window." Borrowing from the Fed increases reserves and thereby expands the money supply, other things being equal.

For almost 80 years, the Fed tended to keep the discount rate unchanged for weeks at a time. From the late 1960s through the early 2000s, the Fed also typically set the discount rate slightly below the federal funds rate. Because this gave depository institutions an incentive to borrow from the Fed through the discount window instead of from other banks in the federal funds market, the Fed established tough lending conditions. Often, when the Fed changed the discount rate, though, its objective was not necessarily to encourage or discourage depository institutions from borrowing from the Fed. Instead, altering the discount rate would signal to the banking system and financial markets that there had been a change in the Fed's monetary policy.

In 2003, however, the Fed altered the way it lends to depository institutions by setting the discount rate *above* the federal funds rate. In this way, the Fed sought to discourage depository institutions from seeking loans unless they faced significant liquidity problems. Since 2003, the differential between the discount rate and the federal funds rate has ranged from 0.25 percentage point to 1.0 percentage point. An increase in this differential reduces depository institutions' incentive to borrow from the Fed and thereby generates a reduction in discount window borrowings.

THE INTEREST RATE ON RESERVES In October 2008, Congress granted the Fed authority to pay interest on both required reserves and excess reserves of depository institutions. Initially, the Fed paid different rates of interest on required and excess reserves, but since late 2008 the Fed has paid the same interest rate on both categories of reserves.

Varying the interest rate on reserves alters the incentives that banks face when deciding whether to hold any additional reserves they obtain as excess reserves or to lend those reserves out to other banks in the federal funds market. If the Fed raises the interest rate on reserves and thereby reduces the differential between the federal funds rate and the interest rate on reserves, banks have less incentive to lend reserves in the federal funds market. Thus, it is not surprising that excess reserves in the U.S. banking system now amount to more than $1 trillion (see the Issues & Applications feature at the end of this chapter).

The Market for Bank Reserves and the Federal Funds Rate

To see how the Federal Reserve can use open market operations to influence the federal funds rate, consider Figure 16-9 below. This figure depicts the market for bank reserves. The Fed supplies these reserves. Banks demand reserves to hold on reserve as vault cash or reserve deposits at Federal Reserve district banks.

THE EQUILIBRIUM FEDERAL FUNDS RATE Panel (a) depicts the determination of the equilibrium federal funds rate in the market for bank reserves. The quantity of reserves supplied is equal to the accumulated amount of reserves that the Fed has created via past open market operations and loans to banks—$800 billion in panel (a). Fed actions determine this amount of reserves, so the quantity of reserves supplied is unrelated to the federal funds rate. Thus, the supply curve is vertical at $800 billion.

Because banks must satisfy their reserve requirements, the minimum quantity of reserves that they must hold is required reserves—a required reserve ratio set by the Fed times transactions deposits. This is RR = $60 billion in panel (a) of Figure 16-9. In addition, many banks also desire to hold some excess reserves. By holding excess reserves, banks forgo the opportunity to lend the reserves to other banks in the federal funds market and thereby earn interest at the federal funds rate, which usually exceeds the interest rate paid on reserves held with the Fed. Thus, as the opportunity cost of excess reserves, the federal funds rate less the Fed's interest rate on reserves, declines, banks are more willing to hold additional excess reserves. At lower values of the federal funds rate, banks hold more excess reserves. Thus, the demand for reserves

FIGURE 16-9 The Market for Bank Reserves and the Federal Funds Rate

In panel (a), the minimum quantity of reserves demanded by banks is their required reserves, which equal $60 billion. As the federal funds rate declines, the opportunity cost of holding excess reserves falls, and banks are willing to hold more excess reserves. Hence, the demand for reserves is a downward-sloping curve, *D*. At the equilibrium federal funds rate of 2 percent, the total quantity of reserves demanded by banks equals the quantity of reserves supplied by the Fed, which is $800 billion. Panel (b) shows how the Fed can bring about a reduction in the equilibrium federal funds rate. A reserve supply increase of $20 billion increases the supply of reserves from *S* to *S′*, which reduces the equilibrium federal funds rate to 1.9 percent.

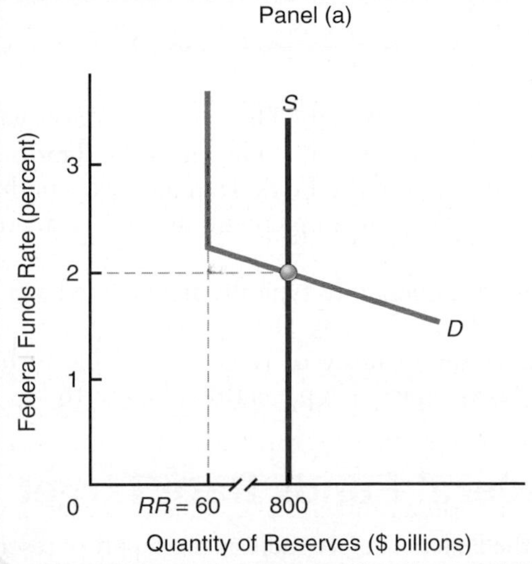

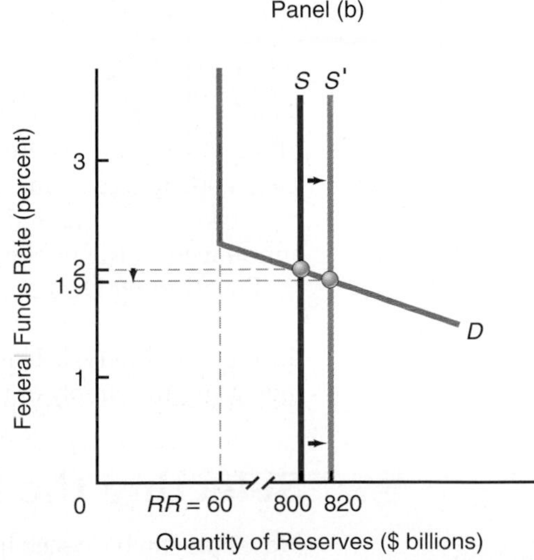

is a downward-sloping curve, as shown in panel (a). At the equilibrium federal funds rate, which is 2 percent, the quantity of reserves demanded by banks is equal to the quantity of reserves supplied by the Fed.

CHANGING THE SUPPLY OF RESERVES TO INFLUENCE THE EQUILIBRIUM FEDERAL FUNDS RATE Panel (b) of Figure 16-9 on the preceding page shows how the Fed can influence the equilibrium federal funds rate by changing the supply of reserves. In panel (b), the initial equilibrium federal funds rate is 2 percent, as in panel (a). Suppose that the Fed desires for the federal funds rate to be 1.9 percent instead of 2 percent. By conducting an open market purchase or making loans in a total amount equal to $20 billion, the Fed can increase the supply of reserves. Consequently, the supply schedule in panel (b) shifts rightward by $20 billion.

Immediately following the Fed's action, at the initial federal funds rate of 2 percent, the quantity of reserves supplied increases to $820 billion in panel (b). The quantity of reserves demanded at the 2 percent rate, however, is still $800 billion. Hence, after the Fed's action, there is an excess quantity of reserves supplied equal to $20 billion, the amount of its purchase or loan. Banks desire to hold fewer reserves than the quantity supplied at the original 2 percent rate. They will offer to lend more reserves to other banks in the federal funds market, and as they do so, the federal funds rate declines to a new equilibrium value of 1.9 percent. At this new equilibrium federal funds rate, the quantity of reserves demanded by banks is again equal to the quantity of reserves supplied by the Fed. In this way, the increase in reserve supply enables the Fed to push the federal funds rate to the desired value, which in this example is the Fed's *target* for the federal funds rate.

Establishing the Fed Policy Strategy

The policy decisions that determine open market operations by which the Fed pursues its announced objective for the federal funds rate are made by the Federal Open Market Committee (FOMC). Every six to eight weeks, the voting members of the FOMC—the seven Fed board governors and five regional bank presidents—determine the Fed's general strategy of open market operations.

FOMC Directive
A document that summarizes the Federal Open Market Committee's general policy strategy, establishes near-term objectives for the federal funds rate, and specifies target ranges for money supply growth.

The FOMC outlines its strategy in a document called the **FOMC Directive.** This document lays out the FOMC's general economic objectives, establishes short-term federal funds rate objectives, and specifies target ranges for money supply growth. After each meeting, the FOMC issues a brief statement to the media, which then publish stories about the Fed's action or inaction and what it is likely to mean for the economy. Typically, these stories have headlines such as "Fed Cuts Key Interest Rate," "Fed Acts to Push Up Interest Rates," or "Fed Decides to Leave Interest Rates Alone."

The Trading Desk

Trading Desk
An office at the Federal Reserve Bank of New York charged with implementing monetary policy strategies developed by the Federal Open Market Committee.

The FOMC leaves the task of implementing the Directive to officials who manage an office at the Federal Reserve Bank of New York known as the **Trading Desk.** The media spend little time considering how the Fed's Trading Desk conducts its activities, taking for granted that the Fed can implement the policy action that it has announced to the public.

The Trading Desk's open market operations typically are confined within a one-hour interval each weekday morning. If the Trading Desk purchases government securities during this interval, it increases the quantity of reserves available to banks, thereby increasing the supply of reserves as depicted in panel (b) of Figure 16-9.

Selecting the Federal Funds Rate Target

Now that you have seen how the Federal Reserve adjusts the supply of reserves to achieve the Federal Open Market Committee's target for the federal funds rate, we can address another question: How does the FOMC select the target value of this interest rate?

The Neutral Federal Funds Rate

The FOMC aims to set the target value of the federal funds rate equal to the **neutral federal funds rate.** At the neutral federal funds rate, the growth rate of real GDP tends neither to speed up nor to slow down in relation to the long-run, or potential, rate of real GDP growth, given the expected rate of inflation.

Neutral federal funds rate
A value of the interest rate on interbank loans at which the growth rate of real GDP tends neither to rise nor to fall relative to the rate of growth of potential, long-run, real GDP, given the expected rate of inflation.

IDENTIFYING THE NEUTRAL FEDERAL FUNDS RATE Suppose, for instance, that the actual equilibrium federal funds rate is 2 percent, but the neutral federal funds rate is 1.9 percent. The higher actual federal funds rate of 2 percent would inhibit growth in interest-sensitive consumption and investment spending. The depressed short-run growth in aggregate demand would, in the short run, cause real GDP to grow at a slower pace than the potential real GDP growth rate.

To boost aggregate demand and increase real GDP growth to the long-run rate of real GDP growth, the Fed would seek to push the equilibrium federal funds rate down to the target level—the neutral federal funds rate of 1.9 percent. The Trading Desk would conduct open market purchases or make loans to raise the supply of reserves sufficiently to attain the 1.9 percent target, as depicted in Figure 16-9 on page 359.

TRYING TO TARGET THE NEUTRAL FEDERAL FUNDS RATE Policymakers on the FOMC face a fundamental problem: The value of the neutral federal funds rate varies over time. The potential rate of growth of real GDP is not constant. It depends on the speed at which the economy's long-run aggregate supply increases over time, which varies with factors such as productivity growth and the pace of technological improvements. Naturally, aggregate supply shocks can suddenly add to or subtract from the natural pace at which aggregate supply rises, thereby causing the potential real GDP growth rate to speed up or slow down unexpectedly.

Whenever the rate of growth of potential real GDP rises or falls, so does the value of the neutral federal funds rate. The FOMC, in turn, must respond by *changing* the target for the federal funds rate that it includes in the FOMC Directive transmitted to the Trading Desk. This explains why you so often see media reports speculating about whether the "Fed has decided to push interest rates up" or to "push interest rates down." The FOMC is always trying to aim at a moving interest rate target—a neutral federal funds rate that varies as economic conditions change.

The Taylor Rule

In light of the difficulties the Fed faces in determining the neutral federal funds rate at any given point in time, could an easier procedure exist for selecting a federal funds rate target? In 1990, John Taylor suggested a relatively simple equation that the Fed might use for this purpose. This equation would direct the Fed to set the federal funds rate target based on an estimated long-run real interest rate (see page 150 in Chapter 7), the current deviation of the actual inflation rate from the Fed's inflation objective, and the proportionate gap between actual real GDP per year and a measure of potential real GDP per year. Taylor and other economists have applied his equation, which has become known as the **Taylor rule,** to actual Fed policy choices. They have concluded that the Taylor rule's recommendations for federal funds rate target values come close to the actual targets the Fed has selected over time.

Taylor rule
An equation that specifies a federal funds rate target based on an estimated long-run real interest rate, the current deviation of the actual inflation rate from the Federal Reserve's inflation objective, and the gap between actual real GDP per year and a measure of potential real GDP per year.

PLOTTING THE TAYLOR RULE ON A GRAPH The Federal Reserve Bank of St. Louis now regularly tracks target levels for the federal funds rate predicted by a basic Taylor-rule equation. Figure 16-10 on the next page displays paths of both the actual federal funds rate (the orange line) and alternative Taylor-rule recommendations under different assumptions about the Fed's inflation objective (represented by green lines consistent with goals of 0, 1, 2, 3, or 4 percent inflation).

FIGURE 16-10 Actual Federal Funds Rates and Values Predicted by a Taylor Rule

This figure displays both the actual path of the federal funds rate since 2002 and the target paths specified by a Taylor-rule equation for alternative annual inflation objectives of 0, 1, 2, 3, and 4 percent.

Source: Federal Reserve Bank of St. Louis; *Monetary Trends,* various issues.

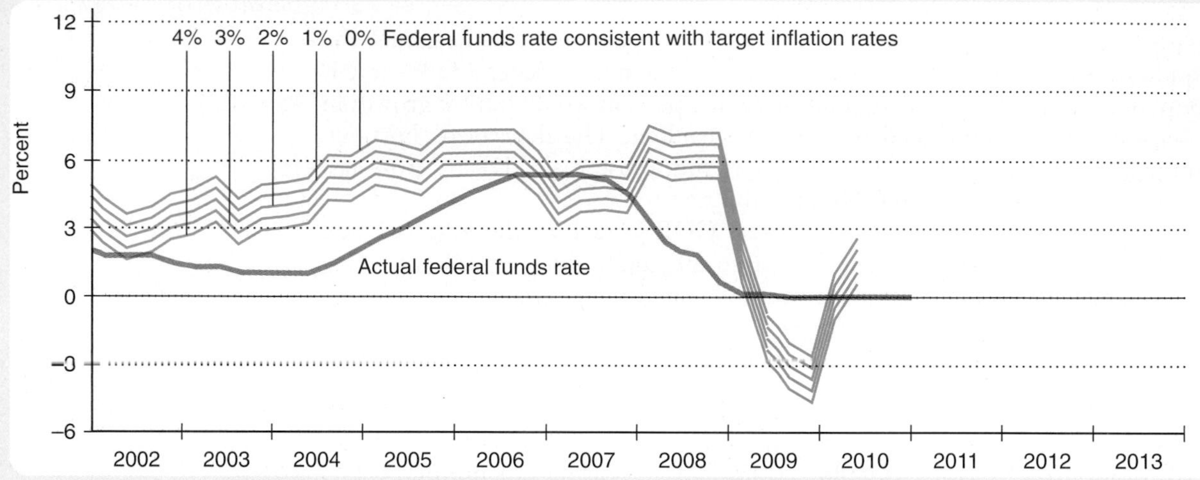

When the actual federal funds rate is at a level consistent with a particular inflation rate goal, then the Taylor rule indicates that Fed policymaking will tend to produce that inflation rate. For instance, at the middle of 2002 the actual federal funds rate was at a level that the Taylor rule specified to be consistent with a 4 percent inflation target.

ASSESSING THE STANCE OF FED POLICY WITH THE TAYLOR RULE Suppose that the actual federal funds rate is *below* the rate implied by a particular inflation goal. In this situation, the Taylor rule implies that the Fed's policymaking is expansionary. As a consequence, the actual inflation rate will rise above the Fed's goal for the inflation rate. Thus, during the 2003–2005 interval, the actual federal funds rate was below the level consistent with a 4 percent inflation rate. This implies that Fed policymaking was very expansionary during this period, sufficiently so as to be expected to yield a long-run inflation rate in excess of 4 percent per year. The Taylor-rule graph implies that in late 2006, the Fed's policy stance became much more contractionary, with the actual federal funds rate above the level consistent with 0 percent inflation. Then, the graph suggests, Fed policymaking became expansionary once more beginning in early 2008.

Until the early 2000s, the actual federal funds rate remained relatively close to the Taylor-rule predictions over time. Since 2003, the Fed has failed to set its federal funds rate target in a manner consistent with the Taylor rule.

Why Not . . . just follow the Taylor rule?

In fact, after 2008, during the Great Recession, following the Taylor rule was not feasible for the Fed. From early 2009 to early 2010, the Fed could not have followed the Taylor rule even if it had desired to do so. As you can see in Figure 16-10 above, the Taylor rule specified a *negative* value for the federal funds rate. Explicit nominal interest rates below 0 percent are very rarely observed, so the closest that the Fed could have come to following the Taylor rule in 2009 and 2010 was to do what it actually did, which was to target the federal funds rate at a value very close to 0 percent.

QUICK QUIZ See page 369 for the answers. Review concepts from this section in MyEconLab.

At present, the policy strategy of the Federal Open Market Committee (FOMC) focuses on aiming for a target value of the __________ __________ rate, which the FOMC seeks to achieve via __________ __________ __________ that alter the supply of reserves to the banking system.

The FOMC outlines the Fed's general monetary policy strategy in the FOMC __________, which it transmits to the Trading Desk of the Federal Reserve Bank of __________ __________ for implementation.

In principle, the appropriate target for the federal funds rate is the __________ federal funds rate. Given the difficulties in determining this rate, some economists have promoted the __________ __________, which is based on an equation involving an estimated long-run real interest rate, the deviation of inflation from the Fed's inflation goal, and the gap between actual real GDP per year and potential real GDP per year.

You Are There

How Zimbabwe Undercut Collectors' Hopes of Profits

Donald MacTavish, a collector of and dealer in currency notes, has acquired notes that he hopes eventually may be prized by money collectors: one-trillion-dollar notes printed during Zimbabwe's *hyperinflation*—an inflation rate so high that the Zimbabwe dollar often lost more than half its value in a single day. MacTavish bought each note at a price of less than 20 U.S. dollars for each one-trillion-dollar Zimbabwe bill. He hopes that only a limited number of the bills will make their way into collectors' hands. Some collectors, he has observed, think that the price of the notes might eventually rise to more than 100 U.S. dollars.

Shortly after acquiring the Zimbabwe notes, however, MacTavish reads some bad news. Zimbabwe's government printed and distributed the notes in very large volumes. Indeed, so many notes were issued that economists have concluded that this helps to explain why Zimbabwe's inflation rate became the second highest in recorded history. To MacTavish's dismay, experts on the values of moneys that have gone out of circulation are suggesting that Zimbabwe's one-trillion-dollar notes are so abundant that their market values may never exceed what he paid for them.

Critical Analysis Questions

1. How did printing and distributing one-trillion-dollar notes help fuel Zimbabwe's hyperinflation?
2. Why do you think that during the hyperinflation, Zimbabwe's residents used currency notes to buy goods and services as rapidly they possibly could?

ISSUES & APPLICATIONS

Explaining the Rise in the Quantity of Bank Reserves

CONCEPTS APPLIED

- ▶ Market for Bank Reserves
- ▶ Trading Desk
- ▶ FOMC Directive

In the late summer of 2008, the equilibrium quantity of reserves determined in the U.S. market for bank reserves was no higher than $45 billion. As you can see in Figure 16-11 on the next page, however, since then the total reserves of depository institutions have increased by nearly 25 times, to a level exceeding $1 trillion.

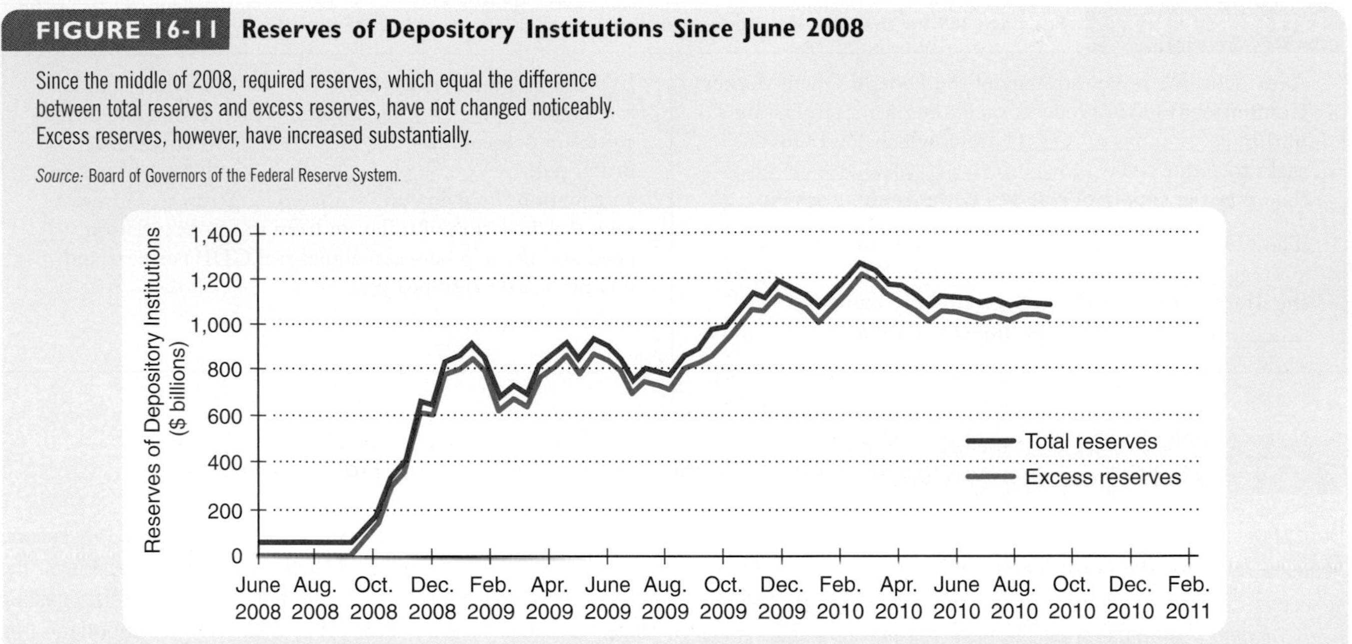

FIGURE 16-11 Reserves of Depository Institutions Since June 2008

Since the middle of 2008, required reserves, which equal the difference between total reserves and excess reserves, have not changed noticeably. Excess reserves, however, have increased substantially.

Source: Board of Governors of the Federal Reserve System.

An Upsurge in Excess Reserves

Take another look at Figure 16-11 above, and you will see that what accounts for the increase in total reserves of depository institutions is a substantial rise in voluntary holdings of excess reserves. Required reserves that the Fed requires banks to hold, which are the difference between total reserves and excess reserves, have not changed much over time. In contrast, excess reserves have risen from an average of just over $2 billion prior to the fall of 2008 to more than $1 trillion today.

A key factor contributing to this substantial increase in depository institutions' holdings of excess reserves is that since October 2008 the Federal Reserve has paid interest on all reserves held at Federal Reserve district banks. What has the Fed done with all of these reserves? The answer is that the Fed has used them to finance programs aimed at assisting a variety of institutions, including lending programs to struggling banks, acquisitions of debts of government-sponsored enterprises, and purchases of debts of private companies. In short, the Fed has created reserves and pays depository institutions to hold them with the Fed, so that in turn the Fed can direct those funds to loans intended to keep struggling financial firms and nonfinancial companies afloat.

A Planned Temporary Departure from Normal Policymaking

As discussed in this chapter, in normal times the Fed influences the quantity of reserves via open market operations. The Trading Desk at the Federal Reserve Bank of New York conducts these operations in accordance with the FOMC Directive.

Currently, however, the Fed is temporarily conducting monetary policy primarily by varying the differential between the federal funds rate and the interest rate it pays on reserves. Since 2008, it has made this differential so small that many depository institutions prefer to hold excess reserves rather than make riskier loans or hold securities. In this way, the Fed obtains the reserves it wishes to lend to struggling banks and nonfinancial companies and simultaneously attains a level of total reserves consistent with its monetary policy goals.

For Critical Analysis

1. Recall the money multiplier analysis discussed in Chapter 15. What would happen to the money supply if many depository institutions suddenly decided to lend out a large portion of their current excess reserves?
2. Assuming that the scenario you described in your answer to Question 1 occurs, what does the quantity theory of money and prices suggest would happen to the level of prices as a consequence?

Web Resources

1. Track changes in total reserves and excess reserves at depository institutions at www.econtoday.com/ch16.
2. To keep tabs on the U.S. money supply, go to www.econtoday.com/ch16.

Research Project

Economists had predicted that the market clearing federal funds rate would never drop to or below the interest rate that the Fed pays on reserves, reasoning that banks could then earn at least the same rate of interest by holding reserves with the

Fed instead of making federal funds loans. In fact, government-supported and foreign financial institutions, which do not hold reserves with the Fed but can borrow or lend in the federal funds market, have made loans to U.S. banks at market clearing federal funds rates *below* the Fed's interest rate on reserves. How can banks profit from borrowing at a federal funds rate lower than the interest rate that the Fed pays on reserves?

For more questions on this chapter's Issues & Applications, go to **MyEconLab**. In the Study Plan for this chapter, select Section N: News.

Here is what you should know after reading this chapter. **MyEconLab** will help you identify what you know, and where to go when you need to practice.

WHAT YOU SHOULD KNOW		WHERE TO GO TO PRACTICE
Key Factors That Influence the Quantity of Money That People Desire to Hold People generally make more transactions with money when nominal GDP rises. Thus, they desire to hold more money when nominal GDP increases. In addition, money is a store of value that people may hold alongside bonds, stocks, and other interest-earning assets. The opportunity cost of holding money as an asset is the interest rate, so the quantity of money demanded declines as the market interest rate increases.	money balances, 346 transactions demand, 346 precautionary demand, 346 asset demand, 347 **KEY FIGURE** Figure 16-1, 347	• **MyEconLab** Study Plan 16.1 • Audio introduction to Chapter 16 • Video: Why People Wish to Hold Money
How the Federal Reserve's Open Market Operations Influence Market Interest Rates When the Fed sells U.S. government bonds, it must offer them for sale at a lower price to induce buyers to purchase the bonds. The market price of existing bonds and the prevailing interest rate in the economy are inversely related, so the market interest rate rises when the Fed sells bonds. When the Fed buys bonds, it must offer a higher price to induce sellers to part with the bonds. Because of the inverse relationship between the market price of existing bonds and the prevailing rate of interest, the market interest rate declines when the Fed purchases bonds.	**KEY FIGURE** Figure 16-2, 348	• **MyEconLab** Study Plan 16.2 • Animated Figure 16-2 • ABC News Videos: The Federal Reserve
How Expansionary and Contractionary Monetary Policies Affect Equilibrium Real GDP and the Price Level in the Short Run An expansionary monetary policy action increases the money supply and causes a decrease in market interest rates. The aggregate demand curve shifts rightward, which can eliminate a short-run recessionary gap in real GDP. In contrast, a contractionary monetary policy action reduces the money supply and causes an increase in market interest rates. This results in a leftward shift in the aggregate demand curve, which can eliminate a short-run inflationary gap.	**KEY FIGURES** Figure 16-3, 350 Figure 16-4, 351	• **MyEconLab** Study Plan 16.3 • Animated Figures 16-3, 16-4

(*continued*)

MyEconLab continued

WHAT YOU SHOULD KNOW		WHERE TO GO TO PRACTICE
The Equation of Exchange and the Quantity Theory of Money and Prices The equation of exchange states that the quantity of money times the average number of times a unit of money is used in exchange—the income velocity of money—must equal the price level times real GDP. The quantity theory of money and prices assumes that the income velocity of money is constant and real GDP is relatively stable. Thus, a rise in the quantity of money leads to an equiproportional increase in the price level.	equation of exchange, 353 income velocity of money (V), 353 quantity theory of money and prices, 353	• **MyEconLab** Study Plan 16.3 • Video: The Quantity Theory of Money
The Interest-Rate-Based Transmission Mechanism of Monetary Policy, and Why the Federal Reserve Cannot Stabilize the Money Supply and the Interest Rate Simultaneously The interest-rate-based approach to the monetary policy transmission mechanism operates through effects of monetary policy actions on market interest rates, which bring about changes in desired investment and thereby affect equilibrium real GDP via the multiplier effect. To target the money supply, the Fed must let the market interest rate vary whenever the demand for money rises or falls. Thus, stabilizing the money supply entails some interest rate volatility. To target the interest rate, however, the Federal Reserve must be willing to adjust the money supply when there are variations in the demand for money. Hence, stabilizing the interest rate requires variations in the money supply.	**KEY FIGURES** Figure 16-6, 355 Figure 16-7, 356 Figure 16-8, 357	• **MyEconLab** Study Plans 16.3, 16.4, 16.5 • Animated Figures 16-6, 16-7, 16-8 • ABC News Video: The Federal Reserve
How the Federal Reserve Achieves a Target Value for the Federal Funds Rate and Issues the Fed Confronts in Selecting This Target At present, the Fed uses an interest rate target, which is the federal funds rate. This interest rate is at an equilibrium level when the quantity of reserves demanded by banks equals the quantity of reserves supplied by the Fed. The Trading Desk at the Federal Reserve Bank of New York conducts open market purchases or sales to alter the supply of reserves as necessary to keep the equilibrium federal funds rate at the target. In principle, the Federal Open Market Committee's target is the neutral federal funds rate, at which the growth rate of real GDP tends neither to rise above nor fall below the rate of growth of long-run potential real GDP. Some economists favor using a Taylor rule, which specifies an equation for the federal funds rate target based on an estimated long-run real interest rate, the current deviation of actual inflation from the Fed's inflation goal, and the gap between actual real GDP and a measure of potential real GDP.	federal funds market, 358 federal funds rate, 358 discount rate, 358 FOMC Directive, 360 Trading Desk, 360 neutral federal funds rate, 361 Taylor rule, 361	• **MyEconLab** Study Plans 16.5, 16.6 • ABC News Videos: The Federal Reserve

Log in to MyEconLab, take a chapter test, and get a personalized Study Plan that tells you which concepts you understand and which ones you need to review. From there, MyEconLab will give you further practice, tutorials, animations, videos, and guided solutions.
Log in to www.myeconlab.com

PROBLEMS

All problems are assignable in myeconlab. *Answers to odd-numbered problems appear at the back of the book.*

16-1. Let's denote the price of a nonmaturing bond (called a *consol*) as P_b. The equation that indicates this price is $P_b = I/r$, where I is the annual net income the bond generates and r is the nominal market interest rate.

a. Suppose that a bond promises the holder $500 per year forever. If the nominal market interest rate is 5 percent, what is the bond's current price?

b. What happens to the bond's price if the market interest rate rises to 10 percent?

16-2. Based on Problem 16-1, imagine that initially the market interest rate is 5 percent and at this interest rate you have decided to hold half of your financial wealth as bonds and half as holdings of non-interest-bearing money. You notice that the market interest rate is starting to rise, however, and you become convinced that it will ultimately rise to 10 percent.

a. In what direction do you expect the value of your bond holdings to go when the interest rate rises?

b. If you wish to prevent the value of your financial wealth from declining in the future, how should you adjust the way you split your wealth between bonds and money? What does this imply about the demand for money?

16-3. You learned in Chapter 11 that if there is an inflationary gap in the short run, then in the long run a new equilibrium arises when input prices and expectations adjust upward, causing the aggregate supply curve to shift upward and to the left and pushing equilibrium real GDP back to its long-run potential value. In this chapter, however, you learned that the Federal Reserve can eliminate an inflationary gap in the short run by undertaking a policy action that reduces aggregate demand.

a. Propose one monetary policy action that could eliminate an inflationary gap in the short run.

b. In what way might society gain if the Fed implements the policy you have proposed instead of simply permitting long-run adjustments to take place?

16-4. Explain why the net export effect of a contractionary monetary policy reinforces the usual impact that monetary policy has on equilibrium real GDP per year in the short run.

16-5. Suppose that, initially, the U.S. economy was in an aggregate demand–aggregate supply equilibrium at point A along the aggregate demand curve AD in the diagram on the top of the next column. Now, however, the value of the U.S. dollar has suddenly appreciated relative to foreign currencies. This appreciation happens to have no measurable effects on either the short-run or the long-run aggregate supply curve in the United States. It does, however, influence U.S. aggregate demand.

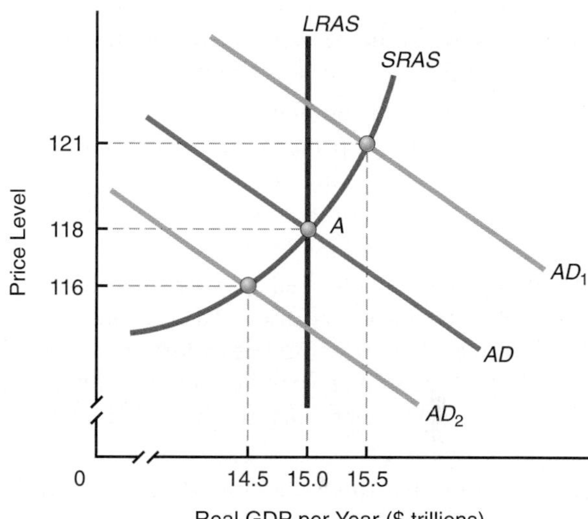

a. Explain in your own words how the dollar appreciation will affect U.S. net export expenditures.

b. Of the alternative aggregate demand curves depicted in the figure—AD_1 versus AD_2—which could represent the aggregate demand effect of the U.S. dollar's appreciation? What effects does the appreciation have on real GDP and the price level?

c. What policy action might the Federal Reserve take to prevent the dollar's appreciation from affecting equilibrium real GDP in the short run?

16-6. Suppose that the quantity of money in circulation is fixed but the income velocity of money doubles. If real GDP remains at its long-run potential level, what happens to the equilibrium price level?

16-7. Suppose that following the events in Problem 16-6, the Fed cuts the money supply in half. How does the price level now compare with its value before the income velocity and the money supply changed?

16-8. Consider the following data: The money supply is $1 trillion, the price level equals 2, and real GDP is $5 trillion in base-year dollars. What is the income velocity of money?

16-9. Consider the data in Problem 16-8. Suppose that the money supply increases by $100 billion and real GDP and the income velocity remain unchanged.

a. According to the quantity theory of money and prices, what is the new price level after the increase in the money supply?

b. What is the percentage increase in the money supply?

c. What is the percentage change in the price level?

d. How do the percentage changes in the money supply and price level compare?

16-10. Assuming that the Fed judges inflation to be the most significant problem in the economy and that it wishes to employ all of its policy instruments except interest on reserves, what should the Fed do with its three policy tools?

16-11. Suppose that the Fed implements each of the policy changes you discussed in Problem 16-10. Now explain how the net export effect resulting from these monetary policy actions will reinforce their effects that operate through interest rate changes.

16-12. Suppose that the Federal Reserve wishes to keep the nominal interest rate at a target level of 4 percent. Draw a money supply and demand diagram in which the current equilibrium interest rate is 4 percent. Explain a specific policy action, except for a change in the interest rate paid on reserves, that the Fed could take to keep the interest rate at its target level if the demand for money suddenly declines.

16-13. Imagine working at the Trading Desk at the New York Fed. Explain whether you would conduct open market purchases or sales in response to each of the following events. Justify your recommendation.

a. The latest FOMC Directive calls for an increase in the target value of the federal funds rate.

b. For a reason unrelated to monetary policy, the Fed's Board of Governors has decided to raise the differential between the discount rate and the federal funds rate. Nevertheless, the FOMC Directive calls for maintaining the present federal funds rate target.

16-14. Consider the following diagram of the market for bank reserves, in which the current equilibrium value of the federal funds rate, 2.50 percent, also corresponds to the Federal Open Market Committee's target for this interest rate.

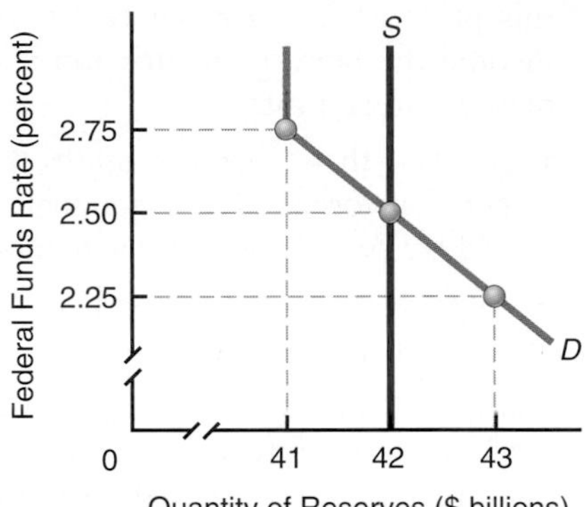

a. Suppose that the FOMC issues a new Directive to the Trading Desk at the Federal Reserve Bank of New York specifying a new federal funds rate target of 2.25 percent. What policy action should the Trading Desk implement to comply with the new FOMC Directive?

b. Explain the adjustments that will take place in the above diagram following the policy action you identified in part (a).

16-15. Explain the concept of the neutral federal funds rate in your own words, and then answer the following questions.

a. Suppose that the Federal Open Market Committee's current target for the federal funds rate is lower than the neutral federal funds rate that Fed staff economists are confident they have correctly identified. If the FOMC is convinced that the Fed staff economists are correct, what new policy strategy should the FOMC implement with its next Directive to the Trading Desk?

b. What action should the Trading Desk undertake to carry out the new FOMC policy strategy you identified in part (a)?

ECONOMICS ON THE NET

The Fed's Policy Report to Congress Congress requires the Fed to make periodic reports on its recent activities. In this application, you will study recent reports to learn about what factors affect Fed decisions.

Title: Monetary Policy Report to the Congress

Navigation: Go to **www.econtoday.com/ch16** to view the Federal Reserve's Monetary Policy Report to the Congress (formerly called the Humphrey-Hawkins Report).

Application Read the report; then answer the following questions.

1. According to the report, what economic events were most important in shaping recent monetary policy?
2. Based on the report, what are the Fed's current monetary policy goals?

For Group Study and Analysis Divide the class into "domestic" and "foreign" groups. Have each group read the past four monetary policy reports and then explain to the class how domestic and foreign factors, respectively, appear to have influenced recent Fed monetary policy decisions. Which of the two types of factors seems to have mattered most during the past year?

ANSWERS TO QUICK QUIZZES

p. 347: (i) demand; (ii) transactions . . . precautionary . . . asset; (iii) opportunity . . . downward
p. 349: (i) lower . . . higher; (ii) inverse; (iii) decrease . . . increase . . . increase . . . decrease
p. 351: (i) direct; (ii) indirect . . . reduction . . . lower
p. 352: (i) exports; (ii) negative . . . more . . . more; (iii) fewer . . . decrease . . . increase
p. 355: (i) equation . . . exchange; (ii) true . . . spent . . . received; (iii) money supply . . . price level
p. 357: (i) interest rates . . . investment; (ii) interest rate . . . money . . . money; (iii) interest rate . . . money supply
p. 363: (i) federal funds . . . open market operations; (ii) Directive . . . New York; (iii) neutral . . . Taylor rule

APPENDIX E Monetary Policy: A Keynesian Perspective

According to the traditional Keynesian approach to monetary policy, changes in the money supply can affect the level of aggregate demand only through their effect on interest rates. Moreover, interest rate changes act on aggregate demand solely by changing the level of real planned investment spending. Finally, the traditional Keynesian approach argues that there are plausible circumstances under which monetary policy may have little or no effect on interest rates and thus on aggregate demand.

Figure E-1 below measures real GDP per year along the horizontal axis and total planned expenditures (aggregate demand) along the vertical axis. The components of aggregate demand are real consumption (C), investment (I), government spending (G), and net exports (X). The height of the schedule labeled $C + I + G + X$ shows total real planned expenditures (aggregate demand) as a function of real GDP per year. This schedule slopes upward because consumption depends positively on real GDP. All along the line labeled $Y = C + I + G + X$, real planned spending equals real GDP per year. At point Y^*, where the $C + I + G + X$ line intersects this 45-degree reference line, real planned spending is consistent with real GDP. At any real GDP level less than Y^*, spending exceeds real GDP, so real GDP and thus spending will tend to rise. At any level of real GDP greater than Y^*, real planned spending is less than real GDP, so real GDP and thus spending will tend to decline. Given the determinants of C, I, G, and X, total spending (aggregate demand) will be Y^*.

Increasing the Money Supply

According to the Keynesian approach, an increase in the money supply pushes interest rates down. This induces firms to increase the level of investment spending from I to I'. As a result, the $C + I + G + X$ line shifts upward in Figure E-1 by the full amount of the rise in investment spending, thus yielding the line $C + I' + G + X$. The rise in investment spending causes real GDP to rise, which in turn causes real

FIGURE E-1 An Increase in the Money Supply

An increase in the money supply increases real GDP by lowering interest rates and thus increasing investment from I to I'.

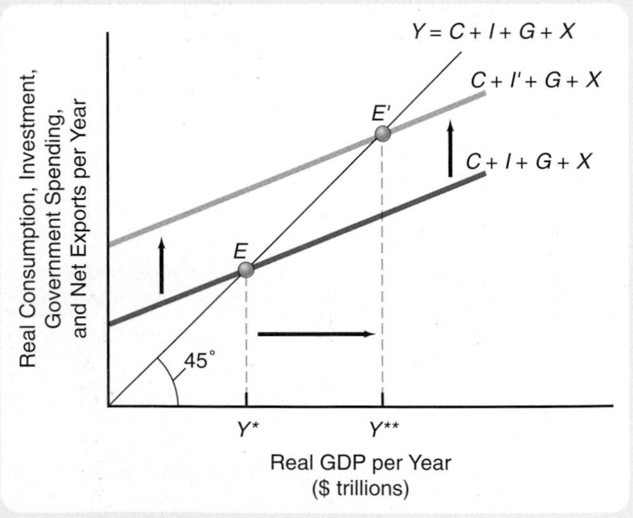

consumption spending to rise, which further increases real GDP. Ultimately, aggregate demand rises to Y^{**}, where spending again equals real GDP. A key conclusion of the Keynesian analysis is that total spending rises by *more* than the original rise in investment spending because consumption spending depends positively on real GDP.

Decreasing the Money Supply

Not surprisingly, contractionary monetary policy works in exactly the reverse manner. A reduction in the money supply pushes interest rates up. Firms respond by reducing their investment spending, and this pushes real GDP downward. Consumers react to the lower real GDP by scaling back on their real consumption spending, which further depresses real GDP. Thus, the ultimate decline in real GDP is larger than the initial drop in investment spending. Indeed, because the change in real GDP is a multiple of the change in investment, Keynesians note that changes in investment spending (similar to changes in government spending) have a *multiplier* effect on the economy.

Arguments Against Monetary Policy

It might be thought that this multiplier effect would make monetary policy a potent tool in the Keynesian arsenal, particularly when it comes to getting the economy out of a recession. In fact, however, many traditional Keynesians argue that monetary policy is likely to be relatively ineffective as a recession fighter. According to their line of reasoning, although monetary policy has the potential to reduce interest rates, changes in the money supply have little *actual* impact on interest rates. Instead, during recessions, people try to build up as much as they can in liquid assets to protect themselves from risks of unemployment and other losses of income. When the monetary authorities increase the money supply, individuals are willing to allow most of it to accumulate in their bank accounts. This desire for increased liquidity thus prevents interest rates from falling very much, which in turn means that there will be almost no change in investment spending and thus little change in aggregate demand.

PROBLEMS

All problems are assignable in myeconlab. *Answers to odd-numbered problems appear at the back of the book.*

E-1. Suppose that each 0.1-percentage-point decrease in the equilibrium interest rate induces a $10 billion increase in real planned investment spending by businesses. In addition, the investment multiplier is equal to 5, and the money multiplier is equal to 4. Furthermore, every $20 billion increase in the money supply brings about a 0.1-percentage-point reduction in the equilibrium interest rate. Use this information to answer the following questions under the assumption that all other things are equal.

a. How much must real planned investment increase if the Federal Reserve desires to bring about a $100 billion increase in equilibrium real GDP?

b. How much must the money supply change for the Fed to induce the change in real planned investment calculated in part (a)?

c. What dollar amount of open market operations must the Fed undertake to bring about the money supply change calculated in part (b)?

E-2. Suppose that each 0.1-percentage-point increase in the equilibrium interest rate induces a $5 billion decrease in real planned investment spending by businesses. In addition, the investment multiplier is equal to 4, and the money multiplier is equal to 3. Furthermore, every $9 billion decrease in the money supply brings about a 0.1-percentage-point increase in the equilibrium interest rate. Use this information to answer the following questions under the assumption that all other things are equal.

a. How much must real planned investment decrease if the Federal Reserve desires to bring about an $80 billion decrease in equilibrium real GDP?

b. How much must the money supply change for the Fed to induce the change in real planned investment calculated in part (a)?

c. What dollar amount of open market operations must the Fed undertake to bring about the money supply change calculated in part (b)?

E-3. Assume that the following conditions exist:

a. All banks are fully loaned up—there are no excess reserves, and desired excess reserves are always zero.

b. The money multiplier is 3.

c. The planned investment schedule is such that at a 6 percent rate of interest, investment is $1,200 billion; at 5 percent, investment is $1,225 billion.

d. The investment multiplier is 3.

e. The initial equilibrium level of real GDP is $12 trillion.

f. The equilibrium rate of interest is 6 percent.

Now the Fed engages in expansionary monetary policy. It buys $1 billion worth of bonds, which increases the money supply, which in turn lowers the market rate of interest by 1 percentage point. Determine how much the money supply must have increased, and then trace out the numerical consequences of the associated reduction in interest rates on all the other variables mentioned.

E-4. Assume that the following conditions exist:

a. All banks are fully loaned up—there are no excess reserves, and desired excess reserves are always zero.

b. The money multiplier is 4.

c. The planned investment schedule is such that at a 4 percent rate of interest, investment is $1,400 billion. At 5 percent, investment is $1,380 billion.

d. The investment multiplier is 5.

e. The initial equilibrium level of real GDP is $13 trillion.

f. The equilibrium rate of interest is 4 percent.

Now the Fed engages in contractionary monetary policy. It sells $2 billion worth of bonds, which reduces the money supply, which in turn raises the market rate of interest by 1 percentage point. Determine how much the money supply must have decreased, and then trace out the numerical consequences of the associated increase in interest rates on all the other variables mentioned.

Predict Future Inflation Rates

an eHow Contributing Writer

cle Rating: ★★☆☆☆ (5 Ratings)

17

Stabilization in an Integrated World Economy

Today, many financial market participants pay close attention to something called the "5yr5yr rate"—a measure of the average annual expected inflation rate 5 to 10 years hence, derived from interest rates on certain government bonds. If there is an increase in this measure of the annual inflation rate that people anticipate will prevail several years into the *future*, financial market participants interpret that increase as a signal that inflation is likely to rise in the *current* year. In this chapter, you will learn that this interpretation is consistent with predictions offered by a theory proposed by economists known as "new Keynesians." You will also learn why this theory also suggests that monetary and fiscal policies may have considerable ability to promote greater stability for the U.S. economy.

LEARNING OBJECTIVES

After reading this chapter, you should be able to:

- ▶ Explain why the actual unemployment rate might depart from the natural rate of unemployment
- ▶ Describe why there may be an inverse relationship between the inflation rate and the unemployment rate, reflected by the Phillips curve
- ▶ Evaluate how expectations affect the actual relationship between the inflation rate and the unemployment rate
- ▶ Understand the rational expectations hypothesis and its implications for economic policymaking
- ▶ Distinguish among alternative modern approaches to strengthening the case for active policymaking

myeconlab

MyEconLab helps you master each objective and study more efficiently. See end of chapter for details.

Did You Know That?

a number of economists have determined from data collected from U.S. retail price scanners that prices of most items remain unchanged for longer intervals during holiday periods than at other times of the year? These researchers argue that during holiday seasons—especially the weeks from Thanksgiving to Christmas—retailers' opportunity cost of devoting time to changing prices increases. Harried retailers opt instead to restock shelves, help customers locate products, and scan prices and bag items at checkout counters. Even though the opportunity cost of time allocated to changing prices remains relatively small during holiday seasons, it is higher than at other times of the year, so retailers change prices less often during holiday periods.

As you will learn in this chapter, a key modern economic theory suggests that even relatively small costs of changing prices can lead to widespread price stickiness. A consequence, they suggest, is that macroeconomic policies intentionally aimed at stabilizing the economy become more potent.

Active versus Passive Policymaking

Active (discretionary) policymaking
All actions on the part of monetary and fiscal policymakers that are undertaken in response to or in anticipation of some change in the overall economy.

Passive (nondiscretionary) policymaking
Policymaking that is carried out in response to a rule. It is therefore not in response to an actual or potential change in overall economic activity.

If it is true that monetary and fiscal policy actions aimed at exerting significant stabilizing effects on overall economic activity are likely to succeed, then this would be a strong argument for **active (discretionary) policymaking.** This is the term for actions that monetary and fiscal policymakers undertake in reaction to or in anticipation of a change in economic performance. On the other side of the debate is the view that the best way to achieve economic stability is through **passive (nondiscretionary) policymaking,** in which there is no deliberate stabilization policy at all. Policymakers follow a rule and do not attempt to respond in a discretionary manner to actual or potential changes in economic activity. Recall from Chapter 13 that there are lags between the time when the national economy enters a recession or a boom and the time when that fact becomes known and acted on by policymakers. Proponents of passive policy argue that such time lags often render short-term stabilization policy ineffective or, worse, procyclical.

To take a stand on this debate concerning active versus passive policymaking, you first need to know the potential trade-offs that policymakers believe they face. Then you need to see what the data actually show. The most important policy trade-off appears to be between price stability and unemployment. Before exploring that, however, we need to look at the economy's natural, or long-run, rate of unemployment.

You Are There

To contemplate a possible problem with the Fed's activist policymaking before and during the Great Recession, read **Fed Discretion—Based on What the Fed Forecasts or What It Observes?** on page 391.

The Natural Rate of Unemployment

Recall from Chapter 7 that there are different types of unemployment: frictional, cyclical, structural, and seasonal. *Frictional unemployment* arises because individuals take the time to search for the best job opportunities. Much unemployment is of this type, except when the economy is in a recession or a depression, when cyclical unemployment rises.

Note that we did not say that frictional unemployment was the *sole* form of unemployment during normal times. *Structural unemployment* is caused by a variety of "rigidities" throughout the economy. Structural unemployment results from factors such as these:

1. Government-imposed minimum wage laws, laws restricting entry into occupations, and welfare and unemployment insurance benefits that reduce incentives to work
2. Union activity that sets wages above the equilibrium level and also restricts the mobility of labor

All of these factors reduce individuals' abilities or incentives to choose employment rather than unemployment.

Consider the effect of unemployment insurance benefits on the probability of an unemployed person's finding a job. When unemployment benefits run out, according to economists Lawrence Katz and Bruce Meyer, the probability of an unemployed person's finding a job doubles. The conclusion is that unemployed workers are more serious about finding a job when they are no longer receiving such benefits.

Frictional unemployment and structural unemployment both exist even when the economy is in long-run equilibrium—they are a natural consequence of costly information (the need to conduct a job search) and the existence of rigidities such as those noted above. Because these two types of unemployment are a natural consequence of imperfect and costly information and rigidities, they are components of what economists call the **natural rate of unemployment.** As we discussed in Chapter 7, this is defined as the rate of unemployment that would exist in the long run after everyone in the economy fully adjusted to any changes that have occurred. Recall that real GDP per year tends to return to the level implied by the long-run aggregate supply curve (*LRAS*). Thus, whatever rate of unemployment the economy tends to return to in long-run equilibrium can be called the natural rate of unemployment.

Natural rate of unemployment
The rate of unemployment that is estimated to prevail in long-run macroeconomic equilibrium, when all workers and employers have fully adjusted to any changes in the economy.

How has the natural rate of unemployment changed over the years?

EXAMPLE The U.S. Natural Rate of Unemployment

In 1982, the unemployment rate was nearly 10 percent. By the late 2000s and early 2010s, it was at this level once again. These two nearly matching unemployment rates prove nothing by themselves. But look at Figure 17-1 below. There you see not only what has happened to the unemployment rate since 1950 but an estimate of the natural rate of unemployment. The line labeled "Natural rate of unemployment" is produced by averaging unemployment rates from five years earlier to five years later at each point in time (except for the end period, which is estimated). This computation reveals that until the late 1980s, the natural rate of unemployment was rising. Then it trended downward until the late 2000s, when it began to rise once more, exceeding 7 percent by 2011.

FOR CRITICAL ANALYSIS

Why does the natural rate of unemployment differ from the actual rate of unemployment?

FIGURE 17-1 Estimated Natural Rate of Unemployment in the United States

As you can see, the actual rate of unemployment has varied widely in the United States in recent decades. If we generate the natural rate of unemployment by averaging unemployment rates from five years earlier to five years later at each point in time, we get the line so labeled. It rose from the 1950s until the late 1980s and then declined until the late 2000s, when it began to rise again.

Sources: Economic Report of the President; Economic Indicators, various issues; author's estimates.

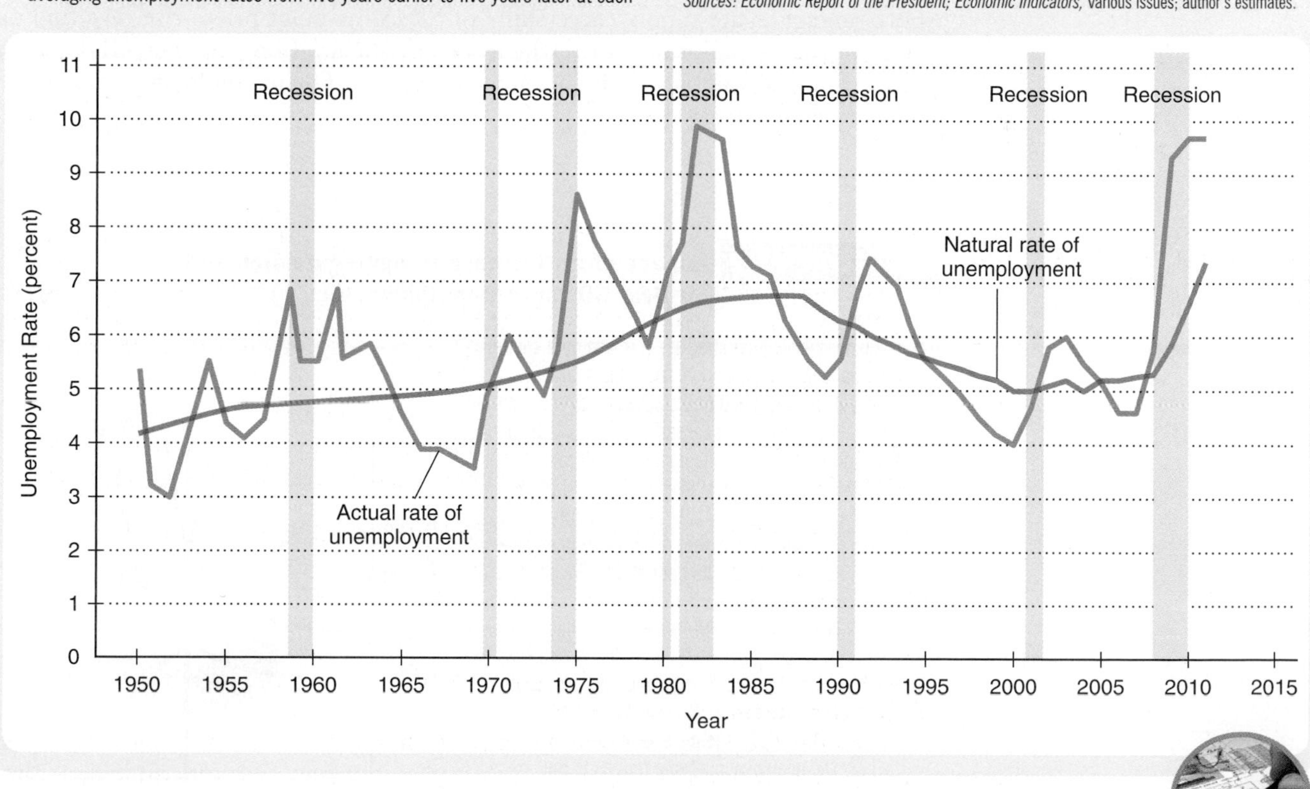

Departures from the Natural Rate of Unemployment

Even though the unemployment rate has a strong tendency to stay at and return to the natural rate, it is possible for other factors, such as changes in private spending or fiscal and monetary policy actions, to move the actual unemployment rate away from the natural rate, at least in the short run. Deviations of the actual unemployment rate from the natural rate are called *cyclical unemployment* because they are observed over the course of nationwide business fluctuations. During recessions, the overall unemployment rate exceeds the natural rate, so cyclical unemployment is positive. During periods of economic booms, the overall unemployment rate can go below the natural rate. At such times, cyclical unemployment is negative.

To see how departures from the natural rate of unemployment can occur, let's consider two examples. In Figure 17-2 below, we begin in equilibrium at point E_1 with the associated price level 117 and real GDP per year of $15 trillion.

THE IMPACT OF EXPANSIONARY POLICY Now imagine that the government decides to use fiscal or monetary policy to stimulate the economy. Further suppose, for reasons that will soon become clear, that this policy surprises decision makers throughout the economy in the sense that they did not anticipate that the policy would occur.

As shown in Figure 17-2, the expansionary policy action causes the aggregate demand curve to shift from AD_1 to AD_2. The price level rises from 117 to 120. Real GDP, measured in base-year dollars, increases from $15 trillion to $15.4 trillion.

In the labor market, individuals find that conditions have improved markedly relative to what they expected. Firms seeking to expand output want to hire more workers. To accomplish this, they recruit more actively and possibly ask workers to work overtime, so individuals in the labor market find more job openings and more possible hours they can work. Consequently, as you learned in Chapter 7, the average duration of unemployment falls, and so does the unemployment rate.

The *SRAS* curve does not stay at $SRAS_1$ indefinitely, however. Input owners, such as workers and owners of capital and raw materials, revise their expectations. The short-run aggregate supply curve shifts to $SRAS_2$ as input prices rise. We find ourselves at a new equilibrium at E_3, which is on the *LRAS*. Long-run real GDP per year is $15 trillion again, but at a higher price level, 122. The unemployment rate returns to its original, natural level.

FIGURE 17-2 Impact of an Increase in Aggregate Demand on Real GDP and Unemployment

If the economy is operating at E_1, it is in both short-run and long-run equilibrium. Here the actual rate of unemployment is equal to the natural rate of unemployment. Subsequent to expansionary monetary or fiscal policy, the aggregate demand curve shifts outward to AD_2. The price level rises from 117 to 120 at point E_2, and real GDP per year increases to $15.4 trillion in base-year dollars. The unemployment rate is now below its natural rate. We are at a short-run equilibrium at E_2. In the long run, expectations of input owners are revised. The short-run aggregate supply curve shifts from $SRAS_1$ to $SRAS_2$ because of higher prices and higher resource costs. Real GDP returns to the *LRAS* level of $15 trillion per year, at point E_3. The price level increases to 122. The unemployment rate returns to the natural rate.

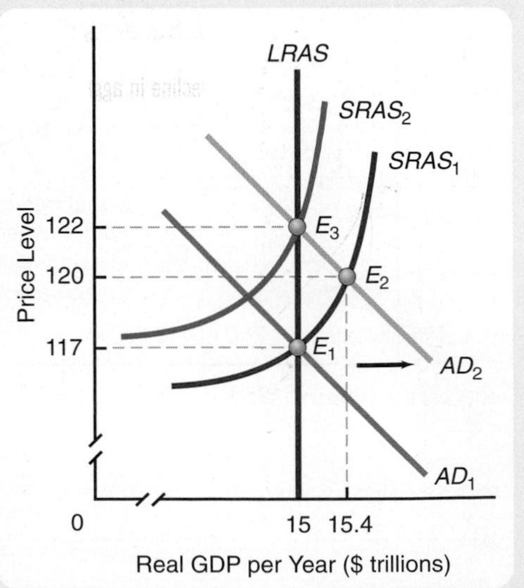

THE CONSEQUENCES OF CONTRACTIONARY POLICY Instead of expansionary policy, the government could have decided to engage in contractionary (or deflationary) policy. As shown in Figure 17-3 below, the sequence of events would have been in the opposite direction of those in Figure 17-2 on the facing page.

Beginning from an initial equilibrium E_1, an unanticipated reduction in aggregate demand puts downward pressure on both prices and real GDP. The price level falls from 120 to 118, and real GDP declines from $15 trillion to $14.7 trillion. Fewer firms are hiring, and those that are hiring offer fewer overtime possibilities. Individuals looking for jobs find that it takes longer than predicted. As a result, unemployed individuals remain unemployed longer. The average duration of unemployment rises, and so does the rate of unemployment.

The equilibrium at E_2 is only a short-run situation, however. As input owners change their expectations about future prices, $SRAS_1$ shifts to $SRAS_2$, and input prices fall. The new long-run equilibrium is at E_3, which is on the long-run aggregate supply curve, *LRAS*. In the long run, the price level declines farther, to 116, as real GDP returns to $15 trillion. Thus, in the long run the unemployment rate returns to its natural level.

The Phillips Curve: A Rationale for Active Policymaking?

Let's recap what we have just observed. In the short run, an *unexpected increase* in aggregate demand causes the price level to rise and the unemployment rate to fall. Conversely, in the short run, an *unexpected decrease* in aggregate demand causes the price level to fall and the unemployment rate to rise. Moreover, although not shown explicitly in either diagram, two additional points are true:

1. The greater the unexpected increase in aggregate demand, the greater the amount of inflation that results in the short run, and the lower the unemployment rate.
2. The greater the unexpected decrease in aggregate demand, the greater the deflation that results in the short run, and the higher the unemployment rate.

THE NEGATIVE SHORT-RUN RELATIONSHIP BETWEEN INFLATION AND UNEMPLOYMENT Figure 17-4 on the following page summarizes these findings. The inflation rate (*not* the price level) is measured along the vertical axis, and the unemployment rate is measured along the horizontal axis. Panel (a) shows the unemployment rate at a sample natural rate, U^*, that is assumed to be 6.6 percent at point A. At this point, the actual inflation rate and anticipated inflation rate are both equal to 0 percent.

FIGURE 17-3 Impact of a Decline in Aggregate Demand on Real GDP and Unemployment

Starting from equilibrium at E_1, a decline in aggregate demand to AD_2 leads to a lower price level, 118, and real GDP declines to $14.7 trillion. The unemployment rate will rise above the natural rate of unemployment. Equilibrium at E_2 is temporary, however. At the lower price level, the expectations of input owners are revised. $SRAS_1$ shifts to $SRAS_2$. The new long-run equilibrium is at E_3, with real GDP equal to $15 trillion and a price level of 116. The actual unemployment rate is once again equal to the natural rate of unemployment.

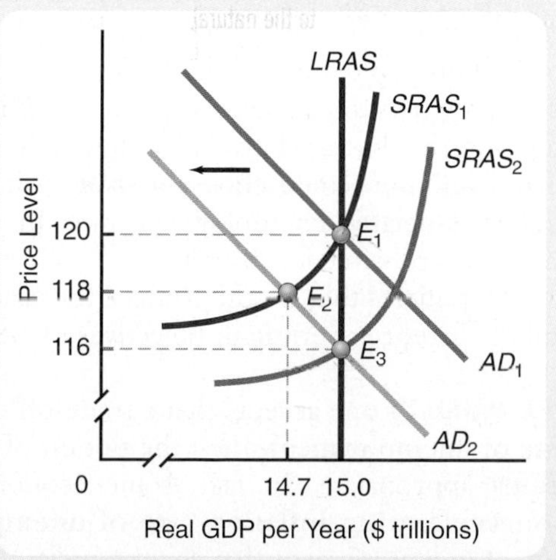

FIGURE 17-4 The Phillips Curve

Unanticipated changes in aggregate demand produce a negative relationship between the inflation rate and unemployment. U^* is the natural rate of unemployment.

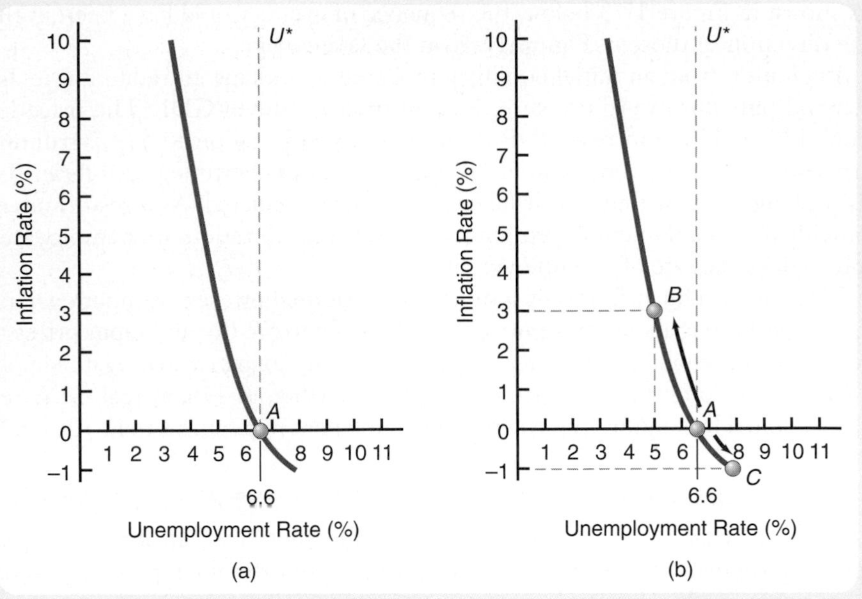

Panel (b) of Figure 17-4 above depicts the effects of unanticipated changes in aggregate demand. In panel (b), an unexpected increase in aggregate demand causes the price level to rise—the inflation rate rises to 3 percent—and causes the unemployment rate to fall, to 5 percent. Thus, the economy moves upward to the left from *A* to *B*.

Conversely, in the short run, unexpected decreases in aggregate demand cause the price level to fall and the unemployment rate to rise above the natural rate. In panel (b), the price level declines—the *deflation* rate is −1 percent—and the unemployment rate rises to 8 percent. The economy moves from point *A* to point *C*. If we look at both increases and decreases in aggregate demand, we see that high inflation rates tend to be associated with low unemployment rates (as at *B*) and that low (or negative) inflation rates tend to be accompanied by high unemployment rates (as at *C*).

Phillips curve
A curve showing the relationship between unemployment and changes in wages or prices. It was long thought to reflect a trade-off between unemployment and inflation.

IS THERE A TRADE-OFF? The apparent negative relationship between the inflation rate and the unemployment rate shown in panels (a) and (b) of Figure 17-4 has come to be called the **Phillips curve,** after A. W. Phillips, who discovered that a similar relationship existed historically in Great Britain. Although Phillips presented his findings only as an empirical regularity, economists quickly came to view the relationship as representing a *trade-off* between inflation and unemployment. In particular, policymakers who favored active policymaking believed that they could *choose* alternative combinations of unemployment and inflation. Thus, it seemed that a government that disliked unemployment could select a point like *B* in panel (b) of Figure 17-4, with a positive inflation rate but a relatively low unemployment rate. Conversely, a government that feared inflation could choose a stable price level at *A*, but only at the expense of a higher associated unemployment rate. Indeed, the Phillips curve seemed to suggest that it was possible for discretionary policymakers to fine-tune the economy by selecting the policies that would produce the exact mix of unemployment and inflation that suited current government objectives. As it turned out, matters are not so simple.

Nonaccelerating inflation rate of unemployment (NAIRU)
The rate of unemployment below which the rate of inflation tends to rise and above which the rate of inflation tends to fall.

THE NAIRU If one accepts that a trade-off exists between the rate of inflation and the rate of unemployment, then the notion of "noninflationary" rates of unemployment seems appropriate. In fact, some economists have proposed what they call the **nonaccelerating inflation rate of unemployment (NAIRU).** The NAIRU is the rate of unemployment that corresponds to a stable rate of inflation. When the unemployment rate is less than the NAIRU, the rate of inflation tends to increase. When the unemployment rate is more than the NAIRU, the rate of inflation tends to decrease. When the rate of unemployment is equal to the NAIRU, inflation continues at an unchanged rate. If the Phillips curve trade-off exists and if the NAIRU can be estimated, that estimate will define the potential short-run trade-off between the rate of unemployment and the rate of inflation.

DISTINGUISHING BETWEEN THE NATURAL UNEMPLOYMENT RATE AND THE NAIRU The NAIRU is not always the same as the natural rate of unemployment. Recall that the natural rate of unemployment is the unemployment rate that is observed whenever all cyclical factors have played themselves out. Thus, the natural unemployment rate applies to a long-run equilibrium in which any short-run adjustments have concluded. It depends on structural factors in the labor market and typically changes gradually over relatively lengthy intervals.

In contrast, the NAIRU is simply the rate of unemployment that is consistent at present with a steady rate of inflation. The unemployment rate consistent with a steady inflation rate can potentially change during the course of cyclical adjustments in the economy. Thus, the NAIRU typically varies by a relatively greater amount and relatively more frequently than the natural rate of unemployment.

The Importance of Expectations

The reduction in unemployment that takes place as the economy moves from *A* to *B* in Figure 17-4 on the facing page occurs because the wage offers encountered by unemployed workers are unexpectedly high. As far as the workers are concerned, these higher *nominal* wages appear, at least initially, to be increases in *real* wages. It is this perception that induces them to reduce the duration of their job search. This is a sensible way for the workers to view the world if aggregate demand fluctuates up and down at random, with no systematic or predictable variation one way or another. But if activist policymakers attempt to exploit the apparent trade-off in the Phillips curve, according to economists who support passive policymaking, aggregate demand will no longer move up and down in an *unpredictable* way.

THE EFFECTS OF AN UNANTICIPATED POLICY Consider, for example, Figure 17-5 below. If the Federal Reserve attempts to reduce the unemployment rate to 5 percent, it must

FIGURE 17-5 A Shift in the Phillips Curve

When there is a change in the expected inflation rate, the Phillips curve (*PC*) shifts to incorporate the new expectations. PC_0 shows expectations of zero inflation. PC_5 reflects a higher expected inflation rate, such as 3 percent.

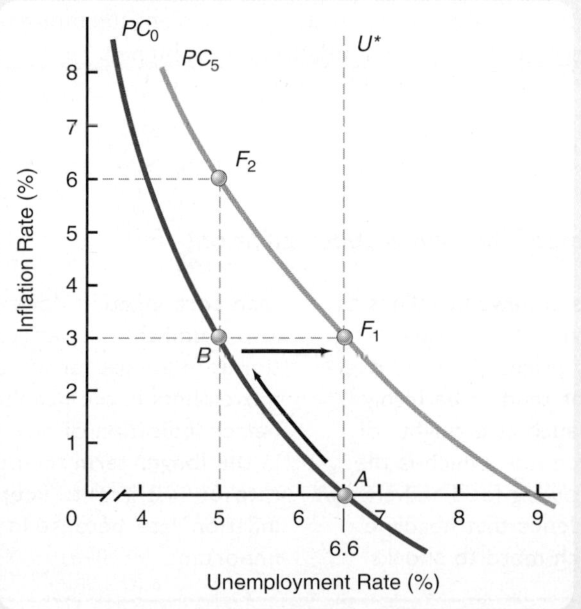

increase the rate of growth of the money supply enough to produce an inflation rate of 3 percent. If this is an unexpected one-shot action in which the rate of growth of the money supply is first increased and then returned to its previous level, the inflation rate will temporarily rise to 3 percent, and the unemployment rate will temporarily fall to 5 percent. Proponents of passive policymaking contend that past experience with active policies indicates that after the money supply stops growing, the inflation rate will soon return to zero and unemployment will return to 6.6 percent, its natural rate. Thus, an unexpected temporary increase in money supply growth will cause a movement from point *A* to point *B*, and the economy will move on its own back to *A*.

ADJUSTING EXPECTATIONS AND A SHIFTING PHILLIPS CURVE Why do those advocating passive policymaking argue that variations in the unemployment rate from its natural rate typically are temporary? If activist authorities wish to prevent the unemployment rate from returning to $U^* = 6.6$ percent in Figure 17-5 on the previous page, they will conclude that the money supply must grow fast enough to keep the inflation rate up at 3 percent. But if the Fed does this, argue those who favor passive policymaking, all of the economic participants in the economy—workers and job seekers included—will come to *expect* that inflation rate to continue. This, in turn, will change their expectations about wages.

To try out the "biz/ed" Web site's virtual economy and use the Phillips curve as a guide for policymaking in the United Kingdom, go to www.econtoday.com/ch17.

For example, when the expected inflation rate was zero, a 3 percent rise in nominal wages meant a 3 percent expected rise in real wages, and this was sufficient to induce some individuals to take jobs rather than remain unemployed. It was this expectation of a rise in *real* wages that reduced search duration and caused the unemployment rate to drop from $U^* = 6.6$ percent to 5 percent. But if the expected inflation rate becomes 3 percent, a 3 percent rise in nominal wages means *no* rise in *real* wages. Once workers come to expect the higher inflation rate, rising nominal wages will no longer be sufficient to entice them out of unemployment. As a result, as the *expected* inflation rate moves up from 0 percent to 3 percent, the unemployment rate will move up also.

In terms of Figure 17-5 on the previous page, as authorities initially increase aggregate demand, the economy moves from point *A* to point *B*. If the authorities continue the stimulus in an effort to keep the unemployment rate down, workers' expectations will adjust, causing the unemployment rate to rise. In this second stage, the economy moves from *B* to point F_1. The unemployment rate returns to the natural rate, $U^* = 6.6$ percent, but the inflation rate is now 3 percent instead of zero. Once the adjustment of expectations has taken place, any further changes in policy will have to take place along a curve such as PC_5, say, a movement from F_1 to F_2. This new schedule is also a Phillips curve, differing from the first, PC_0, in that the actual inflation rate consistent with a 5 percent unemployment rate is higher, at 6 percent, because the expected inflation rate is higher.

Why Not . . . ignore media headlines about inflation?

Policymakers regard inflation rates in news headlines as exaggerations. Before computing the inflation rate, they prefer to remove food and energy prices from the overall price index because these prices tend to be highly volatile due to short-term events such as droughts or floods. The result is the *core inflation rate,* which is the rate of change in average prices *excluding* food and energy prices. Economists have found evidence that headline inflation does initially respond much more to shocks than core inflation does. Nevertheless, economists have also found that the effects of shocks on the core inflation rate persist for an excessively long time. Therefore, movements in the headline inflation rate provide a better indication of how much the price level will rise in the longer term than changes in the core inflation rate. So it is best to keep looking at the headline inflation rate, because in the long run it is what is really important.

QUICK QUIZ See page 396 for the answers. Review concepts from this section in MyEconLab.

The **natural rate of unemployment** is the rate that exists in __________-run equilibrium, when workers' __________ are consistent with actual conditions.

Departures from the natural rate of unemployment can occur when individuals encounter unanticipated changes in fiscal or monetary policy. An unexpected __________ in aggregate demand will reduce unemployment below the natural rate, whereas an unanticipated __________ in aggregate demand will push unemployment above the natural rate.

The __________ curve exhibits a negative short-run relationship between the inflation rate and the unemployment rate that can be observed when there are *unanticipated* changes in aggregate __________.

__________ policymakers seek to take advantage of a proposed Phillips curve trade-off between inflation and unemployment.

Rational Expectations, the Policy Irrelevance Proposition, and Real Business Cycles

You already know that economists assume that economic participants act *as though* they were rational and calculating. We assume that firms rationally maximize profits when they choose today's rate of output and that consumers rationally maximize satisfaction when they choose how much of what goods to consume today. One of the pivotal features of current macro policy research is the assumption that economic participants think rationally about the future as well as the present. This relationship was developed by Robert Lucas, who won the Nobel Prize in 1995 for his work. In particular, there is widespread agreement among many macroeconomics researchers that the **rational expectations hypothesis** extends our understanding of the behavior of the macroeconomy. This hypothesis has two key elements:

Rational expectations hypothesis A theory stating that people combine the effects of past policy changes on important economic variables with their own judgment about the future effects of current and future policy changes.

1. Individuals base their forecasts (expectations) about the future values of economic variables on all readily available past and current information.
2. These expectations incorporate individuals' understanding about how the economy operates, including the operation of monetary and fiscal policy.

In essence, the rational expectations hypothesis holds that Abraham Lincoln was correct when he said, "You can fool all the people some of the time. You can even fool some of the people all of the time. But you can't fool *all* of the people *all* the time."

If we further assume that there is pure competition in all markets and that all prices and wages are flexible, we obtain what many call the *new classical* approach to evaluating the effects of macroeconomic policies. To see how rational expectations operate in the new classical perspective, let's take a simple example of the economy's response to a change in monetary policy.

Flexible Wages and Prices, Rational Expectations, and Policy Irrelevance

Consider Figure 17-6 on the next page, which shows the long-run aggregate supply curve (*LRAS*) for the economy, as well as the initial aggregate demand curve (AD_1) and the short-run aggregate supply curve ($SRAS_1$). The money supply (assumed to be the M2 measure) is initially given by M_1 = \$9 trillion, and the price level and real GDP are equal to 110 and \$15 trillion, respectively. Thus, point *A* represents the initial long-run equilibrium.

Suppose now that the money supply is unexpectedly increased to M_2 = \$10 trillion, thereby causing the aggregate demand curve to shift outward to AD_2. Given the location of the short-run aggregate supply curve, this increase in aggregate demand will cause the price level and real GDP to rise to 120 and \$15.3 trillion, respectively. The new short-run equilibrium is at *B*. Because real GDP is *above* the long-run equilibrium level of \$15 trillion, unemployment must be below long-run levels (the natural rate),

FIGURE 17-6 Responses to Anticipated and Unanticipated Increases in Aggregate Demand

A $1 trillion increase in the money supply causes the aggregate demand curve to shift rightward. If people anticipate the increase in the money supply, then workers will insist on higher nominal wages, which causes the short-run aggregate supply curve to shift leftward immediately, from $SRAS_1$ to $SRAS_2$. Hence, there is a direct movement, indicated by the green arrow, from point *A* to point *C*. In contrast, an unanticipated increase in the money supply causes an initial upward movement along $SRAS_1$ from point *A* to point *B*, indicated by the black arrow. Thus, in the short run, real GDP rises from $15 trillion to $15.3 trillion. In the long run, workers recognize that the price level has increased and demand higher wages, causing the *SRAS* curve to shift leftward, resulting in a movement from point *B* to point *C*.

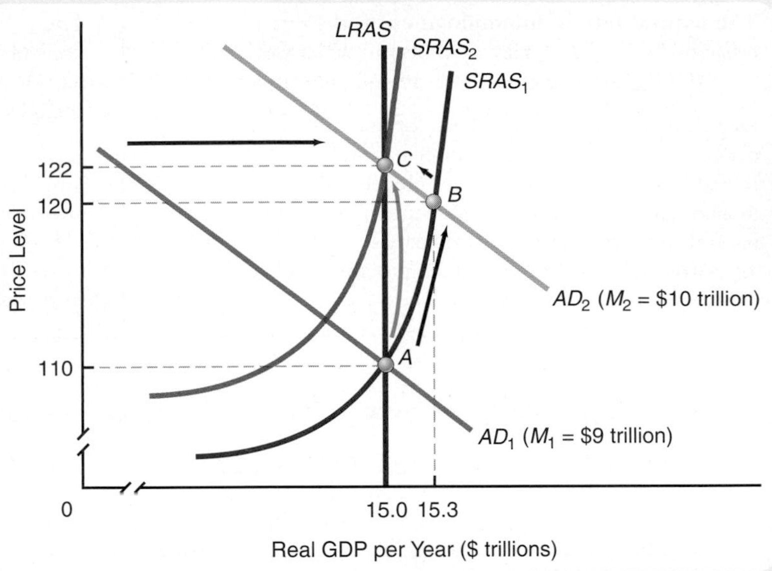

and so workers will soon respond to the higher price level by demanding higher nominal wages. This will cause the short-run aggregate supply curve to shift upward vertically. As indicated by the black arrow, the economy moves from point *B* to a new long-run equilibrium at *C*. The price level thus continues its rise to 122, even as real GDP declines back down to $15 trillion (and unemployment returns to the natural rate). So, as we have seen before, even though an increase in the money supply can raise real GDP and lower unemployment in the short run, it has no effect on either variable in the long run.

THE RESPONSE TO ANTICIPATED POLICY Now let's look at this disturbance with the perspective given by the rational expectations hypothesis when wages and prices are flexible in a purely competitive environment. Suppose that workers (and other input owners) know ahead of time that this increase in the money supply is about to take place. Assume also that they know when it is going to occur and understand that its ultimate effect will be to push the price level from 110 to 122. Will workers wait until after the price level has increased to insist that their nominal wages go up? The rational expectations hypothesis says that they will not. Instead, they will go to employers and insist that their nominal wages move upward in step with the higher prices. From the workers' perspective, this is the only way to protect their real wages from declining due to the anticipated increase in the money supply.

THE POLICY IRRELEVANCE PROPOSITION As long as economic participants behave in this manner, we must take their expectations into account when we consider the *SRAS* curve. Let's look again at Figure 17-6 above to do this. In the initial equilibrium at point *A* of the figure, the short-run aggregate supply curve $SRAS_1$ corresponds to a situation in which the expected money supply and the actual money supply are equal. When the money supply changes in a way that is anticipated by economic participants, the aggregate supply curve will shift to reflect this expected change in the money supply. The new short-run aggregate supply curve $SRAS_2$ reflects this. According to the rational expectations hypothesis, the short-run aggregate supply curve will shift upward *simultaneously* with the rise in aggregate demand. As a result, the economy will move directly from point *A* to point *C*, without passing through *B*, as depicted by the green arrow in Figure 17-6. The *only* response to the rise in the money supply is a rise in the price level from 110 to 122. Neither output nor unemployment changes at all. This conclusion—that fully anticipated monetary policy is irrelevant in determining the levels of real variables—is called the **policy irrelevance proposition:**

Policy irrelevance proposition
The conclusion that policy actions have no real effects in the short run if the policy actions are anticipated and none in the long run even if the policy actions are unanticipated.

> ***Under the assumption of rational expectations on the part of decision makers in the economy,* anticipated *monetary policy cannot alter either the rate of unemployment or the level of real GDP. Regardless of the nature of the anticipated policy, the unemployment rate will equal the natural rate, and real GDP will be determined solely by the economy's long-run aggregate supply curve.***

WHAT MUST PEOPLE KNOW? There are two important matters to keep in mind when considering this proposition. First, our discussion has assumed that economic participants know in advance exactly what the change in monetary policy is going to be and precisely when it is going to occur. In fact, the Federal Reserve does not announce exactly what the future course of monetary policy is going to be. Instead, the Fed tries to keep most of its plans secret, announcing only in general terms what policy actions are intended for the future.

It is tempting to conclude that because the Fed's intended policies are not fully known, they are not available at all. But such a conclusion would be wrong. Economic participants have great incentives to learn how to predict the future behavior of the monetary authorities, just as businesses try to forecast consumer behavior and college students do their best to forecast what their next economics exam will look like. Even if the economic participants are not perfect at forecasting the course of policy, they are likely to come a lot closer than they would in total ignorance. The policy irrelevance proposition really assumes only that *people don't persistently make the same mistakes in forecasting the future*.

WHAT HAPPENS IF PEOPLE DON'T KNOW EVERYTHING? This brings us to our second point. Once we accept the fact that people's ability to predict the future is not perfect, the possibility emerges that some policy actions will have systematic effects that look much like the movements, depicted by black arrows, from *A* to *B* to *C* in Figure 17-6 on the facing page. For example, just as other economic participants sometimes make mistakes, it is likely that the Federal Reserve sometimes makes mistakes—meaning that the money supply may change in ways that even the Fed does not predict. And even if the Fed always accomplished every policy action it intended, there is no guarantee that other economic participants would fully forecast those actions.

What happens if the Fed makes a mistake or if firms and workers misjudge the future course of policy? Looking back at Figure 17-6 on the facing page once more, suppose that economic participants' expectation of the money supply is M_1 = \$9 trillion, but the actual money supply turns out to be M_2 = \$10 trillion. Because $M_2 > M_1$, aggregate demand shifts relative to aggregate supply. The result is a rise in real GDP in the short run, from \$15 trillion to \$15.3 trillion. Corresponding to this rise in real GDP will be an increase in employment and hence a fall in the unemployment rate. So, even under the rational expectations hypothesis, monetary policy *can* have an effect on real variables in the short run, but only if the policy is unsystematic and therefore unanticipated.

In the long run, this effect on real variables will disappear because people will figure out that the Fed either accidentally increased the money supply or intentionally increased it in a way that somehow fooled individuals. Either way, people will soon revise their money supply expectation to match the actual money supply of \$10 trillion, and as a result the short-run aggregate supply curve will shift upward. As shown in Figure 17-6, real GDP will return to its long-run level of \$15 trillion, meaning that so will the employment and unemployment rates.

Another Challenge to Policy Activism: Real Business Cycles

When confronted with the policy irrelevance proposition, many economists began to reexamine the first principles of macroeconomics with fully flexible wages and prices.

THE DISTINCTION BETWEEN REAL AND MONETARY SHOCKS Some economists argue that real, as opposed to purely monetary, forces might help explain aggregate economic fluctuations. These shocks may take various forms such as technological advances that improve productivity, changes in the composition of the labor force, or changes in availability of a key resource. Consider Figure 17-7 below, which illustrates the concept of *real business cycles*. We begin at point E_1 with the economy in both short- and long-run equilibrium, with the associated supply curves, $SRAS_1$ and $LRAS_1$. Initially, the level of real GDP is $15 trillion, and the price level is 118. Because the economy is in long-run equilibrium, the unemployment rate must be at the natural rate.

A reduction in the supply of a key productive resource, such as oil, causes the *SRAS* curve to shift to the left to $SRAS_2$ because fewer goods will be available for sale due to the reduced supplies. If the reduction in, for example, oil supplies is (or is believed to be) permanent, the *LRAS* shifts to the left also. This assumption is reflected in Figure 17-7, where $LRAS_2$ shows the new long-run aggregate supply curve associated with the lowered output of oil.

In the short run, two adjustments begin to occur simultaneously. First, the prices of oil and petroleum-based products begin to rise, so the overall price level rises to 121. Second, the higher costs of production occasioned by the rise in oil prices induce firms to cut back production, so real GDP falls to $14.7 trillion in the short run. The new temporary short-run equilibrium occurs at E_2, with a higher price level (121) and a lower level of real GDP ($14.7 trillion).

This is not the full story, however. Owners of nonoil inputs, such as labor, are also affected by the reduction in oil supplies. For instance, individuals who are employed experience real wage reductions as the price level increases following the movement from point E_1 to point E_2. Even though most individuals may be willing to put up with reduced real payments in the short run, not every worker will tolerate them in the long run. Thus, some workers who were willing to continue on the job at lower real wages in the short run will eventually decide to switch from full-time to part-time employment or to drop out of the labor force altogether. In effect, there will be a fall in the supply of nonoil inputs, reflected in an upward shift in the *SRAS* curve from $SRAS_2$ to $SRAS_3$. This puts additional upward pressure on the price level and exerts a

FIGURE 17-7 Effects of a Reduction in the Supply of Resources

The position of the *LRAS* depends on our endowments of all types of resources. Hence, a permanent reduction in the supply of one of those resources, such as oil, causes a reduction—an inward shift—in the aggregate supply curve from $LRAS_1$ to $LRAS_2$. In addition, there is a rise in the equilibrium price level and a fall in the equilibrium rate of real GDP per year.

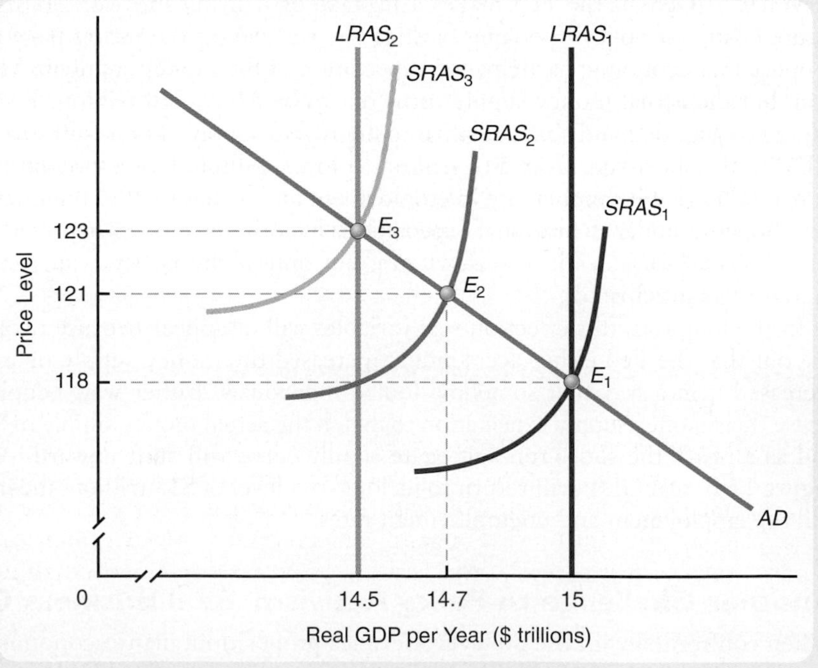

downward force on real GDP. Thus, the final long-run equilibrium occurs at point E_3, with the price level at 123 and real GDP at $14.5 trillion.

STAGFLATION Notice that in the example depicted in Figure 17-7 on the facing page, real GDP declines over the same interval that the price level increases. This decline in real GDP is associated with lower employment and a higher unemployment rate. At the same time, there is higher inflation. Such a situation involving lower real GDP and increased inflation is called **stagflation.**

Stagflation
A situation characterized by lower real GDP, lower employment, and a higher unemployment rate during the same period that the rate of inflation increases.

The most recent prolonged periods of stagflation in the United States occurred during the 1970s and early 1980s. One factor contributing to stagflation episodes during those years was sharp reductions in the supply of oil, as in the example illustrated in Figure 17-7. In addition, Congress enacted steep increases in marginal tax rates and implemented a host of new federal regulations on firms in the early 1970s. All these factors together acted to reduce long-run aggregate supply and hence contributed to stagflation. Increases in oil supplies, cuts in marginal tax rates, and deregulation during the 1980s and 1990s helped to prevent stagflation episodes from occurring after the early 1980s.

QUICK QUIZ See page 396 for the answers. Review concepts from this section in MyEconLab.

The __________ __________ hypothesis assumes that individuals' forecasts incorporate all readily available information, including an understanding of government policy and its effects on the economy.

If the **rational expectations hypothesis** is valid, there is pure competition, and all prices and wages are flexible, then the __________ __________ proposition follows: Fully anticipated monetary policy actions cannot alter either the rate of unemployment or the level of real GDP.

Even if all prices and wages are perfectly flexible, aggregate __________ shocks such as sudden changes in technology or in the supplies of factors of production can cause national economic fluctuations. To the extent that these __________ __________ cycles predominate as sources of economic fluctuations, the case for active policymaking is weakened.

Modern Approaches to Justifying Active Policymaking

The policy irrelevance proposition and the idea that real shocks are important causes of business cycles are major attacks on the desirability of trying to stabilize economic activity with activist policies. Both anti-activism suggestions arise from combining the rational expectations hypothesis with the assumptions of pure competition and flexible wages and prices. It should not be surprising, therefore, to learn that economists who see a role for activist policymaking do not believe that market clearing models of the economy can explain business cycles. They contend that the "sticky" wages and prices assumed by Keynes in his major work (see Chapter 11) remain important in today's economy. To explain how aggregate demand shocks and policies can influence a nation's real GDP and unemployment rate, these economists, who are sometimes called *new Keynesians*, have tried to refine the theory of aggregate supply.

Small Menu Costs and Sticky Prices

One approach to explaining why many prices might be sticky in the short run supposes that much of the economy is characterized by imperfect competition and that it is costly for firms to change their prices in response to changes in demand. The costs associated with changing prices are called *menu costs*. These include the costs of renegotiating contracts, printing price lists (such as menus), and informing customers of price changes.

Many such costs may not be very large, so economists call them **small menu costs.** Some of the costs of changing prices, however, such as those incurred in bringing together business managers from points around the nation or the world for meetings on price changes or renegotiating deals with customers, may be significant.

Small menu costs
Costs that deter firms from changing prices in response to demand changes—for example, the costs of renegotiating contracts or printing new price lists.

Just how "small" are small menu costs in the market for beer imported into the United States?

EXAMPLE Small Menu Costs in the U.S. Market for Imported Beer

How significant are costs of changing prices? Pinelopi Goldberg and Rebecca Hellerstein of the Federal Reserve Bank of New York have estimated the costs of changing prices in the market for beer imported into the United States. They find that for beer retailers, the cost of changing prices of imported beers is only about 0.1 percent of revenues from retail sales of the beers. For the manufacturers of the beers, the cost of changing prices is somewhat higher but still only approximately 0.4 percent of the manufacturers' revenues.

Goldberg and Hellerstein note that rates of exchange of the U.S. dollar for currencies of nations from which U.S. beers are imported often vary considerably from week to week. This causes dollar-denominated revenues from sales of imported beers to change every week. Nevertheless, retailers and manufacturers of the beers often leave their prices unchanged for many weeks at a time. Retailers change their prices slightly more often than manufacturers, consistent with the lower menu costs retailers face, but both retailers and manufacturers allow lengthy intervals—typically one year or longer—to pass before adjusting the prices of imported beers.

FOR CRITICAL ANALYSIS

When retailers of imported beers opt to leave their prices unchanged even when exchange rate changes cause dollar revenues to vary, what must be true of the magnitude of those changes in revenues?

Real GDP and the Price Level in a Sticky-Price Economy

According to the new Keynesians, sticky prices strengthen the argument favoring active policymaking as a means of preventing substantial short-run swings in real GDP and, as a consequence, employment.

NEW KEYNESIAN INFLATION DYNAMICS To see why the idea of price stickiness strengthens the case for active policymaking, consider panel (a) of Figure 17-8 on the facing page. If a significant portion of all prices do not adjust rapidly, then in the short run the aggregate supply curve effectively is horizontal, as assumed in the traditional Keynesian theory discussed in Chapter 11. This means that a decline in aggregate demand, such as the shift from AD_1 to AD_2 shown in panel (a), will induce the largest possible decline in equilibrium real GDP, from $15 trillion to $14.7 trillion. When prices are sticky, economic contractions induced by aggregate demand shocks are as severe as they can be.

As panel (a) shows, in contrast to the traditional Keynesian theory, the new Keynesian sticky-price theory indicates that the economy will find its own way back to a long-run equilibrium. The theory presumes that small menu costs induce firms not to change their prices in the short run. In the long run, however, the profit gains to firms from reducing their prices to induce purchases of more goods and services cause them to cut their prices. Thus, in the long run, the price level declines in response to the decrease in aggregate demand. As firms reduce their prices, the horizontal aggregate supply curve shifts downward, from $SRAS_1$ to $SRAS_2$, and equilibrium real GDP returns to its former level, other things being equal.

Of course, an increase in aggregate demand would have effects opposite to those depicted in panel (a) of Figure 17-8 on the facing page. A rise in aggregate demand would cause real GDP to rise in the short run. In the long run, firms would gain sufficient profits from raising their prices to compensate for incurring menu costs, and the short-run aggregate supply curve would shift upward. Consequently, an economy with growing aggregate demand should exhibit so-called **new Keynesian inflation dynamics:** initial sluggish adjustment of the price level in response to aggregate demand increases followed by higher inflation later on.

New Keynesian inflation dynamics
In new Keynesian theory, the pattern of inflation exhibited by an economy with growing aggregate demand—initial sluggish adjustment of the price level in response to increased aggregate demand followed by higher inflation later.

WHY ACTIVE POLICYMAKING CAN PAY OFF WHEN PRICES ARE STICKY To think about why the new Keynesian sticky-price theory supports the argument for active policymaking, let's return to the case of a decline in aggregate demand illustrated in panel (a) of Figure 17-8. Panel (b) shows the same decline in aggregate demand as in panel (a) and the resulting maximum contractionary effect on real GDP.

FIGURE 17-8 Short- and Long-Run Adjustments in the New Keynesian Sticky-Price Theory

Panel (a) shows that when prices are sticky, the short-run aggregate supply curve is horizontal, here at a price level of 118. As a consequence, the short-run effect of a fall in aggregate demand from AD_1 to AD_2 generates the largest possible decline in real GDP, from \$15 trillion at point E_1 to \$14.7 trillion at point E_2. In the long run, producers perceive that they can increase their profits sufficiently by cutting prices and incurring the menu costs of doing so. The resulting decline in the price level implies a downward shift of the *SRAS* curve, so that the price level falls to 116 and real GDP returns to \$15 trillion at point E_3. Panel (b) illustrates the argument for active policymaking based on the new Keynesian theory. Instead of waiting for long-run adjustments to occur, policymakers can engage in expansionary policies that shift the aggregate demand curve back to its original position, thereby shortening or even eliminating a recession.

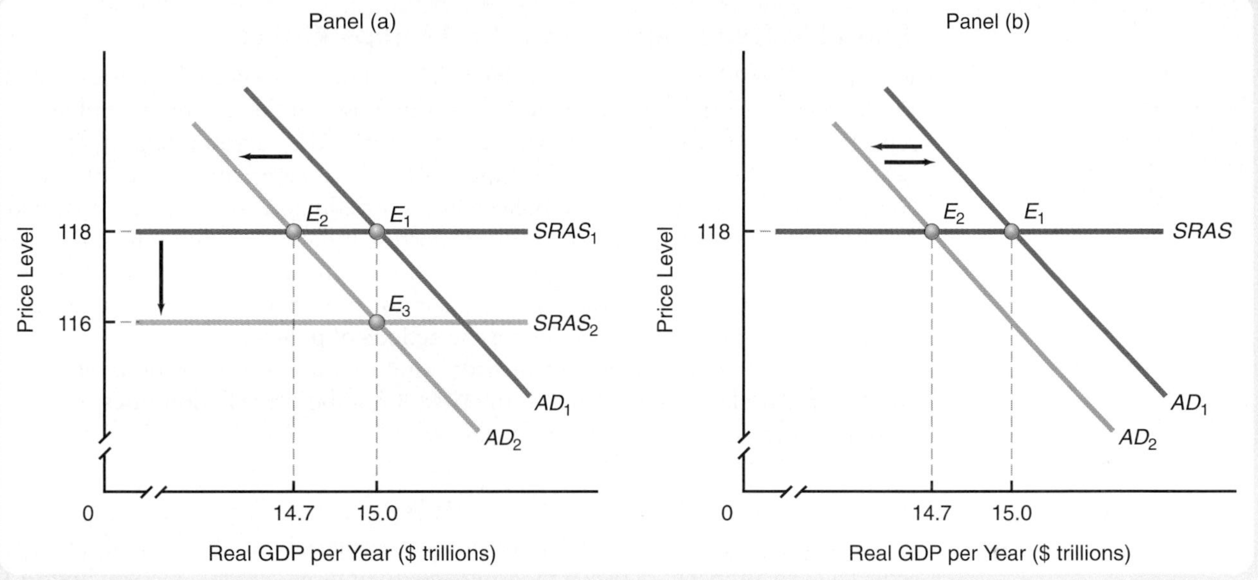

Monetary and fiscal policy actions that influence aggregate demand are as potent as possible when prices are sticky and short-run aggregate supply is horizontal. In principle, therefore, all that a policymaker confronted by the leftward shift in aggregate demand depicted in panel (b) must do is to conduct the appropriate policy to induce a rightward shift in the *AD* curve back to its previous position. Indeed, if the policymaker acts rapidly enough, the period of contraction experienced by the economy may be very brief. Active policymaking can thereby moderate or even eliminate recessions.

Did extremely active fiscal policymaking moderate the Great Recession?

POLICY EXAMPLE **Moderating the Great Recession Is Harder Than Anticipated**

Early in 2009, the federal government increased its spending by the largest percentage in a single year since World War II. Prior to the initiation of this policy action by Congress and President Obama, the president's Council of Economic Advisers (CEA) issued a report that provided a justification for very active fiscal policymaking. The CEA suggested that the ultimate payoff would be an increase in real GDP of \$1.60 for every \$1.00 of government expenditures.

Exactly one year later, Robert Barro of Harvard University provided an evaluation of the effect of the active fiscal expansion on real GDP to that point. His judgment was that the government spending had failed to boost real GDP significantly. At best, he found, each \$1 of government expenditures replaced \$1 of private spending that otherwise would have occurred and thus exerted no *net* stimulative impact on real GDP. Barro concluded, therefore, that the government's very active fiscal policymaking aimed at moderating the Great Recession failed to accomplish its objective.

FOR CRITICAL ANALYSIS

Can you think of reasons that private spending declined when public spending rose?

Is There a New Keynesian Phillips Curve?

A fundamental thrust of the new Keynesian theory is that activist policymaking can promote economic stability. Assessing this implication requires evaluating whether policymakers face an *exploitable* relationship between the inflation rate and the unemployment rate and between inflation and real GDP. By "exploitable," economists mean a relationship that is sufficiently predictable and long-lived to allow enough time for policymakers to reduce unemployment or to push up real GDP when economic activity falls below its long-run level.

The U.S. Experience with the Phillips Curve

For more than 40 years, economists have debated the existence of a policy-exploitable Phillips curve relationship between the inflation rate and the rate of unemployment. In separate articles in 1968, the late Milton Friedman and Edmond Phelps published pioneering studies suggesting that the apparent trade-off suggested by the Phillips curve could *not* be exploited by activist policymakers. Friedman and Phelps both argued that any attempt to reduce unemployment by boosting inflation would soon be thwarted by the incorporation of the new higher inflation rate into the public's expectations. The Friedman-Phelps research thus implies that for any given unemployment rate, *any* inflation rate is possible, depending on the actions of policymakers.

Figure 17-9 below appears to provide support for the propositions of Friedman and Phelps. It clearly shows that in the past, a number of inflation rates have proved feasible at the same rates of unemployment.

The New Keynesian Phillips Curve

Today's new Keynesian theorists are not concerned about the lack of an apparent long-lived relationship between inflation and unemployment revealed by Figure 17-9. From their point of view, the issue is not whether a relationship between inflation and

FIGURE 17-9 The Phillips Curve: Theory versus Data

If we plot points representing the rate of inflation and the rate of unemployment for the United States from 1953 to the present, there does not appear to be any trade-off between the two variables.

Sources: Economic Report of the President; Economic Indicators, various issues.

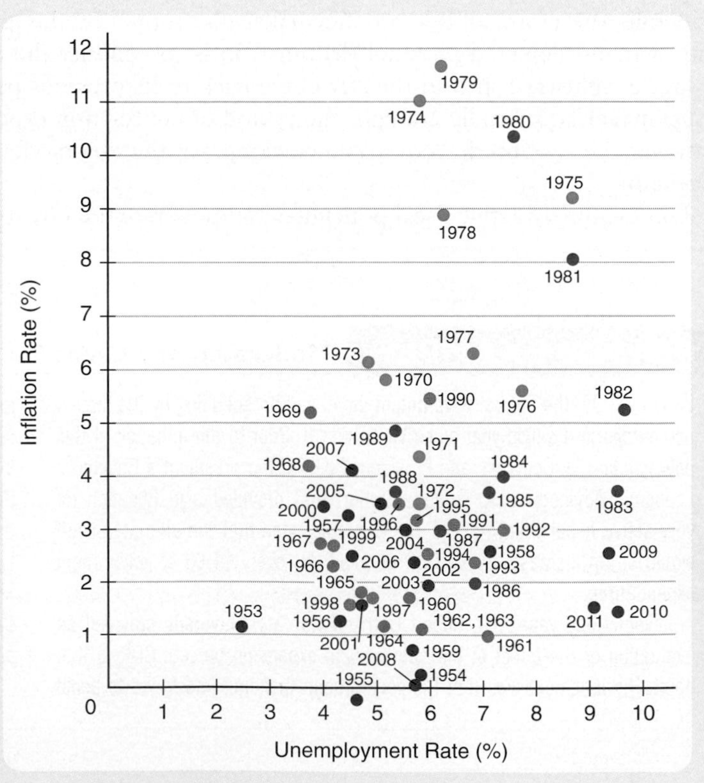

unemployment or between inflation and real GDP breaks down over a period of years. All that matters for policymakers, the new Keynesians suggest, is whether such a relationship is exploitable in the near term. If so, policymakers can intervene in the economy as soon as actual unemployment and real GDP vary from their long-run levels. Appropriate activist policies, new Keynesians conclude, can dampen cyclical fluctuations and make them shorter-lived.

EVALUATING NEW KEYNESIAN INFLATION DYNAMICS To assess the predictions of new Keynesian inflation dynamics, economists seek to evaluate whether inflation is closely related to two key factors that theory indicates should determine the inflation rate. The first of these factors is anticipated future inflation. The new Keynesian theory implies that menu costs reduce firms' incentive to adjust their prices. When some firms *do* adjust their prices, however, they will seek to set prices at levels based on expected future positions of demand curves for their products. The expected future inflation rate signals to firms how much equilibrium prices are likely to increase during future months, so firms will take into account the expected future inflation rate when setting prices at the present time.

The second key factor that new Keynesian theory indicates should affect current inflation is the average inflation-adjusted (real) per-unit costs that firms incur in producing goods and services. Thus, new Keynesians propose a positive relationship between inflation and an aggregate measure of real per-unit costs faced by firms throughout the economy. If firms' average inflation-adjusted per-unit costs increase, the prediction is that there will be higher prices charged by that portion of firms that do adjust their prices in the current period and, hence, greater current inflation.

Empirical evidence does indicate that increases in expected future inflation and greater real per-unit production costs are indeed associated with higher observed rates of inflation. In light of this support for these key predictions of the new Keynesian theory, the theory is exerting increasing influence on U.S. policymakers. For instance, media reports commonly refer to Fed officials' careful attention to changes in inflation expectations and firms' production costs that they interpret as signals of altered inflationary pressures.

JUST HOW EXPLOITABLE IS THE NEW KEYNESIAN PHILLIPS CURVE? Not all economists are persuaded that the new Keynesian theory is correct. They point out that new classical theory already indicates that when prices are *flexible*, higher inflation expectations should reduce short-run aggregate supply. Such a decline in aggregate supply should, in turn, contribute to increased inflation.

Even if one were convinced that new Keynesian theory is correct, a fundamental issue is whether the new Keynesian theory has truly identified *exploitable* relationships. At the heart of this issue is just how often firms adjust their prices.

WHY THE AMOUNT OF PRICE STICKINESS MATTERS If the average interval between firms' price adjustments is relatively long, then the horizontal new Keynesian aggregate supply curve will remain in position for a longer interval. As a result, a decline in aggregate demand will have a longer-lasting negative effect on real GDP. Then there will be a greater potential scope for activist policymaking to be able to boost aggregate demand and stabilize real GDP and unemployment. In contrast, if the average interval between changes in prices is short, then prices will adjust relatively quickly to a change in aggregate demand. There will be less scope for activist policies to stabilize the economy, because speedier adjustments of prices will automatically tend to dampen movements in real GDP and the unemployment rate.

Naturally, economists are hard at work trying to determine the average interval between price changes in national economies. So far, conclusions are mixed. Initially, studies of new Keynesian inflation dynamics yielded estimates of average price-adjustment intervals for the United States as long as two years. More recent studies, however, have produced estimated price-adjustment intervals no longer than one year. Some suggest that average periods between price adjustments are even shorter. At present, therefore, little agreement exists about just how much scope activist policymakers might have to stabilize real GDP and the unemployment rate under the new Keynesian theory.

Summing Up: Economic Factors Favoring Active versus Passive Policymaking

To many people who have never taken a principles of economics course, it seems apparent that the world's governments should engage in active policymaking aimed at achieving high and stable real GDP growth and a low and stable unemployment rate. As you have learned in this chapter, the advisability of policy activism is not so obvious.

Several factors are involved in assessing whether policy activism is really preferable to passive policymaking. Table 17-1 below summarizes the issues involved in evaluating the case for active policymaking versus the case for passive policymaking.

The current state of thinking on the relative desirability of active or passive policymaking may leave you somewhat frustrated. On the one hand, most economists agree that active policymaking is unlikely to exert sizable long-run effects on any nation's economy. Most also agree that aggregate supply shocks contribute to business cycles.

TABLE 17-1

Issues That Must Be Assessed in Determining the Desirability of Active versus Passive Policymaking

Economists who contend that active policymaking is justified argue that for each issue listed in the first column, there is evidence supporting the conclusions listed in the second column. In contrast, economists who suggest that passive policymaking is appropriate argue that for each issue in the first column, there is evidence leading to the conclusions in the third column.

Issue	Support for Active Policymaking	Support for Passive Policymaking
Phillips curve inflation–unemployment trade-off	Stable in the short run; perhaps predictable in the long run	Varies with inflation expectations; at best fleeting in the short run and nonexistent in the long run
Aggregate demand shocks	Induce short-run and perhaps long-run effects on real GDP and unemployment	Have little or no short-run effects and certainly no long-run effects on real GDP and unemployment
Aggregate supply shocks	Can, along with aggregate demand shocks, influence real GDP and unemployment	Cause movements in real GDP and unemployment and hence explain most business cycles
Pure competition	Is not typical in most markets, where imperfect competition predominates	Is widespread in markets throughout the economy
Price flexibility	Is uncommon because factors such as small menu costs induce firms to change prices infrequently	Is common because firms adjust prices immediately when demand changes
Wage flexibility	Is uncommon because labor market adjustments occur relatively slowly	Is common because nominal wages adjust speedily to price changes, making real wages flexible

Consequently, there is general agreement that there are limits on the effectiveness of monetary and fiscal policies. On the other hand, a number of economists continue to argue that there is evidence indicating stickiness of prices and wages. They argue, therefore, that monetary and fiscal policy actions can offset, at least in the short run and perhaps even in the long run, the effects that aggregate demand shocks would otherwise have on real GDP and unemployment.

These diverging perspectives help explain why economists reach differing conclusions about the advisability of pursuing active or passive approaches to macroeconomic policymaking. Different interpretations of evidence on the issues summarized in Table 17-1 on the facing page will likely continue to divide economists for years to come.

QUICK QUIZ

See page 396 for the answers. Review concepts from this section in MyEconLab.

Some new Keynesian economists suggest that __________ __________ costs inhibit many firms from making speedy changes in their prices and that this price stickiness can make the short-run aggregate supply curve __________. Variations in aggregate demand have the largest possible effects on real GDP in the short run, so policies that influence aggregate demand also have the greatest capability to stabilize real GDP in the face of aggregate demand shocks.

Even though there is little evidence supporting a long-run trade-off between inflation and unemployment, new Keynesian theory suggests that activist policymaking may be able to stabilize real GDP and employment in the __________ run. This is possible, according to the theory, if stickiness of __________ adjustment is sufficiently great that policymakers can exploit a __________-run trade-off between inflation and real GDP.

You Are There

Fed Discretion—Based on What the Fed Forecasts or What It Observes?

It is January 2010, and a crowd of economists attending the American Economic Association annual meetings has gathered to listen to Ben Bernanke discuss Fed policymaking prior to and during the Great Recession. The Fed's policies, Bernanke argues, were fully appropriate before, during, and after the onset of the crisis. The Fed, Bernanke states, adjusted the growth of the money supply in a way that moved market interest rates to levels that the Fed's inflation forecasts suggested would hold down inflation while stabilizing real GDP as well as possible. Bernanke concludes that the Fed's discretionary policies prevented a more severe downturn.

One point that Bernanke did not mention in his talk, however, sets many economists abuzz during the hours, days, and weeks that follow. If the Fed was basing its policy actions on its inflation forecasts, these economists realize, discretionary policies probably could not have been formulated as well as Bernanke claimed. The reason is that during the years leading up to and including the start of the financial meltdown, the Fed's forecasts of inflation were persistently incorrect. *Actual* inflation was almost always *higher* than the Fed's *forecasts* of inflation. Thus, it is likely that Fed policymaking would have been more effective if the Fed had based its discretionary policies on the inflation rates it actually observed instead of on inflation forecasts that were nearly always wrong.

Critical Analysis Questions

1. How might the Fed have a theoretical advantage over individuals and firms in forecasting inflation?
2. Why might the Fed have an incentive to issue artificially low inflation forecasts?

ISSUES & APPLICATIONS

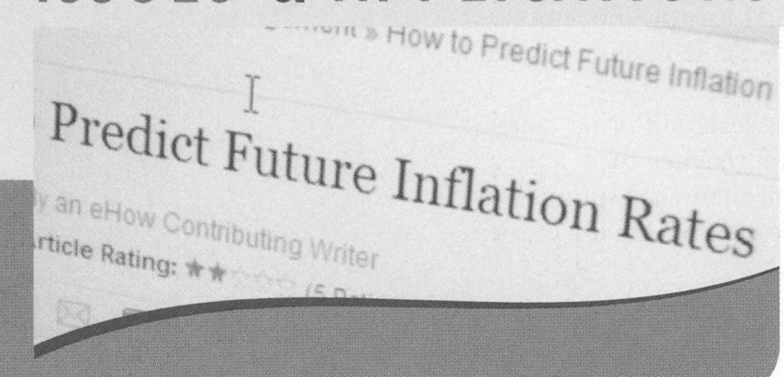

Inflation Expectations and the "5yr5yr Rate"

CONCEPTS APPLIED

- New Keynesian Inflation Dynamics
- Small Menu Costs
- Rational Expectations Hypothesis

The theory of new Keynesian inflation dynamics suggests that widespread price stickiness arising from small menu costs of changing prices provides policymakers with the capability to stabilize the economy via active policymaking. Nevertheless, this theory indicates that if aggregate demand increases quickly enough—perhaps because the Fed permits rapid growth in the money supply—anticipated revenue gains from changing prices can predominate over small menu costs. As a consequence, most firms will adjust their prices, and inflation will occur.

For this reason, the theory of new Keynesian inflation dynamics indicates that when expected future inflation rises, actual current inflation will also increase. Thus, this theory predicts that upticks in measures of expectations of future inflation will exert upward pressure on the current inflation rate.

Measuring Expected Future Inflation with "TIPS"

Treasury inflation-protected securities, or TIPS, offer a method for measuring inflation expectations. People who hold TIPS are guaranteed a fixed inflation-adjusted return, so the interest rate they require from these securities is lower than the rate people require to hold non-inflation-protected (traditional) Treasury securities.

The difference between the interest rate on a traditional U.S. government security maturing in one year and the rate on a one-year TIPS provides a gauge of what people expect the inflation rate will be over the coming year. Thus, this difference should approximately equal the rate of inflation that people anticipate over the next year.

The "5yr5yr Rate" and Longer-Term Expectations

Economists have found that current swings in food and energy prices can bias the measures of inflation expectations derived from TIPS maturing just a year or so in the future. For this reason, many economists look at a statistic called the "5yr5yr rate." This is a measure of the average annual expected inflation rate implied by differences between interest rates on traditional securities and TIPS maturing between 5 and 10 years from now. Essentially, the 5yr5yr rate is the average anticipated rate of inflation over a 5-year interval that starts 5 years from now.

Recently, the 5yr5yr rate has increased considerably. To many economists, this fact signals that people anticipate that ongoing active monetary and fiscal policymaking will fuel inflation throughout the coming decade. According to the theory of new Keynesian inflation dynamics, a consequence of these expectations of higher future inflation will be higher near-term inflation as firms respond by raising their prices today.

For Critical Analysis

1. Why does it make sense that people who hold government securities require higher interest rates on traditional Treasury securities than on TIPS?
2. If the market interest rate on traditional Treasury securities declines while the market interest rate on TIPS remains unchanged, what could you conclude about people's expectation of future inflation?

Web Resources

1. For more information about Treasury inflation-protected securities, go to www.econtoday.com/ch17.
2. To see TIPS-based estimates of inflation expectations calculated by the Federal Reserve Bank of Cleveland, go to www.econtoday.com/ch17.

Research Project

Explain in your own words why the new Keynesian theory of inflation dynamics suggests that a decrease in the 5yr5yr rate indicates that the current actual inflation rate should begin to decline, other things being equal.

For more questions on this chapter's Issues & Applications, go to **MyEconLab**. In the Study Plan for this chapter, select Section N: News.

Here is what you should know after reading this chapter. **MyEconLab** will help you identify what you know, and where to go when you need to practice.

WHAT YOU SHOULD KNOW		WHERE TO GO TO PRACTICE
Why the Actual Unemployment Rate Might Depart from the Natural Rate of Unemployment An unexpected increase in aggregate demand can cause real GDP to rise in the short run, which results in a reduction in the unemployment rate below the natural rate of unemployment. Likewise, an unanticipated reduction in aggregate demand can push down real GDP in the short run, thereby causing the actual unemployment rate to rise above the natural unemployment rate.	active (discretionary) policymaking, 374 passive (nondiscretionary) policymaking, 374 natural rate of unemployment, 375 **KEY FIGURES** Figure 17-1, 375 Figure 17-2, 376 Figure 17-3, 377	• **MyEconLab** Study Plans 17.1, 17.2 • Audio introduction to Chapter 17 • Animated Figures 17-1, 17-2, 17-3 • Video: The Natural Rate of Unemployment
The Phillips Curve An unexpected increase in aggregate demand that causes a drop in the unemployment rate also induces a rise in the equilibrium price level and, hence, inflation. Thus, other things being equal, there should be an inverse relationship between the inflation rate and the unemployment rate. This downward-sloping relationship is called the Phillips curve.	Phillips curve, 378 nonaccelerating inflation rate of unemployment (NAIRU), 378 **KEY FIGURES** Figure 17-4, 378 Figure 17-5, 379	• **MyEconLab** Study Plan 17.2 • Animated Figures 17-4, 17-5
How Expectations Affect the Actual Relationship Between the Inflation Rate and the Unemployment Rate A Phillips curve relationship will exist only when expectations are unchanged. If people anticipate policymakers' efforts to exploit the Phillips curve trade-off via inflationary policies aimed at pushing down the unemployment rate, then input prices such as nominal wages will adjust more rapidly to an increase in the price level. As a result, the Phillips curve will shift outward, and the economy will adjust more speedily toward the natural rate of unemployment.		• **MyEconLab** Study Plan 17.2

(continued)

MyEconLab continued

WHAT YOU SHOULD KNOW		WHERE TO GO TO PRACTICE
Rational Expectations, Policy Ineffectiveness, and Real-Business-Cycle Theory The rational expectations hypothesis suggests that people form expectations of inflation using all available past and current information and an understanding of how the economy functions. If pure competition prevails and wages and prices are flexible, then only unanticipated policy actions can induce even short-run changes in real GDP per year. If people completely anticipate the actions of policymakers, wages and other input prices adjust immediately, so real GDP remains unaffected. Technological changes and labor market shocks such as variations in the composition of the labor force can induce business fluctuations, called real business cycles, which weaken the case for active policymaking.	rational expectations hypothesis, 381 policy irrelevance proposition, 383 stagflation, 385 **KEY FIGURES** Figure 17-6, 382 Figure 17-7, 384	• **MyEconLab** Study Plan 17.3 • Animated Figures 17-6, 17-7
Modern Approaches to Bolstering the Case for Active Policymaking New Keynesian approaches suggest that firms may be slow to change prices in the face of variations in demand. Thus, the short-run aggregate supply curve is horizontal, and changes in aggregate demand have the largest possible effects on real GDP in the short run. If prices and wages are sufficiently inflexible in the short run that there is an exploitable trade-off between inflation and real GDP, discretionary policy actions can stabilize real GDP.	small menu costs, 385 new Keynesian inflation dynamics, 386	• **MyEconLab** Study Plans 17.4, 17.5, 17.6 • Video: The New Keynesian Economics

Log in to MyEconLab, take a chapter test, and get a personalized Study Plan that tells you which concepts you understand and which ones you need to review. From there, MyEconLab will give you further practice, tutorials, animations, videos, and guided solutions. Log in to www.myeconlab.com

PROBLEMS

All problems are assignable in myeconlab. *Answers to odd-numbered problems appear at the back of the book.*

17-1. Suppose that the government altered the computation of the unemployment rate by including people in the military as part of the labor force.

a. How would this affect the actual unemployment rate?

b. How would such a change affect estimates of the natural rate of unemployment?

c. If this computational change were made, would it in any way affect the logic of the short-run and long-run Phillips curve analysis and its implications for policymaking? Why might the government wish to make such a change?

17-2. The natural rate of unemployment depends on factors that affect the behavior of both workers and firms. Make lists of possible factors affecting workers and firms that you believe are likely to influence the natural rate of unemployment.

17-3. What distinguishes the nonaccelerating inflation rate of unemployment (NAIRU) from the natural rate of unemployment? (Hint: Which is easier to quantify?)

17-4. When will the natural rate of unemployment and the NAIRU differ? When will they be the same?

17-5. Suppose that more unemployed people who are classified as part of frictional unemployment decide to stop looking for work and start their own businesses instead. What is likely to happen to each of the following, other things being equal?

a. The natural unemployment rate

b. The NAIRU

c. The economy's Phillips curve

17-6. People called "Fed watchers" earn their living by trying to forecast what policies the Federal Reserve will implement within the next few weeks and months. Suppose that Fed watchers discover that the current group of Fed officials is following very systematic and predictable policies intended to reduce the unemployment rate. The Fed watchers then sell this information to firms, unions, and others in the private sector. If pure competition prevails, prices and wages are flexible, and people form rational expectations, are the Fed's policies enacted after the information sale likely to have their intended effects on the unemployment rate?

17-7. Suppose that economists were able to use U.S. economic data to demonstrate that the rational expectations hypothesis is true. Would this be sufficient to demonstrate the validity of the policy irrelevance proposition?

17-8. Evaluate the following statement: "In an important sense, the term *policy irrelevance proposition* is misleading because even if the rational expectations hypothesis is valid, economic policy actions can have significant effects on real GDP and the unemployment rate."

17-9. Consider the diagram below, which is drawn under the assumption that the new Keynesian sticky-price theory of aggregate supply applies. Assume that at present, the economy is in long-run equilibrium at point *A*. Answer the following questions.

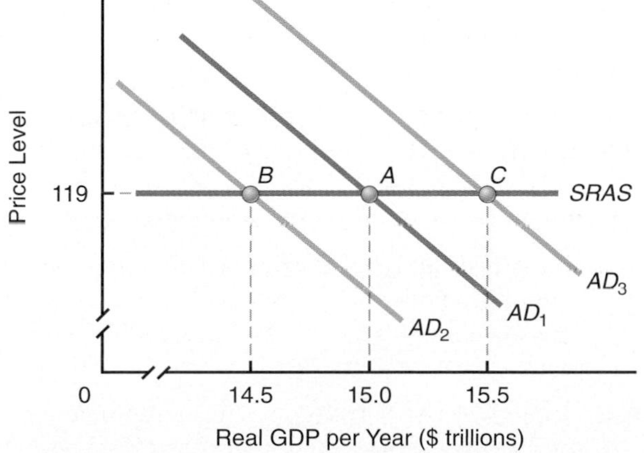

a. Suppose that there is a sudden increase in desired investment expenditures. Which of the alternative aggregate demand curves—AD_2 or AD_3—will apply after this event occurs? Other things being equal, what will happen to the equilibrium price level and to equilibrium real GDP in the *short run*? Explain.

b. Other things being equal, after the event and adjustments discussed in part (a) have taken place, what will happen to the equilibrium price level and to equilibrium real GDP in the *long run*? Explain.

17-10. Both the traditional Keynesian theory discussed in Chapter 11 and the new Keynesian theory considered in this chapter indicate that the short-run aggregate supply curve is horizontal.

a. In terms of their *short-run* implications for the price level and real GDP, is there any difference between the two approaches?

b. In terms of their *long-run* implications for the price level and real GDP, is there any difference between the two approaches?

17-11. The real-business-cycle approach attributes even short-run increases in real GDP largely to aggregate supply shocks. Rightward shifts in aggregate supply tend to push down the equilibrium price level. How could the real-business-cycle perspective explain the low but persistent inflation that the United States experienced until 2007?

17-12. Normally, when aggregate demand increases, firms find it more profitable to raise prices than to leave prices unchanged. The idea behind the small-menu-cost explanation for price stickiness is that firms will leave their prices unchanged if their profit gain from adjusting prices is less than the menu costs they would incur if they change prices. If firms anticipate that a rise in demand is likely to last for a long time, does this make them more or less likely to adjust their prices when they face small menu costs? (Hint: Profits are a flow that firms earn from week to week and month to month, but small menu costs are a one-time expense.)

17-13. The policy relevance of new Keynesian inflation dynamics based on the theory of small menu costs and sticky prices depends on the exploitability of the implied relationship between inflation and real GDP. Explain in your own words why the average time between price adjustments by firms is a crucial determinant of whether policymakers can actively exploit this relationship to try to stabilize real GDP.

ECONOMICS ON THE NET

The Inflation–Unemployment Relationship According to the basic aggregate demand and aggregate supply model, the unemployment rate should be inversely related to changes in the inflation rate, other things being equal. This application allows you to take a direct look at unemployment and inflation data to judge for yourself whether the two variables appear to be related.

Title: Bureau of Labor Statistics: Economy at a Glance

Navigation: Go to **www.econtoday.com/ch17** to visit the Bureau of Labor Statistics Economy at a Glance home page.

Application Perform the indicated operations, and then answer the following questions.

1. Click on the "back data" box next to *Consumer Price Index*. Has the U.S. economy consistently experienced inflation since 2008? Was there consistently inflation prior to 2008?
2. Back up to *Economy at a Glance*, and now click on the "back data" box next to *Unemployment Rate*. Was the unemployment rate lower or higher before 2008? Do you note any appearance of an inverse relationship between the unemployment rate and the inflation rate?

For Group Study and Analysis Divide the class into groups, and have each group search through the *Economy at a Glance* site to develop an explanation for the key factors accounting for the recent behavior of the unemployment rate. Have each group report on its explanation. Is there any one factor that best explains the recent behavior of the unemployment rate?

ANSWERS TO QUICK QUIZZES

p. 381: (i) long . . . expectations; (ii) increase . . . decrease; (iii) Phillips . . . demand; (iv) Activist
p. 385: (i) rational expectations; (ii) policy irrelevance; (iii) supply . . . real business

p. 391: (i) small menu . . . horizontal; (ii) short . . . price . . . short

18

Policies and Prospects for Global Economic Growth

Government officials in many nations realize that they have no special talent for identifying new or improved ways of producing and distributing goods and services. A number of governments, therefore, have sought to promote higher rates of economic growth by helping to jump-start businesses operating in the private sector. Toward this end, government officials have developed programs that provide public funds to help entrepreneurs open new businesses. Many observers, though, question whether government officials are better able than private investors to identify entrepreneurial ideas worthy of funding. Indeed, some observers contend that governments are at a disadvantage compared with private investors. Studying this chapter will help you to understand the basis of these criticisms of government programs that provide public funds to entrepreneurs.

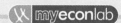

LEARNING OBJECTIVES

After reading this chapter, you should be able to:

- Explain why population growth can have uncertain effects on economic growth
- Understand why the existence of dead capital retards investment and economic growth in much of the developing world
- Describe how government inefficiencies have contributed to the creation of relatively large quantities of dead capital in the world's developing nations
- Discuss the sources of international investment funds for developing nations and identify obstacles to international investment in these nations
- Identify the key functions of the World Bank and the International Monetary Fund
- Explain the problems faced by policy-makers at the World Bank and the International Monetary Fund and discuss some proposals for dealing with these problems

myeconlab

MyEconLab helps you master each objective and study more efficiently. See end of chapter for details.

Did You Know That ? in Zimbabwe, the cost of registering business property to meet the legal requirements for operating a business is nearly 25 percent of the value of that property? In comparison, in the United States the cost of registering business property to meet legal requirements is only about 0.5 percent of the property's value. Obtaining licenses to operate a business generally takes about two and a half years in Zimbabwe, but fewer than three weeks in the United States.

Economists' understanding of the determinants of economic growth suggests that in light of the above figures, it is not surprising that the long-run average rate of economic growth is much lower in Zimbabwe than in the United States. After reading this chapter, you will be equipped to undertake your own evaluation of the prospects for global economic growth.

Labor Resources and Economic Growth

You learned in Chapter 9 that the main determinants of economic growth are the growth of labor and capital resources and the rate of increase of labor and capital productivity. Human resources are abundant around the globe. Currently, the world's population increases by more than 70 million people each year. This population growth is not spread evenly over the earth's surface. Among the relatively wealthy nations of Europe, women bear an average of just over one child during their lifetimes. In the United States, a typical woman bears about 1.5 children. But in the generally poorer nations of Africa, women bear an average of six children.

Population growth does not necessarily translate into an increase in labor resources in the poorest regions of the world. Many people in poor nations do not join the labor force. Many who do so have trouble obtaining employment.

A common assumption is that high population growth in a less developed nation hinders the growth of its per capita GDP. Certainly, this is the presumption in China, where the government has imposed an absolute limit of one child per female resident. In fact, however, the relationship between population growth and economic growth is not really so clear-cut.

Basic Arithmetic of Population Growth and Economic Growth

Does a larger population raise or lower per capita real GDP? If a country has fixed borders and an unchanged level of aggregate real GDP, a higher population directly reduces per capita real GDP. After all, if there are more people, then dividing a constant amount of real GDP by a larger number of people reduces real GDP per capita.

This basic arithmetic works for growth rates too. We can express the growth rate of per capita real GDP in a nation as

$$\begin{array}{c}\text{Rate of growth of}\\ \text{per capita real GDP}\end{array} = \begin{array}{c}\text{rate of growth}\\ \text{in real GDP}\end{array} - \begin{array}{c}\text{rate of growth}\\ \text{of population}\end{array}$$

Hence, if real GDP grows at a constant rate of 4 percent per year and the annual rate of population growth increases from 2 percent to 3 percent, the annual rate of growth of per capita real GDP will decline, from 2 percent to 1 percent.

HOW POPULATION GROWTH CAN CONTRIBUTE TO ECONOMIC GROWTH The arithmetic of the relationship between economic growth and population growth can be misleading. Certainly, it is a mathematical fact that the rate of growth of per capita real GDP equals the difference between the rate of growth in real GDP and the rate of growth of the population. Economic analysis, however, indicates that population growth can affect the rate of growth of real GDP. Thus, these two growth rates generally are not independent.

Recall from Chapter 9 that a higher rate of labor force participation by a nation's population contributes to increased growth of real GDP. If population growth is also accompanied by growth in the rate of labor force participation, then population growth can positively contribute to *per capita* real GDP growth. Even though population growth by itself tends to reduce the growth of per capita real GDP, greater labor force participation by an enlarged population can boost real GDP growth sufficiently to more than compensate for the increase in population. On balance, the rate of growth of per capita real GDP can thereby increase.

WHETHER POPULATION GROWTH HINDERS OR CONTRIBUTES TO ECONOMIC GROWTH DEPENDS ON WHERE YOU LIVE On net, does an increased rate of population growth detract from or add to the rate of economic growth? Table 18-1 below indicates that the answer depends on which nation one considers. In some nations that have experienced relatively high rates of population growth, such as Egypt, Indonesia, and Malaysia, and, to a lesser extent, Chile and China, economic growth has accompanied population growth. In contrast, in nations such as the Congo Democratic Republic, Liberia, and Togo, there has been a negative relationship between population growth and per capita real GDP growth. Other factors apparently must affect how population growth and economic growth ultimately interrelate.

The Role of Economic Freedom

A crucial factor influencing economic growth is the relative freedom of a nation's residents. Particularly important is the degree of **economic freedom**—the rights to own private property and to exchange goods, services, and financial assets with minimal government interference—available to the residents of a nation.

Economic freedom
The rights to own private property and to exchange goods, services, and financial assets with minimal government interference.

Approximately two-thirds of the world's people reside in about three dozen nations with governments unwilling to grant residents significant economic freedom. The economies of these nations, even though they have the majority of the world's population, produce only 13 percent of the world's total output. Some of these countries have experienced rates of economic growth at or above the 1.2 percent annual average for the world's nations during the past 30 years, but many are growing much more slowly. More than 30 of these countries have experienced negative rates of per capita income growth.

Go to **www.econtoday.com/ch18** to review the Heritage Foundation's evaluations of the degree of economic freedom in different nations.

Only 17 nations, with 17 percent of the world's people, grant their residents high degrees of economic freedom. These nations, some of which have very high population densities, together account for 81 percent of total world output. All of the countries that grant considerable economic freedom have experienced positive rates of

TABLE 18-1

Population Growth and Growth in Per Capita Real GDP in Selected Nations Since 1970

Country	Average Annual Population Growth Rate (%)	Average Annual Rate of Growth of Per Capita Real GDP (%)
Central African Republic	2.4	−1.1
Chile	1.5	2.7
China	1.3	7.2
Congo Democratic Republic	3.0	−3.3
Egypt	2.4	3.4
Haiti	1.8	0.0
Indonesia	1.8	4.1
Liberia	2.4	−1.3
Madagascar	2.9	−0.4
Malaysia	2.3	4.7
Togo	2.9	−1.0
United States	1.0	1.9

Source: Penn World Tables, International Monetary Fund.

economic growth, and most are close to or above the world's average rate of economic growth.

How has increased freedom for farmers to obtain information about soybean prices helped contribute to economic growth in India?

INTERNATIONAL POLICY EXAMPLE

Freedom of Information and Growth in Developing Nations

The Indian government requires farmers to sell soybeans to middlemen who, in turn, resell the beans in wholesale markets. In years past, this restriction has given the middlemen an advantage in price negotiations because they always have up-to-the-minute data about wholesale soybean prices. As a consequence, many Indian farmers who might otherwise produce soybeans have been dissuaded from doing so, for fear of being "taken" by middlemen. This has depressed the rate of increase of agricultural production in a nation in which a significant fraction of the population suffers from malnourishment.

Recently, ITC Limited, a wholesale buyer of soybeans in India, has established a network of more than 1,700 Internet kiosks in villages in key agricultural regions of the country. At these kiosks, farmers can obtain the current day's minimum and maximum wholesale soybean prices paid to market middlemen. With this information in their possession, farmers are able to bargain for better prices on their crops. In areas served by ITC's kiosks, the result has been a 33 increase in Indian soybean farmers' profits and a 19 percent increase in soybean production. The resulting boost in the supply of soybeans has contributed to lower prices and an increase in soybean consumption by the nation's residents.

FOR CRITICAL ANALYSIS

What do you suppose has happened to the profits of soybean market middlemen?

The Role of Political Freedom

Interestingly, *political freedom*—the right to openly support and democratically select national leaders—appears to be less important than economic freedom in determining economic growth. Some countries that grant considerable economic freedom to their citizens have relatively strong restrictions on their residents' freedoms of speech and the press.

When nondemocratic countries have achieved high standards of living through consistent economic growth, they tend to become more democratic over time. This suggests that economic freedom tends to stimulate economic growth, which then leads to more political freedom.

QUICK QUIZ **See page 414 for the answers.** **Review concepts from this section in MyEconLab.**

For a given rate of growth of aggregate real GDP, higher population growth tends to __________ the growth of per capita real GDP.

To the extent that increased population growth leads to greater __________ __________ participation that raises the growth of total real GDP, a higher population growth rate can potentially __________ the rate of growth in per capita real GDP.

In general, the extent of __________ freedom does not necessarily increase the rate of economic growth. A greater degree of __________ freedom, however, does have a positive effect on a nation's growth prospects.

Capital Goods and Economic Growth

Dead capital
Any capital resource that lacks clear title of ownership.

A fundamental problem developing countries face is that a significant portion of their capital goods, or manufactured resources that may be used to produce other items in the future, is what economists call **dead capital,** a term coined by economist Hernando de Soto. This term describes a capital resource lacking clear title of ownership. Dead capital may actually be put to some productive purpose, but individuals and firms face difficulties in exchanging, insuring, and legally protecting their rights to this resource. Thus, dead capital is a resource that people cannot readily allocate to its *most efficient* use. As economists have dug deeper into the difficulties confronting residents of the world's poorest nations, they have found that dead capital is among the most significant impediments to growth of per capita incomes in these countries.

Dead Capital and Inefficient Production

Physical structures used to house both business operations and labor resources are forms of capital goods. Current estimates indicate that unofficial, nontransferable physical structures valued at more than $9 trillion are found in developing nations around the world. Because people in developing countries do not officially own this huge volume of capital goods, they cannot easily trade these resources. Thus, it is hard for many of the world's people to use capital goods in ways that will yield the largest feasible output of goods and services.

Consider, for instance, a hypothetical situation faced by an individual in Cairo, Egypt, a city in which an estimated 90 percent of all physical structures are unofficially owned. Suppose this person unofficially owns a run-down apartment building but has no official title of ownership for this structure. Also suppose that the building is better suited for use as a distribution center for a new import-export firm. The individual would like to sell or lease the structure to the new firm, but because he does not formally own the building, he is unable to do so. If the costs of obtaining formal title to the property are sufficiently high relative to the potential benefit—as they apparently are at present for about 9 out of every 10 Cairo businesses and households—this individual's capital resource will likely not be allocated to its highest-valued use.

This example illustrates a basic problem of dead capital. People who unofficially own capital goods are commonly constrained in their ability to use them efficiently. As a result, large quantities of capital goods throughout the developing world are inefficiently employed.

You Are There

To contemplate how ownership of even a small quantity of capital goods affects the economic prospects of a resident of a developing country, read **Putting Meager Capital to Work in India,** on page 408.

Dead Capital and Economic Growth

Recall from Chapter 2 that when we take into account production choices over time, any society faces a trade-off between consumption goods and capital goods. Whenever we make a choice to produce more consumption goods today, we incur an opportunity cost of fewer goods in the future. This means that when we make a choice to aim for more future economic growth to permit consumption of more goods in the future, we must allocate more resources to producing capital goods today. This entails incurring an opportunity cost today because society must allocate fewer resources to the current production of consumption goods.

This growth trade-off applies to any society, whether in a highly industrialized nation or a developing country. In a developing country, however, the inefficiencies of dead capital greatly reduce the rate of return on investment by individuals and firms. The resulting disincentives to invest in new capital goods can greatly hinder economic growth.

GOVERNMENT INEFFICIENCIES, INVESTMENT, AND GROWTH A major factor contributing to the problem of dead capital in many developing nations is significant and often highly inefficient government regulation. Governments in many of the world's poorest nations place tremendous obstacles in the way of entrepreneurs interested in owning capital goods and directing them to profitable opportunities.

In addition to creating dead capital, overzealously administered government regulations that impede private resource allocation tend to reduce investment in new capital goods. If newly produced capital goods cannot be easily devoted to their most efficient uses, there is less incentive to invest. In a nation with a stifling government bureaucracy regulating the uses of capital goods, newly created capital will all too likely become dead capital.

Thus, government inefficiency can be a major barrier to economic growth. Figure 18-1 on the next page depicts the relationship between average growth of per capita incomes and index measures of governmental inefficiency for various nations. As you can see, the economies of countries with less efficient governments tend to grow at relatively slower rates. The reason is that bureaucratic inefficiencies in these nations complicate efforts to direct capital goods to their most efficient uses.

ACCESS TO CREDIT MATTERS The 2006 Nobel Peace Prize went to Muhammad Yunus of Bangladesh. Yunus contends that access to private credit is vital for promoting

FIGURE 18-1 Bureaucratic Inefficiency and Economic Growth

Inefficiencies in government bureaucracies reduce the incentive to invest and thereby detract from economic growth.

Sources: International Monetary Fund; World Bank.

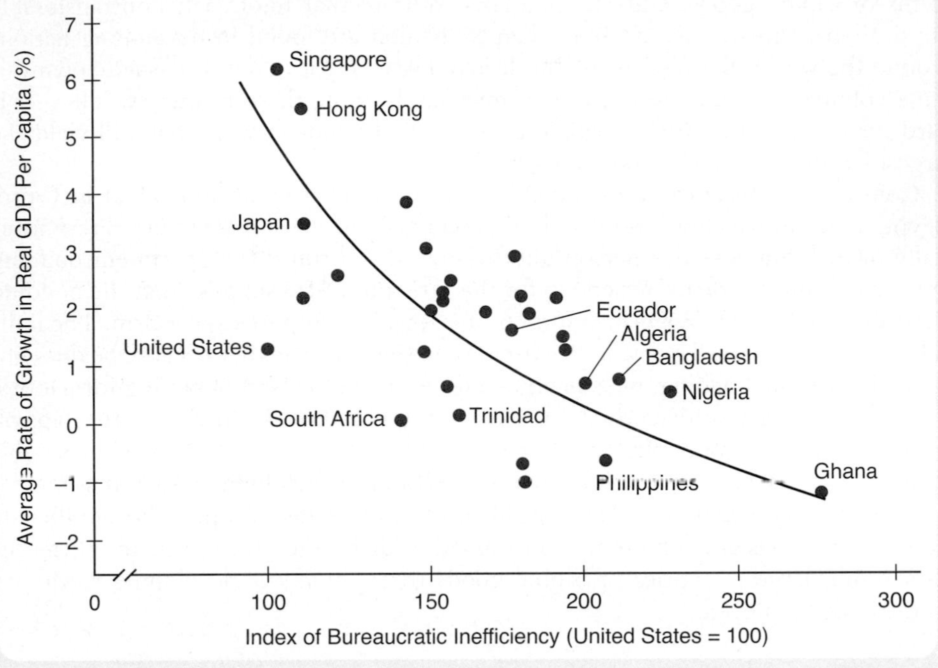

economic growth in poverty-stricken countries, where, in his view, present credit arrangements are inadequate.

Private lenders, Yunus suggests, are more likely to grant loans if borrowers can provide marketable collateral in the form of capital assets that lenders can obtain if a borrower defaults. Loan applicants cannot offer as collateral capital assets that they do not officially own, however. Even if an applicant has legal title to capital assets, a lender is unlikely to accept them as collateral if government rules and inefficiencies inhibit the marketability of those assets in the event that the borrower defaults.

Figure 18-2 below displays both the top five and the bottom five nations of the world ranked by their ratios of private credit to GDP. Common features of the bottom five nations are significant stocks of informally used but officially unowned capital goods and very inefficient government bureaucracies. Access to credit in these nations is very limited, so ratios of private credit to GDP are low.

FIGURE 18-2 The Ratio of Private Credit to GDP in Selected Nations

This figure displays the top five and bottom five nations of the world ranked according to ratios of private credit to GDP.

Source: Federal Reserve Bank of St. Louis.

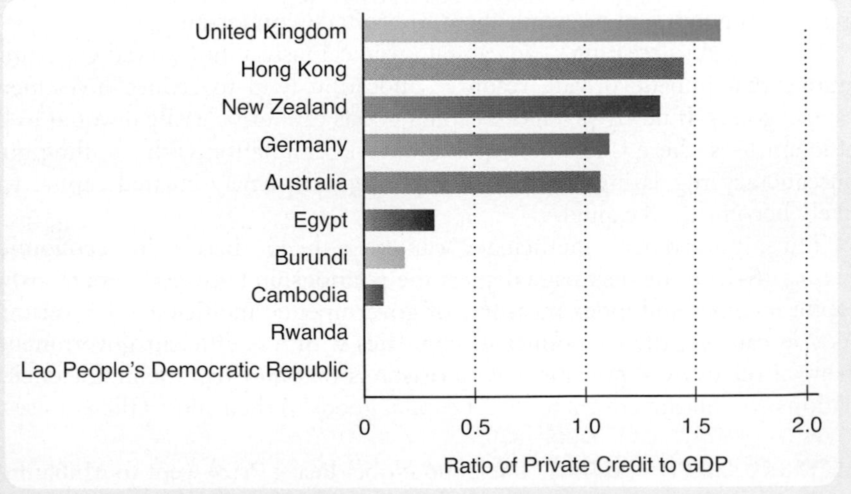

Yunus received the Nobel Peace Prize for his efforts to operate a *microlender*—a banking institution that specializes in making very small loans to entrepreneurs seeking to lift themselves up from the lowest rungs of poverty. In some of the poorest nations in which microlending activities are beginning to flourish, tens of millions of people are obtaining access to credit for the first time in their lives. As a consequence, ratios of private credit to GDP are climbing.

QUICK QUIZ See page 414 for the answers. **Review concepts from this section in MyEconLab.**

Dead capital is a capital resource without clear title of _________. It is difficult for a buyer to trade, insure, or maintain a right to use dead capital.

The inability to put dead capital to its most efficient use contributes to _________ economic growth, particularly in _________ nations, where dead capital can be a relatively large portion of total capital goods.

Inefficient government _________ contribute to the dead capital problem, which reduces the incentive to invest in additional capital goods.

Private International Financial Flows as a Source of Global Growth

Given the large volume of inefficiently employed capital goods in developing nations, what can be done to promote greater global growth? One approach is to rely on private markets to find ways to direct capital goods toward their best uses in most nations. Another is to entrust the world's governments with the task of developing and implementing policies that enhance economic growth in developing nations. Let's begin by considering the market-based approach to promoting global growth.

Private Investment in Developing Nations

Between 1995 and 2007, at least $150 billion per year in private funds flowed to developing nations in the form of loans or purchases of bonds or stock. Of course, in some years, as during the Panic of 2008, international investors stop lending to developing countries or sell off government-issued bonds and private-company stocks of those countries. When these international outflows of funds are taken into account, the *net* flows of funds to developing countries have averaged just over $80 billion per year since 1995. This is nearly 5 percent of the annual net investment within the United States.

Nearly all the funds that flow into developing countries do so to finance investment projects in those nations. Economists group these international flows of investment funds into three categories. One is loans from banks and other sources. The second is **portfolio investment,** or purchases of less than 10 percent of the shares of ownership in a company. The third is **foreign direct investment,** or the acquisition stocks to obtain more than a 10 percent share of a firm's ownership.

Portfolio investment
The purchase of less than 10 percent of the shares of ownership in a company in another nation.

Foreign direct investment
The acquisition of more than 10 percent of the shares of ownership in a company in another nation.

Figure 18-3 on the following page displays percentages of each type of international investment financing provided to developing nations since 1981. As you can see, three decades ago, bank loans accounted for the bulk of international funding of investment in the world's less developed nations. Today, direct ownership shares in the form of portfolio investment and foreign direct investment together account for most international investment financing.

Obstacles to International Investment

There is an important difficulty with depending on international flows of funds to finance capital investment in developing nations. The markets for loans, bonds, and stocks in developing countries are particularly susceptible to problems relating to *asymmetric information* (see Chapter 15). International investors are well aware of the informational problems to which they are exposed in developing nations, so many stand ready to withdraw their financial support at a moment's notice.

For a link to an Asian Development Bank analysis of the effects of foreign direct investment on developing nations, go to **www.econtoday.com/ch18**.

FIGURE 18-3 Sources of International Investment Funds

Since 1981, international funding of capital investment in developing nations has shifted from lending by banks to ownership shares via portfolio investment and foreign direct investment.

Source: International Monetary Fund (including estimates).

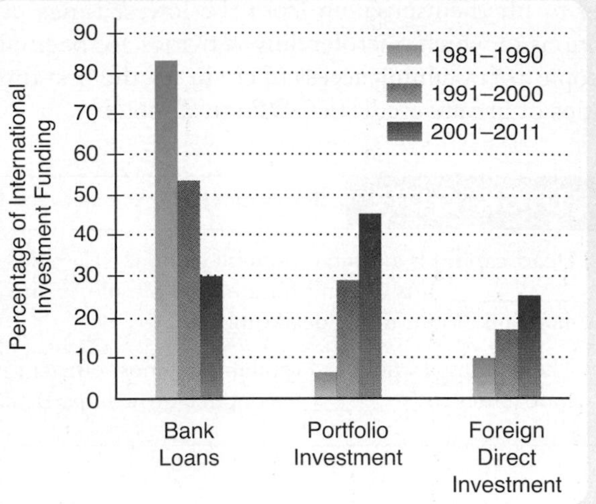

ASYMMETRIC INFORMATION AS A BARRIER TO FINANCING GLOBAL GROWTH Recall from Chapter 15 that asymmetric information in financial markets exists when institutions that make loans or investors who hold bonds or stocks have less information than those who seek to use the funds. *Adverse selection* problems arise when those who wish to obtain funds for the least worthy projects are among those who attempt to borrow or issue bonds or stocks. If banks and investors have trouble identifying these higher-risk individuals and firms, they may be less willing to channel funds to even creditworthy borrowers. Another asymmetric information problem is *moral hazard.* This is the potential for recipients of funds to engage in riskier behavior after receiving financing.

In light of the adverse selection problem, anyone thinking about funding a business endeavor in any locale must study the firm carefully before extending financial support. The potential for moral hazard requires a lender to a firm or someone who has purchased the firm's bonds or stock to continue to monitor the company's performance after providing financial support.

By definition, financial intermediation is still relatively undeveloped in less advanced regions of the world. Consequently, individuals interested in financing potentially profitable investments in developing nations typically cannot rely on financial intermediaries based in these countries. Asymmetric information problems may be so great in some developing nations that very few private lenders or investors will wish to direct their funds to worthy capital investment projects. In some countries, therefore, concerns about adverse selection and moral hazard can be a significant obstacle to economic growth.

Why Not . . . direct more foreign aid to poor nations to help them grow faster?

The U.S. government confronts the same asymmetric information problems that private individuals and firms face when they consider lending to firms in developing nations. It is not apparent that the U.S. government is any more likely than private parties, other things being equal, to direct funds to worthy projects in developing countries. In fact, other things are not equal. Private individuals and firms have a strong incentive to do their best to evaluate risks arising from asymmetric information problems: They will earn lower private returns or even incur private losses if they fail to do so. In contrast, when U.S. government officials disburse foreign aid, they are using "other people's money"—namely, the funds of taxpayers—and hence do not have strong personal incentives to avoid funding projects with uncertain and riskier returns. Thus, government officials distributing foreign aid have fewer incentives than do private parties to correctly identify worthy projects.

INCOMPLETE INFORMATION AND INTERNATIONAL FINANCIAL CRISES Those who are willing to contemplate making loans or buying bonds or stocks issued in developing nations must either do their own careful homework or follow the example of other lenders or investors whom they regard as better informed. Many relatively unsophisticated lenders and investors, such as relatively small banks and individual savers, rely on larger lenders and investors to evaluate risks in developing nations.

This has led some economists to suggest that a follow-the-leader mentality can influence international flows of funds. In extreme cases, they contend, the result can be an **international financial crisis.** This is a situation in which lenders rapidly withdraw loans made to residents of developing nations and investors sell off bonds and stocks issued by firms and governments in those countries. Of course, an international financial crisis began in 2008. Unlike the crisis during the early 2000s that radiated outward from Southeast Asia, Central Asia, and Latin America, the more recent crisis began in the United States. It then spread to Europe before adversely affecting most developing nations. Although economies of several Asian nations have weathered the crisis relatively well so far, the world economy shrank for the first time in decades. Undoubtedly, this has contributed to a decline in flows of private funds to developing nations.

International financial crisis
The rapid withdrawal of foreign investments and loans from a nation.

QUICK QUIZ See page 414 for the answers. Review concepts from this section in MyEconLab.

The three main categories of international flows of investment funds are loans by __________, __________ investment that involves purchasing less than 10 percent of the shares of ownership in a company, and __________ __________ investment that involves purchasing more than 10 percent of a company's ownership shares.

On net, an average of about $__________ billion in international investment funds flows to developing nations each year. In years past, bank loans were the source of most foreign funding of investment in developing countries, but recently __________ investment and __________ __________ investment have increased.

Obstacles to private financing of capital accumulation and growth in developing nations include __________ __________ and __________ __________ problems caused by asymmetric information, which can restrain and sometimes destabilize private flows of funds.

International Institutions and Policies for Global Growth

There has long been a recognition that adverse selection and moral hazard problems can both reduce international flows of private funds to developing nations and make these flows relatively variable. Since 1945, the world's governments have taken an active role in supplementing private markets. Two international institutions, the World Bank and the International Monetary Fund, have been at the center of government-directed efforts to attain higher rates of global economic growth.

The World Bank

The **World Bank** specializes in extending relatively long-term loans for capital investment projects that otherwise might not receive private financial support. When the World Bank was first formed in 1945, it provided assistance in the post–World War II rebuilding period. In the 1960s, the World Bank broadened its mission by widening its scope to encompass global antipoverty efforts.

World Bank
A multinational agency that specializes in making loans to about 100 developing nations in an effort to promote their long-term development and growth.

Today, the World Bank makes loans solely to about 100 developing nations containing roughly half the world's population. Governments and firms in these countries typically seek loans from the World Bank to finance specific projects, such as better irrigation systems, road improvements, and better hospitals.

The World Bank is actually composed of five separate institutions: the International Development Association, the International Bank for Reconstruction and Development, the International Finance Corporation, the Multinational Investment

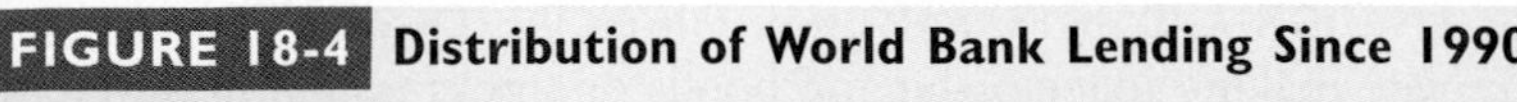

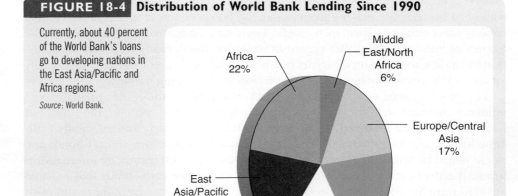

FIGURE 18-4 Distribution of World Bank Lending Since 1990

Currently, about 40 percent of the World Bank's loans go to developing nations in the East Asia/Pacific and Africa regions.

Source: World Bank.

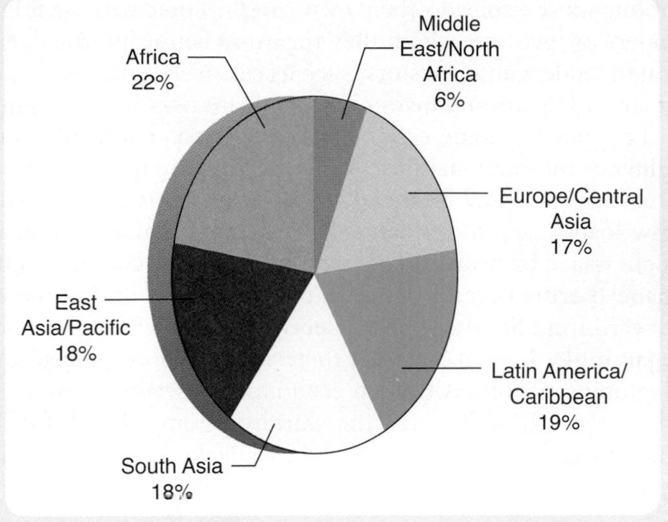

Guarantee Agency, and the International Center for Settlement of Investment Disputes. These World Bank organizations each have between 144 and 186 member nations, and on their behalf, the approximately 10,000 people employed by World Bank institutions coordinate the funding of investment activities undertaken by various governments and private firms in developing nations. Figure 18-4 above displays the current regional distribution of about $20 billion in World Bank lending. Governments of the world's wealthiest countries provide most of the funds that the World Bank lends each year, although the World Bank also raises some of its funds in private financial markets.

Might low-income nations be better off if the World Bank made fewer loans to their governments and instead devoted more of its resources to funding construction of private cellphone networks?

INTERNATIONAL EXAMPLE

How Cellphones Are Fueling Economic Development

In many developing nations, firms have trouble communicating effectively with customers and employees. Roads are poor, and government-operated postal and telecommunications services are inefficient. All that is required for communication by cellphone, however, is the construction of towers to transmit signals among handsets. World Bank economists have found that once cellular communications networks have been established, business communications flourish, and so do firms and markets, even in the lowest-income nations. Indeed, a recent World Bank study found that adding an extra 10 cellphones per 100 people in a typical developing country raises the nation's average annual rate of economic growth by 0.8 percentage point.

FOR CRITICAL ANALYSIS

Why do you suppose that the fact that 75 percent of the world's cellphones are in use in lower-income nations is raising development economists' optimism about the potential for higher economic growth in these countries?

The International Monetary Fund

International Monetary Fund (IMF) A multinational organization that aims to promote world economic growth through more financial stability.

The **International Monetary Fund (IMF)** is an international organization that aims to promote global economic growth by fostering financial stability. Currently, the IMF has more than 180 member nations.

When a country joins the IMF, it deposits funds to an account called its **quota subscription.** These funds are measured in terms of an international unit of accounting called *special drawing rights (SDRs)*, which have a value based on a weighted average of a basket of four key currencies: the euro, the pound sterling, the yen, and the dollar. At present, one SDR is equivalent to just over $1.50.

Quota subscription
A nation's account with the International Monetary Fund, denominated in special drawing rights.

The IMF assists developing nations primarily by making loans to their governments. Originally, the IMF's primary function was to provide short-term loans, and it continues to offer these forms of assistance.

After the 1970s, however, nations' demands for short-term credit declined, and the IMF adapted by expanding its other lending programs. It now provides certain types of credit directly to poor and heavily indebted countries, either as long-term loans intended to support growth-promoting projects or as short- or long-term assistance aimed at helping countries experiencing problems in repaying existing debts. Under these funding programs, the IMF seeks to assist any qualifying member experiencing an unusual fluctuation in exports or imports, a loss of confidence in its own financial system, or spillover effects from financial problems originating elsewhere.

The World Bank and the IMF: Problems and Proposals

Among the World Bank's client nations, meager economic growth in recent decades shows up in numerous ways. The average resident in a nation receiving World Bank assistance lives on less than $2 per day. Hundreds of millions of people in nations receiving its financial support will never attend school, and about 40,000 people in these countries die of preventable diseases every day. Thus, there is an enormous range of areas where World Bank funds might be put to use.

The International Monetary Fund also continues to deal with an ongoing string of major international financial crisis situations. Countries most notably involved in such crises have included Mexico in 1995; Thailand, Indonesia, Malaysia, and South Korea in 1997; Russia in 1998; Brazil in 1999 and 2000; Turkey in 2001; Argentina in 2001 and 2002; and Greece, Spain, and other European nations since 2008.

ASYMMETRIC INFORMATION AND THE WORLD BANK AND IMF Like any other lenders, the World Bank and IMF encounter adverse selection and moral hazard problems. In an effort to address these problems, both institutions impose conditions that borrowers must meet to receive funds.

Officials of these organizations do not publicly announce all terms of lending agreements, however, so it is largely up to the organizations to monitor whether borrower nations are wisely using funds donated by other countries. In addition, the World Bank and IMF tend to place very imprecise initial conditions on the loans they extend. They typically toughen conditions only after a borrowing nation has violated the original arrangement. By giving nations that are most likely to try to take advantage of vague conditions a greater incentive to seek funding, this policy worsens the adverse selection problem the World Bank and IMF face.

RETHINKING LONG-TERM DEVELOPMENT LENDING Since the early 1990s, one of the main themes of development economics has been the reform of market processes in developing nations. Markets work better at promoting growth when a developing nation has more effective institutions, such as basic property rights, well-run legal systems, and uncorrupt government agencies.

Hence, there is considerable agreement that a top priority of the World Bank and the IMF should be to identify ways to put basic market foundations into place by guaranteeing property and contract rights. Doing so would require constructing legal systems that can credibly enforce laws protecting these rights. Another key requirement is simplifying the processes for putting capital goods to work most efficiently in developing countries.

To learn about the International Monetary Fund's view on its role in international financial crises, go to www.econtoday.com/ch18.

ALTERNATIVE INSTITUTIONAL STRUCTURES FOR LIMITING FINANCIAL CRISES In recent years, economists have advanced a wide variety of proposals on the appropriate role for the International Monetary Fund in anticipating and reacting to international financial crises. Many of these proposals share common features, such as more frequent and in-depth releases of information both by the IMF and by countries that borrow from this institution. Nearly all economists also recommend improved financial and accounting standards for those receiving funds from the World Bank and the IMF, as well as other changes that might help reduce moral hazard problems in such lending.

Nevertheless, proposals for change diverge sharply. The IMF and its supporters have suggested maintaining its current structure but working harder to develop so-called early warning systems of financial crises so that aid can be provided to head off crises before they develop. Some economists have proposed establishing an international system of rules restricting capital outflows that might threaten international financial stability.

Other economists call for more dramatic changes. For instance, one proposal suggests creating a board composed of finance ministers of member nations to be directly in charge of day to day management of the IMF. Another recommends providing government incentives, in the form of tax breaks and subsidies, for increased private-sector lending that would supplement or even replace loans now made by the IMF.

QUICK QUIZ See page 414 for the answers. Review concepts from this section in MyEconLab.

The **World Bank** is an umbrella institution for __________ international organizations, each of which has more than 140 member nations, which coordinate __________-term loans to governments and private firms in developing nations.

The **International Monetary Fund** is an organization with more than 180 member nations. It coordinates mainly __________-term and some longer-term financial assistance to developing nations in an effort to __________ international flows of funds.

Like other lenders, the World Bank and the IMF confront __________ __________ and __________ __________ problems. Recently, there have been suggestions for restructuring the operations of both institutions, but so far there is little agreement about how to do so.

You Are There

Putting Meager Capital to Work in India

Surajben Babubhai Patni is a 58-year-old woman who makes a living selling corn, nuts, and tomatoes in a wooden stall covered by a makeshift tarp on a street in the village of Ahmedabad, India. In the next stall, a man sharpens nails with a blade attached to a spinning bicycle wheel. Farther down the row of aged wooden stalls that constitutes the village marketplace, other vendors peddle various items such as beans and brass pots.

Patni earns as much as $5 per day, which is enough to pay for food for her household. Its nine members include her son, who just joined the approximately 60 million people who have lost jobs worldwide in the aftermath of the U.S. and European financial meltdown. She and the neighboring nail sharpener have noticed that a number of village residents who have lost their jobs are now selling their own products in newly opened street businesses. Consequently, market clearing prices in the street market are declining faster than Patni's quantities sold are rising, and her revenues and profits are falling. In addition, as the street is becoming more crowded with wooden stalls, police officers are soliciting higher bribes in exchange for not enforcing the laws limiting street selling. Thus, even though Patni is grateful that her informal business is helping her family weather tough economic times, she worries about the future of her business.

Critical Analysis Questions

1. What form of capital are the wooden stalls used by vendors in this Indian street market?
2. How might access to microcredit enable Patni to expand her revenues and profits?

ISSUES & APPLICATIONS

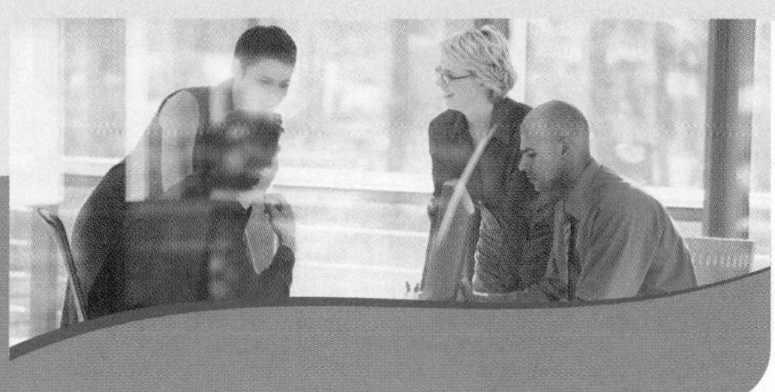

Supporting Private Entrepreneurs with Public Funds

CONCEPTS APPLIED

- Economic Freedom
- Dead Capital
- Asymmetric Information

The same two conclusions emerge in study after study: (1) providing economic freedom that enables entrepreneurs to start and maintain businesses is a precondition for nations to experience sustained economic growth; and (2) the dead capital problem hinders growth, so governments seeking to boost economic growth should make it easier for entrepreneurs to utilize capital goods. Governments in a number of nations around the globe are responding to these conclusions by trying to promote more entrepreneurship among their residents. In many cases, government officials try to jump-start entrepreneurship in the only way they know how—by providing public support to the entrepreneurs that the *officials* conclude are most likely to succeed. Typically, however, these government officials fall victim to asymmetric information problems, so their efforts rarely succeed in promoting economic growth.

Problem #1: Identifying Entrepreneurs Most Likely to Succeed

The first difficulty that government officials confront when they try to identify deserving entrepreneurs is determining which entrepreneurs' business plans are likely to succeed and promote economic growth. In this respect, government bureaucrats and private investors who consider funding entrepreneurs face the same problem: the adverse selection problem, or the likelihood that at least some of the entrepreneurs seeking public support know that their potential for success is low.

Government bureaucrats are notoriously bad at identifying entrepreneurs most likely to succeed. Malaysia's government financed a massive "Biovalley" complex intended to be a biological sciences version of the U.S. Silicon Valley region. Today, many Malaysian residents refer to the Biovalley as the "Valley of the BioGhosts." The Dubai government recently funded an entire "entrepreneurial hub"—a collection of business startups based in a specific urban area—that to date has experienced nothing but steady losses. In Australia, a public program to fund high-tech entrepreneurs called BITS—Building on Information Technology Strengths—so far has yielded few strong companies.

Problem #2: Publicly Funded Entrepreneurs Often Go Astray

Also like private investors, governments that provide entrepreneurship financing aimed at promoting more economic growth can fall victim to moral hazard problems. In other words, they discover that some entrepreneurs with good business plans ultimately decide to redirect government funds to more risky activities. In Norway, for instance, many government funds aimed at financing oil production entrepreneurs ended up being wasted on projects that mainly benefited friends and family members of government officials.

Governments face even more substantial exposure to moral hazard difficulties than private investors, however. Once entrepreneurs know that they have access to a risk-free stream of taxpayer funds, projects that previously appeared unworthy can become more tempting to contemplate. After all, when government funds are already in hand, entrepreneurs know that they will reap any gains, while taxpayers' funds will cover any losses.

For Critical Analysis

1. How might differences in incentives faced by private investors and government bureaucrats lead to diverging decisions regarding which types of entrepreneurial projects merit support?
2. Is it possible that governments could overcome adverse selection difficulties and select worthy entrepreneurs to support yet still experience moral hazard problems?

Web Resources

1. To learn more about the Malaysian Biovalley, go to www.econtoday.com/ch18.
2. For more information about the Australian government's BITS-based growth dreams, go to www.econtoday.com/ch18.

Research Project

Develop a short list of methods that governments might employ in an effort to reduce their exposure to asymmetric information problems when attempting to identify entrepreneurial projects to support with public funds.

For more questions on this chapter's Issues & Applications, go to **MyEconLab**. In the Study Plan for this chapter, select Section N: News.

Here is what you should know after reading this chapter. **MyEconLab** will help you identify what you know, and where to go when you need to practice.

WHAT YOU SHOULD KNOW		WHERE TO GO TO PRACTICE
Effects of Population Growth on Economic Growth Increased population growth has contradictory effects on economic growth. On the one hand, for a given growth rate of real GDP, increased population growth tends to reduce growth of per capita real GDP. On the other hand, if increased population growth is accompanied by higher labor productivity, the growth rate of real GDP can increase.	economic freedom, 399	• **MyEconLab** Study Plan 18.1 • Audio introduction to Chapter 18
Why Dead Capital Deters Investment and Slows Economic Growth Relatively few people in less developed countries establish legal ownership of capital goods. These unofficially owned resources are known as dead capital. Inability to trade, insure, and enforce rights to dead capital makes it difficult for unofficial owners to use these resources most efficiently, and this tends to limit economic growth.	dead capital, 400	• **MyEconLab** Study Plan 18.2
Government Inefficiencies and Dead Capital in Developing Nations In many developing nations, government regulations and red tape impose very high costs on those who officially register capital ownership. The dead capital problem that these government inefficiencies create reduces investment and growth. Thus, there is a negative relationship between measures of government inefficiency and economic growth.	**KEY FIGURE** Figure 18-1, 402	• **MyEconLab** Study Plan 18.2 • Animated Figure 18-1

MyEconLab continued

WHAT YOU SHOULD KNOW		WHERE TO GO TO PRACTICE
Sources of International Investment Funds and Obstacles to Investing in Developing Nations International flows of funds to developing nations promote global economic growth. There are three basic categories of these flows of funds: (1) bank loans; (2) portfolio investment, or purchases of less than 10 percent of the shares of ownership in a company; and (3) foreign direct investment, or purchases of more than 10 percent of the shares of ownership in a company. Asymmetric information problems, such as adverse selection and moral hazard problems, hinder international flows of funds and thereby slow economic growth in developing nations.	portfolio investment, 403 foreign direct investment, 403 international financial crisis, 405 **KEY FIGURE** Figure 18-3, 404	• **MyEconLab** Study Plan 18.3 • Animated Figure 18-3 • Economics Video: Understanding Entry Modes into the Chinese Market
The Functions of the World Bank and the International Monetary Fund Adverse selection and moral hazard problems faced by private investors can both limit and destabilize international flows of funds to developing countries. The World Bank finances capital investment in countries that have trouble attracting funds from private sources. The International Monetary Fund stabilizes international financial flows by extending loans to countries caught up in international financial crises.	World Bank, 405 International Monetary Fund (IMF), 406 quota subscription, 407	• **MyEconLab** Study Plan 18.4 • Economics Video: Understanding Entry Modes into the Chinese Market
Problems Faced by Policymakers at the World Bank and IMF Both the World Bank and the IMF face adverse selection and moral hazard problems that may be worsened by the imprecise initial conditions they impose on the loans they extend. Development economists generally agree that both institutions should emphasize reforms such as basic property rights that give domestic residents more incentive to invest.		• **MyEconLab** Study Plan 18.4

Log in to MyEconLab, take a chapter test, and get a personalized Study Plan that tells you which concepts you understand and which ones you need to review. From there, MyEconLab will give you further practice, tutorials, animations, videos, and guided solutions.
Log in to www.myeconlab.com

PROBLEMS

All problems are assignable in myeconlab. *Answers to odd-numbered problems appear at the back of the book.*

18-1. A country's real GDP is growing at an annual rate of 3.1 percent, and the current rate of growth of per capita real GDP is 0.3 percent. What is the population growth rate in this nation?

18-2. The annual rate of growth of real GDP in a developing nation is 0.3 percent. Initially, the country's population was stable from year to year. Recently, however, a significant increase in the nation's birthrate has raised the annual rate of population growth to 0.5 percent.

a. What was the rate of growth of per capita real GDP before the increase in population growth?

b. If the rate of growth of real GDP remains unchanged, what is the new rate of growth of per capita real GDP following the increase in the birthrate?

18-3. A developing country has determined that each additional $1 billion of investment in capital goods adds 0.01 percentage point to its long-run average annual rate of growth of per capita real GDP.

a. Domestic entrepreneurs recently began to seek official approval to open a range of businesses employing capital resources valued at $20 billion. If the entrepreneurs undertake these investments, by what fraction of a percentage point will the nation's long-run average annual rate of growth of per capita real GDP increase, other things being equal?

b. After weeks of effort trying to complete the first of 15 stages of bureaucratic red tape necessary to obtain authorization to start their businesses, a number of entrepreneurs decide to drop their investment plans completely, and the amount of official investment that actually takes place turns out to be $10 billion. Other things being equal, by what fraction of a percentage point will this decision reduce the nation's long-run average annual rate of growth of per capita real GDP from what it would have been if investment had been $20 billion?

18-4. Consider the estimates that the World Bank has assembled for the following nations:

Country	Legal Steps Required to Start a Business	Days Required to Start a Business	Cost of Starting a Business as a Percentage of Per Capita GDP
Angola	14	146	838%
Bosnia-Herzegovina	12	59	52%
Morocco	11	36	19%
Togo	14	63	281%
Uruguay	10	27	47%

Rank the nations in order starting with the one you would expect to have the highest rate of economic growth, other things being equal. Explain your reasoning.

18-5. Suppose that every $500 billion of dead capital reduces the average rate of growth in worldwide per capita real GDP by 0.1 percentage point. If there is $10 trillion in dead capital in the world, by how many percentage points does the existence of dead capital reduce average worldwide growth of per capita real GDP?

18-6. Assume that each $1 billion in investment in capital goods generates 0.3 percentage point of the average percentage rate of growth of per capita real GDP, given the nation's labor resources. Firms have been investing exactly $6 billion in capital goods each year, so the annual average rate of growth of per capita real GDP has been 1.8 percent. Now a government that fails to consistently adhere to the rule of law has come to power, and firms must pay $100 million in bribes to gain official approval for every $1 billion in investment in capital goods. In response, companies cut back their total investment spending to $4 billion per year. If other things are equal and companies maintain this rate of investment, what will be the nation's new average annual rate of growth of per capita real GDP?

18-7. During the past year, several large banks extended $200 million in loans to the government and several firms in a developing nation. International investors also purchased $150 million in bonds and $350 million in stocks issued by domestic firms. Of the stocks that foreign investors purchased, $100 million were shares that amounted to less than a 10 percent interest in domestic firms. This was the first year this nation had ever permitted inflows of funds from abroad.

a. Based on the investment category definitions discussed in this chapter, what was the amount of portfolio investment in this nation during the past year?

b. What was the amount of foreign direct investment in this nation during the past year?

18-8. Last year, $100 million in outstanding bank loans to a developing nation's government were not renewed, and the developing nation's government paid off $50 million in maturing government bonds that had been held by foreign residents. During that year, however, a new group of banks participated in a $125 million loan to help finance a major government construction project in the capital city. Domestic firms also issued $50 million in bonds and $75 million in stocks to foreign investors. All of the stocks issued gave the foreign investors more than 10 percent shares of the domestic firms.

a. What was gross foreign investment in this nation last year?

b. What was net foreign investment in this nation last year?

18-9. Identify which of the following situations currently faced by international investors are examples of adverse selection and which are examples of moral hazard.

a. Among the governments of several developing countries that are attempting to issue new bonds this year, it is certain that a few will fail to collect taxes to repay the bonds when they mature. It is difficult, however, for investors considering buying government bonds to predict which governments will experience this problem.

b. Foreign investors are contemplating purchasing stock in a company that, unknown to them, may have failed to properly establish legal ownership over a crucial capital resource.

c. Companies in a less developed nation have already issued bonds to finance the purchase of new capital goods. After receiving the funds from the bond issue, however, the company's managers pay themselves large bonuses instead.

d. When the government of a developing nation received a bank loan three years ago, it ultimately repaid the loan but had to reschedule its payments after officials misused the funds for unworthy projects. Now the government, which still has many of the same officials, is trying to raise funds by issuing bonds to foreign investors, who must decide whether or not to purchase them.

18-10. Identify which of the following situations currently faced by the World Bank or the International Monetary Fund are examples of adverse selection and which are examples of moral hazard.

a. The World Bank has extended loans to the government of a developing country to finance construction of a canal with a certain future flow of earnings. Now, however, the government has decided to redirect those funds to build a casino that may or may not generate sufficient profits to allow the government to repay the loan.

b. The IMF is considering extending loans to several nations that failed to fully repay loans they received from the IMF during the past decade but now claim to be better credit risks. Now the IMF is not sure in advance which of these nations are unlikely to fully repay new loans.

c. The IMF recently extended a loan to a government directed by democratically elected officials that would permit the nation to adjust to an abrupt reduction in private flows of funds from abroad. A coup has just occurred, however, in response to newly discovered corruption within the government's elected leadership. The new military dictator has announced tentative plans to disburse some of the funds in equal shares to all citizens.

18-11. For each of the following situations, explain which of the policy issues discussed in this chapter is associated with the stance the institution has taken.

a. The World Bank offers to make a loan to a company in an impoverished nation at a lower interest rate than the company had been about to agree to pay to borrow the same amount from a group of private banks.

b. The World Bank makes a loan to a company in a developing nation that has not yet received formal approval to operate there, even though the government approval process typically takes 15 months.

c. The IMF extends a loan to a developing nation's government, with no preconditions, to enable the government to make already overdue payments on a loan it had previously received from the World Bank.

18-12. For each of the following situations, explain which of the policy issues discussed in this chapter is associated with the stance the institution has taken.

a. The IMF extends a long-term loan to a nation's government to help it maintain publicly supported production of goods and services that the government otherwise would have turned over to private companies.

b. The World Bank makes a loan to companies in an impoverished nation in which government officials typically demand bribes equal to 50 percent of companies' profits before allowing them to engage in any new investment projects.

c. The IMF offers to make a loan to banks in a country in which the government's rulers commonly require banks to extend credit to finance high-risk investment projects headed by the rulers' friends and relatives.

18-13. Answer the following questions concerning proposals to reform long-term development lending programs currently offered by the IMF and World Bank.

a. Why might the World Bank face moral hazard problems if it were to offer to provide funds to governments that promise to allocate the funds to major institutional reforms aimed at enhancing economic growth?

b. How does the IMF face an adverse selection problem if it is considering making loans to governments in which the ruling parties have already shown predispositions to try to "buy" votes by creating expensive public programs in advance of elections? How might following an announced rule in which the IMF cuts off future loans to governments that engage in such activities reduce this problem and promote increased economic growth in nations that do receive IMF loans?

ECONOMICS ON THE NET

The International Monetary Fund The purpose of this exercise is to evaluate the IMF's role in promoting global economic growth.

Title: International Monetary Fund

Navigation: Go to the home page of the IMF on the Web at **www.econtoday.com/ch18**.

Application Read each entry, and then answer the question.

1. Click on the link on the Web page titled *Our Work*. Which of the IMF's purposes are most directly related to promoting a higher rate of global economic growth? Are any related more indirectly to this goal?
2. Click on *Surveillance*. Based on this discussion, what type of asymmetric information problem does IMF surveillance attempt to address?
3. Click on *Lending by the IMF*, and then click on *Main Lending Facilities*. Which IMF lending "facilities" appear to be aimed at maintaining stability of international flows of funds? Which appear to be longer-term loans similar to those extended by the World Bank?

For Group Study and Analysis The full reading entitled *Lending by the IMF* discusses terms of lending that the IMF imposes on different groups of nations. What are the likely rationales for charging some nations lower interest rates than others? Are there any potential problems with this policy? (Hint: Consider the adverse selection and moral hazard problems faced by the IMF.)

ANSWERS TO QUICK QUIZZES

p. 400: (i) reduce; (ii) labor force . . . increase; (iii) political . . . economic
p. 403: (i) ownership; (ii) lower . . . developing; (iii) bureaucracies
p. 405: (i) banks . . . portfolio . . . foreign direct; (ii) 80 . . . portfolio . . . foreign direct; (iii) adverse selection . . . moral hazard
p. 408: (i) five . . . long; (ii) short . . . stabilize; (iii) adverse selection . . . moral hazard

19

Demand and Supply Elasticity

When the price of one type of television delivery service falls, people tend to switch in favor of buying that form of TV service and substitute away from alternative TV delivery services. Economists have estimated that if the price of satellite-delivered TV services decreases by a certain percentage, the demand for cable TV falls by about the same percentage. A given percentage decline in the price of cable TV, however, causes a percentage decrease in the demand for satellite TV that is typically less than half as large. What does this smaller percentage change in satellite TV consumption in response to a change in the price of cable TV services tell us about how consumers perceive consumption of cable TV versus satellite TV? The answer is provided by a concept called the *cross price elasticity of demand,* which is one of several elasticity concepts you will encounter in this chapter.

LEARNING OBJECTIVES

After reading this chapter, you should be able to:

- Express and calculate price elasticity of demand
- Understand the relationship between the price elasticity of demand and total revenues
- Discuss the factors that determine the price elasticity of demand
- Describe the cross price elasticity of demand and how it may be used to indicate whether two goods are substitutes or complements
- Explain the income elasticity of demand
- Classify supply elasticities and explain how the length of time for adjustment affects the price elasticity of supply

MyEconLab helps you master each objective and study more efficiently. See end of chapter for details.

Did You Know That?

Federal Reserve economists have estimated that when bank debit-card transaction fees increase by 10 percent, the number of debit-card transactions that people wish to utilize declines by nearly 67 percent? Thus, an increase as small as 1 percent in the price of debit-card usage generates a significant proportionate reduction in the quantity of transactions demanded by debit-card users.

Businesses must constantly take into account consumers' response to changing fees and prices. If Dell reduces its prices by 10 percent, will consumers respond by buying so many more computers that the company's revenues rise? At the other end of the spectrum, can Ferrari dealers "get away" with a 2 percent increase in prices? That is, will Ferrari purchasers respond so little to the relatively small increase in price that the total revenues received for Ferrari sales will not fall and may actually rise? The only way to answer these questions is to know how responsive consumers in the real world will be to changes in prices. Economists have a special name for quantity responsiveness—*elasticity*, which is the subject of this chapter.

Price Elasticity

To begin to understand what elasticity is all about, just keep in mind that it means "responsiveness." Here we are concerned with the price elasticity of demand. We wish to know the extent to which a change in the price of, say, petroleum products will cause the quantity demanded to change, other things held constant. We want to determine the percentage change in quantity demanded in response to a percentage change in price.

Price Elasticity of Demand

Price elasticity of demand (E_p) The responsiveness of the quantity demanded of a commodity to changes in its price; defined as the percentage change in quantity demanded divided by the percentage change in price.

We will formally define the **price elasticity of demand**, which we will label E_p, as follows:

$$E_p = \frac{\text{percentage change in quantity demanded}}{\text{percentage change in price}}$$

What will price elasticity of demand tell us? It will tell us the *relative* amount by which the quantity demanded will change in response to a change in the price of a particular good.

Consider an example in which a 10 percent rise in the price of oil leads to a reduction in quantity demanded of only 1 percent. Putting these numbers into the formula, we find that the price elasticity of demand for oil in this case equals the percentage change in quantity demanded divided by the percentage change in price, or

$$E_p = \frac{-1\%}{+10\%} = -0.1$$

An elasticity of −0.1 means that a 1 percent *increase* in the price would lead to a mere 0.1 percent *decrease* in the quantity demanded. If you were now told, in contrast, that the price elasticity of demand for oil was −1, you would know that a 10 percent increase in the price of oil would lead to a 10 percent decrease in the quantity demanded.

RELATIVE QUANTITIES ONLY Notice that in our elasticity formula, we talk about *percentage* changes in quantity demanded divided by *percentage* changes in price. We focus on relative amounts of price changes, because percentage changes are independent of the units chosen. This means that it doesn't matter if we measure price changes in terms of cents, dollars, or hundreds of dollars. It also doesn't matter whether we measure quantity changes in ounces, grams, or pounds.

Go to www.econtoday.com/ch19 for additional review of the price elasticity of demand.

ALWAYS NEGATIVE The law of demand states that quantity demanded is *inversely* related to the relative price. An *increase* in the price of a good leads to a *decrease* in the quantity demanded. If a *decrease* in the relative price of a good should occur, the quantity demanded would *increase* by some percentage. The point is that price elasticity of demand will always be negative. By convention, however, *we will ignore the minus sign in our discussion from this point on.*

Basically, the greater the *absolute* price elasticity of demand (disregarding the sign), the greater the demand responsiveness to relative price changes—a small change in price has a great impact on quantity demanded. Conversely, the smaller the absolute price elasticity of demand, the smaller the demand responsiveness to relative price changes—a large change in price has little effect on quantity demanded.

Calculating Elasticity

To calculate the price elasticity of demand, we must compute percentage changes in quantity demanded and in price. To calculate the percentage change in quantity demanded, we might divide the absolute change in the quantity demanded by the original quantity demanded:

$$\frac{\text{change in quantity demanded}}{\text{original quantity demanded}}$$

To find the percentage change in price, we might divide the change in price by the original price:

$$\frac{\text{change in price}}{\text{original price}}$$

There is an arithmetic problem, though, when we calculate percentage changes in this manner. The percentage change, say, from 2 to 3—50 percent—is not the same as the percentage change from 3 to 2—$33\frac{1}{3}$ percent. In other words, it makes a difference where you start. One way out of this dilemma is simply to use average values.

To compute the price elasticity of demand, we take the *average* of the two prices and the two quantities over the range we are considering and compare the change with these averages. Thus, the formula for computing the price elasticity of demand is as follows:

$$E_p = \frac{\text{change in quantity}}{\text{sum of quantities/2}} \div \frac{\text{change in price}}{\text{sum of prices /2}}$$

We can rewrite this more simply if we do two things: (1) We can let Q_1 and Q_2 equal the two different quantities demanded before and after the price change and let P_1 and P_2 equal the two different prices. (2) Because we will be dividing a percentage by a percentage, we simply use the ratio, or the decimal form, of the percentages. Therefore,

$$E_p = \frac{\Delta Q}{(Q_1 + Q_2)/2} \div \frac{\Delta P}{(P_1 + P_2)/2}$$

where the Greek letter Δ (delta) stands for "change in."

How can we use actual changes in the price of natural gas and associated changes in the quantity of natural gas demanded to calculate the price elasticity of demand for natural gas (all other things held constant) with this formula? (See the next page.)

EXAMPLE **The Price Elasticity of Demand for Natural Gas**

During a recent three-month period, the price of natural gas decreased from \$4.81 per 1,000 cubic feet to \$4.44 per 1,000 cubic feet. As a consequence, during this three-month period the total quantity of natural gas consumed in the United States increased from 62.21 billion cubic feet per day to 62.64 billion cubic feet per day.

Assuming other things were equal, we can calculate the price elasticity of demand for natural gas during this period:

$$E_p = \frac{\text{change in } Q}{\text{sum of quantities/2}} \div \frac{\text{change in } P}{\text{sum of prices/2}}$$

$$= \frac{62.64 \text{ billion} - 62.21 \text{ billion}}{(62.64 \text{ billion} + 62.21 \text{ billion})/2} \div \frac{\$4.81 - \$4.44}{(\$4.81 + \$4.44)/2}$$

$$= \frac{0.43 \text{ billion}}{124.85 \text{ billion}/2} \div \frac{\$0.37}{\$9.25/2} = 0.09$$

The price elasticity of 0.09 means that a 1 percent decrease in price generated a 0.09 percent increase in the quantity of natural gas demanded. Thus, during this three-month period, the quantity of natural gas demanded was not very responsive to a decrease in the price of natural gas.

FOR CRITICAL ANALYSIS

Would the estimated price elasticity of demand for natural gas have been different if we had not used the average-values formula? How?

Price Elasticity Ranges

We have names for the varying ranges of price elasticities, depending on whether a 1 percent change in price elicits more or less than a 1 percent change in the quantity demanded.

- We say that a good has an **elastic demand** whenever the price elasticity of demand is greater than 1. A change in price of 1 percent causes a greater than 1 percent change in the quantity demanded.
- In a situation of **unit elasticity of demand**, a change in price of 1 percent causes exactly a 1 percent change in the quantity demanded.
- In a situation of **inelastic demand**, a change in price of 1 percent causes a change of less than 1 percent in the quantity demanded.

Elastic demand
A demand relationship in which a given percentage change in price will result in a larger percentage change in quantity demanded.

Unit elasticity of demand
A demand relationship in which the quantity demanded changes exactly in proportion to the change in price.

Inelastic demand
A demand relationship in which a given percentage change in price will result in a less-than-proportionate percentage change in the quantity demanded.

When we say that a commodity's demand is elastic, we are indicating that consumers are relatively responsive to changes in price. When we say that a commodity's demand is inelastic, we are indicating that its consumers are relatively unresponsive to price changes. When economists say that demand is inelastic, it does not necessarily mean that quantity demanded is *totally* unresponsive to price changes. Remember, the law of demand implies that there will almost always be some responsiveness in quantity demanded to a price change. The question is how much. That's what elasticity attempts to determine.

Extreme Elasticities

There are two extremes in price elasticities of demand. One extreme represents total unresponsiveness of quantity demanded to price changes, which is referred to as **perfectly inelastic demand,** or zero elasticity. The other represents total responsiveness, which is referred to as infinitely or **perfectly elastic demand.**

Perfectly inelastic demand
A demand that exhibits zero responsiveness to price changes. No matter what the price is, the quantity demanded remains the same.

Perfectly elastic demand
A demand that has the characteristic that even the slightest increase in price will lead to zero quantity demanded.

We show perfect inelasticity in panel (a) of Figure 19-1 on the facing page. Notice that the quantity demanded per year is 8 million units, no matter what the price. Hence, for any price change, the quantity demanded will remain the same, and thus the change in the quantity demanded will be zero. Look back at our formula for computing elasticity. If the change in the quantity demanded is zero, the numerator is also zero, and a nonzero number divided into zero results in a value of zero too. This is true at any point along the demand curve. Hence, there is perfect inelasticity.

FIGURE 19-1 Extreme Price Elasticities

In panel (a), we show complete price unresponsiveness. The demand curve is vertical at the quantity of 8 million units per year. This means that the price elasticity of demand is zero. In panel (b), we show complete price responsiveness. At a price of 30 cents, in this example, consumers will demand an unlimited quantity of the particular good in question, over the relevant range of quantities. This is a case of infinite price elasticity of demand.

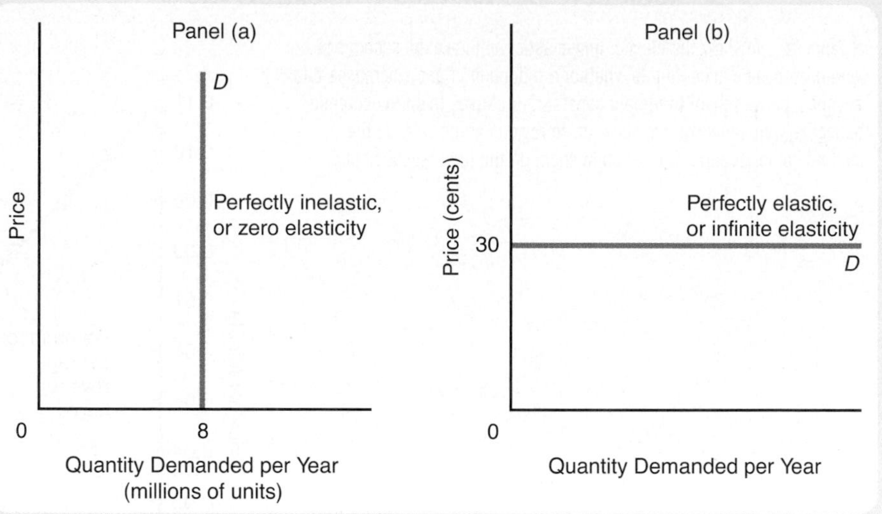

At the opposite extreme is the situation depicted in panel (b) of Figure 19-1. Here we show that at a price of 30 cents, an unlimited quantity will be demanded over the relevant range of quantities. At a price that is only slightly above 30 cents, no quantity will be demanded. There is perfect, or infinite, responsiveness at each point along this curve, and hence we call the demand schedule in panel (b) perfectly elastic.

QUICK QUIZ See page 434 for the answers. Review concepts from this section in MyEconLab.

The **price elasticity of demand** is equal to the percentage change in __________ __________ divided by the percentage change in __________.

Price elasticity of demand is calculated in terms of __________ changes in quantity demanded and in price. Thus, it is expressed as a unitless, dimensionless number that is __________ of units of measurement.

The price elasticity of demand is always __________, because an increase in price will lead to a __________ in quantity demanded and a decrease in price will lead to an __________ in quantity demanded. By convention, we ignore the negative sign in discussions of the price elasticity of demand.

One extreme elasticity occurs when a demand curve is vertical. It has __________ price elasticity of demand. It is completely __________. Another extreme elasticity occurs when a demand curve is horizontal. It has completely __________ demand. Its price elasticity of demand is __________.

Elasticity and Total Revenues

Suppose that you are an employee of a firm in the cellular phone service industry. How would you know when a rise in the market clearing price of cellular phone services will result in an increase in the total revenues, or the total receipts, of firms in the industry? It is commonly thought that the way for total receipts to rise is for the price per unit to increase. But is it possible that a rise in price per unit could lead to a decrease in total revenues? The answer to this question depends on the price elasticity of demand.

Let's look at Figure 19-2 on the next page. In panel (a), column 1 shows the price of cellular phone service in cents per minute, and column 2 represents billions of minutes per year. In column 3, we multiply column 1 times column 2 to derive total revenue because total revenue is always equal to the number of units (quantity) sold times the price per unit. In column 4, we calculate values of elasticity. Notice what happens to total revenues throughout the schedule. They rise steadily as the price rises from 1 cent to 5 cents per minute. When the price rises further to 6 cents per minute, total revenues remain constant at $3 billion. At prices per minute higher than

FIGURE 19-2 The Relationship Between Price Elasticity of Demand and Total Revenues for Cellular Phone Service

In panel (a), we show the elastic, unit-elastic, and inelastic sections of the demand schedule according to whether a reduction in price increases total revenues, causes them to remain constant, or causes them to decrease, respectively. In panel (b), we show these regions graphically on the demand curve. In panel (c), we show them on the total revenue curve.

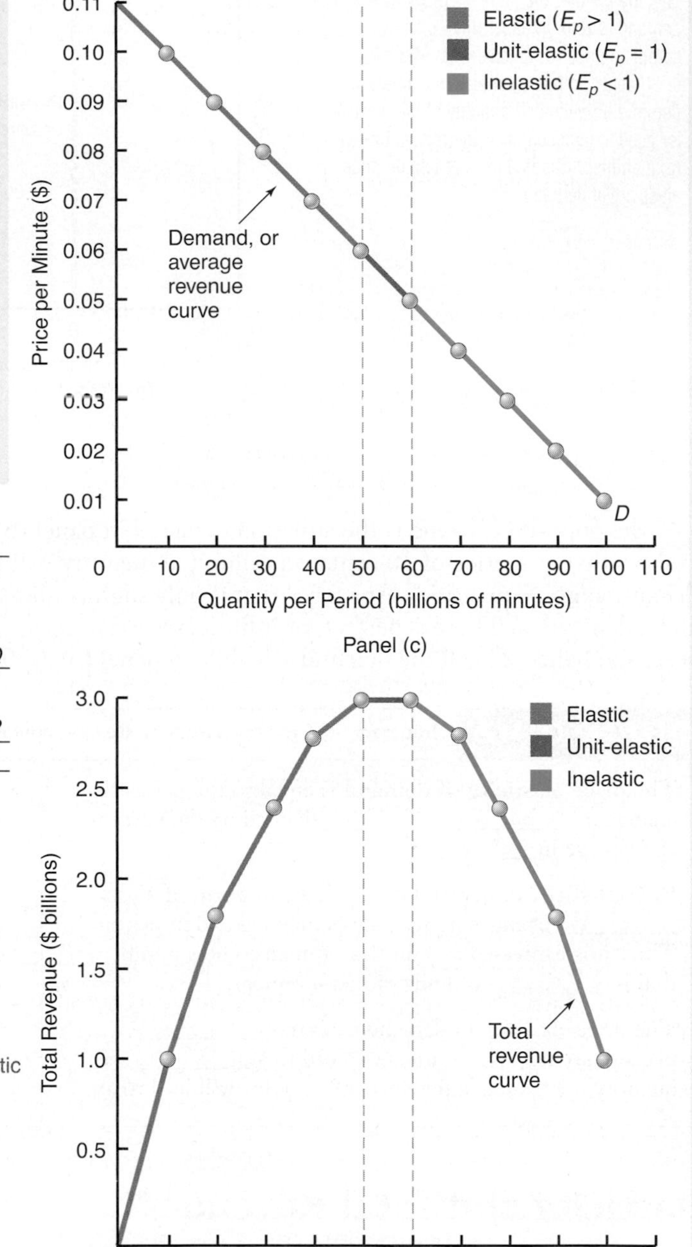

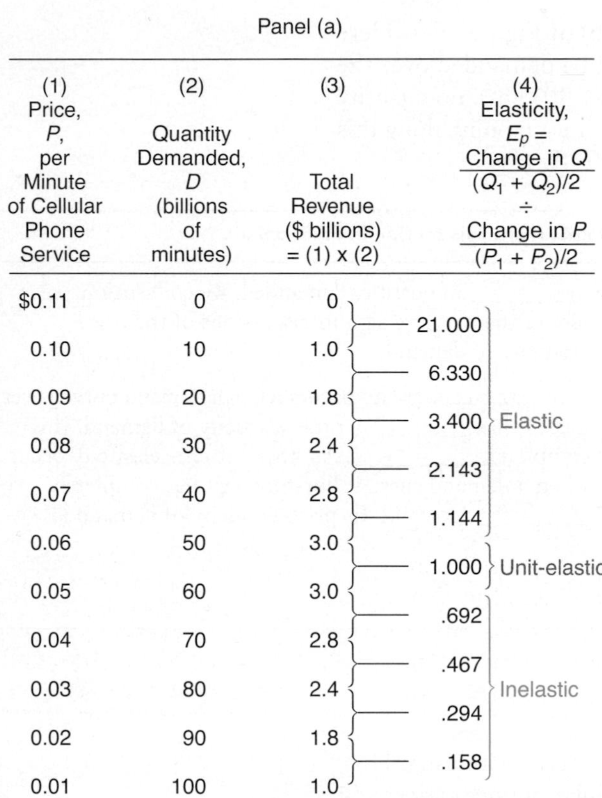

Panel (a)

(1) Price, P, per Minute of Cellular Phone Service	(2) Quantity Demanded, D (billions of minutes)	(3) Total Revenue ($ billions) = (1) x (2)	(4) Elasticity, $E_p = \dfrac{\text{Change in } Q}{(Q_1 + Q_2)/2} \div \dfrac{\text{Change in } P}{(P_1 + P_2)/2}$	
$0.11	0	0		
			21.000	Elastic
0.10	10	1.0		
			6.330	Elastic
0.09	20	1.8		
			3.400	Elastic
0.08	30	2.4		
			2.143	Elastic
0.07	40	2.8		
			1.144	Elastic
0.06	50	3.0		
			1.000	Unit-elastic
0.05	60	3.0		
			.692	Inelastic
0.04	70	2.8		
			.467	Inelastic
0.03	80	2.4		
			.294	Inelastic
0.02	90	1.8		
			.158	Inelastic
0.01	100	1.0		

6 cents, total revenues fall as price increases. Indeed, if prices are above 6 cents per minute, total revenues will increase only if the price *declines*, not if the price rises.

Labeling Elasticity

The relationship between price and quantity on the demand schedule is given in columns 1 and 2 of panel (a) in Figure 19-2 above. In panel (b), the demand curve, *D*, representing that schedule is drawn. In panel (c), the total revenue curve representing the data in column 3 is drawn. Notice first the level of these curves at small quantities. The demand curve is at a maximum height, but total revenue is zero, which makes sense according to this demand schedule—at a price of 11 cents per minute and above, no units will be purchased, and therefore total revenue will be zero. As price is lowered, we travel down the demand curve, and total revenues increase until price is 6 cents per minute, remain constant from 6 cents to 5 cents per minute, and then fall at lower unit prices. Corresponding to those three sections, demand is elastic, unit-elastic, and inelastic. Hence, we have three relationships among the three types of price elasticity and total revenues.

- *Elastic demand.* A negative relationship exists between changes in price and changes in total revenues. That is to say, when market demand for an item is elastic, total revenues will rise if the market price decreases. Total revenues will fall if the market price increases.
- *Unit-elastic demand.* Changes in price do not change total revenues. When market demand is unit-elastic and the market price increases, total revenues will not change, nor will total revenues change if the market price decreases.
- *Inelastic demand.* A positive relationship exists between changes in price and total revenues. When market demand is inelastic and the market price increases, total revenues will go up. When the market price decreases, total revenues will fall. We therefore conclude that if demand is inelastic, price and total revenues move in the *same* direction.

GRAPHIC PRESENTATION The elastic, unit-elastic, and inelastic areas of the demand curve are shown in Figure 19-2 on the facing page. For prices from 11 cents per minute of cellular phone time to 6 cents per minute, as price decreases, total revenues rise from zero to $3 billion. Demand is elastic. When price changes from 6 cents to 5 cents, however, total revenues remain constant at $3 billion. Demand is unit-elastic. Finally, when price falls from 5 cents to 1 cent, total revenues decrease from $3 billion to $1 billion. Demand is inelastic. In panels (b) and (c) of Figure 19-2, we have labeled the sections of the demand curve accordingly, and we have also shown how total revenues first rise, then remain constant, and finally fall.

THE ELASTICITY-REVENUE RELATIONSHIP The relationship between price elasticity of demand and total revenues brings together some important microeconomic concepts. Total revenues, as we have noted, are the product of price per unit times number of units purchased. The law of demand states that along a given demand curve, price and quantity changes will move in opposite directions: One increases as the other decreases. Consequently, what happens to the product of price times quantity depends on which of the opposing changes exerts a greater force on total revenues. But this is just what price elasticity of demand is designed to measure—responsiveness of quantity demanded to a change in price. The relationship between price elasticity of demand and total revenues is summarized in Table 19-1 below.

You Are There

To consider how the price elasticity of demand for Internet-ready gadgets influences the prices at which companies offer them for sale, read **Pricing the iPad: Learning Lessons from the iPhone,** on page 430.

TABLE 19-1

Relationship Between Price Elasticity of Demand and Total Revenues

Price Elasticity of Demand (E_p)		Effect of Price Change on Total Revenues (TR)	
		Price Decrease	Price Increase
Inelastic	($E_p < 1$)	TR ↓	TR ↑
Unit-elastic	($E_p = 1$)	No change in TR	No change in TR
Elastic	($E_p > 1$)	TR ↑	TR ↓

QUICK QUIZ See page 434 for the answers. Review concepts from this section in MyEconLab.

Price elasticity of demand is related to total __________.

When demand is *elastic*, the change in price elicits a change in total revenues in the __________ direction from the price change.

When demand is *unit-elastic*, a change in price elicits __________ change in total revenues (or in total consumer expenditures).

When demand is *inelastic*, a change in price elicits a change in total revenues (and in consumer expenditures) in the __________ direction as the price change.

Determinants of the Price Elasticity of Demand

We have learned how to calculate the price elasticity of demand. We know that theoretically it ranges numerically from zero (completely inelastic) to infinity (completely elastic). What we would like to do now is to come up with a list of the determinants of the price elasticity of demand. The price elasticity of demand for a particular commodity at any price depends, at a minimum, on the following factors:

- The existence, number, and quality of substitutes
- The percentage of a consumer's total budget devoted to purchases of that commodity
- The length of time allowed for adjustment to changes in the price of the commodity

Existence of Substitutes

The closer the substitutes for a particular commodity and the more substitutes there are, the greater will be its price elasticity of demand. At the limit, if there is a perfect substitute, the elasticity of demand for the commodity will be infinity. Thus, even the slightest increase in the commodity's price will cause a dramatic reduction in the quantity demanded: Quantity demanded will fall to zero.

Keep in mind that in this extreme example, we are really talking about two goods that the consumer believes are exactly alike and equally desirable, like dollar bills whose only difference is their serial numbers. When we talk about less extreme examples, we can speak only in terms of the number and the similarity of substitutes that are available.

Thus, we will find that the more narrowly we define a good, the closer and greater will be the number of substitutes available. For example, the demand for diet soft drinks may be relatively elastic because consumers can switch to other low-calorie liquid refreshments. The demand for diet drinks (as a single group), however, is relatively less elastic because there are fewer substitutes.

Share of Budget

We know that the greater the share of a person's total budget that is spent on a commodity, the greater that person's price elasticity of demand is for that commodity. A key reason that the demand for pepper is very inelastic is because individuals spend so little on it relative to their total budgets. In contrast, the demand for items such as transportation and housing is far more elastic because they occupy a large part of people's budgets—changes in their prices cannot easily be ignored without sacrificing a lot of other alternative goods that could be purchased.

Consider a numerical example. A household spends $40,000 a year. It purchases $4 of pepper per year and $4,000 of transportation services. Now consider the spending power of this family when the price of pepper and the price of transportation both double. If the household buys the same amount of pepper, it will now spend $8. It will thus have to reduce other expenditures by $4. This $4 represents only 0.01 percent of the entire household budget. By contrast, if transportation costs double, the family will have to spend $8,000, or $4,000 more on transportation, if it is to purchase the same quantity. That increased expenditure on transportation of $4,000 represents 10 percent of total expenditures that must be switched from other purchases. We would therefore predict that the household will react differently if the price of pepper doubles than it will if transportation prices double. It will reduce its transportation purchases by a proportionately greater amount.

Time for Adjustment

When the price of a commodity changes and that price change persists, more people will learn about it. Further, consumers will be better able to revise their consumption patterns the longer the time period they have to do so. And in fact, the longer the time they do take, the less costly it will be for them to engage in this revision of consumption patterns. Consider a price decrease. The longer the price decrease persists, the greater will be the number of new uses that consumers will discover for the particular commodity, and the greater will be the number of new users of that particular commodity.

It is possible to make a very strong statement about the relationship between the price elasticity of demand and the time allowed for adjustment:

> ***The longer any price change persists, the greater the elasticity of demand, other things held constant. Elasticity of demand is greater in the long run than in the short run.***

SHORT-RUN VERSUS LONG-RUN ADJUSTMENTS Let's consider an example. Suppose that the price of electricity goes up 50 percent. How do you adjust in the short run? You can turn the lights off more often, you can stop using your personal computer as much as you usually do, and similar measures. Otherwise it's very difficult to cut back on your consumption of electricity.

In the long run, though, you can devise other methods to reduce your consumption. Instead of using only electric heaters, the next time you have a house built you will install solar panels. You will purchase fluorescent bulbs because they use less electricity. The more time you have to think about it, the more ways you will find to cut your electricity consumption.

DEMAND ELASTICITY IN THE SHORT RUN AND IN THE LONG RUN We would expect, therefore, that the short-run demand curve for electricity would be relatively less elastic (in the price range around P_e), as demonstrated by D_1 in Figure 19-3 on the next page. The long-run demand curve, however, will exhibit more elasticity (in the neighborhood of P_e), as demonstrated by D_3. Indeed, we can think of an entire family of demand curves such as those depicted in the figure. The short-run demand curve is for the period when there is little time for adjustment. As more time is allowed, the demand curve goes first to D_2 and then all the way to D_3. Thus, in the neighborhood of P_e, elasticity differs for each of these curves. It is greater for the less steep curves (but slope alone does not measure elasticity for the entire curve).

Why Not . . . always raise prices when demand Is Inelastic?

Certain products, such as baby food, exhibit inelastic demand. So if you are a baby food manufacturer, why not raise your prices all the time? The problem is that even if the demand for all baby food is inelastic, you have competitors. If you increase the price of your product, but your competitors do not raise the prices of their products, your competitors will pick off your customers. Consequently, unless you have no competitors, you cannot raise your price just because market demand is inelastic.

FIGURE 19-3

Short-Run and Long-Run Price Elasticity of Demand

Consider a situation in which the market price is P_e and the quantity demanded is Q_e. Then there is a price increase to P_1. In the short run, as evidenced by the demand curve D_1, we move from equilibrium quantity demanded, Q_e, to Q_1. After more time is allowed for adjustment, the demand curve rotates at original price P_e to D_2. Quantity demanded falls again, now to Q_2. After even more time is allowed for adjustment, the demand curve rotates at price P_e to D_3. At the higher price P_1 in the long run, the quantity demanded falls all the way to Q_3.

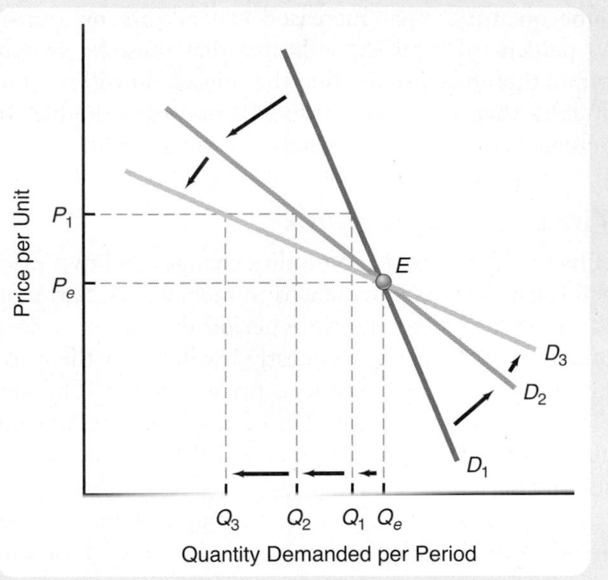

EXAMPLE What Do Real-World Price Elasticities of Demand Look Like?

In Table 19-2 below, we present demand elasticities for selected goods. None of them is zero, and the largest is 4.6. Remember that even though we are omitting the negative sign, there is an inverse relationship between price and quantity demanded. Also remember that these elasticities are measured over given price ranges. Recall from the example of the demand curve in Figure 19-2 on page 420 that choosing different price ranges could yield different elasticity estimates for these goods.

Economists have consistently found that estimated price elasticities of demand are greater in the long run than in the short run, as seen in Table 19-2. There you see that all available estimates indicate that the long-run price elasticity of demand for vacation air travel is 2.7, whereas the estimate for the short run is 1.1. Throughout the table, you see that all estimates of long-run price elasticities of demand exceed their short-run counterparts.

FOR CRITICAL ANALYSIS

Explain the intuitive reasoning behind the difference between long-run and short-run price elasticity of demand.

TABLE 19-2

Price Elasticities of Demand for Selected Goods

Here are estimated demand elasticities for selected goods. All of them are negative, although we omit the minus sign. We have given some estimates of the long-run price elasticities of demand. The long run is associated with the time necessary for consumers to adjust fully to any given price change. (Note: "N.A." indicates that no estimate is available.)

	Estimated Elasticity	
Category	**Short Run**	**Long Run**
Air travel (business)	0.4	1.2
Air travel (vacation)	1.1	2.7
Beef	0.6	N.A.
Cheese	0.3	N.A.
Electricity	0.1	1.7
Fresh tomatoes	4.6	N.A.
Gasoline	0.2	0.5
Hospital services	0.1	0.7
Intercity bus service	0.6	2.2
Physician services	0.1	0.6
Private education	1.1	1.9
Restaurant meals	2.3	N.A.
Tires	0.9	1.2

HOW TO DEFINE THE SHORT RUN AND THE LONG RUN We've mentioned the short run and the long run. Is the short run one week, two weeks, one month, two months? Is the long run three years, four years, five years? There is no single answer. The long run is the period of time necessary for consumers to make a full adjustment to a given price change, all other things held constant. In the case of the demand for electricity, the long run will be however long it takes consumers to switch over to cheaper sources of heating, to buy houses and appliances that are more energy-efficient, and so on. The long-run elasticity of demand for electricity therefore relates to a period of at least several years. The short run—by default—is any period less than the long run.

Cross Price Elasticity of Demand

In Chapter 3, we discussed the effect of a change in the price of one good on the demand for a related good. We defined substitutes and complements in terms of whether a reduction in the price of one caused a decrease or an increase, respectively, in the demand for the other. If the price of Blu-ray discs is held constant, the number of discs purchased (at any price) will certainly be influenced by the price of a close substitute such as Internet digital movie downloads. If the price of computer printers is held constant, the amount of computer printers demanded (at any price) will certainly be affected by changes in the price of computers. (These goods are complements.)

Measuring the Cross Price Elasticity of Demand

What we now need to do is come up with a numerical measure of the responsiveness of the amount of an item demanded to the prices of related goods. This is called the **cross price elasticity of demand (E_{xy})**, which is defined as the percentage change in the amount of a particular item demanded at the item's current price (a shift in the demand curve) divided by the percentage change in the price of the related good. In equation form, the cross price elasticity of demand between good X and good Y is

Cross price elasticity of demand (E_{xy}) The percentage change in the amount of an item demanded (holding its price constant) divided by the percentage change in the price of a related good.

$$E_{xy} = \frac{\text{percentage change in the amount of good X demanded}}{\text{percentage change in price of good Y}}$$

Alternatively, the cross price elasticity of demand between good Y and good X would use the percentage change in the amount of good Y demanded as the numerator and the percentage change in the price of good X as the denominator.

Substitutes and Complements

When two goods are substitutes, the cross price elasticity of demand will be positive. For example, when the price of portable hard drives goes up, the amount of flash memory drives demanded at their current price will rise—the demand curve for flash drives will shift horizontally rightward—in response as consumers shift away from the now relatively more expensive portable hard drives to flash memory drives. A producer of flash memory drives could benefit from a numerical estimate of the cross price elasticity of demand between portable hard drives and flash memory drives. For example, if the price of portable hard drives goes up by 10 percent and the producer of flash memory drives knows that the cross price elasticity of demand is 1, the flash drive producer can estimate that the amount of flash memory drives demanded will also go up by 10 percent at any given price of flash memory drives. Plans for increasing production of flash memory drives can then be made.

When two related goods are complements, the cross price elasticity of demand will be negative (and we will *not* disregard the minus sign). For example, when the price of personal computers declines, the amount of computer printers demanded will rise. This is because as prices of computers decrease, the number of printers purchased at any given price of printers will naturally increase, because computers and printers are often used together. Any manufacturer of computer printers must take this into account in making production plans.

If goods are completely unrelated, their cross price elasticity of demand will, by definition, be zero.

Income Elasticity of Demand

In Chapter 3, we discussed the determinants of demand. One of those determinants was income. We can apply our understanding of elasticity to the relationship between changes in income and changes in the amount of a good demanded at that good's current price.

Measuring the Income Elasticity of Demand

Income elasticity of demand (E_i) The percentage change in the amount of a good demanded, holding its price constant, divided by the percentage change in income; the responsiveness of the amount of a good demanded to a change in income, holding the good's relative price constant.

We measure the responsiveness of the amount of an item demanded at that item's current price to a change in income by the **income elasticity of demand (E_i):**

$$E_i = \frac{\text{percentage change in amount of a good demanded}}{\text{percentage change in income}}$$

holding relative price constant.

Income elasticity of demand refers to a *horizontal shift* in the demand curve in response to changes in income, whereas price elasticity of demand refers to a *movement along* the curve in response to price changes. Thus, income elasticity of demand is calculated at a given price, and price elasticity of demand is calculated at a given income.

Calculating the Income Elasticity of Demand

To get the same income elasticity of demand over the same range of values regardless of the direction of change (increase or decrease), we can use the same formula that we used in computing the price elasticity of demand. When doing so, we have

$$E_i = \frac{\text{change in quantity}}{\text{sum of quantities/2}} \div \frac{\text{change in income}}{\text{sum of incomes/2}}$$

A simple example will demonstrate how income elasticity of demand can be computed. Table 19-3 below gives the relevant data. The product in question is prerecorded Blu-ray discs. We assume that the price of Blu-ray discs remains constant relative to other prices. In period 1, six Blu-ray discs per month are purchased. Income per month is $4,000. In period 2, monthly income increases to $6,000, and the number of Blu-ray discs demanded per month increases to eight. We can apply the following calculation:

$$E_i = \frac{2/[(6 + 8)/2]}{\$2{,}000/[(\$4{,}000 + \$6{,}000)/2]} = \frac{2/7}{2/5} = 0.71$$

Hence, measured income elasticity of demand for Blu-ray discs for the individual represented in this example is 0.71.

TABLE 19-3

How Income Affects Quantity of Blu-Ray Discs Demanded

Period	Number of Blu-Ray Discs Demanded per Month	Income per Month
1	6	$4,000
2	8	6,000

How responsive is the amount of dental services demanded to a change in income in the United States?

EXAMPLE **The Income Elasticity of Demand for Dental Services**

During a few weeks in the depths of the Great Recession of the late 2000s, U.S. household income declined by 1 percent. In the same period, the amount of dental services that people purchased nationwide fell by 5.8 percent. Thus, the income elasticity of demand for U.S. dental services was equal to -5.8 percent $\div -1$ percent $= +5.8$. Thus, the amount of dental services demanded at the current price of such services varies directly with income.

FOR CRITICAL ANALYSIS

What do you think happened to the amount of dental services demanded when U.S. personal income rose in 2010?

You have just been introduced to three types of elasticities. All three elasticities are important in influencing the consumption of most goods. Reasonably accurate estimates of these elasticities can go a long way toward making accurate forecasts of demand for goods or services.

QUICK QUIZ See page 434 for the answers. Review concepts from this section in MyEconLab.

Some determinants of price elasticity of demand are (1) the existence, number, and quality of _________; (2) the _________ of the total budget spent on the good in question; and (3) the length of time allowed for _________ to a change in prices.

_________ price elasticity of demand measures the responsiveness of the amount of one good demanded to another's price changes. For substitutes, the cross price elasticity of demand is ____________. For complements, it is ____________.

Income elasticity of demand tells you by what percentage the amount of a good _________ will change for a particular percentage change in _________.

Price Elasticity of Supply

The **price elasticity of supply (E_s)** is defined similarly to the price elasticity of demand. Supply elasticities are generally positive. The reason is that at higher prices, larger quantities will generally be forthcoming from suppliers. The definition of the price elasticity of supply is as follows:

Price elasticity of supply (E_s)
The responsiveness of the quantity supplied of a commodity to a change in its price; the percentage change in quantity supplied divided by the percentage change in price.

$$E_s = \frac{\text{percentage change in quantity supplied}}{\text{percentage change in price}}$$

Classifying Supply Elasticities

Just as with demand, there are different ranges of supply elasticities. They are similar in definition to the ranges of demand elasticities.

If a 1 percent increase in price elicits a greater than 1 percent increase in the quantity supplied, we say that at the particular price in question on the supply schedule, *supply is elastic*. The most extreme elastic supply is called **perfectly elastic supply**—the slightest reduction in price will cause quantity supplied to fall to zero.

Perfectly elastic supply
A supply characterized by a reduction in quantity supplied to zero when there is the slightest decrease in price.

If, conversely, a 1 percent increase in price elicits a less than 1 percent increase in the quantity supplied, we refer to that as an *inelastic supply*. The most extreme inelastic supply is called **perfectly inelastic supply**—no matter what the price, the quantity supplied remains the same.

Perfectly inelastic supply
A supply for which quantity supplied remains constant, no matter what happens to price.

If the percentage change in the quantity supplied is just equal to the percentage change in the price, we call this *unit-elastic supply*.

FIGURE 19-4

The Extremes in Supply Curves

Here we have drawn two extremes of supply schedules: S is a perfectly elastic supply curve; S' is a perfectly inelastic one. In the former, an unlimited quantity will be supplied within the relevant range of quantities at price P_1. In the latter, no matter what the price, the quantity supplied will be Q_1. An example of S' might be the supply curve for fresh (unfrozen) fish on the morning the boats come in.

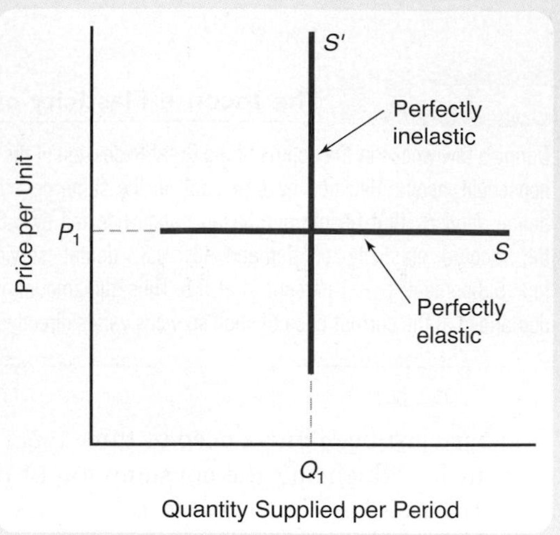

Figure 19-4 above shows two supply schedules, S and S'. You can tell at a glance, even without reading the labels, which one is perfectly elastic and which one is perfectly inelastic. As you might expect, most supply schedules exhibit elasticities that are somewhere between zero and infinity.

Price Elasticity of Supply and Length of Time for Adjustment

We pointed out earlier that the longer the time period allowed for adjustment, the greater the price elasticity of demand. It turns out that the same proposition applies to supply. The longer the time for adjustment, the more elastic the supply curve. Consider why this is true:

1. The longer the time allowed for adjustment, the more resources can flow into (or out of) an industry through expansion (or contraction) of existing firms. As an example, suppose that there is a long-lasting, significant increase in the demand for gasoline. The result is a sustained rise in the market price of gasoline. Initially, gasoline refiners will be hampered in expanding their production with the operating refining equipment available to them. Over time, however, some refining companies might be able to recondition old equipment that had fallen into disuse. They can also place orders for construction of new gasoline-refining equipment, and once the equipment arrives, they can also put it into place to expand their gasoline production. Given sufficient time, therefore, existing gasoline refiners can eventually respond to higher gasoline prices by adding new refining operations.

2. The longer the time allowed for adjustment, the entry (or exit) of firms increases (or decreases) production in an industry. Consider what happens if the price of gasoline remains higher than before as a result of a sustained rise in gasoline demand. Even as existing refiners add to their capability to produce gasoline by retooling old equipment, purchasing new equipment, and adding new refining facilities, additional businesses may seek to earn profits at the now-higher gasoline prices. Over time, the entry of new gasoline-refining companies adds to the productive capabilities of the entire refining industry, and the quantity of gasoline supplied increases.

We therefore talk about short-run and long-run price elasticities of supply. The short run is defined as the time period during which full adjustment has not yet taken place.

The long run is the time period during which firms have been able to adjust fully to the change in price.

How different are the short- and long-run price elasticities of salmon supply?

INTERNATIONAL EXAMPLE Price Elasticities of Salmon Supply in Norway

Researchers at Norway's University of Stavanger recently studied data on prices and quantities of salmon supplied by Norwegian salmon-farming firms between the 1980s and the 2000s. They estimated that in the short run, when salmon firms were unable to vary inputs such as types and quantities of feed and capital equipment used in producing farm-raised salmon, the price elasticity of salmon supply was only 0.05. In the long run, however, the estimated price elasticity of supply was 1.4, or 28 times larger than the estimated short-run elasticity. Thus, when firms have sufficient time to respond to a price increase by changing varieties and amounts of feed and capital equipment, a 1 percent rise in the price of salmon induces a percentage increase in quantity supplied that is 28 times greater.

FOR CRITICAL ANALYSIS

How would a technological improvement that enabled salmon firms to increase yields of salmon raised in fisheries affect the short-run price elasticity of supply?

A GRAPHIC PRESENTATION We can show a whole set of supply curves similar to the ones we generated for demand. As Figure 19-5 below shows, when nothing can be done in the immediate run, the supply curve is vertical, S_1. As more time is allowed for adjustment, the supply curve rotates to S_2 and then to S_3, becoming more elastic as it rotates.

QUICK QUIZ

See page 434 for the answers. Review concepts from this section in MyEconLab.

Price elasticity of supply is calculated by dividing the percentage change in the __________ __________ by the percentage change in __________.

Usually, price elasticities of supply are __________—higher prices yield __________ quantities supplied.

Long-run supply curves are __________ elastic than short-run supply curves because the __________ the time allowed, the more resources can flow into or out of an industry when price changes.

FIGURE 19-5

Short-Run and Long-Run Price Elasticity of Supply

Consider a situation in which the price is P_e and the quantity supplied is Q_e. In the immediate run, we hypothesize a vertical supply curve, S_1. With the price increase to P_1, therefore, there will be no change in the short run in quantity supplied, which will remain at Q_e. Given some time for adjustment, the supply curve will rotate to S_2. The new amount supplied will increase to Q_1. The long-run supply curve is shown by S_3. The amount supplied again increases to Q_2.

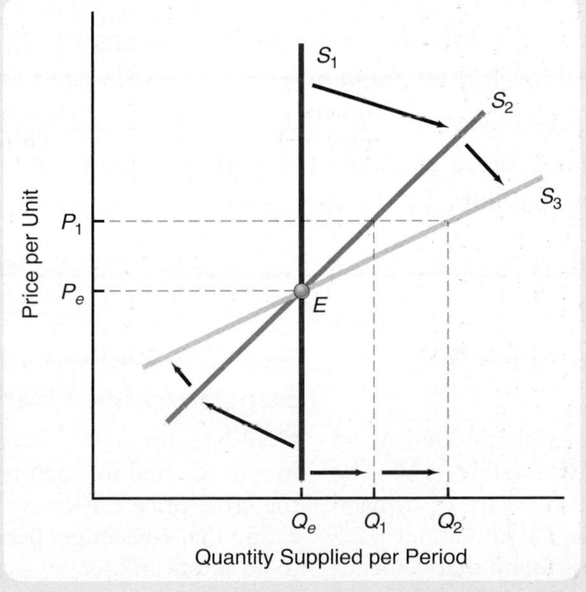

You Are There Pricing the iPad: Learning Lessons from the iPhone

It is January 2010, and Steve Jobs has just made his first big pitch for Apple's latest high-tech gadget, the iPad, which can perform a variety of functions from playing computer games to displaying animated figures from college textbooks. According to media reports, industry observers expect that the company will offer the device at a relatively high price.

Jobs and Apple, however, have learned a lesson from their experience with the iPhone in mid-2007. At that time, Jobs and Apple had anticipated inelastic demand for the iPhone and other Internet-ready, "smart" cellphones, so they set a relatively high price for the iPhone in an effort to generate maximum revenues. In fact, the estimated price elasticity of demand for smart cellphones turned out to be about 1.4. Hence, revenues received by Apple and other manufacturers of smart cellphones increased only after the market clearing price of smart cellphones *declined* in late 2007 and early 2008.

Thus, although most industry observers anticipated that a basic iPad would be priced at $1,000, Apple's initial price is only $499. The company has set this lower price in anticipation that the demand for the new gadget will turn out to be elastic, so a lower price will ultimately yield higher revenues.

Critical Analysis Questions

1. By setting the iPad's price at half the expected level, did Apple signal that it anticipated a price elasticity of demand below or above 1? Explain.
2. Why is the price elasticity of demand for Apple's iPhone greater than the price elasticity of the market demand for *all* smart cellphones?

ISSUES & APPLICATIONS

Measuring the Substitutability of Satellite and Cable TV

CONCEPTS APPLIED

- Price Elasticity of Demand
- Elastic Demand
- Cross Price Elasticity of Demand

Is access to television programming essentially the same good whether it is delivered by cable or satellite? To find out, Austan Goolsbee of the University of Chicago and Amil Petrin of the University of Minnesota estimated price elasticities and cross price elasticities of demand for cable and satellite TV delivery services.

Price Elasticities of Demand for TV Delivery Services

Goolsbee and Petrin estimated price elasticities of demand for cable TV and direct broadcast satellite TV. The researchers estimated that the price elasticity of demand was between −1.5 and −3.0 for cable TV and about −2.5 for satellite TV. Thus, the researchers found that demands for both types of TV delivery services were elastic.

Satellite Delivery Is Slightly Less Substitutable Than Cable

Goolsbee and Petrin also estimated the cross price elasticities of demand for each type of TV service. The values of the cross price elasticities of demand were positive, indicating that consumers perceive cable TV and satellite TV to be substitutes.

The cross price elasticities were not the same, however. Goolsbee and Petrin found that a 1 percent decrease in the price of satellite TV caused the amount of cable TV services demanded to decline by about 1 percent. In contrast, they found that the amount of satellite TV services demanded fell by only 0.3 to 0.5 percent in response to a 1 percent decrease in the price of cable TV. Apparently, consumers of satellite TV perceive cable TV to be less substitutable for satellite TV services than do cable TV consumers.

For Critical Analysis

1. If the market clearing prices of cable and satellite TV services were to decrease, what would happen to the revenues earned by sellers of these services?
2. Based on the information above, what was the range of estimates of the value of the cross price elasticity of demand for satellite TV with respect to the price of cable TV?

Web Resources

1. For information about why cable and satellite services are typically viewed as imperfectly substitutable, go to www.econtoday.com/ch19.
2. To learn about how satellite TV services can now be accessed using personal computers, go to www.econtoday.com/ch19.

Research Project

Providers of satellite TV services have already developed ways for people to capture TV programming on personal computing devices as well as via traditional television sets, while cable TV providers have been slower to offer such services. Discuss whether this difference might, at least in theory, help explain the differing estimates of cross price elasticities of demand for cable versus satellite TV.

For more questions on this chapter's Issues & Applications, go to **MyEconLab**. In the Study Plan for this chapter, select Section N: News.

Here is what you should know after reading this chapter. **MyEconLab** will help you identify what you know, and where to go when you need to practice.

WHAT YOU SHOULD KNOW		WHERE TO GO TO PRACTICE
Expressing and Calculating the Price Elasticity of Demand The price elasticity of demand is the percentage change in quantity demanded divided by the percentage change in price. To calculate the price elasticity of demand for relatively small changes in price, the percentage change in quantity demanded is equal to the change in the quantity resulting from a price change divided by the average of the initial and final quantities, and the percentage change in price is equal to the price change divided by the average of the initial and final prices.	price elasticity of demand (E_p), 416	• **MyEconLab** Study Plan 19.1 • Audio introduction to Chapter 19
The Relationship Between the Price Elasticity of Demand and Total Revenues Demand is elastic when the price elasticity of demand exceeds 1, and over the elastic range of a demand curve, an increase in price reduces total revenues. Demand is inelastic when the price elasticity of demand is less than 1, and over this range of a demand curve, an increase in price raises total revenues. Finally, demand is unit-elastic when the price elasticity of demand equals 1, and over this range of a demand curve, an increase in price does not affect total revenues.	elastic demand, 418 unit elasticity of demand, 418 inelastic demand, 418 perfectly inelastic demand, 418 perfectly elastic demand, 418 **KEY FIGURES** Figure 19-1, 419 Figure 19-2, 420	• **MyEconLab** Study Plans 19.2, 19.3 • Animated Figures 19-1, 19-2

(continued)

MyEconLab continued

WHAT YOU SHOULD KNOW		WHERE TO GO TO PRACTICE
Factors That Determine the Price Elasticity of Demand Three factors affect the price elasticity of demand. If there are more close substitutes, the price elasticity of demand increases. The price elasticity of demand also tends to be higher when a larger portion of a person's budget is spent on the good. In addition, if people have a longer period of time to adjust to a price change, the price elasticity of demand tends to be higher.	**KEY FIGURE** Figure 19-3, 424	• **MyEconLab** Study Plan 19.4 • Video: The Determinants of the Price Elasticity of Demand • Animated Figure 19-3
The Cross Price Elasticity of Demand and Using It to Determine Whether Two Goods Are Substitutes or Complements The cross price elasticity of demand for a good is the percentage change in the amount of that good demanded divided by the percentage change in the price of a related good. If two goods are substitutes, an increase in the price of one of the goods induces an increase in the amount of the other good demanded, so the cross price elasticity of demand is positive. In contrast, if two goods are complements, an increase in the price of one of the goods brings about a decrease in the amount of the other good demanded, so the cross price elasticity of demand is negative.	cross price elasticity of demand (E_{xy}), 425	• **MyEconLab** Study Plan 19.5 • Video: Cross Price Elasticity of Demand
The Income Elasticity of Demand The income elasticity of demand for any good is equal to the percentage change in the amount of the good demanded divided by the percentage change in income, holding the good's relative price unchanged.	income elasticity of demand (E_i), 426	• **MyEconLab** Study Plan 19.6 • Video: Income Elasticity of Demand
Classifying Supply Elasticities and How the Length of Time for Adjustment Affects the Price Elasticity of Supply The price elasticity of supply is equal to the percentage change in quantity supplied divided by the percentage change in price. If the price elasticity of supply is greater than 1, supply is elastic, and if the price elasticity of supply is less than 1, supply is inelastic. Supply is unit-elastic if the price elasticity of supply equals 1. Supply is more likely to be elastic when sellers have more time to adjust to price changes.	price elasticity of supply (E_s), 427 perfectly elastic supply, 427 perfectly inelastic supply, 427 **KEY FIGURE** Figure 19-5, 429	• **MyEconLab** Study Plan 19.7 • Animated Figure 19-5

Log in to MyEconLab, take a chapter test, and get a personalized Study Plan that tells you which concepts you understand and which ones you need to review. From there, MyEconLab will give you further practice, tutorials, animations, videos, and guided solutions.
Log in to www.myeconlab.com

PROBLEMS

All problems are assignable in myeconlab. *Answers to odd-numbered problems appear at the back of the book.*

19-1. When the price of shirts emblazoned with a college logo is $10, consumers buy 150 per week. When the price declines to $9, consumers purchase 200 per week. Based on this information, calculate the price elasticity of demand for logo-emblazoned shirts.

19-2. Table 19-2 on page 424 indicates that the short-run price elasticity of demand for tires is 0.9. If an increase in the price of petroleum (used in producing tires) causes the market prices of tires to rise from $50 to $60, by what percentage would you expect the quantity of tires demanded to change?

19-3. The diagram below depicts the demand curve for "miniburgers" in a local fast-food market. Use the information in this diagram to answer the questions that follow.

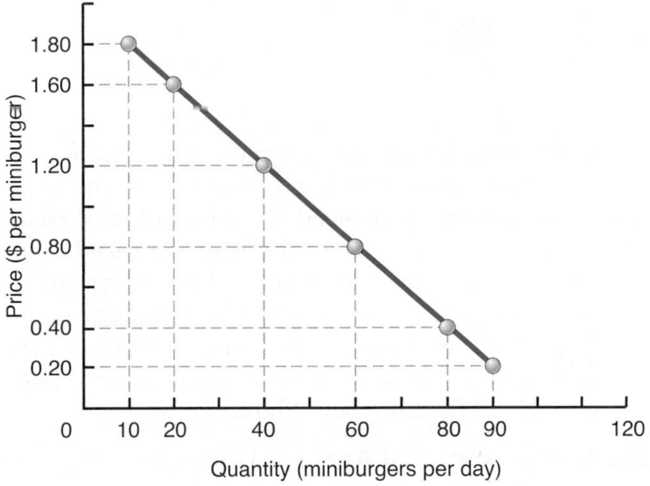

a. What is the price elasticity of demand along the range of the demand curve between a price of $0.20 per miniburger and a price of $0.40 per miniburger? Is demand elastic or inelastic over this range?

b. What is the price elasticity of demand along the range of the demand curve between a price of $0.80 per miniburger and a price of $1.20 per miniburger? Is demand elastic or inelastic over this range?

c. What is the price elasticity of demand along the range of the demand curve between a price of $1.60 per miniburger and a price of $1.80 per miniburger? Is demand elastic or inelastic over this range?

19-4. In a local market, the monthly price of Internet access service decreases from $20 to $10, and the total quantity of monthly accounts across all Internet access providers increases from 100,000 to 200,000. What is the price elasticity of demand? Is demand elastic, unit-elastic, or inelastic?

19-5. At a price of $27.50 to play 18 holes on local golf courses, 1,200 consumers pay to play a game of golf each day. A rise in the price to $32.50 causes the number of consumers to decline to 800. What is the price elasticity of demand? Is demand elastic, unit-elastic, or inelastic?

19-6. It is very difficult to find goods with perfectly elastic or perfectly inelastic demand. We can, however, find goods that lie near these extremes. Characterize demands for the following goods as being near perfectly elastic or near perfectly inelastic.

a. Corn grown and harvested by a small farmer in Iowa

b. Heroin for a drug addict

c. Water for a desert hiker

d. One of several optional textbooks in a pass-fail course

19-7. In the market for hand-made guitars, when the price of guitars is $800, annual revenues are $640,000. When the price falls to $700, annual revenues decline to $630,000. Over this range of guitar prices, is the demand for hand-made guitars elastic, unit-elastic, or inelastic?

19-8. Suppose that over a range of prices, the price elasticity of demand varies from 15.0 to 2.5. Over another range of prices, the price elasticity of demand varies from 1.5 to 0.75. What can you say about total revenues and the total revenue curve over these two ranges of the demand curve as price falls?

19-9. Based solely on the information provided below, characterize the demands for the following goods as being more elastic or more inelastic.

a. A 45-cent box of salt that you buy once a year

b. A type of high-powered ski boat that you can rent from any one of a number of rental agencies

c. A specific brand of bottled water

d. Automobile insurance in a state that requires autos to be insured but has only a few insurance companies

e. A 75-cent guitar pick for the lead guitarist of a major rock band

19-10. The value of cross price elasticity of demand between goods X and Y is 1.25, while the cross price elasticity of demand between goods X and Z is −2.0. Characterize X and Y and X and Z as substitutes or complements.

19-11. Suppose that the cross price elasticity of demand between eggs and bacon is −0.5. What would you expect to happen to purchases of bacon if the price of eggs rises by 10 percent?

19-12. Assume that the income elasticity of demand for hot dogs is −1.25 and that the income elasticity of demand for lobster is 1.25. Based on the fact that the measure for hot dogs is negative while that for lobster is positive, are these normal or inferior goods? (Hint: You may want to refer to the discussion of normal and inferior goods in Chapter 3.)

19-13. At a price of $25,000, producers of midsized automobiles are willing to manufacture and sell 75,000 cars per month. At a price of $35,000, they are willing to produce and sell 125,000 a month. Using the same type of calculation method used to compute the price elasticity of demand, what is the price elasticity of supply? Is supply elastic, unit-elastic, or inelastic?

19-14. The price elasticity of supply of a basic commodity that a nation imports from producers in other countries is 2. What would you expect to happen to the volume of imports if the price of this commodity rises by 10 percent?

19-15. A 20 percent increase in the price of skis induces ski manufacturers to increase production of skis by 10 percent in the short run. In the long run, other things being equal, the 20 percent price increase generates a production increase of 40 percent. What is the short-run price elasticity of supply? What is the long-run price elasticity of supply?

19-16. An increase in the market price of men's haircuts, from $15 per haircut to $25 per haircut, initially causes a local barbershop to have its employees work overtime to increase the number of daily haircuts provided from 35 to 45. When the $25 market price remains unchanged for several weeks and all other things remain equal as well, the barbershop hires additional employees and provides 65 haircuts per day. What is the short-run price elasticity of supply? What is the long-run price elasticity of supply?

ECONOMICS ON THE NET

Price Elasticity and Consumption of Illegal Drugs Making the use of certain drugs illegal drives up their market prices, so the price elasticity of demand is a key factor affecting the use of illegal drugs. This application applies concepts from this chapter to analyze how price elasticity of demand affects drug consumption.

Title: The Demand for Illicit Drugs

Navigation: Go to **www.econtoday.com/ch19**, and follow the link to the summary of this paper published by the National Bureau of Economic Research.

Application Read the summary of the results of this study of price elasticities of participation in use of illegal drugs, and answer the following questions.

1. Based on the results of the study, is the demand for cocaine more or less price elastic than the demand for heroin? For which drug, therefore, will quantity demanded fall by a greater percentage in response to a proportionate increase in price?
2. The study finds that decriminalizing currently illegal drugs would bring about sizable increases both in overall consumption of heroin and cocaine and in the price elasticity of demand for both drugs. Why do you suppose that the price elasticity of demand would rise? (Hint: At present, users of cocaine and heroin are restricted to only a few illegal sources of the drugs, but if the drugs could legally be produced and sold, there would be many more suppliers providing a variety of different types of both drugs.)

For Group Study and Analysis Discuss ways that government officials might use information about the price elasticities of demand for illicit drugs to assist in developing policies intended to reduce the use of these drugs. Which of these proposed policies might prove most effective? Why?

ANSWERS TO QUICK QUIZZES

p. 419: (i) quantity demanded . . . price; (ii) percentage . . . independent; (iii) negative . . . decrease . . . increase; (iv) zero . . . inelastic . . . elastic . . . infinite

p. 422: (i) revenues; (ii) opposite; (iii) zero; (iv) same

p. 427: (i) substitutes . . . share . . . adjustment; (ii) Cross . . . positive . . . negative; (iii) demanded . . . income

p. 429: (i) quantity supplied . . . price; (ii) positive . . . greater; (iii) more . . . longer

20 Consumer Choice

According to some economists who perceive that consumers have limited ability to make rational choices, credit cards are "bad." These economists reason that being able to use credit cards to obtain items immediately makes consumers more satisfied until they receive their credit-card bills. Then, the economists argue, consumers discover that they have to pay some of their income to the credit-card issuers and forgo spending that amount of their income on other goods and services. The net result is that people are less happy than they would have been if they had not used the credit cards—which these economists suggest is justification for governments to ban credit cards. Before you can contemplate this proposal to try to make people better off by banning credit cards, you first must understand how economists study the way people make choices intended to maximize their levels of satisfaction. That is the key topic of this chapter.

LEARNING OBJECTIVES

After reading this chapter, you should be able to:

- Distinguish between total utility and marginal utility
- Discuss why marginal utility first rises but ultimately tends to decline as a person consumes more of a good or service
- Explain why an individual's optimal choice of how much to consume of each good or service entails equalizing the marginal utility per dollar spent across all goods and services
- Describe the substitution effect of a price change on the quantity demanded of a good or service
- Understand how the real-income effect of a price change affects the quantity demanded of a good or service

Did You Know That ?

the human brain does its intelligent computing with 10^{11} (100,000,000,000) neurons? These neurons are interconnected in a complex network of about 10^{16} (10,000,000,000,000,000) electrochemical connections called synapses, each of which performs about 1,000 operations per second. Evidence indicates that all this computing power makes the human brain at least 10,000 times more intelligent than most artificially constructed supercomputers. Thus, there is general agreement that the human brain is thousands of times better at making choices among desirable alternatives than the computing machines available today. Human beings have considerable capability to evaluate choices and determine the quantities of different goods and services they wish to consume.

In Chapter 3, you learned that a determinant of the quantity demanded of any particular item is the price of that item. The law of demand implies that at a lower overall price, there will be a higher quantity demanded. Understanding the derivation of the law of demand is useful because it allows us to examine the relevant variables, such as price, income, and tastes, in such a way as to make better sense of the world and even perhaps generate predictions about it. One way of deriving the law of demand involves an analysis of the logic of consumer choice in a world of limited resources. In this chapter, therefore, we discuss what is called *utility analysis*.

Utility Theory

When you buy something, you do so because of the satisfaction you expect to receive from having and using that good. For everything that you like to have, the more you have of it, the higher the level of total satisfaction you receive. Another term that can be used for satisfaction is **utility,** or want-satisfying power. This property is common to all goods that are desired. The concept of utility is purely subjective, however. There is no way that you or I can measure the amount of utility that a consumer might be able to obtain from a particular good, for utility does not imply "useful" or "utilitarian" or "practical." Thus, there can be no accurate scientific assessment of the utility that someone might receive by consuming a fast-food dinner or a movie relative to the utility that another person might receive from that same good or service.

Utility
The want-satisfying power of a good or service.

The utility that individuals receive from consuming a good depends on their tastes and preferences. These tastes and preferences are normally assumed to be given and stable for a particular individual. An individual's tastes determine how much utility that individual derives from consuming a good, and this in turn determines how that individual allocates his or her income to purchases of that good. But we cannot explain why tastes are different between individuals. For example, we cannot explain why some people like yogurt but others do not.

We can analyze in terms of utility the way consumers decide what to buy, just as physicists have analyzed some of their problems in terms of what they call force. No physicist has ever seen a unit of force, and no economist has ever seen a unit of utility. In both cases, however, these concepts have proved useful for analysis.

Throughout this chapter, we will be discussing **utility analysis,** which is the analysis of consumer decision making based on utility maximization—that is, making choices with the aim of attaining the highest feasible satisfaction.

Utility analysis
The analysis of consumer decision making based on utility maximization.

Utility and Utils

Economists once believed that utility could be measured. In fact, there is a philosophical school of thought based on utility theory called *utilitarianism*, developed by the English philosopher Jeremy Bentham (1748–1832). Bentham held that society should seek the greatest happiness for the greatest number. He sought to apply an arithmetic formula for measuring happiness. He and his followers developed the notion of measurable utility and invented the **util** to measure it. For the moment, we will also assume that we can measure satisfaction using this representative unit. Our

Util
A representative unit by which utility is measured.

assumption will allow us to quantify the way we examine consumer behavior. Thus, the first chocolate bar that you eat might yield you 4 utils of satisfaction. The first peanut cluster, might yield 6 utils, and so on. Today, no one really believes that we can actually measure utils, but the ideas forthcoming from such analysis will prove useful in understanding how consumers choose among alternatives.

Total and Marginal Utility

Consider the satisfaction, or utility, that you receive each time that you download and listen to digital music albums. To make the example straightforward, let's say that there are thousands of downloadable music albums to choose from each year and that each of them is of the same quality. Let's say that you normally download and listen to one music album per week. You could, of course, download two, or three, or four per week. Presumably, each time you download and listen to another music album per week, you will get additional satisfaction, or utility. The question that we must ask though, is, given that you are already downloading and listening to one album per week, will the next one downloaded and listened to during that week give you the same amount of additional utility?

That additional, or incremental, utility is called **marginal utility,** where *marginal* means "incremental" or "additional." (Marginal changes also refer to decreases, in which cases we talk about *decremental* changes.) The concept of marginality is important in economics because we can think of people comparing additional (marginal) benefits with additional (marginal) costs.

Marginal utility
The change in total utility due to a one-unit change in the quantity of a good or service consumed.

Applying Marginal Analysis to Utility

The example in Figure 20-1 on the following page will clarify the distinction between total utility and marginal utility. The table in panel (a) shows the total utility and the marginal utility of downloading and listening to digital music albums each week. Marginal utility is the difference between total utility derived from one level of consumption and total utility derived from another level of consumption within a given time interval. A simple formula for marginal utility is this:

$$\text{Marginal utility} = \frac{\text{change in total utility}}{\text{change in number of units consumed}}$$

In our example, when a person has already downloaded and listened to two music albums in one week and then downloads and listens to another, total utility increases from 16 utils to 19 utils. Therefore, the marginal utility (of downloading and listening to one more album of Internet music after already having downloaded and listened to two in one week) is equal to 3 utils.

Graphical Analysis

We can transfer the information in panel (a) onto a graph, as we do in panels (b) and (c) of Figure 20-1 on the next page. Total utility, which is represented in column 2 of panel (a), is transferred to panel (b).

Total utility continues to rise until four digital music albums are downloaded and listened to per week. This measure of utility remains at 20 utils through the fifth album, and at the sixth album per week it falls to 18 utils. We assume that at some quantity consumed per unit time period, boredom with consuming more digital music albums begins to set in. Thus, at some quantity consumed, the additional utility from consuming an additional album begins to fall, so total utility first rises and then declines in panel (b).

FIGURE 20-1 Total and Marginal Utility of Downloading and Listening to Digital Music Albums

If we were able to assign specific values to the utility derived from downloading and listening to digital music albums each week, we could obtain a marginal utility schedule similar in pattern to the one shown in panel (a). In column 1 is the number of music albums downloaded and listened to per week; in column 2, the total utility derived from each quantity; and in column 3, the marginal utility derived from each additional quantity, which is defined as the change in total utility due to a change of one unit of listening to downloaded albums per week. Total utility from panel (a) is plotted in panel (b). Marginal utility is plotted in panel (c), where you see that it reaches zero where total utility hits its maximum at between 4 and 5 units.

Panel (a)

(1) Number of Music Albums Downloaded and Listened to per Week	(2) Total Utility (utils per week)	(3) Marginal Utility (utils per week)
0	0	
		10 (10 – 0)
1	10	
		6 (16 – 10)
2	16	
		3 (19 – 16)
3	19	
		1 (20 – 19)
4	20	
		0 (20 – 20)
5	20	
		–2 (18 – 20)
6	18	

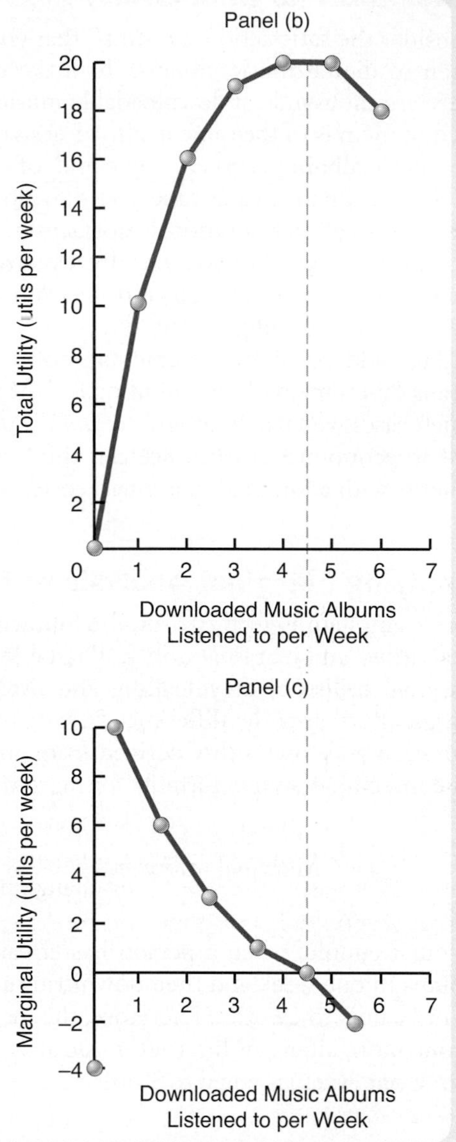

Marginal Utility

If you look carefully at panels (b) and (c) of Figure 20-1 above, the notion of marginal utility becomes clear. In economics, the term *marginal* always refers to a *change* in the total. The marginal utility of listening to three downloaded digital music albums per week instead of two albums per week is the increment in total utility and is equal to 3 utils per week. All of the points in panel (c) are taken from column 3 of the table in panel (a). Notice that marginal utility falls throughout the graph. A special point occurs after four albums are downloaded and listened to per week because the total utility curve in panel (b) is unchanged after the consumption of the fourth album. That means that the consumer receives no additional (marginal) utility from downloading and listening to five albums rather than four. This is shown in panel (c) as *zero* marginal utility. After that point, marginal utility becomes negative.

In our example, when marginal utility becomes negative, it means that the consumer is tired of downloading and listening to digital music albums and would require some form of compensation to listen to any more. When marginal utility is negative, an additional unit consumed actually lowers total utility by becoming a nuisance. Rarely does a consumer face a situation of negative marginal utility. Whenever this point is reached, goods in effect become "bads." Consuming more units actually causes total utility to *fall* so that marginal utility is negative. A rational consumer will stop consuming at the point at which marginal utility becomes negative, even if the good is available at a price of zero.

QUICK QUIZ See page 452 for the answers. Review concepts from this section in MyEconLab.

_________ is defined as want-satisfying power. It is a power common to all desired goods and services.

We arbitrarily measure **utility** in units called _________.

It is important to distinguish between **total utility** and **marginal utility.** _________ utility is the total satisfaction derived from the consumption of a given quantity of a good or service. _________ utility is the *change* in total utility due to a one-unit change in the consumption of the good or service.

Diminishing Marginal Utility

Notice that in panel (c) of Figure 20-1 on the facing page, marginal utility is continuously declining. This property has been named the principle of **diminishing marginal utility.** There is no way that we can prove diminishing marginal utility. Nevertheless, diminishing marginal utility has even been called a law. This supposed law concerns a psychological, or subjective, utility that you receive as you consume more and more of a particular good. Stated formally, the law is as follows:

Diminishing marginal utility The principle that as more of any good or service is consumed, its extra benefit declines. Otherwise stated, increases in total utility from the consumption of a good or service become smaller and smaller as more is consumed during a given time period.

> ***As an individual consumes more of a particular commodity, the total level of utility, or satisfaction, derived from that consumption usually increases. Eventually, however, the rate at which it increases diminishes as more is consumed.***

Take a hungry individual at a dinner table. The first serving is greatly appreciated, and the individual derives a substantial amount of utility from it. Consumption of the second serving does not have quite as much pleasurable impact as the first one, and consumption of the third serving is likely to be even less satisfying. This individual experiences diminishing marginal utility of food until he or she stops eating, and this is true for most people. All-you-can-eat restaurants count on this fact. A second helping of ribs may provide some marginal utility, but the third helping would have only a little or even negative marginal utility.

Consider for a moment the opposite possibility—increasing marginal utility. Under such a situation, the marginal utility after consuming, say, one hamburger would increase. Consuming the second hamburger would yield more utility to you, and consuming the third would yield even more. If increasing marginal utility existed, each of us would consume only one good or service! Rather than observing that "variety is the spice of life," we would see that monotony in consumption was preferred. We do not observe such single-item consumption, and therefore we have great confidence in the concept of diminishing marginal utility.

Can diminishing marginal utility explain why newspaper vending machines rarely prevent people from taking more than the one current issue they have paid to purchase?

EXAMPLE Newspaper Vending Machines versus Candy Vending Machines

Have you ever noticed that newspaper vending machines nearly everywhere in the United States allow you to put in the correct change, lift up the door, and—if you were willing to violate the law—take as many newspapers as you want? Contrast this type of vending machine with candy machines. They are securely locked at all times. You must designate the candy that you wish, normally by using some type of keypad. The candy then drops down so that you can retrieve it but cannot grab any other candy.

The difference between these two types of vending machines is explained by diminishing marginal utility. Newspaper companies dispense newspapers from coin-operated boxes that allow dishonest people to take more copies than they pay for. What would a dishonest person do with more than one copy of a newspaper, however? The marginal utility of reading a second newspaper is normally zero. The benefit of storing excessive newspapers is usually nil because yesterday's news has no value. But the same analysis does not hold for candy. The marginal utility of consuming a second candy bar is certainly less than the marginal utility of consuming the first, but it is normally not zero. Moreover, one can store candy for relatively long periods of time at relatively low cost. Consequently, food vending machine companies have to worry about dishonest users of their equipment and must make that equipment more theftproof than newspaper vending machines.

FOR CRITICAL ANALYSIS

Can you think of a circumstance under which a substantial number of newspaper purchasers might be inclined to take more than one newspaper out of a vending machine?

Optimizing Consumption Choices

Every consumer has a limited income, so choices must be made. When a consumer has made all of his or her choices about what to buy and in what quantities, and when the total level of satisfaction, or utility, from that set of choices is as great as it can be, we say that the consumer has *optimized.* When the consumer has attained an optimum consumption set of goods and services, we say that he or she has reached **consumer optimum.**

Consumer optimum
A choice of a set of goods and services that maximizes the level of satisfaction for each consumer, subject to limited income.

A Two-Good Example

Consider a simple two-good example. The consumer has to choose between spending income on downloads of digital music albums at $5 per download and on purchasing cappuccinos at $3 each. Let's say that when the consumer has spent all income on music album downloads and cappuccinos, the last dollar spent on a cappuccino yields 3 utils of utility but the last dollar spent on downloading music albums yields 10 utils. Wouldn't this consumer increase total utility if some dollars were taken away from consumption of cappuccinos and allocated to music album downloads? The answer is yes. More dollars spent downloading music albums will reduce marginal utility per last dollar spent, whereas fewer dollars spent on consumption of cappuccinos will increase marginal utility per last dollar spent. The loss in utility from spending fewer dollars purchasing fewer cappuccinos is more than made up by spending additional dollars on more album downloads. As a consequence, total utility increases. The consumer optimum—where total utility is maximized—occurs when the satisfaction per last dollar spent on both cappuccinos and music album downloads per week is equal for the two goods. Thus, the amount of goods consumed depends on the prices of the goods, the income of the consumer, and the marginal utility derived from the amounts of each good consumed.

Table 20-1 on the facing page presents information on utility derived from consuming various quantities of music album downloads and cappuccinos. Columns 4 and 8 show the marginal utility per dollar spent on music downloads and cappuccinos, respectively. If the prices of both goods are zero, individuals will consume each as long as their respective marginal utility is positive (at least five units of each and probably much more). It is also true that a consumer with unlimited income will continue consuming goods until the marginal utility of each is equal to zero. When the price is zero or the consumer's income is unlimited, there is no effective constraint on consumption.

A Two-Good Consumer Optimum

Consumer optimum is attained when the marginal utility of the last dollar spent on each good yields the same utility and income is completely exhausted. In the situation

TABLE 20-1

Total and Marginal Utility from Consuming Music Album Downloads and Cappuccinos on an Income of $26

(1) Music Album Downloads per Period	(2) Total Utility of Music Album Downloads per Period (utils)	(3) Marginal Utility (utils) MU_d	(4) Marginal Utility per Dollar Spent (MU_d/P_d) (price = $5)	(5) Cappuccinos per Period	(6) Total Utility of Cappuccinos per Period (utils)	(7) Marginal Utility (utils) MU_c	(8) Marginal Utility per Dollar Spent (MU_c/P_c) (price = $3)
0	0	–	–	0	0	–	–
1	50.0	50.0	10.0	1	25	25	8.3
2	95.0	45.0	9.0	2	47	22	7.3
3	135.0	40.0	8.0	3	65	18	6.0
4	171.5	36.5	7.3	4	80	15	5.0
5	200.0	28.5	5.7	5	89	9	3.0

in Table 20-1 above, the individual's income is $26. From columns 4 and 8 of Table 20-1, equal marginal utilities per dollar spent occur at the consumption level of four music album downloads and two cappuccinos (the marginal utility per dollar spent equals 7.3). Notice that the marginal utility per dollar spent for both goods is also (approximately) equal at the consumption level of three music album downloads and one cappuccino, but here total income is not completely exhausted. Likewise, the marginal utility per dollar spent is (approximately) equal at five music album downloads and three cappuccinos, but the expenditures necessary for that level of consumption ($34) exceed the individual's income.

Table 20-2 below shows the steps taken to arrive at consumer optimum. Listening to the first downloaded music album would yield a marginal utility per dollar of

TABLE 20-2

Steps to Consumer Optimum

In each purchase situation described here, the consumer always purchases the good with the higher marginal utility per dollar spent (*MU/P*). For example, at the time of the third purchase, the marginal utility per last dollar spent on downloads of music albums is 8, but it is 8.3 for cappuccinos, and $16 of income remains, so the next purchase will be a cappuccino. Here $P_d = \$5$, $P_c = \$3$, MU_d is the marginal utility of consumption of music album downloads, and MU_c is the marginal utility of consumption of cappuccinos.

	Choices					
	Music Album Downloads		Cappuccinos			
Purchase	Unit	MU_d/P_d	Unit	MU_c/P_c	Buying Decision	Remaining Income
1	First	10.0	First	8.3	First music album download	$26 – $5 = $21
2	Second	9.0	First	8.3	Second music album download	$21 – $5 = $16
3	Third	8.0	First	8.3	First cappuccino	$16 – $3 = $13
4	Third	8.0	Second	7.3	Third music album download	$13 – $5 = $8
5	Fourth	7.3	Second	7.3	Fourth music album download and second cappuccino	$8 – $5 = $3 $3 – $3 = $0

10 (50 units of utility divided by $5 per music album), while consuming the first cappuccino would yield a marginal utility of only 8.3 per dollar (25 units of utility divided by $3 per cappuccino). Because it yields the higher marginal utility per dollar, the music album is purchased. This leaves $21 of income. Downloading and listening to the second music album yield a higher marginal utility per dollar (9, versus 8.3 for a cappuccino), so this album is also purchased, leaving an unspent income of $16. Purchasing and consuming the first cappuccino now yield a higher marginal utility per dollar than listening to the next music album (8.3 versus 8), so the first cappuccino is purchased. This leaves income of $13 to spend. The process continues until all income is exhausted and the marginal utility per dollar spent is equal for both goods.

To restate, consumer optimum requires the following:

A consumer's money income should be allocated so that the last dollar spent on each good purchased yields the same amount of marginal utility (when all income is spent), because this rule yields the largest possible total utility.

Does the price of an item ever affect how much utility people experience from consuming that item?

EXAMPLE **Does Consuming More Expensive Items Make People Happier?**

Antonio Rangel of the California Institute of Technology conducted experiments in which he offered to let people taste wines. He sometimes told people that the wine they were drinking had been poured from a bottle purchased at a price of $90 when he actually had poured it from a bottle priced at $5. Other times, he told people the true price of the wine. As subjects drank the wines, their brains were subjected to magnetic resonance imaging (MRI). The images revealed that many people enjoyed the wine tasting more when they were told that the wine was expensive.

Thus, the experiment showed that when people receive a good at no explicit charge, they derive greater satisfaction from consuming the good when they *believe* that it has a higher explicit price. Of course, in real-world market settings, people do pay explicit prices for items. In all normal situations, the additional satisfaction they derive from consuming higher-priced items naturally increases when they *choose* to pay the higher prices. After all, this must be true for the marginal utility per dollar spent to be equalized across all items consumed.

FOR CRITICAL ANALYSIS

Why do you suppose that some firms now use magnetic resonance imaging of people consuming new products when the firms decide what price to charge for the items?

A Little Math

We can state the rule of consumer optimum in algebraic terms by examining the ratio of marginal utilities and prices of individual products. The rule simply states that a consumer maximizes personal satisfaction when allocating money income in such a way that the last dollars spent on good A, good B, good C, and so on, yield equal amounts of marginal utility. Marginal utility (*MU*) from good A is indicated by "*MU* of good A." For good B, it is "*MU* of good B." Our algebraic formulation of this rule, therefore, becomes

$$\frac{MU \text{ of good A}}{\text{Price of good A}} = \frac{MU \text{ of good B}}{\text{price of good B}} = \cdots = \frac{MU \text{ of good Z}}{\text{price of good Z}}$$

The letters A, B, . . . , Z indicate the various goods and services that the consumer might purchase.

We know, then, that in order for the consumer to maximize utility, the marginal utility of good A divided by the price of good A must equal the marginal utility of any other good divided by its price. Note, though, that the application of the rule of equal marginal utility per dollar spent does not necessarily describe an explicit or conscious act on the part of consumers. Rather, this is a *model* of consumer optimum.

You Are There

To consider how companies are using "free" trial offers to induce people to include their products within a typical consumer optimum, read **Signing Up for "Free" Trial Offers with TrialPay,** on page 447.

Why Not . . . make consumers happier by requiring them to purchase the quantities the government chooses?

At consumers' optimal allocations of their incomes to expenditures on goods and services, the marginal utility per dollar spent is equalized across all purchases. If the government required individuals to reallocate their incomes to purchase larger quantities of certain items, then the marginal utilities from consuming those items would decline. In addition, consumers would have less remaining income available to purchase as many units of other items, so the marginal utilities derived from buying those items would rise. Consequently, at current prices of goods and services, consumers' marginal utility per dollar spent would no longer be equal, meaning that consumers would be *less satisfied*. Thus, a government requirement for consumers to reallocate their incomes to different quantities of goods and services might please government officials but would *not* make consumers happier.

QUICK QUIZ See page 452 for the answers. Review concepts from this section in MyEconLab.

The principle of **diminishing marginal utility** tells us that each successive marginal unit of a good consumed adds __________ extra utility.

The consumer maximizes total utility by __________ the marginal utility of the last dollar spent on one good with the marginal utility per last dollar spent on all other goods. That is the state of consumer __________.

To remain in **consumer optimum,** a price decrease requires an __________ in consumption. A price increase requires a __________ in consumption.

How a Price Change Affects Consumer Optimum

Consumption decisions are summarized in the law of demand, which states that the amount purchased is inversely related to price. We can now see why by using utility analysis.

A Consumer's Response to a Price Change

When a consumer has optimally allocated all her income to purchases, the marginal utility per dollar spent at current prices of goods and services is the same for each good or service she buys. No consumer will, when optimizing, buy 10 units of a good per unit of time when the marginal utility per dollar spent on the tenth unit of that good is less than the marginal utility per dollar spent on a unit of some other item.

If we start out at a consumer optimum and then observe a good's price decrease, we can predict that consumers will respond to the price decrease by consuming more of that good. This is because before the price change, the marginal utility per dollar spent on each good or service consumed was the same. Now, when a specific good's price is lower, it is possible to consume more of that good while continuing to equalize the marginal utility per dollar spent on that good with the marginal utility per dollar spent on other goods and services. The purchase and consumption of additional units of the lower-priced good will cause the marginal utility from consuming the good to fall. Eventually, it will fall to the point at which the marginal utility per dollar spent on the good is once again equal to the marginal utility per dollar spent on other goods and services. At this point, the consumer will stop buying additional units of the lower-priced good.

A hypothetical demand curve for music downloads per week for a typical consumer is presented in Figure 20-2 on the next page. Suppose that at point *A*, at which the price per music download is $5, the marginal utility of the last music album downloaded per week is MU_A. At point *B*, at which the price is $4 per music download per week, the marginal utility is represented by MU_B. With the consumption of more downloaded digital music, the marginal utility of the last unit of these additional

FIGURE 20-2 Digital Music Download Prices and Marginal Utility

When consumers respond to a reduction in music download prices from \$5 per download to \$4 per download by increasing consumption, marginal utility falls. The movement is from point *A*, at which marginal utility is MU_A, to point *B*, at which marginal utility is MU_B, which is less than MU_A. This brings about the equalization of the marginal utility per dollar spent across all purchases.

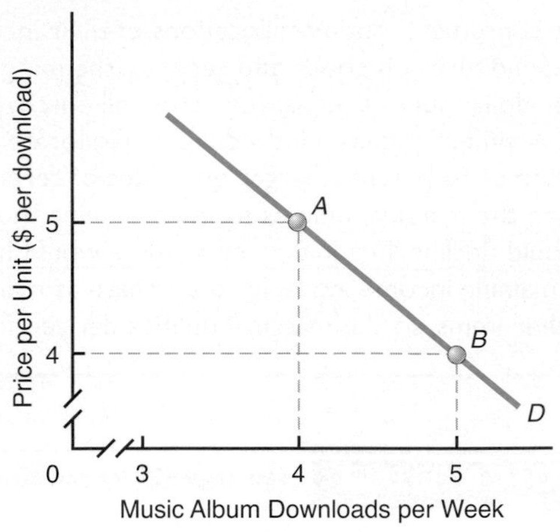

music downloads is lower—MU_B must be less than MU_A. What has happened is that at a lower price, the number of music album downloads per week increased from four to five. Marginal utility must have fallen. At a higher consumption rate, the marginal utility falls in response to the rise in downloadable music consumption so that the marginal utility per dollar spent is equalized across all purchases.

The Substitution Effect

What is happening as the price of music downloads falls is that consumers are substituting the now relatively cheaper music downloads for other goods and services, such as restaurant meals and live concerts. We call this the **substitution effect** of a change in the price of a good because it occurs when consumers substitute relatively cheaper goods for relatively more expensive ones.

Substitution effect
The tendency of people to substitute cheaper commodities for more expensive commodities.

We assume that people desire a variety of goods and pursue a variety of goals. That means that few, if any, goods are irreplaceable in meeting demand. We are generally able to substitute one product for another to satisfy demand. This is commonly referred to as the **principle of substitution.**

Principle of substitution
The principle that consumers shift away from goods and services that become priced relatively higher in favor of goods and services that are now priced relatively lower.

AN EXAMPLE Let's assume now that there are several goods, not exactly the same, and perhaps even very different from one another, but all contributing to consumers' total utility. If the relative price of one particular good falls, we will substitute in favor of the now lower-priced good and against the other goods that we might have been purchasing. Conversely, if the price of that good rises relative to the price of the other goods, we will substitute in favor of them and not buy as much of the now higher-priced good. An example is the growth in purchases of Internet-ready cellphones, or smartphones, since the mid-2000s. As the relative price of smartphones has plummeted, people have substituted away from other, now relatively more expensive goods in favor of purchasing additional smartphones.

PURCHASING POWER AND REAL INCOME If the price of some item that you purchase goes down while your money income and all other prices stay the same, your ability to purchase goods goes up. That is to say, your effective **purchasing power** has increased, even though your money income has stayed the same. If you purchase 20 gallons of gas a week at \$5 per gallon, your total outlay for gas is \$100. If the price goes down by 50 percent, to \$2.50 per gallon, you would have to spend only \$50 a week to purchase the same number of gallons of gas. If your money income and the prices

Purchasing power
The value of money for buying goods and services. If your money income stays the same but the price of one good that you are buying goes up, your effective purchasing power falls, and vice versa.

of other goods remain the same, it would be possible for you to continue purchasing 20 gallons of gas a week *and* to purchase more of other goods. You will feel richer and will indeed probably purchase more of a number of goods, including perhaps even more gasoline.

The converse will also be true. When the price of one good you are purchasing goes up, without any other change in prices or income, the purchasing power of your income will drop. You will have to reduce your purchases of either the now higher-priced good or other goods (or a combination).

In general, this **real-income effect** is usually quite small. After all, unless we consider broad categories, such as housing or food, a change in the price of one particular item that we purchase will have a relatively small effect on our total purchasing power. Thus, we expect that the substitution effect will be more important than the real-income effect in causing us to purchase more of goods that have become cheaper and less of goods that have become more expensive.

Real-income effect
The change in people's purchasing power that occurs when, other things being constant, the price of one good that they purchase changes. When that price goes up, real income, or purchasing power, falls, and when that price goes down, real income increases.

The Demand Curve Revisited

Linking the law of diminishing marginal utility and the rule of equal marginal utilities per dollar gives us a negative relationship between the quantity demanded of a good or service and its price. As the relative price of digital music downloads goes up, for example, the quantity demanded will fall, and as the relative price of music downloads goes down, the quantity demanded will rise. Figure 20-2 on the facing page showed this demand curve for music downloads. As the price of music downloads falls, the consumer can maximize total utility only by purchasing more music, and vice versa. In other words, the relationship between price and quantity desired is simply a downward-sloping demand curve. Note, though, that this downward-sloping demand curve (the law of demand) is derived under the assumption of constant tastes and incomes. You must remember that we are keeping these important determining variables constant when we look at the relationship between price and quantity demanded.

Marginal Utility, Total Utility, and the Diamond-Water Paradox

Even though water is essential to life and diamonds are not, water is relatively cheap and diamonds are relatively expensive. The economist Adam Smith in 1776 called this the "diamond-water paradox." The paradox is easily understood when we make the distinction between total utility and marginal utility. The total utility of water greatly exceeds the total utility derived from diamonds. What determines the price, though, is what happens on the margin. We have relatively few diamonds, so the marginal utility of the last diamond consumed is relatively high. The opposite is true for water. Total utility does not determine what people are willing to pay for a unit of a particular commodity—marginal utility does. Look at the situation graphically in Figure 20-3 on the next page. We show the demand curve for diamonds, labeled D_{diamonds}. The demand curve for water is labeled D_{water}. We plot quantity in terms of kilograms per unit time period on the horizontal axis. On the vertical axis, we plot price in dollars per kilogram. We use kilograms as our common unit of measurement for water and for diamonds. We could just as well have used pounds or liters.

Notice that the demand for water is many, many times the demand for diamonds (even though we really can't show this in the diagram). We draw the supply curve of water as S_1 at a quantity of Q_{water}. The supply curve for diamonds is given as S_2 at quantity Q_{diamonds}. At the intersection of the supply curve of water with the demand curve of water, the price per kilogram is P_{water}. The intersection of the supply curve of diamonds with the demand curve of diamonds is at P_{diamonds}. Notice that P_{diamonds} exceeds P_{water}. Diamonds sell at a higher price than water.

FIGURE 20-3 The Diamond-Water Paradox

We pick kilograms as a common unit of measurement for both water and diamonds. To demonstrate that the demand for and supply of water are immense, we have put a break in the horizontal quantity axis. Although the demand for water is much greater than the demand for diamonds, the marginal valuation of water is given by the marginal value placed on the *last* unit of water consumed. To find that, we must know the supply of water, which is given as S_1. At that supply, the price of water is P_{water}. But the supply for diamonds is given by S_2. At that supply, the price of diamonds is $P_{diamonds}$. The total valuation that consumers place on water is tremendous relative to the total valuation consumers place on diamonds. What is important for price determination, however, is the marginal valuation, or the marginal utility received.

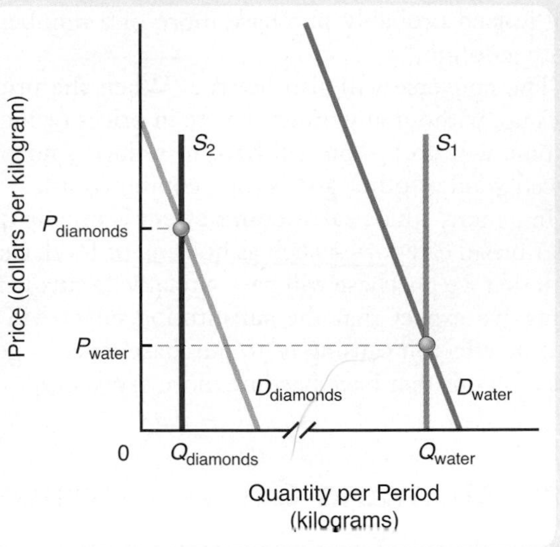

Behavioral Economics and Consumer Choice Theory

Utility analysis has long been appealing to economists because it makes clear predictions about how individuals will adjust their consumption of different goods and services based on the prices of those items and their incomes. Traditionally, another attraction of utility analysis to many economists has been its reliance on the assumption that consumers behave *rationally*, or that they do not intentionally make decisions that would leave them worse off. As we discussed in Chapter 1, proponents of behavioral economics have doubts about the rationality assumption, which causes them to question the utility-based theory of consumer choice.

Does Behavioral Economics Better Predict Consumer Choices?

Advocates of behavioral economics question whether utility theory is supported by the facts, which they argue are better explained by applying the assumption of *bounded rationality*. Recall from Chapter 1 that this assumption states that human limitations prevent people from examining every possible choice available to them and thereby thwart their efforts to effectively pursue long-term personal interests.

As evidence favoring the bounded rationality assumption, proponents of behavioral economics point to real-world examples that they claim violate rationality-based utility theory. For instance, economists have found that when purchasing electric appliances such as refrigerators, people sometimes buy the lowest-priced, energy-inefficient models even though the initial purchase-price savings often fail to compensate for higher future energy costs. There is also evidence that people who live in earthquake- or flood-prone regions commonly fail to purchase sufficient insurance against these events. In addition, experiments have shown that when people are placed in situations in which strong emotions come into play, they may be willing to pay different amounts for items than they would pay in calmer settings.

These and other observed behaviors, behavioral economists suggest, indicate that consumers do not behave as if they are rational. If the rationality assumption does not apply to actual behavior, they argue, it follows that utility-based consumer choice theory cannot, either.

Consumer Choice Theory Remains Alive and Well

In spite of the doubts expressed by proponents of behavioral economics, most economists continue to apply the assumption that people behave *as if* they act rationally with an aim to maximize utility. These economists continue to utilize utility theory because of a fundamental strength of this approach: it yields clear-cut predictions regarding consumer choices.

In contrast, if the rationality assumption is rejected, any number of possible human behaviors might be considered. To proponents of behavioral economics, ambiguities about actual outcomes make the bounded rationality approach to consumer choice more realistic than utility-based consumer choice theory. Nevertheless, a major drawback is that no clearly testable predictions emerge from the many alternative behaviors that people might exhibit if they fail to behave *as if* they are rational.

Certainly, arguments among economists about the "reasonableness" of rational consumers maximizing utility are likely to continue. So far, however, the use of utility-based consumer choice theory has allowed economists to make a wide array of predictions about how consumers respond to changes in prices, incomes, and other factors. In general, these key predictions continue to be supported by the actual choices that consumers make.

QUICK QUIZ **See page 452 for the answers. Review concepts from this section in MyEconLab.**

Each change in price has a **substitution effect.** When the price of a good __________, the consumer __________ in favor of that relatively cheaper good.

Each change in price also has a **real-income effect.** When price __________, the consumer's real purchasing power increases, causing the consumer to purchase __________ of most goods. Assuming that the principle of diminishing marginal utility holds, the demand curve must slope downward.

The price of water is lower than the price of diamonds because people consume __________ water than diamonds, which results in a __________ marginal utility of water compared with the marginal utility of diamonds.

You Are There

Signing Up for "Free" Trial Offers with TrialPay

Alex Rampell operates a Web-based company called TrialPay. He is now in his late 20s, but he started his business while in high school. Rampell and TrialPay offer "freebies"—items obtainable at no explicit charge. Instead of paying for an item, such as a software download, a TrialPay customer agrees to sign up for a trial offer for a product offered by another firm. For instance, TrialPay might provide a "free" copy of a downloadable video game that the customer otherwise would have had to purchase from PopCap Games at a price of $25. To obtain the right to download the video game, the customer may be required to sign up for a "free" trial membership with the movie service Netflix.

Rampell knows that even if the marginal utility that a consumer gets from a package of "freebies" is small, the *effective* price—the dollar value of the time and effort expended at TrialPay's Web page—is also very low. This ensures that the marginal utility per dollar spent will be high enough to make a trial membership part of the consumer optimum for TrialPay's customers. Rampell has convinced Netflix and 7,500 other merchants that many of these consumers are likely to continue buying their products after trying them. Thus, these merchants can anticipate earning future revenues from TrialPay's customers, which is why the merchants are willing to pay fees to TrialPay as compensation for operating its online service.

Critical Analysis Questions

1. Why is the effective price of a TrialPay "freebie" greater than zero?
2. What does Netflix anticipate that TrialPay customers will discover about the marginal utility experienced from trial consumption of Netflix's movie service?

ISSUES & APPLICATIONS

Is the Utility from Using Credit Cards Really Negative?

CONCEPTS APPLIED

- Bounded Rationality
- Utility
- Marginal Utility

According to behavioral economists, a consumer's rationality is bounded, meaning that people often are unable to assess all aspects of choices that they confront. Behavioral economists contend that as a result, people sometimes make near-term decisions that ultimately turn out to reduce their well-being. A good example, the economists suggest, is the decision that many people make to use credit cards.

Credit Cards: Short-Term Gain but Long-Term Pain?

George Loewenstein of Carnegie Mellon University and Ted O'Donoghue of Cornell University realize that using a credit card initially increases a consumer's satisfaction by enabling the consumer to obtain an item immediately. But they note that consumers experience "negative emotion" when it is time to submit payment.

This, they suggest, creates a problem: People use their cards to obtain too many items. Loewenstein and O'Donoghue argue that the solution to this perceived problem is to "ban credit cards as they currently exist."

Assessing the Marginal Utility of Credit Cards

Loewenstein and O'Donoghue contend that the positive utility people derive from using credit cards to obtain immediate use of an item is overwhelmed by a utility decrease from having to give up other items when they must pay their credit-card bill. On *net*, therefore, the utility from credit-card use is negative. Economists refer to negative utility from consuming an item as *disutility*. Goods and services from which people derive disutility are "economic bads"—items that people are better off not consuming. This is the logic that leads Loewenstein and O'Donoghue to propose that the government should prevent anyone from obtaining a credit card.

One difficulty with this analysis is that it assumes that *everyone* who uses a credit card suffers from a bounded rationality problem. Economists have long recognized that many people utilize credit cards as a convenient means of payment and happily pay their bills each month. For these people, credit-card use could be viewed as entirely rational. Another difficulty is that even if bounded rationality prevails, it is unlikely that the disutility from having to give up other items later *always* outweighs the additional utility of immediate access to items obtained using credit cards.

Thus, if the government banned credit cards, a consumer optimum in which positive marginal utility per dollar spent is equalized for all items would no longer include credit-card services among those items. Such a policy would reduce the well-being of people who otherwise could use the cards to generate higher total utility.

For Critical Analysis

1. Why does any effective government prohibition on the sale of a good or service likely result in reduced total utility for at least some people?
2. If credit cards were banned and, as a result, some people's utility dropped while the total utility of others rose, could we necessarily reach any conclusion about whether society as a whole was better off? Explain.

Web Resources

1. To read the analysis provided by Loewenstein and O'Donoghue, go to www.econtoday.com/ch20.
2. For a discussion of proposals to ban credit cards, go to www.econtoday.com/ch20.

Research Project

Suppose that Loewenstein and O'Donoghue are correct that some people derive negative net utility from using a credit card to obtain an item today by having to give up other items later as a result. In addition, however, suppose that other people rationally use credit cards and always derive positive utility from using the cards as a means of payment. Can you suggest any policies that the government might implement that could benefit people suffering from bounded rationality without harming those who do not?

For more questions on this chapter's Issues & Applications, go to **MyEconLab**. In the Study Plan for this chapter, select Section N: News.

myeconlab

Here is what you should know after reading this chapter. **MyEconLab** will help you identify what you know, and where to go when you need to practice.

WHAT YOU SHOULD KNOW		WHERE TO GO TO PRACTICE
Total Utility versus Marginal Utility Total utility is the total satisfaction that an individual derives from consuming a given amount of a good or service during a given period. Marginal utility is the additional satisfaction that a person gains by consuming an additional unit of the good or service.	utility, 436 utility analysis, 436 util, 436 marginal utility, 437 **KEY FIGURE** Figure 20-1, 438	• **MyEconLab** Study Plans 20.1, 20.2 • Audio introduction to Chapter 20 • Animated Figure 20-1 • Economics Video: No Frills Grocery Shopping
The Law of Diminishing Marginal Utility For at least the first unit of consumption of a good or service, a person's total utility increases with increased consumption. Eventually, however, the rate at which an individual's utility rises with greater consumption tends to fall. Thus, marginal utility ultimately declines as the person consumes more and more of the good or service.	diminishing marginal utility, 439	• **MyEconLab** Study Plan 20.3
The Consumer Optimum An individual optimally allocates available income to consumption of all goods and services when the marginal utility per dollar spent on the last unit consumed of each good is equalized. Thus, a consumer optimum occurs when (1) the ratio of the marginal utility derived from an item to the price of that item is equal across all items that the person consumes and (2) when the person spends all available income.	consumer optimum, 440	• **MyEconLab** Study Plan 20.4 • Video: Optimizing Consumption Choices • Economics Video: Cash for Trash • Economics Video: Kraft Leading the Way
The Substitution Effect of a Price Change One effect of a change in the price of a good or service is that the price change induces people to substitute among goods. For example, if the price of a good rises, the individual will tend to consume some other good that has become relatively less expensive as a result. In addition, the individual will tend to reduce consumption of the good whose price increased.	substitution effect, 444 principle of substitution, 444 **KEY FIGURE** Figure 20-2, 444	• **MyEconLab** Study Plan 20.5 • Animated Figure 20-2

(continued)

MyEconLab continued

WHAT YOU SHOULD KNOW		WHERE TO GO TO PRACTICE
The Real-Income Effect of a Price Change If the price of a good increases, a person responds to the loss of purchasing power of available income by reducing purchases of either the now higher-priced good or other goods (or a combination of both of these responses). Normally, we anticipate that the real-income effect is smaller than the substitution effect, so that when the price of a good or service increases, people will purchase more of goods or services that have lower relative prices as a result.	purchasing power, 444 real-income effect, 445 **KEY FIGURES** Figure 20-2, 444 Figure 20-3, 446	• **MyEconLab** Study Plan 20.5 • Animated Figures 20-2, 20-3 • Video: The Substitution Effect and the Real-Income Effect

Log in to MyEconLab, take a chapter test, and get a personalized Study Plan that tells you which concepts you understand and which ones you need to review. From there, MyEconLab will give you further practice, tutorials, animations, videos, and guided solutions.
Log in to www.myeconlab.com

PROBLEMS

All problems are assignable in myeconlab. *Answers to odd-numbered problems appear at the back of the book.*

20-1. The campus pizzeria sells a single pizza for $12. If you order a second pizza, however, the pizzeria charges a price of only $5 for the additional pizza. Explain how an understanding of marginal utility helps to explain the pizzeria's pricing strategy.

20-2. As an individual consumes more units of an item, the person eventually experiences diminishing marginal utility. This means that to increase marginal utility, the person must consume less of an item. Explain the logic of this behavior using the example in Problem 20-1.

20-3. Where possible, complete the missing cells in the table.

Number of Cheese-burgers	Total Utility of Cheese-burgers	Marginal Utility of Cheese-burgers	Bags of French Fries	Total Utility of French Fries	Marginal Utility of French Fries
0	0	—	0	0	—
1	20	—	1	—	10
2	36	—	2	—	8
3	—	12	3	—	2
4	—	8	4	21	—
5	—	4	5	21	—

20-4. From the data in Problem 20-3, if the price of a cheeseburger is $2, the price of a bag of french fries is $1, and you have $6 to spend (and you spend all of it), what is the utility-maximizing combination of cheeseburgers and french fries?

20-5. Return to Problem 20-4. Suppose that the price of cheeseburgers falls to $1. Determine the new utility-maximizing combination of cheeseburgers and french fries.

20-6. Suppose that you observe that total utility rises as more of an item is consumed. What can you say for certain about marginal utility? Can you say for sure that it is rising or falling or that it is positive or negative?

20-7. After monitoring your daily consumption patterns, you determine that your daily consumption of soft drinks is 3 and your daily consumption of tacos is 4 when the prices per unit are 50 cents and $1, respectively. Explain what happens to your consumption bundle, the marginal utility of soft drinks, and the marginal utility of tacos when the price of soft drinks rises to 75 cents.

20-8. At a consumer optimum, for all goods purchased, marginal utility per dollar spent is equalized. A high school student is deciding between attending Western State University and Eastern State University. The student cannot attend both universities simultaneously. Both are fine universities, but the reputation of Western is slightly higher, as is the tuition. Use the rule of consumer optimum to explain how the student will go about deciding which university to attend.

20-9. Consider the movements that take place from one point to the next (*A* to *B* to *C* and so on) along the total utility curve below as the individual successively increases consumption by one more unit, and answer the questions that follow.

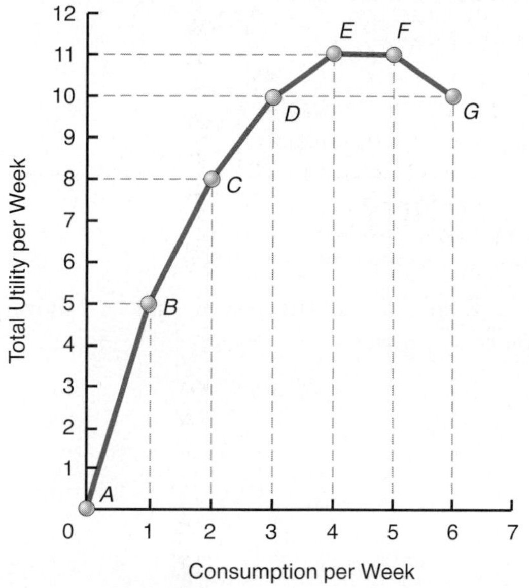

a. Which one-unit increase in consumption from one point to the next along the total utility curve generates the highest marginal utility?

b. Which one-unit increase in consumption from one point to the next along the total utility curve generates zero marginal utility?

c. Which one-unit increase in consumption from one point to the next along the total utility curve generates negative marginal utility?

20-10. Draw a marginal utility curve corresponding to the total utility curve depicted in Problem 20-9.

20-11. Refer to the table on the top of the next column. If the price of a fudge bar is $2, the price of a Popsicle is $1, and a student has $9 to spend, what quantities will she purchase at a consumer optimum?

Quantity of Fudge Bars per Week	Marginal Utility (utils)	Quantity of Popsicles per Week	Marginal Utility (utils)
1	1,200	1	1,700
2	1,000	2	1,400
3	800	3	1,100
4	600	4	800
5	400	5	500
6	100	6	200

20-12. Refer to the following table for a different consumer, and assume that each week this consumer buys only hot dogs and tickets to baseball games. The price of a hot dog is $2, and the price of a baseball game is $60. If the consumer's income is $128 per week, what quantity of each item will he purchase each week at a consumer optimum?

Quantity of Hot Dogs per Week	Total Utility (utils)	Quantity of Baseball Games per Week	Total Utility (utils)
1	40	1	400
2	60	2	700
3	76	3	850
4	86	4	950
5	91	5	1,000
6	93	6	1,025

20-13. In Problem 20-12, if the consumer's income rises to $190 per week, what new quantities characterize the new consumer optimum?

20-14. At a consumer optimum involving goods A and B, the marginal utility of good A is twice the marginal utility of good B. The price of good B is $3.50. What is the price of good A?

20-15. At a consumer optimum involving goods X and Y, the marginal utility of good X equals 3 utils. The price of good Y is three times the price of good X. What is the marginal utility of good Y?

ECONOMICS ON THE NET

Book Prices and Consumer Optimum This application helps you see how a consumer optimum can be attained when one engages in Internet shopping.

Title: Amazon.com Web site

Navigation: Go to **www.econtoday.com/ch20** to start at Amazon.com's home page. Click on the *Books* tab.

Application

1. At the top of the page, find the list of the top books in the Amazon.com "Bestsellers" section. Click on the number one book. Record the price of the book. Then locate the Search window. Type in *Economics Today*. Scroll down until you find your class text listed. Record the price.
2. Suppose you are an individual who has purchased both the number one book and *Economics Today* through Amazon.com. Describe how economic analysis would explain this choice.
3. Using the prices you recorded for the two books, write an equation that relates the prices and your marginal utilities of the two books. Use this equation to explain verbally how you might quantify the magnitude of your marginal utility for the number one book relative to your marginal utility for your class text.

For Group Study and Analysis Discuss what changes might occur if the price of the number one book were lowered but the student remains enrolled in this course. Discuss what changes might take place regarding the consumer optimum if the student were not enrolled in this course.

ANSWERS TO QUICK QUIZZES

p. 439: (i) Utility; (ii) utils; (iii) Total . . . Marginal

p. 443: (i) less; (ii) equating . . . optimum; (iii) increase . . . decrease

p. 447: (i) falls . . . substitutes; (ii) falls . . . more; (iii) more . . . lower

More Advanced Consumer Choice Theory

APPENDIX F

It is possible to analyze consumer choice verbally, as we did for the most part in Chapter 20. The theory of diminishing marginal utility can be fairly well accepted on intuitive grounds and by introspection. If we want to be more formal and perhaps more elegant in our theorizing, however, we can translate our discussion into a graphical analysis with what we call *indifference curves* and the *budget constraint*. Here we discuss these terms and their relationship and demonstrate consumer equilibrium in geometric form.

On Being Indifferent

What does it mean to be indifferent? It usually means that you don't care one way or the other about something—you are equally disposed to either of two alternatives. With this interpretation in mind, we will turn to two choices, viewing films at theaters and consuming fast-food meals. In panel (a) of Figure F-1 below, we show several combinations of fast food and movie tickets per week that a representative consumer considers equally satisfactory. That is to say, for each combination, *A*, *B*, *C*, and *D*, this consumer will have exactly the same level of total utility.

The simple numerical example that we have used happens to concern the consumption of fast-food meals and visits to movie theaters (both of which we assume this consumer enjoys) per week. This example is used to illustrate general features of indifference curves and related analytical tools that are necessary for deriving the demand curve. Obviously, we could have used any two commodities. Just remember that we are using a *specific* example to illustrate a *general* analysis.

We plot these combinations graphically in panel (b) of Figure F-1, with movie tickets per week on the horizontal axis and fast-food meals per week on the vertical

FIGURE F-1 Combinations That Yield Equal Levels of Satisfaction

A, *B*, *C*, and *D* represent combinations of fast-food meals and movie tickets per week that give an equal level of satisfaction to this consumer. In other words, the consumer is indifferent among these four combinations.

Panel (a)

Combination	Fast-Food Meals per Week	Movie Tickets per Week
A	7	1
B	4	2
C	2	3
D	1	4

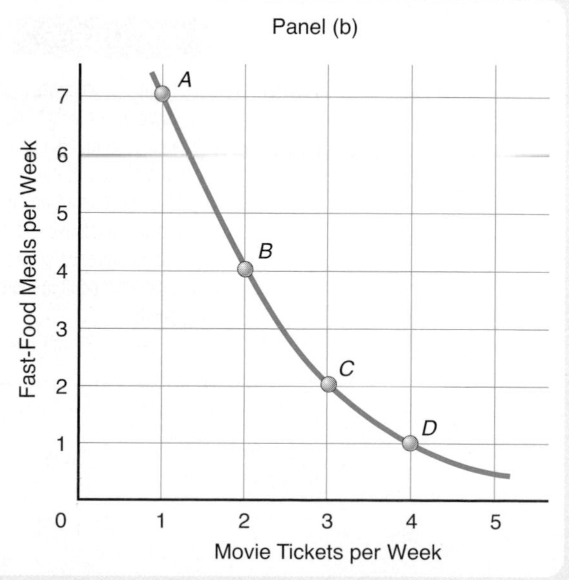

axis. These are our consumer's indifference combinations—the consumer finds each combination as acceptable as the others. These combinations lie along a smooth curve that is known as the consumer's **indifference curve.** Along the indifference curve, every combination of the two goods in question yields the same level of satisfaction. Every point along the indifference curve is equally desirable to the consumer. For example, one fast-food meal per week and four movie tickets per week will give our representative consumer exactly the same total satisfaction as consuming four fast-food meals per week and viewing two movies per week.

Indifference curve
A curve composed of a set of consumption alternatives, each of which yields the same total amount of satisfaction.

Properties of Indifference Curves

Indifference curves have special properties relating to their slope and shape.

Downward Slope

The indifference curve shown in panel (b) of Figure F-1 on the preceding page slopes downward. That is, the indifference curve has a negative slope. Now consider Figure F-2 below. Here we show two points, *A* and *B*. Point *A* represents four fast-food meals per week and two movie tickets per week. Point *B* represents five fast-food meals per week and six movie viewings per week. Clearly, *B* is always preferred to *A* for a consumer who enjoys both fast-food meals and movies, because *B* represents more of everything. If *B* is always preferred to *A*, it is impossible for points *A* and *B* to be on the same indifference curve because the definition of the indifference curve is a set of combinations of two goods that are preferred equally.

Curvature

The indifference curve that we have drawn in panel (b) of Figure F-1 on the previous page is special. Notice that it is curved. Why didn't we just draw a straight line, as we have usually done for a demand curve?

IMAGINING A STRAIGHT-LINE INDIFFERENCE CURVE To find out why we don't posit straight-line indifference curves, consider the implications. We show such a straight-line indifference curve in Figure F-3 on the facing page. Start at point *A*. The consumer has no movie tickets and five fast-food meals per week. Now the consumer wishes to go to point *B*. She is willing to give up only one fast-food meal in order to

FIGURE F-2 Indifference Curves: Impossibility of an Upward Slope

Point *B* represents a consumption of more movie tickets per week and more fast-food meals per week than point *A*. *B* is always preferred to *A*. Therefore, *A* and *B* cannot be on the same *positively* sloped indifference curve. An indifference curve shows *equally preferred* combinations of the two goods.

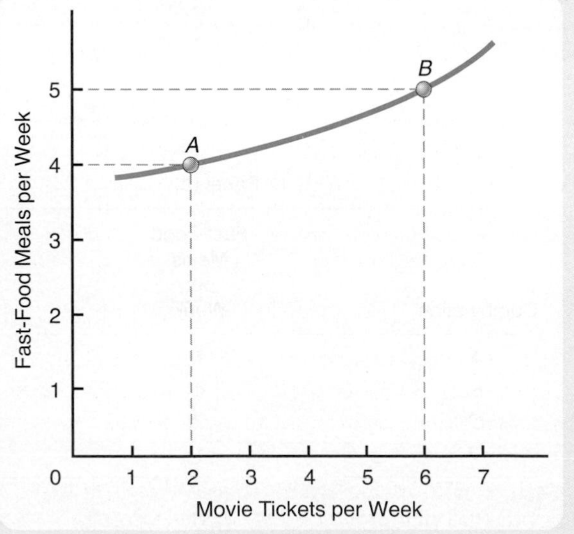

FIGURE F-3 Implications of a Straight-Line Indifference Curve

This straight-line indifference curve indicates that the consumer will always be willing to give up the same number of fast-food meals to get one more movie ticket per week. For example, the consumer at point *A* consumes five fast-food meals and views no movies at theaters per week. She is willing to give up one fast-food meal in order to get one movie ticket per week. At point *C*, however, the consumer has only one fast-food meal and views four movies per week. Because of the straight-line indifference curve, this consumer is willing to give up the last fast-food meal in order to get one more movie ticket per week, even though she already has four.

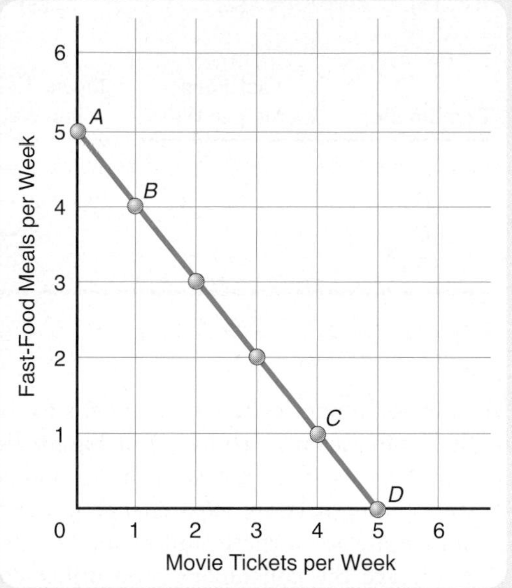

get one ticket to a movie. Now let's assume that the consumer is at point *C*, consuming one fast-food meal per week and viewing four movies at a theater per week. If the consumer wants to go to point *D*, she is again willing to give up one fast-food meal in order to get one more movie ticket per week.

In other words, no matter how many times the consumer consumes a fast-food meal, she is willing to give up one fast-food meal to get one movie viewing per week—which does not seem plausible. Doesn't it make sense to hypothesize that the more times the consumer consumes fast-food meals per week, the less she will value an *additional* fast-food meal that week? Presumably, when the consumer has five fast-food meals and no movie tickets per week, she should be willing to give up *more than* one fast-food meal in order to get one movie ticket. Therefore, a straight-line indifference curve as shown in Figure F-3 above no longer seems plausible.

CONVEXITY OF THE INDIFFERENCE CURVE In mathematical jargon, an indifference curve is convex with respect to the origin. Let's look at this in panel (a) of Figure F-1 on page 453. Starting with combination *A*, the consumer has one movie ticket but seven fast-food meals per week. To remain indifferent, the consumer would have to be willing to give up three fast-food meals to obtain one more ticket to a movie (as shown in combination *B*). To go from combination *C* to combination *D*, however, notice that the consumer would have to be willing to give up only one fast-food meal for an additional movie ticket per week. The quantity of the substitute considered acceptable changes as the rate of consumption of the original item changes.

Consequently, the indifference curve in panel (b) of Figure F-1 on page 453 will be convex when viewed from the origin.

The Marginal Rate of Substitution

Instead of using marginal utility, we can talk in terms of the *marginal rate of substitution* between fast-food meals and movie tickets per week. We can formally define the consumer's marginal rate of substitution as follows:

The marginal rate of substitution is equal to the change in the quantity of one good that just offsets a one-unit change in the consumption of another good, such that total satisfaction remains constant.

TABLE F-1

Calculating the Marginal Rate of Substitution

As we move from combination *A* to combination *B*, we are still on the same indifference curve. To stay on that curve, the number of fast-food meals decreases by three and the number of movie tickets increases by one. The marginal rate of substitution is 3:1. A three-unit decrease in fast-food meals requires an increase in one movie ticket to leave the consumer's total utility unaltered.

(1) Combination	(2) Fast-Food Meals per Week	(3) Movie Tickets per Week	(4) Marginal Rate of Substitution of Fast-Food Meals for Movie Tickets
A	7	1	
			3:1
B	4	2	
			2:1
C	2	3	
			1:1
D	1	4	

We can see numerically what happens to the marginal rate of substitution in our example if we rearrange panel (a) of Figure F-1 on page 453 into Table F-1 above. Here we show fast-food meals in the second column and movie tickets in the third. Now we ask the question, what change in the number of movie tickets per week will just compensate for a three-unit change in the consumption of fast-food meals per week and leave the consumer's total utility constant? The movement from *A* to *B* increases the number of weekly movie tickets by one. Here the marginal rate of substitution is 3:1—a three-unit decrease in fast-food meals requires an increase of one movie ticket to leave the consumer's total utility unaltered. Thus, the consumer values the three fast-food meals as the equivalent of one movie ticket.

We do this for the rest of the table and find that as fast-food meals decrease, the marginal rate of substitution goes from 3:1 to 2:1 to 1:1. The marginal rate of substitution of fast-food meals for movie tickets per week falls as the consumer views more films at theaters. That is, the consumer values successive movie viewings less and less in terms of fast-food meals. The first movie ticket is valued at three fast-food meals. The last (fourth) movie ticket is valued at only one fast-food meal. The fact that the marginal rate of substitution falls is sometimes called the *law of substitution*.

In geometric language, the slope of the consumer's indifference curve (actually, the negative of the slope of the indifference curve) measures the consumer's marginal rate of substitution.

The Indifference Map

Let's now consider the possibility of having both more movie tickets *and* more fast-food meals per week. When we do this, we can no longer stay on the same indifference curve that we drew in Figure F-1 on page 453. That indifference curve was drawn for equally satisfying combinations of movie tickets and fast-food meals per week. If the individual can now obtain more of both, a new indifference curve will have to be drawn, above and to the right of the one shown in panel (b) of Figure F-1. Alternatively, if the individual faces the possibility of having less of both movie tickets and fast-food meals per week, an indifference curve will have to be drawn below and to the left of the one in panel (b) of Figure F-1. We can map out a whole set of indifference curves corresponding to these possibilities.

Figure F-4 at the top of the facing page shows three possible indifference curves. Indifference curves that are higher than others necessarily imply that for every given quantity of one good, more of the other good can be obtained on a higher indifference curve. Looked at one way, if one goes from curve I_1 to I_2, it is possible to view the same number of movies *and* be able to consume more fast-food meals each week. This is shown as a movement from point *A* to point *B* in Figure F-4. We could do it the other way. When we move from a lower to a higher indifference curve, it is possible to consume the same number of fast-food meals *and* to view more movies each week. Thus, the higher an indifference curve is for a consumer, the greater that consumer's total level of satisfaction.

FIGURE F-4 A Set of Indifference Curves

An infinite number of indifference curves can be drawn. We show three possible ones. Realize that a higher indifference curve represents the possibility of higher rates of consumption of both goods. Hence, a higher indifference curve is preferred to a lower one because more is preferred to less. Look at points *A* and *B*. Point *B* represents more fast-food meals than point *A*. Therefore, bundles on indifference curve I_2 have to be preferred over bundles on I_1 because the number of tickets for movie viewings per week is the same at points *A* and *B*.

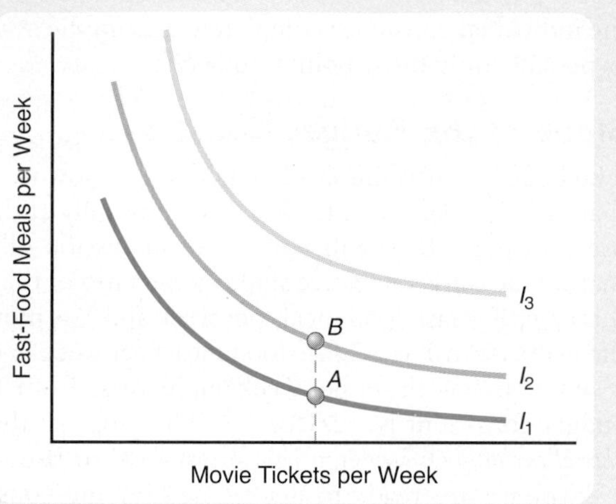

The Budget Constraint

Our problem here is to find out how to maximize consumer satisfaction. To do so, we must consult not only our *preferences*—given by indifference curves—but also our *market opportunities*, which are given by our available income and prices, called our **budget constraint.** We might want more of everything, but for any given budget constraint, we have to make choices, or trade-offs, among possible goods. Everyone has a budget constraint. That is, everyone faces a limited consumption potential. How do we show this graphically? We must find the prices of the goods in question and determine the maximum consumption of each allowed by our budget.

Budget constraint
All of the possible combinations of goods that can be purchased (at fixed prices) with a specific budget.

For example, let's assume that there is a $5 price for each fast-food meal and that a ticket to a movie costs $10. Let's also assume that our representative consumer has a total budget of $30 per week. What is the maximum number of fast-food meals this individual can consume? Six. And the maximum number of films per week she can view? Three. So now, as shown in Figure F-5 below, we have two points on our budget line, which is sometimes called the *consumption possibilities curve*. These anchor points of the budget line are obtained by dividing money income by the price of each product. The first point is at *b* on the vertical axis. The second point is at *b′* on the horizontal axis. The budget line is linear because prices are constant.

FIGURE F-5 The Budget Constraint

The line *bb′* represents this individual's budget constraint. Assuming that meals at fast-food restaurants cost $5 each, movie tickets cost $10 each, and the individual has a budget of $30 per week, a maximum of six fast-food meals or three movie tickets can be bought each week. These two extreme points are connected to form the budget constraint. All combinations within the colored area and on the budget constraint line are feasible.

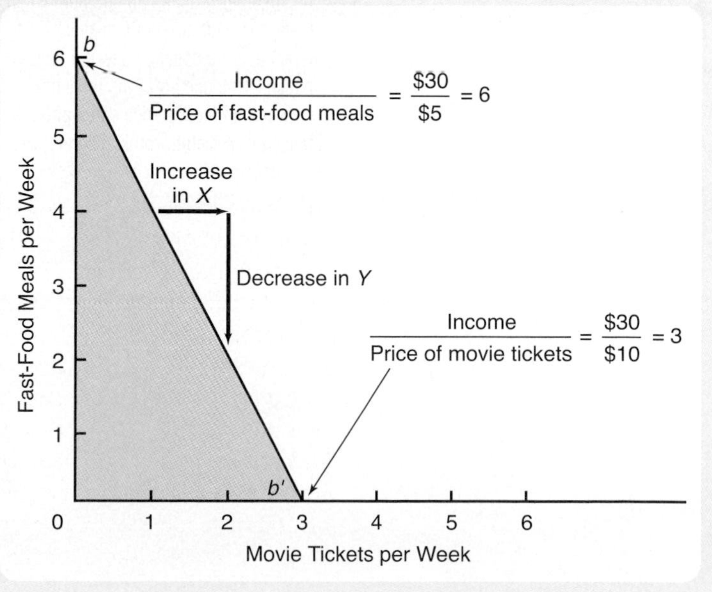

Any combination along line *bb′* is possible; in fact, any combination in the colored area is possible. We will assume, however, that there are sufficient goods available that the individual consumer completely uses up the available budget, and we will consider as possible only those points along *bb′*.

Slope of the Budget Constraint

The budget constraint is a line that slopes downward from left to right. The slope of that line has a special meaning. Look carefully at the budget line in Figure F-5 on the previous page. Remember from our discussion of graphs in Appendix A on page 21 that we measure a negative slope by the ratio of the decrease in Y over the run in X. In this case, Y is fast-food meals per week and X is movie tickets per week. In Figure F-5, the decrease in Y is -2 fast-food meals per week (a drop from 4 to 2) for an increase in X of one movie ticket per week (an increase from 1 to 2). Therefore, the slope of the budget constraint is $-2/1$ or -2. This slope of the budget constraint represents the *rate of exchange* between meals at fast-food restaurants and tickets to movies.

Now we are ready to determine how the consumer achieves the optimum consumption rate.

Consumer Optimum Revisited

Consumers will try to attain the highest level of total utility possible, given their budget constraints. How can this be shown graphically? We draw a set of indifference curves similar to those in Figure F-4 on the preceding page, and we bring in reality—the budget constraint *bb′*. Both are drawn in Figure F-6 below. Because a higher level of total satisfaction is represented by a higher indifference curve, we know that the consumer will strive to be on the highest indifference curve possible. The consumer cannot get to indifference curve I_3, however, because the budget will be exhausted before any combination of fast-food meals and movie tickets represented on indifference curve I_3 is attained. This consumer can maximize total utility, subject to the budget constraint, only by being at point E on indifference curve I_2 because here the consumer's income is just being exhausted. Mathematically, point E is called the *tangency point* of the curve I_2 to the straight line *bb′*.

Go to www.econtoday.com/ch20 for a numerical example illustrating the consumer optimum.

Consumer optimum is achieved when the marginal rate of substitution (which is subjective) is just equal to the feasible rate of exchange between meals at fast-food restaurants and tickets to movies. This rate is the ratio of the two prices of the goods

FIGURE F-6 Consumer Optimum

A consumer reaches an optimum when he or she ends up on the highest indifference curve possible, given a limited budget. This occurs at the tangency between an indifference curve and the budget constraint. In this diagram, the tangency is at *E*.

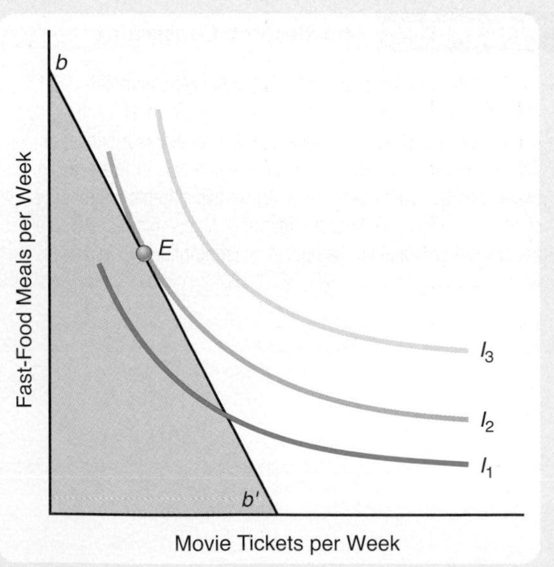

involved. It is represented by the absolute value of the slope of the budget constraint (i.e., ignoring the negative signs). At point *E*, the point of tangency between indifference curve I_2 and budget constraint *bb*′, the rate at which the consumer wishes to substitute fast-food meals for movie tickets (the numerical value of the slope of the indifference curve) is just equal to the rate at which the consumer *can* substitute fast-food meals for tickets to movies (the slope of the budget line).

Deriving the Demand Curve

We are now in a position to derive the demand curve using indifference curve analysis. In panel (a) of Figure F-7 below, we show what happens when the price of tickets to movies decreases, holding both the price of meals at fast-food restaurants and income constant. If the price of movie tickets decreases, the budget line rotates from *bb*′ to *bb*″. The two optimum points are given by the tangency at the highest indifference curve that just touches those two budget lines. This is at *E* and *E*′. But those two points give us two price-quantity pairs. At point *E*, the price of movie tickets

FIGURE F-7 Deriving the Demand Curve

In panel (a), we show the effects of a decrease in the price of movie tickets from $10 to $5. At $10, the highest indifference curve touches the budget line *bb*′ at point *E*. The number of movies viewed is two. We transfer this combination—price, $10; quantity demanded, 2—down to panel (b). Next we decrease the price of movie tickets to $5. This generates a new budget line, or constraint, which is *bb*″. Consumer optimum is now at *E*′. The optimum quantity of movie tickets demanded at a price of $5 is five. We transfer this point—price, $5; quantity demanded, 5—down to panel (b). When we connect these two points, we have a demand curve, *D*, for tickets to movies.

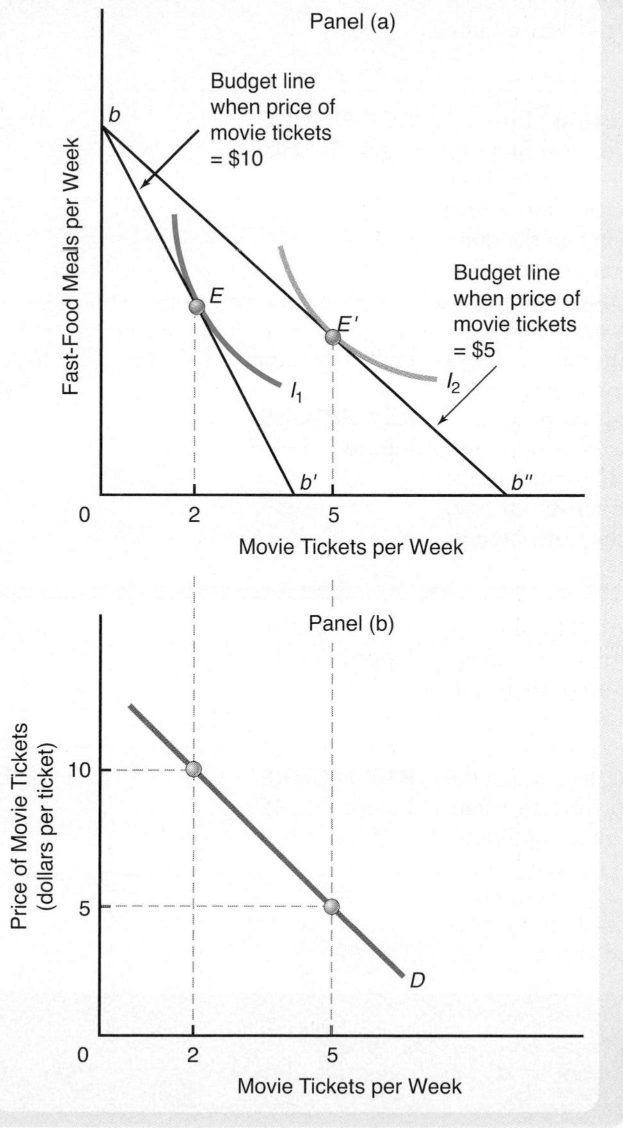

is \$10; the quantity demanded is 2. Thus, we have one point that we can transfer to panel (b) of Figure F-7 on the preceding page. At point E', we have another price-quantity pair. The price has fallen to \$5, and the quantity demanded has increased to 5. We therefore transfer this other point to panel (b). When we connect these two points (and all the others in between), we derive the demand curve for tickets to movies, which slopes downward.

Here is what you should know after reading this appendix. **MyEconLab** will help you identify what you know, and where to go when you need to practice.

WHAT YOU SHOULD KNOW		WHERE TO GO TO PRACTICE
On Being Indifferent Along an indifference curve, the consumer experiences equal levels of satisfaction. That is to say, along any indifference curve, every combination of the two goods in question yields exactly the same level of satisfaction.	indifference curve, 454	• **MyEconLab** Study Plan 20.8
Properties of Indifferent Curves Indifference curves typically slope downward and are usually convex to the origin.		• **MyEconLab** Study Plan 20.9
The Marginal Rate of Substitution To measure the marginal rate of substitution, we find out how much of one good has to be given up in order to allow the consumer to consume one more unit of the other good while still remaining on the same indifference curve. The marginal rate of substitution falls as one moves down an indifference curve.	**KEY FIGURE** Figure F-1, 453	• **MyEconLab** Study Plan 20.10
The Budget Constraint Indifference curves represent preferences. A budget constraint represents opportunities—how much can be purchased with a given level of income. Consumer optimum is obtained when the highest feasible indifference curve is just tangent to the budget constraint line. At that point, the consumer reaches the highest feasible indifference curve.	budget constraint, 457 **KEY FIGURE** Figure F-5, 457	• **MyEconLab** Study Plans 20.9, 20.10, 20.11, 20.12
Slope of the Budget Constraint The slope of the budget constraint is the rate of exchange between two goods, which is the ratio of their dollar prices.	**KEY FIGURE** Figure F-5, 457	• **MyEconLab** Study Plan 20.10
Deriving the Demand Curve A decrease in the price of an item causes the budget line to rotate outward. This generates a new consumer optimum, at which the individual chooses to consume more units of the item. Hence, a decrease in price generates an increase in quantity demanded, or a movement down along a derived demand curve.	**KEY FIGURE** Figure F-7, 459	• **MyEconLab** Study Plan 20.13

Log in to MyEconLab, take an appendix test, and get a personalized Study Plan that tells you which concepts you understand and which ones you need to review. From there, MyEconLab will give you further practice, tutorials, animations, videos, and guided solutions. Log in to www.myeconlab.com

PROBLEMS

All problems are assignable in myeconlab. *Answers to odd-numbered problems appear at the back of the book.*

F-1. Consider the indifference curve illustrated in Figure F-1 on page 453. Explain, in economic terms, why the curve is convex to the origin.

F-2. Your classmate tells you that he is indifferent between three soft drinks and two hamburgers or two soft drinks and three hamburgers.

a. Draw a rough diagram of an indifference curve containing your classmate's consumption choices.

b. Suppose that your classmate states that he is also indifferent between two soft drinks and three hamburgers or one soft drink and four hamburgers, but that he prefers three soft drinks and two hamburgers to one soft drink and four hamburgers. Use your diagram from part (a) to reason out whether he can have these preferences.

F-3. The following table represents Sue's preferences for bottled water and soft drinks, the combination of which yields the same level of utility.

Combination of Bottled Water and Soft Drinks	Bottled Water per Month	Soft Drinks per Month
A	5	11
B	10	7
C	15	4
D	20	2
E	25	1

Calculate Sue's marginal rate of substitution of soft drinks for bottled water at each rate of consumption of water (or soft drinks). Relate the marginal rate of substitution to marginal utility.

F-4. Using the information provided in Problem F-3, illustrate Sue's indifference curve, with water on the horizontal axis and soft drinks on the vertical axis.

F-5. Sue's monthly budget for bottled water and soft drinks is $23. The price of bottled water is $1 per bottle, and the price of soft drinks is $2 per bottle. Calculate the slope of Sue's budget constraint. Given this information and the information provided in Problem F-3, find the combination of goods that satisfies Sue's utility maximization problem in light of her budget constraint.

F-6. Using the indifference curve diagram you constructed in Problem F-4, add in Sue's budget constraint using the information in Problem F-5. Illustrate the utility-maximizing combination of bottled water and soft drinks.

F-7. Suppose that at a higher satisfaction level than in Problem F-3, Sue's constant-utility preferences are as shown in the table below. Calculate the slope of Sue's new budget constraint using the information provided in Problem F-5. Supposing now that the price of a soft drink falls to $1, find the combination of goods that satisfies Sue's utility maximization problem in light of her budget constraint.

Combination of Bottled Water and Soft Drinks	Bottled Water per Month	Soft Drinks per Month
A	5	22
B	10	14
C	15	8
D	20	4
E	25	2

F-8. Illustrate Sue's new budget constraint and indifference curve in a diagram from the data in Problem F-3. Illustrate also the utility-maximizing combination of goods.

F-9. Given your answers to Problems F-5 and F-7, are Sue's preferences for soft drinks consistent with the law of demand?

F-10. Using your answer to Problem F-8, draw Sue's demand curve for soft drinks.

21

Rents, Profits, and the Financial Environment of Business

The Dow Jones Industrial Average (DJIA) is a commonly utilized measure of the average prices of U.S. *stocks,* which are shares of ownership in U.S. corporations. In early October 2007, the DJIA had a value exceeding 14,000. Just 17 months later, the value of the DJIA was close to 6,000. Overall, average U.S. stock prices dropped by about 57 percent during this period, an eerie parallel to the aftermath of the Great Crash of 1929, when average stock prices also plummeted by about 57 percent within 17 months. Was the meltdown in stock prices after October 2007 ultimately as substantial as the decline over the same period after the 1929 crash? Before you can consider determinants of declines in prices of stocks and other types of securities, such as bonds, you must first learn about interest rates and discounted present value. These concepts are key topics of this chapter.

LEARNING OBJECTIVES

After reading this chapter, you should be able to:

- Understand the concept of economic rent
- Distinguish among the main organizational forms of business and explain the chief advantages and disadvantages of each
- Explain the difference between accounting profits and economic profits
- Discuss how the interest rate performs a key role in allocating resources
- Calculate the present discounted value of a payment to be received at a future date
- Identify the main sources of corporate funds and differentiate between stocks and bonds

MyEconLab helps you master each objective and study more efficiently. See end of chapter for details.

during 2008, there were 42 days when average prices of shares of stock in U.S. companies gained or lost more than 3 percent of their value? As a consequence, there was greater volatility in U.S. stock prices in 2008 than in any other year since 1933. Between October 9, 2007, and March 9, 2009—with all of 2008 sandwiched within the intervening period—a key index measure of U.S. stock prices lost more than 50 percent of its value. Of course, during one particularly infamous interval, the stock market crash of 1929, the average level of stock prices declined by about 50 percent much more rapidly—within a period encompassing less than two months.

How do markets for shares of stock function? What are shares of stock? In this chapter, you will learn the answers to these questions. First, however, you must learn about the important function of *economic rent.*

Did You Know That ?

Economic Rent

When you hear the term *rent*, you are accustomed to having it mean the payment made to property owners for the use of land or dwellings. The term *rent* has a different meaning in economics. **Economic rent** is payment to the owner of a resource in excess of its *opportunity cost*—that is, the minimum payment that would be necessary to call forth production of that amount (and quality) of the resource.

Economic rent
A payment for the use of any resource over and above its opportunity cost.

Determining Land Rent

Economists originally used the term *rent* to designate payment for the use of land. What was thought to be important about land was that its supply was completely inelastic. That is, the supply curve for land was thought to be a vertical line, so that no matter what the prevailing market price for land, the quantity supplied would remain the same.

The concept of economic rent is associated with the British economist David Ricardo (1772–1823). Here is how Ricardo analyzed economic rent for land. He first simplified his model by assuming that all land is equally productive. Then Ricardo assumed that the quantity of land in a country is *fixed* so that land's opportunity cost is equal to zero. Graphically, then, in terms of supply and demand, we draw the supply curve for land vertically (zero price elasticity). In Figure 21-1 below, the supply curve of land is represented by S. If the demand curve is D_1, it intersects the supply curve, S, at price P_1. The entire amount of revenues obtained, $P_1 \times Q_1$, is labeled "Economic rent." If the demand for land increases to D_2, the equilibrium price will rise to P_2. Additions to economic rent are labeled "More economic rent." Notice that the

FIGURE 21-1 Economic Rent

If indeed the supply curve of land were completely price-inelastic in the long run, it would be depicted by S. The opportunity cost of land is zero, so the same quantity of land is forthcoming at any constant-quality price. Thus, at the quantity in existence, Q_1, any and all revenues are economic rent. If demand is D_1, the price will be P_1. If demand is D_2, price will rise to P_2. Economic rent would be $P_1 \times Q_1$ and $P_2 \times Q_1$, respectively.

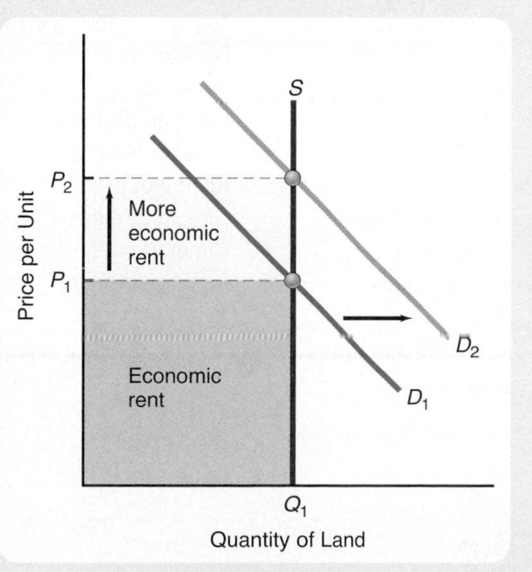

quantity of land remains insensitive to the change in price. Another way of stating this is that the supply curve is perfectly inelastic.

Economic Rent to Labor

Land and natural resources are not the only factors of production to which the analysis of economic rent can be applied. In fact, the analysis is probably more often applicable to labor. Here is a list of people who provide different labor services, some of whom probably receive large amounts of economic rent:

- Professional sports superstars
- Rock stars
- Movie stars
- World-class models
- Successful inventors and innovators
- World-famous opera stars

Just apply the definition of economic rent to the phenomenal earnings that these people make. They would undoubtedly work for considerably less than they earn. Therefore, much of their earnings constitutes economic rent (but not all, as we shall see). Economic rent occurs because specific resources cannot be replicated exactly. No one can duplicate today's most highly paid entertainment figures, and therefore they receive economic rent. How much do top performers earn?

EXAMPLE Do Entertainment Superstars Make Super Economic Rents?

Superstars certainly do well financially. Table 21-1 below shows the earnings of selected individuals in the entertainment industry as estimated by *Forbes* magazine. Earnings are totaled for a two-year period. How much of these earnings can be called economic rent? The question is not easy to answer, because an entertainment newcomer would almost certainly work for much less than she or he earns, implying that the newcomer is making high economic rent. The same cannot necessarily be said for entertainers who have been raking in millions for years. They probably have very high accumulated wealth and also a more jaded outlook about their work. It is therefore not clear how much they would work if they were not offered those huge sums of income.

FOR CRITICAL ANALYSIS

Even if some superstar entertainers would work for less, what forces cause them to make so much income anyway?

TABLE 21-1

Superstar Earnings

Name	Occupation	Two-Year Earnings
Oprah Winfrey	Talk show host and owner, author	$315,000,000
James Cameron	Director, producer	210,000,000
U2	Rock group	130,000,000
Tyler Perry	Director, producer	125,000,000
Michael Bay	Director, producer	120,000,000
AC/DC	Rock group	114,000,000
Jerry Bruckheimer	Director, producer	100,000,000
Steven Spielberg	Director, producer	100,000,000
George Lucas	Director, producer	95,000,000
Beyoncé Knowles	Musician	87,000,000

Source: Forbes, 2010.

Economic Rent and the Allocation of Resources

Suppose that a highly paid movie star would make the same number of movies at half his or her current annual earnings. Why, then, does the superstar receive a higher income? Look again at Figure 21-1 on page 463, but substitute *entertainment activities of the superstars* for the word *land*. The high "price" received by the superstar is due to the demand for his or her services. If Anne Hathaway announces that she will work for a million dollars per movie and do two movies a year, how is she going to know which production company values her services the most highly? Hathaway and other movie stars let the market decide where their resources should be used. In this sense, we can say the following:

Economic rent allocates resources to their highest-valued use.

Otherwise stated, economic rent directs resources to the people who can use them most efficiently.

QUICK QUIZ **See page 482 for the answers. Review concepts from this section in MyEconLab.**

Economic rent is defined as payment for a factor of production that is completely __________ in supply.	Economic rent __________ resources to their __________-valued use.

Firms and Profits

Firms or businesses, like individuals, seek to earn the highest possible returns. We define a **firm** as follows:

A firm is an organization that brings together factors of production—labor, land, physical capital, human capital, and entrepreneurial skill—to produce a product or service that it hopes to sell at a profit.

Firm
A business organization that employs resources to produce goods or services for profit. A firm normally owns and operates at least one "plant" or facility in order to produce.

A typical firm will have an organizational structure consisting of an entrepreneur, managers, and workers. The entrepreneur is the person who takes the risks, mainly of losing his or her personal wealth. In compensation, the entrepreneur will get any profits that are made. Recall from Chapter 2 that entrepreneurs take the initiative in combining land, labor, and capital to produce a good or a service. Entrepreneurs are the ones who innovate in the form of new production and new products. The entrepreneur also decides whom to hire to manage the firm. Some economists maintain that the true quality of an entrepreneur becomes evident with his or her selection of managers.

Managers, in turn, decide who else should be hired and fired and how the business should be operated on a day-to-day basis. The workers ultimately use the other inputs to produce the products or services that are being sold by the firm. Workers and managers are paid contractual wages. They receive a specified amount of income for a specified time period. Entrepreneurs are not paid contractual wages. They receive no reward specified in advance. The entrepreneurs make profits if there are any, for profits accrue to those who are willing to take risks. (Because the entrepreneur gets only what is left over after all expenses are paid, she or he is often referred to as a *residual claimant*. The entrepreneur lays claim to the residual—whatever is left.)

The Legal Organization of Firms

We all know that firms differ from one another. Some sell frozen yogurt, others make automobiles. Some advertise, some do not. Some have annual sales of a few thousand dollars, others have sales in the billions of dollars. The list of differences is probably endless. Yet for all this diversity, the basic organization of *all* firms can be thought of in terms of a few simple structures, the most important of which are the proprietorship, the partnership, and the corporation.

TABLE 21-2

Forms of Business Organization

Type of Firm	Percentage of U.S. Firms	Average Size (annual sales in dollars)	Percentage of Total Business Revenues
Proprietorship	71.5	58,000	4.1
Partnership	9.5	1,402,000	13.1
Corporation	19.0	4,463,000	82.8

Sources: U.S. Bureau of the Census; *2010 Statistical Abstract.*

Proprietorship
A business owned by one individual who makes the business decisions, receives all the profits, and is legally responsible for the debts of the firm.

PROPRIETORSHIP The most common form of business organization is the **proprietorship.** As shown in Table 21-2 above, close to 72 percent of all firms in the United States are proprietorships. Each is owned by a single individual who makes the business decisions, receives all the profits, and is legally responsible for all the debts of the firm. Although proprietorships are numerous, they are generally rather small businesses, with annual sales averaging about $58,000. For this reason, even though there are more than 22 million proprietorships in the United States, they account for only 4.1 percent of all business revenues.

Advantages of Proprietorships. Proprietorships offer several advantages as a form of business organization. First, they are *easy to form and to dissolve*. In the simplest case, all one must do to start a business is to start working. To dissolve the firm, one simply stops working. Second, *all decision-making power resides with the sole proprietor*. No partners, shareholders, or board of directors need be consulted. The third advantage is that its *profit is taxed only once*. All profit is treated by law as the net income of the proprietor and as such is subject only to personal income taxation.

Unlimited liability
A legal concept whereby the personal assets of the owner of a firm can be seized to pay off the firm's debts.

Disadvantages of Proprietorships. The most important disadvantage of a proprietorship is that the proprietor faces **unlimited liability** *for the debts of the firm*. This means that the owner is personally responsible for all of the firm's debts. The second disadvantage is that many lenders are reluctant to lend large sums to a proprietorship. Consequently, a proprietorship may have a *limited ability to raise funds*, to expand the business or even simply to help it survive bad times. The third disadvantage of proprietorships is that they normally *end with the death of the proprietor*, which creates added uncertainty for prospective lenders or employees.

Partnership
A business owned by two or more joint owners, or partners, who share the responsibilities and the profits of the firm and are individually liable for all the debts of the partnership.

PARTNERSHIP The second important form of business organization is the **partnership.** As shown in Table 21-2 above, partnerships are far less numerous than proprietorships but tend to be larger businesses—about 24 times greater on average. A partnership differs from a proprietorship chiefly in that there are two or more co-owners, called partners. They share the responsibilities of operating the firm and its profits, and they are *each* legally responsible for *all* of the debts incurred by the firm. In this sense, a partnership may be viewed as a proprietorship with more than one owner.

Advantages of Partnerships. The first advantage of a partnership is that it is *easy to form*. In fact, it is almost as easy to form as a proprietorship. Second, partnerships, like proprietorships, often help *reduce the costs of monitoring job performance*. This is particularly true when interpersonal skills are important for successful performance and in lines of business in which, even after the fact, it is difficult to measure performance objectively. Thus, attorneys and physicians often organize themselves as partnerships. A third advantage of the partnership is that it *permits more effective specialization* in occupations in which, for legal or other reasons, the multiple talents required for success are unlikely to be uniform across individuals. Finally, the income of the partnership is treated as personal income and thus is *subject only to personal taxation*.

Disadvantages of Partnerships. Partnerships also have their disadvantages. First, the *partners each have unlimited liability*. Thus, the personal assets of *each* partner are at risk due to debts incurred on behalf of the partnership by *any* of the partners. Second, *decision making is generally more costly* in a partnership than in a proprietorship. More people are involved in making decisions, and they may have differences of opinion that must be resolved before action is possible. Finally, *dissolution of the partnership* often occurs when a partner dies or voluntarily withdraws or when one or more partners wish to remove someone from the partnership. This creates potential uncertainty for creditors and employees.

CORPORATION A **corporation** is a legal entity that may conduct business in its own name just as an individual does. The owners of a corporation are called *shareholders* because they own shares of the profits earned by the firm. By law, shareholders have **limited liability,** meaning that if the corporation incurs debts that it cannot pay, the shareholders' personal property is shielded from claims by the firm's creditors. As shown in Table 21-2 on the facing page, corporations are far less numerous than proprietorships, but because of their large size, they are responsible for nearly 83 percent of all business revenues in the United States.

Corporation
A legal entity that may conduct business in its own name just as an individual does. The owners of a corporation, called shareholders, own shares of the firm's profits and have the protection of limited liability.

Limited liability
A legal concept in which the responsibility, or liability, of the owners of a corporation is limited to the value of the shares in the firm that they own.

Advantages of Corporations. Perhaps the greatest advantage of corporations is that their owners (the shareholders) have *limited liability*. The liability of shareholders is limited to the value of their shares. The second advantage is that, legally, the corporation *continues to exist* even if one or more owners cease to be owners. A third advantage of the corporation stems from the first two: Corporations are well positioned to *raise large sums of financial capital*. People are able to buy ownership shares or lend funds to the corporation knowing that their liability is limited to the amount of funds they invest and confident that the corporation's existence does not depend on the life of any one of the firm's owners.

Disadvantages of Corporations. The chief disadvantage of the corporation is that corporate income is subject to *double taxation*. The profits of the corporation are subject first to corporate taxation. Then, if any of the after-tax profits are distributed to shareholders as **dividends,** such payments are treated as personal income to the shareholders and subject to personal taxation. Because the corporate income is also taxed at the corporate level, owners of corporations generally pay higher taxes on corporate income than on other forms of income.

Dividends
Portion of a corporation's profits paid to its owners (shareholders).

A second disadvantage of the corporation is that corporations are potentially subject to problems associated with the *separation of ownership and control*. The owners and managers of a corporation are typically different persons and may have different incentives. The problems that can result are discussed later in the chapter.

What benefits have various British law firms hoped to gain from becoming corporations?

INTERNATIONAL EXAMPLE British Law Firms Adopt Corporate Structures

In 2011, law firms in the United Kingdom were authorized to restructure themselves as corporations instead of remaining private partnerships. A number of British law firms have already engaged in *initial public offerings (IPOs),* or first-time issues of shares of stock to outside investors. Some law firms have used the proceeds of the IPOs to expand their operations by buying up smaller law firms.

In addition to the possibility of using the corporate structure to raise more financial capital, operating as a corporation instead of a private partnership can offer a law firm additional advantages. One of these, of course, is limited liability. The other key advantage is that the firm will be able to continue as a business concern following the death of a top attorney. In years past, many highly successful British law firms had to dissolve when a key legal partner died. The threat of this possibility is removed for law firms that have switched to the new corporate structure.

FOR CRITICAL ANALYSIS

What are some possible disadvantages that corporate law firms in the United Kingdom may encounter?

The Profits of a Firm

Most people think of a firm's profit as the difference between the amount of revenues the firm takes in and the amount it spends for wages, materials, and so on. In a bookkeeping sense, the following formula could be used:

$$\text{Accounting profit} = \text{total revenues} - \text{explicit costs}$$

Explicit costs
Costs that business managers must take account of because they must be paid. Examples are wages, taxes, and rent.

Accounting profit
Total revenues minus total explicit costs.

Implicit costs
Expenses that managers do not have to pay out of pocket and hence normally do not explicitly calculate, such as the opportunity cost of factors of production that are owned. Examples are owner-provided capital and owner-provided labor.

where **explicit costs** are expenses that must actually be paid out by the firm. This definition of profit is known as **accounting profit.** It is appropriate when used by accountants to determine a firm's taxable income. Economists are more interested in how firm managers react not just to changes in explicit costs but also to changes in **implicit costs,** defined as expenses that business managers do not have to pay out of pocket but are costs to the firm nonetheless because they represent an opportunity cost. They do not involve any direct cash outlay by the firm and must therefore be measured by the *opportunity cost principle*. That is to say, they are measured by what the resources (land, capital) currently used in producing a particular good or service could earn in other uses. Consequently, a better definition of implicit cost is the opportunity cost of using factors that a producer does not buy or hire but already owns. Economists use the full opportunity cost of all resources (including both explicit and implicit costs) as the figure to subtract from revenues to obtain a definition of profit.

Opportunity Cost of Capital

Normal rate of return
The amount that must be paid to an investor to induce investment in a business. Also known as the *opportunity cost of capital*.

Firms enter or remain in an industry if they earn, at minimum, a **normal rate of return.** People will not invest their wealth in a business unless they obtain a positive normal (competitive) rate of return—that is, unless their invested wealth pays off. Any business wishing to attract capital must expect to pay at least the same rate of return on that capital as all other businesses (of similar risk) are willing to pay. Put another way, when a firm requires the use of a resource in producing a particular product, it must bid against alternative users of that resource. Thus, the firm must offer a price that is at least as much as other potential users are offering to pay.

For example, if individuals can invest their wealth in almost any publishing firm and get a rate of return of 10 percent per year, each firm in the publishing industry must *expect* to pay 10 percent as the normal rate of return to present and future investors. This 10 percent is a *cost to the firm*, the **opportunity cost of capital.** The opportunity cost of capital is the amount of income, or yield, that could have been earned by investing in the next-best alternative. Capital will not stay in firms or industries in which the expected rate of return falls below its opportunity cost—that is, what could be earned elsewhere. If a firm owns some capital equipment, it can either use it or lease it out and earn a return. If the firm uses the equipment for production, part of the cost of using that equipment is the forgone revenue that the firm could have earned had it leased out that equipment.

Opportunity cost of capital
The normal rate of return, or the available return on the next-best alternative investment. Economists consider this a cost of production, and it is included in our cost examples.

Opportunity Cost of Owner-Provided Labor and Capital

Single-owner proprietorships often grossly exaggerate their profit rates because they understate the opportunity cost of the labor that the proprietor provides to the business. Here we are referring to the opportunity cost of labor. For example, you may know people who run a small grocery store. These people will sit down at the end of the year and figure out what their "profits" are. They will add up all their sales and subtract what they had to pay to other workers, what they had to pay to their suppliers, what they had to pay in taxes, and so on. The end result they will call "profit." They normally will not, however, have figured into their costs the salary that they could have made if they had worked for somebody else in a similar type of job. By working for themselves, they become residual claimants—they receive what is left after all explicit costs have been accounted for. Part of the costs, however, should include the salary the owner-operator could have received working for someone else.

Consider a simple example of a skilled auto mechanic working 14 hours a day at his own service station, six days a week. Compare this situation to how much he could earn working 84 hours a week as a trucking company mechanic. This self-employed auto mechanic might have an opportunity cost of about $35 an hour. For his 84-hour week in his own service station, he is forfeiting $2,940. Unless his service station shows accounting profits of more than that per week, he is incurring losses in an economic sense.

Another way of looking at the opportunity cost of running a business is that opportunity cost consists of all explicit and implicit costs. Accountants only take account of explicit costs. Therefore, accounting profit ends up being the residual after only explicit costs are subtracted from total revenues.

Go to **www.econtoday.com/ch21** for a link to Internal Revenue Service reports on U.S. annual revenues and expenses of proprietorships, partnerships, and corporations based on tax returns. Click on recent quarters and choose relevant reports.

This same analysis can apply to owner-provided capital, such as land or buildings. The fact that the owner owns the building or the land with which he or she operates a business does not mean that it is "free." Rather, use of the building and land still has an opportunity cost—the value of the next-best alternative use for those assets.

Accounting Profits versus Economic Profits

The term *profits* in economics means the income that entrepreneurs earn, over and above all costs including their own opportunity cost of time, plus the opportunity cost of the capital they have invested in their business. Profits can be regarded as total revenues minus total costs—which is how accountants think of them—but we must now include *all* costs. Our definition of **economic profits** will be the following:

Economic profits
Total revenues minus total opportunity costs of all inputs used, or the total of all implicit and explicit costs.

$$\text{Economic profits} = \text{total revenues} - \text{total opportunity cost of all inputs used}$$

or

$$\text{Economic profits} = \text{total revenues} - (\text{explicit} + \text{implicit costs})$$

Remember that implicit costs include a normal rate of return on invested capital. We show this relationship in Figure 21-2 below.

FIGURE 21-2 Simplified View of Economic and Accounting Profit

We see on the right column that accounting profit is the difference between total revenues and total explicit accounting costs. Conversely, we see on the left column that economic profit is equal to total revenues minus economic costs. Economic costs equal explicit accounting costs plus all implicit costs, including a normal rate of return on invested capital.

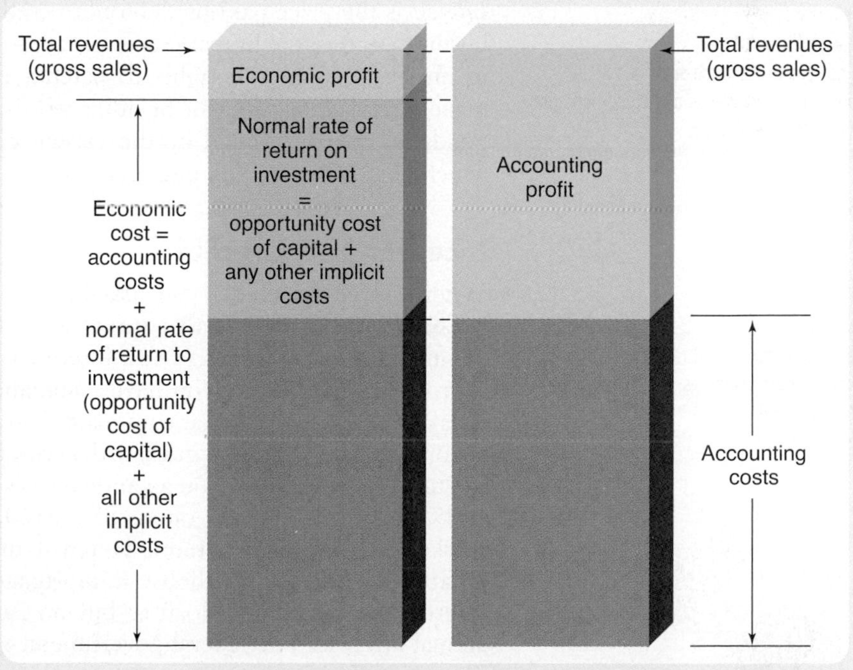

The Goal of the Firm: Profit Maximization

When we examined the theory of consumer demand, utility (or satisfaction) maximization by the individual provided the basis for the analysis. In the theory of the firm and production, *profit maximization* is the underlying hypothesis of our predictive theory. The goal of the firm is to maximize economic profits, and the firm is expected to make the positive difference between total revenues and total costs as large as it can.

Our justification for assuming profit maximization by firms is similar to our assumption concerning utility maximization by individuals (see Chapter 20). To obtain labor, capital, and other resources required to produce commodities, firms must first obtain financing from investors. Although investors typically monitor managers' performances to ensure that the funds they provide are not misused, they are most interested in the earnings on these funds and the risk of obtaining lower returns or losing the funds they have invested. Firms that can provide relatively higher risk-corrected returns will therefore have an advantage in obtaining the financing needed to continue or expand production. Over time, we would expect a policy of profit maximization to become the dominant mode of behavior for firms that survive.

QUICK QUIZ See page 482 for the answers. **Review concepts from this section in MyEconLab.**

__________ are the most common form of business organization, comprising close to 72 percent of all firms. Each is owned by a single individual who makes all business decisions, receives all the profits, and has __________ liability for the firm's debts.

__________ are much like proprietorships, except that two or more individuals, or partners, share the decisions and the profits of the firm. In addition, each partner has __________ liability for the debts of the firm.

Corporations are responsible for the largest share of business revenues. The owners, called __________, share in the firm's profits but normally have little responsibility for the firm's day-to-day operations. They enjoy __________ liability for the debts of the firm.

Accounting profits differ from **economic profits,** which are defined as total revenues minus total costs, where costs include the full __________ cost of all of the factors of production plus all other implicit costs.

The full opportunity cost of capital invested in a business is generally not included as a cost when accounting profits are calculated. Thus, accounting profits often are __________ than economic profits. We assume throughout that the goal of the firm is to __________ economic profits.

Interest

Financial capital
Funds used to purchase physical capital goods, such as buildings and equipment, and patents and trademarks.

Interest is the price paid by debtors to creditors for the use of loanable funds. Often businesses go to credit markets to obtain so-called **financial capital** in order to invest in physical capital and rights to patents and trademarks from which they hope to make a satisfactory return. In other words, in our society, the production of capital goods is often facilitated by the existence of credit markets. These are markets in which borrowing and lending take place.

Interest and Credit

Interest
The payment for current rather than future command over resources; the cost of obtaining credit.

When you obtain credit, you actually obtain funds to have command over resources today. We can say, then, that **interest** is the payment for current rather than future command over resources. Thus, interest is the payment for obtaining credit. If you borrow $100 from me, you have command over $100 worth of goods and services today. I no longer have that command. You promise to pay me back $100 plus interest at some future date. The interest that you pay is usually expressed as a percentage of the total loan, calculated on an annual basis. If at the end of one year you pay me back $105, the annual interest rate is $5 ÷ $100, or 5 percent. When you go out into the marketplace to obtain credit, you will find that the interest rate charged differs greatly. A loan to buy a house (a mortgage) may cost you 4 to 6 percent in annual interest. An installment loan to buy an automobile may cost you 6 to 8 percent in annual interest. The federal government, when it wishes to obtain credit (issue U.S. Treasury securities), may have to pay only 0.5 to 4 percent in annual interest. Variations in the rate of annual interest that must be paid for credit depend on the following factors.

1. *Length of loan.* In many (but not all) cases, the longer the loan will be outstanding, other things being equal, the greater will be the interest rate charged.
2. *Risk.* The greater the risk of nonrepayment of the loan, other things being equal, the greater the interest rate charged. Risk is assessed on the basis of the creditworthiness of the borrower and whether the borrower provides collateral for the loan. Collateral consists of any asset that will automatically become the property of the lender should the borrower fail to comply with the loan agreement.
3. *Handling charges.* It takes resources to set up a loan. Papers have to be filled out and filed, credit references have to be checked, collateral has to be examined, and so on. The larger the amount of the loan, the smaller the handling (or administrative) charges as a percentage of the total loan. Therefore, we would predict that, other things being equal, the larger the loan, the lower the interest rate.

Go to www.econtoday.com/ch21 for Federal Reserve data on U.S. interest rates.

Real versus Nominal Interest Rates

We have been assuming that there is no inflation. In a world of inflation—a persistent rise in an average of all prices—the **nominal rate of interest** will be higher than it would be in a world with no inflation. Nominal, or market, rates of interest rise to take account of the anticipated rate of inflation. If, for example, no inflation is expected, the nominal rate of interest might be 5 percent for home mortgages. If the rate of inflation goes to 4 percent a year and stays there, everybody will anticipate that inflation rate. The nominal rate of interest will rise to about 9 percent to take account of the anticipated rate of inflation. If the interest rate did not rise to 9 percent, the principal plus interest earned at 5 percent would have lower purchasing power in the future because inflation would have eroded its real value. We can therefore say that the nominal, or market, rate of interest is approximately equal to the real rate of interest plus the anticipated rate of inflation, or

Nominal rate of interest
The market rate of interest expressed in today's dollars.

$$i_n = i_r + \text{anticipated rate of inflation}$$

where i_n equals the nominal rate of interest and i_r equals the real rate of interest. In short, you can expect to see high nominal rates of interest in periods of high inflation rates. The **real rate of interest** may not necessarily be high, though. We must first correct the nominal rate of interest for the anticipated rate of inflation before determining whether the real interest rate is in fact higher than normal.

Real rate of interest
The nominal rate of interest minus the anticipated rate of inflation.

The Allocative Role of Interest

In Chapter 4, we talked about the price system and the role that prices play in the allocation of resources. Interest is a price that allocates loanable funds (credit) to consumers and to businesses. Within the business sector, interest allocates funds to different firms and therefore to different investment projects. An investment, or capital, project with a rate of return—an annual payoff as a percentage of the investment—higher than the market rate of interest in the credit market will be undertaken, given an unrestricted market for loanable funds. For example, if the expected rate of return on the purchase of a new factory or of intellectual property—patents or copyrights—in some industry is 10 percent and funds can be acquired for 6 percent, the investment project will proceed. If, however, that same project had an expected rate of return of only 4 percent, it would not be undertaken. In sum, the interest rate allocates funds to industries whose investments yield the highest (risk-adjusted) returns—where resources will be the most productive.

It is important to realize that the interest rate performs the function of allocating financial capital and that this ultimately allocates real physical capital to various firms for investment projects.

Interest Rates and Present Value

Businesses make investments in which they often incur large costs today but don't make any profits until some time in the future. Somehow they have to be able to compare their investment cost today with a stream of future profits. How can they relate present cost to future benefits?

Interest rates are used to link the present with the future. After all, if you have to pay $105 at the end of the year when you borrow $100, that 5 percent interest rate gives you a measure of the premium on the earlier availability of goods and services. If you want to have things today, you have to pay the 5 percent interest rate in order to have current purchasing power.

The question could be put this way: What is the present value (the value today) of $105 that you could receive one year from now? That depends on the market rate of interest, or the rate of interest that you could earn in some appropriate savings institution, such as in a savings account. To make the arithmetic simple, let's assume that the rate of interest is 5 percent. Now you can figure out the **present value** of $105 to be received one year from now. You figure it out by asking, What sum must I put aside today at the market interest rate of 5 percent to receive $105 one year from now? Mathematically, we represent this equation as

Present value
The value of a future amount expressed in today's dollars; the most that someone would pay today to receive a certain sum at some point in the future.

$$(1 + 0.05)PV_1 = \$105$$

where PV_1 is the sum that you must set aside now.

Let's solve this simple equation to obtain PV_1:

$$PV_1 = \frac{\$105}{1.05} = \$100$$

That is, $100 will accumulate to $105 at the end of one year with a market rate of interest of 5 percent. Thus, the present value of $105 one year from now, using a rate of interest of 5 percent, is $100. The formula for present value of any sums to be received one year from now thus becomes

$$PV_1 = \frac{FV_1}{1 + i}$$

where

PV_1 = present value of a sum one year hence
FV_1 = future sum paid or received one year hence
i = market rate of interest

Go to www.econtoday.com/ch21 to utilize an MFM Communication Software, Inc., manual providing additional review of present value.

PRESENT VALUES FOR MORE DISTANT PERIODS The present-value formula for figuring out today's worth of dollars to be received at a future date can now be determined. How much would have to be put in the same savings account today to have $105 *two years* from now if the account pays a rate of 5 percent per year compounded annually?

After one year, the sum that would have to be set aside, which we will call PV_2, would have grown to $PV_2 \times 1.05$. This amount during the second year would increase to $PV_2 \times 1.05 \times 1.05$, or $PV_2 \times (1.05)^2$. To find the PV_2 that would grow to $105 over two years, let

$$PV_2 \times (1.05)^2 = \$105$$

and solve for PV_2:

$$PV_2 = \frac{\$105}{(1.05)^2} = \$95.24$$

You Are There

To consider how a city government sometimes weighs current expenses against the discounted present value of future costs, read **Why New York City Provides the Homeless with One-Way Tickets,** on page 477.

TABLE 21-3

Present Value of a Future Dollar

This table shows how much a dollar received at the end of a certain number of years in the future is worth today. For example, at 5 percent a year, a dollar to be received 20 years in the future is worth 37.7 cents. If received in 50 years, it isn't even worth a dime today. To find out how much $10,000 would be worth a certain number of years from now, just multiply the figures in the table by 10,000. For example, $10,000 received at the end of 10 years discounted at a 5 percent rate of interest would have a present value of $6,140.

	Discounted Present Values of $1				
Year	3%	5%	8%	10%	20%
1	.971	.952	.926	.909	.833
2	.943	.907	.857	.826	.694
3	.915	.864	.794	.751	.578
4	.889	.823	.735	.683	.482
5	.863	.784	.681	.620	.402
6	.838	.746	.630	.564	.335
7	.813	.711	.583	.513	.279
8	.789	.677	.540	.466	.233
9	.766	.645	.500	.424	.194
10	.744	.614	.463	.385	.162
15	.642	.481	.315	.239	.0649
20	.554	.377	.215	.148	.0261
25	.478	.295	.146	.0923	.0105
30	.412	.231	.0994	.0573	.00421
40	.307	.142	.0460	.0221	.000680
50	.228	.087	.0213	.00852	.000109

Thus, the present value of $105 to be paid or received two years hence, discounted at an interest rate of 5 percent per year compounded annually, is equal to $95.24. In other words, $95.24 put into a savings account yielding 5 percent per year compounded interest would accumulate to $105 in two years.

THE GENERAL FORMULA FOR DISCOUNTING The general formula for **discounting** becomes

$$PV_t = \frac{FV_t}{(1 + i)^t}$$

where t refers to the number of periods in the future the money is to be paid or received.

Table 21-3 above gives the present value of $1 to be received in future years at various interest rates. The interest rate used to derive the present value is called the **rate of discount.**

Why did a number of U.S. corporations suddenly report significant reductions in the estimated discounted present values of their after-tax profits following passage of federal health care legislation in 2010?

Discounting
The method by which the present value of a future sum or a future stream of sums is obtained.

Rate of discount
The rate of interest used to discount future sums back to present value.

EXAMPLE Higher Future Taxes Reduce the Discounted Present Value of Profits

On March 24, 2010, President Obama signed the new health care legislation into law. One of the provisions in the new law reduced the amount that companies can deduct from their federal income taxes for providing prescription-drug benefits for their retired employees. As a result, within 48 hours, several U.S. corporations, including AT&T, Deere & Company, and Caterpillar, announced that the discounted present value of future tax bills that the new law would impose on their firms would amount to a combined $2 billion. During the next weeks, many other firms announced that they also would enter into their accounting statements higher discounted present values of estimated future tax payments, which together amounted to nearly $12 billion. Thus, in one fell swoop, congressional passage of the health care program reduced U.S. companies' discounted present value of anticipated after-tax profits by about $14 billion.

FOR CRITICAL ANALYSIS

If all of U.S. companies' higher annual expected future tax payments to pay for the health care program were added together without computing their discounted present values, would this sum be greater or less than $14 billion? Explain your reasoning.

QUICK QUIZ See page 482 for the answers. Review concepts from this section in MyEconLab.

Interest is the price of obtaining credit. In the credit market, the rate of interest paid depends on the __________ of the loan, the __________, and the handling charges, among other things.

Nominal interest rates include a factor to take account of the __________ rate of inflation. Therefore, during periods of high __________ inflation, nominal interest rates will be relatively high.

Payments received or costs incurred in the future are worth less than those received or incurred today. The __________ __________ of any future sum is lower the farther it occurs in the future and the greater the discount rate used.

Corporate Financing Methods

When the Dutch East India Company was founded in 1602, it raised financial capital by selling shares of its expected future profits to investors. The investors thus became the owners of the company, and their ownership shares eventually became known as "shares of stock," or simply *stocks*. The company also issued notes of indebtedness, which involved borrowing funds in return for interest paid on the funds, plus eventual repayment of the principal amount borrowed. In modern parlance, these notes of indebtedness are called *bonds*. As the company prospered over time, some of its revenues were used to pay lenders the interest and principal owed them. Of the profits that remained, some were paid to shareholders in the form of dividends. Some were retained by the company for reinvestment in further enterprises. The methods of financing used by the Dutch East India Company four centuries ago—stocks, bonds, and reinvestment—remain the principal methods of financing for today's corporations.

Stocks

Share of stock
A legal claim to a share of a corporation's future profits. If it is *common stock*, it incorporates certain voting rights regarding major policy decisions of the corporation. If it is *preferred stock*, its owners are accorded preferential treatment in the payment of dividends but do not have any voting rights.

A **share of stock** in a corporation is simply a legal claim to a share of the corporation's future profits. If there are 100,000 shares of stock in a company and you own 1,000 of them, you own the right to 1 percent of that company's future profits. If the stock you own is *common stock*, you also have the right to vote on major policy decisions affecting the company, such as the selection of the corporation's board of directors. Your 1,000 shares would entitle you to cast 1 percent of the votes on such issues.

If the stock you own is *preferred stock*, you own a share of the future profits of the corporation but do *not* have regular voting rights. You do, however, get something in return for giving up your voting rights: preferential treatment in the payment of dividends. Specifically, the owners of preferred stock generally must receive at least a certain amount of dividends in each period before the owners of common stock can receive *any* dividends.

Bonds

Bond
A legal claim against a firm, usually entitling the owner of the bond to receive a fixed annual coupon payment, plus a lump-sum payment at the bond's maturity date. Bonds are issued in return for funds lent to the firm.

A **bond** is a legal claim against a firm, entitling the owner of the bond to receive a fixed annual *coupon* payment, plus a lump-sum payment at the maturity date of the bond. Bonds are issued in return for funds lent to the firm. The coupon payments represent interest on the amount borrowed by the firm, and the lump-sum payment at maturity of the bond generally equals the amount originally borrowed by the firm.

Bonds are *not* claims on the future profits of the firm. Legally, bondholders must be paid whether the firm prospers or not. To help ensure this, bondholders generally receive their coupon payments each year, along with any principal that is due, before *any* shareholders can receive dividend payments.

Reinvestment

Reinvestment
Profits (or depreciation reserves) used to purchase new capital equipment.

Reinvestment takes place when the firm uses some of its profits to purchase new capital equipment rather than paying the profits out as dividends to shareholders.

Although sales of stock are an important source of financing for new firms, reinvestment and borrowing are the primary means of financing for existing firms. Indeed, reinvestment by established firms is such an important source of financing that it dominates the other two sources of corporate finance, amounting to roughly 75 percent of new financial capital for corporations in recent years. Also, small businesses, which are the source of much current growth, commonly cannot rely on the stock market to raise investment funds.

The Markets for Stocks and Bonds

Economists often refer to the "market for wheat" or the "market for labor," but these are concepts rather than actual places. For **securities** (stocks and bonds), however, there really are markets—centralized, physical locations where exchange takes place. The most prestigious of these markets are the New York Stock Exchange (NYSE) and the New York Bond Exchange, both located in New York City. More than 2,500 stocks are traded on the NYSE, which is sometimes called the "Big Board." Numerous other stock and bond markets, or exchanges, exist throughout the United States and in various financial capitals of the world, such as London and Tokyo.

Securities
Stocks and bonds.

Although the exact process by which exchanges are conducted in these markets varies slightly from one to another, the process used on the NYSE is representative of the principles involved. Essentially, brokers earn commissions from volumes of shares traded, while dealers attempt to profit from "buying low and selling high."

Even though the NYSE is traditionally the most prestigious of U.S. stock exchanges, it is no longer the largest. Since the mid-2000s, this title has belonged to the National Association of Securities Dealers Automated Quotations (Nasdaq), which began in 1971 as a tiny electronic network linking about 100 securities firms. Today, the Nasdaq market links about 500 dealers, and Nasdaq is home to nearly 4,000 stocks, including those of such companies as Microsoft, Intel, and Cisco.

The Theory of Efficient Markets

At any point in time, there are tens of thousands, even millions, of persons looking for any bit of information that will enable them to forecast correctly the future prices of stocks. Responding to any information that seems useful, these people try to buy low and sell high. The result is that all publicly available information that might be used to forecast stock prices gets taken into account by those with access to the information and the knowledge and ability to learn from it, leaving no predictable profit opportunities. And because so many people are involved in this process, it occurs quite swiftly. Indeed, there is some evidence that *all* information entering the market is fully incorporated into stock prices within less than a minute of its arrival. One view is that any information about specific stocks will prove to have little value by the time it reaches you.

Consequently, stock prices tend to drift upward following a *random walk*, which is to say that the best forecast of tomorrow's price is today's price plus the effect of any upward drift. This is called the **random walk theory.** Although large values of the random component of stock price changes are less likely than small values, nothing else about the magnitude or direction of a stock price change can be predicted.

Random walk theory
The theory that there are no predictable trends in securities prices that can be used to "get rich quick."

Why Not . . . compare average stock prices today with average stock prices in years past?

Most published charts comparing average stock prices over time indicate that today's average quoted prices of U.S. stocks are more than 20 times higher than those quoted in the late 1920s. Such comparisons, however, fail to account for inflation. Once all past and current stock prices are adjusted to incorporate the effects of inflation, today's average stock prices are about the same as the average stock prices that prevailed in the 1920s. Thus, current average inflation-adjusted U.S. stock prices are no higher than the average inflation-adjusted prices of shares of stocks that were traded 90 years ago.

Inside Information

Inside information
Information that is not available to the general public about what is happening in a corporation.

Go to www.econtoday.com/ch21 to explore how the U.S. Securities and Exchange Commission seeks to prevent the use of inside information.

Isn't there any way to "beat the market"? The answer is yes—but normally only if you have **inside information** that is not available to the public. Suppose that your best friend is in charge of new product development at the world's largest software firm, Microsoft Corporation. Your friend tells you that the company's smartest programmer has just come up with major new software that millions of computer users will want to buy. No one but your friend and the programmer—and now you—is aware of this. You could indeed make a killing using this information by purchasing shares of Microsoft and then selling them (at a higher price) as soon as the new product is publicly announced. There is one problem: Stock trading based on inside information such as this is illegal, punishable by substantial fines and even imprisonment. So, unless you happen to have a stronger-than-average desire for a long vacation in a federal prison, you might be better off investing in Microsoft after the new program is publicly announced.

It is, of course, possible for people to influence stock or bond prices through the accidental release of inside information. For instance, when the U.S. Treasury decided it would discontinue issuing 30-year bonds, it chose to announce its decision on October 31, 2001. Treasury officials told the media that the information of the bond's demise would be public as of 10 a.m. Nevertheless, as a courtesy officials informed reporters in advance in an impromptu 9 a.m. meeting so that the reporters would have time to write stories to release at the later hour. Officials failed to check the credentials of everyone who attended the meeting, however. One of those individuals was a financial consultant who did not understand that this early news of the bond's end was "embargoed" until 10 a.m. After the news conference ended just before 9:30 a.m., the consultant called some of his clients and told them of the media announcement. Within a very few minutes, word of the Treasury's plans had spread widely. Ten minutes before the Treasury's formal announcement, 30-year bond prices rose in response to higher demand for existing bonds.

What agency of the U.S. government would you guess recently had to impose tougher insider-trading rules on its staff?

POLICY EXAMPLE The Insider-Trading Regulator's Insiders Require Regulating

The U.S. government agency charged with enforcing insider-trading laws is the Securities and Exchange Commission (SEC). Recently, SEC officials discovered that members of the commission's own staff had failed to report stock trades. The SEC has long had rules prohibiting staff members from trading the stocks of firms against which it might bring charges—actions that likely would affect those companies' stock prices. Unlike most private firms that have responded to SEC regulations by establishing automatic surveillance systems intended to help prevent insider trading, the SEC had no systems to monitor its own staff's stock trading. When SEC officials found that some employees were conducting hundreds of stock trades per year and not reporting all of the trades, the officials realized that the individuals could have profited from insider trading. The officials found no evidence that any SEC employees had actually done this. Nevertheless, the officials decided that it would be prudent to put into place the kinds of monitoring systems aimed at preventing insider trading that the SEC has long encouraged the firms that it regulates to implement.

FOR CRITICAL ANALYSIS

How could an employee of a government regulatory agency potentially profit from engaging in stock trading based on inside information available only to people working at that agency?

QUICK QUIZ

See page 482 for the answers. Review concepts from this section in MyEconLab.

The three primary sources of corporate funds are __________, __________, and __________ of profits.

A **share of stock** is a share of __________ providing a legal claim to a corporation's future profits. A __________ is a legal claim entitling the owner to a fixed annual coupon payment and to a lump-sum payment on the date it matures.

Many economists believe that asset markets, especially the stock market, are __________, meaning that one cannot make a higher-than-normal rate of return without having inside information (information that the general public does not possess). Stock prices normally drift upward following a __________ __________, meaning that you cannot predict changes in future stock prices based on information about stock price behavior in the past.

You Are There Why New York City Provides the Homeless with One-Way Tickets

New York City's mayor, Michael Bloomberg, has made his decision. Henceforth, he announces, the city government will pay to send a homeless person anywhere in the world that the individual wishes to go. There are no explicit limits on distance or on the market price of a plane ticket that the city government will pay. The city will provide transportation to the airport and will even cover any unavoidable hotel expenses. There are two conditions on the city's offer. First, there must be relatives at the destination who are willing to take the individual into their home. Second, he or she must be willing to accept a *one-way* plane ticket. Although the city will fully reimburse travel agencies for their services in booking trips, the city will permit no tickets involving return flights.

Why are Mayor Bloomberg and the New York City government willing to foot the bill for up to several thousand dollars' worth of travel expenses for each homeless person in the city who wishes to depart? The answer is that the city faces an even higher discounted present value of anticipated future expenses to shelter and feed a typical homeless person year after year. Paying for the city's homeless people to depart, Bloomberg has determined, is the lower-cost alternative.

Critical Analysis Questions

1. If New York City's cost of sheltering and feeding a homeless person is the same each year, why is the discounted present value of this expense two years from now lower than the discounted present value of the expense one year from now?
2. Why might Bloomberg rethink his plan if the market interest rate were to rise substantially?

ISSUES & APPLICATIONS

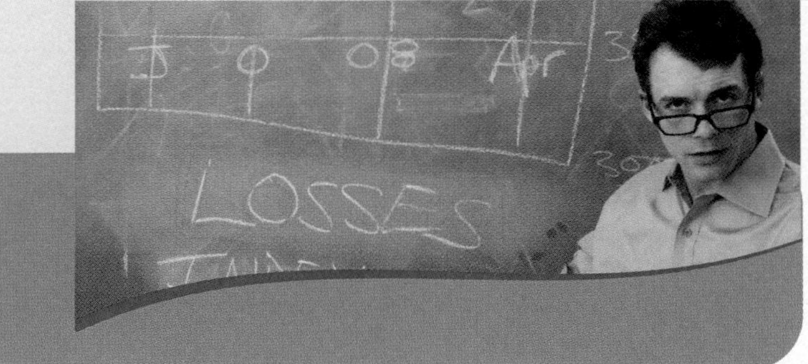

The Recent Stock Market Meltdown versus Past Meltdowns

CONCEPTS APPLIED

- ▶ Securities
- ▶ Markets for Stocks and Bonds
- ▶ Stock Prices

Many people have compared the downturn in average U.S. securities prices that occurred in the late 2000s to the stock market crash that began in late 1929 and ushered in the Great Depression of the 1930s. Let's evaluate whether such a comparison is reasonable.

Similarities for the First 17 Months

As you can see in Figure 21-3 on the next page, the initial decrease in stock prices was much greater in the crash that began in early September 1929 than in the meltdown that began in October 2007. Once the Great Crash of 1929 was under way, share prices plunged by nearly 48 percent in only two months' time, whereas average stock prices dropped by only about 10 percent in the first two months of the late-2000s meltdown.

In September 2008, however, more than 11 months after the downturn of the late 2000s began, a plunge in stock prices did occur. As a consequence, the percentage decline 17 months after October 2007 was very close to the overall percentage decrease 17 months after stock prices began

FIGURE 21-3 Comparing Four U.S. Downturns in Stock Prices

During the first 17 months of the drop in U.S. stock prices in the late 2000s, average share prices fell as dramatically as during the Great Crash of 1929. In later months, however, the stock price downturn of the late 2000s began to look more like those of the 1973–1974 and 2000–2002 periods.

Source: Securities and Exchange Commission.

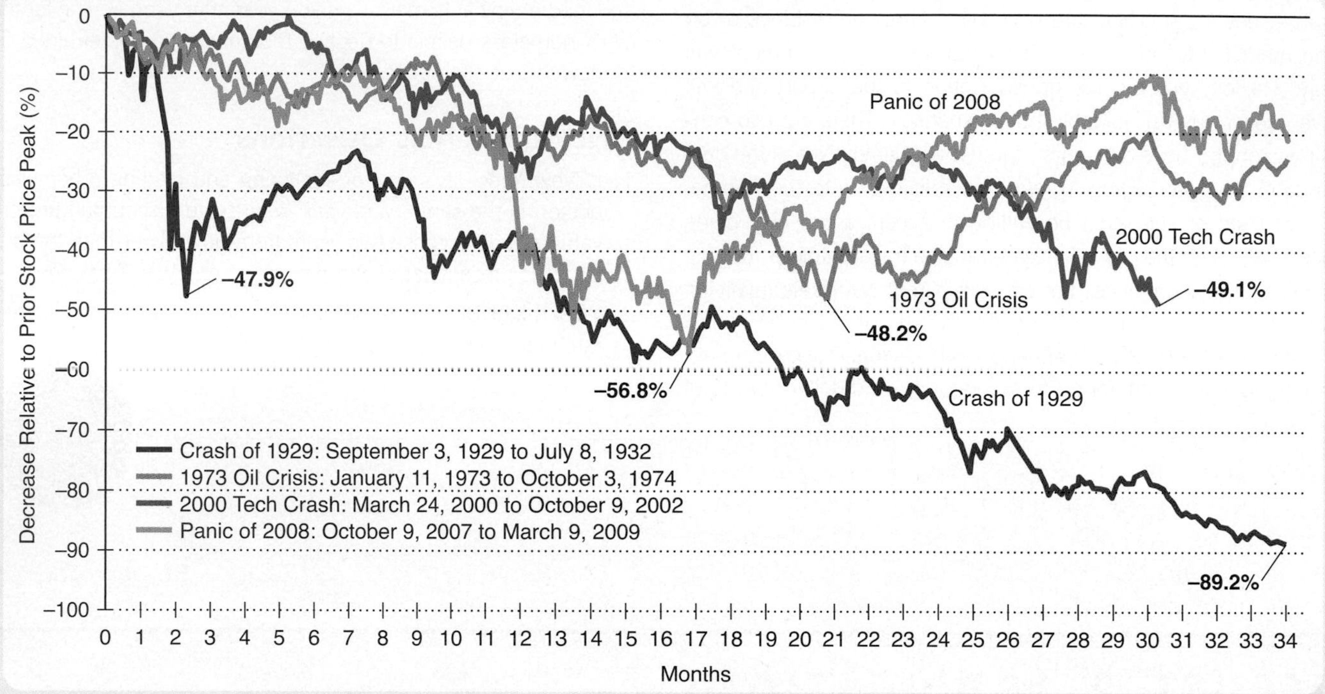

dropping in September 1929. By February 2009, the stock price decline appeared to be on its way to rivaling the post-1929 crash in severity.

Lately More Similar to Other Recent Stock Price Meltdowns

Figure 21-3 above also shows that since February 2009, the stock price meltdown of the late 2000s has looked less like the downturn that followed the Great Crash of 1929. After dropping by 57 percent from the average level of stock prices that had prevailed in October 2007, during the spring of 2009 average share prices began to level off and then recover.

More than 20 months into the downturn of the late 2000s, the behavior of average prices of shares of stock began to appear less similar to that observed following 1929. Instead, the pattern of U.S. stock prices in 2009 and 2010 looked more like that observed during the 1973–1974 and 2000–2002 periods. Thus, whereas the first half of the downturn of the late 2000s was comparable to the Great Crash of 1929, the overall behavior of stock prices during the second half was similar to other more recent declines.

For Critical Analysis

1. If you had held stocks with a market value of $10,000 in early September 1929 or in early October 2007, about how much would those shares have been worth 17 months later?
2. If you had held stocks with a market value of $10,000 in both September 1929 and September 2008, about how much would those shares have been worth 34 months later?

Web Resources

1. To read about the Great Crash of 1929, use the link available at www.econtoday.com/ch21.
2. To learn more about the biggest stock price drops that occurred during the late-2000s downturn, go to www.econtoday.com/ch21.

Research Project

When most U.S. stock prices decline simultaneously, what can we infer about what most people perceive is happening to the discounted present value of profits that most U.S. companies can anticipate earning in the future? Explain your reasoning.

For more questions on this chapter's Issues & Applications, go to **MyEconLab**. In the Study Plan for this chapter, select Section N: News.

Here is what you should know after reading this chapter. **MyEconLab** will help you identify what you know, and where to go when you need to practice.

WHAT YOU SHOULD KNOW		WHERE TO GO TO PRACTICE
Economic Rent and Resource Allocation Owners of a resource in fixed supply, meaning that the resource supply curve is perfectly inelastic, are paid economic rent. In general, economic rent is a payment for the use of any resource that exceeds the opportunity cost of the resource. The economic rents received by the owners of such a resource reflect the maximum market valuation of the resource's value. Thus, economic rent allocates resources to their highest-valued use.	economic rent, 463 **KEY FIGURE** Figure 21-1, 463	• **MyEconLab** Study Plan 21.1 • Audio introduction to Chapter 21 • Animated Figure 21-1 • Video: Economic Rent and the Allocation of Resources
The Main Organizational Forms of Business and the Chief Advantages and Disadvantages of Each A proprietorship is owned by a single person, who makes the business decisions, is entitled to all the profits, and is subject to unlimited liability. A partnership has two or more owners, who share the responsibility for decision making, share the firm's profits, and individually bear unlimited liability for the firm's debts. Owners of corporations have limited liability, so their responsibility for the debts of the corporation is limited to the value of their ownership shares. Corporate income is subject to double taxation—corporate taxation when income is earned by the corporation and personal taxation when after-tax profits are paid as dividends to the owners. Corporations do not legally cease to exist due to a change of ownership or the death of an owner.	firm, 465 proprietorship, 466 unlimited liability, 466 partnership, 466 corporation, 467 limited liability, 467 dividends, 467	• **MyEconLab** Study Plan 21.2 • Video: The Goal of the Firm Is Profit Maximization
Accounting Profits versus Economic Profits A firm's accounting profits equal its total revenues minus its total explicit costs, which are expenses directly paid out by the firm. Economic profits equal accounting profits minus implicit costs, which are expenses that managers do not have to pay out of pocket, such as the opportunity cost of factors of production dedicated to the firm's production process. Owners of a firm seek to maximize the firm's economic profits to ensure that they earn at least a normal rate of return, meaning that the firm's total revenues at least cover explicit costs and implicit opportunity costs.	explicit costs, 468 accounting profit, 468 implicit costs, 468 normal rate of return, 468 opportunity cost of capital, 468 economic profits, 469 **KEY FIGURE** Figure 21-2, 469	• **MyEconLab** Study Plan 21.2 • Animated Figure 21-2 • Video: The Goal of the Firm Is Profit Maximization

(continued)

MyEconLab continued

WHAT YOU SHOULD KNOW		WHERE TO GO TO PRACTICE
Interest Rates Interest is a payment for the ability to use resources today instead of in the future. The nominal interest rate includes a factor that takes into account the anticipated inflation rate, so during periods of high anticipated inflation, current market (nominal) interest rates are high. The interest rate allocates funds to industries whose investments yield the highest (risk-adjusted) returns, and available resources are put to their most productive uses.	financial capital, 470 interest, 470 nominal rate of interest, 471 real rate of interest, 471	• **MyEconLab** Study Plan 21.3 • Video: Interest Rates and Present Value
Calculating the Present Discounted Value of a Payment to Be Received at a Future Date The present value of a future payment is the value of the future amount expressed in today's dollars, and it is equal to the most that someone would pay today to receive that amount in the future. The method by which the present value of a future sum is calculated is called *discounting*. This method implies that the present value of a sum to be received a year from now is equal to the future amount divided by 1 plus the appropriate rate of interest, which is called the *rate of discount*.	present value, 472 discounting, 473 rate of discount, 473	• **MyEconLab** Study Plan 21.3 • Video: Interest Rates and Present Value
The Main Sources of Corporate Funds Stocks are ownership shares, promising a share of profits, sold to investors. Common stocks also embody voting rights regarding the major decisions of the firm. Preferred stocks typically have no voting rights but enjoy priority status in the payment of dividends. Bonds are notes of indebtedness, issued in return for the loan of funds. They typically promise to pay interest in the form of annual coupon payments, plus repayment of the original principal amount upon maturity. Bondholders are generally promised payment before any payment of dividends to shareholders, and for this reason bonds are less risky than stocks.	share of stock, 474 bond, 474 reinvestment, 474 securities, 475 random walk theory, 475 inside information, 476	• **MyEconLab** Study Plans 21.4, 21.5 • Video: The Theory of Efficient Markets and Inside Information • Economics Video: Amy's Ice Cream

Log in to MyEconLab, take a chapter test, and get a personalized Study Plan that tells you which concepts you understand and which ones you need to review. From there, MyEconLab will give you further practice, tutorials, animations, videos, and guided solutions.
Log in to www.myeconlab.com

PROBLEMS

All problems are assignable in myeconlab*. Answers to odd-numbered problems appear at the back of the book.*

21-1. Which of the following individuals would you expect to have a high level of economic rent, and which would you expect to have a low level of economic rent? Explain why for each.

a. Bob has a highly specialized medical skill shared by very few individuals.

b. Sally has never attended school. She is 25 years old and is an internationally known supermodel.

c. Tim is a high school teacher and sells insurance part time.

21-2. A British pharmaceutical company spent several years and considerable funds on the development of a treatment for HIV patients. Now, with the protection afforded by patent rights, the company has the potential to reap enormous gains. The government, in response, has threatened to tax away any economic rents the company may earn. Is this an advisable policy? Why or why not? (Hint: Contrast the short-run and long-run effects of taxing away the economic rents.)

21-3. Write a brief explanation of the differences among a sole proprietorship, a partnership, and a corporation. In addition, list one advantage and one disadvantage of a proprietorship, a partnership, and a corporation.

21-4. After graduation, you face a choice. One option is to work for a multinational consulting firm and earn a starting salary (benefits included) of $40,000. The other option is to use $5,000 in savings to start your own consulting firm. You could earn an interest return of 5 percent on your savings. You choose to start your own consulting firm. At the end of the first year, you add up all of your expenses and revenues. Your total includes $12,000 in rent, $1,000 in office supplies, $20,000 for office staff, and $4,000 in telephone expenses. What are your total explicit costs and total implicit costs?

21-5. Suppose, as in Problem 21-4, that you have now operated your consulting firm for a year. At the end of the first year, your total revenues are $77,250. Based on the information in Problem 21-4, what is the accounting profit, and what is your economic profit?

21-6. An individual leaves a college faculty, where she was earning $80,000 a year, to begin a new venture. She invests her savings of $20,000, which were earning 10 percent annually. She then spends $40,000 renting office equipment, hires two students at $60,000 a year each, rents office space for $24,000, and has other variable expenses of $80,000. At the end of the year, her revenues are $400,000. What are her accounting profit and her economic profit for the year?

21-7. Classify the following items as either financial capital or physical capital.

a. A computer server owned by an information-processing company

b. $100,000 set aside in an account to purchase a computer server

c. Funds raised through a bond offer to expand plant and equipment

d. A warehouse owned by a shipping company

21-8. Explain the difference between the dividends of a corporation and the profits of a proprietorship or partnership, particularly in their tax treatment.

21-9. The owner of WebCity is trying to decide whether to remain a proprietorship or to incorporate. Suppose that the corporate tax rate on profits is 20 percent and the personal income tax rate is 30 percent. For simplicity, assume that all corporate profits (after corporate taxes are paid) are distributed as dividends in the year they are earned and that such dividends are subject to tax at the personal income tax rate.

a. If the owner of WebCity expects to earn $100,000 in before-tax profits this year, regardless of whether the firm is a proprietorship or a corporation, which method of organization should be chosen?

b. What is the dollar value of the after-tax advantage of the form of organization determined in part (a)?

c. Suppose that the corporate form of organization has cost advantages that will raise before-tax profits by $50,000. Should the owner of WebCity incorporate?

d. Based on parts (a) and (c), by how much will after-tax profits change due to incorporation?

e. Suppose that tax policy is changed to completely exempt from personal taxation the first $40,000 per year in dividends. Would this change in policy affect the decision made in part (a)?

f. How can you explain the fact that even though corporate profits are subject to double taxation, most business in the United States is conducted by corporations rather than by proprietorships or partnerships?

21-10. Explain how the following events would likely affect the relevant interest rate.

a. A major bond-rating agency has improved the risk rating of a developing nation.

b. The government has passed legislation requiring bank regulators to significantly increase the paperwork required when a bank makes a loan.

21-11. Suppose that the interest rate in Japan is only 2 percent, while the comparable rate in the United States is 4 percent. Japan's rate of inflation is 0.5 percent, while the U.S. inflation rate is 3 percent. Which economy has the higher real interest rate?

21-12. You expect to receive a payment of $104 one year from now.

a. Your discount rate is 4 percent. What is the present value of the payment to be received?

b. Suppose that your discount rate rises to 5 percent. What is the present value of the payment to be received?

21-13. Outline the differences between common stock and preferred stock.

21-14. Explain the basic differences between a share of stock and a bond.

21-15. Suppose that one of your classmates informs you that he has developed a method of forecasting stock market returns based on past trends. With a monetary investment from you, he claims that the two of you could profit handsomely from this forecasting method. How should you respond to your classmate?

21-16. Suppose that you are trying to decide whether to spend $1,000 on stocks issued by WildWeb or on bonds issued by the same company. There is a 50 percent chance that the value of the stock will rise to $2,200 at the end of the year and a 50 percent chance that the stock will be worthless at the end of the year. The bonds promise an interest rate of 20 percent per year, and it is certain that the bonds and interest will be repaid at the end of the year.

a. Assuming that your time horizon is exactly one year, will you choose the stocks or the bonds?

b. By how much is your expected end-of-year wealth reduced if you make the wrong choice?

c. Suppose the odds of success improve for WildWeb: Now there is a 60 percent chance that the value of the stock will be $2,200 at year's end and only a 40 percent chance that it will be worthless. Should you now choose the stocks or the bonds?

d. By how much did your expected end-of-year wealth rise as a result of the improved outlook for WildWeb?

ECONOMICS ON THE NET

How the New York Stock Exchange Operates This application gives you the chance to learn about how the New York Stock Exchange functions.

Title: The New York Stock Exchange: How a Stock Is Bought and Sold

Navigation: Follow the link at **www.econtoday.com/ch21** to visit the New York Stock Exchange. Click on "About us" in the left margin for a pop-up menu, and then click on *Education.* Select the tab named *Educational Materials.* Under "Publications for Investors," click on *How a Stock Is Bought and Sold.* Read the article.

Application Answer the following questions.

1. Why might companies contemplating issuing stock value the relatively low costs of trading shares on the New York Stock Exchange?
2. Why might people who buy and sell stocks value the relatively faster speeds of trade execution that the NYSE has achieved in recent years?

For Group Study and Analysis Go back up to "Publications for Investors," click on *NYSE Indexes,* and read the article. Divide the class into groups, and assign each group to examine one of the six NYSE indexes discussed in the article. Ask each group to evaluate how stock traders might use the specific index as a "benchmark" when evaluating whether to buy or sell stocks.

ANSWERS TO QUICK QUIZZES

p. 465: (i) inelastic; (ii) allocates . . . highest
p. 470: (i) Proprietorships . . . unlimited; (ii) Partnerships . . . unlimited; (iii) shareholders . . . limited; (iv) opportunity; (v) greater . . . maximize

p. 474: (i) length . . . risk; (ii) anticipated . . . anticipated; (iii) present value
p. 476: (i) stocks . . . bonds . . . reinvestment; (ii) ownership . . . bond; (iii) efficient . . . random walk

22

The Firm: Cost and Output Determination

The last commercial nuclear reactor plant built in the United States was completed in 1996. Since then, most media reports have suggested that concerns about safety and waste disposal have prevented energy firms from constructing additional nuclear power plants. In fact, the economics of electricity generation has probably been more important in dissuading electric companies from building more nuclear plants. During the late 1990s and the 2000s, energy firms found lower-cost ways of generating additional electricity using traditional power plants. Hence, they had less incentive to undertake the significant expenditures required to build nuclear plants. In contrast, recent technological developments in nuclear power generation may induce energy firms to start building electricity-generating nuclear reactors once again. To understand why this is so, you must first study production and cost concepts covered in this chapter.

LEARNING OBJECTIVES

After reading this chapter, you should be able to:

- Discuss the difference between the short run and the long run from the perspective of a firm
- Understand why the marginal physical product of labor eventually declines as more units of labor are employed
- Explain the short-run cost curves a typical firm faces
- Describe the long-run cost curves a typical firm faces
- Identify situations of economies and diseconomies of scale and define a firm's minimum efficient scale

myeconlab

MyEconLab helps you master each objective and study more efficiently. See end of chapter for details.

Did You Know That ? the average single-item cash register receipt has grown more than 2 inches longer since 1990? This has happened because most retailers now print additional information on receipts, such as savings from use of reward cards, discount coupons, and information about special offers. Retailers have provided receipts since the advent of cash registers in 1884. Recently, however, many companies have determined that they can save hundreds of dollars per store each year if they reduce the amount of paper devoted to receipts. Wal-Mart is testing two-sided receipts, and CVS is using loyalty cards that track customer information instead of printing the data on physical receipts. Lowe's has made its receipts wider to allow for 56 characters per line instead of 38 characters, deleted all white space at the top and bottom of receipts, and put its return policy on the back—all in an effort to use less paper and reduce costs. Some retailers, such as Apple, hope to eliminate the expense of paper receipts entirely by encouraging customers to accept electronic receipts sent via e-mail.

What are the determinants of a company's expenses? To understand the answer to this question, you must learn about the nature of the costs that firms incur in their productive endeavors, which in turn requires contemplating how firms employ inputs in the production of goods and services. This chapter considers each of these important topics.

Short Run versus Long Run

In Chapter 19, we discussed short-run and long-run price elasticities of supply and demand. As you will recall, for consumers, the long run means the time period during which all adjustments to a change in price can be made, and anything shorter than that is considered the short run. For suppliers, the long run is the time in which all adjustments can be made, and anything shorter than that is the short run. Now that we are discussing firms only, we will maintain a similar distinction between the short and the long run, but we will be more specific.

The Short Run

Short run
The time period during which at least one input, such as plant size, cannot be changed.

Plant size
The physical size of the factories that a firm owns and operates to produce its output. Plant size can be defined by square footage, maximum physical capacity, and other physical measures.

In the theory of the firm, the **short run** is defined as any time period that is so short that there is at least one input, such as current **plant size,** that the firm cannot alter. In other words, during the short run, a firm makes do with whatever big machines and factory size it already has, no matter how much more it wants to produce because of increased demand for its product. We consider the plant and heavy equipment, the size or amount of which cannot be varied in the short run, as *fixed* resources. In agriculture and in some other businesses, land may be a fixed resource.

There are, of course, variable resources that the firm can alter when it wants to change its rate of production. These are called *variable inputs* or *variable factors of production*. Typically, the variable inputs of a firm are its labor and its purchases of raw materials. In the short run, in response to changes in demand, the firm can, by definition, change only the amounts of its variable inputs.

The Long Run

Long run
The time period during which all factors of production can be varied.

The **long run** can now be considered the period of time in which *all* inputs can be varied. Specifically, in the long run, the firm can alter its plant size. How long is the long run? That depends on each individual industry. For Wendy's or McDonald's, the long run may be four or five months, because that is the time it takes to add new franchises. For a steel company, the long run may be several years, because that's how long it takes to plan and build a new plant. An electric utility might need more than a decade to build a new plant.

Short run and *long run* in our discussion are terms that apply to planning decisions made by managers. Managers routinely take account of both the short-run and the long-run consequences of their behavior. While always making decisions about what to do today, tomorrow, and next week—the short run as it were—they keep an eye on the long-run net benefits of all short-run actions. As an individual, you have long-run plans, such as going to graduate school or having a successful career, and you make a series of short-run decisions with these long-run plans in mind.

The Relationship Between Output and Inputs

A firm takes numerous inputs, combines them using a technological production process, and ends up with an output. There are, of course, a great many factors of production, or inputs. Keeping the quantity of land fixed, we classify production inputs into two broad categories—capital and labor. The relationship between output and these two inputs is as follows:

Output per time period = some function of capital and labor inputs

We have used the word *production* but have not defined it. **Production** is any process by which resources are transformed into goods or services. Production includes not only making things but also transporting them, retailing, repackaging them, and so on. Notice that the production relationship tells nothing about the worth or value of the inputs or the output.

Production
Any activity that results in the conversion of resources into products that can be used in consumption.

The Production Function: A Numerical Example

The relationship between maximum physical output and the quantity of capital and labor used in the production process is sometimes called the **production function.** The production function is a technological relationship between inputs and output.

Production function
The relationship between inputs and maximum physical output. A production function is a technological, not an economic, relationship.

PROPERTIES OF THE PRODUCTION FUNCTION The production function specifies the maximum possible output that can be produced with a given amount of inputs. It also specifies the minimum amount of inputs necessary to produce a given level of output. Firms that are inefficient or wasteful in their use of capital and labor will obtain less output than the production function will show. No firm can obtain more output than the production function allows, however. The production function also depends on the technology available to the firm. It follows that an improvement in technology that allows the firm to produce more output with the same amount of inputs (or the same output with fewer inputs) results in a new production function.

How are new techniques for utilizing various types of computer software allowing companies to produce more output using the same inputs?

EXAMPLE Virtualization Expands Feasible Production at Many Firms

Database management programs, spreadsheets, and media players are examples of application software that firms commonly employ as part of the process of producing goods and services. Traditionally, firms have installed such software applications on the hard drives of their computers. Today, however, many firms are using a procedure called *application virtualization* to effectively "fool" the operating system of a computer into running application software even though the software is installed on a different computer. Hence, application virtualization frees up disc space on the "fooled" computers that the company can devote to other computing tasks.

In addition, through application virtualization, an operating system can often be used to run previously incompatible software applications side-by-side on the same computer. This allows firms to deploy the same computers and software application programs to complete more production tasks within the same period of time. Thus, application virtualization enables firms to produce a larger flow of goods and services per unit of time.

FOR CRITICAL ANALYSIS

Why do you suppose that business managers regard the process of developing the best production procedures as a fundamental requirement for operating at an (efficient) point on a firm's production function?

Panel (a) of Figure 22-1 on the next page shows a production function relating maximum output in column 2 to the quantity of labor in column 1. Zero workers per week produce no output. Five workers per week of input produce a total output of 50 computer servers per week. (Ignore for the moment the rest of that panel.) Panel (b) of Figure 22-1 displays this production function. It relates to the short run, because plant size is fixed, and it applies to a single firm.

FIGURE 22-1 The Production Function and Marginal Product: A Hypothetical Case

Marginal product is the addition to the total product that results when one additional worker is hired (for a week in this example). Thus, in panel (a), the marginal product of adding the fourth worker is eight computer servers. With four workers, 44 servers are produced, but with three workers, only 36 are produced. The difference is 8. In panel (b), we plot the numbers from columns 1 and 2 of panel (a). In panel (c), we plot the numbers from columns 1 and 4 of panel (a). When we go from 0 to 1, marginal product is 10. When we go from one worker to two workers, marginal product increases to 16. After two workers, marginal product declines, but it is still positive. Total product (output) reaches its peak at about seven workers, so after seven workers, marginal product is negative. When we move from seven to eight workers, marginal product becomes −1 computer server per week.

Panel (a)

(1) Input of Labor (number of worker-weeks)	(2) Total Product (output in computer servers per week)	(3) Average Physical Product (total product ÷ number of worker-weeks) [servers per week]	(4) Marginal Physical Product (output in servers per week)
0	—	—	
			10
1	10	10.00	
			16
2	26	13.00	
			10
3	36	12.00	
			8
4	44	11.00	
			6
5	50	10.00	
			4
6	54	9.00	
			2
7	56	8.00	
			−1
8	55	6.88	
			−2
9	53	5.89	
			−3
10	50	5.00	
			−4
11	46	4.18	

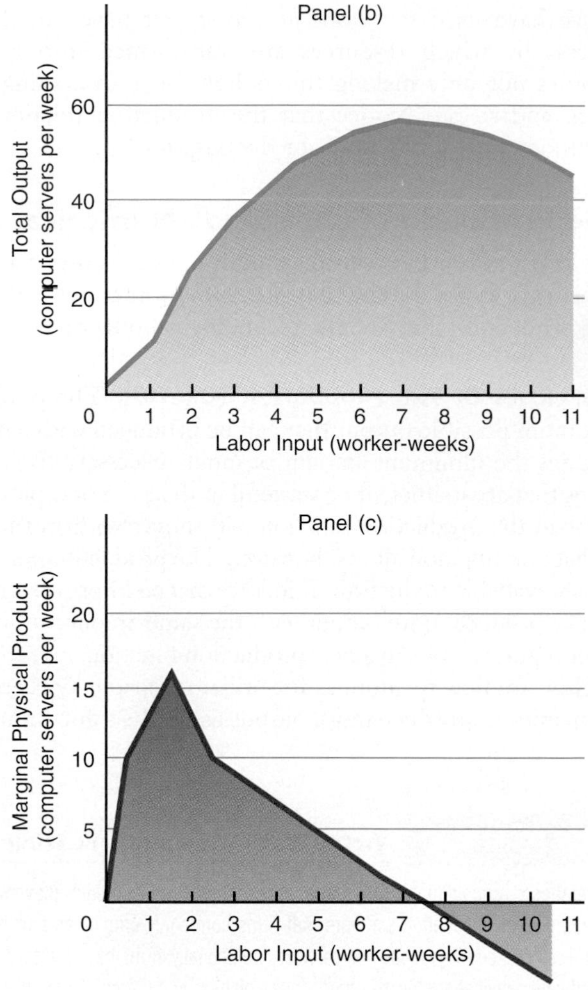

Panel (b)

Total Output (computer servers per week)

Labor Input (worker-weeks)

Panel (c)

Marginal Physical Product (computer servers per week)

Labor Input (worker-weeks)

TOTAL PHYSICAL PRODUCT Panel (b) shows a total physical product curve, or the maximum feasible output when we add successive equal-sized units of labor while holding all other inputs constant. The graph of the production function in panel (b) is not a straight line. It peaks at about seven workers per week and then starts to go down.

Average and Marginal Physical Product

Average physical product
Total product divided by the variable input.

Marginal physical product
The physical output that is due to the addition of one more unit of a variable factor of production. The change in total product occurring when a variable input is increased and all other inputs are held constant. It is also called *marginal product*.

To understand the shape of the total physical product curve, let's examine columns 3 and 4 of panel (a) of Figure 22-1 above—that is, average and marginal physical products. **Average physical product** is the total product divided by the number of worker-weeks. You can see in column 3 of panel (a) of Figure 22-1 that the average physical product of labor first rises and then steadily falls after two workers are hired.

Marginal means "additional," so the **marginal physical product** of labor is the *change* in total product that occurs when a worker is added to a production process for a given interval. (The term *physical* here emphasizes the fact that we are measuring in terms of material quantities of goods or tangible amounts of services, not in dollar terms.) The marginal physical product of labor therefore refers to the *change in output caused by a one-unit change in the labor input* as shown in column 4 of panel (a) of Figure 22-1 on the facing page. (Marginal physical product is also referred to as *marginal product*.)

Diminishing Marginal Product

Note that in Figure 22-1, when three workers instead of two are employed each week, marginal product declines. The concept of diminishing marginal product applies to many situations. If you put a seat belt across your lap, a certain amount of safety is obtained. If you add another seat belt over your shoulder, some additional safety is obtained, but less than when the first belt was secured. When you add a third seat belt over the other shoulder, the amount of *additional* safety obtained is even smaller.

Measuring Diminishing Marginal Product

How do we measure diminishing marginal product? First, we limit the analysis to only one variable factor of production (or input)—let's say the factor is labor. Every other factor of production, such as machines, must be held constant. Only in this way can we calculate the marginal product from adding more workers and know when we reach the point of diminishing marginal product.

SPECIALIZATION AND MARGINAL PRODUCT The marginal productivity of labor may increase rapidly at the very beginning. A firm starts with no workers, only machines. The firm then hires one worker, who finds it difficult to get the work started. But when the firm hires more workers, each is able to *specialize* in performing different tasks, and the marginal product of those additional workers may actually be greater than the marginal product of the previous few workers.

DIMINISHING MARGINAL PRODUCT Beyond some point, diminishing marginal product must set in—*not* because new workers are less qualified but because each worker has, on average, fewer machines with which to work (remember, all other inputs are fixed). In fact, eventually the firm's plant will become so crowded that workers will start to get in each other's way. At that point, marginal physical product becomes negative, and total production declines.

Using these ideas, we can define the **law of diminishing marginal product:**

Law of diminishing marginal product The observation that after some point, successive equal-sized increases in a variable factor of production, such as labor, added to fixed factors of production will result in smaller increases in output.

As successive equal increases in a variable factor of production are added to fixed factors of production, there will be a point beyond which the extra, or marginal, product that can be attributed to each additional unit of the variable factor of production will decline.

Note that the law of diminishing marginal product is a statement about the *physical* relationships between inputs and outputs that we have observed in many firms. If the law of diminishing marginal product were not a fairly accurate statement about the world, what would stop firms from hiring additional workers forever?

An Example of the Law of Diminishing Marginal Product

Production of computer servers provides an example of the law of diminishing marginal product. With a fixed amount of factory space, assembly equipment, and quality-control diagnostic software, the addition of more workers eventually yields successively smaller increases in output. After a while, when all the assembly equipment and quality-control diagnostic software are being used, additional workers will have to start assembling and troubleshooting quality problems manually. They obviously won't be as productive as the first workers, who had access to other productive inputs. The marginal physical product of an additional worker, given a specified amount of capital, must eventually be less than that for the previous workers.

GRAPHING THE MARGINAL PRODUCT OF LABOR A hypothetical set of numbers illustrating the law of diminishing marginal product is presented in panel (a) of Figure 22-1 on page 486. The numbers are presented graphically in panel (c). Marginal productivity (returns from adding more workers during a week) first increases, then decreases, and finally becomes negative.

When one worker is hired, total output goes from 0 to 10. Thus, marginal physical product is 10 computer servers per week. When two workers instead of one are hired, total product goes from 10 to 26 servers per week. Marginal physical product therefore increases to 16 servers per week. When three workers rather than two are hired, total product again increases, from 26 to 36 servers per week. This represents a marginal physical product of only 10 servers per week. Therefore, the point of diminishing marginal product occurs after two workers are hired.

THE POINT OF SATURATION Notice that after seven workers per week, marginal physical product becomes negative. That means that eight workers instead of seven would reduce total product. Sometimes this is called the *point of saturation*, indicating that given the amount of fixed inputs, there is no further positive use for more of the variable input. We have entered the region of negative marginal product.

QUICK QUIZ See page 506 for the answers. Review concepts from this section in MyEconLab.

The technological relationship between output and inputs is called the _________ function. It relates _________ per time period to several inputs, such as capital and labor.

After some rate of output, the firm generally experiences diminishing marginal _________.

The law of diminishing marginal product states that if all factors of production are held constant except one, equal increments in that one variable factor will eventually yield _________ increments in _________.

Short-Run Costs to the Firm

You will see that costs are the extension of the production ideas just presented. Let's consider the costs the firm faces in the short run. To make this example simple, assume that there are only two factors of production, capital and labor. Our definition of the short run will be the time during which capital is fixed but labor is variable.

Total costs
The sum of total fixed costs and total variable costs.

In the short run, a firm incurs certain types of costs. We label all costs incurred **total costs.** Then we break total costs down into total fixed costs and total variable costs, which we will explain shortly. Therefore,

Total costs (TC) = total fixed costs (TFC) + total variable costs (TVC)

Remember that these total costs include both explicit and implicit costs, including the normal rate of return on investment.

After we have looked at the elements of total costs, we will find out how to compute average and marginal costs.

Total Fixed Costs

Let's look at an ongoing business such as Hewlett-Packard (HP). The decision makers in that corporate giant can look around and see big machines, thousands of parts, huge buildings, and a multitude of other components of plant and equipment that have already been bought and are in place. HP has to take into account expenses to replace some worn-out equipment, no matter how many digital devices it produces. The opportunity costs of any fixed resources that HP owns will all be identical, regardless of the rate of output. In the short run, these costs are the same for HP no matter how many digital devices it produces.

We also have to point out that the opportunity cost (or normal rate of return) of capital must be included along with other costs. Remember that we are dealing in the short run, during which capital is fixed. This leads us to a very straightforward definition of fixed costs: All costs that do not vary—that is, all costs that do not depend on the rate of production—are called **fixed costs.**

Fixed costs
Costs that do not vary with output. Fixed costs typically include such expenses as rent on a building. These costs are fixed for a certain period of time (in the long run, though, they are variable).

Let's now take as an example the fixed costs incurred by a producer of titanium batteries used with digital cameras, computer accessories, and other devices. This firm's total fixed costs will usually include the cost of the rent for its plant and equipment and the insurance it has to pay. We see in panel (a) of Figure 22-2 on the next page that total fixed costs per hour are $10. In panel (b), these total fixed costs are represented by the horizontal line at $10 per hour. They are invariant to changes in the daily output of titanium batteries—no matter how many are produced, fixed costs will remain at $10 per hour.

Total Variable Costs

Total **variable costs** are costs whose magnitude varies with the rate of production. Wages are an obvious variable cost. The more the firm produces, the more labor it has to hire. Therefore, the more wages it has to pay. Parts are another variable cost. To manufacture titanium batteries, for example, titanium must be bought. The more batteries that are made, the more titanium that must be bought. A portion of the rate of depreciation (wear and tear) on machines that are used in the assembly process can also be considered a variable cost if depreciation depends partly on how long and how intensively the machines are used. Total variable costs are given in column 3 in panel (a) of Figure 22-2. These are translated into the total variable cost curve in panel (b). Notice that the total variable cost curve lies below the total cost curve by the vertical distance of $10. This vertical distance of course, represents, total fixed costs.

Variable costs
Costs that vary with the rate of production. They include wages paid to workers and purchases of materials.

Why Not . . . force firms to reduce their fixed and, hence, total costs by cutting their energy use?

The level of energy that firms use in their operations usually cannot be adjusted in the short run, so firms' energy expenses are fixed costs. Thus, if firms were to find ways to operate using less energy, their fixed costs would fall. Nevertheless, requiring companies to cut back on their use of short-run energy would not necessarily reduce their *total* costs. The reason is that current levels of energy use already reflect firms' efforts to balance inputs in a way that minimizes total costs. If firms were forced to cut back on energy utilization, then overall cost minimization could require them to increase their use of labor or other variable inputs to maintain their output rates, which would cause their variable costs to increase. Therefore, it is possible that requiring firms to reduce energy expenses could, on net, *raise* their total costs.

Short-Run Average Cost Curves

In panel (b) of Figure 22-2 on the next page, we see total costs, total variable costs, and total fixed costs. Now we want to look at average cost. With the average cost concept, we are measuring cost per unit of output. It is a matter of simple arithmetic to figure the averages of these three cost concepts. We can define them as follows:

$$\text{Average total costs (ATC)} = \frac{\text{total costs (TC)}}{\text{output } (Q)}$$

$$\text{Average variable costs (AVC)} = \frac{\text{total variable costs (TVC)}}{\text{output } (Q)}$$

$$\text{Average fixed costs (AFC)} = \frac{\text{total fixed costs (TFC)}}{\text{output } (Q)}$$

You Are There

To contemplate why higher variable costs depressed profits of firms that specialize in repossessing vehicles, even though the demand for their services increased during the recent economic downturn, read **During Hard Times for Borrowers, a Repo Man Also Has It Tough,** on page 501.

FIGURE 22-2 Cost of Production: An Example

In panel (a), the derivations of columns 4 through 9 are given in parentheses in each column heading. For example, in column 6, average variable costs are derived by dividing column 3, total variable costs, by column 1, total output per hour. Note that marginal cost (MC) in panel (c) intersects average variable costs (AVC) at the latter's minimum point. Also, MC intersects average total costs (ATC) at that latter's minimum point. It is a little more difficult to see that MC equals AVC and ATC at their respective minimum points in panel (a) because we are using discrete one-unit changes. You can see, though, that the marginal cost of going from 4 units per hour to 5 units per hour is $2 and increases to $3 when we move to 6 units per hour. Somewhere in between it equals AVC of $2.60, which is in fact the minimum average variable cost. The same analysis holds for ATC, which hits its respective minimum at 7 units per day at $4.28 per unit. MC goes from $4 to $5 and just equals ATC somewhere in between.

Panel (a)

(1) Total Output (*Q*/hour)	(2) Total Fixed Costs (TFC)	(3) Total Variable Costs (TVC)	(4) Total Costs (TC) (4) = (2) + (3)	(5) Average Fixed Costs (AFC) (5) = (2) ÷ (1)	(6) Average Variable Costs (AVC) (6) = (3) ÷ (1)	(7) Average Total Costs (ATC) (7) = (4) ÷ (1)	(8) Total Costs (TC) (4)	(9) Marginal Cost (MC) (9) = $\frac{\text{Change in (8)}}{\text{Change in (1)}}$
0	$10	$ 0	$10	—	—	—	$10	
								$5
1	10	5	15	$10.00	$5.00	$15.00	15	
								3
2	10	8	18	5.00	4.00	9.00	18	
								2
3	10	10	20	3.33	3.33	6.67	20	
								1
4	10	11	21	2.50	2.75	5.25	21	
								2
5	10	13	23	2.00	2.60	4.60	23	
								3
6	10	16	26	1.67	2.67	4.33	26	
								4
7	10	20	30	1.43	2.86	4.28	30	
								5
8	10	25	35	1.25	3.12	4.38	35	
								6
9	10	31	41	1.11	3.44	4.56	41	
								7
10	10	38	48	1.00	3.80	4.80	48	
								8
11	10	46	56	.91	4.18	5.09	56	

Panel (b)

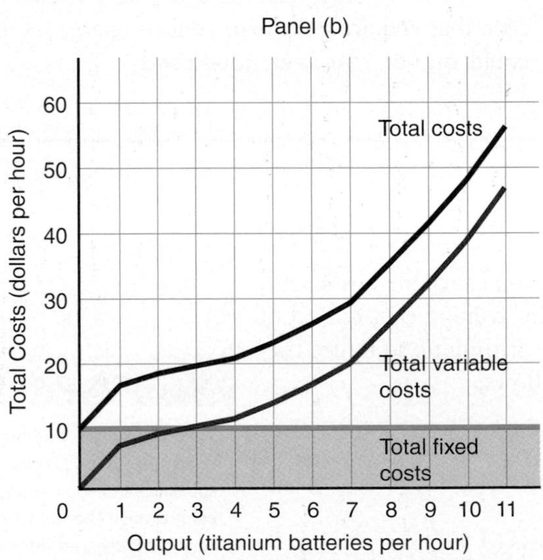

Panel (c)

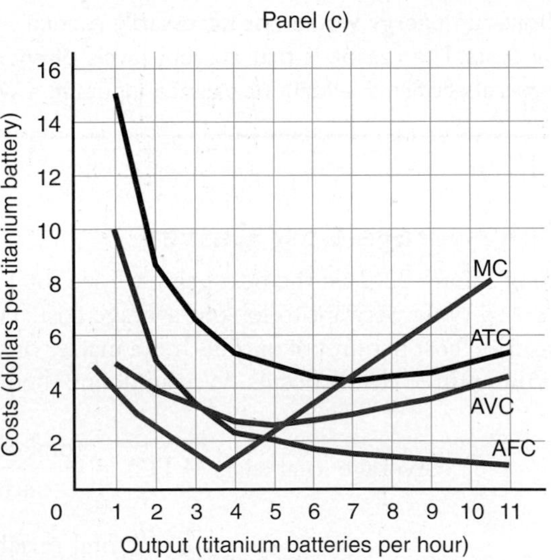

The arithmetic is done in columns 5, 6, and 7 in panel (a) of Figure 22-2 on the facing page. The numerical results are translated into a graphical format in panel (c). Because total costs (TC) equal variable costs (TVC) plus fixed costs (TFC), the difference between average total costs (ATC) and average variable costs (AVC) will always be identical to average fixed costs (AFC). That means that average total costs and average variable costs move together as output expands.

Now let's see what we can observe about the three average cost curves in Figure 22-2.

AVERAGE FIXED COSTS (AFC) **Average fixed costs** continue to fall throughout the output range. In fact, if we were to continue panel (c) of Figure 22-2 farther to the right, we would find that average fixed costs would get closer and closer to the horizontal axis. That is because total fixed costs remain constant. As we divide this fixed number by a larger and larger number of units of output, the resulting AFC becomes smaller and smaller. In business, this is called "spreading the overhead."

Average fixed costs
Total fixed costs divided by the number of units produced.

AVERAGE VARIABLE COSTS (AVC) We assume a particular form of the curve for **average variable costs.** The form that it takes is U-shaped: First it falls; then it starts to rise. (It is possible for the AVC curve to take other shapes in the long run.)

Average variable costs
Total variable costs divided by the number of units produced.

AVERAGE TOTAL COSTS (ATC) This curve has a shape similar to that of the AVC curve. Nevertheless, it falls even more dramatically in the beginning and rises more slowly after it has reached a minimum point. It falls and then rises because **average total costs** are the vertical summation of the AFC curve and the AVC curve. Thus, when AFC and AVC are both falling, ATC must fall too. At some point, however, AVC starts to increase while AFC continues to fall. Once the increase in the AVC curve outweighs the decrease in the AFC curve, the ATC curve will start to increase and will develop a U shape, just like the AVC curve.

Average total costs
Total costs divided by the number of units produced; sometimes called *average per-unit total costs*.

How has the U.S. military reduced the average total costs of developing and producing electronic weapons systems?

POLICY EXAMPLE **Pulling New Weapons off the Computer Games Shelf**

In recent years, the U.S. military has procured thousands of everyday electronic products, including Sony PlayStation and Microsoft Xbox consoles, Panasonic Toughbook computers, and Apple iPods, iPhones, and iPads. The U.S. military uses these everyday electronic gadgets to assist in developing new weapons. In the past, the creation of new weapons technologies required new types of computer hardware specifically geared to military purposes. In recent years, however, computing technologies have advanced so rapidly that "new" military computer hardware has been outdated by the time it has been developed. Weapons developers have found that by employing components from electronic gadgets produced by firms such as Sony, Microsoft, and Apple, they can incorporate the most up-to-date computing technologies.

The developers have also found that the costs incurred in developing weapons are reduced if they use the latest equipment produced by commercial firms. The costs incurred in producing each additional unit of military hardware, such as robotic reconnaissance vehicles, are also lower when readily available products are utilized as components. Thus, employing electronic products available to anyone—friend and foe alike—has reduced average total costs incurred in designing and producing new military hardware.

FOR CRITICAL ANALYSIS

Has the U.S. military's use of widely available electronic products reduced its average fixed costs, its average variable costs, or both? Explain.

Marginal Cost

We have stated repeatedly that the basis of decisions is always on the margin—movement in economics is always determined at the margin. This dictum also holds true within the firm. Firms, according to the analysis we use to predict their behavior, are very concerned with their **marginal costs.** Because the term *marginal* means "additional" or "incremental" (or "decremental," too) here, *marginal costs* refer to costs that result from a one-unit change in the production rate. For example, if the

Marginal costs
The change in total costs due to a one-unit change in production rate.

production of 10 titanium batteries per hour costs a firm $48 and the production of 11 of these batteries costs $56 per hour, the marginal cost of producing 11 rather than 10 batteries per hour is $8.

Marginal costs can be measured by using the formula

$$\text{Marginal cost} = \frac{\text{change in total cost}}{\text{change in output}}$$

We show the marginal costs of production of titanium batteries per hour in column 9 of panel (a) in Figure 22-2 on page 490, computed according to the formula just given. In our example, we have changed output by one unit every time, so the denominator in that particular formula always equals one.

This marginal cost schedule is shown graphically in panel (c) of Figure 22-2. Just like average variable costs and average total costs, marginal costs first fall and then rise. The U shape of the marginal cost curve is a result of increasing and then diminishing marginal product. At lower levels of output, the marginal cost curve declines. The reasoning is that as marginal physical product increases with each addition of output, the marginal cost of this last unit of output must fall.

Conversely, when diminishing marginal product sets in, marginal physical product decreases (and eventually becomes negative). It follows that the marginal cost must rise when the marginal product begins its decline. These relationships are clearly reflected in the geometry of panels (b) and (c) of Figure 22-2.

In summary:

As long as marginal physical product rises, marginal cost will fall. When marginal physical product starts to fall (after reaching the point of diminishing marginal product), marginal cost will begin to rise.

The Relationship Between Average and Marginal Costs

Let us now examine the relationship between average costs and marginal costs. There is always a definite relationship between averages and marginals. Consider the example of 10 football players with an average weight of 250 pounds. An eleventh player is added. His weight is 300 pounds. That represents the marginal weight. What happens now to the average weight of the team? It must increase. That is, when the marginal player weighs more than the average, the average must increase. Likewise, if the marginal player weighs less than 250 pounds, the average weight will decrease.

AVERAGE VARIABLE COSTS AND MARGINAL COSTS There is a similar relationship between average variable costs and marginal costs. When marginal costs are less than average costs, the latter must fall. Conversely, when marginal costs are greater than average costs, the latter must rise. When you think about it, the relationship makes sense. The only way average variable costs can fall is if the extra cost of the marginal unit produced is less than the average variable cost of all the preceding units. For example, if the average variable cost for two units of production is $4.00 a unit, the only way for the average variable cost of three units to be less than that of two units is for the variable costs attributable to the last unit—the marginal cost—to be less than the average of the past units. In this particular case, if average variable cost falls to $3.33 a unit, total variable cost for the three units would be three times $3.33, or almost exactly $10.00. Total variable cost for two units is two times $4.00 (average variable cost), or $8.00. The marginal cost is therefore $10.00 minus $8.00, or $2.00, which is less than the average variable cost of $3.33.

A similar type of computation can be carried out for rising average variable costs. The only way average variable costs can rise is if the average variable cost of additional units is more than that for units already produced. But the incremental cost is the marginal cost. In this particular case, the marginal costs have to be higher than the average variable costs.

AVERAGE TOTAL COSTS AND MARGINAL COSTS There is also a relationship between marginal costs and average total costs. Remember that average total cost is equal to total costs divided by the number of units produced. Also remember that marginal cost does not include any fixed costs. Fixed costs are, by definition, fixed and cannot influence marginal costs. Our example can therefore be repeated substituting *average total costs* for *average variable costs*.

These rising and falling relationships can be seen in panel (c) of Figure 22-2 on page 490, where MC intersects AVC and ATC at their respective minimum points.

Minimum Cost Points

At what rate of output of titanium batteries per hour does our representative firm experience the minimum average total costs? Column 7 in panel (a) of Figure 22-2 shows that the minimum average total cost is $4.28, which occurs at an output rate of seven of these batteries per hour. We can also find this minimum cost by finding the point in panel (c) of Figure 22-2 where the marginal cost curve intersects the average total cost curve. This should not be surprising. When marginal cost is below average total cost, average total cost falls. When marginal cost is above average total cost, average total cost rises. At the point where average total cost is neither falling nor rising, marginal cost must then be equal to average total cost. When we represent this graphically, the marginal cost curve will intersect the average total cost curve at the latter's minimum.

The same analysis applies to the intersection of the marginal cost curve and the average variable cost curve. When are average variable costs at a minimum? According to panel (a) of Figure 22-2, average variable costs are at a minimum of $2.60 at an output rate of five titanium batteries per hour. This is where the marginal cost curve intersects the average variable cost curve in panel (c) of Figure 22-2.

QUICK QUIZ See page 506 for the answers. Review concepts from this section in MyEconLab.

Total costs equal total __________ costs plus total __________ costs. Fixed costs are those that do not vary with the rate of production. Variable costs are those that do vary with the rate of production.

__________ total costs equal total costs divided by output (__________ = TC/Q).

Average __________ costs equal total variable costs divided by output (__________ = TVC/Q).

Average __________ costs equal total fixed costs divided by output (__________ = TFC/Q).

__________ cost equals the change in __________ cost divided by the change in output (__________ = Δ __________/ΔQ, where the Greek letter Δ, delta, means "change in").

The marginal cost curve intersects the __________ point of the average total cost curve and the __________ point of the average variable cost curve.

The Relationship Between Diminishing Marginal Product and Cost Curves

There is a unique relationship between output and the shape of the various cost curves we have drawn. Let's consider Internet access service calls and the relationship between marginal cost and diminishing marginal physical product shown in panel (a) of Figure 22-3 on the next page. It turns out that if wage rates are constant, the shape of the marginal cost curve in panel (d) of Figure 22-3 is both a reflection of and a consequence of the law of diminishing marginal product.

Marginal Cost and Marginal Physical Product

Let's assume that each unit of labor can be purchased at a constant price. Further assume that labor is the only variable input. We see that as more workers are hired, marginal physical product first rises and then falls. Thus, the marginal cost of each

Panel (a)

(1) Labor Input	(2) Total Product (number of Internet access accounts serviced per week)	(3) Average Physical Product (accounts per technician) (3) = (2) ÷ (1)	(4) Marginal Physical Product	(5) Average Variable Cost (5) = *W* ($1,000) ÷ (3)	(6) Marginal Cost (6) = *W* ($1,000) ÷ (4)
0	0	—	—	—	—
1	50	50	50	$20.00	$20.00
2	110	55	60	18.18	16.67
3	180	60	70	16.67	14.29
4	240	60	60	16.67	16.67
5	290	58	50	17.24	20.00
6	330	55	40	18.18	25.00
7	360	51	30	19.61	33.33

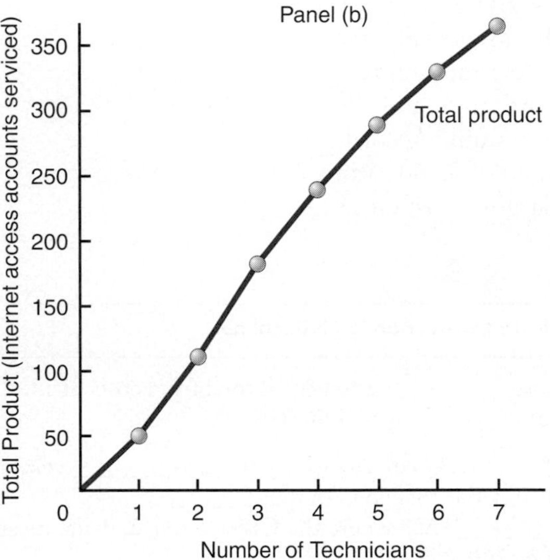

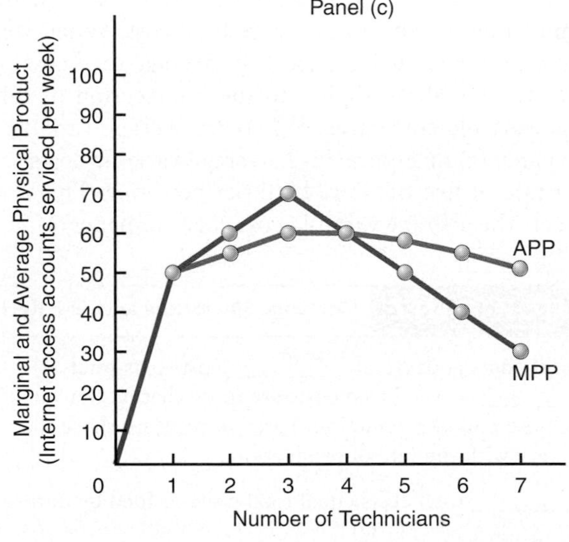

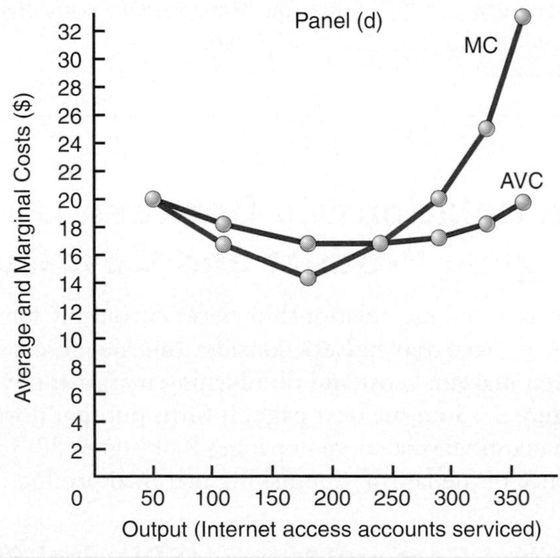

FIGURE 22-3 The Relationship Between Output and Costs

As the number of skilled technicians increases, the total number of Internet access accounts serviced each week rises, as shown in panels (a) and (b). In panel (c), marginal physical product (MPP) first rises and then falls. Average physical product (APP) follows. The near mirror image of panel (c) is shown in panel (d), in which MC and AVC first fall and then rise.

extra unit of output will first fall as long as marginal physical product is rising, and then it will rise as long as marginal physical product is falling. Recall that marginal cost is defined as

$$\text{MC} = \frac{\text{change in total cost}}{\text{change in output}}$$

Because the price of labor is assumed to be constant, the change in total cost depends solely on the unchanged price of labor, W. The change in output is simply the marginal physical product (MPP) of the one-unit increase in labor. Therefore, we see that

$$\text{Marginal cost} = \frac{W}{\text{MPP}}$$

This means that initially, when marginal physical product is increasing, marginal cost falls (we are dividing W by increasingly larger numbers), and later, when marginal product is falling, marginal cost must increase (we are dividing W by smaller numbers). So, as marginal physical product increases, marginal cost decreases, and as marginal physical product decreases, marginal cost must increase. Thus, when marginal physical product reaches its maximum, marginal cost necessarily reaches its minimum.

An Illustration

To illustrate this, let's return to Figure 22-1 on page 486 and consider specifically panel (a). Assume that a skilled worker assembling computer servers is paid $1,000 a week. When we go from zero labor input to one unit, output increases by 10 computer servers. Each of those 10 servers has a marginal cost of $100. Now the second unit of labor is hired, and this individual costs $1,000 per week. Output increases by 16. Thus, the marginal cost is $1,000 ÷ 16 = $62.50. We continue the experiment. We see that adding another unit of labor yields only 10 additional computer servers, so marginal cost starts to rise again back to $100. The following unit of labor yields a marginal physical product of only 8, so marginal cost becomes $1,000 ÷ 8 = $125.

All of the foregoing can be restated in relatively straightforward terms:

> ***Firms' short-run cost curves are a reflection of the law of diminishing marginal product. Given any constant price of the variable input, marginal costs decline as long as the marginal physical product of the variable resource is rising. At the point at which marginal product begins to diminish, marginal costs begin to rise as the marginal physical product of the variable input begins to decline.***

The result is a marginal cost curve that slopes down, hits a minimum, and then slopes up.

Average Costs and Average Physical Product

Of course, average total costs and average variable costs are affected. The ATC and AVC curves will have their familiar U shape in the short run. Recall that

$$\text{AVC} = \frac{\text{total variable costs}}{\text{total output}}$$

As we move from zero labor input to one unit in panel (a) of Figure 22-1 on page 486, output increases from zero to 10 computer servers. The total variable costs are the price per worker, W ($1,000), times the number of workers (1). Because the average product of one worker (column 3) is 10, we can write the total product, 10, as the average product, 10, times the number of workers, 1. Thus, we see that

$$\text{AVC} = \frac{\$1{,}000 \times 1}{10 \times 1} = \frac{\$1{,}000}{10} = \frac{W}{\text{AP}}$$

From column 3 in panel (a) of Figure 22-1, we see that the average product increases, reaches a maximum, and then declines. Because AVC = W/AP, average variable cost decreases as average product increases, and increases as average product decreases. AVC reaches its minimum when average product reaches its maximum. Furthermore, because ATC = AVC + AFC, the average total cost curve inherits the relationship between the average variable cost and diminishing returns.

To illustrate, consider an Internet service provider that employs skilled technicians to provide access services within a given geographic area. In panel (a) of Figure 22-3 on page 494, column 2 shows the total number of Internet access accounts serviced as the number of technicians increases. Notice that the total product first increases at an increasing rate and later increases at a decreasing rate. This is reflected in column 4, which shows that the marginal physical product increases at first and then falls. The average physical product too first rises and then falls. The marginal and average physical products are graphed in panel (c) of Figure 22-3.

Our immediate interest here is the average variable and marginal costs. Because we can define average variable cost as $1,000/AP (assuming that the wage paid is constant at $1,000), as the average product rises from 50 to 55 to 60 Internet access accounts, the average variable cost falls from $20.00 to $18.18 to $16.67. Conversely, as average product falls from 60 to 51, average variable cost rises from $16.67 to $19.61. Likewise, because marginal cost can also be defined as *W*/MPP, we see that as marginal physical product rises from 50 to 70, marginal cost falls from $20.00 to $14.29. As marginal physical product falls to 30, marginal cost rises to $33.33. These relationships are also expressed in panels (b), (c), and (d) of Figure 22-3 on page 494.

Long-Run Cost Curves

Planning horizon
The long run, during which all inputs are variable.

The long run is defined as a time period during which full adjustment can be made to any change in the economic environment. Thus, in the long run, *all* factors of production are variable. Long-run curves are sometimes called *planning curves*, and the long run is sometimes called the **planning horizon.** We start our analysis of long-run cost curves by considering a single firm contemplating the construction of a single plant. The firm has three alternative plant sizes from which to choose on the planning horizon. Each particular plant size generates its own short-run average total cost curve. Now that we are talking about the difference between long-run and short-run cost curves, we will label all short-run curves with an *S* and long-run curves with an *L*. Short-run average (total) costs will be labeled SAC. Long-run average cost curves will be labeled LAC.

Panel (a) of Figure 22-4 on the facing page shows short-run average cost curves for three successively larger plants. Which is the optimal size to build, if we can only choose among these three? That depends on the anticipated normal, sustained rate of output per time period. Assume for a moment that the anticipated normal, sustained rate is Q_1. If a plant of size 1 is built, average cost will be C_1. If a plant of size 2 is built, we see on SAC_2 that average cost will be C_2, which is greater than C_1. Thus, if the anticipated rate of output is Q_1, the appropriate plant size is the one from which SAC_1 was derived.

If the anticipated sustained rate of output per time period increases from Q_1 to a higher level such as Q_2, however, and a plant of size 1 is selected, average cost will be C_4. If a plant of size 2 is chosen, average cost will be C_3, which is clearly less than C_4.

In choosing the appropriate plant size for a single-plant firm during the planning horizon, the firm will pick the size whose short-run average cost curve generates an average cost that is lowest for the expected rate of output.

Long-Run Average Cost Curve

If we now assume that the entrepreneur faces an infinite number of choices of plant sizes in the long run, we can conceive of an infinite number of SAC curves similar to the three in panel (a) of Figure 22-4. We are not able, of course, to draw an infinite number, but we have drawn quite a few in panel (b) of Figure 22-4. We then draw the

FIGURE 22-4 Preferable Plant Size and the Long-Run Average Cost Curve

If the anticipated sustained rate of output per unit time period is Q_1, the optimal plant to build is the one corresponding to SAC_1 in panel (a) because average cost is lower. If the sustained rate of output increases toward the higher level Q_2, however, it will be more profitable to have a plant size corresponding to SAC_2. If we draw all the possible short-run average cost curves that correspond to different plant sizes and then draw the envelope (a curve tangent to each member of a set of curves) to these various curves, $SAC_1 - SAC_8$, we obtain the long-run average cost (LAC) curve as shown in panel (b).

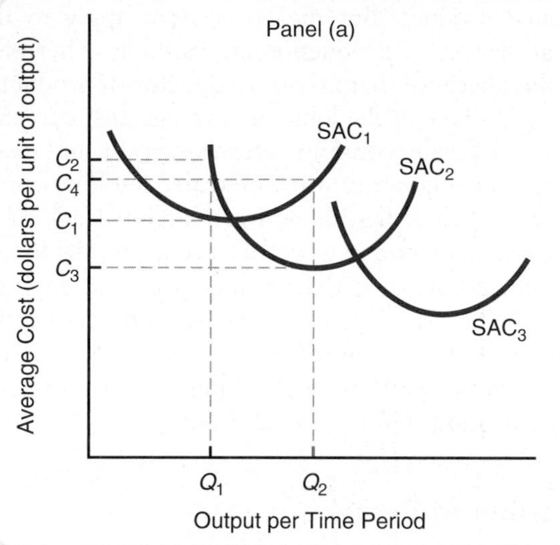

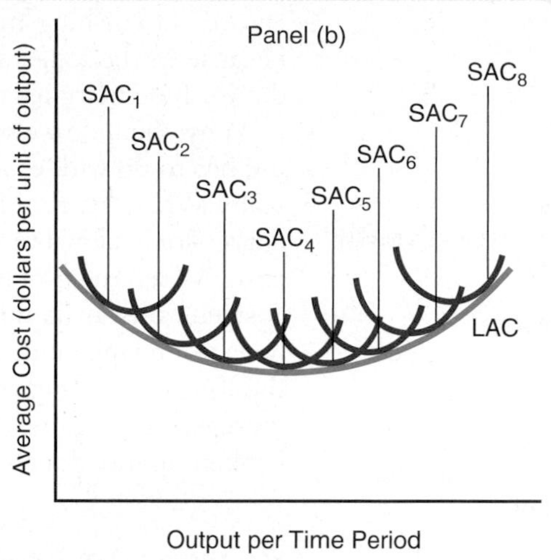

"envelope" to all these various short-run average cost curves. The resulting envelope is the **long-run average cost curve.** This long-run average cost curve is sometimes called the **planning curve,** for it represents the various average costs attainable at the planning stage of the firm's decision making. It represents the locus (path) of points giving the least unit cost of producing any given rate of output. Note that the LAC curve is *not* tangent to each individual SAC curve at the latter's minimum points, except at the minimum point of the LAC curve. Then and only then are minimum long-run average costs equal to minimum short-run average costs.

Long-run average cost curve
The locus of points representing the minimum unit cost of producing any given rate of output, given current technology and resource prices.

Planning curve
The long-run average cost curve.

How is the shape of the long-run average cost curve changing in the book-publishing industry?

EXAMPLE New Technologies Reshape the LAC Curve in Book Publishing

A "print-on-demand" (POD) apparatus can print a book in the same time that it takes a Starbucks employee to prepare a cappuccino. The device's black-and-white printer processes the book's pages, a color printer produces the book's cover, and a special mechanism glues the pages and cover together into a book.

In the past, book publishers traditionally utilized offset-print machines, which can be used to print books at lowest average cost only if large numbers of copies are produced. Indeed, for many years publishers have routinely printed individual books in such large numbers that a significant percentage of copies end up being discarded. Today, publishers can use POD devices to produce many fewer copies of a book at an average cost at least as low as that incurred using traditional offset printing.

Thus, publishers can produce fewer copies of individual books at the lowest feasible average cost, which is why the percentage of books printed by POD devices is projected to rise from 6 percent today to 25 percent in 2018. Short-run cost curves associated with lower rates of book output have shifted downward and thereby pushed the minimum point of publishers' long-run average cost curves leftward.

FOR CRITICAL ANALYSIS

If the minimum point of the LAC curve for POD printing is at a lower position than the old minimum point for offset printing, what is true of the minimum long-run average cost of POD printing compared with offset printing?

Why the Long-Run Average Cost Curve Is U-Shaped

Notice that the long-run average cost curve, LAC, in panel (b) of Figure 22-4 on the preceding page is U-shaped, similar to the U shape of the short-run average cost curve developed earlier in this chapter. The reason behind the U shape of the two curves is not the same, however. The short-run average cost curve is U-shaped because of the law of diminishing marginal product. But the law cannot apply to the long run, because in the long run, all factors of production are variable. There is no point of diminishing marginal product because there is no fixed factor of production.

Why, then, do we see the U shape in the long-run average cost curve? The reasoning has to do with economies of scale, constant returns to scale, and diseconomies of scale. When the firm is experiencing **economies of scale,** the long-run average cost curve slopes downward—an increase in scale and production leads to a fall in unit costs. When the firm is experiencing **constant returns to scale,** the long-run average cost curve is at its minimum point, such that an increase in scale and production does not change unit costs. When the firm is experiencing **diseconomies of scale,** the long-run average cost curve slopes upward—an increase in scale and production increases unit costs. These three sections of the long-run average cost curve are broken up into panels (a), (b), and (c) in Figure 22-5 below.

Economies of scale
Decreases in long-run average costs resulting from increases in output.

Constant returns to scale
No change in long-run average costs when output increases.

Diseconomies of scale
Increases in long-run average costs that occur as output increases.

Reasons for Economies of Scale

We shall examine three of the many reasons why a firm might be expected to experience economies of scale: specialization, the dimensional factor, and improvements in productive equipment.

SPECIALIZATION As a firm's scale of operation increases, the opportunities for specialization in the use of resource inputs also increase. This is sometimes called *increased division of tasks* or *operations*. Cost reductions generated by productivity enhancements from such division of labor or increased specialization are well known. When we consider managerial staffs, we also find that larger enterprises may be able to put together more highly specialized staffs.

FIGURE 22-5 Economies of Scale, Constant Returns to Scale, and Diseconomies of Scale Shown with the Long-Run Average Cost Curve

The long-run average cost curve will fall when there are economies of scale, as shown in panel (a). It will be constant (flat) when the firm is experiencing constant returns to scale, as shown in panel (b). It will rise when the firm is experiencing diseconomies of scale, as shown in panel (c).

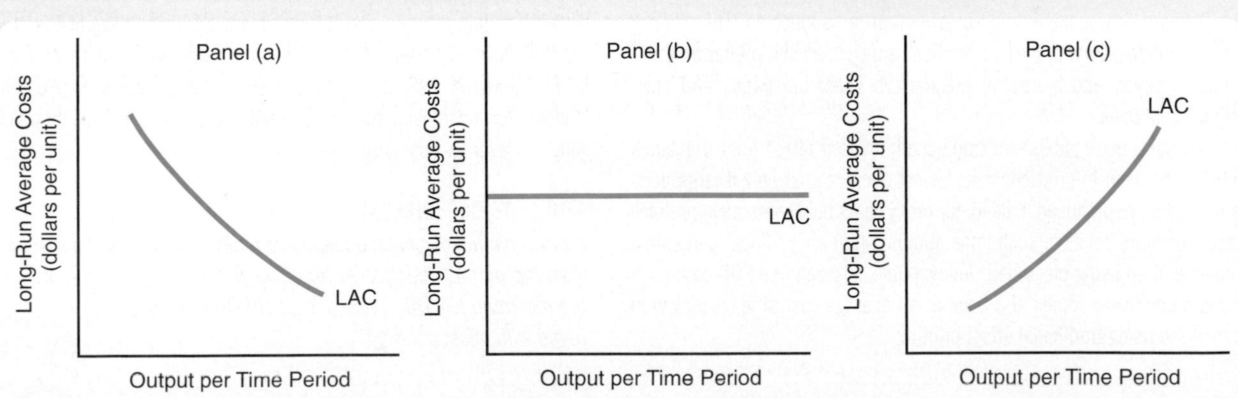

DIMENSIONAL FACTOR Large-scale firms often require proportionately less input per unit of output simply because certain inputs do not have to be physically doubled in order to double the output. Consider an oil-storage firm's cost of storing oil. The cost of storage is related to the cost of steel that goes into building the storage container. The amount of steel required, however, goes up less than in proportion to the volume (storage capacity) of the container (because the volume of a container increases more than proportionately with its surface area).

IMPROVEMENTS IN PRODUCTIVE EQUIPMENT The larger the scale of the enterprise, the more the firm is able to take advantage of larger-volume (output capacity) types of machinery. Small-scale operations may not be able to profitably use large-volume machines that can be more efficient per unit of output. Also, smaller firms often cannot use technologically more advanced machinery because they are unable to spread out the high cost of such sophisticated equipment over a large output.

For any of these reasons, the firm may experience economies of scale, which means that equal percentage increases in output result in a decrease in average cost. Thus, output can double, but total costs will less than double. Hence, average cost falls. Note that the factors listed for causing economies of scale are all *internal* to the firm. They do not depend on what other firms are doing or what is happening in the economy.

Why a Firm Might Experience Diseconomies of Scale

One of the basic reasons that a firm can expect to run into diseconomies of scale is that there are limits to the efficient functioning of management. This is so because larger levels of output imply successively larger *plant* size, which in turn implies successively larger *firm* size. Thus, as the level of output increases, more people must be hired, and the firm gets bigger. As this happens, however, the support, supervisory, and administrative staff and the general paperwork of the firm all increase. As the layers of supervision grow, the costs of information and communication grow more than proportionately. Hence, the average unit cost will start to increase.

Some observers of corporate giants claim that many of them have been experiencing some diseconomies of scale. Witness the difficulties that firms such as Dell and General Motors have experienced in recent years. Some analysts say that the profitability declines they have encountered are at least partly a function of their size relative to their smaller, more flexible competitors, which can make decisions more quickly and then take advantage of changing market conditions more rapidly.

Minimum Efficient Scale

Economists and statisticians have obtained actual data on the relationship between changes in all inputs and changes in average cost. It turns out that for many industries, the long-run average cost curve does not resemble the curve shown in panel (b) of Figure 22-4 on page 497. Rather, it more closely resembles Figure 22-6 on the next page. What you observe there is a small portion of declining long-run average costs (economies of scale) and then a wide range of outputs over which the firm experiences relatively constant economies of scale.

At the output rate when economies of scale end and constant economies of scale start, the **minimum efficient scale (MES)** for the firm is encountered. It occurs at point A. The minimum efficient scale is defined as the lowest rate of output at which long-run average costs are minimized. In any industry with a long-run average cost curve similar to the one in Figure 22-6, larger firms will have no cost-saving

Minimum efficient scale (MES)
The lowest rate of output per unit time at which long-run average costs for a particular firm are at a minimum.

FIGURE 22-6 Minimum Efficient Scale

This long-run average cost curve reaches a minimum point at *A*. After that point, long-run average costs remain horizontal, or constant, and then rise at some later rate of output. Point *A* is called the minimum efficient scale for the firm because that is the point at which it reaches minimum costs. It is the lowest rate of output at which average long-run costs are minimized. At point *B*, diseconomies of scale arise, so long-run average cost begins to increase with further increases in output.

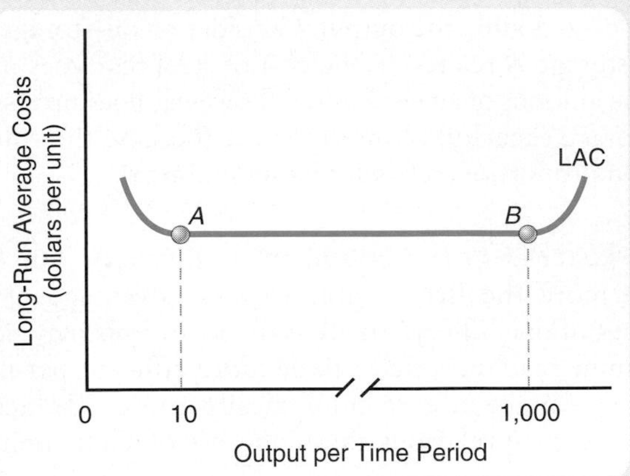

advantage over smaller firms as long as the smaller firms have at least obtained the minimum efficient scale at point *A*.

What accounts for the smaller minimum efficient scale of stores operated by a major electronics retailer?

EXAMPLE Why "Big-Box" Retailer Best Buy Has Begun to Shrink Its Stores

Discount retailers that typically operate stores of at least 30,000 square feet, such as Wal-Mart and Costco, are often called "big-box" retailers. Among the traditional big-box retailers is Best Buy, which sells a wide range of electronic goods such as flat screen televisions, Blu-ray disc players, and audio systems. Traditionally, the average size of a Best Buy store has been 40,000 square feet. Soon, however, this average size will be shrinking because the average scale of operations for most of Best Buy's newer stores will be less than one-tenth as large. The company has determined that it can sell many of today's most sought-after items, such as Internet-ready smart phones, at lower average cost in stores with only 3,000 square feet. Thus, the minimum efficient scale of Best Buy stores will be decreasing in the years to come.

FOR CRITICAL ANALYSIS

If Best Buy's overall sales of electronic equipment do not change but the minimum efficient scale of its stores drops closer to 3,000 square feet, what will happen to the total number of stores at which it sells these goods?

QUICK QUIZ See page 506 for the answers. Review concepts from this section in MyEconLab.

The __________ run is often called the **planning horizon.** The __________-run average cost curve is the planning curve. It is found by drawing a curve tangent to one point on a series of __________-run average cost curves, each corresponding to a different plant size.

The firm can experience **economies of scale, diseconomies of scale,** or **constant returns to scale,** all according to whether the long-run average cost curve slopes __________, slopes __________, or is __________. Economies of scale refer to what happens to average cost when all factors of production are increased.

We observe economies of scale for a number of reasons, including specialization, improved productive equipment, and the __________ factor, because large-scale firms require proportionately less input per unit of output. The firm may experience __________ of scale primarily because of limits to the efficient functioning of management.

The **minimum efficient scale** occurs at the __________ rate of output at which long-run average costs are __________.

You Are There

During Hard Times for Borrowers, a Repo Man Also Has It Tough

Tony Cooper is a "repo man"—he earns his income repossessing vehicles from individuals who have failed to make required payments to lenders. Difficult times for so many during the recession of the late 2000s have resulted in an increase in orders for repossession of vehicles. Nevertheless, Cooper's profits have dropped, and he has just had to tell two of his tow truck drivers that he must lay them off.

"People are doing everything they can to hold onto what they've got," Cooper explains. "Do you think that they're going to wait around to give up their cars? They hide them. They fight over them." Indeed, on one recent day Cooper spent almost 11 hours traversing 350 miles in search of nine autos, but he was able to repossess only three of them. Many of his days are even less productive. Compared with years past, the expense incurred in repossessing an additional vehicle has risen considerably. Thus, Cooper has experienced increases in his average total costs of repossessing cars, which is why his profits have fallen.

Critical Analysis Questions

1. What variable factors of production does Cooper utilize?
2. Why do you suppose that when a car is purchased with borrowed funds, many auto dealers now install a device called "The Disabler," which prevents the vehicle from starting if the buyer gets too far behind on loan payments?

ISSUES & APPLICATIONS

Why Small Nuclear Reactors Are Fueling Big Dreams

CONCEPTS APPLIED

- Long-Run Average Cost Curve
- Minimum Efficient Scale
- Diseconomies of Scale

The first nuclear reactor intended for commercial electricity production—at a level of about 60 megawatts of power—was constructed in Shippingport, Pennsylvania, in 1957. By the late 1980s and early 1990s, commercial nuclear power plants were much larger and generated 1,000 megawatts of electricity. Today, however, energy firms are planning to downsize nuclear power generation to levels closer to the original Shippingport reactor's output. The reason is a change in the shape of the nuclear power industry's long-run average cost curve.

Production Enhancement with Modular Nuclear Reactors

The technology of nuclear power generation is still such that smaller reactors produce less power. The latest reactors produce about 125 to 145 megawatts—less than the massive reactors constructed in the 1970s through the 1990s.

Nevertheless, today's smaller reactors are more sophisticated than the original low-wattage reactors, so they can generate the same power using less nuclear fuel. For instance, the latest modular nuclear reactors, Energy

Multiplier Modules, use nuclear waste by-products to produce yet more energy. Modular reactors can be manufactured faster and installed as individual modules in space now occupied by traditional coal- and oil-fired turbines at existing power plants or by outdated reactors in current nuclear plants. Thus, eight 125-megawatt modular reactors could replace a 1,000-megawatt plant. Their combined energy output would be the same as the old plant's but would be produced at lower average cost.

The Economic Incentives for Downsizing Nuclear Power

Because the newer, smaller nuclear reactors enable more power to be produced at lower average cost, the shape of the long-run average cost curve for the nuclear power industry has changed. The average cost of producing electricity with huge reactors of yesteryear now exceeds the lowest feasible average cost available from smaller-scale reactors. This means that the bottom of the curve's U shape has moved to the left.

Because the minimum point of the long-run average cost curve for the nuclear power industry has shifted leftward, individual 1,000-megawatt reactors now experience diseconomies of scale. Smaller reactors producing less output per reactor today produce the lowest-average-cost scale of output. This means that the minimum efficient scale for nuclear reactors has decreased. Thus, the days of massive nuclear power plants using large reactors are probably over.

For Critical Analysis

1. What has happened to the position of a short-run average total cost curve associated with a nuclear reactor power output of 125 megawatts?
2. Along the new long-run average total cost curve for the nuclear power industry, are economies or diseconomies of scale available if a company increases the size of a nuclear reactor above a capacity output of 145 megawatts? Explain.

Web Resources

1. For a discussion of the technological advantages of modular nuclear reactors, go to www.econtoday.com/ch22.
2. To learn how use of a new type of modular reactor—a gas-turbine modular helium reactor—may reduce long-run costs of generating power, go to www.econtoday.com/ch22.

Research Project

Explain why technological improvements can sometimes cause *both* a downward shift of *and* a change in the shape of an industry's long-run average cost curve.

For more questions on this chapter's Issues & Applications, go to **MyEconLab**. In the Study Plan for this chapter, select Section N: News.

Here is what you should know after reading this chapter. **MyEconLab** will help you identify what you know, and where to go when you need to practice.

WHAT YOU SHOULD KNOW		WHERE TO GO TO PRACTICE
The Short Run versus the Long Run from a Firm's Perspective The short run for a firm is a period during which at least one input, such as plant size, cannot be altered. Inputs that cannot be changed in the short run are fixed inputs, whereas inputs that may be adjusted in the short run are variable inputs. The long run is a period in which a firm may vary all inputs.	short run, 484 plant size, 484 long run, 484	• **MyEconLab** Study Plan 22.1 • Audio introduction to Chapter 22 • ABC News Videos: The Space Shuttle: Cost vs. Benefit

MyEconLab continued

WHAT YOU SHOULD KNOW		WHERE TO GO TO PRACTICE
The Law of Diminishing Marginal Product The production function is the relationship between inputs and the maximum physical output, or total product, that a firm can produce. Typically, a firm's marginal physical product—the physical output resulting from the addition of one more unit of a variable factor of production—increases with the first few units of the variable input that it employs. Eventually, as the firm adds more and more units of the variable input, the marginal physical product begins to decline. This is the law of diminishing marginal product.	production, 485 production function, 485 average physical product, 486 marginal physical product, 486 law of diminishing marginal product, 487 **KEY FIGURE** Figure 22-1, 486	• **MyEconLab** Study Plans 22.2, 22.3 • Animated Figure 22-1
A Firm's Short-Run Cost Curves The expenses for a firm's fixed inputs are its fixed costs, and the expenses for its variable inputs are variable costs. The total costs of a firm are the sum of its fixed costs and variable costs. Average fixed cost equals total fixed cost divided by total product. Average variable cost equals total variable cost divided by total product, and average total cost equals total cost divided by total product. Finally, marginal cost is the change in total cost resulting from a one-unit change in production.	total costs, 488 fixed costs, 489 variable costs, 489 average fixed costs, 491 average variable costs, 491 average total costs, 491 marginal costs, 491 **KEY FIGURE** Figure 22-2, 490	• **MyEconLab** Study Plans 22.4, 22.5 • Animated Figure 22-2 • Video: Short-Run Costs to the Firm • Economics Video: Government Should Leave Farm Business • Economics Video: 'Gray Googlers' Work from Home
A Firm's Long-Run Cost Curves Over a firm's long-run, or planning, horizon, it can choose all inputs, including plant size. Thus, it can choose a long-run scale of production along a long-run average cost curve. The long-run average cost curve, which for most firms is U-shaped, is traced out by the short-run average cost curves corresponding to various plant sizes.	planning horizon, 496 long-run average cost curve, 497 planning curve, 497 **KEY FIGURES** Figure 22-3, 494 Figure 22-4, 497	• **MyEconLab** Study Plans 22.6, 22.7 • Animated Figures 22-3, 22-4
Economies and Diseconomies of Scale and a Firm's Minimum Efficient Scale Along the downward-sloping range of a firm's long-run average cost curve, the firm experiences economies of scale, meaning that its long-run production costs decline as it raises its output scale. In contrast, along the upward-sloping portion of the long-run average cost curve, the firm encounters diseconomies of scale, so that its long-run costs of production rise as it increases its output scale. The minimum point of the long-run average cost curve occurs at the firm's minimum efficient scale, which is the lowest rate of output at which the firm can achieve minimum long-run average cost.	economies of scale, 498 constant returns to scale, 498 diseconomies of scale, 498 minimum efficient scale (MES), 499 **KEY FIGURES** Figure 22-5, 498 Figure 22-6, 500	• **MyEconLab** Study Plans 22.7, 22.8 • Animated Figures 22-5, 22-6 • Video: Reasons for Economies of Scale • Economics Video: No Smoking Employees • Economics Video: Whirlpool

Log in to MyEconLab, take a chapter test, and get a personalized Study Plan that tells you which concepts you understand and which ones you need to review. From there, MyEconLab will give you further practice, tutorials, animations, videos, and guided solutions.
Log in to www.myeconlab.com

PROBLEMS

All problems are assignable in myeconlab. *Answers to odd-numbered problems appear at the back of the book.*

22-1. The academic calendar for a university is August 15 through May 15. A professor commits to a contract that binds her to a teaching position at this university for this period. Based on this information, explain the short run and long run that the professor faces.

22-2. The short-run production function for a manufacturer of flash memory drives is shown in the table below. Based on this information, answer the following questions.

Input of Labor (workers per week)	Total Output of Flash Memory Drives
0	0
1	25
2	60
3	85
4	105
5	115
6	120

a. Calculate the average physical product at each quantity of labor.

b. Calculate the marginal physical product of labor at each quantity of labor.

c. At what point does marginal product begin to diminish?

22-3. At the end of the year, a firm produced 10,000 laptop computers. Its total costs were $5 million, and its fixed costs were $2 million. What are the average variable costs of this firm?

22-4. The cost structure of a manufacturer of microchips is described in the following table. The firm's fixed costs equal $10 per day. Calculate the average variable cost, average fixed cost, and average total cost at each output level.

Output (microchips per day)	Total Cost of Output ($ thousands)
0	10
25	60
50	95
75	150
100	220
125	325
150	465

22-5. The diagram below displays short-run cost curves for a facility that produces liquid crystal display (LCD) screens for cellphones:

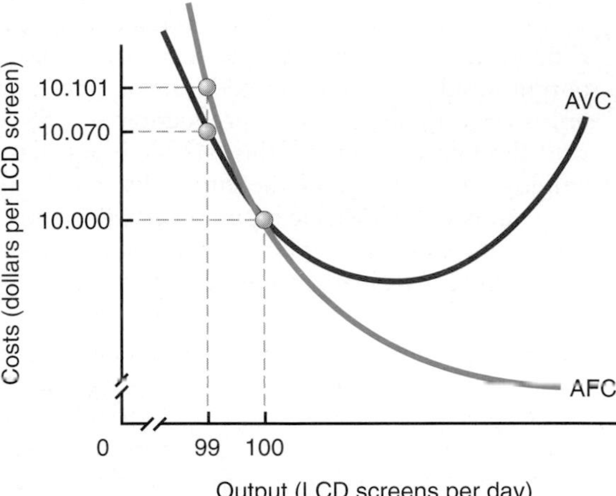

a. What are the daily total fixed costs of producing LCD screens?

b. What are the total variable costs of producing 100 LCD screens per day?

c. What are the total costs of producing 100 LCD screens per day?

d. What is the marginal cost of producing 100 LCD screens instead of 99? (Hint: To answer this question, you must first determine the total costs—or, alternatively, the total variable costs—of producing 99 LCD screens.)

22-6. A watch manufacturer finds that at 1,000 units of output, its marginal costs are below average total costs. If it produces an additional watch, will its average total costs rise, fall, or stay the same?

22-7. At its current short-run level of production, a firm's average variable costs equal $20 per unit, and its average fixed costs equal $30 per unit. Its total costs at this production level equal $2,500.

a. What is the firm's current output level?

b. What are its total variable costs at this output level?

c. What are its total fixed costs?

22-8. In an effort to reduce their total costs, many companies are now replacing paychecks with payroll cards, which are stored-value cards onto which the companies can download employees' wages and salaries electronically. If the only factor of production that a company varies in the short run is the number of hours worked by people already on its payroll, would shifting from paychecks to payroll cards reduce the firm's total fixed costs or its total variable costs? Explain your answer.

22-9. During autumn months, passenger railroads across the globe deal with a condition called slippery rail. It results from a combination of water, leaf oil, and pressure from the train's weight, which creates a slippery black ooze that prevents trains from gaining traction.

a. One solution for slippery rail is to cut back trees from all of a rail firm's rail network on a regular basis, thereby helping prevent the problem from developing. If incurred, would this railroad expense be a better example of a fixed cost or a variable cost? Why?

b. Another way of addressing slippery rail is to wait until it begins to develop. Then the company purchases sand and dumps it on the slippery tracks so that trains already en route within the rail network can proceed. If incurred, would this railroad expense be a better example of a fixed cost or a variable cost? Why?

22-10. In the short run, a firm's total costs of producing 100 units of output equal $10,000. If it produces one more unit, its total costs will increase to $10,150.

a. What is the marginal cost of the 101st unit of output?

b. What is the firm's average total cost of producing 100 units?

c. What is the firm's average total cost of producing 101 units?

22-11. Suppose that a firm's only variable input is labor, and the constant hourly wage rate is $20 per hour. The last unit of labor hired enabled the firm to increase its hourly production from 250 units to 251 units. What was the marginal cost of producing 251 units of output instead of 250?

22-12. Suppose that a firm's only variable input is labor. The firm increases the number of employees from four to five, thereby causing weekly output to rise by two units and total costs to increase from $3,000 per week to $3,300 per week.

a. What is the marginal physical product of hiring five workers instead of four?

b. What is the weekly wage rate earned by the fifth worker?

22-13. Suppose that a company currently employs 1,000 workers and produces 1 million units of output per month. Labor is its only variable input, and the company pays each worker the same monthly wage. The company's current total variable costs equal $2 million.

a. What are average variable costs at this firm's current output level?

b. What is the average physical product of labor?

c. What monthly wage does the firm pay each worker?

22-14. A manufacturing firm with a single plant is contemplating changing its plant size. It must choose from among seven alternative plant sizes. In the table, plant size A is the smallest it might build, and size G is the largest. Currently, the firm's plant size is B.

Plant Size	Average Total Cost ($)
A (smallest)	4,250
B	3,600
C	3,100
D	3,100
E	3,100
F	3,250
G (largest)	4,100

a. At plant site B, is this firm currently experiencing economies of scale or diseconomies of scale?

b. What is the firm's minimum efficient scale?

22-15. An electricity-generating company confronts the following long-run average total costs associated with alternative plant sizes. It is currently operating at plant size G.

Plant Size	Average Total Cost ($)
A (smallest)	2,000
B	1,800
C	1,600
D	1,550
E	1,500
F	1,500
G (largest)	1,500

a. What is this firm's minimum efficient scale?

b. If damage caused by a powerful hurricane generates a reduction in the firm's plant size from its current size to B, would there be a leftward or rightward movement along the firm's long-run average total cost curve?

ECONOMICS ON THE NET

Industry-Level Capital Expenditures In this chapter, you learned about the explicit and implicit costs that firms incur in the process of producing goods and services. This Internet application gives you an opportunity to consider one type of cost—expenditures on capital goods.

Title: U.S. Census Bureau's Annual Capital Expenditures Survey

Navigation: Follow the link at **www.econtoday.com/ch22**, and select the most recent *Annual Capital Spending Report.*

Application Read the introductory summary of the report, and then answer the following questions.

1. What types of business expenditures does the Census Bureau include in this report?
2. Are the inputs that generate these business expenditures more likely to be inputs that firms can vary in the short run or in the long run?
3. Which inputs account for the largest portion of firms' capital expenditures? Why do you suppose this is so?

For Group Discussion and Analysis Review reports for the past several years. Do capital expenditures vary from year to year? What factors might account for such variations? Are there noticeable differences in capital expenditures from industry to industry?

ANSWERS TO QUICK QUIZZES

p. 488: (i) production . . . output; (ii) product; (iii) decreasing . . . output

p. 493: (i) fixed . . . variable; (ii) Average . . . ATC; (iii) variable . . . AVC; (iv) fixed . . . AFC; (v) Marginal . . . total . . . MC . . . TC; (vi) minimum . . . minimum

p. 500: (i) long . . . long . . . short; (ii) downward . . . upward . . . horizontal; (iii) dimensional . . . diseconomies; (iv) lowest . . . minimized

23 Perfect Competition

More than 160 years ago, miners in California found a rich vein of gold running through the earth's surface, and the great California Gold Rush began. For more than a century afterward, mines in that state continued to produce gold, but by the 1960s most mines had ceased operations. Since 2007, however, a number of mining companies have been modernizing some of these gold mines, and a few firms have recently begun extracting gold from the mines once again. To understand what key economic conditions in the gold mining industry resulted in the past closures and recent reopenings of California's aged gold mines, you must learn about the theory of perfect competition, which is the topic of this chapter.

LEARNING OBJECTIVES

After reading this chapter, you should be able to:

- Identify the characteristics of a perfectly competitive market structure
- Discuss the process by which a perfectly competitive firm decides how much output to produce
- Understand how the short-run supply curve for a perfectly competitive firm is determined
- Explain how the equilibrium price is determined in a perfectly competitive market
- Describe what factors induce firms to enter or exit a perfectly competitive industry
- Distinguish among constant-, increasing-, and decreasing-cost industries based on the shape of the long-run industry supply curve

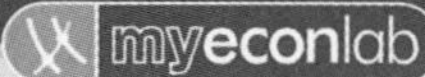

MyEconLab helps you master each objective and study more efficiently. See end of chapter for details.

Did You Know That ?

more than 1,600 U.S. auto dealerships—in excess of 8 percent of all of the firms in the industry—closed during 2009? Ease of exit from an industry is a fundamental characteristic of the theory of *perfect competition,* the topic of this chapter. In common speech, *competition* simply means "rivalry." In the extreme, perfectly competitive situation, individual buyers and sellers cannot affect the market price—it is determined by the market forces of demand and supply. Firms in a perfectly competitive industry that have been earning economic losses for a time begin to return to profitability as other firms respond to negative economic profits by leaving the industry. In this chapter, we examine these and other implications of the theory of perfect competition.

Characteristics of a Perfectly Competitive Market Structure

Perfect competition
A market structure in which the decisions of *individual* buyers and sellers have no effect on market price.

Perfectly competitive firm
A firm that is such a small part of the total *industry* that it cannot affect the price of the product it sells.

Price taker
A perfectly competitive firm that must take the price of its product as given because the firm cannot influence its price.

We are interested in studying how a firm acting within a perfectly competitive market structure makes decisions about how much to produce. In a situation of **perfect competition,** each firm is such a small part of the total industry that it cannot affect the price of the product in question. That means that each **perfectly competitive firm** in the industry is a **price taker**—the firm takes price as a given, something determined *outside* the individual firm.

This definition of a competitive firm is obviously idealized, for in one sense the individual firm *has* to set prices. How can we ever have a situation in which firms regard prices as set by forces outside their control? The answer is that even though every firm sets its own prices, a firm in a perfectly competitive situation will find that it will eventually have no customers at all if it sets its price above the competitive price. The best example is in agriculture. Although the individual farmer can set any price for a bushel of wheat, if that price doesn't coincide with the market price of a bushel of similar-quality wheat, no one will purchase the wheat at a higher price. Nor would the farmer be inclined to reduce revenues by selling below the market price.

Let's examine why a firm in a perfectly competitive industry is a price taker.

1. *There are large numbers of buyers and sellers.* When this is the case, the quantity demanded by one buyer or the quantity supplied by one seller is negligible relative to the market quantity. No one buyer or seller has any influence on price.
2. *The product sold by the firms in the industry is homogeneous.* The product sold by each firm in the industry is a perfect substitute for the product sold by every other firm. Buyers are able to choose from a large number of sellers of a product that the buyers regard as being the same.
3. *Both buyers and sellers have access to all relevant information.* Consumers are able to find out about lower prices charged by competing firms. Firms are able to find out about cost-saving innovations that can lower production costs and prices, and they are able to learn about profitable opportunities in other industries.
4. *Any firm can enter or leave the industry without serious impediments.* Firms in a competitive industry are not hampered in their ability to get resources or reallocate resources. In pursuit of profit-making opportunities, they move labor and capital to whatever business venture gives them their highest expected rate of return on their investment.

The Demand Curve of the Perfect Competitor

When we discussed substitutes in Chapter 19, we pointed out that the more substitutes there are and the more similar they are to the commodity in question, the greater is the price elasticity of demand. Here we assume that the perfectly competitive firm is producing a homogeneous commodity that has perfect substitutes. That means that if the individual firm raises its price one penny, it will lose all of its business. This, then, is how we characterize the demand schedule for a perfectly competitive firm: It is the going market price as determined by the forces of market supply and market

FIGURE 23-1 The Demand Curve for a Producer of Titanium Batteries

At \$5—where market demand, *D*, and market supply, *S*, intersect—the individual firm faces a perfectly elastic demand curve, *d*. If the firm raises its price even one penny, it will sell no titanium batteries, measured from its point of view in hourly production, at all. Notice the difference in the quantities of batteries represented on the horizontal axes of panels (a) and (b).

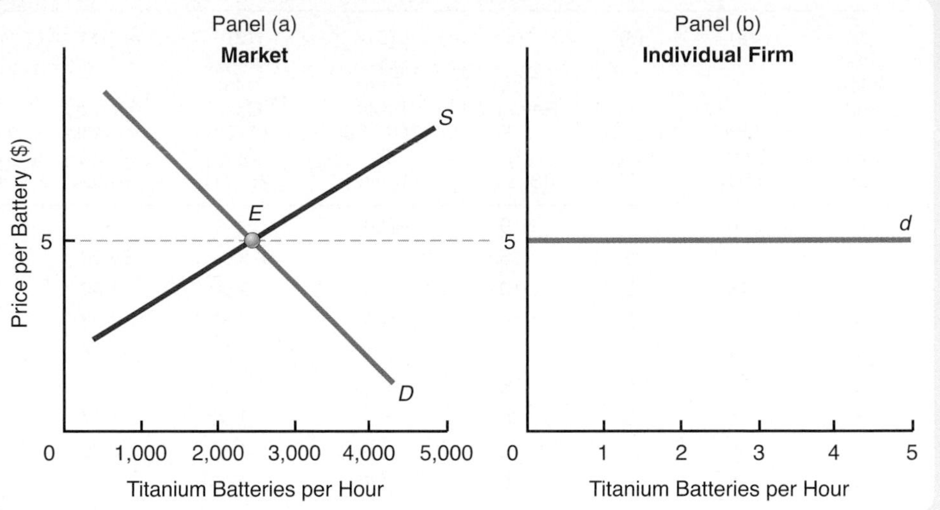

demand—that is, where the market demand curve intersects the market supply curve. The demand curve for the product of an individual firm in a perfectly competitive industry is perfectly elastic at the going market price. Remember that with a perfectly elastic demand curve, any increase in price leads to zero quantity demanded.

We show the market demand and supply curves in panel (a) of Figure 23-1 above. Their intersection occurs at the price of \$5. The commodity in question is titanium batteries. Assume for the purposes of this exposition that all of these batteries are perfect substitutes for all others. At the going market price of \$5 apiece, an individual demand curve for a producer of titanium batteries who sells a very, very small part of total industry production is shown in panel (b). At the market price, this firm can sell all the output it wants. At the market price of \$5 each, which is where the demand curve for the individual producer lies, consumer demand for the titanium batteries of that one producer is perfectly elastic.

This can be seen by noting that if the firm raises its price, consumers, who are assumed to know that this supplier is charging more than other producers, will buy elsewhere, and the producer in question will have no sales at all. Thus, the demand curve for that producer is perfectly elastic. We label the individual producer's demand curve *d*, whereas the *market* demand curve is always labeled *D*.

How Much Should the Perfect Competitor Produce?

As we have shown, from the perspective of a perfectly competitive firm deciding how much to produce, the firm has to accept the price of the product as a given. If the firm raises its price, it sells nothing. If it lowers its price, it earns lower revenues per unit sold than it otherwise could. The firm has one decision left: How much should it produce? We will apply our model of the firm to this question to come up with an answer. We'll use the *profit-maximization model*, which assumes that firms attempt to maximize their total profits—the positive difference between total revenues and total costs. This also means that firms seek to minimize any losses that arise in times when total revenues may be less than total costs.

Total Revenues

Every firm has to consider its *total revenues*. **Total revenues** are defined as the quantity sold multiplied by the price per unit. (They are the same as total receipts from the sale of output.) The perfect competitor must take the price as a given.

Total revenues
The price per unit times the total quantity sold.

Panel (a)

(1) Total Output and Sales per Hour (*Q*)	(2) Total Costs (TC)	(3) Market Price (*P*)	(4) Total Revenues (TR) (4) = (3) x (1)	(5) Total Profit (TR – TC) (5) = (4) – (2)	(6) Average Total Cost (ATC) (6) = (2) ÷ (1)	(7) Average Variable Cost (AVC)	(8) Marginal Cost (MC) (8) = Change in (2) / Change in (1)	(9) Marginal Revenue (MR) (9) = Change in (4) / Change in (1)
0	$10	$5	$ 0	–$10	—	—		
1	15	5	5	–10	$15.00	$5.00	$5	$5
2	18	5	10	–8	9.00	4.00	3	5
3	20	5	15	–5	6.67	3.33	2	5
4	21	5	20	–1	5.25	2.75	1	5
5	23	5	25	2	4.60	2.60	2	5
6	26	5	30	4	4.33	2.67	3	5
7	30	5	35	**5**	4.28	2.86	4	5
8	35	5	40	**5**	4.38	3.12	5	5
9	41	5	45	4	4.56	3.44	6	5
10	48	5	50	2	4.80	3.80	7	5
11	56	5	55	–1	5.09	4.18	8	5

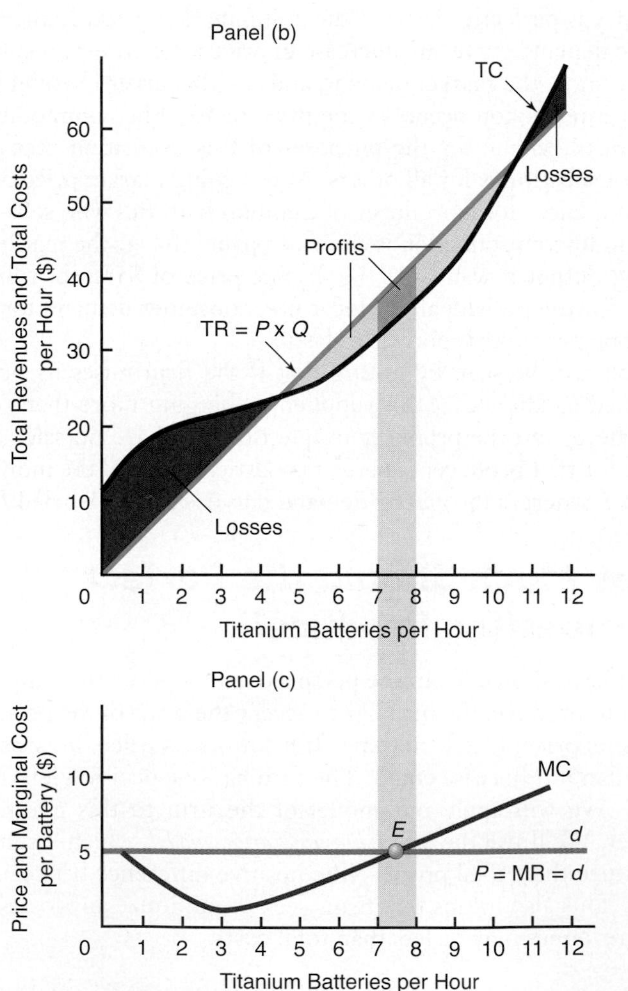

FIGURE 23-2 Profit Maximization

Profit maximization occurs where marginal revenue equals marginal cost. Panel (a) indicates that this point occurs at a rate of sales of between seven and eight titanium batteries per hour. In panel (b), we find maximum profits where total revenues exceed total costs by the largest amount. This occurs at a rate of production and sales per hour of seven or eight batteries. In panel (c), the marginal cost curve, MC, intersects the marginal revenue curve at the same rate of output and sales of somewhere between seven and eight batteries per hour.

Look at Figure 23-2 on the facing page. The information in panel (a) comes from panel (a) of Figure 22-2 on page 490, but we have added some essential columns for our analysis. Column 3 is the market price, *P*, of $5 per titanium battery. Column 4 shows the total revenues, or TR, as equal to the market price, *P*, times the total output per hour, or *Q*. Thus, TR = *PQ*.

For the perfect competitor, price is also equal to average revenue (AR) because

$$\text{AR} = \frac{\text{TR}}{Q} = \frac{PQ}{Q} = P$$

where *Q* stands for quantity. If we assume that all units sell for the same price, it becomes apparent that another name for the demand curve is the *average revenue curve* (this is true regardless of the type of market structure under consideration).

We are assuming that the market supply and demand schedules intersect at a price of $5 and that this price holds for all the firm's production. We are also assuming that because our maker of titanium batteries is a small part of the market, it can sell all that it produces at that price. Thus, panel (b) of Figure 23-2 shows the total revenue curve as a straight green line. For every additional battery sold, total revenue increases by $5.

Comparing Total Costs with Total Revenues

Total costs are given in column 2 of panel (a) of Figure 23-2 and plotted in panel (b). Remember, the firm's costs always include a normal rate of return on investment. So, whenever we refer to total costs, we are talking not about accounting costs but about economic costs. When the total cost curve is above the total revenue curve, the firm is experiencing losses. When total costs are less than total revenues, the firm is making profits.

By comparing total costs with total revenues, we can figure out the number of titanium batteries the individual competitive firm should produce per hour. Our analysis rests on the assumption that the firm will attempt to maximize total profits. In panel (a) of Figure 23-2, we see that total profits reach a maximum at a production rate of between seven and eight batteries per hour. We can see this graphically in panel (b) of the figure. The firm will maximize profits where the total revenue curve lies above the total cost curve by the greatest amount. That occurs at a rate of output and sales of between seven and eight batteries per hour. This rate is called the **profit-maximizing rate of production.** (If output were continuously divisible or there were extremely large numbers of titanium batteries, we would get a unique profit-maximizing output.)

Profit-maximizing rate of production The rate of production that maximizes total profits, or the difference between total revenues and total costs. Also, it is the rate of production at which marginal revenue equals marginal cost.

We can also find the profit-maximizing rate of production for the individual competitive firm by looking at marginal revenues and marginal costs.

Using Marginal Analysis to Determine the Profit-Maximizing Rate of Production

It is possible—indeed, preferable—to use marginal analysis to determine the profit-maximizing rate of production. We end up with the same results derived in a different manner, one that focuses more on where decisions are really made—on the margin. Managers examine changes in costs and relate them to changes in revenues. In fact, whether the question is how much more or less to produce, how many more workers to hire or fire, or how much more to study or not study, we compare changes in costs with changes in benefits, where change is occurring at the margin.

Marginal Revenue

Marginal revenue
The change in total revenues resulting from a one-unit change in output (and sale) of the product in question.

Marginal revenue represents the change in total revenues attributable to changing production of an item by one unit. Hence, a more formal definition of marginal revenue is

$$\text{Marginal revenue} = \frac{\text{change in total revenues}}{\text{change in output}}$$

In a perfectly competitive market, the marginal revenue curve is exactly equivalent to the price line, which is the individual firm's demand curve. Each time the firm produces and sells one more unit, total revenues rise by an amount equal to the (constant) market price of the good. Thus, in Figure 23-1 on page 509, the demand curve, *d*, for the individual producer is at a price of $5—the price line is coincident with the demand curve. But so is the marginal revenue curve, for marginal revenue in this case also equals $5.

The marginal revenue curve for our competitive producer of titanium batteries is shown as a line at $5 in panel (c) of Figure 23-2 on page 510. Notice again that the marginal revenue curve is the price line, which is the firm's demand, or average revenue, curve, *d*. This equality of MR, *P*, and *d* for an individual firm is a general feature of a perfectly competitive industry. The price line shows the quantity that consumers desire to purchase from this firm at each price—which is *any* quantity that the firm provides at the market price—and hence is the demand curve, *d*, faced by the firm. The market clearing price per unit does not change as the firm varies its output, so the average revenue and marginal revenue also are equal to this price. Thus, MR is identically equal to *P* along the firm's demand curve.

When Are Profits Maximized?

Now we add the marginal cost curve, MC, taken from column 8 in panel (a) of Figure 23-2 on page 510. As shown in panel (c) of that figure, because of the law of diminishing marginal product, the marginal cost curve first falls and then starts to rise, eventually intersecting the marginal revenue curve and then rising above it. Notice that the numbers for both the marginal cost schedule, column 8 in panel (a), and the marginal revenue schedule, column 9 in panel (a), are printed *between* the rows on which the quantities appear. This indicates that we are looking at a *change* between one rate of output and the next rate of output.

EQUALIZING MARGINAL REVENUE AND MARGINAL COST In panel (c) of Figure 23-2 on page 510, the marginal cost curve intersects the marginal revenue curve somewhere between seven and eight batteries per hour. The firm has an incentive to produce and sell until the amount of the additional revenue received from selling one more battery just equals the additional costs incurred for producing and selling that battery. This is how the firm maximizes profit. Whenever marginal cost is less than marginal revenue, the firm will always make more profit by increasing production.

Now consider the possibility of producing at an output rate of 10 titanium batteries per hour. The marginal cost at that output rate is higher than the marginal revenue. The firm would be spending more to produce that additional output than it would be receiving in revenues. It would be foolish to continue producing at this rate.

THE PROFIT-MAXIMIZING OUTPUT RATE But how much should the firm produce? It should produce at point *E* in panel (c) of Figure 23-2, where the marginal cost curve intersects the marginal revenue curve from below. The firm should continue production until the cost of increasing output by one more unit is just equal to the revenues obtainable from that extra unit. This is a fundamental rule in economics:

Profit maximization occurs at the rate of output at which marginal revenue equals marginal cost.

For a perfectly competitive firm, this rate of output is at the intersection of the demand schedule, *d*, which is identical to the MR curve, and the marginal cost curve, MC. When MR exceeds MC, each additional unit of output adds more to total revenues than to total costs, so the additional unit should be produced. When MC is greater than MR, each unit produced adds more to total cost than to total revenues, so this unit should not be produced. Therefore, profit maximization occurs when MC equals MR. In our particular example, our profit-maximizing, perfectly competitive producer of titanium batteries will produce at a rate of between seven and eight batteries per hour.

QUICK QUIZ See page 531 for the answers. Review concepts from this section in MyEconLab.

Four fundamental characteristics of the market in **perfect competition** are (1) __________ numbers of buyers and sellers, (2) a __________ product, (3) good information in the hands of both buyers and sellers, and (4) __________ exit from and entry into the industry by other firms.

A perfectly competitive firm is a **price taker.** It has __________ control over price and consequently has to take price as a given, but it can sell __________ that it wants at the going market price.

The demand curve for a perfect competitor is perfectly elastic at the going market price. The demand curve is also the perfect competitor's __________ revenue curve because __________ revenue is defined as the change in total revenue due to a one-unit change in output.

Profit is maximized at the rate of output at which the positive difference between total revenues and total costs is the greatest. This is the same level of output at which marginal __________ equals marginal __________. The perfectly competitive firm produces at an output rate at which marginal cost equals the __________ per unit of output, because MR is always equal to *P*.

Short-Run Profits

To find what our competitive individual producer of titanium batteries is making in terms of profits in the short run, we have to add the average total cost curve to panel (c) of Figure 23-2 on page 510. We take the information from column 6 in panel (a) and add it to panel (c) to get Figure 23-3 at the top of the following page. Again the profit-maximizing rate of output is between seven and eight titanium batteries per hour. If we have production and sales of seven batteries per hour, total revenues will be $35 per hour. Total costs will be $30 per hour, leaving a profit of $5 per hour. If the rate of output and sales is eight batteries per hour, total revenues will be $40 and total costs will be $35, again leaving a profit of $5 per hour.

A Graphical Depiction of Maximum Profits

In Figure 23-3, the lower boundary of the rectangle labeled "Profits" is determined by the intersection of the profit-maximizing quantity line represented by vertical dashes and the average total cost curve. Why? Because the ATC curve gives us the cost per unit, whereas the price ($5), represented by *d*, gives us the revenue per unit, or average revenue. The difference is profit per unit.

Thus, the height of the rectangular box representing profits equals profit per unit, and the length equals the amount of units produced. When we multiply these two quantities, we get total profits. Note, as pointed out earlier, that we are talking about *economic profits* because a normal rate of return on investment plus all opportunity costs is included in the average total cost curve, ATC.

A Graphical Depiction of Minimum Losses

It is also certainly possible for the competitive firm to make short-run losses. We give an example in Figure 23-4 on the next page, where we show the firm's demand curve shifting from d_1 to d_2. The going market price has fallen from $5 to $3 per titanium battery because of changes in market demand conditions. The firm will still do the best it can by producing where marginal revenue equals marginal cost.

FIGURE 23-3 Measuring Total Profits

Profits are represented by the blue-shaded area. The height of the profit rectangle is given by the difference between average total costs and price ($5), where price is also equal to average revenue. This is found by the vertical difference between the ATC curve and the price, or average revenue, line *d*, at the profit-maximizing rate of output of between seven and eight titanium batteries per hour.

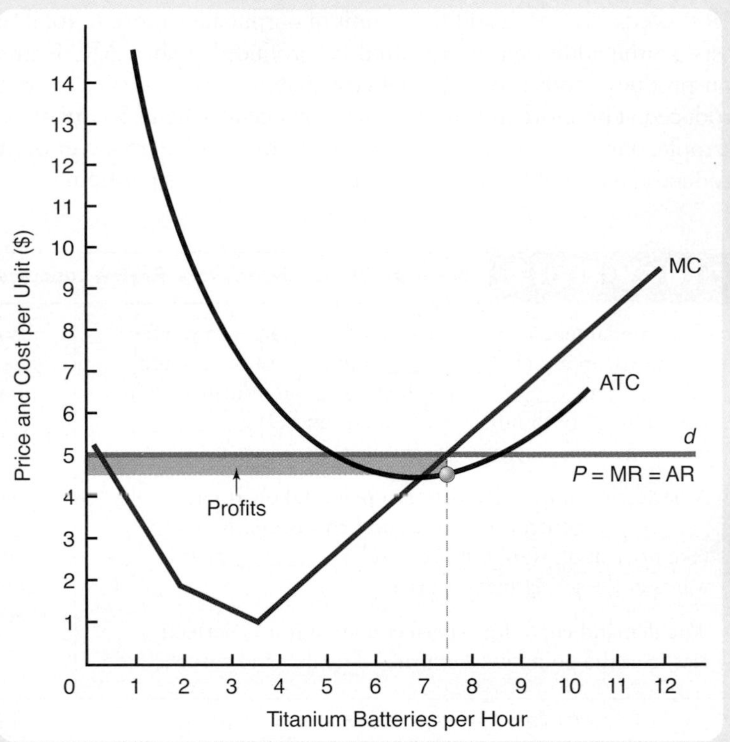

We see in Figure 23-4 below that the marginal revenue (d_2) curve is intersected (from below) by the marginal cost curve at an output rate of about $5\frac{1}{2}$ batteries per hour. The firm is clearly not making profits because average total costs at that output rate are greater than the price of $3 per battery. The losses are shown in the shaded area. By producing where marginal revenue equals marginal cost, however, the firm is minimizing its losses. That is, losses would be greater at any other output.

FIGURE 23-4 Minimization of Short-Run Losses

In situations in which average total costs exceed price, which in turn is greater than or equal to average variable cost, profit maximization is equivalent to loss minimization. This again occurs where marginal cost equals marginal revenue. Losses are shown in the red-shaded area.

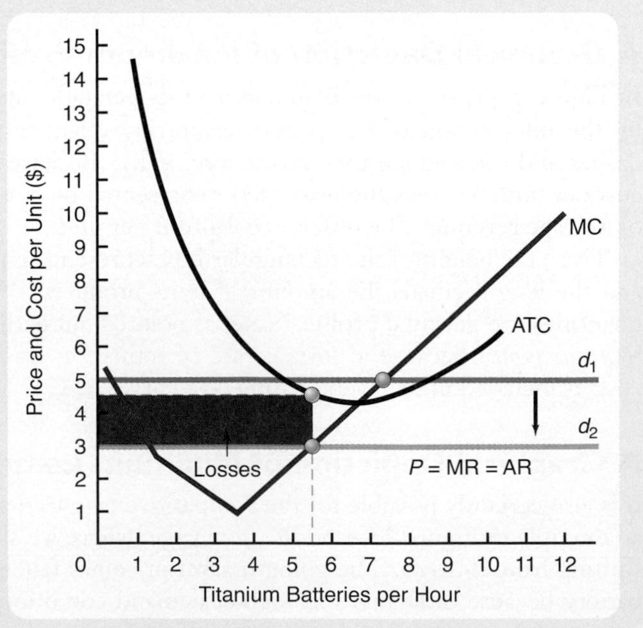

The Short-Run Break-Even Price and the Short-Run Shutdown Price

In Figure 23-4 on the facing page, the firm is sustaining economic losses. Will it go out of business? In the long run it will, but in the short run the firm will not necessarily go out of business. In the short run, as long as the loss from staying in business is less than the loss from shutting down, the firm will remain in business and continue to produce. A firm *goes out of business* when the owners sell its assets to someone else. A firm temporarily *shuts down* when it stops producing, but it still is in business.

Now how can a firm that is sustaining economic losses in the short run tell whether it is still worthwhile *not* to shut down? The firm must compare the loss incurred if it continues producing with the loss it incurs if it ceases production. Looking at the problem on a per-unit basis, as long as average variable cost (AVC) is covered by average revenues (price), the firm is better off continuing to produce. If average variable costs are exceeded even a little bit by the price of the product, staying in production produces some revenues in excess of variable costs. The logic is fairly straightforward:

> ***As long as the price per unit sold exceeds the average variable cost per unit produced, the earnings of the firm's owners will be higher if it continues to produce in the short run than if it shuts down.***

Calculating the Short-Run Break-Even Price

Look at demand curve d_1 in Figure 23-5 below. It just touches the minimum point of the average total cost curve, which is exactly where the marginal cost curve intersects the average total cost curve. At that price, which is about $4.30, the firm will be making exactly zero short-run *economic* profits. That price is called the **short-run break-even price,** and point E_1 therefore occurs at the short-run break-even price for a competitive firm. It is the point at which marginal revenue, marginal cost, and average total cost are all equal (that is, at which P = MC and P = ATC). The break-even price is the one that yields zero short-run *economic* profits or losses.

Short-run break-even price
The price at which a firm's total revenues equal its total costs. At the break-even price, the firm is just making a normal rate of return on its capital investment. (It is covering its explicit and implicit costs.)

FIGURE 23-5 Short-Run Break-Even and Shutdown Prices

We can find the short-run break-even price and the short-run shutdown price by comparing price with average total costs and average variable costs. If the demand curve is d_1, profit maximization occurs at output E_1, where MC equals marginal revenue (the d_1 curve). Because the ATC curve includes all relevant opportunity costs, point E_1 is the break-even point, and zero economic profits are being made. The firm is earning a normal rate of return. If the demand curve falls to d_2, profit maximization (loss minimization) occurs at the intersection of MC and MR (the d_2 curve), or E_2. Below this price, it does not pay for the firm to continue in operation because its average variable costs are not covered by the price of the product.

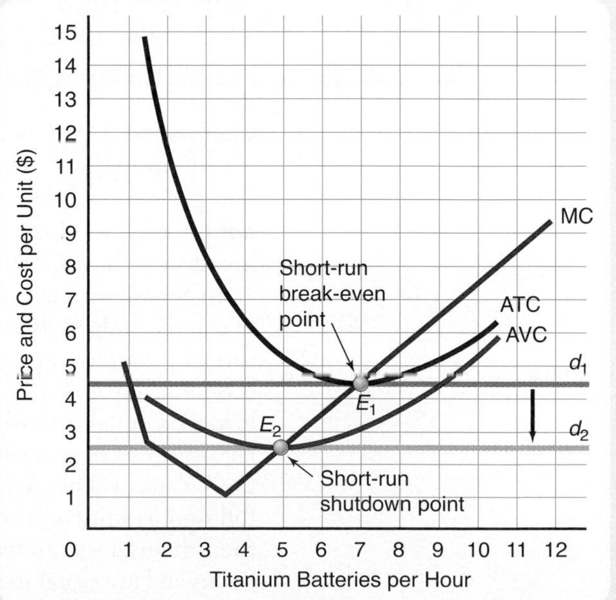

Calculating the Short-Run Shutdown Price

To calculate the firm's shutdown price, we must introduce the average variable cost (AVC) to our graph. In Figure 23-5 on the preceding page, we have plotted the AVC values from column 7 in panel (a) of Figure 23-2 on page 510. For the moment, consider two possible demand curves, d_1 and d_2, which are also the firm's respective marginal revenue curves. If demand is d_1, the firm will produce at E_1, where that curve intersects the marginal cost curve. If demand falls to d_2, the firm will produce at E_2. The special feature of the hypothetical demand curve, d_2, is that it just touches the average variable cost curve at the latter's minimum point, which is also where the marginal cost curve intersects it. This price is the **short-run shutdown price.** Why? Below this price, the firm would be paying out more in variable costs than it is receiving in revenues from the sale of its product. Each unit it sold would generate losses that could be avoided if it shut down operations.

Short-run shutdown price
The price that covers average variable costs. It occurs just below the intersection of the marginal cost curve and the average variable cost curve.

The intersection of the price line, the marginal cost curve, and the average variable cost curve is labeled E_2. The resulting short-run shutdown price is valid only for the short run because, of course, in the long run the firm will not stay in business if it is earning less than a normal rate of return (zero economic profits).

What accounted for abrupt shutdowns of iron ore production around the globe in the late 2000s?

INTERNATIONAL EXAMPLE A Global Plunge in the Price of Iron Ore Leads to Shutdowns

A global contagion appeared to have struck the iron ore industry. First, Brazil-based Companhia Vale do Rio Doce closed down some of its operations. Within a couple of days, Rio Tinto Minerals had also cut 10 percent of its iron ore production by shutting down facilities in Montana and elsewhere in North America. During the next week, companies in Australia, Canada, South Africa, and Russia had announced that they, too, had closed many of their iron-ore-producing operations. All of these firms responded to the same event: the fastest-ever decline in the market clearing price of iron ore. Within just a few months at the end of the 2000s, the equilibrium price of iron ore dropped by more than 45 percent. The lower market clearing price that resulted was below the short-run shutdown price applicable to operations at most companies. This fact explained the rapid worldwide cutback in iron-ore-producing operations.

FOR CRITICAL ANALYSIS

Even though the iron ore firms laid off tens of thousands of employees at the closed plants, why do you suppose the companies said that they hoped to call the employees back to work within a year or two?

The Meaning of Zero Economic Profits

The fact that we labeled point E_1 in Figure 23-5 on the previous page, the break-even point may have disturbed you. At point E_1, price is just equal to average total cost. If this is the case, why would a firm continue to produce if it were making no profits whatsoever? If we again make the distinction between accounting profits and economic profits, you will realize that at that price, the firm has zero economic profits but positive accounting profits. Recall that accounting profits are total revenues minus total explicit costs. But such accounting ignores the reward offered to investors—the opportunity cost of capital—plus all other implicit costs.

In economic analysis, the average total cost curve includes the full opportunity cost of capital. Indeed, the average total cost curve includes the opportunity cost of *all* factors of production used in the production process. At the short-run break-even price, economic profits are, by definition, zero. Accounting profits at that price are not, however, equal to zero. They are positive. Consider an example. A baseball bat manufacturer sells bats at some price. The owners of the firm have supplied all the funds in the business. They have not borrowed from anyone else, and they explicitly pay the full opportunity cost to all factors of production, including any managerial labor that they themselves contribute to the business. Their salaries show up as a cost in the books and are equal to what they could have earned in the next-best alternative occupation. At the end of the year, the owners find that after they subtract all explicit costs from total revenues, accounting profits are $100,000. If their investment was $1 million, the rate of return on that investment is 10 percent per year. We will assume that this turns out to be equal to the market rate of return.

This $100,000, or 10 percent rate of return, is actually, then, a competitive, or normal, rate of return on invested capital in all industries with similar risks. If the owners had made only $50,000, or 5 percent on their investment, they would have been able to make higher profits by leaving the industry. The 10 percent rate of return is the opportunity cost of capital. Accountants show it as a profit. Economists call it a cost. We include that cost in the average total cost curve, similar to the one shown in Figure 23-5 on page 515. At the short-run break-even price, average total cost, including this opportunity cost of capital, will just equal that price. The firm will be making zero economic profits but a 10 percent *accounting profit.*

Why did aluminum firms' production initially continue unabated for a few months during the late 2000s even though the equilibrium price of aluminum had declined substantially?

EXAMPLE **Why Firms Stubbornly Produced Aluminum in the Late 2000s**

Between the summer of 2008 and the end of the winter of 2009, the market clearing price of aluminum fell by more than 50 percent. Nevertheless, almost all aluminum firms maintained their production operations until early in the spring of 2009. They did so because, even though the equilibrium price fell below the short-run break-even price, for several months the price remained above the short-run shutdown price. During that period, the firms continued to employ variable inputs in the production of aluminum to sell at the prevailing market clearing price. By doing so, they generated sufficient revenues to more than cover costs that were variable in the short run.

By the middle of the spring of 2009, however, most aluminum firms were earning negative economic profits. A number of firms responded by closing down some of their operations and cutting back on production. A few firms even exited the industry. Thus, even though the firms continued to produce aluminum while the price remained above the short-run shutdown price, in the long run the companies curtailed some of their operations and reduced sales of aluminum.

FOR CRITICAL ANALYSIS

Why does the level of the actual equilibrium price in relation to the short-run break-even price determine whether aluminum firms are able to earn positive, zero, or negative economic profits?

The Supply Curve for a Perfectly Competitive Industry

As you learned in Chapter 3, the relationship between a product's price and the quantity produced and offered for sale is a supply curve. Let's now examine the supply curve for a perfectly competitive industry.

The Perfect Competitor's Short-Run Supply Curve

What does the supply curve for the individual firm look like? Actually, we have been looking at it all along. We know that when the price of titanium batteries is $5, the firm will supply seven or eight of them per hour. If the price falls to $3, the firm will supply five or six batteries per hour. And if the price falls below $3, the firm will shut down. Hence, in Figure 23-6 at the top of the next page, the firm's supply curve is the marginal cost curve above the short-run shutdown point. This is shown as the solid part of the marginal cost curve.

By definition, then, a firm's short-run supply curve in a competitive industry is its marginal cost curve at and above the point of intersection with the average variable cost curve.

The Short-Run Industry Supply Curve

In Chapter 3, we indicated that the market supply curve was the summation of individual supply curves. At the beginning of this chapter, we drew a market supply curve in Figure 23-1 on page 509. Now we want to derive more precisely a market, or industry, supply curve to reflect individual producer behavior in that industry. First we must ask, What is an industry? It is merely a collection of firms producing a particular product.

FIGURE 23-6 The Individual Firm's Short-Run Supply Curve

The individual firm's short-run supply curve is the portion of its marginal cost curve at and above the minimum point on the average variable cost curve.

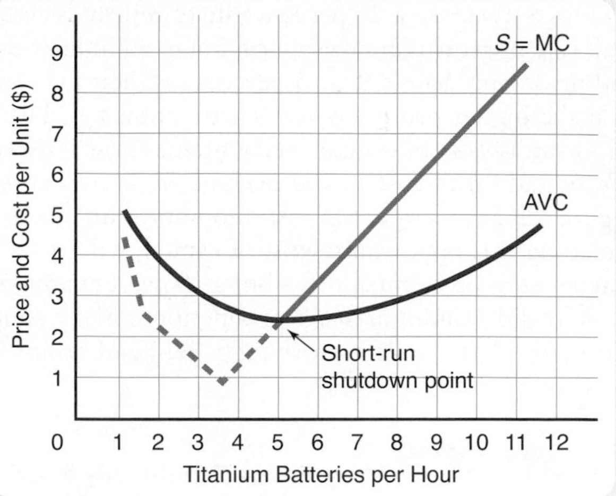

Therefore, we have a way to figure out the total supply curve of any industry: As discussed in Chapter 3, we add the quantities that each firm will supply at every possible price. In other words, we sum the individual supply curves of all the competitive firms *horizontally*. The individual supply curves, as we just saw, are simply the marginal cost curves of each firm.

Consider doing this for a hypothetical world in which there are only two producers of titanium batteries in the industry, firm A and firm B. These two firms' marginal cost curves are given in panels (a) and (b) of Figure 23-7 below. The marginal cost curves for the two separate firms are presented as MC_A in panel (a) and MC_B in panel (b). Those two marginal cost curves are drawn only for prices above the minimum average variable cost for each respective firm. In panel (a), for firm A, at a price of $6 per unit, the quantity supplied would be 7 units. At a price of $10 per unit, the quantity supplied would be 12 units. In panel (b), we see the two different quantities that would be supplied by firm B corresponding to those two prices. Now, at a price of $6, we add

FIGURE 23-7 Deriving the Industry Supply Curve

Marginal cost curves at and above minimum average variable cost are presented in panels (a) and (b) for firms A and B. We horizontally sum the two quantities supplied, 7 units by firm A and 10 units by firm B, at a price of $6. This gives us point *F* in panel (c). We do the same thing for the quantities supplied at a price of $10. This gives us point *G*. When we connect those points, we have the industry supply curve, *S*, which is the horizontal summation—represented by the Greek letter sigma (Σ)—of the firms' marginal cost curves above their respective minimum average variable costs.

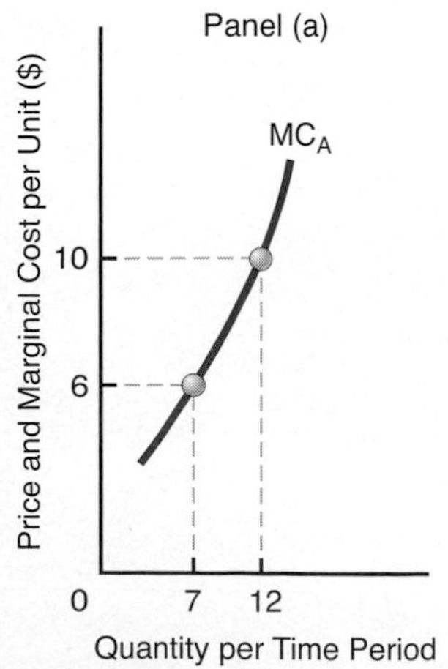

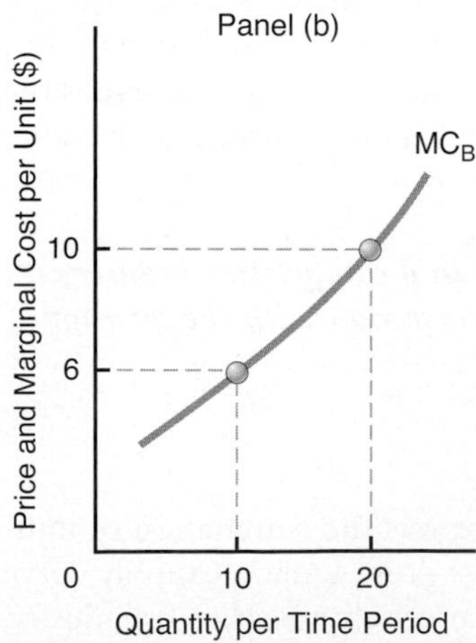

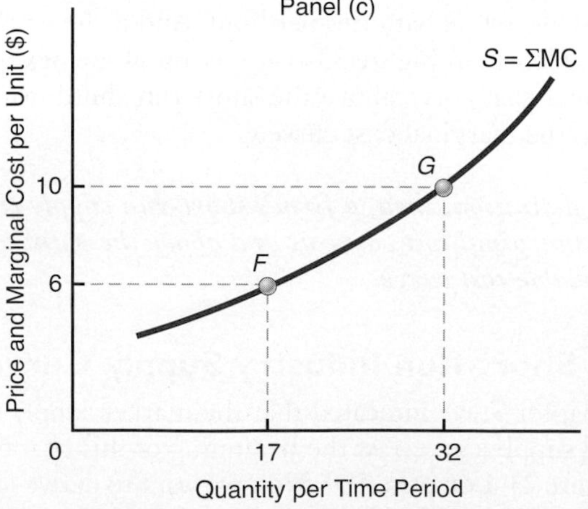

horizontally the quantities 7 and 10 to obtain 17 units. This gives us one point, *F*, for our short-run **industry supply curve,** *S*. We obtain the other point, *G*, by doing the same horizontal adding of quantities at a price of $10 per unit.

When we connect all points such as *F* and *G*, we obtain the industry supply curve *S*, which is also marked ΣMC (where the capital Greek sigma, Σ, is the symbol for summation), indicating that it is the horizontal summation of the marginal cost curves (at and above the respective minimum average variable cost of each firm). Because the law of diminishing marginal product makes marginal cost curves rise as output rises, the short-run supply curve of a perfectly competitive industry must be upward sloping.

Industry supply curve
The locus of points showing the minimum prices at which given quantities will be forthcoming; also called the *market supply curve*.

Factors That Influence the Industry Supply Curve

As you have just seen, the industry supply curve is the horizontal summation of all of the individual firms' marginal cost curves at and above their respective minimum average variable cost points. This means that anything that affects the marginal cost curves of the firm will influence the industry supply curve. Therefore, the individual factors that will influence the supply schedule in a competitive industry can be summarized as the factors that cause the variable costs of production to change. These are factors that affect the individual marginal cost curves, such as changes in the individual firm's productivity, in factor prices (such as wages paid to labor and prices of raw materials), in per-unit taxes, and in anything else that would influence the individual firm's marginal cost curve.

All of these are *ceteris paribus* conditions of supply (see page 62 in Chapter 3). Because they affect the position of the marginal cost curve for the individual firm, they affect the position of the industry supply curve. A change in any of these will shift the firms' marginal cost curves and thus shift the industry supply curve.

QUICK QUIZ **See page 531 for the answers.** **Review concepts from this section in MyEconLab.**

Short-run average profits or losses are determined by comparing __________ total costs with __________ at the **profit-maximizing rate of output.** In the short run, the perfectly competitive firm can make economic profits or economic losses.

The perfectly competitive firm's short-run __________-__________ price equals the firm's minimum average total cost, which is at the point at which the __________ cost curve intersects the average total cost curve.

The perfectly competitive firm's short-run __________ price equals the firm's minimum average variable cost, which is at the point at which the __________ cost curve intersects the average variable cost curve. Shutdown will occur if price falls below average variable cost.

The firm will continue production at a price that exceeds average variable costs because revenues exceed total __________ costs of producing.

At the short-run break-even price, the firm is making __________ economic profits, which means that it is just making a __________ rate of return for industries with similar risks.

The firm's short-run supply curve is the portion of its marginal cost curve at and above its minimum average __________ cost. The industry short-run supply curve is a horizontal __________ of the individual firms' marginal cost curves at and above their respective minimum average __________ costs.

Price Determination Under Perfect Competition

How is the market, or "going," price established in a competitive market? This price is established by the interaction of all the suppliers (firms) and all the demanders (consumers).

The Market Clearing Price

The market demand schedule, *D*, in panel (a) of Figure 23-8 on the following page represents the demand schedule for the entire industry, and the supply schedule, *S*, represents the supply schedule for the entire industry. The market clearing price, P_e,

FIGURE 23-8 Industry Demand and Supply Curves and the Individual Firm Demand Curve

The industry demand curve is represented by D in panel (a). The short-run industry supply curve is S and is equal to ΣMC. The intersection of the demand and supply curves at E determines the equilibrium or market clearing price at P_e. The demand curve faced by the individual firm in panel (b) is perfectly elastic at the market clearing price determined in panel (a). If the producer has a marginal cost curve MC, its profit-maximizing output level is at q_e. For AC_1, economic profits are zero. For AC_2, profits are negative. For AC_3, profits are positive.

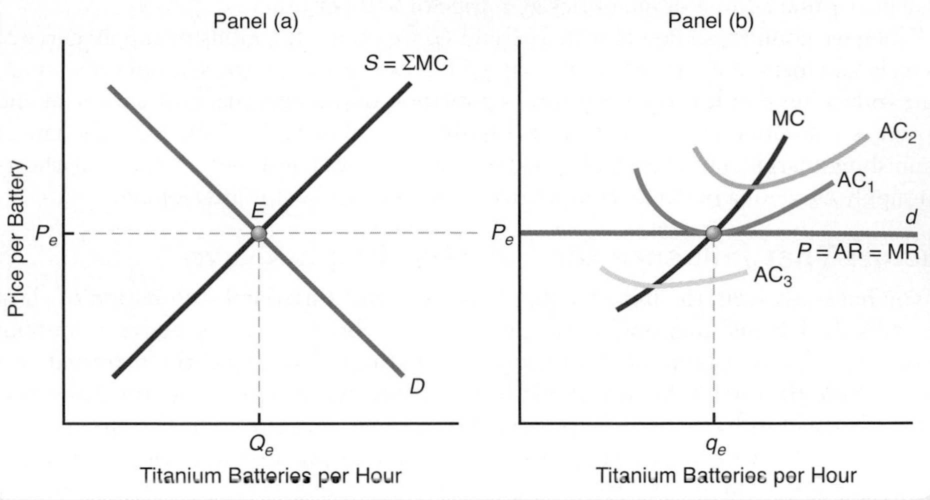

is established by the forces of supply and demand at the intersection of D and the short-run industry supply curve, S. Even though each individual firm has no control or effect on the price of its product in a competitive industry, the interaction of *all* the producers and buyers determines the price at which the product will be sold.

We say that the price P_e and the quantity Q_e in panel (a) of Figure 23-8 above constitute the competitive solution to the resource allocation problem in that particular industry. It is the equilibrium at which quantity demanded equals quantity supplied, and both suppliers and demanders are doing as well as they can. The resulting individual firm demand curve, d, is shown in panel (b) of Figure 23-8 at the price P_e.

Market Equilibrium and the Individual Firm

In a purely competitive industry, the individual producer takes price as a given and chooses the output level that maximizes profits. (This is also the equilibrium level of output from the producer's standpoint.) We see in panel (b) of Figure 23-8 that this is at q_e. If the producer's average costs are given by AC_1, the short-run break-even price arises at q_e (see Figure 23-5 on page 515). If its average costs are given by AC_2, then at q_e, AC exceeds price (average revenue), and the firm is incurring losses. Alternatively, if average costs are given by AC_3, the firm will be making economic profits at q_e. In the former case, we would expect, over time, that some firms will cease production (exit the industry), causing supply to shift inward. In the latter case, we would expect new firms to enter the industry to take advantage of the economic profits, thereby causing supply to shift outward. We now turn to these long-run considerations.

The Long-Run Industry Situation: Exit and Entry

In the long run in a competitive situation, firms will be making zero economic profits. (Actually, this is true only for identical firms. Throughout the remainder of the discussion, we assume firms have the same cost structures.) We surmise, therefore, that in the long run a perfectly competitive firm's price (marginal and average revenue) curve will just touch its average total cost curve. How does this occur? It comes about through an adjustment process that depends on economic profits and losses.

Exit and Entry of Firms

Look back at both Figure 23-3 and Figure 23-4 on page 514. The existence of either profits or losses is a signal to owners of capital both inside and outside the industry. If an industry is characterized by firms showing economic profits as represented in Figure 23-3, these economic profits signal owners of capital elsewhere in the economy that they, too, should enter this industry. In contrast, if some firms in an industry are suffering economic losses as represented in Figure 23-4, these economic losses signal resource owners outside the industry to stay out. In addition, these economic losses signal resource owners within the industry not to reinvest and if possible to leave the industry. It is in this sense that we say that profits direct resources to their highest-valued use. In the long run, capital will flow into industries in which profitability is highest and will flow out of industries in which profitability is lowest.

ALLOCATION OF CAPITAL AND MARKET SIGNALS The price system therefore allocates capital according to the relative expected rates of return on alternative investments. Hence, entry restrictions (such as limits on the numbers of taxicabs and banks permitted to enter the taxi service and banking industries) will hinder economic efficiency by not allowing resources to flow to their highest-valued use. Similarly, exit restrictions (such as laws that require firms to give advance notice of closings) will act to trap resources (temporarily) in sectors in which their value is below that in alternative uses. Such laws will also inhibit the ability of firms to respond to changes in both the domestic and international marketplaces.

Not every industry presents an immediate source of opportunity for every firm. In a brief period of time, it may be impossible for a firm that produces tractors to switch to the production of computers, even if there are very large profits to be made. Over the long run, however, we would expect to see owners of some other resources switch to producing computers. In a market economy, investors supply firms in the more profitable industry with more investment funds, which they take from firms in less profitable industries. (Also, positive economic profits induce existing firms to use internal investment funds for expansion.) Consequently, resources useful in the production of more profitable goods, such as labor, will be bid away from lower-valued opportunities. Investors and other suppliers of resources respond to market **signals** about their highest-valued opportunities.

Signals
Compact ways of conveying to economic decision makers information needed to make decisions. An effective signal not only conveys information but also provides the incentive to react appropriately. Economic profits and economic losses are such signals.

TENDENCY TOWARD EQUILIBRIUM Market adjustment to changes in demand will occur regardless of the wishes of the managers of firms in less profitable markets. They can either attempt to adjust their product line to respond to the new demands, be replaced by managers who are more responsive to new conditions, or see their firms go bankrupt as they find themselves unable to replace worn-out plant and equipment.

In addition, when we say that in a competitive long-run equilibrium situation firms will be making zero economic profits, we must realize that at a particular point in time it would be pure coincidence for a firm to be making *exactly* zero economic profits. Real-world information is not as precise as the curves we use to simplify our analysis. Things change all the time in a dynamic world, and firms, even in a very competitive situation, may for many reasons not be making exactly zero economic profits. We say that there is a *tendency* toward that equilibrium position, but firms are adjusting all the time to changes in their cost curves and in the market demand curves.

Long-Run Industry Supply Curves

In panel (a) of Figure 23-8 on the facing page, we drew the summation of all of the portions of the individual firms' marginal cost curves at and above each firm's respective minimum average variable costs as the upward-sloping supply curve of the entire industry. We should be aware, however, that a relatively inelastic supply curve may be appropriate only in the short run. After all, one of the prerequisites of a competitive industry is freedom of entry.

Long-run industry supply curve A market supply curve showing the relationship between prices and quantities after firms have been allowed the time to enter into or exit from an industry, depending on whether there have been positive or negative economic profits.

Remember that our definition of the long run is a period of time in which all adjustments can be made. The **long-run industry supply curve** is a supply curve showing the relationship between quantities supplied by the entire industry at different prices after firms have been allowed to either enter or leave the industry, depending on whether there have been positive or negative economic profits. Also, the long-run industry supply curve is drawn under the assumption that firms are identical and that entry and exit have been completed. This means that along the long-run industry supply curve, firms in the industry earn zero economic profits.

The long-run industry supply curve can take one of three shapes, depending on whether input prices stay constant, increase, or decrease as the number of firms in the industry changes. In Chapter 22, we assumed that input prices remained constant to the *firm* regardless of the firm's rate of output. When we look at the entire *industry*, however, when all firms are expanding and new firms are entering, they may simultaneously bid up input prices.

Constant-cost industry An industry whose total output can be increased without an increase in long-run per-unit costs. Its long-run supply curve is horizontal.

CONSTANT-COST INDUSTRIES In principle, there are industries that use such a small percentage of the total supply of inputs required for industrywide production that firms can enter the industry without bidding up input prices. In such a situation, we are dealing with a **constant-cost industry.** Its long-run industry supply curve is therefore horizontal and is represented by S_L in panel (a) of Figure 23-9 below.

We can work through the case in which constant costs prevail. We start out in panel (a) with demand curve D_1 and supply curve S_1. The equilibrium price is P_1. Market demand shifts rightward to D_2. In the short run, the equilibrium price rises to P_2. This generates positive economic profits for existing firms in the industry. Such economic profits induce capital to flow into the industry. The existing firms expand or new firms enter (or both). The short-run supply curve shifts outward to S_2. The new intersection with the new demand curve is at E_3. The new equilibrium price is again P_1. The long-run supply curve, labeled S_L, is obtained by connecting the intersections of the corresponding pairs of demand and short-run supply curves, E_1 and E_3. In a constant-cost industry, long-run supply is perfectly elastic. Any shift in demand is eventually met by just enough entry or exit of suppliers that the long-run price is constant at P_1.

FIGURE 23-9 Constant-Cost, Increasing-Cost, and Decreasing-Cost Industries

In panel (a), we show a situation in which the demand curve shifts from D_1 to D_2. Price increases from P_1 to P_2. In time, the short-run supply curve shifts outward because entry occurs in response to positive profits, and the equilibrium shifts from E_2 to E_3. The market clearing price is again P_1. If we connect points such as E_1 and E_3, we come up with the long-run supply curve S_L. This is a constant-cost industry. In panel (b), costs are increasing for the industry, and therefore the long-run supply curve, S'_L, slopes upward and long-run prices rise from P_1 to P_2. In panel (c), costs are decreasing for the industry as it expands, and therefore the long-run supply curve, S''_L, slopes downward such that long-run prices decline from P_1 to P_2.

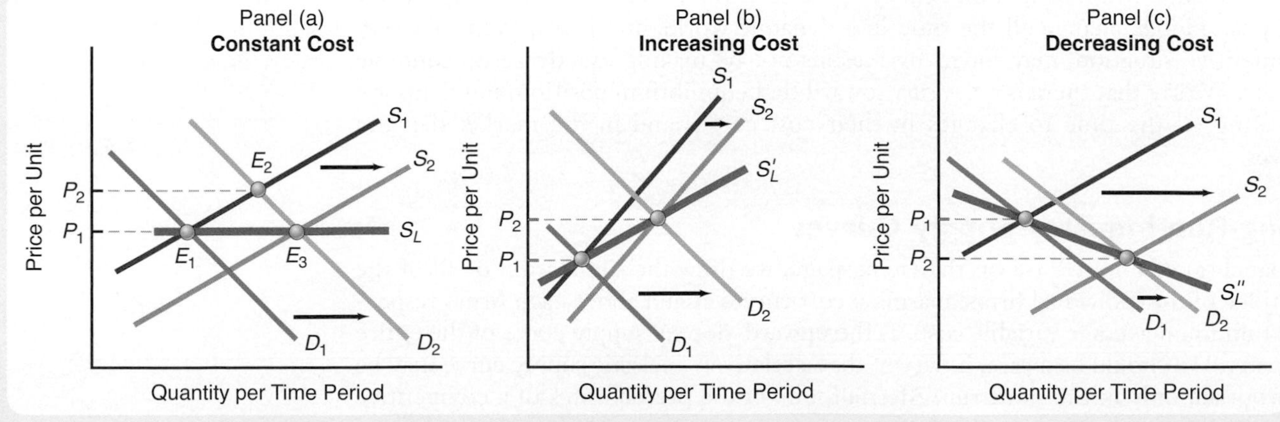

Retail trade is often given as an example of such an industry because output can be expanded or contracted without affecting input prices. Banking is another example.

INCREASING-COST INDUSTRIES In an **increasing-cost industry,** expansion by existing firms and the addition of new firms cause the price of inputs specialized to that industry to be bid up. As costs of production rise, the ATC curve and the firms' MC curves shift upward, causing short-run supply curves (each firm's marginal cost curve) to shift vertically upward. Hence, industry supply shifts out by less than in a constant-cost industry. The result is a long-run industry supply curve that slopes upward, as represented by S_L' in panel (b) of Figure 23-9 on the facing page. Examples are residential construction and coal mining—both use specialized inputs that cannot be obtained in ever-increasing quantities without causing their prices to rise.

Increasing-cost industry
An industry in which an increase in industry output is accompanied by an increase in long-run per-unit costs, such that the long-run industry supply curve slopes upward.

DECREASING-COST INDUSTRIES An expansion in the number of firms in an industry can lead to a reduction in input costs and a downward shift in the ATC and MC curves. When this occurs, the long-run industry supply curve will slope downward. An example, S_L'', is given in panel (c) of Figure 23-9. This is a **decreasing-cost industry.**

Decreasing-cost industry
An industry in which an increase in output leads to a reduction in long-run per-unit costs, such that the long-run industry supply curve slopes downward.

Long-Run Equilibrium

In the long run, the firm can change the scale of its plant, adjusting its plant size in such a way that it has no further incentive to change. It will do so until profits are maximized.

You Are There

To contemplate why the shape of an industry's long-run supply curve might change, take a look at **The Coal Mining Industry Confronts a Changing Cost Structure,** on page 525.

The Firm's Long-Run Situation

Figure 23-10 below shows the long-run equilibrium of the perfectly competitive firm. Given a price of P and a marginal cost curve, MC, the firm produces at output q_e. Because economic profits must be zero in the long run, the firm's short-run average costs (SAC) must equal P at q_e, which occurs at minimum SAC. In addition, because we are in long-run equilibrium, any economies of scale must be exhausted, so we are on the minimum point of the long-run average cost curve (LAC). In other words, the long-run equilibrium position is where "everything is equal," which is at point E in Figure 23-10. There, *price* equals *marginal revenue* equals *marginal cost* equals *average cost* (minimum, short-run, and long-run).

FIGURE 23-10 Long-Run Firm Competitive Equilibrium

In the long run, the firm operates where price, marginal revenue, marginal cost, short-run minimum average cost, and long-run minimum average cost are all equal. This condition is satisfied at point *E*.

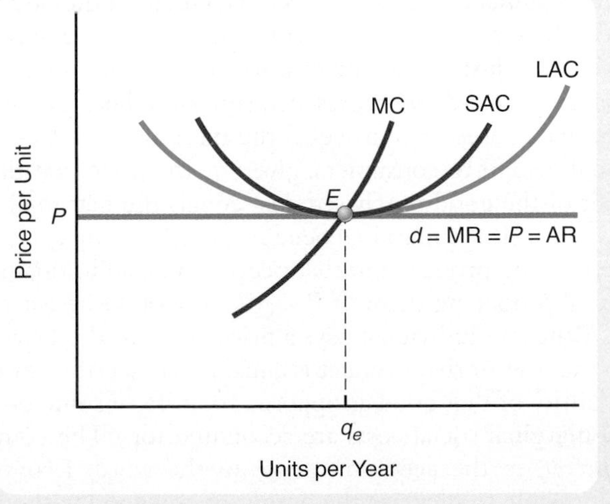

Perfect Competition and Minimum Average Total Cost

Look again at Figure 23-10 on the preceding page. In long-run equilibrium, the perfectly competitive firm finds itself producing at output rate q_e. At that rate of output, the price is just equal to the minimum long-run average cost as well as the minimum short-run average cost. In this sense, perfect competition results in the production of goods and services using the least costly combination of resources. This is an important attribute of a perfectly competitive long-run equilibrium, particularly when we wish to compare the market structure of perfect competition with other market structures that are less than perfectly competitive. We will examine these other market structures in later chapters.

Why Not . . . **eliminate economic profits entirely?**

If companies were unable to earn positive economic profits in the short run, firms and consumers would be deprived of signals about opportunities for adjustments that would yield greater overall welfare for society. For instance, if companies were prohibited from earning more than zero economic profits, entrepreneurs would have little incentive to try new ways of doing things in an effort to reduce costs and gain additional profits. As a consequence, technological advances would grind to a halt. In addition, a mandate that firms must maintain zero economic profits at all times would undercut incentives for new firms to enter an industry experiencing growing demand. Thus, society benefits from the market signals created when firms experience positive short-run economic profits.

Competitive Pricing: Marginal Cost Pricing

In a perfectly competitive industry, each firm produces where its marginal cost curve intersects its marginal revenue curve from below. Thus, perfectly competitive firms always sell their goods at a price that just equals marginal cost. This is said to be the optimal price of this good because the price that consumers pay reflects the opportunity cost to society of producing the good. Recall that marginal cost is the amount that a firm must spend to purchase the additional resources needed to expand output by one unit. Given competitive markets, the amount paid for a resource will be the same in all of its alternative uses. Thus, MC reflects relative resource input use. That is, if the MC of good 1 is twice the MC of good 2, one more unit of good 1 requires twice the resource input of one more unit of good 2.

Marginal Cost Pricing

Marginal cost pricing
A system of pricing in which the price charged is equal to the opportunity cost to society of producing one more unit of the good or service in question. The opportunity cost is the marginal cost to society.

The competitive firm produces up to the point at which the market price just equals the marginal cost. Herein lies the element of the optimal nature of a competitive solution. It is called **marginal cost pricing.** The competitive firm sells its product at a price that just equals the cost to society—the opportunity cost—for that is what the marginal cost curve represents. (But note here that it is the self-interest of firm owners that causes price to equal the marginal cost to society.) In other words, the marginal benefit to consumers, given by the price that they are willing to pay for the last unit of the good purchased, just equals the marginal cost to society of producing the last unit. (If the marginal benefit exceeds the marginal cost, that is, if $P > MC$, too little is being produced in that people value additional units more than the cost to society of producing them. If $P < MC$, the opposite is true.)

When an individual pays a price equal to the marginal cost of production, the cost to the user of that product is equal to the sacrifice or cost to society of producing that quantity of that good as opposed to more of some other good. (We are assuming that all marginal social costs are accounted for.) The competitive solution, then, is called *efficient*, in the economic sense of the word. Economic efficiency means that it is impossible to increase the output of any good without lowering the *value* of the total output produced in the economy. No juggling of resources, such as labor and capital, will result in an output that is higher in total value than the value of all of the goods and services already being produced. In an efficient equilibrium, it is impossible to make one person better off without making someone else worse off. All resources are used in the most advantageous way possible, and society therefore enjoys an efficient allocation of productive resources. All goods and services are sold at their opportunity cost, and marginal cost pricing prevails throughout.

Market Failure

Although perfect competition does offer many desirable results, situations arise when perfectly competitive markets cannot efficiently allocate resources. Either too many or too few resources are used in the production of a good or service. These situations are instances of **market failure.** Externalities arising from failures to fully assign property rights and public goods are examples. For reasons discussed in later chapters, perfectly competitive markets cannot efficiently allocate resources in these situations, and alternative allocation mechanisms are called for. In some cases, alternative market structures or government intervention *may* improve the economic outcome.

Market failure
A situation in which an unrestrained market operation leads to either too few or too many resources going to a specific economic activity.

QUICK QUIZ See page 531 for the answers. **Review concepts from this section in MyEconLab.**

The perfectly competitive price is determined by the __________ of the market demand curve and the market supply curve. The market supply curve is equal to the horizontal summation of the portions of the individual marginal cost curves above their respective minimum average __________ costs.

In the long run, perfectly competitive firms make __________ economic profits because of entry and exit whenever there are industrywide economic profits or losses.

A constant-cost industry has a __________ long-run supply curve. An increasing-cost industry has an __________-sloping long-run supply curve. A decreasing-cost industry has a __________-sloping long-run supply curve.

In the long run, a perfectly competitive firm produces to the point at which price, marginal revenue, marginal cost, short-run minimum average cost, and long-run minimum average cost are all __________.

Perfectly competitive pricing is essentially __________ __________ pricing. Therefore, the perfectly competitive solution is called efficient because __________ __________ represents the social opportunity cost of producing one more unit of the good.

You Are There

The Coal Mining Industry Confronts a Changing Cost Structure

During past decades, the market clearing price of coal steadily declined relative to prices of other goods and services. Coal mining was a decreasing-cost industry. Recently, however, the conditions that the industry confronts have changed. Officials at St. Louis–based Patriot Coal Corporation accept that from now on, extracting coal from beneath the earth's surface is going to require a wider range of—and, as a consequence, costlier—factors of production. Patriot Coal's Janine Orf sums up the situation: "What's left to mine is not as easy as what we mined 20 or even 10 years ago. The seams are getting thinner, and there are more limestone intrusions." As a consequence, Orf notes, Patriot Coal has to dig deeper and move more earth to extract coal from aging mines.

Orf and managers at other coal companies know that the demand for coal to generate the energy that drives turbines in electric power plants will continue to grow in the coming years. They also have little doubt that their firms and others that may enter the industry in the future will be able to boost market supply in response to changes in the equilibrium price. In light of the increasing per-unit cost of mining additional coal, they also have a good idea what will happen to the equilibrium price. Coal mining is now an increasing-cost industry, so in the long run, the equilibrium price will rise as the demand for coal increases.

Critical Analysis Questions

1. What has happened to the shape of the coal industry's long run supply curve?
2. Why might more firms opt to enter coal mining even as input costs rise?

ISSUES & APPLICATIONS

A Higher Price Sets Off a New California Gold Rush

CONCEPTS APPLIED

- Perfect Competition
- Short-Run Shutdown Price
- Short-Run Break-Even Price

Since 2000, as shown in Figure 23-11, both the nominal, current-dollar price and the real, inflation-adjusted price of gold have more than tripled. Consistent with predictions of the theory of perfect competition, the recent increase in the price of gold has touched off renewed interest by mining firms in trying to extract gold from California mines abandoned decades ago.

A Perfectly Competitive Market for a Shiny Metal

Although there are different qualities of gold, units of each type of gold are homogeneous. In addition, many mining firms possess the technology to extract gold from the earth, and the potential output of each of these firms is small relative to total gold production. Furthermore, it is easy for mining firms to enter or leave the industry. Thus, the gold mining industry satisfies the key characteristics of perfect competition.

A New Gold Rush Begins

Since the middle of 2007, the inflation-adjusted price of gold has been above the short-run shutdown price at which most of California's gold mines were closed in the early 1960s. Indeed, the inflation-adjusted gold price shown below in Figure 23-11 is now well above the short-run break-even price. Consequently, a number of mining firms are reopening old California gold mines. Several U.S. and Canadian companies plan to extract gold from hundreds of miles of abandoned mine shafts at various locations

FIGURE 23-11 Index Measures of the Current-Dollar and Inflation-Adjusted Prices of Gold

These index measures of the current-dollar and inflation-adjusted prices of gold indicate that both measures of gold's price generally trended downward between the early 1980s and 2000. Since then, however, both the current-dollar price and the inflation-adjusted price have increased substantially.

Source: U.S. Bureau of Labor Statistics.

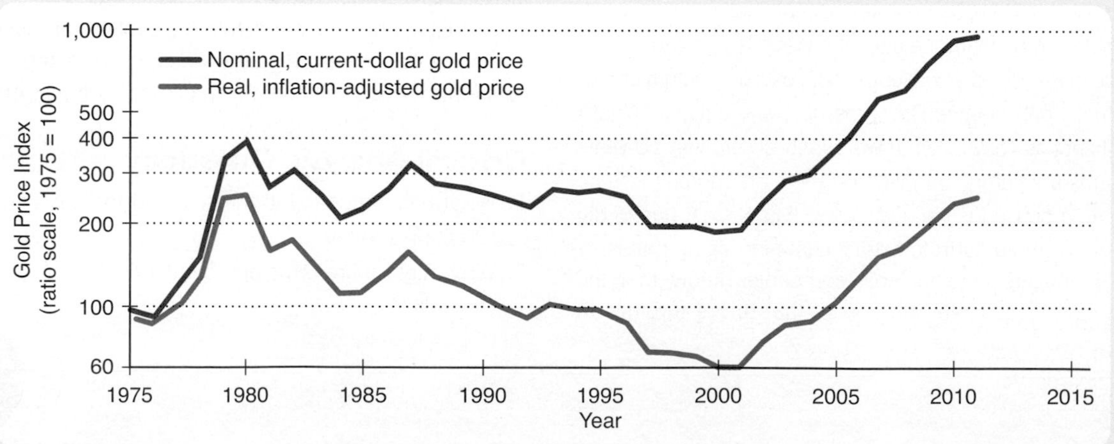

throughout the state. A few have already modernized some of the old mines and begun removing gold that was too costly to extract back when inflation-adjusted prices were much lower than they are today.

For Critical Analysis

1. Based on the data in Figure 23-11 on the facing page, why do you think that some mining firms that initially contemplated reopening Californian gold mines in the late 1970s discarded these plans in the early 1980s?
2. What do you suppose would likely happen to California's gold mines if the current-dollar and inflation-adjusted prices of gold fell during the 2010s?

Web Resources

1. For a brief history of California gold mining, go to www.econtoday.com/ch23.
2. To learn about one mining firm that plans to reopen an abandoned California gold mine, go to www.econtoday.com/ch23.

Research Project

Explain why it is important for mining firms that contemplate reopening old mineral and metal mines to adjust prices for inflation when comparing today's shutdown and break-even prices with those of past years.

For more questions on this chapter's Issues & Applications, go to **MyEconLab**. In the Study Plan for this chapter, select Section N: News.

Here is what you should know after reading this chapter. **MyEconLab** will help you identify what you know, and where to go when you need to practice.

WHAT YOU SHOULD KNOW		WHERE TO GO TO PRACTICE
The Characteristics of a Perfectly Competitive Market Structure A perfectly competitive industry has four fundamental characteristics: (1) there are large numbers of buyers and sellers, (2) firms in the industry produce and sell a homogeneous product, (3) information is equally accessible to both buyers and sellers, and (4) there are insignificant barriers to industry entry or exit. These characteristics imply that each firm in a perfectly competitive industry is a price taker: the firm takes the market price as given and outside its control.	perfect competition, 508 perfectly competitive firm, 508 price taker, 508	• **MyEconLab** Study Plan 23.1 • Audio introduction to Chapter 23 • Economics Video: Government Should Leave Farm Business
How a Perfectly Competitive Firm Decides How Much to Produce Because a perfectly competitive firm sells the amount that it wishes at the market price, the additional revenue it earns from selling an additional unit of output is the market price. Thus, the firm's marginal revenue equals the market price, and its marginal revenue curve is the firm's own perfectly elastic demand curve. The firm maximizes economic profits when marginal cost equals marginal revenue, as long as the market price is not below the short-run shutdown price, where the marginal cost curve crosses the average variable cost curve.	total revenues, 509 profit-maximizing rate of production, 511 marginal revenue, 512 **KEY FIGURES** Figure 23-1, 509 Figure 23-2, 510	• **MyEconLab** Study Plans 23.2, 23.3 • Animated Figures 23-1, 23-2

(continued)

MyEconLab continued

WHAT YOU SHOULD KNOW		WHERE TO GO TO PRACTICE
The Short-Run Supply Curve of a Perfectly Competitive Firm If the market price is below the short-run shutdown price, the firm's total revenues fail to cover its variable costs. The firm would be better off halting production and minimizing its economic loss in the short run. If the market price is above the short-run shutdown price, however, the firm produces the rate of output where marginal revenue, the market price, equals marginal cost. Thus, the range of the firm's marginal cost curve above the short-run shutdown price gives the firm's combinations of market prices and production choices. This range of the marginal cost curve is therefore the firm's short-run supply curve.	short-run break-even price, 515 short-run shutdown price, 516 industry supply curve, 519 **KEY FIGURES** Figure 23-3, 514 Figure 23-4, 514 Figure 23-5, 515 Figure 23-6, 518 Figure 23-7, 518	• **MyEconLab** Study Plans 23.4, 23.5, 23.6, 23.7 • Animated Figures 23-3, 23-4, 23-5, 23-6, 23-7 • Video: The Short-Run Shutdown Price • Video: The Meaning of Zero Economic Profits
The Equilibrium Price in a Perfectly Competitive Market The short-run supply curve for a perfectly competitive industry is obtained by summing the quantities supplied at each price by all firms in the industry. At the equilibrium market price, the total amount of output supplied by all firms is equal to the total amount of output demanded by all buyers.	**KEY FIGURE** Figure 23-8, 520	• **MyEconLab** Study Plan 23.8 • Animated Figure 23-8
Incentives to Enter or Exit a Perfectly Competitive Industry In the short run, a perfectly competitive firm will continue to produce output as long as the market price exceeds the short-run shutdown price. This is so even if the market price is below the short-run break-even point where the marginal cost curve crosses the firm's average total cost curve. Even though the firm earns an economic loss, it minimizes the amount of the loss by continuing to produce in the short run. In the long run, continued economic losses will induce exit from the industry.	signals, 521	• **MyEconLab** Study Plan 23.9
The Long-Run Industry Supply Curve and Constant-, Increasing-, and Decreasing-Cost Industries The long-run industry supply curve in a perfectly competitive industry shows the relationship between prices and quantities after firms have entered or left the industry in response to economic profits or losses. In a constant-cost industry, total output can increase without a rise in long-run per-unit costs, so the long-run industry supply curve is horizontal. In an increasing-cost industry, per-unit costs increase with a rise in industry output, so the long-run industry supply curve slopes upward. In a decreasing-cost industry per-unit costs decline as industry output increases, and the long-run industry supply curve slopes downward.	long-run industry supply curve, 522 constant-cost industry, 522 increasing-cost industry, 523 decreasing-cost industry, 523 marginal cost pricing, 524 market failure, 525 **KEY FIGURE** Figure 23-10, 523	• **MyEconLab** Study Plans 23.10, 23.11 • Animated Figure 23-10

Log in to MyEconLab, take a chapter test, and get a personalized Study Plan that tells you which concepts you understand and which ones you need to review. From there, MyEconLab will give you further practice, tutorials, animations, videos, and guided solutions.
Log in to www.myeconlab.com

PROBLEMS

All problems are assignable in myeconlab. *Answers to odd-numbered problems appear at the back of the book.*

23-1. Explain why each of the following examples is *not* a perfectly competitive industry.

a. One firm produces a large portion of the industry's total output, but there are many firms in the industry, and their products are indistinguishable. Firms can easily exit and enter the industry.

b. There are many buyers and sellers in the industry. Consumers have equal information about the prices of firms' products, which differ moderately in quality from firm to firm.

c. Many taxicabs compete in a city. The city's government requires all taxicabs to provide identical service. Taxicabs are nearly identical, and all drivers must wear a designated uniform. The government also limits the number of taxicab companies that can operate within the city's boundaries.

23-2. Consider a local market for Blu-ray disc movie rentals, which is perfectly competitive. The market supply curve slopes upward, the market demand curve slopes downward, and the equilibrium rental price equals $3.50. Consider each of the following events, and discuss the effects they will have on the market clearing price and on the demand curve faced by the individual rental store.

a. People's tastes change in favor of going to see more movies at cinemas with their friends and family members.

b. National Blu-ray disc rental chains open a number of new stores in this market.

c. There is a significant increase in the price of downloading movies on the Internet.

23-3. Consider the diagram in the next column, which applies to a perfectly competitive firm, which at present faces a market clearing price of $20 per unit and produces 10,000 units of output per week.

a. What is the firm's current average revenue per unit?

b. What are the present economic profits of this firm? Is the firm maximizing economic profits? Explain.

c. If the market clearing price drops to $12.50 per unit, should this firm continue to produce in the short run if it wishes to maximize its economic profits (or minimize its economic losses)? Explain.

d. If the market clearing price drops to $7.50 per unit, should this firm continue to produce in the short run if it wishes to maximize its economic profits (or minimize its economic losses)? Explain.

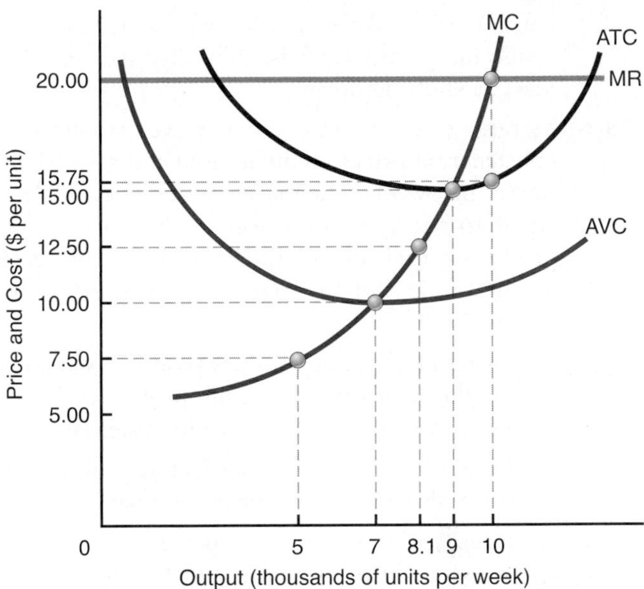

23-4. The following table represents the hourly output and cost structure for a local pizza shop. The market is perfectly competitive, and the market price of a pizza in the area is $10. Total costs include all opportunity costs.

Total Hourly Output and Sales of Pizzas	Total Hourly Cost ($)
0	5
1	9
2	11
3	12
4	14
5	18
6	24
7	32
8	42
9	54
10	68

a. Calculate the total revenue and total economic profit for this pizza shop at each rate of output.

b. Assuming that the pizza shop always produces and sells at least one pizza per hour, does this appear to be a situation of short-run or long-run equilibrium?

c. Calculate the pizza shop's marginal cost and marginal revenue at each rate of output. Based on marginal analysis, what is the profit-maximizing rate of output for the pizza shop?

d. Draw a diagram depicting the short-run marginal revenue and marginal cost curves for this pizza shop, and illustrate the determination of its profit-maximizing output rate.

23-5. Consider the information provided in Problem 23-4. Suppose the market price drops to only $5 per pizza. In the short run, should this pizza shop continue to make pizzas, or will it maximize its economic profits (that is, minimize its economic loss) by shutting down?

23-6. Yesterday, a perfectly competitive producer of construction bricks manufactured and sold 10,000 bricks per week at a market price that was just equal to the minimum average variable cost of producing each brick. Today, all the firm's costs are the same, but the market price of bricks has declined.

a. Assuming that this firm has positive fixed costs, did the firm earn economic profits, economic losses, or zero economic profits yesterday?

b. To maximize economic profits today, how many bricks should this firm produce today?

23-7. Suppose that a perfectly competitive firm faces a market price of $5 per unit, and at this price the upward-sloping portion of the firm's marginal cost curve crosses its marginal revenue curve at an output level of 1,500 units. If the firm produces 1,500 units, its average variable costs equal $5.50 per unit, and its average fixed costs equal 50 cents per unit. What is the firm's profit-maximizing (or loss-minimizing) output level? What is the amount of its economic profits (or losses) at this output level?

23-8. Suppose that the price of a service sold in a perfectly competitive market is $25 per unit. For a firm in this market, the output level corresponding to a marginal cost of $25 per unit is 2,000 units. Average variable costs at this output level equal $15 per unit, and average fixed costs equal $5 per unit. What is the firm's profit-maximizing (or loss-minimizing) output level? What is the amount of its economic profits (or losses) at this output level?

23-9. Suppose that a firm in a perfectly competitive industry finds that at its current output rate, marginal revenue exceeds the minimum average total cost of producing any feasible rate of output. Furthermore, the firm is producing an output rate at which marginal cost is less than the average total cost at that rate of output. Is the firm maximizing its economic profits? Why or why not?

23-10. A perfectly competitive industry is initially in a short-run equilibrium in which all firms are earning zero economic profits but in which firms are operating below their minimum efficient scale. Explain the long-run adjustments that will take place for the industry to attain long-run equilibrium with firms operating at their minimum efficient scale.

23-11. Two years ago, a large number of firms entered a market in which existing firms had been earning positive economic profits. By the end of last year, the typical firm in this industry had begun earning negative economic profits. No other events occurred in this market during the past two years.

a. Explain the adjustment process that occurred last year.

b. Predict what adjustments will take place in this market beginning this year, other things being equal.

23-12. Numerous "hookah bars," at which patrons can pay to utilize water pipes to smoke regular and flavored tobaccos, have popped up around the nation. Hookah bars are particularly popular with college students.

a. Suppose that the market for the services of hookah bars is in long-run equilibrium. Then two events occur: (1) more cities end regulations that had generated fixed costs for hookah bars, and (2) many nonstudent adults discover previously unknown preferences for the services of hookah bars. Use diagrams to trace through the short-run effects on the market price of hookah-bar services, the marginal revenue and marginal cost of these services at a typical hookah bar, and the equilibrium quantity of services provided both by a typical hookah bar and by the hookah-bar industry.

b. Redraw your diagrams showing the situation at the conclusion of your answer to part (a). Use these new diagrams to explain the long-run adjustments that will take place in this industry.

ECONOMICS ON THE NET

The Cost Structure of the Movie Theater Business A key idea in this chapter is that competition among firms in an industry can influence the long-run cost structure within the industry. Here you get a chance to apply this concept to a multinational company that owns movie theaters.

Title: AMC International

Navigation: Follow the link at **www.econtoday.com/ch23** to visit American Multi-Cinema's home page.

Application Answer the following questions.

1. At the bottom of the home page, click on *Investor Relations*, and then click on *Fact Sheet*. What is the average number of screens in an AMC theater? How many theaters does AMC own and manage?
2. Based on the *Fact Sheet* information, which of AMC's theaters serves the largest volume of viewing customers?
3. Back up to the home page, and under "See a Movie," click on *Find a Theater*. Enter a few zip codes and make a list of the numbers of screens at the theaters that appear in each list. Based on the numbers of screens in this sample you have collected and your answers to questions 1 and 2 above, what can you conclude about the likely cost structure of this industry? Illustrate the long-run average cost curve for this industry.

For Group Discussion and Analysis A theater with a particularly large number of screens is called a multiplex. What do you suppose constrains the size of a multiplex theater in a typical locale? What factors do you think determine whether it is likely to be less costly for AMC to have fewer facilities that are larger in size or to have many smaller facilities?

ANSWERS TO QUICK QUIZZES

p. 513: (i) large . . . homogeneous . . . unrestrained; (ii) no . . . all; (iii) marginal . . . marginal; (iv) revenue . . . cost . . . price

p. 519: (i) average . . . price; (ii) break-even . . . marginal; (iii) shutdown . . . marginal; (iv) variable; (v) zero . . . normal; (vi) variable . . . summation . . . variable

p. 525: (i) intersection . . . variable; (ii) zero; (iii) horizontal . . . upward . . . downward; (iv) equal; (v) marginal cost . . . marginal cost

24 Monopoly

A New York City taxi medallion is more than just a decorative metal plate fastened to the hood of each of the city's distinctive yellow taxicabs. Anyone who does not own a taxi medallion cannot lawfully charge fees to transport passengers within the city. In other words, the owner of a medallion has formal legal possession of a license to operate a taxi business. Thus, the medallion ownership requirement constitutes a *barrier to entry* to New York City's taxicab industry. In this chapter, you will learn how governmentally imposed and other types of barriers to entry that protect firms from competition can give rise to *monopolies,* or single-firm industries. Furthermore, by the time you have completed this chapter, you will be able to understand why some people are willing to pay more than $800,000 for a New York City taxi medallion.

LEARNING OBJECTIVES

After reading this chapter, you should be able to:

- Identify situations that can give rise to monopoly
- Describe the demand and marginal revenue conditions a monopolist faces
- Discuss how a monopolist determines how much output to produce and what price to charge
- Evaluate the profits earned by a monopolist
- Understand price discrimination
- Explain the social cost of monopolies

myeconlab

MyEconLab helps you master each objective and study more efficiently. See end of chapter for details.

today the activities of 35 percent of U.S. employees of private businesses are licensed, certified, or regulated by government agencies, up from just 3 percent five decades ago? Typically, the justification for these government licensing, certification, and regulation requirements is that they assure a minimal level of service quality. Such government rules, however, also make it harder for additional service providers to enter industries subjected to the regulations. In this chapter, you will learn that a consequence of such government-established barriers to market entry can be a situation called *monopoly*.

Did You Know That ?

Definition of a Monopolist

The word *monopoly* probably brings to mind notions of a business that gouges the consumer, sells faulty products, and gets unconscionably rich in the process. But if we are to succeed in analyzing and predicting the behavior of imperfectly competitive firms, we will have to be more objective in our definition. Although most monopolies in the United States are relatively large, our definition will be equally applicable to small businesses: A **monopolist** is the *single supplier* of a good or service for which there is no close substitute.

Monopolist
The single supplier of a good or service for which there is no close substitute. The monopolist therefore constitutes its entire industry.

In a monopoly market structure, the firm (the monopolist) and the industry are one and the same. Occasionally, there may be a problem in identifying an industry and therefore determining if a monopoly exists. For example, should we think of aluminum and steel as separate industries, or should we define the industry in terms of basic metals? Our answer depends on the extent to which aluminum and steel can be substituted in the production of a wide range of products.

As we shall see in this chapter, a seller prefers to have a monopoly than to face competitors. In general, we think of monopoly prices as being higher than prices under perfect competition and of monopoly profits as typically being higher than profits under perfect competition (which are, in the long run, merely equivalent to a normal rate of return). How does a firm obtain a monopoly in an industry? Basically, there must be *barriers to entry* that enable firms to receive monopoly profits in the long run. Barriers to entry are restrictions on who can start a business or who can stay in a business.

Barriers to Entry

For any amount of monopoly power to continue to exist in the long run, the market must be closed to entry in some way. Either legal means or certain aspects of the industry's technical or cost structure may prevent entry. We will discuss several of the barriers to entry that have allowed firms to reap monopoly profits in the long run (even if they are not pure monopolists in the technical sense).

Ownership of Resources Without Close Substitutes

Preventing a newcomer from entering an industry is often difficult. Indeed, some economists contend that no monopoly acting without government support has been able to prevent entry into the industry unless that monopoly has had the control of some essential natural resource. Consider the possibility of one firm's owning the entire supply of a raw material input that is essential to the production of a particular commodity. The exclusive ownership of such a vital resource serves as a barrier to entry until an alternative source of the raw material input is found or an alternative technology not requiring the raw material in question is developed. A good example of control over a vital input is the Aluminum Company of America (Alcoa), a firm that prior to World War II owned most world stocks of bauxite, the essential raw material in the production of aluminum. Such a situation is rare, though, and is ordinarily temporary.

Economies of Scale

Sometimes it is not profitable for more than one firm to exist in an industry. This is true if one firm would have to produce such a large quantity in order to realize lower unit costs that there would not be sufficient demand to warrant a second producer of the same product. Such a situation may arise because of a phenomenon we discussed in Chapter 22, economies of scale. When economies of scale exist, total costs increase less than proportionately to the increase in output. That is, proportional increases in output yield proportionately smaller increases in total costs, and per-unit costs drop. When economies of scale exist, larger firms (with larger output) have an advantage in that they have lower costs that enable them to charge lower prices and thereby drive smaller firms out of business.

Natural monopoly
A monopoly that arises from the peculiar production characteristics in an industry. It usually arises when there are large economies of scale relative to the industry's demand such that one firm can produce at a lower average cost than can be achieved by multiple firms.

When economies of scale occur over a wide range of outputs, a **natural monopoly** may develop. A natural monopoly is the first firm to take advantage of persistent declining long-run average costs as scale increases. The natural monopolist is able to underprice its competitors and eventually force all of them out of the market.

Figure 24-1 on the facing page shows a downward-sloping long-run average cost curve (LAC). Recall that when average costs are falling, marginal costs are less than average costs. Thus, when the long-run average cost curve slopes downward, the long-run marginal cost curve (LMC) will be below the LAC.

In our example, long-run average costs are falling over such a large range of production rates that we would expect only one firm to survive in such an industry. That firm would be the natural monopolist. It would be the first one to take advantage of the decreasing average costs. That is, it would construct the large-scale facilities first. As its average costs fell, it would lower prices and get an ever-larger share of the market. Once that firm had driven all other firms out of the industry, it would raise its price to maximize profits.

Legal or Governmental Restrictions

Governments and legislatures can also erect barriers to entry. These include licenses, franchises, patents, tariffs, and specific regulations that tend to limit entry.

Why Not . . . stop erecting government barriers to entry?

Even though many people besides economists understand that government-established entry barriers reduce competition, vested interests often promote insincere public safety rationales for licensing and certification rules. For instance, the American Society of Interior Designers (ASID) has convinced state governments in Alabama, Illinois, and Nevada that the only people qualified to arrange furniture and accessories in office buildings' interiors are ASID members. Other people, the ASID claims, design room interiors in ways that make them more susceptible to fires. To become an ASID member, an individual must earn a college degree in interior design, complete a two-year apprenticeship, and pass a national licensing examination. Only a small portion of this training relates to interior decorating that promotes fire safety. Nevertheless, the ASID requirements constitute a significant entry barrier for many who otherwise might have contemplated entering the market to provide interior design services.

You Are There

For an example of how a government goes about establishing restrictions on market competition, see **A Texas Veterinary Board Whittles Down Vets' Competition,** on page 547.

LICENSES, FRANCHISES, AND CERTIFICATES OF CONVENIENCE It is illegal to enter many industries without a government license, or a "certificate of convenience and public necessity." For example, in some states you cannot form an electrical utility to compete with the electrical utility already operating in your area. You would first have to obtain a certificate of convenience and public necessity from the appropriate authority, which is usually the state's public utility commission. Yet public utility commissions in these states rarely, if ever, issue a certificate to a group of investors who want to compete directly in the same geographic area as an existing electrical utility. Hence, entry into the industry in a particular geographic area is prohibited, and long-run monopoly profits conceivably could be earned by the electrical utility already serving the area.

FIGURE 24-1 The Cost Curves That Might Lead to a Natural Monopoly

Whenever long-run marginal costs (LMC) are less than long-run average costs (LAC), then long-run average costs will be falling. A natural monopoly might arise when this situation exists over most output rates. The first firm to establish low-unit-cost capacity would be able to take advantage of declining average total costs. This firm would drive out all rivals by charging a lower price than the others could sustain at their higher average costs.

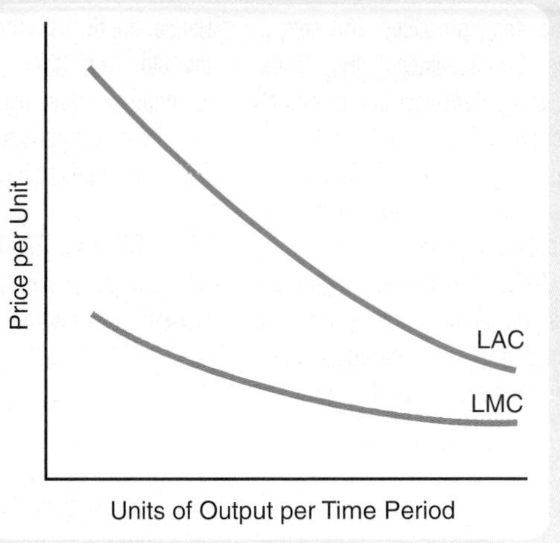

To enter interstate (and also many intrastate) markets for pipelines, television and radio broadcasting, and transmission of natural gas, to cite a few such industries, it is often necessary to obtain similar permits. Because these franchises or licenses are restricted, long-run monopoly profits might be earned by the firms already in the industry.

How have tax preparation firms essentially become public utilities?

POLICY EXAMPLE Congress Decides to License Tax Preparers

Each year, about four out of every five taxpayers obtain assistance filling out their income tax returns, either from paid preparers or from computer programs. Many of the firms offering tax preparation services are unlicensed and uncertified by any governmental authorities. "In most states, anyone can charge to prepare tax returns, regardless of training, education, experience, skill, licensing, or registration," says Doug Shulman, commissioner of the Internal Revenue Service (IRS).

This state of affairs will not last much longer. The IRS has convinced Congress to require all tax preparers to register with the federal government and to satisfy government-defined minimum competency standards. The chief executive of the country's third-largest tax preparation firm, Liberty Tax Services, has publicly stated, "I applaud the IRS in their efforts to require tax preparer certification." He did not add that the success of the IRS in convincing Congress to require federal certification may cause a substantial fraction of Liberty's competition to disappear in a flash. Indeed, under the IRS certification requirements, Liberty and several other large tax preparation firms essentially have become public utilities. Their task is, in IRS Commissioner Shulman's words, "to ensure that the right amount of tax is paid." Naturally, regulated tax preparation firms likely regard their main objective to be to obtain the higher profits made possible by government-erected entry barriers.

FOR CRITICAL ANALYSIS

Who will likely receive higher payments now that tax preparers are required to be licensed?

PATENTS A patent is issued to an inventor to provide protection from having the invention copied or stolen for a period of 20 years. Suppose that engineers working for Ford Motor Company discover a way to build an engine that requires half the parts of a regular engine and weighs only half as much. If Ford is successful in obtaining a patent on this discovery, it can (in principle) prevent others from copying it. The patent holder has a monopoly. It is the patent holder's responsibility to defend the patent, however. That means that Ford—like other patent owners—must expend resources to prevent others from imitating its invention. If the costs of enforcing a particular patent are greater than the benefits, though, the patent may not bestow any monopoly profits on its owner. The policing costs would be too high.

Go to www.econtoday.com/ch24 to learn more about patents and trademarks from the U.S. Patent and Trademark Office and to learn all about copyrights from the U.S. Copyright Office.

Why do some pharmaceutical companies raise the prices of patented drugs substantially just before the patents expire? (See the next page.)

EXAMPLE Inducing Patients to Switch from One Patented Drug to Another

For years, the pharmaceuticals firm Cephalon, Inc., produced and sold a patented narcolepsy (an illness involving excessive sleepiness) drug called Provigil. In the years leading up to 2012 when this patent was due to expire, the company gradually raised the drug's price. By 2012, Provigil's inflation-adjusted price, at more than $9 per tablet, was nearly twice its 2004 level.

Why did the company raise its patented drug's price so much? The answer is that the firm was about to obtain a patent on a new, longer-lasting narcolepsy drug, called Nuvigil. In 2008 and 2009, the company began an early marketing campaign aimed at physicians and patients prior to the new drug's scheduled 2010 introduction. The main theme of the campaign was that the new drug's price would be about half of the price of the old drug. Hence, the firm set the price of the new drug (Nuvigil) at the same price that the old drug (Provigil) had been previously. This pricing strategy was intended to induce existing customers to switch to Nuvigil, in hopes that they would then continue to use that drug until its patent expires in 2023. By then, Cephalon hopes to have yet another narcolepsy drug patented.

FOR CRITICAL ANALYSIS

Why did possession of a patent on Provigil permit Cephalon to raise Provigil's price without losing very many of its customers?

Tariffs
Taxes on imported goods.

TARIFFS Tariffs are special taxes that are imposed on certain imported goods. Tariffs make imports more expensive relative to their domestic counterparts, encouraging consumers to switch to the relatively cheaper domestically made products. If the tariffs are high enough, domestic producers may be able to act together like a single firm and gain monopoly advantage as the sole suppliers. Many countries have tried this protectionist strategy by using high tariffs to shut out foreign competitors.

REGULATIONS Throughout the twentieth century and to the present, government regulation of the U.S. economy has increased, especially along the dimensions of safety and quality. U.S. firms incur hundreds of billions of dollars in expenses each year to comply with federal, state, and local government regulations of business conduct relating to workplace conditions, environmental protection, product safety, and various other activities. Presumably, these large fixed costs of complying with regulations can be spread over a greater number of units of output by larger firms than by smaller firms, thereby putting the smaller firms at a competitive disadvantage. Entry will also be deterred to the extent that the scale of operation of a potential entrant must be sufficiently large to cover the average fixed costs of compliance. We examine regulation in more detail in Chapter 27.

QUICK QUIZ

See page 552 for the answers. Review concepts from this section in MyEconLab.

A **monopolist** is the single seller of a product or good for which there is no _________ substitute.

To maintain a monopoly, there must be barriers to entry. Barriers to entry include _________ of resources without close substitutes; economies of _________; legally required licenses, franchises, and certificates of convenience; patents; tariffs; and safety and quality regulations.

The Demand Curve a Monopolist Faces

A *pure monopolist* is the sole supplier of *one* product. A pure monopolist faces a demand curve that is the demand curve for the entire market for that good or service.

The monopolist faces the industry demand curve because the monopolist is the entire industry.

Because the monopolist faces the industry demand curve, which is by definition downward sloping, its choice regarding how much to produce is not the same as for a perfect competitor. When a monopolist changes output, it does not automatically receive the same price per unit that it did before the change.

Profits to Be Made from Increasing Production

How do firms benefit from changing production rates? What happens to price in each case? Let's first review the situation among perfect competitors.

MARGINAL REVENUE FOR THE PERFECT COMPETITOR Recall that a firm in a perfectly competitive industry faces a perfectly elastic demand curve. That is because the perfectly competitive firm is such a small part of the market that it cannot influence the price of its product. It is a *price taker*. If the forces of supply and demand establish that the price per constant-quality pair of shoes is $50, the individual firm can sell all the pairs of shoes it wants to produce at $50 per pair. The average revenue is $50, the price is $50, and the marginal revenue is also $50.

Let us again define marginal revenue:

> ***Marginal revenue equals the change in total revenue due to a one-unit change in the quantity produced and sold.***

In the case of a perfectly competitive industry, each time a single firm changes production by one unit, total revenue changes by the going price, and price is unchanged. Marginal revenue always equals price, or average revenue. Average revenue was defined as total revenue divided by quantity demanded, or

$$\text{Average revenue} = \frac{\text{TR}}{Q} = \frac{PQ}{Q} = P$$

Hence, marginal revenue, average revenue, and price are all the same for the price-taking firm.

MARGINAL REVENUE FOR THE MONOPOLIST What about a monopoly firm? We begin by considering a situation in which a monopolist charges every buyer the same price for each unit of its product. Because a monopoly is the entire industry, the monopoly firm's demand curve is the market demand curve. The market demand curve slopes downward, just like the other demand curves that we have seen. Therefore, to induce consumers to buy more of a particular product, given the industry demand curve, the monopoly firm must lower the price. Thus, the monopoly firm moves *down* the demand curve. If all buyers are to be charged the same price, the monopoly must lower the price on *all* units sold in order to sell more. It cannot lower the price on just the *last* unit sold in any given time period in order to sell a larger quantity.

Put yourself in the shoes of a monopoly ferryboat owner. You have a government-bestowed franchise, and no one can compete with you. Your ferryboat goes between two islands. If you are charging $1 per crossing, a certain quantity of your services will be demanded. Let's say that you are ferrying 100 people a day each way at that price. If you decide that you would like to ferry more individuals, you must lower your price to all individuals—you must move *down* the existing demand curve for ferrying services. To calculate the marginal revenue of your change in price, you must first calculate the total revenues you received at $1 per passenger per crossing and then calculate the total revenues you would receive at, say, 90 cents per passenger per crossing.

PERFECT COMPETITION VERSUS MONOPOLY It is sometimes useful to compare monopoly markets with perfectly competitive markets. The monopolist is constrained by the demand curve for its product, just as a perfectly competitive firm is constrained by its demand. The key difference is the nature of the demand curve each type of firm faces. We see this in Figure 24-2 on the following page, which compares the demand curves of the perfect competitor and the monopolist.

Here we see the fundamental difference between the monopolist and the perfect competitor. The perfect competitor doesn't have to worry about lowering price to sell more. In a perfectly competitive situation, the perfectly competitive firm accounts for such a small part of the market that it can sell its entire output, whatever that may be, at the same price. The monopolist cannot. The more the monopolist wants to sell,

FIGURE 24-2 Demand Curves for the Perfect Competitor and the Monopolist

The perfect competitor in panel (a) faces a perfectly elastic demand curve, *d*. The monopolist in panel (b) faces the entire industry demand curve, which slopes downward.

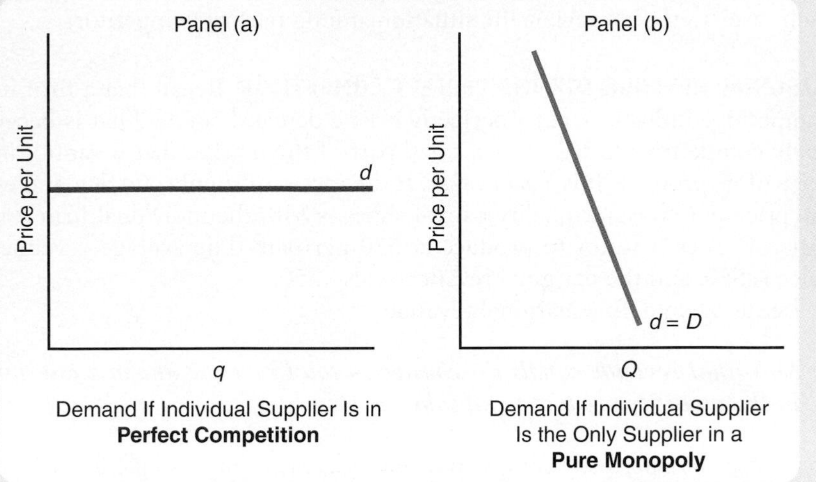

the lower the price it has to charge on the last unit (and on *all* units put on the market for sale). To sell the last unit, the monopolist has to lower the price because it is facing a downward-sloping demand curve, and the only way to move down the demand curve is to lower the price. As long as this price must be the same for all units, the extra revenues the monopolist receives from selling one more unit are going to be smaller than the extra revenues received from selling the next-to-last unit.

The Monopolist's Marginal Revenue: Less Than Price

An essential point is that for the monopolist, marginal revenue is always less than price. To understand why, look at Figure 24-3 on the facing page, which shows a unit increase in output sold due to a reduction from $8 to $7 in the price of ferry crossings provided by a monopolistic ferry company. The new $7 price is the price received for the last unit, so selling this unit contributes $7 to revenues. That is equal to the vertical column (area A). Area A is one unit wide by $7 high.

But price times the last unit sold is *not* the net addition to *total* revenues received from selling that last unit. Why? Because price had to be reduced on the three previous units sold in order to sell the larger quantity—four ferry crossings. The reduction in price is represented by the vertical distance from $8 to $7 on the vertical axis. We must therefore subtract area B from area A to come up with the *change* in total revenues due to a one-unit increase in sales. Clearly, the change in total revenues—that is, marginal revenue—must be less than price because marginal revenue is always the difference between areas A and B in Figure 24-3. Thus, at a price of $7, marginal revenue is $7 − $3 = $4 because there is a $1 per unit price reduction on three previous units. Hence, marginal revenue, $4, is less than price, $7.

Elasticity and Monopoly

The monopolist faces a downward-sloping demand curve (its average revenue curve). That means that it cannot charge just *any* price with no changes in quantity (a common misconception) because, depending on the price charged, a different quantity will be demanded.

Earlier we defined a monopolist as the single seller of a well-defined good or service with no *close* substitute. This does not mean, however, that the demand curve for a monopoly is vertical or exhibits zero price elasticity of demand. After all, consumers have limited incomes and unlimited wants. The market demand curve, which the monopolist alone faces in this situation, slopes downward because individuals compare

FIGURE 24-3 Marginal Revenue: Always Less Than Price

The price received for the last unit sold is equal to $7. The revenues received from selling this last unit are equal to $7 times one unit, or the orange-shaded area of the vertical column. If a single price is being charged for all units, however, total revenues do not go up by the amount of the area represented by that column. The price had to be reduced on all three units that were previously being sold at an $8 price. Thus, we must subtract the green-shaded area B, which is equal to $3, from area A, which is equal to $7, in order to derive marginal revenue. Marginal revenue of $4 is therefore less than the $7 price.

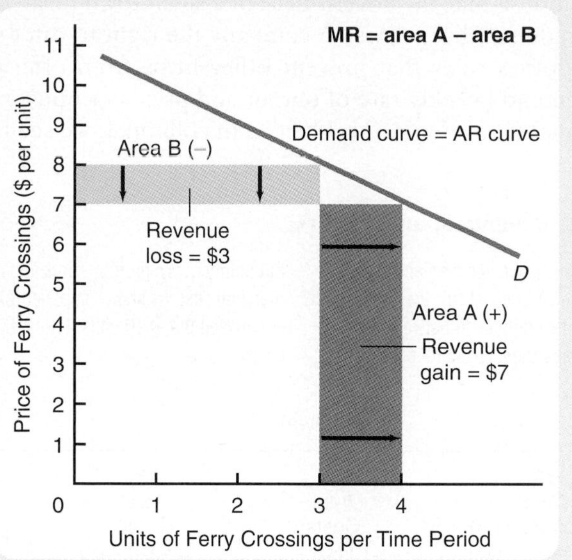

the marginal satisfaction they will receive to the cost of the commodity to be purchased. Take the example of a particular type of sports car. Even if miraculously there were absolutely no substitutes whatsoever for that sports car, the market demand curve would still slope downward. At lower prices, people will purchase more of those sports cars, perhaps buying cars for other family members.

Furthermore, the demand curve for the sports car slopes downward because there are at least several *imperfect* substitutes, such as other types of sports cars, used sports cars, sport utility vehicles, and other stylish vehicles. The more such substitutes there are, and the better these substitutes are, the more elastic will be the monopolist's demand curve, all other things held constant.

QUICK QUIZ **See page 552 for the answers. Review concepts from this section in MyEconLab.**

The monopolist estimates its marginal revenue curve, where marginal revenue is defined as the __________ in __________ revenues due to a one-unit change in quantity sold.

For the perfect competitor, price equals __________ revenue equals average revenue. For the monopolist, __________ revenue is always less than price because price must be reduced on all units to sell more.

The price __________ of demand for the monopolist depends on the number and similarity of substitutes. The more numerous the imperfect substitutes, the greater the price __________ of the monopolist's demand curve.

Costs and Monopoly Profit Maximization

To find the rate of output at which the perfect competitor would maximize profits, we had to add cost data. We will do the same thing now for the monopolist. We assume that profit maximization is the goal of the pure monopolist, just as it is for the perfect competitor. The perfect competitor, however, has only to decide on the profit-maximizing rate of output because price is given. The perfect competitor is a price taker. For the pure monopolist, we must seek a profit-maximizing *price-output combination* because the monopolist is a **price searcher.** We can determine this profit-maximizing price-output combination with either of two equivalent approaches—by looking at total revenues and total costs or by looking at marginal revenues and marginal costs. We shall examine both approaches.

Price searcher
A firm that must determine the price-output combination that maximizes profit because it faces a downward-sloping demand curve.

The Total Revenues–Total Costs Approach

Suppose that the government of a small town located in a remote desert area grants a single satellite television company the right to offer services within its jurisdiction. It enforces rules that prevent other firms from offering television services. We show demand (weekly rate of output and price per unit), revenues, costs, and other data in panel (a) of Figure 24-4 below. In column 3, we see total revenues for this TV service

FIGURE 24-4 Monopoly Costs, Revenues, and Profits

In panel (a), we give demand (weekly satellite television services and price), revenues, costs, and other relevant data. As shown in panel (b), the satellite TV monopolist maximizes profits where the positive difference between TR and TC is greatest. This is at an output rate of between 9 and 10 units per week. Put another way, profit maximization occurs where marginal revenue equals marginal cost, as shown in panel (c). This is at the same weekly service rate of between 9 and 10 units. (The MC curve must cut the MR curve from below.)

Panel (a)

(1) Output (units)	(2) Price per Unit	(3) Total Revenues (TR) (3) = (2) x (1)	(4) Total Costs (TC)	(5) Total Profit (5) = (3) – (4)	(6) Marginal Cost (MC)	(7) Marginal Revenue (MR)
0	$8.00	$ .00	$10.00	–$10.00		
					$4.00	$7.80
1	7.80	7.80	14.00	–6.20		
					3.50	7.40
2	7.60	15.20	17.50	–2.30		
					3.25	7.00
3	7.40	22.20	20.75	1.45		
					3.05	6.60
4	7.20	28.80	23.80	5.00		
					2.90	6.20
5	7.00	35.00	26.70	8.30		
					2.80	5.80
6	6.80	40.80	29.50	11.30		
					2.75	5.40
7	6.60	46.20	32.25	13.95		
					2.85	5.00
8	6.40	51.20	35.10	16.10		
					3.20	4.60
9	6.20	55.80	38.30	17.50		
					4.40	4.20
10	6.00	60.00	42.70	17.30		
					6.00	3.80
11	5.80	63.80	48.70	15.10		
					9.00	3.40
12	5.60	67.20	57.70	9.50		

Panel (b)

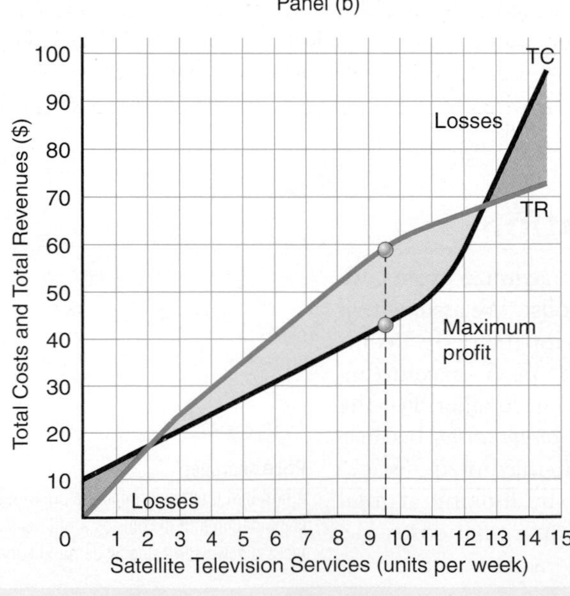

Panel (c)

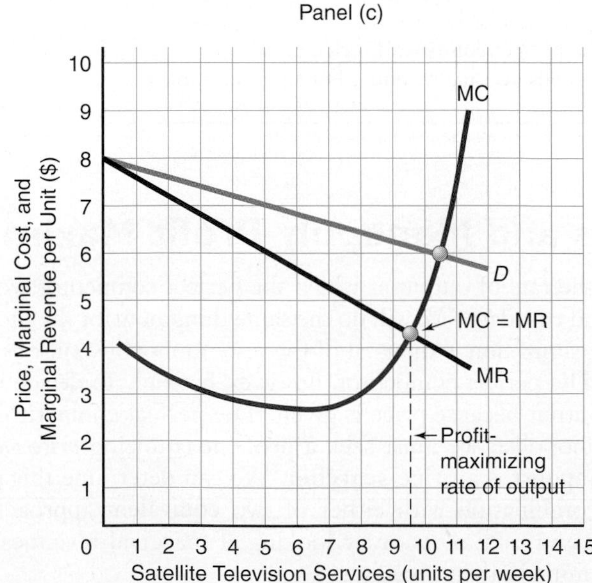

monopolist, and in column 4, we see total costs. We can transfer these two columns to panel (b). The fundamental difference between the total revenue and total cost diagram in panel (b) and the one we showed for a perfect competitor in Chapter 23 is that the total revenue line is no longer straight. Rather, it curves. For any given demand curve, in order to sell more, the monopolist must lower the price. This reflects the fact that the basic difference between a monopolist and a perfect competitor has to do with the demand curve for the two types of firms. The monopolist faces a downward-sloping demand curve.

Profit maximization involves maximizing the positive difference between total revenues and total costs. This occurs at an output rate of between 9 and 10 units per week.

The Marginal Revenue–Marginal Cost Approach

Profit maximization will also occur where marginal revenue equals marginal cost. This is as true for a monopolist as it is for a perfect competitor (but the monopolist will charge a price in excess of marginal revenue). When we transfer marginal cost and marginal revenue information from columns 6 and 7 in panel (a) to panel (c) in Figure 24-4 on the facing page, we see that marginal revenue equals marginal cost at a weekly quantity of satellite TV services of between 9 and 10 units. Profit maximization must occur at the same output as in panel (b).

WHY PRODUCE WHERE MARGINAL REVENUE EQUALS MARGINAL COST? If the monopolist produces past the point where marginal revenue equals marginal cost, marginal cost will exceed marginal revenue. That is, the incremental cost of producing any more units will exceed the incremental revenue. It would not be worthwhile, as was true also in perfect competition. Furthermore, just as in the case of perfect competition, if the monopolist produces less than that, it is not making maximum profits. Look at output rate Q_1 in Figure 24-5 below. Here the monopolist's marginal revenue is at A, but marginal cost is at B. Marginal revenue exceeds marginal cost on the last unit sold. The profit for that *particular* unit, Q_1, is equal to the vertical difference between A and B, or the difference between marginal revenue and marginal cost. The monopolist would be foolish to stop at output rate Q_1 because if output is expanded, marginal revenue will still exceed marginal cost, and therefore total profits will be increased by selling more. In fact, the profit-maximizing monopolist will continue to

FIGURE 24-5 Maximizing Profits

The profit-maximizing production rate is Q_m, and the profit-maximizing price is P_m. The monopolist would be unwise to produce at the rate Q_1 because here marginal revenue would be Q_1A, and marginal cost would be Q_1B. Marginal revenue would exceed marginal cost. The firm will keep producing until the point Q_m, where marginal revenue just equals marginal cost. It would be foolish to produce at the rate Q_2, for here marginal cost exceeds marginal revenue. It would behoove the monopolist to cut production back to Q_m.

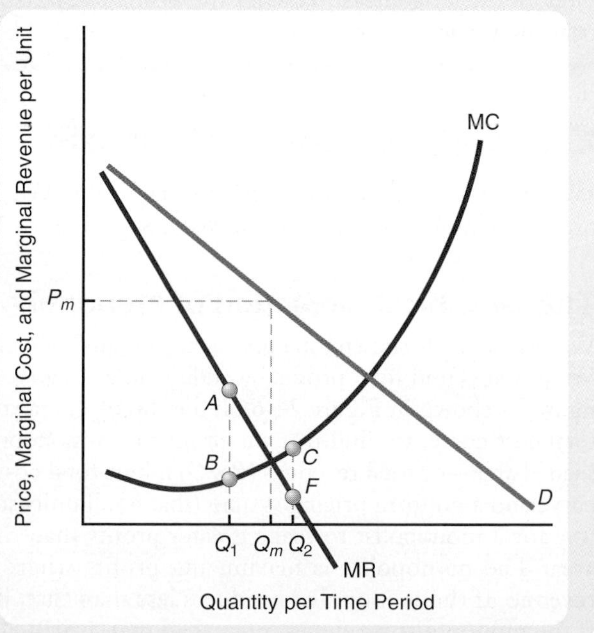

expand output and sales until marginal revenue equals marginal cost, which is at output rate Q_m. The monopolist won't produce at rate Q_2 because here, as we see, marginal costs are C and marginal revenues are F. The difference between C and F represents the *reduction* in total profits from producing that additional unit. Total profits will rise as the monopolist reduces its rate of output back toward Q_m.

What Price to Charge for Output?

How does the monopolist set prices? We know the quantity is set at the point at which marginal revenue equals marginal cost. The monopolist then finds out how much can be charged—how much the market will bear—for that particular quantity, Q_m, in Figure 24-5 on the preceding page.

THE MONOPOLY PRICE We know that the demand curve is defined as showing the *maximum* price for which a given quantity can be sold. That means that our monopolist knows that to sell Q_m, it can charge only P_m because that is the price at which that specific quantity, Q_m, is demanded. This price is found by drawing a vertical line from the quantity, Q_m, to the market demand curve. Where that line hits the market demand curve, the price is determined. We find that price by drawing a horizontal line from the demand curve to the price axis. Doing that gives us the profit-maximizing price, P_m.

In our numerical example, at a profit-maximizing quantity of satellite TV services of between 9 and 10 units in Figure 24-4 on page 540, the firm can charge a maximum price of about $6 and still sell all the services it provides, all at the same price.

The basic procedure for finding the profit-maximizing short-run price-quantity combination for the monopolist is first to determine the profit-maximizing rate of output, by either the total revenue–total cost method or the marginal revenue–marginal cost method. Then it is possible to determine by use of the demand curve, D, the maximum price that can be charged to sell that output.

REAL-WORLD INFORMATIONAL LIMITATIONS Don't get the impression that just because we are able to draw an exact demand curve in Figures 24-4 and 24-5, real-world monopolists have such perfect information. The process of price searching by a less-than-perfect competitor is just that—a process. A monopolist can only estimate the actual demand curve and therefore can make only an educated guess when it sets its profit-maximizing price. This is not a problem for the perfect competitor because price is given already by the intersection of market demand and market supply. The monopolist, in contrast, reaches the profit-maximizing output-price combination by trial and error.

Calculating Monopoly Profit

We have talked about the monopolist's profit. We have yet to indicate how much profit the monopolist makes, which we do in Figure 24-6 on the following page.

The Graphical Depiction of Monopoly Profits

We have actually shown total profits in column 5 of panel (a) in Figure 24-4 on page 540. We can also find total profits by adding an average total cost curve to panel (c) of that figure, as shown in Figure 24-6 on the top of the next page. When we add the average total cost curve, we find that the profit that a monopolist makes is equal to the green-shaded area—or total revenues ($P \times Q$) minus total costs (ATC $\times$ Q). Given the demand curve and a uniform pricing system (that is, all units sold at the same price), there is no way for a monopolist to make greater profits than those shown by the green-shaded area. The monopolist is maximizing profits where marginal cost equals marginal revenue. If the monopolist produces less than that, it will be forfeiting some profits. If the monopolist produces more than that, it will also be forfeiting some profits.

FIGURE 24-6 Monopoly Profit

We find monopoly profit by subtracting total costs from total revenues at a quantity of satellite TV services of between 9 and 10 units per week, labeled Q_m, which is the profit-maximizing rate of output for the satellite TV monopolist. The profit-maximizing price is therefore slightly more than $6 per week and is labeled P_m. Monopoly profit is given by the green-shaded area, which is equal to total revenues ($P \times Q$) minus total costs (ATC $\times$ Q). This diagram is similar to panel (c) of Figure 24-4 on page 540, with the short-run average total cost curve (ATC) added.

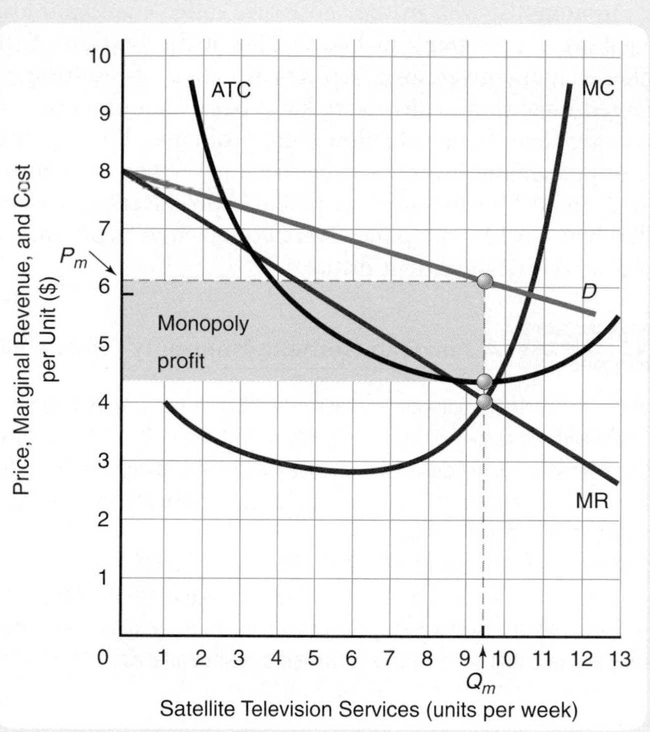

No Guarantee of Profits

The term *monopoly* conjures up the notion of a greedy firm ripping off the public and making exorbitant profits. The mere existence of a monopoly, however, does not guarantee high profits. Numerous monopolies have gone bankrupt. Figure 24-7 below shows the monopolist's demand curve as *D* and the resultant marginal revenue curve as MR. It does not matter at what rate of output this particular monopolist operates. Total costs cannot be covered. Look at the position of the average total cost curve. It lies everywhere above *D* (the average revenue curve). Thus, there is no price-output

FIGURE 24-7 Monopolies: Not Always Profitable

Some monopolists face the situation shown here. The average total cost curve, ATC, is everywhere above the average revenue, or demand, curve, *D*. In the short run, the monopolist will produce where MC = MR at point *A*. Output Q_m will be sold at price P_m, but average total cost per unit is C_1. Losses are the red-shaded rectangle. Eventually, the monopolist will go out of business.

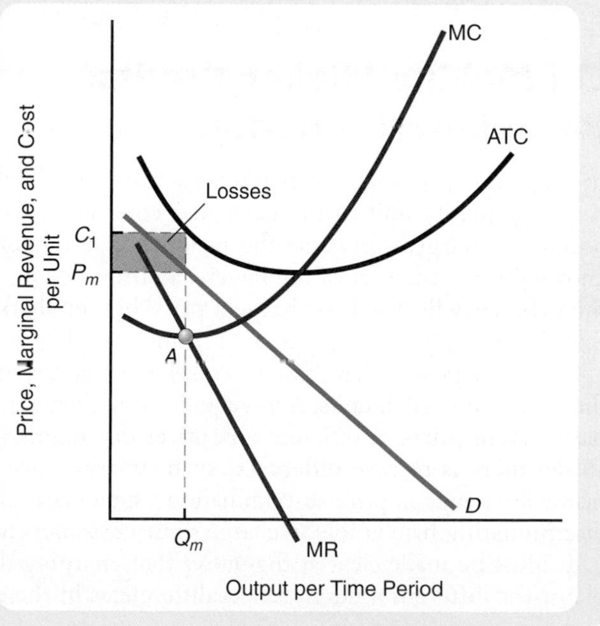

combination that will allow the monopolist even to cover costs, much less earn profits. This monopolist will, in the short run, suffer economic losses as shown by the red-shaded area. The graph in Figure 24-7 at the bottom of the preceding page, which applies to many inventions, depicts a situation of resulting monopoly. The owner of a patented invention or discovery has a pure legal monopoly, but the demand and cost curves are such that production is not profitable. Every year at inventors' conventions, one can see many inventions that have never been put into production because they were deemed "uneconomic" by potential producers and users.

Do real-world monopolies ever earn negative economic profits? Consider the case of a giant Mexican cement firm.

INTERNATIONAL EXAMPLE A Mexican Cement Monopoly Finds a Way to Incur Losses

Cement is made by combining sand or gravel, water, and a mix of aluminum, calcium, iron, and silicon. A number of firms make and sell cement in the United States. In contrast, a single company, Cemex, accounts for almost 80 percent of Mexico's cement production and sales. Cemex sells cement to Mexican consumers at almost twice the U.S. market price, and until the late 2000s, the company's ratio of profits to total revenues was almost twice the average ratio at U.S. cement manufacturers.

Recently, however, Cemex has been incurring losses. When business was booming in the early and middle 2000s, the company relied on short-term bank loans to fund many of its operations. When the demand for cement abruptly plummeted in 2008, the company's debt costs pushed its total expenses above its revenues. Thus, the company's annual profit flow dropped below zero and has remained negative into the early 2010s.

FOR CRITICAL ANALYSIS

What has been true of the position of the demand curve for cement faced by Cemex in relation to the position of the company's average total cost curve?

QUICK QUIZ

See page 552 for the answers. Review concepts from this section in MyEconLab.

The basic difference between a monopolist and a perfect competitor is that a monopolist faces a __________-sloping demand curve, and therefore marginal revenue is __________ than price.

The monopolist must choose the profit-maximizing price-output combination—the output at which __________ revenue equals __________ cost and the highest price possible as given by the __________ curve for that particular output rate.

Monopoly profits are found by looking at average __________ costs compared to price per unit. This difference multiplied by the __________ sold at that price determines monopoly profit.

A monopolist does not necessarily earn a profit. If the average __________ cost curve lies entirely __________ the demand curve for a monopoly, no production rate will be profitable.

On Making Higher Profits: Price Discrimination

In a perfectly competitive market, each buyer is charged the same price for every constant-quality unit of the particular commodity (corrected for differential transportation charges). Because the product is homogeneous and we also assume full knowledge on the part of the buyers, a difference in price cannot exist. Any seller of the product who tried to charge a price higher than the going market price would find that no one would purchase it from that seller.

In this chapter, we have assumed until now that the monopolist charged all consumers the same price for all units. A monopolist, however, may be able to charge different people different prices or different unit prices for successive units sought by a given buyer. When there is no cost difference, such strategies are called **price discrimination.** A firm will engage in price discrimination whenever feasible to increase profits. A price-discriminating firm is able to charge some customers more than other customers.

Price discrimination
Selling a given product at more than one price, with the price difference being unrelated to differences in marginal cost.

It must be made clear at the outset that charging different prices to different people or for different units to reflect differences in the cost of service does not amount to price discrimination. This is **price differentiation:** differences in price that reflect differences in marginal cost.

Price differentiation
Establishing different prices for similar products to reflect differences in marginal cost in providing those commodities to different groups of buyers.

We can also say that a uniform price does not necessarily indicate an absence of price discrimination. Charging all customers the same price when production costs vary by customer is actually a situation of price discrimination.

Necessary Conditions for Price Discrimination

Three conditions are necessary for price discrimination to exist:

1. The firm must face a downward-sloping demand curve.
2. The firm must be able to readily (and cheaply) identify buyers or groups of buyers with predictably different elasticities of demand.
3. The firm must be able to prevent resale of the product or service.

Has it ever occurred to you that most of the other students seated in your college classroom pay different overall tuition rates than you do because your college and others use financial aid packages to engage in price discrimination?

EXAMPLE Why Students Pay Different Prices to Attend College

Out-of-pocket tuition rates for any two college students can differ by considerable amounts, even if the students happen to major in the same subjects and enroll in many of the same courses. The reason is that colleges offer students diverse financial aid packages depending on their "financial need."

To document their "need" for financial aid, students must provide detailed information about family income and wealth. This information, of course, helps the college determine the prices that different families are most likely to be willing and able to pay, so that it can engage in price discrimination. Figure 24-8 alongside shows how this collegiate price-discrimination process works. The college charges the price P_7, which is the college's official posted "tuition rate," to students with families judged to be most willing and able to pay the highest price. Students whose families have the lowest levels of income and wealth are judged to be willing and able to pay a much lower price, such as P_1. To charge these students this lower tuition rate, the college provides them with a financial aid package that reduces the price they pay by the difference between P_7, the full tuition price, and P_1. In this way, the actual price paid by these "neediest" students is only P_1.

Likewise, the college groups other, somewhat less "needy" students into a slightly higher income-and-wealth category and determines that they are likely to be willing to pay a somewhat higher price, P_2. Hence, it grants them a smaller financial aid package, equal to $P_7 - P_2$, so that the students actually pay the price P_2. The college continues this process for other groups, thereby engaging in price discrimination in its tuition charges.

FOR CRITICAL ANALYSIS

Does the educational product supplied by colleges satisfy all three conditions necessary for price discrimination?

FIGURE 24-8 Toward Perfect Price Discrimination in College Tuition Rates

Students that a college determines to be "neediest" and least able to pay the full tuition price, P_7, receive a financial aid package equal to $P_7 - P_1$. These students effectively pay only the price P_1. The college groups the remaining students into categories on the basis of their willingness and ability to pay a higher price, and each group receives a progressively smaller financial aid package. Those students who are willing and able to pay the full price, P_7, receive no financial aid from the college.

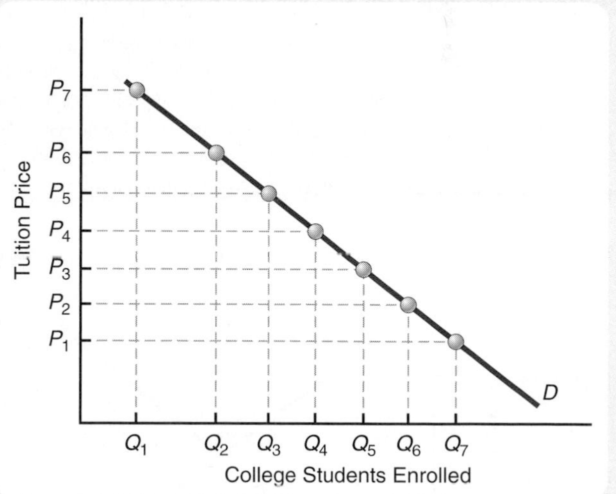

The Social Cost of Monopolies

Let's run a little experiment. We will start with a purely competitive industry with numerous firms, each one unable to affect the price of its product. The supply curve of the industry is equal to the horizontal sum of the marginal cost curves of the individual producers above their respective minimum average variable costs. In panel (a) of Figure 24-9 below, we show the market demand curve and the market supply curve in a perfectly competitive situation. The perfectly competitive price in equilibrium is equal to P_e, and the equilibrium quantity at that price is equal to Q_e. Each individual perfect competitor faces a demand curve (not shown) that is coincident with the price line P_e. No individual supplier faces the market demand curve, *D*.

Comparing Monopoly with Perfect Competition

Now let's assume that a monopolist comes in and buys up every single perfect competitor in the industry. In so doing, we'll assume that monopolization does not affect any of the marginal cost curves or demand. We can therefore redraw *D* and *S* in panel (b) of Figure 24-9, exactly the same as in panel (a).

How does this monopolist decide how much to charge and how much to produce? If the monopolist is profit maximizing, it is going to look at the marginal revenue curve and produce at the output where marginal revenue equals marginal cost. But what is the marginal cost curve in panel (b) of Figure 24-9? It is merely *S*, because we said that *S* was equal to the horizontal summation of the portions of the individual marginal cost curves above each firm's respective minimum average variable cost. The monopolist therefore produces quantity Q_m, and sells it at price P_m. Notice that Q_m is less than Q_e and that P_m is greater than P_e. A monopolist therefore produces a smaller quantity and sells it at a higher price. This is the reason usually given when economists criticize monopolists. Monopolists raise the price and restrict production, compared to a perfectly competitive situation. For a monopolist's product, consumers pay a price that exceeds the marginal cost of production. Resources are misallocated in such a situation—too few resources are being used in the monopolist's industry, and too many are used elsewhere. (See Appendix G on deadweight loss at the end of this chapter.)

FIGURE 24-9 The Effects of Monopolizing an Industry

In panel (a), we show a perfectly competitive situation in which equilibrium is established at the intersection of *D* and *S* at point *E*. The equilibrium price is P_e and the equilibrium quantity is Q_e. Each individual perfectly competitive producer faces a demand curve that is perfectly elastic at the market clearing price, P_e. What happens if the industry is suddenly monopolized? We assume that the costs stay the same. The only thing that changes is that the monopolist now faces the entire downward-sloping demand curve. In panel (b), we draw the marginal revenue curve. Marginal cost is *S* because that is the horizontal summation of all the individual marginal cost curves. The monopolist therefore produces at Q_m and charges price P_m. This price P_m in panel (b) is higher than P_e in panel (a), and Q_m is less than Q_e.

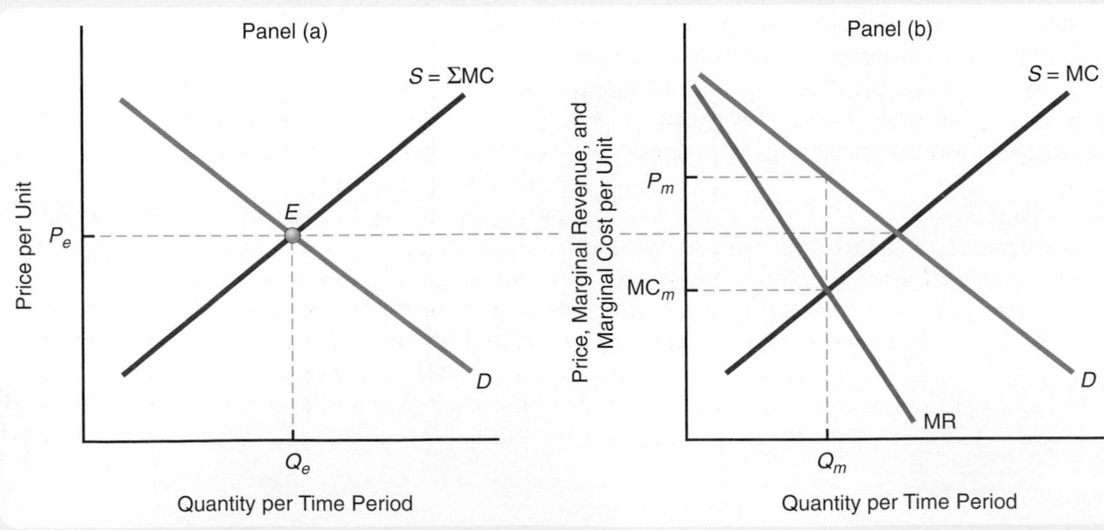

Implications of Higher Monopoly Prices

Notice from Figure 24-9 that by setting MR = MC, the monopolist produces at a rate of output where $P > \text{MC}$ (compare P_m to MC_m). The marginal cost of a commodity (MC) represents what society had to give up in order to obtain the last unit produced. Price, by contrast, represents what buyers are willing to pay to acquire that last unit. Thus, the price of a good represents society's valuation of the last unit produced. The monopoly outcome of $P > \text{MC}$ means that the value to society of the last unit produced is greater than its cost (MC). Hence, not enough of the good is being produced. As we have pointed out before, these differences between monopoly and perfect competition arise not because of differences in costs but rather because of differences in the demand curves the individual firms face. The monopolist faces a downward-sloping demand curve. The individual perfect competitor faces a perfectly elastic demand curve.

Before we leave the topic of the cost to society of monopolies, we must repeat that our analysis is based on a heroic assumption. That assumption is that the monopolization of the perfectly competitive industry does not change the cost structure. If monopolization results in higher marginal cost, the net cost of monopoly to society is even greater.

Conversely, if monopolization results in cost savings, the net cost of monopoly to society is less than we infer from our analysis. Indeed, we could have presented a hypothetical example in which monopolization led to such a dramatic reduction in cost that society actually benefited. Such a situation is a possibility in industries in which economies of scale exist for a very great range of outputs.

QUICK QUIZ **See page 552 for the answers. Review concepts from this section in MyEconLab.**

Three conditions are necessary for price discrimination: (1) The firm must face a __________-sloping demand curve, (2) the firm must be able to identify buyers with predictably different price __________ of demand, and (3) __________ of the product or service must be preventable.

Price __________ should not be confused with price __________, which occurs when differences in price reflect differences in marginal cost.

Monopoly tends to result in a __________ quantity being sold, because the price is __________ than it would be in an ideal perfectly competitive industry in which the cost curves were essentially the same as the monopolist's.

You Are There

A Texas Veterinary Board Whittles Down Vets' Competition

For more than 25 years, Carl Mitz has been a "horse-teeth floater." Mitz charges a $50 fee to farmers and ranchers to spend about three minutes filing down the teeth of each of their horses. Mitz pries open a horse's mouth, grasps its tongue, and saws away at its teeth with power tools. This procedure prevents the horse's teeth from developing sharp points that could damage the horse's cheeks or misalign its jaws. Mitz and other skilled horse-teeth floaters can earn as much as $300,000 per year for providing their services.

Today, Mitz's livelihood is in jeopardy. His problem is that he learned his trade by serving as an apprentice to another horse-teeth floater when he was young. Consequently, Mitz never completed the Texas Institute of Equine Dentistry's 300-hour curriculum of anatomy lectures and laboratory studies. The Texas Board of Veterinary Medical Examiners has determined that Mitz and all other uncertified horse-teeth floaters must either stop practicing their craft or work only under the supervision of a licensed veterinarian. Thus, if the Texas veterinary board has its way, Mitz and other horse-teeth floaters will no longer be able to compete with licensed veterinarians in the business of providing basic dental services for horses.

Critical Analysis Questions

1. If horse-teeth floaters are prohibited from practicing their trade, what will happen to the quantity of services provided in the market for horse dental services?
2. Why can veterinarians anticipate higher profits if horse-teeth floating is banned?

ISSUES & APPLICATIONS

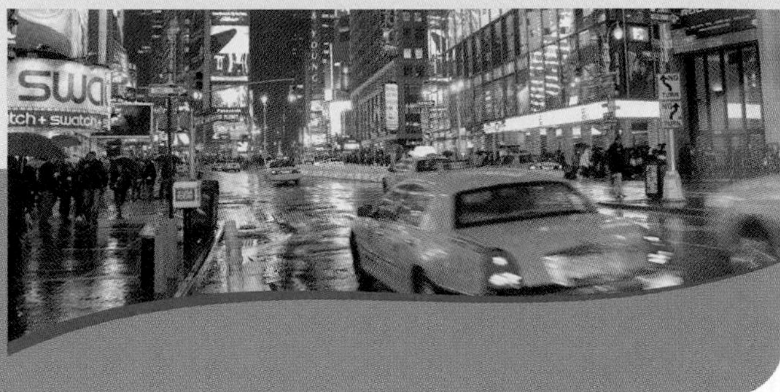

This Medallion Is Not Simply a Decorative Pendant

CONCEPTS APPLIED

- License
- Barrier to Entry
- Monopoly

A New York City taxi medallion adds a decorative element to the hood of a yellow taxicab. The medallion's fundamental purpose, however, is to verify that the owner of the vehicle possesses a government-issued license authorizing the owner to charge passengers fees to transport them around the city.

A Barrier to Entry to a Shared Monopoly

The number of taxi medallions issued by New York City is strictly controlled by the city's Taxi and Limousine Commission. Currently, there are 13,257 commission-issued medallions. Corporations operating fleets of taxis own 60 percent of the medallions, and individual cab drivers own the remaining 40 percent.

The commission's limit on medallions restrains the quantity of taxi services provided to the 8.4 million residents of New York City and thousands of daily visitors to the city. Consequently, this limit serves as a barrier to entry that prevents the quantity of services from reaching a competitive level. Effectively, the city government distributes shares of current and expected future monopoly profits to those owning medallions.

The Value of a Share in the Taxi Monopoly Continues to Rise

New York City taxi medallions can be bought and sold, so the shares in the current and future profits derived from the government-authorized taxi monopoly can be obtained by the highest bidder. As Figure 24-10 on the facing page shows, the market clearing prices of New York City corporate and individual taxi medallions have generally risen since 2004.

As you can see, a share in the current and anticipated future profits available from New York City's government-authorized taxi monopoly has significant value. To an individual taxi medallion owner, this value now exceeds $600,000. For a corporate owner, it is greater than $800,000 per medallion.

For Critical Analysis

1. If the New York City taxicab market were to become perfectly competitive, what would happen to the quantity of taxi services provided?
2. If the New York City taxicab market were to become perfectly competitive, what would happen to current and anticipated profits from providing taxicab services?

Web Resources

1. Learn more about the licensing activities of New York City's Taxi and Limousine Commission at www.econtoday.com/ch24.
2. To take a look at current listings of New York City taxi medallions for sale or lease, go to www.econtoday.com/ch24.

FIGURE 24-10 **Market Prices of New York City Taxi Medallions**

Since 2004, the price of an individual New York City taxi medallion has risen from about $240,000 to just over $600,000, and the price of a corporate medallion has increased from about $290,000 to nearly $800,000.

Source: New York City Taxi and Limousine Commission.

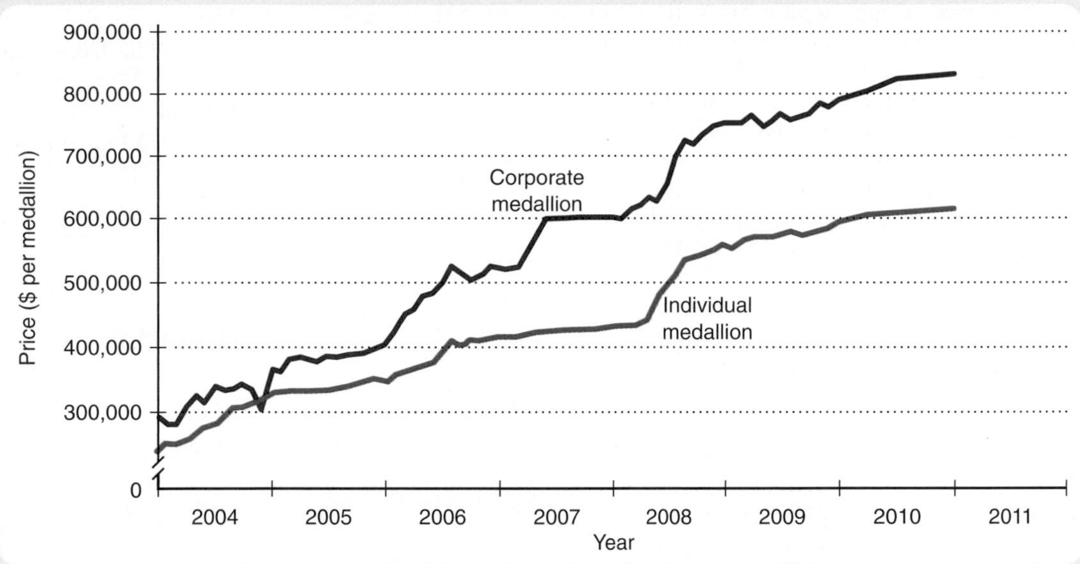

Research Project

The New York City Taxi and Limousine Commission does not necessarily restrain the quantity of taxi services provided to the profit-maximizing level. Suppose that the commission decided to try to achieve this outcome and found that maximizing the total profits shared by taxicab firms and drivers required reducing the number of medallions. If so, what would happen to the quantity of taxi services and the typical taxi fee?

For more questions on this chapter's Issues & Applications, go to **MyEconLab**. In the Study Plan for this chapter, select Section N: News.

Here is what you should know after reading this chapter. **MyEconLab** will help you identify what you know, and where to go when you need to practice.

WHAT YOU SHOULD KNOW		WHERE TO GO TO PRACTICE
Why Monopoly Can Occur Monopoly, a situation in which a single firm produces and sells a good or service, can occur when there are significant barriers to market entry. Examples of barriers to entry include (1) ownership of important resources for which there are no close substitutes, (2) economies of scale for ever-larger ranges of output, and (3) governmental restrictions.	monopolist, 533 natural monopoly, 534 tariffs, 536	• **MyEconLab** Study Plans 24.1, 24.2 • Audio introduction to Chapter 24 • Video: Barriers to Entry • ABC News Video: Optometrists as Monopolists? • ABC News Video: Trade-offs to Higher-Priced Cancer Drugs

(continued)

MyEconLab continued

WHAT YOU SHOULD KNOW		WHERE TO GO TO PRACTICE
Demand and Marginal Revenue Conditions a Monopolist Faces A monopolist faces the entire market demand curve. When it reduces the price of its product, it is able to sell more units at the new price, which boosts revenues, but it also sells other units at this lower price, which reduces revenues somewhat. Thus, the monopolist's marginal revenue at any given quantity is less than the price at which it sells that quantity. Its marginal revenue curve slopes downward and lies below the demand curve.	**KEY FIGURES** Figure 24-2, 538 Figure 24-3, 539	• **MyEconLab** Study Plans 24.3, 24.4 • Video: The Demand Curve Facing a Monopoly Is Not Vertical • Animated Figures 24-2, 24-3
How a Monopolist Determines How Much Output to Produce and What Price to Charge A monopolist is a price searcher, meaning that it seeks to charge the price that maximizes its economic profits. It maximizes its profits by producing to the point at which marginal revenue equals marginal cost. The monopolist then charges the maximum price that consumers are willing to pay for that quantity of output.	price searcher, 539 **KEY FIGURES** Figure 24-4, 540 Figure 24-5, 541	• **MyEconLab** Study Plan 24.5 • Animated Figures 24-4, 24-5 • ABC News Video: What Is a Monopoly?
A Monopolist's Profits A monopolist's profits equal the difference between the price it charges and its average production cost times the quantity it sells. The monopolist's price is at the point on the demand curve corresponding to the profit-maximizing output rate, and its average total cost of producing this output rate is at the corresponding point on the average total cost curve.	**KEY FIGURES** Figure 24-6, 543 Figure 24-7, 543	• **MyEconLab** Study Plan 24.6 • Animated Figures 24-6, 24-7
Price Discrimination A price-discriminating monopolist sells its product at more than one price, with the price difference being unrelated to differences in costs. To be able to price discriminate successfully, a monopolist must be able to sell some of its output at higher prices to consumers with less elastic demand.	price discrimination, 544 price differentiation, 545	• **MyEconLab** Study Plan 24.7 • Video: Price Discrimination
Social Cost of Monopolies A monopoly is able to charge the highest price that people are willing to pay. This price exceeds the marginal cost of producing the output. If the monopolist's marginal cost curve corresponds to the sum of the marginal cost curves for the number of firms that would exist if the industry were perfectly competitive instead, then the monopolist produces and sells less output than perfectly competitive firms would have produced and sold.	**KEY FIGURE** Figure 24-9, 546	• **MyEconLab** Study Plan 24.8 • Animated Figure 24-9 • ABC News Video: What Is a Monopoly?

Log in to MyEconLab, take a chapter test, and get a personalized Study Plan that tells you which concepts you understand and which ones you need to review. From there, MyEconLab will give you further practice, tutorials, animations, videos, and guided solutions.
Log in to www.myeconlab.com

PROBLEMS

All problems are assignable in myeconlab. Answers to odd-numbered problems appear at the back of the book.

24-1. Under federal law, only the U.S. Postal Service has the right to deliver first-class mail. Thus, a consumer can either send a letter via the U.S. Postal Service for less than 50 cents or pay FedEx or UPS $10 or more to deliver it. What is the shape of the demand curve faced by the U.S. Postal Service in the market for first-class mail?

24-2. Recently, a top constitutional law expert who had been licensed to practice law in Massachusetts and was under consideration for nomination to the California Supreme Court failed the California bar examination. In doing so, she joined a long list of accomplished lawyers who have failed to pass the notoriously difficult examination, including a former governor who required four attempts to pass and a Los Angeles mayor who gave up after four tries. In the legal industry, what is a key economic function of the California bar examination?

24-3. Suppose that it is the year 2038. Exclusive ownership of a resource found to be required for the production of fusion power has given a firm monopoly power in the provision of this good. What is true of the relationship between the price of this resource and the marginal revenue the firm receives?

24-4. Consider the resource owner and seller discussed in Problem 24-3. Discuss what would have been true of the price elasticity of demand facing this firm if the firm had been a perfectly competitive seller of this resource. Contrast this with the price elasticity of demand for this firm in its actual role as monopoly provider. Explain why the price elasticities in the two situations are different.

24-5. The following table depicts the daily output, price, and costs of a monopoly dry cleaner located near the campus of a remote college town.

Output (suits cleaned)	Price per Suit ($)	Total Costs ($)
0	8.00	3.00
1	7.50	6.00
2	7.00	8.50
3	6.50	10.50
4	6.00	11.50
5	5.50	13.50
6	5.00	16.00
7	4.50	19.00
8	4.00	24.00

a. Compute revenues and profits at each output rate.

b. What is the profit-maximizing rate of output?

c. Calculate the dry cleaner's marginal revenue and marginal cost at each output level. What is the profit-maximizing level of output?

24-6. A manager of a monopoly firm notices that the firm is producing output at a rate at which average total cost is falling but is not at its minimum feasible point. The manager argues that surely the firm must not be maximizing its economic profits. Is this argument correct?

24-7. Use the following graph to answer the questions below.

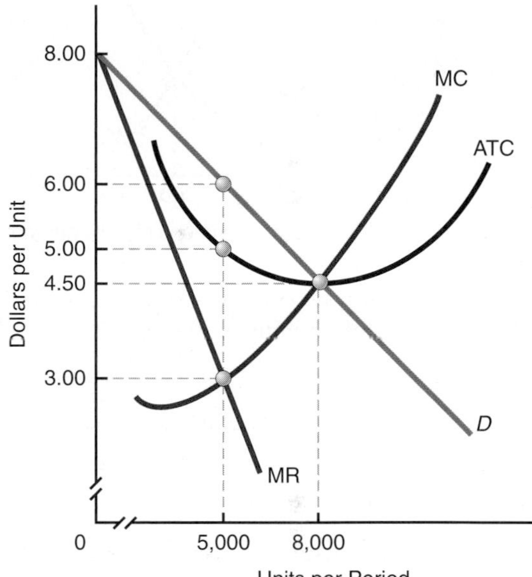

a. What is the monopolist's profit-maximizing output?

b. At the profit-maximizing output rate, what are average total cost and average revenue?

c. At the profit-maximizing output rate, what are the monopolist's total cost and total revenue?

d. What is the maximum profit?

e. Suppose that the marginal cost and average total cost curves in the diagram also illustrate the horizontal summation of the firms in a perfectly competitive industry in the long run. What would the equilibrium price and output be if the market were perfectly competitive? Explain the economic cost to society of allowing a monopoly to exist.

24-8. The marginal revenue curve of a monopoly crosses its marginal cost curve at $30 per unit and an output of 2 million units. The price that consumers are willing to pay for this output is $40 per unit. If it produces this output, the firm's average total cost is $43 per unit, and its average fixed cost is $8 per unit. What is the profit-maximizing (loss-minimizing) output? What are the firm's economic profits (or economic losses)?

24-9. Consider the revenue and cost conditions for a monopolist that are depicted in the figure below.

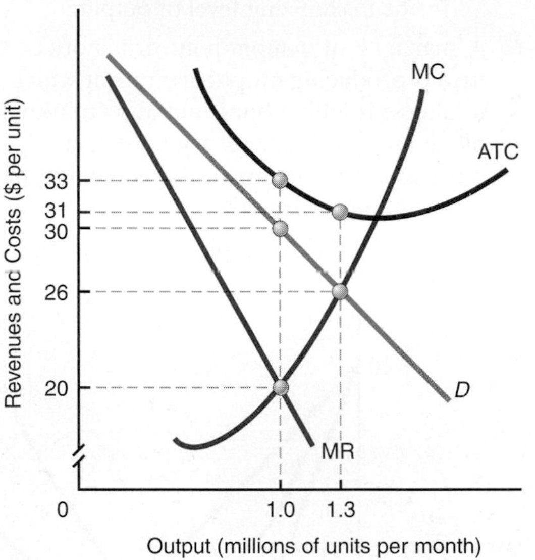

a. What is this producer's profit-maximizing (or loss-minimizing) output?

b. What are the firm's economic profits (or losses)?

24-10. For each of the following examples, explain how and why a monopoly would try to price discriminate.

a. Air transport for businesspeople and tourists

b. Serving food on weekdays to businesspeople and retired people. (Hint: Which group has more flexibility during a weekday to adjust to a price change and, hence, a higher price elasticity of demand?)

c. A theater that shows the same movie to large families and to individuals and couples. (Hint: For which set of people will the overall expense of a movie be a larger part of their budget, so that demand is more elastic?)

24-11. A monopolist's revenues vary directly with price. Is it maximizing its economic profits? Why or why not? (Hint: Recall that the relationship between revenues and price depends on price elasticity of demand.)

24-12. A new competitor enters the industry and competes with a second firm, which had been a monopolist. The second firm finds that although demand is not perfectly elastic, it is now more elastic. What will happen to the second firm's marginal revenue curve and to its profit-maximizing price?

24-13. A monopolist's marginal cost curve has shifted upward. What is likely to happen to the monopolist's price, output rate, and economic profits?

24-14. Demand has fallen. What is likely to happen to the monopolist's price, output rate, and economic profits?

ECONOMICS ON THE NET

Patents, Trademarks, and Intellectual Property This Internet application explores a firm's view on legal protections.

Title: Intellectual Property

Navigation: Follow the link at **www.econtoday.com/ch24** to the GlaxoSmithKline Web site. Select *Investors*, then *Annual Reports*, then the *Report Archive*. View the PDF of Annual Report 2007. Scroll down to Intellectual Property (page 28).

Application Read the statement and table; then answer the following questions.

1. How do patents, trademarks, and registered designs and copyrights differ?

2. What are GlaxoSmithKline's intellectual property goals? Do patents or trademarks seem to be more important?

For Group Discussion and Analysis In 1969, GlaxoSmithKline developed Ventolin, a treatment for asthma symptoms. Though the patent and trademark have long expired, the company still retains over a third of the annual market sales of this treatment. Explain, in economic terms, the source of GlaxoSmithKline's strength in this area. Discuss whether patents and trademarks are beneficial for the development and discovery of new treatments.

ANSWERS TO QUICK QUIZZES

p. 536: (i) close; (ii) ownership . . . scale
p. 539: (i) change . . . total; (ii) marginal . . . marginal; (iii) elasticity . . . elasticity
p. 544: (i) downward . . . less; (ii) marginal . . . marginal . . . demand; (iii) total . . . quantity; (iv) total . . . above
p. 547: (i) downward . . . elasticities . . . resale; (ii) discrimination . . . differentiation; (iii) lower . . . higher

Consumer Surplus and the Deadweight Loss Resulting from Monopoly

APPENDIX G

You have learned that a monopolist produces fewer units than would otherwise be produced in a perfectly competitive market and that it sells these units at a higher price. It seems that consumers surely must be worse off under monopoly than they would be under perfect competition. This appendix shows that, indeed, consumers are harmed by the existence of a monopoly in a market that otherwise could be perfectly competitive.

Consumer Surplus in a Perfectly Competitive Market

Consider the determination of consumer surplus in a perfectly competitive market (for consumer surplus, see page 94 in Appendix B). Take a look at the market diagram depicted in Figure G-1 below. In the figure, we assume that all firms producing in this market incur no fixed costs. We also assume that each firm faces the same marginal cost, which does not vary with its output. These assumptions imply that the marginal cost curve is horizontal and that marginal cost is the same as average total cost at any level of output. Thus, if many perfectly competitive firms operate in this market, the horizontal summation of all firms' marginal cost curves, which is the market supply curve, is this same horizontal curve, labeled MC = ATC.

Under perfect competition, the point at which this market supply curve crosses the market demand curve, D, determines the equilibrium quantity, Q_{pc}, and the market clearing price, P_{pc}. Thus, in a perfectly competitive market, consumers obtain Q_{pc} units at the same per-unit price of P_{pc}. Consumers gain surplus values—vertical distances between the demand curve and the level of the market clearing price—for each unit consumed, up to the total of Q_{pc} units. This totals to the entire striped area under the demand curve above the market clearing price. Consumer surplus is the difference between the total amount that consumers would have been willing to pay and the total amount that they actually pay, given the market clearing price that prevails in the perfectly competitive market.

FIGURE G-1 Consumer Surplus in a Perfectly Competitive Market

If all firms in this market incur no fixed costs and face the same, constant marginal costs, then the marginal cost curve, MC, and the average total cost curve, ATC, are equivalent and horizontal. Under perfect competition, the horizontal summation of all firms' marginal cost curves is this same horizontal curve, which is the market supply curve, so the market clearing price is P_{pc}, and the equilibrium quantity is Q_{pc}. The total consumer surplus in a perfectly competitive market is the striped area.

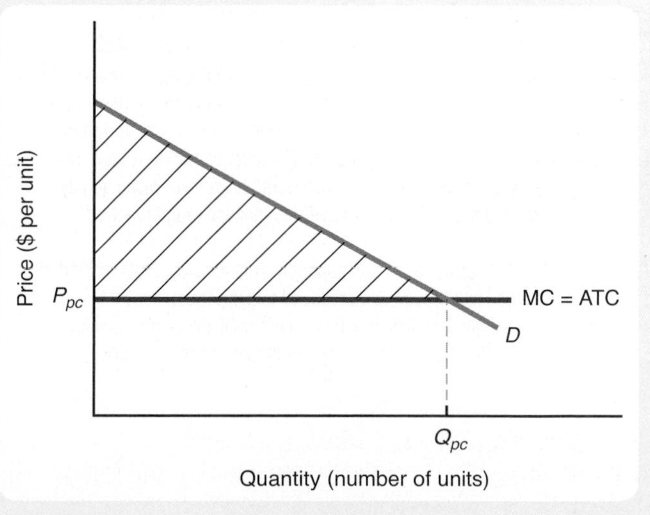

How Society Loses from Monopoly

Now let's think about what happens if a monopoly situation arises in this market, perhaps because a government licenses the firms to conduct joint operations as a single producer. These producers respond by acting as a single monopoly firm, which searches for the profit-maximizing quantity and price.

In this altered situation, which is depicted in Figure G-2 below, the new monopolist (which we assume is unable to engage in price discrimination—see pages 544–545) will produce to the point at which marginal revenue equals marginal cost. This rate of output is Q_m units. The demand curve indicates that consumers are willing to pay a price equal to P_m for this quantity of output. Consequently, as you learned in this chapter, the monopolist will produce fewer units of output than the quantity, Q_{pc}, that firms would have produced in a perfectly competitive market. The monopolist also charges a higher price than the market clearing price, P_{pc}, that would have prevailed under perfect competition.

Recall that the monopolist's maximized economic profits equal its output times the difference between price and average total cost, or the yellow-shaded rectangular area equal to $Q_m \times (P_m - \text{ATC})$. By setting its price at P_m, therefore, the monopolist is able to transfer this portion of the competitive level of consumer surplus to itself in the form of monopoly profits. Consumers are still able to purchase Q_m units of output at a per-unit price, P_m, below the prices they would otherwise have been willing to pay. Hence, the blue-shaded triangular area above this monopoly-profit rectangle is consumer surplus that remains in the new monopoly situation.

Once the monopoly is formed, what happens to the green-shaded portion of the competitive consumer surplus? The answer is that this portion of consumer surplus is lost to society. The monopolist's failure to produce the additional $Q_{pc} - Q_m$ units of output that would have been forthcoming in a perfectly competitive market eliminates this portion of the original consumer surplus. This lost consumer surplus resulting from monopoly production and pricing is called a **deadweight loss** because it is a portion of the competitive level of consumer surplus that no one in society can obtain in a monopoly situation.

Deadweight loss
The portion of consumer surplus that no one in society is able to obtain in a situation of monopoly.

Thus, as a result of monopoly, consumers are worse off in two ways. First, the monopoly profits that result constitute a transfer of a portion of consumer surplus away from consumers to the monopolist. Second, the failure of the monopoly to produce as many units as would have been produced under perfect competition eliminates consumer surplus that otherwise would have been a benefit to consumers. No one in society, not even the monopoly, can obtain this deadweight loss.

FIGURE G-2 Losses Generated by Monopoly

If firms are able to act as a single monopoly, then the monopolist will produce only Q_m units at the point at which marginal revenue equals marginal cost and charge the price P_m. Economic profits, $Q_m \times (P_m - \text{ATC})$, equal the yellow-shaded rectangular area, which is a portion of the competitive level of consumer surplus (the original striped area) transferred to the monopolist. Consumers can now purchase Q_m units of output at a per-unit price, P_m, below the prices they otherwise would have been willing to pay, so the blue-shaded triangular area above this monopoly-profit rectangle is remaining consumer surplus. The green-shaded triangular area is lost consumer surplus that results from the monopoly producing Q_m units instead of the Q_{pc} units that would have been produced under perfect competition. This is called a *deadweight loss* because it is a portion of the competitive level of consumer surplus that no one in society can obtain under monopoly.

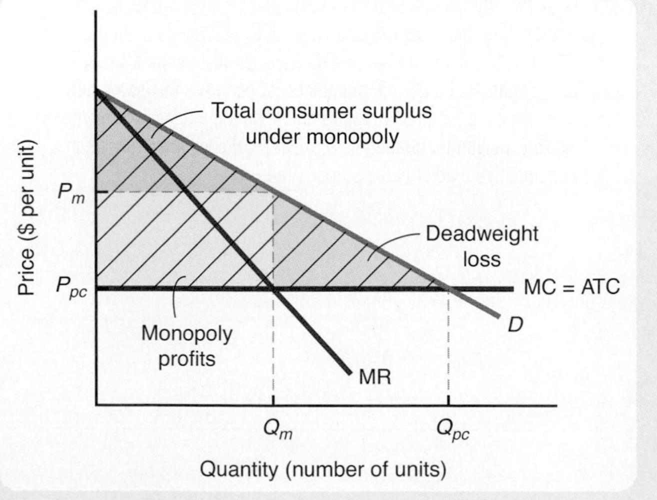

25

Monopolistic Competition

As you scan through the song titles offered for download by the latest rock bands, you cannot help wondering why so many of the newest groups have such unusual names. After all, what you care about as a consumer is the quality of a band's original songs, the style of the band's arrangements of those songs, and the musical talents of the band members who sing and play the songs. Why then do so many rock bands adopt names that involve odd combinations of everyday words? To find out the answer to this question, you must learn about the market structure in which today's rock bands interact, known as *monopolistic competition*.

LEARNING OBJECTIVES

After reading this chapter, you should be able to:

- ▶ Discuss the key characteristics of a monopolistically competitive industry
- ▶ Contrast the output and pricing decisions of monopolistically competitive firms with those of perfectly competitive firms
- ▶ Explain why brand names and advertising are important features of monopolistically competitive industries
- ▶ Describe the fundamental properties of information products and evaluate how the prices of these products are determined under monopolistic competition

myeconlab

MyEconLab helps you master each objective and study more efficiently. See end of chapter for details.

Did You Know That?

by the time Dan Brown's novel *The Lost Symbol,* a sequel to the *The Da Vinci Code,* appeared on retailers' shelves, its price had fallen so much that retailers earned very few profits from selling the book? The book's cover jacket indicated a price of $28.95, but on the day the book appeared on booksellers' shelves, its price had fallen to about $16. That price was just barely high enough to compensate for the book's production and distribution costs and for retailers' opportunity costs. This outcome occurred even though there was no other book quite like *The Lost Symbol* and the book's publisher conducted an expensive marketing campaign.

Product heterogeneity and advertising did not show up in our analysis of perfect competition. They play large roles, however, in industries that cannot be described as perfectly competitive but cannot be described as pure monopolies, either. A combination of consumers' preferences for variety and competition among producers has led to similar but *differentiated* products in the marketplace. This situation has been described as *monopolistic competition,* the subject of this chapter.

Monopolistic Competition

Monopolistic competition
A market situation in which a large number of firms produce similar but not identical products. Entry into the industry is relatively easy.

In the 1920s and 1930s, economists became increasingly aware that there were many industries to which both the perfectly competitive model and the pure monopoly model did not apply and did not seem to yield very accurate predictions. Theoretical and empirical research was instituted to develop some sort of middle ground. Two separately developed models of **monopolistic competition** resulted. At Harvard, Edward Chamberlin published *Theory of Monopolistic Competition* in 1933. The same year, Britain's Joan Robinson published *The Economics of Imperfect Competition*. In this chapter, we will outline the theory as presented by Chamberlin.

Chamberlin defined monopolistic competition as a market structure in which a relatively large number of producers offer similar but differentiated products. Monopolistic competition therefore has the following features:

1. Significant numbers of sellers in a highly competitive market
2. Differentiated products
3. Sales promotion and advertising
4. Easy entry of new firms in the long run

Even a cursory look at the U.S. economy leads to the conclusion that monopolistic competition is an important form of market structure in the United States. Indeed, that is true of all developed economies.

Number of Firms

In a perfectly competitive industry, there are an extremely large number of firms. In pure monopoly, there is only one. In monopolistic competition, there are a large number of firms, but not so many as in perfect competition. This fact has several important implications for a monopolistically competitive industry.

1. *Small share of market.* With so many firms, each firm has a relatively small share of the total market.
2. *Lack of collusion.* With so many firms, it is very difficult for all of them to get together to collude—to cooperate in setting a pure monopoly price (and output). Collusive pricing in a monopolistically competitive industry is nearly impossible. Also, barriers to entry are minor, and the flow of new firms into the industry makes collusive agreements less likely. The large number of firms makes the monitoring and detection of cheating very costly and extremely difficult. This difficulty is compounded by differentiated products and high rates of innovation. Collusive agreements are easier for a homogeneous product than for heterogeneous ones.

Follow the link at **www.econtoday.com/ch25** to *Wall Street Journal* articles about real-world examples of monopolistic competition.

3. *Independence*. Because there are so many firms, each one acts independently of the others. No firm attempts to take into account the reaction of all of its rival firms—that would be impossible with so many rivals. Thus, an individual producer does not try to take into account possible reactions of rivals to its own output and price changes.

Product Differentiation

Product differentiation
The distinguishing of products by brand name, color, and other minor attributes. Product differentiation occurs in other than perfectly competitive markets in which products are, in theory, homogeneous, such as wheat or corn.

Perhaps the most important feature of the monopolistically competitive market is **product differentiation.** We can say that each individual manufacturer of a product has an absolute monopoly over its own product, which is slightly differentiated from other similar products. This means that the firm has some control over the price it charges. Unlike the perfectly competitive firm, it faces a downward-sloping demand curve.

Consider the abundance of brand names for toothpaste, soap, gasoline, vitamins, shampoo, and most other consumer goods and a great many services. We are not obliged to buy just one type of video game, just one type of jeans, or just one type of footwear. We can usually choose from a number of similar but differentiated products. The greater a firm's success at product differentiation, the greater the firm's pricing options.

Are all groundhogs alike? Not according to at least some people in Punxsutawny, Pennsylvania.

EXAMPLE Is Punxsutawny Phil Hogging Too Much Attention?

According to U.S. folklore, if a groundhog emerges from its den on February 2—the official Groundhog Day—and sees its shadow, there will be six more weeks of winter. Most U.S. residents associate Groundhog Day with Punxsutawny Phil, the groundhog residing in the Pennsylvania town of that name. Since 1887 a local group has been using Phil to predict the weather. Today, there are at least 17 "groundhog lodges" in Pennsylvania and nearby states, each of which promotes its own groundhog's weather-forecasting talents on February 2. Among Punxsutawny Phil's competitors are Dunkirk Dave, General Beauregard Lee, Octorara Orphie, and Staten Island Chuck. Every Groundhog Day, the various groundhog lodges promote the allegedly differentiated weather-forecasting talents of their groundhogs in an effort to attract tourists to their communities.

FOR CRITICAL ANALYSIS

Why do you suppose that businesses in communities where groundhog lodges are located contribute to the expenses of caring for the lodges' celebrity groundhogs?

Each separate differentiated product has numerous similar substitutes. This clearly has an impact on the price elasticity of demand for the individual firm. Recall that one determinant of price elasticity of demand is the availability of substitutes: The greater the number and closeness of substitutes available, other things being equal, the greater the price elasticity of demand. If the consumer has a vast array of alternatives that are just about as good as the product under study, a relatively small increase in the price of that product will lead many consumers to switch to one of the many close substitutes. Thus, the ability of a firm to raise the price above the price of *close* substitutes is very small. At a given price, the demand curve is highly elastic compared to a monopolist's demand curve. In the extreme case, with perfect competition, the substitutes are perfect because we are dealing with only one particular undifferentiated product. In that case, the individual firm has a perfectly elastic demand curve.

Sales Promotion and Advertising

Monopolistic competition differs from perfect competition in that no individual firm in a perfectly competitive market will advertise. A perfectly competitive firm, by definition, can sell all that it wants to sell at the going market price anyway. Why, then, would it spend even one penny on advertising? Furthermore, by definition, the perfect competitor is selling a product that is identical to the product that all other firms in the industry are selling. Any advertisement that induces consumers to buy more of that product will, in effect, be helping all the competitors too. A perfect competitor therefore cannot be expected to incur any advertising costs (except when all firms in an industry collectively agree to advertise to urge the public to buy more beef or drink more milk, for example).

The monopolistic competitor, however, has at least *some* monopoly power. Because consumers regard the monopolistic competitor's product as distinguishable from the products of the other firms, the firm can search for the most profitable price that consumers are willing to pay for its differentiated product. Advertising, therefore, may result in increased profits. Advertising is used to increase demand and to differentiate one's product. How much advertising should be undertaken? It should be carried to the point at which the additional revenue from one more dollar of advertising just equals that one dollar of additional cost.

Ease of Entry

For any current monopolistic competitor, potential competition is always lurking in the background. The easier—that is, the less costly—entry is, the more a current monopolistic competitor must worry about losing business.

A good example of a monopolistic competitive industry is the computer software industry. Many small firms provide different programs for many applications. The fixed capital costs required to enter this industry are small. All you need are skilled programmers. In addition, there are few legal restrictions. The firms in this industry also engage in extensive advertising in more than 150 computer publications.

QUICK QUIZ **See page 572 for the answers. Review concepts from this section in MyEconLab.**

In a **monopolistically competitive** industry, a relatively __________ number of firms interact in a __________ competitive market.

Because monopolistically competitive firms sell __________ products, sales promotion and advertising are common features of a monopolistically competitive industry.

There is __________ entry (or exit) of new firms in a monopolistically competitive industry.

Price and Output for the Monopolistic Competitor

Now that we are aware of the assumptions underlying the monopolistic competition model, we can analyze the price and output behavior of each firm in a monopolistically competitive industry. We assume in the analysis that follows that the desired product type and quality have been chosen. We further assume that the budget and the type of promotional activity have already been chosen and do not change.

The Individual Firm's Demand and Cost Curves

Because the individual firm is not a perfect competitor, its demand curve slopes downward, as in all three panels of Figure 25-1 on the next page. Hence, it faces a marginal revenue curve that is also downward sloping and below the demand curve. To find the profit-maximizing rate of output and the profit-maximizing price, we go to the output where the marginal cost (MC) curve intersects the marginal revenue (MR) curve from below. That gives us the profit-maximizing output rate. Then we draw a vertical line up to the demand curve. That gives us the price that can be charged to sell

FIGURE 25-1 Short-Run and Long-Run Equilibrium with Monopolistic Competition

In panel (a), the typical monopolistic competitor is shown making economic profits. In this situation, there would be entry into the industry, forcing the demand curve for the individual monopolistic competitor leftward. Eventually, firms would find themselves in the situation depicted in panel (c), where zero *economic* profits are being made. In panel (b), the typical firm is in a monopolistically competitive industry making economic losses. In this situation, firms would leave the industry. Each remaining firm's demand curve would shift outward to the right. Eventually, the typical firm would find itself in the situation depicted in panel (c).

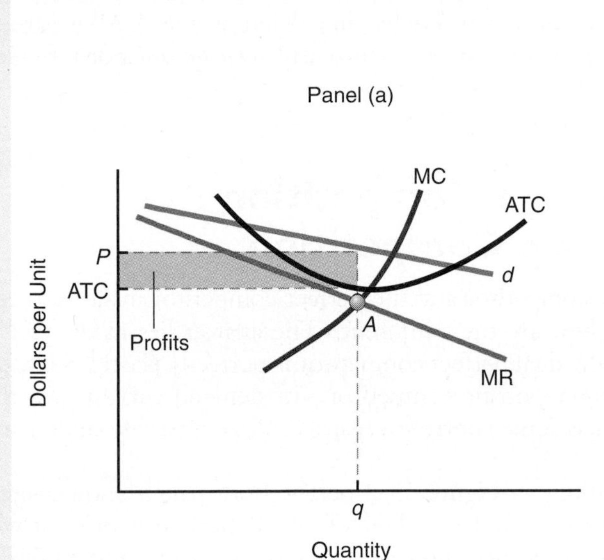

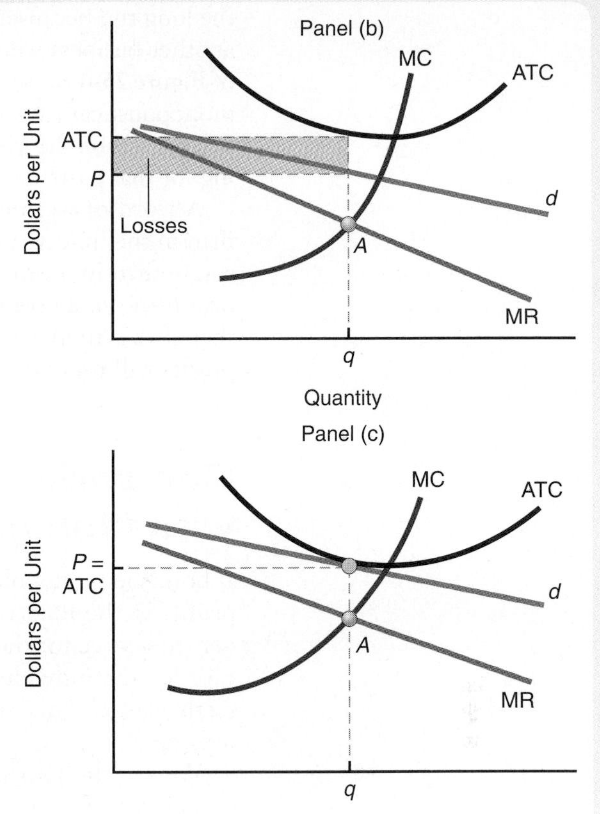

exactly that quantity produced. This is what we have done in Figure 25-1 above. In each panel, a marginal cost curve intersects the marginal revenue curve at *A*. The profit-maximizing rate of output is *q*, and the profit-maximizing price is *P*.

Short-Run Equilibrium

In the short run, it is possible for a monopolistic competitor to make economic profits—profits over and above the normal rate of return or beyond what is necessary to keep that firm in that industry. We show such a situation in panel (a) of Figure 25-1. The average total cost (ATC) curve is drawn below the demand curve, *d*, at the profit-maximizing rate of output, *q*. Economic profits are shown by the blue-shaded rectangle in that panel.

Losses in the short run are clearly also possible. They are presented in panel (b) of Figure 25-1. Here the average total cost curve lies everywhere above the individual firm's demand curve, *d*. The losses are indicated by the red-shaded rectangle.

Just as with any market structure or any firm, in the short run it is possible to observe either economic profits or economic losses. In either case, the price does not equal marginal cost but rather is above it.

The Long Run: Zero Economic Profits

The long run is where the similarity between perfect competition and monopolistic competition becomes more obvious. In the long run, because so many firms produce substitutes for the product in question, any economic profits will disappear with competition. They will be reduced to zero either through entry by new firms seeing a chance to make a higher rate of return than elsewhere or by changes in product quality and advertising outlays by existing firms in the industry. (Profitable products will be imitated by other firms.) As for economic losses in the short run, they will disappear in the long run because the firms that suffer them will leave the industry. They will go into another business where the expected rate of return is at least normal. Panels (a) and (b) of Figure 25-1 on the preceding page therefore represent only short-run situations for a monopolistically competitive firm. In the long run, the individual firm's demand curve *d* will just touch the average total cost curve at the particular price that is profit maximizing for that particular firm. This is shown in panel (c) of Figure 25-1.

A word of warning: This is an idealized, long-run equilibrium situation for each firm in the industry. It does not mean that even in the long run we will observe every single firm in a monopolistically competitive industry making *exactly* zero economic profits or *just* a normal rate of return. We live in a dynamic world. All we are saying is that if this model is correct, the rate of return will *tend toward* normal—economic profits will *tend toward* zero.

Comparing Perfect Competition with Monopolistic Competition

If both the monopolistic competitor and the perfect competitor make zero economic profits in the long run, how are they different? The answer lies in the fact that the demand curve for the individual perfect competitor is perfectly elastic. Such is not the case for the individual monopolistic competitor—its demand curve is less than perfectly elastic. This firm has some control over price. Price elasticity of demand is not infinite.

We see the two situations in Figure 25-2 below. Both panels show average total costs just touching the respective demand curves at the particular price at which the firm is selling the product. Notice, however, that the perfect competitor's average total costs are at a minimum. This is not the case with the monopolistic competitor.

FIGURE 25-2 Comparison of the Perfect Competitor with the Monopolistic Competitor

In panel (a), the perfectly competitive firm has zero economic profits in the long run. The price is set equal to marginal cost, and the price is P_1. The firm's demand curve is just tangent to the minimum point on its average total cost curve. With the monopolistically competitive firm in panel (b), there are also zero economic profits in the long run. The price is greater than marginal cost, though. The monopolistically competitive firm does not find itself at the minimum point on its average total cost curve. It is operating at a rate of output, q_2, to the left of the minimum point on the ATC curve.

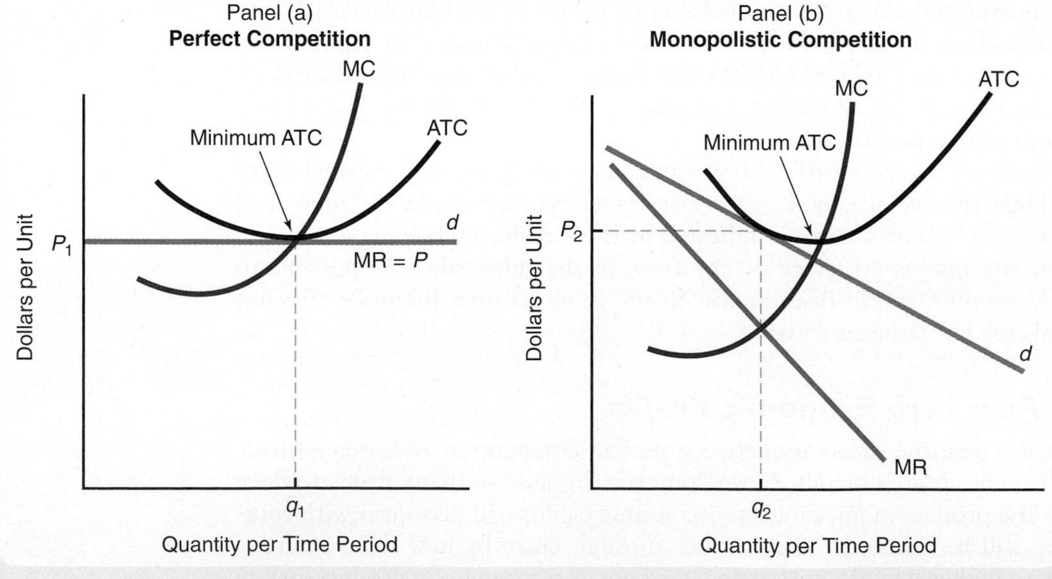

The equilibrium rate of output is to the left of the minimum point on the average total cost curve where price is greater than marginal cost. The monopolistic competitor cannot expand output to the point of minimum costs without lowering price, and then marginal cost would exceed marginal revenue. A monopolistic competitor at profit maximization charges a price that exceeds marginal cost. In this respect it is similar to the monopolist.

It has consequently been argued that monopolistic competition involves *waste* because minimum average total costs are not achieved and price exceeds marginal cost. There are too many firms, each with excess capacity, producing too little output. According to critics of monopolistic competition, society's resources are being wasted.

Chamberlin had an answer to this criticism. He contended that the difference between the average cost of production for a monopolistically competitive firm in an open market and the minimum average total cost represented what he called the cost of producing "differentness." Chamberlin did not consider this difference in cost between perfect competition and monopolistic competition a waste. In fact, he argued that it is rational for consumers to have a taste for differentiation. Consumers willingly accept the resultant increased production costs in return for more choice and variety of output.

You Are There

Contemplate how candy companies seek to obtain economic profits by incorporating new ingredients into their sugary morsels in **Stimulating Candy Sales by Adding Caffeine,** on page 567.

QUICK QUIZ See page 572 for the answers. Review concepts from this section in MyEconLab.

In the __________ run, it is possible for monopolistically competitive firms to make economic profits or economic losses.

In the __________ run, monopolistically competitive firms will make __________ economic profits—that is, they will make a __________ rate of return.

Because the monopolistic competitor faces a downward-sloping demand curve, it does not produce at the minimum point on its average __________ cost curve. Hence, we say that a monopolistic competitor has higher average __________ costs per unit than a perfect competitor would have.

Chamberlin argued that the difference between the __________ __________ cost of production for a monopolistically competitive firm and the __________ average total cost at which a perfectly competitive firm would produce is the cost of producing "differentness."

Brand Names and Advertising

Because "differentness" has value to consumers, monopolistically competitive firms regard their brand names as valuable. Firms use trademarks—words, symbols, and logos—to distinguish their product brands from goods or services sold by other firms. Consumers associate these trademarks with the firms' products. Thus, companies regard their brands as valuable private (intellectual) property, and they engage in advertising to maintain the differentiation of their products from those of other firms.

Brand Names and Trademarks

A firm's ongoing sales generate current profits and, as long as the firm is viable, the prospect of future profits. A company's value in the marketplace, or its purchase value, depends largely on its current profitability and perceptions of its future profitability.

Table 25-1 at the top of the following page gives the market values of the world's most valuable product brands. Each valuation is calculated as the market price of shares of stock in a company times the number of shares traded. Brand names, symbols, logos, and unique color schemes such as the color combinations trademarked by FedEx relate to consumers' perceptions of product differentiation and hence to the market values of firms. Companies protect their trademarks from misuse by registering them with the U.S. Patent and Trademark Office. Once its trademark application is approved, a company has the right to seek legal damages if someone makes unauthorized use of its brand name, spreads false rumors about the company, or engages in other devious activities that can reduce the value of its brand.

TABLE 25-1

Values of the Top Ten Brands

The market value of a company is equal to the number of shares of stock issued by the company times the market price of each share. To a large extent, the company's value reflects the value of its brand.

Brand	Market Value ($ billions)
Coca-Cola	70.5
International Business Machines (IBM)	64.7
Microsoft	60.9
Google	43.6
General Electric (GE)	42.8
McDonald's	33.6
Intel	32.0
Nokia	29.5
Disney	28.7
Hewlett-Packard	26.9

Source: Interbrand Annual Survey, 2010.

Advertising

To help ensure that consumers differentiate their product brands from those of other firms, monopolistically competitive firms commonly engage in advertising. Advertising comes in various forms, and the nature of advertising can depend considerably on the types of products that firms wish to distinguish from competing brands.

Direct marketing
Advertising targeted at specific consumers, typically in the form of postal mailings, telephone calls, or e-mail messages.

Mass marketing
Advertising intended to reach as many consumers as possible, typically through television, newspaper, radio, or magazine ads.

Interactive marketing
Advertising that permits a consumer to follow up directly by searching for more information and placing direct product orders.

METHODS OF ADVERTISING Figure 25-3 below shows the current distribution of advertising expenses among the various advertising media. Today, as in the past, firms primarily rely on two approaches to advertising their products. One is **direct marketing,** in which firms engage in personalized advertising using postal mailings, phone calls, and e-mail messages (excluding so-called banner and pop-up ads on Web sites). The other is **mass marketing,** in which firms aim advertising messages at as many consumers as possible via media such as television, newspapers, radio, and magazines.

A third advertising method is called **interactive marketing.** This advertising approach allows a consumer to respond directly to an advertising message. Often the consumer is able to search for more detailed information and place an order as part of the response. Sales booths and some types of Internet advertising, such as banner ads with links to sellers' Web pages, are forms of interactive marketing.

FIGURE 25-3 Distribution of U.S. Advertising Expenses

Direct marketing accounts for more than half of advertising expenses in the United States.

Sources: Advertising Today; Direct Marketing Today; and Internet Advertising Bureau.

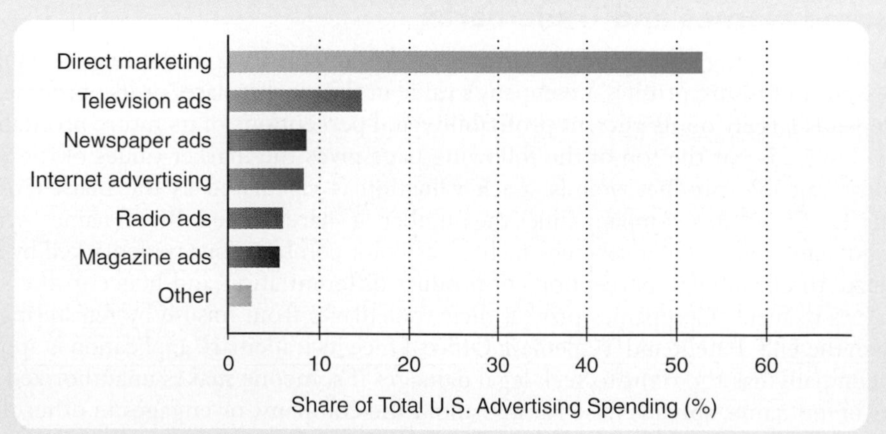

SEARCH, EXPERIENCE, AND CREDENCE GOODS The qualities and characteristics of a product determine how the firm should advertise that product. Some types of products, known as **search goods,** possess qualities that are relatively easy for consumers to assess in advance of their purchase. Clothing and music are common examples of items that have features that a consumer may assess, or perhaps even sample, before purchasing.

Search good
A product with characteristics that enable an individual to evaluate the product's quality in advance of a purchase.

Other products, known as **experience goods,** are products that people must actually consume before they can determine their qualities. Soft drinks, restaurant meals, and haircutting services are examples of experience goods.

Experience good
A product that an individual must consume before the product's quality can be established.

A third category of products, called **credence goods,** includes goods and services with qualities that might be difficult for consumers who lack specific expertise to evaluate without assistance. Products such as pharmaceuticals and services such as health care and legal advice are examples of credence goods.

Credence good
A product with qualities that consumers lack the expertise to assess without assistance.

INFORMATIONAL VERSUS PERSUASIVE ADVERTISING The forms of advertising that firms use vary considerably depending on whether the item being marketed is a search good or an experience good. If the item is a search good, a firm is more likely to use **informational advertising** that emphasizes the features of its product. A video trailer for the latest movie starring Shia LaBeouf will include snippets of the film, which help potential buyers assess the quality of the movie.

Informational advertising
Advertising that emphasizes transmitting knowledge about the features of a product.

In contrast, if the product is an experience good, a firm is more likely to engage in **persuasive advertising** intended to induce a consumer to try the product and, as a consequence, discover a previously unknown taste for it. For example, a soft-drink ad is likely to depict happy people drinking the clearly identified product during breaks from enjoyable outdoor activities on a hot day.

Persuasive advertising
Advertising that is intended to induce a consumer to purchase a particular product and discover a previously unknown taste for the item.

If a product is a credence good, producers commonly use a mix of informational and persuasive advertising. For instance, an ad for a pharmaceutical product commonly provides both detailed information about the product's curative properties and side effects and suggestions to consumers to ask physicians to help them assess the drug.

ADVERTISING AS SIGNALING BEHAVIOR Recall from Chapter 23 that *signals* are compact gestures or actions that convey information. For example, high profits in an industry are signals that resources should flow to that industry. Individual companies can explicitly engage in signaling behavior. A firm can do so by establishing brand names or trademarks and then promoting them heavily. This is a signal to prospective consumers that this is a company that plans to stay in business. Before the modern age of advertising, U.S. banks needed a way to signal their soundness. To do this, they constructed large, imposing bank buildings using marble and granite. Stone structures communicated permanence. The effect was to give bank customers confidence that they were not doing business with fly-by-night operations.

When Ford Motor Company advertises its brand name heavily, it incurs substantial costs. The only way it can recoup those costs is by selling many Ford vehicles over a long period of time. Heavy advertising in the company's brand name thereby signals to car buyers that Ford intends to stay in business a long time and wants to develop a loyal customer base—because loyal customers are repeat customers.

Why Not . . . outlaw persuasive advertising?

Companies run persuasive ads to induce consumers to try a product to find out if they have a previously unknown taste for it. Because the purpose of persuasive advertising is more to attract consumers' attention and less to provide product information, many people think that persuasive advertising offers no clear benefits to society at large and argue for government limits on such ads. Nevertheless, when a company such as Coca-Cola launches new ad campaigns, the company also signals to consumers that it intends to remain in business indefinitely. Coca-Cola's spending on expensive persuasive ads demonstrates that the company intends to expand its customer base and thereby perpetuate its operations for years to come. In this way, even persuasive advertising offers some information to consumers. Banning such ads would impose a cost on society.

QUICK QUIZ See page 572 for the answers. Review concepts from this section in MyEconLab.

_________ such as words, symbols, and logos distinguish firms' products from those of other firms. Firms seek to differentiate their brands through advertising, via _________ marketing, _________ marketing, or _________ marketing.

A firm is more likely to use _________ advertising that emphasizes the features of its product if the item is a **search good** with features that consumers can assess in advance.

A firm is more likely to use _________ advertising to affect consumers' tastes and preferences if it sells an **experience good.** This is an item that people must actually consume before they can determine its qualities.

A firm that sells a _________ good, which is an item possessing qualities that consumers lack the expertise to fully assess, typically uses a combination of informational and persuasive advertising.

Information Products and Monopolistic Competition

Information product
An item that is produced using information intensive inputs at a relatively high fixed cost but distributed for sale at a relatively low marginal cost.

A number of industries sell **information products,** which entail relatively high fixed costs associated with the use of knowledge and other information-intensive inputs as key factors of production. Once the first unit has been produced, however, it is possible to produce additional units at a relatively low per-unit cost. Most information products can be put into digital form. Good examples are computer games, computer operating systems, digital music and videos, educational and training software, electronic books and encyclopedias, and office productivity software.

Special Cost Characteristics of Information Products

Creating the first copy of an information product often entails incurring a relatively sizable up-front cost. Once the first copy is created, however, making additional copies can be very inexpensive. For instance, a firm that sells a computer game can simply make properly formatted copies of the original digital file of the game available for consumers to download, at a price, via the Internet.

COSTS OF PRODUCING INFORMATION PRODUCTS To think about the cost conditions faced by the seller of an information product, consider the production and sale of a computer game. The company that creates a computer game must devote many hours of labor to developing and editing its content. Each hour of labor and each unit of other resources devoted to performing this task entail an opportunity cost. The sum of all these up-front costs constitutes a relatively sizable *fixed cost* that the company must incur to generate the first copy of the computer game.

Once the company has developed the computer game in a form that is readable by personal computers, the marginal cost of making and distributing additional copies is very low. In the case of a computer game, it is simply a matter of incurring a minuscule cost to place the required files on a DVD or on the company's Web site.

COST CURVES FOR AN INFORMATION PRODUCT Suppose that a manufacturer decides to produce and sell a computer game. Creating the first copy of the game requires incurring a total fixed cost equal to $250,000. The marginal cost that the company incurs to place the computer game on a DVD or in downloadable format is a constant amount equal to $2.50 per computer game.

Figure 25-4 on the facing page displays the firm's cost curves for this information product. By definition, average fixed cost is total fixed cost divided by the quantity produced and sold. Hence, the average fixed cost of the first computer game is $250,000. But if the company sells 5,000 copies, the average fixed cost drops to $50 per game. If the total quantity sold is 50,000, average fixed cost declines to $5 per game. The average fixed cost (AFC) curve slopes downward over the entire range of possible quantities of computer games.

Average variable cost equals total variable cost divided by the number of units of a product that a firm sells. If this company sells only one copy, then the total variable

FIGURE 25-4 Cost Curves for a Producer of an Information Product

The total fixed cost of producing a computer game is $250,000. If the producer sells 5,000 copies, average fixed cost falls to $50 per copy. If quantity sold rises to 50,000, average fixed cost decreases to $5 per copy. Thus, the producer's average fixed cost (AFC) curve slopes downward. If the per-unit cost of producing each copy of the game is $2.50, then both the marginal cost (MC) and average variable cost (AVC) curves are horizontal at $2.50 per copy. Adding the AFC and AVC curves yields the ATC curve. Because the ATC curve slopes downward, the producer of this information product experiences short-run economies of operation.

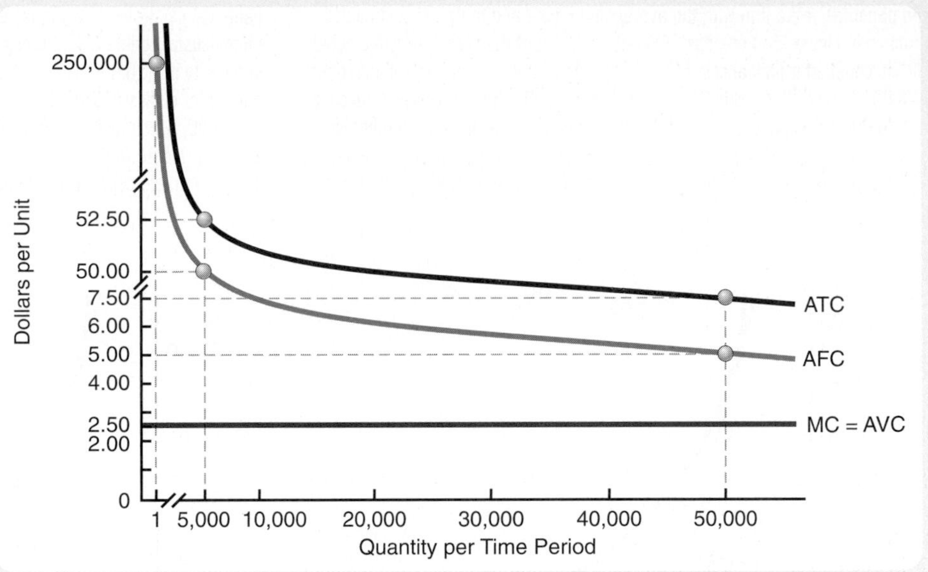

cost it incurs is the per-unit cost of $2.50, and this is also the average variable cost of producing one unit. Because the per-unit cost of producing the computer game is a constant $2.50, producing two games entails a total variable cost of $5.00, and the average variable cost of producing two games is $5.00 ÷ 2 = $2.50. Thus, as shown in Figure 25-4 above, the average variable cost of producing and selling this computer game is always equal to the constant marginal cost of $2.50 per game that the company incurs. The average variable cost (AVC) curve is the same as the marginal cost (MC) curve, which for this company is the horizontal line depicted in Figure 25-4.

SHORT-RUN ECONOMIES OF OPERATION By definition, average total cost equals the sum of average fixed cost and average variable cost. The average total cost (ATC) curve for this computer game company slopes downward over its entire range.

Recall from Chapter 22 that along the downward-sloping range of an individual firm's *long-run* average cost curve, the firm experiences *economies of scale*. For the producer of an information product such as a computer game, the *short-run* average total cost curve slopes downward. Consequently, sellers of information products typically experience **short-run economies of operation.** The average total cost of producing and selling an information product declines as more units of the product are sold. Short-run economies of operation are a distinguishing characteristic of information products that sets them apart from most other goods and services.

Short-run economies of operation
A distinguishing characteristic of an information product arising from declining short-run average total cost as more units of the product are sold.

Monopolistic Competition and Information Products

In the example depicted in Figure 25-4 above, the information product is a computer game. There are numerous computer games among which consumers can choose. Hence, there are many products that are close substitutes in the market for computer games. Yet no two computer games are exactly the same. This means that the particular computer game product sold by the company in our example is distinguishable from other competing products.

For the sake of argument, therefore, let's suppose that this company participates in a monopolistically competitive market for this computer game. Panels (a) and (b) of Figure 25-5 on the next page display a possible demand curve for the computer game manufactured and sold by this particular company.

MARGINAL COST PRICING AND INFORMATION PRODUCTS What if the company making this particular computer game were to behave *as if* it were a perfectly competitive firm by setting the price of its product equal to marginal cost? Panel (a) of Figure 25-5

FIGURE 25-5 The Infeasibility of Marginal Cost Pricing of an Information Product

In panel (a), if the firm with the average total cost and marginal cost curves shown in Figure 25-4 on page 565 sets the price of the computer game equal to its constant marginal cost of $2.50 per copy, then consumers will purchase 20,000 copies. This yields $50,000 in revenues. The firm's average total cost of 20,000 games is $15 per copy, so its total cost of selling that number of copies is $15 × 20,000 = $300,000. Marginal cost pricing thereby entails a $250,000 loss, which is the total fixed cost of producing the computer game.

Panel (b) illustrates how the price of the game is ultimately determined under monopolistic competition. Setting a price of $27.50 per game induces consumers to buy 10,000 copies, and the average total cost of producing this number of copies is also $27.50. Consequently, total revenues equal $275,000, which just covers the sum of the $250,000 in total fixed costs and $25,000 (the 10,000 copies times the constant $2.50 average variable cost) in total variable costs. The firm earns zero economic profits.

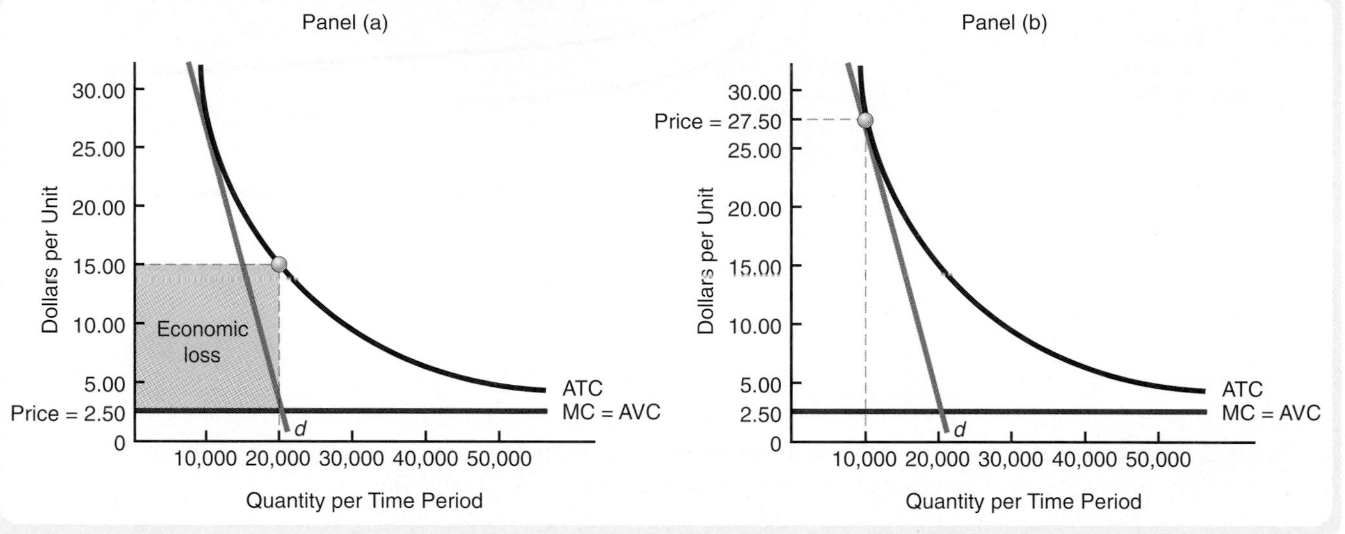

provides the answer to this question. If the company sets the price of the computer game equal to marginal cost, it will charge only $2.50 per game it sells. Naturally, a larger number of people desire to purchase computer games at this price, and given the demand curve in the figure, the company could sell 20,000 copies of this game.

The company would face a problem, however. At a price of $2.50 per computer game, it would earn $50,000 in revenues on sales of 20,000 copies. The average fixed cost of 20,000 copies equals $250,000/20,000, or $12.50 per computer game. Adding this to the constant $2.50 average variable cost implies an average total cost of selling 20,000 copies of $15 per game. Under marginal cost pricing, therefore, the company would earn an average loss of $12.50 (price − average total cost = $2.50 − $15.00 = −$12.50) per computer game for all 20,000 copies sold. The company's total economic loss from selling 20,000 computer games at a price equal to marginal cost would amount to $250,000. Hence, the company would fail to recoup the $250,000 total fixed cost of producing the computer game. If the company had planned to set its price equal to the computer game's marginal cost, it would never have developed the computer game in the first place!

The failure of marginal cost pricing to allow firms selling information products to cover the fixed costs of producing those products is intrinsic to the nature of such products. In the presence of short-run economies of operation in producing information products, marginal cost pricing is simply not feasible in the marketplace.

Recall that marginal cost pricing is associated with perfect competition. An important implication of this example is that markets for information products cannot function as perfectly competitive markets. Imperfect competition is the rule, not the exception, in the market for information products.

THE CASE IN WHICH PRICE EQUALS AVERAGE TOTAL COST Panel (b) of Figure 25-5 above illustrates how the *price* of the computer game is ultimately determined in a monopolistically competitive market. After all entry or exit from the market has occurred, the price of the computer game will equal the producer's average cost of production, including all implicit opportunity costs. The price charged for the game generates total revenues sufficient to cover all explicit and implicit costs and therefore is consistent with earning a normal return on invested capital.

Given the demand curve depicted in Figure 25-5, at a price of $27.50 per computer game, consumers are willing to purchase 10,000 copies. The company's average total cost of offering 10,000 copies for sale is also equal to $27.50 per computer game. Consequently, the price of each copy equals the average total cost of producing the game.

At a price of $27.50 per computer game, the company's revenues from selling 10,000 copies equal $275,000. This amount of revenues is just sufficient to cover the company's total fixed cost (including the opportunity cost of capital) of $250,000 and the $25,000 total variable cost it incurs in producing 10,000 copies at an average variable cost of $2.50 per game. Thus, the company earns zero economic profits.

LONG-RUN EQUILIBRIUM FOR AN INFORMATION PRODUCT INDUSTRY When competition drives the price of an information product to equality with average total cost, sellers charge the minimum price required to cover their production costs, including the relatively high initial costs they must incur to develop their products in the first place. Consumers thereby pay the lowest price necessary to induce sellers to provide the item.

The situation illustrated in panel (b) of Figure 25-5 on the facing page corresponds to a long-run equilibrium for this particular firm in a monopolistically competitive market for computer games. If this and other companies face a situation such as the diagram depicts, there is no incentive for additional companies to enter or leave the computer game industry. Consequently, the product price naturally tends to adjust to equality with average total cost as a monopolistically competitive industry composed of sellers of information products moves toward long-run equilibrium.

QUICK QUIZ

See page 572 for the answers. Review concepts from this section in MyEconLab.

Firms that sell **information products** experience relatively __________ fixed costs, but once they have produced the first unit, they can sell additional units at a relatively __________ per-unit cost. Consequently, the manufacturer of an information product experiences short-run __________ of __________.

If a firm sets the price of an information product equal to marginal cost, it earns only sufficient revenues to cover its __________ costs. Engaging in marginal cost pricing, therefore, fails to cover the relatively high fixed costs of making an information product.

In a long-run equilibrium outcome under monopolistic competition, the price of an information product equals __________ __________ cost. The seller's total revenues exactly cover __________ costs, including the opportunity cost of capital.

You Are There

Stimulating Candy Sales by Adding Caffeine

Jason Kensey, president of Vroom Foods, likes to say that his company offers "the most caffeinated products out there." Vroom's two main products are Buzz Bites and Foosh Energy Mints. One piece of either product contains 100 milligrams of caffeine. Thus, only three pieces of either candy provide more than the 250 milligrams of caffeine that mental health guides indicate are sufficient to induce nervousness and insomnia.

Nevertheless, Vroom's customers are looking for that extra surge of vigor offered by the growing category of "energy candy." Vroom's biggest problem is disguising the bitter taste of caffeine in its sugary morsels, but as Kensey remarks, "Our customers realize that the Buzz Bites aren't going to taste like Godiva Chocolate." Among Vroom's competitors in the energy candy business are Crackheads, Extreme Sport Beans, Ice Breakers Energy Mints, Jolt Gum and Mints, and Snickers Charged candy bars. In addition to differentiating its product from other candies by including caffeine, Vroom increasingly is seeking to differentiate Buzz Bites and Foosh Energy Mints from the caffeine-laden products of other energy candy makers.

Critical Analysis Questions

1. How is it possible for candy companies to earn short-run economic profits each time they create slightly differentiated brands of candy?
2. Why do you suppose that firms offering energy candy products typically engage primarily in persuasive advertising instead of informational advertising?

ISSUES & APPLICATIONS

Finding a Band Name Between ABBA and ZZ Top

CONCEPTS APPLIED

- ▶ Product Differentiation
- ▶ Monopolistic Competition
- ▶ Trademarks

For a group of musicians bringing together their voices, guitars, and drums in a commercial venture, the single most important issue might seem to be the quality of their music. Although a rock band's musical quality undoubtedly is *one* of the more important issues, finding a name may be equally crucial. Increasingly, this is one of the hardest problems for bands to solve.

Musical Monopolistic Competition and Trademarked Brands

There are many thousands of rock bands, and it is easy for bands to enter or exit the musical performance industry. Most bands seek to differentiate themselves by writing their own novel songs, developing their own styles, and offering uniquely blended sounds. Thus, the industry is monopolistically competitive.

A key product characteristic is a band's name, as evidenced by names such as the Beatles, Coldplay, Grateful Dead, Herman Düne, LCD Soundsystem, Led Zeppelin, Modest Mouse, Metallica, Pink Floyd, Spoon, and Vampire Weekend. Therefore, one of the first agenda items for a band after its formation is to find a unique name and obtain a trademark for it.

A Trademark Battle of the Bands

Sometimes, a band that is starting to make headway on the musical aspect of product differentiation discovers that the name it has been using could be subject to a legal challenge by a band that has already trademarked that name. In this situation, the up-and-coming band usually has to look for a new, untrademarked name that will not alienate its fan base.

Unfortunately, there are already about 1.4 million trademarked names of musical artists, and 6,000 additional names receive trademarks every month. Among the most common words appearing in names of rock bands are *bliss*, *mirage*, *one*, *gemini*, *legacy*, *paradox*, *rain*, and *discovery*. Most of these and other common words are already trademarked as single-word band names. Thus, bands typically mix words together in different combinations in an effort to create unique names that have not already been trademarked by other bands.

Sometimes, bands face challenges to their names from nonmusical trademark holders. One of the more commercially successful rock bands of all time, Chicago, originally tried going by the name Chicago Transit Authority. The group opted to shorten its name when the city of Chicago's actual transit authority threatened a trademark battle. During the 1990s, a Scottish group called Captain America had just signed a recording deal with Atlantic Records when Marvel Comics went to court to block the use of the name of its trademarked superhero. More recently, a group tried to call itself Jane Deere but withdrew the proposed name when confronted by a potential legal challenge from the maker of John Deere tractors.

For Critical Analysis

1. What is the economic objective behind any rock band's efforts to come up with a unique name?
2. Why do you suppose that names of rock bands are sometimes similar but not quite the same, just as the actual products that the bands produce have analogous but not quite identical features?

Web Resources

1. To take a look at a Web site that randomly combines words to help develop names for rock bands, go to www.econtoday.com/ch25.
2. Learn about the issues that rock bands confront in finding names at www.econtoday.com/ch25.

Research Project

Consider a monopolistically competitive rock band that is in an initial long-run equilibrium. The band's members are contemplating changing the band's name in hopes of attracting new fans. What are two ways that a new name for the band might succeed in boosting its economic profits? (Hint: What two changes in a product demand curve can enable a firm to boost its product's price?) Why are these economic profits likely to disappear in the long run?

For more questions on this chapter's Issues & Applications, go to **MyEconLab**. In the Study Plan for this chapter, select Section N: News.

Here is what you should know after reading this chapter. **MyEconLab** will help you identify what you know, and where to go when you need to practice.

WHAT YOU SHOULD KNOW		WHERE TO GO TO PRACTICE
The Key Characteristics of a Monopolistically Competitive Industry A monopolistically competitive industry consists of a large number of firms that sell differentiated products that are close substitutes. Firms can easily enter or exit the industry. Monopolistically competitive firms can increase their profits if they can successfully distinguish their products from those of their rivals. Thus, they have an incentive to advertise.	monopolistic competition, 556 product differentiation, 557	• **MyEconLab** Study Plan 25.1 • Audio introduction to Chapter 25 • Video: Characteristics of Monopolistic Competition • Economics Video: 'Gray Googlers' Work from Home • Economics Video: No Frills Grocery Shopping
Contrasting the Output and Pricing Decisions of Monopolistically Competitive Firms with Those of Perfectly Competitive Firms In the short run, a monopolistically competitive firm produces to the point at which marginal revenue equals marginal cost. The price it charges can exceed both marginal cost and average total cost in the short run. The resulting economic profits induce new firms to enter the industry. In the long run, therefore, monopolistically competitive firms earn zero economic profits, but price exceeds marginal cost.	**KEY FIGURES** Figure 25-1, 559 Figure 25-2, 560	• **MyEconLab** Study Plans 25.2, 25.3 • Animated Figures 25-1, 25-2 • Economics Video: Doc Martens
Why Brand Names and Advertising Are Important Features of Monopolistically Competitive Industries Monopolistically competitive firms engage in advertising. If the product is a search good with features that consumers can evaluate prior to purchase, the seller is more likely to use advertising to transmit information about product features. If the firm sells an experience good, with features that are apparent only when consumed, it is more likely to use persuasive advertising to induce consumers to discover unknown tastes. If the product is a credence good with characteristics that consumers cannot readily assess unaided, then the firm often uses a mix of informational and persuasive advertising.	direct marketing, 562 mass marketing, 562 interactive marketing, 562 search good, 563 experience good, 563 credence good, 563 informational advertising, 563 persuasive advertising, 563	• **MyEconLab** Study Plan 25.4 • Economics Video: Amy's Ice Cream • Economics Video: Pizza for Pesos • Economics Video: Skechers

(continued)

MyEconLab continued

WHAT YOU SHOULD KNOW		WHERE TO GO TO PRACTICE
Properties of Information Products and Determining Their Prices Providing an information product entails high fixed costs but a relatively low per-unit cost. Hence, the average total cost curve for a firm that sells an information product slopes downward, meaning that the firm experiences short-run economies of operation. In a long-run equilibrium, price adjusts to equality with average total cost.	information product, 564 short-run economies of operation, 565 **KEY FIGURES** Figure 25-4, 565 Figure 25-5, 566	• **MyEconLab** Study Plan 25.5 • Animated Figures 25-4, 25-5

Log in to MyEconLab, take a chapter test, and get a personalized Study Plan that tells you which concepts you understand and which ones you need to review. From there, MyEconLab will give you further practice, tutorials, animations, videos, and guided solutions. Log in to www.myeconlab.com

PROBLEMS

All problems are assignable in myeconlab. *Answers to odd-numbered problems appear at the back of the book.*

25-1. Explain why the following are examples of monopolistic competition.

a. There are a number of fast-food restaurants in town, and they compete fiercely. Some restaurants cook their hamburgers over open flames. Others fry their hamburgers. In addition, some serve broiled fish sandwiches, while others serve fried fish sandwiches. A few serve ice cream cones for dessert, while others offer frozen ice cream pies.

b. There are a vast number of colleges and universities across the country. Each competes for top students. All offer similar courses and programs, but some have better programs in business, while others have stronger programs in the arts and humanities. Still others are academically stronger in the sciences.

25-2. Consider the diagram at the right depicting the demand and cost conditions faced by a monopolistically competitive firm.

a. What are the total revenues, total costs, and economic profits experienced by this firm?

b. Is this firm more likely in short- or long-run equilibrium? Explain.

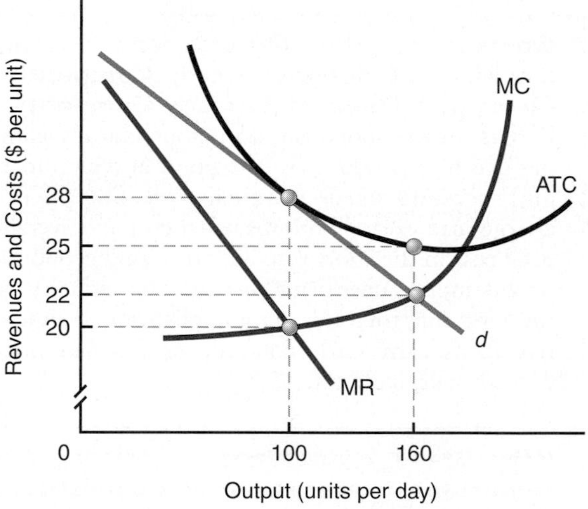

25-3. The table at the top of the facing page depicts the prices and total costs a local used-book store faces. The bookstore competes with a number of similar stores, but it capitalizes on its location and the word-of-mouth reputation of the coffee it serves to its customers. Calculate the store's total revenue, total profit, marginal revenue, and marginal cost at each level of output, beginning with the first unit. Based on marginal analysis, what is the approximate profit-maximizing level of output for this business?

Output	Price per Book ($)	Total Costs ($)
0	6.00	2.00
1	5.75	5.25
2	5.50	7.50
3	5.25	9.60
4	5.00	12.10
5	4.75	15.80
6	4.50	20.00
7	4.00	24.75

25-4. Calculate total average costs for the bookstore in Problem 25-3. Illustrate the store's short-run equilibrium by plotting demand, marginal revenue, average total costs, and marginal costs. What is its total profit?

25-5. Suppose that after long-run adjustments take place in the used-book market, the business in Problem 25-3 ends up producing 4 units of output. What are the market price and economic profits of this monopolistic competitor in the long run?

25-6. It is a typical Christmas electronics shopping season, and makers of flat-panel TVs are marketing the latest available models through their own Web sites as well as via retailers such as Best Buy and Wal-Mart. Each manufacturer offers its own unique versions of flat-panel TVs in differing arrays of shapes and sizes. As usual, each is hoping to maintain a stream of economic profits earned since it first introduced these most recent models late last year or perhaps just a few months before Christmas. Nevertheless, as sales figures arrive at the headquarters of companies such as Dell, Samsung, Sharp, and Sony, it is clear that most of the companies will end up earning only a normal rate of return this year.

a. How can makers of flat-panel TVs earn economic profits during the first few months after the introduction of new models?

b. What economic forces result in the dissipation of economic profits earned by manufacturers of flat-panel TVs?

25-7. Classify each of the following as an example of direct, interactive, and/or mass marketing.

a. The sales force of a pharmaceutical company visits physicians' offices to promote new medications and to answer physicians' questions about treatment options and possible side effects.

b. A mortgage company targets a list of specific low-risk borrowers for a barrage of e-mail messages touting its low interest rates and fees.

c. An online bookseller pays fees to an Internet search engine to post banner ads relating to each search topic chosen by someone conducting a search. In part, this helps promote the bookseller's brand, but clicking on the banner ad also directs the person to a Web page displaying books on the topic that are available for purchase.

d. A national rental car chain runs advertisements on all of the nation's major television networks.

25-8. Classify each of the following as an example of direct, interactive, and/or mass marketing.

a. A cosmetics firm pays for full-page display ads in a number of top women's magazines.

b. A magazine distributor mails a fold-out flyer advertising its products to the addresses of all individuals it has identified as possibly interested in magazine subscriptions.

c. An online gambling operation arranges for pop-up ads to appear on the computer screen every time a person uses a media player to listen to digital music or play video files, and clicking on the ads directs an individual to its Web gambling site.

d. A car dealership places advertisements in newspapers throughout the region where potential customers reside.

25-9. Categorize each of the following as an experience good, a search good, or a credence good or service, and justify your answer.

a. A heavy-duty filing cabinet

b. A restaurant meal

c. A wool overcoat

d. Psychotherapy

25-10. Categorize each of the following as an experience good, a search good, or a credence good or service, and justify your answer.

a. Services of a carpet cleaning company

b. A new cancer treatment

c. Athletic socks

d. A silk necktie

25-11. In what ways do credence goods share certain characteristics of both experience goods and search goods? How do credence goods differ from both experience goods and search goods? Why does advertising of credence goods commonly contain both informational and persuasive elements? Explain your answers.

25-12. Is each of the following items more likely to be the subject of an informational or a persuasive advertisement? Why?

a. An office copying machine

b. An automobile loan

c. A deodorant

d. A soft drink

25-13. Discuss the special characteristics of an information product, and explain the implications for a producer's short-run average and marginal cost curves. In addition, explain why having a price equal to marginal cost is not feasible for the producer of an information product.

25-14. A firm that sells e-books—books in digital form downloadable from the Internet—sells all e-books relating to do-it-yourself topics (home plumbing, gardening, and the like) at the same price. At present, the company can earn a maximum annual profit of \$25,000 when it sells 10,000 copies within a year's time. The firm incurs a 50-cent expense each time a consumer downloads a copy, but the company must spend \$100,000 per year developing new editions of the e-books. The company has determined that it would earn zero economic profits if price were equal to average total cost, and in this case it could sell 20,000 copies. Under marginal cost pricing, it could sell 100,000 copies.

a. In the short run, what is the profit-maximizing price of e-books relating to do-it-yourself topics?

b. At the profit-maximizing quantity, what is the average total cost of producing e-books?

ECONOMICS ON THE NET

Legal Services on the Internet A number of legal firms now offer services on the Internet, and in this application you contemplate features of the market for Web-based legal services.

Title: Nolo.com—Law for All

Navigation: Link to the Nolo.com site via **www.econtoday.com/ch25**.

Application Answer the following questions.

1. In what respects does the market for legal services, such as those provided online by Nolo.com, have the characteristics of a monopolistically competitive industry?
2. How can providers of legal services differentiate their products? How does Nolo.com attempt to do this?

For Group Discussion and Analysis Assign groups to search the Web for at least three additional online legal firms and compare the services these firms offer. Reconvene the entire class and discuss whether it is reasonable to classify the market for online legal services as monopolistically competitive.

ANSWERS TO QUICK QUIZZES

p. 558: (i) large . . . highly; (ii) differentiated; (iii) easy

p. 561: (i) short; (ii) long . . . zero . . . normal; (iii) total . . . total; (iv) average total . . . minimum

p. 564: (i) Trademarks . . . direct . . . mass . . . interactive; (ii) informational; (iii) persuasive; (iv) credence

p. 567: (i) high . . . low . . . economies . . . operation; (ii) variable; (iii) average total . . . total

26 Oligopoly and Strategic Behavior

In the last few decades, many U.S. companies decided to specialize in specific aspects of production. Some companies concentrated on procuring raw materials. They sold these materials to other firms, which utilized the raw materials to manufacture inputs that other firms, in turn, assembled into final products. Other companies specialized in distributing the assembled products to retailers, which then sold the products to consumers. Recently, however, a number of U.S. firms have engaged in *vertical mergers,* combining firms that previously specialized in various stages of production into a single, larger company. Mergers that form a few large companies can contribute to an industry structure called *oligopoly,* in which an industry has only a few competitors. This type of market structure is the subject of the present chapter.

LEARNING OBJECTIVES

After reading this chapter, you should be able to:

- Outline the fundamental characteristics of oligopoly
- Understand how to apply game theory to evaluate the pricing strategies of oligopolistic firms
- Identify features of an industry that help or hinder efforts to form a cartel that seeks to restrain output and earn economic profits
- Illustrate how network effects and market feedback can explain why some industries are oligopolies
- Explain why multiproduct firms selling complementary sets of products may or may not want their products to be compatible with those of their competitors

myeconlab

MyEconLab helps you master each objective and study more efficiently. See end of chapter for details.

Did You Know That?

executives at EMI, one of the largest producers of recorded music, recently invited some teenagers to visit its London headquarters? The firm's top managers wished to learn about the teens' music-listening habits and preferences. At the conclusion of the meeting, the managers thanked the teens for their insights and invited them to select CDs for themselves, at no charge, from a pile of music CDs on a table. Yet not a single teen left with a CD. At that moment, one EMI manager said later, "We realized the game was completely up when it came to distributing music via CDs." The teens, he noted, had responded to the fact that most other teens were not listening to music on CDs by halting their own use of CDs, even at an explicit price of zero. In this chapter, you will learn about how firms in industries with just a few competitors can benefit—or lose out—when a consumer's willingness to purchase their products is influenced by other consumers' decisions about whether to buy them.

Oligopoly

An important market structure that we have yet to discuss involves a situation in which a few large firms comprise essentially an entire industry. They are not perfectly competitive in the sense that we have used the term. They are not even monopolistically competitive. And because there are several of them, a pure monopoly does not exist. We call such a situation an **oligopoly,** which consists of a small number of *interdependent* sellers. Each firm in the industry knows that other firms will react to its changes in prices, quantities, and qualities. An oligopoly market structure can exist for either a homogeneous or a differentiated product.

Oligopoly
A market structure in which there are very few sellers. Each seller knows that the other sellers will react to its changes in prices, quantities, and qualities.

Characteristics of Oligopoly

Oligopoly is characterized by a small number of interdependent firms that constitute the entire market.

SMALL NUMBER OF FIRMS How many is "a small number of firms"? More than two but less than a hundred? The question is not easy to answer. Basically, though, oligopoly exists when the top few firms in the industry account for an overwhelming percentage of total industry output.

Oligopolies often involve three to five big companies that produce the bulk of industry output. Between World War II and the 1970s, three firms—General Motors, Chrysler, and Ford—produced and sold nearly all the output of the U.S. automobile industry. Among manufacturers of chewing gum and coin-operated amusement games, four large firms produce and sell essentially the entire output of each industry.

INTERDEPENDENCE All markets and all firms are, in a sense, interdependent. But only when a few large firms produce most of the output in an industry does the question of **strategic dependence** of one on the others' actions arise. In this situation, when any one firm changes its output, its product price, or the quality of its product, other firms notice the effects of its decisions. The firms must recognize that they are interdependent and that any action by one firm with respect to output, price, quality, or product differentiation will cause a reaction by other firms. A model of such mutual interdependence is difficult to build, but examples of such behavior are not hard to find in the real world. Oligopolists in the cigarette industry, for example, are constantly reacting to each other.

Strategic dependence
A situation in which one firm's actions with respect to price, quality, advertising, and related changes may be strategically countered by the reactions of one or more other firms in the industry. Such dependence can exist only when there are a limited number of major firms in an industry.

Recall that in the model of perfect competition, each firm ignores the behavior of other firms because each firm is able to sell all that it wants at the going market price. At the other extreme, the pure monopolist does not have to worry about the reaction of current rivals because there are none. In an oligopolistic market structure, the managers of firms are like generals in a war: *They must attempt to predict the reaction of rival firms.* It is a strategic game.

Why Oligopoly Occurs

Why are some industries composed chiefly of a few large firms? What causes an industry that might otherwise be competitive to tend toward oligopoly? We can provide some partial answers here.

Follow the link at **www.econtoday.com/ch26** to *Wall Street Journal* articles about real-world examples involving oligopoly.

ECONOMIES OF SCALE Perhaps the most common reason that has been offered for the existence of oligopoly is economies of scale. Recall that economics of scale exist when a doubling of output results in less than a doubling of total costs. When economies of scale exist, the firm's long-run average total cost curve will slope downward as the firm produces more and more output. Average total cost can be reduced by continuing to expand the scale of operation to the *minimum efficient scale*, or the output rate at which long-run average cost is minimized. (See page 499 in Chapter 22.) Smaller firms in a situation in which the minimum efficient scale is relatively large will have average total costs greater than those incurred by large firms. Little by little, they will go out of business or be absorbed into larger firms.

BARRIERS TO ENTRY It is possible that certain barriers to entry have prevented more competition in oligopolistic industries. They include legal barriers, such as patents, and control and ownership of critical supplies. Indeed, we can find periods in the past when firms were able not only to erect a barrier to entry but also to keep it in place year after year. In principle, the chemical, electronics, and aluminum industries have been at one time or another either monopolistic or oligopolistic because of the ownership of patents and the control of strategic inputs by specific firms.

OLIGOPOLY BY MERGER Another reason that oligopolistic market structures may sometimes develop is that firms merge. A merger is the joining of two or more firms under single ownership or control. The merged firm naturally becomes larger, enjoys greater economies of scale as output increases, and may ultimately have a greater ability to influence the market price for the industry's output.

There are two key types of mergers, vertical and horizontal. A **vertical merger** occurs when one firm merges with either a firm from which it purchases an input or a firm to which it sells its output. Vertical mergers occur, for example, when a coal-using electrical utility purchases a coal-mining firm or when a shoe manufacturer purchases retail shoe outlets.

Vertical merger
The joining of a firm with another to which it sells an output or from which it buys an input.

Obviously, vertical mergers cannot *create* oligopoly as we have defined it. But that can indeed occur via a **horizontal merger,** which involves firms selling a similar product. If two shoe manufacturing firms merge, that is a horizontal merger. If a group of firms, all producing steel, merge into one, that is also a horizontal merger.

Horizontal merger
The joining of firms that are producing or selling a similar product.

So far we have been talking about oligopoly in a theoretical manner. Now it is time to look at the actual oligopolies in the United States.

Measuring Industry Concentration

As we have stated, oligopoly is a market structure in which a few interdependent firms produce a large part of total output in an industry. This situation is often called one of high *industry concentration*. Before we show the concentration statistics in the United States, let's determine how industry concentration can be measured.

CONCENTRATION RATIO The most common way to compute industry concentration is to determine the percentage of total sales or production accounted for by the top four or top eight firms in an industry. This gives the four- or eight-firm **concentration ratio,** also known as the *industry concentration ratio*. An example of an industry with 25 firms is given in Table 26-1 at the top of the following page. We can see in that table that the four largest firms account for almost 90 percent of total output in the hypothetical industry. This is an example of an oligopoly because a few firms will recognize the interdependence of their output, pricing, and quality decisions.

Concentration ratio
The percentage of all sales contributed by the leading four or leading eight firms in an industry; sometimes called the *industry concentration ratio*.

TABLE 26-1

Computing the Four-Firm Concentration Ratio

Firm	Annual Sales ($ millions)		
1	150	= 400 (firms 1–4)	Total number of firms in industry = 25
2	100		
3	80		
4	70		
5 through 25	50		
Total	450		

Four-firm concentration ratio = 400/450 = 88.9%

U.S. CONCENTRATION RATIOS Table 26-2 below shows the four-firm *domestic* concentration ratios for various industries. Is there any way that we can show or determine which industries to classify as oligopolistic? There is no definite answer. If we arbitrarily picked a four-firm concentration ratio of 75 percent, we could infer that cigarettes and breakfast cereals were oligopolistic. But we would always be dealing with an arbitrary definition.

How concentrated is the U.S. cellphone service provider industry?

EXAMPLE **Market Concentration in the Cellphone Industry**

The U.S. cellphone service provider industry generated a total of $117.1 billion in revenues in a recent year. Of these revenues, AT&T received $30.8 billion; Verizon, $29.0 billion; Sprint/Nextel, $22.8 billion; and T-Mobile, $13.3 billion. Based on these figures, AT&T's market share was 26.3 percent, Verizon's was 24.8 percent, Sprint/Nextel's was 19.5 percent, and T-Mobile's was 11.4 percent. Consequently, the four-firm concentration ratio for the cellphone service provider industry was 82.0 percent.

FOR CRITICAL ANALYSIS

Given that cellphone service provider Alltel received the fifth-largest amount of revenues, about $4.9 billion, during this particular year, what was the five-firm concentration ratio in the U.S. cellphone industry?

Oligopoly, Efficiency, and Resource Allocation

Although oligopoly is not the dominant form of market structure in the United States, oligopolistic industries do exist. To the extent that oligopolists have *market power*—the ability to *individually* affect the *market* price for the industry's output—they lead to resource misallocations, just as monopolies do. Oligopolists charge prices that exceed

TABLE 26-2

Four-Firm Domestic Concentration Ratios for Selected U.S. Industries

Industry	Share of Total Sales Accounted for by the Top Four Firms (%)
Cigarettes	95
Breakfast cereals	78
Household vacuum cleaners	62
Primary aluminum	51
Computers	50
Soft drinks	48
Printing and publishing	38
Commercial banking	29.5

Source: U.S. Bureau of the Census.

marginal cost. But what about oligopolies that occur because of economies of scale? Consumers might actually end up paying lower prices than if the industry were composed of numerous smaller firms.

All in all, there is no definite evidence of serious resource misallocation in the United States because of oligopolies. In any event, *the more U.S. firms face competition from the rest of the world, the less any current oligopoly will be able to exercise market power.*

QUICK QUIZ See page 593 for the answers. Review concepts from this section in MyEconLab.

An **oligopoly** is a market situation with a __________ number of __________ sellers.

Oligopoly may result from __________ of scale, barriers to entry, and __________.

__________ mergers involve the merging of one firm with either the supplier of an input or the purchaser of its output.

__________ mergers involve the joining of firms selling a similar product.

Industry concentration can be measured by the combined __________ of total __________ accounted for by the top four firms in the industry.

Strategic Behavior and Game Theory

At this point, we would like to be able to show oligopoly price and output determination in the way we did for perfect competition, pure monopoly, and monopolistic competition, but we cannot. Whenever there are relatively few firms competing in an industry, each can and does react to the price, quantity, quality, and product innovations that the others undertake. In other words, each oligopolist has a **reaction function.** Oligopolistic competitors are interdependent. Consequently, the decision makers in such firms must employ strategies. And we must be able to model their strategic behavior if we wish to predict how prices and outputs are determined in oligopolistic market structures. In general, we can think of reactions of other firms to one firm's actions as part of a *game* that is played by all firms in the industry. Economists have developed **game theory** models to describe firms' rational interactions. Game theory is the analytical framework in which two or more individuals, companies, or nations compete for certain payoffs that depend on the strategy that the others employ. Poker is such a game situation because it involves a strategy of reacting to the actions of others.

Reaction function
The manner in which one oligopolist reacts to a change in price, output, or quality made by another oligopolist in the industry.

Game theory
A way of describing the various possible outcomes in any situation involving two or more interacting individuals when those individuals are aware of the interactive nature of their situation and plan accordingly. The plans made by these individuals are known as *game strategies*.

Some Basic Notions About Game Theory

Games can be either cooperative or noncooperative. If firms work together to obtain a jointly shared objective, such as maximizing profits for the industry as a whole, then they participate in a **cooperative game.** Whenever it is too costly for firms to coordinate their actions to obtain cooperative outcomes, they are in a **noncooperative game** situation. Most strategic behavior in the marketplace is best described as a noncooperative game.

Games can be classified by whether the payoffs are zero, negative, or positive. In a **zero-sum game,** one player's losses are offset by another player's gains. If two retailers have an absolutely fixed total number of customers, for example, the customers that one retailer wins over are exactly equal to the customers that the other retailer loses. In a **negative-sum game,** players as a group lose during the process of the game (although one perhaps by more than the other, and it's possible for one or more players to win). In a **positive-sum game,** players as a group end up better off. Some economists describe all voluntary exchanges as positive-sum games. After an exchange, both the buyer and the seller are better off than they were prior to the exchange.

Cooperative game
A game in which the players explicitly cooperate to make themselves jointly better off. As applied to firms, it involves companies colluding in order to make higher than perfectly competitive rates of return.

Noncooperative game
A game in which the players neither negotiate nor cooperate in any way. As applied to firms in an industry, this is the common situation in which there are relatively few firms and each has some ability to change price.

Zero-sum game
A game in which any gains within the group are exactly offset by equal losses by the end of the game.

Negative-sum game
A game in which players as a group lose during the process of the game.

Positive-sum game
A game in which players as a group are better off at the end of the game.

STRATEGIES IN NONCOOPERATIVE GAMES Players, such as decision makers in oligopolistic firms, have to devise a **strategy,** which is defined as a rule used to make a choice. The goal of the decision maker is to devise a strategy that is more successful than alternative strategies. Whenever a firm's decision makers can come up with certain

Strategy
Any rule that is used to make a choice, such as "Always pick heads."

Dominant strategies
Strategies that always yield the highest benefit. Regardless of what other players do, a dominant strategy will yield the most benefit for the player using it.

strategies that are generally successful no matter what actions competitors take, these are called **dominant strategies.** The dominant strategy always yields the unique best action for the decision maker no matter what action the other "players" undertake. Relatively few business decision makers over a long period of time have successfully devised dominant strategies. We know this by observation: Few firms in oligopolistic industries have maintained relatively high profits consistently over time.

How can a real-world situation faced by two captured bank robbers help to illustrate basic principles of game theory?

EXAMPLE The Prisoners' Dilemma

An example of game theory occurs when two people involved in a bank robbery are caught. What should they do when questioned by police? Their situation has been called the **prisoners' dilemma.** The two suspects, Sam and Carol, are interrogated separately (they cannot communicate with each other) and are given various alternatives. The interrogator indicates separately to Sam and Carol the following:

1. If both confess to the bank robbery, they will both go to prison for 5 years.
2. If neither confesses, they will each be given a sentence of 2 years on a lesser charge.
3. If one prisoner turns state's evidence and confesses, that prisoner goes free and the other one, who did not confess, will serve 10 years for bank robbery.

You can see the prisoners' alternatives in the **payoff matrix** in Figure 26-1 below. The two possibilities for each prisoner are "confess" and "don't confess." There are four possibilities:

1. Both confess.
2. Neither confesses.
3. Sam confesses (turns state's evidence) but Carol doesn't.
4. Carol confesses (turns state's evidence) but Sam doesn't.

In Figure 26-1, all of Sam's possible outcomes are shown on the upper half of each rectangle, and all of Carol's possible outcomes are shown on the lower half.

By looking at the payoff matrix, you can see that if Carol confesses, Sam's best strategy is to confess also—he'll get only 5 years instead of 10. Conversely, if Sam confesses, Carol's best strategy is also to confess—she'll get 5 years instead of 10. Now let's say that Sam is being interrogated and Carol doesn't confess. Sam's best strategy is still to confess, because then he goes free instead of serving 2 years. Conversely, if Carol is being interrogated, her best strategy is still to confess even if Sam hasn't. She'll go free instead of serving 2 years. To confess is a dominant strategy for Sam. To confess is also a dominant strategy for Carol. The situation is exactly symmetrical. So this is the prisoners' dilemma. The prisoners know that both of them will be better off if neither confesses. Yet it is in each individual prisoner's interest to confess, even though the *collective* outcome of each prisoner's pursuit of his or her own interest is inferior for both.

FOR CRITICAL ANALYSIS

Can you apply the prisoners' dilemma to the firms in a two-firm industry that agree to share market sales equally? (Hint: Think about the payoff to cheating on the market-sharing agreement.)

Prisoners' dilemma
A famous strategic game in which two prisoners have a choice between confessing and not confessing to a crime. If neither confesses, they serve a minimum sentence. If both confess, they serve a longer sentence. If one confesses and the other doesn't, the one who confesses goes free. The dominant strategy is always to confess.

Payoff matrix
A matrix of outcomes, or consequences, of the strategies available to the players in a game.

FIGURE 26-1 The Prisoners' Dilemma Payoff Matrix

Regardless of what the other prisoner does, each prisoner is better off if he or she confesses. So confessing is the dominant strategy, and each ends up behind bars for 5 years.

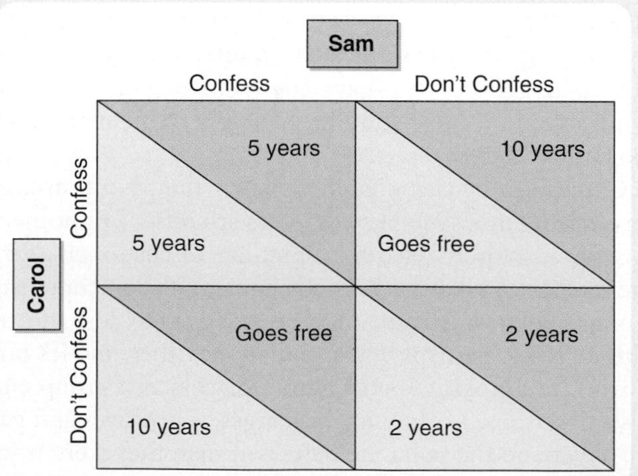

FIGURE 26-2 Game Theory and Pricing Strategies

This payoff matrix shows that if both oligopolists choose a high price, each makes $6 million. If they both choose a low price, each makes $4 million. If one chooses a low price and the other doesn't, the low-priced firm will make $8 million. Unless they collude, they will end up at the low-priced solution, because charging a low price is the dominant strategy.

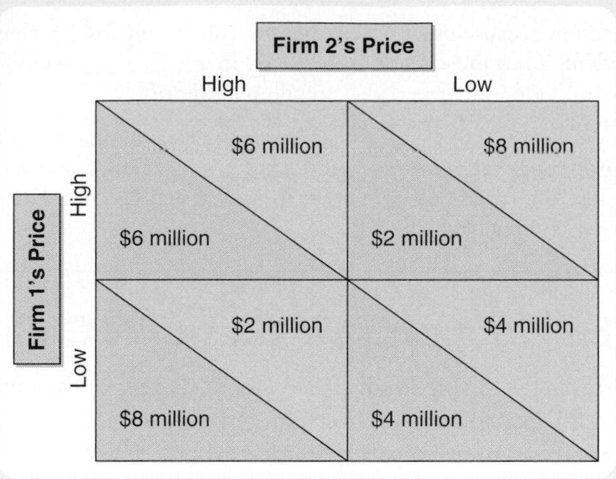

Applying Game Theory to Pricing Strategies

We can apply game strategy to two firms—oligopolists—that have to decide on their pricing strategy. Each can choose either a high or a low price. Their payoff matrix is shown in Figure 26-2 above. If they both choose a high price, each will make $6 million, but if they both choose a low price, each will make only $4 million. If one sets a high price and the other a low one, the low-priced firm will make $8 million, but the high-priced firm will make only $2 million. As in the prisoners' dilemma, in the absence of collusion, they will end up choosing low prices.

Opportunistic Behavior

In the prisoners' dilemma, it is clear that cooperative behavior—both parties standing firm without admitting to anything—leads to the best outcome for both players. But each prisoner (player) stands to gain by cheating. Such action is called **opportunistic behavior.** Our daily economic activities involve the potential for the prisoners' dilemma all the time. We could engage in opportunistic behavior. You could write a check for a purchase knowing that it is going to bounce because you have just closed that bank account. When you agree to perform a specific task for pay, you could perform your work in a substandard way. When you go to buy a product, the seller might be able to cheat you by selling you a defective item.

Opportunistic behavior
Actions that focus solely on short-run gains because long-run benefits of cooperation are perceived to be smaller.

In short, if all of us—sellers and buyers—engaged in opportunistic behavior all of the time, we would constantly be acting in a world of noncooperative behavior. That is not the world in which most of us live, however. Why not? Because most of us engage in *repeat transactions*. Manufacturers would like us to keep purchasing their products. Sellers would like us to keep coming back to their stores. As sellers of labor services, we all would like to keep our jobs, get promotions, or be hired away by another firm at a higher wage rate. Therefore, we engage in **tit-for-tat strategic behavior.** A consumer using a tit-for-tat strategy may, for instance, continue to purchase items from a firm each period as long as the firm provides products of the same quality and abides by any guarantees. If the firm fails in any period to provide high-quality products and honor its product guarantees, the consumer purchases items elsewhere.

Tit-for-tat strategic behavior
In game theory, cooperation that continues as long as the other players continue to cooperate.

QUICK QUIZ See page 593 for the answers. Review concepts from this section in MyEconLab.

Each oligopolist has a _________ function because oligopolistic competitors are interdependent. They must therefore engage in _________ behavior. One way to model this behavior is to use **game theory.**

Games can be either **cooperative** or **noncooperative.** In a _________-sum game, one player's losses are exactly offset by another player's gains. In a _________-sum game, all players collectively lose, perhaps one player more than the others. In a _________-sum game, the players as a group end up better off.

Decision makers in oligopolistic firms must devise a strategy. A _________ strategy is one that is generally successful no matter what actions competitors take.

The Cooperative Game: A Collusive Cartel

According to Adam Smith (1723–1790), "People of the same trade seldom meet together, even for merriment and diversion, but the conversation ends in a conspiracy against the public, or in some contrivance to raise prices." Why can firms profit from engaging in a "conspiracy against the public"? How can firms work together to create a "contrivance to raise prices"? Why does accomplishing this task turn out to be a feat only occasionally achieved by certain industries? Let's consider each of these questions in turn.

The Rationale for a Cartel and the Seeds of Its Undoing

Cartel
An association of producers in an industry that agree to set common prices and output quotas to prevent competition.

If all the firms in an industry can find a way to cooperatively determine how much to produce to maximize their combined profits, then they can form a **cartel** and jointly act as a single producer. This means that they *collude*. They act together to attain the same outcome that a monopoly firm would aim to achieve: producing to the point at which marginal revenue derived from the *market* demand curve is equal to marginal cost. To do so, they must set common prices and output quotas for their members. If the firms are able to accomplish this task, they can all charge the same profit-maximizing price that a monopoly would have charged. Then they can share in the maximized monopoly profits.

CUTTING BACK ON PRODUCTION Although the prospect of monopoly profits provides a strong incentive to collude, a fledgling cartel faces two fundamental problems. First, recall that a monopoly producer maximizes economic profits by restraining its production to a rate below the competitive output rate. Thus, the first problem for the members of the cartel is to determine how much each producer will restrain its output.

Once the first problem is solved, another immediately appears. As soon as all producers in the cartel begin restraining production and charging a higher price, each individual member could increase its revenues and profits by charging a slightly lower price, raising production, and selling more units. Hence, if all other cartel members honor their agreement to reduce production, one member could boost its economic profits by reneging on its promise to the rest of the cartel and increasing its production.

Enforcing a Cartel Agreement

Go to www.econtoday.com/ch26 to find out from WTRG Economics how effective the Organization of Petroleum Exporting Countries has been in acting as an oil market cartel.

There are four conditions that make it more likely that firms will be able to coordinate their efforts to restrain output and detect cheating, thereby reducing the temptation for participating firms to cheat:

1. *A small number of firms in the industry*. If an industry consists of only a few firms, it is easier to assess how much each firm should restrain production to yield the monopoly output and hence maximum industry profits. In addition, it is easier for each cartel member to monitor other firms' output rates for signs of cheating. For instance, when a cartel has only a few members, they might agree to keep their sales a certain percentage below pre-cartel levels. Failure to do so could be regarded as evidence of cheating.
2. *Relatively undifferentiated products*. If cartel members sell nearly homogeneous products, it is easier for them to agree on how much each firm should reduce its production. In contrast, if each firm sells a highly differentiated product, then

some members can reasonably claim that the prices of their products should differ from the prices of other firms' products to reflect differences in costs of production. Thus, a firm with a differentiated product can reasonably claim that it is selling at a lower price for its differentiated good because its good is less valued by consumers—when in fact the firm may simply be using this claim as an excuse to cheat on the cartel agreement.

3. *Easily observable prices*. Naturally, one way to make sure that a producer is abiding by a cartel agreement is to look at the prices at which it actually sells its output. If the terms of industry transactions are publicly available, cartel members can more readily spot a firm's efforts to cheat.
4. *Little variation in prices*. If the industry's market is susceptible to frequent shifts in demand for firms' products or in prices of key inputs, the firms' prices will tend to fluctuate. Establishing a cartel agreement and monitoring cheating consequently will be more difficult. Hence, stable demand and cost conditions help a cartel form and continue to operate effectively.

Sometimes cartels prevent cheating on prices by using mechanisms that masquerade as contracts that are favorable to buyers. For example, all members of a cartel might agree to offer buyers contracts that permit a buyer to switch to another seller if that seller offers the product at a lower price. Naturally, if a customer can provide evidence that a lower price is available from another firm claiming to participate in the cartel, this fact would constitute evidence that the other firm is cheating. In this way, cartel members use their customers to police other cartel participants!

Why Cartel Agreements Usually Break Down

Studies have shown that it is very rare for cartel agreements to last more than 10 years. In many cases, cartel agreements break down more quickly than that. Even industries that usually satisfy the four conditions listed above have difficulty keeping cartels together over time.

One reason that cartels tend to break down is that the economic profits that existing firms obtain from holding prices above competitive levels provide an incentive for new firms to enter the market. Effectively, market entrants can earn profits by acting as a cheating cartel firm would behave. Their entry then provides incentives to cartel members to reduce their own prices and boost their production, and ultimately the cartel unravels.

Variations in overall economic activity also tend to make cartels unsustainable. During general business downturns, market demands tend to decline across all industries as consumers' incomes fall. So do profits of firms participating in a cartel. This increases the incentive for individual firms to cheat on a cartel agreement.

Do U.S. government agencies help perpetuate a securities-rating cartel?

POLICY EXAMPLE The U.S. Government Protects an Oligopoly—Or Is It a Cartel?

When the U.S. financial meltdown occurred at the end of the 2000s, many people were taken by surprise when securities rated as having low risk turned out to be highly risky—so risky that their market values fell very close to zero. The risk ratings of all of the securities traded in U.S. financial markets were assigned by three firms: Fitch, Moody's, or Standard & Poor's. All three firms assigned essentially identical risk ratings to similar securities, and they charged almost identical fees to do so—characteristics that some critics have alleged amounted to cartel-like behavior.

Yet after the financial crash of the late 2000s, no new ratings firms entered the securities-rating industry. The reason was that U.S. government agencies maintain rules that protect the three incumbent ratings firms from competition. For instance, the Federal Reserve will not allow collateral—securities pledged to back up loans—offered by financial institutions on interbank loans to be rated by firms *other* than Fitch, Moody's, or Standard & Poor's. Likewise, the U.S. Securities and Exchange Commission will allow only securities rated by these firms—which it has designated Nationally Recognized Statistical Rating Organizations—to be held by mutual funds and brokerage firms. Thus, agencies of the U.S. government have erected high barriers that have perpetuated an oligopoly, which some observers allege functions as a cartel.

FOR CRITICAL ANALYSIS

Why is the existence of high barriers to entry important to perpetuating a cartel arrangement?

QUICK QUIZ See page 593 for the answers. Review concepts from this section in MyEconLab.

A __________ is a group of firms in an industry that agree to set common prices and output quotas to restrict competition.

Characteristics of an industry that make it more likely that firms can coordinate efforts to restrain output and earn economic profits are a __________ number of firms, relatively __________ products, easily __________ prices, and little __________ in prices.

Factors that contribute to the breakdown of a cartel are the __________ of firms seeking the economic profits earned by the cartel members and __________ in economic activity.

Network Effects

Network effect
A situation in which a consumer's willingness to purchase a good or service is influenced by how many others also buy or have bought the item.

A feature sometimes present in oligopolistic industries is **network effects,** or situations in which a consumer's willingness to use an item depends on how many others use it. Commonplace examples are telephones and fax machines. Ownership of a phone or fax machine is not particularly useful if no one else has one, but once a number of people own a phone or fax machine, the benefits that others gain from consuming these devices increases.

In like manner, people who commonly work on joint projects within a network of fellow employees, consultants, or clients naturally find it useful to share computer files. Trading digital files is an easier process if all use common spreadsheet programs and office productivity software. The benefit that each person receives from using spreadsheet programs and office productivity software increases when others use the same software.

Network Effects and Market Feedback

Industries in which firms produce goods or services subject to network effects can experience sudden surges in growth, but the fortunes of such industries can also undergo significant and sometimes sudden reversals.

Positive market feedback
A tendency for a good or service to come into favor with additional consumers because other consumers have chosen to buy the item.

POSITIVE MARKET FEEDBACK When network effects are an important characteristic of an industry's product, an industry can experience **positive market feedback.** This is the potential for a network effect to arise when an industry's product catches on with consumers. Increased use of the product by some consumers then induces other consumers to purchase the product.

Positive market feedback can affect the prospects of an entire industry. The market for Internet service provider (ISP) servers is an example. The growth of this industry has roughly paralleled the rapid growth of Internet servers worldwide. Undoubtedly, positive market feedback resulting from network effects associated with Internet communications and interactions resulted in additional people desiring to obtain access to the Internet.

Negative market feedback
A tendency for a good or service to fall out of favor with more consumers because other consumers have stopped purchasing the item.

NEGATIVE MARKET FEEDBACK Network effects can also result in **negative market feedback,** in which a speedy downward spiral of product sales occurs for a product subject to network effects. If a sufficient number of consumers cut back on their use of the product, others are induced to reduce their consumption as well, and the product can rapidly become a "has-been."

An example of an industry that has experienced negative market feedback of late is the telecommunications industry. Traditional telecommunications firms such as AT&T, WorldCom, and Sprint experienced positive market feedback during the late 1980s and early 1990s as cellphones and fax machines proliferated and individuals and firms began making long-distance phone calls from cellphones or via fax machines. Since the mid-1990s, as more people have acquired Internet access via cable and satellite Internet service providers, e-mail communications and e-mail document attachments have supplanted large volumes of phone and fax communications. For the telecommunications industry, the greater use of e-mail and e-mail attachments by some individuals induced others to follow suit. This resulted in negative market feedback that reduced the overall demand for traditional long-distance phone services.

Network Effects and Industry Concentration

In some industries, a few firms can potentially reap most of the benefits of positive market feedback. Suppose that firms in an industry sell differentiated products that are subject to network effects. If the products of two or three firms catch on, these firms will capture the bulk of the sales due to industry network effects.

A good example is the market for online auction services. An individual is more likely to use the services of an auction site if there is a significant likelihood that many other potential buyers or sellers also trade items at that site. Hence, there is a network effect present in the online auction industry, in which eBay and Overstock account for more than 80 percent of total sales. eBay in particular has experienced positive market feedback, and its share of sales of online auction services has increased to more than 50 percent.

Consequently, in an industry that produces and sells products subject to network effects, a small number of firms may be able to secure the bulk of the payoffs resulting from positive market feedback. In such an industry, oligopoly is likely to emerge as the prevailing market structure.

QUICK QUIZ See page 593 for the answers. Review concepts from this section in MyEconLab.

__________ effects exist when a consumer's demand for an item depends in part on how many other consumers also use the product.

__________ market feedback arises if consumption of a product by a sufficient number of individuals induces others to purchase it. __________ market feedback can take place if a falloff in usage of a product by some consumers causes others to stop purchasing the item.

In an industry with differentiated products subject to **network effects,** an oligopoly may arise if a few firms can reap most of the sales __________ resulting from __________ market feedback.

Product Compatibility in Multiproduct Oligopolies Facing Network Effects

In addition to helping make industries more concentrated, network effects influence decisions that firms make regarding **product compatibility.** That is, firms must take into account the longer-term implications of network effects when deciding whether to offer products that function when used together with complementary products of competitors.

Product compatibility The capability of a product sold by one firm to function together with another firm's complementary product.

Why Firms Face Product Compatibility Issues

Should a company share the computer code for its new office productivity software program with another software producer so that consumers will be able to use either firm's program, separately or together? Is the answer to this question altered if both companies sell hardware products that consumers regard as complements to their software products? How does the potential existence of network effects further complicate the issue? In today's information-technology-intensive economy, a growing number of firms must address these kinds of questions regularly.

THE BETA-VHS BATTLE Questions about product compatibility are not new. More than two decades ago, when the possibility of recording television shows and renting and selling movies for home viewing was a new idea, firms battled over two videocassette formats known as Beta and VHS. The Beta format was the brainchild of Sony, which also offered a line of videocassette recorders and players compatible only with the Beta videocassette format. In the meantime, another firm, JVC, developed the rival VHS format, a bulkier videocassette that could hold more videotape. VHS videocassettes had room for longer movies and more recorded programming than Beta videocassettes.

Soon people were sharing lengthy VHS videotapes of children at play, complete sporting events, and the like with friends and relatives—as long as they had access to VHS players, which other consumer electronics firms were willing to produce. Within a few years, Sony realized that it had erred by opting to make its products compatible only with Beta videocassettes. Sony's decision had harmed its sales of video recorders and players and, ultimately, its sales of videocassettes. Eventually, Sony discontinued the production of all Beta-format products and switched to the VHS format.

WHY PRODUCT COMPATIBILITY MATTERS The Beta-VHS format battle involved three key economic features. First, the products involved—lines of videocassettes, recorders, players, and related accessories—were items that consumers regarded as *complementary*. Second, these complementary goods were manufactured and sold by **multiproduct firms,** or firms that produce more than one product. Third, network effects were present. Because people shared their videotapes, the fact that most people preferred the VHS longer-play format led others to prefer VHS over Beta as well.

Multiproduct firm
A firm that produces and sells two or more different items.

These features figure in many interactions in oligopolistic industries today, as new information technologies have led to the development of many complementary products sold by multiproduct firms and subject to network effects. In such situations, firms face a crucial product compatibility issue. Should a firm that produces two or more products that consumers regard as complements sell each one in a form that allows consumers to use the products only as a set? Or should the firm sell the items in a form that permits consumers to utilize each product individually, perhaps in conjunction with a complementary product offered by a competing firm?

DIFFERENT COMPATIBILITY DECISIONS, DIFFERENT PAYOFFS In the battle between Beta and VHS formats, Sony opted for incompatibility with an intent to earn higher economic profits. What actually happened was that the demand for its VHS-incompatible products eventually disappeared as consumers substituted away from Beta videocassettes into VHS videocassettes. Consequently, Sony's profits from its video-related businesses plummeted, and the firm ultimately had to completely abandon its Beta-format video product line.

Does this mean that multiproduct firms should always make complementary products compatible with those of other firms? The answer is no. Sometimes firms lose, as Sony did, from making complementary products incompatible with those offered by other firms. Other times, however, firms reap exactly the same types of gains that Sony sought. Consider, for instance, Apple's experience with its iPod and iPad products since the early 2000s. Apple offered a number of complementary products, such as iTunes downloadable music products, downloadable videos, and various accessories, in forms that were incompatible with products sold by other firms. In contrast to Sony, Apple boosted its profits by making its complementary products incompatible with those of its competitors.

Product Compatibility and Network Effects

The fact that Sony and Apple experienced such different outcomes indicates that multiproduct firms could experience either losses or gains by offering their products in forms that are incompatible with those sold by competing firms. Before we consider how firms' product compatibility choices affect oligopoly outcomes, let's consider why network effects matter to individual firms.

HOW A FIRM CAN GAIN FROM OPTING FOR INCOMPATIBILITY To see how a multiproduct firm might gain from making the complementary products it sells incompatible with those of competitors, again consider Apple's strategy of intentionally making its iPod-related product line incompatible with many other items sold by competitors. Alongside the iPod, Apple—or firms that paid Apple licensing royalties—offered a variety of complementary speaker systems, memory storage devices, and accessories.

For Apple, the main objective of opting for incompatibility was to sharply differentiate its own line of products. This tended to reduce price elasticities of demand for Apple's complementary product set. In addition, when its iPod-related products experienced positive market feedback, demand for these products increased. Consequently, Apple was able to charge higher prices for its entire line of complementary iPod products, and the firm's profits soared.

HOW A FIRM CAN LOSE FROM MAKING INCOMPATIBLE PRODUCTS Given how well product incompatibility turned out for Apple, why did things go wrong for Sony back in the days of videocassettes? After all, Sony also sought to differentiate its complementary Beta video products by making them incompatible with the products offered by competing firms.

The answer is that whereas Apple experienced positive market feedback in the downloadable-media industry, Sony's Beta-format video products suffered *negative* market feedback in the videocassette industry. Sony certainly succeeded in differentiating its products by making them incompatible with those offered by competitors. As more consumers opted for the larger-capacity VHS videocassettes, however, a bandwagon effect led other consumers to choose VHS as well, which led to a wave of substitutions away from Sony's Beta-format video products.

Product Compatibility, Oligopolies, and Prices

Of course, oligopolistic multiproduct firms cannot make choices about product compatibility in isolation from the decisions of their competitors. In light of their strategic dependence, they must also take into account the reactions of other firms.

HOW INDUSTRY PRODUCT INCOMPATIBILITY CAN EMERGE To see how *industry* outcomes with regard to product compatibility can differ, begin by taking a look at Figure 26-3 below. This figure displays a payoff matrix for an industry composed of two multiproduct firms, Firm 1 and Firm 2, which are contemplating offering

FIGURE 26-3 Payoffs Yielding a Product Format Conflict

If two firms face the depicted payoff matrix, known as a *Tweedle Dee–Tweedle Dum game* situation, Firm 1 expects to earn the highest profits if it adopts Format A, and Firm 2 anticipates earning the highest profits if it opts for Format B. Hence, the firms choose these incompatible product formats (the lower right-hand quadrant).

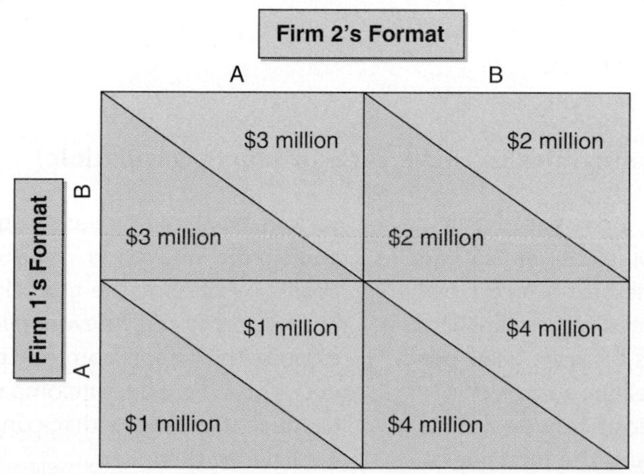

Firm 1's Format \ Firm 2's Format	A	B
B	$3 million (Firm 2) / $3 million (Firm 1)	$2 million (Firm 2) / $2 million (Firm 1)
A	$1 million (Firm 2) / $1 million (Firm 1)	$4 million (Firm 2) / $4 million (Firm 1)

sets of complementary products in one of two incompatible formats, Format A or Format B. We also assume that, at the outset, neither firm believes that network effects are likely to prove to be important to the industry in which they operate.

If both firms offer their products in Format A, each firm anticipates that the resulting homogeneity of their product lines will yield only $1 million in profits during the relevant period. If both firms offer their products in Format B, each expects to earn only $2 million in profits. If Firm 1 differentiates its product set by offering it in Format B while Firm 2 selects Format A, then each firm anticipates earning $3 million in profits. If Firm 1 uses Format A while Firm 2 selects Format B, then each firm expects to earn $4 million in profits. Firm 1, therefore, will opt for Format A, and Firm 2 will opt for Format B. Thus, the firms favor mutual incompatibility that differentiates their product sets and yields the highest anticipated profits. Each firm opts to go its separate way with its own different format. In game theory, the configuration of payoffs depicted in Figure 26-3 on the preceding page is often known as the *Tweedle Dee–Tweedle Dum game*, after the British nursery rhyme characters who choose to disagree.

You Are There

To contemplate a recent real-world product-compatibility issue, read **Apple Puts Adobe on Hold,** on page 588.

THE COMPLICATING IMPACTS OF NETWORK EFFECTS If both of the firms with the payoffs depicted in Figure 26-3 are correct in assuming that network effects are minuscule in their industry, then they can achieve anticipated profit levels. What happens if their shared supposition about network effects is incorrect? Once the presence of network effects is discovered, Firm 1 will fight for Format A to be the industry standard, and Firm 2 will battle for Format B. That is, *after* opting for an incompatible format, each firm actually is likely to expend more resources than previously anticipated to promote its format and achieve positive market feedback.

For instance, suppose that Firms 1 and 2 manufacture videogame systems and various complementary accessories. After the firms have opted for incompatible formats, consumers unexpectedly develop an interest in remote multiplayer gaming via the Internet. Each firm may respond by offering inducements to creators of multiplayer games to produce games compatible only with its selected format. Each may also "preannounce" forthcoming complementary products in its selected format that allow multiplayer gaming in an effort to discourage consumers from purchasing items in the other firm's product line. Either of these actions would push up each firm's operating costs. In addition, the firms may try to induce consumers to opt for their product formats by cutting prices, which would reduce the competitors' revenues.

Thus, during the current period, both firms likely will earn lower profits than they anticipated when they selected their formats. If one firm ultimately loses the battle to become the industry standard, its profits likely will plummet, much as Sony's did when it lost the Beta-VHS battle. The profits of its competitor will then rise, much as Apple's profits soared when its iPod product line became a predominant downloadable-media system since the early 2000s.

Why Not . . . require companies to make their products compatible?

Requiring product compatibility would not necessarily be in the best interest of consumers. For some types of applications, product compatibility is in the best interest of both firms and consumers, as evidenced by a relatively recent decision by all cellphone firms to make their products compatible with standardized cellphone battery chargers. For other types of applications, however, such as interfaces between smartphones and the Internet or various types of software, requiring product compatibility could stifle innovation. Firms hope to reap short-term profits by offering the next "killer app" and could lose the motivation to offer new applications if they could not exclude their apps from functioning on competing products. Thus, if product incompatibility were illegal, many product applications that consumers desire would not be available to them.

FIGURE 26-4 Payoffs Inducing Firms to Seek to Coordinate Product Formats

If two firms face the payoff matrix in panel (a), then both firms earn the highest profits by utilizing Format A, and they will gain by coordinating their choice of this compatible product format (the lower left-hand quadrant). In panel (b), both firms earn greater profits if their products have the same formats. Nevertheless, Firm 1 earns the highest profits if both firms opt for Format A, while Firm 2 earns the highest profits if both agree to use Format B. Hence, both parties wish to coordinate but may not agree on how to do so, which is why this game situation is called the *Battle of the Sexes*.

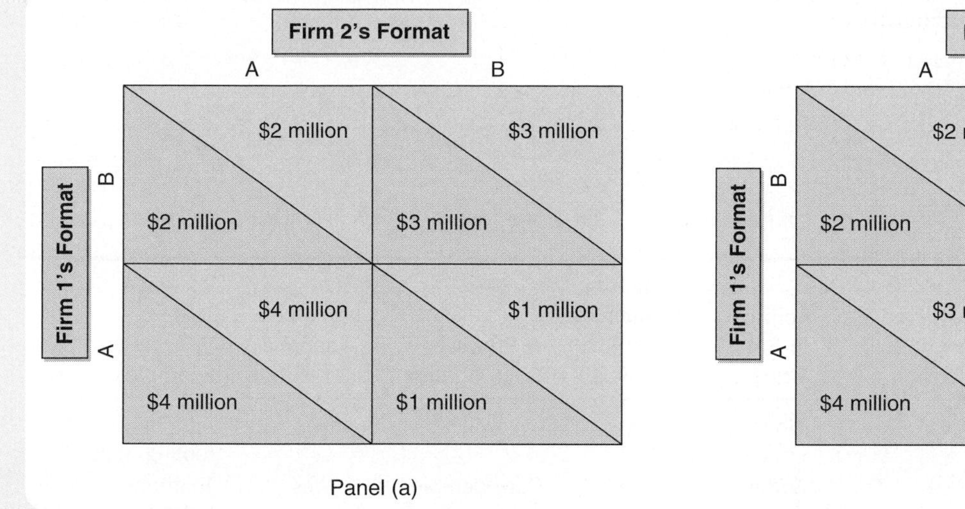

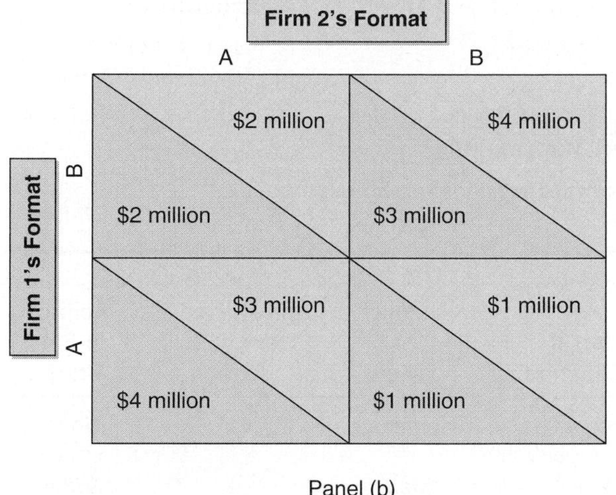

WHY PRODUCT COMPATIBILITY MIGHT BE AN INDUSTRY OUTCOME Now consider a different industry situation, depicted by the payoff matrices in Figure 26-4 above, in which Firm 1 and Firm 2 recognize in advance that network effects will result in one of the two formats winning out over the other with consumers. Panel (a) displays the simplest possible outcome, in which Firm 1 and Firm 2 each anticipate earning the most profits if both choose the same format. In this example, both firms earn the highest profits, $4 million during the relevant period, by mutually adopting the compatible Format A.

Panel (b) of Figure 26-4 depicts a more complicated situation. It is still true that both firms earn the most profits if they each choose the same format. Nevertheless, Firm 1 earns the highest profits if the firms mutually adopt the compatible Format A, but Firm 2 earns the highest profits if the firms agree to choose Format B. The fact that each party desires to coordinate with the other but agreement is not immediately forthcoming is why in game theory this payoff configuration is often referred to as the *Battle of the Sexes*.

As with the payoff matrix in Figure 26-3 on page 585, one result could be a battle between the firms over which format to adopt. Another possible result, given that both firms recognize the role of network effects, is that the firms might work together to develop one common format and arrange to share the profits.

QUICK QUIZ See page 593 for the answers. Review concepts from this section in MyEconLab.

Product compatibility is the capability of an item sold by one firm to function with another firm's __________ product.

Product compatibility is an industrywide issue for __________ firms selling two or more complementary products subject to __________ effects.

An industry battle between incompatible product formats can occur if competing firms selling sets of __________ products fail to take into account __________ effects.

Comparing Market Structures

Now that we have looked at perfect competition, pure monopoly, monopolistic competition, and oligopoly, we are in a position to compare the attributes of these four different market structures. We do this in summary form in Table 26-3 below, in which we compare the number of sellers, their ability to set price, and the degree of product differentiation and also give some examples of each of the four market structures.

TABLE 26-3

Comparing Market Structures

Market Structure	Number of Sellers	Unrestricted Entry and Exit	Ability to Set Price	Long-Run Economic Profits Possible	Product Differentiation	Nonprice Competition	Examples
Perfect competition	Numerous	Yes	None	No	None	None	Agriculture, roofing nails
Monopolistic competition	Many	Yes	Some	No	Considerable	Yes	Toothpaste, toilet paper, soap, retail trade
Oligopoly	Few	Partial	Some	Yes	Frequent	Yes	Recorded music, college textbooks
Pure monopoly	One	No (for entry)	Considerable	Yes	None (product is unique)	Yes	Some electric companies, some local telephone companies

You Are There

Apple Puts Adobe on Hold

Kevin Lynch, chief technology officer at Adobe Systems, is frustrated with Apple, the manufacturer of the Macintosh computer and the iPod, iPhone, and iPad devices. When Apple introduced the iPhone a few years earlier, the company would not make the iPhone compatible with Adobe's Flash video technology. At that time, Apple officials justified the decision by complaining that Adobe's Flash software was prone to "bugs" that had caused its Mac computers to crash frequently.

After years of effort to improve the Flash software, Lynch says that it is "ready to go" for use with Apple products, especially the company's new iPad. The only hurdle, Lynch indicates, is that Adobe "requires Apple's cooperation to get on the device." Nevertheless, to the dismay of Lynch and other Adobe executives, Apple has announced that for now it will not allow compatibility of the Flash software with the iPad. Adobe managers wonder if Apple's policy is aimed at preventing development of software applications that can operate on devices that compete with the iPhone and iPad. The main purpose of the Flash software is to allow videos to be viewed on digital devices, but in principle software developers could use Flash to design applications that could help competing devices function more like the iPhone or the iPad. Consequently, Lynch suspects that perhaps Apple never really intended to make its products compatible with Adobe's Flash software.

Critical Analysis Questions

1. Why would Adobe likely gain if Apple devices were compatible with Flash?
2. Why might it not be a profit-maximizing choice for Apple to make its digital devices compatible with Adobe's Flash software?

ISSUES & APPLICATIONS

More Companies Are "Going Vertical"

CONCEPTS APPLIED

- ▶ Vertical Mergers
- ▶ Oligopoly
- ▶ Strategic Dependence

Recently, there has been an upswing in vertical mergers, or mergers between firms that previously bought and sold items used as inputs. Vertical mergers cannot *create* oligopolies, but they often involve firms operating in oligopolistic industries.

Reversing a Prior Trend Toward Specialized Functions

During the late twentieth and early twenty-first centuries, companies often opted to specialize in particular tasks. Many firms shifted functions such as procuring raw materials and manufacturing to other companies and then specialized in assembling and distributing final products. Thus, steelmakers sold off mining operations in the 1980s. Automakers separated themselves from parts suppliers in the 1990s. In the 2000s, information technology companies specialized in making any one of the following: microchips, hardware, or software.

In recent years, however, there has been a movement back toward incorporating multiple functions within a single company. The result has been a wave of vertical mergers, such as those listed in Table 26-4 on the next page.

The Rationale for Vertical Mergers: Vertical Integration

Table 26-4 lists the reasons that the companies involved in large vertical mergers gave for combining their firms. Although each rationale is specific to a particular merger, a common theme is a desire to combine business operations to create what economists refer to as a *vertical integrated* structure. That is, the firms sought to integrate several different aspects of the production process within one firm instead of multiple firms.

Another common theme is that most of the companies that merged are in traditionally oligopolistic industries. These include staging and ticketing of events production, bottling of soft drinks, and large-scale manufacturing and distribution of vehicles, aircraft, and steel. Consequently, the companies' decisions to engage in vertical mergers reflected an understanding of strategic dependence vis-à-vis competitors in their industry. For example, PepsiCo's decision to merge with the company that bottles most of its soft drinks took into account likely reactions of its main competitors, Coca-Cola and Dr Pepper Snapple. Likewise, Boeing's decision to merge with a key manufacturer of aircraft components reflected Boeing's anticipation of the reaction of its primary competitor, Airbus. Like their choices of how much to produce and what prices to charge, these firms' decisions about mergers that vertically integrate their operations are strategically dependent on reactions of their competitors.

For Critical Analysis

1. How might a vertical merger help to reduce the costs of producing a final product and thereby give a firm a competitive edge over a competitor?
2. In principle, how could a vertical merger that removes a competitor's access to a supplier of raw materials or other required inputs potentially provide the merging firm with a competitive edge over that competitor?

Web Resources

1. For a brief discussion of possible rationales for vertical mergers, go to www.econtoday.com/ch26.
2. To learn about policy issues associated with vertical mergers, go to www.econtoday.com/ch26.

TABLE 26-4

Recent Vertical Mergers Involving Large Global Enterprises

Although each merger listed had its own particular rationale, all of the mergers resulted in the integration of various productive activities within a single firm.

Companies Merged	Year	Motivation for Vertical Merger
Ticketmaster–Live Nation	2010	Combine the functions of event promotion and ticketing.
PepsiCo–Pepsi Bottling	2010	Link the functions of soft-drink production and distribution.
Oracle–Sun Microsystems	2010	Integrate the production and sale of hardware and software.
GM–Delphi Automotive	2009	Combine the production of auto parts and final auto assembly.
Boeing–Vought Aircraft	2009	Join aircraft parts production and final aircraft assembly.
Apple–P.A. Semi	2008	Combine the production of microchips and computing devices.
Nucor–SHV North America	2008	Incorporate raw materials acquisition into production.

Research Project

Contrast a vertical merger with a horizontal merger, and explain why a vertical merger typically is less likely than a horizontal merger to directly reduce the degree of competition among firms selling the same product.

For more questions on this chapter's Issues & Applications, go to **MyEconLab**. In the Study Plan for this chapter, select Section N: News.

Here is what you should know after reading this chapter. **MyEconLab** will help you identify what you know, and where to go when you need to practice.

WHAT YOU SHOULD KNOW		WHERE TO GO TO PRACTICE
The Fundamental Characteristics of Oligopoly Economies of scale, barriers to entry, and horizontal mergers among firms that sell similar products can result in an oligopoly, a situation in which a few firms produce most of an industry's output. To measure the extent to which a few firms account for an industry's production and sales, economists calculate concentration ratios, which are the percentages of total sales or production by the top few firms. Strategic dependence is an important characteristic of oligopoly. One firm's decisions concerning price, product quality, or advertising can bring about responses by other firms.	oligopoly, 574 strategic dependence, 574 vertical merger, 575 horizontal merger, 575 concentration ratio, 575	• **MyEconLab** Study Plan 26.1 • Audio introduction to Chapter 26 • Economics Video: Record Job Losses
Applying Game Theory to Evaluate the Pricing Strategies of Oligopolistic Firms Game theory is the analytical framework used to evaluate how two or more firms compete for payoffs that depend on the strategies that others employ.	reaction function, 577 game theory, 577 cooperative game, 577 noncooperative game, 577 zero-sum game, 577	• **MyEconLab** Study Plan 26.2 • Video: Opportunistic Behavior • Animated Figures 26-1, 26-2

MyEconLab continued

WHAT YOU SHOULD KNOW		WHERE TO GO TO PRACTICE
When firms work together for a common objective such as maximizing industry profits, they participate in cooperative games, but when they cannot work together, they engage in noncooperative games. One important type of game is the prisoners' dilemma, in which the inability to cooperate in determining prices of their products can cause firms to choose lower prices than they otherwise would prefer.	negative-sum game, 577 positive-sum game, 577 strategy, 577 dominant strategies, 578 prisoners' dilemma, 578 payoff matrix, 578 opportunistic behavior, 579 tit-for-tat strategic behavior, 579 **KEY FIGURES** Figure 26-1, 578 Figure 26-2, 579	
Industry Features That Contribute to or Detract from Efforts to Form a Cartel A cartel is an organization of firms in an industry that collude to earn economic profits by producing a combined output consistent with monopoly profit maximization. Four conditions make a collusive cartel agreement easier to create and enforce: (1) a small number of firms in the industry, (2) relatively undifferentiated products, (3) easily observable prices, and (4) little variation in prices.	cartel, 580	• **MyEconLab** Study Plan 26.3
Why Network Effects and Market Feedback Encourage Oligopoly Network effects arise when a consumer's demand for an item is affected by how many other consumers also use it. There is positive market feedback when enough people consume a product to induce others to do so. Negative market feedback occurs when decreased purchases of an item by some consumers give others an incentive to stop buying it. Oligopoly can develop because a few firms may be able to capture most of the growth in demand induced by positive market feedback.	network effect, 582 positive market feedback, 582 negative market feedback, 582	• **MyEconLab** Study Plan 26.4 • Video: Price Leadership and Price Wars
Why Multiproduct Firms Selling Complementary Sets of Products May or May Not Wish for Their Products to Be Compatible with Those of Competitors Product compatibility refers to the capability of an item sold by one firm to function with another firm's complementary product. A multiproduct firm selling two or more complementary products may opt for incompatibility with competing firms' products if it anticipates that lack of compatibility will differentiate its product set and maximize its profits.	product compatibility, 583 multiproduct firm, 584 **KEY TABLE** Table 26-3, 588	• **MyEconLab** Study Plans 26.5, 26.6 • Animated Table 26-3

Log in to MyEconLab, take a chapter test, and get a personalized Study Plan that tells you which concepts you understand and which ones you need to review. From there, MyEconLab will give you further practice, tutorials, animations, videos, and guided solutions.
Log in to www.myeconlab.com

PROBLEMS

All problems are assignable in myeconlab. *Answers to odd-numbered problems appear at the back of the book.*

26-1. Suppose that the distribution of sales within an industry is as shown in the table.

Firm	Share of Total Market Sales
A	15%
B	14
C	12
D	11
E	10
F	10
G	8
H	7
All others	13
Total	100%

a. What is the four-firm concentration ratio for this industry?

b. What is the eight-firm concentration ratio for this industry?

26-2. The table below shows recent worldwide market shares of producers of inkjet printers.

Firm	Share of Worldwide Market Sales
Brother	3%
Canon	17
Dell	6
Epson	18
Hewlett-Packard	41
Lexmark	13
Samsung	1
Other	1

a. In this year, what was the four-firm concentration ratio in the inkjet-printer industry?

b. In this year, what was the seven-firm concentration ratio in the inkjet-printer industry?

26-3. Characterize each of the following as a positive-sum game, a zero-sum game, or a negative-sum game.

a. Office workers contribute $10 each to a pool of funds, and whoever best predicts the winners in a professional sports playoff wins the entire sum.

b. After three years of fighting with large losses of human lives and materiél, neither nation involved in a war is any closer to its objective than it was before the war began.

c. Two collectors who previously owned incomplete and nearly worthless sets of trading cards exchange several cards, and as a result both end up with completed sets with significant market value.

26-4. Characterize each of the following as a positive-sum game, a zero-sum game, or a negative-sum game.

a. You play a card game in your dorm room with three other students. Each player brings $5 to the game to bet on the outcome, winner take all.

b. Two nations exchange goods in a mutually beneficial transaction.

c. A thousand people buy $1 lottery tickets with a single payoff of $800.

26-5. Last weekend, Bob attended the university football game. At the opening kickoff, the crowd stood up. Bob therefore realized that he would have to stand up as well to see the game. For the crowd (not the football team), explain the outcomes of a cooperative game and a noncooperative game. Explain what Bob's "tit-for-tat strategic behavior" would be if he wished to see the game.

26-6. Consider two strategically dependent firms in an oligopolistic industry, Firm A and Firm B. Firm A knows that if it offers extended warranties on its products but Firm B does not, it will earn $6 million in profits, and Firm B will earn $2 million. Likewise, Firm B knows that if it offers extended warranties but Firm A does not, it will earn $6 million in profits, and Firm A will earn $2 million. The two firms know that if they both offer extended warranties on their products, each will earn $3 million in profits. Finally, the two firms know that if neither offers extended warranties, each will earn $5 million in profits.

a. Set up a payoff matrix that fits the situation faced by these two firms.

b. What is the dominant strategy for each firm in this situation? Explain.

26-7. Take a look back at the data regarding the inkjet-printer industry in Problem 26-2, and answer the following questions.

a. Suppose that consumer demands for inkjet printers, the prices of which are readily observable in office supply outlets and at Internet sites, are growing at a stable pace. Discuss whether circumstances are favorable to an effort by firms in this industry to form a cartel.

b. If the firms successfully establish a cartel, why will there naturally be pressures for the cartel to break down, either from within or from outside?

26-8. Consider the following payoff matrix. Firm 1 and Firm 2 are seeking to choose between Format A and Format B for their products, under the assumption that there are *not* any network effects. Will they desire to produce and sell compatible product formats?

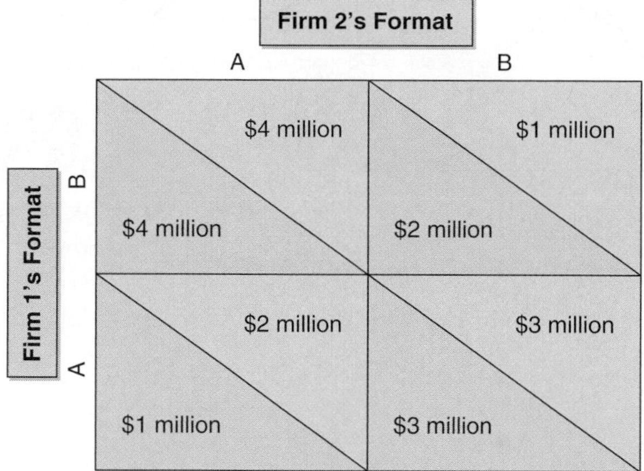

26-9. Consider the payoff matrix at the right, in which Firm 1 and Firm 2 seek to choose between product Format A and Format B, under the assumption that there *are* network effects. Will they desire to produce and sell compatible product formats?

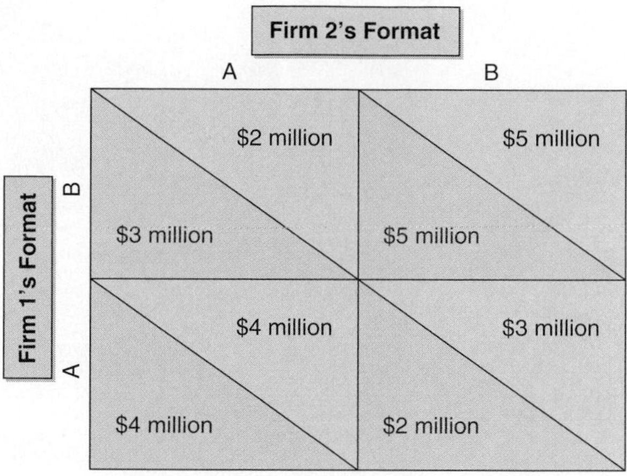

26-10. Explain why network effects can cause the demand for a product *either* to expand *or* to contract relative to what it would be if there were no network effects.

26-11. List three products that you think are subject to network effects. For each product, indicate whether, in your view, all or just a few firms within the industry that produces each product experience market feedback effects. In your view, are any market feedback effects in these industries currently positive or negative?

ECONOMICS ON THE NET

Current Concentration Ratios in U.S. Manufacturing Industries As you learned in this chapter, economists sometimes use concentration ratios to evaluate whether industries are oligopolies. In this application, you will make your own determination using the most recent data available.

Title: Concentration Ratios in Manufacturing

Navigation: Follow the link at **www.econtoday.com/ch26** to get to the U.S. Census Bureau's report on Concentration Ratios in Manufacturing.

Application Answer the following questions.

1. Select the report for the most recent year. Find the four-firm concentration ratios for the following industries: fluid milk (311511), women's and girls' cut & sew dresses (315233), envelopes (322232), electronic computers (334111).
2. Which industries are characterized by a high level of competition? Which industries are characterized by a low level of competition? Which industries qualify as oligopolies?
3. Name some of the firms that operate in the industries that qualify as oligopolies.

For Group Study and Analysis Discuss whether the four-firm concentration ratio is a good measure of competition. Consider some of the firms you named in item 3. Do you consider these firms to be "competitive" in their pricing and output decisions? Consider the four-firm concentration ratio for ready-mix concrete (327320). Do you think that on a local basis, this industry is competitive? Why or why not?

ANSWERS TO QUICK QUIZZES

p. 577: (i) small . . . interdependent; (ii) economies . . . mergers; (iii) Vertical; (iv) Horizontal; (v) percentage . . . sales

p. 580: (i) reaction . . . strategic; (ii) zero . . . negative . . . positive; (iii) dominant

p. 582: (i) cartel; (ii) small . . . undifferentiated . . . observable . . . variation; (iii) entry . . . variations

p. 583: (i) Network; (ii) Positive . . . Negative; (iii) gains . . . positive

p. 587: (i) complementary; (ii) multiproduct . . . network; (iii) complementary . . . network

27 Regulation and Antitrust Policy in a Globalized Economy

Recently, the Food and Drug Administration (FDA) and the U.S. Department of Agriculture (USDA) asked Congress to increase their operating budgets. Among the justifications they offered was that Congress has assigned the agencies to enforce new food-labeling regulations. Congress has ordered the USDA to administer a new rule requiring large supermarkets to label all fruit, vegetable, and meat items with their nation of origin. Congress has also ordered the FDA to issue a regulation requiring restaurant chains to add calorie counts to their menus. The USDA and the FDA argued that enforcing these regulations would boost the agencies' operating costs. Of course, supermarkets and restaurants faced costs of complying with the new regulations, but the agencies do not have to pay those expenses. In this chapter, you will learn about both the costs and the benefits of government regulation.

LEARNING OBJECTIVES

After reading this chapter, you should be able to:

- Distinguish between economic regulation and social regulation
- Recognize the practical difficulties in regulating the prices charged by natural monopolies
- Explain the main rationales for regulation of industries that are not inherently monopolistic
- Identify alternative theories aimed at explaining the behavior of regulators
- Understand the foundations of antitrust laws and regulations
- Discuss basic issues in enforcing antitrust laws

myeconlab

MyEconLab helps you master each objective and study more efficiently. See end of chapter for details.

Did You Know That ?

in a recent year not only did 285 laws enacted by the U.S. Congress go into effect, but U.S. federal agencies also imposed 3,830 new regulatory rules? Many of these rules are intended to induce U.S. industries to operate in ways that government regulators contend will promote economic efficiency and benefit consumers. Nevertheless, some critics have estimated that the annual cost of complying with these regulations exceeds $1 trillion. Consequently, how regulations and other forms of government oversight *should act* to promote greater economic efficiency and how they *actually act* are important topics for understanding how every economy works. Nevertheless, before you can begin your study of the economic effects of regulation, it is important to understand the various ways in which the government oversees the activities of U.S. businesses.

Forms of Industry Regulation

The U.S. government began regulating social and economic activity early in the nation's history. The amount of government regulation began increasing in the twentieth century and has grown considerably since 1970. Figure 27-1 below displays two common measures of regulation in the United States. Panel (a) shows that regulatory spending by federal agencies (in 2005 dollars) has generally trended upward since 1970 and has risen considerably since 2000. New national security regulations following the 2001 terrorist attacks in New York City and Washington, D.C., have fueled a significant portion of this growth. The remainder of the increase in spending is related to a general upswing in regulatory enforcement by the federal government during this period. Panel (b) of Figure 27-1 depicts the number of pages in the *Federal Register*, a government publication that lists all new regulatory rules. According to this measure, the scope of new federal regulations increased sharply during the 1970s, dropped off in the 1980s, and has generally increased since then.

There are two basic types of government regulation. One is *economic regulation* of natural monopolies and of specific nonmonopolistic industries. For instance, some state

FIGURE 27-1 Regulation on the Rise

Panel (a) shows that federal government regulatory spending is now more than $50 billion per year. State and local spending is not shown. As panel (b) shows, the number of pages in the *Federal Register* per year rose sharply in the 1970s, dropped off somewhat in the 1980s, and then began to rise once more.

Sources: Institute for University Studies; *Federal Register*, various issues.

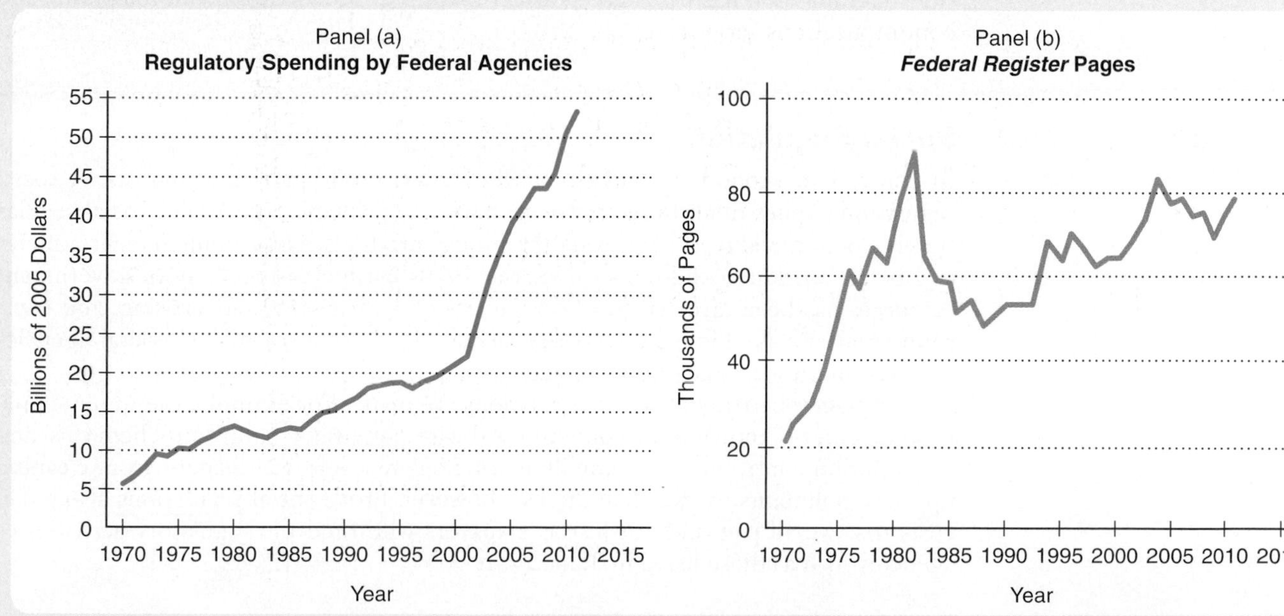

commissions regulate the prices and quality of services provided by electric power companies, which are considered natural monopolies that experience lower long-run average costs as their output increases. Financial services industries and interstate transportation industries are examples of nonmonopolistic industries that are subjected to considerable government regulation. The other form of government regulation is *social regulation*, which covers all industries. Examples include various occupational, health, and safety rules that federal and state governments impose on most businesses.

Economic Regulation

Initially, most economic regulation in the United States was aimed at controlling prices in industries considered to be natural monopolies. Over time, federal and state governments have also sought to influence the characteristics of products or processes of firms in a variety of industries without inherently monopolistic features.

REGULATION OF NATURAL MONOPOLIES The regulation of natural monopolies has tended to emphasize restrictions on product prices. Various public utility commissions throughout the United States regulate the rates (prices) of electrical utility companies and some telephone operating companies. This *rate regulation*, as it is usually called, officially has been aimed at preventing such industries from earning monopoly profits.

REGULATION OF NONMONOPOLISTIC INDUSTRIES The prices charged by firms in many other industries that do not have steadily declining long-run average costs, such as financial services industries, have also been subjected to regulations. Every state in the United States, for instance, has a government agency devoted to regulating the prices that insurance companies charge.

More broadly, government regulations establish rules pertaining to production, product (or service) features, and entry and exit within a number of specific nonmonopolistic industries. The federal government is heavily involved, for instance, in regulating the securities, banking, transportation, and communications industries. The Securities and Exchange Commission regulates securities markets. The Federal Reserve, Office of the Comptroller of the Currency, and Federal Deposit Insurance Corporation regulate commercial banks and savings banks. The National Credit Union Administration supervises credit unions. The Federal Aviation Administration supervises the airline industry, and the Federal Motor Carrier Safety Administration regulates the trucking industry. The Federal Communications Commission has oversight powers relating to broadcasting and telephone and communications services.

Social Regulation

In contrast to economic regulation, which covers only particular industries, social regulation applies to all firms in the economy. In principle, the aim of social regulation is a better quality of life through improved products, a less polluted environment, and better working conditions. Since the 1970s, an increasing array of government resources has been directed toward regulating product safety, advertising, and environmental effects. Table 27-1 on the facing page lists some major federal agencies involved in these broad regulatory activities.

The *possible* benefits of social regulations are many. For example, the water supply in some cities is known to be contaminated with potentially hazardous chemicals, and air pollution contributes to many illnesses. Society might well benefit from cleaning up these pollutants. As we shall discuss, however, broad social regulations also entail costs that we all pay, and not just as taxpayers who fund the regulatory activities of agencies such as those listed in Table 27-1.

TABLE 27-1

Federal Agencies Engaged in Social Regulation

Agency	Jurisdiction	Date Formed	Major Regulatory Functions
Federal Trade Commission (FTC)	Product markets	1914	Responsible for preventing businesses from engaging in misleading advertising, unfair trade practices, and monopolistic actions, as well as for protecting consumer rights.
Food and Drug Administration (FDA)	Food and pharmaceuticals	1938	Regulates the quality and safety of foods, health and medical products, pharmaceuticals, cosmetics, and animal feed.
Equal Employment Opportunity Commission (EEOC)	Labor markets	1964	Investigates complaints of discrimination based on race, religion, gender, or age in hiring, promotion, firing, wages, testing, and all other conditions of employment.
Environmental Protection Agency (EPA)	Environment	1970	Develops and enforces environmental standards for air, water, waste, and noise.
Occupational Safety and Health Administration (OSHA)	Health and safety	1970	Regulates workplace safety and health conditions.
Consumer Product Safety Commission (CPSC)	Consumer product safety	1972	Responsible for protecting consumers from products posing fire, electrical, chemical, or mechanical hazards or dangers to children.
Mining Enforcement and Safety Administration	Mining and oil drilling safety	1973	Establishes and enforces operational safety rules for mines and oil rigs.

QUICK QUIZ See page 617 for the answers. **Review concepts from this section in MyEconLab.**

__________ regulation applies to specific industries, whereas __________ regulation applies to businesses throughout the economy.

Governments commonly regulate the prices and quality of services provided by electric, gas, and other utilities, which traditionally have been considered __________ monopolies.

Governments also single out various nonmonopolistic industries, such as the financial and transportation industries, for special forms of __________ regulation.

Among the common forms of __________ regulation covering all industries are the occupational, health, and safety rules that federal and state governments impose on producers.

Regulating Natural Monopolies

At one time, much government regulation of business purportedly aimed to solve the so-called monopoly problem. Of particular concern was implementing appropriate regulations for natural monopolies.

The Theory of Natural Monopoly Regulation

Recall from Chapter 24 that a natural monopoly arises whenever a single firm can produce all of an industry's output at a lower per-unit cost than other firms attempting to produce less than total industry output. In a natural monopoly, therefore, economies of large-scale production exist, leading to a single-firm industry.

THE UNREGULATED NATURAL MONOPOLY Like any other firm, an unregulated natural monopolist will produce to the point at which marginal revenue equals marginal cost. Panel (a) of Figure 27-2 below depicts a situation in which a monopolist faces the market demand curve, *D*, and the marginal revenue curve, MR. The monopolist searches along the demand curve for the profit-maximizing price and quantity. The profit-maximizing quantity is at point *A*, at which the marginal revenue curve crosses the long-run marginal cost curve, LMC, and the unregulated monopolist maximizes profits by producing the quantity Q_m. Consumers are willing and able to pay the price per unit P_m for this quantity at point *F*. This price is above marginal cost, so it leads to a socially inefficient allocation of resources by restricting production to a rate below that at which price equals marginal cost.

THE IMPRACTICALITY OF MARGINAL COST PRICING What would happen if the government were to require the monopolist in Figure 27-2 below to produce to the point at which price equals marginal cost, which is point *B* in panel (b)? Then it would produce

FIGURE 27-2 Profit Maximization and Regulation Through Marginal Cost Pricing

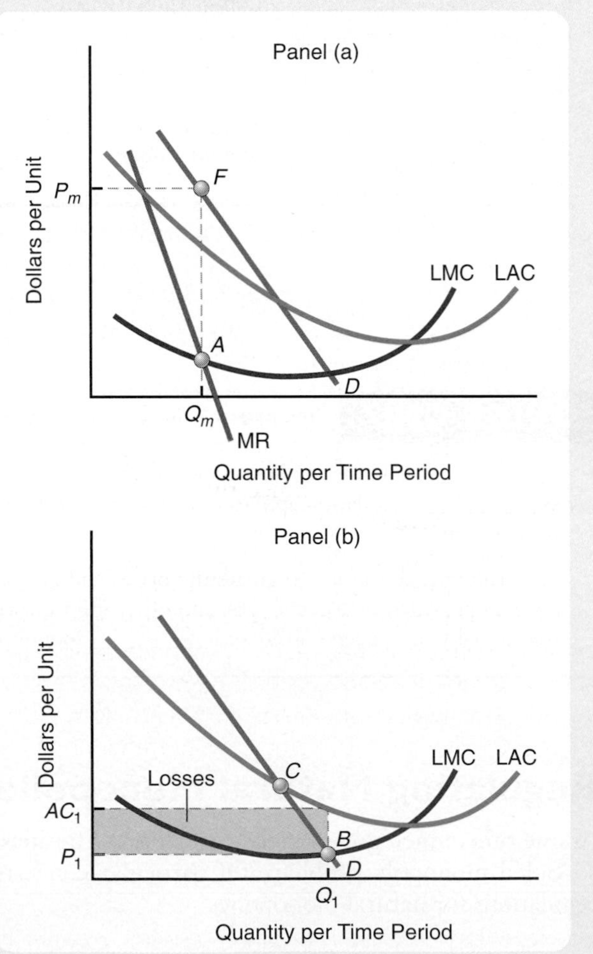

The profit-maximizing natural monopolist here would produce at the point in panel (a) at which marginal costs equal marginal revenue—that is, at point *A*, which gives the quantity of production Q_m. The per-unit price charged would be P_m at point *F*, which is the price consumers would be willing to pay for the quantity produced. If a regulatory commission attempted to regulate natural monopolies so that price equaled long-run marginal cost, the commission would make the monopolist set production at the point where the long-run marginal cost (LMC) curve intersects the demand schedule. This is shown in panel (b). The quantity produced would be Q_1, and the per-unit price would be P_1. Average costs at output rate Q_1 are equal to AC_1, however. Losses would ensue, equal to the shaded area. It would be self-defeating for a regulatory commission to force a natural monopolist to produce at an output rate at which MC $=$ *P* without subsidizing some of its costs because losses would eventually drive the natural monopolist out of business.

a larger output rate, Q_1. Consumers, however, would pay only the price per unit P_1 for this quantity, which would be less than the average cost of producing this output rate, AC_1. Consequently, requiring the monopolist to engage in marginal cost pricing would yield a loss for the firm equal to the shaded rectangular area in panel (b). The profit-maximizing monopolist would go out of business rather than face such regulation.

AVERAGE COST PRICING Regulators cannot practically force a natural monopolist to engage in marginal cost pricing. Thus, regulation of natural monopolies has often taken the form of allowing the firm to set price at the point at which the long-run average cost (LAC) curve intersects the demand curve. In panel (b) of Figure 27-2 on the facing page, this is point *C*. In this situation, the regulator forces the firm to engage in *average cost pricing*, with average cost including what the regulators deem a "fair" rate of return on investment. For instance, a regulator might impose **cost-of-service regulation,** which requires a natural monopoly to charge only prices that reflect the actual average cost of providing products to consumers. Alternatively, although in a similar vein, a regulator might use **rate-of-return regulation,** which allows firms to set prices that ensure a normal return on investment.

Cost-of-service regulation
Regulation that allows prices to reflect only the actual average cost of production and no monopoly profits.

Rate-of-return regulation
Regulation that seeks to keep the rate of return in an industry at a competitive level by not allowing prices that would produce economic profits.

Natural Monopolies No More?

For years, the electricity, natural gas, and telecommunications industries have been subjected to regulations intended to induce firms in these industries to engage in average cost pricing. Traditionally, a feature common to all three industries has been that they utilize large networks of wires or pipelines to transmit their products to consumers. Federal, state, and local governments concluded that the average costs of providing electricity, natural gas, and telecommunications declined as the output rates of firms in these industries increased. Consequently, governments treated these industries as natural monopolies and established regulatory commissions to subject the industries to forms of cost-of-service and rate-of-return regulation.

ELECTRICITY AND NATURAL GAS: SEPARATING PRODUCTION FROM DELIVERY Today, 15 different companies provide electricity to homes, office buildings, and factories in Houston. Eight different firms compete to sell electricity in New York City, and six companies provide electricity in Philadelphia. Similarly, various producers of natural gas vie to market their product in a number of cities across the country. In nearly half of the U.S. states, there is active competition in the production of electricity and natural gas.

What circumstances led to this transformation? The answer is that regulators of electricity and natural gas companies figured out that the function of *producing* electricity or natural gas did not necessarily have to be combined with the *delivery* of the product. Until the mid-1980s, producers of natural gas and electricity had exclusive ownership of the pipeline and wire networks that provided energy for homes, office buildings, and factories. Since then, various regulators have gradually implemented policies that have separated production of electricity and natural gas from the distribution of these items to consumers.

Thus, in a growing number of U.S. locales, multiple producers now pay to use wire and pipeline networks to get their products to buyers. Economies of scale still exist in these distribution networks, and regulatory commissions impose cost-of-service or rate-of-return regulations on the network owners. Individual producers of electricity and natural gas openly compete, nonetheless, in the markets for the products that consumers actually utilize in their homes and businesses. The market clearing rates that consumers pay to consume electricity and natural gas reflect both the costs of producing these items and the transportation costs that producers pay to deliver them via regulated distribution networks.

TELECOMMUNICATIONS SERVICES MEET THE INTERNET As the production and sale of electricity and natural gas began to become more competitive undertakings, regulators started to apply the same principles to telecommunications services.

In the 1980s, the Federal Communications Commission (FCC) required AT&T to open its existing phone networks to competing providers of long-distance phone services. Gradually, during the 1990s and 2000s, federal, state, and local regulators applied the same principles to local telecommunications services. Today, many U.S. cities and towns are served by two or more competing producers of wired phone services.

At the same time, other forces reshaped the cost structure of the telecommunications industry. First, during the 1990s, significant technological advances drastically reduced the costs of providing wireless telecommunications. Most individuals and businesses regarded cellphone services as imperfect substitutes for wire-based telecommunications. Nevertheless, the growing use of cellphones slowed growth in the demand for services delivered over traditional wire networks.

Go to www.econtoday.com/ch27 to learn about the latest broadband regulations proposed by the Federal Communications Commission.

Second, since 2000, Internet phone service has become more widely available. Most cable television companies that provide Internet access now offer Web-based telephone services as well. Many other companies also offer Web phone services for purchase by anyone who already has access to the Internet.

ARE NATURAL MONOPOLIES RELICS OF THE PAST? Clearly, the scope of the government's role as regulator of natural monopolies has decreased with the unraveling of conditions that previously created this particular market structure. In many U.S. electricity and natural gas markets, government agencies now apply traditional cost-of-service or rate-of-return regulations primarily to wire and pipeline owners. Otherwise, the government's main role in many regional markets is to serve as a "traffic cop," enforcing property rights and rules governing the regulated networks that serve competing electricity and natural gas producers.

In telecommunications, any natural monopoly rationale for a governmental regulator role is rapidly dissipating as more and more households and businesses substitute cellular and Web-based phone services for wired phone services. Since 2000, consumers have stopped using more than 35 million land phone lines. At present, phone signals stop flowing on an additional 3 percent of existing lines each year. Telecommunications has become a technology-driven, competitive free-for-all. This industry is now far from being a natural monopoly.

QUICK QUIZ See page 617 for the answers. **Review concepts from this section in MyEconLab.**

A **natural monopoly** arises when one firm can produce all of an industry's output at a __________ per-unit cost than other firms. A profit-maximizing natural monopolist produces to the point at which marginal __________ equals long-run marginal __________ and charges the price that people are willing to pay for the quantity produced.

Because a natural monopolist that is required to set price equal to long-run marginal cost will sustain long-run losses and shut down, regulators typically allow natural monopolists to charge prices that just cover __________ costs. Normally, regulators have done this through **cost-of-service regulation,** in which prices are based on actual production costs, or **rate-of-return regulation,** in which prices are set to yield a rate of return consistent with __________ economic profits.

Technological and regulatory innovations have made the concept of natural monopoly less relevant. In the electricity, natural gas, and telecommunications industries, production increasingly is accomplished by numerous competing firms that __________ their products through regulated __________.

Regulating Nonmonopolistic Industries

Traditionally, one of the fundamental purposes of governments has been to provide a coordinated system of safeguarding the interests of their citizens. Not surprisingly, protecting consumer interests is the main rationale offered for governmental regulatory functions.

Rationales for Consumer Protection in Nonmonopolistic Industries

The Latin phrase *caveat emptor*, or "let the buyer beware," was once the operative principle in most consumer dealings with businesses. The phrase embodies the idea that the buyer alone is ultimately responsible for assessing a producer and the quality of the items it sells before agreeing to purchase the firm's product. Today, various federal agencies require companies to meet specific minimal standards in their dealings with consumers. For instance, a few years ago, the U.S. Federal Trade Commission assessed monetary penalties on Toys "Я" Us and KB Toys because they failed to ship goods sold on their Web sites in time for a pre-Christmas delivery. Such a government action would have been unheard of a few decades ago.

In some industries, federal agencies dictate the rules of the game for firms' interactions with consumers. The Federal Aviation Administration (FAA), for example, oversees almost every aspect of the delivery of services by airline companies. The FAA regulates the process by which tickets for flights are sold and distributed, oversees all flight operations, and even establishes rules governing the procedures for returning luggage after flights are concluded.

Go to **www.econtoday.com/ch27** to view a full list of the regulations put into place by the Federal Aviation Administration.

REASONS FOR GOVERNMENT-ORCHESTRATED CONSUMER PROTECTION Two rationales are commonly advanced for heavy government involvement in overseeing and supervising nonmonopolistic industries. One, which you encountered in Chapter 5, is the possibility of *market failures*. For example, the presence of negative externalities such as pollution may induce governments to regulate industries that create such externalities.

The second common rationale is *asymmetric information*. In the context of many producer-consumer interactions, this term refers to situations in which a producer has information about a product that the consumer lacks. For instance, administrators of your college or university may know that another school in your vicinity offers better-quality degree programs in certain fields. If so, it would not be in your college or university's interest to transmit this information to applicants who are interested in pursuing degrees in those fields.

For certain products, asymmetric information problems can pose special difficulties for consumers trying to assess product quality in advance of purchase. In unregulated financial markets, for example, individuals contemplating buying a company's stock, a municipality's bond, or a bank's certificate of deposit might struggle to assess the associated risks of financial loss. If the air transportation industry were unregulated, a person might have trouble determining if one airline's planes were less safe than those of competing airlines. In an unregulated market for pharmaceuticals, parents might worry about whether one company's childhood-asthma medication could have more dangerous side effects than medications sold by other firms.

ASYMMETRIC INFORMATION AND PRODUCT QUALITY In extreme cases, asymmetric information can create situations in which most of the available products are of low quality. A commonly cited example is the market for used automobiles. Current owners of cars that *appear* to be in good condition know the autos' service records. Some owners know that their cars have been well maintained and really do run great. Others, however, have not kept their autos in good repair and thus are aware that they will be susceptible to greater-than-normal mechanical or electrical problems.

Suppose that in your local used-car market, half of all used cars offered for sale are high-quality autos. The other half are low-quality cars, commonly called "lemons," that are likely to break down within a few months or perhaps even weeks. In addition, suppose that a consumer is willing to pay $20,000 for a particular car model if it is in excellent condition but is willing to pay only $10,000 if it is a lemon. Finally, suppose that people who own truly high-quality used cars are only willing to sell at a price of at least $20,000, but people who own lemons are willing to sell at any price at or above $10,000.

Because there is a 50–50 chance that a given car up for sale is of either quality, the average amount that a prospective buyer is willing to pay equals $(\frac{1}{2} \times \$20{,}000) + (\frac{1}{2} \times \$10{,}000) = \$15{,}000$. Owners of low-quality used cars are willing to sell them at this price, but owners of high-quality used cars are not. In this example, only lemons will be traded, at a price of $10,000, because owners of cars in excellent condition will not sell their cars at a price that prospective buyers are willing to pay.

Lemons problem
The potential for asymmetric information to bring about a general decline in product quality in an industry.

THE LEMONS PROBLEM Economists refer to the possibility that asymmetric information can lead to a general reduction in product quality in an industry as the **lemons problem.** This problem does not apply only to the used-car industry. In principle, any product with qualities that are difficult for consumers to fully assess is susceptible to the same problem. *Credence goods*, which as you learned in Chapter 25 are items such as pharmaceuticals, health care, and professional services, also may be particularly vulnerable to the lemons problem.

MARKET SOLUTIONS TO THE LEMONS PROBLEM Firms offering truly high-quality products for sale can address the lemons problem in a variety of ways. They can offer product guarantees and warranties. In addition, to help consumers separate high-quality producers from incompetent or unscrupulous competitors, the high-quality producers may work together to establish industry standards.

In some cases, firms in an industry may even seek external product certification. They may, for example, solicit scientific reports supporting proposed industry standards and bearing witness that products of certain firms in the industry meet those standards. To legitimize a product-certification process, firms may hire outside companies or groups to issue such reports.

Implementing Consumer Protection Regulation

Governments offering asymmetric information and lemons problems as rationales for regulation presumably have concluded that private market solutions such as warranties, industry standards, and product certification are insufficient. To address asymmetric information problems, governments may offer legal remedies to consumers or enforce licensing requirements in an effort to provide minimum product standards. In some cases, governments go well beyond simple licensing requirements by establishing a regulatory apparatus for overseeing all aspects of an industry's operations.

Go to www.econtoday.com/ch27 to see how the Federal Trade Commission imposes regulations intended to protect consumers.

LIABILITY LAWS AND GOVERNMENT LICENSING Sometimes liability laws, which specify penalties for product failures, provide consumers with protections similar to guarantees and warranties. When the Federal Trade Commission (FTC) charged Toys "Я" Us and KB Toys with failing to meet pre-Christmas delivery dates for Internet toy orders, it operated under a mail-order statute Congress passed in the early 1970s. The mail-order law effectively made the toy companies' delivery guarantees legally enforceable. Although the FTC applied the law in this particular case, any consumer could have filed suit for damages under the terms of the statute.

Federal and state governments also get involved in consumer protection by issuing licenses granting only "qualifying" firms the legal right to produce and sell certain products. For instance, governments of nearly half of the states give the right to sell caskets only to people who have a mortuary or funeral director's license, allegedly to ensure that bodies of deceased individuals are handled with care and dignity.

Although government licensing may successfully limit the sale of low-quality goods, licensing requirements also often limit the number of providers. As you learned in Chapter 24, such requirements can ease efforts by established firms to act as monopolists. In addition, if governments rely on the expertise of established firms for assistance in drafting licensing requirements, these firms certainly have strong incentives to recommend low standards for themselves but high standards for prospective entrants.

DIRECT ECONOMIC AND SOCIAL REGULATION In some instances, governments determine that liability laws and licensing requirements are insufficient to protect the interests of consumers. A government may decide that lemons problems in banking are so severe that without an extensive banking regulatory apparatus, consumers will lose confidence in banks, and bank runs may ensue. It may rely on similar rationales to establish economic regulation of other financial services industries. Eventually, it may apply consumer protection rationales to justify the economic regulation of additional industries such as trucking or air transportation.

The government may establish an oversight authority to make certain that consumers are protected from incompetent producers of foods and pharmaceuticals. Eventually, the government may determine that a host of other products should meet government consumer protection standards. It may also decide that the people who produce the products also require government agencies to ensure workplace safety. In this way, widespread social regulation emerges, as it has in the United States and most other developed nations.

QUICK QUIZ See page 617 for the answers. Review concepts from this section in MyEconLab.

Governments tend to regulate industries in which they think market __________ and __________ information problems are most severe.

A common justification for government regulation is to protect consumers from adverse effects of __________ information.

To address the __________ problem, or the potential for __________-quality products to predominate when asymmetric information is widespread, governments often supplement private firms' guarantees, warranties, and certification standards with liability laws and licensing requirements.

Incentives and Costs of Regulation

Abiding by government regulations is a costly undertaking for firms. Consequently, businesses engage in a number of activities intended to avoid the true intent of regulations or to bring about changes in the regulations that government agencies establish.

Creative Response and Feedback Effects: Results of Regulation

Sometimes individuals and firms respond to a regulation in a way that conforms to the letter of the law but undermines its spirit. When they do so, they engage in **creative response** to regulations.

Creative response
Behavior on the part of a firm that allows it to comply with the letter of the law but violate the spirit, significantly lessening the law's effects.

One type of creative response has been labeled a *feedback effect*. Individuals' behaviors may change after a regulation has been put into effect. If a regulation requires fluoridated water, then parents know that their children's teeth have significant protection against tooth decay. Consequently, the feedback effect is that parents become less concerned about how many sweets their children eat.

How has a Food and Drug Administration (FDA) regulation that requires disclosure of trans fats in food items created an unanticipated feedback effect? (See the next page.)

POLICY EXAMPLE Food Makers Respond to Regulation by Replacing Trans Fats

During the mid-2000s, a flurry of media stories exposed the food industry's widespread use of *trans fats*—fats created when hydrogen is added to vegetable oil. Because trans fats induce the human body to boost production of unhealthful cholesterol, the FDA decided to require companies to disclose the amounts of trans fats in their food products. Many companies worried that having *any* trans fats in their products would lead to lower sales, so they began to remove them. In fact, many consumers responded to labels indicating that no trans fats were present in foods by increasing their purchases of those food items. This, of course, encouraged more companies to eliminate trans fats.

To maintain product consistency and flavor, however, companies replaced the trans fats with ingredients such as coconut oil, palm oil, and palm kernel oil. The net effect was that the total fat content of the food remained the same but with no trans fats. The new ingredients, however, are higher in *saturated fats*—which, like trans fats, generate production of harmful cholesterol in the human body. Some nutritionists suggest that by encouraging many people to buy more foods containing saturated fats, the FDA's regulation on trans fat may be leading to consumption of even *more* unhealthful fats.

FOR CRITICAL ANALYSIS

What feedback effect might occur if companies were required to include very lengthy package labels explaining the dangers of all *fats contained in food items?*

Explaining Regulators' Behavior

Those charged with enforcing government regulations operate outside the market, so their decisions are determined by nonmarket processes. A number of theories have emerged to describe the behavior of regulators. These theories explain how regulation can harm consumers by generating higher prices and fewer product choices while benefiting producers by reducing competitive forces and allowing higher profits. Two of the best-known theories of regulatory behavior are the *capture hypothesis* and the *share-the-gains, share-the-pains theory*.

Capture hypothesis
A theory of regulatory behavior that predicts that regulators will eventually be captured by special interests of the industry being regulated.

THE CAPTURE HYPOTHESIS Regulators often end up becoming champions of the firms they are charged with regulating. According to the **capture hypothesis,** regardless of why a regulatory agency was originally established, eventually special interests of the industry it regulates will capture it. After all, the people who know the most about a regulated industry are the people already in the industry. Thus, people who have been in the industry and have allegiances and friendships with others in the industry will most likely be asked to regulate the industry.

According to the capture hypothesis, individual consumers of a regulated industry's products and individual taxpayers who finance a regulatory agency have interests too diverse to be greatly concerned with the industry's actions. In contrast, special interests of the industry are well organized and well defined. These interests also have more to offer political entrepreneurs within a regulatory agency, such as future employment with one of the regulated firms. Therefore, regulators have a strong incentive to support the position of a well-organized special-interest group within the regulated industry.

Why do U.S. tobacco companies want to be regulated by the Food and Drug Administration (FDA)?

POLICY EXAMPLE The Tobacco Industry Sees Benefits in Regulation

Recently, the U.S. Congress granted the FDA the authority to regulate the tobacco industry. Under the legislation, the FDA can require reductions of tar and nicotine, ban the use of certain flavors and ingredients, and restrict the distribution and sale of cigarettes and smokeless tobacco products.

Among the strongest supporters of these actual and proposed regulatory changes have been tobacco firms. One reason is that the existing and proposed laws do not permit the FDA to consider banning existing tobacco products. Another reason is that the FDA would have the authority to decide whether any new tobacco products could be introduced into U.S. markets. Incumbent tobacco firms know that the FDA is unlikely to approve any new tobacco products. Therefore, regulation would eliminate threats of entry by new competitors. Finally, another source of competition would be removed because the FDA would be required to stop the distribution of counterfeit cigarettes. Thus, FDA regulation of the tobacco industry promises to constrain the FDA to act in the interests of current tobacco firms by perpetuating existing tobacco products and protecting the firms selling these products from competition. In other words, the actual and proposed laws effectively require the FDA to pursue some of the industry's key interests.

FOR CRITICAL ANALYSIS

Why might the wording of a law imposing regulation on an industry influence that industry's ability to capture its regulator? (Hint: Often, a law's wording spells out how a regulator is required to interact with the firms that it supervises.)

"SHARE THE GAINS, SHARE THE PAINS" The **share-the-gains, share-the-pains theory** offers a somewhat different view of regulators' behavior. This theory focuses on the specific aims of regulators. It proposes that a regulator's main objective is simply to keep his or her job as a regulator. To do so, the regulator must obtain the approval of both the legislators who originally established and continue to oversee the regulatory agency and the regulated industry. The regulator must also take into account the views of the industry's customers.

Share-the-gains, share-the-pains theory A theory of regulatory behavior that holds that regulators must take account of the demands of three groups: legislators, who established and oversee the regulatory agency; firms in the regulated industry; and consumers of the regulated industry's products.

In contrast to the capture hypothesis, which holds that regulators must take into account only industry special interests, the share-the-gains, share-the-pains theory contends that regulators must worry about legislators and consumers as well. After all, if industry customers who are hurt by improper regulation complain to legislators, the regulators might lose their jobs. Whereas the capture theory predicts that regulators will quickly allow electric utilities to raise their rates in the face of higher fuel costs, the share-the-gains, share-the-pains theory predicts a slower, more measured regulatory response. Ultimately, regulators will permit an increase in utility rates, but the allowed adjustment will not be as speedy or complete as predicted by the capture hypothesis. The regulatory agency is not completely captured by the industry. It also has to consider the views of consumers and legislators.

The Benefits and Costs of Regulation

As noted earlier, regulation offers many *potential* benefits. *Actual* benefits, however, are difficult to measure. Putting a dollar value on safer products, a cleaner environment, and better working conditions is a difficult proposition. Furthermore, the benefits of most regulations accrue to society over a long time.

THE DIRECT COSTS OF REGULATION TO TAXPAYERS Measuring the costs of regulation is also a challenging undertaking. After all, about 5,000 new federal and state regulations are issued each year. One cost, though, is certain: U.S. federal and state taxpayers pay more than $50 billion per year to staff regulatory agencies with more than 250,000 employees and to fund their various activities. Figure 27-3 below displays the distribution of total federal government outlays for economic and social regulation of various areas of the economy.

The *total* cost of regulation is much higher than just the explicit government outlays to fund the administration of various regulations, however. After all, businesses must expend resources complying with regulations, developing creative responses to regulations, and funding special-interest lobbying efforts directed at legislators and regulatory officials. Sometimes companies find that it is impossible to comply with one regulation without violating another, and determining how to avoid the resulting legal entanglements can entail significant expenditures.

FIGURE 27-3 The Distribution of Federal Regulatory Spending

This figure shows the areas of the economy to which more than $50 billion of taxpayer-provided funds are distributed to finance economic and social regulation.

Source: Office of Management and Budget.

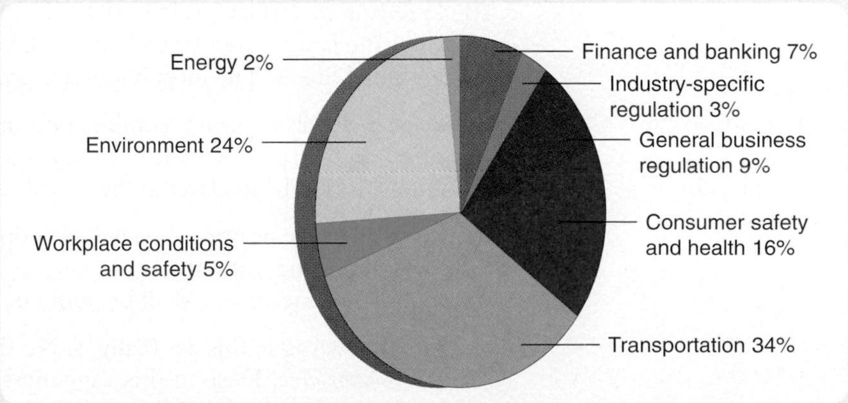

THE TOTAL SOCIAL COST OF REGULATION According to the Office of Management and Budget, annual expenditures that U.S. businesses must make solely to comply with regulations issued by various federal agencies amount to more than $700 billion per year. Nevertheless, this estimate encompasses only the explicit costs of satisfying regulatory demands placed on businesses. It ignores relevant opportunity costs. After all, owners, managers, and employees of companies could be doing other things with their time and resources than complying with regulations. Economists estimate that the opportunity costs of complying with federal regulations may be as high as $300 billion per year. A portion of this amount is passed on to consumers in the form of higher prices.

All told, therefore, the total social cost associated with satisfying federal regulations in the United States probably exceeds $1 trillion per year. This figure, of course, applies only to federal regulations. It does not include the explicit and implicit opportunity costs associated with regulations issued by 50 different state governments and tens of thousands of municipalities. Undoubtedly, the annual cost of regulation throughout the United States exceeds $1.75 trillion per year.

You Are There

To envision why government regulation typically imposes costs on regulated firms, take a look at **A Church Loses a Pie Fight with Pennsylvania,** on page 611.

QUICK QUIZ See page 617 for the answers. Review concepts from this section in MyEconLab.

The **capture hypothesis** holds that regulatory agencies will eventually be captured by industry special interests because __________ individually are not greatly influenced by regulation, whereas regulated __________ are directly affected.

According to the **share-the-gains, share-the-pains theory** of regulation, regulators must take into account the interests of three groups: the __________, __________, and __________.

Regulation has benefits that are difficult to quantify in dollars. The costs of regulation include direct __________ expenditures on regulatory agencies and __________ explicit and implicit opportunity costs of complying.

Antitrust Policy

An expressed aim of the U.S. government is to foster competition. To this end, Congress has made numerous attempts to legislate against business practices that Congress has perceived to be anticompetitive. This is the general idea behind antitrust legislation. If the courts can prevent collusion among sellers of a product, there will be no restriction of output, and monopoly prices will not result. Instead, prices of goods and services will be close to their marginal social opportunity costs.

Antitrust Policy in the United States

Congress has enacted four key antitrust laws, which are summarized in Table 27-2 on the facing page. The most important of these is the original U.S. antitrust law, called the Sherman Act.

THE SHERMAN ANTITRUST ACT OF 1890 The Sherman Antitrust Act, which was passed in 1890, was the first attempt by the federal government to control the growth of monopoly in the United States. The most important provisions of that act are as follows:

> *Section 1*: Every contract, combination in the form of a trust or otherwise, or conspiracy, in restraint of trade or commerce among the several states, or with foreign nations, is hereby declared to be illegal.
>
> *Section 2*: Every person who shall monopolize, or attempt to monopolize, or combine or conspire with any other person or persons to monopolize any part of the trade or commerce . . . shall be guilty of a misdemeanor [now a felony].

Notice how vague this act really is. No definition is given for the terms *restraint of trade* or *monopolize*. Despite this vagueness, however, the act was used to prosecute the infamous Standard Oil Trust of New Jersey. This company was charged with

TABLE 27-2

Key U.S. Antitrust Laws

Law	Provisions
Sherman Antitrust Act of 1890	Forbids any contract, combination, or conspiracy to restrain trade or commerce within the United States or across U.S. borders. Holds any person who attempts to monopolize trade or commerce criminally liable.
Clayton Act of 1914	Prohibits specific business practices deemed to restrain trade or commerce. Bans discrimination in prices charged to various purchasers when price differences are not due to actual differences in selling or transportation costs. Also forbids a company from selling goods on the condition that the purchaser must deal exclusively with that company. Finally, it prevents corporations from holding stock in other companies when this may lessen competition.
Federal Trade Commission Act of 1914 (and 1938 Amendment)	Outlaws business practices that reduce the extent of competition, such as alleged cutthroat pricing intended to drive rivals from the marketplace. Also established the Federal Trade Commission and empowered it to issue cease and desist orders in situations in which it determines "unfair methods of competition in commerce" exist. The 1938 amendment added deceptive business practices to the list of illegal acts.
Robinson-Patman Act of 1936	Bans selected discriminatory price cuts by chain stores that allegedly drive smaller competitors from the marketplace. In addition, forbids price discrimination through special concessions in the form of price or quantity discounts, free advertising, or promotional allowances granted to one buyer but not to others, if these actions substantially reduce competition.

and convicted of violations of Sections 1 and 2 of the Sherman Antitrust Act in 1906. At the time it controlled more than 80 percent of the nation's oil-refining capacity. In addressing the company's legal appeal, the U.S. Supreme Court ruled that Standard Oil's predominance in the oil market created "a *prima facie* presumption of intent and purpose to control and maintain dominancy . . . not as a result from normal methods of industrial development, but by means of combinations." Here the word *combination* meant entering into associations and preferential arrangements with the intent of restraining competition. The Supreme Court forced Standard Oil of New Jersey to break up into many smaller companies that would have no choice but to compete.

The Sherman Act applies today just as it did more than a century ago. Recently, Samsung and other producers of DRAM computer chips admitted that they had violated the Sherman Act by conspiring to fix the price of DRAM chips by holding down production. Samsung paid a $300 million fine for this Sherman Act violation.

OTHER IMPORTANT ANTITRUST LEGISLATION Table 27-2 above lists three other important antitrust laws. In 1914, Congress passed the Clayton Act to clarify some of the vague provisions of the Sherman Act by identifying specific business practices that were to be legally prohibited.

Congress also passed the Federal Trade Commission Act in 1914. In addition to establishing the Federal Trade Commission to investigate unfair trade practices, this law enumerated certain business practices that, according to Congress, involved overly aggressive competition. A 1938 amendment to this law expressly prohibited "unfair or deceptive acts or practices in commerce" and empowered the FTC to regulate advertising and marketing practices by U.S. firms.

The Robinson-Patman Act of 1936 amended the Clayton Act by singling out specific business practices, such as selected price cuts, aimed at driving smaller competitors out of business. The act is often referred to as the "Chain Store Act" because it was intended to protect *independent* retailers and wholesalers from "unfair competition" by chain stores.

EXEMPTIONS FROM ANTITRUST LAWS Numerous laws exempt the following industries and business practices from antitrust legislation:

- Labor unions
- Public utilities—electric, gas, and telephone companies
- Professional baseball
- Cooperative activities among U.S. exporters
- Hospitals
- Public transit and water systems
- Suppliers of military equipment
- Joint publishing arrangements in a single city by two or more newspapers

Thus, not all U.S. businesses are subject to antitrust laws.

International Discord in Antitrust Policy

What, if anything, should U.S. antitrust authorities do if AT&T decides that it wishes to merge with British Telecommunications or if Germany's Deutsche Telecom wants to acquire Sprint Nextel? What, if anything, should they do if Time Warner, the largest U.S. entertainment company, attempts to merge with London-based EMI, one of the world's largest recorded-music companies? These are not just rhetorical questions, as U.S. and European antitrust authorities learned in the 2000s when these issues actually surfaced. Growing international linkages among markets for many goods and services have increasingly made antitrust policy a global undertaking.

Go to **www.econtoday.com/ch27** to take a look at the guidelines the U.S. Department of Justice uses to decide whether to challenge proposed mergers under antitrust laws.

The international dimensions of antitrust pose a problem for U.S. antitrust authorities in the Department of Justice and the Federal Trade Commission. In the United States, the overriding goal of antitrust policies has traditionally been protecting the interests of consumers. This is also a formal objective of European Union (EU) antitrust authorities. In the EU, however, policymakers are also required to reject any business combination that "creates or strengthens a dominant position as a result of which effective competition would be significantly impeded."

This additional clause has sometimes created tension between U.S. and EU policymaking. In the United States, increasing dominance of a market by a single firm arouses the concern of antitrust authorities. Nevertheless, U.S. authorities typically will remain passive if they determine that the increased market dominance arises from factors such as exceptional management and greater cost efficiencies that ultimately benefit consumers by reducing prices. In contrast, under EU rules antitrust authorities are obliged to block *any* business combination that increases the dominance of any producer. They must do so regardless of what factors might have caused the business's preeminence in the marketplace or whether the antitrust action might have adverse implications for consumers.

QUICK QUIZ **See page 617 for the answers. Review concepts from this section in MyEconLab.**

The first national antitrust law was the __________ Antitrust Act of 1890, which made illegal every contract and combination in restraint of trade. It remains the single most important antitrust law in the United States.

The __________ Act of 1914 made illegal various specific business practices, such as price discrimination.

The __________ __________ __________ Act of 1914 and its 1938 amendment established the Federal Trade Commission and prohibited "unfair or deceptive acts or practices in commerce."

The __________-__________ Act of 1936 aimed to prevent large producers from driving out small competitors by means of selective discriminatory price cuts.

Why did European antitrust authorities recently rule that Intel's microprocessor prices were too *low*?

INTERNATIONAL POLICY EXAMPLE

Antitrust Authorities Fine Intel for Its Low Prices

Intel produces and sells 80 percent of the microprocessors that power desktop and laptop computers, netbooks, cellphones, and other computing devices. The second-largest producer, Advanced Micro Devices (AMD), accounts for between 10 and 11 percent of the microprocessors produced worldwide.

Between 2000 and 2008, the average price of microprocessors fell by more than 40 percent. AMD responded by filing an antitrust suit in Europe alleging that microprocessor prices fell because Intel had been setting its prices below the average total costs faced by Intel's competitors. Intel's goal, AMD alleged, was to force its competitors to operate at a loss and induce them to exit the market.

Europe's antitrust authority, the European Commission, responded by launching an antitrust investigation. Ultimately, the European Commission imposed a $1.45 billion fine on Intel—the largest in the history of antitrust enforcement. Later, Intel paid another $1.25 billion directly to AMD as part of a legal settlement. Soon, the profits of AMD and other microprocessor firms increased because microprocessor prices increased. As a result, by the 2010s, consumers were also paying higher prices for microprocessor-equipped computing devices.

FOR CRITICAL ANALYSIS

What is your evaluation of the European Commission's argument that its ruling against Intel would prevent microprocessor prices from increasing even more in the future?

Antitrust Enforcement

How are antitrust laws enforced? In the United States, most enforcement continues to be based on the Sherman Act. The Supreme Court has defined the offense of **monopolization** as involving the following elements: "(1) the possession of monopoly power in the relevant market and (2) the willful acquisition or maintenance of that power, as distinguished from growth or development as a consequence of a superior product, business acumen, or historical accident."

Monopolization
The possession of monopoly power in the relevant market and the willful acquisition or maintenance of that power, as distinguished from growth or development as a consequence of a superior product, business acumen, or historical accident.

Monopoly Power and the Relevant Market

The Sherman Act does not define monopoly. Monopoly need not be a single entity. Also, monopoly is not a function of size alone. For example a "mom and pop" grocery store located in an isolated town can function as a monopolist.

It is difficult to define and measure market power precisely. As a workable proxy, courts often look to the firm's percentage share of the "relevant market." This is the so-called **market share test.** A firm is generally considered to have monopoly power if its share of the relevant market is 70 percent or more. This is only a rule of thumb, however, not an absolute requirement. In some cases, a smaller share may be held to constitute monopoly power.

Market share test
The percentage of a market that a particular firm supplies; used as the primary measure of monopoly power.

The relevant market consists of two elements: a relevant *product* market and a relevant *geographic* market. What should the relevant product market include? It must include all items produced by different firms that have identical attributes, such as sugar. Yet products that are not identical may sometimes be substituted for one another. Coffee may be substituted for tea, for example. In defining the relevant product market, the key issue is the degree to which products are interchangeable. If one product is sufficiently substitutable for another, then the two products are considered to be part of the same product market.

The second component of the relevant market is the geographic boundaries of the market. For items that are sold nationwide, the geographic boundaries of the market encompass the entire United States. If a producer and its competitors sell in only a limited area (one in which customers have no access to other sources of the product), the geographic market is limited to that area. A national firm may thus compete in several distinct areas and have monopoly power in one area but not in another.

Why Not . . . outlaw all mergers between firms that sell similar items?

One way to prevent monopoly power would be to prevent all mergers. But not all mergers lead to reductions in quantities and increases in prices in the markets in which the mergers take place. A number of mergers actually result in the combined firm incurring lower marginal cost than the individual firms incurred before their merger. Other things being equal, a reduction in marginal cost generates increased profit-maximizing production by the merged firm. A rise in production results in an increase in the total quantity available for sale in the market. Consequently, in many markets in which mergers occur, the mergers result in lower equilibrium prices.

Product Packaging and Antitrust Enforcement

A particular problem in U.S. antitrust enforcement is determining whether a firm has engaged in "willful acquisition or maintenance" of market power. Actions that appear to some observers to be good business look like antitrust violations to others. To illustrate why quandaries can arise in antitrust enforcement, let's consider two examples: *versioning* and *bundling*.

Versioning
Selling a product in slightly altered forms to different groups of consumers.

PRODUCT VERSIONING A firm engages in product **versioning** when it sells an item in slightly altered forms to different groups of consumers. A typical method of versioning is to remove certain features from an item and offer what remains as a somewhat stripped-down version of the product at a different price.

Consider an office-productivity software program, such as Adobe Acrobat or Microsoft Word. Firms selling such programs typically offer both a "professional" version containing a full range of features and a "standard" version providing only basic functions. One perspective on this practice regards it as a form of price discrimination, or selling essentially the same product at different prices to different consumers. People who desire to use the full range of features in Adobe Acrobat or Microsoft Word are likely to be computing professionals. Compared to most other consumers, their demand for the full-featured version of an office-productivity software program is likely to be less elastic. In principle, therefore, Adobe and Microsoft can earn higher profits by offering "professional" versions at higher prices and selling a "standard" version at a lower price.

Price discrimination—charging varying prices to different consumers when the price differences are not a result of different production or transportation costs—is illegal under the Clayton Act of 1914. Are Adobe, Microsoft, and other companies engaging in illegal price discrimination? Another perspective on versioning indicates that they are not. According to this point of view, consumers regard "professional" and "standard" versions of software packages as imperfect substitutes. Consequently, each version is a distinctive product sold in a unique market. If so, versioning increases overall consumer satisfaction because consumers who are not computing professionals are able to utilize certain features of software products at a lower price. So far, antitrust authorities in the United States and elsewhere have been inclined toward this view of the economic effects of versioning, rather than perceiving it as a form of price discrimination.

Bundling
Offering two or more products for sale as a set.

Tie-in sales
Purchases of one product that are permitted by the seller only if the consumer buys another good or service from the same firm.

PRODUCT BUNDLING Antitrust authorities have been less tolerant of another form of product packaging, known as **bundling,** which involves the joint sale of two or more products as a set. Antitrust authorities usually are not concerned if a firm allows consumers to purchase the products either individually or as a set. They are more likely to investigate a firm's business practices, however, when it allows consumers to purchase one product only when it is bundled with another. Antitrust officials often view this form of bundling as a method of price discrimination known as **tie-in sales,** in which a firm requires consumers who wish to buy one of its products to purchase another item the firm sells as well.

To understand their reasoning, consider a situation in which one group of consumers is willing to pay \$200 for a computer operating system but only \$100 for an

Internet-browsing program. A second group of consumers is willing to pay only $100 for the same operating system but is willing to pay $200 for the same Internet-browsing program. If the same company that sells both types of software offers the operating system at a price above $100, then only consumers in the first group will buy this software. Likewise, if it sells the Internet-browsing program at a price above $100, then only the second group of consumers will purchase that program.

But if the firm sells both products as a bundled set, it can charge $300 and generate sales of both products to both groups. One interpretation is that the first group pays $200 for the operating system, but for the second group, the operating system's price is $100. At the same time, the first group has paid $100 for the Internet-browsing program, while the second group perceives the price of the program to be $200. Effectively, bundling enables the software company to engage in price discrimination by charging different prices to different groups.

Antitrust enforcers in the Justice Department applied this interpretation in their prosecution of Microsoft, which for years had bundled its Internet-browsing program, Internet Explorer, together with its Windows operating system. Enforcement officials added another twist by contending that Microsoft also had monopoly power in the market for computer operating systems. By bundling the two products, they argued, Microsoft had sought both to price-discriminate and to extend its monopoly power to the market for Internet-browsing software. The remedy that the courts imposed was for Microsoft to alter some of its business practices. As part of this legal remedy, Microsoft was required to unbundle its Windows and Internet Explorer products.

QUICK QUIZ **See page 617 for the answers.** **Review concepts from this section in MyEconLab.**

As part of the enforcement of antitrust laws, officials at the U.S. Department of Justice and the Federal Trade Commission often apply __________ __________ tests to determine if a few firms account for most of industry __________.

Antitrust enforcers must decide whether producers seek to monopolize the relevant market, which involves determining both the relevant __________ market and the relevant __________ market.

Antitrust authorities generally have not considered product __________, or offering different versions of essentially the same product for sale at different prices, to be illegal price discrimination. U.S. authorities have, however, raised antitrust concerns about product __________, which they view as a method of engaging in **tie-in sales** that require consumers to purchase one product in order to obtain another.

You Are There A Church Loses a Pie Fight with Pennsylvania

The gathering on a recent Friday evening did not go well at St. Cecilia Catholic Church, in Rochester, Pennsylvania. According to Josie Read, a retired schoolteacher, by the end of the evening, "Everyone was devastated." The gathering at the church had started off well when a large number of parishioners turned out for the fish-fry dinner. Read had brought her highly regarded pumpkin and berry pies, which were set out beside Louise Humbert's raisin pie, Marge Murtha's apple pie, and Mary Pratte's coconut-cream pie. All of the pies were for sale, with the proceeds slated for church upkeep and charity work. Then, an inspector from the Pennsylvania Department of Agriculture arrived for an annual check on the church's adherence to the state's food safety rules. He immediately noticed the pies and declared them off limits for sale because they had been baked in the women's homes instead of the church's state-approved kitchen.

For the church, one consequence of the ban on pies was the loss of what had been a regular inflow of revenues from pie sales. Another consequence, however, was that the media attention given to the state inspector's action—dubbed "piegate" by a local reporter—raised public awareness of the church's Friday night fish-fry dinners. Thus, more people began to attend, boosting revenues from the dinners, which provide funds for the church's charity work.

Critical Analysis Questions

1. How does the experience of this nonprofit church help to illustrate the types of costs that firms face in complying with government regulations?
2. Was the state inspector enforcing economic or social regulations?

ISSUES & APPLICATIONS

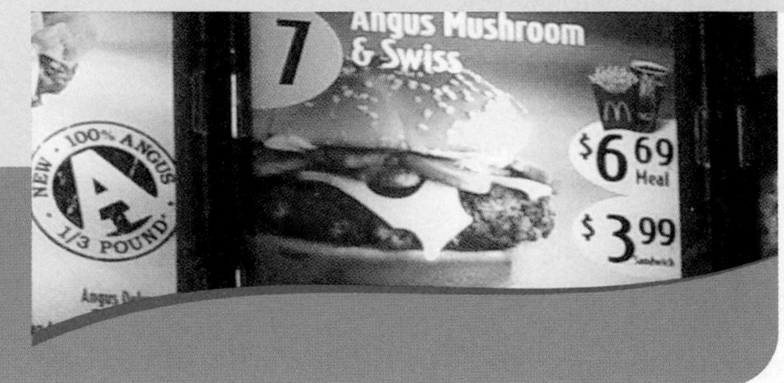

Food-Labeling Regulations Multiply

CONCEPTS APPLIED

- Economic Regulation
- Regulation Compliance Costs
- Feedback Effects

During the late 2000s, the federal government added to an already long list of regulations of the food industry. Among the new regulations being phased in during the early 2010s are rules governing food labeling at grocery stores and restaurants.

Label Changes Generate Significant Compliance Costs for Groceries

The grocery food-labeling regulation, which is administered by the U.S. Department of Agriculture (USDA), covers companies operating large supermarkets. These firms must add labels indicating the country of origin of all beef, chicken, fruit, lamb, pork, and vegetable products. When the USDA implemented the rule as required by law, it issued a statement saying that the benefits to consumers "will be small and will accrue mainly to those consumers who desire the information."

The costs of complying with the rule are not "small," however. The USDA estimates that grocers will spend more than $26,000 per store to put systems into place to assure compliance with the labeling requirement. It also estimates that the first-year cost of complying with the regulation for meats will be 7 cents per pound of beef and 4 cents per pound of lamb and pork. The total compliance cost for society as a whole is estimated to be more than $2.7 billion.

Restaurant Calorie Labels, Creative Response, and Feedback Effects

The labeling regulation imposed on restaurants was included in the health care legislation passed in March 2010. The rule applies to chains with at least 20 restaurants and covers more than 200,000 restaurants nationwide. The rule, which is administered by the Food and Drug Administration (FDA), requires these restaurant chains to include the calorie content for food items on all paper menus, menu boards, drive-through menu displays, and vending-machine menus. Compliance costs for a typical chain will include the cost of FDA-approved calorie-counting software priced at $1,000 and the costs of redoing menus to include calorie counts.

The benefits of this labeling law are even more nebulous than those associated with the food-labeling law faced by supermarkets. Most studies offered in support of adding calorie counts to restaurant menus only examined how this information affected each consumer's decision about what to buy for a *single meal*. Follow-up studies of the total *daily* calorie consumption of consumers when they were provided calorie data at restaurants have discovered evidence of a significant regulatory feedback effect.

These studies found that consumers who responded to calorie information in restaurant menus by limiting their calorie intake at the restaurant meal often gave themselves a "reward" later that same day. This "self-reward" typically would entail either consuming more calories—often in extra desserts—at a subsequent meal or adding high-calorie treats between meals that the consumers otherwise would not have eaten. On net, the subsequent studies found, offering calorie information on restaurant menus did not significantly reduce a typical consumer's *daily* intake of calories.

For Critical Analysis

1. As long as demand and supply curves have their typical shapes, who besides supermarkets will pay for the food-labeling compliance costs of 7 cents per pound of beef and 4 cents per pound of lamb and pork? (Hint: A higher per-unit cost of offering an item for sale shifts the market supply curve upward.)

2. Is it possible that for some people, the "self-reward" feedback effect of requiring calorie information on restaurant menus could actually lead to the consumption of more calories in a day's time? Explain briefly.

Web Resources

1. For more information about country-of-origin food label requirements faced by groceries, go to www.econtoday.com/ch27.
2. Read about the gradual phase-in of the federal rule requiring the addition of calorie counts to restaurant menus at www.econtoday.com/ch27.

Research Project

Evaluate how regulatory feedback effects make it harder to assess the benefits of a regulation in relation to the regulation's costs.

For more questions on this chapter's Issues & Applications, go to **MyEconLab**. In the Study Plan for this chapter, select Section N: News.

Here is what you should know after reading this chapter. **MyEconLab** will help you identify what you know, and where to go when you need to practice.

WHAT YOU SHOULD KNOW		WHERE TO GO TO PRACTICE
Government Regulation of Business There are two basic forms of government regulation of business: economic regulation and social regulation. Economic regulation applies to specific industries and includes the regulation of prices charged by natural monopolies and the regulation of certain activities of specific nonmonopolistic industries. Social regulations affect nearly all businesses and encompass a broad range of objectives concerning such issues as product safety, environmental quality, and working conditions.	**KEY FIGURE** Figure 27-1, 595	• **MyEconLab** Study Plan 27.1 • Audio introduction to Chapter 27 • Animated Figure 27-1
Practical Difficulties in Regulating the Prices Charged by Natural Monopolies For a natural monopoly, long-run marginal cost is typically less than long-run average total cost, so requiring marginal cost pricing forces the firm to incur an economic loss. Hence, regulators normally aim for a natural monopoly to charge a price equal to average total cost so that the firm earns zero economic profits. In recent years, uncoupling production of electricity, natural gas, and telecommunications from their distribution has enabled regulators to promote competition in these industries.	cost-of-service regulation, 599 rate-of-return regulation, 599 **KEY FIGURE** Figure 27-2, 598	• **MyEconLab** Study Plan 27.2 • Animated Figure 27-2

(*continued*)

MyEconLab continued

WHAT YOU SHOULD KNOW		WHERE TO GO TO PRACTICE
Rationales for Regulating Nonmonopolistic Industries The two most common rationales for regulation of nonmonopolistic industries relate to addressing market failures and protecting consumers from problems arising from information asymmetries they face in some markets. Asymmetric information can also create a lemons problem, which occurs when uncertainty about product quality leads to markets containing mostly low-quality items. Governments may seek to reduce the lemons problem by establishing liability laws and business licensing requirements.	lemons problem, 602	• **MyEconLab** Study Plan 27.3
Regulators' Incentives and the Costs of Regulation The capture theory of regulator behavior predicts that regulators will eventually find themselves supporting the positions of the firms that they regulate. The share-the-gains, share-the-pains theory predicts that a regulator will try to satisfy all constituencies, at least in part. The costs of regulation, which include both the direct costs to taxpayers of funding regulatory agencies and the explicit and implicit opportunity costs that businesses must incur to comply, are easier to quantify in dollar terms than the benefits.	creative response, 603 capture hypothesis, 604 share-the-gains, share-the-pains theory, 605 **KEY FIGURE** Figure 27-3, 605	• **MyEconLab** Study Plan 27.4 • Animated Figure 27-3 • Video: Creative Response and Feedback Effects: Results of Regulation
Foundations of Antitrust There are four key antitrust laws. The Sherman Act of 1890 forbids attempts to monopolize an industry. The Clayton Act of 1914 clarified antitrust law by prohibiting specific types of business practices. The Federal Trade Commission Act of 1914, as amended in 1938, seeks to prohibit deceptive business practices and to prevent "cutthroat pricing." The Robinson-Patman Act of 1936 outlawed price cuts deemed to be discriminatory and predatory.		• **MyEconLab** Study Plan 27.5 • Video: Antitrust Laws
Issues in Enforcing Antitrust Laws The Supreme Court has defined monopolization as possessing or seeking monopoly pricing power in the "relevant market." Authorities charged with enforcing antitrust laws use a market share test, which involves determining the percentage of market production or sales supplied by a firm within a defined relevant market. In recent years, antitrust officials have raised questions about whether product packaging, either in the form of different versions or as bundled sets, is a type of price discrimination involving tie-in sales.	monopolization, 609 market share test, 609 versioning, 610 bundling, 610 tie-in sales, 610	• **MyEconLab** Study Plan 27.6 • Video: Theory of Contestable Markets

Log in to MyEconLab, take a chapter test, and get a personalized Study Plan that tells you which concepts you understand and which ones you need to review. From there, MyEconLab will give you further practice, tutorials, animations, videos, and guided solutions.
Log in to www.myeconlab.com

PROBLEMS

All problems are assignable in myeconlab. *Answers to odd-numbered problems appear at the back of the book.*

27-1. Local cable television companies are sometimes granted monopoly rights to service a particular territory of a metropolitan area. The companies typically pay special taxes and licensing fees to local municipalities. Why might a municipality give monopoly rights to a cable company?

27-2. A local cable company, the sole provider of cable television service, is regulated by the municipal government. The owner of the company claims that she is normally opposed to regulation by government, but asserts that regulation is necessary because local residents would not want a large number of different cables crisscrossing the city. Why do you think the owner is defending regulation by the city?

27-3. The table below depicts the cost and demand structure a natural monopoly faces.

Quantity	Price ($)	Long-Run Total Cost ($)
0	100	0
1	95	92
2	90	177
3	85	255
4	80	331
5	75	406
6	70	480

a. Calculate total revenues, marginal revenue, and marginal cost at each output level. If this firm is allowed to operate as a monopolist, what will be the quantity produced and the price charged by the firm? What will be the amount of monopoly profit? [Hint: Recall that marginal revenue equals the change in total revenues ($P \times Q$) from each additional unit and that marginal cost equals the change in total costs from each additional unit.]

b. If regulators require the firm to practice marginal cost pricing, what quantity will it produce, and what price will it charge? What is the firm's profit under this regulatory framework? [Hint: Recall that average total cost equals total cost divided by quantity and that profits equal ($P -$ ATC) $\times Q$.]

c. If regulators require the firm to practice average cost pricing, what quantity will it produce, and what price will it charge? What is the firm's profit under this regulatory framework?

27-4. As noted in the chapter, separating the *production* of electricity from its *delivery* has led to considerable deregulation of producers.

a. Briefly explain which of these two aspects of the sale of electricity remains susceptible to natural monopoly problems.

b. Suppose that the potential natural monopoly problem you identified in part (a) actually arises. Why is marginal cost pricing not a feasible solution? What makes average cost pricing a feasible solution?

c. Discuss two approaches that a regulator could use to try to implement an average-cost-pricing solution to the problem identified in part (a).

27-5. Are lemons problems likely to be more common in some industries and less common in others? Based on your answer to this question, should government regulatory activities designed to reduce the scope of lemons problems take the form of economic regulation or social regulation? Take a stand, and support your reasoning.

27-6. Research into genetically modified crops has led to significant productivity gains for countries such as the United States that employ these techniques. Countries such as the European Union's member nations, however, have imposed controls on the import of these products, citing concern for public health. Is the European Union's regulation of genetically modified crops social regulation or economic regulation?

27-7. Do you think that the regulation described in Problem 27-6 is more likely an example of the capture hypothesis or the share-the-gains, share-the-pains theory? Why?

27-8. Prices of tickets for seats on commercial passenger planes are typically in the hundreds of dollars, whereas trips can be made by automobile at much lower cost. Accident rates per person per trip in the airline industry are considerably lower than auto accident rates per person per trip. Based on these facts, discuss how regulatory costs and benefits may help to explain why government regulations require children to be placed in safety seats in automobiles but not on commercial passenger planes.

27-9. In 2003, the U.S. government created a "Do Not Call Registry" and forbade marketing firms from calling people who placed their names on this list. Today, an increasing number of companies are sending mail solicitations to individuals inviting them to send back an enclosed postcard for more information about the firms' products. What these solicitations fail to mention is that they are worded in such a way that someone who returns the postcard gives up protection from telephone solicitations, even if they are on the government's "Do Not Call Registry." In what type of behavior are these companies engaging? Explain your answer. (Hint: Are these firms meeting the letter of the law but violating its spirit?)

27-10. Suppose that a business has developed a very high-quality product and operates more efficiently in producing that product than any other potential competitor. As a consequence, at present it is the only seller of this product, for which there are few close substitutes. Is this firm in violation of U.S. antitrust laws? Explain.

27-11. Consider the following fictitious sales data (in thousands of dollars) for books sold both over the Internet and in physical retail establishments. Firms have numbers instead of names, and Firm 1 generates book sales only over the Internet. Antitrust authorities judge that a single firm possesses "monopoly power" if its share of sales in the relevant market exceeds 70 percent.

Internet Book Sales		Book Sales in Physical Stores		Combined Book Sales	
Firm	Sales	Firm	Sales	Firm	Sales
1	$ 750	2	$4,200	2	$ 4,250
2	50	3	2,000	3	2,050
3	50	4	1,950	4	2,000
4	50	5	450	1	750
5	50	6	400	5	500
6	50			6	450
Total	$1,000		$9,000		$10,000

a. Suppose that the antitrust authorities determine that bookselling in physical retail stores and Internet bookselling are individually separate relevant markets. Does any single firm have monopoly power, as defined by the antitrust authorities?

b. Suppose that in fact there is really only a single book industry, in which firms compete both in physical retail stores and via the Internet. According to the antitrust authorities' measure of monopoly power, is there actually cause for concern?

27-12. A package delivery company provides both overnight and second-day delivery services. It charges almost twice as much to deliver an overnight package to any world location as it does to deliver the same package to the same location in two days. Often, second-day packages arrive at company warehouses in destination cities by the next day, but drivers intentionally do not deliver these packages until the following day. What is this business practice called? Briefly summarize alternative perspectives concerning whether this activity should or should not be viewed as a form of price discrimination.

27-13. A firm that sells both Internet-security software and computer antivirus software will sell the antivirus software as a stand-alone product. It will only sell the Internet-security software to consumers in a combined package that also includes the antivirus software. What is this business practice called? Briefly explain why an antitrust authority might view this practice as a form of price discrimination.

27-14. Recently, a food retailer called Whole Foods sought to purchase Wild Oats, a competitor in the market for organic foods. When the Federal Trade Commission (FTC) sought to block this merger on antitrust grounds, FTC officials argued that such a merger would dramatically increase concentration in the market for "premium organic foods." Whole Foods' counterargument was that it considered itself to be part of the broadly defined supermarket industry that includes retailers such as Albertson's, Kroger, and Safeway. What key issue of antitrust regulation was involved in this dispute? Explain.

ECONOMICS ON THE NET

Guidelines for U.S. Antitrust Merger Enforcement How does the U.S. government apply antitrust laws to mergers? This application gives you the opportunity to learn about the standards applied by the Antitrust Division of the U.S. Department of Justice when it evaluates a proposed merger.

Title: U.S. Department of Justice Antitrust Merger Enforcement Guidelines

Navigation: Go to **www.econtoday.com/ch27** to access the home page of the Antitrust Division of the U.S. Department of Justice.

Application Answer the following questions.

1. Click on *Horizontal Merger Guidelines*. In section 1, click on *Overview*, and read this section. What factors do U.S. antitrust authorities consider when evaluat-

ing the potential for a horizontal merger to "enhance market power"—that is, to place the combination in a monopoly situation?

2. Back up to the page titled *Merger Enforcement*, and click on *Non-Horizontal Merger Guidelines*. Read the guidelines. In what situations will the antitrust authorities most likely question a nonhorizontal merger?

For Group Study and Analysis Have three groups of students from the class examine sections 1, 2, and 3 of the *Horizontal Merger Guidelines* discussed in item 1. After each group reports on all the factors that the antitrust authorities consider when evaluating a horizontal merger, discuss why large teams of lawyers and many economic consultants are typically involved when the Antitrust Division of the Department of Justice alleges that a proposed merger would be "anticompetitive."

ANSWERS TO QUICK QUIZZES

p. 597: (i) Economic . . . social; (ii) natural . . . economic; (iii) social

p. 600: (i) lower . . . revenue . . . cost; (ii) average . . . zero; (iii) deliver . . . networks

p. 603: (i) failures . . . asymmetric; (ii) asymmetric; (iii) lemons . . . low

p. 606: (i) consumers . . . firms; (ii) industry . . . legislators . . . consumers; (iii) government . . . firms'

p. 608: (i) Sherman; (ii) Clayton; (iii) Federal Trade Commission; (iv) Robinson-Patman

p. 611: (i) market share . . . sales; (ii) product . . . geographic; (iii) versioning . . . bundling

28 The Labor Market: Demand, Supply, and Outsourcing

International Business Machines (IBM) Corporation recently announced that it was eliminating 5,000 jobs in the United States. The company said that it would replace almost all of the positions by hiring workers located outside the United States. Since the mid-1990s, a long list of companies, from computer manufacturers to commercial banks, have been engaging in international *outsourcing* by hiring workers in foreign countries to engage in various tasks. Why are IBM and so many other U.S. firms hiring thousands of workers abroad instead of here in the United States? In this chapter, you will learn the answer to this question.

LEARNING OBJECTIVES

After reading this chapter, you should be able to:

- Understand why a firm's marginal revenue product curve is its labor demand curve
- Explain in what sense the demand for labor is a "derived" demand
- Identify the key factors influencing the elasticity of demand for inputs
- Describe how equilibrium wage rates are determined for perfectly competitive firms
- Explain what labor outsourcing is and how it is ultimately likely to affect U.S. workers' earnings and employment prospects
- Contrast the demand for labor and wage determination by a product market monopolist with outcomes that would arise under perfect competition

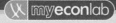

MyEconLab helps you master each objective and study more efficiently. See end of chapter for details.

Did You Know That in Ukraine, when politicians want to have a large crowd at a political rally, they sometimes turn to a company called Easy Work, which pays college students to cheer for politicians? According to the head of the company, who is also a college student, "We'll do business with any political party. Ideology doesn't matter to us. We rally only for the money." Easy Work pays an hourly wage of about $4 per hour, which is more than four times the nation's minimum hourly wage rate.

The demand for participants at political rallies by politicians or for all types of inputs by businesses can be studied in much the same manner as we studied the demand for output. Our analysis will always end with the same conclusion: A firm will hire employees up to the point beyond which it isn't profitable to hire any more. It will hire employees to the point at which the marginal benefit of hiring a worker will just equal the marginal cost. Indeed, in every profit-maximizing situation, it is most profitable to carry out an activity up to the point at which the marginal benefit equals the marginal cost. Remembering that guideline will help you in analyzing decision making at the firm level, which is where we will begin our discussion of the demand for labor.

Labor Demand for a Perfectly Competitive Firm

We will start our analysis under the assumption that the market for input factors is perfectly competitive. We will further assume that the output market is perfectly competitive. This provides a benchmark against which to compare other situations in which labor markets or product markets are not perfectly competitive.

Competition in the Product Market

Let's take as our example a firm that sells titanium batteries and is in competition with many companies selling the same kind of product. Assume that the laborers hired by this manufacturing firm do not need any special skills. This firm sells titanium batteries in a perfectly competitive market. It also buys labor (its variable input) in a perfectly competitive market. A firm that hires labor under perfectly competitive conditions hires only a minuscule proportion of all the workers who are potentially available to the firm. By "potentially available," we mean all the workers in a given geographic area who possess the skills demanded by our perfect competitor.

In such a market, it is always possible for the individual firm to hire extra workers without having to offer a higher wage. Thus, the supply of labor to the firm is perfectly elastic at the going wage rate established by the forces of supply and demand in the entire labor market. The firm is a *price taker* in the labor market.

Marginal Physical Product

Look at panel (a) of Figure 28-1 on the following page. In column 1, we show the number of workers per week that the firm can employ. In column 2, we show total physical product (TPP) per week, the total *physical* production of titanium batteries that different quantities of the labor input (in combination with a fixed amount of other inputs) will generate in a week's time. In column 3, we show the additional output gained when the company adds workers to its existing manufacturing facility. This column, the **marginal physical product (MPP) of labor,** represents the extra (additional) output attributed to employing additional units of the variable input factor. If this firm employs seven workers rather than six, the MPP is 118. The law of diminishing marginal product predicts that additional units of a variable factor will, after some point, cause the MPP to decline, other things held constant.

Marginal physical product (MPP) of labor The change in output resulting from the addition of one more worker. The MPP of the worker equals the change in total output accounted for by hiring the worker, holding all other factors of production constant.

We are assuming that all other nonlabor factors of production are held constant. So, if our manufacturing firm wants to add one more worker to its production line, it has to crowd all the existing workers a little closer together because it does not increase its capital stock (the production equipment). Therefore, as we add more

FIGURE 28-1 Marginal Revenue Product

In panel (a), column 4 shows marginal revenue product (MRP), which is the additional revenue the firm receives for the sale of that additional output. Marginal revenue product is simply the revenue the additional worker brings in—the combination of that worker's contribution to production and the revenue that that production will bring to the firm. For this perfectly competitive firm, marginal revenue is equal to the price of the product, or $10 per unit. At a weekly wage of $830, the profit-maximizing employer will pay for only 12 workers because then the marginal revenue product is just equal to the wage rate or weekly salary.

Panel (a)

(1) Labor Input (workers per week)	(2) Total Physical Product (TPP) (titanium batteries per week)	(3) Marginal Physical Product (MPP) (titanium batteries per week)	(4) Marginal Revenue (MR = P = $10) x MPP = Marginal Revenue Product (MRP) ($ per additional worker)	(5) Wage Rate ($ per week) = Marginal Factor Cost (MFC) = Change in Total Costs ÷ Change in Labor
6	882			
		118	$1,180	$830
7	1,000			
		111	1,110	830
8	1,111			
		104	1,040	830
9	1,215			
		97	970	830
10	1,312			
		90	900	830
11	1,402			
		83	830	830
12	1,485			
		76	760	830
13	1,561			

In panel (b), we find the number of workers the firm will want to hire by observing the wage rate that is established by the forces of supply and demand in the entire labor market. We show that this employer is hiring labor in a perfectly competitive labor market and therefore faces a perfectly elastic supply curve represented by *s* at a constant marginal factor cost (MFC) of $830 per week. As in other situations, we have a supply and demand model. In this example, the demand curve is represented by MRP, and the supply curve is *s*. Profit maximization occurs at their intersection, which is the point at which MRP = MFC.

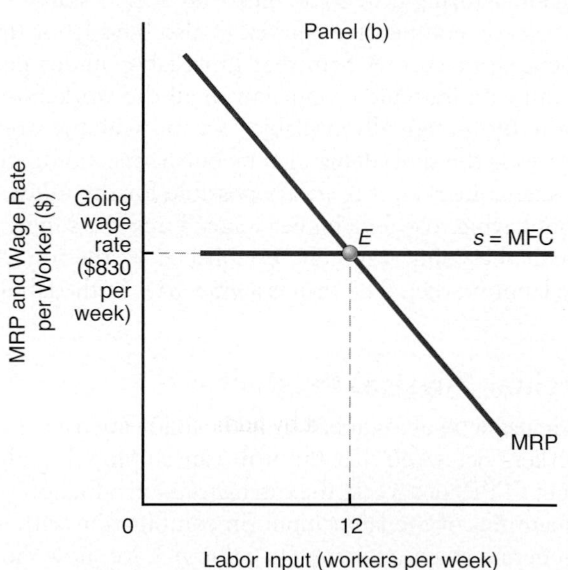

workers, each one has a smaller and smaller fraction of the available capital stock with which to work. If one worker uses one machine, adding another worker usually won't double the output because the machine can run only so fast and for so many hours per day. In other words, MPP declines because of the law of diminishing marginal product (see Chapter 22).

Marginal Revenue Product

We now need to translate into a dollar value the physical product that results from hiring an additional worker. This is done by multiplying the marginal physical product by the marginal revenue of the firm. Because this firm sells titanium batteries in a perfectly competitive market, marginal revenue is equal to the price of the product. If employing seven workers rather than six yields an MPP of 118 and the marginal revenue is $10 per flash memory drive, the **marginal revenue product (MRP)** is $1,180 (118 × $10). The MRP is shown in column 4 of panel (a) of Figure 28-1 on the facing page. *The marginal revenue product represents the incremental worker's contribution to the firm's total revenues.*

Marginal revenue product (MRP)
The marginal physical product (MPP) times marginal revenue (MR). The MRP gives the additional revenue obtained from a one-unit change in labor input.

When a firm operates in a perfectly competitive product market, the marginal physical product times the product price is also referred to as the *value of marginal product (VMP)*. Because price and marginal revenue are the same for a perfectly competitive firm, the VMP is also the MRP for such a firm.

In column 5 of panel (a) of Figure 28-1, we show the wage rate, or *marginal factor cost*, of each worker. The marginal cost of workers is the extra cost incurred in employing an additional unit of that factor of production. We call that cost the **marginal factor cost (MFC).** Otherwise stated,

Marginal factor cost (MFC)
The cost of using an additional unit of an input. For example, if a firm can hire all the workers it wants at the going wage rate, the marginal factor cost of labor is that wage rate.

$$\text{Marginal factor cost} = \frac{\text{change in total cost}}{\text{change in amount of resource used}}$$

Because each worker is paid the same competitively determined wage of $830 per week, the MFC is the same for all workers. And because the firm is buying labor in a perfectly competitive labor market, the wage rate of $830 per week really represents the supply curve of labor to the firm. That supply curve is perfectly elastic because the firm can purchase all labor at the same wage rate, considering that it is a minuscule part of the entire labor-purchasing market. (Recall the definition of perfect competition.) We show this perfectly elastic supply curve as *s* in panel (b) of Figure 28-1.

GENERAL RULE FOR HIRING Nearly every optimizing rule in economics involves comparing marginal benefits with marginal cost. Because the benefit from added workers is extra output and consequently more revenues, the general rule for the hiring decision of a firm is this:

> ***The firm hires workers up to the point at which the additional cost associated with hiring the last worker is equal to the additional revenue generated by hiring that worker.***

In a perfectly competitive market, this is the point at which the wage rate just equals the marginal revenue product. If the firm were to hire more workers, the additional wages would not be covered by additional increases in total revenue. If the firm were to hire fewer workers, it would be forfeiting the contributions that those workers otherwise could make to total profits.

Therefore, referring to columns 4 and 5 in panel (a) of Figure 28-1 on the preceding page, we see that this firm would certainly employ at least seven workers because the MRP is $1,180 while the MFC is only $830. The firm would continue to add workers up to the point at which MFC = MRP because as workers are added, those additional workers contribute more to revenue than to cost.

THE MRP CURVE: DEMAND FOR LABOR We can also use panel (b) of Figure 28-1 to find how many workers our firm should hire. First, we draw a line at the going wage rate, which is determined by demand and supply in the labor market. The line is labeled *s* to indicate that it is the supply curve of labor for the *individual* firm purchasing labor in a perfectly competitive labor market. That firm can purchase all the labor

FIGURE 28-2 Demand for Labor, a Derived Demand

The demand for labor is derived from the demand for the final product being produced. Therefore, the marginal revenue product curve will shift whenever the price of the product changes. If we start with the marginal revenue product curve MRP_0 at the going wage rate of $830 per week, 12 workers will be hired. If the price of titanium batteries goes down, the marginal revenue product curve will shift to MRP_1, and the number of workers hired will fall, in this case to 10. If the price of titanium batteries goes up, the marginal revenue product curve will shift to MRP_2, and the number of workers hired will increase, in this case to 15.

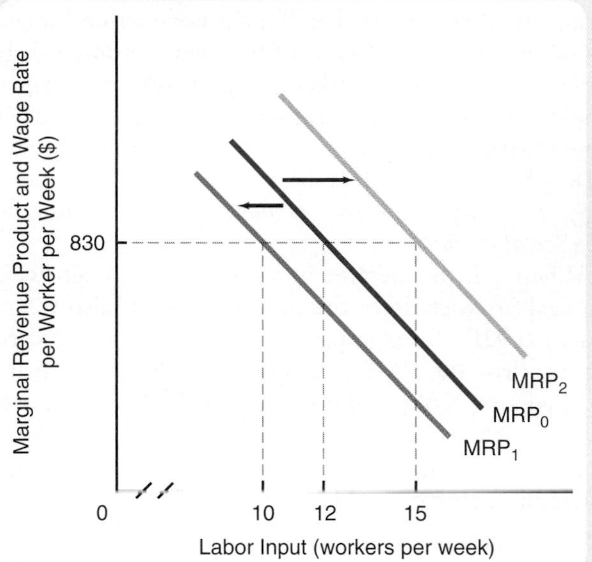

it wants of equal quality at $830 per worker. This perfectly elastic supply curve, *s*, intersects the marginal revenue product curve at 12 workers per week. At the intersection, *E*, in panel (b) in Figure 28-1 on page 620, the wage rate is equal to the marginal revenue product. The firm maximizes profits where its demand curve for labor, which turns out to be its MRP curve, intersects the firm's supply curve for labor, shown as *s*. The firm in our example would not hire 13 workers, because using 13 rather than 12 would add only $760 to revenue but $830 to cost. If the price of labor should fall to, say, $760 per worker per week, the firm would hire an additional worker. Thus, the quantity of labor demanded increases as the wage decreases.

Derived Demand for Labor

We have identified an individual firm's demand for labor curve, which shows the quantity of labor that the firm will wish to hire at each wage rate, as its MRP curve. Under conditions of perfect competition in both product and labor markets, MRP is determined by multiplying MPP times the product's price. This suggests that the demand for labor is a **derived demand.** Factors of production are rented or purchased not because they give any intrinsic satisfaction to the firms' owners but because they can be used to manufacture output that is expected to be sold at a profit.

Derived demand
Input factor demand derived from demand for the final product being produced.

We know that an increase in the market demand for a given product raises the product's price (all other things held constant), which in turn increases the marginal revenue product, or demand for the resource. Figure 28-2 above illustrates the effective role played by changes in product demand in a perfectly competitive product market. The MRP curve shifts whenever there is a change in the price of the final product that the workers are producing.

Suppose, for example, that the market price of titanium batteries declines. In that case, the MRP curve will shift to the left from MRP_0 to MRP_1. We know that $MRP \equiv MPP \times MR$. If marginal revenue (here the output price) falls, so does the demand for labor. At the initial equilibrium, therefore, the price of labor (here the MFC) becomes greater than MRP. At the same going wage rate, the firm will hire fewer workers. This is because at various levels of labor use, the marginal revenue product of labor is now lower. Thus, the firm would reduce the number of workers hired. Conversely, if marginal revenue (the output price) rises, the demand for labor will also rise, and the firm will want to hire more workers at each and every possible wage rate.

We just pointed out that MRP ≡ MPP × MR. Clearly, then, a change in marginal productivity, or in the marginal physical product of labor, will shift the MRP curve. If the marginal productivity of labor decreases, the MRP curve, or demand curve, for labor will shift inward to the left. Again, this is because at every quantity of labor used, the MRP will be lower. A lower amount of labor will be demanded at every possible wage rate.

QUICK QUIZ See page 641 for the answers. Review concepts from this section in MyEconLab.

The change in total __________ due to a one-unit change in one variable __________, holding all other __________ constant, is called the **marginal physical product (MPP).** When we multiply marginal physical product times __________ __________, we obtain the **marginal revenue product (MRP).**

A firm will hire workers up to the point at which the additional cost of hiring one more worker is equal to the additional revenue generated. For the individual firm, therefore, its MRP of labor curve is also its __________ __________ labor curve.

The demand for labor is a __________ demand, __________ from the demand for final output. Therefore, a change in the price of the final output will cause a __________ in the MRP curve (which is also the firm's demand for labor curve).

The Market Demand for Labor

The downward-sloping portion of each individual firm's marginal revenue product curve is also its demand curve for the one variable factor of production—in our example, labor. When we go to the entire market for a particular type of labor in a particular industry, we will also find that the quantity of labor demanded will vary inversely as the wage rate changes.

Constructing the Market Labor Demand Curve

Given that the market demand curve for labor is made up of the individual firms' downward-sloping demand curves for labor, we can safely infer that the market demand curve for labor will look like D in panel (b) of Figure 28-3 on the following page: It will slope downward. That market demand curve for labor in the titanium battery industry shows the quantities of labor demanded by all of the firms in the industry at various wage rates.

Nevertheless, the market demand curve for labor is *not* a simple horizontal summation of the labor demand curves of all individual firms. Remember that the demand for labor is a derived demand. Even if we hold labor productivity constant, the demand for labor still depends on both the wage rate and the price of the final output.

For instance, suppose that we start at a wage rate of $20 per hour and employment level 10 in panel (a) of Figure 28-3 on the next page. If we sum all such employment levels—point a in panel (a)—across 200 firms, we get a market quantity demanded of 2,000, or point A in panel (b), at the wage rate of $20. A decrease in the wage rate to $10 per hour would induce individual firms' employment levels to increase toward a quantity demanded of 22 *if product price did not change.*

As all 200 firms simultaneously increase employment, total industry output also increases at the present price. Indeed, this would occur at *any* price, meaning that the industry product supply curve will shift rightward, and the market clearing price of the product must fall. The fall in the output price in turn causes a downward shift of each firm's MRP curve (d_0) to MRP_1 (d_1) in panel (a). Thus, each firm's employment of labor increases to 15 rather than to 22 at the wage rate of $10 per hour. A summation of all such 200 employment levels gives us 3,000—point B—in panel (b).

Determinants of Demand Elasticity for Inputs

Just as we were able to discuss the price elasticity of demand for different commodities in Chapter 19, we can discuss the price elasticity of demand for inputs. The price elasticity of demand for labor is defined in a manner similar to the price elasticity of

FIGURE 28-3 Derivation of the Market Demand Curve for Labor

The market demand curve for labor is not simply the horizontal summation of each individual firm's demand curve for labor. If wage rates fall from $20 to $10, all 200 firms will increase employment and therefore output, causing the price of the product to fall. This causes the marginal revenue product curve of each firm to shift inward, from d_0 to d_1 in panel (a). The resulting market demand curve, *D,* in panel (b) is therefore less elastic around prices from $10 to $20 than it would be if the output price remained constant.

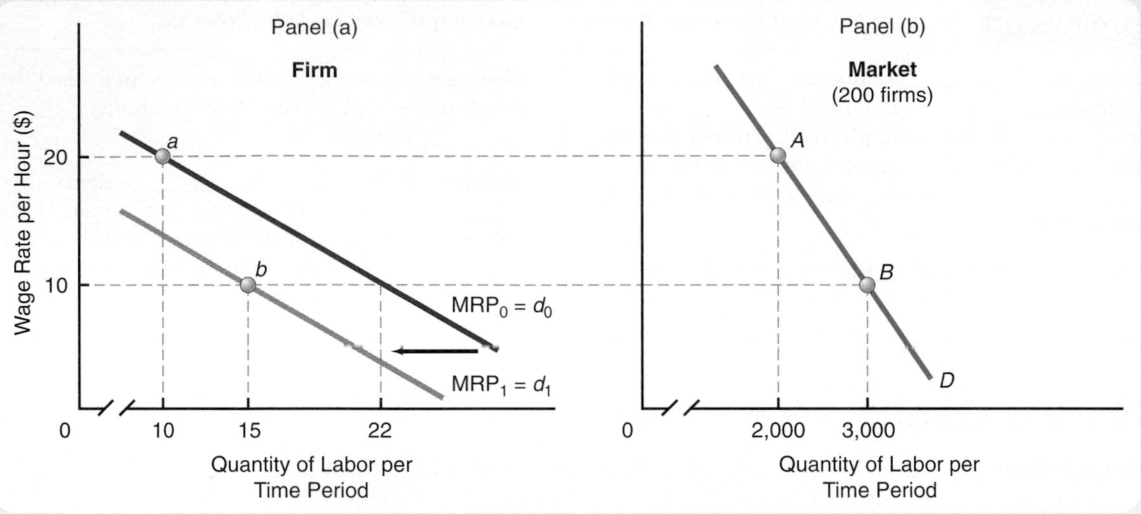

demand for goods: the percentage change in the quantity of labor demanded divided by the percentage change in the price of labor. When the *numerical* (or absolute) value of this ratio is less than 1, demand is inelastic. When it is 1, demand is unit-elastic. When it is greater than 1, demand is elastic.

There are four principal determinants of the price elasticity of demand for an input. The price elasticity of demand for a variable input will be greater:

1. The greater the price elasticity of demand for the final product
2. The easier it is to employ substitute inputs in production
3. The larger the proportion of total costs accounted for by the particular variable input
4. The longer the time period available for adjustment

FINAL PRODUCT PRICE ELASTICITY An individual radish farmer faces an extremely elastic demand for radishes, given the existence of many competing radish growers. If the farmer's laborers tried to obtain a significant wage increase, the farmer couldn't pass on the resultant higher costs to radish buyers. So any wage increase would lead to a large reduction in the quantity of labor demanded by the individual radish farmer.

EASE OF SUBSTITUTION Clearly, the easier it is for producers to switch to using another factor of production, the more responsive those producers will be to an increase in an input's price. If plastic can easily substitute for chrome plating in the production of, say, car bumpers, then a rise in the price of chrome plating will cause automakers to greatly reduce the quantity of chrome plating they demand.

How has U.S. firms' increased ability to have labor performed by workers in other nations affected the elasticity of the demand for labor in the United States?

INTERNATIONAL EXAMPLE **Globalization of Tasks and the Elasticity of U.S. Labor Demand**

During the past two decades, U.S. companies have hired more foreign workers to perform tasks, such as operating customer service call centers and tabulating bank records, that previously were performed by workers located in the United States. (See pages 628–631 for a more detailed discussion of this phenomenon, which is known as international *outsourcing* of labor.) The economist Mine Senses of Johns Hopkins University has examined how this increased substitutability of foreign labor for U.S. labor has affected U.S. labor demand elasticities. She finds evidence that a shift toward using foreign labor to perform more tasks has boosted labor demand elasticities in the United States by at least 20 percent on average. Thus, greater ease of substitution of foreign labor for labor based within U.S. borders has increased elasticities of U.S. labor demand.

FOR CRITICAL ANALYSIS

Many foreign firms also have increased their employment of U.S. workers to perform tasks over the past 20 years. What do you predict has happened to the elasticity of demand for labor in countries where these firms are located?

PORTION OF TOTAL COST When a particular input's costs account for a very large share of total costs, any increase in that input's price will affect total costs relatively more. If labor costs are 80 percent of total costs, companies will cut back on employment more aggressively than if labor costs are only 8 percent of total costs, for any given wage increase.

ADJUSTMENT PERIOD Finally, over longer periods, firms have more time to figure out ways to economize on the use of inputs whose prices have gone up. Furthermore, over time, technological change will allow for easier substitution in favor of relatively cheaper inputs and against inputs whose prices went up. At first, a pay raise obtained by a strong telephone industry union may not result in many layoffs, but over time, the telephone companies will use new technology to replace many of the now more expensive workers.

QUICK QUIZ **See page 641 for the answers. Review concepts from this section in MyEconLab.**

Because the demand for labor is a derived demand that depends on both the __________ rate and the __________ of final output, the market demand curve for labor is not a simple horizontal summation of the labor demand curves of all individual firms. The market demand curve for labor does slope __________, however.

Input price elasticity of demand depends on the final product's __________ of demand, the ease of substituting other __________, the relative importance of the input's cost in total __________, and the time available for __________.

Wage Determination in a Perfectly Competitive Labor Market

Having developed the demand curve for labor (and all other variable inputs) in a particular industry, let's turn to the labor supply curve. By adding supply to the analysis, we can determine the equilibrium wage rate that workers earn in an industry. We can think in terms of a supply curve for labor that slopes upward in a particular industry. At higher wage rates, more workers will want to enter that particular industry. The individual firm, however, does not face the entire *market* supply curve. Rather, in a perfectly competitive case, the individual firm is such a small part of the market that it can hire all the workers that it wants at the going wage rate. We say, therefore, that the industry faces an upward-sloping supply curve but that the individual *firm* faces a perfectly elastic supply curve for labor.

FIGURE 28-4 The Equilibrium Wage Rate and the Titanium Battery Industry

The industry demand curve for labor is D. We put in a hypothetical upward-sloping labor supply curve for the titanium battery industry, S. The intersection is at point E, giving an equilibrium wage rate of $830 per week and an equilibrium quantity of labor demanded of Q_1. At a wage above $830 per week, there will be an excess quantity of workers supplied. At a wage below $830 per week, there will be an excess quantity of workers demanded.

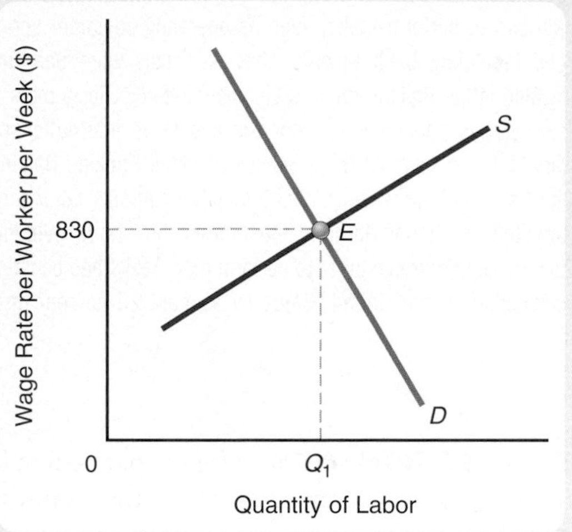

Labor Market Equilibrium

The demand curve for labor in the titanium battery industry is D in Figure 28-4 above, and the supply curve of labor is S. The equilibrium wage rate of $830 a week is established at the intersection of the two curves. The quantity of workers both supplied and demanded at that rate is Q_1. If for some reason the wage rate fell to $800 a week, in our hypothetical example, there would be an excess number of workers demanded at that wage rate. Conversely, if the wage rate rose to $900 a week, there would be an excess quantity of workers supplied at that wage rate. In either case, competition would quickly force the wage back to the equilibrium level.

We have just found the equilibrium wage rate for the entire titanium battery industry. The individual firm must take that equilibrium wage rate as given in the perfectly competitive model used here because the individual firm is a very small part of the total demand for labor. Thus, each firm purchasing labor in a perfectly competitive market can purchase all of the input it wants at the going market price.

Shifts in the Market Demand for and the Supply of Labor

Just as we discussed shifts in the supply curve and the demand curve for various products in Chapter 3, we can discuss the effects of shifts in supply and demand in labor markets.

REASONS FOR LABOR DEMAND CURVE SHIFTS Many factors can cause the demand curve for labor to shift. We have already discussed a number of them. Clearly, because the demand for labor or any other variable input is a derived demand, the labor demand curve will shift if there is a shift in the demand for the final product. There are two other important determinants of the position of the demand curve for labor: changes in labor's productivity and changes in the price of related factors of production (substitute inputs and complementary inputs).

1. *Changes in the demand for the final product.* The demand for labor or any other variable input is derived from the demand for the final product. The marginal revenue product is equal to marginal physical product times marginal revenue. Therefore, any change in the demand for the final product will change its price and hence the MRP of the input. The rule of thumb is as follows:

   A change in the demand for the final product that labor (or any other variable input) is producing will shift the market demand curve for labor in the same direction.

What lies behind the surge in the demand for people who can translate the Icelandic language into English and other languages?

INTERNATIONAL EXAMPLE An Increase in the Demand for Services of Icelandic Translators

A financial crisis and a volcano might not seem to be related to the demand for translators. Nevertheless, in Iceland they are. In 2008 and 2009, Iceland experienced the largest banking crisis, in relation to the size of the country's national income, ever experienced by a country in all of recorded history. This event induced European and U.S. customers of banks in Iceland to seek assistance from financial professionals and attorneys. To provide these services, many financial advisers and lawyers had to obtain translations of financial and legal documents written in the Icelandic language.

Then, in the spring of 2010, Iceland's Eyjafjallajökull volcano began to erupt, emitting plumes of ash that grounded tens of thousands of airline flights in and around Europe. The eruption brought about an increased demand for media coverage of the history, present condition, and likely future of Iceland's 22 active volcanoes. For their reports on the eruption, media people relied considerably on interpretations provided by Icelandic translators. Thus, as a result of these two events, the derived demand for services provided by Icelandic translators increased considerably between 2008 and 2010.

FOR CRITICAL ANALYSIS

Why did the derived demand for the services of Icelandic translators increase even though the translators' marginal physical product probably did not increase? (Hint: Recall that the derived demand for labor depends on marginal revenue product.)

2. *Changes in labor productivity.* The second part of the MRP equation is MPP, which relates to labor productivity. We can surmise, then, that, other things being equal:

A change in labor productivity will shift the market labor demand curve in the same direction.

Labor productivity can increase because labor has more capital or land to work with, because of technological improvements, or because labor's quality has improved. Such considerations explain why the real standard of living of workers in the United States is higher than in most other countries. U.S. workers generally work with a larger capital stock, have more natural resources, are in better physical condition, and are better trained than workers in many countries. Hence the demand for labor in the United States is, other things held constant, greater.

3. *Change in the price of related factors.* Labor is not the only resource that firms use. Some resources are substitutes and some are complements in the production process. If we hold output constant, we have the following general rule:

A change in the price of a substitute input will cause the demand for labor (or any other input) to change in the same direction.

Thus, if the price of an input for which labor can substitute as a factor of production decreases, the demand for labor falls. For instance, if the price of mechanized ditch-digging equipment decreases, the demand for workers who, in contrast, can use shovels to dig ditches decreases.

Suppose that a particular type of capital equipment and labor are complementary. In general, we predict the following:

A change in the price of a complementary input will cause the demand for labor to change in the opposite direction.

If the price of machines goes up but they must be used with labor, fewer machines will be purchased and therefore fewer workers will be used.

You Are There

To learn how developments in robotics are creating substitutes for human labor, read **At Staples, the Demand for Robotic Inputs Is Increasing,** on page 636.

DETERMINANTS OF THE SUPPLY OF LABOR Labor supply curves may shift in a particular industry for a number of reasons. For example, if wage rates for factory workers in the digital camera industry remain constant while wages for factory workers in the computer industry go up dramatically, the supply curve of factory workers in the digital camera industry will shift inward to the left as these workers move to the computer industry.

Changes in working conditions in an industry can also affect its labor supply curve. If employers in the digital camera industry discover a new production technique that makes working conditions much more pleasant, the supply curve of labor to the digital camera industry will shift outward to the right.

Job flexibility also determines the position of the labor supply curve. For example, when an industry allows workers more flexibility, such as the ability to work at home via computer, the workers are likely to provide more hours of labor. That is to say, their supply curve will shift outward to the right. Some industries in which firms offer *job sharing*, particularly to people raising families, have found that the supply curve of labor has shifted outward to the right.

QUICK QUIZ See page 641 for the answers. Review concepts from this section in MyEconLab.

The individual perfectly competitive firm faces a perfectly __________ labor supply curve—it can hire all the labor it wants at the going market wage rate. The industry supply curve of labor slopes __________.

By plotting an industrywide supply curve for labor and an industrywide demand curve for labor on the same graph, we obtain the __________ wage rate in the industry.

The labor demand curve can shift because the __________ for the final product shifts, labor __________ changes, or the price of a related (__________ or __________) factor of production changes.

Labor Outsourcing, Wages, and Employment

In addition to making it easier for people to work at home, computer technology has made it possible for them to provide labor services to companies located in another country. Some companies based in Canada regularly transmit financial records—often via the Internet—to U.S. accountants so that they can process payrolls and compile income statements. Meanwhile, some U.S. manufacturers of personal computers and peripheral devices arrange for customers' calls for assistance to be directed to call centers in India, where English-speaking technical-support specialists help the customers with their problems.

Outsourcing
A firm's employment of labor outside the country in which the firm is located.

A firm that employs labor located outside the country in which it is based engages in labor **outsourcing.** Canadian companies that hire U.S. accountants outsource accounting services to the United States. U.S. computer manufacturers that employ Indian call-center staff outsource technical-support services to India. How does outsourcing affect employment and wages in the United States? Who loses and who gains from outsourcing? Let's consider each of these questions in turn.

Wage and Employment Effects of Outsourcing

Equilibrium wages and levels of employment in U.S. labor markets are determined by the demands for and supplies of labor in those markets. As you have learned, one of the determinants of the market demand for labor is the price of a substitute input. Availability of a lower-priced substitute, you also learned, causes the demand for labor to fall. Thus, the *immediate* economic effects of labor outsourcing are straightforward. When a home industry's firms can obtain *foreign* labor services that are a close substitute for *home* labor services, the demand for labor services provided by home workers will decrease. What this economic reasoning ultimately implies for U.S. labor markets, however, depends on whether we view the United States as the "home" country or the "foreign" country.

FIGURE 28-5 Outsourcing of U.S. Computer Technical-Support Services

Initially, the market wage for U.S. workers providing technical support for customers of U.S. computer manufacturers is $19 per hour at point E_1 in panel (a), while the market wage for Indian workers who provide the same service is $8 per hour in panel (b). Then, improvements in communications technologies enable U.S. firms to substitute away from U.S. workers in favor of Indian workers. The market demand for U.S. labor decreases in panel (a), generating a new equilibrium at point E_2 at a lower U.S. market wage and employment level. The market demand for Indian labor increases in panel (b), bringing about higher wages and employment at point E_2.

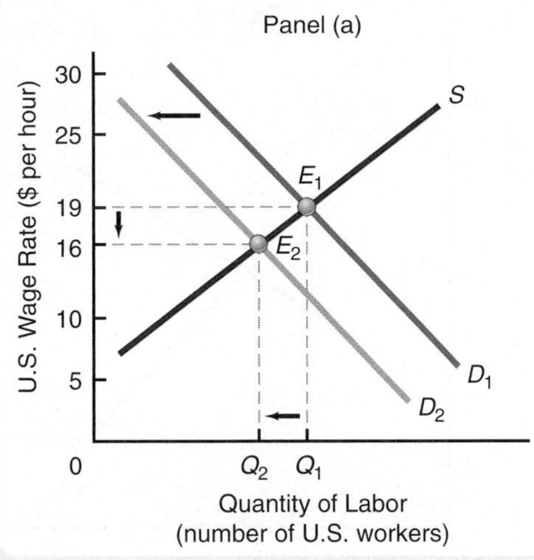

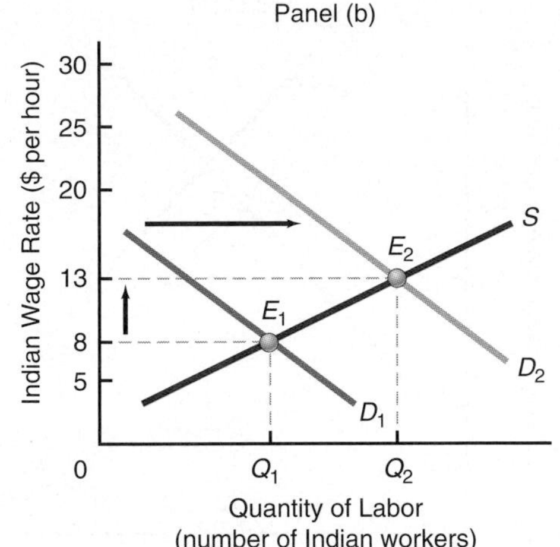

U.S. LABOR MARKET EFFECTS OF OUTSOURCING BY U.S. FIRMS To begin, let's view the United States as the home country. Suppose that initially all U.S. firms employ only U.S. workers. Then developments in computer, communications, and transportation technologies enable an increasing number of U.S. firms to regard the labor of foreign workers as a close substitute for labor provided by U.S. workers. Take a look at Figure 28-5 above. Panel (a) depicts demand and supply curves in the U.S. market for workers who handle calls for technical support for U.S. manufacturers of personal computers. Suppose that before technological change makes foreign labor substitutable for U.S. labor, point E_1 is the initial equilibrium. At this point, the market wage rate in this U.S. labor market is $19 per hour.

Now suppose that improvements in communications technologies enable U.S. personal computer manufacturers to consider foreign labor as a substitute input for U.S. labor. Panel (b) displays demand and supply curves in a market for substitutable labor services in India. At the initial equilibrium point E_1, the wage rate denominated in U.S. dollars is $8 per hour. Firms in this U.S. industry will respond to the lower price of substitute labor in India by increasing their demand for labor services in that country and reducing their demand for U.S. labor. Thus, in panel (b), the market demand for the substitute labor services available in India rises. The market wage in India rises to $13 per hour, at point E_2, and Indian employment increases. In panel (a), the market demand for U.S. labor services decreases. At the new equilibrium point E_2, the U.S. market wage has fallen to $16 per hour, and equilibrium employment has decreased.

Consequently, when U.S. firms are the home firms engaging in labor outsourcing, the effects are lower wages and decreased employment in the relevant U.S. labor markets. In those nations where workers providing the outsourced labor reside, the effects are higher wages and increased employment.

U.S. LABOR MARKET EFFECTS OF OUTSOURCING BY FOREIGN FIRMS U.S. firms are not the only companies that engage in outsourcing. Consider the Canadian companies that hire U.S. accountants to calculate their payrolls and maintain their financial records. Figure 28-6 on the following page shows the effects in the Canadian and U.S. markets for labor services provided by accountants before and after *Canadian*

FIGURE 28-6 Outsourcing of Accounting Services by Canadian Firms

Suppose that the market wage for accounting services in Canada is initially \$29 per hour, at point E_1 in panel (a), but in the United States accountants earn just \$21 per hour at point E_1 in panel (b). Then, Internet access enables Canadian firms to substitute labor services provided by U.S. accountants for the services of Canadian accountants. The market demand for the services of Canadian accountants decreases in panel (a), and at point E_2 fewer Canadian accountants are employed at a lower market wage. The market demand for U.S. accounting services increases in panel (b). This generates higher wages and employment for U.S. accountants at point E_2.

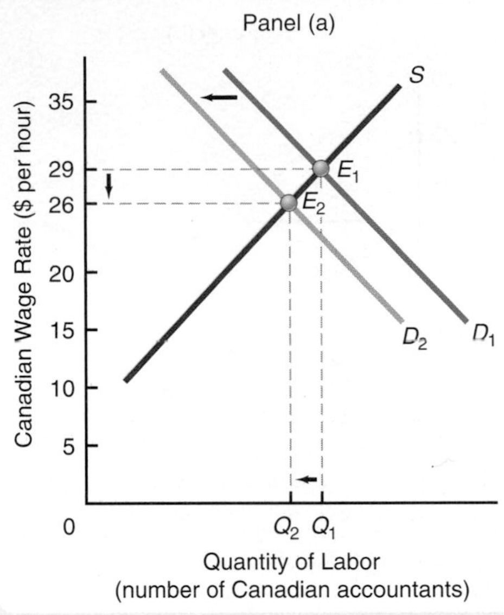

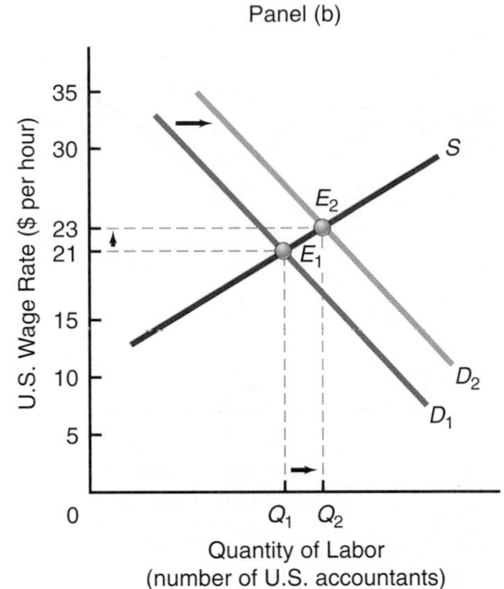

outsourcing of accountants' labor. At point E_1 in panel (a), before any outsourcing takes place, the initial market wage for qualified accountants in Canada is \$29 per hour. In panel (b), the market wage for similarly qualified U.S. accountants is \$21 per hour.

After Internet access allows companies in Canada to transfer financial data electronically, the services of U.S. accountants become available as a less expensive substitute for those provided by Canadian accountants. When Canadian firms respond by seeking to outsource to U.S. accountants, the demand for U.S. accountants' labor services rises in panel (b). This causes the market wage earned by U.S. accountants to increase to \$23 per hour. Canadian firms substitute away from the services of Canadian accountants, so in panel (a) the demand for the labor of accountants in Canada declines. Canadian accountants' wages decline to \$26 per hour.

In contrast to the situation in which U.S. firms are the home firms engaging in labor outsourcing, when foreign firms outsource by hiring workers in the United States, wages and employment levels rise in the affected U.S. markets. In the nations where the firms engaging in outsourcing are located, the effects are lower wages and decreased employment.

Gauging the Net Effects of Outsourcing on the U.S. Economy

In the example depicted in Figure 28-5 on the preceding page, the market wage and employment level for U.S. technical-support workers declined as a result of outsourcing by U.S. firms. In contrast, in the example shown in Figure 28-6 above, U.S. accountants earned higher wages and experienced increased employment as a result of outsourcing by Canadian firms. Together, these examples illustrate a fundamental conclusion concerning the short-run effects of global labor outsourcing in U.S. labor markets:

To read a Heritage Foundation lecture about the net effects of outsourcing on U.S. jobs, use the link at **www.econtoday.com/ch28**.

> ***Labor outsourcing by U.S. firms tends to reduce U.S. wages and employment. Whenever foreign firms engage in labor outsourcing in the United States, however, U.S. wages and employment tend to increase.***

Consequently, the immediate effects of increased worldwide labor outsourcing are lower wages and employment in some U.S. labor markets and higher wages and employment in others. In this narrow sense, some U.S. workers "lose" from outsourcing while others "gain," just as some Canadian workers "lose" while some Indian workers "gain."

SUMMING UP THE ECONOMIC IMPLICATIONS OF OUTSOURCING Even in the best of times, workers in labor markets experience short-run ups and downs in wages and jobs. During normal times in the United States, after all, about 4 million jobs typically come and go every month.

Certainly, various groups of U.S. workers earn lower pay or experience reduced employment opportunities, at least for a time, as a result of labor outsourcing. Nevertheless, outsourcing is a two-way street. Labor outsourcing does not just involve U.S. firms purchasing the labor services of residents located abroad. This phenomenon also entails the purchase of labor services from U.S. workers who provide outsourcing services to companies located in other nations.

Indeed, outsourcing really amounts to another way for residents of different nations to conduct trade with one another. As you learned in Chapter 2 (also see Chapter 32 for a more detailed look), trade allows nations' residents to specialize according to their *comparative advantages* and thereby obtain gains from exchanging items across country boundaries. To be sure, not all workers gain equally from the trade of outsourced labor services, and some people temporarily lose, in the form of either lower wages or reduced employment opportunities. Nevertheless, specialization and trade of labor services through outsourcing generate overall gains from trade for participating nations, such as India, Canada, and the United States.

Why Not . . . prohibit U.S. firms from outsourcing?

Barring U.S. companies from engaging in international labor outsourcing likely would have two negative consequences for the U.S. economy. First, with outsourcing prohibited, the equilibrium wages that U.S. firms would have to pay to obtain labor that they had previously outsourced would increase, which would boost their operating costs. These firms would respond by reducing the quantities of goods and services supplied at any given prices, and the reduction in supply in affected markets would lead to higher equilibrium prices for consumers. Second, other nations' governments probably would respond by prohibiting their own companies from outsourcing to U.S. workers. This response would generate a decrease in the demand for U.S. labor, which would result in lower market clearing wages and reduced equilibrium employment in the affected U.S. labor markets.

QUICK QUIZ

See page 641 for the answers. Review concepts from this section in MyEconLab.

Advances in telecommunications and computer networking are making foreign labor more easily __________ for home labor. Home firms' __________ of foreign labor for home labor is known as labor **outsourcing.**

In the short run, outsourcing by U.S. firms __________ the demand for labor, market wages, and equilibrium employment in U.S. labor markets. Outsourcing by foreign firms that hire U.S. labor __________ the demand for labor, market wages, and equilibrium employment in U.S. labor markets. The net short-run effects on U.S. wages and employment are mixed.

In the long run, outsourcing enables U.S. firms to operate more efficiently and this activity generates overall __________ __________ __________ for U.S. residents.

Monopoly in the Product Market

So far we've considered only perfectly competitive markets, both in selling the final product and in buying factors of production. We will continue our assumption that the firm purchases its factors of production in a perfectly competitive factor market. Now, however, we will assume that the firm sells its product in an *imperfectly* competitive output market. In other words, we are considering the output market structures of monopoly, oligopoly, and monopolistic competition. In all such cases, the firm, be it a monopolist, an oligopolist, or a monopolistic competitor, faces a downward-sloping demand curve for its product.

Throughout the rest of this chapter, we will simply refer to a monopoly situation for ease of analysis. The analysis holds for all industry structures that are less than perfectly competitive. In any event, the fact that our firm now faces a downward-sloping demand curve for its product means that if it wants to sell more of its product (at a uniform price), it has to lower the price, *not just on the last unit, but on all preceding units.* The *marginal revenue* received from selling an additional unit is continuously falling (and is less than price) as the firm attempts to sell more and more. This is certainly different from our earlier discussions in this chapter in which the firm could sell all it wanted at a constant price. Why? Because the firm we discussed until now was a perfect competitor.

Constructing the Monopolist's Input Demand Curve

In reconstructing our demand schedule for an input, we must account for the facts that (1) the marginal *physical* product falls because of the law of diminishing marginal product as more workers are added and (2) the price (and marginal revenue) received for the product sold also falls as more is produced and sold. That is, for the monopolist, we have to account for both the diminishing marginal physical product and the diminishing marginal revenue. Marginal revenue is always less than price for the monopolist. The marginal revenue curve always lies below the downward-sloping product demand curve.

MARGINAL REVENUE PRODUCT FOR A PERFECTLY COMPETITIVE FIRM Marginal revenue for the perfect competitor is equal to the price of the product because all units can be sold at the going market price. In our example involving the production of titanium batteries, we assumed that the perfect competitor could sell all it wanted at $10 per unit. A one-unit change in sales always led to a $10 change in total revenues. Hence, marginal revenue was always equal to $10 for that perfect competitor. Multiplying this unchanging marginal revenue by the marginal physical product of labor then yielded the perfectly competitive firm's marginal revenue product.

MARGINAL REVENUE PRODUCT FOR A MONOPOLY FIRM The monopolist, however, cannot simply calculate marginal revenue by looking at the price of the product. To sell the additional output from an additional unit of input, the monopolist has to cut prices on all previous units of output. As output is increasing, then, marginal revenue is falling. The underlying concept is, of course, the same for both the perfect competitor and the monopolist. We are asking exactly the same question in both cases: When an additional worker is hired, what is the benefit? In either case, the benefit is obviously the change in total revenues due to the one-unit change in the variable input, labor. In our discussion of the perfect competitor, we were able simply to multiply the marginal physical product by the *constant* per-unit price of the product because the price of the product never changed (for the perfect competitor, $P \equiv MR$).

A single monopolist ends up hiring fewer workers than would all of the perfectly competitive firms added together. To see this, we must consider the marginal revenue product for the monopolist, which varies with each one-unit change in the monopolist's labor input. This is what we do in panel (a) of Figure 28-7 on the facing page, where column 5, "Marginal Revenue Product," gives the monopolist a quantitative notion of how additional workers and additional production generate additional revenues. The marginal revenue product curve for this monopolist has been plotted in panel (b) of the figure. To emphasize the lower elasticity of the monopolist's MRP curve (MRP_m) around the wage rate $830, the labor demand curve for a perfectly competitive industry (labeled *D*) has been plotted on the same graph in Figure 28-7 on the facing page. Recall that this curve is not simply the sum of the marginal revenue product curves of all perfectly competitive firms,

FIGURE 28-7 A Monopolist's Marginal Revenue Product

The monopolist hires just enough workers to make marginal revenue product equal to the going wage rate. If the going wage rate is \$830 per week, as shown by the labor supply curve, *s*, in panel (b), the monopolist would want to hire approximately 10 workers per week. That is the profit-maximizing amount of labor. The labor demand curve for a perfectly competitive industry from Figure 28-4 on page 626 is also plotted (*D*). The monopolist's MRP curve will always be less elastic around the going wage rate than it would be if marginal revenue were constant.

Panel (a)

(1) Labor Input (workers per week)	(2) Marginal Physical Product (MPP) (titanium batteries per week)	(3) Price of Product (*P*)	(4) Marginal Revenue (MR)	(5) Marginal Revenue Product (MRP_m) = (2) x (4)
8	111	\$11.60	\$9.40	\$1,043.40
9	104	11.40	9.00	936.00
10	97	11.20	8.60	834.20
11	90	11.00	8.20	738.00
12	83	10.80	7.80	647.40
13	76	10.60	7.40	562.40

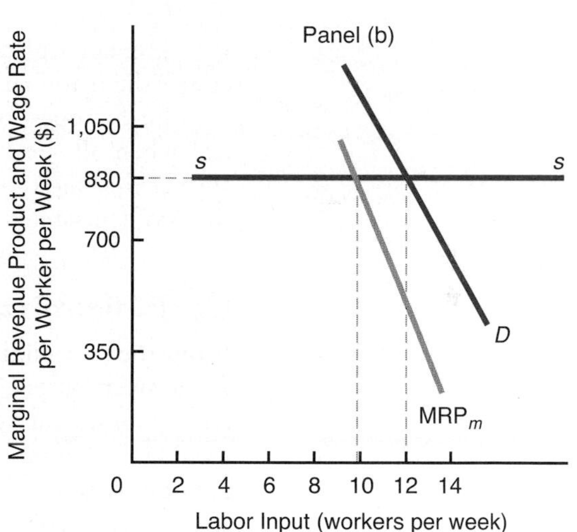

because when competitive firms together increase employment, their output expands and the product price declines. Nevertheless, at any given wage rate, the quantity of labor demanded by the monopoly is still less than the quantity of labor demanded by a perfectly competitive industry.

Why does MRP_m represent the monopolist's input demand curve? As always, our profit-maximizing monopolist will continue to hire labor as long as additional profits result. Profits are made as long as the additional cost of more workers is outweighed by the additional revenues made from selling the output of those workers. When the wage rate equals these additional revenues, the monopolist stops hiring. That is, the firm stops hiring when the wage rate is equal to the marginal revenue product because additional workers would add more to cost than to revenue.

Why the Monopolist Hires Fewer Workers

Because we have used the same numbers as in Figure 28-1 on page 620, we can see that the monopolist hires fewer workers per week than firms in a perfect competitive market would. That is to say, if we could magically change the titanium battery industry in our example from one in which there is perfect competition in the output market to one in which there is monopoly in the output market, the amount of employment would fall. Why? Because the monopolist must take account of the declining product price that must be charged in order to sell a larger number of titanium batteries. Remember that every firm hires up to the point at which marginal benefit equals marginal cost. The marginal benefit to the monopolist of hiring an additional worker is not simply the additional output times the price of the product. Rather, the monopolist faces a reduction in the price charged on *all* units sold in order to be able to sell more.

So the monopolist ends up hiring fewer workers than all of the perfect competitors taken together, assuming that all other factors remain the same for the two hypothetical examples. But this should not come as a surprise. In considering product markets, by implication we saw that a monopolized titanium battery industry would produce less output than a competitive one. Therefore, the monopolized industry would hire fewer workers.

The Utilization of Other Factors of Production

The analysis in this chapter has been given in terms of the demand for the variable input labor. The same analysis holds for any other variable factor input. We could have talked about the demand for fertilizer or the demand for the services of tractors by a farmer instead of the demand for labor and reached the same conclusions. The entrepreneur will hire or buy any variable input up to the point at which its price equals the marginal revenue product.

A further question remains: How much of each variable factor should the firm utilize when all the variable factors are combined to produce the product? We can answer this question by looking at either the cost-minimizing side of the question or the profit-maximizing side.

Cost Minimization and Factor Utilization

From the cost minimization point of view, how can the firm minimize its total costs for a given output? Assume that you are an entrepreneur attempting to minimize costs. Consider a hypothetical situation in which if you spend $1 more on labor, you would get 20 more units of output, but if you spend $1 more on machines, you would get only 10 more units of output. What would you want to do in such a situation? You would wish to hire more workers or sell off some of your machines, for you are not getting as much output per *last* dollar spent on machines as you are per *last* dollar spent on labor. You would want to employ factors of production so that the marginal products per last dollar spent on each are equal. Thus, the least-cost, or cost minimization, rule will be as follows:

> ***To minimize total costs for a particular rate of production, the firm will hire factors of production up to the point at which the marginal physical product per last dollar spent on each factor of production is equalized.***

That is,

$$\frac{\text{MPP of labor}}{\text{price of labor (wage rate)}} = \frac{\text{MPP of capital}}{\text{price of capital (cost per unit of service)}} = \frac{\text{MPP of land}}{\text{price of land (rental rate per unit)}}$$

All we are saying here is that the cost-minimizing firm will always utilize *all* resources in such combinations that cost will be minimized for any given output rate. This is commonly called the *least-cost combination of resources.*

How does the ratio of marginal physical product to the price of labor of full-time employees compared to the same ratio for independent contractors help to explain why firms are choosing to hire fewer full-time employees and more independent contractors?

POLICY EXAMPLE **Payroll Regulations Spur the Hiring of Independent Contractors**

More than 10 million U.S. workers are classified as independent contractors who sell skilled labor services. Firms typically regard the marginal physical product of the labor of independent contractors as greater than that of regular full-time employees. Thus, equalization of the MPP/wage rate ratios for independent contractors and full-time employees in the past resulted in hiring fewer independent contractors at higher wages compared with full-time employees.

In recent years, in contrast, U.S. firms have been hiring more independent contractors relative to the number of full-time employees. A key reason is that the federal government has gradually been requiring firms to provide more benefits—overtime pay, family leave, and health benefits—for full-time employees. This legislation has pushed up the effective wage rate—*inclusive* of benefits—that firms must pay to full-time employees. The result of this increase in the denominator of the MPP/wage rate ratio for full-time employees has been to push that ratio down relative to the ratio for independent contractors. Firms have responded by hiring fewer full-time employees and more independent contractors.

FOR CRITICAL ANALYSIS

How does hiring fewer full-time employees and more independent contractors push the MPP/wage rate ratios back to equality?

Profit Maximization Revisited

If a firm wants to maximize profits, how much of each factor should be hired (or bought)? As you have learned, the firm will never utilize a factor of production unless the marginal benefit from hiring that factor is at least equal to the marginal cost. What is the marginal benefit? As we have pointed out several times, the marginal benefit is the change in total revenues due to a one-unit change in utilization of the variable input. What is the marginal cost? In the case of a firm buying in a perfectly competitive market, it is the price of the variable factor—the wage rate if we are referring to labor.

The profit-maximizing combination of resources for the firm will be where, in a perfectly competitive market structure,

MRP of labor = price of labor (wage rate)
MRP of capital = price of capital (cost per unit of service)
MRP of land = price of land (rental rate per unit)

To attain maximum profits, the marginal revenue product of each of a firm's resources must be exactly equal to its price. If the MRP of labor is \$20 and its price is only \$15, the firm will expand its employment of labor.

There is an exact match between the profit-maximizing combination of resources and the least-cost combination of resources discussed above. In other words, either rule can be used to yield the same cost-minimizing rate of utilization of each variable resource.

QUICK QUIZ **See page 641 for the answers. Review concepts from this section in MyEconLab.**

When a firm sells its output in a monopoly market, marginal revenue is __________ than price.

Just as the MRP is the perfectly competitive firm's input demand curve, the MRP is also the __________ input demand curve.

The profit-maximizing combination of factors will occur when each factor is used up to the point at which its MRP is equal to its unit __________.

To minimize total costs for a given output, the profit-maximizing firm will hire each factor of production up to the point at which the marginal __________ product per last dollar spent on each factor is equal to the marginal __________ product per last dollar spent on each of the other factors of production.

To maximize profits, the marginal __________ product of each resource must equal the resource's __________.

You Are There

At Staples, the Demand for Robotic Inputs Is Increasing

At warehouses operated by Staples, the office supply retailer, a key input in the distribution process is the "Kiva bot," a 250-pound, orange robot that is 2.5 feet long, 2 feet wide, and 1 foot tall. The Kiva bot is powered by a rechargeable lead-acid battery and moves around a warehouse at about 3 miles per hour. The robot negotiates its path by scanning a grid of floor stickers, and it broadcasts its location and receives routing directions via wireless signals from a central computer. At any given moment, some Kiva bots are transporting items in holding containers to human workers, who remove items from the containers, pack the items into delivery boxes, and load the boxes onto trucks. Other Kiva bots shift some containers toward the front of the packaging area and other containers to the rear as the company's order-processing system adjusts to changes in items' popularity as revealed by recent orders.

Laurence Plourde, a Staples executive, says that Kiva, the company that produces the robots, "has made robotic technology useful for smaller and smaller tasks" previously performed by humans. So far, Kiva and other robot manufacturers have not been able to design robots that can pack items into boxes as well as humans can, but Plourde wonders if such a breakthrough might come soon.

Critical Analysis Questions

1. What will happen to the demand for human warehouse workers at Staples if a cost-reducing technological improvement generates a lower price of Kiva bots?
2. What will happen to the demand for Kiva bots if there is a decline in the prices that Staples receives for its products?

ISSUES & APPLICATIONS

The Incentives to Outsource Labor Internationally

CONCEPTS APPLIED

- ▶ Outsourcing
- ▶ Marginal Revenue Product
- ▶ Derived Demand for Labor

Recently, International Business Machines (IBM) Corporation announced plans to lay off about 5,000 U.S. employees and move most of those jobs to India. Many of the affected positions involved customer support via call centers. IBM joined a long list of U.S. firms, including personal computer manufacturers, financial services companies, and media firms, that have opted to outsource labor abroad.

Evaluating the Marginal Revenue Product of Labor

What elements influence a firm's decision regarding international labor outsourcing? As always, a firm first considers the input's marginal revenue product, which equals marginal revenue times the marginal physical product of labor. Marginal revenue depends on conditions in a firm's product market, so it typically does not influence an outsourcing decision.

Thus, a key consideration in whether to outsource is differences in the marginal physical product of labor in different countries. To compare the levels of marginal physical product of labor in various nations, firms must try to measure these levels in constant-quality terms. One reason that Indian workers often "win out" over, say, Chinese workers in call-center outsourcing deals with U.S. firms is that a larger fraction of Indian workers are fluent in English. This greater familiarity with English increases Indian workers' constant-quality marginal physical product of labor and hence raises the derived U.S. demand for Indian-based labor. Another concern when making international comparisons of the constant-quality marginal physical product of labor is distance. The greater the distance between a firm's location and the outsourced labor that it hires, the more miscommunications and other problems that may occur.

Comparing Wage Rates

Firms always hire labor to the point at which the marginal revenue product of labor equals the market clearing wage rate. Consequently, the other fundamental factor influencing a firm's outsourcing decision is wage differences across countries.

Figure 28-8 below displays the average hourly U.S. dollar wage rate received by call-center agents in selected countries. The figure provides another reason that Indian call-center workers often gain outsourcing employment from U.S. firms: they receive lower wages than call-center workers in most other nations.

FIGURE 28-8 Average Hourly Wages of Call-Center Agents in Selected Nations

There are significant differences across nations in wages paid to call-center agents.

Source: International Labor Organization.

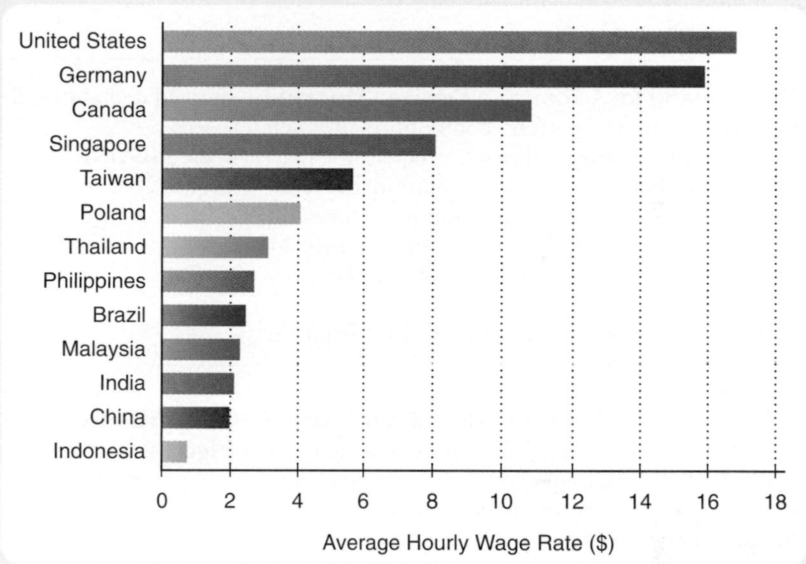

For Critical Analysis

1. Given that Indonesian call-center workers' wages are lower than those of call center workers in India, why do you suppose that U.S. firms nonetheless hire proportionately more Indian than Indonesian workers?
2. In light of the large differences between wages of call-center workers in the United States and wages of workers in a number of other countries, why do you think that some U.S. firms continue to employ U.S. call-center workers?

Web Resources

1. For a discussion of how to compare wages internationally by measuring the amount of time that people have to work to earn sufficient wages to buy a McDonald's Big Mac sandwich, go to www.econtoday.com/ch28.
2. To read in more detail about how different countries' wage rates can be measured in terms of Big Mac sandwiches, go to www.econtoday.com/ch28.

Research Project

Discuss key issues that a U.S. firm faces when attempting to compare constant-quality marginal physical product of workers in different nations.

For more questions on this chapter's Issues & Applications, go to **MyEconLab**. In the Study Plan for this chapter, select Section N: News.

Here is what you should know after reading this chapter. **MyEconLab** will help you identify what you know, and where to go when you need to practice.

WHAT YOU SHOULD KNOW		WHERE TO GO TO PRACTICE
Why a Firm's Marginal Revenue Product Curve Is Its Labor Demand Curve The marginal revenue product of labor equals marginal revenue times the marginal physical product of labor. Because of the law of diminishing marginal product, for a perfectly competitive producer the marginal revenue product curve slopes downward. To maximize profits, a firm hires labor to the point where the marginal factor cost of labor—the addition to total input costs resulting from employing an additional unit of labor—equals the marginal revenue product.	marginal physical product (MPP) of labor, 619 marginal revenue product (MRP), 621 marginal factor cost (MFC), 621 **KEY FIGURE** Figure 28-1, 620	• **MyEconLab** Study Plan 28.1 • Audio introduction to Chapter 28 • Animated Figure 28-1 • Economics Video: Myth: Outsourcing Is Bad for America
The Demand for Labor as a Derived Demand For firms that are perfect competitors in their product markets, marginal revenue equals the market price of their output, so the marginal revenue product of labor equals the product price times the marginal physical product of labor. As product market conditions vary and cause the market price to change, marginal revenue product curves shift. Hence, the demand for labor is derived from the demand for final products.	derived demand, 622 **KEY FIGURE** Figure 28-2, 622	• **MyEconLab** Study Plan 28.2 • Animated Figure 28-2 • Economics Video: No Smoking Employees
Key Factors Affecting the Elasticity of Demand for Inputs The price elasticity of demand for an input equals the percentage change in the quantity of the input demanded divided by the percentage change in the input's price. An input's price elasticity of demand is relatively high when any one of the following is true: (1) the price elasticity of demand for the final product is relatively high; (2) it is relatively easy to substitute other inputs in production; (3) the proportion of total costs accounted for by the input is relatively large; or (4) the firm has a longer time period to adjust to the change in the input's price.	**KEY FIGURE** Figure 28-3, 624	• **MyEconLab** Study Plan 28.2 • Animated Figure 28-3 • Video: Determinants of Demand Elasticity for Inputs • Economics Video: Doc Martens
How Equilibrium Wage Rates at Perfectly Competitive Firms Are Determined In a competitive labor market, at the equilibrium wage rate, the quantity of labor demanded by all firms is equal to the quantity of labor supplied by all workers. At this wage rate, each firm looks to its own labor demand curve to determine how much labor to employ.	**KEY FIGURE** Figure 28-4, 626	• **MyEconLab** Study Plan 28.3 • Animated Figure 28-4 • Video: Shifts in the Market Demand for Labor • Economics Video: Rust Belt City's Brighter Future

MyEconLab continued

WHAT YOU SHOULD KNOW		WHERE TO GO TO PRACTICE
U.S. Wage and Employment Effects of Labor Outsourcing The immediate, short-run effects of labor outsourcing on wages and employment in U.S. labor markets are mixed. Outsourcing by U.S. firms reduces the demand for labor in affected U.S. labor markets and thereby pushes down wages and employment. Outsourcing by foreign firms that hire U.S. labor, however, raises the demand for labor in related U.S. labor markets, which boosts U.S. wages and employment.	outsourcing, 628 **KEY FIGURES** Figure 28-5, 629 Figure 28-6, 630	• **MyEconLab** Study Plan 28.4 • Animated Figures 28-5, 28-6 • ABC News Video: How Outsourcing Affects Our Lives • Economics Video: Doc Martens • Economics Video: Myth: Outsourcing Is Bad for America • Economics Video: No Smoking Employees
Contrasting the Demand for Labor and Wage Determination Under Monopoly with Outcomes Under Perfect Competition If a product market monopolist competes for labor in a competitive labor market, it takes the market wage rate as given. Its labor demand curve, however, lies to the left of the labor demand curve that would have arisen in a competitive industry. Thus, at the competitively determined wage rate, a monopolized industry employs fewer workers than the industry otherwise would if it were perfectly competitive.	**KEY FIGURE** Figure 28-7, 633	• **MyEconLab** Study Plans 28.5, 28.6 • Animated Figure 28-7

Log in to MyEconLab, take a chapter test, and get a personalized Study Plan that tells you which concepts you understand and which ones you need to review. From there, MyEconLab will give you further practice, tutorials, animations, videos, and guided solutions.
Log in to www.myeconlab.com

PROBLEMS

All problems are assignable in myeconlab. Answers to the odd-numbered problems appear at the back of the book.

28-1. The following table depicts the output of a firm that manufactures computer printers. The printers sell for $100 each.

Labor Input (workers per week)	Total Physical Output (printers per week)
10	200
11	218
12	234
13	248
14	260
15	270
16	278

Calculate the marginal physical product and marginal revenue product at each input level above 10 units.

28-2. Refer back to your answers to Problem 28-1 in answering the following questions.

a. What is the maximum wage the firm will be willing to pay if it hires 15 workers?

b. The weekly wage paid by computer printer manufacturers in a perfectly competitive market is $1,200. How many workers will the profit-maximizing employer hire?

c. Suppose that there is an increase in the demand for personal computer systems. Explain the likely effects on marginal revenue product, marginal factor cost, and the number of workers hired by the firm.

28-3. Explain what happens to the elasticity of demand for labor in a given industry after each of the following events.

a. A new manufacturing technique makes capital easier to substitute for labor.

b. There is an increase in the number of substitutes for the final product that labor produces.

c. After a drop in the prices of capital inputs, labor accounts for a larger portion of a firm's factor costs.

28-4. Explain how the following events would affect the demand for labor.

a. A new education program administered by the company increases labor's marginal product.

b. The firm completes a new plant with a larger workspace and new machinery.

28-5. The following table depicts the product market and labor market an MP3 player manufacturer faces.

Labor Input (workers per day)	Total Physical Product	Product Price ($)
10	100	50
11	109	49
12	116	48
13	121	47
14	124	46
15	125	45

a. Calculate the firm's marginal physical product, total revenue, and marginal revenue product at each input level above 10 units.

b. The firm competes in a perfectly competitive labor market, and the market wage it faces is $100 per worker per day. How many workers will the profit-maximizing employer hire?

28-6. Recently, there has been an increase in the market demand for products of firms in manufacturing industries. The production of many of these products requires the skills of welders. Because welding is a dirty and dangerous job compared with other occupations, in recent years fewer people have sought employment as welders. Draw a diagram of the market for the labor of welders. Use this diagram to explain the likely implications of these recent trends for the market clearing wage earned by welders and the equilibrium quantity of welding services hired.

28-7. Since the early 2000s, there has been a significant increase in the price of corn-based ethanol.

a. A key input in the production of corn-based ethanol is corn. Use an appropriate diagram to explain what has likely occurred in the market for corn.

b. In light of your answer to part (a), explain why many hog farmers, who in the past used corn as the main feed input in hog production, have switched to cookies, licorice, cheese curls, candy bars, and other human snack foods instead of corn as food for their hogs.

28-8. A firm hires labor in a perfectly competitive labor market. Its current profit-maximizing hourly output is 100 units, which the firm sells at a price of $5 per unit. The marginal physical product of the last unit of labor employed is 5 units per hour. The firm pays each worker an hourly wage of $15.

a. What marginal revenue does the firm earn from sale of the output produced by the last worker employed?

b. Does this firm sell its output in a perfectly competitive market?

28-9. Explain why the short-term effects of outsourcing on U.S. wages and employment tend to be more ambiguous than the long-term effects.

28-10. A profit-maximizing monopolist hires workers in a perfectly competitive labor market. Employing the last worker increased the firm's total weekly output from 110 units to 111 units and caused the firm's weekly revenues to rise from $25,000 to $25,750. What is the current prevailing weekly wage rate in the labor market?

28-11. A monopoly firm hires workers in a perfectly competitive labor market in which the market wage rate is $20 per day. If the firm maximizes profit, and if the marginal revenue from the last unit of output produced by the last worker hired equals $10, what is the marginal physical product of that worker?

28-12. The current market wage rate is $10, the rental rate of land is $1,000 per unit, and the rental rate of capital is $500. Production managers at a firm find that under their current allocation of factors of production, the marginal physical product of labor is 100, the marginal physical product of land is 10,000, and the marginal physical product of capital is 4,000. Is the firm minimizing costs? Why or why not?

28-13. The current wage rate is $10, and the rental rate of capital is $500. A firm's marginal physical product of labor is 200, and its marginal physical product of capital is 20,000. Is the firm maximizing profits for the given cost outlay? Why or why not?

ECONOMICS ON THE NET

Current Trends in U.S. Labor Markets The Federal Reserve's "Beige Book," which summarizes regional economic conditions around the United States, provides a wealth of information about the current status of U.S. labor markets. This Internet application helps you assess developments in employment and wages in the United States.

Title: The Beige Book—Summary

Navigation: Go to **www.econtoday.com/ch28** to access the home page of the Federal Reserve's Board of Governors. Click on *A–Z Index*, and then click on *Beige Book*. Then select the report for the most recent period.

Application Read the section entitled "Prices and Wages," and answer the following questions.

1. Has overall employment been rising or falling during the most recent year? Based on what you learned in this chapter, what factors might account for this pattern? Does the Beige Book summary bear out any of these explanations for changes in U.S. employment?
2. Have U.S. workers' wages been rising or falling during the most recent year?

For Group Study and Analysis The left-hand margin of the Beige Book site lists the reports of the 12 Federal Reserve districts. Divide the class into two groups, and have each group develop brief summaries of the main conclusions of one district's report concerning employment and wages within that district. Reconvene and compare the reports. Are there pronounced regional differences?

ANSWERS TO QUICK QUIZZES

p. 623: (i) output . . . input . . . inputs . . . marginal revenue; (ii) demand for; (iii) derived . . . derived . . . shift
p. 625: (i) wage . . . price . . . downward; (ii) elasticity . . . inputs . . . costs . . . adjustment
p. 628: (i) elastic . . . upward; (ii) equilibrium; (iii) demand . . . productivity . . . substitute . . . complementary
p. 631: (i) substitutable . . . substitution; (ii) reduces . . . increases; (iii) gains from trade
p. 635: (i) less; (ii) monopolist's; (iii) price; (iv) physical . . . physical; (v) revenue . . . price

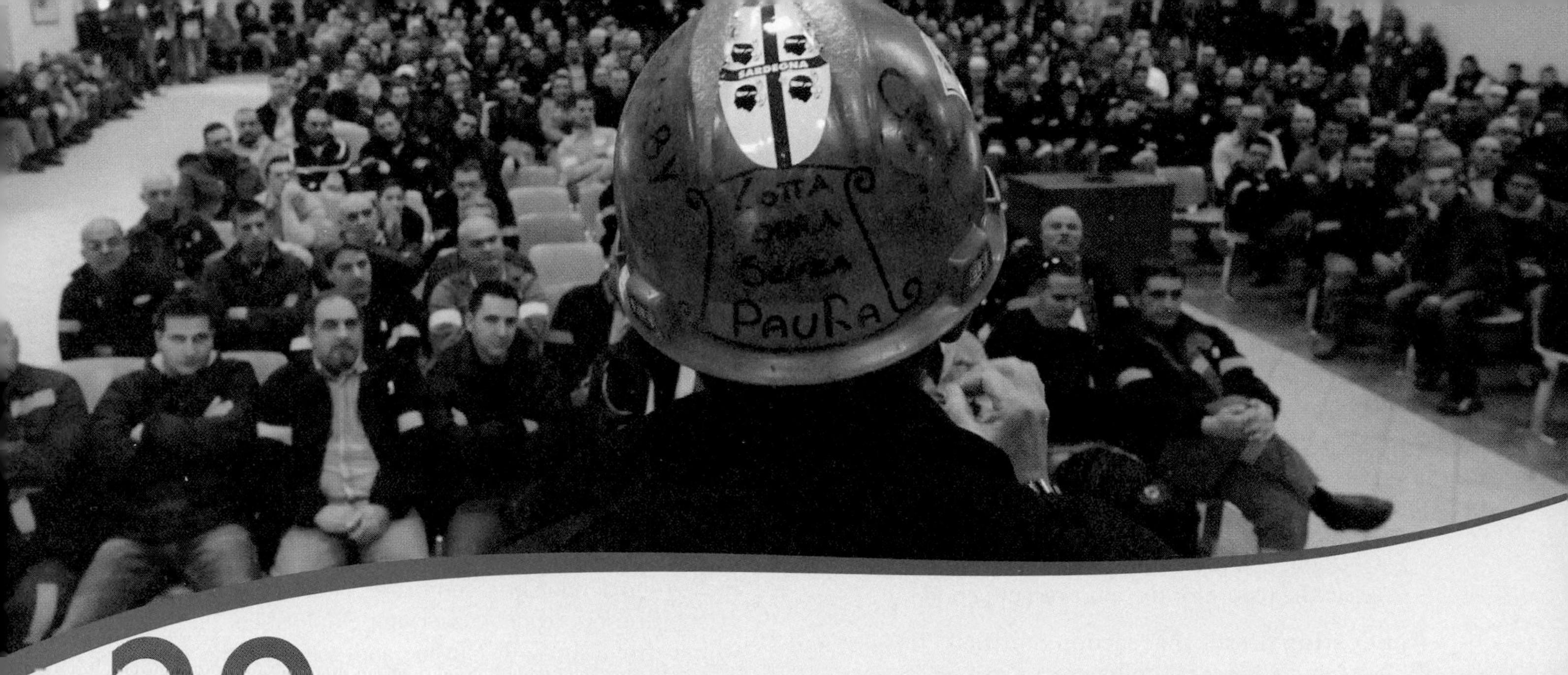

29

Unions and Labor Market Monopoly Power

Today, fewer than 8 percent of all U.S. workers employed by private firms are members of unions. In contrast, nearly 40 percent of local, state, and federal government employees belong to unions. Recently, government employment has grown more rapidly than private-sector employment—a trend that has contributed to the growth in the number of union members employed by governments. Indeed, in the late 2000s, the number of unionized workers in the government sector surpassed the number of unionized workers in the private sector for the first time in U.S. history. In this chapter, you will learn about the goals of unions and about their place in the U.S. economy.

LEARNING OBJECTIVES

After reading this chapter, you should be able to:

- Outline the essential history of the labor union movement
- Discuss the current status of labor unions
- Describe the basic economic goals and strategies of labor unions
- Evaluate the potential effects of labor unions on wages and productivity
- Explain how a monopsonist determines how much labor to employ and what wage rate to pay
- Compare wage and employment decisions by a monopsonistic firm with the choices made by firms in industries with alternative market structures

MyEconLab helps you master each objective and study more efficiently. See end of chapter for details.

the average employee of state and local governments in the United States receives 45 percent more in combined wages and benefits than the average worker in the private sector? The explanation for this differential is that an increasing percentage of state and local government workers belong to **labor unions**—organizations that seek to secure economic improvements for their members. Nonunion employees of state and local governments receive approximately the same wages and benefits as private workers. In contrast, *unionized* employees of state and local governments receive wages that are at least 20 percent higher and benefits that are more than *70 percent* greater.

Did You Know That?

Traditionally, one rationale for forming a union was that members might be able to earn more than they would in a competitive labor market by obtaining a type of monopoly power. Because the entire supply of a particular group of workers is controlled by a single source when a union bargains as a single entity with management, a certain monopoly element enters into the determination of employment. In such situations, we can no longer talk about a perfectly competitive supply of labor. Later in the chapter, we will examine the converse—a single employer who is the sole employer of a particular group of workers.

Labor unions
Worker organizations that seek to secure economic improvements for their members. They also seek to improve the safety, health, and other benefits (such as job security) of their members.

Industrialization and Labor Unions

In most parts of the world, labor movements began with local **craft unions.** These were groups of workers in individual trades, such as shoemaking, printing, or baking. Beginning around the middle of the eighteenth century, new technologies permitted reductions in unit production costs through the formation of larger-scale enterprises that hired dozens or more workers. By the late 1790s, workers in some British craft unions began trying to convince employers to engage in **collective bargaining,** in which business management negotiates with representatives of all union members about wages and hours of work.

Craft unions
Labor unions composed of workers who engage in a particular trade or skill, such as baking, carpentry, or plumbing.

Collective bargaining
Negotiation between the management of a company or of a group of companies and the management of a union or a group of unions for the purpose of reaching a mutually agreeable contract that sets wages, fringe benefits, and working conditions for all employees in all the unions involved.

In 1799 and 1800, the British Parliament passed laws called the Combination Acts aimed at prohibiting the formation of unions. In 1825, Parliament enacted a replacement Combination Act allowing unions to exist and to engage in limited collective bargaining. Unions on the European continent managed to convince most governments throughout Europe to enact similar laws during the first half of the nineteenth century.

Unions in the United States

The development of unions in the United States lagged several decades behind events in Europe. In the years between the Civil War and World War I (1861–1914), the Knights of Labor, an organized group of both skilled and unskilled workers, pushed for an eight-hour workday and equal pay for women and men. In 1886, a dissident group split from the Knights of Labor to form the American Federation of Labor (AFL) under the leadership of Samuel Gompers. During World War I, union membership increased to more than 5 million. But after the war, the government decided to stop protecting labor's right to organize. Membership began to fall.

THE FORMATION OF INDUSTRIAL UNIONS The Great Depression was a landmark event in U.S. labor history. Franklin Roosevelt's National Industrial Recovery Act of 1933 gave labor the federal right to bargain collectively, but that act was declared unconstitutional. The 1935 National Labor Relations Act (NLRA), otherwise known as the Wagner Act, took its place. The NLRA guaranteed workers the right to form unions, to engage in collective bargaining, and to be members of any union.

In 1938, the Congress of Industrial Organizations (CIO) was formed by John L. Lewis, the president of the United Mine Workers. Prior to the formation of the CIO, most labor organizations were craft unions. The CIO was composed of **industrial unions,** which drew their membership from an entire industry such as steel or automobiles. In 1955, the CIO and the AFL merged because the leaders of both associations thought a merger would help organized labor grow faster.

Industrial unions
Labor unions that consist of workers from a particular industry, such as automobile manufacturing or steel manufacturing.

Go to www.econtoday.com/ch29 to link to the Legal Information Institute's review of all the key U.S. labor laws.

Right-to-work laws
Laws that make it illegal to require union membership as a condition of continuing employment in a particular firm.

Closed shop
A business enterprise in which employees must belong to the union before they can be hired and must remain in the union after they are hired.

Union shop
A business enterprise that may hire nonunion members, conditional on their joining the union by some specified date after employment begins.

CONGRESSIONAL CONTROL OVER LABOR UNIONS Since the Great Depression, Congress has occasionally altered the relationship between labor and management through significant legislation. One of the most important pieces of legislation was the Taft-Hartley Act of 1947 (the Labor Management Relations Act). In general, the Taft-Hartley Act outlawed certain labor practices of unions, such as imposing make-work rules and forcing unwilling workers to join a particular union. Among other things, it allowed individual states to pass their own **right-to-work laws.** A right-to-work law makes it illegal for union membership to be a requirement for continued employment in any establishment.

The Taft-Hartley Act also made a **closed shop** illegal. A closed shop requires union membership before employment can be obtained. A **union shop,** however, is legal. A union shop does not require membership as a prerequisite for employment, but it can, and usually does, require that workers join the union after a specified amount of time on the job. (Even a union shop is illegal in states with right-to-work laws.)

What group benefits most from a Chinese labor law that allows a closed shop?

INTERNATIONAL EXAMPLE

The Chinese Union Monopoly Expands to Include Employees of Foreign Firms

Chinese firms have operated within a closed shop environment for many years. In an important sense, so have Chinese workers. There is only a single union in China—the appropriately named All-China Federation of Trade Unions (ACFTU), which has 193 million members. Whenever groups of workers have tried to establish their own, separate bargaining arrangements with Chinese employers, the union has successfully filed lawsuits to require employers to deal only with the ACFTU.

In recent years, the ACFTU has sought to expand its membership by requiring firms based outside China to recognize the ACFTU as the sole bargaining agent for their Chinese employees. The ACFTU is phasing in agreements covering all 50,000 Chinese employees of Wal-Mart, which in most other nations usually has chosen not to operate rather than hire union workers. Today, more than 90 percent of all U.S. firms operating in China, including McDonald's and FedEx, must require their employees to join the ACFTU when they accept their positions.

FOR CRITICAL ANALYSIS

If Chinese workers at covered foreign firms were permitted to work for a few months before joining the ACFTU, what type of legal structure governing union membership would exist?

Jurisdictional dispute
A disagreement involving two or more unions over which should have control of a particular jurisdiction, such as a particular craft or skill or a particular firm or industry.

Sympathy strike
A work stoppage by a union in sympathy with another union's strike or cause.

Secondary boycott
A refusal to deal with companies or purchase products sold by companies that are dealing with a company being struck.

Jurisdictional disputes, sympathy strikes, and secondary boycotts were also made illegal by the Taft-Hartley Act. In a **jurisdictional dispute,** two or more unions fight (and strike) over which should have control in a particular jurisdiction. For example, should carpenters working for a steel manufacturer be members of the steelworkers' union or the carpenters' union? A **sympathy strike** occurs when one union strikes in sympathy with another union's cause or strike. For example, if the retail clerks' union in a city is striking grocery stores, Teamsters union members may refuse to deliver products to those stores in sympathy with the retail clerks' demands for higher wages or better working conditions. A **secondary boycott** is a boycott of a company that deals with a struck company. For example, if union workers strike a baking company, a boycott of grocery stores that continue to sell that company's products is a secondary boycott. A secondary boycott brings pressure on third parties to force them to stop dealing with an employer who is being struck.

Perhaps the most famous provision of the Taft-Hartley Act allows the president to obtain a court injunction that will stop a strike for an 80-day cooling-off period if the strike is expected to imperil the nation's safety or health.

You Are There

To contemplate an atypical jurisdictional dispute involving only one union, read **Caught Up in an Unusual Jurisdictional Dispute in Michigan,** on page 656.

The Current Status of U.S. Labor Unions

As shown in Figure 29-1 on the facing page, union membership has been declining in the United States since the 1960s. At present, only about 12 percent of U.S. workers are union members. Fewer than 8 percent of workers in the private sector belong to unions.

FIGURE 29-1 Decline in Union Membership

Numerically, union membership in the United States has increased dramatically since the 1930s, but as a percentage of the labor force, union membership peaked around 1960 and has been falling ever since. Most recently, the absolute number of union members has also diminished.

Sources: L. Davis et al., *American Economic Growth* (New York: HarperCollins, 1972), p. 220; U.S. Department of Labor, Bureau of Labor Statistics.

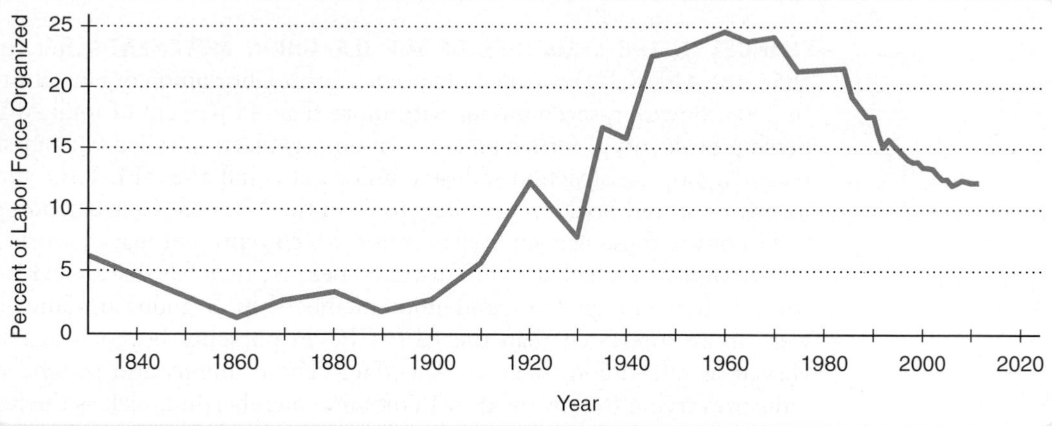

A DECLINE IN MANUFACTURING EMPLOYMENT A large part of the explanation for the decline in union membership has to do with the shift away from manufacturing. In 1948, workers in manufacturing industries, transportation, and utilities, which traditionally have been among the most heavily unionized industries, constituted more than half of private nonagricultural employment. Today, that fraction is less than one-fifth.

The relative decline in manufacturing employment helps explain why most of the largest U.S. unions now draw their members primarily from workers in service industries and governments. As you can see in Table 29-1 below, five of the ten largest unions now represent workers in these areas. The remaining five largest unions represent the manufacturing industries, transportation, and utilities that once dominated the U.S. union movement.

TABLE 29-1

The Ten Largest Unions in the United States

Half of the top ten U.S. unions have members who work in service and government occupations.

Union	Industry	Members
National Education Association	Education	2,731,000
Service Employees International Union	Health care, public, and janitorial services	1,505,000
American Federation of State, County, and Municipal Employees	Government services	1,460,000
International Brotherhood of Teamsters	Trucking, delivery	1,396,000
United Food and Commercial Workers International Union	Food and grocery services	1,312,000
American Federation of Teachers	Education	829,000
United Steelworkers of America	Steel	755,000
International Brotherhood of Electrical Workers	Electrical	705,000
Laborers' International Union of North America	Construction, utilities	670,000
International Association of Machinists and Aerospace Workers	Machine and aerospace	654,000

Source: U.S. Department of Labor.

DEREGULATION AND IMMIGRATION The trend away from manufacturing is the main reason for the decline in unionism. Nevertheless, the deregulation of certain industries, such as airlines and trucking, has also contributed, as has increased global competition. In addition, immigration has weakened the power of unions. Much of the unskilled and typically nonunionized work in the United States is done by foreign-born workers, and immigrant workers who are undocumented cannot legally join a union.

CHANGES IN THE STRUCTURE OF THE U.S. UNION MOVEMENT After its founding in 1955, the AFL-CIO remained the predominant labor union organization for 50 years. In 2005, however, seven unions with more than 45 percent of total AFL-CIO membership broke off to form a separate union organization called Change to Win. More recently, two construction industry unions also left the AFL-CIO and joined with ironworkers and bricklayers unions to form the National Construction Alliance.

Unions in these new umbrella groups, which represent mainly workers in growing service industries, had become frustrated because they felt that the AFL-CIO was not working hard enough to expand union membership. In addition, some of these unions were more interested than the AFL-CIO in pursuing boycotts against companies viewed as anti-union, such as Wal-Mart. These unions also sought strikes against industries trying to slow the growth of union membership, such as the hotel industry.

QUICK QUIZ See page 662 for the answers. Review concepts from this section in MyEconLab.

The _________ _________ of _________, composed of **craft unions,** was formed in 1886 under the leadership of Samuel Gompers. Membership increased until after World War I, when the government temporarily stopped protecting labor's right to organize.

During the Great Depression, legislation was passed that allowed for **collective bargaining.** The _________ _________ _________ Act of 1935 guaranteed workers the right to form unions. The Congress of Industrial Organizations (CIO), composed of _________ unions, was formed during the Great Depression. The AFL and the CIO merged in 1955.

In the United States, union membership as a percentage of the labor force peaked at nearly _________ percent in 1960 and has declined since then to only about _________ percent.

Union Goals and Strategies

Through collective bargaining, unions establish the wages below which no individual worker may legally offer his or her services. Each year, union representatives and management negotiate collective bargaining contracts covering wages as well as working conditions and fringe benefits for about 5 million workers. If approved by the members, a union labor contract sets wage rates, maximum workdays, working conditions, fringe benefits, and other matters, usually for the next two or three years.

Strike: The Ultimate Bargaining Tool

Whenever union-management negotiations break down, union negotiators may turn to their ultimate bargaining tool, the threat or the reality of a strike. Strikes make headlines, but a strike occurs in less than 2 percent of all labor-management disputes before the contract is signed. In the other 98 percent, contracts are signed without much public fanfare.

The purpose of a strike is to impose costs on stubborn management to force it to accept the union's proposed contract terms. Strikes disrupt production and interfere with a company's or an industry's ability to sell goods and services. The strike works both ways, though, because workers receive no wages while on strike (though they may be partly compensated out of union strike funds). Striking union workers may also be eligible to draw state unemployment benefits.

The impact of a strike is closely related to the ability of striking unions to prevent nonstriking (and perhaps nonunion) employees from continuing to work for the targeted company or industry. Therefore, steps are usually taken to prevent others from working for the employer. **Strikebreakers** can effectively destroy whatever bargaining power rests behind a strike. Numerous methods have been used to prevent strikebreakers from breaking strikes. Violence has been known to erupt, almost always in connection with union attempts to prevent strikebreaking.

Strikebreakers
Temporary or permanent workers hired by a company to replace union members who are striking.

In recent years, companies have had less incentive to hire strikebreakers because work stoppages have become much less common. From 1945 until 1990, on average more than 200 union strikes took place in the United States each year. Since 1990, however, the average has been closer to 25 strikes per year.

Union Goals with Direct Wage Setting

We have already pointed out that one of the goals of unions is to set minimum wages. The effects of setting a wage rate higher than a competitive market clearing wage rate can be seen in Figure 29-2 below. The market for labor is perfectly competitive. The market demand curve is *D*, and the market supply curve is *S*. The market clearing wage rate is W_e. The equilibrium quantity of labor is Q_e. If the union establishes by collective bargaining a minimum wage rate that exceeds W_e, an excess quantity of labor will be supplied (assuming no change in the labor demand schedule). If the minimum wage established by union collective bargaining is W_U, the quantity supplied will be Q_S. The quantity demanded will be Q_D. The difference is the excess quantity supplied, or surplus. Hence, the following point becomes clear:

> ***One of the major roles of a union that establishes a wage rate above the market clearing wage rate is to ration available jobs among the excess number of workers who wish to work in the unionized industry.***

Note also that the surplus of labor is equivalent to a shortage of jobs at wage rates above equilibrium.

To ration jobs, the union may use a seniority system, lengthen the apprenticeship period to discourage potential members from joining, or institute other rationing methods. This has the effect of shifting the supply of labor curve to the left in order to support the higher wage, W_U.

FIGURE 29-2 Unions Must Ration Jobs

The market clearing wage rate is W_e, at point *E*, at which the equilibrium quantity of labor is Q_e. If the union succeeds in obtaining wage rate W_U, the quantity of labor demanded will be Q_D, at point *A* on the labor demand curve, but the quantity of labor supplied will be Q_S, at point *B* on the labor supply curve. The union must ration a limited number of jobs among a greater number of workers. The surplus of labor is equivalent to a shortage of jobs at that wage rate.

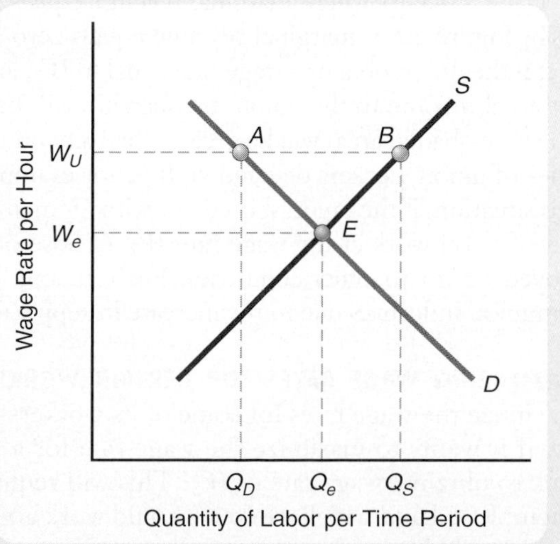

FIGURE 29-3 What Do Unions Maximize?

Assume that the union wants to employ all its Q_1 members. It will attempt to get wage rate W_1. If the union wants to maximize total wage receipts (income) of members who have jobs in this industry, it will do so at wage rate W_2, where the elasticity of the demand for labor is equal to 1. (The blue-shaded area represents the maximum total income that the union membership would earn at W_2.) If the union wants to maximize the wage rate for a given number of workers, say, Q_3, it will set the wage rate at W_3.

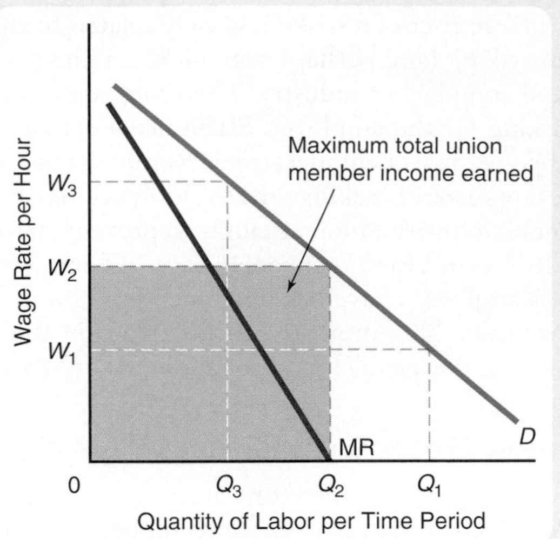

There is a trade-off here that any union's leadership must face: Higher wages inevitably mean a reduction in total union employment—fewer union positions. When facing higher wages, management may replace part of the workforce with machinery or may even seek to hire nonunion workers.

If we view unions as monopoly sellers of a service, we can identify three different types of goals that they may pursue: ensuring employment for all members of the union, maximizing aggregate income of workers, and maximizing wage rates for some workers.

EMPLOYING ALL MEMBERS IN THE UNION Assume that the union has Q_1 workers. If it faces a labor demand curve such as D in Figure 29-3 above, the only way it can "sell" all of those workers' services is to accept a wage rate of W_1. This is similar to any other market. The demand curve tells the maximum price that can be charged to sell any particular quantity of a good or service. Here the service happens to be labor.

MAXIMIZING MEMBER INCOME If the union is interested in maximizing the gross income of its members, it will normally want a smaller membership than Q_1—namely, Q_2 workers, all employed and paid a wage rate of W_2. The aggregate income to all members of the union is represented by the wages of only the ones who work. Total income earned by union members is maximized where the price elasticity of demand is numerically equal to 1. That occurs where marginal revenue equals zero.

In Figure 29-3, marginal revenue equals zero at a quantity of labor Q_2. So we know that if the union obtains a wage rate equal to W_2, and therefore Q_2 workers are demanded, the total income to the union membership will be maximized. In other words, $Q_2 \times W_2$ (the blue-shaded area) will be greater than any other combination of wage rates and quantities of union workers demanded. It is, for example, greater than $Q_1 \times W_1$. Note that in this situation, if the union started out with Q_1 members, there would be $Q_1 - Q_2$ members out of *union* work at the wage rate W_2. (Those out of union work either remain unemployed or go to other industries. Such actions have a depressing effect on wages in nonunion industries due to the increase in supply of workers there.)

MAXIMIZING WAGE RATES FOR CERTAIN WORKERS Assume that the union wants to maximize the wage rates for some of its workers—perhaps those with the most seniority. If it wants to maximize the wage rate for a given quantity of workers, Q_3, it will seek to obtain a wage rate of W_3. This will require deciding which workers should be unemployed and which workers should work and for how long each week or each year they should be employed.

FIGURE 29-4 Restricting Supply over Time

When the union was formed, it didn't affect wage rates or employment, which remained at \$19 and Q_1 (the equilibrium wage rate and quantity at point E_1). As demand increased—that is, as the demand schedule shifted outward from D_1 to D_2—the union restricted membership to its original level of Q_1, however. The new supply curve is S_1S_2, which intersects D_2 at E_2, or at a wage rate of \$21. Without the union, equilibrium would be at E_3, with a wage rate of \$20 and employment of Q_2.

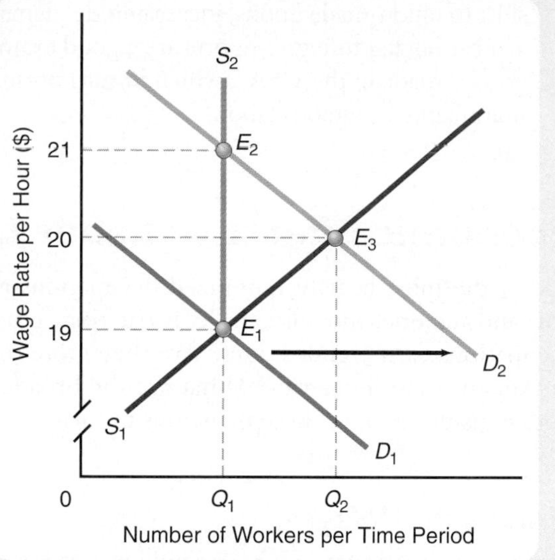

Union Strategies to Raise Wages Indirectly

One way or another, unions seek above-market wages for some or all of their members. Sometimes unions try to achieve this goal without making wage increases direct features of contract negotiations.

LIMITING ENTRY OVER TIME One way to raise wage rates without specifically setting wages is for a union to limit the size of its membership to the size of its employed workforce at the time the union was first organized. No workers are put out of work when the union is formed. Over time, as the demand for labor in the industry increases, the union prevents any net increase in membership, so larger wage increases are obtained than would otherwise be the case. We see this in Figure 29-4 above. In this example, union members freeze entry into their union, thereby obtaining a wage rate of \$21 per hour instead of allowing a wage rate of only \$20 per hour with no restriction on labor supply.

ALTERING THE DEMAND FOR UNION LABOR Another way that unions can increase wages is to shift the demand curve for labor outward to the right. This approach has the advantage of increasing both wage rates and the employment level. The demand for union labor can be increased by increasing worker productivity, increasing the demand for union-made goods, and decreasing the demand for non-union-made goods.

1. *Increasing worker productivity*. Supporters of unions have argued that unions provide a good system of industrial jurisprudence. The presence of unions may induce workers to feel that they are working in fair and just circumstances. If so, they work harder, increasing labor productivity. Productivity is also increased when unions resolve differences and reduce conflicts between workers and management, thereby providing a more peaceful administrative environment.
2. *Increasing demand for union-made goods*. Because the demand for labor is a derived demand, a rise in the demand for products produced by union labor will increase the demand for union labor itself. One way that unions attempt to increase the demand for goods produced by union labor is by advertising "Look for the union label."

3. *Decreasing the demand for non-union-made goods.* When the demand for goods that are competing with (or are substitutes for) union-made goods is reduced, consumers shift to union-made goods, increasing the demand. The campaigns of various unions against buying foreign imports are a good example. The result is greater demand for goods "made in the USA," which in turn presumably increases the demand for U.S. union (and nonunion) labor.

Economic Effects of Labor Unions

Today, the most heavily unionized occupations are government service, transportation and material moving, and construction. Do union members in these and other occupations earn higher wages? Are they more or less productive than nonunionized workers in their industries? What are the broader economic effects of unionization? Let's consider each of these questions in turn.

Unions and Wages

You have learned that unions are able to raise the wages of their members if they can successfully limit the supply of labor in a particular industry. Unions are also able to raise wages if they can induce increases in the demand for union labor.

Economists have extensively studied the differences between union wages and nonunion wages. They have found that the average *hourly* wage (not including benefits) earned by a typical private-sector union worker is about $2.25 higher than the hourly wage earned by a typical worker who is not a union member. Adjusted for inflation, this union-nonunion hourly wage differential is only about half as large as it was two decades ago, however.

Comparisons of the *annual* earnings of union and nonunion workers indicate that in recent years, unions have not succeeded in raising the annual incomes of their members. In 1985, workers who belonged to unions earned nearly 7 percent more per year than nonunion workers, even though union workers worked fewer hours per week. Today, a typical nonunion employee still works slightly longer each week, but the average nonunion worker also has a higher annual income than the average union worker.

Even the $2.25 hourly wage differential already mentioned is somewhat misleading because it is an average across *all* U.S. workers. In the private sector, union workers earn only about 4 percent more than nonunion workers, or a little less than 60 cents per hour. The hourly wage gain for government workers is more than six times higher at about $3.55 per hour. A state government employee who belongs to a union currently earns an hourly wage more than 20 percent higher than a state government worker who is not a union member.

Why Not . . . require firms to pay union wages to nonunionized workers?

Requiring employers to pay the average nonunionized U.S. worker about $2.25 per hour more would bring the average nonunion wage into line with the average union wage. Such a rule, however, would subject nonunionized labor markets to the same problem of surplus labor that confronts unionized industries. Requiring firms to boost their wages above the current equilibrium levels would induce the firms to cut back on the quantity of labor demanded. At the same time, more people would desire to supply additional labor at the higher, government-mandated union wage rate. Across all nonunionized labor markets, the result would be excess quantities of labor supplied, or surpluses of labor. Thus, more people would be unemployed.

Unions and Labor Productivity

A traditional view of union behavior is that unions decrease productivity by artificially shifting the demand curve for union labor outward through excessive staffing and make-work requirements. For example, some economists have traditionally argued that unions tend to bargain for excessive use of workers, as when an airline union requires an engineer on all flights. This is called **featherbedding.** Many painters' unions, for example, resisted the use of paint sprayers and required that their members use only brushes. They even specified the maximum width of the brush. Moreover, whenever a union strikes, productivity drops, and this reduction in productivity in one sector of the economy can spill over into other sectors.

Featherbedding
Any practice that forces employers to use more labor than they would otherwise or to use existing labor in an inefficient manner.

Economic Benefits and Costs of Labor Unions

As should be clear by now, there are two opposing views of unions. One sees them as monopolies whose main effect is to raise the wage rate of high-seniority members at the expense of low-seniority members (and nonunion workers). The other contends that unions can increase labor productivity by promoting safer working conditions and generally better work environments. According to this view, unions contribute to workforce stability by providing arbitration and grievance procedures.

Critics point out that the positive view of unionism overlooks the fact that many of the benefits that unions provide do not require that unions engage in restrictive labor practices, such as the closed shop. Unions could still provide benefits for their members without restricting the labor market.

Consequently, a key issue that economists seek to assess when judging the social costs of unions is the extent to which their existence has a negative effect on employment growth. Most evidence indicates that while unions do significantly reduce employment in some of the most heavily unionized occupations, the overall effects on U.S. employment are modest. On the whole, therefore, the social costs of unions in the U.S. *private* sector are probably relatively low.

QUICK QUIZ See page 662 for the answers. Review concepts from this section in MyEconLab.

When unions set wage rates __________ market clearing prices, they face the problem of __________ a restricted number of jobs to workers who desire to earn the higher wages.

Unions may pursue any one of three goals: (1) to employ __________ union members, (2) to maximize total __________ of the union's members, or (3) to __________ wages for certain, usually high-seniority, workers.

Unions can increase the wage rate of members by engaging in practices that shift the union labor supply curve __________ or shift the demand curve for union labor __________ (or both).

Some economists believe that unions can increase __________ by promoting safer working conditions and generally better work environments.

Monopsony: A Buyer's Monopoly

Let's assume that a firm is a perfect competitor in the product market. The firm cannot alter the price of the product it sells, and it faces a perfectly elastic demand curve for its product. We also assume that the firm is the only buyer of a particular input. Although this situation may not occur often, it is useful to consider. Let's think in terms of a factory town, like those dominated by textile mills or those in the mining industry. One company not only hires the workers but also owns the businesses in the community, owns the apartments that workers live in, and hires the clerks, waiters, and all other personnel. This buyer of labor is called a **monopsonist,** the only buyer in the market.

Monopsonist
The only buyer in a market.

What does this situation mean to a monopsonist in terms of the costs of hiring extra workers? It means that if the monopsonist wants to hire more workers, it has to offer higher wages. Our monopsonist firm cannot hire all the labor it wants at the going wage rate. Instead, it faces an upward-sloping supply curve. If it wants to hire more workers, it has to raise wage rates, including the wages of all its current workers (assuming a non-wage-discriminating monopsonist). It therefore has to take account of these increased costs when deciding how many more workers to hire.

Marginal Factor Cost

The monopsonist faces an upward-sloping supply curve of the input in question because as the only buyer, it faces the entire market supply curve. Each time the monopsonist buyer of labor, for example, wishes to hire more workers, it must raise wage rates. Thus, the marginal cost of another unit of labor is rising. In fact, the marginal cost of increasing its workforce will always be greater than the wage rate. This is because the monopsonist must pay the same wage rate to everyone in order to obtain another unit of labor. Consequently, the higher wage rate has to be offered not only to the last worker but also to *all* its other workers. We call the additional cost to the monopsonist of hiring one more worker the marginal factor cost (MFC).

The marginal factor cost of hiring the last worker is therefore that worker's wages plus the increase in the wages of all other existing workers. As we pointed out in Chapter 28, marginal factor cost is equal to the change in total variable costs due to a one-unit change in the one variable factor of production—in this case, labor. In Chapter 28, marginal factor cost was simply the competitive wage rate because the employer could hire all workers at the same wage rate.

Derivation of a Marginal Factor Cost Curve

Panel (a) of Figure 29-5 on the facing page shows the quantity of labor purchased, the wage rate per hour, the total cost of the quantity of labor supplied per hour, and the marginal factor cost per hour for the additional labor bought.

We translate the columns from panel (a) to the graph in panel (b) of the figure. We show the supply curve as *S*, which is taken from columns 1 and 2. (Note that this is the same as the *average* factor cost curve. Hence, you can view Figure 29-5 as showing the relationship between average factor cost and marginal factor cost.) The marginal factor cost curve (MFC) is taken from columns 1 and 4. The MFC curve must be above the supply curve whenever the supply curve is upward sloping. If the supply curve is upward sloping, the firm must pay a higher wage rate in order to attract a larger amount of labor. This higher wage rate must be paid to all workers. Thus, the increase in total costs due to an increase in the labor input will exceed the wage rate. (Recall from Chapter 28 that in a perfectly competitive input market, the supply curve facing the firm is perfectly elastic and the marginal factor cost curve is identical to the supply curve.)

Employment and Wages Under Monopsony

To determine the number of workers that a monopsonist desires to hire, we compare the marginal benefit to the marginal cost of each hiring decision. The marginal cost is the marginal factor cost (MFC) curve, and the marginal benefit is the marginal revenue product (MRP) curve. In Figure 29-6 on page 654, we assume competition in the output market and monopsony in the input market. A monopsonist finds its profit-maximizing quantity of labor demanded at *A*, where the marginal revenue product is just equal to the marginal factor cost. The monopsonist will therefore desire to hire exactly Q_m workers.

FIGURE 29-5 Derivation of a Marginal Factor Cost Curve

The supply curve, *S*, in panel (b) is taken from columns 1 and 2 of panel (a). The marginal factor cost curve (MFC) is taken from columns 1 and 4. It is the increase in the total wage bill resulting from a one-unit increase in labor input.

Panel (a)

(1) Quantity of Labor Supplied to Management	(2) Required Hourly Wage Rate	(3) Total Wage Bill (3) = (1) x (2)	(4) Marginal Factor Cost (MFC) = Change in (3) / Change in (1)
0	—	—	
			$12
1	$12	$12	
			16
2	14	28	
			20
3	16	48	
			24
4	18	72	
			28
5	20	100	
			32
6	22	132	

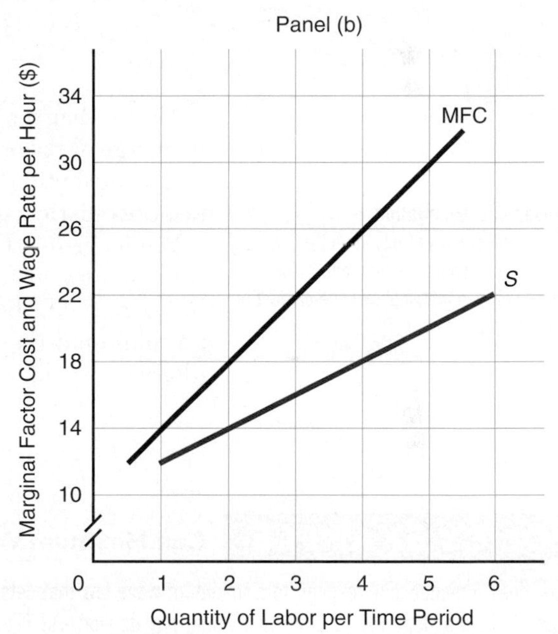

THE INPUT PRICE PAID BY A MONOPSONY How much is the firm going to pay these workers? The monopsonist sets the wage rate so that it will get exactly the quantity, Q_m, supplied to it by its "captive" labor force. We find that wage rate is W_m. There is no reason to pay the workers any more than W_m because at that wage rate, the firm can get exactly the quantity it wants. The actual quantity used is determined by the intersection of the marginal factor cost curve and the marginal revenue product curve for labor—that is, at the point at which the marginal revenue from expanding employment just equals the marginal cost of doing so (point *A* in Figure 29-6 on the following page).

FIGURE 29-6 Wage and Employment Determination for a Monopsonist

The monopsonist firm looks at a marginal cost curve, MFC, that slopes upward and lies above its labor supply curve, *S*. The marginal benefit of hiring additional workers is given by the firm's MRP curve (its demand-for-labor curve). The intersection of MFC with MRP, at point *A*, determines the number of workers hired. The firm hires Q_m workers but has to pay them only W_m in order to attract them.

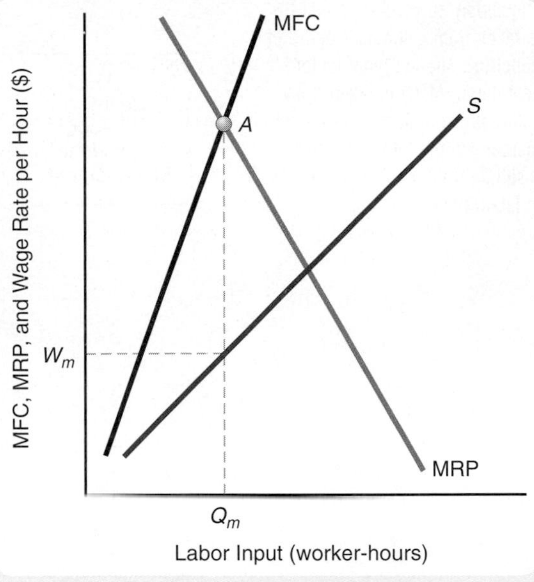

Notice that the profit-maximizing wage rate paid to workers (W_m) is lower than the marginal revenue product. That is to say, workers are paid a wage that is less than their contribution to the monopsonist's revenues. This is sometimes referred to as **monopsonistic exploitation** of labor.

Monopsonistic exploitation
Paying a price for the variable input that is less than its marginal revenue product; the difference between marginal revenue product and the wage rate.

You learned in Chapter 4 that in a perfectly competitive labor market, establishing a minimum wage rate above the market clearing wage rate causes employers to reduce the quantity of labor demanded, resulting in a decline in employment. What happens if a minimum wage rate is established above the wage rate that a *monopsony* would otherwise pay its workers?

POLICY EXAMPLE Can Minimum Wage Laws Ever Boost Employment?

How does a monopsony respond to a minimum wage law that sets a wage floor above the wage rate it otherwise would pay its workers? Figure 29-7 on the facing page provides the answer to this question. In the figure, the entire upward-sloping curve labeled *S* is the labor supply curve in the absence of a minimum wage. Given the associated MFC curve and the firm's MRP curve, Q_m is the quantity of labor hired by a monopsony in the absence of a minimum wage law. The profit-maximizing wage rate is W_m.

If the government establishes a minimum wage equal to W_{min}, however, then the supply of labor to the firm becomes horizontal at the minimum wage and includes only the upward-sloping portion of the curve *S* above this legal minimum. In addition, the wage rate W_{min} becomes the monopsonist's marginal factor cost along the horizontal portion of this new labor supply curve, because when the firm hires one more unit of labor, it must pay each unit of labor the same wage rate, W_{min}.

To maximize its economic profits under the minimum wage, the monopsony equalizes the minimum wage rate with marginal revenue product and hires Q_{min} units of labor. This quantity exceeds the amount of labor, Q_m, that the monopsony would have hired in the absence of the minimum wage law. Thus, establishing a minimum wage can generate a rise in employment at a monopsony firm.

FOR CRITICAL ANALYSIS

If a government establishes a minimum wage law covering all firms within its jurisdiction, including firms operating in both perfectly competitive and monopsonistic labor markets, will overall employment necessarily increase?

FIGURE 29-7 A Monopsony's Response to a Minimum Wage

In the absence of a minimum wage law, a monopsony faces the upward-sloping labor supply curve, *S*, and the marginal factor cost curve, MFC. To maximize its profits, the monopsony hires Q_m units of labor, at which MFC is equal to MRP, and it pays the wage rate W_m. Once the minimum wage rate, W_{min}, is established, the supply of labor becomes horizontal at the minimum wage and includes only the upward-sloping portion of the labor supply curve above this legal minimum. Because the monopsony must pay the same wage rate W_{min} for each unit of labor along this horizontal portion of the new labor supply curve, its marginal factor cost is also equal to the minimum wage rate, W_{min}. Thus, the monopsony hires Q_{min} units of labor. Employment at the monopsony firm increases.

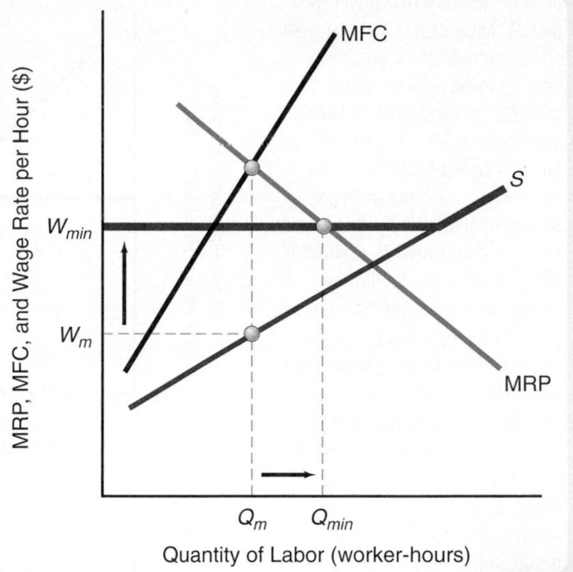

BILATERAL MONOPOLY We have studied the pricing of labor in various situations, including perfect competition in both the output and input markets and monopoly in both the output and input markets. Figure 29-8 on the following page shows four possible situations graphically.

The organization of workers into a union normally creates a monopoly supplier of labor, which gives the union some power to bargain for higher wages. What happens when a monopsonist meets a monopolist? This situation is called **bilateral monopoly,** defined as a market structure in which a single buyer faces a single seller. An example of bilateral monopoly is a county education employer facing a single teachers' union in that labor market. Another example is a players' union facing an organized group of team owners, as has occurred in professional baseball and football. To analyze bilateral monopoly, we would have to look at the interaction of both sides, buyer and seller. The wage outcome turns out to be indeterminate.

Bilateral monopoly
A market structure consisting of a monopolist and a monopsonist.

QUICK QUIZ See page 662 for the answers. Review concepts from this section in MyEconLab.

A **monopsonist** is the __________ __________ in a market. The monopsonist faces an __________-sloping supply curve of labor.

Because the monopsonist faces an __________-sloping supply curve of labor, the marginal factor cost of increasing the labor input by one unit is __________ than the wage rate.

Thus, the marginal factor cost curve always lies __________ the supply curve.

A monopsonist will hire workers up to the point at which marginal __________ cost equals marginal __________ product. Then the monopsonist will find the lowest necessary wage to attract that number of workers, as indicated by the supply curve.

FIGURE 29-8 Pricing and Employment Under Various Market Conditions

In panel (a), the firm operates in perfect competition in both the input and output markets. It purchases labor up to the point where the going rate W_e is equal to MRP_c. It hires quantity Q_e of labor. In panel (b), the firm is a perfect competitor in the input market but has a monopoly in the output market. It purchases labor up to the point where W_e is equal to MRP_m. In panel (c), the firm is a monopsonist in the input market and a perfect competitor in the output market. It hires labor up to the point where $MFC = MRP_c$. It will hire quantity Q_1 and pay wage rate W_c. Panel (d) shows a situation in which the firm is both a monopolist in the market for its output and a monopsonist in its labor market. It hires the quantity of labor Q_2 at which $MFC = MRP_m$ and pays the wage rate W_m.

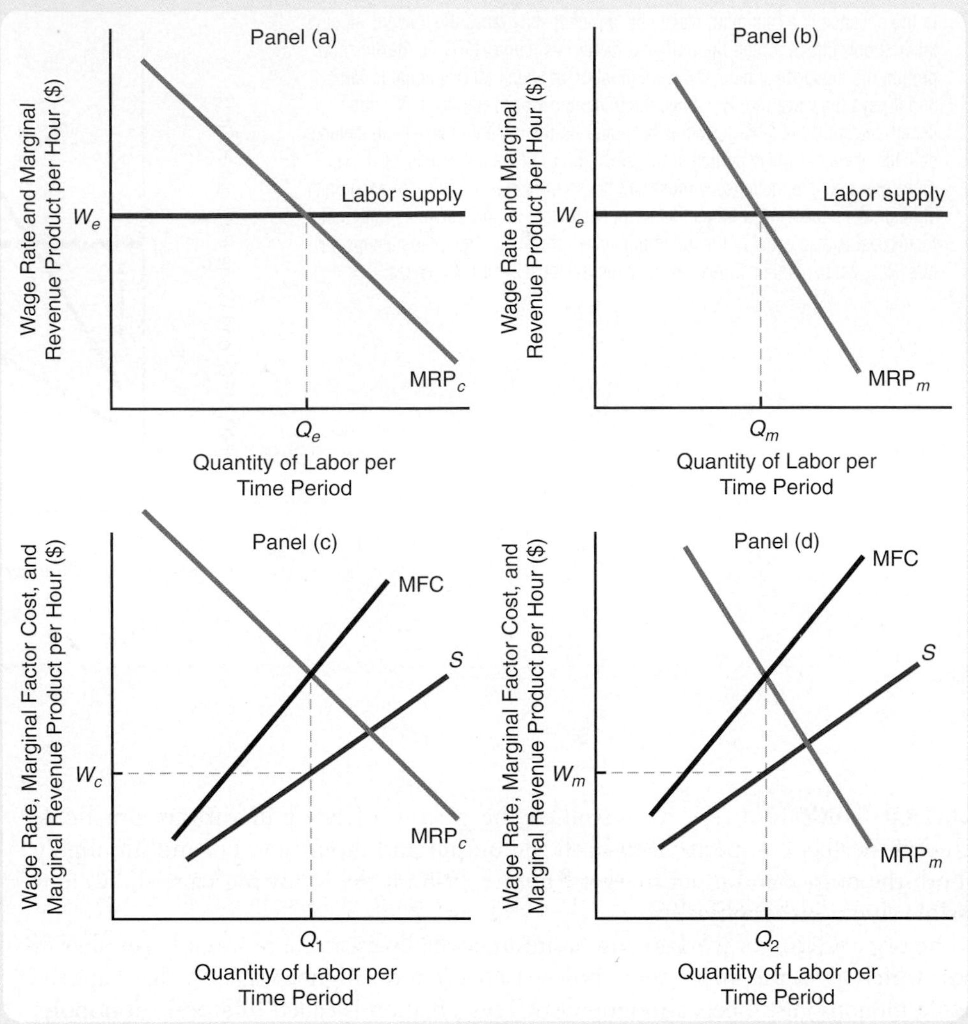

You Are There

Caught Up in an Unusual Jurisdictional Dispute in Michigan

Michele Berry operates a private day-care service from her home in Flint, Michigan. Recently, she was shocked to learn that the Michigan Department of Human Services had classified her as a government employee and a union member and was withholding union dues from payments that the state government makes on behalf of low-income families to whom Berry provides child-care services. The union dues go to Child Care Providers Together Michigan (CCPTM), a union established in 2006 by the American Federation of State, County, and Municipal Employees and the United Auto Workers.

The CCPTM was certified by the state of Michigan following an election involving 6,000 day-care providers. Afterward, the state's Department of Human Services decided that Berry and about 34,000 other home-based day-care providers who accepted state payments were public employees who were required to join the CCPTM. Berry, however, regards herself as self-employed and says that she "wants nothing to do with the union." This unusual jurisdictional dispute—unusual because it involves only a single union that people do not wish to join—is under review in a court. Meanwhile, a portion of Berry's income still goes to the CCPTM. The union, in turn, uses her dues to help cover expenses of lobbying the Michigan legislature for higher payments to day-care operators.

Critical Analysis Questions

1. Does Berry appear to be facing a right-to-work law or a law establishing a closed shop?
2. Based on this information, what are the CCPTM's main goals?

ISSUES & APPLICATIONS

Tax Dollars Increasingly Pay Union Wages

CONCEPTS APPLIED

- Industrial Unions
- Collective Bargaining
- Union Goals and Strategies

For many industrial unions today, the relevant "industry" is the public—that is, government—sector of the U.S. economy. An increasing percentage of collective bargaining agreements now cover government workers. A declining share of such agreements cover workers employed by private companies.

Changing U.S. Unionization Trends

Panel (a) of Figure 29-9 below shows that unionization rates of private-sector workers have dropped steadily since the early 1970s. Meanwhile, the public-sector unionization rate has generally trended very slightly upward since the early 1980s.

The number of government workers at all levels—local, state, and federal—has also increased. Panel (b) shows an effect of more government workers together with falling private-sector and relatively steady public-sector unionization rates. The percentage of unionized workers employed in the public sector now exceeds 50 percent.

FIGURE 29-9 Private- versus Public-Sector Unionization Rates

Panel (a) indicates that the percentage of unionized workers in the public sector has remained stable since the early 1980s, while the percentage of unionized private-sector workers has steadily declined. Panel (b) shows that as a consequence of this trend, the total percentage of all unionized workers who are employed in the public sector now exceeds the percentage employed in the private sector.

Source: Bureau of Labor Statistics.

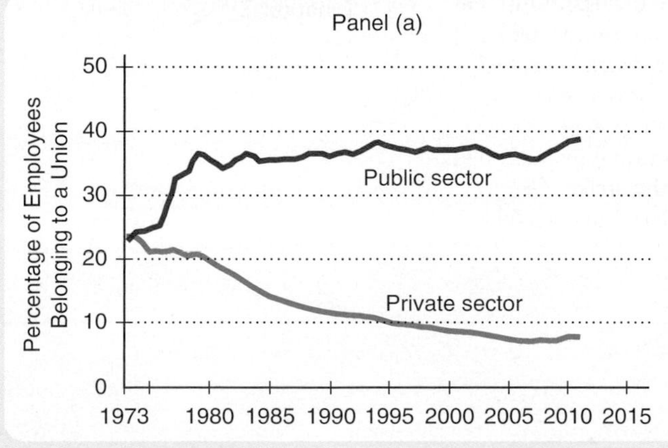

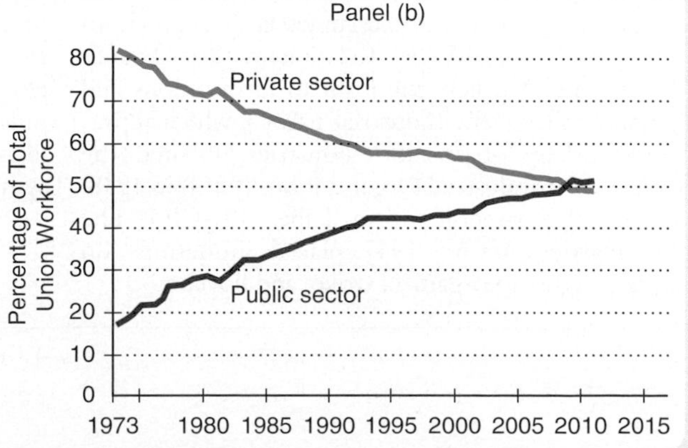

A Union Goal of the 2010s: Increased Access to Tax Dollars

Since 2009, several firms employing many unionized workers have effectively been under the control of the federal government. An example is General Motors, which is largely owned by the U.S. government and employs more than 70,000 unionized workers. Naturally, if unionized workers at these and other government-controlled firms were reclassified as employed within the public sector, the true share of unionized employees would rise further.

Key proponents of the U.S. government's bailout and effective takeover of these companies included unions representing their employees. Unions whose jurisdictions potentially encompass government workers actively seek to recruit those workers into their ranks. These unions have determined that tax revenues provide a more stable source of income to unions and their members than do private-sector firms' revenues, which vary with changing market conditions.

For Critical Analysis

1. Why do you think that jurisdictional disputes tend to be more common among unions representing government employees than among unions representing workers at private firms?
2. Who do you suppose represents the interests of taxpayers during collective bargaining with unions that represent public-sector employees?

Web Resources

1. To find out more about unionization rates in both the private and the public sectors, go to www.econtoday.com/ch29.
2. To compare average earnings of union workers by occupation, go to www.econtoday.com/ch29.

Research Project

Evaluate why a union that wishes both to maximize its members' incomes and to keep their incomes as stable as possible might desire to bring in members who are employed by local, state, and federal governments. Why are public-sector union members' incomes still subject to some variability?

For more questions on this chapter's Issues & Applications, go to **MyEconLab**. In the Study Plan for this chapter, select Section N: News.

Here is what you should know after reading this chapter. **MyEconLab** will help you identify what you know, and where to go when you need to practice.

WHAT YOU SHOULD KNOW		WHERE TO GO TO PRACTICE
Labor Unions The first labor unions were craft unions, representing workers in specific trades. In the United States, the American Federation of Labor (AFL) emerged in the late nineteenth century. In 1935, the National Labor Relations Act (or Wagner Act) granted workers the right to form unions and bargain collectively. Industrial unions, which represent workers of specific industries, formed the Congress of Industrial Organizations (CIO) in 1938, and in 1955 a merger formed the AFL-CIO. The Taft-Hartley Act of 1947 placed limitations on unions' rights to organize, strike, and boycott.	labor unions, 643 craft unions, 643 collective bargaining, 643 industrial unions, 643 right-to-work laws, 644 closed shop, 644 union shop, 644 jurisdictional dispute, 644 sympathy strike, 644 secondary boycott, 644	• **MyEconLab** Study Plan 29.1 • Audio introduction to Chapter 29

MyEconLab continued

WHAT YOU SHOULD KNOW		WHERE TO GO TO PRACTICE
The Current Status of Labor Unions A key reason for an ongoing decline in U.S. union membership rates is the relative decline in manufacturing jobs as a share of total employment. In addition, many workers are undocumented and foreign-born (i.e., illegal immigrants). Greater domestic and global competition has also had a part in bringing about a decline in unions.		• **MyEconLab** Study Plan 29.1
Basic Goals and Strategies of Labor Unions A key goal of most unions is to achieve higher wages. Often this entails bargaining for wages above competitive levels, which produces surplus labor. Thus, a major task of many unions is to ration available jobs among the excess number of individuals who desire to work at the wages established by collective bargaining agreements. Unions often address this trade-off between wages and the number of jobs by maximizing the total income of members. Strategies to raise wages indirectly include placing limits on the entry of new workers, increasing worker productivity, and lobbying consumers to increase their demands for union-produced goods.	strikebreakers, 647 **KEY FIGURES** Figure 29-2, 647 Figure 29-3, 648 Figure 29-4, 649	• **MyEconLab** Study Plan 29.2 • Video: Union Goals • Animated Figures 29-2, 29-3, 29-4
Effects of Labor Unions on Wages and Productivity On average, union hourly wages are higher than wages of nonunionized workers. Unionized employees typically work fewer hours per year, however, so their average annual earnings are lower than those of nonunionized employees. Some collective bargaining rules specifying how jobs are performed appear to reduce productivity, but unionization promotes generally better work environments, which may enhance productivity.	featherbedding, 651	• **MyEconLab** Study Plan 29.3 • Video: The Benefits of Labor Unions
How a Monopsonist Determines How Much Labor to Employ and What Wage Rate to Pay For a monopsonist, which is the only buyer of an input such as labor, paying a higher wage to attract an additional unit of labor increases total factor costs for all other labor employed. The labor market monopsonist employs labor to the point at which the marginal factor cost of labor equals the marginal revenue product of labor. It then pays workers the wage at which they are willing to work, as determined by the labor supply curve, which lies below the marginal factor cost curve. As a result, the monopsonist pays workers a wage that is less than their marginal revenue product.	monopsonist, 651 monopsonistic exploitation, 654 bilateral monopoly, 655 **KEY FIGURES** Figure 29-5, 653 Figure 29-6, 654 Figure 29-7, 655	• **MyEconLab** Study Plan 29.4 • Video: The Buyer's Monopoly—Monopsony • Animated Figures 29-5, 29-6, 29-7

(continued)

MyEconLab continued

WHAT YOU SHOULD KNOW		WHERE TO GO TO PRACTICE
Comparing a Monopsonist's Wage and Employment Decisions with Choices by Firms in Industries with Other Market Structures Firms that hire workers in perfectly competitive labor markets take the wage rate as market determined. A product market monopolist tends to employ fewer workers than would be employed if the monopolist's industry were perfectly competitive, but the product market monopolist nonetheless cannot affect the market wage rate. In contrast, a monopsonist is the only employer of labor, so it searches for the wage rate that maximizes its profit. This wage rate is less than the marginal revenue product of labor. If a firm is both a product market monopolist and a labor market monopsonist, its demand for labor is also lower than it would be if the firm's product market were competitive, so the firm hires fewer workers as well.	**KEY FIGURE** Figure 29-8, 656	• **MyEconLab** Study Plan 29.4 • Animated Figure 29-8

Log in to MyEconLab, take a chapter test, and get a personalized Study Plan that tells you which concepts you understand and which ones you need to review. From there, MyEconLab will give you further practice, tutorials, animations, videos, and guided solutions.
Log in to www.myeconlab.com

PROBLEMS

All problems are assignable in myeconlab. *Answers to the odd-numbered problems appear at the back of the book.*

29-1. Discuss three aspects of collective bargaining that society might deem desirable.

29-2. Give three reasons why a government might seek to limit the power of a union.

29-3. Recently, the Writers Guild of America (WGA), which represents TV and film screenwriters, called for a strike, and most screenwriters stopped working. Nevertheless, writers for certain TV soap operas, such as *The Young and Restless*—which have had shrinking audiences for years, draw small numbers of viewers for repeat shows, and rarely sell on Blu-ray discs—opted to drop their WGA memberships and tried to continue working during the strike. Why do you suppose that the WGA posted on its Web site a phone number for union members to report "strike-breaking activities and 'scab writing'" to the union's 12-person Strike Rules Compliance Committee? What effect do strikebreakers have on the collective bargaining power of a union?

29-4. Suppose that the objective of a union is to maximize the total dues paid to the union by its membership. Explain the union's strategy, in terms of the wage level and employment level, under the following two scenarios.

a. Union dues are a percentage of total earnings of the union membership.

b. Union dues are paid as a flat amount per union member employed.

29-5. Explain why, in economic terms, the total income of union membership is maximized when marginal revenue is zero. (Hint: How much more revenue is forthcoming when marginal revenue is equal to zero?)

29-6. Explain the impact of each of the following events on the market for union labor.

a. Union-produced TV and radio commercials convince consumers to buy domestically manufactured clothing instead of imported clothing.

b. The union sponsors periodic training programs that instruct union laborers about the most efficient use of machinery and tools.

29-7. Why are unions in industries in which inputs such as machines are poor substitutes for labor more likely to be able to bargain for wages higher than market levels?

29-8. How is it possible for the average annual earnings of nonunionized workers to exceed those of unionized workers even though unionized workers' hourly wages are more than $2 higher?

29-9. In the short run, a tool manufacturer has a fixed amount of capital. Labor is a variable input. The cost and output structure that the firm faces is depicted in the following table:

Labor Supplied	Total Physical Product	Hourly Wage Rate ($)
10	100	5
11	109	6
12	116	7
13	121	8
14	124	9
15	125	10

Derive the firm's total wage costs and marginal factor cost at each level of labor supplied.

29-10. Suppose that for the firm in Problem 29-9, the goods market is perfectly competitive. The market price of the product the firm produces is $4 at each quantity supplied by the firm. What is the amount of labor that this profit-maximizing firm will hire, and what wage rate will it pay?

29-11. The price and wage structure that a firm faces is depicted in the following table.

Labor Supplied	Total Physical Product	Hourly Wage Rate ($)	Product Price ($)
10	100	5	3.11
11	109	6	3.00
12	116	7	2.95
13	121	8	2.92
14	124	9	2.90
15	125	10	2.89

The firm finds that the price of its product changes with the rate of output. In addition, the wage it pays its workers varies with the amount of labor it employs. This firm maximizes profits. How many units of labor will it hire? What wage will it pay?

29-12. What is the amount of monopsonistic exploitation that takes place at the firm examined in Problem 29-11?

29-13. A profit-maximizing clothing producer in a remote area is the only employer of people in that area. It sells its clothing in a perfectly competitive market. The firm pays each worker the same weekly wage rate. The last worker hired raised the firm's total weekly wage expenses from $105,600 to $106,480. What is the marginal revenue product of the last worker hired by this firm if it is maximizing profits?

29-14. A single firm is the only employer in a labor market. The marginal revenue product, labor supply, and marginal factor cost curves that it faces are displayed in the diagram below. Use this information to answer the following questions.

a. How many units of labor will this firm employ in order to maximize its economic profits?

b. What hourly wage rate will this firm pay its workers?

c. What is the total amount of wage payments that this firm will make to its workers each hour?

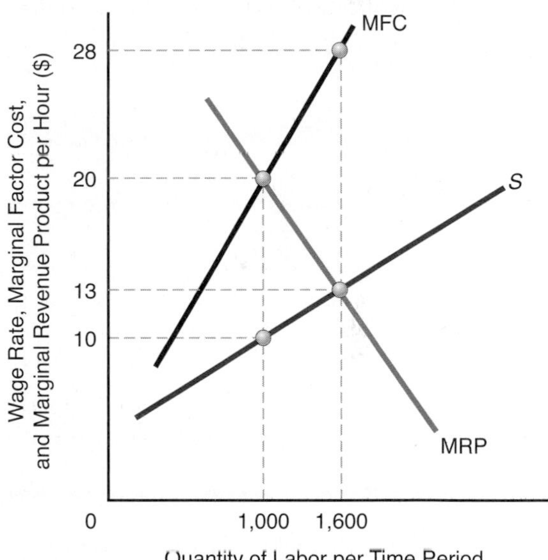

ECONOMICS ON THE NET

Evaluating Union Goals As discussed in this chapter, unions can pursue any of a number of goals. The AFL-CIO's home page provides links to the Web sites of several unions, and reviewing these sites can help you determine the objectives these unions have selected.

Title: American Federation of Labor–Congress of Industrial Organizations

Navigation: Go to **www.econtoday.com/ch29** to visit the AFL-CIO's home page.

Application Perform the indicated operations, and answer the following questions.

1. Click on *About Us*, then click on *Mission Statement*. Does the AFL-CIO claim to represent the interests of all workers or just workers in specific firms

or industries? Can you discern what broad wage and employment strategy the AFL-CIO pursues?

2. Click on *Unions of the AFL-CIO*. Explore two or three of these Web sites. Do these unions appear to represent the interests of all workers or just workers in specific firms or industries? What general wage and employment strategies do these unions appear to pursue?

For Group Study and Analysis Divide up all the unions affiliated with the AFL-CIO among groups, and have each group explore the Web sites listed under *Unions of the AFL-CIO* at the AFL-CIO Web site. Have each group report on the wage and employment strategies that appear to prevail for the unions it examined.

ANSWERS TO QUICK QUIZZES

p. 646: (i) American Federation . . . Labor; (ii) National Labor Relations . . . industrial; (iii) 25 . . . 12
p. 651: (i) above . . . rationing; (ii) all . . . income . . . maximize, (iii) inward . . . outward; (iv) productivity

p. 655: (i) only buyer . . . upward; (ii) upward . . . greater . . . above; (iii) factor . . . revenue

30

Income, Poverty, and Health Care

A number of U.S. colleges advertise that a college graduate can anticipate earning at least $1 million more over a working lifetime than someone who has only a high school diploma. The colleges' ads base this claim on U.S. census data showing that a college graduate earns about $26,000 more per year on average than a high school graduate. Multiplying this amount by 40 years yields $1,040,000. One problem with this calculation is that the discounted present value (see Chapter 21) of the difference in lifetime earnings is much smaller than $1 million. Another problem is that the colleges fail to deduct the significant explicit and implicit costs that people incur to obtain college degrees. Thus, the expected lifetime earnings differential is less than $1 million. Nevertheless, as you will learn in this chapter, there are substantial lifetime income gains from higher education, which is a key determinant of differences in people's incomes.

LEARNING OBJECTIVES

After reading this chapter, you should be able to:

- Describe how to use a Lorenz curve to represent a nation's income distribution
- Identify the key determinants of income differences across individuals
- Discuss theories of desired income distribution
- Distinguish among alternative approaches to measuring and addressing poverty
- Recognize the role played by third-party payments in rising health care costs
- Explain the key elements of the new U.S. national health insurance program and evaluate its potential economic effects

myeconlab

MyEconLab helps you master each objective and study more efficiently. See end of chapter for details.

Did You Know That ?

during 2008, the wealth of the world's richest people—those with at least $1 million in wealth—declined by $33 trillion, or about two and a half times annual U.S. national income? Prior to 2008, U.S. families with the highest 1 percent of incomes—those earning annual incomes equal to $400,000 or more—accounted for nearly 24 percent of total annual U.S. income. Today, the top 1 percent of families receive less than 19 percent of all U.S. income.

Clearly, in recent years there have been changes in the **distribution of income**—the way that income is allocated among the population. What are the determinants of the distribution of income? Economists have devised various theories to explain income distribution. We will present some of these theories in this chapter. We will also present some of the more obvious institutional reasons why income is not distributed equally in the United States. In addition, we will examine the health care problems confronting individuals in all income groups and how the federal government's new health care program proposes to solve these problems.

Distribution of income
The way income is allocated among the population based on groupings of residents.

Income

Income provides each of us with the means of consuming and saving. Income can be the result of a payment for labor services or a payment for ownership of one of the other factors of production besides labor—land, physical capital, or entrepreneurship. In addition, individuals obtain spendable income from gifts and government transfers. (Some individuals also obtain income by stealing, but we will not treat this matter here.) Right now, let's examine how money income is distributed across classes of income earners within the United States.

Measuring Income Distribution: The Lorenz Curve

We can represent the distribution of money income graphically with what is known as the **Lorenz curve,** named after a U.S.-born statistician, Max Otto Lorenz, who proposed it in 1905. The Lorenz curve shows what share of total money income is accounted for by different proportions of the nation's households. Look at Figure 30-1 below. On the horizontal axis, we measure the *cumulative* percentage of households, lowest-income households first. Starting at the left corner, there are zero households. At the right corner, we have 100 percent of households. In the middle, we have 50 percent of households. The vertical axis represents the cumulative percentage of money income.

Lorenz curve
A geometric representation of the distribution of income. A Lorenz curve that is perfectly straight represents complete income equality. The more bowed a Lorenz curve, the more unequally income is distributed.

FIGURE 30-1 The Lorenz Curve

The horizontal axis measures the cumulative percentage of households, with lowest-income households first, from 0 to 100 percent. The vertical axis measures the cumulative percentage of money income from 0 to 100. A straight line at a 45-degree angle cuts the box in half and represents a line of complete income equality, along which 25 percent of the families get 25 percent of the money income, 50 percent get 50 percent, and so on. The observed Lorenz curve, showing the actual U.S. money income distribution, is not a straight line but rather a curved line as shown. The difference between complete money income equality and the Lorenz curve is the inequality gap.

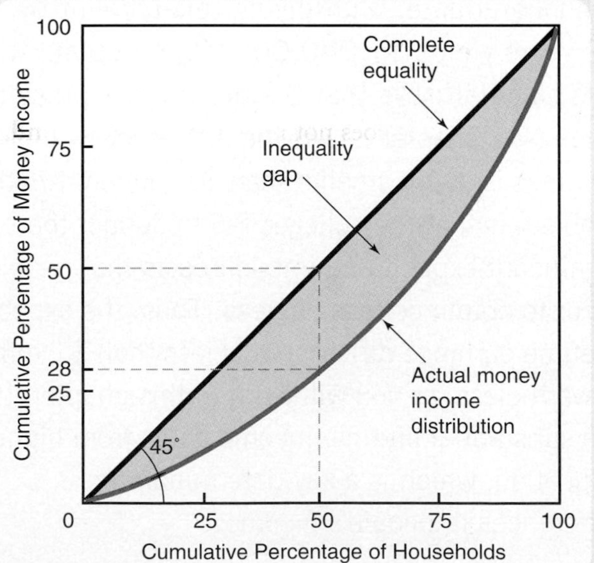

FIGURE 30-2 Lorenz Curves of Income Distribution, 1929 and 2011

Since 1929, the Lorenz curve has moved inward toward the straight line of perfect income equality.

Source: U.S. Department of Commerce.

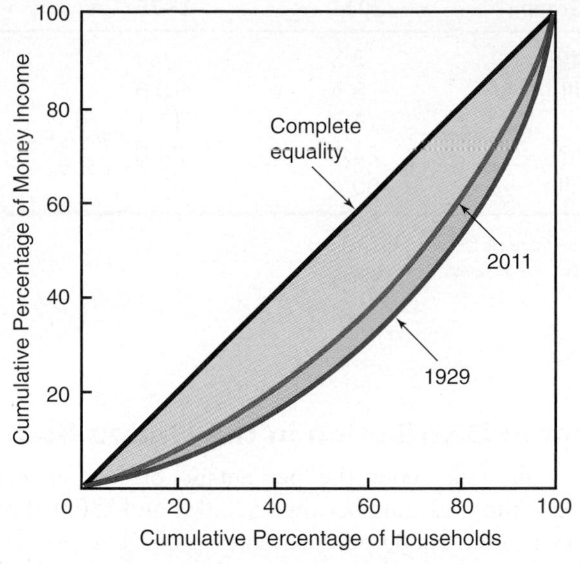

The 45-degree line represents complete equality: 50 percent of the households obtain 50 percent of total income, 60 percent of the households obtain 60 percent of total income, and so on. Of course, in no real-world situation is there such complete equality of income. No actual Lorenz curve would be a straight line. Rather, it would be some curved line, like the one labeled "Actual money income distribution" in Figure 30-1 on the previous page. For example, the bottom 50 percent of households in the United States receive about 23 percent of total money income.

In Figure 30-2 above, we again show the actual money income distribution Lorenz curve for the United States, and we also compare it to the distribution of money income in 1929. Since that year, the Lorenz curve has generally become less bowed. That is, it has moved closer to the line of complete equality.

CRITICISMS OF THE LORENZ CURVE In recent years, economists have placed less and less emphasis on the shape of the Lorenz curve as an indication of the degree of income inequality in a country. There are five basic reasons why the Lorenz curve has been criticized:

1. The Lorenz curve is typically presented in terms of the distribution of *money* income only. It does not include **income in kind,** such as government-provided food stamps, education, medical care, or housing aid, and goods or services produced and consumed in the home or on the farm.
2. The Lorenz curve does not account for differences in the size of households or the number of wage earners they contain.
3. It does not account for age differences. Even if all families in the United States had exactly the same *lifetime* incomes, chances are that young families would have modest incomes, middle-aged families would have relatively high incomes, and retired families would have lower incomes. Because the Lorenz curve is drawn at a moment in time, it can never tell us anything about the inequality of *lifetime* income.
4. The Lorenz curve ordinarily reflects money income *before* taxes.
5. It does not measure unreported income from the underground economy, a substantial source of income for some individuals.

Income in kind
Income received in the form of goods and services, such as housing or medical care. Income in kind differs from money income, which is simply income in dollars, or general purchasing power, that can be used to buy *any* goods and services.

TABLE 30-1

Percentage Share of Money Income for Households Before Direct Taxes

Income Group	2011	1975	1960	1947
Lowest fifth	3.3	4.4	4.8	5.1
Second fifth	8.5	10.5	12.2	11.8
Third fifth	14.7	17.1	17.8	16.7
Fourth fifth	23.1	24.8	24.0	23.2
Highest fifth	50.4	43.2	41.3	43.3

Note: Figures may not sum to 100 percent due to rounding.
Sources: U.S. Bureau of the Census; author's estimates.

Income Distribution in the United States

Go to www.econtoday/ch30 to view the U.S. Census Bureau's most recent data on the U.S. income distribution. Click on the most recent year next to "Money Income in the United States."

We could talk about the percentage of income earners within specific income classes—those earning between $20,001 and $30,000 per year, those earning between $30,001 and $40,000 per year, and so on. The problem with this type of analysis is that we live in a growing economy. Income, with infrequent exceptions, is going up all the time. If we wish to compare the relative shares of total income going to different income classes, we cannot look at specific amounts of money income. Instead, we talk about a distribution of income over five groups. Then we can talk about how much the bottom fifth (or quintile) makes compared with the top fifth, and so on.

In Table 30-1 above, we see the percentage share of income for households before direct taxes. The table groups households according to whether they are in the lowest 20 percent of the income distribution, the second lowest 20 percent, and so on. We see that in 2011, the lowest 20 percent had an estimated combined money income of 3.3 percent of the total money income of the entire population. This is less than the lowest 20 percent had at the end of World War II.

Accordingly, some have concluded that the distribution of money income has become slightly more unequal. *Money* income, however, understates *total* income for individuals who receive in-kind transfers from the government in the form of food stamps, public housing, education, and the like. In particular, since World War II, the share of *total* income—money income plus in-kind benefits—going to the bottom 20 percent of households has more than doubled.

The Distribution of Wealth

When referring to the distribution of income, we must realize that income—a flow—can be viewed as a return on wealth (both human and nonhuman)—a stock. A discussion of the distribution of income is not necessarily the same thing as a discussion of the distribution of wealth, however. A complete concept of wealth would include not only tangible objects, such as buildings, machinery, land, cars, and houses—nonhuman wealth—but also people who have skills, knowledge, initiative, talents, and the like—human wealth. The total of human and nonhuman wealth in the United States makes up our nation's capital stock.

Figure 30-3 on the next page shows that the richest 10 percent of U.S. households hold more than two-thirds of all measured wealth. The problem with those data, gathered by the Federal Reserve System, however, is that they do not include many important assets. One of these is workers' claims on private pension plans, which equal at least $4 trillion. If you add the value of these pensions, household wealth increases by almost 25 percent and reveals that many more U.S. households are middle-wealth households (popularly known as the *middle class*). Another asset excluded from the data is anticipated claims on the Social Security system, which tend to comprise a larger share of the wealth of lower-income individuals.

FIGURE 30-3 Measured Total Wealth Distribution

The top 10 percent of households have 69 percent of all *measured* wealth. This distribution changes dramatically if other nonmeasured components of wealth, such as claims on private pension plans and on government-guaranteed Social Security commitments, are taken into account.

Source: Board of Governors of the Federal Reserve.

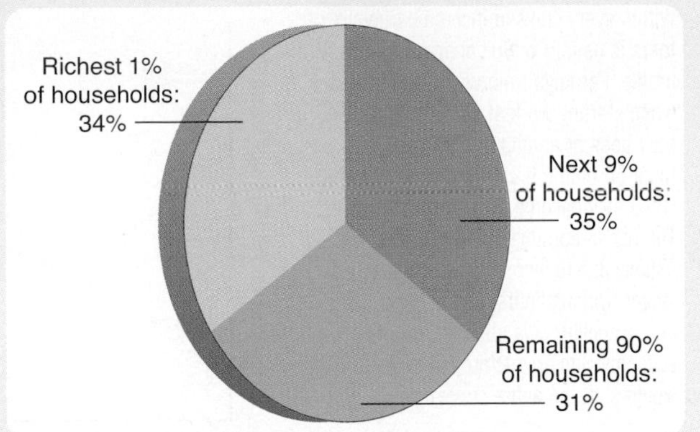

QUICK QUIZ See page 687 for the answers. Review concepts from this section in MyEconLab.

The **Lorenz curve** graphically represents the distribution of _________. If it is a straight line, there is complete _________ of income. The more it is bowed, the more _________ income is distributed.

The distribution of wealth is not the same as the distribution of income. Wealth includes _________ such as houses, stocks, and bonds. Although the apparent distribution of wealth seems to be _________ concentrated at the top than income, the data used are not very accurate, and most summary statistics fail to take account of workers' claims on private and public pensions, which are substantial.

Determinants of Income Differences

We know that there are income differences—that is not in dispute. A more important question is why these differences in income occur. We will look at four determinants of income differences: age, marginal productivity, inheritance, and discrimination.

Age

Age turns out to be a determinant of income because with age come, usually, more education, more training, and more experience. It is not surprising that within every class of income earners, there seem to be regular cycles of earning behavior. Most individuals earn more when they are middle-aged than when they are younger or older. We call this the **age-earnings cycle.**

Age-earnings cycle
The regular earnings profile of an individual throughout his or her lifetime. The age-earnings cycle usually starts with a low income, builds gradually to a peak at around age 50, and then gradually curves down until it approaches zero at retirement.

THE AGE-EARNINGS CYCLE Every occupation has its own age-earnings cycle, and every individual will probably experience some variation from the average. Nonetheless, we can characterize the typical age-earnings cycle graphically in Figure 30-4 on the following page. Here we see that at age 18, earnings from wages are relatively low. As a person's productivity increases through more training and experience, earnings gradually rise until they peak at about age 50. Then they fall until retirement, when they become zero (that is, currently earned wages become zero, although retirement payments may then commence).

Note that general increases in overall productivity for the entire workforce will result in an upward shift in the typical age-earnings profile depicted in Figure 30-4. Thus, even at the end of the age-earnings cycle, when just about to retire, the worker would receive a relatively high wage compared with the starting wage 45 years earlier. The wage would be higher due to factors that contribute to rising real wages for everyone, regardless of the stage in the age-earnings cycle.

FIGURE 30-4 Typical Age-Earnings Profile

Within every class of income earners there is usually a typical age-earnings profile. Earnings from wages are lowest when starting work at age 18, reach their peak at around age 50, and then taper off until retirement around age 65, when they become zero for most people. The rise in earnings up to age 50 is usually due to increased experience, longer working hours, and better training and schooling. (We abstract from economywide productivity changes that would shift the entire curve upward.)

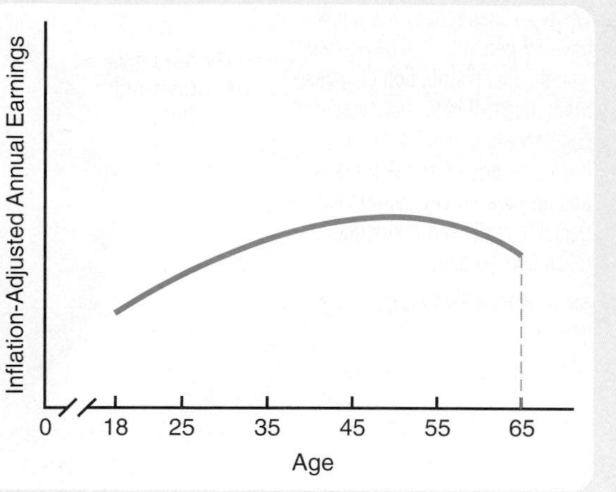

Now we have some idea why specific individuals earn different incomes at different times in their lives, but we have yet to explain why different people are paid different amounts for their labor. One way to explain this is to recall the marginal productivity theory developed in Chapter 28.

Marginal Productivity

When trying to determine how many workers a firm would hire, we had to construct a marginal revenue product curve. We found that as more workers were hired, the marginal revenue product fell due to diminishing marginal product. If the forces of demand and supply established a certain wage rate, workers would be hired until their marginal physical product times marginal revenue (which equals the market price under perfect competition) was equal to the going wage rate. Then the hiring would stop. This analysis suggests what workers can expect to be paid in the labor market: As long as there are low-cost information flows and the labor and product markets are competitive, each worker can expect to be paid his or her marginal revenue product.

DETERMINANTS OF MARGINAL PRODUCTIVITY According to marginal revenue product theory, if people can increase their marginal physical product, they can expect to earn higher incomes. Key determinants of marginal physical product are talent, experience, and training.

Talent. Talent is the easiest factor to explain, but it is difficult to acquire if you don't have it. Innate abilities and attributes can be very strong, if not overwhelming, determinants of a person's potential productivity. Strength, coordination, and mental alertness are facets of nonacquired human capital and thus have some bearing on the ability to earn income. Someone who is tall and agile has a better chance of being a basketball player than someone who is short and unathletic. A person born with a superior talent for abstract thinking has a better chance of earning a relatively high income as a mathematician or a physicist than someone who is not born with that capability.

Experience. Additional experience at particular tasks is another way to increase productivity. Experience can be linked to the well-known *learning curve* that applies when the same task is done over and over. The worker repeating a task becomes more efficient: The worker can do the same task in less time or in the same amount of time but better. Take an example of a person going to work on an automobile assembly line.

At first she is able to fasten only three bolts every two minutes. Then the worker becomes more adept and can fasten four bolts in the same time plus insert a rubber guard on the bumper. After a few more weeks, another task can be added. Experience allows this individual to improve her productivity. The more effectively people learn to do something, the more productive they are.

Training. Training is similar to experience but is more formal. Much of a person's increased productivity is due to on-the-job training. Many companies have training programs for new workers.

Why is the U.S. income distribution shifting in favor of women?

EXAMPLE **Women Discover Payoffs from Extra Education and Training**

Since 2007, for every 100 bachelor's degrees earned by men in the United States, U.S. women have earned 135. For every 100 associate's degrees earned by U.S. men, women have earned 166. As a result, although employed men still earn higher wages than employed women, since 2007 the wages of female workers have increased by nearly 2 percentage points more than the wages of male workers. Hence, the male-female wage differential, which had already declined from nearly 37 percent in 1980 to just below 20 percent in 2010, is likely to continue to narrow. In addition, in the aftermath of the Great Recession of the late 2000s, female workers with their better education and training now hold nearly 700,000 more jobs in the U.S. labor market than do male workers.

The consequence of higher-paying and increased employment opportunities for women has been a gradual shift in the U.S. income distribution in favor of women. Female workers in the United States have discovered that obtaining more education and training pays off in the form of higher incomes.

FOR CRITICAL ANALYSIS

How do you suppose that the fact that most lower-income families are now sending more young women than young men to college will affect the future distribution of income between males and females?

INVESTMENT IN HUMAN CAPITAL Investment in human capital is just like investment in anything else. If you invest in yourself by going to college, rather than going to work after high school and earning more current income, you will presumably be rewarded in the future with a higher income or a more interesting job (or both). This is exactly the motivation that underlies the decision of many college-bound students to obtain a formal higher education.

As with other investments, we can determine the rate of return on an investment in a college education. To do so, we first have to figure out the marginal cost of going to school. The cost is not simply what you have to pay for books, fees, and tuition but also includes the income you forgo. *A key cost of education is the income forgone—the opportunity cost of not working*. In addition, the direct expenses of college must be paid for. Certainly, not all students forgo all income during their college years. Many work part time. Taking account of those who work part time and those who are supported by tuition grants and other scholarships, the average rate of return on going to college ranges between 6 and 8 percent per year. The gain in lifetime income has a present value ranging from $200,000 to more than $500,000.

Inheritance

It is not unusual to inherit cash, jewelry, stocks, bonds, homes, or other real estate. Yet only about 10 percent of income inequality in the United States can be traced to differences in inherited wealth. If for some reason the government confiscated all property that had been inherited, the immediate result would be only a modest change in the distribution of income in the United States. In any event, at both federal and state levels substantial inheritance taxes generally are levied on the estates of relatively wealthy deceased Americans (although there are some legally valid ways to avoid certain estate taxes).

Discrimination

Economic discrimination occurs whenever workers with the same marginal revenue product receive unequal pay due to some noneconomic factor such as their race, gender, or age. It is possible—and indeed quite obvious—that discrimination affects the distribution of income. Certain groups in our society are not paid wages at rates comparable to those received by other groups, even when we correct for productivity. Differences in income remain between whites and nonwhites and between men and women. For example, the median income of black families is about 65 percent that of white families. The median wage rate of women is about 80 percent that of men. Some people argue that all of these differences are due to discrimination against nonwhites and against women.

We cannot simply accept *any* differences in income as due to discrimination, though. What we need to do is discover why differences in income between groups exist and then determine if factors other than discrimination in the labor market can explain them. The unexplained part of income differences can rightfully be considered the result of discrimination.

ACCESS TO EDUCATION African Americans and other minorities have faced discrimination in the acquisition of human capital. The amount and quality of schooling offered black U.S. residents has generally been inferior to that offered whites. As a result, among other things, African Americans and certain other minority groups, such as Hispanics, suffer from reduced investment in human capital. Even when this difference in human capital is taken into account, however, there still appears to be an income differential that cannot be explained.

The unexplained income differential between whites and blacks is often attributed to discrimination in the labor market. Because no better explanation is offered, we will infer that discrimination in the labor market does indeed still exist.

Theories of Desired Income Distribution

We have talked about the factors affecting the distribution of income, but we have not yet mentioned the normative issue of how income *ought* to be distributed. This, of course, requires a value judgment. We are talking about the problem of economic justice. We can never completely resolve this problem because there are always going to be conflicting values. It is impossible to give all people what each thinks is just. Nonetheless, two particular normative standards for the distribution of income have been popular with economists. These are income distribution based on productivity and income distribution based on equality.

Productivity

The *productivity standard* for the distribution of income can be stated simply as "To each according to what he or she produces." This is also called the *contributive standard* because it is based on the principle of rewarding according to the contribution to society's total output. It is also sometimes referred to as the *merit standard* and is one of the oldest concepts of justice. People are rewarded according to merit, and merit is judged by one's ability to produce what is considered useful by society.

We measure a person's productive contribution in a capitalist system by the market value of that person's output. We have already referred to this as the marginal revenue product theory of wage determination.

Equality

The *egalitarian principle* of income distribution is simply "To each exactly the same." Everyone would have exactly the same amount of income. This criterion of income distribution has been debated as far back as biblical times. This system of income distribution has been considered equitable, meaning that presumably everybody is dealt with fairly and equally. There are problems, however, with an income distribution that is completely equal.

Some jobs are more unpleasant or more dangerous than others. Should the people undertaking these jobs be paid exactly the same as everyone else? Indeed, under an equal distribution of income, what incentive would there be for individuals to take risky, hazardous, or unpleasant jobs at all? What about overtime? Who would be willing to work overtime without additional pay? There is another problem: If everyone earned the same income, what incentive would there be for individuals to invest in their own human capital—a costly and time-consuming process?

Just consider the incentive structure within a corporation. Within corporations, much of the differential between, say, the pay of the CEO and the pay of all of the vice presidents is meant to create competition among the vice presidents for the CEO's job. The result is higher productivity. If all incomes were the same, much of this competition would disappear, and productivity would fall.

There is some evidence that differences in income lead to higher rates of economic growth. Future generations are therefore made better off. Elimination of income differences may reduce the rate of economic growth and cause future generations to be poorer than they otherwise might have been.

QUICK QUIZ See page 687 for the answers. **Review concepts from this section in MyEconLab.**

Most people follow an __________-__________ cycle in which they earn relatively small incomes when they first start working, increase their incomes until about age 50, and then slowly experience a decrease in their real incomes as they approach retirement.

According to the marginal __________ theory of wages, workers can expect to be paid their marginal __________ product.

Marginal physical productivity depends on __________, __________, __________, and __________.

Going to school and receiving on-the-job training can be considered an investment in __________ capital. A key cost of education is the __________ cost of not working.

Two normative standards for income distribution are income distribution based on __________ and income distribution based on __________.

Poverty and Attempts to Eliminate It

Throughout the history of the world, mass poverty has been accepted as inevitable. This nation and others, particularly in the Western world, however, have sustained enough economic growth in the past several hundred years so that *mass* poverty can no longer be said to be a problem for these fortunate countries. As a matter of fact, the residual of poverty in the United States strikes us as bizarre, an anomaly. How can there still be so much poverty in a nation of such abundance? Having talked about the determinants of the distribution of income, we now have at least some ideas of why some people are destined to remain low-income earners throughout their lives.

Income can be transferred from the relatively well-to-do to the relatively poor by various methods, and as a nation we have been using them for a long time. Today, we have a vast array of welfare programs set up for the purpose of redistributing income. As we know, however, these programs have not been entirely successful. Are there alternatives to our current welfare system? Is there a better method of helping the poor? Before we answer these questions, take a look at Figure 30-5 on the following page, which displays the percentage of the U.S. population determined to be in a state of poverty by the U.S. government. This percentage, called the *poverty rate*, has varied between roughly 11 percent and 16 percent since 1965.

FIGURE 30-5 The Official Poverty Rate in the United States

The official poverty rate, or the number of people in poverty as a percentage of the U.S. population, has remained in a range of roughly 11 to 16 percent since 1965.

Source: U.S. Department of Labor.

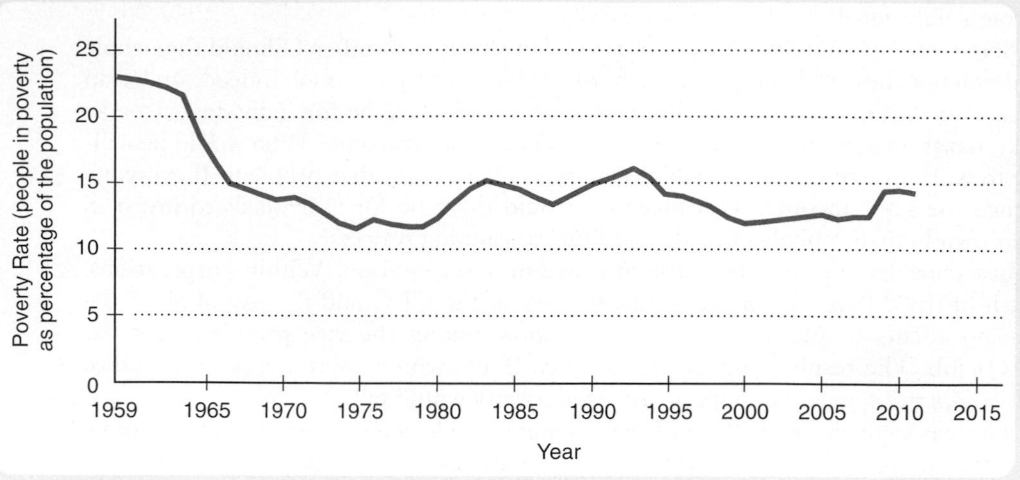

Defining Poverty

The threshold income level, which is used to determine who falls into the poverty category, was originally based on the cost of a nutritionally adequate food plan designed by the U.S. Department of Agriculture. The threshold was determined by multiplying the food plan cost by 3 on the assumption that food expenses comprise approximately one-third of a poor family's income. Annual revisions of the threshold level were based only on price changes in the food budget. In 1969, a federal interagency committee looked at the calculations of the threshold and decided to set new standards, with adjustments made on the basis of changes in the Consumer Price Index. For example, in 2011, the official poverty level for an urban family of four was around $22,000. It typically goes up each year to reflect whatever inflation has occurred.

Absolute Poverty

Go to **www.econtoday.com/ch30** to learn about the World Bank's programs intended to combat global poverty.

Because the low-income threshold is an absolute measure, we know that if it never changes in real terms, we will reduce poverty even if we do nothing. How can that be? The reasoning is straightforward. Real incomes in the United States have been growing at a compounded annual rate of almost 2 percent per capita for at least the past century and at about 2.5 percent since World War II. If we define the poverty line at a specific real income level, more and more individuals will make incomes that exceed that poverty line. Thus, in absolute terms, we will eliminate poverty (assuming continued per capita growth and no change in income distribution).

Relative Poverty

Be careful with this analysis, however. Poverty can also be defined in relative terms, that is, in terms of the income levels of individuals or families relative to the rest of the population. As long as the distribution of income is not perfectly equal, there will always be some people who make less income than others, even if their relatively low income is high by historical standards. Thus, in a relative sense, the problem of poverty will always exist.

Transfer Payments as Income

The official poverty level is based on pretax income, including cash but not in-kind subsidies—food stamps, housing vouchers, and the like. If we correct poverty levels for such benefits, the percentage of the population that is below the poverty line

FIGURE 30-6 Relative Poverty: Comparing Household Income and Household Spending

On the vertical axis, this graph shows the ratio of the top 20 percent of income-earning households to the bottom 20 percent. When we look at measured household income, there appears to be increasing income inequality. If we look at household *spending*, though, inequality is more nearly constant.

Sources: U.S. Bureau of Labor Statistics; U.S. Bureau of the Census.

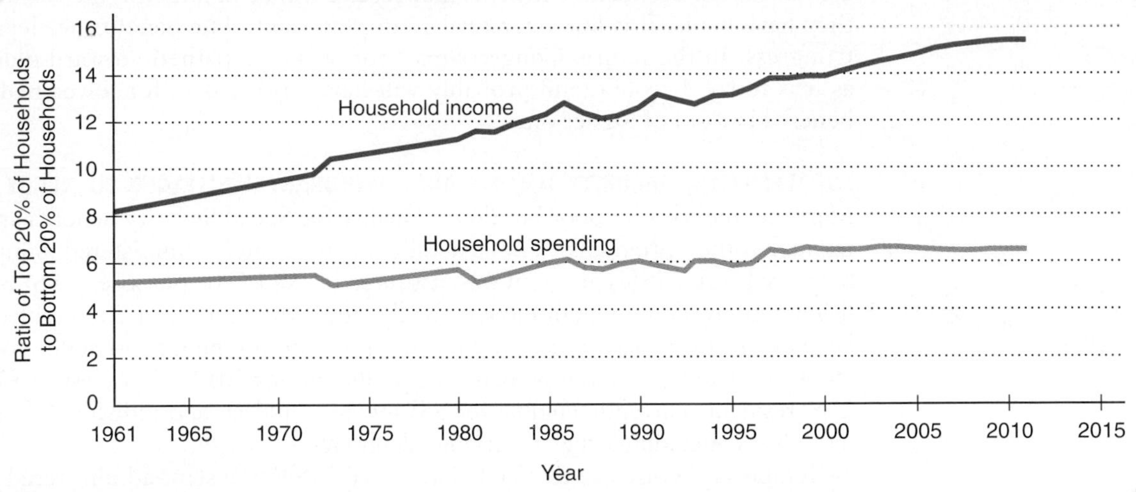

drops dramatically. Some economists argue that the way the official poverty level is calculated makes no sense in a nation that redistributed more than $1.4 trillion in cash and noncash transfers in 2010.

Furthermore, some of the nation's official poor partake in the informal, or underground, sectors of the economy without reporting their income from these sources. And some of the officially defined poor obtain benefits from owning their own home (40 percent of all poor households do own their own homes). Look at Figure 30-6 above for two different views of what has happened to the relative position of this nation's poor. The graph shows the ratio of the top fifth of the nation's households to the bottom fifth of the nation's households. If we look only at measured income, it appears that the poor are getting relatively poorer compared to the rich (the top line). If we compare household spending (consumption), however, a different picture emerges. The nation's poorest households are in fact holding their own in relative terms.

Attacks on Poverty: Major Income Maintenance Programs

There are a variety of income maintenance programs designed to help the poor. We examine a few of them here.

SOCIAL SECURITY For the retired, the unemployed, and the disabled, social insurance programs provide income payments in prescribed situations. The best known is Social Security, which includes what has been called old-age, survivors', and disability insurance (OASDI). As discussed in Chapter 6, this was originally supposed to be a program of compulsory saving financed from payroll taxes levied on both employers and employees. Workers pay for Social Security while working and receive the benefits after retirement. The benefit payments are usually made to people who have reached retirement age. When the insured worker dies, benefits accrue to the survivors, including widows and children. Special benefits provide for disabled workers.

More than 90 percent of all employed persons in the United States are covered by OASDI. Today, Social Security is an intergenerational income transfer that is only vaguely related to past earnings. It transfers income from U.S. residents who work (the young through the middle-aged) to those who do not work—older retired persons.

In 2011, more than 55 million people were receiving OASDI checks averaging about $1,000 a month. Benefit payments from OASDI redistribute income to some degree. Benefit payments, however, are not based on recipient need. Participants' contributions give them the right to benefits even if they would be financially secure without the benefits. Social Security is not really an insurance program because people are not guaranteed that the benefits they receive will be in line with the "contributions" they have made. It is not a personal savings account. The benefits are legislated by Congress. In the future, Congress may not be as sympathetic toward older people as it is today. It could (and probably will have to) legislate for lower real levels of benefits instead of higher ones.

SUPPLEMENTAL SECURITY INCOME AND TEMPORARY ASSISTANCE TO NEEDY FAMILIES Many people who are poor but do not qualify for Social Security benefits are assisted through other programs. The federally financed and administered Supplemental Security Income (SSI) program was instituted in 1974. The purpose of SSI is to establish a nationwide minimum income for the aged, the blind, and the disabled. SSI has become one of the fastest-growing transfer programs in the United States. Whereas in 1974 less than $8 billion was spent, the prediction for 2012 is in excess of $50 billion. U.S. residents currently eligible for SSI include children and individuals with mental disabilities, including drug addicts and alcoholics.

Temporary Assistance to Needy Families (TANF) is a state-administered program, financed in part by federal grants. The program provides aid to families in need. TANF payments are intended to be temporary. Projected expenditures for TANF in 2011 are $23 billion.

FOOD STAMPS Food stamps are government-issued, electronic debit cards that can be used to purchase food. In 1964, some 367,000 Americans were receiving food stamps. For 2011, the estimate is more than 42 million recipients. The annual cost has jumped from $860,000 to more than $36 billion. In 2011, almost one in every seven citizens (including children) was using food stamps.

THE EARNED INCOME TAX CREDIT PROGRAM In 1975, the Earned Income Tax Credit (EITC) Program was created to provide rebates of Social Security taxes to low-income workers. More than one-fifth of all tax returns claim an earned income tax credit. Each year the federal government grants more than $43 billion in these credits. In some states, such as Mississippi, nearly half of all families are eligible for an EITC. The program works as follows: Single-income households with two children that report income of about $39,000 (exclusive of welfare payments) receive EITC benefits up to about $5,000. There is a catch, though. Those with earnings up to a threshold of about $13,000 receive higher benefits as their incomes rise.

But families earning more than this threshold income are penalized about 18 cents for every dollar they earn above the income threshold. Thus, on net the EITC discourages work by low- or moderate-income earners more than it rewards work. In particular, it discourages low-income earners from taking on second jobs. The Government Accountability Office estimates that hours worked by working wives in EITC-beneficiary households have consequently decreased by 15 percent. The average EITC recipient works 1,700 hours a year compared to a normal work year of about 2,000 hours.

No Apparent Reduction in Poverty Rates

In spite of the numerous programs in existence and the trillions of dollars transferred to the poor, the officially defined rate of poverty in the United States has shown no long-run tendency to decline. From 1945 until the 1970s, the percentage of U.S. residents in poverty fell steadily every year. As Figure 30-5 on page 672 shows, it reached a low of around 11 percent in 1974, shot back up beyond 15 percent in 1983, fell to nearly 12 percent by 2007, and has since risen above 14 percent. Why this pattern has emerged is a puzzle. Since the War on Poverty was launched under President

Lyndon B. Johnson in 1965, more than $13 trillion has been transferred to the poor, and yet more U.S. residents are poor today than ever before. This fact created the political will to pass the Welfare Reform Act of 1996, putting limits on people's use of welfare. The law's goal has been to get people off public assistance and into jobs.

QUICK QUIZ **See page 687 for the answers. Review concepts from this section in MyEconLab.**

If poverty is defined in __________ terms, economic growth eventually decreases the number of officially defined poor. If poverty is defined in __________ terms, however, we will never eliminate it.

Although the relative position of the __________ measured by household __________ seems to have worsened, household spending by the bottom 20 percent of households compared to that of the top 20 percent has shown little change since the 1960s.

Major attacks on poverty have been made through social insurance programs, including __________ Security, __________ Security Income (SSI), Temporary Assistance to Needy Families, the __________ __________ tax credit, and __________ stamps.

Health Care

It may seem strange to be reading about health care in a chapter on the distribution of income and poverty. Yet health care is intimately related to those two topics. For example, sometimes people become poor because they do not have adequate health insurance (or have none at all), fall ill, and deplete all of their wealth in obtaining medical care. Moreover, some individuals remain in certain jobs simply because their employer's health care package seems so good that they are afraid to change jobs and risk not being covered by health insurance in the process.

As you will see, much of the cause of the increased health care spending in the United States can be attributed to a change in the incentives that U.S. residents face. Finally, we will examine the economic impact of the new national health care program.

The U.S. Health Care Situation

Spending for health care is estimated to account for about 17 percent of U.S. real GDP. You can see from Figure 30-7 below that in 1965, about 6 percent of annual income was spent on health care, but that percentage has been increasing ever since.

FIGURE 30-7 Percentage of Total National Income Spent on Health Care in the United States

The portion of total national income spent on health care has risen steadily since 1965.

Sources: U.S. Department of Commerce; U.S. Department of Health and Human Services, Deloitte and Touche LLP, VHA, Inc.

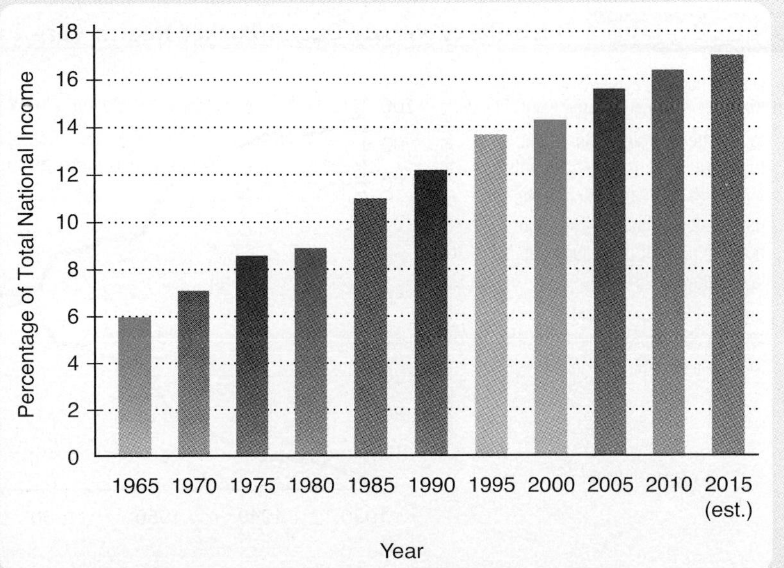

WHY HAVE HEALTH CARE COSTS RISEN SO MUCH? There are numerous explanations for why health care costs have risen so much. At least one has to do with changing demographics: The U.S. population is getting older.

The Age–Health Care Expenditure Equation. The top 5 percent of health care users incur more than 50 percent of all health costs. The bottom 70 percent of health care users account for only 10 percent of health care expenditures. Not surprisingly, the elderly make up most of the top users of health care services. Nursing home expenditures are made primarily by people older than 70. The use of hospitals is also dominated by the aged.

The U.S. population is aging steadily. More than 13 percent of the 310 million U.S. residents are over 65. It is estimated that by the year 2035, senior citizens will comprise about 22 percent of our population. This aging population stimulates the demand for health care. The elderly consume more than four times as much per capita health care services as the rest of the population. In short, whatever the demand for health care services is today, it is likely to be considerably higher in the future as the U.S. population ages.

New Technologies. Another reason that health care costs have risen so dramatically is advancing technology. Each CT (computerized tomography) scanner costs at least $100,000. An MRI (magnetic resonance imaging) scanner can cost over $2 million. A PET (positron emission tomography) scanner costs around $4 million. All of these machines have become increasingly available in recent decades and are desired throughout the country. Typical fees for procedures using them range from $300 to $400 for a CT scan to as high as $2,000 for a PET scan. The development of new technologies that help physicians and hospitals prolong human life is an ongoing process in an ever-advancing industry. New procedures at even higher prices can be expected in the future.

Third-Party Financing. Currently, government spending on health care constitutes more than 40 percent of total health care spending (of which the *federal* government pays about 70 percent). Private insurance accounts for a little over 35 percent of payments for health care. The remainder—less than 20 percent—is paid directly by individuals. Figure 30-8 below shows the change in the payment scheme for medical care in the United States since 1930. Medicare and Medicaid are the main sources

FIGURE 30-8 Third-Party versus Out-of-Pocket Health Care Payments

Out-of-pocket payments for health care services have been falling steadily since the 1930s. In contrast, third-party payments for health care have risen to the point that they account for more than 80 percent of all such outlays today.

Sources: Health Care Financing Administration; U.S. Department of Health and Human Services.

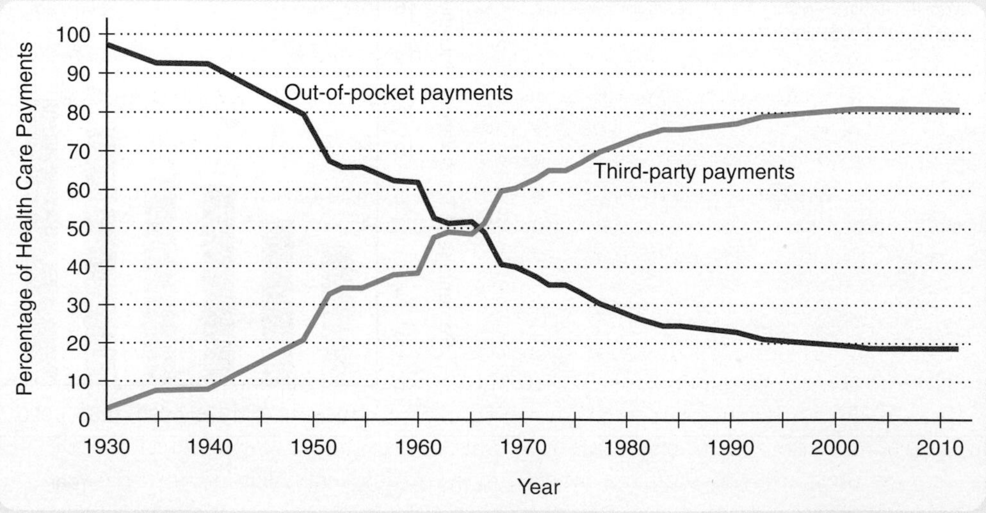

FIGURE 30-9 The Demand for Health Care Services

At price P_1, the quantity of health care services demanded per year would hypothetically be Q_1. If the price fell to zero (third-party payment with zero deductible), the quantity demanded would expand to Q_2.

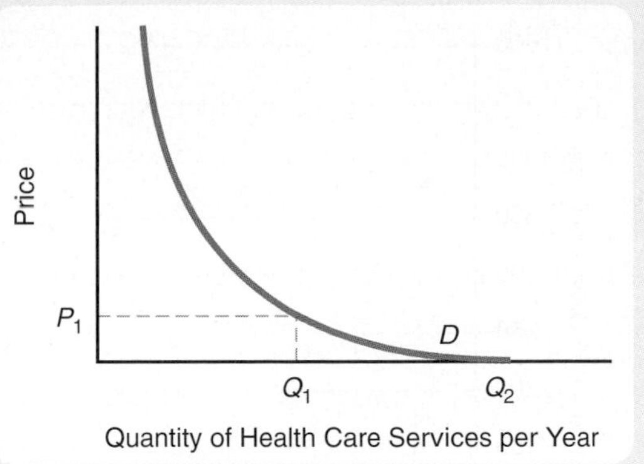

of hospital and other medical benefits for more than 40 million U.S. residents, most of whom are over 65. Medicaid—the joint state-federal program—provides long-term health care, particularly for people living in nursing homes.

Medicare, Medicaid, and private insurance companies are considered **third parties** in the medical care equation. Caregivers and patients are the two primary parties. When third parties step in to pay for medical care, the quantity demanded of those services increases. For example, within four years after Medicare went into effect in 1966, the volume of federal government–reimbursed medical services increased to a level 65 percent higher than anticipated when the program was enacted.

Third parties
Parties who are not directly involved in a given activity or transaction. For example, in the relationship between caregivers and patients, fees may be paid by third parties (insurance companies, government).

PRICE, QUANTITY DEMANDED, AND THE QUESTION OF MORAL HAZARD Although some people may think that the demand for health care is insensitive to price changes, significant increases in quantities of medical services demanded follow reductions in people's out-of-pocket costs. Look at Figure 30-9 above. There you see a hypothetical demand curve for health care services. To the extent that third parties—whether government or private insurance—pay for health care, the out-of-pocket cost, or net price, to the individual decreases. If all medical expenses were paid for by third parties, dropping the price to zero in Figure 30-9, the quantity demanded would increase.

One of the issues here has to do with the problem of *moral hazard*. Consider two individuals with two different health insurance policies. The first policy pays for all medical expenses, but under the second, the individual has to pay the first $1,000 a year (this amount is known as the *deductible*). Will the behavior of the two individuals be different? Generally, the answer is yes.

The individual with no deductible is more likely to seek treatment for health problems after they develop rather than try to avoid them and will generally seek medical attention on a more regular basis. In contrast, the individual who faces the first $1,000 of medical expenses each year will tend to engage in more wellness activities and will be less inclined to seek medical care for minor problems. The moral hazard here is that the individual with the zero deductible for medical care expenses will tend to engage in a less healthful lifestyle than will the individual with the $1,000 deductible.

MORAL HAZARD AS IT AFFECTS PHYSICIANS AND HOSPITALS The issue of moral hazard also has a direct effect on the behavior of physicians and hospital administrators. Due to third-party payments, patients rarely have to worry about the expense of operations and other medical procedures. As a consequence, both physicians and hospitals order more procedures. Physicians are typically reimbursed on the basis of medical procedures. Thus, they have no financial interest in trying to keep hospital costs down. Indeed, many have an incentive to raise costs.

FIGURE 30-10 Federal Medicare Spending

Federal spending on Medicare has increased about 10 percent per year, *after adjusting for inflation,* since its inception in 1966. (All figures expressed in constant 2005 dollars per year.)

Sources: Economic Report of the President; U.S. Bureau of Labor Statistics.

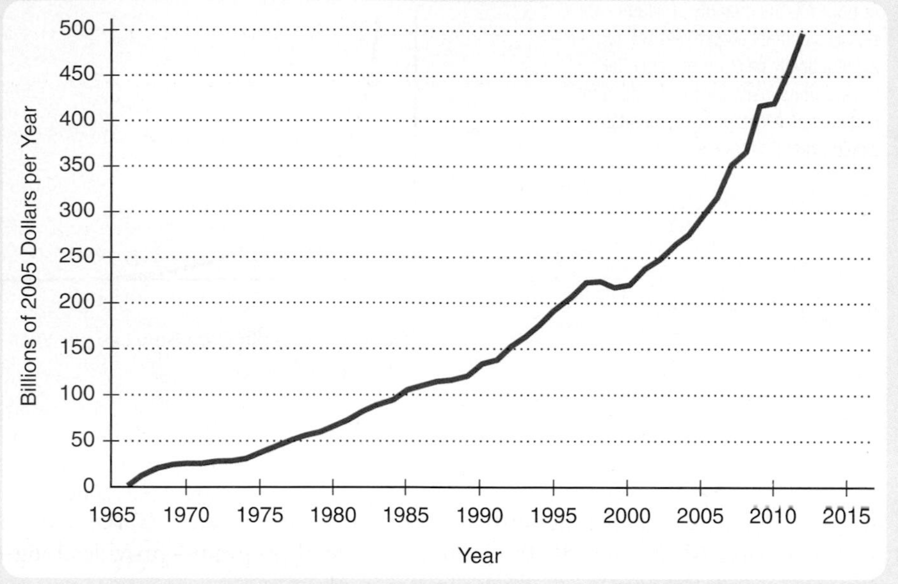

Such actions are most evident with terminally ill patients. A physician may order a CT scan and other costly procedures for a terminally ill patient. The physician knows that Medicare or some other type of insurance will pay. Then the physician can charge a fee for analyzing the CT scan. Fully 30 percent of Medicare expenditures are for U.S. residents who are in the last six months of their lives.

Rising Medicare expenditures are one of the most serious problems facing the federal government today. The number of beneficiaries has increased from 19.1 million in 1966 (first year of operation) to more than 40 million in 2011. Figure 30-10 above shows that federal spending on Medicare has been growing at an average of about 10 percent per year, adjusted for inflation. The rate of growth in Medicare spending will be even higher in the future as a result of the Medicare prescription drug benefit that was implemented in 2006.

The Nationalization of U.S. Health Care Spending

In March 2010, President Barack Obama signed a roughly 2,000-page law that will govern the future operation of U.S. health care markets. Before we contemplate the law's likely effect on the economics of health care, let's review its key features.

GOVERNMENT HEALTH INSURANCE MANDATES Table 30-2 on the facing page summarizes the fundamental components of the federal government's new national health care program, which is to be phased in through the mid-2010s. The first two elements of the program are restraints on choices of individuals and families and on decisions of employers. People must either purchase health insurance or pay a fine to the federal government. Thus, a young person in good health who otherwise might have opted not to purchase health insurance must buy insurance or pay a penalty.

In addition, firms with more than 50 employees must either provide health insurance or pay fines when uninsured employees receive tax subsidies to purchase insurance. A firm that otherwise would have hired another worker but determines that the additional cost imposed by the health care program pushes the overall cost above the individual's marginal revenue product will choose not to hire that person.

TABLE 30-2

Key Components of the Federal Government's National Health Care Program

Individual mandate	Nearly all U.S. residents must either purchase health insurance coverage or pay a fine of up to $750 per year for an individual (up to $2,250 per year for a family).
Employer mandate	Firms with more than 50 employees must offer health insurance coverage or pay an annual fine of up to $750 per employee who obtains federal subsidies for coverage.
Health care insurance subsidies	1. Families with incomes up to 133% of the federal poverty level are eligible for federal Medicaid coverage. 2. Families with incomes up to 400% of the federal poverty level are eligible for thousands of dollars in tax subsidies per year (amounts vary with family incomes). 3. Tax credits are available to businesses providing health insurance to 25 or fewer workers and paying annual salaries averaging no more than $50,000.
National health insurance exchanges	Government-directed exchanges will assist in matching individuals and small businesses with health insurance policies that satisfy government requirements.
Health insurance regulations	1. All private health insurance plans must satisfy a number of federal rules and regulations. 2. Health insurers must cover all who apply, including people who already have health problems. 3. Ceilings are placed on health insurance premium increases for elderly people.
Higher tax rates to help fund the program	A special tax rate of 3.8% is applied to nearly all income earnings above $200,000 for individuals or $250,000 for married couples.

GOVERNMENT HEALTH CARE SUBSIDIES Another fundamental feature is federal health care subsidies. The government's subsidies vary based on individual and family incomes. The national health care program directs more relatively low-income people into the Medicaid program by raising the maximum-income threshold for government-provided health care to 133 percent of the official poverty level. As a result, millions of people now qualify for the Medicaid program's coverage of health care with very few out-of-pocket payments.

Other individuals and families earning incomes as high as four times the official poverty income level receive *tax subsidies*. These are reductions in federal tax payments intended to assist these people in covering required expenditures on health insurance. Thus, some families with incomes exceeding $100,000 per year will receive tax breaks of about $2,400—some of their own income that the government will allow them to keep and direct to satisfying its requirement to buy health insurance. Lower-income families not eligible for Medicaid coverage receive larger tax subsidies. Finally, the program also offers tax credits to businesses that provide health insurance to 25 or fewer workers who receive an average salary of no more than $50,000 per year.

GOVERNMENT HEALTH INSURANCE EXCHANGES Under the new program, the federal government will coordinate the establishment of **health insurance exchanges.** These are government agencies tasked with helping individuals and families—especially the roughly 30 million additional people who will obtain health insurance—find policies to buy. The exchanges, which state governments are charged with operating, also will assist small businesses in finding health insurance they can purchase for employees.

Health insurance exchanges
Government agencies to which the national health care program assigns the task of assisting individuals, families, and small businesses in identifying health insurance policies to purchase.

REGULATIONS AND TAXES The national health care program also imposes new federal regulations on health care insurers and assesses special tax rates on higher-income families to help finance the tax subsidies extended to lower-income families. All health insurance policies now must satisfy a variety of requirements. For example, insurers cannot deny anyone health insurance, and a ceiling is imposed on the rate of increase in health insurance prices charged to elderly people.

Finally, the national health care plan imposes a special health care tax. A tax rate of 3.8 percent will be assessed on nearly all earnings above $200,000 per year for individuals and above $250,000 per year for married couples.

Why Not . . . have all physicians work for the federal government?

This certainly would simplify payments to physicians under the new national health care program. A difficulty with this idea, though, is that the government would have to determine what the equilibrium payments to physicians in various specializations otherwise *would be* in a private market. If the government were to set the payments too low, then physicians' overall wages would end up below the market clearing levels. The result would be physician shortages, and there would be insufficient physicians to deliver the care promised by the national health care program.

Economic Effects of the National Health Care Program

Naturally, the new U.S. health care program will have significant effects on health care markets. In addition, the program will also have effects on labor markets, product markets, and government budgets.

HIGHER HEALTH CARE SPENDING AND A WORSENED MORAL HAZARD PROBLEM The government's national health care program enlarges the scope of third-party payments for health care services. As we noted earlier, health care expenditures already consume about 17 percent of national income. The program promises to boost that spending and to expand the size of the moral hazard problem in U.S. health care markets.

Once the national health care program goes into effect during the mid-2010s, tens of millions of people will pay fewer of their health care expenses out of their own pockets than they did previously. This change will have three primary consequences. First, because the price people actually pay out of their own pockets to consume health care services will decline, the quantity of health care services demanded will increase. Second, because health insurers will be required to cover this expanded quantity demanded of services, total expenditures on health care will increase. Third, there will be an increased moral hazard problem. Because people will pay a smaller portion of the actual cost of treating health problems, more individuals will have reduced incentives to make decisions that promote better health. As people have more health problems as a consequence of this rise in moral hazard, the demand for health care will increase.

You Are There

To contemplate possible lessons that the recent experience of a U.S. state with a similar program may offer for the new national health care program, consider **In Massachusetts, Public Health Care Means Price Controls,** on page 682.

IMPACTS ON THE REST OF THE U.S. ECONOMY Implementation of the new national health care program will have effects on labor markets, markets for goods and services, and budgets of federal and state governments:

1. *Labor market impacts.* In labor markets, the requirement for many firms to provide health insurance will raise the effective wage rate that they must pay for each unit of labor. Recall from Chapter 28 that firms employ labor to the point at which the marginal revenue product of labor—marginal revenue times the marginal physical product—equals the wage rate. The increase in the effective wage rate will induce firms to move upward along their downward-sloping

marginal-revenue-product-of-labor curves. Thus, the quantity of labor demanded by firms will decline. Other things being equal, U.S. employment will be lower than it otherwise would have been.

2. *Markets for goods and services.* In markets for goods and services, the increase in labor costs firms incur in hiring each unit of labor will raise their marginal costs. Because each firm maximizes profits by producing to the point at which marginal revenue equals marginal cost, the increase in marginal costs will induce firms to decrease their output at all prices. Other things being equal, this will place pressure on equilibrium prices to rise in a number of markets. Consequently, consumers will pay higher prices for many goods and services.
3. *Effects on government budgets.* The new tax rate applied to higher-income individuals goes into effect in 2013, so tax revenues will begin flowing into the new program at that time. Federal government expenditures on the program are being phased in more gradually, so the program initially will be financed by the revenues collected in advance. Most observers agree, however, that the new tax revenues will be insufficient to cover the increases in government health care spending that surely will occur in future years. Hence, the federal government ultimately will have to search for ways to reduce its health care expenditures or to raise more tax revenues to fund the program. The federal program does not include revenues for states to cover the higher expenses of the additional people admitted to the Medicaid program, which state governments administer. Thus, state governments will also face pressures to boost tax revenues.

Who are the thousands of foreign workers who are indirectly benefiting from implementation of the new U.S. health care program?

INTERNATIONAL EXAMPLE The U.S. Health Care Program's Benefits for Indian Workers

As discussed in Chapter 28, many U.S. firms engage in international labor *outsourcing* by hiring foreign workers to perform certain tasks. Among U.S. firms that outsource labor are health insurers, most of which hire workers in India to perform a variety of record-keeping tasks. The 2,000-page health care law has imposed many new record-keeping requirements on health insurers. Thus, implementation of the new U.S. health care program has increased demand for outsourced Indian labor. As a result, there are more jobs for Indian workers, and the market clearing wages paid to these workers by U.S. health insurers are higher.

FOR CRITICAL ANALYSIS

Who ultimately pays for the extra costs that U.S. health insurers incur in additional record keeping?

QUICK QUIZ

See page 687 for the answers. Review concepts from this section in MyEconLab.

The U.S. national health care program adopted in 2010 expands the scope of health care coverage across millions of additional people by covering more lower-income people under the existing __________ program and by subsidizing health care expenses for people with incomes up to __________ percent of the poverty income level.

Key elements of the national health care program include __________ for individuals to buy health insurance and for firms employing more than 50 workers to provide insurance access or pay fines; establishment of government-operated __________ to assist individuals and small businesses in finding health insurance plans; a requirement for health insurers to accept __________ applicants; and imposition of a new __________ on high-income earners.

Economic analysis suggests that likely effects of the adoption of the national health care program include __________ employment in U.S. labor markets, __________ prices of goods and services for consumers, and a __________ shortfall of federal and state tax revenues in relation to government expenses.

You Are There

In Massachusetts, Public Health Care Means Price Controls

Massachusetts governor Deval Patrick looks at the data and shakes his head. He must determine how to address the state government's rapidly increasing health care costs. A state program adopted in 2006 requires all state residents to buy health insurance or pay a penalty. It also requires insurers to cover all applicants and to charge everyone very nearly the same premiums, which the state subsidizes for many residents. Patrick sees that since 2008, about 40 percent of all who purchased insurance enrolled for less than five months—long enough to incur about $12,000 per person in expenses. After receiving treatment, these people dropped their health care insurance coverage. A consequence of this behavior is that health care spending in Massachusetts is growing at an annual rate of nearly 7 percent. This experience contradicts forecasts back in 2006 that adopting the program would *reduce* the state's health care spending.

After hours of study, Patrick decides to recommend a revision to the program. Henceforth, Patrick concludes, a state health care regulator must have the power to review the prices charged by physicians and hospitals. If the regulator determines that current prices are too high, then the state government will establish ceilings on health care prices in an effort to contain the government's health care expenses.

Critical Analysis Questions

1. What will happen in the Massachusetts health care market in the future if the state regulator sets ceiling prices below equilibrium prices?
2. Based on your answer to Question 1, could setting ceiling prices below equilibrium prices succeed in reducing health care expenses in Massachusetts?

ISSUES & APPLICATIONS

Is Your College Degree Worth $1 Million?

CONCEPTS APPLIED

- Income
- Determinants of Income
- Distribution of Income

Ads placed by a number of colleges across the United States include the claim that a college degree can be expected to yield $1 million more in lifetime income than would be earned with only a high school diploma. As you have learned in this chapter, the amount of education and training that people obtain does indeed have a significant influence on their incomes and, consequently, the distribution of incomes across society. But from the perspective of an entering college student, is a college degree really worth $1 million?

Discounting Matters

To obtain the $1 million lifetime income differential claimed by colleges' ads, the colleges subtract the $32,000 per year earned by a typical high school graduate from the $58,000 per year earned by a typical college graduate. This yields an annual income boost of $26,000 (or more than 80 percent) from attending college. Multiplying this amount by 40 years yields a total slightly exceeding $1 million—hence, the claims in the colleges' ads.

TABLE 30-3

Estimated Lifetime Income Gains from Obtaining a College Degree

	Assumed Annual Interest Rate		
	2 Percent	4 Percent	6 Percent
Discounted present value of $26,000 per year for 40 years	$711,243	$514,612	$391,204
Explicit college expenses: Present value of tuition, fees, books, and room and board for 4 years	−128,000	−121,847	−116,157
Opportunity cost: Present value of $32,000 per year in forgone income for 4 years	−72,000	−68,539	−65,338
Net anticipated lifetime income differential	$511,243	$324,226	$209,709

As you learned in Chapter 21, however, people discount the future. The first line of Table 30-3 above displays the discounted present value of the income differential of $26,000 over 40 years. Assuming an annual interest rate of just 2 percent, the anticipated extra average lifetime earnings from obtaining a college degree drop to $711,243, or $288,757 below $1 million. If a 6 percent interest rate is used to discount the future, the expected additional lifetime earnings from obtaining a college degree are only $391,204, or $608,796 less than $1 million!

Taking College Expenses into Account

Another important element missing from the colleges' calculation of the expected lifetime income gain from a college degree is the expenses that an individual incurs to obtain a degree. These costs, of course, include spending on tuition and fees, books, room and board, and other miscellaneous expenses that naturally vary from student to student and from college to college. Currently, the annual average of these expenses at a public college is about $12,000. At a private college, the average annual cost is about $26,000. To compute the discounted present value of costs for four years in Table 30-3, $18,000 is used as an approximate average annual explicit expense across all U.S. colleges.

Naturally, instead of attending college classes and earning a degree, a typical student could work for four years at the average annual income earned by high school graduates of $32,000. Table 30-3 lists discounted present values of the opportunity cost of attending college for four years instead of working for these annual earnings. The table shows that, depending on the interest rate used to compute discounted present values, the *net* lifetime income gain from obtaining a college degree ranges from almost $210,000 to just over $511,000. Thus, the higher expected lifetime earnings boost from earning a college degree is well below the $1 million claimed by a number of colleges. Nevertheless, the expected lifetime income gain is still substantial, which explains why so many young people seek a college degree.

For Critical Analysis

1. At annual interest rates higher than 6 percent, would computed net lifetime income gains from obtaining a college degree be higher or lower than the values computed in Table 30-3?
2. If the calculations in Table 30-3 were revised to take into account each year's small but positive probability of death, which increases with age, would the net anticipated income gain from a college degree rise or fall? Explain briefly.

Web Resources

1. To see an example of a claim that a college degree is worth as much as $1 million in additional lifetime earnings, go to www.econtoday.com/ch30.
2. For updated estimates of the average annual expenses to attend college in the United States, go to www.econtoday.com/ch30.

Research Project

Evaluate other aspects of a college education, besides simply obtaining a degree, that contribute to increasing a student's anticipated lifetime income gain.

For more questions on this chapter's Issues & Applications, go to **MyEconLab**. In the Study Plan for this chapter, select Section N: News.

Here is what you should know after reading this chapter. **MyEconLab** will help you identify what you know, and where to go when you need to practice.

WHAT YOU SHOULD KNOW		WHERE TO GO TO PRACTICE
Using a Lorenz Curve to Represent a Nation's Income Distribution A Lorenz curve is a diagram that illustrates the distribution of income geometrically by measuring the percentage of households in relation to the cumulative percentage of income earnings. A perfectly straight Lorenz curve depicts perfect income equality because at each percentage of households measured along a straight-line Lorenz curve, those households earn exactly the same percentage of income. The more bowed a Lorenz curve is, the more unequally income is distributed.	distribution of income, 664 Lorenz curve, 664 income in kind, 665 **KEY FIGURES** Figure 30-1, 664 Figure 30-2, 665	• **MyEconLab** Study Plan 30.1 • Audio introduction to Chapter 30 • Animated Figures 30-1, 30-2 • ABC News Video: Tradeoffs to High-Priced Cancer Drugs
Key Determinants of Income Differences Across Individuals Because of the age-earnings cycle, in which people typically begin working at relatively low incomes when young, age is an important factor influencing income differences. So are marginal productivity differences, which arise from differences in talent, experience, and training due to different investments in human capital. Discrimination likely plays a role as well.	age-earnings cycle, 667 **KEY FIGURE** Figure 30-4, 668	• **MyEconLab** Study Plan 30.2 • Video: The Determinants of Income Differences • Animated Figure 30-4
Theories of Desired Income Distribution One theory of desired income distribution is the productivity standard (also called the contributive or merit standard), according to which each person receives income based on the value of what he or she produces. The other is the egalitarian principle of income distribution, which proposes that each person should receive exactly the same income.		• **MyEconLab** Study Plan 30.3
Alternative Approaches to Measuring and Addressing Poverty One approach to measuring poverty is to define an absolute poverty standard, such as a specific and unchanging income level. Another approach defines poverty in terms of income levels relative to the rest of the population. Currently, the U.S. government seeks to address poverty via income maintenance programs such as Social Security, Supplemental Security Income, Temporary Assistance to Needy Families, food stamps, and the Earned Income Tax Credit Program.	**KEY FIGURES** Figure 30-5, 672 Figure 30-6, 673	• **MyEconLab** Study Plan 30.4 • Video: Defining Poverty • Animated Figures 30-5, 30-6
Rising Health Care Costs and Third-Party Payments Spending on health care as a percentage of total U.S. national income has increased during recent decades. Third-party financing of health care expenditures by private and government insurance programs gives covered individuals an incentive to purchase more health care than they would if they paid all expenses out of pocket.	third parties, 677 **KEY FIGURES** Figure 30-7, 675 Figure 30-8, 676 Figure 30-9, 677	• **MyEconLab** Study Plan 30.5 • Animated Figures 30-7, 30-8, 30-9

MyEconLab continued

WHAT YOU SHOULD KNOW		WHERE TO GO TO PRACTICE
Key Provisions of the New U.S. National Health Insurance Program The national health care program adopted in March 2010 requires all individuals to purchase health insurance and mandates that firms with more than 50 employees either provide health insurance or pay penalties. The program insures health care for nearly all U.S. residents by placing more lower-income people in the Medicaid program and subsidizing health insurance for families with incomes up to 400 percent of the official poverty level. Under the program, health insurers must provide coverage to all who apply. To help finance the program, people earning incomes above relatively high thresholds will face a special 3.8 percent tax rate applied to nearly all sources of income above those thresholds.	health insurance exchanges, 679	• **MyEconLab** Study Plan 30.5

Log in to MyEconLab, take a chapter test, and get a personalized Study Plan that tells you which concepts you understand and which ones you need to review. From there, MyEconLab will give you further practice, tutorials, animations, videos, and guided solutions.
Log in to www.myeconlab.com

PROBLEMS

All problems are assignable in myeconlab. *Answers to the odd-numbered problems appear at the back of the book.*

30-1. Consider the graph below, which depicts Lorenz curves for countries X, Y, and Z.

a. Which country has the least income inequality?

b. Which country has the most income inequality?

c. Countries Y and Z are identical in all but one respect: population distribution. The share of the population made up of children below working age is much higher in country Z. Recently, however, birthrates have declined in country Z and risen in country Y. Assuming that the countries remain identical in all other respects, would you expect that in 20 years the Lorenz curves for the two countries will be closer together or farther apart? (Hint: According to the age-earnings cycle, what typically happens to income as an individual begins working and ages?)

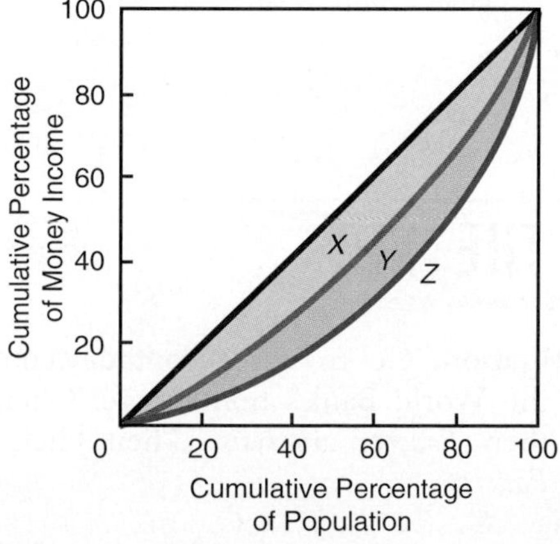

30-2. Consider the following estimates from the late 2000s of shares of income to each group. Use graph paper or a hand-drawn diagram to draw rough Lorenz curves for each country. Which has the most nearly equal distribution, based on your diagram?

Country	Poorest 40%	Next 30%	Next 20%	Richest 10%
Bolivia	13	21	26	40
Chile	13	20	26	41
Uruguay	22	26	26	26

30-3. Suppose that the 20 percent of people with the highest incomes decide to increase their annual giving to charities, which pass nearly all the funds on to the 20 percent of people with the lowest incomes. What is the effect on the shape of the Lorenz curve?

30-4. Suppose that a nation has implemented a system for applying a tax rate of 2 percent to the incomes earned by the 10 percent of its residents with the highest incomes. All funds collected are then transferred directly to the 10 percent of the nation's residents with the lowest incomes.

- **a.** What is the general effect on the shape of a Lorenz curve based on incomes prior to collection and redistribution of the tax?
- **b.** What is the general effect on the shape of a Lorenz curve based on incomes after collection and redistribution of the tax?

30-5. Estimates indicate that during the late 2000s, the poorest 40 percent of the population earned about 15 percent of total income in Argentina. In Brazil, the poorest 40 percent earned about 10 percent of total income. The next-highest 30 percent of income earners in Argentina received roughly 25 percent of total income. In Brazil, the next-highest 30 percent of income earners received approximately 20 percent of total income. Can you determine, without drawing a diagram (though you can if you wish), which country's Lorenz curve was bowed out farther to the right?

30-6. Explain why the productivity standard for the distribution of income entails rewarding people based on their contribution to society's total output. Why does the productivity standard typically fail to yield an equal distribution of income?

30-7. Identify whether each of the following proposed poverty measures is an absolute or relative measure of poverty, and discuss whether poverty could ever be eliminated if that measure were utilized.

- **a.** An inflation-adjusted annual income of $25,000 for an urban family of four
- **b.** Individuals with annual incomes among the lowest 15 percent
- **c.** An inflation-adjusted annual income of $10,000 per person

30-8. Some economists have argued that if the government wishes to subsidize health care, it should instead provide predetermined amounts of payments (based on the type of health care problems experienced) directly to patients, who then would be free to choose their health care providers. Whether or not you agree, can you give an economic rationale for this approach to governmental health care funding?

30-9. Suppose that a government agency guarantees to pay all of an individual's future health care expenses after the end of this year, so that the effective price of health care for the individual will be zero from that date onward. In what ways might this well-intended policy induce the individual to consume "excessive" health care services in future years?

30-10. Suppose that a group of physicians establishes a joint practice in a remote area. This group provides the only health care available to people in the local community, and its objective is to maximize total economic profits for the group's members. Draw a diagram illustrating how the price and quantity of health care will be determined in this community. (Hint: How does a single producer of any service determine its output and price?)

30-11. A government agency determines that the entire community discussed in Problem 30-10 qualifies for a special program in which the government will pay for a number of health care services that most residents previously had not consumed. Many residents immediately make appointments with the community physicians' group. Given the information in Problem 30-10, what is the likely effect on the profit-maximizing price and the equilibrium quantity of health care services provided by the physicians' group in this community?

30-12. A government agency notifies the physicians' group in Problem 30-10 that to continue providing services in the community, the group must document its activities. The resulting paperwork expenses raise the cost of each unit of health care services that the group provides. What is the likely effect on the profit-maximizing price and the equilibrium quantity of health care services provided by the physicians' group in this community?

ECONOMICS ON THE NET

Measuring Poverty In this application, you will learn why poverty can be difficult to measure.

Title: World Bank PovertyNet: Understanding Poverty

Navigation: Go to **www.econtoday.com/ch30** to visit the World Bank's home page. Click on *Topics* and then *Poverty Analysis*. Then click on *Measuring Poverty*.

Application Perform the indicated operations, and answer the following questions.

1. Click on "Defining welfare measures." Why does this discussion suggest that measures of consumption are more useful to use in measuring poverty than income measures? Does the U.S. government's use of income thresholds for its official definition of poverty accord with this discussion?
2. Click on "Choose and estimate a poverty line." What alternative absolute poverty definitions are discussed? If the U.S. government were to adopt any of these absolute measures for its official poverty definition, what would happen to the U.S. poverty rate as real incomes and living standards rise over time?

For Group Study and Analysis Click on "Choose and estimate poverty indicators." What are the advantages and disadvantages of the poverty indicators that are discussed? Which indicator does the U.S. government utilize?

ANSWERS TO QUICK QUIZZES

p. 667: (i) income . . . equality . . . unequally; (ii) assets . . . more

p. 671: (i) age-earnings; (ii) productivity . . . revenue; (iii) talent . . . education . . . experience . . . training; (iv) human . . . opportunity; (v) productivity . . . equality

p. 675: (i) absolute . . . relative; (ii) poor . . . income; (iii) Social . . . Supplemental . . . earned income . . . food

p. 681: (i) Medicaid . . . 400; (ii) mandates . . . exchanges . . . all . . . tax; (iii) lower . . . higher . . . larger

31 Environmental Economics

The United Nations Food and Agriculture Organization is spending about $28 million to study why the world's honeybee population appears to be rapidly shrinking, thereby potentially depriving planet earth of a key agent for pollination of farmers' crops. In recent years, honeybees have suffered a variety of maladies, such as parasitic infections and viruses. These problems may or may not be related to a phenomenon called "colony collapse disorder," in which colonies of honeybees suddenly shrink or disappear altogether for reasons not fully understood. There is growing evidence, however, that human activities may contribute to colony collapse disorder—and also that forces at work in human markets may help to revive the global honeybee population. In this chapter, you will learn about the relationship between markets and the environment.

LEARNING OBJECTIVES

After reading this chapter, you should be able to:

- Distinguish between private costs and social costs
- Understand market externalities and possible ways to correct externalities
- Explain how economists can conceptually determine the optimal quantity of pollution
- Contrast the roles of private and common property rights in alternative approaches to addressing the problem of pollution
- Describe how many of the world's governments are seeking to reduce pollution by capping and controlling the use of pollution-generating resources
- Discuss how the assignment of property rights may influence the fates of endangered species

myeconlab

MyEconLab helps you master each objective and study more efficiently. See end of chapter for details.

in the 1970s, many news magazines ran cover stories about how the world was descending into a new ice age? These stories reported that scientists were convinced that the average world temperature had been dropping since the late 1940s. Some climatologists speculated that the earth might be entering a full-blown 10,000-year ice age and that glaciers might expand across much of the Northern Hemisphere. Of course, today a contrary scientific consensus suggests that global *warming* is a more likely scenario. Now some scientists worry that glaciers eventually will melt. Political leaders convinced by this argument have proposed a wide range of policies aimed at reducing emissions of "greenhouse gases," such as carbon dioxide, that may be contributing to a worldwide warming trend.

Did You Know That

The economic way of thinking about policies intended to reduce greenhouse gases requires that the costs of such policies be considered. Likewise, the economic way of thinking about nonrenewable resources or endangered species requires that we take into account the costs of resource conservation and protection of wildlife. How much of your weekly wages are you willing to sacrifice to be used to reduce aggregate emissions of carbon dioxide, a gas that you exhale every time you breathe? To some people, framing questions in terms of the dollars-and-cents costs of environmental improvement sounds anti-ecological. But this is not so. Economists want to help citizens and policymakers opt for informed policies that have the maximum possible *net* benefits (benefits minus costs). As you will see, every decision made in favor of "the environment" involves a trade-off.

Private versus Social Costs

Human actions often give rise to unwanted side effects—the destruction of our environment is one. Human actions generate pollutants that go into the air and the water. The question that is often asked is, Why do individuals and businesses continue to create pollution without necessarily paying directly for the negative consequences?

Until now, we've been dealing with settings in which the costs of an individual's actions are borne directly by the individual. When a business has to pay wages to workers, it knows exactly what its labor costs are. When it has to buy materials or build a plant, it knows quite well what these will cost. An individual who has to pay for car repairs or a theater ticket knows exactly what the cost will be. These costs are what we term *private costs*. **Private costs** are borne solely by the individuals who incur them. They are *internal* in the sense that the firm or household must explicitly take account of them.

Private costs
Costs borne solely by the individuals who incur them. Also called *internal costs*.

Now consider the actions of a business that dumps the waste products from its production process into a nearby river or an individual who litters a public park or beach. Obviously, these actions involve a cost. When the firm pollutes the water, people downstream suffer the consequences. They may not want to swim in or drink the polluted water. They may catch fewer fish than before because of the pollution. In the case of littering, the people who come along after the litterer has cluttered the park or the beach are the ones who bear the costs. The cost of these actions is borne by people other than those who commit the actions. The creator of the cost is not the sole bearer. The costs are not internalized by the individual or firm—they are external.

When we add *external* costs to *internal*, or private, costs, we obtain **social costs.** Pollution problems—indeed, all problems pertaining to the environment—may be viewed as situations in which social costs exceed private costs. Because some economic participants pay only the smaller private costs of their actions, not the full social costs, their actions ultimately contribute to higher external costs on the rest of society. Therefore, in such situations in which social and private costs diverge, we see "too much" steel production, automobile driving, or beach littering, to name only a few of the many possible examples.

Social costs
The full costs borne by society whenever a resource use occurs. Social costs can be measured by adding external costs to private, or internal, costs.

The Costs of Polluted Air

Why is the air in cities so polluted with automobile exhaust fumes? When automobile drivers step into their cars, they bear only the private costs of driving. That is, they must pay for the gas, maintenance, depreciation, and insurance on their automobiles.

But they cause an additional cost—air pollution—which they are not forced to take into account when they make the decision to drive. Air pollution is a cost because it causes harm to individuals—burning eyes, respiratory ailments, and dirtier clothes, cars, and buildings—and adds to accumulations of various gases that may contribute to global warming. The air pollution created by automobile exhausts is a cost that individual operators of automobiles do not yet bear directly. The social cost of driving includes all the private costs plus at least the cost of air pollution, which society bears. Decisions made only on the basis of private costs lead to too much automobile driving. Clean air is a scarce resource used by automobile drivers free of charge. They use more of it than they would if they had to pay the full social costs.

Externalities

Externality
A situation in which a private cost (or benefit) diverges from a social cost (or benefit); a situation in which the costs (or benefits) of an action are not fully borne (or gained) by the decision makers engaged in an activity that uses scarce resources.

When a private cost differs from a social cost, we say that there is an **externality** because individual decision makers are not paying (internalizing) all the costs. (We briefly covered this topic in Chapter 5.) Some of these costs remain external to the decision-making process. Remember that the full cost of using a scarce resource is borne one way or another by all who live in the society. That is, members of society must pay the full opportunity cost of any activity that uses scarce resources. The individual decision maker is the firm or the customer, and external costs and benefits will not enter into that individual's or firm's decision-making processes.

We might want to view the problem as it is presented in Figure 31-1 below. Here we have the market demand curve, D, for product X and the supply curve, S_1, for product X. The supply curve, S_1, includes only internal, or private, costs. The intersection of the demand and supply curves as drawn will be at price P_1 and quantity Q_1 (at E_1). We now assume that the production of good X involves externalities that the private firms did not take into account. Those externalities could be air pollution, water pollution, scenery destruction, or anything of that nature.

We know that the social costs of producing product X exceed the private costs. We show this by drawing curve S_2. It is above the original supply curve S_1 because it includes the full social costs of producing the product. If firms could be made to bear these costs, their willingness to supply the good would be reduced, so the

FIGURE 31-1 Reckoning with Full Social Costs

The supply curve, S_1, is equal to the horizontal summation (represented by the capital Greek letter sigma, Σ) of the individual marginal cost curves above the respective minimum average variable costs of all the firms producing good X. These individual marginal cost curves include only internal, or private, costs. If the external costs were included and added to the private costs, we would have social costs. The supply curve would shift upward to S_2. In the uncorrected situation, the equilibrium price is P_1, and the equilibrium quantity is Q_1. In the corrected situation, the equilibrium price would rise to P_2, and the equilibrium quantity would fall to Q_2.

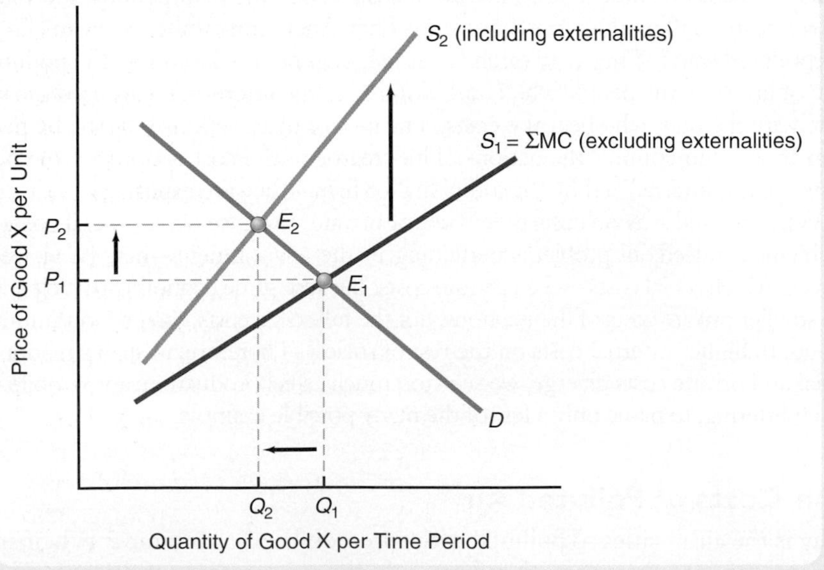

price would be P_2 and the quantity Q_2 (at E_2). The inclusion of external costs in the decision-making process would lead to a higher-priced product and a decline in quantity produced. Thus, we see that when social costs are not fully borne by the creators of those costs, the quantity produced is "excessive" because the price to consumers is too low.

Correcting for Externalities

We can see here a method for reducing pollution and environmental degradation. Somehow the signals in the economy must be changed so that decision makers will take into account *all* the costs of their actions. In the case of automobile pollution, we might want to devise some method of taxing motorists according to the amount of pollution they cause. In the case of a firm, we might want to devise a system of taxing businesses according to the amount of pollution for which they are responsible. They might then have an incentive to install pollution abatement equipment.

The Polluters' Choice

Facing an additional private cost for polluting, firms will be induced to (1) install pollution abatement equipment or otherwise change production techniques so as to reduce the amount of pollution, (2) reduce pollution-causing activity, or (3) simply pay a government-mandated cost for the right to pollute. The relative costs and benefits of each option for each polluter will determine which one or combination will be chosen. Allowing the choice is the efficient way to decide who pollutes and who doesn't. In principle, just as with the use of all other scarce resources, each polluter faces the full social cost of its actions and makes a production decision accordingly. No matter what each firm decides, the cost of pollution-causing activity is now higher, so pollution will be reduced.

You Are There

To consider how the U.S. government uses fuel economy standards to try to reduce carbon emissions, read **Fuel Efficiency Rules and the "Rebound Effect,"** on page 698.

Is a Uniform Tax Appropriate?

It may not be appropriate to levy a *uniform* tax according to physical quantities of pollution. After all, we're talking about external costs. Such costs are not necessarily the same everywhere in the United States for the same action.

Essentially, we must establish the amount of the *economic damages* rather than the amount of the physical pollution. A polluting electrical plant in New York City will cause much more damage than the same plant in Montana. There are already innumerable demands on the air in New York City, so the pollution from smokestacks will not be cleansed away naturally. Millions of people will breathe the polluted air and thereby incur the costs of sore throats, sickness, emphysema, and even early death. Buildings will become dirtier faster because of the pollution, as will cars and clothes. A given quantity of pollution will cause more harm in concentrated urban environments than it will in less dense rural environments. If we were to establish some form of taxation to align private costs with social costs and to force people to internalize externalities, we would somehow have to come up with a measure of *economic* costs instead of *physical* quantities. But the tax, in any event, would fall on the private sector and modify individuals' and firms' behavior. Therefore, because the economic cost for the same physical quantity of pollution would be different in different locations depending on population density, natural formations of mountains and rivers, and the like, so-called optimal taxes on pollution would vary from location to location. (Nonetheless, a uniform tax might make sense when administrative costs, particularly the cost of ascertaining the actual economic costs, are relatively high.)

Why might a uniform tax on cigarettes protect people from external spillovers of cigarette smoke while avoiding the unintended negative consequences created by smoking bans? (See the next page.)

POLICY EXAMPLE **Why Higher Cigarette Taxes Might Be Preferable to Smoking Bans**

Many locales have attempted to protect people from secondhand smoke by prohibiting smoking in public places. Often, however, these bans do not include bars in which alcoholic beverages are served. Studies have found that some smokers respond by spending more time in bars, where they end up drinking more and then driving. The result is an increase in deaths in accidents involving drunk drivers. Other studies have found that each 10 percent increase in a uniform tax on cigarettes is associated with a 3 to 4 percent reduction in nonsmokers' exposure to cigarette smoke. A possible explanation is that when smokers cut back on cigarette consumption in response to higher taxes, they smoke the smaller number of cigarettes alone, rather than in the presence of nonsmokers. Thus, well-intended partial bans on smoking contribute to an unintended but deadly spillover effect, whereas imposing higher uniform taxes on cigarettes may be effective in shielding nonsmokers from cigarette smoke.

FOR CRITICAL ANALYSIS

Why do you suppose that evidence suggests that exempting bars from smoking bans increases the degree to which people regard cigarettes and alcohol as complements?

QUICK QUIZ **See page 704 for the answers. Review concepts from this section in MyEconLab.**

__________ costs are costs that are borne directly by consumers and producers when they engage in any resource-using activity.

Social costs are __________ costs plus any other costs that are external to the decision maker. For example, the social costs of driving include all the __________ costs plus, at a minimum, any pollution caused.

When __________ costs differ from social costs, __________ exist because individual decision makers are not internalizing all the costs that society is bearing.

Pollution

The term *pollution* is used quite loosely and can refer to a variety of by-products of any activity. Industrial pollution involves mainly air and water but can also include noise and even aesthetic pollution, as when a landscape is altered in a negative way. For the most part, we will be analyzing the most common forms—air and water pollution.

Assessing the Appropriate Amount of Pollution

When asked how much pollution there should be in the economy, many people will respond, "None." But if we ask those same people how much starvation or deprivation of consumer products should exist in the economy, many will again say, "None." Growing and distributing food or producing consumer products creates pollution, however. There is no correct answer to how much pollution should be in an economy because when we ask how much pollution there *should* be, we are entering the realm of normative economics. We are asking people to express values. There is no way to disprove somebody's value system scientifically.

One way we can approach a discussion of the "correct" amount of pollution is to set up the same type of marginal analysis we used in our discussion of a firm's employment and output decisions. That is, we can consider pursuing measures to reduce pollution only up to the point at which the marginal benefit from pollution reduction equals the marginal cost of pollution reduction.

THE MARGINAL BENEFIT OF A LESS POLLUTED ENVIRONMENT Look at Figure 31-2 on the facing page. On the horizontal axis, we show the degree of air cleanliness. A vertical line is drawn at 100 percent cleanliness—the air cannot become any cleaner. Consider the benefits of obtaining a greater degree of air cleanliness. The benefits of obtaining cleaner air are represented by the marginal benefit curve, which slopes downward.

When the air is very dirty, the marginal benefit from air that is a little cleaner appears to be relatively high, as shown on the vertical axis. As the air becomes cleaner, however, the marginal benefit of a little bit more air cleanliness falls.

FIGURE 31-2 The Optimal Quantity of Air Pollution

As we attempt to achieve a greater degree of air cleanliness, the marginal cost rises until trying to increase air cleanliness even slightly leads to a very high marginal cost, as can be seen at the upper right of the graph. Conversely, the marginal benefit curve slopes downward: The more pure air we have, the less we value an additional unit of pure air. Marginal cost and marginal benefit intersect at point *E*. The optimal degree of air cleanliness is something less than 100 percent at Q_0. The price that we should pay for the last unit of air cleanup is no greater than P_0, for that is where marginal cost equals marginal benefit.

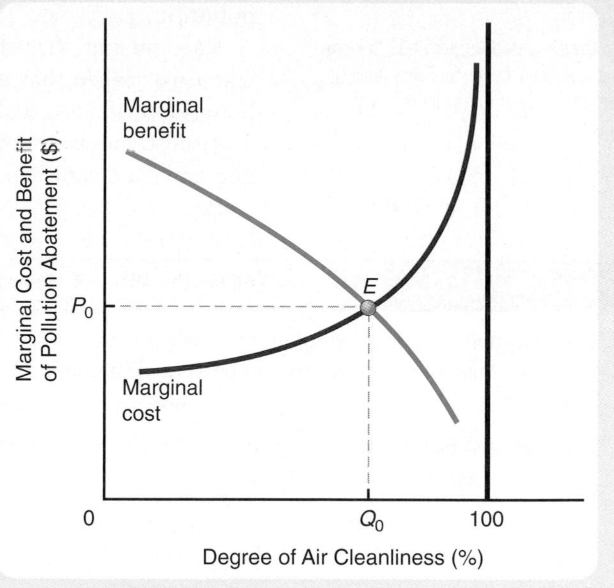

THE MARGINAL COST OF POLLUTION ABATEMENT Consider the marginal cost of pollution abatement—that is, the marginal cost of obtaining cleaner air. In the 1960s, automobiles had no pollution abatement devices. Eliminating only 20 percent of the pollutants emitted by internal-combustion engines entailed a relatively small cost per unit of pollution removed. The per-unit cost of eliminating the next 20 percent increased, though. Finally, as we now get to the upper limits of removal of pollutants from the emissions of internal-combustion engines, we find that the elimination of one more percentage point of the amount of pollutants becomes astronomically expensive. In the short run, moving from 97 percent cleanliness to 98 percent cleanliness involves a marginal cost that is many times greater than the marginal cost of going from 10 percent cleanliness to 11 percent cleanliness.

It is realistic, therefore, to draw the marginal cost of pollution abatement as an upward-sloping curve, as shown in Figure 31-2 above. (The marginal cost curve slopes up because of the law of diminishing marginal product.)

The Optimal Quantity of Pollution

The **optimal quantity of pollution** is the level of pollution at which the marginal benefit equals the marginal cost of pollution abatement. This occurs at the intersection of the marginal benefit curve and the marginal cost curve in Figure 31-2, at point *E*. This solution is analytically exactly the same as for every other economic activity. If we increased pollution control by one unit beyond Q_0, the marginal cost of that small increase in the degree of air cleanliness would be greater than the marginal benefit to society.

Optimal quantity of pollution
The level of pollution for which the marginal benefit of one additional unit of pollution abatement just equals the marginal cost of that additional unit of pollution abatement.

As is usually the case in economic analysis, the optimal quantity occurs when marginal cost equals marginal benefit. That is, the optimal quantity of pollution occurs at the point at which the marginal cost of reducing (or abating) pollution is just equal to the marginal benefit of doing so. The marginal cost of pollution abatement rises as more and more abatement is achieved (as the environment becomes cleaner and cleaner, the *extra* cost of cleansing rises). Early units of pollution abatement are easily achieved (at low cost), but attaining higher and higher levels of environmental quality becomes progressively more difficult (as the extra cost rises to prohibitive levels). At the same time, the marginal benefits of an increasingly cleaner environment fall. The marginal benefit of pollution abatement declines as our notion of a cleaner environment moves from the preservation of human life to recreation to beauty to a perfectly pure environment.

The point at which the increasing marginal cost of pollution abatement equals the decreasing marginal benefit of pollution abatement defines the optimal quantity of pollution.

Go to www.econtoday.com/ch31 to learn from the National Center for Policy Analysis about alternative programs for reducing pollution.

Recognizing that the optimal quantity of pollution is not zero becomes easier when we realize that it takes scarce resources to reduce pollution. A trade-off exists between producing a cleaner environment and producing other goods and services. In that sense, environmental cleanliness is a good that can be analyzed like any other good, and a cleaner environment must take its place with other human wants.

QUICK QUIZ See page 704 for the answers. **Review concepts from this section in MyEconLab.**

The marginal cost of cleaning up the environment __________ as we get closer to 100 percent cleanliness. Indeed, it __________ at an __________ rate.

The marginal benefit of environmental cleanliness __________ as we have more of it.

The **optimal quantity of pollution** is the quantity at which the __________ __________ of cleanup equals the __________ __________ of cleanup.

Pollution abatement is a trade-off. We trade off __________ and __________ for cleaner air and water, and vice versa.

Common Property

Private property rights
Exclusive rights of ownership that allow the use, transfer, and exchange of property.

Common property
Property that is owned by everyone and therefore by no one. Air and water are examples of common property resources.

In most cases, you do not have **private property rights,** or exclusive ownership rights, to the air surrounding you, nor does anyone else. Air is a **common property,** or a nonexclusive resource. Therein lies the crux of the problem. When no one owns a particular resource, no one has any incentive (conscience aside) to consider externality spillovers associated with that resource. If one person decides not to add to externality spillovers and avoids polluting the air, normally there will not be any significant effect on the total level of pollution. If one person decides not to pollute the ocean, there will still be approximately the same amount of ocean pollution—provided, of course, that the individual was previously responsible for only a small part of the total amount of ocean pollution.

Basically, pollution and other activities that create spillovers occur when we have poorly defined private property rights, as in air and common bodies of water. We do not, for example, have a visual pollution problem in people's attics. That is their own property, which they choose to keep as clean as they want, depending on their preferences for cleanliness weighed against the costs of keeping the attic neat and tidy.

When private property rights exist, individuals have legal recourse for any damages sustained through the use of their property. When private property rights are well defined, the use of property—that is, the use of resources—will generally involve contracts between the owners of those resources. If you own land, you might contract with another person who wants to use your land for raising cattle. The contract would most likely take the form of a written lease agreement.

Voluntary Agreements and Transaction Costs

Is it possible for externalities to be internalized via voluntary agreement? Take a simple example. You live in a house with a nice view of a lake. The family living below you plants a tree. The tree grows so tall that it eventually starts to cut off your view. In most cities, no one has property rights to views, so you usually cannot go to court to obtain relief. You do have the option of contracting with your neighbors, however.

VOLUNTARY AGREEMENTS: CONTRACTING You have the option of paying your neighbors (contracting) to trim the tree. You could start out by offering a small amount and keep going up until your neighbors agree or until you reach your limit. Your limit will equal the value you place on having an unobstructed view of the lake. Your neighbors will be willing if the payment is at least equal to the reduction in their intrinsic property value due to a stunted tree. Your offer of the payment makes your neighbors aware of the social cost of their actions. The social cost here is equal to the care of the tree plus the cost suffered by you from an impeded view of the lake.

In essence, then, your offer of money income to your neighbors indicates to them that there is an opportunity cost to their actions. If they don't comply, they forfeit the payments that you are offering them. The point here is that *opportunity cost always exists, no matter who has property rights*. Therefore, we would expect that under some circumstances voluntary contracting will occur to internalize externalities. The question is, When will voluntary agreements occur?

TRANSACTION COSTS One major condition for the outcome just outlined is that the **transaction costs**—all costs associated with making and enforcing agreements—must be low relative to the expected benefits of reaching an agreement. (We already looked at this topic briefly in Chapter 4.) If we expand our example to a much larger one such as air pollution, the transaction costs of numerous homeowners trying to reach agreements with the individuals and companies that create the pollution are relatively high. Consequently, people may not always engage in voluntary contracting, even though it can be an effective way to internalize the externality of air pollution.

Transaction costs
All costs associated with making, reaching, and enforcing agreements.

Changing Property Rights

We can approach the problem of property rights by assuming that initially in a society, many property rights to resources are not defined. But this situation does not cause a problem so long as no one wants to use the resources for which there are no property rights or resources are available in desired quantities at a zero price. Only if and when a use is found for a resource at a zero price does a problem develop. Unless some decision then is made about property rights, the resource will be wasted and possibly even destroyed. Property rights can be assigned to individuals who will then assert control. Alternatively, the rights may be assigned to government, which can maintain and preserve the resource, charge for its use, or implement some other rationing device.

Another way of viewing the problem of pollution spillovers is to argue that it cannot continue to arise if a way can be found to assign private property rights for all resources. We can then say that each individual does not have the right to act on anything that is not his or her property. Hence, no individual has the right to create pollution spillovers on property that the individual does not specifically own.

Clearly, we must fill the gap between private costs and social costs in situations in which property rights are not well defined or assigned. There are three ways to fill this gap: taxation, subsidization, and regulation. Government is involved in all three. Unfortunately, government does not have perfect information and may not pick the appropriate tax, subsidy, or type of regulation. Furthermore, in some situations, it may be difficult to enforce taxes or direct subsidies to "worthy" recipients. In such cases, outright prohibition of the polluting activity may be the optimal solution to a particular pollution spillover. For example, if it is difficult to monitor the level of a particular type of pollution that even in small quantities can cause severe environmental damage, outright prohibition of activities that cause such pollution may be the best alternative.

QUICK QUIZ See page 704 for the answers. Review concepts from this section in MyEconLab.

A **common property** resource is one that __________ __________ owns—or, otherwise stated, that __________ owns. Common property exists when property rights are indefinite or nonexistent.

When no __________ __________ rights exist, pollution occurs because no one individual or firm has a sufficient economic incentive to care for the common property in question, be it air, water, or scenery.

Private costs will equal __________ costs for common property only if a few individuals or companies are involved and they are able to voluntarily __________ among themselves.

Reducing Humanity's Carbon Footprint: Restraining Pollution-Causing Activities

In light of the costs arising from spillovers that polluting activities create, one solution might seem to be for governments to try to stop them from taking place. Why don't more governments simply *require* businesses and households to cut back on pollution-causing activities?

How the European Union Mixes Government Controls and Market Processes

In fact, many governments are implementing schemes aimed at capping and controlling the use of pollution-generating resources. In recent years, certain scientific research has suggested that emissions of carbon dioxide, sulfur dioxide, and various other so-called *greenhouse gases* might be contributing to atmospheric warming. The result, some scientists fear, might be global climate changes harmful to people inhabiting various regions of the planet. In response, the governments of more than three dozen nations agreed to participate in the *Kyoto Protocol* of a broader set of international treaties called the Framework Convention on Climate Change. Under this 1997 agreement, the governments of participating nations agreed to reduce their overall emissions of greenhouse gases by 2020 to as much as 20 percent below 1990 levels.

EMISSIONS CAPS AND PERMITS TRADING The members of the European Union (EU) are among the key participants in the Kyoto Protocol. In January 2005, the EU established a set of rules called the *Emissions Trading Scheme*. Under this program, each nation in the EU seeks to cap its aggregate greenhouse gas emissions at a level consistent with its target under the Kyoto Protocol. Thus, for instance, the French government specified limits on aggregate emissions of carbon dioxide and other greenhouse gases that would enable France to meet its Kyoto target.

Once an overall national cap was set, each EU nation established an *allowance* of metric tons of a gas, such as carbon dioxide, that a company is permitted to release. If a company's emissions of carbon dioxide exceed its allowance—that is, if its "carbon footprint" in the atmosphere is too large—then the company must buy more allowances through a trading system. These allowances can be obtained, at the current market clearing price, from companies that are emitting less carbon dioxide than their permitted amounts and therefore have unutilized allowances.

THEORY CONFRONTS EUROPEAN POLICY AND MARKET REALITIES In theory, if EU governments had set the national emissions caps low enough to force companies to reduce greenhouse gases, the market clearing price of emissions allowances should have reflected this constraint. In addition, as governments continue to tighten the caps to meet the Kyoto limits that require greenhouse gas emissions to be reduced to 20 percent below 1990 levels by 2020, more firms should respond by purchasing allowances. Then the market clearing price of allowances would rise. Rather than paying a higher price for emissions allowances, many firms would instead opt to develop methods of reducing their emissions. In this way, this market-based mechanism established by the Emissions Trading Scheme would induce firms to reduce their emissions, and the EU nations would achieve the targets set under the Kyoto Protocol.

In fact, in the spring of 2006, the market clearing price of EU emissions allowances dropped by more than 60 percent. The reason that prices dropped, many economists agree, is that most EU governments issued more allowances than were consistent with capping emissions at the Kyoto target levels. Indeed, the price drop was consistent with an initial surplus of more than 200 million allowances.

Most observers suspect that the Emissions Trading Scheme's fundamental weakness was that each nation's government was permitted to establish the emissions target and allowances for its own country. Each government feared making its own nation's firms less cost-competitive than those in other nations, so every government inflated its estimate of its mid-2000s emissions of greenhouse gases. Doing so allowed each government to set its overall emissions cap at a level that actually failed to constrain emissions. One result was the big drop in prices of emissions allowances, which have remained substantially lower than when the Emissions Trading Scheme was first established. Another outcome is that instead of declining, greenhouse gas emissions by companies based in the EU actually *increased* during the late 2000s and early 2010s.

Are There Alternatives to Pollution-Causing Resource Use?

Some people cannot understand why, if pollution is bad, we still use pollution-causing resources such as coal and oil to generate electricity. Why don't we forgo the use of such polluting resources and opt for one that apparently is pollution-free, such as solar energy? The plain fact is that the cost of generating solar power in many circumstances is much higher than generating that same power through conventional means. We do not yet have the technology that allows us the luxury of driving solar-powered cars. Moreover, with current technology, the solar panels necessary to generate the electricity for the average town would cover massive sections of the countryside, and the manufacturing of those solar panels would itself generate pollution.

Why Not . . . eliminate nearly all U.S. carbon emissions?

The official carbon emissions target of the U.S. government already calls for total U.S. carbon emissions to be reduced to 80 percent of 2010 levels by the year 2050. To attain this target, the carbon emissions of the typical U.S. resident in 2050 will have to fall to levels not observed since the eighteenth century, when many fewer colonial Americans burned wood to generate heat. In the world today, the only nations with per capita carbon emissions this low are some of the poorest, such as Belize, Haiti, Mauritius, and Somalia. Thus, costly investments in new energy technologies will be required to meet the official U.S. target while continuing to generate energy for a much larger—and growing—U.S. population. To reduce carbon emissions even further, greater expenses would have to be incurred.

Wild Species, Common Property, and Trade-Offs

One common property problem that receives considerable media attention involves endangered species, usually in the wild. Few are concerned about not having enough dogs, cats, cattle, sheep, and horses. The reason is that those species are almost always private property. People have economic incentives—satisfaction from pet ownership, desire for food products, or preference for animal-borne transport—to protect members of these species. In contrast, spotted owls, bighorn mountain sheep, condors, and the like are typically common property. Therefore, no one has a vested interest in making sure that they perpetuate in good health.

Go to **www.econtoday.com/ch31** to contemplate the issue of endangered species via a link to the National Center for Policy Analysis.

In 1973, the federal government passed the Endangered Species Act in an attempt to prevent species from dying out. Initially, few individuals were affected by the rulings of the Interior Department regarding which species were listed as endangered. Eventually, however, as more and more species were put on the endangered list, a trade-off became apparent. Nationwide, the trade-off was brought to the public's attention when the snail darter was declared an endangered species in the Tennessee valley. Ultimately, thousands of construction jobs were lost when the courts halted completion of a dam in the snail darter's habitat. Then two endangered small birds, the spotted owl and marbled murrelet, were found in the Pacific Northwest, inducing lumber companies to cut back their logging practices. In 1995, the U.S. Supreme Court ruled that the federal government has the right to regulate activities on private land in order to save endangered species.

The issues are not straightforward. Today, the earth has only 0.02 percent of all of the species that have ever lived, and nearly all the 99.98 percent of extinct species became extinct before humans appeared. Every year, 1,000 to 3,000 new species are discovered and classified. Estimates of how many species are actually dying out range from a high of 50,000 a year (based on the assumption that undiscovered insect species are dying off before being discovered) to a low of one every four years.

How are some governments using private property rights to prevent depletion of fish populations?

INTERNATIONAL EXAMPLE Fisheries Hook a Solution to the Common Property Problem

In many regions of the world, specified areas of large lakes, seas, and oceans—called *fisheries*—are open to fishing by everyone. Because the fish in these bodies of water are common property, no one has a vested interest in preventing depletion of fish populations. In fact, the reverse is true: Fishermen have an incentive to fill their boats with as many fish as their holds can store.

In recent years, some of the world's fisheries have developed a means of conferring private property rights to fish called individual transferable quotas (ITQs). With an ITQ system, the government determines how many total fish can be removed from a given area during each fishing season. Then shares in this total—the ITQs—are auctioned off to fishermen, who receive the right to catch no more than their shares during that season. Fishermen can sell their ITQs, or they can purchase others' ITQs if they wish to expand their individual production. Each fisherman also can decide, based on prevailing market clearing prices of fish, when to bring the largest volumes of fish back to port. Recent economic studies have found evidence of stabilized and even expanding fish populations in fisheries using ITQs, whereas populations continue to shrink in fisheries where fish are common property.

FOR CRITICAL ANALYSIS

Why do you suppose that the market value of an ITQ depends in part on the equilibrium price of fish?

QUICK QUIZ

See page 704 for the answers. Review concepts from this section in MyEconLab.

The more than three dozen countries that participated in the 1997 Kyoto Protocol of the Framework Convention on Climate Change agreed to reduce their emissions of greenhouse gases by the year __________ to at least __________ percent below the levels that prevailed in the year __________.

Under a program called the Emissions Trading Scheme, the governments of European Union member nations established overall targets for greenhouse gas emissions and issued __________, or permits, authorizing companies to emit certain amounts. In theory, an increase in the market clearing price of __________ should induce firms to develop methods of __________ their emissions of greenhouse gases.

In contrast to domesticated animals that are __________ property, most endangered species are __________ property. Consequently, there is a problem in perpetuating these species that the federal government has sought to address through legislation governing use of lands where such species reside.

You Are There Fuel Efficiency Rules and the "Rebound Effect"

David Greene of Oak Ridge National Laboratory is studying the "rebound effect" associated with the U.S. government's requirement that vehicles meet minimum fuel efficiency standards. These rules presume that if vehicles burn less gasoline, they will generate fewer emissions. Nevertheless, these standards create the rebound effect of interest to Greene: When vehicle fuel efficiency improves, the per-mile cost of driving falls, and people drive more. The result is additional carbon emissions—the rebound effect. The *net* reduction in emissions depends on the size of the rebound effect.

Greene knows that the government has estimated that when average fuel efficiency of vehicles rises by 10 miles per gallon (mpg), people drive 6 percent more miles. Now, however, a few economists have found evidence that a 10 mpg increase in fuel efficiency induces people to drive only about 2 percent more. When he examines the data, Greene obtains the same result.

Why has the rebound effect declined? Greene thinks that he has an answer. Every 10 mpg increase in minimum fuel economy standards now pushes up a typical new vehicle's price by about $1,000. This additional expense has cut into budgets for buying fuel, so people are driving less. "What we're seeing," Greene concludes, "is that the increased cost of [new] vehicles has compensated for higher fuel economy."

Critical Analysis Questions

1. Why do you think that many economists argue that a higher uniform tax on gasoline might reduce emissions more than tougher fuel economy standards?
2. Could assessing a uniform tax on new vehicle purchases reduce carbon emissions?

ISSUES & APPLICATIONS

Human Activities and Honeybee Colony Collapse Disorder

CONCEPTS APPLIED

- Common Property
- Social Costs
- Private Property Rights

Honeybees are important to humans, because in their search for nectar and pollen, the bees pollinate flowering plants, many of which produce fruits, vegetables, and grains that humans consume. Beginning in the late 1990s, beekeepers began to observe that honeybee colonies were shrinking during winter months. By spring, many colonies were gone. Parasites, funguses, and viruses have all played a role in reducing honeybee populations, but during the 2000s, an apparent epidemic of "colony collapse disorder" (CCD) began to devastate honeybee colonies.

Human Activities and Honeybees

Although many honeybees live in the wilds, where they are common property, many other colonies of honeybees are managed by humans. These beekeepers earn fees from farmers to place colonies of bees within range of the farmers' orchards and fields.

During honeybees' continuous searches for nectar and pollen in flowering plants, the bees help to ensure that crops are more widely pollinated. In this way, the presence of honeybees boosts farmers' agricultural yields. Thus, the CCD epidemic that appeared to become more widespread during the 2000s has threatened to reduce agricultural yields worldwide.

How Humans May Have Accidentally Reduced—and Now May Revive—Honeybee Populations

Recently, scientists have discovered that honeybees in the wilds forage so widely that they typically encounter many sources of nectar and pollen. Hence, the bees ingest a surprisingly wide variety of nutrients. In contrast, colonies of honeybees managed by beekeepers typically are placed near more limited sources of nutrients—mainly the plants that farmers wish to have pollinated. Consequently, honeybees in human-managed colonies may fail to ingest some key nutrients. One prevailing theory is that deficiencies of these nutrients may have contributed to the CCD epidemic.

This information provides beekeepers whose livelihoods depend on sustaining their honeybee colonies with an incentive to provide supplemental nutrition to their bees. Indeed, there is already evidence that beekeepers who regularly feed nutrient supplements to their colonies experience much lower CCD rates. Although gauging the world's population of honeybees is an inexact science, there is growing evidence that in areas where beekeepers are incurring the costs for supplemental nutrition, bee populations are recovering.

For Critical Analysis

1. The beekeeping industry grew rapidly in many nations during the 1980s and 1990s. How might this development have contributed to the CCD epidemic? (Hint: How did the expansion of beekeeping alter bees' exposure to a range of nutrients?)
2. What types of economic policies might governments implement in an effort to help counter the CCD epidemic and contribute to a larger honeybee population?

Web Resources

1. To learn more about the importance of honeybees to the human economy, go to www.econtoday.com/ch31.
2. For a detailed discussion of the costs to humans resulting from the CCD epidemic, go to www.econtoday.com/ch31.

Research Project

Evaluate how incurring new expenses to provide nutrient supplements to honeybees has likely affected the supply of beekeeping services, the market clearing price of these services, and the market clearing prices of items grown by farmers who pay for beekeepers' services.

For more questions on this chapter's Issues & Applications, go to **MyEconLab**. In the Study Plan for this chapter, select Section N: News.

Here is what you should know after reading this chapter. **MyEconLab** will help you identify what you know, and where to go when you need to practice.

WHAT YOU SHOULD KNOW		WHERE TO GO TO PRACTICE
Private Costs versus Social Costs Private, or internal, costs are borne solely by individuals who use resources. Social costs are the full costs that society bears whenever resources are used. Problems related to the environment arise when individuals take into account only private costs instead of the broader social costs arising from their use of resources.	private costs, 689 social costs, 689	• **MyEconLab** Study Plan 31.1 • Audio introduction to Chapter 31 • ABC News Video: Coca-Cola in India
Market Externalities and Ways to Correct Them A market externality arises if a private cost (or benefit) differs from the social cost (or benefit) associated with a market transaction between two parties or from the use of a scarce resource. An externality can be corrected by forcing individuals to take all the social costs (or benefits) of their actions into account.	externality, 690 **KEY FIGURE** Figure 31-1, 690	• **MyEconLab** Study Plan 31.2 • Video: Correcting for Externalities • Animated Figure 31-1

MyEconLab continued

WHAT YOU SHOULD KNOW		WHERE TO GO TO PRACTICE
Determining the Optimal Amount of Pollution The marginal benefit of pollution abatement declines as the quality of the environment improves. At the same time, the marginal cost of pollution abatement increases as more and more resources are devoted to achieving an improved environment. The optimal quantity of pollution is the amount of pollution for which the marginal benefit of pollution abatement just equals the marginal cost of pollution abatement.	optimal quantity of pollution, 693 **KEY FIGURE** Figure 31-2, 693	• **MyEconLab** Study Plan 31.3 • Animated Figure 31-2
Private and Common Property Rights and the Pollution Problem Private property rights permit the use and exchange of a resource. Common property is owned by everyone and therefore by no single individual. A pollution problem often arises because air and many water resources are common property, and private property rights relating to them are not well defined. This is a common rationale for using taxes, subsidies, or regulations to address the pollution problem.	private property rights, 694 common property, 694 transaction costs, 695	• **MyEconLab** Study Plan 31.4
Restraining Pollution-Causing Activities Through Caps and Allowances The European Union (EU) has established a program called the Emissions Trading Scheme. Each EU nation's government established an overall target level of greenhouse gas emissions and distributed allowances, or permits, granting companies the right to emit a certain amount of gases. If a firm's greenhouse gas emissions exceed its allowances, it must purchase a sufficient number of allowances from firms emitting less than the allowances they possess. In theory, the market clearing price of allowances will increase, giving EU companies incentives to develop methods of restraining their emissions of greenhouse gases.		• **MyEconLab** Study Plan 31.5
Endangered Species and the Assignment of Property Rights Many members of such species as dogs, pigs, and horses are the private property of human beings. Thus, people have economic incentives to protect members of these species. In contrast, most members of species such as spotted owls, condors, or tigers are common property, so no specific individuals have incentives to keep these species in good health. A possible way to address the endangered species problem is government involvement via regulations.		• **MyEconLab** Study Plan 31.6

Log in to MyEconLab, take a chapter test, and get a personalized Study Plan that tells you which concepts you understand and which ones you need to review. From there, MyEconLab will give you further practice, tutorials, animations, videos, and guided solutions.
Log in to www.myeconlab.com

PROBLEMS

All problems are assignable in myeconlab. *Answers to the odd-numbered problems appear at the back of the book.*

31-1. The market price of insecticide is initially $10 per unit. To address a negative externality in this market, the government decides to charge producers of insecticide for the privilege of polluting during the production process. A fee that fully takes into account the social costs of pollution is determined, and once it is put into effect, the market supply curve for insecticide shifts upward by $4 per unit. The market price of insecticide also increases, to $12 per unit. What fee is the government charging insecticide manufacturers?

31-2. One possible method for reducing emissions of greenhouse gases such as carbon dioxide is to inject the gases into deep saltwater-laden rock formations where they would be trapped for thousands of years. Suppose that the federal government provides a fixed per-unit subsidy to firms that utilize this technology in West Virginia and other locales where such rock formations are known to exist.

a. Use an appropriate diagram to examine the effects of the government subsidy on the production and sale of equipment that injects greenhouse gases into underground rock formations. What happens to the market clearing price of such pollution abatement equipment?

b. Who pays to achieve the results discussed in part (a)?

31-3. Examine the following marginal costs and marginal benefits associated with water cleanliness in a given locale:

Quantity of Clean Water (%)	Marginal Cost ($)	Marginal Benefit ($)
0	3,000	200,000
20	15,000	120,000
40	50,000	90,000
60	85,000	85,000
80	100,000	40,000
100	Infinite	0

a. What is the optimal degree of water cleanliness?

b. What is the optimal degree of water pollution?

c. Suppose that a company creates a food additive that offsets most of the harmful effects of drinking polluted water. As a result, the marginal benefit of water cleanliness declines by $40,000 at each degree of water cleanliness at or less than 80 percent. What is the optimal degree of water cleanliness after this change?

31-4. Consider the diagram below, which displays the marginal cost and marginal benefit of water pollution abatement in a particular city, and answer the following questions.

a. What is the optimal percentage degree of water cleanliness?

b. When the optimal percentage degree of water cleanliness has been attained, what cost will be incurred for the last unit of water cleanup?

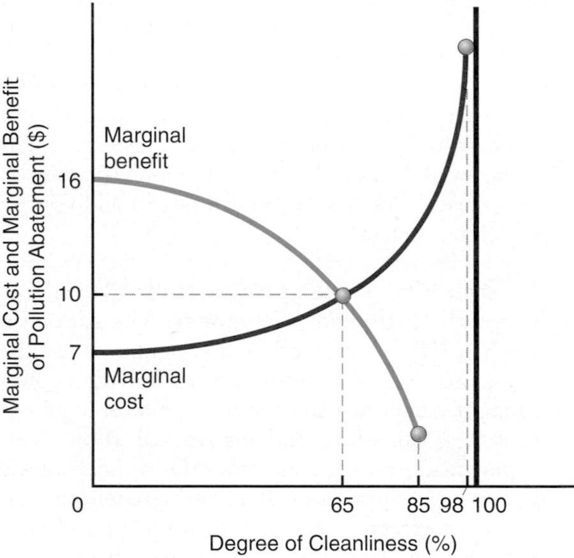

31-5. Consider the diagram in Problem 31-4, and answer the following questions.

a. Suppose that a new technology for reducing water pollution generates a reduction in the marginal cost of pollution abatement at every degree of water cleanliness. After this event occurs, will the optimal percentage degree of water cleanliness rise or fall? Will the cost incurred for the last unit of water cleanup increase or decrease? Provide a diagram to assist in your explanation.

b. Suppose that the event discussed in part (a) occurs and that, in addition, medical studies determine that the marginal benefit from water pollution abatement is higher at every degree of water cleanliness. Following *both* events, will the optimal percentage degree of water cleanliness increase or decrease? In comparison with the *initial* optimum, can you determine whether the cost incurred for the last unit of water cleanup will increase or decrease? Use a new diagram to assist in explaining your answers.

31-6. Under an agreement with U.S. regulators, American Electric Power Company of Columbus, Ohio, has agreed to offset part of its 145 million metric tons of carbon dioxide emissions by paying another company to lay plastic tarps. These tarps cover farm lagoons holding rotting livestock wastes that emit methane gas 21 times more damaging to the atmosphere than carbon dioxide. The annual methane produced by a typical 1,330-pound cow translates into about 5 metric tons of carbon dioxide emissions per year.

a. How many cows' worth of manure would have to be covered to offset the carbon dioxide emissions of this single electric utility?

b. Given that there are about 9 million cows in the United States in a typical year, what percentage of its carbon dioxide emissions could this firm offset if it paid for all cow manure in the entire nation to be covered with tarps?

31-7. The following table displays hypothetical annual total costs and total benefits of conserving wild tigers at several possible worldwide tiger population levels.

Population of Wild Tigers	Total Cost ($ millions)	Total Benefit ($ millions)
0	0	40
2,000	25	90
4,000	35	130
6,000	50	160
8,000	75	185
10,000	110	205
12,000	165	215

a. Calculate the marginal costs and benefits.

b. Given the data, what is the socially optimal world population of wild tigers?

c. Suppose that tiger farming is legalized and that this has the effect of reducing the marginal cost of tiger conservation by $15 million for each 2,000-tiger population increment in the table. What is the new socially optimal population of wild tigers?

31-8. The following table gives hypothetical annual total costs and total benefits of maintaining alternative populations of Asian elephants.

Population of Asian Elephants	Total Cost ($ millions)	Total Benefit ($ millions)
0	0	0
7,500	20	100
15,000	45	185
22,500	90	260
30,000	155	325
37,500	235	375
45,000	330	410

a. Calculate the marginal costs and benefits, and draw marginal benefit and cost schedules.

b. Given the data, what is the socially optimal world population of Asian elephants?

c. Suppose that two events occur simultaneously. Technological development allows machines to do more efficiently much of the work that elephants once did, which reduces by $10 million the marginal benefit of maintaining the elephant population for each 7,500 increment in the elephant population. In addition, new techniques for breeding, feeding, and protecting elephants reduce the marginal cost by $40 million for each 7,500 increment in the elephant population. What is the new socially optimal population of Asian elephants?

ECONOMICS ON THE NET

Economic Analysis at the Environmental Protection Agency In this chapter, you learned how to use economic analysis to think about environmental problems. Does the U.S. government use economic analysis? This application helps you learn the extent to which the government uses economics in its environmental policymaking.

Title: National Center for Environmental Economics (NCEE)

Navigation: Go to **www.econtoday.com/ch31** to view the NCEE's link to "Environmental Protection: Is It Bad for the Economy? A Non-Technical Summary of the Literature." Download the article and read the section entitled "What Do We Spend on Environmental Protection?"

Application Read this section of the article. Then answer the following questions.

1. According to the article, what are the key objectives of the Environmental Protection Agency (EPA)? What role does cost-benefit analysis appear to play in the EPA's efforts? Does the EPA appear to take other issues into account in its policymaking?

2. Read the next section, entitled "Regardless of the Cost of Environmental Protection, Is It Still Money Well Spent?" In what ways does this discussion help clarify your answers in Question 1?

For Group Study and Analysis Have a class discussion of the following question: Should the EPA apply economic analysis in all aspects of its policymaking? If not, why not? If so, in what manner should economic analysis be applied?

ANSWERS TO QUICK QUIZZES

p. 692: (i) Private; (ii) private . . . private; (iii) private . . . externalities

p. 694: (i) rises . . . rises . . . increasing; (ii) falls; (iii) marginal cost . . . marginal benefit; (iv) goods . . . services

p. 695: (i) no one . . . everyone; (ii) private property; (iii) social . . . contract

p. 698: (i) 2020 . . . 20 . . . 1990; (ii) allowances . . . allowances . . . reducing; (iii) private . . . common

32 Comparative Advantage and the Open Economy

In early 2010, President Barack Obama announced that his administration intended to double U.S. exports of goods and services by 2015. The president said that achieving this goal would help to preserve existing jobs and create new jobs for U.S. workers. Just six months earlier, the president had also acted to protect U.S. jobs by imposing a *tariff*—a tax on imported items—on Chinese tires. Ironically, during the same week that the president announced his goal of doubling U.S. exports, a report documented barriers that the Chinese government had established to hinder U.S. exports from entering China. Indeed, China had created a few of these barriers in retaliation for the U.S. tariff on Chinese tires. In this chapter, you will learn how nations can gain from *both* exporting *and* importing goods and services. You will also learn about tariffs and other mechanisms that governments often utilize to reduce imports.

LEARNING OBJECTIVES

After reading this chapter, you should be able to:

- Discuss the worldwide importance of international trade
- Explain why nations can gain from specializing in production and engaging in international trade
- Understand common arguments against free trade
- Describe ways that nations restrict foreign trade
- Identify key international agreements and organizations that adjudicate trade disputes among nations

myeconlab

MyEconLab helps you master each objective and study more efficiently. See end of chapter for details.

Did You Know That ?

Ford Motor Company produces small *passenger* vans in a factory located in Turkey and ships them to Baltimore, Maryland, where employees strip out the vehicles' rear seats and replace their rear windows with metal panels? Ford then sells the vehicles in the United States as *commercial* vans intended for business use. By reconfiguring the vehicles in this way, Ford can avoid paying a 25 percent *tariff*—an import tax—that applies to imports of *passenger* vans with rear seats and windows but not to imports of *commercial* vans.

What effects do restrictions on imports have on quantities and prices of domestically produced goods and services? You will learn the answer to this question in this chapter. First, however, you must learn more about international trade.

The Worldwide Importance of International Trade

Look at panel (a) of Figure 32-1 below. Since the end of World War II, world output of goods and services (world real gross domestic product, or world real GDP) has increased almost every year. It is now almost 10 times what it was then. Look at the

FIGURE 32-1 The Growth of World Trade

In panel (a), you can see the growth in world trade in relative terms because we use an index of 100 to represent real world trade in 1950. By the late 2000s, that index had increased to more than 2,800 before dropping during the recent economic downturn. At the same time, the index of world real GDP (annual world real income) had gone up to only around 900 before turning downward. Thus, until recently, world trade has been on the rise: In the United States, both imports and exports, expressed as a percentage of annual national income (GDP) in panel (b), generally rose after 1950 until the Great Recession.

Sources: Steven Husted and Michael Melvin, *International Economics*, 3rd ed. (New York: HarperCollins, 1995), p. 11, used with permission; World Trade Organization; Federal Reserve System; U.S. Department of Commerce.

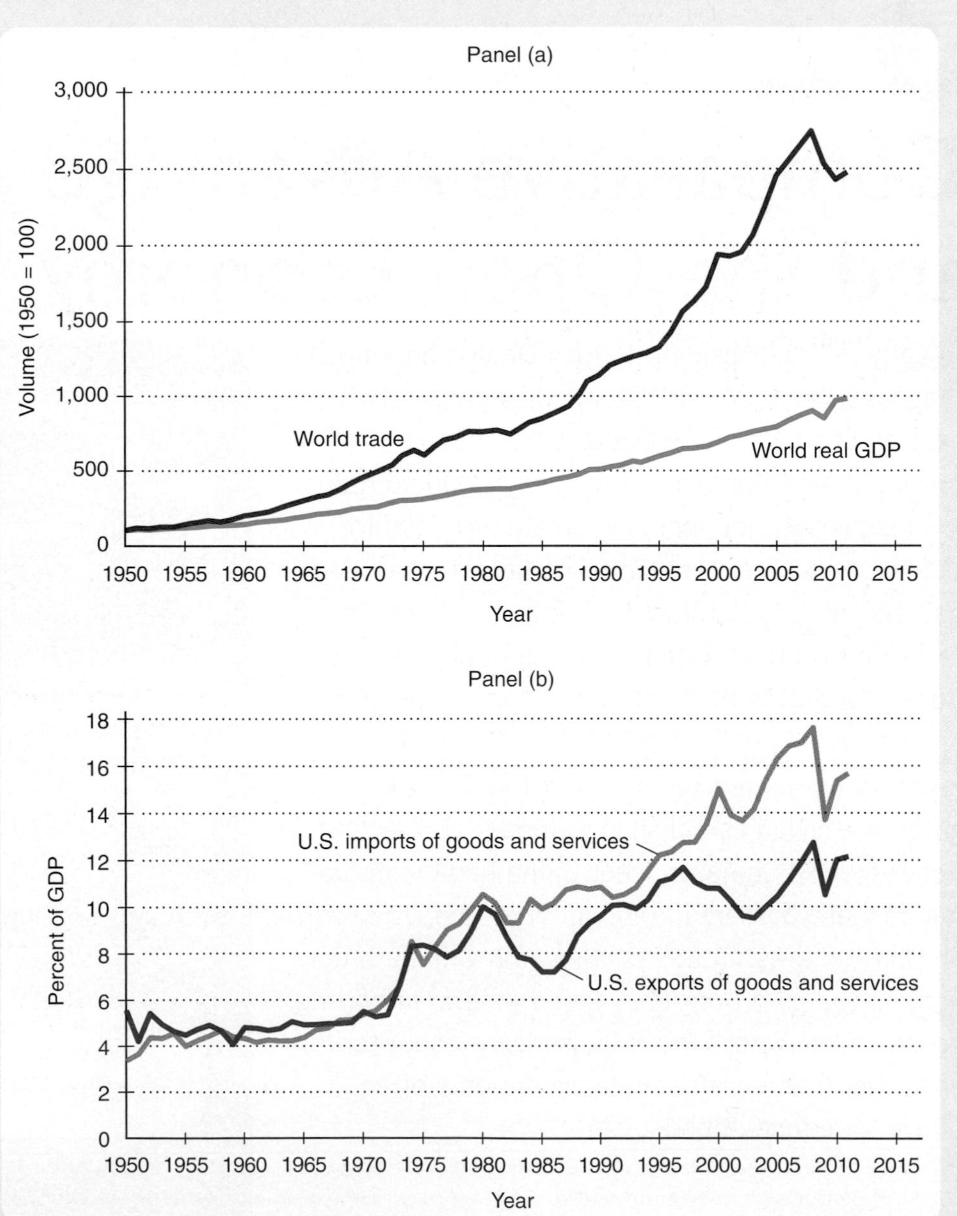

top line in panel (a) of Figure 31-1 on the facing page. Even taking into account its recent dip, world trade has increased to about 25 times its level in 1950.

The United States has figured prominently in this expansion of world trade. In panel (b) of Figure 32-1, you see imports and exports expressed as a percentage of total annual yearly income (GDP). Whereas imports amounted to barely 4 percent of annual U.S. GDP in 1950, today they account for almost 16 percent. Despite the recent drop, international trade has become more important to the U.S. economy, and it may become even more so as other countries loosen their trade restrictions.

Go to **www.econtoday.com/ch32** for the World Trade Organization's most recent data on world trade.

Why We Trade: Comparative Advantage and Mutual Gains from Exchange

You have already been introduced to the concept of specialization and mutual gains from trade in Chapter 2. These concepts are worth repeating because they are essential to understanding why the world is better off because of more international trade. The best way to understand the gains from trade among nations is first to understand the output gains from specialization between individuals.

The Output Gains from Specialization

Suppose that a creative advertising specialist can come up with two pages of ad copy (written words) an hour or generate one computerized art rendering per hour. At the same time, a computer art specialist can write one page of ad copy per hour or complete one computerized art rendering per hour. Here the ad specialist can come up with more pages of ad copy per hour than the computer specialist and seemingly is just as good as the computer specialist at doing computerized art renderings. Is there any reason for the ad specialist and the computer specialist to "trade"? The answer is yes because such trading will lead to higher output.

Consider the scenario of no trading. Assume that during each eight-hour day, the ad specialist and the computer whiz devote half of their day to writing ad copy and half to computerized art rendering. The ad specialist would create eight pages of ad copy (4 hours × 2) and four computerized art renderings (4 × 1). During that same period, the computer specialist would create four pages of ad copy (4 hours × 1) and four computerized art renderings (4 × 1). Each day, the combined output for the ad specialist and the computer specialist would be 12 pages of ad copy and eight computerized art renderings.

Go to **www.econtoday.com/ch32** for data on U.S. trade with all other nations of the world.

If the ad specialist specialized only in writing ad copy and the computer whiz specialized only in creating computerized art renderings, their combined output would rise to 16 pages of ad copy (8 × 2) and eight computerized art renderings (8 × 1). Overall, production would increase by four pages of ad copy per day with no decline in art renderings.

Note that this example implies that to create one additional computerized art rendering during a day, the ad specialist has to sacrifice the creation of two pages of ad copy. The computer specialist, in contrast, has to give up the creation of only one page of ad copy to generate one more computerized art rendering. Thus, the ad specialist has a comparative advantage in writing ad copy, and the computer specialist has a comparative advantage in doing computerized art renderings. **Comparative advantage** is simply the ability to produce something at a lower *opportunity* cost than other producers, as we pointed out in Chapter 2.

Comparative advantage
The ability to produce a good or service at a lower opportunity cost than other producers.

Specialization Among Nations

To demonstrate the concept of comparative advantage for nations, let's consider a simple two-country, two-good world. As a hypothetical example, let's suppose that the nations in this world are India and the United States.

TABLE 32-1

Maximum Feasible Hourly Production Rates of Either Commercial Software or Personal Computers Using All Available Resources

This table indicates maximum feasible rates of production of software and personal computers if all available resources are allocated to producing either one item or the other. If U.S. residents allocate all resources to producing a single good, they can produce either 90 units of software per hour or 225 PCs per hour. If residents of India allocate all resources to manufacturing one good, they can produce either 100 units of software per hour or 50 PCs per hour.

Product	United States	India
Units of software	90	100
Personal computers	225	50

PRODUCTION AND CONSUMPTION CAPABILITIES IN A TWO-COUNTRY, TWO-GOOD WORLD In Table 32-1 above, we show maximum feasible quantities of computer software and personal computers (PCs) that may be produced during an hour using all resources—labor, capital, land, and entrepreneurship—available in the United States and in India. As you can see from the table, U.S. residents can utilize all their resources to produce either 90 units of software per hour or 225 PCs per hour. If residents of India utilize all their resources, they can produce either 100 units of software per hour or 50 PCs per hour.

COMPARATIVE ADVANTAGE Suppose that in each country, there are constant opportunity costs of producing software and PCs. Table 32-1 implies that to allocate all available resources to production of 50 PCs, residents of India would have to sacrifice the production of 100 units of software. Thus, the opportunity cost in India of producing 1 PC is equal to 2 units of software. At the same time, the opportunity cost of producing 1 unit of software in India is 0.5 PC.

In the United States, to allocate all available resources to production of 225 PCs, U.S. residents would have to give up producing 90 units of software. This means that the opportunity cost in the United States of producing 1 PC is equal to 0.4 unit of software. Alternatively, we can say that the opportunity cost to U.S. residents of producing 1 unit of software is 2.5 PCs (225 ÷ 90 = 2.5).

The opportunity cost of producing a PC is lower in the United States than in India. At the same time, the opportunity cost of producing software is lower in India than in the United States. Consequently, the United States has a comparative advantage in manufacturing PCs, and India has a comparative advantage in producing software.

PRODUCTION WITHOUT TRADE Table 32-2 on the facing page tabulates two possible production choices in a situation in which U.S. and Indian residents choose not to engage in international trade. Let's suppose that in the United States, residents choose to produce and consume 30 units of software. To produce this amount of software requires that 75 fewer PCs (30 units of software times 2.5 PCs per unit of software) be produced than the maximum feasible PC production of 225 PCs, or 150 PCs. Thus, in the absence of trade, 30 units of software and 150 PCs are produced and consumed in the United States.

Table 32-2 indicates that during an hour's time in India, residents choose to produce and consume 37.5 PCs. Obtaining this amount of PCs entails the production of 75 fewer units of software (37.5 PCs times 2 units of software per PC) than the maximum of 100 units, or 25 units of software. Hence, in the absence of trade, 37.5 PCs and 25 units of software are produced and consumed in India.

TABLE 32-2

U.S. and Indian Production and Consumption Without Trade

This table indicates two possible hourly combinations of production and consumption of software and personal computers in the absence of trade in a "world" encompassing the United States and India. U.S. residents produce 30 units of software, and residents of India produce 25 units of software, so the total amount of software that can be consumed worldwide is 55 units. In addition, U.S. residents produce 150 PCs, and Indian residents produce 37.5 PCs, so worldwide production and consumption of PCs amount to 187.5 PCs per hour.

Product	United States	India	Actual World Output
Units of software (per hour)	30	25	55
Personal computers (per hour)	150	37.5	187.5

Finally, Table 32-2 above displays production of software and PCs for this two-country world given the nations' production (and, implicitly, consumption) choices in the absence of trade. In an hour's time, U.S. software production is 30 units, and Indian software production is 25 units, so the total amount of software produced and available for consumption worldwide is 55 units. Hourly U.S. PC production is 150 PCs, and Indian PC production is 37.5 PCs, so a total of 187.5 PCs per hour is produced and available for consumption in this two-country world.

SPECIALIZATION IN PRODUCTION More realistically, residents of the United States will choose to specialize in the activity for which they experience a lower opportunity cost. In other words, U.S. residents will specialize in the activity in which they have a comparative advantage, which is the production of PCs, which they can offer in trade to residents of India. Likewise, Indian residents will specialize in the manufacturing industry in which they have a comparative advantage, which is the production of commercial software, which they can offer in trade to U.S. residents.

By specializing, the two countries can gain from engaging in international trade. To see why, suppose that U.S. residents allocate all available resources to producing 225 PCs, the good in which they have a comparative advantage. In addition, residents of India utilize all resources they have on hand to produce 100 units of commercial software, the good in which they have a comparative advantage.

CONSUMPTION WITH SPECIALIZATION AND TRADE U.S. residents will be willing to buy a unit of Indian commercial software as long as they must provide in exchange no more than 2.5 PCs, which is the opportunity cost of producing 1 unit of software at home. At the same time, residents of India will be willing to buy a U.S. PC as long as they must provide in exchange no more than 2 units of software, which is their opportunity cost of producing a PC.

Suppose that residents of both countries agree to trade at a rate of exchange of 1 PC for 1 unit of software and that they agree to trade 75 U.S. PCs for 75 units of Indian software. Table 32-3 at the top of the following page displays the outcomes that result in both countries. By specializing in PC production and engaging in trade, U.S. residents can continue to consume 150 PCs. In addition, U.S. residents are also able to import and consume 75 units of software produced in India. At the same time, specialization and exchange allow residents of India to continue to consume 25 units of software. Producing 75 more units of software for export to the United States allows India to import 75 PCs.

TABLE 32-3

U.S. and Indian Production and Consumption with Specialization and Trade

In this table, U.S. residents produce 225 personal computers and no software, and Indian residents produce 100 units of software and no PCs. Residents of the two nations then agree to a rate of exchange of 1 PC for 1 unit of software and proceed to trade 75 U.S. PCs for 75 units of Indian software. Specialization and trade allow U.S. residents to consume 75 units of software imported from India and to consume 150 PCs produced at home. By specializing and engaging in trade, Indian residents consume 25 units of software produced at home and import 75 PCs from the United States.

Product	U.S. Production and Consumption with Trade		Indian Production and Consumption with Trade	
Units of software (per hour)	U.S. production	0	Indian production	100
	+Imports from India	75	−Exports to U.S.	75
	Total U.S. consumption	75	Total Indian consumption	25
Personal computers (per hour)	U.S. production	225	Indian production	0
	−Exports to India	75	+Imports from U.S.	75
	Total U.S. consumption	150	Total Indian consumption	75

GAINS FROM TRADE Table 32-4 below summarizes the rates of consumption of U.S. and Indian residents with and without trade. Column 1 displays U.S. and Indian software and PC consumption rates with specialization and trade from Table 32-3 above, and it sums these to determine total consumption rates in this two-country world. Column 2 shows U.S., Indian, and worldwide consumption rates without international trade from Table 32-2 on the previous page. Column 3 gives the differences between the two columns.

Table 32-4 indicates that by producing 75 additional PCs for export to India in exchange for 75 units of software, U.S. residents are able to expand their software consumption from 30 units to 75 units. Thus, the U.S. gain from specialization and trade is 45 units of software. This is a net gain in software consumption for the two-country world as a whole, because neither country had to give up consuming any PCs for U.S. residents to realize this gain from trade.

TABLE 32-4

National and Worldwide Gains from Specialization and Trade

This table summarizes the consumption gains experienced by the United States, India, and the two-country world. U.S. and Indian software and PC consumption rates with specialization and trade from Table 32-3 above are listed in column 1, which sums the national consumption rates to determine total worldwide consumption with trade. Column 2 shows U.S., Indian, and worldwide consumption rates without international trade, as reported in Table 32-2 on the previous page. Column 3 gives the differences between the two columns, which are the resulting national and worldwide gains from international trade.

Product	(1) National and World Consumption with Trade		(2) National and World Consumption without Trade		(3) Worldwide Consumption Gains from Trade	
Units of software (per hour)	U.S. consumption	75	U.S. consumption	30	Change in U.S. consumption	+45
	+Indian consumption	25	+Indian consumption	25	Change in Indian consumption	+0
	World consumption	100	World consumption	55	**Change in world consumption**	**+45**
Personal computers (per hour)	U.S. consumption	150	U.S. consumption	150	Change in U.S. consumption	+0
	+Indian consumption	75	+Indian consumption	37.5	Change in Indian consumption	+37.5
	World consumption	225	World consumption	187.5	**Change in world consumption**	**+37.5**

In addition, without trade residents of India could have used all resources to produce and consume only 37.5 PCs and 25 units of software. By using all resources to specialize in producing 100 units of software and engaging in trade, residents of India can consume 37.5 *more* PCs than they could have produced and consumed alone without reducing their software consumption. Thus, the Indian gain from trade is 37.5 PCs. This represents a worldwide gain in PC consumption, because neither country had to give up consuming any PCs for Indian residents to realize this gain from trade.

Can even international exchange of used items generate gains from trade?

INTERNATIONAL EXAMPLE Gains from International Trade in Used Merchandise

Sofronis Clerides of the University of Cyprus has estimated the gains to residents of Cyprus from a decision several years ago by the Cypriot government to legalize imports of used Japanese cars. He finds that the typical buyer of a used imported vehicle realized a gain from trade of about $2,000. Clerides concludes that considerable gains could be realized if governments of more countries would allow people to engage in international trade of used merchandise.

FOR CRITICAL ANALYSIS

Could it be feasible for a country to establish a comparative advantage in exporting used commodities that initially were produced in other nations? (Hint: Consider that there are car dealers who sell only used vehicles.)

SPECIALIZATION IS THE KEY This example shows that when nations specialize in producing goods for which they have a comparative advantage and engage in international trade, considerable consumption gains are possible for those nations and hence for the world. Why is this so? The answer is that specialization and trade enable Indian residents to obtain each PC at an opportunity cost of 1 unit of software instead of 2 units of software and permit U.S. residents to obtain each unit of software at an opportunity cost of 1 PC instead of 2.5 PCs. Indian residents effectively experience a gain from trade of 1 unit of software for each PC purchased from the United States, and U.S. residents experience a gain from trade of 1.5 PCs for each unit of software purchased from India. Thus, specializing in producing goods for which the two nations have a comparative advantage allows both nations to produce more efficiently. As a consequence, worldwide production capabilities increase. This makes greater worldwide consumption possible through international trade.

Of course, not everybody in our example is better off when free trade occurs. In our example, the U.S. software industry and Indian computer industry have disappeared. Thus, U.S. software makers and Indian computer manufacturers are worse off.

Some people worry that the United States (or any country, for that matter) might someday "run out of exports" because of overaggressive foreign competition. The analysis of comparative advantage tells us the contrary. No matter how much other countries compete for our business, the United States (or any other country) will always have a comparative advantage in something that it can export. In 10 or 20 years, that something may not be what we export today, but it will be exportable nonetheless because we will have a comparative advantage in producing it. Consequently, the significant flows of world trade shown in Figure 32-2 on the following page will continue because the United States and other nations will retain comparative advantages in producing various goods and services.

Other Benefits from International Trade: The Transmission of Ideas

Beyond the fact that comparative advantage results in an overall increase in the output of goods produced and consumed, there is another benefit to international trade. International trade also aids in the transmission of ideas. According to economic historians, international trade has been the principal means by which new goods, services, and processes have spread around the world. For example, coffee was initially grown in

FIGURE 32-2 World Trade Flows

International merchandise trade amounts to about $15 trillion worldwide. The percentage figures show the proportion of trade flowing in the various directions throughout the globe.

Sources: World Trade Organization and author's estimates (data are for 2011).

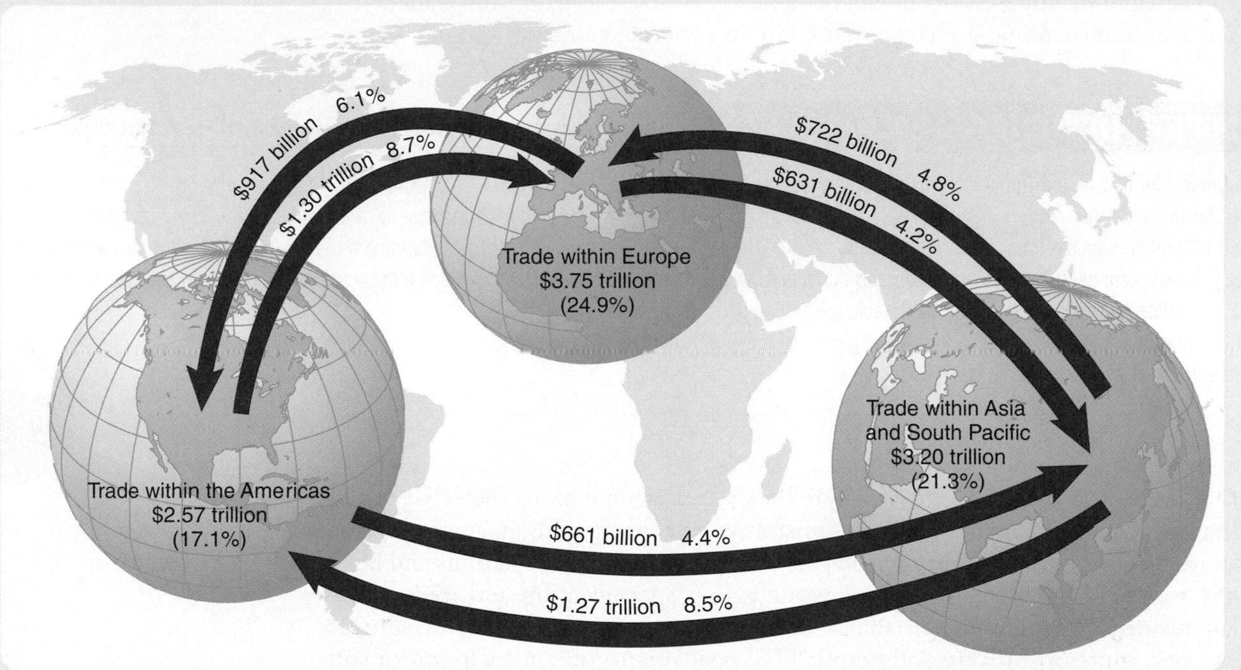

Arabia near the Red Sea. Around AD 675, it began to be roasted and consumed as a beverage. Eventually, it was exported to other parts of the world, and the Dutch started cultivating it in their colonies during the seventeenth century and the French in the eighteenth century. The lowly potato is native to the Peruvian Andes. In the sixteenth century, it was brought to Europe by Spanish explorers. Thereafter, its cultivation and consumption spread rapidly. Finally, it became part of the North American agricultural scene in the early eighteenth century.

New processes have also been transmitted through international trade. An example is the Japanese manufacturing innovation that emphasized redesigning the system rather than running the existing system in the best possible way. Inventories were reduced to just-in-time levels by reengineering machine setup methods.

In addition, international trade has enabled *intellectual property* to spread throughout the world. New music, such as rock and roll in the 1950s and 1960s and hip-hop in the 1990s and 2000s, has been transmitted in this way, as have the software applications and computer communications tools that are common for computer users everywhere.

Why Not . . . obtain gains from trade by subsidizing exports and discouraging imports?

Gains from trade arise naturally from voluntary specialization and exchange. Government subsidies for exports and policies that discourage imports distort the assessment of opportunity costs and, hence, of comparative advantages. In fact, government-created distortions can be so large that domestic and foreign industries may choose to specialize in production of items based on government incentives or disincentives rather than actual opportunity costs. As a consequence, industries receive transfers from taxpayers, but society as a whole does not experience true gains from trade in the form of expanded production and consumption possibilities.

The Relationship Between Imports and Exports

The basic proposition in understanding all of international trade is this:

In the long run, imports are paid for by exports.

The reason that imports are ultimately paid for by exports is that foreign residents want something in exchange for the goods that are shipped to the United States. For the most part, they want U.S.-made goods. From this truism comes a remarkable corollary:

Any restriction of imports ultimately reduces exports.

This is a shocking revelation to many people who want to restrict foreign competition to protect domestic jobs. Although it is possible to "protect" certain U.S. jobs by restricting foreign competition, it is impossible to make *everyone* better off by imposing import restrictions. Why? The reason is that ultimately such restrictions lead to a reduction in employment and output—and hence incomes—in the export industries of the nation.

International Competitiveness

"The United States is falling behind." "We need to stay competitive internationally." Statements such as these are often heard when the subject of international trade comes up. There are two problems with such talk. The first has to do with a simple definition. What does "global competitiveness" really mean? When one company competes against another, it is in competition. Is the United States like one big corporation, in competition with other countries? Certainly not. The standard of living in each country is almost solely a function of how well the economy functions *within that country*, not relative to other countries.

Another point relates to real-world observations. According to the Institute for Management Development in Lausanne, Switzerland, the United States continues to lead the pack in overall productive efficiency, ahead of Japan, Germany, and the rest of the European Union. According to the report, the top ranking of the United States over the years has been due to widespread entrepreneurship, more than a decade of economic restructuring, and information-technology investments. Other factors include the open U.S. financial system and large investments in scientific research.

Why are few African nations internationally competitive, even though Africa possesses fertile lands rich in minerals and has many labor resources?

INTERNATIONAL EXAMPLE Can Africa's International Competitiveness Be Improved?

Even though countries in the heart of Africa are endowed with abundant resources, these nations are not internationally competitive. One problem is that most African railways and many roads are in a poor state of repair, and often they are blocked by rockslides. As a result, it takes as long to transport a shipping container filled with grain between the African nations of Uganda and Kenya as it does to transport the container from Kenya to Chicago. Similarly, it costs more to move the container from Uganda to Kenya than to transport it from Kenya to Chicago.

A French firm called Bolloré is trying to improve Africa's international competitiveness by creating "trade corridors" linking long stretches of the Congo, Niger, and Nile rivers and their widest and deepest tributaries. Bolloré uses these riverways to transport shipping containers on barges over long distances and employs trains and trucks only over shorter stretches. By utilizing these trade corridors, Bolloré has been able to reduce average container shipping times by about 75 percent and to cut shipping costs dramatically.

FOR CRITICAL ANALYSIS

How can a nation's international competitiveness be reduced when a longer time is required to ship its traded goods, other things being equal?

QUICK QUIZ See page 725 for the answers. Review concepts from this section in MyEconLab.

A nation has a **comparative advantage** when its residents are able to produce a good or service at a __________ opportunity cost than residents of another nation.

Specializing in production of goods and services for which residents of a nation have a __________ __________ allows the nation's residents to __________ more of all goods and services.

__________ from trade arise for all nations in the world that engage in international trade because specialization and trade allow countries' residents to __________ more goods and services without necessarily giving up consumption of other goods and services.

Arguments Against Free Trade

Numerous arguments are raised against free trade. These arguments focus mainly on the costs of trade. They do not consider the benefits or the possible alternatives for reducing the costs of free trade while still reaping benefits.

The Infant Industry Argument

A nation may feel that if a particular industry is allowed to develop domestically, it will eventually become efficient enough to compete effectively in the world market. Therefore, the nation may impose some restrictions on imports in order to give domestic producers the time they need to develop their efficiency to the point where they can compete in the domestic market without any restrictions on imports. In graphic terminology, we would expect that if the protected industry truly does experience improvements in production techniques or technological breakthroughs toward greater efficiency in the future, the supply curve will shift outward to the right so that the domestic industry can produce larger quantities at each and every price. National policymakers often assert that this **infant industry argument** has some merit in the short run. They have used it to protect a number of industries in their infancy around the world.

Infant industry argument
The contention that tariffs should be imposed to protect from import competition an industry that is trying to get started. Presumably, after the industry becomes technologically efficient, the tariff can be lifted.

Such a policy can be abused, however. Often the protective import-restricting arrangements remain even after the infant has matured. If other countries can still produce more cheaply, the people who benefit from this type of situation are obviously the stockholders (and specialized factors of production that will earn economic rents—see pages 463–465 in Chapter 21) in the industry that is still being protected from world competition. The people who lose out are the consumers, who must pay a price higher than the world price for the product in question. In any event, because it is very difficult to know beforehand which industries will eventually survive, it is possible, perhaps even likely, that policymakers will choose to protect industries that have no reasonable chance of competing on their own in world markets. Note that when we speculate about which industries "should" be protected, we are in the realm of *normative economics*. We are making a value judgment, a subjective statement of what *ought to be*.

Countering Foreign Subsidies and Dumping

Go to www.econtoday.com/ch32 for a Congressional Budget Office review of antidumping actions in the United States and around the world.

Another common argument against unrestricted foreign trade is that a nation must counter other nations' subsidies to their own producers. When a foreign government subsidizes its producers, our producers claim that they cannot compete fairly with these subsidized foreign producers. To the extent that such subsidies fluctuate, it can be argued that unrestricted free trade will seriously disrupt domestic producers. They will not know when foreign governments are going to subsidize their producers and when they are not. Our competing industries will be expanding and contracting too frequently.

The phenomenon called *dumping* is also used as an argument against unrestricted trade. **Dumping** is said to occur when a producer sells its products abroad below the price that is charged in the home market or at a price below its cost of production.

Dumping
Selling a good or a service abroad below the price charged in the home market or at a price below its cost of production.

Often, when a foreign producer is accused of dumping, further investigation reveals that the foreign nation is in the throes of a recession. The foreign producer does not want to slow down its production at home. Because it anticipates an end to the recession and doesn't want to hold large inventories, it dumps its products abroad at prices below home prices. U.S. competitors may also allege that the foreign producer sells its output at prices below its full costs to be assured of covering variable costs of production.

Protecting Domestic Jobs

Perhaps the argument used most often against free trade is that unrestrained competition from other countries will eliminate jobs in the United States because other countries have lower-cost labor than we do. (Less restrictive environmental standards in other countries might also lower their private costs relative to ours.) This is a compelling argument, particularly for politicians from areas that might be threatened by foreign competition. For example, a representative from an area with shoe factories would certainly be upset about the possibility of constituents' losing their jobs because of competition from lower-priced shoe manufacturers in Brazil and Italy. But, of course, this argument against free trade is equally applicable to trade between the states within the United States.

Economists David Gould, G. L. Woodbridge, and Roy Ruffin examined the data on the relationship between increases in imports and the unemployment rate. They concluded that there is no causal link between the two. Indeed, in half the cases they studied, when imports increased, the unemployment rate fell.

Another issue involves the cost of protecting U.S. jobs by restricting international trade. The Institute for International Economics examined the restrictions on foreign textiles and apparel goods. The study found that U.S. consumers pay $9 billion a year more than they would otherwise pay for those goods to protect jobs in those industries. That comes out to $50,000 *a year* for each job saved in an industry in which the average job pays only $20,000 a year. Similar studies have yielded similar results: Restrictions on imports of Japanese cars have cost $160,000 *per year* for every job saved in the auto industry. Every job preserved in the glass industry has cost $200,000 each and every year. Every job preserved in the U.S. steel industry has cost an astounding $750,000 per year.

Emerging Arguments Against Free Trade

In recent years, two new antitrade arguments have been advanced. One of these focuses on environmental and safety concerns. For instance, many critics of free trade have suggested that genetic engineering of plants and animals could lead to accidental production of new diseases and that people, livestock, and pets could be harmed by tainted foods imported for human and animal consumption. These worries have induced the European Union to restrain trade in such products.

Another argument against free trade arises from national defense concerns. Major espionage successes by China in the late 1990s and 2000s led some U.S. strategic experts to propose sweeping restrictions on exports of new technology.

Free trade proponents counter that at best these are arguments for the judicious regulation of trade. They continue to argue that, by and large, broad trade restrictions mainly harm the interests of the nations that impose them.

QUICK QUIZ **See page 725 for the answers. Review concepts from this section in MyEconLab.**

The __________ industry argument against free trade contends that new industries should be __________ against world competition so that they can become technologically efficient in the long run.

Unrestricted foreign trade may allow foreign governments to subsidize exports or foreign producers to engage in __________, or selling products in other countries below their cost of production. Critics claim that to the extent that foreign export subsidies and __________ create more instability in domestic production, they may impair our well-being.

Ways to Restrict Foreign Trade

International trade can be stopped or at least stifled in many ways. These include quotas and taxes (the latter are usually called *tariffs* when applied to internationally traded items). Let's talk first about quotas.

Quotas

Quota system
A government-imposed restriction on the quantity of a specific good that another country is allowed to sell in the United States. In other words, quotas are restrictions on imports. These restrictions are usually applied to one or several specific countries.

Under a **quota system,** individual countries or groups of foreign producers are restricted to a certain amount of trade. An import quota specifies the maximum amount of a commodity that may be imported during a specified period of time. For example, the government might allow no more than 200 million barrels of foreign crude oil to enter the United States in a particular month.

Consider the example of quotas on textiles. Figure 32-3 below presents the demand and supply curves for imported textiles. In an unrestricted import market, the equilibrium quantity imported is 900 million yards at a price of $1 per yard (expressed in constant-quality units). When an import quota is imposed, the supply curve is no longer *S*. Instead, the supply curve becomes vertical at some amount less than the equilibrium quantity—here, 800 million yards per year. The price to the U.S. consumer increases from $1.00 to $1.50.

Clearly, the output restriction generated by a quota on foreign imports of a particular item has the effect of raising the domestic price of the imported item. Two groups benefit. One group is importers that are able to obtain the rights to sell imported items domestically at the higher price, which raises their revenues and boosts their profits. The other group is domestic producers. Naturally, a rise in the price of an imported item induces an increase in the demand for domestic substitutes. Thus, the domestic prices of close substitutes for the item subject to the import restriction also increase, which generates higher revenues and profits for domestic producers.

Voluntary restraint agreement (VRA)
An official agreement with another country that "voluntarily" restricts the quantity of its exports to the United States.

VOLUNTARY QUOTAS Quotas do not have to be explicit and defined by law. They can be "voluntary." Such a quota is called a **voluntary restraint agreement (VRA).** In the early 1980s, Japanese automakers voluntarily restrained exports to the United States. These restraints stayed in place into the 1990s. Today, there are VRAs on machine tools and textiles.

FIGURE 32-3 The Effect of Quotas on Textile Imports

Without restrictions, at point E_1, 900 million yards of textiles would be imported each year into the United States at the world price of $1.00 per yard. If the federal government imposes a quota of only 800 million yards, the effective supply curve becomes vertical at that quantity. It intersects the demand curve at point E_2, so the new equilibrium price is $1.50 per yard.

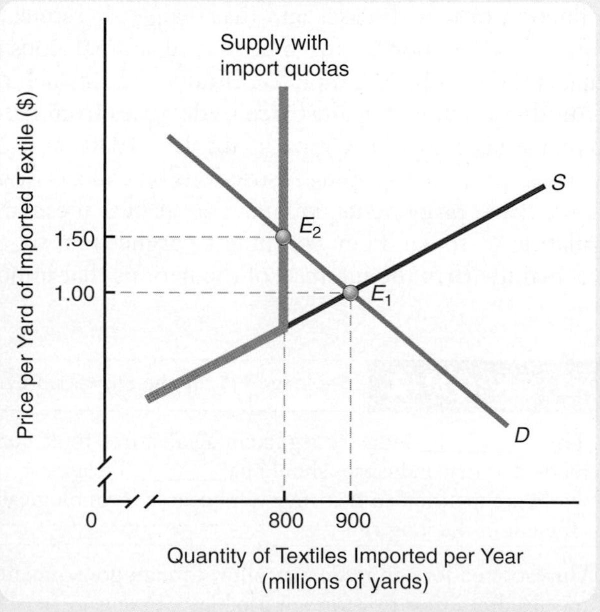

The opposite of a VRA is a **voluntary import expansion (VIE).** Under a VIE, a foreign government agrees to have its companies import more foreign goods from another country. The United States almost started a major international trade war with Japan in 1995 over just such an issue. The U.S. government wanted Japanese automobile manufacturers to voluntarily increase their imports of U.S.-made automobile parts. Ultimately, Japanese companies did make a token increase in their imports of U.S. auto parts.

Voluntary import expansion (VIE)
An official agreement with another country in which it agrees to import more from the United States.

Tariffs

We can analyze tariffs by using standard supply and demand diagrams. Let's use as our commodity laptop computers, some of which are made in Japan and some of which are made domestically. In panel (a) of Figure 32-4 below, you see the demand for and supply of Japanese laptops. The equilibrium price is $500 per constant-quality unit, and the equilibrium quantity is 10 million per year. In panel (b), you see the same equilibrium price of $500, and the *domestic* equilibrium quantity is 5 million units per year.

Go to **www.econtoday.com/ch32** to take a look at the U.S. State Department's reports on economic policy and trade practices.

Now a tariff of $250 is imposed on all imported Japanese laptops. The supply curve shifts upward by $250 to S_2. For purchasers of Japanese laptops, the price increases to $625. The quantity demanded falls to 8 million per year. In panel (b), you see that at the higher price of imported Japanese laptops, the demand curve for U.S.-made laptops shifts outward to the right to D_2. The equilibrium price increases to $625, and the equilibrium quantity increases to 6.5 million units per year. So the tariff benefits domestic laptop producers because it increases the demand for their products due to the higher price of a close substitute, Japanese laptops. This causes a redistribution of income from Japanese producers and U.S. consumers of laptops to U.S. producers of laptops.

TARIFFS IN THE UNITED STATES In Figure 32-5 on the following page, we see that tariffs on all imported goods have varied widely. The highest rates in the twentieth century occurred with the passage of the Smoot-Hawley Tariff in 1930.

FIGURE 32-4 The Effect of a Tariff on Japanese-Made Laptop Computers

Without a tariff, the United States buys 10 million Japanese laptops per year at an average price of $500, at point E_1 in panel (a). U.S. producers sell 5 million domestically made laptops, also at $500 each, at point E_1 in panel (b). A $250 tariff per laptop will shift the Japanese import supply curve to S_2 in panel (a), so that the new equilibrium is at E_2 with price increased to $625 and quantity sold reduced to 8 million per year. The demand curve for U.S.-made laptops (for which there is no tariff) shifts to D_2, in panel (b). Domestic sales increase to 6.5 million per year, at point E_2.

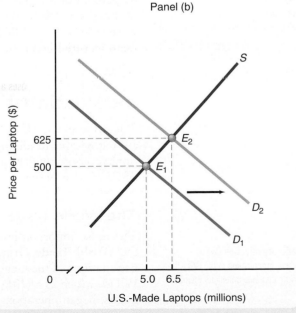

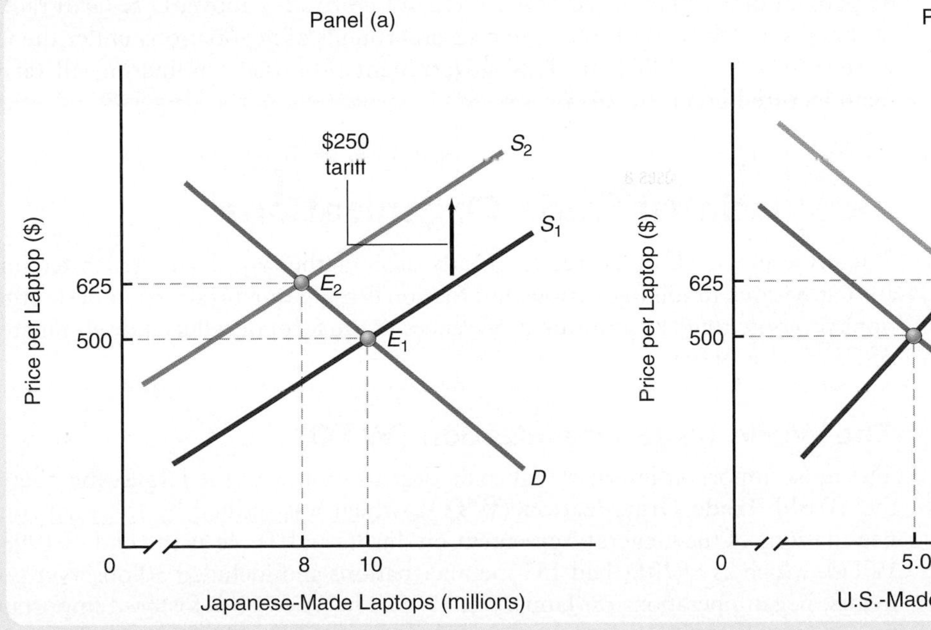

FIGURE 32-5 Tariff Rates in the United States Since 1820

Tariff rates in the United States have bounced around like a football. Indeed, in Congress, tariffs are a political football. Import-competing industries prefer high tariffs. In the twentieth century, the highest tariff was the Smoot-Hawley Tariff of 1930, which was about as high as the "tariff of abominations" in 1828.

Source: U.S. Department of Commerce.

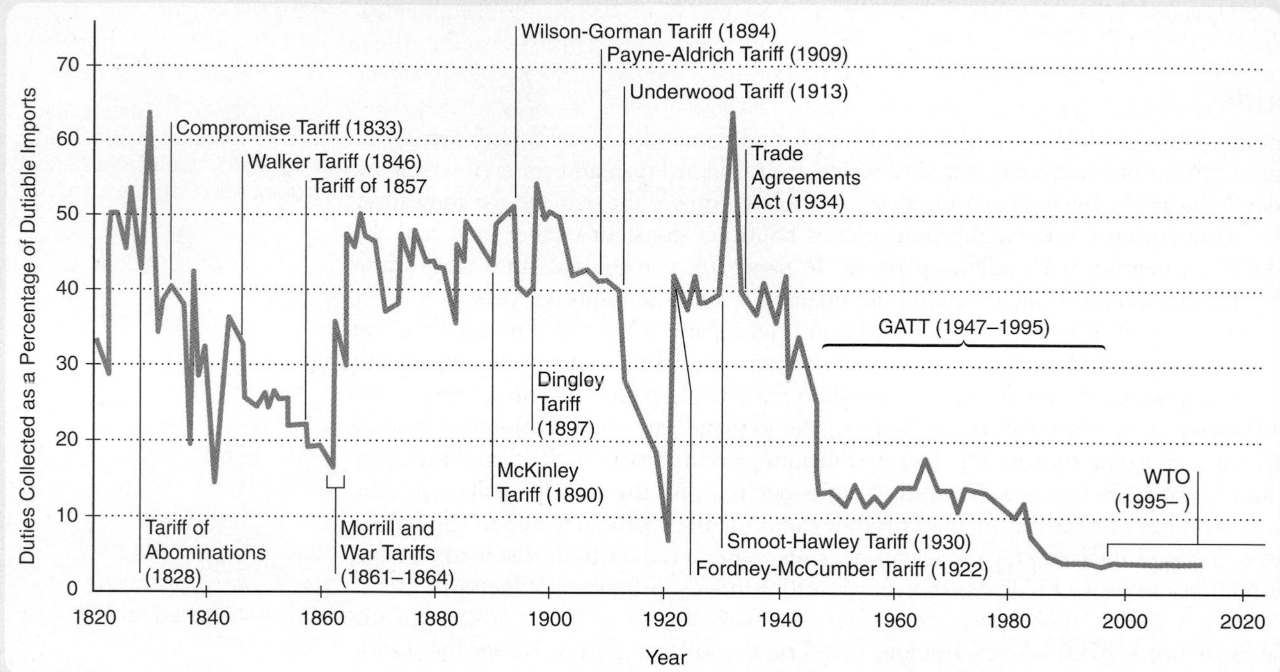

You Are There

To consider how some U.S. workers may lose from the imposition of a tariff while others gain, read **Union Workers Find Themselves on Opposing Sides on Trade,** on page 720.

General Agreement on Tariffs and Trade (GATT)
An international agreement established in 1947 to further world trade by reducing barriers and tariffs. The GATT was replaced by the World Trade Organization in 1995.

CURRENT TARIFF LAWS The Trade Expansion Act of 1962 gave the president the authority to reduce tariffs by up to 50 percent. Subsequently, tariffs were reduced by about 35 percent. In 1974, the Trade Reform Act allowed the president to reduce tariffs further. In 1984, the Trade and Tariff Act resulted in the lowest tariff rates ever. All such trade agreement obligations of the United States were carried out under the auspices of the **General Agreement on Tariffs and Trade (GATT),** which was signed in 1947. Member nations of the GATT account for more than 85 percent of world trade. As you can see in Figure 32-5 above, U.S. tariff rates have declined since the early 1960s, when several rounds of negotiations under the GATT were initiated. In 2002, the U.S. government proposed eliminating all tariffs on manufactured goods by 2015.

International Trade Organizations

The widespread effort to reduce tariffs around the world has generated interest among nations in joining various international trade organizations. These organizations promote trade by granting preferences in the form of reduced or eliminated tariffs, duties, or quotas.

The World Trade Organization (WTO)

World Trade Organization (WTO)
The successor organization to the GATT that handles trade disputes among its member nations.

The most important international trade organization with the largest membership is the **World Trade Organization (WTO),** which was ratified by the final round of negotiations of the General Agreement on Tariffs and Trade at the end of 1993. The WTO, which as of 2011 had 153 member nations and included 30 observer governments, began operations on January 1, 1995. The WTO has fostered important and far-reaching global trade agreements. There is considerable evidence that since the WTO was formed, many of its member nations have adopted policies promoting international trade. The WTO also adjudicates trade disputes between nations in an effort to reduce the scope of protectionism around the globe.

Regional Trade Agreements

Numerous other international trade organizations exist alongside the WTO. Sometimes known as **regional trade blocs,** these organizations are created by special deals among groups of countries that grant trade preferences only to countries within their groups. Currently, more than 475 bilateral or regional trade agreements are in effect around the globe. Examples include groups of industrial powerhouses, such as the European Union, the North American Free Trade Agreement, and the Association of Southeast Asian Nations. Nations in South America with per capita real GDP nearer the world average have also formed regional trade blocs called Mercosur and the Andean Community. Less developed nations have also formed regional trade blocs, such as the Economic Community of West African States and the Community of East and Southern Africa.

Regional trade bloc
A group of nations that grants members special trade privileges.

DO REGIONAL TRADE BLOCS SIMPLY DIVERT TRADE? Figure 32-6 below shows that the formation of regional trade blocs, in which the European Union and the United States are often key participants, is on an upswing. An average African nation participates in four separate regional trading agreements. A typical Latin American country belongs to eight different regional trade blocs.

In the past, economists worried that the formation of regional trade blocs could mainly result in **trade diversion,** or the shifting of trade from countries outside a regional trade bloc to nations within a bloc. Indeed, a study by Jeffrey Frankel of Harvard University found evidence that some trade diversion does take place. Nevertheless, Frankel and other economists have concluded that the net effect of regional trade agreements has been to boost overall international trade, in some cases considerably.

Trade diversion
Shifting existing international trade from countries outside a regional trade bloc to nations within the bloc.

THE TRADE DEFLECTION ISSUE Today, the primary issue associated with regional trade blocs is **trade deflection.** This occurs when a company located in a nation outside a regional trade bloc moves goods that are not quite fully assembled into a member country, completes assembly of the goods there, and then exports them to other nations in the bloc. To try to reduce incentives for trade deflection, regional trade agreements often include **rules of origin,** which are regulations carefully defining categories of products that are eligible for trading preferences under the agreements. Some rules of origin, for instance, require any products trading freely among members of a bloc to be composed mainly of materials produced within a member nation.

Trade deflection
Moving partially assembled products into a member nation of a regional trade bloc, completing assembly, and then exporting them to other nations within the bloc, so as to benefit from preferences granted by the trade bloc.

Rules of origin
Regulations that nations in regional trade blocs establish to delineate product categories eligible for trading preferences.

Proponents of free trade worry, however, about the potential for parties to regional trade agreements to use rules of origin to create barriers to trade. Sufficiently complex

FIGURE 32-6 The Percentage of World Trade Within Regional Trade Blocs

As the number of regional trade agreements has increased since 1990, the share of world trade undertaken among nations that are members of regional trade blocs—involving the European Union (EU), the United States, and developing nations—has also increased.

Source: World Bank.

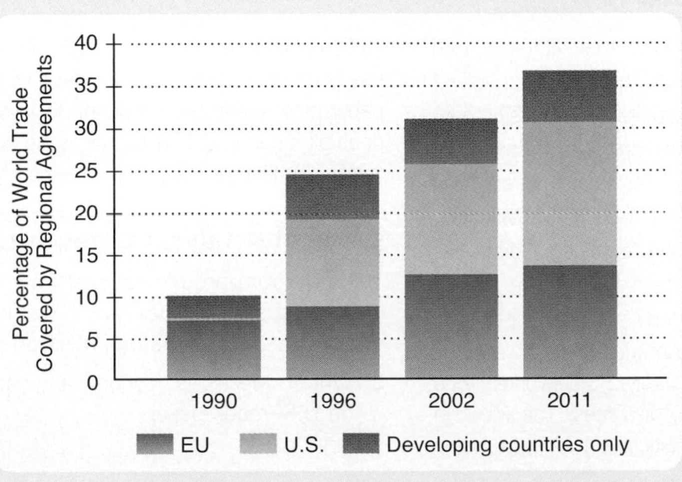

rules of origin, they suggest, can provide disincentives for countries to utilize the trade-promoting preferences that regional trade agreements ought to provide. Indeed, some free trade proponents applaud successful trade deflection. They contend that it helps to circumvent trade restrictions and thus allows nations within regional trade blocs to experience additional gains from trade.

Could the establishment of regional trade blocs help to promote more international trade by making governments less protectionist?

INTERNATIONAL POLICY EXAMPLE

Does the Spread of Regional Trade Blocs Reduce Protectionism?

Scott Baier of Clemson University and Jeffrey Bergstrand of the University of Notre Dame have examined the extent to which nations' governments adjust their trade policies up to 10 years after the nations become members of regional trade blocs. They found that within a few years after nations join regional trade blocs, their governments gradually tend to become less protectionist. Thus, the overall net effect of joining a regional trade bloc is greater trade with nations *outside* the bloc as well as with countries that are co-members of the bloc.

FOR CRITICAL ANALYSIS

Why might the shedding of protectionist policies by members of regional trade blocs help to reduce the extent of trade diversion?

QUICK QUIZ

See page 725 for the answers. Review concepts from this section in MyEconLab.

One means of restricting foreign trade is an import quota, which specifies a _________ amount of a good that may be imported during a certain period. The resulting increase in import prices benefits domestic _________ that receive higher prices resulting from substitution to domestic goods.

Another means of restricting imports is a **tariff,** which is a _________ on imports only. An import tariff _________ import-competing industries and harms consumers by raising prices.

The main international institution created to improve trade among nations was the General Agreement on Tariffs and Trade (GATT). The last round of trade talks under the GATT led to the creation of the _________ _________ _________.

_________ _________ agreements among numerous nations of the world have established more than 475 bilateral and _________ _________ blocs, which grant special trade privileges such as reduced tariff barriers and quota exemptions to member nations.

You Are There

Union Workers Find Themselves on Opposing Sides on Trade

Recently, a U.S. law that prohibits Mexican commercial trucks from traveling on U.S. highways went into effect. The stated purpose of the law is to protect U.S. drivers from potentially unsafe foreign drivers. Nevertheless, a side effect of the law—and in the opinion of some critics, its true intent—is to prevent Mexican truckers from competing head to head with U.S. truckers. For DuWayne Marshall, a Wisconsin trucker who is a member of the Teamsters Union, this law is wonderful news. "Why should I have to compete against 'Third World' drivers within my own borders?" asks Marshall. "By closing down the borders, we are saving American jobs."

Elizabeth Villagomez, a member of the United Steelworkers who is employed by a Wisconsin paper plant, disagrees. The Mexican government has retaliated for the ban on Mexican trucks by imposing tariffs on Mexican imports of U.S.-manufactured paper. The result has been sharp reductions in Mexican purchases of paper that her paper plant produces. According to Villagomez, "The company has done all it can to cut costs. I'm at the bottom of the list if they have layoffs. It's kind of scary, not knowing if you're going to have a job."

Critical Analysis Questions

1. Solely from an international trade standpoint—without considering safety issues—who besides workers like Villagomez is harmed by the ban on Mexican trucks?
2. Who in Mexico is economically harmed by the Mexican tariff on U.S.-made paper?

ISSUES & APPLICATIONS

A U.S. Effort to Expand Exports While Reducing Imports

CONCEPTS APPLIED

- Tariffs and Quotas
- Gains from Trade
- Comparative Advantage

The U.S. government is formally committed to bringing about a significant expansion of the nation's exports. Yet it has imposed tariffs on Chinese tires to reduce U.S. imports. The intent of both policies is to increase U.S. gains from trade, but in reality these policies are likely to reduce such gains.

Subsidizing Exports

The key objective of U.S. trade policy is to double U.S. exports by 2015. Toward this end, the president established two panels to advise him on how to achieve this goal: an "export promotion cabinet" and a private-sector advisory board.

Some members of the private-sector advisory board have suggested that the government should increase export subsidies. This would enable U.S. firms to offer goods for sale abroad at lower prices, which would boost export sales and thereby help fulfill the U.S. government's plan to double the nation's exports.

Exports, Imported Tires, and Confusion About Gains from Trade

A few months before the U.S. government announced its intent to increase exports, it imposed a new 35 percent tariff on low-priced Chinese-manufactured tires for passenger vehicles and light trucks. The main rationale for implementing the tariff was to push up the price of Chinese tires and increase U.S. purchases of U.S.-manufactured tires.

The basic idea behind the U.S. government's efforts to promote exports and discourage imports is to "create U.S. jobs" by raising exports while "saving U.S. jobs" by reducing import competition. Gains from trade are not achieved by promoting certain industries and protecting others, however. Such gains arise when each nation's industries specialize in providing items that they can produce at lower opportunity cost. Policies to promote exports, such as subsidies, give the appearance of reducing domestic opportunity costs. In reality, however, subsidies transfer resources from taxpayers to subsidized firms. Furthermore, policies to reduce imports, such as tariffs on Chinese tires, directly inhibit the realization of gains from trade by restraining domestic consumption possibilities.

For Critical Analysis

1. Why are public subsidies received by exporting firms not gains from trade?
2. Were high-, middle-, or low-income U.S. consumers most likely to have been harmed by the imposition of the 35 percent U.S. tariff on low-priced Chinese tires? Why?

Web Resources

1. To read the presidential executive order announcing the goal of doubling U.S. exports by 2015, go to www.econtoday.com/ch32.
2. View the formal presidential proclamation of the imposition of the tariff on Chinese tires at www.econtoday.com/ch32.

Research Project

Suppose that governments around the globe subsidize exports. International trade takes place, but there is no net expansion of the overall production and consumption possibilities of the world's nations. Are there gains from trade? Explain.

For more questions on this chapter's Issues & Applications, go to **MyEconLab**. In the Study Plan for this chapter, select Section N: News.

Here is what you should know after reading this chapter. **MyEconLab** will help you identify what you know, and where to go when you need to practice.

WHAT YOU SHOULD KNOW		WHERE TO GO TO PRACTICE
The Worldwide Importance of International Trade Total trade among nations has been growing faster than total world GDP. The growth of U.S. exports and imports relative to U.S. GDP parallels this global trend. Today, exports constitute more than 10 percent of total national production. In some countries, trade accounts for a much higher share of total economic activity.	**KEY FIGURE** Figure 32-1, 706	• **MyEconLab** Study Plan 32.1 • Audio introduction to Chapter 32 • Animated Figure 32-1 • ABC News Video: How Outsourcing Affects Our Lives
Why Nations Can Gain from Specializing in Production and Engaging in Trade A country has a comparative advantage in producing a good if it can produce that good at a lower opportunity cost, in terms of forgone production of a second good, than another nation. Both nations can gain by specializing in producing the goods in which they have a comparative advantage and engaging in international trade. Together, they can consume more than they would have in the absence of specialization and trade.	comparative advantage, 707 **KEY FIGURE** Figure 32-2, 712	• **MyEconLab** Study Plan 32.2 • Animated Figure 32-2 • Video: The Gains from Trade
Arguments Against Free Trade One argument against free trade is that temporary import restrictions might permit an "infant industry" to develop. Another argument concerns dumping, in which foreign firms allegedly sell some of their output in domestic markets at prices below the prices in their home markets or even below their costs of production. In addition, some environmentalists support restrictions on foreign trade to protect their nations from exposure to environmental hazards. Finally, some contend that countries should limit exports of technologies that could pose a threat to their national defense.	infant industry argument, 714 dumping, 714	• **MyEconLab** Study Plans 32.3, 32.4, 32.5 • Video: Arguments Against Free Trade
Ways That Nations Restrict Foreign Trade One way to restrain trade is to impose a quota, or a limit on imports of a good. This action restricts the supply of the good in the domestic market, thereby pushing up the equilibrium price of the good. Another way to reduce trade is to place a tariff on imported goods. This reduces the supply of foreign-made goods and increases the demand for domestically produced goods, thereby bringing about a rise in the price of the good.	quota system, 716 voluntary restraint agreement (VRA), 716 voluntary import expansion (VIE), 717 General Agreement on Tariffs and Trade (GATT), 718 **KEY FIGURES** Figure 32-3, 716 Figure 32-4, 717	• **MyEconLab** Study Plan 32.6 • Animated Figures 32-3, 32-4

MyEconLab continued

WHAT YOU SHOULD KNOW		WHERE TO GO TO PRACTICE
Key International Trade Agreements and Organizations From 1947 to 1995, nations agreed to abide by the General Agreement on Tariffs and Trade (GATT), which laid an international legal foundation for relaxing quotas and reducing tariffs. Since 1995, the World Trade Organization (WTO) has adjudicated trade disputes that arise between or among nations. Now there are also more than 475 bilateral and regional trade blocs, including the North American Free Trade Agreement and the European Union, that provide special trade preferences to member nations.	World Trade Organization, 718 regional trade bloc, 719 trade diversion, 719 trade deflection, 719 rules of origin, 719 **KEY FIGURE** Figure 32-5, 718	• **MyEconLab** Study Plan 32.7 • Animated Figure 32-5

PROBLEMS

All problems are assignable in myeconlab. Answers to the odd-numbered problems appear at the back of the book.

32-1. To answer the questions below, consider the following table for the neighboring nations of Northland and West Coast. The table lists maximum feasible hourly rates of production of pastries if no sandwiches are produced and maximum feasible hourly rates of production of sandwiches if no pastries are produced. Assume that the opportunity costs of producing these goods are constant in both nations.

Product	Northland	West Coast
Pastries (per hour)	50,000	100,000
Sandwiches (per hour)	25,000	200,000

a. What is the opportunity cost of producing pastries in Northland? Of producing sandwiches in Northland?

b. What is the opportunity cost of producing pastries in West Coast? Of producing sandwiches in West Coast?

32-2. Based on your answers to Problem 32-1, which nation has a comparative advantage in producing pastries? Which nation has a comparative advantage in producing sandwiches?

32-3. Suppose that the two nations in Problems 32-1 and 32-2 choose to specialize in producing the goods for which they have a comparative advantage. They agree to trade at a rate of exchange of 1 pastry for 1 sandwich. At this rate of exchange, what are the maximum possible numbers of pastries and sandwiches that they could agree to trade?

32-4. Residents of the nation of Border Kingdom can forgo production of digital televisions and utilize all available resources to produce 300 bottles of high-quality wine per hour. Alternatively, they can forgo producing wine and instead produce 60 digital TVs per hour. In the neighboring country of Coastal Realm, residents can forgo production of digital TVs and use all resources to produce

150 bottles of high-quality wine per hour, or they can forgo wine production and produce 50 digital TVs per hour. In both nations, the opportunity costs of producing the two goods are constant.

a. What is the opportunity cost of producing digital TVs in Border Kingdom? Of producing bottles of wine in Border Kingdom?

b. What is the opportunity cost of producing digital TVs in Coastal Realm? Of producing bottles of wine in Coastal Realm?

32-5. Based on your answers to Problem 32-4, which nation has a comparative advantage in producing digital TVs? Which nation has a comparative advantage in producing bottles of wine?

32-6. Suppose that the two nations in Problem 32-4 decide to specialize in producing the good for which they have a comparative advantage and to engage in trade. Will residents of both nations agree to trade wine for digital TVs at a rate of exchange of 4 bottles of wine for 1 digital TV? Why or why not?

To answer Problems 32-7 and 32-8, refer to the following table, which shows possible combinations of hourly outputs of modems and flash memory drives in South Shore and neighboring East Isle, in which opportunity costs of producing both products are constant.

South Shore		East Isle	
Modems	Flash Drives	Modems	Flash Drives
75	0	100	0
60	30	80	10
45	60	60	20
30	90	40	30
15	120	20	40
0	150	0	50

32-7. Consider the above table and answer the questions that follow.

a. What is the opportunity cost of producing modems in South Shore? Of producing flash memory drives in South Shore?

b. What is the opportunity cost of producing modems in East Isle? Of producing flash memory drives in East Isle?

c. Which nation has a comparative advantage in producing modems? Which nation has a comparative advantage in producing flash memory drives?

32-8. Refer to your answers to Problem 32-7 when answering the following questions.

a. Which *one* of the following rates of exchange of modems for flash memory drives will be acceptable to *both* nations: (i) 3 modems for 1 flash drive; (ii) 1 modem for 1 flash drive; or (iii) 1 flash drive for 2.5 modems? Explain.

b. Suppose that each nation decides to use all available resources to produce only the good for which it has a comparative advantage and to engage in trade at the single feasible rate of exchange you identified in part (a). Prior to specialization and trade, residents of South Shore chose to produce and consume 30 modems per hour and 90 flash drives per hour, and residents of East Isle chose to produce and consume 40 modems per hour and 30 flash drives per hour. Now, residents of South Shore agree to export to East Isle the same quantity of South Shore's specialty good that East Isle residents were consuming prior to engaging in international trade. How many units of East Isle's specialty good does South Shore import from East Isle?

c. What is South Shore's hourly consumption of modems and flash drives after the nation specializes and trades with East Isle? What is East Isle's hourly consumption of modems and flash drives after the nation specializes and trades with South Shore?

d. What consumption gains from trade are experienced by South Shore and East Isle?

32-9. Critics of the North American Free Trade Agreement (NAFTA) suggest that much of the increase in exports from Mexico to the United States now involves goods that Mexico otherwise would have exported to other nations. Mexican firms choose to export the goods to the United States, the critics argue, solely because the items receive preferential treatment under NAFTA tariff rules. What term describes what these critics are claiming is occurring with regard to U.S.-Mexican trade as a result of NAFTA? Explain your reasoning.

ECONOMICS ON THE NET

How the World Trade Organization Settles Trade Disputes A key function of the WTO is to adjudicate trade disagreements that arise among nations. This application helps you learn about the process that the WTO follows when considering international trade disputes.

Title: The World Trade Organization: Settling Trade Disputes

Navigation: Go to **www.econtoday.com/ch32** to access the WTO's Web page titled *Dispute Settlement*. Under "Introduction to dispute settlement in the WTO," click on *How does the WTO settle disputes?*

Application Read the article. Then answer the following questions.

1. As the article discusses, settling trade disputes often takes at least a year. What aspects of the WTO's dispute settlement process take the longest time?
2. Does the WTO actually "punish" a country it finds has broken international trading agreements? If not, who does impose sanctions?

For Group Study and Analysis Go to the WTO's main site at **www.econtoday.com/ch32**, and click on *The WTO*. Divide the class into groups, and have the groups explore this information on areas of WTO involvement. Have a class discussion of the pros and cons of WTO involvement in these areas. Which are most important for promoting world trade? Which are least important?

ANSWERS TO QUICK QUIZZES

p. 714: (i) lower; (ii) comparative advantage . . . consume; (iii) Gains . . . consume

p. 715: (i) infant . . . protected; (ii) dumping . . . dumping

p. 720: (i) maximum . . . producers; (ii) tax . . . benefits; (iii) World Trade Organization; (iv) Regional trade . . . regional trade

33

Exchange Rates and the Balance of Payments

Some economists call the U.S. dollar the world's "reserve currency," which means that people in other nations hold significant portions of their wealth as dollars. Other economists refer to the dollar as the world's "vehicle currency," which means that people in other countries often provide dollar-denominated payments to one another when engaging in international trade. More generally, the dollar is the predominant *global currency* that many people throughout the world utilize to conduct transactions relating to international trade and finance. During the 2000s, the dollar's position appeared to be weakening, and some observers suggested that the euro, the currency used by a number of European nations, might replace the dollar. Nevertheless, today the euro's status is in doubt, and the dollar remains the predominant global currency. To consider why this is so, you must first understand the determination of exchange rates, which is a key topic of this chapter.

LEARNING OBJECTIVES

After reading this chapter, you should be able to:

- Distinguish between the balance of trade and the balance of payments
- Identify the key accounts within the balance of payments
- Outline how exchange rates are determined in the markets for foreign exchange
- Discuss factors that can induce changes in equilibrium exchange rates
- Understand how policymakers can go about attempting to fix exchange rates

myeconlab

MyEconLab helps you master each objective and study more efficiently. See end of chapter for details.

in the spring of 2010, a pair of Levi's 505 jeans priced at about 30 U.S. dollars in a U.S. Sears store could be purchased at a Sears Canada store at a price equivalent to 68 U.S. dollars? Hence, Canadians could trade 60 Canadian dollars for just over 60 U.S. dollars, drive across the U.S border, and buy two pairs of jeans for the price of one pair in Canada. This situation came about because of a change in the U.S. dollar–Canadian dollar *exchange rate,* which is the price of the Canadian dollar in terms of the U.S. dollar. Between late 2009 and mid-2010, the amount of U.S. dollars that could be obtained with a Canadian dollar rose significantly. This made U.S. items less expensive to Canadians, who responded by trading more of their Canadian dollars for U.S. dollars. Thus, the rising value of the Canadian dollar in terms of U.S. dollars—or, alternatively stated, the declining value of the U.S. dollar in terms of Canadian dollars—generated an increase in the amount of Canadian dollars that Canadian residents desired to trade for U.S. dollars. In this chapter, you will examine the relationships between the exchange rate and desired foreign currency holdings. You will learn that these relationships are key elements in the determination of exchange rates.

Did You Know That ?

The Balance of Payments and International Capital Movements

Governments typically keep track of each year's economic activities by calculating the gross domestic product—the total of expenditures on all newly produced final domestic goods and services—and its components. A summary information system has also been developed for international trade. It covers the balance of trade and the balance of payments. The **balance of trade** refers specifically to exports and imports of physical goods, or merchandise, as discussed in Chapter 32. When international trade is in balance, the value of exports equals the value of imports. When the value of imports exceeds the value of exports, we are running a deficit in the balance of trade. When the value of exports exceeds the value of imports, we are running a surplus.

Balance of trade
The difference between exports and imports of physical goods.

The **balance of payments** is a more general concept that expresses the total of all economic transactions between a nation and the rest of the world, usually for a period of one year. Each country's balance of payments summarizes information about that country's exports and imports of services as well as physical goods, earnings by domestic residents on assets located abroad, earnings on domestic assets owned by foreign residents, international capital movements, and official transactions by central banks and governments. In essence, then, the balance of payments is a record of all the transactions between households, firms, and the government of one country and the rest of the world. Any transaction that leads to a *payment* by a country's residents (or government) is a deficit item, identified by a negative sign (−) when the actual numbers are given for the items listed in the second column of Table 33-1 on the following page. Any transaction that leads to a *receipt* by a country's residents (or government) is a surplus item and is identified by a plus sign (+) when actual numbers are considered. Table 33-1 provides a list of the surplus and deficit items on international accounts.

Balance of payments
A system of accounts that measures transactions of goods, services, income, and financial assets between domestic households, businesses, and governments and residents of the rest of the world during a specific time period.

Accounting Identities

Accounting identities—definitions of equivalent values—exist for financial institutions and other businesses. We begin with simple accounting identities that must hold for families and then go on to describe international accounting identities.

Accounting identities
Values that are equivalent by definition.

If a family unit is spending more than its current income, the family unit must necessarily be doing one of the following:

1. Reducing its money holdings or selling stocks, bonds, or other assets
2. Borrowing
3. Receiving gifts from friends or relatives
4. Receiving public transfers from a government, which obtained the funds by taxing others (a transfer is a payment, in money or in goods or services, made without receiving goods or services in return)

TABLE 33-1

Surplus (+) and Deficit (−) Items on the International Accounts

Surplus Items (+)	Deficit Items (−)
Exports of merchandise	Imports of merchandise
Private and governmental gifts from foreign residents	Private and governmental gifts to foreign residents
Foreign use of domestically operated travel and transportation services	Use of foreign-operated travel and transportation services
Foreign tourists' expenditures in this country	U.S. tourists' expenditures abroad
Foreign military spending in this country	Military spending abroad
Interest and dividend receipts from foreign entities	Interest and dividends paid to foreign residents
Sales of domestic assets to foreign residents	Purchases of foreign assets
Funds deposited in this country by foreign residents	Funds placed in foreign depository institutions
Sales of gold to foreign residents	Purchases of gold from foreign residents
Sales of domestic currency to foreign residents	Purchases of foreign currency

We can use this information to derive an identity: If a family unit is currently spending more than it is earning, it must draw on previously acquired wealth, borrow, or receive either private or public aid. Similarly, an identity exists for a family unit that is currently spending less than it is earning: It must be increasing its money holdings or be lending and acquiring other financial assets, or it must pay taxes or bestow gifts on others. When we consider businesses and governments, each unit in each group faces its own identities or constraints. Ultimately, *net* lending by households must equal *net* borrowing by businesses and governments.

DISEQUILIBRIUM Even though our individual family unit's accounts must balance, in the sense that the identity discussed previously must hold, sometimes the item that brings about the balance cannot continue indefinitely. *If family expenditures exceed family income and this situation is financed by borrowing, the household may be considered to be in disequilibrium because such a situation cannot continue indefinitely*. If such a deficit is financed by drawing on previously accumulated assets, the family may also be in disequilibrium because it cannot continue indefinitely to draw on its wealth. Eventually, the family will find it impossible to continue that lifestyle. (Of course, if the family members are retired, they may well be in equilibrium by drawing on previously acquired assets to finance current deficits. This example illustrates that it is necessary to understand all circumstances fully before pronouncing an economic unit in disequilibrium.)

EQUILIBRIUM Individual households, businesses, and governments, as well as the entire group of households, businesses, and governments, must eventually reach equilibrium. Certain economic adjustment mechanisms have evolved to ensure equilibrium. Deficit households must eventually increase their income or decrease their expenditures. They will find that they have to pay higher interest rates if they wish to borrow to finance their deficits. Eventually, their credit sources will dry up, and they will be forced into equilibrium. Businesses, on occasion, must lower costs or prices—or go bankrupt—to reach equilibrium.

AN ACCOUNTING IDENTITY AMONG NATIONS When people from different nations trade or interact, certain identities or constraints must also hold. People buy goods from people in other nations. They also lend to and present gifts to people in other nations. If residents of a nation interact with residents of other nations, an accounting identity ensures a balance (but not necessarily an equilibrium, as will soon become clear). Let's look at the three categories of balance of payments transactions: current account transactions, capital account transactions, and official reserve account transactions.

Current Account Transactions

During any designated period, all payments and gifts that are related to the purchase or sale of both goods and services constitute the **current account** in international trade. Major types of current account transactions include the exchange of merchandise, the exchange of services, and unilateral transfers.

Current account
A category of balance of payments transactions that measures the exchange of merchandise, the exchange of services, and unilateral transfers.

MERCHANDISE TRADE EXPORTS AND IMPORTS The largest portion of any nation's balance of payments current account is typically the importing and exporting of merchandise. During 2011, for example, as shown in lines 1 and 2 of Table 33-2 below, the United States exported an estimated $1,222.6 billion of merchandise and imported $1,824.8 billion. The balance of merchandise trade is defined as the difference between the value of merchandise exports and the value of merchandise imports. For 2011, the United States had a balance of merchandise trade deficit because the value of its merchandise imports exceeded the value of its merchandise exports. This deficit was about $602.2 billion (line 3).

SERVICE EXPORTS AND IMPORTS The balance of (merchandise) trade involves tangible items—things you can feel, touch, and see. Service exports and imports involve invisible or intangible items that are bought and sold, such as shipping, insurance, tourist expenditures, and banking services. Also, income earned by foreign residents on U.S. investments and income earned by U.S. residents on foreign investments are part of service imports and exports. As shown in lines 4 and 5 of Table 33-2, in 2011, estimated service exports were $524.8 billion, and service imports were $387.3 billion. Thus, the balance of services was about $137.5 billion in 2011 (line 6). Exports constitute receipts or inflows into the United States and are positive. Imports constitute payments abroad or outflows of money and are negative.

When we combine the balance of merchandise trade with the balance of services, we obtain a balance on goods and services equal to −$464.7 billion in 2011 (line 7).

TABLE 33-2

U.S. Balance of Payments Account, Estimated for 2011 (in billions of dollars)

Current Account		
(1) Exports of merchandise goods	+1,222.6	
(2) Imports of merchandise goods	−1,824.8	
(3) Balance of merchandise trade		−602.2
(4) Exports of services	+524.8	
(5) Imports of services	−387.3	
(6) Balance of services		+137.5
(7) Balance on goods and services [(3) + (6)]		−464.7
(8) Net unilateral transfers	−148.2	
(9) Balance on current account		−612.9
Capital Account		
(10) U.S. private capital going abroad	−1,238.6	
(11) Foreign private capital coming into the United States	+1,551.4*	
(12) Balance on capital account [(10) + (11)]		+312.8
(13) Balance on current account plus balance on capital account [(9) + (12)]		−300.1
Official Reserve Transactions Account		
(14) Official transactions balance		+300.1
(15) Total (balance)		0

Sources: U.S. Department of Commerce, Bureau of Economic Analysis; author's estimates.
*Includes an approximately $28 billion statistical discrepancy, probably uncounted capital inflows, many of which relate to the illegal drug trade.

UNILATERAL TRANSFERS U.S. residents give gifts to relatives and others abroad, the federal government makes grants to foreign nations, foreign residents give gifts to U.S. residents, and in the past some foreign governments have granted funds to the U.S. government. In the current account, we see that net unilateral transfers—the total amount of gifts given by U.S. residents and the government minus the total amount received from abroad by U.S. residents and the government—came to an estimated –$148.2 billion in 2011 (line 8). The minus sign before the number for unilateral transfers means that U.S. residents and the U.S. government gave more to foreign residents than foreign residents gave to U.S. residents.

BALANCING THE CURRENT ACCOUNT The balance on current account tracks the value of a country's exports of goods and services (including income on investments abroad) and transfer payments (private and government) relative to the value of that country's imports of goods and services and transfer payments (private and government). In 2011, it was estimated to be –$612.9 billion (line 9).

Go to www.econtoday.com/ch33 for the latest U.S. balance of payments data from the Bureau of Economic Analysis.

If the sum of net exports of goods and services plus net unilateral transfers plus net investment income exceeds zero, a* current account surplus *is said to exist. If this sum is negative, a current account deficit is said to exist. A* current account deficit *means that we are importing more goods and services than we are exporting. Such a deficit must be paid for by the export of financial assets.

Capital Account Transactions

Capital account
A category of balance of payments transactions that measures flows of financial assets.

In world markets, it is possible to buy and sell not only goods and services but also financial assets. These international transactions are measured in the **capital account.** Capital account transactions occur because of foreign investments—either by foreign residents investing in the United States or by U.S. residents investing in other countries. The purchase of shares of stock in British firms on the London stock market by a U.S. resident causes an outflow of funds from the United States to Britain. The construction of a Japanese automobile factory in the United States causes an inflow of funds from Japan to the United States. Any time foreign residents buy U.S. government securities, there is an inflow of funds from other countries to the United States. Any time U.S. residents buy foreign government securities, there is an outflow of funds from the United States to other countries. Loans to and from foreign residents cause outflows and inflows.

Line 10 of Table 33-2 on the preceding page indicates that in 2011, the value of private capital going out of the United States was an estimated –$1,238.6 billion, and line 11 shows that the value of private capital coming into the United States (including a statistical discrepancy) was $1,551.4 billion. U.S. capital going abroad constitutes payments or outflows and is therefore negative. Foreign capital coming into the United States constitutes receipts or inflows and is therefore positive. Thus, there was a positive net capital movement of $312.8 billion into the United States (line 12). This net private flow of capital is also called the balance on capital account.

There is a relationship between the current account balance and the capital account balance, assuming no interventions by the finance ministries or central banks of nations.

In the absence of interventions by finance ministries or central banks, the current account balance and the capital account balance must sum to zero. Stated differently, the current account deficit must equal the capital account surplus when governments or central banks do not engage in foreign exchange interventions. In this situation, any nation experiencing a current account deficit, such as the United States, must also be running a capital account surplus.

This basic relationship is apparent in the United States, as you can see in Figure 33-1 on the facing page. As the figure shows, U.S. current account deficits experienced since the early 1980s have largely been balanced by private capital inflows, but there are exceptions, for reasons that we explain in the next section.

FIGURE 33-1 The Relationship Between the Current Account and the Capital Account

The current account balance is the mirror image of the sum of the capital account balance and the official transactions balance. We can see this in years since 1970. When the current account balance was in surplus, the sum of the capital account balance and the official transactions balance was negative. When the current account balance was in deficit, the sum of the current account balance and the official transactions balance was positive.

Sources: International Monetary Fund; *Economic Indicators*.

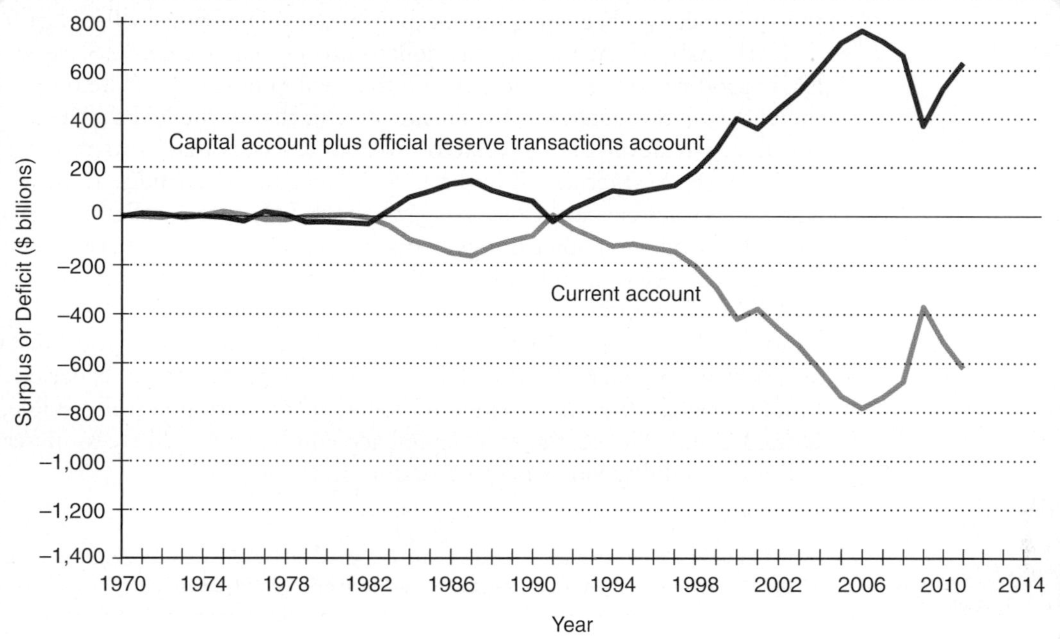

Official Reserve Account Transactions

The third type of balance of payments transaction concerns official reserve assets, which consist of the following:

1. Foreign currencies
2. Gold
3. **Special drawing rights (SDRs),** which are reserve assets that the **International Monetary Fund** created to be used by countries to settle international payment obligations
4. The reserve position in the International Monetary Fund
5. Financial assets held by an official agency, such as the U.S. Treasury Department

Special drawing rights (SDRs)
Reserve assets created by the International Monetary Fund for countries to use in settling international payment obligations.

International Monetary Fund
An agency founded to administer an international foreign exchange system and to lend to member countries that had balance of payments problems. The IMF now functions as a lender of last resort for national governments.

To consider how official reserve account transactions occur, look again at Table 33-2 on page 729. The surplus in the U.S. capital account was $312.8 billion. But the deficit in the U.S. current account was −$612.9 billion, so the United States had a net deficit on the combined accounts (line 13) of −$300.1 billion. In other words, the United States obtained less in foreign funds in all its international transactions than it used. How is this deficiency made up? By foreign central banks and governments adding to their U.S. funds, shown by the +$300.1 billion in official transactions on line 14 in Table 33-2. There is a plus sign on line 14 because this represents an *inflow* of foreign exchange in our international transactions.

The U.S. balance of payments deficit is measured by the official transactions figure on line 14. The balance (line 15) in Table 33-2 is zero, as it must be with double-entry bookkeeping. Hence, as shown in Figure 33-1 above, the current account balance is a mirror image of the sum of the official reserve transactions account and the capital account balance.

What Affects the Distribution of Account Balances Within the Balance of Payments?

A major factor affecting the distribution of account balances within any nation's balance of payments is its rate of inflation relative to that of its trading partners. Assume that the rates of inflation in the United States and in the European Monetary Union (EMU)—the nations that use the euro as their currency—are equal. Now suppose that all of a sudden, the U.S. inflation rate increases. EMU residents will find that U.S. products are becoming more expensive, and U.S. firms will export fewer of them to EMU nations. At the current dollar-euro exchange rate, U.S. residents will find EMU products relatively cheaper, and they will import more. The reverse will occur if the U.S. inflation rate suddenly falls relative to that of the EMU. All other things held constant, whenever the U.S. rate of inflation exceeds that of its trading partners, we expect to see a larger deficit in the U.S. balance of merchandise trade and in the U.S. current account balance. Conversely, when the U.S. rate of inflation is less than that of its trading partners, other things being constant, we expect to see a smaller deficit in the U.S. balance of merchandise trade and in the U.S. current account balance.

Another important factor that sometimes influences account balances within a nation's balance of payments is its relative political stability. Political instability causes *capital flight*. Owners of capital in countries anticipating or experiencing political instability will often move assets to countries that are politically stable, such as the United States. Hence, the U.S. capital account balance is likely to increase whenever political instability looms in other nations in the world.

QUICK QUIZ See page 748 for the answers. Review concepts from this section in MyEconLab.

The __________ of __________ reflects the value of all transactions in international trade, including goods, services, financial assets, and gifts.

The merchandise trade balance gives us the difference between exports and imports of __________ items.

Included in the __________ account along with merchandise trade are service exports and imports relating to commerce in intangible items, such as shipping, insurance, and tourist expenditures. The __________ account also includes income earned by foreign residents on U.S. investments and income earned by U.S. residents on foreign investments.

__________ __________ involve international private gifts and federal government grants or gifts to foreign nations.

When we add the balance of merchandise trade and the balance of services and take account of net unilateral transfers and net investment income, we come up with the balance on the __________ account, a summary statistic.

There are also __________ account transactions that relate to the buying and selling of financial assets. Foreign capital is always entering the United States, and U.S. capital is always flowing abroad. The difference is called the balance on the __________ account.

Another type of balance of payments transaction concerns the __________ __________ assets of individual countries, or what is often simply called official transactions. By standard accounting convention, official transactions are exactly equal to but opposite in sign from the sum of the current account balance and the capital account balance.

Account balances within a nation's balance of payments can be affected by its relative rate of __________ and by its __________ stability relative to other nations.

Determining Foreign Exchange Rates

When you buy foreign products, such as European pharmaceuticals, you have dollars with which to pay the European manufacturer. The European manufacturer, however, cannot pay workers in dollars. The workers are European, they live in Europe, and they must have euros to buy goods and services in nations that are members of the European Monetary Union (EMU) and use the euro as their currency. There must therefore be a way to exchange dollars for euros that the pharmaceuticals manufacturer will accept. That exchange occurs in a **foreign exchange market,** which in this case involves the exchange of euros and dollars.

Foreign exchange market
A market in which households, firms, and governments buy and sell national currencies.

The particular **exchange rate** between euros and dollars that prevails—the dollar price of the euro—depends on the current demand for and supply of euros and dollars. In a sense, then, our analysis of the exchange rate between dollars and euros will be familiar, for we have used supply and demand throughout this book. If it costs you $1.20 to buy 1 euro, that is the foreign exchange rate determined by the current demand for and supply of euros in the foreign exchange market. The European person going to the foreign exchange market would need about 0.83 euro to buy 1 dollar.

Exchange rate
The price of one nation's currency in terms of the currency of another country.

Now let's consider what determines the demand for and supply of foreign currency in the foreign exchange market. We will continue to assume that the only two regions in the world are Europe and the United States.

Demand for and Supply of Foreign Currency

You wish to purchase European-produced pharmaceuticals directly from a manufacturer located in Europe. To do so, you must have euros. You go to the foreign exchange market (or your U.S. bank). Your desire to buy the pharmaceuticals therefore causes you to offer (supply) dollars to the foreign exchange market. Your demand for euros is equivalent to your supply of dollars to the foreign exchange market.

> ***Every U.S. transaction involving the importation of foreign goods constitutes a supply of dollars and a demand for some foreign currency, and the opposite is true for export transactions.***

In this case, the import transaction constitutes a demand for euros.

In our example, we will assume that only two goods are being traded, European pharmaceuticals and U.S. computer printers. The U.S. demand for European pharmaceuticals creates a supply of dollars and a demand for euros in the foreign exchange market. Similarly, the European demand for U.S. computer printers creates a supply of euros and a demand for dollars in the foreign exchange market. Under a system of **flexible exchange rates,** the supply of and demand for dollars and euros in the foreign exchange market will determine the equilibrium foreign exchange rate. The equilibrium exchange rate will tell us how many euros a dollar can be exchanged for—that is, the euro price of dollars—or how many dollars a euro can be exchanged for—the dollar price of euros.

Flexible exchange rates
Exchange rates that are allowed to fluctuate in the open market in response to changes in supply and demand. Sometimes called *floating exchange rates*.

The Equilibrium Foreign Exchange Rate

To determine the equilibrium foreign exchange rate, we have to find out what determines the demand for and supply of foreign exchange. We will ignore for the moment any speculative aspect of buying foreign exchange. That is, we assume that there are no individuals who wish to buy euros simply because they think that their price will go up in the future.

Go to **www.econtoday.com/ch33** for recent data from the Federal Reserve Bank of St. Louis on the exchange value of the U.S. dollar relative to the major currencies of the world.

The idea of an exchange rate is no different from the idea of paying a certain price for something you want to buy. Suppose that you have to pay about $1.50 for a cup of coffee. If the price goes up to $2.50, you will probably buy fewer cups. If the price goes down to 50 cents, you will likely buy more. In other words, the demand curve for cups of coffee, expressed in terms of dollars, slopes downward following the law of demand. The demand curve for euros slopes downward also, and we will see why.

Let's think more closely about the demand schedule for euros. If it costs you $1.10 to purchase 1 euro, that is the exchange rate between dollars and euros. If tomorrow you have to pay $1.25 for the same euro, the exchange rate would have changed. Looking at such a change, we would say that there has been an **appreciation** in the value of the euro in the foreign exchange market. But another way to view this increase in the value of the euro is to say that there has been a **depreciation** in the value of the dollar in the foreign exchange market. The dollar used to buy almost 0.91 euro, but tomorrow the dollar will be able to buy only 0.80 euro at a price of $1.25 per euro. If the dollar price of euros rises, you will probably demand fewer euros. Why? The answer lies in the reason you and others demand euros in the first place.

Appreciation
An increase in the exchange value of one nation's currency in terms of the currency of another nation.

Depreciation
A decrease in the exchange value of one nation's currency in terms of the currency of another nation.

APPRECIATION AND DEPRECIATION OF EUROS Recall that in our example, you and others demand euros to buy European pharmaceuticals. The demand curve for European pharmaceuticals follows the law of demand and therefore slopes downward. If it costs more U.S. dollars to buy the same quantity of European pharmaceuticals, presumably you and other U.S. residents will not buy the same quantity. Your quantity demanded will be less. We say that your demand for euros is *derived from* your demand for European pharmaceuticals. In panel (a) of Figure 33-2 below, we present

Panel (a)
Demand Schedule for Packages of European Pharmaceuticals in the United States per Week

Price per Package	Quantity Demanded
$130	100
125	300
120	500
115	700

Panel (b)
U.S. Demand Curve for European Pharmaceuticals

Panel (c)
Euros Required to Purchase Quantity Demanded (at P = 100 euros per package of pharmaceuticals)

Quantity Demanded	Euros Required
100	10,000
300	30,000
500	50,000
700	70,000

Panel (d)
Derived Demand Schedule for Euros in the United States with Which to Pay for Imports of Pharmaceuticals

Dollar Price of One Euro	Dollar Price of Pharmaceuticals	Quantity of Pharmaceuticals Demanded	Quantity of Euros Demanded per Week
$1.30	$130	100	10,000
1.25	125	300	30,000
1.20	120	500	50,000
1.15	115	700	70,000

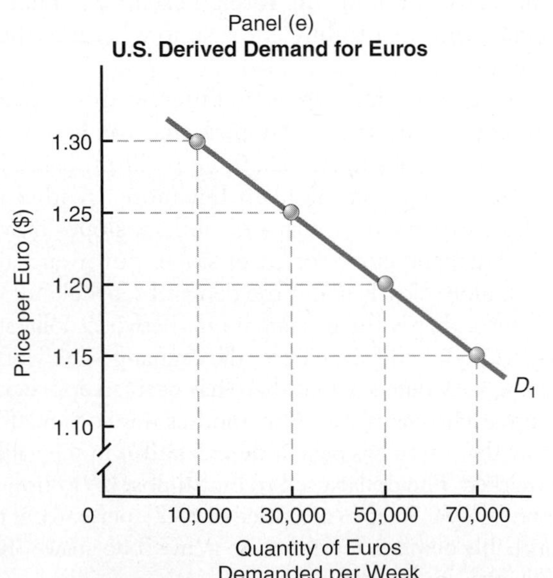

FIGURE 33-2 Deriving the Demand for Euros

In panel (a), we show the demand schedule for European pharmaceuticals in the United States, expressed in terms of dollars per package of pharmaceuticals. In panel (b), we show the demand curve, D, which slopes downward. In panel (c), we show the number of euros required to purchase up to 700 packages of pharmaceuticals. If the price per package of pharmaceuticals is 100 euros, we can now find the quantity of euros needed to pay for the various quantities demanded. In panel (d), we see the derived demand for euros in the United States in order to purchase the various quantities of pharmaceuticals given in panel (a). The resultant demand curve, D_1, is shown in panel (e). This is the U.S. derived demand for euros.

the hypothetical demand schedule for packages of European pharmaceuticals by a representative set of U.S. consumers during a typical week. In panel (b) of Figure 33-2 on the facing page, we show graphically the U.S. demand curve for European pharmaceuticals in terms of U.S. dollars taken from panel (a).

AN EXAMPLE OF DERIVED DEMAND Let us assume that the price of a package of European pharmaceuticals in Europe is 100 euros. Given that price, we can find the number of euros required to purchase 500 packages of European pharmaceuticals. That information is given in panel (c) of Figure 33-2 on the facing page. If purchasing one package of European pharmaceuticals requires 100 euros, 500 packages require 50,000 euros. Now we have enough information to determine the derived demand curve for euros. If 1 euro costs $1.20, a package of pharmaceuticals would cost $120 (100 euros per package × $1.20 per euro = $120 per package). At $120 per package, the representative group of U.S. consumers would, we see from panel (a) of Figure 33-2, demand 500 packages of pharmaceuticals.

From panel (c), we see that 50,000 euros would be demanded to buy the 500 packages of pharmaceuticals. We show this quantity demanded in panel (d). In panel (e), we draw the derived demand curve for euros. Now consider what happens if the price of euros goes up to $1.25. A package of European pharmaceuticals priced at 100 euros in Europe would now cost $125. From panel (a), we see that at $125 per package, 300 packages of pharmaceuticals will be imported from Europe into the United States by our representative group of U.S. consumers. From panel (c), we see that 300 packages of pharmaceuticals would require 30,000 euros to be purchased. Thus, in panels (d) and (e), we see that at a price of $1.25 per euro, the quantity demanded will be 30,000 euros.

We continue similar calculations all the way up to a price of $1.30 per euro. At that price, a package of European pharmaceuticals costing 100 euros in Europe would cost $130, and our representative U.S. consumers would import only 100 packages of pharmaceuticals.

DOWNWARD-SLOPING DERIVED DEMAND As can be expected, as the price of the euro rises, the quantity demanded will fall. The only difference here from the standard demand analysis developed in Chapter 3 and used throughout this text is that the demand for euros is derived from the demand for a final product—European pharmaceuticals in our example.

SUPPLY OF EUROS Assume that European pharmaceutical manufacturers buy U.S. computer printers. The supply of euros is a derived supply in that it is derived from the European demand for U.S. computer printers. We could go through an example similar to the one for pharmaceuticals to come up with a supply schedule of euros in Europe. It slopes upward. Obviously, Europeans want dollars to purchase U.S. goods. European residents will be willing to supply more euros when the dollar price of euros goes up, because they can then buy more U.S. goods with the same quantity of euros. That is, the euro would be worth more in exchange for U.S. goods than when the dollar price for euros was lower.

AN EXAMPLE Let's take an example. Suppose a U.S.-produced computer printer costs $200. If the exchange rate is $1.20 per euro, a European resident will have to come up with 166.67 euros ($200 ÷ $1.20 per euro = 166.67 euros) to buy one computer printer. If, however, the exchange rate goes up to $1.25 per euro, a European resident must come up with only 160 euros ($200 ÷ $1.25 per euro = 160 euros) to buy a U.S. computer printer. At this lower price (in euros) of U.S. computer printers, Europeans will demand a larger quantity. In other words, as the price of euros goes up in terms of dollars, the quantity of U.S. computer printers demanded will go up, and hence the quantity of euros supplied will go up. Therefore, the supply schedule of euros, which is derived from the European demand for U.S. goods, will slope upward, as seen in Figure 33-3 at the top of the following page.

FIGURE 33-3 The Supply of Euros

If the market price of a U.S.-produced computer printer is $200, then at an exchange rate of $1.20 per euro, the price of the printer to a European consumer is 167.67 euros. If the exchange rate rises to $1.25 per euro, the European price of the printer falls to 160 euros. This induces an increase in the quantity of printers demanded by European consumers and consequently an increase in the quantity of euros supplied in exchange for dollars in the foreign exchange market. In contrast, if the exchange rate falls to $1.15 per euro, the European price of the printer rises to 173.91 euros. This causes a decrease in the quantity of printers demanded by European consumers. As a result, there is a decline in the quantity of euros supplied in exchange for dollars in the foreign exchange market. Hence, the euro supply curve slopes up.

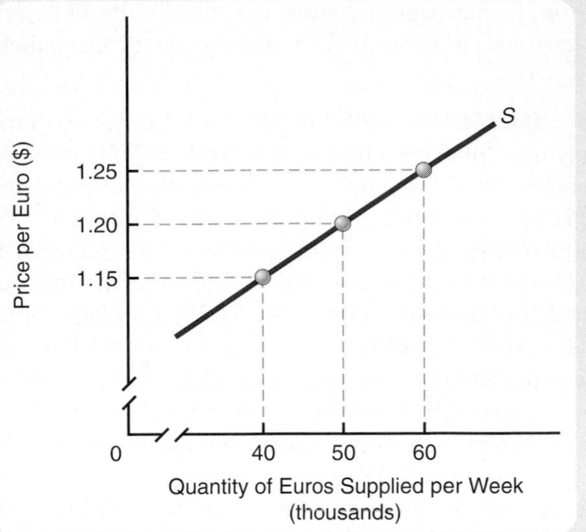

TOTAL DEMAND FOR AND SUPPLY OF EUROS Let us now look at the total demand for and supply of euros. We take all U.S. consumers of European pharmaceuticals and all European consumers of U.S. computer printers and put their demands for and supplies of euros together into one diagram. Thus, we are showing the total demand for and total supply of euros. The horizontal axis in Figure 33-4 below represents the quantity of foreign exchange—the number of euros per year. The vertical axis represents the exchange rate—the price of foreign currency (euros) expressed in dollars (per euro). The foreign currency price of $1.25 per euro means it will cost you $1.25 to buy 1 euro. At the foreign currency price of $1.20 per euro, you know that it will cost you $1.20 to buy 1 euro. The equilibrium, *E*, is again established at $1.20 for 1 euro.

In our hypothetical example, assuming that there are only representative groups of pharmaceutical consumers in the United States and computer printer consumers in Europe, the equilibrium exchange rate will be set at $1.20 per euro.

This equilibrium is not established because U.S. residents like to buy euros or because Europeans like to buy dollars. Rather, the equilibrium exchange rate depends on how many computer printers Europeans want and how many European pharma-

FIGURE 33-4 Total Demand for and Supply of Euros

The market supply curve for euros results from the total European demand for U.S. computer printers. The demand curve, *D*, slopes downward like most demand curves, and the supply curve, *S*, slopes upward. The foreign exchange price, or the U.S. dollar price of euros, is given on the vertical axis. The number of euros is represented on the horizontal axis. If the foreign exchange rate is $1.25—that is, if it takes $1.25 to buy 1 euro—U.S. residents will demand 20 billion euros. The equilibrium exchange rate is at the intersection of *D* and *S*, or point *E*. The equilibrium exchange rate is $1.20 per euro. At this point, 30 billion euros are both demanded and supplied each year.

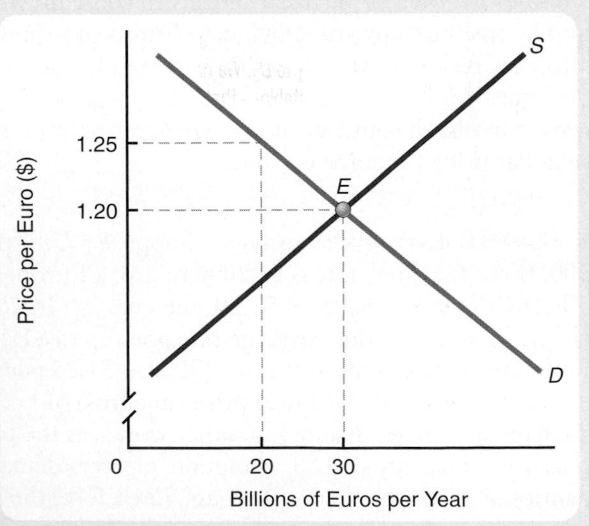

ceuticals U.S. residents want (given their respective incomes, their tastes, and, in our example, the relative prices of pharmaceuticals and computer printers).

A SHIFT IN DEMAND Assume that a successful advertising campaign by U.S. pharmaceutical importers has caused U.S. demand for European pharmaceuticals to rise. U.S. residents demand more pharmaceuticals at all prices. Their demand curve for European pharmaceuticals has shifted outward to the right.

The increased demand for European pharmaceuticals can be translated into an increased demand for euros. All U.S. residents clamoring for European pharmaceuticals will supply more dollars to the foreign exchange market while demanding more euros to pay for the pharmaceuticals. Figure 33-5 below presents a new demand schedule, D_2, for euros. This demand schedule is to the right of the original demand schedule. If Europeans do not change their desire for U.S. computer printers, the supply schedule for euros will remain stable.

A new equilibrium will be established at a higher exchange rate. In our particular example, the new equilibrium is established at an exchange rate of \$1.25 per euro. It now takes \$1.25 to buy 1 euro, whereas formerly it took \$1.20. This will be translated into an increase in the price of European pharmaceuticals to U.S. residents and into a decrease in the price of U.S. computer printers to Europeans. For example, a package of European pharmaceuticals priced at 100 euros that sold for \$120 in the United States will now be priced at \$125. Conversely, a U.S. printer priced at \$200 that previously sold for 166.67 euros will now sell for 160 euros.

You Are There

To think about how people try to earn currency-trading profits based on their predictions about the future positions of the demand and supply curves in the foreign exchange market, consider **Trading in the Real Estate Business for Trading Currencies,** on page 743.

Why Not . . . encourage U.S. exports by forcing the dollar's value to fall?

A lower value for the U.S. dollar in terms of foreign currencies makes U.S. exports less expensive to foreign residents. Thus, a decrease in the dollar's exchange value would indeed encourage U.S. exports, which would be consistent with the U.S. government's official goal of doubling exports by 2015. Economists who study foreign exchange markets have estimated that, other things being equal, the U.S. dollar's value would have to decline by nearly 40 percent to generate a doubling of U.S. exports.

So far, however, the interaction of supply and demand in foreign exchange markets has not yielded such a dramatic reduction in the dollar's value. In fact, shortly after the U.S. government announced its 2015 export target, the value of the dollar *increased* in relation to most of the world's currencies. As a consequence, U.S. goods and services became more expensive to people in other nations, which discouraged foreign purchases and thereby contributed to a slight *drop* in U.S. exports.

FIGURE 33-5 A Shift in the Demand Schedule

The demand schedule for European pharmaceuticals shifts to the right, causing the derived demand schedule for euros to shift to the right also. We have shown this as a shift from D_1 to D_2. We have assumed that the supply schedule for euros has remained stable—that is, European demand for U.S. computer printers has remained constant. The old equilibrium foreign exchange rate was \$1.20 per euro. The new equilibrium exchange rate will be E_2. It will now cost \$1.25 to buy 1 euro. The higher price of euros will be translated into a higher U.S. dollar price for European pharmaceuticals and a lower euro price for U.S. computer printers.

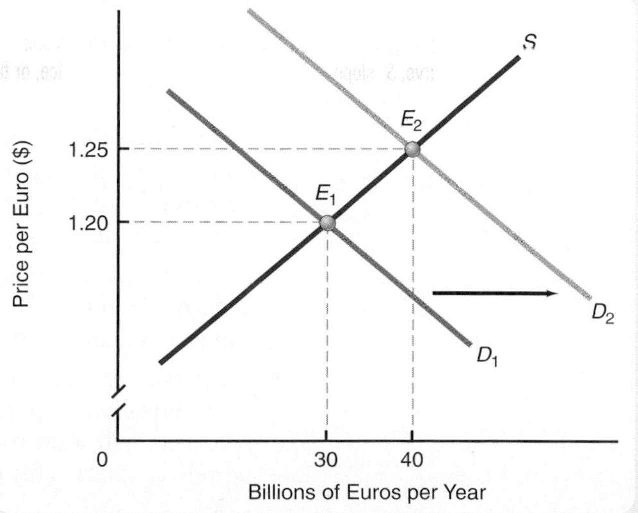

FIGURE 33-6 A Shift in the Supply of Euros

There has been a shift in the supply curve for euros. The new equilibrium will occur at E_1, meaning that \$1.15, rather than \$1.20, will now buy 1 euro. After the exchange rate adjustment, the annual amount of euros demanded and supplied will increase from 30 billion to 60 billion.

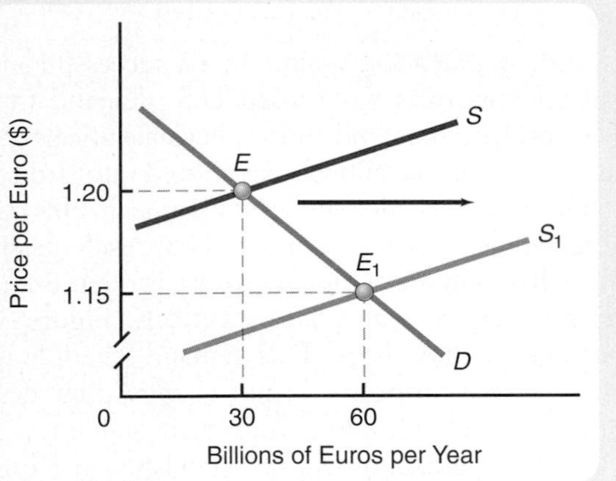

A SHIFT IN SUPPLY We just assumed that the U.S. demand for European pharmaceuticals shifted due to a successful ad campaign. The demand for euros is derived from the demand by U.S. residents for pharmaceuticals. This change in pharmaceuticals demand is translated into a shift in the demand curve for euros. As an alternative exercise, we might assume that the supply curve of euros shifts outward to the right. Such a supply shift could occur for many reasons, one of which is a relative rise in the European price level. For example, if the prices of all European-manufactured computer peripherals went up 20 percent in euros, U.S. computer printers would become relatively cheaper. That would mean that European residents would want to buy more U.S. computer printers. But remember that when they want to buy more U.S. printers, they supply more euros to the foreign exchange market.

Thus, we see in Figure 33-6 above that the supply curve of euros moves from S to S_1. In the absence of restrictions—that is, in a system of flexible exchange rates—the new equilibrium exchange rate will be \$1.15 equals 1 euro. The quantity of euros demanded and supplied will increase from 30 billion per year to 60 billion per year. We say, then, that in a flexible international exchange rate system, shifts in the demand for and supply of foreign currencies will cause changes in the equilibrium foreign exchange rates. Those rates will remain in effect until world supply or demand shifts.

Market Determinants of Exchange Rates

The foreign exchange market is affected by many other variables in addition to changes in relative price levels, including the following:

- *Changes in real interest rates.* Suppose that the U.S. interest rate, corrected for people's expectations of inflation, increases relative to the rest of the world. Then international investors elsewhere seeking the higher returns now available in the United States will increase their demand for dollar-denominated assets, thereby increasing the demand for dollars in foreign exchange markets. An increased demand for dollars in foreign exchange markets, other things held constant, will cause the dollar to appreciate and other currencies to depreciate.
- *Changes in consumer preferences.* If Germany's citizens suddenly develop a taste for U.S.-made automobiles, this will increase the derived demand for U.S. dollars in foreign exchange markets.
- *Perceptions of economic stability.* As already mentioned, if the United States looks economically and politically more stable relative to other countries, more foreign residents will want to put their savings into U.S. assets rather than in their own domestic assets. This will increase the demand for dollars.

Why are changes in countries' currency values positively related to the nations' current account balances?

INTERNATIONAL EXAMPLE Current Account Balances and Currency Values

Figure 33-7 below shows that there is a positive relationship between nations' current account balances and percentage changes in the values of those nations' currencies. Recall that in a country with a current account surplus, spending by residents of other nations on that country's exports of goods and services exceeds expenditures by that country's residents on imported items. It is likely, therefore, that the net outcome will be an appreciation of the country's currency. Thus, as depicted in Figure 33-7, countries with current account surpluses have a tendency to experience currency appreciations. In contrast, the currencies of nations with current account deficits tend to depreciate.

FOR CRITICAL ANALYSIS

Why is the value of a nation's current account balance not the only determinant of whether its currency appreciates or depreciates? (Hint: Flows of financial assets also affect the demand for and supply of a currency, and these flows are measured in a country's capital account and official reserve transactions account.)

FIGURE 33-7 Percentage Changes in Currency Values and Current Account Balances as Percentages of GDP for Selected Nations in the 2000s

The currencies of nations with current account surpluses tend to experience appreciations, and the currencies of nations with current account deficits tend to experience depreciations.

Source: Bank for International Settlements.

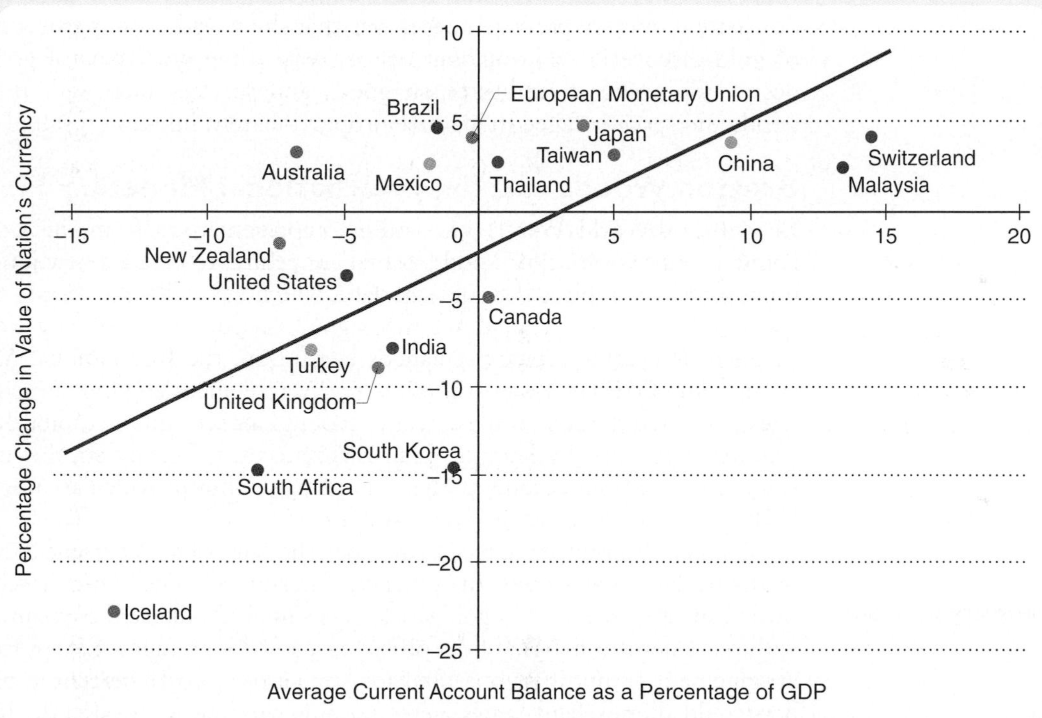

QUICK QUIZ

See page 748 for the answers. Review concepts from this section in MyEconLab.

The foreign __________ __________ is the rate at which one country's currency can be exchanged for another's.

The __________ for foreign exchange is a derived __________, which is derived from the demand for foreign goods and services (and financial assets). The __________ of foreign exchange is derived from foreign residents' demands for U.S. goods and services.

The demand curve of foreign exchange slopes __________, and the supply curve of foreign exchange slopes __________. The equilibrium foreign exchange rate occurs at the intersection of the demand and supply curves for a currency.

A __________ in the demand for foreign goods will result in a shift in the __________ for foreign exchange, thereby changing the equilibrium foreign exchange rate. A shift in the supply of foreign currency will also cause a change in the equilibrium exchange rate.

The Gold Standard and the International Monetary Fund

The current system of more or less freely floating exchange rates is a relatively recent development. In the past, we have had periods of a gold standard, fixed exchange rates under the International Monetary Fund, and variants of the two.

The Gold Standard

Until the 1930s, many nations were on a gold standard. The value of their domestic currency was fixed, or *pegged*, in units of gold. Nations operating under this gold standard agreed to redeem their currencies for a fixed amount of gold at the request of any holder of that currency. Although gold was not necessarily the means of exchange for world trade, it was the unit to which all currencies under the gold standard were pegged. And because all currencies in the system were pegged to gold, exchange rates between those currencies were fixed.

Two problems plagued the gold standard, however. One was that by fixing the value of its currency in relation to the amount of gold, a nation gave up control of its domestic monetary policy. Another was that the world's commerce was at the mercy of gold discoveries. Throughout history, each time new veins of gold were found, desired domestic expenditures on goods and services increased. If production of goods and services failed to increase proportionately, inflation resulted.

Bretton Woods and the International Monetary Fund

In 1944, as World War II was ending, representatives from the world's capitalist countries met in Bretton Woods, New Hampshire, to create a new international payment system to replace the gold standard, which had collapsed during the 1930s. The Bretton Woods Agreement Act was signed on July 31, 1945, by President Harry Truman. It created a new permanent institution, the International Monetary Fund (IMF). The IMF's task was to administer the agreement and to lend to member countries for which the sum of the current account balance and the capital account balance was negative, thereby helping them maintain an offsetting surplus in their official reserve transactions accounts. The arrangements thus provided are now called the old IMF system or the Bretton Woods system.

Par value
The officially determined value of a currency.

Member governments agreed to maintain the value of their currencies within 1 percent of the declared **par value**—the officially determined value. The United States, which owned most of the world's gold stock, was similarly obligated to maintain gold prices within a 1 percent margin of the official rate of $35 an ounce. Except for a transitional arrangement permitting a one-time adjustment of up to 10 percent in par value, members could alter exchange rates thereafter only with the approval of the IMF.

On August 15, 1971, President Richard Nixon suspended the convertibility of the dollar into gold. On December 18, 1971, the United States officially devalued the dollar—that is, lowered its official value—relative to the currencies of 14 major industrial nations. Finally, on March 16, 1973, the finance ministers of the European Economic Community (now the European Union) announced that they would let their currencies float against the dollar, something Japan had already begun doing with its yen. Since 1973, the United States and most other trading countries have had either freely floating exchange rates or managed ("dirty") floating exchange rates, in which their governments or central banks intervene from time to time to try to influence world market exchange rates.

Fixed versus Floating Exchange Rates

The United States went off the Bretton Woods system of fixed exchange rates in 1973. As Figure 33-8 at the top of the next page indicates, many other nations of the world have been less willing to permit the values of their currencies to vary in the foreign exchange markets.

FIGURE 33-8 Current Foreign Exchange Rate Arrangements

Today, 21 percent of the member nations of the International Monetary Fund have an independent float, and 24 percent have a managed float exchange rate arrangement. Another 12 percent of all nations use the currencies of other nations instead of issuing their own currencies.

Source: International Monetary Fund.

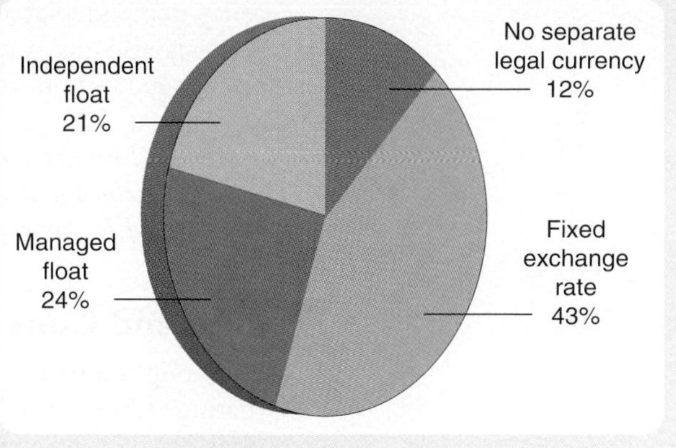

Fixing the Exchange Rate

How did nations fix their exchange rates in years past? How do many countries accomplish this today? Figure 33-9 below shows the market for dinars, the currency of Bahrain. At the initial equilibrium point E_1, U.S. residents had to give up \$2.66 to obtain 1 dinar. Suppose now that there is an increase in the supply of dinars for dollars, perhaps because Bahraini residents wish to buy more U.S. goods. Other things being equal, the result would be a movement to point E_2 in Figure 33-9. The dollar value of the dinar would fall to \$2.00.

To prevent a dinar depreciation from occurring, however, the Central Bank of Bahrain could increase the demand for dinars in the foreign exchange market by purchasing dinars with dollars. The Central Bank of Bahrain can do this using dollars that it has on hand as part of its *foreign exchange reserves*. All central banks hold reserves of foreign currencies. Because the U.S. dollar is a key international currency, the Central Bank of Bahrain and other central banks typically hold billions of dollars in reserve so that they can make transactions such as the one in this example.

Note that a sufficiently large purchase of dinars could, as shown in Figure 33-9, cause the demand curve to shift rightward to achieve the new equilibrium point E_3, at which the dinar's value remains at \$2.66. Provided that it has enough dollar reserves on hand, the Central Bank of Bahrain could maintain—effectively fix—the exchange rate in the face of the rise in the supply of dinars.

FIGURE 33-9 A Fixed Exchange Rate

This figure illustrates how the Central Bank of Bahrain could fix the dollar-dinar exchange rate in the face of an increase in the supply of dinars caused by a rise in the demand for U.S. goods by Bahraini residents. In the absence of any action by the Central Bank of Bahrain, the result would be a movement from point E_1 to point E_2. The dollar value of the dinar would fall from \$2.66 to \$2.00. The Central Bank of Bahrain can prevent this exchange rate change by purchasing dinars with dollars in the foreign exchange market, thereby increasing the demand for dinars. At the new equilibrium point, E_3, the dinar's value remains at \$2.66.

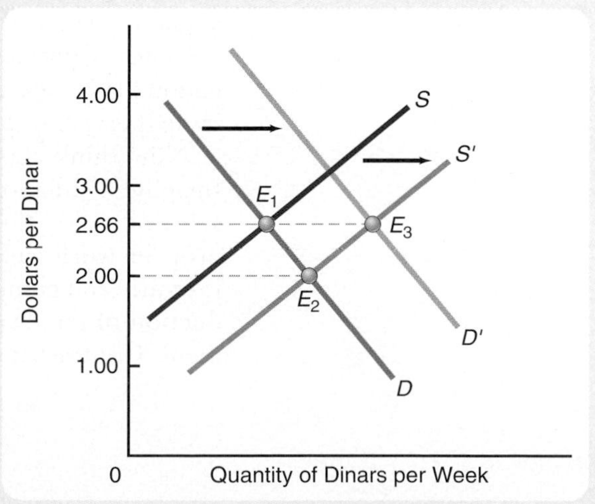

The Central Bank of Bahrain has maintained the dollar-dinar exchange rate in this manner since 2001. This basic approach—varying the amount of the national currency demanded at any given exchange rate in foreign exchange markets when necessary—is also the way that *any* central bank seeks to keep its nation's currency value unchanged in light of changing market forces.

Central banks can keep exchange rates fixed as long as they have enough foreign exchange reserves to deal with potentially long-lasting changes in the demand for or supply of their nation's currency.

Pros and Cons of a Fixed Exchange Rate

Why might a nation such as Bahrain wish to keep the value of its currency from fluctuating? One reason is that changes in the exchange rate can affect the market values of assets that are denominated in foreign currencies. This can increase the financial risks that a nation's residents face, thereby forcing them to incur costs to avoid these risks.

Foreign exchange risk
The possibility that changes in the value of a nation's currency will result in variations in the market value of assets.

FOREIGN EXCHANGE RISK The possibility that variations in the market value of assets can take place due to changes in the value of a nation's currency is the **foreign exchange risk** that residents of a country face because their nation's currency value can vary. For instance, if companies in Bahrain had many loans denominated in dollars but earned nearly all their revenues in dinars from sales within Bahrain, a decline in the dollar value of the dinar would mean that Bahraini companies would have to allocate a larger portion of their earnings to make the same *dollar* loan payments as before. Thus, a fall in the dinar's value would increase the operating costs of these companies, thereby reducing their profitability and raising the likelihood of eventual bankruptcy.

Hedge
A financial strategy that reduces the chance of suffering losses arising from foreign exchange risk.

Limiting foreign exchange risk is a classic rationale for adopting a fixed exchange rate. Nevertheless, a country's residents are not defenseless against foreign exchange risk. In what is known as a **hedge,** they can adopt strategies intended to offset the risk arising from exchange rate variations. For example, a company in Bahrain that has significant euro earnings from sales in Germany but sizable loans from U.S. investors could arrange to convert its euro earnings into dollars via special types of foreign exchange contracts called *currency swaps*. The Bahraini company could likewise avoid holdings of dinars and shield itself—*hedge*—against variations in the dinar's value.

THE EXCHANGE RATE AS A SHOCK ABSORBER If fixing the exchange rate limits foreign exchange risk, why do so many nations allow the exchange rates to float? The answer must be that there are potential drawbacks associated with fixing exchange rates. One is that exchange rate variations can actually perform a valuable service for a nation's economy. Consider a situation in which residents of a nation speak only their own nation's language. As a result, the country's residents are very *immobile*: They cannot trade their labor skills outside their own nation's borders.

Now think about what happens if this nation chooses to fix its exchange rate. Imagine a situation in which other countries begin to sell products that are close substitutes for the products its people specialize in producing, causing a sizable drop in worldwide demand for that nation's goods. If wages and prices do not instantly and completely adjust downward, the result will be a sharp decline in production of goods and services, a falloff in national income, and higher unemployment. Contrast this situation with one which the exchange rate floats. In this case, a sizable decline in outside demand for the nation's products will cause it to experience a trade deficit, which will lead to a significant drop in the demand for that nation's currency. As a result, the nation's currency will experience a sizable depreciation, making the goods that the nation offers to sell abroad much less expensive in other countries. People abroad who continue to consume the nation's products will increase their purchases, and the nation's exports will increase. Its production will begin to recover somewhat, as will its residents' incomes. Unemployment will begin to fall.

This example illustrates how exchange rate variations can be beneficial, especially if a nation's residents are relatively immobile. It can be difficult, for example, for a Polish resident who has never studied Portuguese to move to Lisbon, even if she is highly qualified for available jobs there. If many residents of Poland face similar linguistic or cultural barriers, Poland could be better off with a floating exchange rate even if its residents must incur significant costs hedging against foreign exchange risk as a result.

QUICK QUIZ See page 748 for the answers. **Review concepts from this section in MyEconLab.**

The International Monetary Fund was developed after World War II as an institution to maintain __________ exchange rates in the world. Since 1973, however, __________ exchange rates have disappeared in most major trading countries. For these nations, exchange rates are largely determined by the forces of demand and supply in global foreign exchange markets.

Central banks can fix exchange rates by buying or selling foreign __________ and thereby adding to or subtracting from their foreign exchange __________.

Although fixing the exchange rate helps protect a nation's residents from foreign exchange __________, this policy makes less mobile residents susceptible to greater volatility in income and employment.

You Are There

Trading in the Real Estate Business for Trading Currencies

Ray Firetag, a former real estate agent in Elk Grove, California, now earns most of his income from currency trading. Today, he bought Australian dollars with Japanese yen at a high rate of exchange in terms of dollars and then traded those dollars back for yen at a lower exchange rate. On other days, Firetag may seek to profit by buying and selling a different set of currencies.

Firetag is one of thousands of individuals who now trade foreign currencies online from their homes. Firetag and other currency traders attempt to predict changes in the positions of demand and supply curves in the foreign exchange markets. For instance, Firetag initially purchased Australian dollars because he anticipated that the market demand for Japanese yen in exchange for Australian dollars would fall during the day, thereby pushing down the exchange rate measured in dollars per yen. This enabled him to buy more yen later in the day with his dollars, thereby earning profits measured in yen.

All told, the daily foreign exchange trading by individual traders such as Firetag amounts to about $120 billion. This amount is minuscule, however, compared with the volume of trading by financial institutions and multinational companies, which typically exceeds $4 *trillion* each day.

Critical Analysis Questions

1. What would have happened to Firetag's ability to earn trading profits on this particular day if the demand for yen had risen later in the day?
2. If Firetag expects the supply of yen to increase tomorrow morning (all other things held constant), should he trade yen for dollars or vice versa before the end of today's trading?

ISSUES & APPLICATIONS

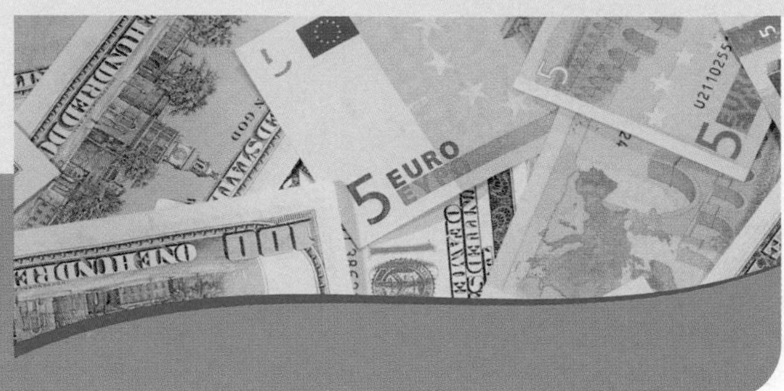

Will the Euro's Global Currency Status Be Short-Lived?

CONCEPTS APPLIED

- Foreign Exchange Market
- Foreign Exchange Risk
- Exchange Rate

As Table 33-3 below indicates, the U.S. dollar is only the latest in a long line of *global currencies* that people in *other* nations widely utilize in international trade and finance. During the 2000s, the European *euro* emerged to rival the dollar as the preeminent global currency. A few short years later, however, the euro's status has become in doubt. Let's consider why this is so.

TABLE 33-3

Key Currencies Throughout World History

The U.S. dollar is only the most recent of many currencies that have figured predominantly in the world economy.

Source: Robert Mundell, "The International Impact of the Euro and Its Implications for Transition Economies," in *Central Banking, Monetary Policies, and the Implications for Transition Economies,* ed. Mario Blejer and Marko Skreb (Boston: Kluwer Academic Publishers, 1999), pp. 403–428.

Period	Nation	Currencies
Pre–7th century BC	Babylonia	Shekel
7th–6th centuries BC	Persia	Daric
5th–3rd centuries BC	Greece, Macedonia	Drachma, stater
3rd century BC–4th century AD	Rome	Solidus, denarius, seterce, aureus
4th–13th centuries	Byzantium	Solidus, besant
7th–13th centuries	Mecca/Damascus/Baghdad	Dirham, dinar
9th–13th centuries	China	Tael, chuen
13th–16th centuries	Italy	Florin, grosso, sequin, ducat
16th–17th centuries	Spain	Real, escudo
17th–18th centuries	France	Denier, sol, louis d'or
18th century	India	Rupee, mohur
19th century	France	Franc
19th–20th centuries	Britain	Pound
20th–early 21st centuries	United States	Dollar

Features Possessed by a Global Currency

A nation's currency typically must possess two key characteristics before it can emerge as a global currency. One characteristic is that the currency must be widely traded in foreign exchange markets, typically because the nation that issues the currency generates substantial flows of exports and imports relative to other nations. In the past, this condition was satisfied for the currencies and nations listed in Table 33-3.

The second key feature that a currency must possess to attain *and* maintain the status of vehicle currency is a low level of foreign exchange risk. If the currency's exchange rate is expected to retain its value relative to the currencies of other nations, then people residing in other nations will be more likely to be willing to hold large volumes of the currency for use in trade and finance.

Why the Euro's Global Currency Status Is Shaky

European nations introduced the euro in 1999. These countries constitute a combined economy that is among the world's largest. Hence, people regularly exchange their own currencies for euros in all major foreign exchange markets. During the 2000s, therefore, the euro satisfied the first key condition for a global currency.

In the immediate aftermath of the U.S. financial meltdown between 2007 and 2009, many people regarded the euro as an alternative currency that might have lower foreign exchange risk. By the end of 2009, therefore, some observers were arguing that the euro's prospects of displacing the dollar as the key global currency had brightened. Since early 2010, however, the euro's value has been prone to sudden drops. This has induced individuals and businesses in many nations to shift funds away from euro-denominated bank deposit accounts, bonds, and stocks. Many of those funds are finding their way to dollar-denominated accounts, bonds, and stocks instead. Thus, as the euro's fortunes have darkened, the dollar's prospects for maintaining its current position as the preeminent global currency have brightened.

For Critical Analysis

1. Could multiple currencies function as global currencies simultaneously?
2. Why would savers in other nations desire to avoid holding a currency whose value is subject to unexpected decreases in value relative to other currencies?

Web Resources

1. See an assessment of the euro's fortunes at one particularly low point during the spring of 2010 at www.econtoday.com/ch33.
2. To read a European perspective on the pros and cons associated with the euro becoming a global currency, go to www.econtoday.com/ch33.

Research Project

Evaluate whether a national currency might be able to possess one of the characteristics typically possessed by a global currency without have the other characteristic. Is it possible that a currency could exhibit both features yet fail to emerge as a global currency? Why or why not? Can you provide any real-world, present-day examples?

For more questions on this chapter's Issues & Applications, go to **MyEconLab**. In the Study Plan for this chapter, select Section N: News.

Here is what you should know after reading this chapter. **MyEconLab** will help you identify what you know, and where to go when you need to practice.

WHAT YOU SHOULD KNOW		WHERE TO GO TO PRACTICE
The Balance of Trade versus the Balance of Payments The balance of trade is the difference between exports and imports of physical goods, or merchandise, during a given period. The balance of payments is a system of accounts for all transactions between a nation's residents and the residents of other countries of the world.	balance of trade, 727 balance of payments, 727 accounting identities, 727	• **MyEconLab** Study Plan 33.1 • Audio introduction to Chapter 33

(*continued*)

MyEconLab continued

WHAT YOU SHOULD KNOW		WHERE TO GO TO PRACTICE
The Key Accounts Within the Balance of Payments There are three accounts within the balance of payments. The current account measures net exchanges of goods and services, transfers, and income flows across a nation's borders. The capital account measures net flows of financial assets. The official reserve transactions account tabulates exchanges of financial assets involving the home nation's and foreign nations' governments and central banks. Because each international exchange generates both an inflow and an outflow, the sum of the balances on all three accounts must equal zero.	current account, 729 capital account, 730 special drawing rights (SDRs), 731 International Monetary Fund, 731 **KEY FIGURE** Figure 33-1, 731	• **MyEconLab** Study Plan 33.1 • Animated Figure 33-1
Exchange Rate Determination in the Market for Foreign Exchange From the perspective of the United States, the demand for a nation's currency by U.S. residents is derived largely from the demand for imports from that nation. Likewise, the supply of a nation's currency is derived mainly from the supply of U.S. exports to that country. The equilibrium exchange rate is the rate of exchange between the dollar and the other nation's currency at which the quantity of the currency demanded is equal to the quantity supplied.	foreign exchange market, 732 exchange rate, 733 flexible exchange rates, 733 appreciation, 733 depreciation, 733 **KEY FIGURES** Figure 33-2, 734 Figure 33-3, 736 Figure 33-4, 736 Figure 33-5, 737	• **MyEconLab** Study Plan 33.2 • Animated Figures 33-2, 33-3, 33-4, 33-5 • Video: Market Determinants of Foreign Exchange Rates
Factors That Can Induce Changes in Equilibrium Exchange Rates The equilibrium exchange rate changes in response to changes in the demand for or supply of another nation's currency. Changes in desired flows of exports or imports, real interest rates, tastes and preferences of consumers, and perceptions of economic stability affect the positions of the demand and supply curves in foreign exchange markets and induce variations in equilibrium exchange rates.	**KEY FIGURE** Figure 33-6, 738	• **MyEconLab** Study Plan 33.2 • Animated Figure 33-6 • Video: Market Determinants of Foreign Exchange Rates
How Policymakers Can Attempt to Keep Exchange Rates Fixed If the current price of the home currency in terms of another nation's currency starts to fall below the level where the home country wants it to remain, the home country's central bank can use reserves of the other nation's currency to purchase the home currency in foreign exchange markets. This raises the demand for the home currency and thereby pushes up the currency's value in terms of the other nation's currency.	par value, 740 foreign exchange risk, 742 hedge, 742 **KEY FIGURE** Figure 33-9, 741	• **MyEconLab** Study Plans 33.3, 33.4 • Animated Figure 33-9 • Video: Pros and Cons of a Fixed Exchange Rate

Log in to MyEconLab, take a chapter test, and get a personalized Study Plan that tells you which concepts you understand and which ones you need to review. From there, MyEconLab will give you further practice, tutorials, animations, videos, and guided solutions.
Log in to www.myeconlab.com

PROBLEMS

All problems are assignable in myeconlab. *Answers to the odd-numbered problems appear at the back of the book.*

33-1. Over the course of a year, a nation tracked its foreign transactions and arrived at the following amounts:

Merchandise exports	500
Service exports	75
Net unilateral transfers	10
Domestic assets abroad (capital outflows)	−200
Foreign assets at home (capital inflows)	300
Changes in official reserves	−35
Merchandise imports	600
Service imports	50

What are this nation's balance of trade, current account balance, and capital account balance?

33-2. Identify whether each of the following items creates a surplus item or a deficit item in the current account of the U.S. balance of payments.

a. A Central European company sells products to a U.S. hobby-store chain.

b. Japanese residents pay a U.S. travel company to arrange hotel stays, ground transportation, and tours of various U.S. cities, including New York, Chicago, and Orlando.

c. A Mexican company pays a U.S. accounting firm to audit its income statements.

d. U.S. churches and mosques send relief aid to Pakistan following a major earthquake in that nation.

e. A U.S. microprocessor manufacturer purchases raw materials from a Canadian firm.

33-3. Explain how the following events would affect the market for the Mexican peso, assuming a floating exchange rate.

a. Improvements in Mexican production technology yield superior guitars, and many musicians around the world buy these guitars.

b. Perceptions of political instability surrounding regular elections in Mexico make international investors nervous about future business prospects in Mexico.

33-4. Explain how the following events would affect the market for South Africa's currency, the rand, assuming a floating exchange rate.

a. A rise in U.S. inflation causes many U.S. residents to seek to buy gold, which is a major South African export good, as a hedge against inflation.

b. Major discoveries of the highest-quality diamonds ever found occur in Russia and Central Asia, causing a significant decline in purchases of South African diamonds.

33-5. Suppose that the following two events take place in the market for China's currency, the yuan: U.S. parents are more willing than before to buy action figures and other Chinese toy exports, and China's government tightens restrictions on the amount of U.S. dollar–denominated financial assets that Chinese residents may legally purchase. What happens to the dollar price of the yuan? Does the yuan appreciate or depreciate relative to the dollar?

33-6. On Wednesday, the exchange rate between the Japanese yen and the U.S. dollar was $0.010 per yen. On Thursday, it was $0.009. Did the dollar appreciate or depreciate against the yen? By how much, expressed as a percentage change?

33-7. On Wednesday, the exchange rate between the euro and the U.S. dollar was $1.20 per euro, and the exchange rate between the Canadian dollar and the U.S. dollar was U.S. $1.05 per Canadian dollar. What is the exchange rate between the Canadian dollar and the euro?

33-8. Suppose that signs of an improvement in the Japanese economy lead international investors to resume lending to the Japanese government and businesses. Policymakers, however, are worried about how this will influence the yen. How would this event affect the market for the yen? How should the central bank, the Bank of Japan, respond to this event if it wants to keep the value of the yen unchanged?

33-9. Briefly explain the differences between a flexible exchange rate system and a fixed exchange rate system.

33-10. Suppose that under a gold standard, the U.S. dollar is pegged to gold at a rate of $35 per ounce and the pound sterling is pegged to gold at a rate of £17.50 per ounce. Explain how the gold standard constitutes an exchange rate arrangement between the dollar and the pound. What is the exchange rate between the U.S. dollar and the pound sterling?

33-11. Suppose that under the Bretton Woods system, the dollar is pegged to gold at a rate of $35 per ounce and the pound sterling is pegged to the dollar at a rate of $2 = £1. If the dollar is devalued against gold and the pegged rate is changed to $40 per ounce, what does this imply for the exchange value of the pound in terms of dollars?

33-12. Suppose that the People's Bank of China wishes to peg the rate of exchange of its currency, the yuan, in terms of the U.S. dollar. In each of the following situations, should it add to or subtract from its dollar foreign exchange reserves? Why?

a. U.S. parents worrying about safety begin buying fewer Chinese-made toys for their children.

b. U.S. interest rates rise relative to interest rates in China, so Chinese residents seek to purchase additional U.S. financial assets.

c. Chinese furniture manufacturers produce high-quality early American furniture and successfully export large quantities of the furniture to the United States.

ECONOMICS ON THE NET

Daily Exchange Rates It is easy to keep up with daily changes in exchange rates by using the Web site of Oanda.com. In this application, you will learn how hard it is to predict exchange rate movements, and you will get some practice thinking about what factors can cause exchange rates to change.

Title: Oanda Currency Converter

Navigation: Go to **www.econtoday.com/ch33** to visit the Oanda.com's currency converter home page. Click on *Foreign Exchange 12 PM Rates.*

Application Answer the following questions.

1. Choose a currency from the many available in the drop-down menu. How many dollars does it take to purchase a unit of the currency in the spot foreign exchange market?
2. For the currency you chose in part 1, keep track of its value relative to the dollar over the course of several days. Based on your tabulations, try to predict the value of the currency at the end of the week *following* your data collections. Use any information you may have, or just do your best without any additional information. How far off did your prediction turn out to be?

For Group Study and Analysis Divide the class into groups, and assign a currency to each group. Ask the group to track the currency's value over the course of two days and to determine whether the currency's value appreciated or depreciated relative to the dollar from one day to the next. In addition, ask each group to discuss what kinds of demand or supply shifts could have caused the change that occurred during this interval.

ANSWERS TO QUICK QUIZZES

p. 732: (i) balance . . . payments; (ii) physical; (iii) current . . . current; (iv) Unilateral transfers; (v) current; (vi) capital . . . capital; (vii) official reserve; (viii) inflation . . . political

p. 739: (i) exchange rate; (ii) demand . . . demand . . . supply; (iii) downward . . . upward; (iv) shift . . . demand

p. 743: (i) fixed . . . fixed; (ii) currencies . . . reserves; (iii) risk

Answers to the Odd-Numbered Problems

Chapter 1

1-1. Economics is the study of how individuals allocate limited resources to satisfy unlimited wants.

a. Among the factors that a rational, self-interested student will take into account are her income, the price of the textbook, her anticipation of how much she is likely to study the textbook, and how much studying the book is likely to affect her grade.

b. A rational, self-interested government official will, for example, recognize that higher taxes will raise more funds for mass transit while making more voters, who have limited resources, willing to elect other officials.

c. A municipality's rational, self-interested government will, for instance, take into account that higher hotel taxes will produce more funds if as many visitors continue staying at hotels, but that the higher taxes will also discourage some visitors from spending nights at hotels.

1-3. Because wants are unlimited, the phrase applies to very high-income households as well as low- and middle-income households. Consider, for instance, a household with a low income and unlimited wants at the beginning of the year. The household's wants will still remain unlimited if it becomes a high-income household later in the year.

1-5. Sally is displaying rational behavior if all of these activities are in her self-interest. For example, Sally likely derives intrinsic benefit from volunteer and extracurricular activities and may believe that these activities, along with good grades, improve her prospects of finding a job after she completes her studies. Hence, these activities are in her self interest even though they reduce some available study time.

1-7. The rationality assumption states that people do not intentionally make choices that leave them worse off. The bounded rationality hypothesis suggests that people are *almost*, but not completely, rational.

1-9. Suppose that there is a change in the environment that a person faces, and the person adjusts to this change as predicted by the rationality assumption. If the new environment becomes predictable, then the individual who actually behaves as predicted by the traditional rationality assumption may settle into behavior that *appears* to involve repetitive applications of a rule of thumb.

1-11. a. The model using prices from the Iowa Electronic Market is more firmly based on the rationality assumption, because people who trade assets on this exchange based on poor forecasts actually experience losses. This gives them a strong incentive to make the best possible forecasts. Unpaid respondents to opinion polls have less incentive to give truthful answers about whether and how they will vote.

b. An economist would develop a means of evaluating whether prices in the Iowa Electronic Market or results of opinion polls did a better job of matching actual electoral outcomes.

1-13. a. Positive

b. Normative

c. Normative

d. Positive

APPENDIX A

A-1. a. Independent: price of a notebook; Dependent: quantity of notebooks

b. Independent: work-study hours; Dependent: credit hours

c. Independent: hours of study; Dependent: economics grade

A-3. a. above x axis, to left of y axis

b. below x axis, to right of y axis

c. on x axis, to right of y axis

A-5.

y	x
−20	−4
−10	−2
0	0
10	2
20	4

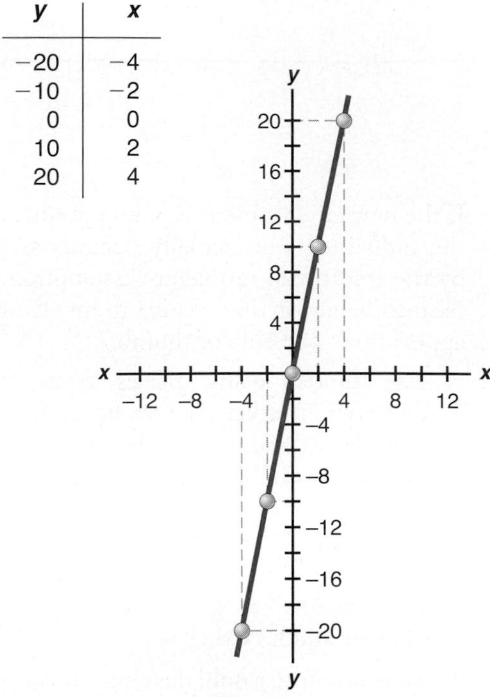

A-7. Each one-unit increase in x yields a 5-unit increase in y, so the slope given by the change in y corresponding to the change in x is equal to 5.

Chapter 2

2-1. The opportunity cost of attending a class at 11:00 a.m. is the next-best use of that hour of the day. Likewise, the opportunity cost of attending an 8:00 a.m. class is the next-best use of that particular hour of the day. If you are an early riser, it is arguable that the opportunity cost of the 8:00 a.m. hour is lower, because you will already be up at that time but have fewer choices compared with the 11:00 a.m. hour when shops, recreation centers, and the like are open. If you are a late riser, it may be that the opportunity cost of the 8:00 a.m. hour is higher, because you place a relatively high value on an additional hour of sleep in the morning.

2-3. The bank apparently determined that the net gain that it anticipated receiving from trying to sell the house to someone else, taking into account the opportunity cost of resources that the bank would have had to devote to renovating the house, was less than \$10.

2-5. If the student allocates additional study time to economics in order to increase her score from 90 to 100, her biology score declines from 50 to 40, so the opportunity cost of earning 10 additional points in economics is 10 fewer points in biology.

2-7.

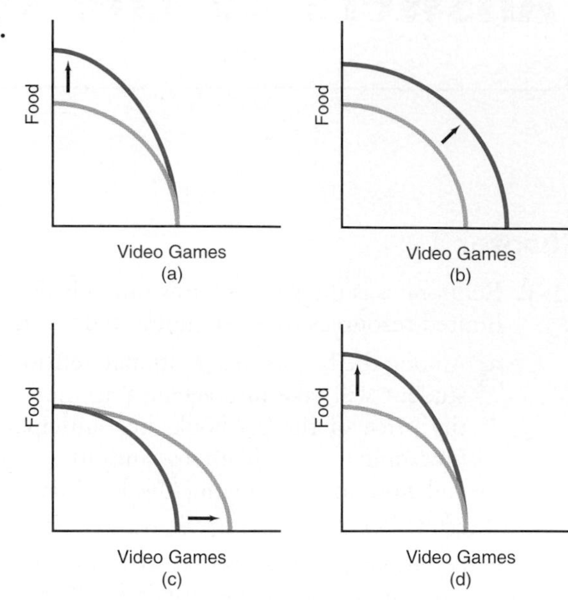

2-9. D

2-11. a. If the nation's residents increase production of consumption goods from 0 units to 10 units, the opportunity cost is 3 units of human capital forgone. If the nation's residents increase production of consumption goods from 0 units to 60 units, the opportunity cost is 100 units of human capital.

b. Yes, because successive 10-unit increases in production of consumption goods generate larger sacrifices of human capital, equal to 3, 7, 15, 20, 25, and 30.

2-13. Because it takes you less time to do laundry, you have an absolute advantage in laundry. Neither you nor your roommate has an absolute advantage in meal preparation. You require 2 hours to fold a basket of laundry, so your opportunity cost of folding a basket of laundry is 2 meals. Your roommate's opportunity cost of folding a basket of laundry is 3 meals. Hence, you have a comparative advantage in laundry, and your roommate has a comparative advantage in meal preparation.

2-15. It may be that the professor is very proficient at doing yard work relative to teaching and research activities, so in fact the professor may have a comparative advantage in doing yard work.

Chapter 3

3-1. The equilibrium price is \$21 per Blu-ray disc, and the equilibrium quantity is 80 million Blu-ray discs (see the figure on the facing page). At a price of \$20 per Blu-ray disc, the quantity of Blu-ray discs demanded is 90 million, and the quantity of Blu-ray discs supplied is 60 million. Hence, there is a shortage of 30 million Blu-ray discs at a price of \$20 per Blu-ray disc.

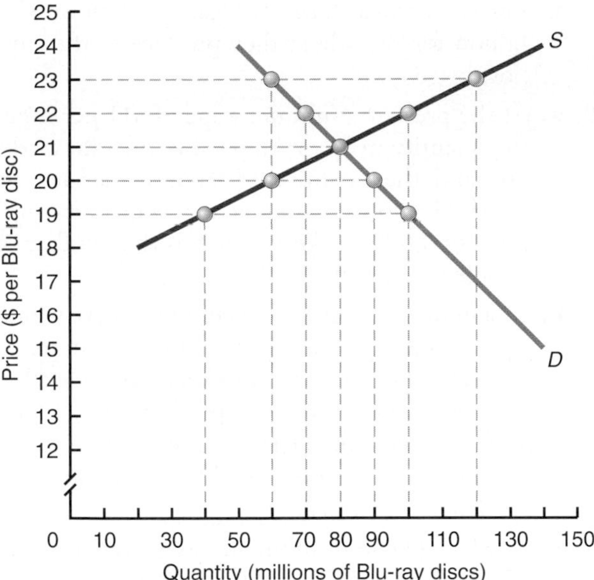

3-3. a. Satellite and cable Internet access services are substitutes, so a reduction in the price of cable Internet access services causes a decrease in the demand for satellite high-speed Internet access services.

b. A decrease in the price of satellite Internet access services generates an increase in the quantity of these services demanded.

c. Satellite high-speed Internet access services are a normal good, so a fall in the incomes of consumers reduces the demand for these services.

d. If consumers' tastes shift away from cable Internet access services in favor of satellite high-speed Internet services, then the demand for these services increases.

3-5. a. Complement: eggs; Substitute: sausage

b. Complement: tennis balls; Substitute: racquetball racquets

c. Complement: cream; Substitute: tea

d. Complement: gasoline; Substitute: city bus

3-7. a. At the $1,000 rental rate, the quantity of one bedroom apartments supplied is 8,500 per month, but the quantity demanded is only 7,000 per month. Thus, there is an excess quantity of one-bedroom apartments supplied equal to 1,500 apartments per month.

b. To induce consumers to lease unrented one-bedroom apartments, some landlords will reduce their rental rates. As they do so, the quantity demanded will increase. In addition, some landlords will choose not to offer apartments for rent at lower rates, and the quantity supplied will decrease. At the equilibrium rental rate of $800 per month, there will be no excess quantity supplied.

c. At the $600 rental rate, the quantity of one-bedroom apartments demanded is 8,000 per month, but the quantity supplied is only 6,500 per month. Thus, there is an excess quantity of one-bedroom apartments demanded equal to 1,500 apartments per month.

d. To induce landlords to make additional onc-bedroom apartments available for rent, some consumers will offer to pay higher rental rates. As they do so, the quantity supplied will increase. In addition, some consumers will choose not to try to rent apartments at higher rates, and the quantity demanded will decrease. At the equilibrium rental rate of $800 per month, there will be no excess quantity demanded.

3-9. a. Because memory chips are an input in the production of laptop computers, a decrease in the price of memory chips causes an increase in the supply of laptop computers. The market supply curve shifts to the right, which causes the market price of laptop computers to fall and the equilibrium quantity of laptop computers to increase.

b. Machinery used to produce laptop computers is an input in the production of these devices, so an increase in the price of machinery generates a decrease in the supply of laptop computers. The market supply curve shifts to the left, which causes the market price of laptop computers to rise and the equilibrium quantity of laptop computers to decrease.

c. An increase in the number of manufacturers of laptop computers causes an increase in the supply of laptop computers. The market supply curve shifts rightward. The market price of laptop computers declines, and the equilibrium quantity of laptop computers increases.

d. The demand curve for laptop computers shifts to the left along the supply curve, so there is a decrease in the quantity supplied. The market price falls, and the equilibrium quantity declines.

3.11. The decline in the price of palladium, a substitute for platinum, will cause a decrease in the demand for platinum, so the platinum demand curve will shift leftward. Both the market clearing price and the equilibrium quantity of platinum will decrease.

3-13. Because processor chips are an input in the production of personal computers, a decrease in the price of processor chips generates an increase in the supply of personal computers. The market price of personal computers will decrease, and the equilibrium quantity will increase.

Chapter 4

4-1. The ability to produce music CDs at lower cost and the entry of additional producers shift the supply curve rightward, from S_1 to S_2. At the same time, reduced prices of substitute goods result in a leftward shift in the demand for music CDs, from D_1 to D_2. Consequently, the equilibrium price of music CDs declines, from P_1 to P_2. The equilibrium quantity may rise, fall, or, as shown in the diagram, remain unchanged.

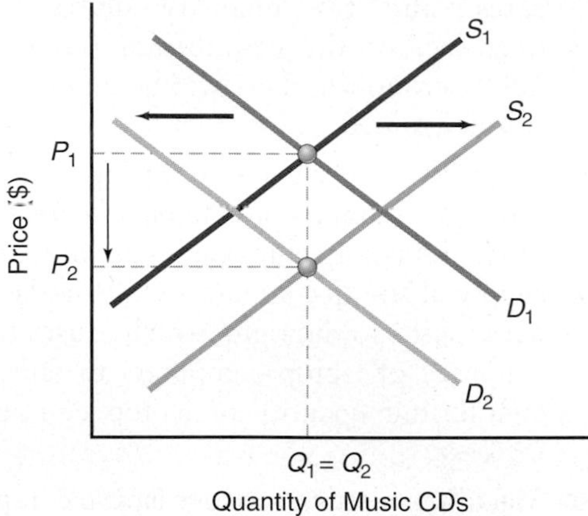

4-3. The market rental rate is $700 per apartment, and the equilibrium quantity of apartments rented to tenants is 2,000. At a ceiling price of $650 per month, the number of apartments students desire to rent increases to 2,500 apartments. At the ceiling price, the number of apartments that owners are willing to supply decreases to 1,800 apartments. Thus, there is a shortage of 700 apartments at the ceiling price, and only 1,800 are rented at the ceiling price.

4.5. The market price is $400, and the equilibrium quantity of seats is 1,600. If airlines cannot sell tickets to more than 1,200 passengers, then passengers are willing to pay $600 per seat. Normally, airlines would be willing to sell each ticket for $200, but they will be able to charge a price as high as $600 for each of the 1,200 tickets they sell. Hence, the quantity of tickets sold declines from 1,600, and the price of a ticket rises from $400 to as high as $600.

4-7. **a.** Consumers buy 10 billion kilograms at the support price of $0.20 per kilogram and hence spend $2 billion on wheat.

b. The amount of surplus wheat at the support price is 8 billion kilograms, so at the $0.20-per-kilogram support price, the government must spend $1.6 billion to purchase this surplus wheat.

c. Pakistani wheat farmers receive a total of $3.6 billion for the wheat they produce at the support price.

4-9. **a.** At the present minimum wage of $11 per hour, the quantity of labor supplied is 102,000 workers, and the quantity of labor demanded by firms is 98,000. There is an excess quantity supplied of 4,000 workers, which is the number of people who are unemployed.

b. At a minimum wage of $9 per hour, there would be nothing to prevent market forces from pushing the wage rate to the market clearing level of $10 per hour. This $10-per-hour wage rate would exceed the legal minimum and hence would prevail. There would be no unemployed workers.

c. At a $12-per-hour minimum wage, the quantity of labor supplied would increase to 104,000 workers, and the quantity of labor demanded would decline to 96,000. There would be an excess quantity of labor supplied equal to 8,000 workers, which would then be the number of people unemployed.

4-11. **a.** The rise in the number of wheat producers causes the market supply curve to shift rightward, so more wheat is supplied at the support price.

b. The quantity of wheat demanded at the same support price is unchanged.

c. Because quantity demanded is unchanged while quantity supplied has increased, the amount of surplus wheat that the government must purchase has risen.

Chapter 5

5-1. In the absence of laws forbidding cigar smoking in public places, people who are bothered by the odor of cigar smoke will experience costs not borne by cigar producers. Because the supply of cigars will not reflect these costs, from society's perspective the market supply curve for cigars will be in a position too far to the right. The market price of cigars will be too low, and too many cigars will be produced and consumed.

5-3. Imposing the tax on pesticides causes an increase in the price of pesticides, which are an input in the production of oranges (see the diagram at the top of the facing page). Hence, the supply curve in the orange market shifts leftward. The market price of oranges increases, and the equilibrium quantity of oranges declines. Hence, orange consumers indirectly help to pay for dealing with the spillover costs of pesticide production by paying more for oranges.

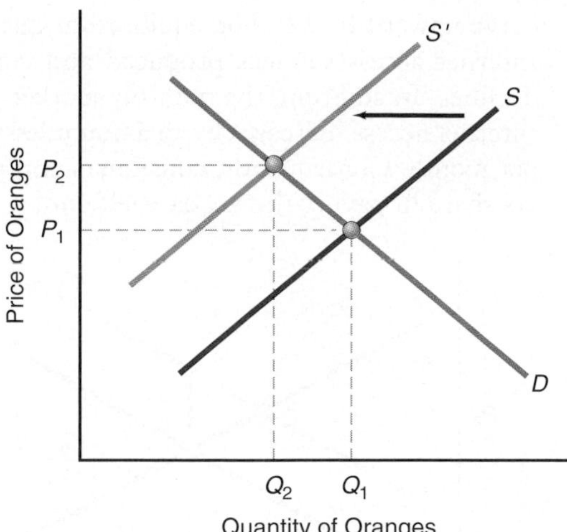

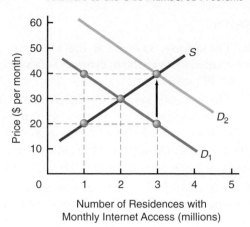

5-5. **a.** As shown in the figure below, if the social benefits associated with bus ridership were taken into account, the demand schedule would be D' instead of D, and the market price would be higher. The equilibrium quantity of bus rides would be higher.

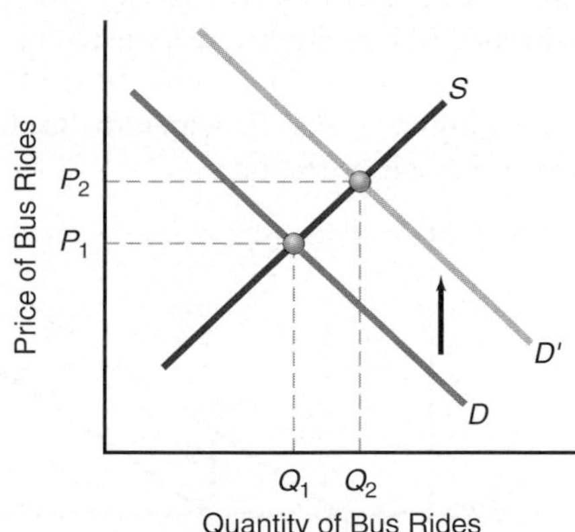

b. The government could pay commuters a subsidy to ride the bus, thereby shifting the demand curve outward and to the right. This would increase the market price and equilibrium number of bus rides.

5-7. At present, the equilibrium quantity of residences with Internet access is 2 million (see the diagram at the top of the next column). To take into account the external benefit of Internet access and boost the quantity of residences with access to 3 million, the demand curve would have to shift upward by $20 per month at any given quantity, to D_2 from D_1. Thus, the government would have to offer a $20-per-month subsidy to raise the quantity of residences with Internet access to 3 million.

Price ($ per month)
60
50
40
30
20
10
0
S
D_2
D_1
1 2 3 4 5
Number of Residences with Monthly Internet Access (millions)

5-9. No, the outcome will be different. If the government had simply provided grants to attend private schools at the current market tuition rate, parents and students receiving the grants would have paid a price equal to the market valuation of the last unit of educational services provided. Granting a subsidy to private schools allows the private schools to charge parents and students a price less than the market price. Private schools thereby will receive a higher-than-market price for the last unit of educational services they provide. Consequently, they will provide a quantity of educational services in excess of the market equilibrium quantity. At this quantity, parents and students place a lower value on the services than the price received by the private schools. Public schools will lose students to private schools. The prices that public schools receive will also decline. Both of these changes will result in lower revenues for public schools.

5-11. **a.** $40 million

b. The effective price of a memory-storage drive to consumers will be lower after the government pays the subsidy, so people will purchase a larger quantity.

c. $60 million

d. $90 million

5-13. **a.** $60 − $50 = $10

b. Expenditures after the program expansion are $2.4 million. Before the program expansion, expenditures were $1 million. Hence, the increase in expenditures is $1.4 million.

c. At a per-unit subsidy of $50, the share of the per-unit $60 price paid by the government is 5/6, or 83.3 percent. Hence, this is the government's share of total expenditures on the 40,000 devices that consumers purchase.

Chapter 6

6-1. a. The average tax rate is the total tax of \$40 divided by the \$200 in income: \$40/\$200 = 0.2, or 20 percent

b. The marginal tax rate for the last hour of work is the change in taxes, \$3, divided by the change in income, \$8: \$3/\$8 = 0.375, or 37.5 percent

6-3. 2003: \$300 million; 2005: \$350 million; 2007: \$400 million; 2009: \$400 million; 2011: \$420 million

6-5. During 2010, the tax base was an amount of income equal to \$20 million/0.05 = \$400 million. During 2011, the income tax base was equal to \$19.2 million/0.06 = \$320 million. Although various factors could have contributed to the fall in taxable income, dynamic tax analysis suggests that the higher income tax rate induced people to reduce their reported income. For instance, some people might have earned less income subject to city income taxes, and others might even have moved outside the city to avoid paying the higher income tax rate.

6-7. a. The supply of tickets for flights into and out of London shifts upward by \$154, as shown in the diagram below. The equilibrium quantity of flights in and out of London declines. The market clearing price of London airline tickets rises by an amount less than the tax.

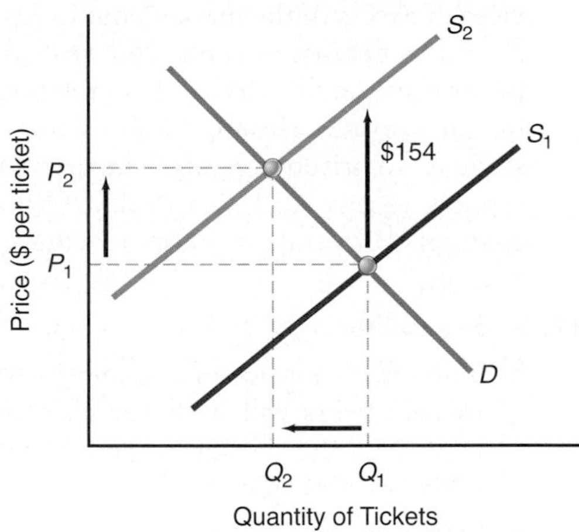

b. Tickets for flights into or out of London are substitutes for tickets for flights into and out of nearby cities. Thus, the demand for tickets for flights into and out of these cities will increase. This will cause an increase in the equilibrium quantities of these tickets and an increase in the market clearing prices.

6-9. As shown in the diagram at the top of the next column, if the supply and demand curves have their normal shapes, then the \$2-per-month tax on Internet access services shifts the market supply curve upward by \$2. The equilibrium quantity of Internet access services produced and consumed declines. In addition, the monthly market price of Internet access increases by an amount less than \$2 per month. Consequently, consumers and producers share in paying the tax on each unit.

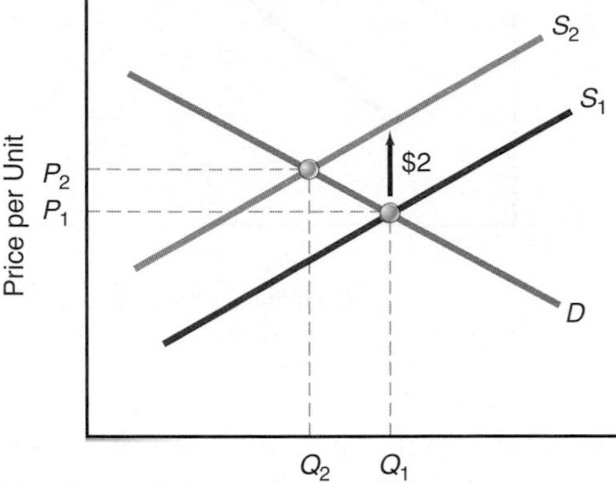

6-11. If the market price of Internet access for businesses does not change, then as shown in the diagram below, over the relevant range the demand for Internet access services by businesses is horizontal. The quantity of services demanded by businesses is very highly responsive to the tax, so Internet access providers must bear the tax in the form of higher costs. Providers of Internet access services pay all of the tax.

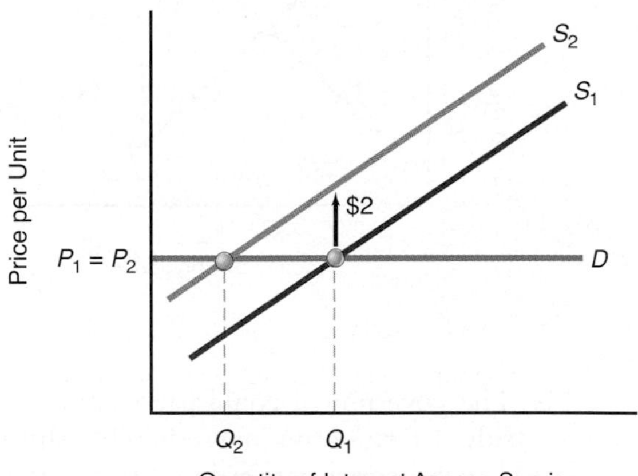

Chapter 7

7-1. a. Multiplying the fraction of people who participate in the labor force, 0.7, times the adult, noninstitutionalized, nonmilitary population of 200.0 million yields a labor force of 140.0 million.

b. Subtracting the 7.5 million unemployed from the labor force of 140.0 million yields 132.5 million people who are employed.

c. Dividing the 7.5 million unemployed by the 140.0 million in the labor force and multiplying by 100 yields an unemployment rate of about 5.36 percent.

7-3. a. The labor force equals the number employed plus the number unemployed, or 156 million + 8 million = 164 million. In percentage terms, therefore, the unemployment rate is 100 times 8 million/164 million, or 4.9 percent.

b. These 60 million people are not in the labor force. The labor force participation rate is, in percentage terms, 100 times 164 million/224 million, or 73.2 percent.

7-5. a. Four of the 100 people are always continuously unemployed because they are between jobs, so the frictional unemployment rate is (4/100) × 100 = 4 percent.

b. Three of the 100 people are always unemployed as a result of government regulations, so the structural unemployment rate is (3/100) × 100 = 3 percent.

c. The unemployment rate is the sum of the frictional and structural rates of unemployment, or 7 percent.

7-7. The overall unemployment rate is 8 percent, and the natural rate of unemployment is 5 percent.

7-9. a. 2012

b. 10 percent

c. 10 percent

d. $1,800 in 2011; $3,000 in 2014

7-11. The expected rate of inflation is equal to 100 × [(99 − 90)/90] = 10 percent. Hence, the real interest rate equals the difference between the 12 percent nominal interest rate and the 10 percent anticipated inflation rate, or 2 percent.

7-13. a. The homeowner gains; the savings bank loses.

b. The tenants gain; the landlord loses.

c. The auto buyer gains; the bank loses.

d. The employer gains; the pensioner loses.

Chapter 8

8-1. a. When Maria does all the work herself, only purchases of the materials in markets (magazines, texturing materials, paint brushes, and paints), which total to $280 per year, count in GDP.

b. She must pay the market price of $200 for the texturing, so her contribution to annual GDP from this project, including the materials, is $480.

c. Because Maria now pays for the entire project via market transactions, her total contribution to GDP equals the sum of the $280 material purchases from part (a), $200 for the texturing from part (b), and $350 for the painting, or $830 per year.

8-3. a. GDP = $16.6 trillion; NDP = $15.3 trillion; NI = $14.5 trillion.

b. GDP in 2015 will equal $15.5 trillion.

8-5. a. Gross domestic income = $14.6 trillion; GDP = $14.6 trillion.

b. Gross private domestic investment = $2.0 trillion.

c. Personal income = $12.0 trillion; personal disposable income = $10.3 trillion.

8-7. a. Measured GDP declines.

b. Measured GDP increases.

c. Measured GDP does not change (the firearms are not newly produced).

8-9. a. The chip is an intermediate good, so its purchase in June is not included in GDP; only the final sale in November is included.

b. This is a final sale of a good that is included in GDP for the year.

c. This is a final sale of a service that is included in GDP for the year.

8-11. a. Nominal GDP for 2011 is $2,300; for 2015, nominal GDP is $2,832.

b. Real GDP for 2011 is $2,300; for 2015, real GDP is $2,229.

8-13. The price index is (2014 nominal GDP/2014 real GDP) × 100 = ($88,000/$136,000) × 100 = 64.7.

8-15. The $1 billion expended to pay for employees and equipment and the additional $1 billion paid to clean up the oil spill would be included in GDP, for a total of $2 billion added to GDP in 2015. The rise in oil reserves increases the stock of wealth but is not included in the current flow of newly produced goods and services. In addition, the welfare loss relating to the deaths of wildlife is also not measured in the marketplace and therefore is not included in GDP.

Chapter 9

9-1. a. Y

b. X

9-3. The nation will maintain its stock of capital goods at its current level, so its rate of economic growth will be zero.

9-5. A: $8,250 per capita; B: $4,500 per capita; C: $21,000 per capita

9-7. 1.77 times higher after 20 years; 3.16 times higher after 40 years

9-9. 5 years

9-11. 4 percent

9-13. Per capita real GDP in 2012 was 10 percent higher than in 2011, or $2,200. The level of real GDP is $2,200 per person × 5 million people = $11 billion.

Chapter 10

10-1. The amount of unemployment would be the sum of frictional, structural, and seasonal unemployment.

10-3. The real value of the new full-employment level of nominal GDP is ($17.7 trillion/1.15) = $15.39 trillion, so the long-run aggregate supply curve has shifted rightward by $2.35 trillion, in base-year dollars.

10-5. This change implies a rightward shift of the long-run aggregate supply curve along the unchanged aggregate demand curve, so the long-run equilibrium price level will decline.

10-7. There are three effects. First, there is a real-balance effect, because the rise in the price level reduces real money balances, inducing people to cut back on their spending. In addition, there is an interest rate effect as a higher price level pushes up interest rates, thereby reducing the attractiveness of purchases of autos, houses, and plants and equipment. Finally, there is an open-economy effect as home residents respond to the higher price level by reducing purchases of domestically produced goods in favor of foreign-produced goods, while foreign residents cut back on their purchases of home-produced goods. All three effects entail a reduction in purchases of goods and services, so the aggregate demand curve slopes downward.

10-9. a. At the price level P_2 above the equilibrium price level P_1, the total quantity of real goods and services that people plan to consume is less than the total quantity that is consistent with firms' production plans. One reason is that at the higher-than-equilibrium price level, real money balances are lower, which reduces real wealth and induces lower planned consumption. Another is that interest rates are higher at the higher-than-equilibrium price level, which generates a cutback in consumption spending. Finally, at the higher-than-equilibrium price level P_2, people tend to cut back on purchasing domestic goods in favor of foreign-produced goods, and foreign residents reduce purchases of domestic goods. As unsold inventories of output accumulate, the price level drops toward the equilibrium price level P_1, which ultimately causes planned consumption to rise toward equality with total production.

b. At the price level P_3 below the equilibrium price level P_1, the total quantity of real goods and services that people plan to consume exceeds the total quantity that is consistent with firms' production plans. One reason is that at the lower-than-equilibrium price level, real money balances are higher, which raises real wealth and induces higher planned consumption. Another is that interest rates are lower at the lower-than-equilibrium price level, which generates an increase in consumption spending. Finally, at the lower-than-equilibrium price level P_3, people tend to raise their purchases of domestic goods and cut back on buying foreign-produced goods, and foreign residents increase purchases of domestic goods. As inventories of output are depleted, the price level begins to rise toward the equilibrium price level P_1, which ultimately causes planned consumption to fall toward equality with total production.

10-11. a. When the price level falls with deflation, there is a movement downward along the *AD* curve.

b. The decline in foreign real GDP levels reduces incomes of foreign residents, who cut back on their spending on domestic exports. Thus, the domestic *AD* curve shifts leftward.

c. The fall in the foreign exchange value of the nation's currency makes domestic-produced goods and services less expensive to foreign residents, who increase their spending on domestic exports. Thus, the domestic *AD* curve shifts rightward.

d. An increase in the price level causes a movement upward along the *AD* curve.

10-13. a. The aggregate demand curve shifts leftward along the long-run aggregate supply curve. The equilibrium price level falls, and equilibrium real GDP remains unchanged.

b. The aggregate demand curve shifts rightward along the long-run aggregate supply curve. The equilibrium price level rises, and equilibrium real GDP remains unchanged.

c. The long-run aggregate supply curve shifts rightward along the aggregate demand curve. The equilibrium price level falls, and equilibrium real GDP increases.

d. The aggregate demand curve shifts rightward along the long-run aggregate supply curve. The equilibrium price level rises, and equilibrium real GDP remains unchanged.

10-15. a. The income flows are mainly influencing relatives' consumption, so the main effect is on the aggregate demand curve.

b. A rise in aggregate demand will lead to an increase in the equilibrium price level.

Chapter 11

11-1. a. Because saving increases at any given interest rate, the desired saving curve shifts rightward. This causes the equilibrium interest rate to decline.

b. There is no effect on current equilibrium real GDP, because in the classical model the vertical long-run aggregate supply curve always applies.

c. A change in the saving rate does not directly affect the demand for labor or the supply of labor in the classical model, so equilibrium employment does not change.

d. The decrease in the equilibrium interest rate generates a rightward and downward movement along the demand curve for investment. Consequently, desired investment increases.

e. The rise in current investment implies greater capital accumulation. Other things being equal, this will imply increased future production and higher equilibrium real GDP in the future.

11-3. False. In fact, there is an important distinction. The classical model of short-run real GDP determination applies to an interval short enough that some factors of production, such as capital, are fixed. Nevertheless, the classical model implies that even in the short run the economy's aggregate supply curve is the same as its long-run aggregate supply curve.

11-5. a. The labor supply curve shifts rightward, and equilibrium employment increases.

b. The rise in employment causes the aggregate supply curve to shift rightward, and real GDP rises.

c. Because the immigrants have higher saving rates, the nation's saving supply curve shifts to the right along its investment curve, and the equilibrium interest rate declines.

d. The fall in the equilibrium interest rate induces a rise in investment, and equilibrium saving also rises.

e. Capital accumulation rises, and more real GDP will be forthcoming in future years.

11-7. In the long run, the aggregate supply curve is vertical because all input prices adjust fully and people are fully informed in the long run. Thus, the short-run aggregate supply curve is more steeply sloped if input prices adjust more rapidly and people become more fully informed within a short-run interval.

11-9. This event would cause the aggregate demand curve to shift leftward. In the short run, the equilibrium price level would decline, and equilibrium real GDP would fall.

11-11. To prevent a short-run decrease in real GDP from taking place after the temporary rise in oil prices shifts the *SRAS* curve leftward, policymakers should increase the quantity of money in circulation. This will shift the *AD* curve rightward and prevent equilibrium real GDP from declining in the short run.

11-13. a. *E*: The union wage boost causes the *SRAS* curve to shift leftward, from $SRAS_1$ to $SRAS_3$. The reduction in incomes abroad causes import spending in this nation to fall, which induces a leftward shift in the *AD* curve, from AD_1 to AD_3.

b. *B*: The short-term reduction in production capabilities causes the *SRAS* curve to shift leftward, from $SRAS_1$ to $SRAS_3$, and the increase in money supply growth generates a rightward shift in the *AD* curve, from AD_1 to AD_2.

c. *C*: The strengthening of the value of this nation's currency reduces the prices of imported inputs that domestic firms utilize to produce goods and services, which causes the *SRAS* curve to shift rightward, from $SRAS_1$ to $SRAS_2$. At the same time, the currency's strengthening raises the prices of exports and reduces the prices of imports, so net export spending declines, thereby inducing a leftward shift in the *AD* curve, from AD_1 to AD_3.

Chapter 12

12-1. a. Flow

b. Flow

c. Stock

d. Flow

e. Stock

f. Flow

g. Stock

12-3. a. The completed table follows (all amounts in dollars):

Real GDP	Consumption	Saving	Investment
2,000	2,000	0	1,200
4,000	3,600	400	1,200
6,000	5,200	800	1,200
8,000	6,800	1,200	1,200
10,000	8,400	1,600	1,200
12,000	10,000	2,000	1,200

MPC = 1,600/2,000 = 0.8; MPS = 400/2,000 = 0.2.

b. The graph appears below.

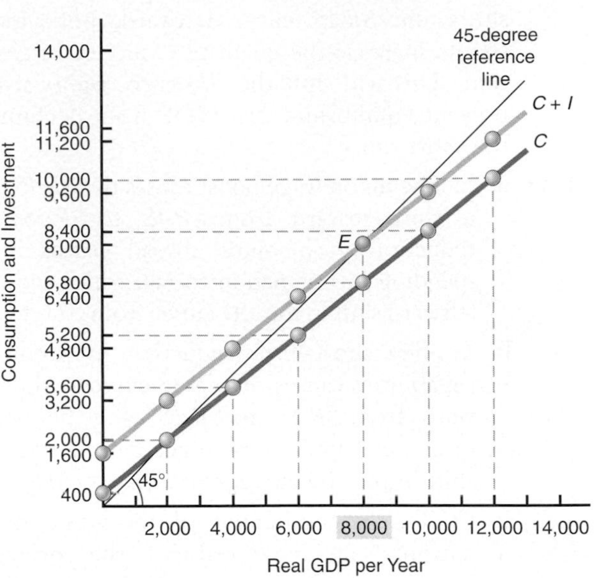

c. The graph appears below. Equilibrium real GDP on both graphs equals $8,000.

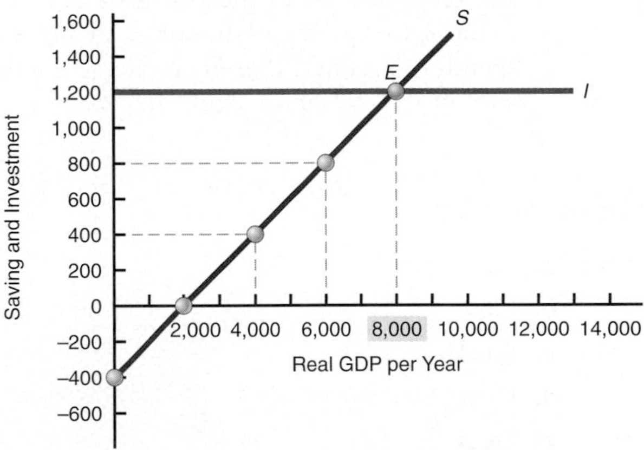

d. APS = $1,200/$8,000 = 0.15.

e. The multiplier is 1/(1 – MPC) = 1/(1 – 0.8) = 1/0.2 = 5. Thus, if autonomous consumption were to rise by $100, then equilibrium real GDP would increase by $100 times 5, or $500.

12-5. The multiplier is 1/(1 – MPC) = 4, so 1 – MPC = 0.25, which implies that MPC = 0.75. Thus, when real GDP equals $15 trillion, consumption is $1 trillion + (0.75 × $15 trillion) = $12.25 trillion.

12-7. The multiplier is 1/(1 – MPC) = 1/(1 – 0.75) = 4, so the increase in equilibrium real GDP is $250 billion × 4 = $1 trillion, and the level of real GDP at the new point on the aggregate demand curve is $16 trillion.

12-9. a. The MPS is equal to 1/3.

b. $0.1 trillion

Chapter 13

13-1. a. A key factor that could help explain why the actual effect may have turned out to be lower is the crowding-out effect. Some government spending may have entailed direct expenditure offsets that reduced private expenditures on a dollar-for-dollar basis. In addition, indirect crowding out may have occurred. Because the government did not change taxes, it probably sold bonds to finance its increased expenditures, and this action likely pushed up interest rates, thereby discouraging private investment. Furthermore, the increase in government spending likely pushed up aggregate demand, which may have caused a short-run increase in the price level. This, in turn, may have induced foreign residents to reduce their expenditures on U.S. goods. It also could have reduced real money holdings sufficiently to discourage consumers from spending as much as before. On net, therefore, real GDP rose in the short run but not by the full amount predicted by the basic multiplier effect.

b. In the long run, as the increased spending raised aggregate demand, wages and other input prices likely increased in proportion to the resulting increase in the price level. Thus, in the long run the aggregate supply schedule was vertical, and the increase in government spending induced only a rise in the price level.

13-3. Because of the recognition time lag entailed in gathering information about the economy, policymakers may be slow to respond to a downturn in real GDP. Congressional approval of policy actions to address the downturn may be delayed. Hence, an action time lag may also arise. Finally, there is an effect time lag, because policy actions take time to exert their full effects on the economy. If these lags are sufficiently long, it is possible that by the time a policy to address a downturn has begun to have its effects, real GDP may already be rising. If so, the policy action may push real GDP up faster than intended, thereby making real GDP less stable.

13-5. Situation *b* is an example of indirect crowding out because the reduction in private expenditures takes place indirectly in response to a change in the interest rate. In contrast, situations *a* and *c* are examples of direct expenditure offsets.

13-7. Situation *b* is an example of a discretionary fiscal policy action because this is a discretionary action by Congress. So is situation *d* because the president uses discretionary authority. Situation *c* is an example of monetary policy, not fiscal policy, and situation *a* is an example of an automatic stabilizer.

13-9. There is a recessionary gap, because at point *A* equilibrium real GDP of $15.5 trillion is below the long-run level of $16.0 trillion. To eliminate the recessionary gap of $0.5 trillion, government spending must increase sufficiently to shift the *AD* curve rightward to a long-run equilibrium, which will entail a price level increase from 115 to 120. Hence, the spending increase must shift the *AD* curve rightward by $1 trillion, or by the multiplier, which is 1/0.20 = 5, times the increase in spending. Government spending must rise by $200 billion, or $0.2 trillion.

13-11. Because the MPC is 0.80, the multiplier equals 1/(1 − MPC) = 1/0.2 = 5. Net of indirect crowding out, therefore, total autonomous expenditures must rise by $40 billion in order to shift the aggregate demand curve rightward by $200 billion. If the government raises its spending by $50 billion, the market interest rate rises by 0.5 percentage point and thereby causes planned investment spending to fall by $10 billion, which results in a net rise in total autonomous expenditures equal to $40 billion. Consequently, to accomplish its objective the government should increase its spending by $50 billion.

13-13. A cut in the tax rate should induce a rise in consumption and, consequently, a multiple short-run increase in equilibrium real GDP. In addition, however, a tax-rate reduction reduces the automatic-stabilizer properties of the tax system, so equilibrium real GDP would be less stable in the face of changes in autonomous spending.

APPENDIX D

D-1. a. The marginal propensity to consume is equal to 1 − MPS, or 6/7.

b. The required increase in equilibrium real GDP is $0.35 trillion, or $350 billion. The multiplier equals 1/(1 − MPC) = 1/MPS = 1/(1/7) = 7. Hence, investment or government spending must increase by $50 billion to bring about a $350 billion increase in equilibrium real GDP.

c. The multiplier relevant for a tax change equals −MPC/(1 − MPC) = −MPC/MPS = −(6/7)/(1/7) = −6. Thus, the government would have to cut taxes by $58.33 billion to induce a rise in equilibrium real GDP equal to $350 billion.

D-3. a. The aggregate expenditures curve shifts up by $1 billion. Equilibrium real GDP increases by $5 billion.

b. The aggregate expenditures curve shifts down by the MPC times the tax increase, or by 0.8 × $1 billion = $0.8 billion. Equilibrium real income falls by $4 billion.

c. The aggregate expenditures curve shifts upward by (1 − MPC) times $1 billion = $0.2 billion. Equilibrium real income rises by $1 billion.

d. No change; no change.

Chapter 14

14-1. $0.4 trillion

14-3. A higher deficit creates a higher public debt.

14-5. The net public debt is obtained by subtracting government interagency borrowing from the gross public debt.

14-7. When foreign dollar holders hold more domestic government bonds issued to finance higher domestic government budget deficits, they purchase fewer domestic exports, so the domestic trade deficit rises, other things being equal.

14-9. As shown in the diagram below, the increase in government spending and/or tax reduction that creates the budget deficit also causes the aggregate demand curve to shift rightward, from *AD* to AD_2. Real GDP rises to its long-run equilibrium level of $15 trillion at point *B*. The equilibrium price level increases to a value of 130 at this point. As real GDP rises, the government's tax collections increase and benefit payouts fall, both of which will help ultimately reduce the deficit.

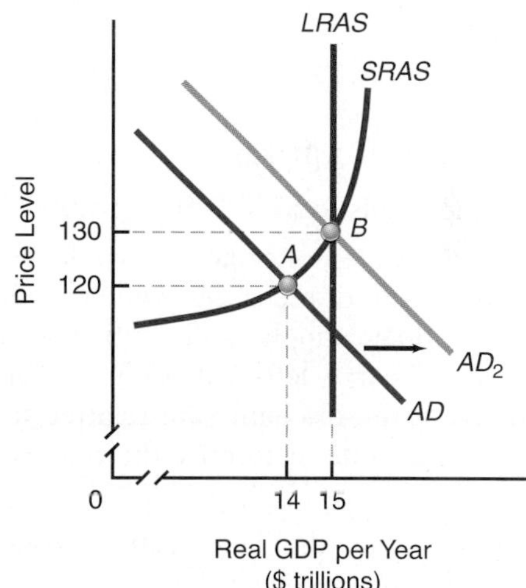

14-11. "The rich" are likely to respond to higher tax rates by reducing their activities that generate taxable income, so actual tax collections from "the rich" will not turn out to be as high as the politician suggests.

Chapter 15

15-1. medium of exchange; store of value; standard of deferred payment

15-3. store of value; standard of deferred payment

15-5. **a.** M1 and M2
b. neither
c. M2 only
d. M1 and M2
e. M2 only

15-7. **a.** moral hazard problem
b. adverse selection problem
c. moral hazard problem

15-9. The Fed provides banking services such as check clearing services and large-value payment services for other banks and for the U.S. Treasury, just as a private bank provides such services for its customers. Unlike a private bank, however, the Federal Reserve serves as a lender of last resort, a regulator, and a policymaker.

15-11. **a.** asset
b. liability
c. asset
d. asset
e. asset
f. liability

15-13. 25 percent (or 0.25)

15-15. The maximum potential money multiplier is 1/0.01 = 100, so total deposits in the banking system will increase by \$5 million × 100 = \$500 million.

Chapter 16

16-1. **a.** \$500/0.05 = \$10,000.
b. Its price falls to \$500/0.10 = \$5,000.

16-3. **a.** One possible policy action would be an open market sale of securities, which would reduce the money supply and shift the aggregate demand curve leftward. Others would be to increase the discount rate relative to the federal funds rate or to raise the required reserve ratio.
b. In principle, the Fed's action would reduce inflation more quickly.

16-5. **a.** The dollar appreciation will raise the prices of U.S. goods and services from the perspective of foreign residents, so they will reduce their spending on U.S. exports. It will reduce the prices of foreign goods and services from the perspective of U.S. residents, so they will increase their spending on foreign imports. Thus, net export expenditures will decline.
b. The fall in net export expenditures will bring about a decrease in U.S. aggregate demand, so the aggregate demand curve AD_2 will apply to this situation. In the short run, the equilibrium price level will fall from 118 to 116, and equilibrium real GDP, measured in base-year dollars, will fall from \$15.0 trillion to \$14.5 trillion.
c. The Federal Reserve could engage in a policy action, such as open market purchases, that increase aggregate demand to its original level.

16-7. The price level remains at its original value. Because $M_sV = PY$, V has doubled, and Y is unchanged, cutting M_s in half leaves P unchanged.

16-9. **a.** $M_sV = PY$, so $P = M_sV/Y$ = (\$1.1 trillion × 10)/\$5 trillion = 2.2.
b. \$100 billion/\$1 trillion = 0.1, or 10 percent
c. 0.2/2 = 0.1, or 10 percent
d. Both the money supply and the price level increased by 10 percent.

16-11. Any one of these contractionary actions will tend to raise interest rates, which in turn will induce international inflows of financial capital. This pushes up the value of the dollar and makes U.S. goods less attractive abroad. As a consequence, real planned total expenditures on U.S. goods decline even further.

16-13. **a.** To push the equilibrium federal funds rate up to the new target value, the Trading Desk will have to reduce the money supply by selling U.S. government securities.
b. The increase in the differential between the discount rate and the federal funds rate will induce fewer depository institutions to borrow reserves from Federal Reserve banks. In the absence of a Trading Desk action, this would cause the equilibrium interest rate to increase. To prevent this from occurring, the Trading Desk will have to boost the money supply by purchasing U.S. government securities.

16-15. The neutral federal funds rate is the level of the interest rate on interbank loans at which, given current inflation expectations, the growth rate of real GDP tends neither to rise nor to fall relative to the rate of growth of potential, long-run, real GDP.
a. The FOMC should instruct the Trading Desk to aim to achieve a higher target for the federal funds rate.
b. The Trading Desk should engage in open market sales and thereby reduce the quantity of reserves supplied, which will bring about an increase in the equilibrium federal funds rate.

APPENDIX E

E-1. **a.** \$20 billion increase
b. \$40 billion increase
c. \$10 billion open market purchase

E-3. Through its purchase of $1 billion in bonds, the Fed increased reserves by $1 billion. This ultimately caused a $3 billion increase in the money supply after full multiple expansion of the money supply. The 1 percentage-point drop in the interest rate, from 6 percent to 5 percent, caused investment to rise by $25 billion, from $1,200 billion to $1,225 billion. An investment multiplier of 3 indicates that equilibrium real GDP rose by $75 billion, to $12,075 billion, or $12.075 trillion.

Chapter 17

17-1. a. The actual unemployment rate, which equals the number of people unemployed divided by the labor force, would decline, because the labor force would rise while the number of people unemployed would remain unchanged.

b. Natural unemployment rate estimates also would be lower.

c. The logic of the short- and long-run Phillips curves would not be altered. The government might wish to make this change if it feels that those in the military "hold jobs" and therefore should be counted as employed within the U.S. economy.

17-3. The natural rate of unemployment is the rate of unemployment that would exist after full adjustment has taken place in response to any changes that have occurred. In contrast, the nonaccelerating inflation rate of unemployment is the rate of unemployment that corresponds to a stable rate of inflation, which is easier to quantify.

17-5. a. The measured unemployment rate when all adjustments have occurred will now always be lower than before, so the natural unemployment rate will be smaller.

b. The unemployment rate consistent with stable inflation will now be reduced, so the NAIRU will be smaller.

c. The Phillips curve will shift inward.

17-7. No. It could still be true that wages and other prices of factors of production adjust sluggishly to changes in the price level. Then a rise in aggregate demand that boosts the price level brings about an upward movement along the short-run aggregate supply curve, causing equilibrium real GDP to rise.

17-9. a. An increase in desired investment spending induces an increase in aggregate demand, so AD_3 applies. The price level is unchanged in the short run, and equilibrium real GDP rises from $15 trillion at point *A* to $15.5 trillion at point *C*.

b. Over time, firms perceive that they can increase their profits by adjusting prices upward in response to the increase in aggregate demand. Thus, firms eventually will incur the menu costs required to make these price adjustments. As they do so, the aggregate supply curve will shift upward, from *SRAS* to $SRAS_2$, as shown in the diagram below. Real GDP will return to its original level of $15 trillion, in base-year dollars. The price level will increase to a level above 119, such as 124.

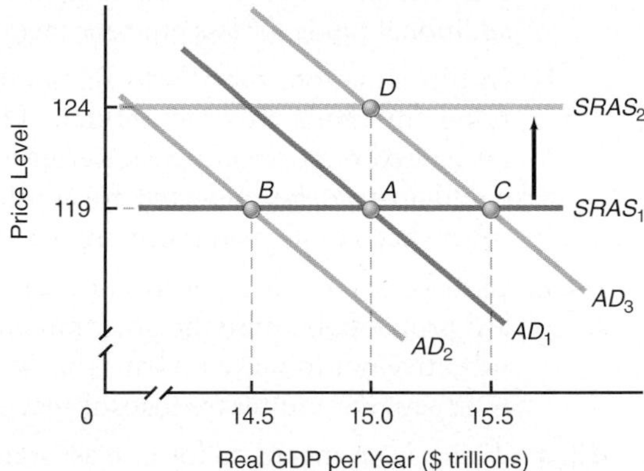

17-11. The explanation would be that aggregate demand increased at a faster pace than the rise in aggregate supply caused by economic growth. On net, therefore, the price level rose during those years.

17-13. If the average time between price adjustments by firms is significant, then the short-run aggregate supply curve could be regarded as horizontal, as hypothesized by the new Keynesian theorists. As a consequence, there would be a short-run trade-off between inflation and real GDP that policymakers potentially could exploit.

Chapter 18

18-1. Population growth rate = real GDP growth rate − rate of growth of per capita real GDP = 3.1 percent − 0.3 percent = 2.8 percent.

18-3. a. 20 × 0.01 percent = 0.2 percent.

b. 10 × 0.01 percent = 0.1 percent.

18-5. $10 trillion/$0.5 trillion × 0.1 = 2 percentage points.

18-7. a. Portfolio investment is equal to $150 million in bonds plus $100 million in stocks representing ownership of less than 10 percent, or $250 million. (Bank loans are neither portfolio investment nor foreign direct investment.)

b. Foreign direct investment is equal to $250 million in stocks representing an ownership share of at least 10 percent. (Bank loans are neither portfolio investment nor foreign direct investment.)

18-9. **a.** adverse selection
b. adverse selection
c. moral hazard
d. adverse selection

18-11. **a.** The company had already qualified for funding at a market interest rate, so the World Bank is interfering with functioning private markets for credit. In addition, by extending credit to the company at a below-market rate, the World Bank provides an incentive for the company to borrow additional funds for less efficient investment.
b. In this situation, the World Bank effectively is tying up funds in dead capital. There is an associated opportunity cost, because the funds could instead be allocated to another investment that would yield more immediate returns.
c. In this case, the IMF contributes to a moral hazard problem, because the government has every incentive not to make reforms that will enable it to repay this and future loans it may receive.

18-13. **a.** There is an incentive for at least some governments to fail to follow through with reforms, even if those governments might have had good intentions when they applied for World Bank loans.
b. National governments most interested in obtaining funds to "buy" votes will be among those most interested in obtaining IMF loans. The proposed IMF rule could help reduce the number of nations whose governments seek to obtain funds to try to "buy" votes.

Chapter 19

19-1. −[(200 − 150)/(350/2)]/[(9 − 10)/(19/2)], which is approximately equal to −2.7. Thus, the absolute price elasticity of demand equals 2.7.

19-3. **a.** −[(90 − 80)/(85)]/[(0.20 − 0.40)/(0.30)], which is approximately equal to −0.18. Consequently, the absolute price elasticity of demand is 0.18, so demand is inelastic over this range.
b. −[(60 − 40)/(50)]/[(0.80 − 1.20)/(1.00)] = −1.00. The absolute price elasticity of demand, therefore, equals 1.00, which implies that demand is unit-elastic over this range.
c. −[(20 − 10)/(15)]/[(1.60 − 1.80)/(1.70)], which is approximately equal to −5.67. Thus, the absolute price elasticity of demand is 5.67, so demand is elastic over this range.

19-5. −[(800 − 1,200)/(2,000/2)]/[($32.50 − $27.50)/($60.00/2)] = −2.4. Hence, the absolute price elasticity of demand equals 2.4. Demand is elastic over this range.

19-7. Because price and total revenue move in the same direction, then over this range of demand, the demand for hand-made guitars is inelastic.

19-9. **a.** More inelastic, because it represents a smaller portion of the budget
b. More elastic, because there are many close substitutes
c. More elastic, because there are a number of substitutes
d. More inelastic, because there are few close substitutes
e. More inelastic, because it represents a small portion of the budget

19-11. Let *X* denote the percentage change in the quantity of bacon. Then *X*/10 percent = −0.5. *X*, therefore, is −5 percent.

19-13. [(125,000 − 75,000)/(200,000/2)]/[($35,000 − $25,000)/($60,000/2)] = 1.5. Supply is elastic.

19-15. The short-run price elasticity of supply is 10 percent/20 percent = 0.5, and the long-run price elasticity of supply is 40 percent/20 percent = 2.0.

Chapter 20

20-1. The campus pizzeria indicates by its pricing policy that it recognizes the principle of diminishing marginal utility. As shown in Figure 20-1 on page 438, a customer's marginal utility for the second pizza is typically lower than for the first. Thus, the customer is likely to value the second pizza less and, therefore, only be willing to pay less for it.

20-3. The total utility of the third, fourth, and fifth cheeseburgers is 48, 56, and 60, respectively. The marginal utility of the first and second cheeseburgers is 20 and 16, respectively. The total utility of the first, second, and third bags of french fries is 10, 18, and 20, respectively. The marginal utility of the fourth and fifth bags of french fries is 1 and 0, respectively.

20-5. The new utility-maximizing combination is four cheeseburgers and two orders of french fries, at which the marginal utility per dollar spent is 2 units per dollar and the entire $6 is spent.

20-7. Other things being equal, when the price of soft drinks rises, the substitution effect comes into play, and the individual tends to consume less of the more expensive item, soft drinks, and more of the item with the unchanged price, tacos. Hence, the marginal utility of soft drinks rises, and the marginal utility of tacos falls.

20-9. **a.** Of all the possible one-unit increases in consumption displayed, the movement from point *A* to point *B* generates the highest marginal utility. Total utility rises by 5 units between these points, so the marginal utility of the first unit consumed is 5 units.

b. Between points E and F, a one-unit increase in the quantity consumed leaves total utility unchanged at 11 units, so marginal utility is equal to zero.

c. Between points F and G, a one-unit increase in the quantity consumed causes total utility to decline from 11 units to 10 units, so marginal utility is negative and equal to −1 unit.

20-11. For this consumer, at these prices the marginal utility per dollar spent on 2 fudge bars is 500 units of utility per dollar, and the marginal utility per dollar spent on 5 Popsicles is also 500 units of utility per dollar. In addition, the entire budget of $9 is spent at this combination, which is the consumer optimum.

20-13. The marginal utility per dollar spent is equalized at 2.50 if 5 hot dogs and 3 baseball games are consumed, and this consumption combination just exhausts the now-available $190 in income.

20-15. The marginal utility of good Y is three times the marginal utility of good X, or 3 × 3 utils = 9 utils.

APPENDIX F

F-1. The indifference curve is convex to the origin because of a diminishing marginal rate of substitution. As an individual consumes more and more of an item, the less the individual is willing to forgo of the other item. The diminishing marginal rate of substitution is due to diminishing marginal utility.

F-3. Sue's marginal rate of substitution is calculated below:

Combination of Bottled Water and Soft Drinks	Bottled Water per Month	Soft Drinks per Month	MRS
A	5	11	
B	10	7	5:4
C	15	4	5:3
D	20	2	5:2
E	25	1	5:1

The diminishing marginal rate of substitution of soft drinks for water shows Sue's diminishing marginal utility of bottled water. She is willing to forgo fewer and fewer soft drinks to get an additional five bottles of water.

F-5. Given that water is measured along the horizontal axis and soft drinks are measured along the vertical axis, the slope of Sue's budget constraint is the price of water divided by the price of soft drinks, or $P_W/P_S = \frac{1}{2}$. The only combination of bottled water and soft drinks that is on Sue's indifference curve and budget constraint is combination C. For this combination, total expenditures on water and soft drinks equal (15 × $1) + (4 × $2) = $15 + $8 = $23.

F-7. With the quantity of bottled water measured along the horizontal axis and the quantity of soft drinks measured along the vertical axis, the slope of Sue's budget constraint is the price of water divided by the price of soft drinks. This ratio equals $\frac{1}{2}$. The only combination of bottled water and soft drinks that is on Sue's indifference curve and budget constraint is combination C, where expenditures on water and soft drinks total $23.

F-9. Yes, Sue's revealed preferences indicate that her demand for soft drinks obeys the law of demand. When the price of soft drinks declines from $2 to $1, her quantity demanded rises from 4 to 8.

Chapter 21

21-1. **a.** Bob earns a high economic rent. Because he has a specialized skill that is in great demand, his income is likely to be high, and his opportunity cost relatively low.

b. Sally earns a high economic rent. Because she is a supermodel, her income is likely to be relatively high, and, without any education, her opportunity cost is likely to be relatively low.

c. If Tim were to leave teaching, not a relatively high-paying occupation, he could sell insurance full time. Hence, his opportunity cost is high relative to his income, and his economic rent is low.

21-3. A sole proprietorship is a business entity owned by a single individual, whereas a partnership is a business entity jointly owned by more than one individual. A corporation, in contrast, is a legal entity that is owned by shareholders, who own shares of the profits of the entity. Sole proprietorships and partnerships do not face double taxation, but corporations do. The owners of corporations, however, enjoy limited liability, whereas the sole proprietor or partner does not.

21-5. Accounting profit is total revenue, $77,250, minus explicit costs, $37,000, for a total of $40,250. Economic profit is total revenue, $77,250, less explicit costs, $37,000, and implicit costs, $40,250, for a total equal to zero.

21-7. **a.** Physical capital

b. Financial capital

c. Financial capital

d. Physical capital

21-9. **a.** The owner of WebCity faces both tax rates if the firm is a corporation, but if it is a proprietorship the owner faces only the 30 percent personal income tax rate. Thus, it should choose to be a proprietorship.

b. If WebCity is a corporation, the $100,000 in corporate earnings is taxed at a 20 percent rate, so after-tax dividends are $80,000, and these are taxed at the personal income tax rate of 30 percent, leaving $56,000 in after-tax income for the owner. Hence, the firm should be organized as a proprietorship, with after-tax earnings of $70,000, or a value advantage of $14,000.

c. Yes. In this case, incorporation raises earnings to $150,000, which are taxed at a rate of 20 percent, yielding after-tax dividends of $120,000 that are taxed at the personal rate of 30 percent. This leaves an after-tax income for the owner of $84,000, which is higher than the after-tax earnings of $70,000 if WebCity is a proprietorship that earns lower pre-tax income taxed at the personal rate.

d. After-tax profits rise from $56,000 to $84,000, or by $28,000.

e. This policy change would only increase the incentive to incorporate.

f. A corporate structure provides limited liability for owners, which can be a major advantage. Furthermore, owners may believe that the corporate structure will yield higher pre-tax earnings, as in the above example.

21-11. The real rate of interest in Japan is 2% − 0.5% = 1.5%. The real rate of interest in the United States is 4% − 3% = 1%. Therefore, Japan has the higher *real* rate of interest.

21-13. Ownership of common stock provides voting rights within the firm but also entails immediate loss if assets fall below the value of the firm's liabilities. Preferred stockholders are repaid prior to owners of common stock, but preferred stockholders do not have voting rights.

21-15. You should point out to your classmate that stock prices tend to drift upward following a random walk. That is, yesterday's price plus any upward drift is the best guide to today's price. Therefore, there are no predictable trends that can be used to "beat" the market.

Chapter 22

22-1. The short run is a time period during which the professor cannot enter the job market and find employment elsewhere. This is the nine-month period from August 15 through May 15. The professor can find employment elsewhere after the contract has been fulfilled, so the short run is nine months and the long run is greater than nine months.

22-3. Total variable costs are equal to total costs, $5 million, less total fixed costs, $2 million, which equals $3 million. Average variable costs are equal to total variable costs divided by the number of units produced. Average variable costs, therefore, equal $3 million divided by 10,000, or $300.

22-5. **a.** Total fixed costs equal average fixed costs, $10 per LCD screen, times the quantity produced per day, 100 LCD screens, which equals $1,000 per day.

b. The total variable costs of producing 100 LCD screens equal average variable costs, $10 per unit, times the quantity produced per day, 100 LCD screens, which equals $1,000 per day.

c. The total costs of producing 100 LCD screens equal total fixed costs plus the total variable costs of producing 100 LCD screens, or $1,000 per day plus $1,000 per day, which equals $2,000 per day.

d. The average total costs of producing 99 LCD screens equal the average fixed costs of $10.101 plus the average variable costs of $10.070, or $20.171 per LCD screen. Thus, the total cost of producing 99 LCD screens equals $20.171 times 99, or $1,996.929. The marginal cost of producing the hundredth LCD screen equals the change in total costs from increasing production from 99 to 100, or $2,000 − $1,996.929, or $3.071 per LCD screen.

22-7. **a.** Average total costs are $20 per unit plus $30 per unit, or $50 per unit, and total costs divided by average total costs equal output, which therefore is $2,500/$50 per unit, or 50 units.

b. TVC = AVC × Q = $20 per unit × 50 units = $1,000.

c. TFC = AFC × Q = $30 per unit × 50 units = $1,500; or TFC = TC − TVC = $2,500 − $1,000 = $1,500.

22-9. **a.** The expense incurred in cutting back trees on a regular basis would be unrelated to the quantity of rail services provided on the tracks and hence would represent a fixed cost.

b. The expense of dumping sand on the slippery tracks in advance of trains would vary with the number of trains that run on the tracks and hence would constitute a variable cost.

22-11. Hiring 1 more unit of labor at a wage rate of $20 to increase output by 1 unit causes total costs to rise by $20, so the marginal cost of the 251st unit is $20.

22-13. **a.** AVC = $2 million/1 million units = $2 per unit.

b. APP = 1 million units/1,000 units of labor = 1,000 units of output per unit of labor.

c. Wage rate = \$2 million/1,000 units of labor = \$2,000 per unit of labor.

22-15. a. Plant size E, because this is the minimum output scale at which LRATC is at a minimum level

b. Leftward movement, because the functioning plant size for the firm would decrease

Chapter 23

23-1. a. The single firm producing much of the industry's output can affect price. Therefore, this currently is not a perfectly competitive industry.

b. The output of each firm is not homogeneous, so this is not a perfectly competitive industry.

c. Firms must obtain government permission to enter the industry and hence cannot easily enter, so this is not a perfectly competitive industry.

23-3. a. For a perfectly competitive firm, marginal revenue and average revenue are equal to the market clearing price. Hence, average revenue equals \$20 per unit at each possible output rate.

b. At the present output of 10,000 units per week, the firm's total revenues equal price times output, or \$20 per unit times 10,000 units per week, which equals \$200,000 per week. The firm's total costs equal ATC times output, or \$15.75 per unit times 10,000 units per week, which equals \$157,500 per week. Weekly economic profits equal total revenues minus total costs, or \$200,000 − \$157,500 = \$42,500. The firm is maximizing economic profits, because it is producing the output rate at which marginal revenue equals marginal cost.

c. If the market clearing price were to fall to \$12.50 per unit, the marginal revenue curve would shift down to this level. Average total costs would exceed the price at this output rate, but in the short run the firm would minimize its short-run economic losses by producing 8,100 units per week.

d. If the market clearing price were to fall to \$7.50 per unit, the marginal revenue curve would shift down to this level. Average variable costs at an output rate of 5,000 units per week would exceed the market clearing price, so total variable costs of producing 5,000 units per week would exceed total revenues. The firm should cease production if this event takes place.

23-5. Even though the price of pizzas, and hence marginal revenue, falls to only \$5, this covers average variable costs. Thus, the shop should stay open.

23-7. Because price is less than average variable cost at this rate of output, the firm's total revenues (\$5 per unit × 1,500 units = \$7,500) fail to cover its total variable costs (\$5.50 per unit × 1,500 units = \$8,250). Thus, in the short run the firm should shut down and incur only its fixed costs, which equal AVC × Q, or \$0.50 per unit × 1,500 units = \$750.

23-9. In the described situation, the firm is producing an output rate at a point on the marginal cost curve below the average total cost curve. Marginal revenue is above the minimum point of the average total cost curve, however. Hence, marginal cost at the current rate of production is less than marginal revenue. The firm is not maximizing profit, and it should increase its rate of production.

23-11. a. There was a significant increase in market supply as more firms entered the industry. A consequence for the typical firm was that the market price fell below the minimum average total cost, resulting in negative economic profits.

b. Firms will consider leaving the industry, and some firms probably *will* leave the industry.

Chapter 24

24-1. The alternatives are not close substitutes for first-class mail, so the U.S. Postal Service faces a downward-sloping demand curve for first-class mail.

24-3. The demand curve faced by the firm is the downward-sloping market demand curve, so price exceeds marginal revenue at all quantities beyond the first unit produced.

24-5. a. The total revenue and total profits of the dry cleaner are as follows.

Output (suits cleaned)	Price (\$ per unit)	Total Costs (\$)	Total Revenue (\$)	Total Profit (\$)
0	8.00	3.00	0	−3.00
1	7.50	6.00	7.50	1.50
2	7.00	8.50	14.00	5.50
3	6.50	10.50	19.50	9.00
4	6.00	11.50	24.00	12.50
5	5.50	13.50	27.50	14.00
6	5.00	16.00	30.00	14.00
7	4.50	19.00	31.50	12.50
8	4.00	24.00	32.00	8.00

b. The profit-maximizing rate of output is between 5 and 6 units.

c. The marginal cost and marginal revenue of the dry cleaner are as follows. The profit-maximizing rate of output is 6 units.

Output (suits cleaned)	Price $ per (unit)	Total Costs ($)	Total Revenue ($)	Total Profit ($)	Marginal Cost ($ per unit)	Marginal Revenue ($ per unit)
0	8.00	3.00	0	-3.00	—	—
1	7.50	6.00	7.50	1.50	3.00	7.50
2	7.00	8.50	14.00	5.50	2.50	6.50
3	6.50	10.50	19.50	9.00	2.00	5.50
4	6.00	11.50	24.00	12.50	1.00	4.50
5	5.50	13.50	27.50	14.00	2.00	3.50
6	5.00	16.00	30.00	14.00	2.50	2.50
7	4.50	19.00	31.50	12.50	3.00	1.50
8	4.00	24.00	32.00	8.00	4.00	0.50

24-7. **a.** The profit-maximizing output rate is 5,000 units.

b. Average total cost is $5 per unit. Average revenue is $6 per unit.

c. Total costs equal $5 per unit × 5,000 units = $25,000. Total revenue equals $6 per unit × 5,000 units = $30,000.

d. ($6 per unit – $5 per unit) × 5,000 units = $5,000.

e. In a perfectly competitive market, price would equal marginal cost at $4.50 unit, at which the quantity is 8,000 units. Because the monopolist produces less and charges a higher price than under perfect competition, price exceeds marginal cost at the profit-maximizing level of output. The difference between the price and marginal cost is the per-unit cost to society of a monopolized industry.

24-9. **a.** The monopoly maximizes economic profits or minimizes economic losses by producing to the point at which marginal revenue is equal to marginal cost, which is 1 million units of output per month.

b. The profit-maximizing or loss-minimizing price of 1 million units per month is $30 per unit, so total revenues equal $30 million per month. The average total cost of producing 1 million units per month is $33 per unit, so total costs equal $33 million per month. Hence, in the short run, producing 1 million units minimizes the monopoly's loss at $3 million per month.

24-11. If price varies positively with total revenue, then the monopolist is operating on the inelastic portion of the demand curve. This corresponds to the range where marginal revenue is negative. The monopolist cannot, therefore, be at the point where its profits are maximized. In other words, the monopolist is not producing where marginal cost equals marginal revenue.

24-13. Because marginal cost has risen, the monopolist will be operating at a lower rate of output and charging a higher price. Economic profits are likely to decline because even though the price is higher, its output will be more than proportionately lower.

Chapter 25

25-1. **a.** There are many fast-food restaurants producing and selling differentiated products. Both of these features of this industry are consistent with the theory of monopolistic competition.

b. There are numerous colleges and universities, but each specializes in different academic areas and hence produces heterogeneous products, as in the theory of monopolistic competition.

25-3. The values for marginal cost and marginal revenue appear below. Marginal revenue equals marginal cost at approximately the fifth unit of output, so marginal analysis indicates that 5 units is the profit-maximizing production level.

Output	Price ($ per unit)	Total Costs ($)	Total Revenue ($)	Marginal Cost ($ per unit)	Marginal Revenue ($per unit)	Total Profit ($)
0	6.00	2.00	0	—	—	−2.00
1	5.75	5.25	5.75	3.25	5.75	0.00
2	5.50	7.50	11.00	2.25	5.25	3.50
3	5.25	9.60	15.75	2.10	4.75	6.15
4	5.00	12.10	20.00	2.50	4.25	7.90
5	4.75	15.80	23.75	3.70	3.75	7.95
6	4.50	20.00	27.00	4.20	3.25	7.00
7	4.00	24.75	28.00	4.75	1.00	3.25

25-5. After these long-run adjustments have occurred, the demand curve will have shifted to tangency with the average total cost curve at 4 units of output. At this production level, average total cost is $3.03, so this will be the long-run equilibrium price. Because price and average total cost will be equal, the firm will earn zero economic profits.

25-7. **a.** Interactive

b. Direct

c. Mass and interactive

d. Mass

25-9. a. Search good. Given the knowledge that it is a heavy-duty filing cabinet, a photo and description providing features such as dimensions are sufficient to evaluate the characteristics of a filing cabinct.

b. Experience good. A meal must be eaten for its characteristics to be determined.

c. Search good. Given the knowledge that the coat is made of wool, a photo and description providing size information are sufficient to evaluate the characteristics of the coat.

d. Credence good. Psychotherapy services have characteristics that are likely to be difficult for consumers lacking expertise to assess without assistance from another health care provider, such as a general practitioner who guides someone experiencing depression in seeking psychotherapy treatment from a psychiatrist.

25-11. Consumers may be able to assess certain features of a credence good in advance of purchase, so in this sense a credence good is similar to a search good. Nevertheless, consumers lack expertise to evaluate the full qualities of a credence good until after they have purchased it, which is somewhat analogous to the characteristics of an experience good. The fact that consumers cannot fully evaluate a credence good's qualities in advance of purchase makes it different from a search good. Likewise, the inability to be certain, without assistance, of the qualities of a credence good following purchase of the good also distinguishes a credence good from an experience good. The fact that consumers can evaluate certain aspects of a credence good in advance of purchase, as in the case of a search good, explains why ads for credence goods, such as pharmaceuticals, often have informational elements. At the same time, however, the fact that consumers cannot truly evaluate credence goods until after purchase, and even then only with assistance, explains why ads for credence goods also commonly include persuasive elements.

25-13. Typically, the fixed costs of producing an information product are relatively high, while average variable cost is equal to a very small per-unit amount. As a consequence, the average total cost curve slopes downward with increased output, and average variable cost equals marginal cost at a low, constant amount irrespective of the quantity produced. For an information product, marginal cost is always below average total cost. Consequently, if price were equal to marginal cost, it would always be less than average total cost, so the producer would always earn short-run economic losses.

Chapter 26

26-1. a. 15 percent + 14 percent + 12 percent + 11 percent = 52 percent.

b. 52 percent + 10 percent + 10 percent + 8 percent + 7 percent = 87 percent; or 100 percent − 13 percent = 87 percent.

26-3. a. Zero-sum game

b. Negative-sum game

c. Positive-sum game

26-5. Bob is currently a participant in a noncooperative game, in which some people stand and block his view of the football game. His tit-for-tat strategy is to stand up as well. If he stands, however, he will block the view of another spectator. In a cooperative game, all would sit or stand up simultaneously, so that no individual's view is blocked.

26-7. a. The fact that prices are growing at a stable rate and readily observable favor enforcing a cartel agreement So does the fact that there are only seven firms of significant size in the inkjet-printer industry, which is a relatively small number. Therefore, much depends on degree of heterogeneity of inkjet printers. If these products are relatively homogeneous, then taken together these characteristics of the industry would generally support an effort to form a cartel.

b. Once the cartel is formed, any one of the firms that produce inkjet printers could enlarge its profits by expanding production at the higher cartel price, so there is always an incentive to cheat. In addition, the presence of positive economic profits in the industry could induce firms outside the industry cartel to begin manufacturing and selling inkjet printers.

26-9. If Firm 2 opts for Format A, Firm 1 also prefers Format A, and if Firm 2 opts for Format B, Firm 1 also prefers Format B. At the same time, if Firm 1 opts for Format A, Firm 2 also prefers Format A, and if Firm 1 opts for Format B, Firm 2 also prefers Format B. Thus, both firms will wish to produce compatible formats, although they will have to find a mechanism for settling on a format.

26-11. Possible examples include office productivity software, online auction services, telecommunications services, and Internet payment services. In each case, more people are likely to choose to consume the item when others do, because the inherent usefulness of consuming the item for each person increases as the number of consumers rises.

Chapter 27

27-1. If cable service is an industry that experiences diminishing long-run average total costs, then the city may determine that it is more efficient to have a single, large firm that produces at a lower long-run average cost. The city could then regulate the activity of the firm.

27-3. **a.** As the table below indicates, long-run average cost and long-run marginal cost decline with greater output. If the firm were allowed to operate as a monopolist, it would produce to the point at which marginal cost equals marginal revenue, which is 2 units of output. The price that consumers are willing to pay for this quantity is $90 per unit, and maximum economic profits are $180 − $175 = $5.

Quantity	Price ($ per unit)	Long-Run Total Cost ($)	LRAC ($ per unit)	LRMC ($ per unit)	MR ($ per unit)
0	100	0	—	—	
1	95	92	92.00	92	95
2	90	177	88.50	85	85
3	85	255	85.00	78	75
4	80	331	82.75	76	65
5	75	406	81.20	75	55
6	70	480	80.00	74	45

b. Long-run marginal cost and price both equal $75 per unit at 5 units of output. At a price of $75 per unit, the firm experiences economic losses equal to $375 − $407 = −$32.

c. Long-run average cost and price both equal $85 per unit at 3 units of output. At a price of $85 per unit, the firm's economic profits equal $255 − $255 = $0.

27-5. Lemons problems are likely to be more common in industries in which evaluating the characteristics of goods or services by simple inspection is difficult, as is true of the credence goods discussed in Chapter 25. Unaddressed lemons problems tend to depress the prices that sellers of high-quality items can obtain, which induces them to refrain from selling their high-quality items, resulting in sales of only lower-quality items. The main concern of economic regulation is to balance the trade-off between service and price, with economic regulation aiming to keep price lower than the price a profit-maximizing monopolist would charge. Social regulation seeks to improve working conditions and minimize adverse spillovers of production. The adverse incentives resulting from lemons problems are a form of market spillover, so it is arguable that social regulation is most appropriate for addressing lemons problems.

27-7. If European regulation is designed to protect domestic industries, then this is an example of the capture hypothesis. If, on the other hand, there are legitimate health concerns, then this is an example of the share-the-pain, share-the-gain hypothesis.

27-9. This is a creative response to the do-not-call legislation, in which firms are legally satisfying the terms of the regulation but evading the regulation's intent.

27-11. **a.** In this case, Firm 1 makes 75.0 percent of the sales in the Internet book market, and Firm 2 makes 46.7 percent of the sales in physical retail stores. By the antitrust authority's definition, there is a monopoly situation in the Internet book market.

b. In the combined market, Firm 2 accounts for 42.5 percent of all sales, and Firm 1's share drops to 7.5 percent, so under this alternative definition there is no cause for concern about monopoly.

27-13. This is an example of bundling. Because consumers who purchase the bundled product perceive that they have effectively paid different prices for the bundled products based on their willingness to pay, an antitrust authority might view this practice as charging consumers different prices for the same products, or price discrimination.

Chapter 28

28-1.

Labor Input (workers per week)	Total Physical Output (printers per day)	Marginal Physical Product	Marginal Revenue Product ($)
10	200	—	—
11	218	18	1,800
12	234	16	1,600
13	248	14	1,400
14	260	12	1,200
15	270	10	1,000
16	278	8	800

28-3. **a.** The greater the substitutability of capital, the more elastic is the demand for labor.

b. Because the demand for labor is a derived demand, the greater the elasticity of demand for the final product, the greater is the elasticity of demand for labor.

c. The larger the portion of factor costs accounted for by labor, the larger is the price elasticity of demand for labor.

28-5. a.

Labor Input (workers per week)	Total Physical Product	Product Price ($ per unit)	Marginal Physical Product	Total Revenue ($)	Marginal Revenue Product ($)
10	100	50	—	5,000	—
11	109	49	9	5,341	341
12	116	48	7	5,568	227
13	121	47	5	5,687	119
14	124	46	3	5,704	17
15	125	45	1	5,625	−79

b. The profit-maximizing firm would hire 13 workers, which is the quantity of labor beyond which the marginal revenue product of labor falls below the marginal factor cost.

28-7. a. The rise in the price of ethanol results in an increase in the marginal revenue product of corn, the key input in production of ethanol. Thus, each ethanol producer's marginal revenue product curve shifts rightward, which ultimately translates into an increase in the demand for corn, from D_1 to D_2, as shown in the diagram below. The market clearing price of corn increases, from P_1 to P_2, and the equilibrium quantity of corn rises, from Q_1 to Q_2.

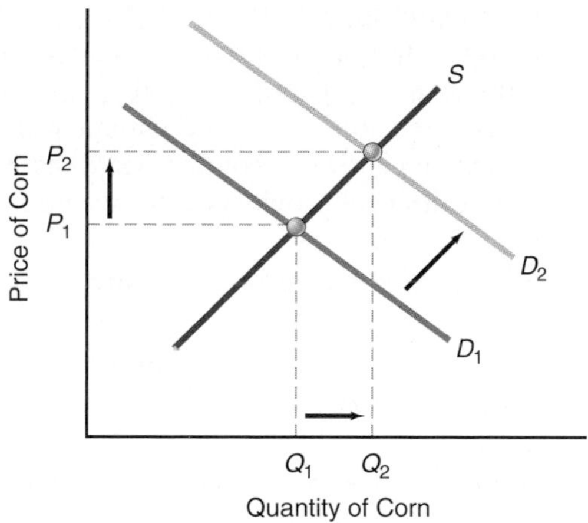

b. Human snack foods are a substitute input in the production of hogs, so the increase in the price of corn induced farmers to substitute in favor of snack foods.

28-9. Labor outsourcing by U.S. firms tends to push down market wages and employment in affected U.S. labor markets, but labor outsourcing by foreign firms that hire U.S. workers tends to push up market wages and employment in affected U.S. labor markets. Consequently, the overall wage and employment effects are ambiguous in the short run. In the long run, however, outsourcing enables U.S. and foreign firms to specialize in producing and trading the goods and services that they can produce most efficiently. The resulting resource saving ultimately expands the ability of U.S. residents to consume more goods and services than they could have otherwise.

28-11. The wage rate, \$20 per unit of labor, equals marginal revenue product, so the marginal physical product of labor is \$20 per unit of labor divided by the marginal revenue, \$10 per unit of output, or 2 units of output per unit of labor.

28-13. In order to maximize profits, the firm should hire inputs up to the point at which the marginal physical product per dollar spent on the input is equalized across all inputs. This is not the case in this example. The marginal physical product of labor per dollar spent on wages is 200/\$10 = 20 units of output per dollar spent on labor, which is less than the marginal physical product of capital per dollar spent on capital, which is 20,000/\$500 or 40 units of output per dollar spent on capital. Thus, the firm should increase the additional output per dollar spent on labor by reducing the number of labor units it hires, and it should reduce the additional output per dollar spent on capital by increasing its use of capital, to the point where these amounts are equalized.

Chapter 29

29-1. Individual workers can air grievances to the collective voice who then takes the issue to the employer. The individual does not run the risk of being singled out by an employer. The individual employee does not waste work time trying to convince the employer that changes are needed in the workplace.

29-3. The reporting system probably was intended to provide information to union officials charged with seeking to impede strikebreaking activities by nonunion workers such as the soap opera writers. Strikebreakers can replace union employees, so they diminish the collective bargaining power of a union.

29-5. When marginal revenue is zero, demand for labor is unit-elastic, and total revenue is neither rising nor falling. No additional revenues can be earned by altering the quantity of labor, so the union's total wage revenues are maximized.

29-7. When unions in these industries attempt to bargain for higher-than-market levels of wages, the firms that employ members of these unions will not be able to readily substitute to alternative inputs. Hence, these unions are more likely to be able to achieve their wage objectives.

29-9.

Quantity of Labor Supplied	Total Physical Product	Required Hourly Wage Rate ($ per unit of labor)	Total Wage Bill ($)	Marginal Factor Cost ($ per unit of labor)
10	100	5	50	—
11	109	6	66	16
12	116	7	84	18
13	121	8	104	20
14	124	9	126	22
15	125	10	150	24

29-11. At 11 units of labor, the marginal revenue product of labor equals $16. This is equal to the marginal factor cost at this level of employment. The firm, therefore, will hire 11 units of labor and pay a wage of $6 an hour.

Quantity of Labor Supplied	Required Hourly Wage Rate ($ per unit of labor)	Total Factor Cost ($)	Marginal Factor Cost ($ per unit of labor)	Total Physical Product	Product Price ($ per unit)	Total Revenue ($)	Marginal Revenue Product ($ per unit of l abor)
10	5	50	—	100	3.11	311.00	—
11	6	66	16.00	109	3.00	327.00	16.00
12	7	84	18.00	116	2.95	342.20	15.20
13	8	104	20.00	121	2.92	353.32	11.12
14	9	126	22.00	124	2.90	359.60	6.28
15	10	150	24.00	125	2.89	361.25	1.65

29-13. The marginal factor cost of the last worker hired was $106,480 − $105,600 = $880, so this is the marginal product of this worker if the firm is maximizing its profits.

Chapter 30

30-1. **a.** X, because for this country the Lorenz curve implies complete income equality.

b. Z, because this country's Lorenz curve is bowed furthest away from the case of complete income equality.

c. Closer, because if all other things including aggregate income remain unchanged, when more people in country Y are children below working age, the share of income to people this age will decline, while the reverse will occur in country Z as more of its people reach working age and begin to earn incomes.

30-3. If the Lorenz curve is based on incomes net of transfer payments, then the Lorenz curve will become less bowed. But if the Lorenz curve does not account for transfer payments, its shape will remain unaffected.

30-5. Brazil

30-7. **a.** Absolute. If economic growth ultimately led to inflation-adjusted annual incomes for all urban families of four rising above $25,000 per year, then by this definition poverty would be ended.

b. Relative. By this definition, the lowest 15 percent of income earners will always be classified as being in a state of poverty.

c. Absolute. If economic growth eventually raised inflation-adjusted annual incomes of all individuals above $10,000, then by this definition poverty would cease to exist.

30-9. First, a moral hazard problem will exist, because government action would reduce the individual's incentive to continue a healthful lifestyle, thereby increasing the likelihood of greater health problems that will require future treatment. Second, an individual who currently has health problems will have an incentive to substitute future care that will be available at a zero price for current care that the individual must purchase at a positive price. Finally, in future years the patient will no longer have an incentive to contain health care expenses, and health care providers will have no incentive to minimize their costs.

30-11. The demand for health care will increase, and the marginal revenue curve will shift rightward. Hence, the profit-maximizing price and equilibrium quantity of health care services will increase.

Chapter 31

31-1. $4 per unit, which exactly accounts for the per-unit social cost of pollution.

31-3. **a.** 60 percent

b. 40 percent

c. 40 percent

31-5. a. There is a downward shift in the position of the marginal cost curve, as shown in the diagram below. The optimal degree of water cleanliness will rise above 65 percent, to a level such as 70 percent, and the cost incurred for the last unit of water clean-up will decrease to less than $10, such as a per-unit cost of $7.

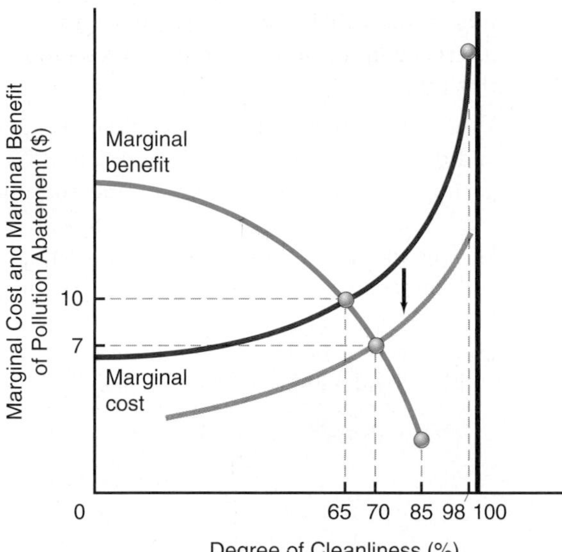

b. The second event induces an upward shift in the marginal benefit curve. Taken together, as shown in the diagram below, the two events unambiguously indicate that the optimal degree of water cleanliness increases to a level above 65 percent, such as 85 percent. The cost incurred for the last unit of water clean-up may rise or fall, however, and could end up at the initial level, which is the situation illustrated in the diagram below.

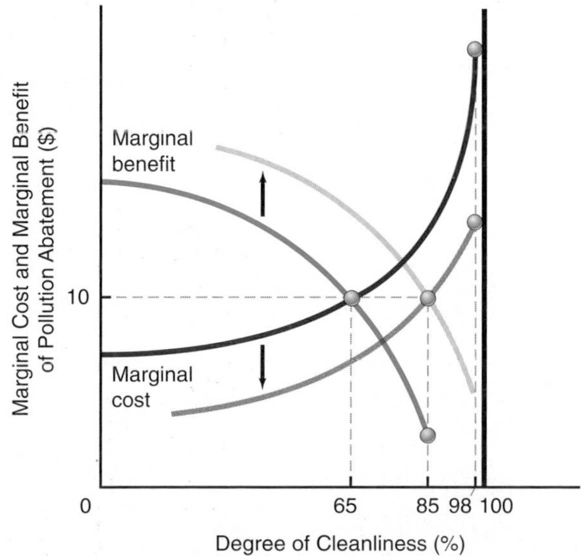

31-7. a. The marginal costs and benefits are tabulated below:

Population of Wild Tigers	Marginal Cost ($)	Marginal Benefit ($)
0	—	—
2,000	25	50
4,000	10	40
6,000	15	30
8,000	25	25
10,000	35	20
12,000	50	10

b. 8,000

c. 10,000

Chapter 32

32-1. a. The opportunity cost of pastries in Northland is 0.5 sandwich per pastry. The opportunity cost of sandwiches in Northland is 2 pastries per sandwich.

b. The opportunity cost of pastries in West Coast is 2 sandwiches per pastry. The opportunity cost of sandwiches in West Coast is 0.5 pastries per sandwich.

32-3. If Northland specializes in producing pastries, the maximum number of pastries it can produce and trade to West Coast is 50,000 pastries. Hence, the maximum number of units of each good that the two countries can trade at a rate of exchange of 1 pastry for 1 sandwich is 50,000.

32-5. Coastal Realm has a comparative advantage in producing digital TVs, and Border Kingdom has a comparative advantage in wine production.

32-7. a. The opportunity cost of modems in South Shore is 2 flash drives per modem. The opportunity cost of flash drives in South Shore is 0.5 modem per flash drive.

b. The opportunity cost of modems in East Isle is 0.5 flash drive per modem. The opportunity cost of flash drives in East Isle is 2 modems per flash drive.

c. Residents of South Shore have a comparative advantage in producing flash drives, and residents of East Isle have a comparative advantage in producing modems.

32-9. The critics are suggesting that Mexican exporters are shifting exports that would have gone to other nations to the United States, a nation within NAFTA, which would constitute trade diversion.

Chapter 33

33-1. The trade balance is merchandise exports minus merchandise imports, which equals 500 − 600 = −100, or a deficit of 100. Adding service exports of 75 and subtracting net unilateral transfers of 10 and service imports of 50 yields −100 + 75 − 10 − 50 = −85, or a current account balance of −85. The capital account balance equals the difference between capital inflows and capital outflows, or 300 − 200 = +100, or a capital account surplus of 100.

33-3. **a.** The increase in demand for Mexican-made guitars increases the demand for Mexican pesos, and the peso appreciates.

b. International investors will remove some of their financial capital from Mexico. The increase in the supply of pesos in the foreign exchange market will cause the peso to depreciate.

33-5. The demand for Chinese yuan increases, and the supply of yuan decreases. The dollar-yuan exchange rate rises, so the yuan appreciates.

33-7. The Canadian dollar–euro exchange rate is found by dividing the U.S. dollar–euro exchange rate by the U.S. dollar–Canadian dollar exchange rate, or (1.45 $US/euro)/(0.94 $US/$C) = 1.54 $C/euro, or 1.54 Canadian dollars per euro.

33-9. A flexible exchange rate system allows the exchange value of a currency to be determined freely in the foreign exchange market with no intervention by the government. A fixed exchange rate pegs the value of the currency, and the authorities responsible for the value of the currency intervene in foreign exchange markets to maintain this value.

33-11. When the dollar is pegged to gold at a rate of $35 and the pound is pegged to the dollar at $2 = £1, an implicit value between gold and the pound is established at £17.50 = 1 ounce of gold. If the dollar falls in value relative to gold, yet the pound is still valued to the dollar at $2 = £1, the pound become undervalued relative to gold. The exchange rate between the dollar and the pound will have to be adjusted to 2.29 $/£.

Glossary

A

45-degree reference line The line along which planned real expenditures equal real GDP per year.

Absolute advantage The ability to produce more units of a good or service using a given quantity of labor or resource inputs. Equivalently, the ability to produce the same quantity of a good or service using fewer units of labor or resource inputs.

Accounting identities Values that are equivalent by definition.

Accounting profit Total revenues minus total explicit costs.

Action time lag The time between recognizing an economic problem and implementing policy to solve it. The action time lag is quite long for fiscal policy, which requires congressional approval.

Active (discretionary) policymaking All actions on the part of monetary and fiscal policymakers that are undertaken in response to or in anticipation of some change in the overall economy.

Ad valorem taxation Assessing taxes by charging a tax rate equal to a fraction of the market price of each unit purchased.

Adverse selection The tendency for high-risk projects and clients to be overrepresented among borrowers.

Age-earnings cycle The regular earnings profile of an individual throughout his or her lifetime. The age-earnings cycle usually starts with a low income, builds gradually to a peak at around age 50, and then gradually curves down until it approaches zero at retirement.

Aggregate demand The total of all planned expenditures in the entire economy.

Aggregate demand curve A curve showing planned purchase rates for all final goods and services in the economy at various price levels, all other things held constant.

Aggregate demand shock Any event that causes the aggregate demand curve to shift inward or outward.

Aggregate supply The total of all planned production for the economy.

Aggregate supply shock Any event that causes the aggregate supply curve to shift inward or outward.

Aggregates Total amounts or quantities. Aggregate demand, for example, is total planned expenditures throughout a nation.

Anticipated inflation The inflation rate that we believe will occur. When it does, we are in a situation of fully anticipated inflation.

Antitrust legislation Laws that restrict the formation of monopolies and regulate certain anticompetitive business practices.

Appreciation An increase in the exchange value of one nation's currency in terms of the currency of another nation.

Asset demand Holding money as a store of value instead of other assets such as corporate bonds and stocks.

Assets Amounts owned; all items to which a business or household holds legal claim.

Asymmetric information Information possessed by one party in a financial transaction but not by the other party.

Automatic, or built-in, stabilizers Special provisions of certain federal programs that cause changes in desired aggregate expenditures without the action of Congress and the president. Examples are the federal progressive tax system and unemployment compensation.

Autonomous consumption The part of consumption that is independent of (does not depend on) the level of disposable income. Changes in autonomous consumption shift the consumption function.

Average fixed costs Total fixed costs divided by the number of units produced.

Average physical product Total product divided by the variable input.

Average propensity to consume (APC) Real consumption divided by real disposable income. For any given level of real income, the proportion of total real disposable income that is consumed.

Average propensity to save (APS) Real saving divided by real disposable income. For any given level of real income, the proportion of total real disposable income that is saved.

Average tax rate The total tax payment divided by total income. It is the proportion of total income paid in taxes.

Average total costs Total costs divided by the number of units produced; sometimes called *average per-unit total costs.*

Average variable costs Total variable costs divided by the number of units produced.

B

Balance of payments A system of accounts that measures transactions of goods, services, income, and financial assets between domestic households, businesses, and governments and residents of the rest of the world during a specific time period.

Balance of trade The difference between exports and imports of physical goods.

Balance sheet A statement of the assets and liabilities of any business entity, including financial institutions and the Federal Reserve System. Assets are what is owned, and liabilities are what is owed.

Balanced budget A situation in which the government's spending is exactly equal to the total taxes and other revenues it collects during a given period of time.

Bank run Attempt by many of a bank's depositors to convert transactions and time deposits into currency out of fear that the bank's liabilities may exceed its assets.

Barter The direct exchange of goods and services for other goods and services without the use of money.

Base year The year that is chosen as the point of reference for comparison of prices in other years.

Base-year dollars The value of a current sum expressed in terms of prices in a base year.

Behavioral economics An approach to the study of consumer behavior that emphasizes psychological limitations and complications that potentially interfere with rational decision making.

Bilateral monopoly A market structure consisting of a monopolist and a monopsonist.

Black market A market in which goods are traded at prices above their legal maximum prices or in which illegal goods are sold.

Bond A legal claim against a firm, usually entitling the owner of the bond to receive a fixed annual coupon payment, plus a lump-sum payment at the bond's maturity date. Bonds are issued in return for funds lent to the firm.

Bounded rationality The hypothesis that people are nearly, but not fully, rational, so that they cannot examine every possible choice available to them but instead use simple rules of thumb to sort among the alternatives that happen to occur to them.

Budget constraint All of the possible combinations of goods that can be purchased (at fixed prices) with a specific budget.

Bundling Offering two or more products for sale as a set.

Business fluctuations The ups and downs in business activity throughout the economy.

C

Capital account A category of balance of payments transactions that measures flows of financial assets.

Capital consumption allowance Another name for depreciation, the amount that businesses would have to save in order to take care of deteriorating machines and other equipment.

Capital gain A positive difference between the purchase price and the sale price of an asset. If a share of stock is bought for $5 and then sold for $15, the capital gain is $10.

Capital goods Producer durables; nonconsumable goods that firms use to make other goods.

Capital loss A negative difference between the purchase price and the sale price of an asset.

Capture hypothesis A theory of regulatory behavior that predicts that regulators will eventually be captured by special interests of the industry being regulated.

Cartel An association of producers in an industry that agree to set common prices and output quotas to prevent competition.

Central bank A banker's bank, usually an official institution that also serves as a bank for a nation's government treasury. Central banks normally regulate commercial banks.

***Ceteris paribus* [KAY-ter-us PEAR-uh-bus] assumption** The assumption that nothing changes except the factor or factors being studied.

***Ceteris paribus* conditions** Determinants of the relationship between price and quantity that are unchanged along a curve. Changes in these factors cause the curve to shift.

Closed shop A business enterprise in which employees must belong to the union before they can be hired and must remain in the union after they are hired.

Collective bargaining Negotiation between the management of a company or of a group of companies and the management of a union or a group of unions for the purpose of reaching a mutually agreeable contract that sets wages, fringe benefits, and working conditions for all employees in all the unions involved.

Collective decision making How voters, politicians, and other interested parties act and how these actions influence nonmarket decisions.

Common property Property that is owned by everyone and therefore by no one. Air and water are examples of common property resources.

Comparative advantage The ability to produce a good or service at a lower opportunity cost than other producers.

Complements Two goods are complements when a change in the price of one causes an opposite shift in the demand for the other.

Concentration ratio The percentage of all sales contributed by the leading four or leading eight firms in an industry; sometimes called the *industry concentration ratio.*

Constant dollars Dollars expressed in terms of real purchasing power using a particular year as the base or standard of comparison, in contrast to current dollars.

Constant returns to scale No change in long-run average costs when output increases.

Constant-cost industry An industry whose total output can be increased without an increase in long-run per-unit costs. Its long-run supply curve is horizontal.

Consumer optimum A choice of a set of goods and services that maximizes the level of satisfaction for each consumer, subject to limited income.

Consumer Price Index (CPI) A statistical measure of a weighted average of prices of a specified set of goods and services purchased by a typical consumer in urban areas.

Consumer surplus The difference between the total amount that consumers would have been willing to pay for an item and the total amount that they actually pay.

Consumption Spending on new goods and services out of a household's current income. Whatever is not consumed is saved. Consumption includes such things as buying food and going to a concert.

Consumption function The relationship between amount consumed and disposable income. A consumption function tells us how much people plan to consume at various levels of disposable income.

Consumption goods Goods bought by households to use up, such as food and movies.

Contraction A business fluctuation during which the pace of national economic activity is slowing down.

Cooperative game A game in which the players explicitly cooperate to make themselves jointly better off. As applied to firms, it involves companies colluding in order to make higher than perfectly competitive rates of return.

Corporation A legal entity that may conduct business in its own name just as an individual does. The owners of a corporation, called shareholders, own shares of the firm's profits and have the protection of limited liability.

Cost-of-living adjustments (COLAs) Clauses in contracts that allow for increases in specified nominal values to take account of changes in the cost of living.

Cost-of-service regulation Regulation that allows prices to reflect only the actual average cost of production and no monopoly profits.

Cost-push inflation Inflation caused by decreases in short-run aggregate supply.

Craft unions Labor unions composed of workers who engage in a particular trade or skill, such as baking, carpentry, or plumbing.

Creative response Behavior on the part of a firm that allows it to comply with the letter of the law but violate the spirit, significantly lessening the law's effects.

Credence good A product with qualities that consumers lack the expertise to assess without assistance.

Cross price elasticity of demand (E_{xy}) The percentage change in the amount of an item demanded (holding its price constant) divided by the percentage change in the price of a related good.

Crowding-out effect The tendency of expansionary fiscal policy to cause a decrease in planned investment or planned consumption in the private sector. This decrease normally results from the rise in interest rates.

Current account A category of balance of payments transactions that measures the exchange of merchandise, the exchange of services, and unilateral transfers.

Cyclical unemployment Unemployment resulting from business recessions that occur when aggregate (total) demand is insufficient to create full employment.

D

Dead capital Any capital resource that lacks clear title of ownership.

Deadweight loss The portion of consumer surplus that no one in society is able to obtain in a situation of monopoly.

Decreasing-cost industry An industry in which an increase in output leads to a reduction in long-run per-unit costs, such that the long-run industry supply curve slopes downward.

Deflation A sustained decrease in the average of all prices of goods and services in an economy.

Demand A schedule showing how much of a good or service people will purchase at any price during a specified time period, other things being constant.

Demand curve A graphical representation of the demand schedule; a negatively sloped line showing the inverse relationship between the price and the quantity demanded (other things being equal).

Demand-pull inflation Inflation caused by increases in aggregate demand not matched by increases in aggregate supply.

Dependent variable A variable whose value changes according to changes in the value of one or more independent variables.

Depository institutions Financial institutions that accept deposits from savers and lend funds from those deposits out at interest.

Depreciation A decrease in the exchange value of one nation's currency in terms of the currency of another nation.

Depression An extremely severe recession.

Derived demand Input factor demand derived from demand for the final product being produced.

Development economics The study of factors that contribute to the economic growth of a country.

Diminishing marginal utility The principle that as more of any good or service is consumed, its extra benefit declines. Otherwise stated, increases in total utility from the consumption of a good or service become smaller and smaller as more is consumed during a given time period.

Direct expenditure offsets Actions on the part of the private sector in spending income that offset government fiscal policy actions. Any increase in government spending in an area that competes with the private sector will have some direct expenditure offset.

Direct marketing Advertising targeted at specific consumers, typically in the form of postal mailings, telephone calls, or e-mail messages.

Direct relationship A relationship between two variables that is positive, meaning that an increase in one variable is associated with an increase in the other and a decrease in one variable is associated with a decrease in the other.

Discount rate The interest rate that the Federal Reserve charges for reserves that it lends to depository institutions. It is sometimes referred to as the *rediscount rate* or, in Canada and England, as the *bank rate.*

Discounting The method by which the present value of a future sum or a future stream of sums is obtained.

Discouraged workers Individuals who have stopped looking for a job because they are convinced that they will not find a suitable one.

Diseconomies of scale Increases in long-run average costs that occur as output increases.

Disposable personal income (DPI) Personal income after personal income taxes have been paid.

Dissaving Negative saving; a situation in which spending exceeds income. Dissaving can occur when a household is able to borrow or use up existing assets.

Distribution of income The way income is allocated among the population based on groupings of residents.

Dividends Portion of a corporation's profits paid to its owners (shareholders).

Division of labor The segregation of resources into different specific tasks. For example, one automobile worker puts on bumpers, another doors, and so on.

Dominant strategies Strategies that always yield the highest benefit. Regardless of what other players do, a dominant strategy will yield the most benefit for the player using it.

Dumping Selling a good or a service abroad below the price charged in the home market or at a price below its cost of production.

Durable consumer goods Consumer goods that have a life span of more than three years.

Dynamic tax analysis Economic evaluation of tax rate changes that recognizes that the tax base eventually declines with ever-higher tax rates, so that tax revenues may eventually decline if the tax rate is raised sufficiently.

E

Economic freedom The rights to own private property and to exchange goods, services, and financial assets with minimal government interference.

Economic goods Goods that are scarce, for which the quantity demanded exceeds the quantity supplied at a zero price.

Economic growth Increases in per capita real GDP measured by its rate of change per year.

Economic profits Total revenues minus total opportunity costs of all inputs used, or the total of all implicit and explicit costs.

Economic rent A payment for the use of any resource over and above its opportunity cost.

Economic system A society's institutional mechanism for determining the way in which scarce resources are used to satisfy human desires.

Economics The study of how people allocate their limited resources to satisfy their unlimited wants.

Economies of scale Decreases in long-run average costs resulting from increases in output.

Effect time lag The time that elapses between the implementation of a policy and the results of that policy.

Efficiency The case in which a given level of inputs is used to produce the maximum output possible. Alternatively, the situation in which a given output is produced at minimum cost.

Effluent fee A charge to a polluter that gives the right to discharge into the air or water a certain amount of pollution; also called a *pollution tax.*

Elastic demand A demand relationship in which a given percentage change in price will result in a larger percentage change in quantity demanded.

Empirical Relying on real-world data in evaluating the usefulness of a model.

Endowments The various resources in an economy, including both physical resources and such human resources as ingenuity and management skills.

Entitlements Guaranteed benefits under a government program such as Social Security, Medicare, or Medicaid.

Entrepreneurship The component of human resources that performs the functions of raising capital, organizing, managing, and assembling other factors of production, making basic business policy decisions, and taking risks.

Equation of exchange The formula indicating that the number of monetary units (M_s) times the number of times each unit is spent on final goods and services (V) is identical to the price level (P) times real GDP (Y).

Equilibrium The situation when quantity supplied equals quantity demanded at a particular price.

Exchange rate The price of one nation's currency in terms of the currency of another country.

Excise tax A tax levied on purchases of a particular good or service.

Expansion A business fluctuation in which the pace of national economic activity is speeding up.

Expenditure approach Computing GDP by adding up the dollar value at current market prices of all final goods and services.

Experience good A product that an individual must consume before the product's quality can be established.

Explicit costs Costs that business managers must take account of because they must be paid. Examples are wages, taxes, and rent.

Externality A consequence of an economic activity that spills over to affect third parties. Pollution is an externality.

F

Featherbedding Any practice that forces employers to use more labor than they would otherwise or to use existing labor in an inefficient manner.

Federal Deposit Insurance Corporation (FDIC) A government agency that insures the deposits held in banks and most other depository institutions. All U.S. banks are insured this way.

Federal funds market A private market (made up mostly of banks) in which banks can borrow reserves from other banks that want to lend them. Federal funds are usually lent for overnight use.

Federal funds rate The interest rate that depository institutions pay to borrow reserves in the interbank federal funds market.

Fiduciary monetary system A system in which money is issued by the government and its value is based uniquely on the public's faith that the currency represents command over goods and services.

Final goods and services Goods and services that are at their final stage of production and will not be transformed into yet other goods or services. For example, wheat ordinarily is not considered a final good because it is usually used to make a final good, bread.

Financial capital Funds used to purchase physical capital goods, such as buildings and equipment, and patents and trademarks.

Financial intermediaries Institutions that transfer funds between ultimate lenders (savers) and ultimate borrowers.

Financial intermediation The process by which financial institutions accept savings from businesses, households, and governments and lend the savings to other businesses, households, and governments.

Firm A business organization that employs resources to produce goods or services for profit. A firm normally owns and operates at least one "plant" or facility in order to produce.

Fiscal policy The discretionary changing of government expenditures or taxes to achieve national economic goals, such as high employment with price stability.

Fixed costs Costs that do not vary with output. Fixed costs typically include such expenses as rent on a building. These costs are fixed for a certain period of time (in the long run, though, they are variable).

Fixed investment Purchases by businesses of newly produced producer durables, or capital goods, such as production machinery and office equipment.

Flexible exchange rates Exchange rates that are allowed to fluctuate in the open market in response to changes in supply and demand. Sometimes called *floating exchange rates.*

Flow A quantity measured per unit of time; something that occurs over time, such as the income you make per week or per year or the number of individuals who are fired every month.

FOMC Directive A document that summarizes the Federal Open Market Committee's general policy strategy, establishes near-term objectives for the federal funds rate, and specifies target ranges for money supply growth.

Foreign direct investment The acquisition of more than 10 percent of the shares of ownership in a company in another nation.

Foreign exchange market A market in which households, firms, and governments buy and sell national currencies.

Foreign exchange rate The price of one currency in terms of another.

Foreign exchange risk The possibility that changes in the value of a nation's currency will result in variations in the market value of assets.

Fractional reserve banking A system in which depository institutions hold reserves that are less than the amount of total deposits.

Free-rider problem A problem that arises when individuals presume that others will pay for public goods so that, individually, they can escape paying for their portion without causing a reduction in production.

Frictional unemployment Unemployment due to the fact that workers must search for appropriate job offers. This activity takes time, and so they remain temporarily unemployed.

Full employment An arbitrary level of unemployment that corresponds to "normal" friction in the labor market. In 1986, a 6.5 percent rate of unemployment was considered full employment. Since the 1990s, it has been assumed to be around 5 percent.

G

Gains from trade The sum of consumer surplus and producer surplus.

Game theory A way of describing the various possible outcomes in any situation involving two or more interacting individuals when those individuals are aware of the interactive nature of their situation and plan accordingly. The plans made by these individuals are known as *game strategies.*

GDP deflator A price index measuring the changes in prices of all new goods and services produced in the economy.

General Agreement on Tariffs and Trade (GATT) An international agreement established in 1947 to further world trade by reducing barriers and tariffs. The GATT was replaced by the World Trade Organization in 1995.

Goods All things from which individuals derive satisfaction or happiness.

Government budget constraint The limit on government spending and transfers imposed by the fact that every dollar the government spends, transfers, or uses to repay borrowed funds must ultimately be provided by the user charges and taxes it collects.

Government budget deficit An excess of government spending over government revenues during a given period of time.

Government budget surplus An excess of government revenues over government spending during a given period of time.

Government-inhibited good A good that has been deemed socially undesirable through the political process. Heroin is an example.

Government-sponsored good A good that has been deemed socially desirable through the political process. Museums are an example.

Government, or political, goods Goods (and services) provided by the public sector.

Gross domestic income (GDI) The sum of all income—wages, interest, rent, and profits—paid to the four factors of production.

Gross domestic product (GDP) The total market value of all final goods and services produced during a year by factors of production located within a nation's borders.

Gross private domestic investment The creation of capital goods, such as factories and machines, that can yield production and hence consumption in the future. Also included in this definition are changes in business inventories and repairs made to machines or buildings.

Gross public debt All federal government debt irrespective of who owns it.

H

Health insurance exchanges Government agencies to which the national health care program assigns the task of assisting individuals, families, and small businesses in identifying health insurance policies to purchase.

Hedge A financial strategy that reduces the chance of suffering losses arising from foreign exchange risk.

Horizontal merger The joining of firms that are producing or selling a similar product.

Human capital The accumulated training and education of workers.

I

Implicit costs Expenses that managers do not have to pay out of pocket and hence normally do not explicitly calculate, such as the opportunity cost of factors of production that are owned. Examples are owner-provided capital and owner-provided labor.

Import quota A physical supply restriction on imports of a particular good, such as sugar. Foreign exporters are unable to sell in the United States more than the quantity specified in the import quota.

Incentive structure The system of rewards and punishments individuals face with respect to their own actions.

Incentives Rewards for engaging in a particular activity.

Income approach Measuring GDP by adding up all components of national income, including wages, interest, rent, and profits.

Income elasticity of demand (E_i) The percentage change in the amount of a good demanded, holding its price constant, divided by the percentage change in income; the responsiveness of the amount of a good demanded to a change in income, holding the good's relative price constant.

Income in kind Income received in the form of goods and services, such as housing or medical care. Income in kind differs from money income, which is simply income in dollars, or general purchasing power, that can be used to buy any goods and services.

Income velocity of money (V) The number of times per year a dollar is spent on final goods and services; identically equal to nominal GDP divided by the money supply.

Increasing-cost industry An industry in which an increase in industry output is accompanied by an increase in long-run per-unit costs, such that the long-run industry supply curve slopes upward.

Independent variable A variable whose value is determined independently of, or outside, the equation under study.

Indifference curve A curve composed of a set of consumption alternatives, each of which yields the same total amount of satisfaction.

Indirect business taxes All business taxes except the tax on corporate profits. Indirect business taxes include sales and business property taxes.

Industrial unions Labor unions that consist of workers from a particular industry, such as automobile manufacturing or steel manufacturing.

Industry supply curve The locus of points showing the minimum prices at which given quantities will be forthcoming; also called the *market supply curve*.

Inefficient point Any point below the production possibilities curve, at which the use of resources is not generating the maximum possible output.

Inelastic demand A demand relationship in which a given percentage change in price will result in a less-than-proportionate percentage change in the quantity demanded.

Infant industry argument The contention that tariffs should be imposed to protect from import competition an industry that is trying to get started. Presumably, after the industry becomes technologically efficient, the tariff can be lifted.

Inferior goods Goods for which demand falls as income rises.

Inflation A sustained increase in the average of all prices of goods and services in an economy.

Inflationary gap The gap that exists whenever equilibrium real GDP per year is greater than full-employment real GDP as shown by the position of the long-run aggregate supply curve.

Information product An item that is produced using information-intensive inputs at a relatively high fixed cost but distributed for sale at a relatively low marginal cost.

Informational advertising Advertising that emphasizes transmitting knowledge about the features of a product.

Innovation Transforming an invention into something that is useful to humans.

Inside information Information that is not available to the general public about what is happening in a corporation.

Interactive marketing Advertising that permits a consumer to follow up directly by searching for more information and placing direct product orders.

Interest The payment for current rather than future command over resources; the cost of obtaining credit.

Interest rate effect One of the reasons that the aggregate demand curve slopes downward: Higher price levels increase the interest rate, which in turn causes businesses and consumers to reduce desired spending due to the higher cost of borrowing.

Intermediate goods Goods used up entirely in the production of final goods.

International financial crisis The rapid withdrawal of foreign investments and loans from a nation.

International Monetary Fund An agency founded to administer an international foreign exchange system and to lend to member countries that had balance of payments problems. The IMF now functions as a lender of last resort for national governments.

Inventory investment Changes in the stocks of finished goods and goods in process, as well as changes in the raw materials that businesses keep on hand. Whenever inventories are decreasing, inventory investment is negative. Whenever they are increasing, inventory investment is positive.

Inverse relationship A relationship between two variables that is negative, meaning that an increase in one variable is associated with a decrease in the other and a decrease in one variable is associated with an increase in the other.

Investment Any use of today's resources to expand tomorrow's production or consumption.

J

Job leaver An individual in the labor force who quits voluntarily.

Job loser An individual in the labor force whose employment was involuntarily terminated.

Jurisdictional dispute A disagreement involving two or more unions over which should have control of a particular jurisdiction, such as a particular craft or skill or a particular firm or industry.

K

Keynesian short-run aggregate supply curve The horizontal portion of the aggregate supply curve in which there is excessive unemployment and unused capacity in the economy.

L

Labor Productive contributions of humans who work.

Labor force Individuals aged 16 years or older who either have jobs or who are looking and available for jobs; the number of employed plus the number of unemployed.

Labor force participation rate The percentage of noninstitutionalized working-age individuals who are employed or seeking employment.

Labor productivity Total real domestic output (real GDP) divided by the number of workers (output per worker).

Labor unions Worker organizations that seek to secure economic improvements for their members. They also seek to improve the safety, health, and other benefits (such as job security) of their members.

Land The natural resources that are available from nature. Land as a resource includes location, original fertility and mineral deposits, topography, climate, water, and vegetation.

Law of demand The observation that there is a negative, or inverse, relationship between the price of any good or service and the quantity demanded, holding other factors constant.

Law of diminishing marginal product The observation that after some point, successive equal-sized increases in a variable factor of production, such as labor, added to fixed factors of production will result in smaller increases in output.

Law of increasing additional cost The fact that the opportunity cost of additional units of a good generally increases as society attempts to produce more of that good. This accounts for the bowed-out shape of the production possibilities curve.

Law of supply The observation that the higher the price of a good, the more of that good sellers will make available over a specified time period, other things being equal.

Leading indicators Events that have been found to occur before changes in business activity.

Lemons problem The potential for asymmetric information to bring about a general decline in product quality in an industry.

Lender of last resort The Federal Reserve's role as an institution that is willing and able to lend to a temporarily illiquid bank that is otherwise in good financial condition to prevent the bank's illiquid position from leading to a general loss of confidence in that bank or in others.

Liabilities Amounts owed; the legal claims against a business or household by nonowners.

Limited liability A legal concept in which the responsibility, or liability, of the owners of a corporation is limited to the value of the shares in the firm that they own.

Liquidity The degree to which an asset can be acquired or disposed of without much danger of any intervening loss in nominal value and with small transaction costs. Money is the most liquid asset.

Liquidity approach A method of measuring the money supply by looking at money as a temporary store of value.

Long run The time period during which all factors of production can be varied.

Long-run aggregate supply curve A vertical line representing the real output of goods and services after full adjustment has occurred. It can also be viewed as representing the real GDP of the economy under conditions of full employment—the full-employment level of real GDP.

Long-run average cost curve The locus of points representing the minimum unit cost of producing any given rate of output, given current technology and resource prices.

Long-run industry supply curve A market supply curve showing the relationship between prices and quantities after firms have been allowed the time to enter into or exit from an industry, depending on whether there have been positive or negative economic profits.

Lorenz curve A geometric representation of the distribution of income. A Lorenz curve that is perfectly straight represents complete income equality. The more bowed a Lorenz curve, the more unequally income is distributed.

Lump-sum tax A tax that does not depend on income. An example is a $1,000 tax that every household must pay, irrespective of its economic situation.

M

M1 The money supply, measured as the total value of currency plus transactions deposits plus traveler's checks not issued by banks.

M2 M1 plus (1) savings deposits at all depository institutions, (2) small-denomination time deposits, and (3) balances in retail money market mutual funds.

Macroeconomics The study of the behavior of the economy as a whole, including such economywide phenomena as changes in unemployment, the general price level, and national income.

Majority rule A collective decision-making system in which group decisions are made on the basis of more than 50 percent of the vote. In other words, whatever more than half of the electorate votes for, the entire electorate has to accept.

Marginal cost pricing A system of pricing in which the price charged is equal to the opportunity cost to society of producing one more unit of the good or service in question. The opportunity cost is the marginal cost to society.

Marginal costs The change in total costs due to a one-unit change in production rate.

Marginal factor cost (MFC) The cost of using an additional unit of an input. For example, if a firm can hire all the workers it wants at the going wage rate, the marginal factor cost of labor is that wage rate.

Marginal physical product The physical output that is due to the addition of one more unit of a variable factor of production. The change in total product occurring when a variable input is increased and all other inputs are held constant. It is also called *marginal product.*

Marginal physical product (MPP) of labor The change in output resulting from the addition of one more worker. The MPP of the worker equals the change in total output accounted for by hiring the worker, holding all other factors of production constant.

Marginal propensity to consume (MPC) The ratio of the change in consumption to the change in disposable income. A marginal propensity to consume of 0.8 tells us that an additional $100 in take-home pay will lead to an additional $80 consumed.

Marginal propensity to save (MPS) The ratio of the change in saving to the change in disposable income. A marginal propensity to save of 0.2 indicates that out of an additional $100 in take-home pay, $20 will be saved. Whatever is not saved is consumed. The marginal propensity to save plus the marginal propensity to consume must always equal 1, by definition.

Marginal revenue The change in total revenues resulting from a one-unit change in output (and sale) of the product in question.

Marginal revenue product (MRP) The marginal physical product (MPP) times marginal revenue (MR). The MRP gives the additional revenue obtained from a one-unit change in labor input.

Marginal tax rate The change in the tax payment divided by the change in income, or the percentage of additional dollars that must be paid in taxes. The marginal tax rate is applied to the highest tax bracket of taxable income reached.

Marginal utility The change in total utility due to a one-unit change in the quantity of a good or service consumed.

Market All of the arrangements that individuals have for exchanging with one another. Thus, for example, we can speak of the labor market, the automobile market, and the credit market.

Market clearing, or equilibrium, price The price that clears the market, at which quantity demanded equals quantity supplied; the price where the demand curve intersects the supply curve.

Market demand The demand of all consumers in the marketplace for a particular good or service. The summation at each price of the quantity demanded by each individual.

Market failure A situation in which an unrestrained market operation leads to either too few or too many resources going to a specific economic activity.

Market share test The percentage of a market that a particular firm supplies; used as the primary measure of monopoly power.

Mass marketing Advertising intended to reach as many consumers as possible, typically through television, newspaper, radio, or magazine ads.

Medium of exchange Any item that sellers will accept as payment.

Microeconomics The study of decision making undertaken by individuals (or households) and by firms.

Minimum efficient scale (MES) The lowest rate of output per unit time at which long-run average costs for a particular firm are at a minimum.

Minimum wage A wage floor, legislated by government, setting the lowest hourly rate that firms may legally pay workers.

Models, or theories Simplified representations of the real world used as the basis for predictions or explanations.

Money Any medium that is universally accepted in an economy both by sellers of goods and services as payment for those goods and services and by creditors as payment for debts.

Money balances Synonymous with money, money stock, money holdings.

Money illusion Reacting to changes in money prices rather than relative prices. If a worker whose wages double when the price level also doubles thinks he or she is better off, that worker is suffering from money illusion.

Money multiplier A number that, when multiplied by a change in reserves in the banking system, yields the resulting change in the money supply.

Money price The price expressed in today's dollars; also called the *absolute* or *nominal price.*

Money supply The amount of money in circulation.

Monopolist The single supplier of a good or service for which there is no close substitute. The monopolist therefore constitutes its entire industry.

Monopolistic competition A market situation in which a large number of firms produce similar but not identical products. Entry into the industry is relatively easy.

Monopolization The possession of monopoly power in the relevant market and the willful acquisition or maintenance of that power, as distinguished from growth or development as a consequence of a superior product, business acumen, or historical accident.

Monopoly A firm that can determine the market price of a good. In the extreme case, a monopoly is the only seller of a good or service.

Monopsonist The only buyer in a market.

Monopsonistic exploitation Paying a price for the variable input that is less than its marginal revenue product; the difference between marginal revenue product and the wage rate.

Moral hazard The possibility that a borrower might engage in riskier behavior after a loan has been obtained.

Multiplier The ratio of the change in the equilibrium level of real GDP to the change in autonomous real expenditures. The number by which a change in autonomous real investment or autonomous real consumption, for example, is multiplied to get the change in equilibrium real GDP.

Multiproduct firm A firm that produces and sells two or more different items.

N

National income (NI) The total of all factor payments to resource owners. It can be obtained from net domestic product (NDP) by subtracting indirect business taxes and transfers and adding net U.S. income earned abroad and other business income adjustments.

National income accounting A measurement system used to estimate national income and its components; one approach to measuring an economy's aggregate performance.

Natural monopoly A monopoly that arises from the peculiar production characteristics in an industry. It usually arises when there are large economies of scale relative to the industry's demand such that one firm can produce at a lower average cost than can be achieved by multiple firms.

Natural rate of unemployment The rate of unemployment that is estimated to prevail in long-run macroeconomic equilibrium, when all workers and employers have fully adjusted to any changes in the economy.

Negative market feedback A tendency for a good or service to fall out of favor with more consumers because other consumers have stopped purchasing the item.

Negative-sum game A game in which players as a group lose during the process of the game.

Net domestic product (NDP) GDP minus depreciation.

Net investment Gross private domestic investment minus an estimate of the wear and tear on the existing capital stock. Net investment therefore measures the change in the capital stock over a one-year period.

Net public debt Gross public debt minus all government interagency borrowing.

Net wealth The stock of assets owned by a person, household, firm, or nation (net of any debts owed). For a household, net wealth can consist of a house, cars, personal belongings, stocks, bonds, bank accounts, and cash (minus any debts owed).

Network effect A situation in which a consumer's willingness to purchase a good or service is influenced by how many others also buy or have bought the item.

Neutral federal funds rate A value of the interest rate on interbank loans at which the growth rate of real GDP tends neither to rise nor to fall relative to the rate of growth of potential, long-run, real GDP, given the expected rate of inflation.

New entrant An individual who has never held a full-time job lasting two weeks or longer but is now seeking employment.

New growth theory A theory of economic growth that examines the factors that determine why technology, research, innovation, and the like are undertaken and how they interact.

New Keynesian inflation dynamics In new Keynesian theory, the pattern of inflation exhibited by an economy with growing aggregate demand—initial sluggish adjustment of the price level in response to increased aggregate demand followed by higher inflation later.

Nominal rate of interest The market rate of interest expressed in today's dollars.

Nominal values The values of variables such as GDP and investment expressed in current dollars, also called *money values;* measurement in terms of the actual market prices at which goods and services are sold.

Nonaccelerating inflation rate of unemployment (NAIRU) The rate of unemployment below which the rate of inflation tends to rise and above which the rate of inflation tends to fall.

Noncontrollable expenditures Government spending that changes automatically without action by Congress.

Noncooperative game A game in which the players neither negotiate nor cooperate in any way. As applied to firms in an industry, this is the common situation in which there are relatively few firms and each has some ability to change price.

Nondurable consumer goods Consumer goods that are used up within three years.

Nonincome expense items The total of indirect business taxes and depreciation.

Nonprice rationing devices All methods used to ration scarce goods that are price-controlled. Whenever the price system is not allowed to work, nonprice rationing devices will evolve to ration the affected goods and services.

Normal goods Goods for which demand rises as income rises. Most goods are normal goods.

Normal rate of return The amount that must be paid to an investor to induce investment in a business. Also known as the *opportunity cost of capital.*

Normative economics Analysis involving value judgments about economic policies; relates to whether outcomes are good or bad. A statement of what ought to be.

Number line A line that can be divided into segments of equal length, each associated with a number.

O

Oligopoly A market structure in which there are very few sellers. Each seller knows that the other sellers will react to its changes in prices, quantities, and qualities.

Open economy effect One of the reasons that the aggregate demand curve slopes downward: Higher price levels result in foreign residents desiring to buy fewer U.S.-made goods, while U.S. residents now desire more foreign-made goods, thereby reducing net exports. This is equivalent to a reduction in the amount of real goods and services purchased in the United States.

Open market operations The purchase and sale of existing U.S. government securities (such as bonds) in the open private market by the Federal Reserve System.

Opportunistic behavior Actions that focus solely on short-run gains because long-run benefits of cooperation are perceived to be smaller.

Opportunity cost The highest-valued, next-best alternative that must be sacrificed to obtain something or to satisfy a want.

Opportunity cost of capital The normal rate of return, or the available return on the next-best alternative investment. Economists consider this a cost of production, and it is included in our cost example.

Optimal quantity of pollution The level of pollution for which the marginal benefit of one additional unit of pollution abatement just equals the marginal cost of that additional unit of pollution abatement.

Origin The intersection of the y axis and the x axis in a graph.

Outsourcing A firm's employment of labor outside the country in which the firm is located.

P

Par value The officially determined value of a currency.

Partnership A business owned by two or more joint owners, or partners, who share the responsibilities and the profits of the firm and are individually liable for all the debts of the partnership.

Passive (nondiscretionary) policymaking Policymaking that is carried out in response to a rule. It is therefore not in response to an actual or potential change in overall economic activity.

Patent A government protection that gives an inventor the exclusive right to make, use, or sell an invention for a limited period of time (currently, 20 years).

Payoff matrix A matrix of outcomes, or consequences, of the strategies available to the players in a game.

Perfect competition A market structure in which the decisions of individual buyers and sellers have no effect on market price.

Perfectly competitive firm A firm that is such a small part of the total industry that it cannot affect the price of the product it sells.

Perfectly elastic demand A demand that has the characteristic that even the slightest increase in price will lead to zero quantity demanded.

Perfectly elastic supply A supply characterized by a reduction in quantity supplied to zero when there is the slightest decrease in price.

Perfectly inelastic demand A demand that exhibits zero responsiveness to price changes. No matter what the price is, the quantity demanded remains the same.

Perfectly inelastic supply A supply for which quantity supplied remains constant, no matter what happens to price.

Personal Consumption Expenditure (PCE) Index A statistical measure of average prices that uses annually updated weights based on surveys of consumer spending.

Personal income (PI) The amount of income that households actually receive before they pay personal income taxes.

Persuasive advertising Advertising that is intended to induce a consumer to purchase a particular product and discover a previously unknown taste for the item.

Phillips curve A curve showing the relationship between unemployment and changes in wages or prices. It was long thought to reflect a trade-off between unemployment and inflation.

Physical capital All manufactured resources, including buildings, equipment, machines, and improvements to land that are used for production.

Planning curve The long-run average cost curve.

Planning horizon The long run, during which all inputs are variable.

Plant size The physical size of the factories that a firm owns and operates to produce its output. Plant size can be defined by square footage, maximum physical capacity, and other physical measures.

Policy irrelevance proposition The conclusion that policy actions have no real effects in the short run if the policy actions are anticipated and none in the long run even if the policy actions are unanticipated.

Portfolio investment The purchase of less than 10 percent of the shares of ownership in a company in another nation.

Positive economics Analysis that is strictly limited to making either purely descriptive statements or scientific predictions; for example, "If A, then B." A statement of what is.

Positive market feedback A tendency for a good or service to come into favor with additional consumers because other consumers have chosen to buy the item.

Positive-sum game A game in which players as a group are better off at the end of the game.

Potential money multiplier The reciprocal of the reserve ratio, assuming no leakages into currency. It is equal to 1 divided by the reserve ratio.

Precautionary demand Holding money to meet unplanned expenditures and emergencies.

Present value The value of a future amount expressed in today's dollars; the most that someone would pay today to receive a certain sum at some point in the future.

Price ceiling A legal maximum price that may be charged for a particular good or service.

Price controls Government-mandated minimum or maximum prices that may be charged for goods and services.

Price differentiation Establishing different prices for similar products to reflect differences in marginal cost in providing those commodities to different groups of buyers.

Price discrimination Selling a given product at more than one price, with the price difference being unrelated to differences in marginal cost.

Price elasticity of demand (E_p) The responsiveness of the quantity demanded of a commodity to changes in its price; defined as the percentage change in quantity demanded divided by the percentage change in price.

Price elasticity of supply (E_s) The responsiveness of the quantity supplied of a commodity to a change in its price; the percentage change in quantity supplied divided by the percentage change in price.

Price floor A legal minimum price below which a good or service may not be sold. Legal minimum wages are an example.

Price index The cost of today's market basket of goods expressed as a percentage of the cost of the same market basket during a base year.

Price searcher A firm that must determine the price-output combination that maximizes profit because it faces a downward-sloping demand curve.

Price system An economic system in which relative prices are constantly changing to reflect changes in supply and demand for different commodities. The prices of those commodities are signals to everyone within the system as to what is relatively scarce and what is relatively abundant.

Price taker A perfectly competitive firm that must take the price of its product as given because the firm cannot influence its price.

Principle of rival consumption The recognition that individuals are rivals in consuming private goods because one person's consumption reduces the amount available for others to consume.

Principle of substitution The principle that consumers shift away from goods and services that become priced relatively higher in favor of goods and services that are now priced relatively lower.

Prisoners' dilemma A famous strategic game in which two prisoners have a choice between confessing and not confessing to a crime. If neither confesses, they serve a minimum sentence. If both confess, they serve a longer sentence. If one confesses and the other doesn't, the one who confesses goes free. The dominant strategy is always to confess.

Private costs Costs borne solely by the individuals who incur them. Also called *internal costs.*

Private goods Goods that can be consumed by only one individual at a time. Private goods are subject to the principle of rival consumption.

Private property rights Exclusive rights of ownership that allow the use, transfer, and exchange of property.

Producer durables, or capital goods Durable goods having an expected service life of more than three years that are used by businesses to produce other goods and services.

Producer Price Index (PPI) A statistical measure of a weighted average of prices of goods and services that firms produce and sell.

Producer surplus Difference between the total amount that producers actually receive for an item and the total amount that they would have been willing to accept for supplying that item.

Product compatibility The capability of a product sold by one firm to function together with another firm's complementary product.

Product differentiation The distinguishing of products by brand name, color, and other minor attributes. Product differentiation occurs in other than perfectly competitive markets in which products are, in theory, homogeneous, such as wheat or corn.

Production Any activity that results in the conversion of resources into products that can be used in consumption.

Production function The relationship between inputs and maximum physical output. A production function is a technological, not an economic, relationship.

Production possibilities curve (PPC) A curve representing all possible combinations of maximum outputs that could be produced assuming a fixed amount of productive resources of a given quality.

Profit-maximizing rate of production The rate of production that maximizes total profits, or the difference between total revenues and total costs. Also, it is the rate of production at which marginal revenue equals marginal cost.

Progressive taxation A tax system in which, as income increases, a higher percentage of the additional income is paid as taxes. The marginal tax rate exceeds the average tax rate as income rises.

Property rights The rights of an owner to use and to exchange property.

Proportional rule A decision-making system in which actions are based on the proportion of the "votes" cast and are in proportion to them. In a market system, if 10 percent of the "dollar votes" are cast for blue cars, 10 percent of automobile output will be blue cars.

Proportional taxation A tax system in which, regardless of an individual's income, the tax bill comprises exactly the same proportion.

Proprietorship A business owned by one individual who makes the business decisions, receives all the profits, and is legally responsible for the debts of the firm.

Public debt The total value of all outstanding federal government securities.

Public goods Goods for which the principle of rival consumption does not apply. They can be jointly consumed by many individuals simultaneously at no additional cost and with no reduction in quality or quantity. Also no one who fails to help pay for the good can be denied the benefit of the good.

Purchasing power The value of money for buying goods and services. If your money income stays the same but the price of one good that you are buying goes up, your effective purchasing power falls, and vice versa.

Purchasing power parity Adjustment in exchange rate conversions that takes into account differences in the true cost of living across countries.

Q

Quantity theory of money and prices The hypothesis that changes in the money supply lead to equiproportional changes in the price level.

Quota subscription A nation's account with the International Monetary Fund, denominated in special drawing rights.

Quota system A government-imposed restriction on the quantity of a specific good that another country is allowed to sell in the United States. In other words, quotas are restrictions on imports. These restrictions are usually applied to one or several specific countries.

R

Random walk theory The theory that there are no predictable trends in securities prices that can be used to "get rich quick."

Rate of discount The rate of interest used to discount future sums back to present value.

Rate-of-return regulation Regulation that seeks to keep the rate of return in an industry at a competitive level by not allowing prices that would produce economic profits.

Rational expectations hypothesis A theory stating that people combine the effects of past policy changes on important economic variables with their own judgment about the future effects of current and future policy changes.

Rationality assumption The assumption that people do not intentionally make decisions that would leave them worse off.

Reaction function The manner in which one oligopolist reacts to a change in price, output, or quality made by another oligopolist in the industry.

Real disposable income Real GDP minus net taxes, or after-tax real income.

Real rate of interest The nominal rate of interest minus the anticipated rate of inflation.

Real values Measurement of economic values after adjustments have been made for changes in the average of prices between years.

Real-balance effect The change in expenditures resulting from a change in the real value of money balances when the price level changes, all other things held constant; also called the *wealth effect.*

Real-income effect The change in people's purchasing power that occurs when, other things being constant, the price of one good that they purchase changes. When that price goes up, real income, or purchasing power, falls, and when that price goes down, real income increases.

Recession A period of time during which the rate of growth of business activity is consistently less than its long-term trend or is negative.

Recessionary gap The gap that exists whenever equilibrium real GDP per year is less than full-employment real GDP as shown by the position of the long-run aggregate supply curve.

Recognition time lag The time required to gather information about the current state of the economy.

Reentrant An individual who used to work full-time but left the labor force and has now reentered it looking for a job.

Regional trade bloc A group of nations that grants members special trade privileges.

Regressive taxation A tax system in which as more dollars are earned, the percentage of tax paid on them falls. The marginal tax rate is less than the average tax rate as income rises.

Reinvestment Profits (or depreciation reserves) used to purchase new capital equipment.

Relative price The money price of one commodity divided by the money price of another commodity; the number of units of one commodity that must be sacrificed to purchase one unit of another commodity.

Rent control Price ceilings on rents.

Repricing, or menu, cost of inflation The cost associated with recalculating prices and printing new price lists when there is inflation.

Reserve ratio The fraction of transactions deposits that banks hold as reserves.

Reserves In the U.S. Federal Reserve System, deposits held by Federal Reserve district banks for depository institutions, plus depository institutions' vault cash.

Resources Things used to produce goods and services to satisfy people's wants.

Retained earnings Earnings that a corporation saves, or retains, for investment in other productive activities; earnings that are not distributed to stockholders.

Ricardian equivalence theorem The proposition that an increase in the government budget deficit has no effect on aggregate demand.

Right-to-work laws Laws that make it illegal to require union membership as a condition of continuing employment in a particular firm.

Rule of 70 A rule stating that the approximate number of years required for per capita real GDP to double is equal to 70 divided by the average rate of economic growth.

Rules of origin Regulations that nations in regional trade blocs establish to delineate product categories eligible for trading preferences.

S

Sales taxes Taxes assessed on the prices paid on most goods and services.

Saving The act of not consuming all of one's current income. Whatever is not consumed out of spendable income is, by definition, saved. Saving is an action measured over time (a flow), whereas savings are a stock, an accumulation resulting from the act of saving in the past.

Say's law A dictum of economist J. B. Say that supply creates its own demand. Producing goods and services generates the means and the willingness to purchase other goods and services.

Scarcity A situation in which the ingredients for producing the things that people desire are insufficient to satisfy all wants at a zero price.

Search good A product with characteristics that enable an individual to evaluate the product's quality in advance of a purchase.

Seasonal unemployment Unemployment resulting from the seasonal pattern of work in specific industries. It is usually due to seasonal fluctuations in demand or to changing weather conditions that render work difficult, if not impossible, as in the agriculture, construction, and tourist industries.

Secondary boycott A refusal to deal with companies or purchase products sold by companies that are dealing with a company being struck.

Secular deflation A persistent decline in prices resulting from economic growth in the presence of stable aggregate demand.

Securities Stocks and bonds.

Services Mental or physical labor or help purchased by consumers. Examples are the assistance of physicians, lawyers, dentists, repair personnel, housecleaners, educators, retailers, and wholesalers; items purchased or used by consumers that do not have physical characteristics.

Share of stock A legal claim to a share of a corporation's future profits. If it is common stock, it incorporates certain voting rights regarding major policy decisions of the corporation. If it is preferred stock, its owners are accorded preferential treatment in the payment of dividends but do not have any voting rights.

Share-the-gains, share-the-pains theory A theory of regulatory behavior that holds that regulators must take account of the demands of three groups: legislators, who established and oversee the regulatory agency; firms in the regulated industry; and consumers of the regulated industry's products.

Short run The time period during which at least one input, such as plant size, cannot be changed.

Short-run aggregate supply curve The relationship between total planned economywide production and the price level in the short run, all other things held constant. If prices adjust incompletely in the short run, the curve is positively sloped.

Short-run break-even price The price at which a firm's total revenues equal its total costs. At the break-even price, the firm is just making a normal rate of return on its capital investment. (It is covering its explicit and implicit costs.)

Short-run economies of operation A distinguishing characteristic of an information product arising from declining short-run average total cost as more units of the product are sold.

Short-run shutdown price The price that covers average variable costs. It occurs just below the intersection of the marginal cost curve and the average variable cost curve.

Shortage A situation in which quantity demanded is greater than quantity supplied at a price below the market clearing price.

Signals Compact ways of conveying to economic decision makers information needed to make decisions. An effective signal not only conveys information but also provides the incentive to react appropriately. Economic profits and economic losses are such signals.

Slope The change in the *y* value divided by the corresponding change in the *x* value of a curve; the "incline" of the curve.

Small menu costs Costs that deter firms from changing prices in response to demand changes—for example, the costs of renegotiating contracts or printing new price lists.

Social costs The full costs borne by society whenever a resource use occurs. Social costs can be measured by adding external costs to private, or internal, costs.

Special drawing rights (SDRs) Reserve assets created by the International Monetary Fund for countries to use in settling international payment obligations.

Specialization The organization of economic activity so that what each person (or region) consumes is not identical to what that person (or region) produces. An individual may specialize, for example, in law or medicine. A nation may specialize in the production of coffee, e-book readers, or digital cameras.

Stagflation A situation characterized by lower real GDP, lower employment, and a higher unemployment rate during the same period that the rate of inflation increases.

Standard of deferred payment A property of an item that makes it desirable for use as a means of settling debts maturing in the future; an essential property of money.

Static tax analysis Economic evaluation of the effects of tax rate changes under the assumption that there is no effect on the tax base, meaning that there is an unambiguous positive relationship between tax rates and tax revenues.

Stock The quantity of something, measured at a given point in time—for example, an inventory of goods or a bank account. Stocks are defined independently of time, although they are assessed at a point in time.

Store of value The ability to hold value over time; a necessary property of money.

Strategic dependence A situation in which one firm's actions with respect to price, quality, advertising, and related changes may be strategically countered by the reactions of one or more other firms in the industry. Such dependence can exist only when there are a limited number of major firms in an industry.

Strategy Any rule that is used to make a choice, such as "Always pick heads."

Strikebreakers Temporary or permanent workers hired by a company to replace union members who are striking.

Structural unemployment Unemployment resulting from a poor match of workers' abilities and skills with current requirements of employers.

Subsidy A negative tax; a payment to a producer from the government, usually in the form of a cash grant per unit.

Substitutes Two goods are substitutes when a change in the price of one causes a shift in demand for the other in the same direction as the price change.

Substitution effect The tendency of people to substitute cheaper commodities for more expensive commodities.

Supply A schedule showing the relationship between price and quantity supplied for a specified period of time, other things being equal.

Supply curve The graphical representation of the supply schedule; a line (curve) showing the supply schedule, which generally slopes upward (has a positive slope), other things being equal.

Supply-side economics The suggestion that creating incentives for individuals and firms to increase productivity will cause the aggregate supply curve to shift outward.

Surplus A situation in which quantity supplied is greater than quantity demanded at a price above the market clearing price.

Sympathy strike A work stoppage by a union in sympathy with another union's strike or cause.

T

Tariffs Taxes on imported goods.

Tax base The value of goods, services, wealth, or incomes subject to taxation.

Tax bracket A specified interval of income to which a specific and unique marginal tax rate is applied.

Tax incidence The distribution of tax burdens among various groups in society.

Tax rate The proportion of a tax base that must be paid to a government as taxes.

Taylor rule An equation that specifies a federal funds rate target based on an estimated long-run real interest rate, the current deviation of the actual inflation rate from the Federal Reserve's inflation objective, and the gap between actual real GDP per year and a measure of potential real GDP per year.

Technology Society's pool of applied knowledge concerning how goods and services can be produced.

The Fed The Federal Reserve System; the central bank of the United States.

Theory of public choice The study of collective decision making.

Third parties Parties who are not directly involved in a given activity or transaction. For example, in the relationship between caregivers and patients, fees may be paid by third parties (insurance companies, government).

Thrift institutions Financial institutions that receive most of their funds from the savings of the public. They include savings banks, savings and loan associations, and credit unions.

Tie-in sales Purchases of one product that are permitted by the seller only if the consumer buys another good or service from the same firm.

Tit-for-tat strategic behavior In game theory, cooperation that continues as long as the other players continue to cooperate.

Total costs The sum of total fixed costs and total variable costs.

Total income The yearly amount earned by the nation's resources (factors of production). Total income therefore includes wages, rent, interest payments, and profits that are received by workers, landowners, capital owners, and entrepreneurs, respectively.

Total revenues The price per unit times the total quantity sold.

Trade deflection Moving partially assembled products into a member nation of a regional trade bloc, completing assembly, and then exporting them to other nations within the bloc, so as to benefit from preferences granted by the trade bloc.

Trade diversion Shifting existing international trade from countries outside a regional trade bloc to nations within the bloc.

Trading Desk An office at the Federal Reserve Bank of New York charged with implementing monetary policy strategies developed by the Federal Open Market Committee.

Transaction costs All costs associated with making, reaching, and enforcing agreements.

Transactions approach A method of measuring the money supply by looking at money as a medium of exchange.

Transactions demand Holding money as a medium of exchange to make payments. The level varies directly with nominal GDP.

Transactions deposits Checkable and debitable account balances in commercial banks and other types of financial institutions, such as credit unions and savings banks. Any accounts in financial institutions from which you can easily transmit debit-card and check payments without many restrictions.

Transfer payments Money payments made by governments to individuals for which no services or goods are rendered in return. Examples are Social Security old-age and disability benefits and unemployment insurance benefits.

Transfers in kind Payments that are in the form of actual goods and services, such as food stamps, subsidized public housing, and medical care, and for which no goods or services are rendered in return.

Traveler's checks Financial instruments obtained from a bank or a nonbanking organization and signed during purchase that can be used in payment upon a second signature by the purchaser.

U

Unanticipated inflation Inflation at a rate that comes as a surprise, either higher or lower than the rate anticipated.

Unemployment The total number of adults (aged 16 years or older) who are willing and able to work and who are actively looking for work but have not found a job.

Union shop A business enterprise that may hire nonunion members, conditional on their joining the union by some specified date after employment begins.

Unit elasticity of demand A demand relationship in which the quantity demanded changes exactly in proportion to the change in price.

Unit of accounting A measure by which prices are expressed; the common denominator of the price system; a central property of money.

Unit tax A constant tax assessed on each unit of a good that consumers purchase.

Unlimited liability A legal concept whereby the personal assets of the owner of a firm can be seized to pay off the firm's debts.

Util A representative unit by which utility is measured.

Utility The want-satisfying power of a good or service.

Utility analysis The analysis of consumer decision making based on utility maximization.

V

Value added The dollar value of an industry's sales minus the value of intermediate goods (for example, raw materials and parts) used in production.

Variable costs Costs that vary with the rate of production. They include wages paid to workers and purchases of materials.

Versioning Selling a product in slightly altered forms to different groups of consumers.

Vertical merger The joining of a firm with another to which it sells an output or from which it buys an input.

Voluntary exchange An act of trading, done on an elective basis, in which both parties to the trade expect to be better off after the exchange.

Voluntary import expansion (VIE) An official agreement with another country in which it agrees to import more from the United States.

Voluntary restraint agreement (VRA) An official agreement with another country that "voluntarily" restricts the quantity of its exports to the United States.

W

Wants What people would buy if their incomes were unlimited.

World Bank A multinational agency that specializes in making loans to about 100 developing nations in an effort to promote their long-term development and growth.

World Trade Organization (WTO) The successor organization to the GATT that handles trade disputes among its member nations.

X

***x* axis** The horizontal axis in a graph.

Y

***y* axis** The vertical axis in a graph.

Z

Zero-sum game A game in which any gains within the group are exactly offset by equal losses by the end of the game.

Index

E

J

Q

R

S

T

X

Y

Z

myeconlab

Cost of Holding Money

The cost of holding money (its opportunity cost) is measured by the alternative interest yield obtainable by holding some other asset.

Policy Irrelevance Proposition

Under the assumption of rational expectations on the part of decision makers in the economy, anticipated monetary policy cannot alter either the rate of unemployment or the level of real GDP. Regardless of the nature of the anticipated policy, the unemployment rate will equal the natural rate, and real GDP will be determined solely by the economy's long-run aggregate supply curve.

Natural Rate of Unemployment

The natural rate of unemployment is the rate of unemployment that exists when workers and employers correctly anticipate the rate of inflation.

Equation of Exchange

$$M_sV = PY$$

where M_s = actual money balances held by the nonbanking public
V = income velocity of money, or the number of times, on average, each monetary unit is spent on final goods and services
P = price level or price index
Y = real GDP

Potential Money Multiplier

The reciprocal of the reserve ratio, assuming no leakages into currency, is the potential money multiplier.

$$\text{Potential money multiplier} = \frac{1}{\text{reserve ratio}}$$

Definition of Money Supply

M1 = currency + transactions deposits + traveler's checks

M2 = M1 +
1. Savings deposits at all depository institutions
2. Small-denomination time deposits
3. Balances in retail money market mutual funds

Relationship Between Imports and Exports

In the long run, imports are paid for by exports.

Therefore, any restriction of imports ultimately reduces exports.

MICROECONOMIC PRINCIPLES

Opportunity Cost

In economics, cost is always a forgone opportunity.

Law of Demand

When the price of a good goes up, people buy less of it, *other things being equal.*

Movement Along, versus Shift in, a Curve

If the relative price changes, we *move along* a curve—there is a change in quantity demanded and/or supplied. If something else changes, we *shift* a curve—there is a change in demand and/or supply.

Income Elasticity of Demand

$$\text{Income elasticity of demand} = \frac{\text{percentage change in amount of a good demanded}}{\text{percentage change in income}}$$

Law of Diminishing Marginal Product

As successive equal increases in a variable factor of production, such as labor, are added to other fixed factors of production, such as capital, there will be a point beyond which the extra, or marginal, product that can be attributed to each additional unit of the variable factor of production will decline.

Supply

At higher prices, a larger quantity will generally be supplied than at lower prices, *all other things held constant.*

Or stated otherwise:

At lower prices, a smaller quantity will generally be supplied than at higher prices, *all other things held constant.*

Profits

$$\text{Accounting profits} = \text{total revenues} - \text{total costs}$$

$$\text{Economic profits} = \text{total revenues} - \text{total opportunity cost of all inputs used}$$

Price Elasticity of Demand

$$E_p = \frac{\text{percentage change in quantity demanded}}{\text{percentage change in price}}$$

Price Elasticity of Supply

$$E_s = \frac{\text{percentage change in quantity supplied}}{\text{percentage change in price}}$$

Monopsony and Monopoly

Input Market Structure	***Output Market Structure***	
	Perfect Competition	**Monopoly**
Perfect Competition	$MC = MR = P$ $W = MFC = MRP_c$	$MC = MR(< P)$ $W = MFC = MRP_m (< MRP_c)$
Monopsony	$MC = MR = P$ $W < MFC = MRP_c$	$MC = MR(< P)$ $W < MFC = MRP_m (< MRP_c)$